Ninth Edition

CompTIA Network+

Guide to Networks

JILL WEST

NETWORKING

CENGAGE

Australia • Brazil • Canada • Mexico • Singapore • United Kingdom • United States

CompTIA Network+
Guide to Networks, Ninth Edition
Jill West

SVP, Higher Education & Skills Product: Erin Joyner

VP, Higher Education & Skills Product: Thais Alencar

Product Director: Mark Santee

Associate Product Manager: Danielle Klahr

Product Assistant: Tom Benedetto

Learning Designer: Natalie Onderdonk

Senior Content Manager: Brooke Greenhouse

Digital Delivery Quality Partner: Jim Vaughey

Technical Editor: Danielle Shaw

Developmental Editor: Ann Shaffer

Vice President, Product Marketing: Jason Sakos

Director, Marketing: Danaë April

Marketing Manager: Mackenzie Paine

IP Analyst: Ashley Maynard

IP Project Manager: Kelli Besse

Production Service: SPi

Senior Designer: Erin Griffin

Cover Image Source: TATYANA Yamshanova/ Shutterstock.com

For product information and technology assistance, contact us at
**Cengage Customer & Sales Support, 1-800-354-9706
or support.cengage.com.**

For permission to use material from this text or product, submit all requests online at **www.cengage.com/permissions.**

Library of Congress Control Number: 2021909679

ISBN: 978-0-357-50813-8
Loose-leaf Edition ISBN: 978-0-357-50814-5

Cengage
200 Pier 4 Boulevard
Boston, MA 02210
USA

Cengage is a leading provider of customized learning solutions with employees residing in nearly 40 different countries and sales in more than 125 countries around the world. Find your local representative at: **www.cengage.com.**

To learn more about Cengage platforms and services, register or access your online learning solution, or purchase materials for your course, visit **www.cengage.com.**

Notice to the Reader

Printed in the United States of America
Print Number: 01   Print Year: 2021

BRIEF CONTENTS

TABLE OF CONTENTS

MODULE 11

SECURITY IN NETWORK DESIGN 607

MODULE 12

PERFORMANCE AND RECOVERY 667

APPENDIX A

COMPTIA NETWORK+ N10-008 CERTIFICATION EXAM OBJECTIVES

PREFACE

Knowing how to install, configure, and troubleshoot a computer network is a highly marketable and exciting skill. This course first introduces the fundamental building blocks that form a modern network, such as hardware, topologies, and protocols, along with an introduction to the OSI model. It then provides in-depth coverage of the most important concepts in contemporary networking, including TCP/IP, Ethernet, wireless transmission, virtual networks, cloud computing, segmentation, security, performance optimization, and troubleshooting. After reading the modules and completing the exercises, you will be prepared to select the network design, hardware, and software that best fit your environment. You will also have the skills to build a network from scratch and maintain, upgrade, troubleshoot, and manage an existing network. Finally, you will be well-prepared to take CompTIA's Network+ N10-008 certification exam.

This course explains technical concepts logically and in a clear, approachable style. In addition, concepts are reinforced by real-world examples of networking issues from a professional's standpoint. Each module opens with an "On the Job" story from a network engineer, technician, or administrator. These insightful stories of actual events, along with Applying Concepts activities, Hands-On Projects, and Capstone Projects in each module, make this text a practical learning tool. The numerous tables and color illustrations, along with the glossary, appendices, and study questions, provide a valuable reference for any networking professional.

INTENDED AUDIENCE

This course is intended to serve the needs of students and professionals who are interested in mastering fundamental, vendor-neutral networking concepts. No previous networking experience is necessary to begin learning from this text, although knowledge of basic computer principles is helpful. Those seeking to pass CompTIA's Network+ certification exam will find the course's content, approach, and numerous study questions especially helpful. For more information on CompTIA® Network+ certification, visit CompTIA's website at *comptia.org*.

The course's pedagogical features are designed to provide a truly interactive learning experience, preparing you for the challenges of the highly dynamic networking industry. In addition to the information presented in the text, each module includes Applying Concepts activities and Hands-On Projects that guide you through software and hardware configuration in a step-by-step fashion. At the end of each module, you will also find progressive Capstone Projects that give you the opportunity to build on previous modules' work and connect ideas from module to module using various virtualized, emulated, and cloud environments.

MODULE DESCRIPTIONS

The following list summarizes the topics covered in each module of this course:

Module 1, "Introduction to Networking," begins by answering the question "What is a network?" Next, it presents the fundamental types of networks and describes the devices and topologies that create a network. This module also introduces the OSI model, best practices for safety when working with networks, and the seven-step troubleshooting model.

Module 2, "Infrastructure and Documentation," begins with a tour through a campus network's data rooms, from the ISP's entry point through to the users' endpoints. The module introduces best practices for managing network and cabling equipment and explains issues related to managing the environment in which networking equipment operates. This module also describes characteristics of documentation and explains how to create a network diagram that can be used in troubleshooting. It ends with a discussion on how to create and follow appropriate change management procedures in an enterprise network environment.

Module 3, "Addressing," describes addressing standards used by devices on a network at various layers of the OSI model, including MAC addresses at the data link layer, IP addresses at the network layer, and ports and sockets at the transport layer. It also explains how host names and domain names work. The module concludes with an introduction to commands used in troubleshooting networks.

Module 4, "Protocols," describes the functions of the core TCP/IP protocols, including TCP, UDP, IP, and others. It compares common encryption protocols, such as IPsec and SSL, and then explores common remote access protocols, such as SSH, RDP, and VPNs. The module finishes with a discussion of TCP/IP utilities used for network discovery and troubleshooting.

Module 5, "Cabling," discusses basic data transmission concepts, including throughput, bandwidth, multiplexing, and common transmission flaws. Next, it describes copper cables, fiber-optic cables, and Ethernet standards, comparing the benefits and limitations of different networking media. The module then concludes with an examination of common cable problems and the tools used for troubleshooting those problems.

Module 6, "Wireless Networking," examines how nodes exchange wireless signals and identifies potential obstacles to successful wireless transmission. The module explores wireless technologies that support the IoT (Internet of Things). It then describes WLAN (wireless LAN) architecture and specifies the characteristics of popular WLAN transmission methods. In this module, you will also learn how to install and configure wireless access points and clients, manage wireless security concerns, and evaluate common problems experienced with wireless networks.

Module 7, "Network Architecture," takes a journey through the progression of abstraction in network architecture. It begins with a description of switch management and a comparison of three-tiered and two-tiered (spine-and-leaf) switch architectures. After some discussion of SDN (software-defined networking) and SAN (storage area network) technologies, the module presents common virtual network connection types and the concept of NFV (Network Functions Virtualization). It then identifies features and benefits of cloud architecture, connectivity, and automation. The module concludes with a discussion of key network availability concepts.

Module 8, "Segmentation," explores the advantages and methods of network segmentation. The module examines the purposes of subnets and their calculations. It then describes techniques for segmenting with VLANs and explains related, advanced features of switches, including VLAN management.

Module 9, "Wide Area Networking," expands your knowledge beyond the LAN with a discussion of WAN (wide area network) concepts and technologies. The module explores how routers work and how various internal and external gateway protocols select and manage routes between networks. The module follows the progression of a fictional company to compare WAN connectivity options, including DSL, cable broadband, leased lines, MPLS (Multiprotocol Label Switching), cloud connectivity options, and SD-WAN (software-defined WAN) so you'll understand how each technology works and what makes each one unique. It then explores common wireless WAN technologies. The module concludes with a discussion of common Internet connectivity issues and interface configuration problems.

Module 10, "Risk Management," covers common security risks and vulnerabilities on a network, including risks associated with people, technology, and malware infections. Here you'll also learn how to assess a network's weaknesses, how to apply appropriate physical security measures, and how to harden devices on the network. Finally, this module teaches you about the kinds of information you should include in security policies for users.

Module 11, "Security in Network Design," examines methods for hardening router and switch configurations, followed by an exploration of common security devices specifically designed to protect a network. The module breaks down AAA (authentication, authorization, and accounting) processes that control users' access to network resources and looks closely at the partnership between authentication and directory services.

Module 12, "Performance and Recovery," presents basic network management concepts and describes how to utilize system and event logs to collect network data. It then explores methods of using this information to evaluate, monitor, manage, and optimize network performance. The module closes with a discussion of threats to network availability and components of a reliable disaster recovery plan and a defensible incident response plan.

The four appendices at the end of this course serve as references for the networking professional:

Appendix A, "CompTIA Network+ N10-008 Certification Exam Objectives," provides a complete list of the latest CompTIA Network+ certification exam objectives, including the percentage of the exam's content that each domain represents and which modules and sections in the text cover material associated with each objective.

Appendix B, "Visual Guide to Connectors," provides a visual connector reference chart for quick identification of connectors and receptacles used in contemporary networking.

Appendix C, "CompTIA Network+ Practice Exam," offers a practice exam containing 100 questions similar in content and presentation to the multiple-choice questions you will find on CompTIA's Network+ examination.

Appendix D, "Project and Discussion Rubrics," gives instructors and students a set of standards for assessing student understanding of and engagement with each module's discussion assignments and project activities.

FEATURES

To aid you in fully understanding networking concepts, this course includes many features designed to enhance your learning experience.

- **On the Job stories**—Each module begins with a real-world story giving context for the technology and concepts presented, providing insight into a variety of modern computing environments from the various perspectives of different professionals in the IT industry.
- **Module Objectives**—Each module lists the learning objectives to be mastered within that module. This list serves as a quick reference to the module's contents and a useful study aid.
- **Applying Concepts activities**—Embedded throughout each module, these "just-in-time" activities help you solidify your understanding of concepts as you read, providing immediate practice of relevant skills with step-by-step instructions.
- **Colorful illustrations, photos, tables, and bullet lists**—Numerous full-color illustrations and photos of network media, protocol behavior, hardware, topology, software screens, peripherals, and components help you visualize common network elements, theories, and concepts. Insightful diagrams provide details and comparisons of both practical and theoretical information. The many tables and bulleted lists make essential information easily accessible for quick reference, presenting condensed information in easy-to-digest chunks.
- **OSI layer icons**—These icons provide visual reinforcement of the link between concepts and the relevant layers of the OSI model. A thorough understanding of where concepts sit on the OSI model makes managing and troubleshooting networks more effective and efficient.
- **CompTIA Network+ Exam Tips and Notes**—Each module's content is supplemented with Note features that provide additional insight and understanding, while CompTIA Network+ Exam Tips guide you in your preparations for taking the CompTIA Network+ certification exam.
- **Legacy Networking features**—Older technology covered by the CompTIA Network+ exam provides historical reference to current technology.
- **Key Terms and Glossary**—Highlighted key terms emphasize the core concepts of networking and are defined in the convenient Glossary.
- **Module Summaries**—Each module's text is followed by a summary of the concepts introduced in that module. These summaries help you revisit the ideas covered in each module.
- **Review Questions**—The end-of-module assessment begins with a set of review questions that reinforce the ideas introduced in each module. Many questions are situational. Rather than simply asking you to repeat what you learned, these questions help you evaluate and apply the material you learned. Answering these questions will help ensure that you have mastered the important concepts and provide valuable practice for taking CompTIA's Network+ exam.
- **Hands-On Projects**—Although it is important to understand the theory behind networking technology, nothing beats real-world experience. To this end, each module provides several Hands-On Projects aimed at providing you with practical software and hardware implementation experience as well as practice in applying critical thinking skills to the concepts learned throughout the module. Requiring only a Windows 10 computer and a typical home network, the projects rely on cloud, virtualization, and simulation technologies to ensure accessibility in a wide variety of learning environments.
- **Capstone Projects**—Each module concludes with two or three in-depth projects where you implement the skills and knowledge gained in the module through real design and implementation scenarios in a variety of networking environments. With the help of sophisticated virtualization and emulation products available

free online, the Capstone Projects introduce you to a multitude of real-world software, hardware, and other solutions that increase your familiarity with these products in preparation for addressing workforce challenges.

- **Support for building good habits**—Supplemental steps in many projects guide you in creating a customized wiki to document information learned and projects completed. A project in the final module gives tips for organizing this wiki as a way to display your new skills for job interviews.
- **User-friendly organization**—Logical arrangement of content consolidates similar concepts for efficient coverage, allowing for deeper investigation of particularly rich concepts and skills that are emphasized in the latest CompTIA Network+ N10-008 exam, including a strong emphasis on security, troubleshooting, and virtualization, with added coverage of cloud, wireless, and switch technologies.

New to this Edition

Just as networking technology continues to evolve, so does learning science and the insights available to course designers. In the interest of providing you with the most effective and durable learning experience, this latest edition is packed with improvements and enriched features.

- **Fully updated**—Content maps completely to CompTIA's Network+ N10-008 exam for productive exam preparation.
- **"Remember this . . ." feature**—Section-specific learning objectives blend the Network+ exam objectives with the material covered in each section to help you focus on the most important points of that section.
- **Self-check questions**—Periodic multiple choice questions sprinkled throughout the readings help you mentally complete the "learning cycle" as you practice recalling the information as you learn it. With answers and thorough explanations at the end of each module, you can check your own learning and assess your progress toward mastering each module's objectives.
- **Project prompts**—"You're ready" boxes in the module indicate at which point you've learned all required concepts to competently complete each project at the end of the module. By embedding this information in your learning path, you can choose to interleave hands-on activities with your reading or continue with your reading and leave the projects for later.
- **Flexible learning environment**—New and updated skills-based projects encourage hands-on exploration of module concepts. These projects include thought-provoking questions that encourage critical thinking and in-depth evaluation of the material. The software tools used in the projects are included in Windows or freely available online, and hardware requirements are kept to a minimum, making these projects accessible to more students in a wide variety of learning environments.
- **Group activities**—Some projects in each module offer optional group work activities to enhance the exploration of various concepts and skills.
- **Cloud, virtualization, and emulation technologies**—Projects at the end of each module challenge you to explore concepts and apply skills with real-world tools. Many projects employ Cisco's network simulator, Packet Tracer, so you can practice setting up a network from start to finish, including device configuration, subnetting, and extensive use of the command line. Other projects guide you in configuring virtual networks so you can experience more complex networking concepts within a single, physical computer. Some new projects also take you into AWS so you can "get your hands dirty in the cloud" and discover why IT as an industry is becoming cloud-centric.

Text and Graphic Conventions

Wherever appropriate, additional information and exercises have been added to this text to help you better understand the topic at hand. The following labels and icons are used throughout the text to alert you to additional materials:

OSI model icons highlight the specific layer(s) of the OSI model being discussed, and they indicate when the layers of interest change throughout the module.

NOTE

Prolific notes draw your attention to helpful material related to the subject being described and offer expanded insights to enrich your understanding.

 The CompTIA Network+ Exam Tip icon provides helpful pointers when studying for the exam.

Legacy Networking

Studying older technologies can help you better understand the ways current technologies developed and what additional challenges future technologies need to overcome. By setting this information apart, you can identify which standards have become obsolete but still offer rich and insightful context for understanding networking and for preparing to take the Network+ exam.

Applying Concepts

Embedded Applying Concepts activities give you "just-in-time" practice with skills and concepts as you read about them.

REMEMBER THIS . . .

The Remember this . . . feature highlights important points from each section as you finish reading that material. This invitation to pause and reflect helps you track your learning and ensure you're absorbing the most relevant concepts as you go.

SELF-CHECK

To complete the learning cycle, these self-check questions help you practice recalling the information you've read. With answers and extensive explanations provided to readers at the end of each module, this low-stakes practice testing helps you assess how well you're learning and what material you might need to review before completing graded work.

You're Ready

These action pointers indicate when you've studied the concepts needed for each Hands-on Project at the end of the module. At each point, you can choose whether to take a break from reading to apply the concepts you've learned, or you can keep reading. These forks in the learning path encourage you to actively engage in choosing how you learn best.

Hands-On Projects

Each Hands-On Project in this course is preceded by the estimated time to complete the project, the relevant exam objective, the required resources, and a description of the project. Hands-On Projects help you understand the theory behind networking with activities using the latest network software and hardware.

Capstone Projects

Capstone Projects give you the opportunity to apply concepts in a more in-depth way than what the Hands-On Projects offer. By building on each other, these Capstones weave concepts from module to module, allowing you to make creative connections and see the big picture. They challenge you to demonstrate a solid understanding and application of skills required for the CompTIA Network+ exam and a career in networking.

✓ CERTIFICATION

Each main section of a module begins with a list of all relevant CompTIA Network+ objectives covered in that section. This unique feature highlights the important information at a glance and helps you better anticipate how deeply you need to understand the concepts covered.

INSTRUCTOR MATERIALS

Everything you need for your course is in one place. This collection of book-specific lecture and class tools is available online. Please visit **login.cengage.com** and log in to access instructor-specific resources on the Instructor Companion Site, which includes the Guide to Teaching Online; Instructor Manual; Solutions to the textbook and MindTap, and live virtual machine labs; Test Bank files; PowerPoint Presentations; Syllabus; and Student Downloads.

- **Guide to Teaching Online**—The Guide to Teaching Online includes two main parts. Part 1 offers general technological and pedagogical considerations and resources, and Part 2 provides discipline-specific suggestions for teaching when you can't be in the same room with students.
- **Electronic Instructor Manual**—The Instructor Manual that accompanies this textbook includes the following items: additional instructional material to assist in class preparation—including suggestions for lecture topics, additional projects, and class discussion topics.
- **Solutions Manuals**—The instructor resources include two solutions guides:
  - The Solution and Answer Guide includes solutions to all of the module activities found in the book, including Applying Concepts, Review Questions, Hands-On Projects, and Capstone Projects. It also provides the MindTap solutions, including grading rubrics for the Networking for Life and Reflection Discussion activities, plus answers to the lab manual review questions.
  - The Live Virtual Machine Labs Solution and Answer Guide includes examples of correct screenshots and answers to the inline questions found within the labs.
- **Test Banks with Cengage Testing Powered by Cognero**—This flexible, online system allows you to do the following:
  - Author, edit, and manage test bank content from multiple Cengage solutions.
  - Create multiple test versions in an instant.
  - Deliver tests from your LMS, your classroom, or wherever you want.

- **PowerPoint Presentations**—This course comes with a set of Microsoft PowerPoint slides for each module. These slides are meant to be used as a teaching aid for classroom presentations, to be made available to students on the network for module review, or to be printed for classroom distribution. Instructors are also at liberty to add their own slides for other topics introduced.
- **Syllabus**—The sample syllabus provides an example of a template for setting up a 14-week course.
- **Student Downloads**—The student downloads include Accessible Launch Text for MindTap Lab Simulations and Accessible Launch Text for MindTap Live Virtual Machine Labs.
- **Packet Tracer Files**—A Packet Tracer solution file is provided for each Packet Tracer project through the Instructors site. Some Packet Tracer projects build on earlier Packet Tracer networks. If needed for one or more students, you can provide a previous project's solution file as a start file for one of these progression projects.

TOTAL SOLUTIONS FOR NETWORKING

To access additional course materials, please visit *www.cengage.com*. At the *www.cengage.com* home page, search for the ISBN of your title (from the back cover of your book) using the search box at the top of the page. This will take you to the product page where these resources can be found.

MINDTAP

MindTap for Network+ Guide to Networks, Ninth Edition, is a personalized, fully online digital learning platform of content, assignments, and services that engages students and encourages them to think critically while allowing you to easily set your course through simple customization options.

MindTap is designed to help students master the skills they need in today's workforce. Research shows employers need critical thinkers, troubleshooters, and creative problem solvers to stay relevant in our fast-paced, technology-driven world. MindTap helps you achieve this with assignments and activities that provide hands-on practice, real-life relevance, and certification test prep. Students are guided through assignments that help them master basic knowledge and understanding before moving on to more challenging problems.

All MindTap activities and assignments are tied to defined learning objectives. Readings support course objectives, while Networking for Life activities encourage learners to read articles, listen to podcasts, or watch videos to stay current with what is happening in the field of IT and networking. You can use these activities to help build student interest in the field of computer networking as well as lifelong learning habits.

Reflection activities encourage self-reflection and open sharing among students to help improve their retention and understanding of the material. Videos help explain and illustrate difficult information technology concepts.

Lab simulations provide students with an opportunity for hands-on experience and problem-solving practice with automatic feedback. The live virtual machine labs provide hands-on practice and give students an opportunity to troubleshoot, explore, and try different real-life solutions in a secure, private sandbox environment.

Practice Test questions in the ATP app allow students to quiz themselves on specific exam domains, and the pre- and post-course assessments measure exactly how much they have learned. CNOW quizzes provide test questions in the style of the Network+ certification exam and help you measure how well learners mastered the material after completing each MindTap module.

MindTap is designed around learning objectives and provides the analytics and reporting to easily see where the class stands in terms of progress, engagement, and completion rates.

Students can access eBook content in the MindTap Reader—which offers highlighting, note taking, search, and audio, as well as mobile access. Learn more at www.cengage.com/mindtap/.

Instant Access Code: (ISBN: 9780357508190)
Printed Access Code: (ISBN: 9780357508206)

Lab Manual

Hands-on learning is necessary to master the networking skills needed for both CompTIA's Network+ Exam and for a career in computer networking. Network+ Guide to Networks Lab Manual, 9th Edition, is included in the MindTap course and contains hands-on exercises that use fundamental computer networking concepts as they are applied in the real world. The labs give students extra practice with challenging concepts (such as subnetting) and expanded experiences with physical, virtual, simulation, and cloud technology (such as VMs, Packet Tracer, and AWS). Each module offers review questions to reinforce mastery of networking topics and to sharpen critical thinking and problem-solving skills.

STATE OF THE INFORMATION TECHNOLOGY (IT) FIELD

Organizations depend on computers and information technology to thrive and grow. Globalization, or connecting with customers and suppliers around the world, is a direct result of the widespread use of the Internet. Rapidly changing technology further affects how companies do business and keeps the demand for skilled and certified IT workers strong across industries. Every sector of the economy requires IT professionals who can establish, maintain, troubleshoot, and extend their business systems.

The latest *Occupational Outlook Handbook* from the Bureau of Labor Statistics (part of the U.S. Department of Labor) reports there were more than 370,000 network and computer systems administrator positions in 2019, the most recent year for which this information is available, with a predicted increase of 4 percent between 2019 and 2029. Median pay for jobs in this sector is over $83,000 annually. A somewhat more advanced job role in the same vein is computer network architect with over 160,000 jobs in 2019, a growth rate of about 5 percent, and a median income of over $112,000 annually. This median pay is the highest of all computer and IT occupations tracked by this site that only require a bachelor's degree, even more than people working as information security analysts. You can find more information about these and related job roles at *bls.gov/ooh*. Overall, people employed in computer and IT occupations make a median wage over $88,000 annually with projected growth of more than 530,000 jobs by 2029.

In any industry, a skilled workforce is important for continually driving business. Finding highly skilled IT workers can be a struggle for employers, given that technologies continue to change quickly. With such a short product life cycle, IT workers must strive to keep up with these changes and continually bring value to their employers.

Certifications

Different levels of education are required for the many jobs in the IT industry. While the level of education and type of training required varies from employer to employer, the need for qualified technicians remains a constant. As the industry continues to evolve, many employers prefer candidates who already have the skills to implement these new technologies. Companies are relying increasingly on technical certifications to adequately identify the quality and skill qualifications of a job applicant, and these certifications can offer job seekers a competitive edge over other applicants.

Certifications fall into one of two categories:

- Vendor-neutral certifications are those that test for the skills and knowledge required in industry job roles and do not subscribe to a vendor's specific technology solutions. Some examples of vendor-neutral certifications include all the CompTIA certifications *(comptia.org)*, Project Management Institute's certifications *(pmi.org)*, and ISACA's certifications *(isaca.org)*.
- Vendor-specific certifications validate the skills and knowledge necessary to be successful while utilizing a specific vendor's technology solution. Some examples of vendor-specific certifications include those offered by Microsoft *(microsoft.com)*, AWS *(aws.amazon.com)*, Red Hat *(redhat.com)*, Oracle *(education.oracle.com)*, and Cisco *(learningnetwork.cisco.com)*.

As employers struggle to fill open IT positions with qualified candidates, certifications are a means of validating the skill sets necessary to be successful within organizations. In most careers, salary and compensation are determined by experience and education, but in the IT field, the number and type of certifications an employee earns also determine salary and wage increases. For example, according to CompTIA, the U.S. Department of Defense and companies such as Apple, Verizon, Dell, HP, and Intel recommend or require their networking technicians attain CompTIA Network+ certification. Global Knowledge reports that certified IT staff earn, on average, 8 percent more than non-certified IT staff. In fact, according to the same report, being certified and adding new certifications is a lifestyle for a majority of IT professionals. Eighty-seven percent of all respondents already hold one certification, nearly 40 percent said they earned their most recent certification in the previous six months, and those with six or more certifications make, on average, $13,000 more than someone with only one certification.

Certification provides job applicants with more than just a competitive edge over their noncertified counterparts competing for the same IT positions. Some institutions of higher education grant college credit to students who successfully pass certification exams, moving them further along in their degree programs. Certification also gives individuals who are interested in careers in the military the ability to move into higher positions more quickly.

Career Planning

Finding a career that fits your personality, skill set, and lifestyle is challenging and fulfilling, but can often be difficult. What are the steps you should take to find that dream career? Is IT interesting to you? Chances are, if you are reading this course, this question has already been answered. What is it about IT that you like? The world of work options in the IT industry is vast. Some questions to ask yourself: Are you a person who likes to work alone, or do you like to work in a group? Do you like speaking directly with customers, or do you prefer to stay behind the scenes? Does your lifestyle encourage a lot of travel, or do you prefer to stay in one location? All these factors influence your job decisions, and all these preferences can find a purpose in IT. Inventory assessments are a good first step to learning more about yourself, your interests, work values, and abilities. A variety of websites can offer assistance with career planning and assessments.

WHAT'S NEW WITH COMPTIA NETWORK+ CERTIFICATION

With its N10-008 Network+ exam, CompTIA has emphasized foundational network concepts and the latest network technologies that can serve as a launching pad for a career in networking, security, cloud, or other specialties. There's a stronger emphasis on security, virtualization, network architecture, and troubleshooting than in past versions of the exam. Some objectives have been added, updated, or expanded, such as coverage of SDN (software-defined networking), SD-WAN (software-defined wide area network), network interface configuration, database protocols, and risk management. Some older technologies have been dropped from the objectives.

As with the previous Network+ exam, the N10-008 version includes many scenario-based questions. Mastering, rather than simply memorizing, the material in this course will help you succeed on the exam and on the job.

Here are the domains covered on the new CompTIA Network+ exam:

Domain	% of Examination
Domain 1.0 Networking Fundamentals	24%
Domain 2.0 Network Implementations	19%
Domain 3.0 Network Operations	16%
Domain 4.0 Network Security	19%
Domain 5.0 Network Troubleshooting	22%

ABOUT THE AUTHOR

Jill West, CIS instructor at Georgia Northwestern Technical College, brings a unique cross-section of experience in business, writing, and education to the development of innovative educational materials. She has taught kindergarten through college using a flipped classroom approach, distance learning, hybrid teaching, and educational counseling. Ms. West has been instrumental in designing and authoring critical-thinking simulations for several of Cengage's computer courses. She regularly presents at regional and national conferences and international webinars on CompTIA certifications for students and train-the-trainer sessions for instructors. She's also a member of the 2019 inaugural cohort of Faculty Ambassadors for AWS Educate and has authored or co-authored several texts, including *Network+ Guide to Networks*, *Cloud+ Guide to Cloud Computing*, *A+ Guide to IT Technical Support*, and *Technology for Success*. Ms. West and her husband, Mike, live in northwest Georgia with three children at home and one off to college.

ACKNOWLEDGMENTS

I never imagined I would develop such beautiful friendships with the people I work with. Some of the folks on this team have been around longer than I have—Ann Shaffer, Developmental Editor, brings an historical perspective to each edition as she tells me stories of earlier contributors and encourages me through late nights and intense deadlines. Brooke Greenhouse, this edition's Senior Content Manager, has worked in some way on this and other projects with me for several editions and runs a tight ship with a friendly laugh that always sets me at ease.

Some folks are newer to this product and also bring their personal, high-quality standards. Natalie Onderdonk, Learning Designer, has provided expert insights from a pedagogical perspective on many other projects and now brings her talents to this book—we love to "geek out" over educational psychology and will fill hours chatting together at conferences. I've enjoyed getting to know Danielle Klahr, Associate Product Manager, as she confidently took the reins at the last minute and navigated us through an intense and quick schedule. And as always, I appreciate technical editor Dani Shaw's attention to detail and helpful suggestions for adding relevant details and concepts. Thank you to Mackenzie Paine, Marketing Manager, and to your entire team for your enthusiastic support in helping instructors and students connect with this resource. And a special thanks to contributors of this edition's new *On the Job* stories as well as other team members who are too numerous to name—it truly takes a community to produce a high-quality course such as this one.

Many more people contributed time, expertise, and advice during this revision. Every contribution has made this course better than it would have been without your help. Thank you to Jeffery Johnson, Georgia Northwestern Technical College, for the enlightening tour and computer geek chit-chat. Thank you to Robert Wilson, McCallie School, for the continued tours, stories, and insights. And thanks to all the amazing instructors who have attended our CompTIA Network+ training sessions and shared their thoughts, creativity, ideas, and concerns. Thank you to each of the reviewers who, driven by your dedication to high-quality education for your students, contributed a great deal of expertise, constantly challenging me to higher levels of insight, accuracy, and clarity. Specifically, thank you to:

Nicholas Pierce, Thomas Nelson Community College

Rebecca Zeng, DeVry University

Brent Ferns, Palm Beach State College

My gratitude would be incomplete without a deeply heartfelt thanks to my husband, Mike, for carrying the family responsibilities while I work long, late hours. This is your accomplishment, too. And thank you to my kids—Winn, Sarah, Daniel, and Zack—for your encouragement and patience with me. I love you more than words can express.

To the instructors and learners who use this course, I invite and encourage you to send suggestions or corrections for future editions. Please write to me at *jillwestauthor@gmail.com*. I never ignore a good idea! And to instructors, if you have ideas that help make a class in CompTIA Network+ preparation a success, please email to share your ideas with other instructors.

DEDICATION

This book is dedicated to every reader working to improve their skills, knowledge, and expertise. What you're doing is amazing, and I'm honored to play a part in your journey.

—Jill West

READ THIS BEFORE YOU BEGIN

The Applying Concepts activities, Hands-On Projects, and Capstone Projects in this course help you to apply what you have learned about computer networking. Although some modern networking components can be expensive, the projects aim to use widely available and moderately priced hardware and software. The following section lists the minimum hardware and software requirements that allow you to complete all the projects in this text (not including the Lab Manual labs). In addition to the following requirements, students must have administrator privileges on their workstations and, for some projects, on a second workstation or device (such as a smartphone), to successfully complete the projects.

Hardware Lab Requirements

Ninety-two percent of all projects can be completed with only a Windows 10 computer with administrative privileges to install software, a smartphone, and a home network with permission from the network owner to perform scanning operations. Most of the other projects require a Bluetooth device (one project), a second computer (part of one project), and cabling supplies (three projects). Detailed hardware requirements include the following:

- Each student needs a computer with at least 8 GB of RAM (preferably 12 GB), a recent Intel or AMD processor, and a minimum of 150 GB of free space on the hard disk to support all the VM projects. Many projects require workstations to have a wired connection to a network, and other projects need a wireless connection.
- Some projects require the use of a second computer to create a network connection between computers—all but one of these projects can be successfully completed between a physical host computer and one or more VMs installed on that host from earlier projects. For part of one project, a second physical computer is required, and this system can be an older device, such as Windows 7, or a different OS, such as macOS.
- For projects with physical transmission media, students require a basic networking toolkit that includes the following cable-making supplies: 1–2 feet of Cat 5 or better cabling, at least five RJ-45 plugs, an RJ-45 data/ phone jack, a wire cutter or snips, a wire stripper, a crimper, and a punchdown tool.
- For projects with wireless transmission, each class (or each group in the class) should have a wireless SOHO router capable of 802.11n or better transmission, compatible wireless NICs in the student workstations, and a patch cable. For students learning at home, a typical home network is sufficient for this requirement providing the student has administrative access to the SOHO router and, if they don't own the network, written permission from the network owner to conduct scans and penetration testing.
- Some projects require each student to have a smartphone (Android or iPhone). Students can do these projects in pairs for those students who don't own a smartphone.
- One project requires a Bluetooth device, such as a Bluetooth speaker, Bluetooth earbuds, or a Bluetooth-enabled car system.
- One project optionally requires a cable modem for the class to examine.
- Many projects require Internet access with a modern browser.

Software Lab Requirements

Most projects are written for workstations running Windows 10. Software requirements include the following:

- Updated Windows 10 Professional (64-bit), Education (64-bit), or Home (64-bit), although Windows 10 Pro is preferred. Many of the projects can be adapted to work on Linux or macOS workstations.
- The latest version of Chrome, Firefox, or Edge web browser.
- A hypervisor—most projects are written for Oracle VirtualBox (any edition of Windows) or Client Hyper-V (Windows 10 Professional/Education only), and they can be adjusted for VMware Workstation Player.
- An installation image for Windows.
- Steps to download installation images for other OSs are given in the projects. These OSs include Ubuntu Desktop, Ubuntu Server, and Kali Linux.
- Some projects use cloud resources in AWS (Amazon Web Services). AWS Educate offers a plethora of helpful and free resources for schools, instructors, and students. At the time of this writing, students can only join AWS Educate when the instructor posts an invitation link in the LMS (learning management system) or when the instructor sends an email invite from an AWS Educate classroom, which provides students with free credits and tools for instructors to help them with their work in AWS. Instructors can allocate free credits to students for every class, and it does not count against their free credits in their own accounts. Creating an instructor's AWS Educate account is easy and free. Creating a classroom in AWS Educate is even easier, and the instructor can allocate free AWS credits for students from the dashboard. For more information, visit **aws.amazon.com/education/awseducate/**. If you have questions or need assistance, contact AWS Educate staff or email the author at *jillwestauthor@gmail.com*.
- Other software that will be downloaded include LastPass, Packet Tracer, Wireshark, ZenMap, Nmap, IP Scanner, PuTTY, TotuSoft's LAN Speed Test, TamoSoft's Throughput Test, iPerf, PRTG Network Monitor, Windows Subsystem for Linux, Advanced Port Scanner, Wi-Fi analyzer app (on smartphone), and THC-IPv6 (in Kali Linux VM).

Cisco's Packet Tracer is now available free to the public. Instructions for downloading and installing Packet Tracer are given in the first Packet Tracer project in Module 2. Abbreviated instructions are repeated here for convenience, as some instructors might want to preview the emulator:

1. Go to **netacad.com/courses/packet-tracer** or search for *packet tracer site:netacad.com* for the latest link. Enter your name, email, and text verification to enroll in the course. Check your email to confirm your email address.
2. Inside the course under *Introductory Chapter*, click **Student Support and Resources**. Scroll down and click **Download and install the latest version of Packet Tracer**. Choose the correct version for your computer. After the download is complete, install Packet Tracer. When the installation is complete, run **Cisco Packet Tracer**. When Packet Tracer asks if you would like to run multi-user, click **No**.
3. When Packet Tracer opens, sign in with your Networking Academy account that you just created. If you see a Windows Security Alert, allow access through your firewall. Cisco Packet Tracer opens.

Note to instructors: A Packet Tracer solution file is provided for each Packet Tracer project through the Instructors site. Some Packet Tracer projects build on earlier Packet Tracer networks. If needed for one or more students, you can provide a previous project's solution file as a start file for one of these progression projects.

INTRODUCTION TO NETWORKING

After reading this module and completing the exercises, you should be able to:

1. Distinguish between peer-to-peer and client-server networks
2. Identify types of applications and protocols used on a network
3. Describe various networking hardware devices and the most common physical topologies
4. Describe the seven layers of the OSI model
5. Explain best practices for safety when working with networks and computers
6. Describe the seven-step troubleshooting model for troubleshooting network problems

On the Job

We were finishing installing computer equipment and setting up network connections in a new building. In the verification phase of the install, I found that one workstation on the second floor had no network connection. All of the other workstations on the floor were connected. I started troubleshooting to figure out why this one workstation had an issue.

Since this was a recent installation, my first thought was that there was no connection at the switch. I checked the patch panel and the network switch number to verify everything was correct. It was.

I then rechecked the physical connections for the PC to make sure the connections were secure. This didn't change anything. Still no connection.

After that, I checked the network settings in the operating system of the PC to make sure these were set correctly. They were correct.

I kept going, checking the VLAN setting on the switch to make sure the port was on. Then I used a known working port on the switch and connected this to the port. Still no network connection.

I was pretty frustrated at this point because one of these troubleshooting steps should have worked. I went back and tried some again. I even tried different cables, thinking that perhaps the cables at the patch panel or from the wall to the PC were bad.

Finally, I tried using a wire toner to trace the wire and make sure the building cabling was not the issue, as is sometimes the case in a new building with an initial install. Sure enough, I could not get a tone on the other end of the cable. None of the cables in that closet received the tone. I thought the cable had been routed to the other wiring closet on the second floor, so I tried the tone generator there. No, that wasn't it. Finally, I tried a downstairs closet and found where the cable had been punched down. I then connected the cable to a switch in the closet, and the PC was able to verify a proper network connection. That was the problem: a wrongly routed cable.

I notified my supervisor who contacted the construction team to see if it could be corrected. In the meantime, I labeled the cable in the patch panel and at the wall so that if/when there were issues again, the cable could be easily identified.

Jeffery Johnson
Technology Support Specialist
Georgia Northwestern Technical College

Loosely defined, a **network** is a group of computers and other devices (such as printers) that are connected by some type of transmission media. Variations on the elements of a network and the way it is designed, however, are nearly infinite. A network can be as small as two computers connected by a cable in a home office or the most complex network of all, the Internet, made up of billions of computers and other devices connected across the world via a combination of cable, phone lines, and wireless links. Networks might link smartphones, personal computers, mainframe computers, printers, corporate phone systems, security cameras, vehicles, and wearable technology devices. They might communicate through copper wires, fiber-optic cable, or radio waves. This module introduces you to the fundamentals of networks and how technicians support them.

NETWORK MODELS

 **CERTIFICATION**

1.2 Explain the characteristics of network topologies and network types.

Average reading time: 15 minutes

A **topology** describes how the parts of a whole work together. When studying networking, you need to understand both the physical topology and the logical topology of a network, as follows:

- **Physical topology**—Mostly refers to a network's hardware and how computers, other devices, and cables or radio signals work together to form the physical network
- **Logical topology**—Mostly refers to how software controls access to network resources (including how users and software initially gain access to the network) and how specific resources such as applications and databases are shared on the network

 EXAM TIP
The CompTIA Network+ exam objectives are developed by industry professionals and cover the concepts and skills they know will be most helpful to you in working with a network. The competency and scope reflect what you would likely learn in about 9–12 months of hands-on experience in a junior network administrator or network support technician job role. These Network+ Exam Tip boxes call your attention to specific concepts known to be commonly tested on the Network+ exam. For example, the Network+ exam expects you to understand the difference between a physical network diagram and a logical network diagram, and the purpose each serves. You might be given a scenario that includes a physical or logical network diagram, and you will need to interpret the information given in that diagram to answer the related question(s). As you read through the text, take a moment to consider the tips given in each of these Network+ Exam Tip boxes to determine whether you understand the material at the level indicated.

Let's begin with a discussion of network models that will help you understand logical topologies and how computers relate to one another in a network. Later in this module, you'll learn about network hardware and physical topologies.

Controlling how users and programs get access to resources on a network is a function of the operating systems used on the network. Each OS (operating system) is configured to use one of two models to connect to network resources: the peer-to-peer model or the client-server model. The peer-to-peer model can be achieved using any assortment of desktop, mobile, or tablet operating systems, but the client-server model requires a **NOS (network operating system)**, which controls access to the entire network. Examples include Windows Server 2019, Ubuntu Server, and Red Hat Enterprise Linux (Ubuntu and Red Hat are versions of Linux).

Applying Concepts 1-1: Explore Network Operating Systems

It's easier to understand what a network operating system is if you've seen one or two in action. For each of the NOSs listed previously (Windows Server 2019, Ubuntu Server, and Red Hat Enterprise Linux), use your favorite search engine to complete the following steps:

1. Search for information about the NOS and write down a short description based on your findings. Include a few features and advantages and identify who develops and publishes each NOS.
2. Search for images of screenshots for the NOS. What are some major elements that you notice on these screens? How are these NOSs managed?
3. Find one or two introductory videos for each NOS and watch the videos. What are some similarities between each NOS? What are some of the differences?

NOTE 1-1

Windows Server 2019, Ubuntu Server, and Red Hat Enterprise Linux are all examples of a specific kind of NOS called a **server operating system**. Other kinds of NOSs exist. For example, network devices such as routers and switches require a NOS that might also be called networking software and are typically managed through a CLI (command-line interface). Examples include IOS (Internetwork OS) on Cisco devices and Junos OS on Juniper devices. You might also refer to other kinds of software, such as a hypervisor that runs virtualized devices or a cloud platform that hosts cloud-based resources, as a type of NOS. You'll learn more about all these platforms throughout this course.

Peer-to-Peer Network Model

In a **P2P (peer-to-peer) network model**, the operating system of each computer on the network is responsible for controlling access to its resources without centralized control. The computers, called nodes or hosts on the network, form a logical group of computers and users that share resources (see Figure 1-1). Each computer on a P2P network controls its own administration, resources, and security.

Examples of operating systems that might be installed on computers in a peer-to-peer network are Windows, Linux, macOS, or Chrome OS on desktop and laptop computers and iOS, Android, or Chrome OS on mobile devices.

NOTE 1-2

When looking at the diagrams in Figure 1-1 and later in Figure 1-2, keep in mind that the connecting lines describe the *logical* arrangement or topology of the group of computers, as opposed to the *physical* arrangement. The physical arrangement in both diagrams may be the same, but the method the OSs use to logically connect the devices differs. The term **physical topology** refers to a network's hardware and how devices and cables fit together. The term **logical topology** refers to the way software controls access to network resources and how those resources are shared on the network.

Devices in a peer-to-peer network can share resources through various techniques of file sharing or user accounts. Most OSs offer options for sharing files with peered devices, even if those devices are running different OSs. If all computers in a peer-to-peer network are running a Windows operating system, resources can be

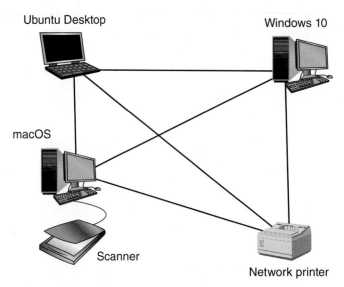

Figure 1-1   In a peer-to-peer network, no computer has more authority than another; each computer controls its own resources and communicates directly with other computers

NOTE 1-3

This course assumes you have mastered the knowledge and skills covered in the CompTIA A+ certification objectives. Using and supporting work-groups and sharing folders and files are part of this content. If you need to learn how folder and file sharing and work-groups are configured and sup-ported, see *CompTIA A+ Guide to IT Technical Support* by Jean Andrews, Joy Dark, and Jill West.

shared using Windows folder and file sharing or a Windows workgroup. In both cases, each computer maintains a list of users and their rights on that computer. Windows allows a user on the network to access local resources based on these assigned rights. You can combine folder and file sharing with workgroups on the same network and even using the same computers. However, it can get confusing to accurately track permissions in this case, so it's best to stick with either folder and file sharing or workgroups.

Generally, if the network supports fewer than about 15 computers, a peer-to-peer network is the way to go. The following are advantages of using peer-to-peer networks:

- They are simple to configure. For this reason, they may be used in environments in which time or technical expertise is scarce.
- They are often less expensive to set up and maintain than other types of networks. A network operating system, such as Windows Server 2019, is much more expensive than a desktop operating system, such as Windows 10.

The following are disadvantages of using traditional peer-to-peer networks:

- They are not **scalable**, which means, as a peer-to-peer network grows larger, adding or changing significant elements of the network may be difficult.
- They are not necessarily secure, meaning that in simple installations, data and other resources shared by network users can be easily discovered and used by unauthorized people.
- They are not practical for connecting more than a few computers because it's too time consuming to manage the resources on the network. For example, suppose you want to set up a file server using P2P file sharing. A **server** is any computer or program that provides a service, such as data or other resources, to other devices. A file server stores files for other computers to access. On this file server, you create a folder named \Shared-Docs and create 20 user accounts, one for each of 20 users who need access to the folder. Then you must set up the workstations with the same user accounts, and the password to each user account on the workstation must match the password for the matching user account on the file server. It can be an organizational night-mare to keep it all straight! If you need to manage that many users and shared resources, it's probably best to implement Windows Server or another NOS.

Client-Server Network Model

In the **client-server network model** (which is sometimes called the client-server architecture or client-server topology), resources are managed by the NOS via a centralized directory database (see Figure 1-2). The database can be managed by one or more servers, so long as they each have a similar NOS installed.

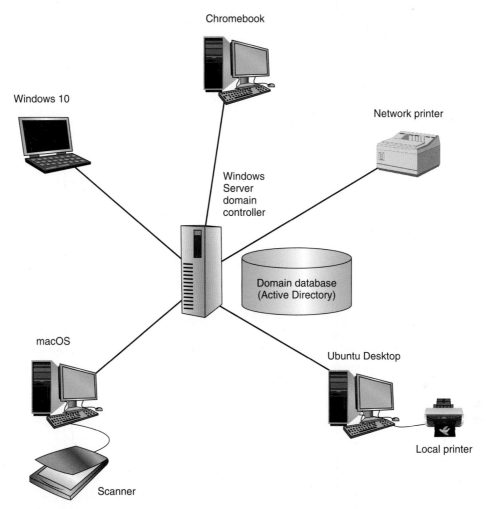

Figure 1-2   A Windows domain uses the client-server model to control access to the network, where security on each computer or device is controlled by a centralized database on a domain controller

When Windows Server controls network access to a group of computers, this logical group is called a Windows **domain**. The centralized directory database that contains user account information and security for the entire group of computers is called **AD (Active Directory)**. Each user on the network has their own domain-level account assigned by the network administrator and kept in Active Directory. This account might be a local account, which is specific to that domain, or a Microsoft account, which links local domain resources with Microsoft cloud resources. A user can sign on to the network from any computer on the network and get access to the resources that Active Directory allows. This process is managed by **AD DS (Active Directory Domain Services)**.

A computer making a request from another is called the **client**. Clients on a client-server network can run applications installed on the desktop and store their own data on local storage devices. Clients don't share their resources directly with each other; instead, access is controlled by entries in the centralized domain database. A client computer accesses resources on another computer by way of the servers controlling this database.

In summary, the NOS (for example, Windows Server 2019, Ubuntu Server, or Red Hat Enterprise Linux) is responsible for the following:

- Managing data and other resources for clients
- Ensuring that only authorized users access the network

- Controlling which types of files a user can open and read
- Restricting when and from where users can access the network
- Dictating which rules computers will use to communicate
- In some situations, supplying applications and data files to clients

Servers that have a NOS installed require more memory, processing power, and storage capacity than clients because servers must handle heavy processing loads and requests from multiple clients. For example, a server might use a RAID (redundant array of independent disks) configuration of hard drives, so that if one hard drive fails, another hard drive automatically takes its place.

Although client-server networks are typically more complex in their design and maintenance than peer-to-peer networks, they offer many advantages over peer-to-peer networks, including the following:

- User accounts and passwords to the network are assigned in one place.
- Access to multiple shared resources (such as data files or printers) can be centrally granted to a single user or groups of users.
- Problems on the network can be monitored, diagnosed, and often fixed from one location.
- Client-server networks are more scalable than peer-to-peer networks. In other words, it's easier to add users and devices to a client-server network.

Now that you have a basic understanding of what a network operating system is and the foundational role it plays, you're ready to look at some of the applications involved in managing the data that travels on a network. These applications allow network devices to establish connections with each other and carry out various tasks.

REMEMBER THIS...

- Compare physical topology with logical topology.
- Describe a client-server network model in contrast with a peer-to-peer network model.
- Explain the role of AD (Active Directory) in a Windows domain.

SELF-CHECK

1. Which of the following is part of a network's physical topology?
   a. A network server's operating system
   b. A printer plugged into a nearby desktop computer
   c. Password for the wireless network
   d. File permission settings on a desktop computer

2. Which of the following is an advantage of P2P file sharing?
   a. Scalable
   b. Centrally controlled
   c. Secure
   d. Inexpensive

3. What group must clients join to access network resources in a client-server network?
   a. Workgroup
   b. Domain
   c. Peer group
   d. RAID

Check your answers at the end of this module.

You're Ready

You're now ready to complete **Project 1-1: IT and Networking Certifications**, or you can wait until you've finished reading this module.

CLIENT-SERVER APPLICATIONS

 **CERTIFICATION**

1.5 Explain common ports and protocols, their application, and encrypted alternatives.

Average reading time: 9 minutes

The resources a network makes available to its users include applications and the data provided by these applications. Collectively, these resources are usually referred to as **network services**. In this section, you'll focus on applications typically found on most networks. These applications involve at least two endpoint devices, such as computers or smartphones, and are known as **client-server applications**. The first computer, a client computer, requests data or a service from the second computer, which is the server. For example, in Figure 1-3, someone uses a web browser to request a web page from a web server. Note that the two computers do not have to reside on the same network—they can communicate across connected networks like the Internet.

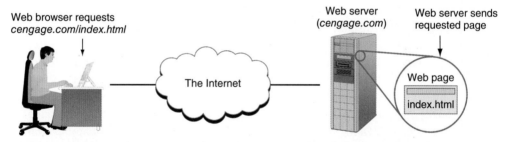

Figure 1-3   A web browser (client application) requests a web page from a web server (server application); the web server returns the requested data to the client

Network Services and Their Protocols

How does the client know how to make the request in a way the server can understand and respond to? These networked devices use methods and rules for communication known as **protocols**. To handle the request for a web page, the client computer must first find the web server. Then, the client and server must agree on the protocols they will use to communicate. Finally, the client makes the request, and the server sends its response in the form of a web page. Hardware, the operating systems, and the applications on both computers are all involved in this process.

The computers on a network communicate with each other via the protocols they have in common. The two primary network protocols are TCP (Transmission Control Protocol) and IP (Internet Protocol), and the suite of all the protocols an OS uses for communication on a network is the **TCP/IP suite** of protocols.

Here's a brief list of several popular client-server applications and their protocols used on networks and the Internet; you'll study many of these protocols more closely in later modules:

- **Web service**—A web server serves up web pages to clients. Many corporations have their own web servers, which are available privately on the corporate network. Other web servers are public, accessible from anywhere on the Internet. The primary protocol used by web servers and browsers (clients) is **HTTP (Hypertext Transfer Protocol)**.

When HTTP is layered on top of an encryption protocol, such as **SSL (Secure Sockets Layer)** or **TLS (Transport Layer Security)**, the result is **HTTPS (HTTP Secure)**, which gives a secure transmission. The most popular web server applications are Apache (see *apache.org*) and Nginx (pronounced *engine-x*, see *nginx.com*), both of which are free and open source and primarily run on Linux systems. **Open source** is the term for software whose code is publicly available for use and modification. Open source applications are often considered more secure because users can evaluate the source code of the software to ensure there are no loopholes left open for attackers to exploit. Note that "open source" is not synonymous with "free," but in this case, Apache and Nginx happen to be both free and open source. Another popular choice is IIS (Internet Information Services), which is embedded in the Windows Server operating system.

NOTE 1-4

To verify that a web-based transmission is secure, look for "https" in the URL in the browser address box, as in *https://www.cengage.com*. Also look for a padlock icon, such as the one shown in Figure 1-4.

Figure 1-4   The lock icon indicates the web page is using HTTPS

- **Email services**—Email is a client-server application that involves two servers. The client uses **SMTP (Simple Mail Transfer Protocol)** to send an email message to the first server, which is sometimes called the SMTP server (see Figure 1-5). The first server sends the message on to the receiver's mail server, where it's stored until the recipient requests delivery. The recipient's mail server delivers the message to the receiving client using one of two protocols: **POP3 (Post Office Protocol, version 3)** or **IMAP4 (Internet Message Access Protocol, version 4)**. Using POP3, email is downloaded to the client computer and typically removed from the server. Using IMAP4, the client application manages the email while it remains stored on the server. Both these protocols are available over SSL or TLS for security. An example of a popular email server application is Microsoft Exchange Server. Outlook, an application in the Microsoft Office suite of applications, is a popular email client application.

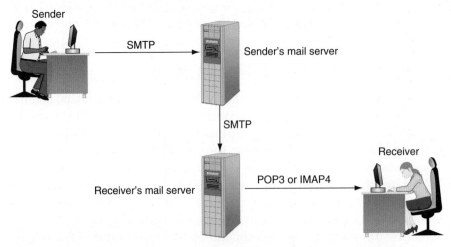

Figure 1-5   SMTP is used to send email to a recipient's email server, and POP3 or IMAP4 is used by the client to receive email

- **DNS service**—DNS (Domain Name System) helps clients find web servers over a network such as the Internet. Often, companies will run their own DNS servers, especially for their employees' computers to find resources within the corporate network. Internet providers also run DNS services for their customers, and many public DNS servers, such as Google's, are available for anyone to use.

- **FTP service**—FTP service is a client-server application that transfers files between two computers, and it primarily uses **FTP (File Transfer Protocol)**. FTP does not provide encryption and is, therefore, not secure. Web browsers can work as FTP clients, although dedicated FTP client applications, such as FileZilla (*filezilla-project.org*) and CuteFTP by Globalscape (*globalscape.com/cuteftp*), offer more features for file transfer than does a browser.

- **Database services**—Not all data is stored in individual files. Databases serve as a container for massive amounts of data that can be organized into tables and records. Users and applications can then access and interact with the data that is stored on a database server. A **DBMS (database management system)** is software installed on the database server. It is responsible for making requested changes to the data and organizing the data for viewing, reporting, or exporting. Many DBMSs use the programming language **SQL (Structured Query Language**, pronounced *S-Q-L* or just *sequel*) to configure and interact with the database's objects and data. Popular examples of SQL database software include **Microsoft SQL Server**, **Oracle Database**, and the open-source **MySQL**.

- **Remote access service**—Some protocols allow an administrator or other user to "remote in," that is, to access a remote computer from the technician's local device to control the computer remotely, as shown in Figure 1-6. The **Telnet** protocol is a command-line application included in many operating systems, but transmissions in Telnet are not encrypted. This has caused Telnet to be largely replaced by other, more secure programs, such as the ssh command in the Linux operating system. The ssh command in Linux uses the **SSH (Secure Shell)** protocol, which creates an encrypted channel or tunnel between two computers and provides security that Telnet lacks. In Windows operating systems, **RDP (Remote Desktop Protocol)** also provides secure, encrypted transmissions. SSH or RDP might be used when a vendor supports software on your corporate network. The vendor's support technician at the vendor's site can connect to a computer on your corporate network and troubleshoot problems with the vendor's installed software. The corporate computer "serves up" its desktop or command line, from which the technician can access any resources on your corporate network. In this situation, the vendor's computer is the client, and the corporate computer is the server or host.

NOTE 1-5

An encrypted and secure file transfer protocol is **SFTP (Secure File Transfer Protocol)**, which is based on the SSH protocol. SSH is discussed below.

NOTE 1-6

Because they can be accessed from outside the local network, remote access servers necessitate strict security measures.

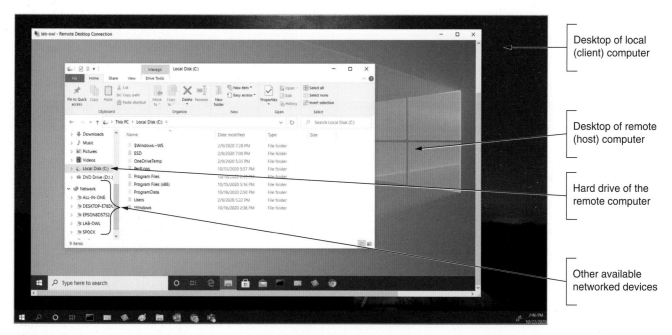

Desktop of local (client) computer

Desktop of remote (host) computer

Hard drive of the remote computer

Other available networked devices

Figure 1-6   Using Remote Desktop, you can access the desktop of the remote computer from your local computer

You can think of applications and their data as the payload traveling on a network and the operating systems as the traffic controllers managing the traffic. The road system itself is the hardware on which the traffic flows. Let's look now at the basics of this networking hardware and the physical topologies they use.

REMEMBER THIS...

- Explain the purposes of various network services.
- Identify important network protocols.
- Notice the key role that encryption protocols play in securing other protocols.
- Distinguish between the functions of various email protocols.
- Identify common DBMSs.

SELF-CHECK

4. Which of the following is a secure protocol?
   a. FTP
   b. HTTP
   c. Telnet
   d. SSH

5. What is an example of an open source DBMS?
   a. MySQL
   b. Microsoft SQL Server
   c. TCP/IP suite
   d. Oracle Database

6. Which of these protocols could *not* be used to access a server in a nearby building?
   a. Telnet
   b. RDP
   c. TLS
   d. SSH

Check your answers at the end of this module.

NETWORK HARDWARE

✓ CERTIFICATION

1.2 Explain the characteristics of network topologies and network types.

2.1 Compare and contrast various devices, their features, and their appropriate placement on the network.

Average reading time: 13 minutes

Technically, two computers connected by an ad hoc Wi-Fi connection are a network. But let's start this discussion of networking hardware with the slightly more complex network shown in Figure 1-7. Keep in mind that every node on a network needs a network address so that other nodes can find it.

NOTE 1-7

Notice the two printers in Figure 1-7. A network printer has a network port and connects directly to the switch. A local printer connects to a computer on the network.

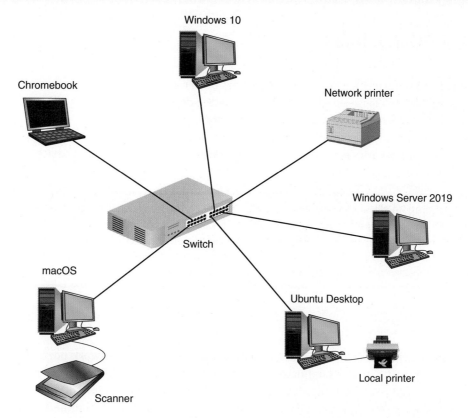

Figure 1-7   This LAN has five computers, a network printer, a local printer, a scanner, and a switch, and uses a star topology

LANs and Their Hardware

The network in Figure 1-7 is a **LAN (local area network)** because each node on the network can communicate directly with others on the network. LANs are usually contained in a small space, such as an office or building. The five computers and the network printer all connect to the switch by way of wired connections. A **switch** (see Figure 1-8) receives

Source: Juniper Networks, Inc.

Vtls/Shutterstock.com

*Mischa Gossen/
Shutterstock.com*

Figure 1-8   Industrial-grade and consumer-grade switches

incoming data from one of its ports and redirects (or switches) it to another port or multiple ports that will send the data to its intended destination(s) within the local network. The physical topology used by this network is called a **star topology** because all devices connect to one central device, the switch. Compare this to the physical topology of the network shown earlier in Figure 1-1 where each device connects to multiple other devices, which is called a **mesh topology**.

Legacy Networking: Hubs

A **hub** is an inefficient and outdated networking device that has been replaced by switches. A hub accepted signals from a transmitting device and repeated those signals to all other connected devices in a broadcast fashion. On Ethernet networks, hubs once served as the central connection point for a star topology.

On today's Ethernet networks, switches have now replaced hubs. Traffic is greatly reduced with switches because, when a switch receives a transmission from a device, the switch sends it only to the destination device or devices rather than broadcasting to all devices connected to the switch.

 EXAM TIP The CompTIA Network+ exam objectives include some older, legacy technologies because, in the real world, not all networks are fully updated. As a network technician, you should be prepared to manage both older and newer technology. And on the exam, you should be ready to identify the benefits offered by newer technology. Studying the historical progression of some technologies can help you better understand modern technology, its benefits, and its limitations.

Computers, network printers, switches, and other network devices have network ports into which you plug a network cable. A network port can be an onboard network port embedded in the computer's motherboard, such as the port on the laptop in Figure 1-9. Another type of port is provided by a modular **NIC (network interface card)**, also called a network adapter (see Figure 1-10), installed in an expansion slot on the motherboard. In reality, whether embedded on a motherboard or attached to an expansion slot, both ports are typically called NICs.

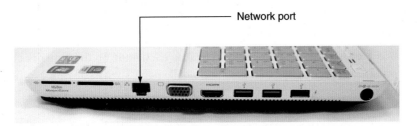

Network port

Figure 1-9   A laptop provides an onboard network port to connect to a wired network

A LAN can have several switches. For example, the network in Figure 1-11 has three switches daisy-chained together. The two thick, yellow lines in the figure connecting the three switches represent the backbone of this network. A **backbone** is a central conduit that connects the segments (pieces) of a network and is sometimes referred to as "a network of networks." The backbone might use higher transmission speeds and different cabling than network cables connected to computers because of the heavier traffic and the longer distances it might span.

Because the three switches are daisy-chained together in a single line, the network is said to use a **bus topology**. However, each switch is connected to its computers via a star topology. Therefore, the topology of the network in Figure 1-11 combines topologies and is called a **hybrid topology**.

Alternatively, a central switch could connect to multiple peripheral switches that each connect to computers in their areas. The network in Figure 1-12 uses a star topology for the switches and also for the computers connected to each switch. In this case, the central switch is referred to as the hub and each peripheral switch is a spoke. Together, this network illustrates an example of a **hub-and-spoke topology**.

Figure 1-10   This Intel Gigabit Ethernet adapter, also called a network interface card or NIC, uses a PCIe x1 slot on a motherboard

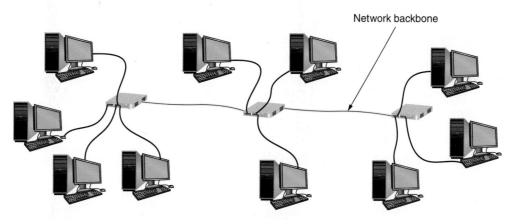

Figure 1-11   This local network has three switches and is using a hybrid topology

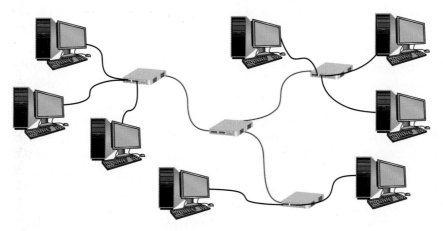

Figure 1-12   Switches connected in a hub-and-spoke topology

Legacy Networking: Ring Topology

In addition to the star, mesh, bus, and hybrid topologies, the CompTIA Network+ exam expects you to know about the ring topology, which is seldom used today. In a **ring topology**, nodes are connected in a ring, with one node connecting only to its two neighboring nodes (see Figure 1-13). A node can put data on the ring only when it holds a token, which is a small group of bits passed around the ring. This is similar to saying "I hold the token, so I get to talk now." The ring topology is rarely used today, primarily because of its slow speed and its vulnerability to failure. If one node fails, the entire ring fails.

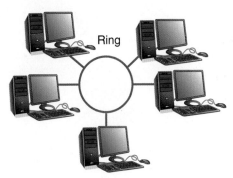

Figure 1-13 Using a ring topology, a computer connects to the two computers adjacent to it in the ring

A LAN needs a way to communicate with other networks, and that's the purpose of a router. A **router** is a device that manages traffic between two or more networks and can help find the best path for traffic to get from one network to another. In **SOHO (small office-home office) networks**, which typically have fewer than 10 computers, a consumer-grade router is used to connect the LAN to the Internet (see Figure 1-14a).

NOTE 1-8

A home network might use a combination device, which is both a router and a switch, and perhaps a wireless access point that creates a Wi-Fi hotspot. For example, the device might provide three network ports and a Wi-Fi hotspot that are part of the local network and one network port to connect to the network belonging to the **ISP (Internet service provider)** and on to the Internet. In this situation (see Figure 1-14b), the three ports for the local network are provided by a switch embedded in the device. The home router belongs to the home's network on one side and the ISP's network on the other. Don't confuse this combo device with a dedicated router device in which each port connects to a different LAN. The key difference here is that a switch belongs to a single LAN, while a router belongs to multiple LANs.

An enterprise or industrial-grade router can have several network ports, one for each of the networks it connects to. In that case, the router belongs to each of these networks. For example, in Figure 1-15, the router connects three LANs and has a network address that belongs to Network A, another network address that belongs to Network B, and a third network address for Network C.

The fundamental difference between a switch and a router is that a switch belongs only to its local network and a router belongs to two or more networks—the router acts as a gateway between multiple networks, but a switch (even if there are multiple switches) can only communicate within a single network. Recall that nodes on a local network communicate directly with one another. However, a node on one LAN cannot communicate with a node on another LAN without a router to manage that communication and to stand as a gateway between the networks. In fact, routers are often referred to as "gateway devices" or just "gateways."

Now that you understand the basic functions of switches and routers, you're ready to make the distinction between the two terms *host* and *node*. A **host** is any endpoint device, such as a computer or printer, connected to a network

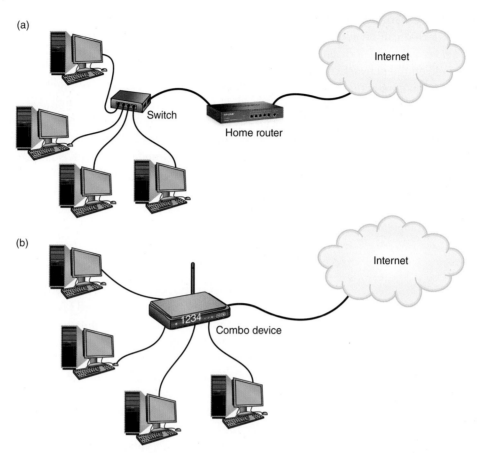

Figure 1-14   (a) A router stands between the LAN and the Internet, connecting the two networks; (b) Home networks often use a combo device that works as both a switch and a router

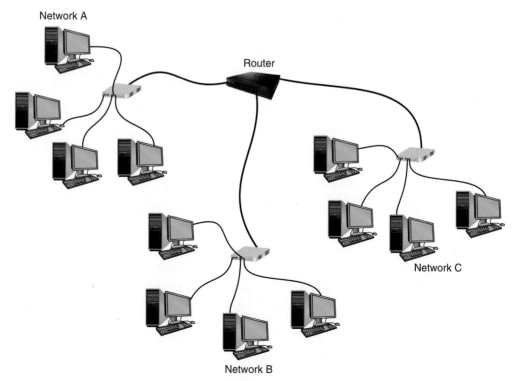

Figure 1-15   Three LANs connected by a router

that hosts or accesses a resource such as an application or data. A **node** is any device, such as a router or switch, connected to a network that can be addressed on the local network or managed through a network connection. A client computer or server is both a node and a host, but a router or switch does not normally host resources and is, therefore, merely a node on the network through which network traffic passes.

A significant distinction here is that hosts are typically *networked* devices—that is, endpoint devices connected to the network to access or provide resources, such as a file server, smartphone, smart thermostat, security camera, or network printer. Cisco standards call these *end devices*. A node that is not a host, such as a router or switch, is a *networking* device—that is, a device that enables connections on the network but does not, itself, provide applications or data resources for networked devices to access. Cisco calls these *intermediary devices*. Hosts are end devices (also called endpoint devices), and nodes can be either end devices or intermediary devices.

So far, you've already learned a great deal about local networks, called LANs. What about networks outside the local network? Let's look at other types of networks, which primarily vary according to the geographic space and the specific connection technologies they use.

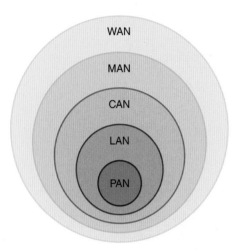

Figure 1-16   Relative sizes of WAN, MAN, CAN, LAN, and PAN networks

MANs and WANs

A group of LANs that spread over a wide geographical area is called a **WAN (wide area network)**. A group of connected LANs in the same geographical area—for example, a handful of government offices surrounding a state capitol building—is known as a **MAN (metropolitan area network)** or **CAN (campus area network)**, although in reality you won't often see those terms used or they might be used interchangeably. WANs and MANs often use different transmission methods and media than LANs do. The Internet is the largest and most varied WAN in the world. A much smaller network type is a **PAN (personal area network)**, which is a network of personal devices, such as the network you use when you sync your smartphone and your computer. Figure 1-16 shows the relative sizes of each of these common network types. Note that these are not drawn to scale—a PAN could cover a very small space (a few inches), while a WAN could cover the entire world!

Figure 1-17 shows a WAN link between two LANs bound by routers. For example, a corporation might have an office in San Francisco and another in Philadelphia. Each office has a LAN, and a WAN link connects the two LANs. The WAN link is most likely provided by a third-party service provider and spans multiple physical network links to traverse the networks between the two cities.

Other network types exist, such as the following:

- **BAN (body area network)**—Made up of personal fitness devices like a smartwatch, fitness tracker, AR (augmented reality) headset, AI (artificial intelligence) hearing aid, or other wearable devices.
- **SAN (storage area network)**—Consists of high capacity data storage devices in a distinctly defined network segment.
- **WLAN (wireless local area network)**—Consists of two or more devices connected wirelessly.

You'll learn more about WANs, SANs, and WLANs in later modules. In the meantime, let's look at how the operating systems, applications, and hardware you've been studying here work together to create and manage a network and its resources.

REMEMBER THIS...

- Compare various network topologies, such as PAN, LAN, and WAN.
- Describe common network types and their characteristics.
- Identify and compare the primary devices used to create a network.

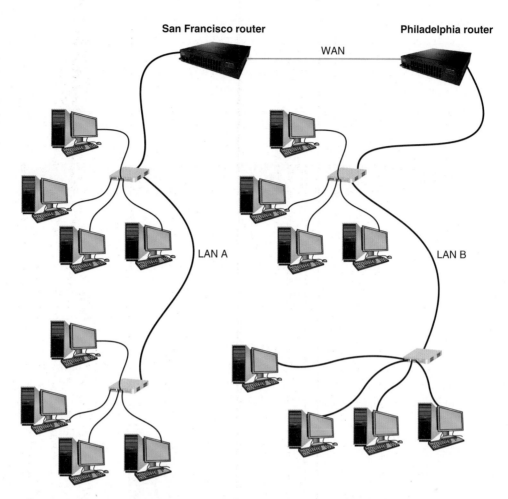

Figure 1-17   A WAN connects two LANs in different geographical areas

SELF-CHECK

7. When you connect your keyboard, mouse, and monitor to your computer, what kind of network topology are you using?
   a. Bus topology
   b. Mesh topology
   c. Star topology
   d. Ring topology

8. Which networking device is best for connecting your network printer to three computers?
   a. Switch
   b. Hub
   c. Router
   d. File server

9. Which network types can your smartphone use?
   a. WAN
   b. LAN
   c. PAN
   d. WAN and LAN
   e. WAN, LAN, and PAN

Check your answers at the end of this module.

You're Ready

You're now ready to complete **Project 1-2: Explore Network Types on a Smartphone**, or you can wait until you've finished reading this module.

THE SEVEN-LAYER OSI MODEL

 **CERTIFICATION**

1.1 Compare and contrast the Open Systems Interconnection (OSI) model layers and encapsulation concepts.

2.1 Compare and contrast various devices, their features, and their appropriate placement on the network.

Average reading time: 21 minutes

Recall that an application, such as a browser, depends on the operating system to communicate across the network. Operating systems, meanwhile, depend on hardware to communicate across the network (see the left side of Figure 1-18). Throughout the entire process, protocols govern each layer of communication.

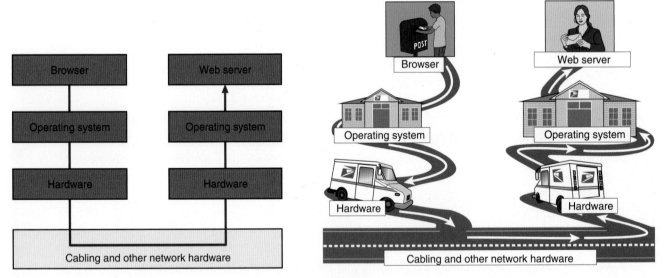

Figure 1-18   A browser and web server communicate by way of the operating system and hardware, similar to how a letter is sent through the mail using the U.S. Postal Service and the road system

To get a better sense of how this works, it's helpful to think of a different type of communication: two people communicating by way of the U.S. Postal Service (see the right side of Figure 1-18). The sender depends on the mailbox to hold their letter until a postal worker picks it up and takes it to the post office. The people at the post office, in turn, depend on truck drivers to transport the letter to the correct city. The truck drivers, for their part, depend on the road system. Throughout the entire process, various protocols govern how people behave. For example, the sender follows basic rules for writing business letters, the mail carriers follow U.S. Postal Service regulations for processing the mail, and the truck drivers follow traffic laws. Think of how complex it might be to explain to someone all the different rules or protocols involved if you were not able to separate or categorize these activities into layers.

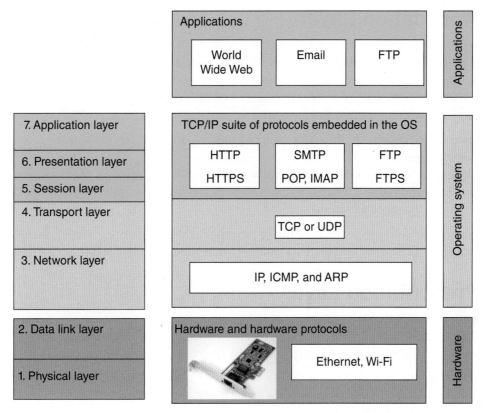

Figure 1-19   How software, protocols, and hardware map to the seven-layer OSI model

Early in the evolution of networking, a seven-layer model was developed to categorize the layers of network communication. This model, which is called the **OSI (Open Systems Interconnection) reference model**, is illustrated on the left side of Figure 1-19. It was first developed by the International Organization for Standardization, also called the ISO. (Its shortened name, *ISO,* is derived from a Greek word meaning *equal.*) Network engineers, hardware technicians, programmers, and network administrators still use the layers of the OSI model to communicate about networking technologies. In this course, you'll learn to use the OSI model to help you understand networking protocols and troubleshoot network problems.

EXAM TIP   The CompTIA Network+ exam expects you to know how to apply the OSI model when troubleshooting network problems.

As you study various protocols used in networking, it will help tremendously to map each protocol onto the OSI model. By doing so, you'll better understand the logistics of which software program or device is initiating and/or receiving the protocol or data and how other protocols are relating to it.

Now let's take a brief look at each layer in the OSI model. The layers are numbered in descending order, starting with layer 7, the application layer, at the top. Figure 1-19 guides you through the layers.

NOTE 1-9

You need to memorize the seven layers of the OSI model. Here's a seven-word, top-to-bottom mnemonic that can help: **A**ll **P**eople **S**eem **T**o **N**eed **D**ata **P**rocessing (Application, Presentation, Session, Transport, Network, Data link, and Physical). A bottom-to-top mnemonic is **P**lease **D**o **N**ot **T**hrow **S**ausage **P**izza **A**way (Physical, Data link, Network, Transport, Session, Presentation, and Application). You can also create your own!

Layer 7: Application Layer

The application layer in the OSI model does not contain applications themselves, such as a web browser, but instead describes the interface between two applications, each on separate computers. Earlier in this module, you learned about several protocols used at this layer, including HTTP, SMTP, POP3, IMAP4, DNS, FTP, Telnet, SSH, and RDP. Application layer protocols are used by applications that fall into two categories:

- Applications that provide services to a user, such as a browser and web server using the HTTP application layer protocol
- Utilities that provide services to the system, such as SNMP (Simple Network Management Protocol) programs that monitor and gather information about network traffic and can alert network administrators about adverse conditions that need attention

Data that is passed between applications or utility programs and the operating system is called a payload and includes control information. The two end-system computers that initiate sending and receiving data are called hosts.

Layer 6: Presentation Layer

In the OSI model, the presentation layer is responsible for reformatting, compressing, and/or encrypting data in a way that the application on the receiving end can read. For example, an email message can be encrypted at the presentation layer by the email client or by the operating system.

Layer 5: Session Layer

The session layer of the OSI model describes how data between applications is synced and recovered if messages don't arrive intact at the receiving application. For example, the Zoom application works with the operating system to establish and maintain a session between two endpoints for as long as a voice conversation or video conference is in progress.

The application, presentation, and session layers are so intertwined that, in practice, it's often difficult to distinguish between them. Also, tasks for each layer may be performed by the operating system or the application. Most tasks are performed by the OS when an application makes an API call to the OS. In general, an API (application programming interface) is an access point into a software's available processes such that a specific type of request will generate a particular kind of response. An API call in this case, then, is the method an application uses when it makes a request of the OS.

Layer 4: Transport Layer

The transport layer is responsible for transporting application layer payloads from one application to another. The two main transport layer protocols are TCP, which guarantees delivery, and UDP, which does not, as described next:

- TCP (Transmission Control Protocol)—Makes a connection with the end host, checks whether the data is received, and resends it if it is not. TCP is, therefore, called a connection-oriented protocol. TCP is used by applications such as web browsers and email. Guaranteed delivery takes longer and is used when it is important to know that the data reached its destination.
- UDP (User Datagram Protocol)—Does not guarantee delivery because it doesn't maintain a connection to check whether data is received; thus, UDP is called a connectionless protocol or best-effort protocol. UDP is used for broadcasting, such as streaming video or audio over the web, where guaranteed delivery is not as important as fast transmission. UDP is also used to monitor network traffic.

Transport-layer protocols add control information in an area at the beginning of the payload called the header to create a message ready to be handed down to the network layer. The process of adding a header to the data inherited from the layer above is called **encapsulation**, which is kind of the same concept as putting a letter in an envelope. The transport layer header addresses the receiving application by a number called a **port**. If the message is too large to transport in one package across the network, TCP divides it into smaller messages called **segments**, and in UDP, they're called **datagrams**.

In the post office analogy, think of a message as a letter. The sender puts the letter in an envelope and adds the name of the sender and receiver, similar to how the transport layer encapsulates the payload into a segment or datagram that identifies both the sending and destination applications. However, this letter needs more addressing information, not just the names of the sender and receiver. That's the job of lower OSI layers.

Layer 3: Network Layer

The **network layer**, sometimes called the Internet layer, is responsible for moving messages from one node to another until they reach the destination host. This is the layer where routers typically function. The principal protocol used by the network layer is **IP (Internet Protocol)**. IP adds its own network layer header to the segment or datagram, and the entire network layer message is now called a **packet**. The network layer header identifies the sending and receiving hosts by their IP addresses. An **IP address** is an address assigned to each node on a network, which the network layer uses to uniquely identify them across multiple networks. In the post office analogy, the network layer would be the trucking system used by the post office and the IP addresses would be the full return and destination addresses written on the envelope.

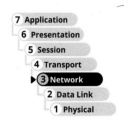

IP relies on several supporting protocols to find the best route for a packet when traversing several networks on its way to its destination. These supporting protocols include ICMP (Internet Control Message Protocol) and ARP (Address Resolution Protocol). You'll learn more about these protocols later.

Along the way, if a network layer protocol is aware that a packet is larger than the maximum size allowed for its network, it will divide the packet into smaller packets in a process called **fragmentation**.

Layer 2: Data Link Layer

Layers 2 and 1 are responsible for interfacing with the physical hardware on the local network. The protocols at these layers are programmed into the firmware of a computer's NIC and other networking hardware. Layer 2, the **data link layer**, is also commonly called the link layer. The type of networking hardware or technology used on a network determines the data link layer protocol used. Examples of data link layer protocols are Ethernet and Wi-Fi. Ethernet is used by switches on wired networks and Wi-Fi is used by access points for wireless networks. As you'll learn in later modules, several types of switches exist. The least intelligent (nonprogrammable) switches, which are called data link layer switches or layer 2 switches, operate only at this layer. More sophisticated switches might combine layer 2 functions with higher-layer functions and are called layer 3 switches.

NOTE 1-10

The term **firmware** refers to programs embedded into hardware devices. This software does not change unless a firmware upgrade is performed.

The data link layer puts its own control information in a data link layer header and also attaches control information to the end of the packet in a **trailer**. The entire data link layer message is then called a **frame**. The frame header contains the hardware addresses of the source and destination NICs. This address is called a **MAC (Media Access Control) address**, physical address, hardware address, or data link layer address and is embedded on every network adapter on the globe (refer back to Figure 1-10). These physical addresses are short-range addresses used only to find nodes on the local network.

In the post office analogy, a truck might travel from one post office to the next en route to its final destination. The address of a post office along the route would be similar to the physical address of each device's NIC that a frame reaches as it traverses each LAN on its way to its destination.

Layer 1: Physical Layer

Layer 1, the **physical layer**, is responsible for sending bits via a wired or wireless transmission. These bits can be transmitted as wavelengths in the air (for example, Wi-Fi), voltage on a copper wire (for example, Ethernet on twisted-pair cabling), or light (for example, Ethernet on fiber-optic cabling).

It's interesting to consider that the higher layers of the OSI model work the same for both wired and wireless transmissions. In fact, the only layers that must deal with the details of wired versus wireless transmissions are the data link layer and physical layer on the firmware of the NIC. In the post office analogy, the data link and physical layers compare with the various road systems a postal truck might use, each with its own speed limits and traffic rules, and any flight systems a postal airplane might use, with its own processes and flight traffic control. Whether a package stays on the ground or spends some time on a plane, the addressing rules for the sender and receiver remain the same.

Protocol Data Unit or PDU

As you've read, there are several different names for a group of bits as it moves from one layer to the next and from one LAN to the next. Although technicians loosely call this group of bits a message or a transmission, the technical name regardless of layer is PDU (protocol data unit). Table 1-1 can help you keep straight all these names for each layer.

Table 1-1   Names for a PDU or message as it moves from one layer to another

OSI model	Name	Technical name
Layer 7, application layer	Payload or data	L7PDU
Layer 6, presentation layer		
Layer 5, session layer		
Layer 4, transport layer	Segment (TCP) or datagram (UDP)	L4PDU
Layer 3, network layer	Packet	L3PDU
Layer 2, data link layer	Frame	L2PDU
Layer 1, physical layer	Bit or transmission	L1PDU

Summary of How the Layers Work Together

Now let's tie the layers together with the simple example shown in Figure 1-20. This transmission involves a browser and web server on their respective hosts, a switch, and a router. As you follow the red line from browser to web server, notice the sending host encapsulates the payload in headers and a trailer before sending it, much like an assistant would place the boss's business letter in an envelope before putting it in the mail.

On the other end, the receiving host removes the headers and trailer in reverse order before the message reaches the web server application, just as the receiver's assistant would remove the letter from the envelope before handing it to the recipient. Removing a header and trailer from a lower layer's PDU is called **decapsulation**.

NOTE 1-11

In conceptual drawings and network maps, symbols are used for switches and routers. In the figure, notice the square symbol representing a switch and the round symbol representing a router.

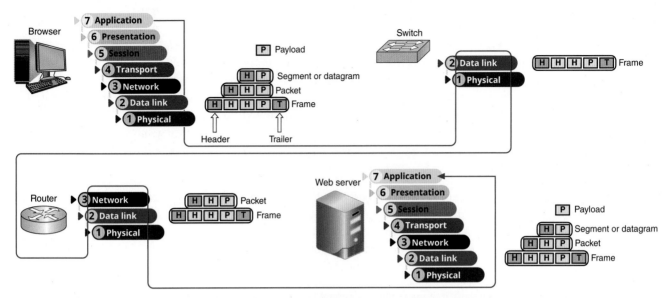

Figure 1-20   Follow the red line to see how the OSI layers work when a browser makes a request to a web server

The steps listed in Table 1-2 summarize the process illustrated in Figure 1-20.

Table 1-2   Steps through the OSI layers during a browser-to-web server transmission

Device	Task
Sending host	1. The browser, involving the application, presentation, and session layers, creates an HTTP message, or payload, on the source computer and passes it down to the transport layer.
Sending host	2. The transport layer (TCP, which is part of the OS) encapsulates the payload by adding its own header and passes the segment down to the network layer.
Sending host	3. IP at the network layer in the OS receives the segment (depicted as two yellow boxes in the figure), adds its header, and passes the packet down to the data link layer.
Sending host	4. The data link layer on the NIC firmware receives the packet (depicted as three yellow boxes in the figure), adds its header and trailer, and passes the frame to the physical layer.
Sending host	5. The physical layer on the NIC hardware places bits on the network.
Switch	6. The network transmission is received by the switch, which passes the frame up to the data link layer (firmware on the switch), looks at the destination MAC address, and decides where to send the frame.
Switch	7. The pass-through frame is sent to the correct port on the switch and on to the next device, which happens to be a router.
Router	8. The router has two NICs, one for each of the two networks to which it belongs. The physical layer of the first NIC receives the frame and passes it up to the data link layer (NIC firmware), which removes the frame header and trailer and passes the packet up to IP at the network layer (firmware program or other software) on the router.
Router	9. This network layer IP program looks at the destination IP address, determines the next node en route for the packet, and passes the packet back down to the data link layer on the second NIC. The data link layer adds a new frame header and trailer appropriate for this second NIC's LAN, including the MAC address of the next destination node. It passes the frame to its physical layer (NIC hardware), which sends the bits on their way.
Destination host	10. After several iterations of this process at various routers and other networking devices, the frame eventually reaches the destination host NIC. The data link layer NIC firmware receives it, removes the frame header and trailer, and passes the packet up to IP at the network layer, which removes its header and passes the segment up to TCP at the transport layer.
Destination host	11. TCP removes its header and passes the payload up to HTTP at the application layer. HTTP presents the message to the web server application.

NOTE 1-12

A four-layer model similar to the OSI model is the TCP/IP model. Using the TCP/IP model, the application, presentation, and session layers are wrapped together and are called the application layer. The physical layer is either ignored or combined with the second layer, which makes for four layers: application layer, transport layer, Internet layer (the network layer in the OSI model), and link layer (the data link layer and physical layer in the OSI model). While the OSI model is typically preferred in reference to theoretical concepts and troubleshooting techniques, the TCP/IP model is most often used to refer to the protocols used at each layer. This course and the CompTIA Network+ exam use the OSI model.

So now you have the big picture of networking and how it works. Throughout this course, you will have several opportunities to work with networking equipment such as switches and routers. Before attempting any of these projects, it's important for you to know about safety procedures and policies. In preparation for the work you'll be doing in this course, let's explore how to stay safe when working around networks and computers.

REMEMBER THIS...

- Compare the seven layers of the OSI model.
- Identify which devices function at each OSI layer, including switch, router, and server.
- Map common protocols to specific layers of the OSI model.

SELF-CHECK

10. At what OSI layer does your browser's web page request begin its journey through the OSI layers?
    a. Application layer
    b. Network layer
    c. Data link layer
    d. Physical layer

11. Which layer holds the address of the target application running on the destination computer?
    a. Application layer
    b. Transport layer
    c. Network layer
    d. Data link layer

12. Which OSI layer adds both a header and a trailer?
    a. Transport layer
    b. Network layer
    c. Data link layer
    d. Physical layer

Check your answers at the end of this module.

SAFETY PROCEDURES AND POLICIES

3.3 Explain high availability and disaster recovery concepts and summarize which is the best solution.

Average reading time: 13 minutes

As a network and computer technician, you need to know how to protect yourself and sensitive electronic components as you work. Let's look at some best practices for safety.

Emergency Procedures

In case of an emergency, such as a fire alert, you need to know the best escape route or emergency exit for you and others around you. Look in the lobby and hallways at your school or workplace for a posted building layout and fire escape plan so that you are prepared in an emergency. You also need to be aware of emergency exit doors, which are usually labeled with battery-powered, lighted exit signs and clearly marked on the posted building layout.

Fire Suppression Systems

A company is likely to have at least one **fire suppression system** in its data center that provides fire protection at the following levels:

- **Building level**—This system protects the building and employees, and it might include both active fire protection, such as fire extinguishers, and passive fire protection, such as firewalls and fire-rated floor assemblies, to slow the spread of fire.
- **Room level**—This system incorporates a sprinkler or gas system with at least two detection points to activate the system, which provides fire suppression in parts of a room or throughout the entire room. Instead of water, data centers often use a gas suppression agent that decreases oxygen levels to suffocate a fire or absorb heat to suppress the fire without damaging sensitive electronics. For example, the popular FM-200 system combines carbon, fluorine, and hydrogen to absorb heat without leaving a residue and without generating any toxic fumes.
- **Rack level** (that is, inside the cabinet that holds network devices)—By offering targeted fire detection and suppression, a fire can be neutralized more quickly with less impact on surrounding equipment and less expense to reset the system.

Other components of a complete fire suppression system might include the following:

- **Emergency alert system**—These systems vary, but they typically generate loud noise and flashing lights. Some send text and voice message alerts to key personnel and post alerts by email, network messages, and other means.
- **Portable fire extinguishers**—Note that electrical fires require a Class C fire extinguisher, as shown in Figure 1-21.
- **Emergency power-off switch**—Don't use a power-off switch unless you really need to; improper shutdowns are hard on computers and their data.

Fail Open or Fail Close

What happens to security when a system responsible for security fails? Does the system allow access during the failure (**fail open**) or deny access during the failure (**fail close**)? For example, during a fire alert using a fail-open policy, all exit doors stay unlocked so that people can safely leave the building and firefighters can enter

NOTE 1-13

In the United States, the national Emergency Alert System (EAS) can only be activated by the president at the national level to address the public within ten minutes during an emergency. It requires TV, radio, cable TV, satellite, and cellular service providers to broadcast the alert. The system can also be used at the state and local levels to alert about missing children (AMBER alert), imminent threats, and dangerous weather conditions.

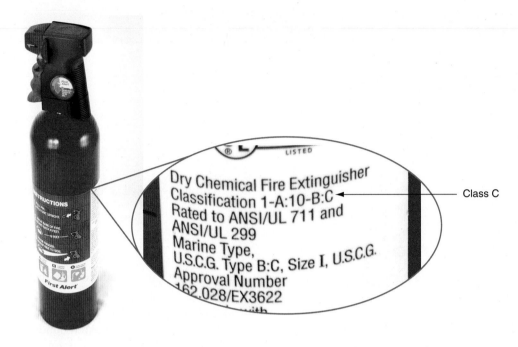

Class C

Figure 1-21   A Class C fire extinguisher is rated to put out electrical fires

NOTE 1-14

The term *open* or *close* takes the opposite meaning in reference to electrical circuits. When a circuit breaker fails, there is a break in the circuit and the circuit is said to be open. The breaker opens the circuit to protect it from out-of-control electricity. Although this sounds like double-talk, an open circuit is, therefore, a fail-close system.

the building, even though this might present a security risk for thieves entering the building. On the other hand, if firewall software protecting access to a database of customer credit card numbers fails, it might be configured to fail close and to deny access to the database until the software is back online.

A fail-open policy is often based on common sense to ensure that, in an emergency, no one is harmed when a system is not working. A fail-close policy is usually based on the need for security to protect private data or other resources even if that means access is denied until the emergency is over.

SDS (Safety Data Sheet)

You might need to use cleaning solutions to clean optical discs, tapes and tape drivers, and other devices. Most of these cleaning solutions contain flammable and poisonous materials. Take care when using them so that they don't get on your skin or in your eyes. To find out what to do if you are accidentally exposed to a dangerous solution, look on the instructions printed on the can or check out the safety data sheet (see Figure 1-22). An SDS (safety data sheet), formerly called an MSDS (material safety data sheet), explains how to properly handle substances such as chemical solvents and how to dispose of them.

An SDS includes information such as identification, first-aid measures, fire-fighting measures, accidental release measures, handling and storage guidelines, exposure controls, and physical and chemical properties. It typically comes packaged with the chemical, but if you can't locate it, you can order one from the manufacturer, or you can find one on the web (see *msdsonline.com/sds-search*).

Safety Precautions

Electrical and tool safety in workplaces is generally regulated by OSHA (Occupational Safety and Health Administration), which is the main federal agency charged with safety and health in the workplace. See *osha.gov*.

OSHA regulations for electrical safety require that electrical devices be turned off and the electrical supply locked out before employees work near these devices. For example, OSHA requires that all devices in a data center cabinet, rack, or panel be turned off and the power locked out before employees work inside of or with these units.

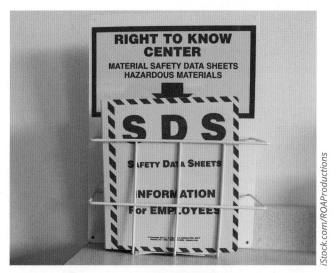

Figure 1-22   Each chemical you use should have a safety data sheet available

Following are some general OSHA guidelines when using power (electric) tools or other hand tools in the workplace. Your employer can give you more details specific to your work environment:

- Wear **PPE (personal protective equipment)** to protect yourself as you work. For example, wear eye protection where dust or fumes are generated by power tools.
- Keep all tools in good condition and properly store tools not in use. Examine a tool for damage before you use it.
- Use the right tool for the job and operate the tool according to the manufacturer's instructions and guidelines. Don't work with a tool unless you are trained and authorized to use it.
- Watch out for trip hazards, so you and others don't stumble on a tool or cord. For example, keep power tool electrical extension cords out from underfoot and don't leave hand tools lying around unattended.

Lifting Heavy Objects

Back injury, caused by lifting heavy objects, is one of the most common injuries that happens at work. Whenever possible, put heavy objects, such as a large laser printer, on a cart to move them. If you do need to lift a heavy object, follow these guidelines to keep from injuring your back:

1. Decide which side of the object to face so that the load is the most balanced.
2. Stand close to the object with your feet apart.
3. Keeping your back straight, bend your knees, and grip the load.
4. Lift with your legs, arms, and shoulders, and not with your back or stomach.
5. Keep the load close to your body and avoid twisting your body while you're holding it.
6. To put the object down, keep your back as straight as you can and lower the object by bending your knees.

Don't try to lift an object that is too heavy for you. Because there are no exact guidelines for when heavy is too heavy, use your best judgment as to when to ask for help.

Protecting against Static Electricity

Computer components are grounded inside a computer case, and computer power cables all use a three-prong plug for this purpose. The third prong is grounded. **Grounding** means that a device is connected directly to the earth so that, in the event of a short circuit, the electricity flows into the earth rather than out of control through the device and back to the power station, which can cause an electrical fire.

In addition, sensitive electronic components (for example, a NIC, motherboard, and memory modules) can be damaged by **ESD (electrostatic discharge)**, commonly known as **static electricity**. Static electricity is an electrical charge at rest. When your body and a component have different static charges and you touch the component, you can discharge up to 1,500 volts of electricity without seeing a spark or feeling the discharge. However, it only takes 10 volts to damage the component. This means you could fry a motherboard and never even feel a shock!

ESD can cause two types of damage in an electronic component: catastrophic failure and upset failure. A catastrophic failure destroys the component beyond use. An upset failure can shorten the life of a component and/or cause intermittent errors. Before touching a component, first ground yourself using one of these methods:

- Wear an ESD strap around your wrist that clips onto a metallic part of the computer case, called a chassis (pronounced "chas-ee"), which eliminates any ESD between you and the chassis and its components (see Figure 1-23).

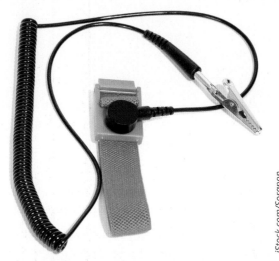

iStock.com/Sorapop

Figure 1-23 An ESD strap, which protects computer components from ESD, can clip to the side of the computer chassis and eliminate ESD between you and the chassis

- If you don't have an ESD strap handy, be sure to keep touching the metal parts of the case before you touch any component inside the case. This is not as effective as wearing an ESD strap, but it can reduce the risk of ESD.
- To protect a sensitive component, always store it *inside* an antistatic bag (but not on top of the bag) when it's not in use.

In addition to protecting against ESD, always shut down and unplug a computer before working inside it. Know which components are considered field-replaceable and which must be sent back to the manufacturer for repair or should simply be replaced.

NOTE 1-15

In this section, you learned about safety procedures and policies to physically protect yourself, other people, and your equipment. In this course, you'll also learn strategies for protecting data and network access. One of the main ways of doing this is using secure passwords for all user accounts. However, it can be challenging to keep up with long and complex passwords for every account. For many projects in this course, you'll store account passwords in a **password manager**. This app provides a secure vault for all your passwords, and you only need to remember one, master password. You'll learn more about secure passwords and other security techniques throughout this course.

REMEMBER THIS...

- Describe major components of fire suppression systems.
- Explain the importance of an SDS (safety data sheet).
- Consistently follow significant safety guidelines and procedures to protect yourself, other people, and your equipment.

SELF-CHECK

13. Which fire suppression level provides the most targeted protection?
- **a.** Desk level
- **b.** Rack level
- **c.** Building level
- **d.** Room level

14. What is the minimum amount of ESD required to damage sensitive electronic equipment?
- **a.** 1,500 volts
- **b.** 800 volts
- **c.** 10 volts
- **d.** 2 volts

Check your answers at the end of this module.

You're Ready

You're now ready to complete **Project 1-3: Create a Password Manager Account**, or you can wait until you've finished reading this module.

TROUBLESHOOTING NETWORK PROBLEMS

✓ CERTIFICATION

5.1 Explain the network troubleshooting methodology.

5.5 Given a scenario, troubleshoot general networking issues.

Average reading time: 11 minutes

Troubleshooting is probably the most significant skill you can learn as a network technician. Throughout your career, you'll be called on to troubleshoot problems with networking hardware, operating systems, applications that use the network, and other network resources. The CompTIA Network+ exam and this course place a significant emphasis on troubleshooting skills. Troubleshooting will come more easily for you once you get a feel for the big picture of how the process works. The flowchart in Figure 1-24 illustrates the method used by most expert network troubleshooters to solve networking problems.

Study the steps in Figure 1-24 carefully so that you understand how each step feeds into the next and how the answers for each step build on the information you've already gathered. Also, it's not uncommon for the Network+ exam to ask you questions about the recommended order of these steps, which step comes next in a given scenario, or which step was missed in a troubleshooting scenario. Here are the steps:

Step 1: Identify the problem and its symptoms—As you gather information about the problem, you'll need to identify the symptoms, question the user, find out what has recently changed, and determine the scope of the problem. If possible, duplicate the problem. For multiple problems, approach each problem individually. Solve one before moving on to the next.

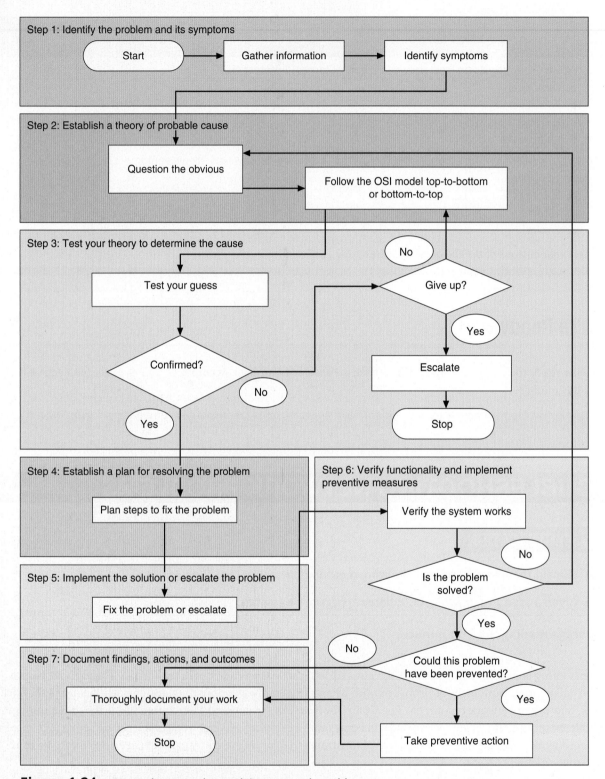

Figure 1-24   General approach to solving network problems

Step 2:   *Establish a theory of probable cause*—As you observe the extent of the problem, make your best guess as to the source of the problem. If symptoms of the problem don't make sense, divide and conquer by searching for the cause of each individual symptom, then look for patterns. Consider multiple approaches to identify the cause, such as working through the layers of the OSI model. Troubleshooters generally follow the bottom-to-top OSI model by first suspecting and eliminating failed hardware as the cause (for example, a loose cable or failed NIC), before moving on to software as the cause of a problem. As you question the obvious and check simple things first, such as plugging the device into a power source, you might solve the problem right on the spot.

Some situations are obviously software related, such as when a user cannot log on to the network and gets an invalid password message. Here, it makes more sense to follow the OSI model top-to-bottom, beginning at the application layer, and suspect the user has forgotten his or her password.

Step 3:   *Test your theory to determine the cause*—For more complicated or expensive solutions, test your theory to assure yourself that it will indeed solve the problem before you implement the solution, and then determine the next steps needed. If your test proves your theory is wrong, move on to another guess or escalate the problem to the next tier of support in your organization. For example, in the *On the Job* story at the beginning of this module, the technician had to test several theories, from the most obvious to the less likely causes, before finding the one that proved correct. Sometimes this process can be frustrating and requires tenacity to press through so you can identify the cause of the problem.

Step 4:   *Establish a plan for resolving the problem*—Changes to a network have the potential for disrupting a lot of people's work. Before you implement a fix, consider the scope of your change, especially how it will affect users, their applications, and their data. Unless the problem poses an emergency, make your changes when the least number of users are on the network. In many cases, you must follow specific change management procedures to implement a change. **Change management** consists of carefully defined processes to evaluate the need for a change, the cost of the change, a plan for making the change with minimal disruption, and a backup plan if the change doesn't work as expected. Check with your organization's policies to determine whether the proposed change falls under the change management requirements.

Step 5:   *Implement the solution or escalate the problem*—Before you make the change, be sure to alert all affected users in advance, create backups of software and data as needed, and save or write down current settings before you change them. Keep good notes as you work so you can backtrack as necessary. Typically, you should make only one change at a time, and then check to see it's working before moving to another change. When finished, test your solution thoroughly, and clean up after yourself after everything is working well. For major changes, it's often best to roll out changes in stages to make sure all is working for a few users before you affect many users. For complex problems, you might need to escalate the problem to someone with access to more technical resources or with more authority to test or implement a solution.

Step 6:   *Verify functionality and implement preventive measures*—At the time you implement your solution, you'll test the system for full system functionality. It's also a good idea to return a few days later and make sure all is working as you expected. Also consider what you can do to make sure the problem doesn't reappear. For example, is more preventive maintenance required? Do you need to implement network monitoring software? You'll learn more about network monitoring techniques later in this course.

Step 7:   *Document findings, actions, and outcomes*—Most organizations use a call tracking system (also called help desk software) to document problems and their resolutions. Your organization is likely to expect you to document the name, department, and contact information of the person who originated the call for help; when the call first came in; information about the problem; the symptoms of the problem; the resolution of the problem; the name of the technician who handled the problem; and perhaps the amount of time spent resolving the problem. Your company may also require you to document lessons learned and unique or insightful solutions to problems in your company's knowledge base for you and others to draw from in the future. A **knowledge base** is a collection of accumulated insights and solutions to the problems encountered on a particular network.

NOTE 1-16

As you work, use a divide-and-conquer approach by eliminating parts of the whole until you zero in on the source of the problem.

NOTE 1-17

As with any computer-related troubleshooting, be sure you choose the least invasive and least expensive solution first before moving on to more drastic or expensive changes to a computer or the network.

Applying Concepts 1-2: Troubleshoot a Failed Network Connection

Suppose your computer cannot connect to the Internet. Here's a simple process for troubleshooting this problem that demonstrates all seven steps in the troubleshooting model:

Step 1: *Identify the problem and its symptoms*—You open your browser on your desktop computer, discover you can't reach any website, and you see an error message on the browser screen. You open File Explorer and find that you can't navigate to resources normally available on your local network. You check with coworkers nearby, who say they're not having problems.

Step 2: *Establish a theory of probable cause*—Because a network technician was working near your desk when you left the evening before, you suspect your network cable might have been left unplugged. In the OSI model, you've started at the bottom layer by suspecting the problem is hardware related.

Step 3: *Test your theory to determine the cause*—You check the cable and discover it is lying on the floor, not connected to your desktop.

Step 4: *Establish a plan for resolving the problem*—You decide to plug in the network cable. This is a very simple resolution that does not affect other users. In other situations, your plan might involve informing coworkers of what is about to happen or possibly filing a request for formal change management.

Step 5: *Implement the solution or escalate the problem*—You plug in the cable.

Step 6: *Verify functionality and implement preventive measures*—You open your browser and find you can surf the web. You verify local network resources are available from File Explorer.

Step 7: *Document findings, actions, and outcomes*—This simple problem and solution don't require formal documentation. However, network technicians are generally expected to document troubleshooting tasks and solutions. In this case, you simply inform your coworkers that your network connection is working now.

REMEMBER THIS...

- Explain the various steps of the troubleshooting method and how each step fits into the process from beginning to end.
- Follow a bottom-to-top or top-to-bottom OSI layers approach when troubleshooting.
- Always document problems and their resolutions, lessons learned, and unique or insightful solutions to problems.

SELF-CHECK

15. What should you do after making a plan to solve a problem and carrying out your plan?
    a. Document your work.
    b. Find out what has recently changed.
    c. Test your theory.
    d. Verify functionality.

16. While exploring the problem and developing a theory about the cause, where can you go to get information on similar problems your coworkers have faced in the past?
    a. Safety data sheet
    b. Knowledge base
    c. Troubleshooting ticket in the call tracking system
    d. Instruction manual

Check your answers at the end of this module.

You're Ready

You're now ready to complete **Project 1-4: Apply Troubleshooting Methodology**, or you can wait until you've finished the Review Questions for this module.

You're Ready

After you finish the Hand-On Projects, you're ready to complete the **Module 1 Capstone Projects**.

MODULE SUMMARY

Network Models

- The term "physical topology" refers to a network's hardware and how devices and cables fit together. Logical topology refers to the way software controls access to network resources and how those resources are shared on the network.
- A peer-to-peer network model allows each computer's operating system to control access to its resources without centralized control. P2P networks are simple to configure and relatively inexpensive. But they are not scalable, not necessarily secure, and not practical for managing more than just a few computers.
- In a client-server network model, resources are managed by the NOS via a centralized directory database. Common examples of NOSs include Windows Server 2019, Ubuntu Server, and Red Hat Enterprise Linux (Ubuntu and Red Hat are versions of Linux).

Client-Server Applications

- Resources a network makes available to its users include applications and data, collectively referred to as network services.
- Networked devices use methods and rules for communication known as protocols. The two primary network protocols are TCP (Transmission Control Protocol) and IP (Internet Protocol), and the suite of all the protocols an OS uses for communication on a network is the TCP/IP suite of protocols.
- The primary protocol used by web servers and browsers (clients) is HTTP (Hypertext Transfer Protocol). When HTTP is layered on top of an encryption protocol, such as SSL (Secure Sockets Layer) or TLS (Transport Layer Security), the result is HTTPS (HTTP Secure), which gives a secure transmission.
- An email client uses SMTP (Simple Mail Transfer Protocol) to send an email message to the first server, which is an SMTP server. The first server sends the message on to the receiver's mail server, which delivers the message to the receiving client using one of two protocols: POP3 (Post Office Protocol, version 3) or IMAP4 (Internet Message Access Protocol, version 4).
- A DBMS (database management system) is software that makes requested changes to data and organizes data for viewing, reporting, or exporting. Many DBMSs use the programming language SQL (Structured Query Language) to configure and interact with the database's objects and data. Popular examples of SQL database software include Microsoft SQL Server, Oracle Database, and the open-source MySQL.

Network Hardware

- In a LAN (local area network), each node on the network can communicate directly with others on the network. LANs are usually contained in a small space, such as an office or building. A switch connects LAN devices; it receives incoming data from one of its ports and redirects (or switches) it to another port or multiple ports that will send the data to its intended destination(s).
- In a star topology, all devices connect to one central device. In a mesh topology, each device connects to multiple other devices.
- A network port can be an onboard network port embedded in the computer's motherboard. Another type of port is provided by a NIC (network interface card), also called a network adapter, installed in an expansion slot on the motherboard.
- A router is a device that manages traffic between two or more networks and can help find the best path for traffic to get from one network to another. In SOHO (small office-home office) networks, which typically have fewer than 10 computers, a consumer-grade router is used to connect the LAN to the Internet. An enterprise or industrial-grade router can have several network ports, one for each of the networks it connects to.
- The fundamental difference between a switch and a router is that a switch belongs only to its local network and a router can belong to two or more networks.
- *Networked* devices connect to the network to access or provide resources, such as a file server, smartphone, smart thermostat, security camera, or network printer. A *networking* device is a device that enables connections on the network but does not, itself, provide applications or data for networked devices to access.
- A group of LANs that spread over a wide geographical area is called a WAN (wide area network). A group of connected LANs in the same geographical area is known as a MAN (metropolitan area network) or CAN (campus area network), and these terms might be used interchangeably. WANs and MANs often use different transmission methods and media than LANs do. A much smaller network type is a PAN (personal area network), which is a network of personal devices, such as the connection between a smartphone and computer.

The Seven-Layer OSI Model

- The seven-layer OSI (Open Systems Interconnection) reference model was developed to categorize the layers of network communication. Mapping each protocol onto the OSI model helps identify the logistics of which software program or device is initiating and/or receiving the protocol or data and how other protocols are relating to it.
- The application layer in the OSI model describes the interface between two applications, each on separate computers. Protocols used at this layer include HTTP, SMTP, POP3, IMAP4, FTP, Telnet, and RDP.
- The presentation layer is responsible for reformatting, compressing, and/or encrypting data in a way that the application on the receiving end can read. The session layer of the OSI model describes how data between applications is synced and recovered if messages don't arrive intact at the receiving application. The application, presentation, and session layers are so intertwined that, in practice, it's often difficult to distinguish between them.
- The transport layer is responsible for transporting application layer payloads from one application to another. The two main transport layer protocols are TCP, which guarantees delivery, and UDP, which does not. Transport-layer protocols add control information in an area at the beginning of the payload called the header to create a message ready to be handed down to the network layer. The process of adding a header to the data inherited from the layer above is called encapsulation.
- The network layer is responsible for moving messages from one node to another until they reach the destination host. The principal protocol used by the network layer is IP (Internet Protocol). IP adds its own network layer header to the segment or datagram, and the entire network layer message is now called a packet. The network layer header identifies the sending and receiving hosts by their IP addresses.
- Layer 2 (the data link layer) and layer 1 (the physical layer) are responsible for interfacing with the physical hardware on the local network. Examples of data link layer protocols are Ethernet and Wi-Fi. The data link

layer puts its own control information in a data link layer header that also contains the hardware addresses of the source and destination NICs; it then attaches control information to the end of the packet in a trailer. The entire data link layer message is called a frame. The physical layer sends the frame's bits via a wired or wireless transmission.

Safety Procedures and Policies

- A fire suppression system is designed to combat the outbreak of a fire and might include an emergency alert system, portable fire extinguishers, an emergency power-off switch, and a suppression agent such as a foaming chemical, gas, or water.
- A fail-open policy is often based on common sense to ensure that, in an emergency, no one is harmed when a system is not working. A fail-close policy is usually based on the need for security to protect private data or other resources even if that means access is denied until the emergency is over.
- An SDS (safety data sheet), formerly called an MSDS (material safety data sheet), explains how to properly handle substances such as chemical solvents and how to dispose of them.
- Electrical and tool safety in workplaces is generally regulated by OSHA (Occupational Safety and Health Administration), which is the main federal agency charged with safety and health in the workplace. OSHA regulations for electrical safety require that electrical devices be turned off and the electrical supply locked out before employees work near these devices.
- Back injury, caused by lifting heavy objects, is one of the most common injuries that happens at work. Don't try to lift an object that is too heavy for you. Because there are no exact guidelines for when heavy is too heavy, use your best judgment as to when to ask for help.
- Sensitive electronic components can be damaged by ESD (electrostatic discharge), commonly known as static electricity. A discharge up to 1,500 volts of ESD won't produce a visible spark or detectable shock. However, it only takes 10 volts to damage some components. Wear an ESD strap clipped to the computer chassis to eliminate ESD between you and the chassis and its components. Always shut down and unplug a computer before working inside it.

Troubleshooting Network Problems

- As you gather information about the problem, identify the symptoms, question the user, find out what has recently changed, and determine the scope of the problem.
- Consider multiple approaches to identify the cause, such as working through the layers of the OSI model. Troubleshooters generally follow the bottom-to-top OSI model by first suspecting and eliminating failed hardware as the cause. Some situations are obviously software related, and it makes more sense to follow the OSI layers top-to-bottom.
- Test your theory to assure yourself that it will indeed solve the problem before you implement the solution, and then determine the next steps needed. If your test proves your theory is wrong, move on to another guess or escalate the problem.
- Before you implement a fix, consider the scope of your change, especially how it will affect users, their applications, and their data. Check with your organization's policies to determine whether the proposed change falls under the change management requirements.
- Before you make the change, be sure to alert all affected users in advance, create backups of software and data as needed, and save or write down current settings before you change them. Test your solution thoroughly, and clean up after yourself when you're finished. For complex problems, you might need to escalate the problem to someone with access to more technical resources or with more authority to test or implement a solution.
- Test the system for full system functionality. Also consider what you can do to make sure the problem doesn't reappear.
- Document problems and their resolutions, lessons learned, and unique or insightful solutions to problems in your company's call tracking system and knowledge base.

Key Terms

For definitions of key terms, see the Glossary.

AD (Active Directory)
AD DS (Active Directory Domain Services)
API (application programming interface)
application layer
backbone
bus topology
CAN (campus area network)
change management
client
client-server application
client-server network model
connectionless protocol
connection-oriented protocol
data link layer
datagram
DBMS (database management system)
decapsulation
DNS (Domain Name System)
domain
encapsulation
ESD (electrostatic discharge)
fail close
fail open
fire suppression system
firewall
firmware
fragmentation
frame
FTP (File Transfer Protocol)
grounding
header
host
HTTP (Hypertext Transfer Protocol)
HTTPS (HTTP Secure)
hub

hub-and-spoke topology
hybrid topology
IMAP4 (Internet Message Access Protocol, version 4)
IP (Internet Protocol)
IP address
ISP (Internet service provider)
knowledge base
LAN (local area network)
logical topology
MAC (Media Access Control) address
MAN (metropolitan area network)
mesh topology
Microsoft SQL Server
MySQL
network
network layer
network service
NIC (network interface card)
node
NOS (network operating system)
open source
Oracle Database
OSHA (Occupational Safety and Health Administration)
OSI (Open Systems Interconnection) reference model
P2P (peer-to-peer) network model
packet
PAN (personal area network)
password manager
payload
physical layer
physical topology
POP3 (Post Office Protocol, version 3)
port

PPE (personal protective equipment)
presentation layer
protocol
RDP (Remote Desktop Protocol)
ring topology
router
SAN (storage area network)
scalable
SDS (safety data sheet)
segment
server
server operating system
session layer
SFTP (Secure File Transfer Protocol)
SMTP (Simple Mail Transfer Protocol)
SNMP (Simple Network Management Protocol)
SOHO (small office-home office) network
SQL (Structured Query Language)
SSH (Secure Shell)
SSL (Secure Sockets Layer)
star topology
static electricity
switch
TCP (Transmission Control Protocol)
TCP/IP suite
Telnet
TLS (Transport Layer Security)
topology
trailer
transport layer
UDP (User Datagram Protocol)
WAN (wide area network)
WLAN (wireless local area network)

Review Questions

1. In the client-server model, what is the primary secure protocol used for communication between a browser and web server?
   a. HTTPS
   b. TLS
   c. HTTP
   d. SSL

2. Which two encryption protocols might be used to provide secure transmissions for email services?
   a. HTTP and HTTPS
   b. SSL and TLS
   c. FTP and SFTP
   d. SSH and RDP

3. Which of the following applications could be used to run a website from a server?
   a. Hypertext Transfer Protocol
   b. FileZilla
   c. Microsoft Exchange Server
   d. Ngnix

4. As you're working to fix a problem with an application, you make multiple changes at once hoping that something will solve the issues you're having. You end up with more problems than when you started. Which step, if followed correctly, would have prevented this complication?
   a. Identify the problem.
   b. Test the theory to determine the cause.
   c. Establish a plan of action to resolve the problem and identify potential effects.
   d. Document findings, actions, outcomes, and lessons learned.

5. In the event of a fire, the most appropriate failure policy is a _____ policy.
   a. power-off
   b. fail-close
   c. fail-open
   d. shutdown

6. A network consists of five computers, all running Windows 10 Professional. All the computers are connected to a switch, which is connected to a router, which is connected to the Internet. Which logical networking model does the network use?
   a. Hub-and-spoke
   b. Ring
   c. Hybrid
   d. Peer-to-peer

7. In Question 6, suppose Windows Server 2019 is installed on one computer. Which networking model can the network now support that it could not support without the upgrade?
   a. Hybrid
   b. Client-server
   c. Hub-and-spoke
   d. Peer-to-peer

8. A network consists of seven computers and a network printer, all connected directly to one switch. Which network topology does this network use?
   a. Client-server
   b. Mesh
   c. Hub-and-spoke
   d. Star

9. You need to access customer records in a database as you're planning a marketing campaign. What language can you use to pull the records most relevant to the campaign?
   a. FTP
   b. SQL
   c. SMTP
   d. TLS

10. Which of the following is an application layer protocol?
    a. IP
    b. RDP
    c. TCP
    d. Apache

11. What is the name of the domain controller database that Windows Server 2019 uses to store data about user access and resources on the network?

12. What is the fundamental distinction between a layer 2 switch and a router?

13. What is the fundamental distinction between a node and a host?

14. What is the fundamental distinction between a MAN and a WAN?

15. List two protocols that function at the transport layer of the OSI model. What type of address do these protocols add to their headers, and what element does that address identify?

16. At the network layer, what type of address is used to identify the receiving host?

17. At the data link layer, which type of network address is used to identify the receiving node?

18. A computer is unable to access the network. When you check the LED lights near the computer's network port, you discover the lights are not lit. Which layer of the OSI model are you using to troubleshoot this problem? At which two layers does the network adapter work?

19. A user complains that their computer cannot access email, although the computer can access websites. At which layer of the OSI model should you begin troubleshooting this problem and why?

20. While troubleshooting a problem, you realize the problem is caused by a complex series of issues that will affect a large number of users even to test your theory as to the cause, and that process won't even solve the problem. What should you do next in the troubleshooting process?

Hands-On Projects

NOTE 1-18

Websites and applications change often. While the instructions given in these projects were accurate at the time of writing, you might need to adjust the steps or options according to later changes.

Note to Instructors and Students: A rubric is provided for evaluating student performance on these projects. Please see Appendix D.

Project 1-1: IT and Networking Certifications

Estimated Time: 20 minutes (+10 minutes for group work, if assigned)
Objective: Explain basic corporate and datacenter network architecture. (Obj. 1.7)
Group Work: This project includes enhancements when assigned as a group project.
Resources:
- Internet access

Context: This course prepares you to take the CompTIA Network+ N10-008 exam, which is considered a fundamental benchmark toward a career in IT. Many other IT certifications will also promote success in your IT and networking career. Use the web to research and answer the following questions:

1. Which certification does CompTIA recommend a candidate for the CompTIA Network+ certification to already have before taking this exam? Include the web address of your authoritative source along with your answer.

 **CAUTION** When you provide a source for your responses, you should always ensure the source is authoritative for the information you are giving. Don't rely solely on hearsay, informal discussion on discussion forums, or second-hand knowledge in blogs, wikis, or articles. For example, an authoritative source about a CompTIA exam would be a CompTIA-published web page.

2. How long does CompTIA recommend you work in networking before you take the CompTIA Network+ exam? Include the web address of your authoritative source along with your answer.
3. Cisco offers a full range of certifications focused on all aspects of networking. How long does Cisco recommend you work in networking before you take the most current CCNA exam for certification? Include the web address of your authoritative source along with your answer.
4. Microsoft network-related certifications have shifted focus toward their cloud-based Azure platform. The entry-level Azure certification is called Azure Fundamentals. Which technology concepts should Azure Fundamentals certification candidates be familiar with before taking the exam? Include the web address of your authoritative source along with your answer.
5. AWS (Amazon Web Services) offers extensive certification options in various areas of cloud computing expertise. The entry-level AWS exam is the Cloud Practitioner certification. How long and in what roles does AWS recommend you work with the AWS cloud before you take the Cloud Practitioner exam? Include the web address of your authoritative source along with your answer.
6. Search online for a job opening in IT networking in your geographical area that requires or recommends a degree, specific IT skills, and at least one IT certification. **Take a screenshot** of the job description and requirements; submit this visual with your answers to this project's questions. (Excellent sites that post IT jobs are **Indeed.com** and **Monster.com.**)
7. Answer the following questions about the job listed:
   a. Which degrees are required or recommended?
   b. What types of skills are required or recommended?
   c. What work experience is required or recommended?
   d. Which IT certifications are required or recommended?
   e. What is the advertised salary range?

8. **For group assignments:** Each member of the group should research online for practice questions for one of the IT certifications discussed in this project. Group members should compare their sources to ensure no one uses the same source as someone else. Each group member quizzes the other group members with the practice questions and tallies their performance. Each group member then lists which exam objectives the group collectively demonstrates sufficient knowledge as required by each objective covered by that exam. Submit the name of the exam, the source of the practice questions, a brief summary of the group's performance on the practice questions, and the list of exam objectives currently mastered by the group collectively.

Project 1-2: Explore Network Types on a Smartphone

Estimated Time: 10 minutes (+10 minutes for group work, if assigned)
Objective: Explain the characteristics of network topologies and network types. (Obj. 1.2)
Group Work: This project includes enhancements when assigned as a group project.
Resources:
- Smartphone with cellular, Wi-Fi, and Bluetooth connection capabilities (you can borrow one from a classmate, friend, or family member)
- Access to a Wi-Fi network, such as at home, school, or a café
- Bluetooth device, such as earbuds, speaker, fitness tracker, vehicle

Context: At first, it can be a little difficult to understand the differences between PANs, LANs, and WANs. However, you most likely own a device that accesses all three of these network types: your smartphone. In this project, you'll explore the various network types your phone can connect to. Complete the following steps:

1. On the smartphone, turn on Airplane mode. Navigate to the network connections screen showing the types of connections available on the smartphone. **Take a screenshot**; submit this visual with your answers to this project's questions.
2. Within range of a Wi-Fi network that you have permission to connect to, turn on Wi-Fi on the smartphone and connect to the network. Using the phone's browser, navigate to **cengage.com**. Does it work? What kind of network are you using to access the web page?
3. Turn off Wi-Fi and turn on Bluetooth. Connect to a nearby Bluetooth device. Does it work? What kind of network are you using to access the Bluetooth device?
4. Without changing any other settings, use the phone's browser to navigate to **google.com**. Does it work? Why or why not?
5. Turn off Bluetooth. Turn off Airplane mode and, if necessary, turn Wi-Fi and Bluetooth off again. Using the phone's browser, try again to navigate to **google.com**. Does it work? Why or why not?
6. What kind of network are you using to access the Internet when Wi-Fi is turned off?
7. **For group assignments:** Select one group member to set up a mobile hotspot using their smartphone. All other group members turn on their Airplane mode. What network connection type is required to connect to the mobile hotspot?
8. **For group assignments:** Each group member turns on the needed network connection for the mobile hotspot and then connects to the mobile hotspot. What network topology is the group using?

Project 1-3: Create a Password Manager Account

Estimated Time: 20 minutes
Objective: Explain common security concepts. (Obj. 4.1)
Resources:
- Internet access
- (Optional) Personal cell phone capable of receiving a text message

Context: Throughout this course, you will create several accounts at different websites to access tools for various projects. As you read in the module, a password manager can help you document those passwords and store them securely.

In this project, you create a LastPass account where you can store all your account information for the projects in this course. LastPass provides a free subscription option, and you can access your information from any device.

If you want, you can also store account information for your other school and personal accounts in LastPass. Just remember to always keep your master password secure.

NOTE 1-19

You'll learn more about how to create a secure password later. For now, keep in mind that the longer the password, the better. A simple and memorable way to do this is to think of an obscure line from a favorite song or movie and use several words of that line to create your master password along with some extra numbers or symbols to add complexity. Here's an example: *Spock$%Transmit@#Now*.

Complete the following steps to create your password manager account:

1. Go to **lastpass.com** and click **Get LastPass Free**.
2. Enter your email address and create a master password (the longer, the better—just make sure you can remember it or store it somewhere else safely because there is only one, somewhat unreliable way to recover the account if you forget the password). Confirm your master password and give yourself a reminder if it's helpful. When you're ready, click **Sign Up – It's Free**.
3. If you're working on your own computer, you can install the LastPass browser extension and log in through the extension. If you're not working on your own computer, you can navigate again to **lastpass.com** and log into your account through the website. Either way, click through to get to your LastPass vault. **Take a screenshot** of your empty vault; submit this visual with your answers to this project's questions. If you already have a LastPass account that you will be using for this course, be sure to obscure any private information from your screenshot. Note that no one, not even your instructor, will need access to your LastPass account for this course.
4. You can take the offered tour or explore the vault on your own. The LastPass vault is shown in Figure 1-25. Click through each menu option in the left pane. Answer the following questions:
   a. What is the difference between saving a note and saving a password?
   b. What is the purpose of the Emergency Access tool? When might this feature become relevant to you?

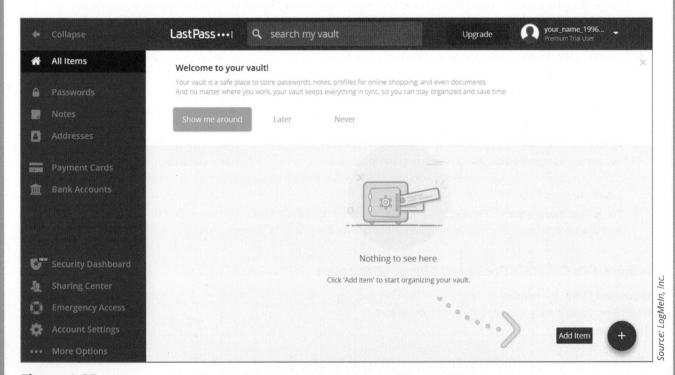

Figure 1-25   Store passwords, notes, and form information in your LastPass vault.

Source: LogMeIn, Inc.

5. When you get to Account Settings, scroll down to SMS Account Recovery and click **Update Phone**. If you have a personal cell phone, add a phone number where you can receive a recovery text message should you forget your master password. The phone must be in your possession to complete this step. Send the test code to your

phone and verify your phone in LastPass after you receive the code. Close the SMS Account Recovery tab in your browser. Close the Account Settings dialog box.

NOTE 1-20

Whenever you change your phone number, be sure to update this information in LastPass right away.

6. Click the **Add Item** button, as shown in the lower right corner of Figure 1-25. Enter information for a site you visit often, such as a social media site or an email service. If you want, you can make up information for this entry and then delete it later.
7. If you added a real account for a real website, move the mouse pointer over the site's tile and click **Launch** to automatically open and sign into that site.
8. Log out of LastPass in your browser. Always remember to log out of your account before walking away from your computer. Store a copy of your master password in a very secure place, such as a lockbox in your home, a safe deposit box at a bank, or an encrypted file on your computer.

NOTE 1-21

You can download and install LastPass as an extension in your favorite browser on each computer that you own. Last-Pass is compatible with Chrome, Firefox, Safari, Opera, Edge, and Internet Explorer. You can also install the LastPass app on your smartphone (Android or iPhone).

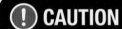 **CAUTION** No password manager is 100 percent reliably secure. Hackers target these services, and occasionally they're successful. LastPass, however, is one of the most reliable password managers currently available for free. KeePass, 1Password, Keeper, and Dashlane are also popular password managers. If you prefer, you can use one of these other password managers for this course.

No password manager is secure if you leave your account open on a computer or device you're not using, or if you write your master password where someone else can find it. Follow these guidelines consistently:

- Never save passwords in your browser, only in a password manager account such as the LastPass browser extension.
- Always log out of your password manager account when you're not using it.
- Always close browser windows where you have been signed into a secure account of any kind.
- Always lock or sign out of Windows before walking away from your computer.

Project 1-4: Apply Troubleshooting Methodology

Estimated Time: 20 minutes
Objective: Explain the network troubleshooting methodology. (Obj. 5.1)
Group Work: This project includes enhancements when assigned as a group project.
Resources:

- A drawing app, such as Paint in Windows or a web app such as jspaint.app, kleki.com, or app.diagrams.net

Context: Most likely at this point in your IT career, you've already encountered some challenging troubleshooting scenarios with computers, mobile devices, and perhaps even with networks. Interestingly, you probably intuitively applied some sound troubleshooting principles to the problem-solving process, and you might even have incorporated a basic understanding of networking layers as you worked through to a solution. Complete the following steps:

1. Think back to one of the more interesting scenarios you've faced, one where you were able to solve the problem. Take a few moments to write down the symptoms you encountered, the information you gathered, and the questions you asked. Try to remember the sense of confusion or concern that this unknowing created.

2. Think through what theories you developed on the possible causes of the problem as well as what attempts you made to solve the problem. Write down as many details as you can remember about how you finally discovered the solution, and how you arrived at that conclusion.

3. Look back at the troubleshooting flowchart in Figure 1-24. Using a drawing app such as Microsoft Paint in Windows or a free web app such as jspaint.app, kleki.com, or app.diagrams.net, map your problem-solving experience to the steps shown in the flowchart and include additional details as they come to you. **Save this image** as a .png file; submit this visual with your answers to this project's questions.

After developing your troubleshooting diagram, answer the following questions:

4. What do you notice about your progression through the OSI model layers? Even without necessarily knowing what the OSI model is, did you naturally take a top-to-bottom or a bottom-to-top approach to the problem?

5. What theories did you test that turned out to be wrong? What information or insights did you learn from those dead ends?

6. Did you involve anyone else in the problem-solving process? If so, who was that person and how did they help?

7. What did you do to test your solution? What measures did you take to ensure the problem didn't happen again?

8. Considering what you've now learned about troubleshooting methodology, what could you have reasonably done differently to discover the solution more quickly?

9. **For group assignments:** Each member of the group should write a summary of the problem experienced in their scenario, steps taken, and outcome of the issue as if they were documenting this information in a knowledge base. Next, exchange this documentation with another member of the group. Each member then reads through the information written by their classmate and lists questions they still have about the events or information gaps that could cause problems in the future. Discuss your concerns with the author of the scenario. Submit this information and a summary of the group discussion.

Capstone Projects

NOTE 1-22

The Capstone Projects in this course are designed to give you a "big picture" experience of networking. While the Capstones don't always map closely to a module's learning objectives, each Capstone adds resources and skills to your toolkit while building on Capstones you completed in earlier modules. For example, in this module, you will create at least one VM (virtual machine) in a hypervisor. In later Capstones, you will revisit this VM to complete other tasks on it. For those Capstones, you won't start from scratch—you'll build on resources you worked on in earlier modules. Over time, your stream of learning will build momentum so that you will accomplish complex tasks in later Capstones that you could not have completed in a single, isolated project.

Sometimes the Capstones will introduce you to concepts you haven't yet learned much about. Don't worry— detailed steps will guide you through each project. Then, when you study these concepts in later modules, you'll already have some familiarity with the concepts. For example, you haven't yet learned about virtualization in this course, and yet, you're working with a hypervisor in this module's Capstone Projects. By the time you get to the virtualization module, you'll have a decent understanding of what a hypervisor is and basically how it works, and that module's material will make a lot more sense to you.

Overall, these Capstones are intended to challenge you and also to provide a fun opportunity to apply what you're learning over time—to link concepts from module to module. In the study of learning science, this technique is called interleaving. Take good notes as you go, think creatively about what you're doing in each Capstone, and look for the ways each module's Capstones connect to other modules. Enjoy!

In Capstone Project 1-1, you will set up a VM (virtual machine) using Client Hyper-V, and in Capstone Project 1-2, you set up a VM using Oracle VirtualBox. You will continue to build your virtual network of VMs in later modules. Client Hyper-V and VirtualBox are client hypervisors, which is software used to manage VMs installed on a workstation. If you don't want to use Client Hyper-V or VirtualBox as your hypervisor of choice, you can substitute another client hypervisor, such as VMware Player, which can be downloaded free from *vmware.com*. Most of the future VM projects in this course can be completed using any of these three hypervisors.

Note that Windows Hyper-V and Oracle VirtualBox don't play well on the same computer and can cause problems, such as failed network connectivity, if used concurrently. For that reason, don't install Hyper-V and VirtualBox on the same computer. If you're choosing only one hypervisor because you only have one computer available, you'll find that future projects will usually work best using VirtualBox.

NOTE 1-23

Websites and applications change often. While the instructions given in these projects were accurate at the time of writing, you might need to adjust the steps or options according to later changes.

Note to Instructors and Students: A rubric is provided for evaluating student performance on these projects. Please see Appendix D.

Capstone Project 1-1: Set Up a Windows Virtual Machine Using Hyper-V

Estimated Time: 45 minutes
Objective: Explain the characteristics of network topologies and network types. (Obj. 1.2)
Resources:
- Windows 10 Pro (64-bit version) host computer
- Windows ISO file to install in a guest VM

Context: In this project, you enable and use Client Hyper-V, which is software embedded in Windows 10 Professional, 64-bit version, to create and manage VMs (virtual machines) and virtual networks on a single workstation. You'll first enable the workstation UEFI to support virtualization and enable Hyper-V. You'll then create a VM in Hyper-V and install a Windows OS in the VM.

NOTE 1-24

If you complete this project, your instructor might not require you to complete Capstone Project 1-2, "Set Up a Windows Virtual Machine Using Oracle VirtualBox." You'll use one of these two hypervisors and its VMs for multiple projects through-out this course, but you won't need both. Be sure to save any user account information or other important information in your LastPass vault for future reference.

Complete the following steps to enable virtualization in UEFI, enable Hyper-V, and configure a virtual switch for the virtual network:

1. For Hyper-V to work, HAV (hardware-assisted virtualization) must be enabled in UEFI setup. If you are not sure it is enabled, click **Start** and **Power**. Hold down the **Shift** key and click **Restart**. When the computer reboots, click **Troubleshoot**, **Advanced options**, and **UEFI Firmware settings**. The computer reboots again, this time into UEFI setup.

NOTE 1-25

Some motherboards might not show "UEFI Firmware settings" as an option on the Advanced options screen. If this is the case for you, you'll need to do a little experimenting and troubleshooting. First, determine your motherboard manu-facturer and model. To do this, continue the boot to Windows, press **Win+R**, and enter **msinfo32**, which will list the motherboard manufacturer and model on the System Summary page. Find the motherboard's documentation online to ensure it supports UEFI. If it does, you can try entering the UEFI settings during boot by pressing the required key, such as Esc, Del, F2, F4, F8, or F12. (If you're not sure which key to try, check your motherboard documentation or watch for a message during boot.) Before pressing the key to successfully access UEFI, you might first need to disable fast startup in the Windows Control Panel's Power Options menu. If you have trouble with any this, be sure to do a search online for the problem you're having and look for information to help you figure it out. Learning how to research a problem online is an important skill for any IT technician.

2. Make sure hardware-assisted virtualization (HAV) is enabled. For the system shown in Figure 1-26, that's done on the CPU Configuration screen. Also make sure that any subcategory items under HAV are enabled. Save your changes, exit UEFI setup, and allow the system to restart to Windows.

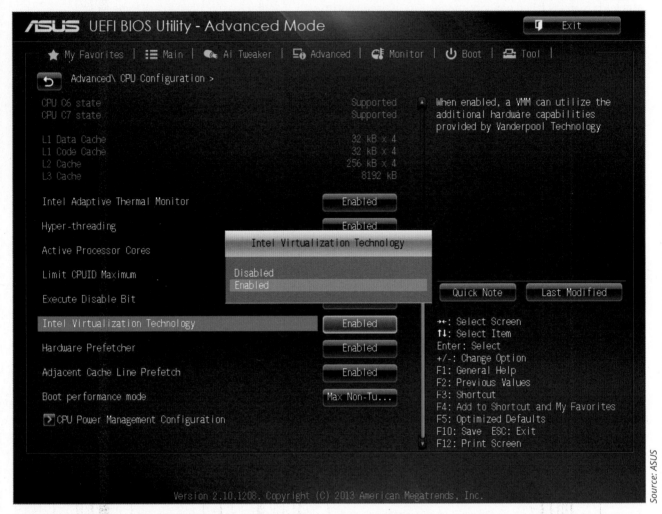

Figure 1-26   Virtualization must be enabled in UEFI setup for Client Hyper-V to work

3. Hyper-V is disabled in Windows 10 Pro by default. To enable it, right-click **Start** and click **Apps and Features**. Scroll down to Related settings and click **Programs and Features**. In the left pane, click **Turn Windows features on or off**. Check **Hyper-V** and click **OK**. When Windows finishes applying changes, click **Restart now** for the changes to take effect.

4. From the Windows Administrative Tools folder on the Start menu, launch the **Hyper-V Manager** application. In the left pane of the Hyper-V Manager, select the name of the host computer, which will be listed underneath Hyper-V Manager.

5. To make sure your VMs have access to the network or the Internet, you need to first install a virtual switch in Hyper-V. To create a new virtual network switch, click **Virtual Switch Manager** in the Actions pane.

6. In the Virtual Switch Manager dialog box, verify **New virtual network switch** is selected in the left pane. Give the switch a name, such as ProjectSwitch. To bind the virtual switch to the physical network adapter so the VMs can access the physical network, select **External** in the right pane. Then click **Create Virtual Switch.** In the next dialog box, make sure **Allow management operating system to share this network adapter** is checked and click **Apply**. In the Apply Networking Changes dialog box, click **Yes**. Your virtual LAN now has a virtual switch. Close the Virtual Switch Manager dialog box.

NOTE 1-26

Your instructor might have special instructions for the following steps. Check with your instructor before proceeding.

To create a VM, follow these steps:

7. In the Actions pane, click **Quick Create**. Use these parameters for the new VM:
   - Click **Local installation source**, and then click **Change installation source**. Browse to the location of the ISO file that contains the Windows operating system setup files made available by your instructor. Select the ISO file and click **Open**.

NOTE 1-27

An ISO file (which has the .iso file extension) is a disc image file. It contains all the files and folders of a virtual CD or DVD merged into a single file. The file can be burned to a physical disc, or it can be mounted to a virtual device, such as a VM.

   - Make sure Windows Secure Boot is enabled.
   - Click **More options** and enter a name for your VM. When naming resources like VMs, be sure to think through what information the resource's name should provide, and think about how this name will compare to other resource names when appearing in a list together. For example, you might want to include the VM's OS in the name, such as "Windows10-64bit," or you might want to reference the project in which you created the VM, such as "CapProj1-1." What did you name your VM?
   - Under Network, specify the VM can use the new virtual switch you created earlier.
   - Click **Create Virtual Machine**.

8. After the VM is created, click **Edit** settings and answer the following questions:
   a. How much memory will the VM have?
   b. How many virtual processors will the VM have?
   c. What device will the VM boot from?

9. Click **Cancel**, click **Connect**, and then click **Start**. If you used an ISO file as the installation source, when you see *Press any key to boot from CD or DVD*, press the spacebar so the VM will boot from the ISO file. Figure 1-27 shows where a Windows 10 installation has begun.

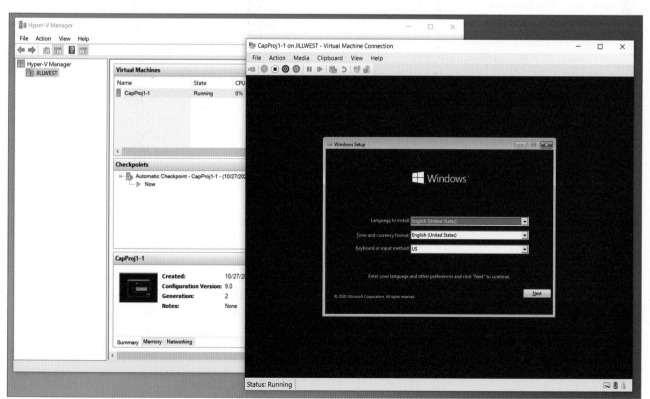

Figure 1-27   Windows 10 setup is running in the VM managed by Hyper-V

NOTE 1-28

If you have trouble booting to the ISO file, consider increasing the VM's available memory in the Settings menu. For example, 64-bit Windows installs more easily with 4 GB of RAM rather than the minimum 2 GB. Keep in mind, though, that any RAM dedicated to a running VM is not available to the host machine.

10. During setup, choose the following options:
    a. Check with your instructor for specific instructions on how to handle the Windows product key.
    b. When prompted, choose the **Windows 10 Home** or **Windows 10 Professional** operating system unless your instructor directs otherwise.
    c. When prompted, choose the **Custom: Install Windows only (advanced)** option.
    d. Otherwise, follow the prompts on-screen and make any adjustments to default settings only as directed by your instructor. How much space is allocated to the VM's Drive 0?
11. After you have installed Windows in the VM, and the VM boots into Windows, you should receive a message asking if you want to allow this computer to be discoverable by other devices on the network. Click **Yes**. Then open the Edge browser to confirm the VM has a good Internet connection. **Take a screenshot** of your desktop showing your Hyper-V Manager, your running VM, and the VM's successful connection with the Internet; submit this visual with your answers to this project's questions. When you're finished, be sure to shut down the VM properly—just like a physical machine, a virtual machine can be corrupted by improper shutdowns.

In later modules, you'll continue to build your virtual network and install resources in the VMs on your network. Make sure you record any relevant information, such as user account password or PIN, in your LastPass vault.

Capstone Project 1-2: Set Up a Windows Virtual Machine Using Oracle VirtualBox

Estimated Time: 45 minutes
Objective: Explain the characteristics of network topologies and network types. (Obj. 1.2)
Resources:
- Any edition of Windows 10 installed on a computer that supports UEFI. Note that instructions for projects using VirtualBox are written for Windows 10 hosts. However, Oracle VirtualBox can also be installed on a Windows 7/8/8.1, Linux, macOS, or Solaris host.
- Windows ISO file to install in a guest VM

Context: In this project, you download and install Oracle VirtualBox, which is a free hypervisor, to create VMs (virtual machines) and a virtual network on a single workstation.

NOTE 1-29

If you completed Capstone Project 1-1, "Set Up a Windows Virtual Machine Using Hyper-V," your instructor might not require you to complete this project. You'll use one of these two hypervisors and its VMs for multiple projects throughout this course, but you won't need both. Be sure to save any user account information or other important information in your LastPass vault for future reference.

Complete the following steps to install VirtualBox:

1. If you are using a 64-bit host computer and want to install a 64-bit OS in the VM, HAV (hardware-assisted virtualization) must be enabled in UEFI setup. If you are not sure it is enabled, click **Start** and **Power**. Hold down the **Shift** key and click **Restart**. When the computer reboots, click **Troubleshoot**, **Advanced options**, and **UEFI Firmware settings**. The computer reboots again, this time into UEFI setup.

NOTE 1-30

Some motherboards might not show "UEFI Firmware settings" as an option on the Advanced options screen. If this is the case for you, you'll need to do a little experimenting and troubleshooting. First, determine your motherboard manufacturer and model. To do this, continue the boot to Windows, press **Win+R**, and enter **msinfo32**, which will list the motherboard manufacturer and model on the System Summary page. Find the motherboard's documentation online to ensure it supports UEFI. If it does, you can try entering the UEFI settings during boot by pressing the required key, such as Esc, Del, F2, F4, F8, or F12. (If you're not sure which key to try, check your motherboard documentation or watch for a message during boot.) For this to work, you might first need to disable fast startup in the Windows Control Panel's Power Options menu. If you have trouble with any this, be sure to do a search online for the problem you're having and look for information to help you figure it out. Learning how to research a problem online is an important skill for any IT technician.

2. Make sure hardware-assisted virtualization (HAV) is enabled. For the system shown earlier in Figure 1-26, that's done on the CPU Configuration screen. Also make sure that any subcategory items under HAV are enabled. Save your changes, exit UEFI setup, and allow the system to restart to Windows.

3. Go to **www.virtualbox.org/wiki/Downloads** and download the most current **VirtualBox platform package** for Windows hosts to your desktop or other folder on your hard drive. Install the software, accepting default settings during the installation. The Oracle VM VirtualBox Manager window opens (see Figure 1-28).

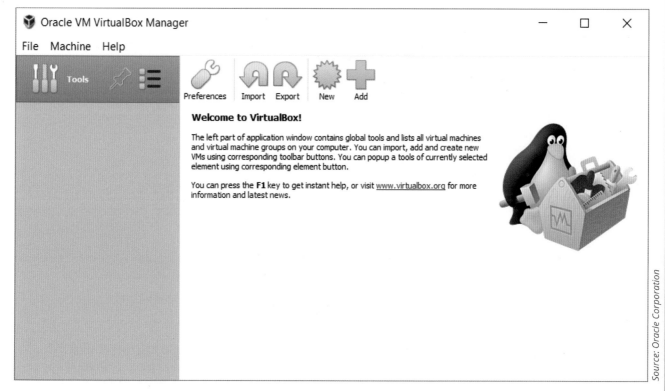

Source: Oracle Corporation

Figure 1-28   Use the VirtualBox Manager to create and manage virtual machines

NOTE 1-31

Your instructor might have special instructions for the following steps. Check with your instructor before proceeding.

To create a virtual machine using VirtualBox, complete the following steps:

4. Click **New** in the toolbar and follow the wizard to create a VM. Give your VM a name. When naming resources like VMs, be sure to think through what information the resource's name should provide, and think about how this name will compare to other resource names when appearing in a list together. For example, you might want to include the VM's OS in the name, such as "Windows10-64bit," or you might want to reference the project in which you created the VM, such as "CapProj1-2." What did you name your VM?

5. Select the Windows OS you will install in the VM, such as Windows 10 (64-bit). You can accept all default settings for the VM unless directed otherwise by your instructor. As you go, notice the resources allocated to the VM and answer the following questions:
   a. How much memory will the VM have?
   b. What kind of file will hold the VM's virtual hard disk?
   c. How much space will the VM's hard disk have?

6. With the VM selected, click **Settings** in the VirtualBox Manager window. In the VM's Settings window, click **Storage** in the left pane.

7. In the Storage Tree area, to the right of *Controller: SATA*, click the **Adds optical drive** icon, which looks like a CD with a plus (+) symbol, as shown in Figure 1-29.

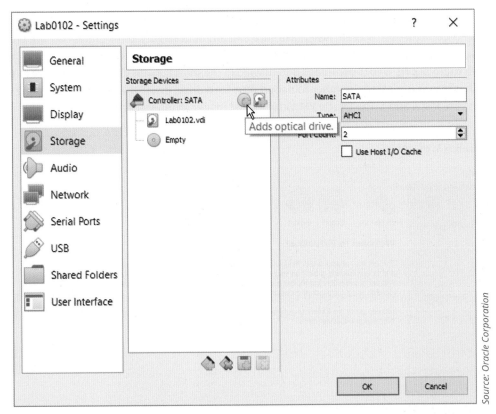

Source: Oracle Corporation

Figure 1-29   Storage Tree options allow you to mount an ISO image as a virtual CD in the VM

8. The Optical Disk Selector window appears. Click **Add**. Browse to the location of the ISO file that contains the Windows operating system setup files made available by your instructor. Select the ISO file, click **Open**, click **Choose**, and click **OK**. You will now return to the VirtualBox Manager window.

NOTE 1-32

An ISO file (which has the .iso file extension) is a disc image file. It contains all the files and folders of a virtual CD or DVD merged into a single file. The file can be burned to a physical disc, or it can be mounted to a virtual device, such as a VM.

9. Click **Start** on the toolbar. When you see *Press any key to boot from CD or DVD*, press the spacebar so the VM will boot from the ISO file. Your VM starts up and begins the process of installing the operating system.

NOTE 1-33

If you have trouble booting to the ISO file, you might need to enable EFI. To do this, go to the VM's **Settings** window and click **System**. In the Extended Features section, select the checkbox for **Enable EFI (special OSs only)**.

Also, if the VM struggles to install Windows, consider increasing the VM's available memory in the Settings menu. For example, 64-bit Windows installs more easily with 4 GB of RAM rather than the minimum 2 GB. Keep in mind, though, that any RAM dedicated to a running VM is not available to the host machine.

10. During setup, choose the following options:
    a. Check with your instructor for specific instructions on how to handle the Windows product key.
    b. When prompted, choose the **Windows 10 Home** operating system unless your instructor directs otherwise.
    c. When prompted, choose the **Custom: Install Windows only (advanced)** option.
    d. Otherwise, follow the prompts on-screen and make any adjustments to default settings only as directed by your instructor.
11. After you have installed Windows in the VM, and the VM boots into Windows, you should receive a message asking if you want to allow this computer to be discoverable by other devices on the network. Click **Yes**. Then open the Edge browser to confirm the VM has a good Internet connection. **Take a screenshot** of your desktop showing your VirtualBox app, your running VM, and the VM's successful connection with the Internet; submit this visual with your answers to this project's questions. When you're finished, be sure to shut down the VM properly—just like a physical machine, a virtual machine can be corrupted by improper shutdowns.

In later modules, you'll continue to build your virtual network and install resources in the VMs on your network. Make sure you record any relevant information, such as user account password or PIN, in your LastPass vault.

Solutions to Self-Check Questions

Network Models

1. Which of the following is part of a network's physical topology?

   Answer: b. A printer plugged into a nearby desktop computer

   Explanation: Physical topology mostly refers to a network's hardware and how computers, other devices (such as **printers**), and cables or radio signals work together to form the physical network. Operating systems, passwords, and file permission settings are all part of a network's logical topology.

2. Which of the following is an advantage of P2P file sharing?

   Answer: d. Inexpensive

   Explanation: Peer-to-peer networks are often **less expensive** to set up and maintain than other types of networks. A network operating system, such as Windows Server 2019, is much more expensive than a desktop operating system, such as Windows 10. P2P networks are not scalable and are not necessarily secure. Client-server networks store user accounts and passwords in one place, and access permissions are centrally granted.

3. What Windows Server group must clients join to access network resources in a client-server network?

   Answer: b. Domain

   Explanation: When Windows Server controls network access to a group of computers, this logical group is called a Windows **domain**. A workgroup is one option for sharing resources in a peer-to-peer network. A server might use a RAID (redundant array of independent disks) configuration of hard drives, so that if one hard drive fails, another hard drive automatically takes its place.

Client-Server Applications

4. Which of the following is a secure protocol?

Answer: d. SSH

Explanation: The **SSH (Secure Shell)** protocol creates an encrypted channel or tunnel between two computers, which provides security that Telnet lacks. HTTP (Hypertext Transfer Protocol) requires another protocol, such as TLS (Transport Layer Security), for security. FTP (File Transfer Protocol) does not provide encryption and is, therefore, not secure. However, an encrypted and secure file transfer protocol is SFTP (Secure File Transfer Protocol), which is based on the SSH protocol.

5. What is an example of an open source DBMS?

Answer: a. MySQL

Explanation: Popular examples of SQL database software include Microsoft SQL Server, Oracle Database, and the open-source **MySQL**. Open source is the term for software whose code is publicly available for use and modification, which is often considered more secure because users can evaluate the source code of the software to ensure there are no loopholes left open for attackers to exploit. Note that "open source" is not synonymous with "free."

6. Which of these protocols could *not* be used to access a server in a nearby building?

Answer: c. TLS

Explanation: **TLS (Transport Layer Security)** adds encryption to other protocols, such as HTTP, but does not provide remote access to a computer. The Telnet protocol is a command-line application included in many operating systems that allows a user to remote into a computer, although its transmissions are not encrypted. The SSH (Secure Shell) protocol creates an encrypted channel or tunnel between two computers, which provides security that Telnet lacks. In Windows operating systems, RDP (Remote Desktop Protocol) also provides secure, encrypted transmissions.

Network Hardware

7. When you connect your keyboard, mouse, and monitor to your computer, what kind of network topology are you using?

Answer: c. Star topology

Explanation: In a **star topology**, all devices connect to one central device. In this case, the keyboard, mouse, and monitor are connecting to the central device, the computer. In a bus topology, the devices would be connected in a line with no device connected to more than two other devices. In a mesh topology, all devices would be connected to each other. In a ring topology, each device would be connected to exactly two other devices.

8. Which networking device is best for connecting your network printer to three computers?

Answer: a. Switch

Explanation: A **switch** receives incoming data from one of its ports and redirects (or switches) it to another port or multiple ports that will send the data to its intended destination(s). The fundamental difference between a switch and a router is that a switch belongs only to its local network and a router belongs to two or more networks. In this case, all the devices belong to the same network. While a hub would work, it's inefficient and outdated so is not the best choice. A file server stores files for other computers to access.

9. Which network types can your smartphone use?

Answer: e. WAN, LAN, and PAN

Explanation: When a smartphone communicates over the cellular network for phone calls, it is using a **WAN** across a wide geographical area. When a smartphone connects with your home network, it is using a **LAN** in your home. When a smartphone connects with Bluetooth ear buds, a fitness tracker, or a Bluetooth weight scale, it is using a **PAN** to connect devices intended for use by one person at a time.

The Seven-Layer OSI Model

10. At what OSI layer does your browser's web page request begin its journey through the OSI layers?

Answer: a. Application layer

Explanation: The **application layer** in the OSI model describes the interface between two applications, each on separate computers. It takes data from an application or utility and creates a payload for lower OSI layers to manage and transport. The lower layers, such as the network, data link, and physical layers, encapsulate the payload from higher layers to add each protocol's information before passing the message down to the next layer.

11. Which layer holds the address of the target application running on the destination computer?

Answer: b. Transport layer

Explanation: The **transport layer** header addresses the receiving application by a number called a port, which identifies a specific application on a computer. The application layer does not include addressing information. The network layer header identifies the sending and receiving host computers on a network by their IP addresses. The data link frame's header contains the hardware addresses of the source and destination NICs. This address is called a MAC (Media Access Control) address.

12. Which OSI layer adds both a header and a trailer?

Answer: c. Data link layer

Explanation: The **data link layer** puts its control information in a data link layer header and also attaches control information to the end of the packet in a trailer. The entire data link layer message is then called a frame. The transport and network layers both add their information in their respective headers but typically do not use trailers. While there is a preamble added in front of the data link layer header, it's not typically considered to be a physical layer header. The physical layer is responsible for sending bits via a wired or wireless transmission.

Safety Procedures and Policies

13. Which fire suppression level provides the most targeted protection?

Answer: b. Rack level

Explanation: **Rack level** fire suppression offers targeted fire detection and suppression inside each cabinet that holds network devices to reduce the impact on surrounding equipment. Room level fire suppression incorporates a sprinkler or gas system that provides fire suppression in parts of a room or throughout the entire room. A building level system protects the entire building and employees throughout that space.

14. What is the minimum amount of ESD required to damage sensitive electronic equipment?

Answer: c. 10 volts

Explanation: When your body and a component have different static charges and you touch the component, you can discharge up to 1,500 volts of static electricity without seeing a spark or feeling the discharge. However, it only takes **10 volts** to damage the component. This means you could fry a motherboard and never even feel a shock.

Troubleshooting Network Problems

15. What should you do after making a plan to solve a problem and carrying out your plan?

Answer: d. Verify functionality

Explanation: After implementing your solution, you'll test the system to **verify full system functionality**. It's also a good idea to return a few days later and make sure all is working as you expected. Also consider what you can do to make sure the problem doesn't reappear. You find out what has recently changed at the beginning of the process. You test your theory of what's causing the problem before developing a plan to solve the problem. You document your work at the end after verifying the solution worked.

16. While exploring the problem and developing a theory about the cause, where can you go to get information on similar problems your coworkers have faced in the past?

Answer: b. Knowledge base

Explanation: A **knowledge base** is a collection of accumulated insights and solutions to the problems encountered on a particular network. A SDS (safety data sheet) explains how to properly handle substances such as chemical solvents and how to dispose of them. The current troubleshooting ticket in the call tracking system will contain information about the current problem but not accumulated insights from previous problems. An instruction manual can provide insights on how a device or application works and possibly troubleshooting help for common problems, but it will not include information on previous problems experienced by your coworkers.

INFRASTRUCTURE AND DOCUMENTATION

After reading this module and completing the exercises, you should be able to:

1 Describe the roles of various network and cabling equipment in commercial buildings and work areas

2 Maintain network documentation

3 Manage changes made to a network

On the Job

Over the years, our need for localized services or "remote" backups has steadily increased. Part of the solution has been to convert several of our larger wiring closets into small server rooms to host the additional equipment. We place climate monitors in these locations to help monitor temperature and humidity conditions. These monitors report climate conditions via SNMP (Simple Network Management Protocol) to our network monitoring system. The network monitoring system then sends notifications to IT staff members if the temperature moves out of a threshold range.

One summer, we placed one of these temperature monitors in a closet where servers had recently been added, and things were good. A few months later, as the temperature cooled outside, we started getting alarms about temperature spikes. The spikes were small at first, but increased as the temperature outside dropped. That was kind of odd.

A little investigation revealed that, although the server room had air conditioning, the room's temperature was not managed independently of the nearby offices. As autumn weather cooled the offices in the building, the staff would turn on the heat, warming themselves and, unfortunately, the servers. A tweak of the air conditioning layout quickly resolved this issue and things were once again good.

Robert Wilson
Information Systems Director
McCallie School

Just as a building architect must decide where to place walls and doors, where to install electrical and plumbing systems, and how to manage traffic patterns through rooms to make a building more livable, a network architect must consider many factors regarding hardware and software when designing a network. You've already learned about physical and logical network models, the OSI model, and the hosts, routers, and switches that manage data on the network. This module details the structural hardware necessary to connect and support these hosts, routers, and switches and connect them to the outside world. You'll learn about cabling, racks, equipment that monitors the environment, and other equipment that supports the physical network in a building or on a campus.

You'll also learn how critical it is to maintain good network documentation, so you can keep track of the complexities of a typical modern network. Finally, you'll learn how to implement clear policies for managing changes to a network. In later modules, you will dig deeper into the various layers of network components, including the details of cabling and wireless networking.

COMPONENTS OF STRUCTURED CABLING

✓ CERTIFICATION

7	Application
6	Presentation
5	Session
4	Transport
3	Network
2	Data Link
▶ **① Physical**

1.2 Explain the characteristics of network topologies and network types.

1.3 Summarize the types of cables and connectors and explain which is the appropriate type for a solution.

1.5 Explain common ports and protocols, their application, and encrypted alternatives.

2.1 Compare and contrast various devices, their features, and their appropriate placement on the network.

3.1 Given a scenario, use the appropriate statistics and sensors to ensure network availability.

3.3 Explain high availability and disaster recovery concepts and summarize which is the best solution.

5.2 Given a scenario, troubleshoot common cable connectivity issues and select the appropriate tools.

Average reading time: 28 minutes

If you were to tour hundreds of data centers and equipment rooms at established enterprises—that is, large organizations or businesses—you would notice some similarities in their equipment and cabling arrangements. That's because organizations tend to follow a family of cabling standards formulated by TIA (Telecommunications Industry Association) and its former parent company EIA (Electronic Industries Alliance) and now accredited by ANSI (American National Standards Institute). These standards, now known as ANSI/TIA-568, or structured cabling, describe uniform, enterprise-wide cabling systems regardless of who manufactures or sells the various parts used in the system. The standards are updated every several years with the most recent version of standards, ANSI/TIA-568-D, published in 2015 through 2017.

 EXAM TIP TIA and EIA are commonly referred to collectively with the acronym TIA/EIA. Occasionally, including on the CompTIA Network+ exam, you might see the acronyms reversed, as follows: EIA/TIA. Many sources now replace the EIA portion with ANSI to reflect ANSI's role in accrediting the standards: ANSI/TIA. All these combinations refer to the same family of standards.

Structured cabling standards describe the best ways to install various types of networking media to maximize performance and minimize upkeep. The principles of structured cabling apply no matter what type of media, transmission technology, or networking speeds are involved. Structured cabling is based on a hierarchical design and assumes a network is set up in a star topology.

From the Demarc to a Workstation

Imagine you're a network technician touring the network on a school or corporate campus where you've just been hired. To get the lay of the land, your trained eye would be on the lookout for the main components that make up the network infrastructure. These components include the demarc, MDF, and locations of various IDFs strategically branched throughout campus. Figure 2-1 diagrams the main components you would look for in a network. Figure 2-2 shows a cross-section view of one building.

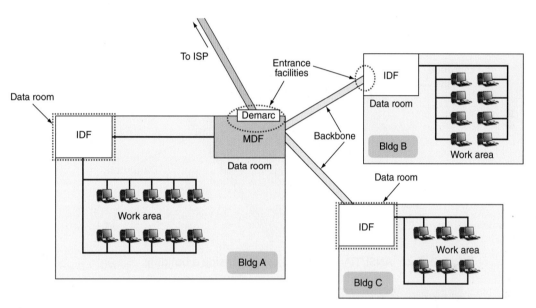

Figure 2-1 ANSI/TIA structured cabling in a campus network with three buildings

Tour Stop 1: Entrance Facility in Building A

A network begins at the demarc and ends at a workstation. Let's begin your tour of the physical network where it begins—at the entrance facility, which contains the demarcation point:

- **EF (entrance facility)**—This is the location where an incoming network, such as the Internet, connects with the school or corporate network and includes all the necessary components to make the transition from the WAN or MAN managed by the ISP (Internet service provider) to the LAN or CAN managed by the customer. It could also refer to the entrance point of cabling from one building to another in a campus network. For large networks, the EF might reside in an equipment room or data closet. For small networks, it might simply be equipment and cabling mounted to the side of a building. The EF is where a telecommunications service provider (whether it is a local phone company, long-distance carrier, dedicated Internet service provider, cable company, or satellite company) accepts responsibility for the external connection. It contains a service provider's equipment, such as cabling and protective boxes. The most important device that belongs to the service provider in the EF is the demarc.
- **Demarc (demarcation point)**—For most situations, the device that marks where an ISP's network ends and the organization's network begins (see Figure 2-3) is the demarc, or demarcation point. For example, the ISP might be responsible for fiber-optic cabling to your building to connect to your LAN. The device where the WAN ends and the LAN begins is the demarc. The ISP is responsible for its network beyond the demarc, and, in most cases, the organization is responsible for devices and services on the campus side of the demarc.

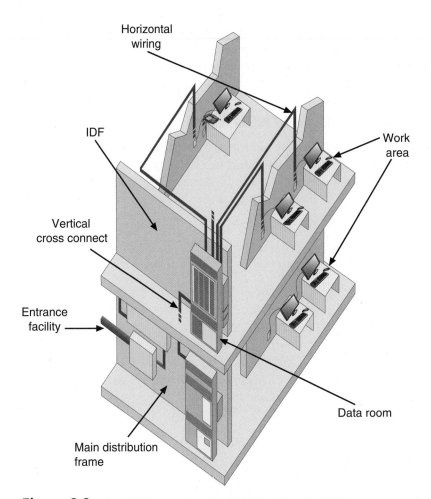

Figure 2-2   ANSI/TIA structured cabling inside a building

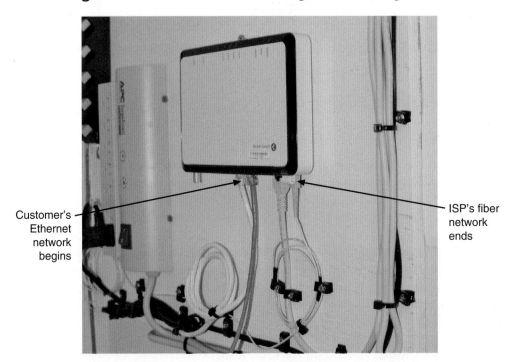

Figure 2-3   Demarc for Internet service to a campus network; this demarc is located inside a small data room and connects the incoming fiber signal from the ISP with the campus's Ethernet network

- **MDF (main distribution frame)**—Also known as the ER (equipment room), the MDF is an environmentally controlled space that hosts the MC (main cross connect) and is the centralized point of interconnection for an organization's LAN, CAN, or WAN. In practice, the term *MDF* can refer either to the racks holding the network equipment or to the room that houses both the racks and the equipment. The MDF and the EF might be in the same room, or they could be in separate rooms, depending on the layout of the building. Connections branching out from the MDF include Ethernet cables connecting to nearby work areas, large or bundles of cables running to IDFs (discussed later in this list) in other buildings or on other floors of the same building, and the incoming connection from the service provider's facility. Imagine a star topology with the MDF at the center, as shown in Figure 2-4. Besides serving as a connection for cables, an MDF might contain the demarc (or an extension from the demarc, if the demarc itself is located outside the building), a transceiver that converts the incoming signal from the ISP into Ethernet, other connectivity devices (such as switches and routers), network servers, and transmission media (such as fiber-optic cable, which is capable of the greatest throughput). Often, it also houses an organization's main servers.

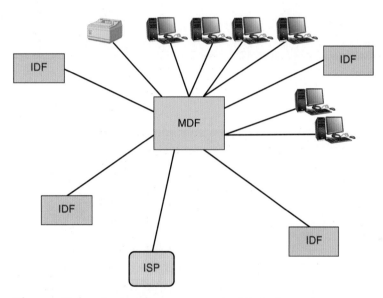

Figure 2-4   The MDF connects to the ISP, IDFs on campus, and nearby workstations

- **Data room**—Also called TR (telecommunications room), TE (telecommunications enclosure), or data closet, a data room is an enclosed space that holds network equipment. These spaces might have requirements for size, clearance around equipment, wall materials, and physical security (such as a locked door). Larger data rooms (also called a TR) and smaller data closets (also called a TE) both require good cooling and ventilation systems for maintaining a constant temperature, as you read about in the *On the Job* story at the beginning of this module.
- **Rack**—A large data room can contain rows of racks to hold various network equipment, such as servers, routers, switches, and firewalls. Rack systems make good use of space in data rooms and ensure adequate spacing, access, and ventilation for the devices they house.
- **Patch panel**—Also called a **patch bay**, this is a panel of data receptors which can be mounted to a wall or a rack and which provides a central termination point when many patch cables converge in a single location. Figure 2-5 shows the front side of a patch panel. Figure 2-6 shows the rear side of a mostly empty patch panel.

Figure 2-5   Patch panel on rack

Empty slots available for more connectors

Figure 2-6   Rear side of a partially filled patch panel, looking in from the back side of the rack

- **VoIP telephone equipment**—**VoIP (Voice over IP)**, also known as IP telephony, is the use of any network (either public or private) to carry voice signals using TCP/IP protocols. In one or more data rooms on a campus network, you might find a **voice gateway** device, which converts signals from a campus's analog phone equipment into IP data that can travel over the Internet, or which converts VoIP data from an internal IP network to travel over a phone company's analog telephone lines. A common application layer protocol used by voice gateways to initiate and maintain connections is the signaling protocol **SIP (Session Initial Protocol)**. You might also find VoIP PBX (private branch exchange) equipment. This is a dedicated telephone switch or a virtual switching device that connects and manages calls within a private organization, and it manages call connections that exit the network through a VoIP gateway. Internally, this equipment connects to **VoIP phones**, which might be telephones sitting at each user's location or applications hosted on a user's computer or other device. See Figure 2-7 for two sample VoIP network layouts.

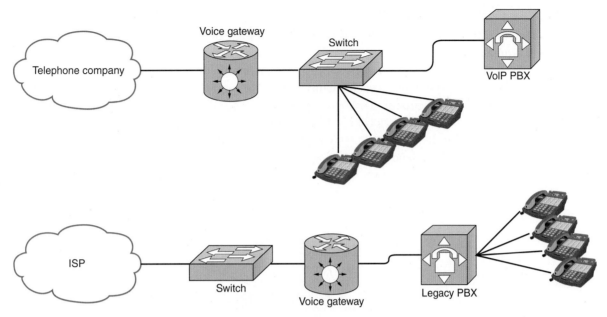

Figure 2-7   VoIP equipment can connect VoIP phones to an analog telephone line or an analog phone system to the Internet; there are pros and cons to each approach

Legacy Networking: Punchdown Blocks

The precursor to the patch panel is another kind of termination point, the punchdown block. This is a panel of voice or data receptors into which twisted-pair wire is inserted, or punched down, using a **punchdown tool** (also called a krone tool) to complete a circuit. The types of punchdown blocks used on data networks were the **110 block**; the similar, European-developed, and -patented **Krone (Krone LSA-PLUS) block**; and the more compact **BIX (Building Industry Cross-connect) block**. These newer blocks are more suitable for data connections than the older **66 block**, which was used primarily for telephone connections. (The numerals 66 and 110 refer to the model numbers of the earliest blocks.) If you do come across punchdown blocks in the field, be careful not to untwist twisted-pair cables more than one-half inch before inserting them into the punchdown block. Figure 2-8 shows a punchdown block.

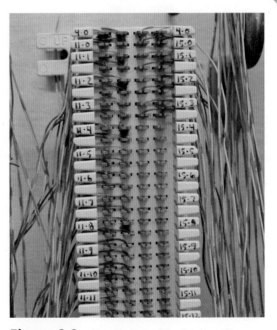

Figure 2-8   Punchdown block on wall

Tour Stop 2: Data Room in Building B

Now that you've seen the MDF in the first building, let's move on to some of the other buildings you'll be responsible for and identify the equipment you'll find there:

- **IDF (intermediate distribution frame)**—The IDF provides an intermediate connection between the MDF and end-user equipment on each floor and in each building. Again, the term *IDF* can refer either to the racks holding the network equipment or to the room that houses both the racks and the equipment. There is only one MDF per campus, but there can be many IDFs connecting internal portions of the network. The ANSI/TIA standards specify at least one IDF per floor, although large organizations may have several data rooms or closets per floor to better manage the data feed from the main data facilities. Connections from the IDF branch out to workstations in an extended star topology, as shown in Figure 2-9.

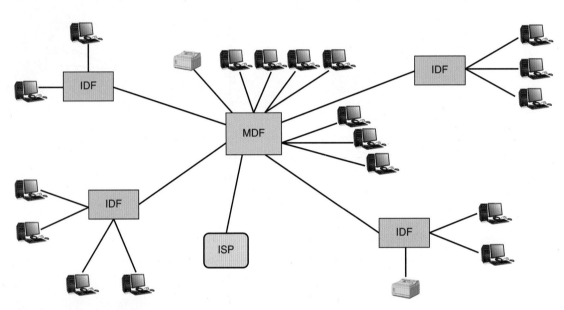

Figure 2-9 Workstations branching off IDFs that branch off an MDF create an extended star topology

Tour Stop 3: Work Areas in All Three Buildings

All these buildings contain work areas where employees and others (students or customers) can access network resources. Each of these work areas contain similar components:

- **Work area**—This area encompasses workstations, printers, and other networked devices, and all the patch cables, wall jacks, and horizontal cabling necessary to connect these devices to a data room.
- **Wall jacks**—A work area often contains wall jacks. The ANSI/TIA standards call for each wall jack to contain at least one voice and one data outlet, as pictured in Figure 2-10. Realistically, you will encounter a variety of wall jacks. For example, in a student computer lab lacking phones, a wall jack with a combination of voice and data outlets is unnecessary.

Rack Systems

By this point in your tour, you've seen a few racks. Generally, racks come in two-post and four-post varieties, though six-post racks are also available. They can also be open-framed, which provides greater accessibility, or enclosed, which provides greater protection. Figure 2-11 shows examples of open two-post racks and enclosed four-post racks.

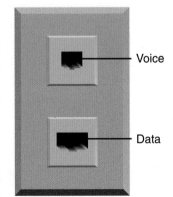

Figure 2-10
A standard ANSI/TIA outlet

Figure 2-11 Open two-post racks and enclosed four-post racks

The side posts in a rack provide bracketing for attaching devices, such as routers, servers, switches, patch panels, audiovisual equipment, or telephony equipment. This equipment often comes with attached or attachable brackets, called rack ears, for securing the device to the posts, as shown in Figure 2-12. Post holes can be round or square, threaded or nonthreaded. Square-hole racks are the most recent attachment innovation, allowing for bolt-free mounting.

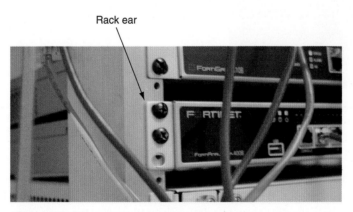

Figure 2-12 Attach network equipment to rack systems by inserting bolts through rack ears

Racks may be wall- or ceiling-mounted, freestanding on the floor, or bolted to the floor. Other features might include power strips, rack fans for cooling, cable trays, or drawers. Carefully consider a rack's dimensions when purchasing racks, as follows:

- **Height**—Rack height is measured in rack units (RU or U) with the industry standard being 42U tall—about 6 feet. Half-racks are usually 18U–22U tall.
- **Width**—Equipment racks come in a standard 19-inch frame, meaning that the front is 19 inches wide. You might also come across 23-inch racks.
- **Depth**—Rack depths vary considerably between manufacturers.

NOTE 2-1

It's impractical to install a separate console for every device on a rack. Typically, racks have one or more **KVM (keyboard, video, and mouse) switches**, which connect to a single console to provide a central control portal for all devices on the rack. Figure 2-13 shows a console that is held in a pull-out tray and that attaches to multiple KVM switches installed in this rack.

Figure 2-13   Here, a single console uses five KVM switches to access and configure multiple devices in a row of racks

Minimizing cable clutter can help prevent airflow blockages and heat buildup. In a typical rack system, airflow through the chassis is designed to move from front to back. In data centers containing multiple rows of racks, a hot aisle/cold aisle layout, as shown in Figure 2-14, pulls cool air from vents in the floor or from nearby, low-lying wall vents into the rows of racks. The hot air aisles are used to direct the heated air away from the racks into exhaust vents for cooling.

Cabling

As you traveled from the entrance facility, demarc, and MDF, then walked through a couple of buildings locating each IDF, and viewed each work area with their workstations, you noticed a variety of cabling types. Some cables are very thin, the Ethernet cables look familiar, and some cables are wrapped in dark insulation and are inches thick. Let's consider each of these cabling types as you work your way back to where you started your network tour. Then you'll explore cable management techniques before rounding out this part of the module with a discussion of the environmental and security needs of network hardware.

Types of Cables

Structured cabling standards allow for three basic types of cable installations, as follows:

- **Patch cable**—A patch cable is a relatively short (usually between 3 and 25 feet) length of cabling with connectors at both ends.

- **Horizontal cabling**—This is the cabling that connects workstations to the closest data room and to switches housed in the room. The maximum allowable distance for horizontal cabling is 100 m. This span includes 90 m to connect the network device in the data room to a data jack on the wall in the work area, plus a maximum of 10 m to connect the wall jack to a workstation. Figure 2-15 depicts an example of a horizontal cabling configuration. Figure 2-16 illustrates a cable installation connecting the data room to the work area. Notice the patch panels in the figure.

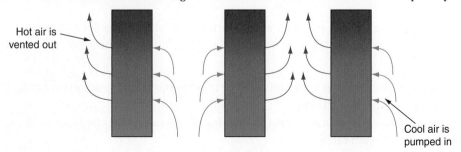

Hot air is vented out

Cool air is pumped in

Figure 2-14   Hot aisle/cold aisle rack layout

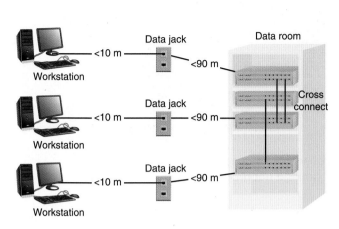

Figure 2-15   Horizontal cabling from a switch in a data room to workstations

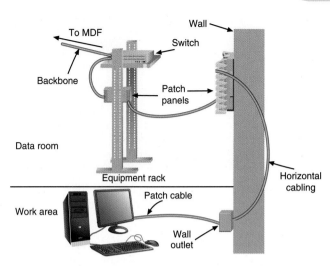

Figure 2-16   A typical UTP cabling installation

NOTE 2-2

ANSI/TIA standards recognize three possible cabling types for horizontal cabling: UTP, STP, or fiber-optic cable. **UTP (unshielded twisted pair)** cable is a type of copper-based cable that consists of one or more insulated twisted-pair wires encased in a plastic sheath. Figure 2-17a shows an example of the twisted pairs inside UTP cable used on local networks. **STP (shielded twisted pair)** cable is a similar type of copper-based cable containing twisted-pair wires with metallic shielding, such as foil around each wire pair or surrounding all four wire pairs. The high-grade STP cable in Figure 2-17b incorporates shielding around the wire pairs *and* around all the pairs for improved performance. **Fiber-optic cable** is a form of cable that contains one or several glass or plastic fibers in its core and comes in two types: SMF (single-mode fiber) or MMF (multimode fiber). Copper-based cable transmits data via electric signals, and fiber-optic cable transmits data via pulsing light sent from a laser or LED (light-emitting diode).

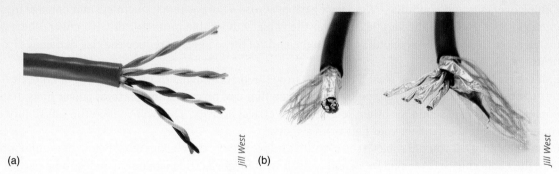

(a)   (b)

Figure 2-17   (a) UTP (unshielded twisted-pair) cable and (b) STP (shielded twisted-pair) cable for local wired networks

---

- **Backbone cabling**—The backbone consists of cables or wireless links that provide interconnection between the entrance facility and MDF and between the MDF and IDFs. One component of the backbone is the vertical cross connect, which runs between a building's floors. For example, it might connect an MDF and IDF or two IDFs within a building. Especially on large, modern networks, backbones are often composed of fiber-optic cable. The cables can be thickly insulated and usually are run through flexible plastic sleeving or sturdier conduit, which are pipes installed overhead or through walls or sometimes underground, as shown in Figure 2-18.

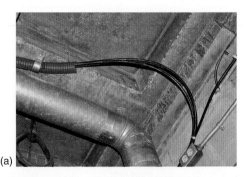

(a)   (b)

Figure 2-18   Sleeving and conduit help protect cabling from damage, but it might also invite rodent traffic and damage along the cables if not properly sealed

Expert network technicians know that many network problems are the result of poor cable installations; they pay close attention to the quality of cable connections and cable management. Let's look at some standards for cable management in a building or enterprise.

Cable Management

As a network professional, you will occasionally add new cables to a data room, repair defective cable ends, or install a data outlet. Following are some cable installation tips that will help prevent physical layer failures:

- **Termination**—When terminating twisted-pair cabling, don't leave more than 1 inch of exposed (stripped) cable before a twisted-pair termination. Doing so increases the possibility of transmission interference between wires, a phenomenon called **crosstalk**.
- **Bend radius**—Each type of cable has a prescribed bend radius, which is the radius of the maximum arc into which you can loop a cable without impairing data transmission. Generally, a twisted-pair cable's bend radius is equal to or greater than four times the diameter of the cable. Be careful to stay within these guidelines.
- **Continuity**—Use a cable tester to verify that each segment of cabling you install transmits data reliably. This practice will prevent you from later having to track down errors in multiple, long stretches of cable.
- **Loosely cinched cables**—Avoid cinching cables so tightly with cable ties that you squeeze their outer covering, a practice that leads to difficult-to-diagnose data errors.
- **Cable coverings and conduits**—Avoid laying cable across a floor where it might sustain damage from rolling chairs or foot traffic. At the very least, cover the cable with a cable protector or cord cover. When possible, install cable through cable conduits and seal the ends of these pipes to reduce the risk of damage from pests or water.
- **EMI sources**—Install cable at least 3 feet away from fluorescent lights or other sources of **EMI (electromagnetic interference)**, which is a type of interference that can be caused by motors, power lines, televisions, copiers, fluorescent lights, or other sources of electrical activity. This will reduce the possibility of noise (interference) that can affect your network's signals.
- **Plenum cabling**—If you run cable in the **plenum**, the area above the ceiling tile or below the subflooring, make sure the cable sheath is plenum-rated and consult with local electric installation codes to be certain you are installing it correctly. A plenum-rated cable is coated with a flame-resistant jacket that produces less smoke than regular cable coated with PVC (polyvinyl chloride), which is made from a cheaper plastic that is toxic when burned. The differences are not visibly obvious, so be sure to check the labels stamped on the cables.
- **Grounding**—Pay attention to grounding requirements and follow them religiously.
- **Slack in cable runs**—Measure first, measure again, and always leave some slack in cable runs. Stringing cable too tightly risks connectivity and data transmission problems.
- **Cable trays**—Use cable management devices such as cable trays and brackets (see Figure 2-19), braided sleeving, and furniture grommets, but don't overfill them.
- **Patch panels**—Use patch panels to organize and connect lines. A patch panel does nothing to the data transmitted on a line other than pass the data along through the connection. But patch panels do help keep lines organized as they run from walls to racks to network devices, and they make it easy to switch out patch cables of variable lengths when devices are moved or changed.

- **Company standards and inventory**—Besides adhering to structured cabling hierarchies and standards, you or your network manager should specify standards for the types of cable used by your organization and maintain a list of approved cabling vendors. Keep a supply room stocked with spare parts so you can easily and quickly replace defective parts.

- **Documentation**—Follow these guidelines to manage documentation at your cabling plant:

  ○ Keep your cable plant documentation in a centrally accessible location. Make sure it includes locations, installation dates, lengths, and grades of installed cable. You'll learn more about what to include in this documentation later in this module.

  ○ Label every data jack or port, patch panel or punchdown block, connector or circuit. You'll learn more about labeling later in this module.

  ○ Use color-coded cables for different purposes and record the color schemes in your documentation. Cables can be purchased in a variety of sheath colors, as shown in Figure 2-20. For example, you might want to use orange for printer cables, green for horizontal cabling, and yellow for vertical (backbone) cabling.

  ○ Be certain to update your documentation as you make changes to the network. The more you document, the easier it will be to troubleshoot, move, or add cable segments in the future.

Figure 2-19   Cable management brackets installed on a rack

Monitoring the Environment and Security

Due to the sensitive nature of the equipment mounted on racks, environmental and security monitoring are both critical preventive measures. Many devices, such as servers and switches, might contain temperature sensors within each device's chassis. These sensors can alert network technicians if a device is becoming overheated. Data rooms are often serviced by HVAC (Heating, Ventilation, and Air Conditioning) systems that are managed separately from the rest of the building to more efficiently cool areas containing heat-sensitive servers and other network devices. The *On the Job* story at the beginning of this module gave a good example of why this is necessary. Specialized products are available that monitor the critical factors of a data room's environment. For example, Vertiv (*vertiv.com*) offers several environmental monitoring products that can alert technicians to unacceptable

Figure 2-20   Different colors of cables can indicate the general purpose of each cable

iStock.com/Liyao Xie

temperature, humidity, or airflow conditions, and can also send text or email alerts when a secure door is left open, when the power supply is compromised, or even when light and sound conditions are unacceptable. To do this, these HVAC sensors are often connected as networked devices themselves. HVAC sensors are an example of an **industrial controls system**, also called **SCADA (supervisory control and data acquisition)**, which acquires real-time data from a physical system and manages the system or presents the data to humans to monitor and manage the system. Other SCADA systems with sensors connected to the network might be monitoring electric utilities, water and sewage, traffic signals, mass transit, manufacturing equipment, refrigeration units, or lighting and entry systems.

Environmental alarms can be programmed to escalate as the severity of the situation increases, alerting higher-level staff if the problem is not resolved. Increasing humidity, for example, is caused by rising levels of water in the air, which can damage sensitive electronic equipment. Of even greater concern is the source of that moisture, which could pose a safety hazard if, say, water is leaking into the room. The monitoring system will likely also record the information so technicians can review recent data to look for patterns of fluctuations.

Security is also a vital priority for data rooms and rack equipment. Every data room should be secured behind a locked door with only limited IT personnel having copies of the keys or entrance code. Never leave the room unlocked, even for a few moments. Many companies place security cameras to monitor any data room entrance—or at least to monitor any access point leading to the area where the data room is located—to serve as a deterrent to tampering and to provide critical information should a break-in ever occur. As you might have anticipated, these security cameras are also connected as networked devices, although typically, security cameras are isolated in a secure network segment.

You've now completed your tour of the campus network. You saw where the Internet connection comes in through the demarc, proceeds to the MDF, and moves out to various IDFs throughout campus. You also learned about different types of cables and the planning that goes into good cable installations. With all this equipment on a network, IT staff need good documentation to track the equipment, software, special configurations, and relevant vendors. This next section explores the types of network documentation you might create, reference, and update while working on a network.

REMEMBER THIS. . .

- Explain the role of a demarcation point.
- Describe the relationship of a network's MDF and IDFs.
- Summarize cable management best practices.
- Identify common networked devices, including VoIP phones, cameras, HVAC sensors, and SCADA sensors.

SELF-CHECK

1. At what point does the ISP hand over responsibility to the customer?
   a. MDF
   b. Patch panel
   c. Demarc
   d. IDF

2. According to structured cabling standards, there must be at least one _____ on each floor.
   a. IDF
   b. MDF
   c. Demarc
   d. Work area

3. Which of the following causes physical layer failures?
   a. SCADA
   b. PVC
   c. STP
   d. EMI

Check your answers at the end of this module.

You're Ready

You're now ready to complete **Project 2-1: Tour MDF and IDF Data Rooms**, or you can wait until you've finished reading this module.

NETWORK DOCUMENTATION

✅ CERTIFICATION

3.2 Explain the purpose of organization documents and policies.

5.3 Given a scenario, use the appropriate network software tools and commands.

Average reading time: 32 minutes

As you work on a network, you collect a lot of valuable information in your mind. Unless you have some good mind-reading technology, documentation is the most reliable way to keep this information safe in case you should be hit by the proverbial bus. Even without a catastrophic event, good documentation makes communication with your coworkers more efficient. It speeds up troubleshooting efforts, and it puts information at your fingertips when you face similar problems or challenges in the future.

Some network documentation, like a network diagram, shows the big picture of a network, while other forms of documentation record more detailed information. Let's start with these visual diagrams and then look at other important aspects of network documentation.

Network Diagrams

You've already learned about the importance of knowledge bases and documenting problem resolutions in a call tracking system. Recall that a knowledge base is a collection of accumulated insights and solutions to the problems encountered on a network. Another critically useful form of documentation is network diagrams, which are graphical representations of a network's devices and connections. These diagrams may show logical topology, IP address reserves, names of major network devices, types of transmission media, and physical layout such as a floor plan or rack diagram. In Figure 2-21, you can see an example of a simple network diagram showing the physical topology of a small network. Figure 2-22 shows the same network's logical topology.

A network diagram is often the product of network mapping, which is the process of discovering and identifying the devices on a network. A network map shows logical connections and addressing information. Several applications are available to assist in this process on your network. One of the simpler and most popular tools is Nmap (Network Mapper), as shown in Figure 2-23. Nmap was originally designed for Linux as a command-line utility, but it has since been expanded for compatibility on several other OSs. It's now also available in a GUI form called Zenmap (see Figure 2-24). At the end of this module, you will install and use Zenmap to discover devices on a network. Network mapping is a fascinating field of study in its own right, and its relevance and importance will only increase as today's networks become more complex. Every network technician can benefit from understanding some general concepts related to network mapping.

You could sketch a diagram or map of your networked devices in a notebook, or you could draw it on your computer using a graphics program. However, many people use software designed for diagramming networks, such as Edraw, SmartDraw, Gliffy, Microsoft Visio, or Network Notepad. Such applications come with icons that represent different types of devices and connections.

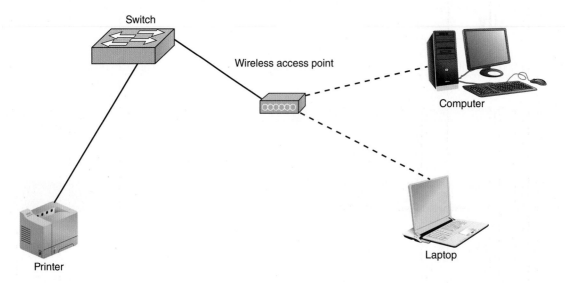

Figure 2-21 A small network's physical topology

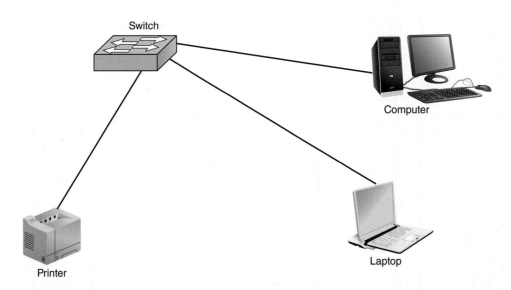

Figure 2-22 A small network's logical topology

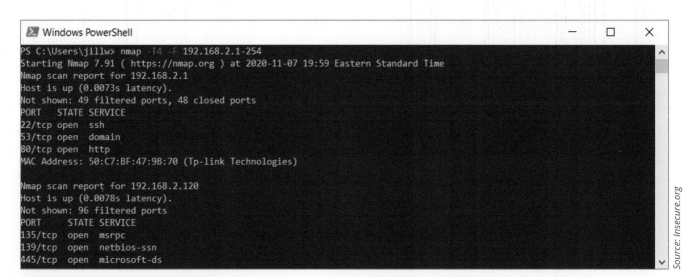

Figure 2-23 Nmap output in PowerShell using the `nmap` command

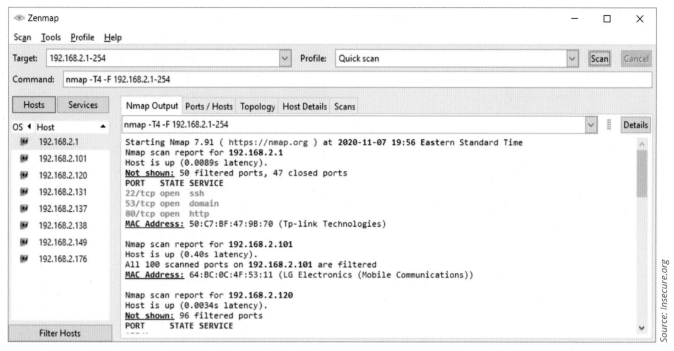

Figure 2-24   Zenmap graphical interface

Cisco Systems long ago set the standard for diagram symbols used to represent routers, switches, firewalls, and other devices. These symbols are widely accepted and understood in the networking field. Figure 2-25 shows a simplified network diagram that uses standard icons based on Cisco's iconography, with each device labeled. Notice that a router is represented by a hockey-puck shape with two arrows pointing inward and two arrows pointing outward. A switch is represented by a small rectangular box, which contains four arrows pointing in opposite directions. A wireless access point is also a rectangular box, but with squiggly lines on the front, and a firewall is a brick wall symbol. The Internet or an undefined portion of a network is represented by a cloud.

There are hundreds of Cisco symbols you might encounter when working with network diagrams. Table 2-1 shows several of the most common symbols that you'll use throughout this course. You can download a copy of Cisco's symbols from their website at *cisco.com/c/en/us/about/brand-center/network-topology-icons.html* to use in your own diagrams, presentations, reports, and documentation.

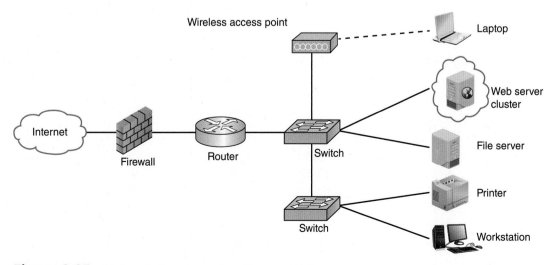

Figure 2-25   Network diagram using Cisco symbols

Table 2-1 Network topology icons

Icon	Device	Icon	Device
	Router	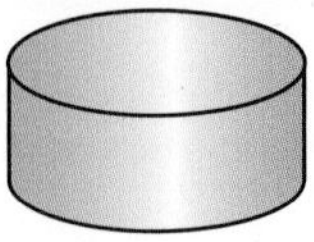	Relational database
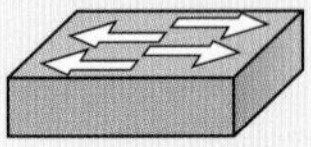	Switch		Radio tower
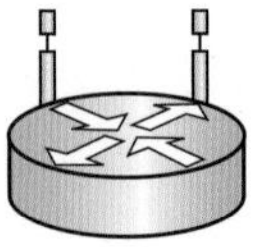	Wireless router		Generic building
	Firewall		Cloud
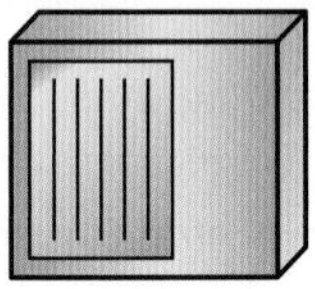	Hub		

Applying Concepts 2-1: Create a Network Diagram

Drawing network diagrams will help you more easily visualize all the various devices and connections on a network. You can choose from several very good, free diagram apps. Here, you'll use one of these apps, *Diagrams.net*, to create your own network diagram. Complete the following steps:

1. In your browser, go to **app.diagrams.net** and select a location to save your diagrams, as shown in Figure 2-26. You might already have an account with Google Drive, Dropbox, or one of the other online storage options, which will simplify this process for you. If you don't want to use one of these online options, click **Device** to download the file to your hard drive when you're finished with it.
2. Click **Create New Diagram**. Give the diagram an informative name, such as **Mod02_NW1**, and click **Create**. What name did you give your diagram? You can save the file to a specific folder on the next screen if you want. You then see the screen shown in Figure 2-27.
3. Click a shape in the left pane to insert it onto the canvas, or drag and drop a shape from the left pane to the canvas. When you do, the format panel on the right changes and gives you many formatting options appropriate to that shape. Experiment with some of the settings, including color, fill, outline, opacity, text options, and arrangement.
4. Add a few more shapes and experiment with layers, labels, connections, and waypoints.

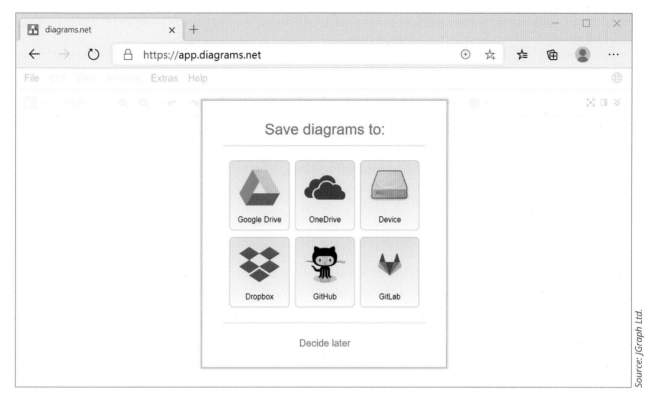

Figure 2-26   Use an account you already have, or store diagrams on your computer

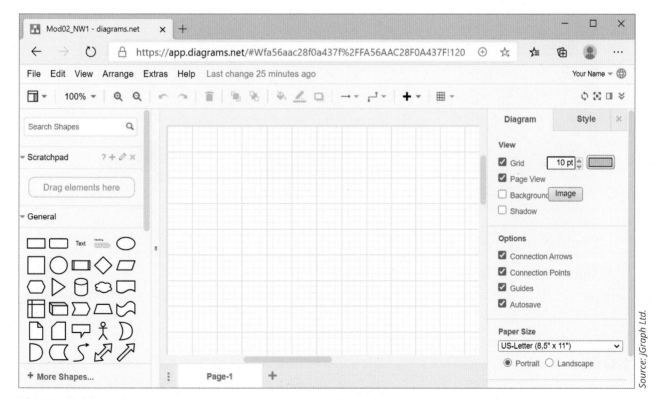

Figure 2-27   A new diagram begins with a blank canvas

   a. To add a label, select a shape and start typing. Select the shape again, and then click the **Text** tab to change the location of that label and other attributes.

   b. To create a connection, move the mouse pointer over a shape, click a blue **X**, and drag the new connection to another location on the canvas. Attach the connection to another shape by dropping it on a blue X on the second shape.

   c. A waypoint is an intermediate point along a connection. To adjust waypoints, select a connection and drag any point on the connection to a different place on the canvas. You can change the waypoint style and endpoint styles on the Style tab.

5. Delete the objects currently on your canvas. You can delete items one at a time or press **Ctrl+A** to select all of them and press **Delete**.

6. At the bottom of the left pane, click **More Shapes**. The Shapes dialog box opens. What are three shape sets listed here that would be helpful drawing a network diagram?

7. In the Networking group, select **Cisco**, and then click **Apply**.

8. In the left pane, scroll down to the Cisco groups. Explore the many icons available here so you have a general understanding of what is included in each group.

9. Recreate the small network shown in Figure 2-28. The solid lines show logical device connections, and the cloud represents the Internet. The shaded boxes show the groupings of different subnets.

10. Export your final diagram as a .png file and save it to your local hard drive. Submit this visual with your answers to this activity's questions.

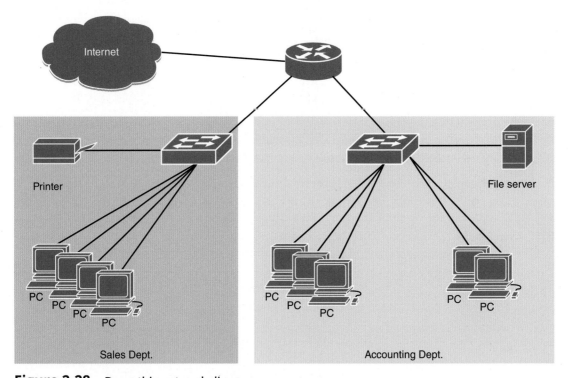

Figure 2-28   Draw this network diagram

NOTE 2-3

Not every device on a network is shown in every diagram of that network. For example, in Figure 2-28, there's no firewall pictured. And yet, there would certainly be at least one firewall in place. The items that are shown in the diagram are selected specifically to illustrate one or a few aspects of the network.

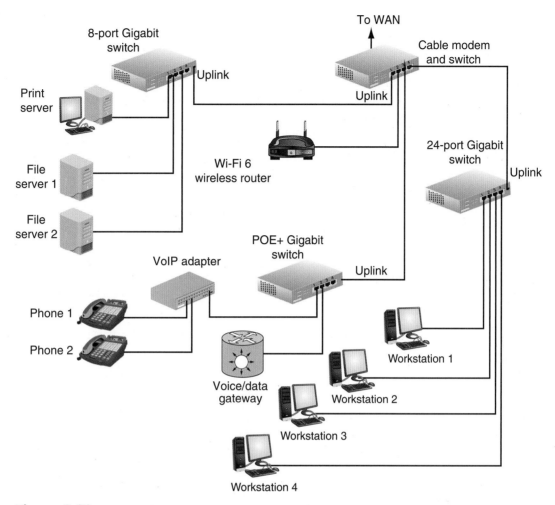

Figure 2-29 Wiring diagram

Most network diagrams provide broad snapshots of a network's physical or logical topology. This type of view is useful for planning where to insert a new switch or determining how particular routers, gateways, and firewalls interact. However, if you're a technician looking for a fault in a client's wired connection to the LAN, a broad overview might be too general. In that case, you'll need a **wiring diagram**, which is a graphical representation of a network's wired infrastructure. In its most detailed form, it shows every wire necessary to interconnect network devices and the locations of those wires. Some less-detailed wiring diagrams might use a single line to represent the group of wires necessary to connect several clients to a switch. Figure 2-29 provides an example of a wiring diagram for a small office network that relies on cable broadband service to access the Internet.

One more diagram type you will come across is the **rack diagram**. These drawings show the devices stacked in a rack system and are typically drawn to scale. You can see a simple rack diagram in Figure 2-30. Rack diagrams are helpful when planning a rack installation. They're also needed when tracking and troubleshooting equipment installed in a rack. Many of the drawing tools used to draw network diagrams, such as *Diagrams.net*, include the symbols needed for drawing simple rack diagrams as well.

Network diagrams give you a visual overview of a network. However, it's impossible for a diagram to include all the information needed for good network documentation. Next, you'll learn about other types of network documentation and consider ways to keep this information up-to-date.

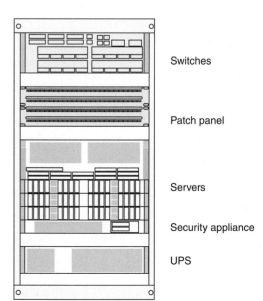

Figure 2-30 Typical devices installed on a rack

Operating Procedures

Essential documentation covers logical and physical connections on a network; inventory management; IP address utilization; vendors (such as contact information, warranty information, service agreements, and troubleshooting instructions); and internal operating procedures, policies, and standards. For example, many corporations establish **SOPs (standard operating procedures)** to ensure consistency as different employees perform the same complex tasks. The way you gather, format, and store your network documentation will depend on company needs, network complexity, and available resources. When creating new documentation, take some time to brainstorm all the elements you want to include, and consider how you'll keep each of these documents updated. Use Table 2-2 to help develop your ideas.

Table 2-2   Items to consider covering in network documentation

Type	What to cover
Hardware	*Includes:*
	Devices, racks, jacks, patch panels, switches, ports, MDF/IDF, floor plans, power and water shutoff locations
	For example:
	Devices: How many of the following devices are connected to your network: switches, routers, firewalls, access points, servers, UPSs, printers, backup devices, and clients? Where are they located? Are they physical or virtual? If physical, what are their model numbers and vendors? Are they owned or leased? What configuration settings does each one require? For servers, specify each type of server hosted on each physical device and any specific configurations of those servers.
Software	*Includes:*
	Operating systems (and their configurations), applications (and their configurations), Active Directory (security groups, domains, etc.)
	For example:
	Which applications are used by clients and servers? What software is required by different departments? Where do you store the applications? From where do they run? Also keep records of leases, product keys, licenses, and licensing restrictions. **Licensing restrictions** might define who is allowed to use an application and for how long, how many users are allowed to install or access it, whether the application can be made available over a company's network or the Internet, and how many backup copies of the application may be stored.
Network configuration	*Includes:*
	Protocols, backups, passwords, IP addressing (static assignments, DHCP scopes), subnets, VLANs, server roles, access methods, transmission details, baseline configurations
	For example:
	Describe how backups are made, what information is included, where they are stored, and how to restore from backup. Also include the **baseline configuration** of network devices and their software, which is a change management concept that defines a stable state to be achieved and maintained before attempting future changes.
Procedures	*Includes:*
	Task details, workflows, role assignments, essential equipment or supplies, compliance requirements, safety restrictions, any scheduling concerns, required minimum training, relevant approval processes, troubleshooting guidelines
	For example:
	Consider all required information needed by the intended audience, depending on their experience and training, to complete a complex but predictable task. Clearly define end goals of the SOP and identify any interrelated processes that might have their own SOP. Also include information about the latest revision date so different versions of the document can be tracked efficiently.

(continues)

Table 2-2   Items to Consider Covering in Network Documentation *(continued)*

Type	What to cover
Contacts	*Includes:* Vendors, decision makers, team members, utilities (alarm, electric, water) *For example:* Include a list of all vendors with contact information, lists of services provided, maintenance agreements, warranties or support subscriptions, and any special troubleshooting instructions from the vendor (or references to where to find that information).
Special instructions	*Includes:* Who to contact in an emergency, how to access backup information, how to meet the requirements of various privacy, security, and safety restrictions *For example:* Medical data is protected by HIPAA (Health Insurance Portability and Accountability Act of 1996). In the event of a network failure or intrusion, certain steps must be taken to notify appropriate parties, minimize data exposure, and remediate any damage.

 **CAUTION**   Obviously, you need to keep password documentation very secure. However, multiple people should have access to it. Otherwise, if the network admin is suddenly incapacitated, you might be unable to retrieve high-security passwords. A password manager, such as KeePass or LastPass, can be invaluable in this situation.

If you have not already collected and centrally stored information for the items just listed, it could take the efforts of several people and several weeks to compile them, depending on the size and complexity of your network. This evaluation would require visits to data rooms, an examination of servers and desktops, a review of receipts for software and hardware purchases, and, potentially, the use of a protocol analyzer or network management software package. Still, all this effort would save you work and mistakes in the future.

As you compile the information, organize it into a database that can be easily updated and searched. That way, staff can access the information in a timely manner and keep it current. Your company might provide an internal website or database for this purpose, or you can use a wiki. A **wiki** is a website that can be edited by users. You can add files and photos, easily create links between pages, group pages by different criteria, and make choices about which users have which privileges on the site. At the end of this module, you'll create your own wiki to track information from several of the projects in this course.

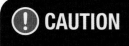 **CAUTION**   If you use a digital format to store your network documentation, consider that this information might be lost or temporarily inaccessible if your network suffers a catastrophic failure. Keep digital backups securely stored off-site, perhaps in the cloud. Also, keep up-to-date, printed copies in multiple, secure locations.

At some point you need to test how thorough and clear your documentation is. Perhaps the CFO, an executive from another department, or a carefully selected consultant can sort through the information, asking questions and pointing out areas of misunderstanding or gaps in coverage. When hiring new technicians, refer them often to your documentation and ask for feedback on how easily they can make sense of it. Also regularly devote time to updating your documentation.

Inventory Management

The process of designing, implementing, and maintaining an entire network is called the system life cycle. Network components progress through the following life cycle phases (see Figure 2-31) so that, collectively, the network is constantly being improved:

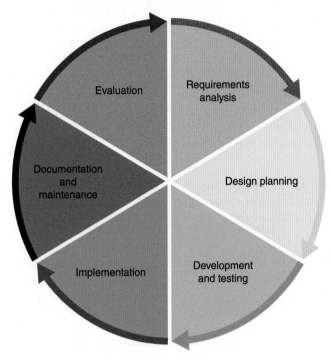

- **Requirements analysis**—Identify network requirements and business needs.
- **Design planning**—Progress from big picture goals to detailed decisions.
- **Development and testing**—Purchase equipment and test before deploying.
- **Implementation**—Deploy new equipment to replace old equipment, and continue testing to achieve a new, stable baseline.
- **Documentation and maintenance**—Apply effective monitoring techniques to detect and address problems, and keep documentation updated.
- **Evaluation**—As improvements are needed or devices break down, perform a cost–benefit analysis to identify devices reaching the end of their life cycle and determine whether to discard, replace, or upgrade.

A major part of this process is the removal and disposal of outdated assets and the addition of compatible, updated devices. This is much easier to oversee and accomplish when you know what devices you have on

Figure 2-31 Phases of a network system life cycle

your network. The term inventory management refers to the monitoring and maintaining of all assets that make up a network. You might create your own documentation for this, such as a spreadsheet or a database, or you might use an inventory management system with features designed to simplify this process. The first step in inventory management is to list all the components on the network, which include the following:

- **Hardware (including virtual hardware)**—Configuration files, model number, serial number, location on the network, and technical support contact
- **Software (including operating systems)**—Version number, vendor, licensing, and technical support contact

Inventory management documentation simplifies maintaining and upgrading a network because it ensures that you know what the network includes. For example, if you discover that a router purchased two years ago requires an upgrade to its operating system to fix a security flaw, you will also need to know how many routers are installed, where they are installed, and whether any have already received the software upgrade. Up-to-date inventory management documentation allows you to avoid searching through old invoices and troubleshooting records to answer these questions.

In addition, inventory documentation provides network administrators with information about the costs and benefits of certain types of hardware or software. For example, if you conclude that 20 percent of your staff's troubleshooting time is spent on workstations with one flawed brand of hard drive, inventory documentation can reveal how many hard drives you would need to purchase if you chose to replace those components and whether it would make sense to replace the entire installed base. Some inventory management applications can also track the length of equipment leases and alert network managers when leases will expire.

NOTE 2-4

The term *inventory management* originally referred to an organization's system for keeping tabs on every piece of equipment it owned. This function was usually handled through the Accounting Department. Some of the accounting-related tasks included under the original definition for inventory management, such as managing the depreciation on network equipment or tracking the expiration of leases, apply to inventory management in networking as well.

Labeling and Naming Conventions

Maintaining up-to-date records about your network devices will reduce your workload and make troubleshooting easier and more efficient. Adequate recordkeeping also saves money by preventing unnecessary purchases. The secret to keeping track of devices is naming them systematically, and then labeling them with those names. A good naming convention can serve double duty by including essential information about the device. Consider the following tips:

- Use names that are as descriptive as possible (without giving away too much information to potential hackers).
- Only include fields that are absolutely essential in identifying the device.
- Don't overcomplicate the name with useless or redundant information.
- Pay attention to any established naming convention already in use by your employer. For example, existing acronyms for the various departments in your corporation are more recognizable for employees.
- Think big-picture-down-to-details when designing device name fields, such as starting with the building name, then floor, then data room number, then rack number. If your company has national locations or international locations, certain names may need to include codes for continent, country, state, city, and so on. Think in terms of "top-down" or "outside-in" and be consistent.
- Consider any security risks from the details you might include in your naming convention. Make sure naming and labeling information is stored behind locked doors and inside secure databases. Don't use names that identify the location (physical or digital) of sensitive information that might alert an attacker to a highly desirable target, such as customer credit card information or protected patient data. When needed, use more obscure names that won't easily attract attention.

Applying Concepts 2-2: Examine a Naming Convention

A good naming convention will save you a lot of time that would otherwise be lost looking up device names. Consider the following device names:

    002-09-03-01-03
    phx-09-nw-01-rtr3

The first name is simply a string of numbers, which many people would have a hard time recognizing as meaningful information. A numeric system like this would force new employees to spend too much time decoding device names.

The second name is easier to interpret on the fly. Some of the numbers have been replaced with abbreviated names, locations, and other identifying information. The first field tells you that the device is located in Phoenix, which is abbreviated as phx. The second field (09) refers to the floor number, so using a number is unavoidable. The third field (nw) refers to the data room's location within the building (the northwest corner) rather than the data room's number, which would also be onerous to memorize. The fourth field contains the rack number (01), and the final field (rtr3) identifies the type of device (a router) and the number of the router (3).

NOTE 2-5

When designing a naming convention, be sure to include enough digits in each field to allow for future expansion. A two-digit field is much more limited than a three- or four-digit field. One digit will work fine for numbering the racks in a small data closet, which can't possibly hold 10 racks. But if you're numbering employees or workstations, your company may quickly outgrow a two-digit workstation field.

Not every company needs long device names; and small devices, such as the ports on a switch, aren't big enough to accommodate long names. For example, when labeling ports on a patch panel or switch in a data room, a connection type (vertical versus horizontal, storage versus workstation, etc.) and possibly a room number may suffice. For jacks on a wall, consider names such as the employee's job title, desk location, or something similar. Avoid using employee names because many of those will change over the lifetime of the device. Ultimately, the name of the game is *consistency*.

A word to the wise network technician: Learn to view good labeling as a beautiful thing! For the meticulous technician, labeling can become an art form. Here are some tips to get started:

- As discussed earlier, you can use color-coded cables for different purposes. However, don't rely on the cable colors alone; use labels on ports or tags on cables to identify each cable's specific purpose, as shown in Figure 2-32.

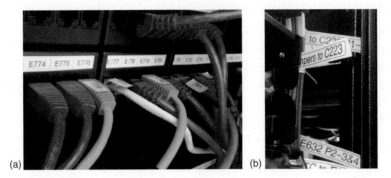

(a) (b)

Figure 2-32   Labels on ports and tags on cables

- In addition to labeling cables, also label the ports and jacks that cables connect to. Place the labels directly on patch panels, switches, routers, wall plates, and computers. Use these labels to identify systems, circuits, and connections.
- Where labels won't fit on the device itself, draw a simple diagram of the device that indicates the purpose of each port, slot, and connector, such as the example in Figure 2-33.

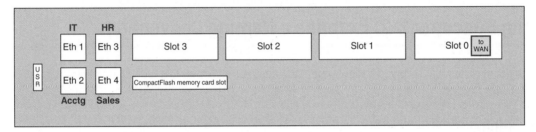

Figure 2-33   Simple diagram of a Cisco router with red labels identifying how five ports are used

- A portable label maker is indispensable for creating labels. Choose labels that are durable and that are designed to stick to plastic and metal, not paper. Keep your label maker handy in your toolbox as you work. Whenever you find a device, wall jack, or port not labeled and you are able to identify its purpose, take the time to label it correctly. Others in your organization will soon see you as the "label champion."

Business Documents

Aside from the documentation you create to track network assets and resources, you will also encounter a variety of standard business documents in the course of your work as a network technician. These documents help define who is responsible for various devices, applications, and expenses. For example, if your organization shares space or networking equipment with another organization, or if your organization leases equipment from a vendor, written documents will define each entity's responsibilities. Although you won't likely be held responsible for creating these documents, it's helpful to be familiar with their purpose and structure, especially if you're involved in making decisions about equipment purchases or software subscriptions. Consider the following documents:

- An **RFP (request for proposal)** is a request to vendors to submit a proposal for a product or service your company wants to purchase. Key parts of an RFP include why your company requires the product or service, how the product or service will be used, how and when the proposals will be evaluated, and a list of items a vendor should include in its proposal (for example, a detailed description of its product or service, technical support, user training, and initial and ongoing costs).
- An **MOU (memorandum of understanding)** documents the intentions of two or more parties to enter into a binding agreement, or contract, and is sometimes used between an informal handshake and the legally binding

signatures on contracts. The MOU can be helpful in pushing along contract negotiations and in defining specific concerns of each party, but it is usually not a
legally binding document, does not grant extensive rights to either party, provides no legal recourse, and is not intended to provide thorough coverage of the
agreement to come.

- An **MSA (master service agreement)** is a contract that defines the terms of future
  contracts between parties, such as payment terms or arbitration arrangements.
- An **SOW (statement of work)** documents in detail the work that must be completed for a particular project, and includes specifics such as tasks, deliverables,
  standards, payment schedule, and work timeline. An SOW is legally binding,
  meaning it can be enforced in a court of law. Many times, an SOW is used to
  define the terms of each new project as an addendum to an existing MSA.
- An **SLA (service-level agreement)** is a legally binding contract or part of a contract that defines, in plain language and in measurable terms, the aspects of a
  service provided to a customer, such as the service provided by an ISP. Details
  specified might include contract duration (minimum or maximum), guaranteed
  uptime, options for compensation if outages exceed defined thresholds, problem management, performance benchmarks, and termination options.
- An **MLA (master license agreement)** grants a license from a creator, developer, or producer, such as a software producer, to a third party for the purposes of marketing, sublicensing, or distributing the product to
  consumers as a stand-alone product or as part of another product.

NOTE 2-6

It's important to understand the specifics covered—and *not* covered—in a particular docu-ment before signing it. For example, although the typical MOU is not intended to serve as a binding contract, there are circumstances under which it could be binding, especially if money is exchanged. Be sure to consult an attorney for advice regarding concerns you might have about any docu-ment before you sign it.

REMEMBER THIS. . .

- Compare common forms of network diagrams.
- Document network configurations and operating procedures.
- Explain the phases of the system life cycle.
- Design effective naming conventions.
- Explain the roles of various business documents in network administration.

SELF-CHECK

4. Which network diagram shows a logical topology?
   a. Rack diagram
   b. Network map
   c. Floor plan
   d. Wiring diagram

5. In which life cycle phase is an old device removed from the network?
   a. Evaluation
   b. Documentation and maintenance
   c. Implementation
   d. Requirement analysis

6. When an Internet connection goes down, what business document defines a customer's options for paying
   a reduced rate?
   a. MOU
   b. SOW
   c. RFP
   d. SLA

Check your answers at the end of this module.

You're Ready

You're now ready to complete **Project 2-2: Create a Wiki**, or you can wait until you've finished reading this module.

You're Ready

You're now ready to complete **Project 2-3: Install and Use Nmap and Zenmap**, or you can wait until you've finished reading this module.

CHANGE MANAGEMENT

✓ CERTIFICATION

3.2 Explain the purpose of organization documents and policies.

4.3 Given a scenario, apply network hardening techniques.

Average reading time: 17 minutes

Network conditions are always in a state of flux. Technology advances, vendors come and go, responsibilities and needs of users change, and attacks from malware and hackers can expose vulnerabilities that require attention. Managing change while maintaining your network's efficiency and availability requires good planning. Even a simple change can result in lengthy downtimes if not instituted properly. Network users need to know when to expect certain network resources to be unavailable. This way, they can plan ahead so as not to lose productivity time. Changes, especially those that affect many users or expensive equipment, must be carefully planned and thoroughly documented. And in most cases, these changes will need to be approved before they can be performed.

The following section describes some of the most common types of software and hardware changes, from installing patches to replacing a network backbone, and explains how to implement those changes. After that, you explore the change management documentation that might be required for an enterprise-scale network.

Software and Hardware Changes

You might be called on to implement the following four types of software changes:

- **Installation**—New software, such as CRM (customer relationship management) software for sales reps or a financial software package for accountants, must be installed on the relevant devices and incorporated with network resources.
- **Patch**—A software patch is a correction, improvement, or enhancement to software. It corrects a bug, closes a vulnerability, or adds minor enhancements to part of the software, leaving most of the code untouched. The process of monitoring the release of new patches, testing them for use on networked devices, and installing them is called patch management.
- **Upgrade**—A software upgrade is a major change to a software package that enhances the functionality and features of the software, while also correcting bugs and vulnerabilities.
- **Rollback**—A software rollback is the process of reverting to a previous version of software after an attempt to patch or upgrade it fails.

Hardware changes could be something as simple as replacing a hard drive or as intensive as upgrading a campus's network backbone cabling. Typical hardware changes include adding new security cameras, replacing old workstations, installing new printers, and upgrading VoIP phone hardware. Hardware changes might also include firmware updates. While these updates can enhance features and functionality of a device, it can also remove features or create compatibility issues. Good firmware management requires that you source the update directly from the manufacturer, confirm you're applying exactly the correct update, carefully test the update before deploying and again after deploying, and fully document any effects on the network. Balance the risks with the potential benefits, especially if the update includes security enhancements that close critical vulnerabilities.

Applying Concepts 2-3: Summarize Steps for Changing Software or Hardware

Although the specifics vary for each type of software or hardware change, the general steps can be summarized as follows:

1. Generally, don't allow patches to be automatically installed in the OS, application, or device. When you're responsible for a computer or network, you need to fully understand the impact of any change before you allow that change.
2. Determine whether the patch or upgrade is necessary. Patches to plug security holes are almost always necessary and should be completed as soon as reasonably possible; however, adding new features or functionality to software might cause more work than it's worth in time and money.
3. Read the vendor's documentation regarding the patch or upgrade to learn its purpose, and make sure you understand how it will affect the system, whether or not it is compatible with current hardware and software, and how to apply or undo the change.
4. Before deploying the patch or upgrade, test it in a testing lab to make sure it acts as expected. A testing lab is a small network that is segmented from the rest of the network. It contains computers, called test beds, that represent the typical hardware and OS configurations in your network, as well as any specialized equipment your company uses (for example, printers, bar-code readers, and biometric devices, such as fingerprint readers or retina scanners) that might interact with the proposed new software or hardware. Also determine whether and how the change can be reversed in case troubles arise. Document your findings.
5. Determine whether the change should apply to some or all users, network segments, or devices. Also decide whether it will be distributed centrally or machine by machine.
6. Schedule the change for completion during off-hours (unless it is an emergency). The time period in which a change will be implemented is called the maintenance window, and many organizations maintain a regularly scheduled maintenance window during which changes can be made. Everyone responsible for those who might be affected by a disruption in service (for example, the technical staff or department directors) must be informed of and agree to the maintenance window in advance.
7. Before the change is made, inform system administrators, help desk personnel, and affected users about the change and the maintenance window, and provide reminders immediately before the maintenance window opens.

NOTE 2-7

If problems arise as maintenance is in progress and you realize that you are about to exceed the maintenance window, be sure to inform technical staff and users of the anticipated delay and what to expect.

8. Back up the current system, software, or hardware configuration before making any modifications. You can typically copy the firmware or OS configuration of a router, switch, or server to a USB flash drive, backup media, or network share.
9. If necessary, throughout the maintenance window, prevent users from accessing the system or the part of the system being altered.

10. Keep the installation instructions and vendor documentation handy as you implement the change.

11. After the change is implemented, test the system in real time, even though you have already tested it in the testing lab. Exercise the software as a typical user would. For hardware devices, put a higher load on the device than it would incur during normal use in your organization. Note any unintended or unanticipated consequences of the modification.

12. If the change was successful, reenable access to the system. If it was unsuccessful, revert to the previous version of the software or hardware according to your rollback plan.

13. Inform system administrators, help desk personnel, and affected users when the change is complete. If you had to reverse it, make this known and explain why.

14. Record your change in the change management system, as described later in this module.

Regardless of how hard you try to make hardware and software changes go smoothly, eventually you will encounter a situation when you must roll back your changes. Although no hard-and-fast rules for rollbacks exist, Table 2-3 summarizes some basic suggestions. Bear in mind that you must always refer to the software vendor's documentation to reverse an upgrade. If you must roll back a network operating system upgrade, you should also consult with experienced professionals about the best approach for your network environment.

Table 2-3   Reversing a software upgrade

Type of upgrade	Options for reversing
Operating system patch	Use the patch's automatic uninstall utility.
Client software upgrade	Use the upgrade's automatic uninstall utility, or reinstall the previous version of the client on top of the upgrade.
Shared application upgrade	Use the application's automatic uninstall utility, or maintain a complete copy of the previous installation of the application and reinstall it over the upgrade.
Operating system upgrade	Prior to the upgrade, make a complete backup of the system; to roll back, restore the entire system from the backup; uninstall an operating system upgrade only as a last resort.

NOTE 2-8

When replacing a device or a component in a device (for example, a hard drive), keep the old component for a while, especially if it is the only one of its kind at your organization. Not only might you need to reinstall the component or device, but you might also need to refer to it later for more information.

Hardware and software are not the only types of changes you might need to implement and manage. Other types include changes to the network (such as when connecting to a new ISP), the environment (such as when installing a new HVAC system), and documentation procedures (such as when upgrading to a more automated call tracking system). The same change management principles apply to any type of change:

- Process all changes through the proper channels.
- Minimize negative impacts on business processes.
- Plan thoroughly to maximize the chances of a successful change on the first attempt.
- Document each change throughout the process.

Change Management Documentation

Generally, the larger an organization, the more documentation is necessary when making hardware and software changes. Required processes and how these processes are documented are designed to protect the person making the change, users, managers, and the organization so that changes don't unnecessarily disrupt normal work flow or put undue responsibility for a problem on any one person. Here is a list of what you may need to do:

1. **Submit a change request document**—Find out who in the organization is responsible for submitting such a document. For example, the lead accountant might be considered the owner of an accounting application and is, therefore, the only one allowed to request an upgrade to the application. On the other hand, IT personnel might be able to request a security patch be applied to the same application. In this case, the change request document might include items listed in Table 2-4.

Table 2-4   Parts of a Change Request Document

Information	Example
Person submitting the change request and person who must authorize the change	The network administrator is submitting the request, and the director of IT must approve it.
Type of change	A software patch is needed for an accounting application.
Reason for change	The application vendor reported a bug that causes errors in printed reports.
Configuration procedures	An upgraded application might require new data file templates be built, settings defined for an entire department of users, or existing data be converted to a new format.
Potential impact	Ten users in the Accounting Department will need three hours of training.
Grounds for rollback	The new application doesn't work as expected, and the Accounting Department head decides it's best to go back to the old way of doing things.
Notification process	Management and users will be informed of the change through email.
Timeline for the change	Anticipated downtime is two hours.

2. **Understand and follow the approval process**—The manager of a department might be able to approve a minor change to an application, hardware device, or OS, whereas major changes might need to go through a review board process. You might be expected to provide additional documentation during this review process. The complexity of the approval process is usually determined by the cost and time involved in making the change, the number of users affected, the potential risk to their work productivity, and the difficulty of rolling back the change. Sometimes a change request is entered into a change management database where many people can access the request, enter supporting documentation and questions, and weigh in with their opinions regarding the change.

3. **Follow project management procedures**—After a major change is approved, a change coordinator is usually assigned to the project. This coordinator is a trained project manager responsible for overseeing all aspects of the change including user training; coordinating between departments involved in the change; documenting how and when notification of the change will happen; negotiating with users, management, and the IT Department regarding the authorized downtime for the change to happen; communicating with management regarding any unforeseen problems that arise during the change; and managing the budget for the change. Technicians and the network administrator work closely with the change coordinator during the change process.

4. **Provide additional documentation**—Depending on the organization, other required documentation might include testing documentation (for example, test data, testing scenarios, and software and hardware used for the testing), step-by-step procedures for applying the change, vendor documentation and vendor contact information, and locations of configuration backups and of backups that will be used in the event

NOTE 2-9

Minor changes, such as applying a security patch to an application that involves only a few users, are sometimes made without going through an official change request process, but are usually documented in some way, such as a technician making entries in the change management database before and after the change is made.

of a rollback. Network administrators should pay particular attention to updating their own documentation regarding the network, including updating the network map you learned about earlier in this module. These network documentation updates might include edits to the following information:

- Network configuration (For example, the network was segmented with three new VLANs and subnets added.)
- IP address utilization (For example, IP address ranges were assigned to the three new subnets.)
- Additions to the network (For example, new routers and switches were installed to accommodate new VLANs to handle additional network traffic.)
- Physical location changes (For example, 20 workstations, a switch, and two printers were moved to a different building on the corporate campus.)

5. **Close the change**—After the change is implemented and tested and users have settled into the change without problems, the change is officially closed. Sometimes the change coordinator will call a debriefing session where all involved can evaluate how well the change went and what can be done to improve future changes.

REMEMBER THIS. . .

- Weigh the potential risks and benefits before applying a patch or firmware update.
- Explain the change management process.

SELF-CHECK

7. Which change is designed to close a security vulnerability without affecting other components of an application?
   a. Patch
   b. Rollback
   c. Upgrade
   d. Installation

8. Which change management principle must you apply to all changes regardless of scope or impact?
   a. Acquire review board approval.
   b. Apply the change as soon as possible.
   c. Submit a change request document.
   d. Document the change.

Check your answers at the end of this module.

You're Ready

You're now ready to complete **Project 2-4: Install and Use Wireshark**, or you can wait until you've finished the Review Questions for this module.

You're Ready

After you finish the Hands-On Projects, you're ready to complete the **Module 2 Capstone Projects**.

MODULE SUMMARY

Components of Structured Cabling

- The ANSI/TIA-568 structured cabling standards describe uniform, enterprise-wide cabling systems regardless of who manufactures or sells the various parts used in the system.
- For most situations, the device that marks where an ISP's network ends and the organization's network begins is the demarc, or demarcation point.
- Connections branching out from the MDF include Ethernet cables connecting to nearby work areas, large cables running to IDFs in other buildings or on other floors of the same building, and the incoming connection from the service provider's facility.
- VoIP (Voice over IP), also known as IP telephony, is the use of any network (either public or private) to carry voice signals using TCP/IP protocols. A voice gateway device converts signals from a campus's analog phone equipment into IP data that can travel over the Internet, or it converts VoIP data from an internal IP network to travel over a phone company's analog telephone lines. A common application layer protocol used by voice gateways to initiate and maintain connections is the signaling protocol SIP (Session Initial Protocol).
- Cable management best practices include minimizing exposed wires at each termination, ensuring continuity, loosely cinching cables, covering cables, organizing cables with cable trays and conduits, reducing cable exposure to EMI, and keeping good documentation.
- HVAC sensors are often connected as networked devices themselves. These HVAC sensors are an example of an industrial controls system, also called SCADA (supervisory control and data acquisition). Other SCADA systems with sensors connected to the network might be monitoring electric utilities, water and sewage, traffic signals, mass transit, manufacturing equipment, refrigeration units, or lighting and entry systems. Security cameras are also connected as networked devices, although typically security cameras are isolated in a secure network segment.

Network Documentation

- Network diagrams are graphical representations of a network's devices and connections. These diagrams may show logical topology, IP address reserves, names of major network devices, types of transmission media, and physical layout such as a floor plan or rack diagram.
- A network diagram is often the product of network mapping, which is the process of discovering and identifying the devices on a network. One of the simpler and most popular tools is Nmap (Network Mapper).
- A wiring diagram is a graphical representation of a network's wired infrastructure. In its most detailed form, it shows every wire necessary to interconnect network devices and the locations of those wires.
- A rack diagram shows the devices stacked in a rack system and is typically drawn to scale. Rack diagrams are helpful when planning a rack installation or when troubleshooting equipment installed in a rack.
- Essential network documentation covers logical and physical connections on a network; inventory management; IP address utilization; vendors (such as contact information, warranty information, service agreements, and troubleshooting instructions); and internal operating procedures, policies, and standards. For example, many corporations establish SOPs (standard operating procedures) to ensure consistency as different employees perform the same complex tasks.
- A baseline configuration of network devices and their software is a change management concept that defines a stable state to be achieved and maintained before attempting future changes.
- The process of designing, implementing, and maintaining an entire network is called the system life cycle. A major part of this process is the removal and disposal of outdated assets, and the addition of compatible, updated devices. The term inventory management refers to the monitoring and maintaining of all the assets that make up a network.

- Systematically name and label network devices and connections. A good naming convention can serve double duty by including essential information about each device while also allowing technicians to identify and track each device more easily.
- Important business documents in network administration include the MOU and the SLA. An MOU (memorandum of understanding) documents the intentions of two or more parties to enter into a binding agreement, or contract, and is sometimes used between an informal handshake and the legally binding signatures on contracts. An SLA (service-level agreement) is a legally binding contract or part of a contract that defines, in plain language and in measurable terms, the aspects of a service provided to a customer.

Change Management

- Four common types of software changes include installations, patch management, software upgrades, and rollbacks after a failed change. Hardware changes might include adding new equipment or replacing old equipment. Hardware changes might also include firmware updates. Good firmware management requires that you source the update directly from the manufacturer, confirm you're applying exactly the correct update, carefully test the update before deploying and again after deploying, and fully document any effects on the network. Balance the risks with the potential benefits, especially if the update includes security enhancements that close critical vulnerabilities.
- Required change management processes and related documentation are designed to protect the person making the change, users, managers, and the organization so that changes don't unnecessarily disrupt normal work flow or put undue responsibility for a problem on any one person.
- Change management steps require a change request document, an approval process, project management, and documentation. The change coordinator is a trained project manager responsible for overseeing all aspects of the change including user training; coordinating between departments involved in the change; documenting how and when notification of the change will happen; negotiating with users, management, and the IT Department regarding the authorized downtime for the change to happen; communicating with management regarding any unforeseen problems that arise during the change; and managing the budget for the change.

Key Terms

For definitions of key terms, see the Glossary.

110 block
66 block
ANSI (American National Standards Institute)
baseline configuration
BIX (Building Industry Cross-connect) block
crosstalk
demarc (demarcation point)
EF (entrance facility)
EMI (electromagnetic interference)
fiber-optic cable
IDF (intermediate distribution frame)
industrial controls system
inventory management
Krone (Krone LSA-PLUS) block
KVM (keyboard, video, and mouse) switch

licensing restrictions
MDF (main distribution frame)
MLA (master license agreement)
MOU (memorandum of understanding)
MSA (master service agreement)
network diagram
Nmap (Network Mapper)
patch
patch bay
patch management
patch panel
plenum
punchdown tool
rack diagram
RFP (request for proposal)
rollback
SCADA (supervisory control and data acquisition)

SIP (Session Initial Protocol)
SLA (service-level agreement)
SOP (standard operating procedure)
SOW (statement of work)
STP (shielded twisted pair)
structured cabling
system life cycle
TIA (Telecommunications Industry Association)
upgrade
UTP (unshielded twisted pair)
voice gateway
VoIP (Voice over IP)
VoIP phone
wiki
wiring diagram

Review Questions

1. A technician from your ISP has arrived to help you troubleshoot a weak WAN connection. To what location do you take them?
   a. IDF
   b. Work area
   c. CEO's office
   d. EF

2. A transceiver was recently damaged by a lightning strike during a storm. How might you decide whether the ISP is responsible for replacing this device, or whether your company must foot the bill?
   a. Look at whether the device is located on the ISP's side of the demarc.
   b. Look at the manufacturer information on the device's label.
   c. Look at purchase records for the device to determine when it was acquired.
   d. Look at what kinds of cables are connected to this device.

3. Which of the following devices are you likely to find in the MDF? Choose all that apply.
   a. Routers
   b. Switches
   c. Network printer
   d. KVM switch

4. Which device converts signals from a campus's analog phone equipment into IP data that can travel over the Internet?
   a. Legacy PBX
   b. VoIP phone
   c. Voice gateway
   d. Dedicated telephone switch

5. If you're shopping for a rack switch, what component on the switch tells you it can be mounted to a rack?
   a. AC adapter
   b. Rack ears
   c. Padded feet
   d. Large fans

6. You need to connect a new network printer to a nearby wall jack. What kind of cable should you use?
   a. Fiber-optic cable
   b. Patch cable
   c. Backbone cable
   d. Plenum-rated cable

7. You've decided to run an Nmap scan on your network. Which apps could you open to perform this task? Choose all that apply.
   a. Zenmap
   b. Microsoft Edge
   c. Command Prompt
   d. PowerShell

8. What type of diagram shows a graphical representation of a network's wired infrastructure?
   a. Rack diagram
   b. Wiring diagram
   c. Network map
   d. Network topology

9. Which of these is considered a secure place to store a list of documented network passwords?
   a. The CEO's smartphone
   b. A sticky note under the keyboard
   c. A password manager
   d. The MDF

10. What is the first step of inventory management?
    a. Interview users.
    b. Identify network requirements.
    c. List an administrative account's username and password for each device on a network.
    d. List all components on the network.

11. Give three examples of *networked* devices that are not computers.

12. Why is it important to use a structured cabling standard when installing and managing cabling systems?

13. Why is it important to use plenum-rated cabling in the area above the ceiling tile?

14. What is the unit of measurement that defines the space available in a rack? How tall are standard racks?

15. Why is it important to minimize cable clutter in a rack?

16. What are some elements that are typically included in network diagrams?

17. How can you go about gathering the information needed to assemble a thorough operations manual?

18. What command invokes Nmap at a command line?

19. For what time period should you schedule a network change?

20. In a large organization, how do you typically request permission to perform a network change?

Hands-On Projects

NOTE 2-10

Websites and applications change often. While the instructions given in these projects were accurate at the time of writing, you might need to adjust the steps or options according to later changes.

Note to Instructors and Students: A rubric is provided for evaluating student performance on these projects. Please see Appendix D.

Project 2-1: Tour MDF and IDF Data Rooms

Estimated Time: 30 minutes
Objective: Compare and contrast various devices, their features, and their appropriate placement on the network. (Obj. 2.1)
Group Work: This project includes enhancements when assigned as a group project.
Resources:

- Internet access

Context: The equipment and spaces discussed in this module come alive when you can see them in real-life situations. Ideally, you would connect with IT departments at schools and businesses in your area and tour their networking facilities so you can see these things for yourself. Additionally, your instructor might be able to give you a tour of the network equipment at your school. In preparation for these real-life tours or as a suitable replacement for them if necessary, find and watch video tours online of various MDF and IDF facilities. Complete the following steps:

1. Do an online search for video tours of MDF and IDF facilities. Good search terms include "MDF IDF tour," "main distribution frame tour," "data room tour," and "MDF data room." Find two to four videos that show you around the MDF or IDF data room, identifying major components and their connections. The best tour videos include a walk to other buildings on the network's campus.
2. **For group assignments:** Each group member should find a video tour that meets the requirements from Step 1. Share each video with all group members to complete the remainder of this project.
3. Answer the following questions:
   a. List the videos you watched. Include a URL for each video or an explanation of how to find it on a particular website.
   b. What network components were shown?
   c. Find a point in one video that shows a good view of the layout of the room. **Take a screenshot**; submit this visual with your answers to this project's questions.
   d. What are three things you learned about the layout of the room, what equipment is there, or how the equipment is installed?

Project 2-2: Create a Wiki

Estimated Time: 30 minutes
Objective: Explain the purpose of organization documents and policies. (Obj. 3.2)
Group Work: This project includes enhancements when assigned as a group project.
Resources:

- Internet access

Context: One way to collect information from members of your team is to use a wiki creator to build your own wiki. There are many good wiki tools that require a purchase or subscription, such as Google Sites and SharePoint. These paid apps provide impressive features that really shine when you're collaborating with several people or making your wiki public as part of your business front. A free app such as Wikidot (*wikidot.com*), though, can give you all the features you need for tracking your own project information in this course. And it will help you better understand which features of a wiki are most important to you.

NOTE 2-11

Websites change. These steps were accurate at the time this text was written. However, you might need to adjust these steps to account for future changes.

Complete the following steps to create your own wiki:

1. Go to **wikidot.com** and create an account. Store your account information in your LastPass vault. Check your email to activate your Wikidot account.
2. Sign into your Wikidot account and click the **Sites** tab. In the left pane, scroll down and click **+ Create site**.
3. Give your wiki a title and web address and make sure the **Standard Template** is selected.

NOTE 2-12

You can choose any template for a later wiki, or you can later change the template for this wiki after completing this project.

4. Select an access policy. Unless directed otherwise by your instructor, choose the **Private** option.
5. Confirm that you have read and agreed to the Terms of Service and then click **Get my Wikidot site**. Your Wikidot site is created with generic information that will help you get started, as shown in Figure 2-34. What title and web address did you give your wiki?

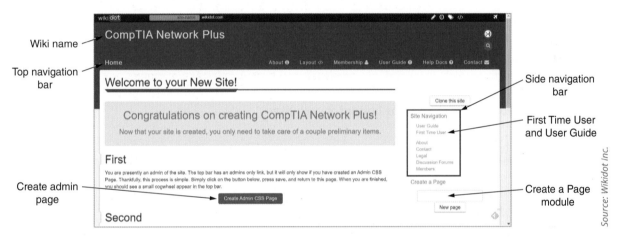

Source: Wikidot Inc.

Figure 2-34   Use a wiki to collect network information that all your team members can access

6. To see the admin link in the top navigation bar, click **Create Admin CSS Page** under the *First* section on the welcome page. Without making any edits to the page, click **Save** at the bottom of the page. There should now be a gear icon in the top navigation bar, as shown in Figure 2-35. Click it to see the admin navigation menu. You'll come back to that soon.

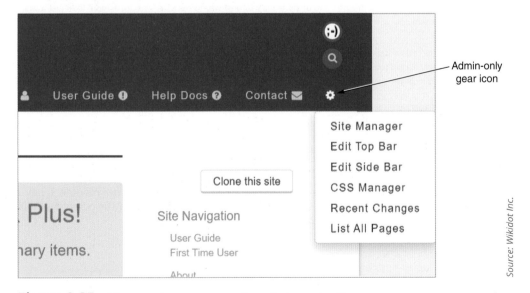

Source: Wikidot Inc.

Figure 2-35   The gear icon accesses the admin navigation menu

7. In the side navigation bar, click **First Time User** and read the information on this page. What feature in the Standard Template makes page creation simple?

8. Click **User Guide** in the side navigation bar and skim through this page to understand how the Site Manager works and how to edit pages. What does the Site Manager let you do?

9. Click each tab along the top navigation bar and skim the contents: **Home, About, Layout, Membership, User Guide, Help Docs,** and **Contact.** This will help you become familiar with the pages included in this template. Each of these pages belongs to your personal wiki site and includes default information you can change later.

10. Click the **Home** link to go back to the Home page. At the bottom of the page, click **Edit,** as shown in Figure 2-36.

Figure 2-36   Page tools at the bottom of each page

11. In the Header box, change the text *Welcome to Wikidot* (See Figure 2-37) to say **This is my Wikidot.** Save your changes. **Take a screenshot** of your new Home page; submit this visual with your answers to this project's questions.

Figure 2-37   Make changes to the text on any page

12. Click the **About** link to go to the About page. In the side navigation bar, in the *Create a Page* module, type **Virtualization:VMclients** (see Figure 2-38). Notice that there is no space before or after the colon. This will create a new page named *VMclients* in the category *Virtualization*. Click **New page.**

Source: Wikidot Inc.

Figure 2-38   Create a new category and page in a wiki

13. You have 15 minutes to complete changes to this page. Type the information for the Capstone Projects you completed in Module 1, as shown in Figure 2-39—substitute the information for your own VMs, such as the names that you gave the VMs and the OSs you installed on them. (Note that you might have only created one VM in one hypervisor because you couldn't complete both Capstone Projects on the same computer.) Click **Save**.

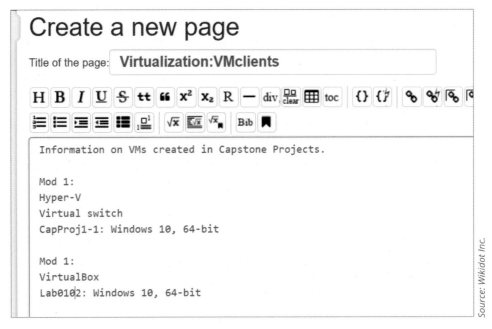

Source: Wikidot Inc.

Figure 2-39   Add information for your Hyper-V and VirtualBox Windows VMs from Module 1

14. To see a list of all pages in your wiki, click the gear icon in the top bar, and then click **List All Pages**. You will continue to add pages and content in later modules. For now, click your new **Virtualization:VMclients** page in the list. **Take a screenshot**; submit this visual with your answers to this project's questions.

15. Click the gear icon and click **Site Manager** to go to the Dashboard.

16. In the left pane, click **Security** and then click **Access policy**. If necessary, scroll up to see your current access policy. What access mode is selected? Scroll down and notice in the blue box that you can apply for a free educational upgrade. This is optional and is not required for this course. Ask your instructor whether you should pursue the upgrade.

17. **For group assignments:** Invite your group members to your wiki. To do this, in the left pane, click **Members** and then click **Invitations**. On the Invite members tab, enter the username of each group member to invite them. Accept your group members' invitations. After each group member accepts your invitation, in the left pane, click the **Members List**. View your page's members, explore the levels of permissions you can manage for each member, and send each member a private message.

18. Click through the other settings and options and make changes as desired. When you're finished, click your wiki's name in the upper-left corner next to the Wikidot logo to return to your wiki.

Project 2-3: Install and Use Nmap and Zenmap

Estimated Time: 45 minutes

Objective: Given a scenario, use the appropriate network software tools and commands. (Obj. 5.3)

Resources:

- Windows computer with ability to scan the local area network
- A computer or user account with application installation rights
- Internet access
- Access to a private network either owned by the student or which the student has explicit permission to scan

Context: In this activity, you install Zenmap, the GUI version of Nmap for Windows, and use it to scan your computer and your local network.

> **(!) CAUTION**   Take note that scanning a network you don't own or don't have permission to scan with Nmap or Zenmap is illegal. Do not use Nmap or Zenmap on public Wi-Fi networks at all. Also don't use Nmap or Zenmap on any network you don't own unless you have written permission from the owner to capture and analyze network communications using Nmap and Zenmap.

NOTE 2-13

Websites change. These steps were accurate at the time this text was written. However, you might need to adjust these steps to account for future changes.

Complete the following steps:

1. Go to **nmap.org** and click **Download** in the grid menu at the top of the page. Scroll down to the Microsoft Windows binaries section which might look similar to Figure 2-40.

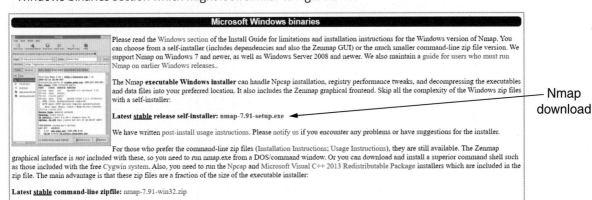

Figure 2-40   Download and install Nmap using the self-installer

Source: Insecure.org

2. Next to the text *Latest stable release self-installer*, click the **nmap-*version*-setup.exe** link. Go to the download location on your computer and run the program to install Nmap. Respond to any system warnings. On the Choose Components window, make sure that all available components are selected, as shown in Figure 2-41. On the Installation Options screen, make sure *Install Npcap in WinPcap API-compatible Mode* is selected, as shown in Figure 2-42. Otherwise, accept all default settings during installation.

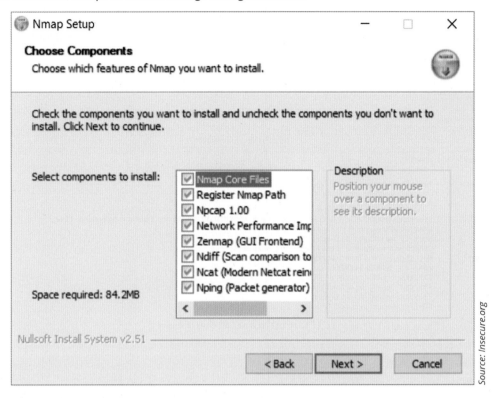

Figure 2-41   Make sure all available components are selected

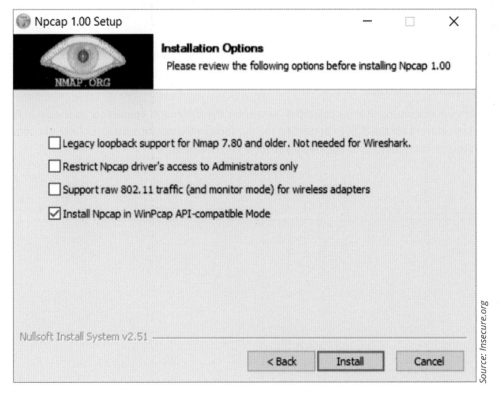

Figure 2-42   Make sure Npcap will be installed using WinPcap API-compatible Mode

3. Once the installation is complete, close all open windows. **Take a screenshot** of the new **Nmap-Zenmap GUI** shortcut on your desktop; submit this visual with your answers to this project's questions. Double-click the shortcut to open **Nmap-Zenmap GUI**.

4. Start with a quick scan of your local computer. To do this, in the Target field, enter **localhost**, and in the Profile field, select **Quick scan.** What command does Zenmap build in the Command field?

5. You could accomplish the same quick scan by entering this command at a CLI (command line interface) such as Command Prompt or PowerShell. For now, click **Scan**. The scan shows a list of open ports on your computer and the services assigned to them, similar to the results shown in Figure 2-43. **Take a screenshot**; submit this visual with your answers to this project's questions.

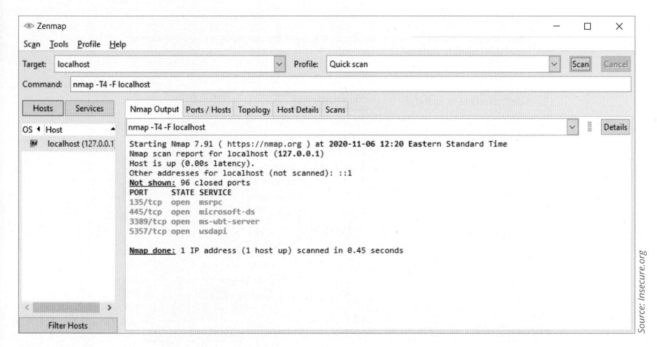

Source: Insecure.org

Figure 2-43   Zenmap localhost scan output

In the following steps, you'll run a scan of your local network and see how the output changes. This time you will target all IP addresses in the same range as your computer's IP address. The easiest way to do this is to first determine your computer's IP address.

6. Open a PowerShell or Command Prompt window and enter the command `ipconfig`, as shown in Figure 2-44. What is the IPv4 address for the active connection to your local network? Be sure to look for the connection for an Ethernet adapter (but not to your hypervisor) or for a Wi-Fi adapter.

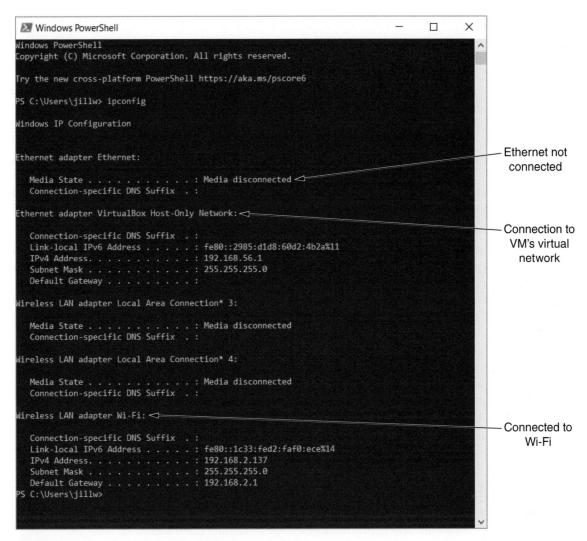

Figure 2-44   The ipconfig command shows the computer's IP address on the local area network

 EXAM TIP

PowerShell natively uses cmdlets (command-lets) to execute tasks. However, native Command Prompt commands, such as `ipconfig`, also work natively in PowerShell or serve as aliases for similar Power-Shell cmdlets. For example, PowerShell cmdlets that generate output similar to that of `ipconfig` are `Get-NetIPConfiguration` or `Get-NetIPAddress`. While familiarity with PowerShell should be a high priority for network technicians, the CompTIA Network+ exam requires Command Prompt and Linux commands such as `ipconfig`, `ifconfig`, and `ip`. You'll learn more about these commands in later modules. This course will also teach you equivalent or similar PowerShell cmdlets to help you prepare for more extensive use of PowerShell in future courses.

7. Go back to Zenmap. In the Target field, type your local computer's IPv4 address. However, so that you can scan a range of IP addresses, replace the final block of digits in your IPv4 address with **1-254**. For example, if your IPv4 address is 192.168.1.106, you would enter **192.168.1.1-254** in the Target field. What command does Zenmap build in the Command field? Click **Scan**.

8. This time, the output shows information about other hosts on your network as well as the information you've already seen for your own computer. Scroll through the output and answer the following questions:

   a. How many IP addresses were scanned? How many hosts are up?

   b. Compared with the information you saw earlier about your own computer, what information is revealed about the other hosts?

   c. Find a host with open ports reported. **Take a screenshot** showing this host's open ports and their services; submit this visual with your answers to this project's questions.

NOTE 2-14

You'll learn more about ports, IP addresses, and MAC addresses later.

9. Copy the command currently listed in the Command field. In a PowerShell or Command Prompt window, paste the command and press **Enter**. How do the results from the CLI compare to the Zenmap results?

10. The command you copied from Zenmap is intended to run a quick scan. Using the resources you've learned about in this project, determine the command to run a regular scan on one of the hosts on your network. Enter that command in the CLI. **Take a screenshot** of the command and its results; submit this visual with your answers to this project's questions.

In Project 2-2, you created a wiki to track information about your work in this course. You started a category called Virtualization and recorded information about the VMs you created in Module 1. App installations for projects is another kind of information you need to track in the wiki, as follows:

11. Go to your Wikidot site and click **User Guide** in the top navigation bar. In the side navigation bar, in the *Create a Page* module, type **Applications:Nmap**. This will create a new page named *Nmap* in a new category named *Applications*. Click **New page**.

12. Under "Create a new page," type some information about your Nmap and Zenmap installation. For example, you could answer the following questions:
    a. What is Nmap? How is Zenmap different than Nmap?
    b. On which computer did you install Nmap?
    c. What problems did you run into, and what solutions did you come up with?
    d. What information did you learn about your network from running scans in Zenmap and Nmap?

13. When you're finished, click **Save**.

14. **Take a screenshot** of your new page; submit this visual with your answers to this project's questions.

15. Click the gear icon and click **List All Pages** to confirm your new page was created. In a later module, you'll streamline your navigation bars and pages.

Project 2-4: Install and Use Wireshark

Estimated Time: 45 minutes
Objective: Given a scenario, use the appropriate network software tools and commands. (Obj. 5.3)
Resources:
- A computer or user account with application installation rights
- Internet access
- Access to a private network either owned by the student or which the student has explicit permission to scan

Context: Wireshark is a free, open-source network protocol analyzer that can help demystify network messages for you and help make the OSI model easier to understand. For some students, using Wireshark for the first time can be an epiphany experience. It allows you to study the OSI layers, all the information that is added to every message, and all the messages that have to go back and forth just to bring up a web page or simply to connect to the network. It all becomes much more real when you see how many messages Wireshark collects during even a short capture.

 **CAUTION** Take note that scanning a network you don't own or don't have permission to scan with Wireshark is illegal. Do not use Wireshark on public Wi-Fi networks at all. Also don't use Wireshark on any network you don't own unless you have written permission from the owner to capture and analyze network communications using Wireshark.

In this project, you will install Wireshark and take a first look at how it works. In a later module, you'll dig deeper into Wireshark's capabilities. Complete the following steps:

1. Open a browser and go to **wireshark.org**. Download and install the current stable release, using the appropriate version for your OS. If you're using the same computer you used for Project 2-3, the Wireshark installer should recognize that you already have Npcap installed and will not offer to install it. If you're using a different computer, accept the Npcap option. In the Wireshark setup window, you do *not* need USBPcap. If needed, reboot your computer to complete the Wireshark installation.

2. When installation is complete, open **Wireshark**.

3. In the Wireshark Network Analyzer window, select your network interface from the list. Then click the shark-fin icon to start the capture, as shown in Figure 2-45.

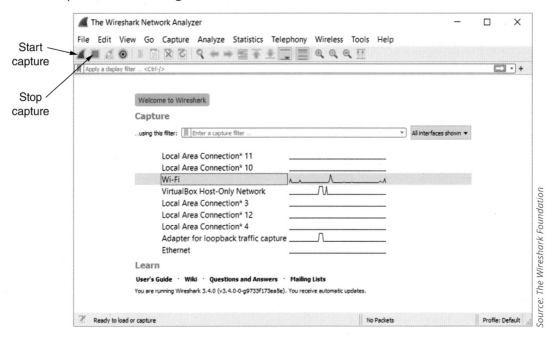

Figure 2-45   The Wireshark Network Analyzer window

Source: The Wireshark Foundation

4. While the capture is running, open your browser and go to **cengage.com**. Then open a PowerShell or Command Prompt window and enter `ping 8.8.8.8`. After the ping completes, click the red box on the command ribbon to stop the capture.

Look at some of the messages you've captured. You can adjust the pane sizes by grabbing a border between them and dragging. Expand the top pane so you can see more of the captured messages at one time. Let's start to decode this blur of numbers and letters.

5. Notice the column headers along the top of the capture, as shown in Figure 2-46. Of particular interest are the Source and Destination columns, the Protocol column, and the Info column. Find a UDP (User Datagram Protocol) message that has an IPv4 Source address and click on it. **Take a screenshot** of your capture with the UDP message selected; submit this visual with your answers to this project's questions.

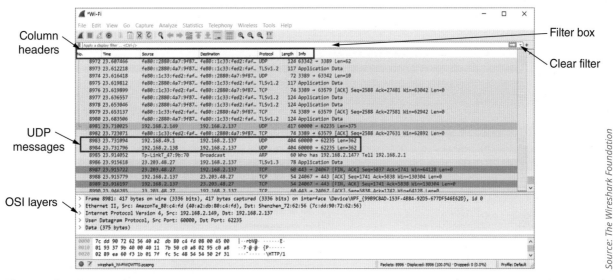

Figure 2-46   A Wireshark capture

Source: The Wireshark Foundation

6. In the middle pane, click on each line to expand that layer's information. What pieces of information stand out to you? Which device on your network do you think sent this message, and which device(s) received it?

Color highlighting can make it easier to spot different protocols. Notice in Figure 2-47 that TCP (Transmission Control Protocol) messages are a light lavender or light green color (when it includes HTTP), and UDP and DNS (Domain Name

Services) messages are a light bluish color. You can see the protocol names in the Protocol column. Note that if you have trouble distinguishing colors, you can choose colors or shades that work for you. For example, you might choose a very dark shade that stands out against lighter shades. If necessary, you could also use a phone app to help, such as Be My Eyes (**bemyeyes.com**) that pairs users with a normally sighted volunteer to help identify colors, Color Blind Pal (**colorblindpal.com**) that provides descriptive information and offers a filter tool, or Pixolor that identifies colors of pixels in an image (website developers often use apps like this to define branding colors).

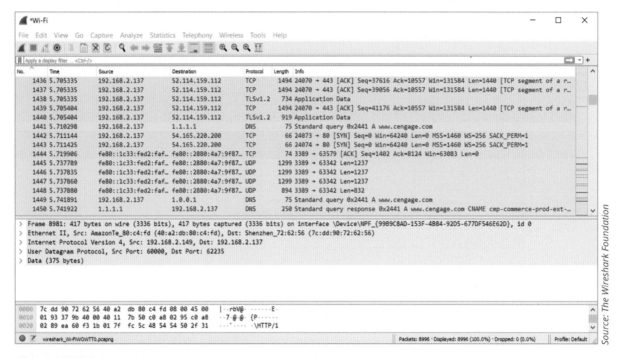

Figure 2-47   Different highlight colors correspond to different protocols

7. To see a list of currently assigned highlight colors and to adjust these assignments, on the main toolbar, click **View** and then click **Coloring Rules**. Here, you can change the priority for matching protocols within a message to colors in the output pane (because more than one protocol is used in each message), and you can assign colors that are easier to spot. In Figure 2-48, the background color for ICMP is changed to a bright green. When you're happy with your color selections, click **OK**.

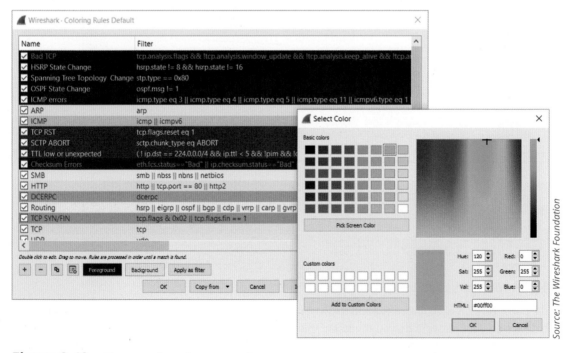

Figure 2-48   Choose colors that are easier to spot

8. To filter for a particular kind of message in your capture, type the name of the protocol in the Filter box (identified in Figure 2-48). Figure 2-49 shows a filter for ICMP messages, which are currently highlighted in bright green. These ICMP messages were generated when pinging another host on the network. Try filtering for other protocols you've read about in this course already, such as HTTP, and see how many different types you can find in your capture. Click the **X** to clear filters between searches. Which protocols did you find?

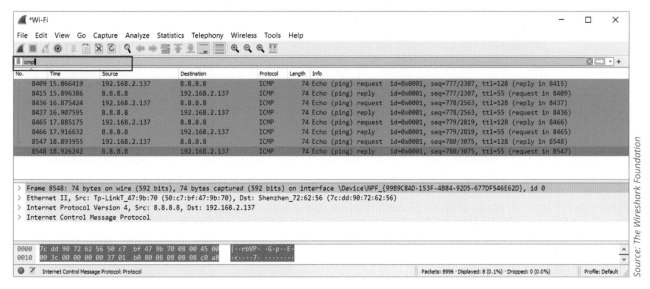

Figure 2-49 Use a filter to narrow your search

9. To compare which OSI layers are represented by each of these protocols, apply a slightly more complicated filter where you can see both HTTP messages and ICMP messages in the same search. Enter the following phrase into the Filter box: **http or icmp**.

10. Click on an ICMP message and count the layers of information available in the middle pane. In Figure 2-50, there are four layers of information, which correspond to layer 2 (Frame and Ethernet II) and layer 3 (Internet Protocol Version 4 and Internet Control Message Protocol).

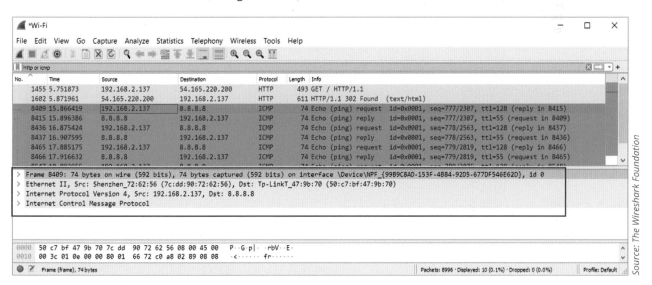

Figure 2-50 Use the middle pane to dig into each layer's headers

11. Examine an HTTP message. Figure 2-51 shows five layers of information in the middle pane. This time, layer 7 (Hypertext Transfer Protocol) and layer 4 (Transmission Control Protocol) are represented, in addition to layer 3 (Internet Protocol Version 4) and layer 2 (Ethernet II and Frame).

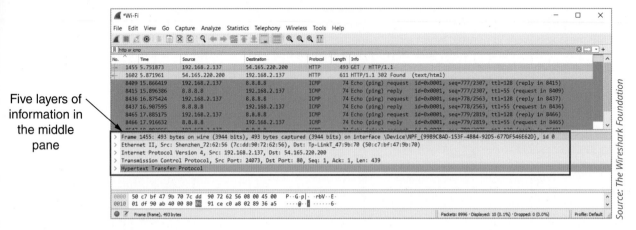

Five layers of information in the middle pane

Figure 2-51 This HTTP message uses TCP at the transport layer and IP at the network layer to contact a Cengage web server

12. Recall that TCP is a connection-oriented protocol. You can filter a capture to follow a TCP stream so you can see how these messages go back and forth for a single session. Clear your filter box and then find a TCP message. Right-click it, point to **Follow**, and click **TCP Stream** (see Figure 2-52). If you picked the right TCP stream, you might see the Cengage URL listed in this conversation, as shown in Figure 2-53. Next, click **Close** to close the Follow TCP Stream window and notice that Wireshark has filtered the capture for this stream's messages. Click the **X** to clear the filter.

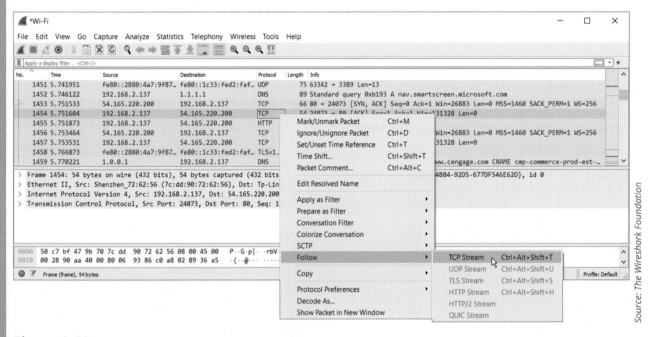

Figure 2-52 Follow the conversation in a TCP stream

Figure 2-53 The stream shows a conversation between the local computer and another device, such as the Cengage web server

13. In your wiki, add a new page titled **Applications:Wireshark**. Indicate the module and project number for this installation, the computer you used for this project, a brief description of what you learned, and any other information you might find helpful when using Wireshark later. You'll return to Wireshark in a later module.

Capstone Projects

NOTE 2-15

Websites and applications change often. While the instructions given in these projects were accurate at the time of writing, you might need to adjust the steps or options according to later changes.

Note to Instructors and Students: A rubric is provided for evaluating student performance on these projects. Please see Appendix D.

Capstone Project 2-1: Set Up an Ubuntu Desktop VM

Estimated Time: 45 minutes

Objective: Explain the characteristics of network topologies and network types. (Obj. 1.2)

Resources:

- Access to the same computer used to complete Capstone Project 1-1 or Capstone Project 1-2
- Internet access
- If desired, instructor can provide Ubuntu Desktop image file

Context: In the Capstone Projects of Module 1, you created a virtual machine using Windows 10 Client Hyper-V and/or Oracle VirtualBox. In this Capstone Project, you create a second VM in your virtual network and install Ubuntu Desktop in the VM. In Module 3, you'll install Ubuntu Server in your network. Ubuntu is a well-known version of Linux and offers both desktop and server editions. For these VM projects, you can use your choice of hypervisor.

Using one of the same computers that you used in Capstone Project 1-1 or 1-2 that has Client Hyper-V or Oracle VirtualBox installed, depending on which hypervisor you prefer, follow these steps:

1. Open the Oracle VM VirtualBox Manager or Hyper-V Manager. Following the directions in the Module 1 Capstone Projects, create a new VM with an informative name. Consider the following tips:
   a. If you're using Hyper-V Manager and you use the Quick Create option, choose the most recent Ubuntu image, such as **Ubuntu 20.04.1 LTS**. After it downloads, click **Connect**.
   b. If you're using VirtualBox, first go to **ubuntu.com** and download the Ubuntu Desktop OS to your hard drive. This is a free download, so you can decline to make any donations. The file that downloads is an ISO file. Back in VirtualBox, choose the **Linux** type and the **Ubuntu (64-bit)** version. When you're ready, mount the ISO file that contains the Ubuntu Desktop image to a virtual DVD in your VM.
2. Start the VM and install Ubuntu Desktop (click **Install Ubuntu**; do *not* click Try Ubuntu). Accept all default settings except, when given the option, don't install any extra software bundled with the OS. Give permission to download updates while installing (see Figure 2-54). Record your user credentials for your Ubuntu VM in a secure note in your LastPass vault. You'll need to restart the VM when the installation is finished.

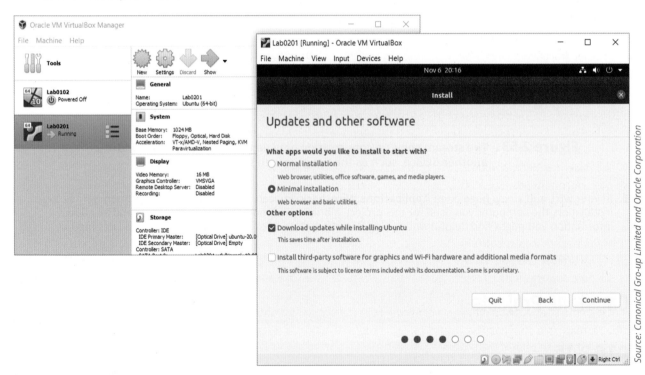

Figure 2-54 Ubuntu Desktop installing in a VM in Oracle VirtualBox

Source: Canonical Gro-up Limited and Oracle Corporation

3. To verify you have an Internet connection, open the Mozilla Firefox browser and surf the web. **Take a screenshot** of your desktop showing your hypervisor, your running VM, and the VM's successful connection with the Internet; submit this visual with your answers to this project's questions.

4. Good network technicians must know how to use many operating systems. Poke around in the Ubuntu Desktop interface and get familiar with it. You can also search the web for tutorials and YouTube videos on how to use Ubuntu Desktop. What are two ways to open the Settings window in Ubuntu Desktop?

5. When you're ready to shut down your VM, click the power icon in the upper-right corner of the Ubuntu Desktop screen, click **Power Off/Log Out**, click **Power Off. . .**, and then click **Power Off**.

6. Before you walk away from this project, take a moment to add the new information to your VMclients page in your wiki. Go to the **Virtualization:VMclients** page, click **Edit** at the bottom of the page, and add the new VM to your list. Include the module number, hypervisor used, VM computer name, and VM operating system. Also note any additional information that you might find helpful when you return to this VM in the future. When you're finished, click **Save**.

7. **Take a screenshot** of the edited wiki page; submit this visual with your answers to this project's questions.

Capstone Project 2-2: Install and Use Packet Tracer

Estimated Time: 1 hour
Objective: Given a scenario, use the appropriate network software tools and commands. (Obj. 5.3)
Resources:
- A computer or user account with application installation rights
- Internet access

Context: If you plan to pursue networking or security as your area of specialty in IT, you might consider earning a few Cisco networking certifications after you complete your CompTIA Network+ certification. The Cisco Networking Academy website provides many useful tools for advancing your networking education. One of those tools is a network simulator called Packet Tracer.

In this Capstone Project, you download and install Packet Tracer and take a tour of the simulator interface. This version of Packet Tracer is free to the public, and your school does not have to be a member of Cisco's Networking Academy for you to download and use it. In later projects, you'll return to Packet Tracer to build networks and even learn some basic Cisco IOS commands. Cisco IOS (Internetworking Operating Systems) is the operating system used on Cisco networking devices, such as routers and switches (with minor variations in the specific IOS for each different type of device). Many other manufacturers of networking devices use the same or similar commands, and those that use different commands typically use very similar functions, even if they call it something a little different.

To get the Packet Tracer download, you must first sign up for the free Introduction to Packet Tracer online course on the Cisco Networking Academy website. Complete the following steps to create your account:

1. Go to **netacad.com/courses/packet-tracer**. If the course is not listed on this page, do a search for *packet tracer site:*netacad.com and follow links to "Download Packet Tracer" or "Introduction to Packet Tracer" to find the current Packet Tracer introduction course. Enter your name, email, and text verification to enroll in the course.

2. Open the confirmation email and confirm your email address. Configure your account and save your account information in your LastPass vault. You will need this information again.

3. Take the brief tour of the course.

Now you're ready to download and install Packet Tracer. If you need help with the download and installation process, use the Course Index to navigate to Page 1.1.2.1 for additional guidance. Complete the following steps:

4. Inside the course, under *Introductory Chapter*, click **Student Support and Resources**. Scroll down and click **Download and install the latest version of Packet Tracer**. Choose the correct version for your computer. After the download is complete, install Packet Tracer. When the installation is complete, run **Cisco Packet Tracer**. When Packet Tracer asks if you would like to run multi-user, click **No**.

5. When Packet Tracer opens, sign in with your Networking Academy account that you just created. If you see a Windows Security Alert, allow access through your firewall. Cisco Packet Tracer opens. The interface window is shown in Figure 2-55.

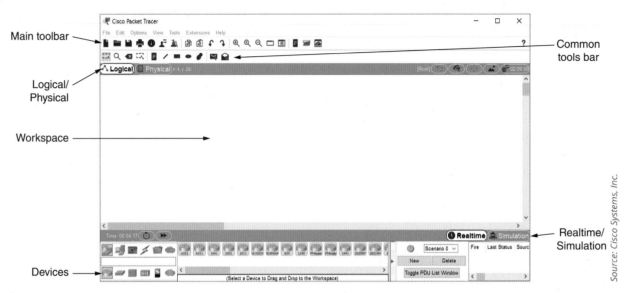

Figure 2-55 Explore the Packet Tracer window

The Introduction to Packet Tracer course presents an excellent introduction to Packet Tracer and provides lab activities. Packet Tracer Activities are interactive labs in which you download a start file, make the changes instructed in the lab, and then grade the activity in Packet Tracer. Complete the following steps to access your course:

6. Return to your Introduction to Packet Tracer course. You've already downloaded Packet Tracer, so you can skip Chapter 1.
7. Complete Chapters 2, 3, and 4, including their videos and labs. The other chapters provide excellent information on Packet Tracer but are not required for this project. Answer the following questions along the way:
   a. What is the first step in deploying a Packet Tracer network?
   b. When looking at a physical device's tabs in Packet Tracer, which tab is considered the learning tab?
   c. What three questions can be answered using the Simulation Mode?
   d. Which Packet Tracer feature do you think will be most helpful for you in learning how to manage a network? Why do you think this?
8. Back in your Packet Tracer window, deploy at least three physical devices into your workspace. You don't need to configure or connect them. **Take a screenshot** of your deployment; submit this visual with your answers to this project's questions.
9. In your wiki, add a new page titled **Applications:PacketTracer**. Remember *not* to include a space after the colon so your PacketTracer page will be collected in the Applications category. Indicate the module and project number for this installation, the computer you used for this project, a brief description of what you learned, and any other information you might find helpful when using Packet Tracer later. You'll return to Packet Tracer many times throughout this course.

Note to Instructors: A Packet Tracer solution file is provided for each Packet Tracer project through the Instructors site. Some Packet Tracer projects build on earlier Packet Tracer networks. If needed for one or more students, you can provide a previous project's solution file as a start file for one of these progression projects.

Solutions to Self-Check Questions

Components of Structured Cabling

1. At what point does the ISP hand over responsibility to the customer?

   Answer: c. Demarc

   Explanation: For most situations, the device that marks where a telecommunications service provider's network ends and the organization's network begins is the **demarc**, or demarcation point. The MDF (main distribution frame) and IDF (intermediate distribution frame) are environmentally controlled spaces holding network equipment. While the demarc might be located inside the MDF, the demarc itself is the cutoff point of responsibility. A patch panel is a panel of data receptors which can be mounted to a wall or a rack and which provides a central termination point when many patch cables converge in a single location.

2. According to structured cabling standards, there must be at least one _____ on each floor.

Answer: a. IDF

Explanation: The ANSI/TIA standard specifies at least one **IDF (intermediate distribution frame)** per floor, although large organizations may have several data rooms or closets per floor to better manage the data feed from the main data facilities. There is only one MDF (main distribution frame) per campus and one demarc per ISP (Internet service provider). There can be none, one, or several work areas per floor, and the number of work areas is not defined by structured cabling standards.

3. Which of the following causes physical layer failures?

Answer: d. EMI

Explanation: Install cable at least 3 feet away from fluorescent lights or other sources of **EMI (electromagnetic interference)** to reduce the possibility of noise (interference) that can affect your network's signals at the physical layer. A SCADA (supervisory control and data acquisition) system acquires real-time data from a physical system and manages the system or presents the data to humans to monitor and manage the system. Regular twisted-pair cables are coated with PVC (polyvinyl chloride), which is made from a cheap plastic that is toxic when burned. STP (shielded twisted pair) cable is a copper-based cable containing twisted-pair wires with metallic shielding, such as foil around each wire pair or surrounding all four wire pairs.

Network Documentation

4. Which network diagram shows a logical topology?

Answer: b. Network map

Explanation: Network mapping is the process of discovering and identifying the devices on a network. A **network map** shows logical connections and addressing information. Diagrams of physical layouts include floor plans, rack diagrams, and wiring diagrams.

5. In which life cycle phase is an old device removed from the network?

Answer: c. Implementation

Explanation: During the **implementation** phase of a system life cycle, you deploy new equipment to replace old equipment, and continue testing to achieve a new, stable baseline. Removing old equipment during normal maintenance, evaluation, or analysis of requirements would leave a gap in the network topology.

6. When an Internet connection goes down, what business document defines a customer's options for paying a reduced rate?

Answer: d. SLA

Explanation: An **SLA (service-level agreement)** specifies options for compensation if outages exceed defined thresholds. An MOU (memorandum of understanding) documents the intentions of two or more parties to enter into a binding agreement. An SOW (statement of work) documents in detail the work that must be completed for a particular project. An RFP (request for proposal) is a request to vendors to submit a proposal for a product or service your company wants to purchase.

Change Management

7. Which change is designed to close a security vulnerability without affecting other components of an application?

Answer: a. Patch

Explanation: A software **patch** is a correction, improvement, or enhancement to software. It corrects a bug, closes a vulnerability, or adds minor enhancements to only part of the software, leaving most of the code untouched.

A software rollback is the process of reverting to a previous version of software after attempting to patch or upgrade it. A software upgrade is a major change to a software package that enhances the functionality and features of the software, while also correcting bugs and vulnerabilities. New software is installed on a device.

8. Which change management principle must you apply to all changes regardless of scope or impact?

Answer: d. Document the change.

Explanation: Some change management principles apply to any type of change, including the requirement to **document each change** throughout the process. More extensive or expensive changes must progress through a formal change management process, which includes submitting a change request document and acquiring review board approval. Patches or upgrades should always be thoroughly tested and planned, although updates that close a critical security vulnerability should be prioritized and applied as soon as reasonably possible.

ADDRESSING

After reading this module and completing the exercises, you should be able to:

1. Work with MAC addresses
2. Configure TCP/IP settings on a computer, including IP address, subnet mask, default gateway, and DNS servers
3. Identify the ports of several common network protocols
4. Describe domain names and the name resolution process
5. Use command-line tools to troubleshoot common network problems

On the Job

I woke up to a message from an on-call engineer, Bill, saying, "Help, I am out of ideas for DNS troubleshooting!" Twenty minutes later, as I walked into the office, he recited a chaotic list of all the troubleshooting steps he took and every possible problem that could have caused the issue at hand. We took a walk to the vending machines so I could get caffeine and the story.

Dying server hardware forced Bill to move a number of services to new hardware. DNS was scheduled to be last, as the configuration was simple, and moving it was supposed to be a quick and easy task. Everything seemed to work fine, but queries for all of the Internet and a test internal domain were not being answered. The OS configuration and DNS server settings all seemed fine, but no matter what we tweaked, the service did not work right.

Because Bill knew more about DNS than I did, there was little reason for a detailed walk-through of the configurations. I took a quick look, in hope of finding something obvious that he had missed, but the configuration was sound. Because no trivial fix was available, I reverted to basic troubleshooting mode and started to work through a simple list of items to check: "ping localhost, ping the interface, ping the router, and a host beyond it, etc."

The last check returned "connect: Network is unreachable." A quick glance at the routing table explained the issue: There was no default route. Without a way to forward traffic, no host outside of a few statically defined internal networks were reachable, including all the root DNS servers.

The fix was simple and, once the service was restored, I helped a bit with moving other services. Another set of eyes is an invaluable asset during late-night work, and I had to work off all that caffeine.

Marcin Antkiewicz

In Module 1, you learned that the OSI model can be used to describe just about every aspect of networking. You saw firsthand the usefulness of working your way up or down the seven layers of the OSI model to troubleshoot networking problems. In Module 2, you toured the elements of a typical network infrastructure and saw the importance of documentation in maintaining and troubleshooting a network. In this module, you will learn the several methods used to address and find software, files, computers, and other devices on a network. You'll take a bottom-up approach to the OSI model to explore these topics, starting at the data link layer and working your way up to the application layer. (The lowest OSI layer, the physical layer, does not require a network address.) At the end of this module, you will learn how to troubleshoot addressing problems by using common command-line utilities.

ADDRESSING OVERVIEW

 **CERTIFICATION**

2.3 Given a scenario, configure and deploy common Ethernet switching features.

Average reading time: 11 minutes

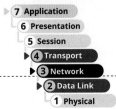

In Module 1, you learned that addressing methods operate at the data link, network, transport, and application layers of the OSI model so that one host or node can find another on a network. Here's a quick overview of the four addressing methods, starting at the lowest layer:

- **Data link layer MAC (Media Access Control) address**—A MAC address is embedded on every NIC on the globe and is assumed to be unique to that NIC. A MAC address is 48 bits, written as six hex (hexadecimal) numbers separated by colons, as in 00:60:8C:00:54:99. Nodes on a LAN find each other using their MAC addresses. Switches, which function at layer 2, check MAC addresses to determine where to send messages on the LAN.

- **Network layer IP (Internet Protocol) address**—An IP address is assigned to nearly every interface, which is a network connection made by a node on a network. An IP address can be used to find any computer in the world if the IP address is public on the Internet. Applications such as browsers can store and retrieve IP addresses. But for routing purposes, an IP address is used only at the network layer. Routers, which function primarily at layer 3, check IP addresses to determine which network a message is destined for. There are two types of IP addresses:

  - IPv4 (Internet Protocol version 4) addresses have 32 bits and are written as four decimal numbers called octets, for example, 92.106.50.200. Each octet, when written in binary, consists of exactly 8 bits. For example, the octet 92 can be written as 0101 1100.

  - IPv6 (Internet Protocol version 6) addresses have 128 bits and are written as eight blocks of hex numbers, for example, 2001:0DB8:0B80:0000:0000:00D3:9C 5A:00CC. Each block, when written in binary, contains 16 bits.

- **Transport layer ports**—A port is a number used by the transport layer to find an application. It identifies one application among several that might be running on a host. For example, a web server application is usually configured to listen for incoming requests at port 80 or port 443.

- **Application layer domain names, computer names, and host names**—Every host on a network is assigned a unique character-based name called the FQDN (fully qualified domain name), for example, *susan.mycompany.com, ftp.mycompany.com,* and *www.mycompany.com.* Collectively, the last two parts of a host's name (for example, *mycompany.com*) are called the domain name, which matches the name of the organization's domain or network. The first part (for example, susan, ftp, and www) is the host name, which identifies the

NOTE 3-1

A hexadecimal number (also called a hex number) is a number written in the base-16 number system, which uses the 16 numerals 0, 1, 2, 3, 4, 5, 6, 7, 8, 9, A, B, C, D, E, and F.

NOTE 3-2

A binary number is a number written in the base-2 number system, which uses only the numerals 0 and 1.

individual computer on the network. Ftp is the host name usually given to an FTP server, and www is often the host name assigned to a computer running a web server. When technicians refer to a "host name," you can usually assume they're referring to the FQDN unless stated otherwise.

NOTE 3-3

Technically, an FQDN ends in a period:

ftp.mycompany.com.

However, in most applications, the terminal period is understood even when it is not typed or shown on the screen.

The organization responsible for tracking the assignments of IP addresses, port numbers, and domain names is IANA (Internet Assigned Numbers Authority) (pronounced "I–anna"). IANA is a department of ICANN (Internet Corporation for Assigned Names and Numbers). ICANN is a nonprofit organization charged with setting many policies that guide how the Internet works. For more information, see *iana.org* and *icann.org*. At *icann.org*, you can download helpful white papers that explain how the Internet works.

Now that you have the big picture of how addressing happens at each layer of the OSI model, you're ready to dig into the details, beginning with MAC addresses at the bottom of the model.

MAC Addresses

You can often find a network adapter's MAC address stamped directly onto the NIC's circuit board or on a sticker attached to some part of the NIC, as shown in Figure 3-1. Later in this module, you'll learn to use TCP/IP utilities to report the MAC address.

MAC addresses contain two parts, are 48 bits long, and are written as hexadecimal numbers separated by colons—for example, 00:60:8C:00:54:99. The first 24 bits (six hex characters, such as 00:60:8C in this example) are known as the OUI (Organizationally Unique Identifier), which identifies the NIC's manufacturer. A manufacturer's OUI is assigned by IEEE (Institute of Electrical and Electronics Engineers). If you know a computer's MAC address, you can determine which company manufactured its NIC by looking up its OUI. IEEE maintains a database of OUIs and their manufacturers, which is accessible via the web. At the time of this writing, the database search page could be found at *standards-oui.ieee.org/oui.txt*. You can also use an OUI lookup tool, such as Wireshark's at *wireshark.org/tools/oui-lookup*.

7 Application
6 Presentation
5 Session
4 Transport
3 Network
▶**2 Data Link**
1 Physical

MAC address

Source: D-Link of North America

Figure 3-1   NIC with MAC address

NOTE 3-4

Links to websites given in this course might become outdated as websites change. If a given link doesn't work, try to search for the item online to find the new link.

The last 24 bits make up the **extension identifier** or **device ID** and identify the device itself. Manufacturers assign each NIC a unique extension identifier, based on the NIC's model and manufacture date, so that, in theory, no two NICs share the same MAC address.

Applying Concepts 3-1: Identify a NIC Manufacturer

Most network packets include the MAC address of the sender, the receiver, or both. When collecting network data on Wireshark using the default settings, some OUIs are automatically resolved, telling you the manufacturer of each device. In Figure 3-2, you can see where Wireshark has identified the manufacturers—TP-Link and ASUS—of two NICs on this network.

The Source NIC's manufacturer and MAC address

The Destination NIC's manufacturer and MAC address

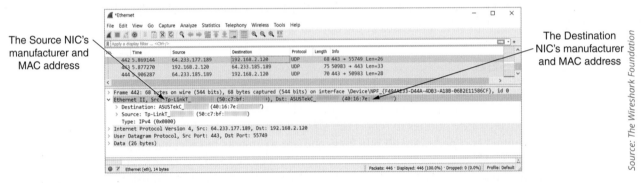

Source: The Wireshark Foundation

Figure 3-2   Wireshark capture shows the manufacturers of the Source and Destination nodes' NICs

Sometimes, however, you might be working with physical addresses provided by a command output, or you might need a little more information than what is provided by a Wireshark capture. For these situations, use an online MAC address lookup table such as Wireshark's OUI Lookup Tool. Complete the following steps:

1. In your browser, go to **wireshark.org/tools/oui-lookup**.
2. Notice earlier in Figure 3-2 that the MAC addresses of the Source and Destination devices are listed in the Ethernet frame. The first three bytes of the Destination device's MAC address, 40:16:7e, make up the OUI of the device's manufacturer. Type those numbers into Wireshark's OUI Lookup Tool and click **Find**. What results did you get?

NOTE 3-5

If you are pulling OUIs from your own Wireshark capture or command-line output, you can copy and paste one or more OUIs into the website search box.

You can perform the same lookup using output from a PowerShell or Command Prompt window:

3. Open a PowerShell or Command Prompt window and enter `ipconfig /all` to identify your NIC's MAC address.
4. From your command output, select the first three bytes of the physical address for the active network connection and press **Ctrl+C**. *Note:* You might need to first press **Ctrl+M** to enable marking.
5. Click in the search box on Wireshark's website, press **Ctrl+V** to paste the information into the Wireshark Lookup Tool, and click **Find**. Who is the manufacturer of your NIC?

Switches use MAC addresses to identify devices on the local area network. As each device communicates on the network, the switch identifies the sending device's MAC address from its transmitted message as shown in Figure 3-3. The MAC address is stored in a **MAC address table** that maps each MAC address to a physical port on the switch.

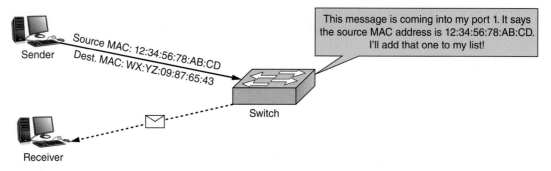

Figure 3-3 The switch learns the sending device's MAC address

Later, when the switch sees a message destined for that MAC address, the switch checks its MAC address table and determines which port leads to the correct device, as shown in Figure 3-4. The information in a MAC address table expires after a short period of time, so the switch is constantly relearning where devices are located on the network. This balances a switch's sensitivity to changes in the network with the switch's ability to quickly and efficiently direct network traffic to its destination. At the end of this module in Capstone Project 3-2, you'll work with a switch in Packet Tracer as it builds a MAC address table.

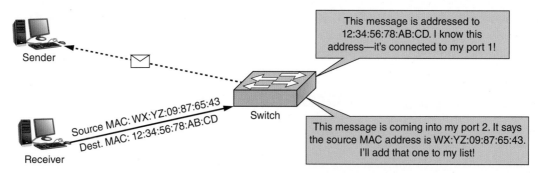

Figure 3-4 The switch learned earlier which port the Destination MAC address is connected to

REMEMBER THIS...

- Describe addressing systems used at the data link, network, transport, and application layers.
- Identify a device's MAC address.
- Interpret the information given in a MAC address.

SELF-CHECK

1. What numbering system do humans use to write MAC addresses?

   a. Decimal

   b. Binary

   c. Base-2

   d. Hexadecimal

2. What Windows command outputs a computer's MAC address?

   a. `ipconfig`

   b. `ping`

   c. `ipconfig /all`

   d. `oui-lookup`

Check your answers at the end of this module.

IP ADDRESSES

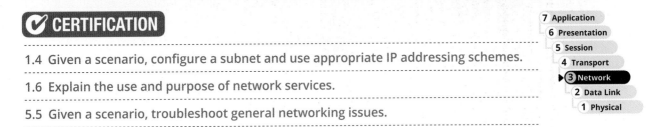

Average reading time: 34 minutes

As you move up to layer 3, recall that IP addresses identify nodes at the network layer. Whereas MAC addresses are used by switches for communication inside a local network, an IP address is required for a device to communicate outside its local network through a gateway device such as a router. While switches need MAC addresses to identify devices in a network, routers rely on IP addresses to locate devices across networks.

You can assign a persistent or **static IP address** to a device, or you can configure the device to request and receive (or lease) a **dynamic IP address** from a DHCP server each time it connects to the network. A **DHCP (Dynamic Host Configuration Protocol)** server manages the dynamic distribution of IP addresses to devices on a network. You'll learn more about DHCP shortly.

Applying Concepts 3-2: Windows TCP/IP Settings

Let's begin with a look at IP addresses and related TCP/IP settings on a Windows 10 computer. Take note that, if you're using a computer with Hyper-V enabled, you might see a few interesting variations as you click through the screens in this module. For example, a computer not running Hyper-V will likely show a direct connection to your LAN, as shown in Figure 3-5a. A computer that is running Hyper-V will likely show a connection to your virtual switch that you created in Module 1, as shown in Figure 3-5b. You'll learn more about why this is the case in a later module when you study virtualization technologies more closely.

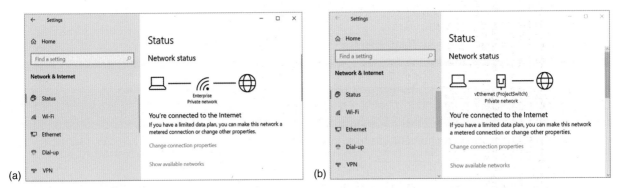

Figure 3-5 (a) A computer not running Hyper-V shows a connection directly to the LAN; (b) A computer running Hyper-V shows a connection with a virtual switch

To check TCP/IP settings on your Windows computer, complete the following steps:

1. Click **Start** and then click the **Settings** gear icon. Click **Network & Internet**. Alternatively, you can right-click the active network connection icon on the right side of your taskbar near the date and time (see Figure 3-6) and then click **Open Network & Internet settings**.
2. Click **Change connection properties** and scroll down to the IP settings and Properties sections. Figure 3-7 shows the TCP/IP settings, including IP assignment source (Automatic from DHCP), IPv6 and IPv4 addresses, DNS servers, and Physical address (MAC).

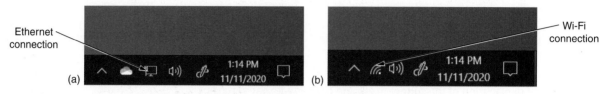

Ethernet connection

Wi-Fi connection

(a)   (b)

Figure 3-6   Right-click the active network connection to see its properties

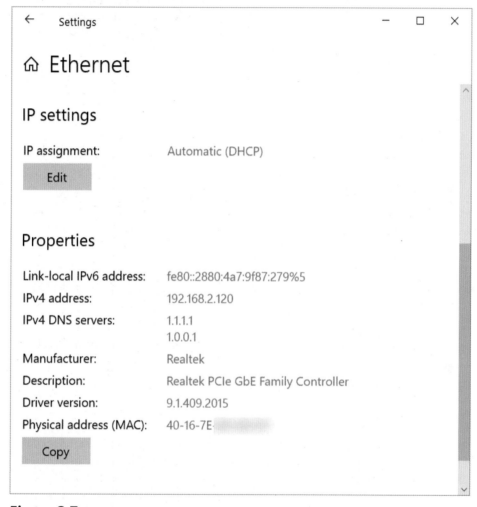

Figure 3-7   View TCP/IP settings

3. You probably have the Automatic (DHCP) option enabled, which dynamically assigns an IP address from a DHCP server. The Properties section shows your IP address, MAC address, and DNS (Domain Name Service) servers. DNS servers are responsible for tracking computer names and their IP addresses. Later in the module, you'll learn more about the various types of DNS servers and how they work together.

You can find similar information and more using the **ipconfig** utility, which you first used in Project 2-3 while working with Nmap. You'll learn more about this utility later in this module. Network technicians need to be comfortable with the CLI (command line interface) because it is quicker and often more powerful and flexible than a GUI (graphical user interface). To see the additional information ipconfig reports, complete the following steps:

4. Open a PowerShell or Command Prompt window and enter **ipconfig**. What are your IPv4 address, subnet mask, and default gateway settings for your active network connection?

NOTE 3-6

Notice that `ipconfig` by itself does not output the MAC address. You must use the `/all` parameter to see the MAC address, which you did earlier in Applying Concepts 3-1.

Here's a brief explanation of the subnet mask and default gateway settings:

- A **subnet mask**, also called a netmask, is a 32-bit number that helps one computer find another. The 32 bits are used to indicate what part of an IP address's bits are the network portion, called the **network ID** or network address, and which bits consist of the host portion, called the **host ID** or **node ID**. Using this information, a computer can determine if another computer with a given IP address is on its own or a different network.
- A **gateway** is a computer, router, firewall, or other device that a host uses to access another network. The **default gateway** is the routing device that nodes on the network turn to for access to the outside world. In the *On the Job* story at the beginning of this module, you read about a problem that appeared to be a DNS issue but was, in fact, a missing default route that prevented network nodes from reaching DNS servers outside the local network. The default gateway provides a connection to all resources outside the local network when static routes aren't available (which is most of the time).

NOTE 3-7

Technically, there is a subtle distinction between the meanings of the terms *subnet mask* and *netmask*. A **subnet** is a smaller network within a larger network. A netmask indicates the bits of an IP address that identify the larger network, while the subnet mask indicates the bits of an IP address that identify a smaller subnet within the larger network. Most of the time, however, these two terms are used interchangeably. You'll learn more about subnets in a later module.

Recall that networks may use two types of IP addresses: IPv4 addresses, which have 32 bits, and IPv6 addresses, which have 128 bits. You'll first learn about how IPv4 addresses are formatted and assigned, and then you'll explore how IPv6 addresses are designed to solve some limitations of IPv4.

IPv4 Addresses

A 32-bit IP address is organized into four groups of 8 bits each, which are presented as four decimal numbers separated by periods, such as 72.56.105.12. Each of these four groups is called an octet. The largest possible 8-bit number is 11111111, which is equal to 255 in decimal. So, the largest possible IP address in decimal is 255.255.255.255. In binary, this number is written 11111111.11111111.11111111.11111111. Each of the four octets can be any number from 0 to 255, making a total of nearly 4.3 billion IPv4 addresses (256 × 256 × 256 × 256). Some IP addresses are reserved, so these numbers are approximations. How are IPv4 addresses determined, and what information do they offer?

Format of IPv4 Addresses

The first part of an IP address identifies the network, and the last part identifies the host. Where this dividing line falls between network and host bits varies according to several factors. When using **classful addressing**, which is an older method of managing IP address ranges, the dividing line between the network and host portions is determined by the numerical range the IP address falls in. Classful IPv4 addresses are categorized into five classes: class A, class B, class C, class D, and class E.

Classes A, B, and C addresses, for the most part, can be used to connect to and access Internet resources. Table 3-1 shows the numerical ranges for these classes of IPv4 addresses. Class D and class E IPv4 addresses are not available for general use. Class D addresses begin with octets 224 through 239 and are used for **multicast** transmissions, in which one host sends messages to multiple hosts. An example of this is when a host transmits a videoconference over the Internet to multiple participants. Class E addresses, which begin with 240 through 254, are reserved for research.

Table 3-1   IP address classes

Class	Network octets*	Approximate number of possible networks	Approximate number of possible hosts in each network
A	1.x.y.z to 126.x.y.z with subnet mask of 255.0.0.0	126	16 million
B	128.0.x.y to 191.255.x.y with subnet mask of 255.255.0.0	16,000	65,000
C	192.0.0.x to 223.255.255.x with subnet mask of 255.255.255.0	2 million	254

*An x, y, or z in the IP address stands for an octet with a value from 0 to 255 that is used to identify hosts on the network

EXAM TIP   The CompTIA Network+ exam expects you to be able to identify the class of any IPv4 address. For the exam, memorize the second column in Table 3-1.

In Table 3-1, notice how each class of addresses defines a different number of octets in its numerical range. For class A, the first octet must fall within a certain range, while the last three octets are undefined. For class B, the first two octets must fall within a certain range, and so on. Each of these three classes—A, B, and C—dedicate different numbers of octets to the network and host portions. Figure 3-8 shows where this dividing line falls for each of these three classes. As you can see, a value of 255 in the corresponding octet of the subnet mask

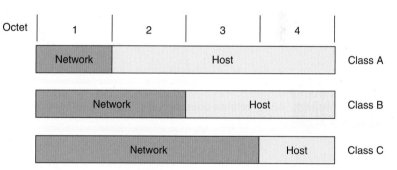

Figure 3-8   The network portion and host portion for each class of IP addresses

indicates that octet of the IP address identifies the network. A value of 0 in the corresponding octet of the subnet mask indicates that octet of the IP address identifies the host. For example, a class A subnet mask (255.0.0.0) contains a value of 255 in the first octet only. Simultaneously, a class A IP address uses information in its first octet to identify the network.

Class A, B, and C licensed IP addresses are available for use on the Internet and are, therefore, called **public IP addresses**. However, even with nearly 4.3 billion IP addresses, the number of devices communicating on the Internet far exceeds this number. To conserve its public IP addresses, a company can instead use **private IP addresses** for devices on its private networks—that is, devices that do not directly connect to the Internet but instead communicate through a representative device such as a router. These addresses were set aside for private use by IANA's **RFC1918 (Request for Comment 1918)** document, released in 1996. IANA allocated the following IP addresses for private networks:

- Class A: 10.0.0.0 through 10.255.255.255
- Class B: 172.16.0.0 through 172.31.255.255
- Class C: 192.168.0.0 through 192.168.255.255

Under these guidelines, a router and a web server might have a public IP address, but laptops, desktops, smartphones, and IoT (Internet of Things) devices might all have private IP addresses. The private devices communicate through the router or similar device as their public representative connected to the Internet. You'll learn more about how this works shortly.

Private IP addresses are not routable on the Internet. In other words, routers will not forward messages addressed to an IP address within one of these private ranges. In addition, the IP addresses listed in Table 3-2 are reserved for special use by TCP/IP and should not be assigned to a public or private device on a network.

Table 3-2   Reserved IP addresses

IP address(es)	Function
255.255.255.255	Used for broadcast messages by TCP/IP background processes. A broadcast message is read by every node on the network. Recall that a LAN is defined as a group of computers and other devices that can directly address each other without going through a router. Technically, a LAN, which consists of all the nodes a broadcast reaches, can be referred to as a broadcast domain. Routers don't forward broadcast messages, thus, creating a boundary for a LAN.
0.0.0.0	Currently unassigned
127.0.0.1 through 127.255.255.254	Used for research or can indicate your own computer, in which case it is called the loopback address. Later in this module, you will learn to use the loopback address to verify that TCP/IP is configured correctly on a computer when it can talk to and hear itself on the loopback interface.
169.254.0.1 through 169.254.255.254	Used to create an APIPA (Automatic Private IP Addressing) address when a computer configured for DHCP first connects to the network and is unable to lease an IPv4 address from the DHCP server. Notice that nearly any IP address starting with 169.254. is identified as an APIPA address.

 EXAM TIP   APIPA-related questions are known to appear often on the CompTIA Network+ exam.

In contrast to classful addressing, classless addressing allows the dividing line between network and host portions to fall anywhere along the string of binary bits in an IP address. Shifting this dividing line allows for segmenting networks within networks in a process called subnetting.

With classless addressing, you can't just look at an IP address's numerical range and know how many octets identify the network and how many octets identify the host. Instead, you rely on a variety of subnet mask values to communicate any number of bits used for the network or host portions. Another option is to use CIDR (Classless Interdomain Routing) notation, devised by the IETF in 1993. (Note that CIDR is pronounced *cider*.) This shorthand method for identifying network and host bits in an IP address is also known as slash notation.

CIDR notation takes the network ID or a host's IP address and follows it with a forward slash (/), which is then followed by the number of bits that are used for the network ID. For example, a private IP address could be written as 192.168.89.127/24, where 24 represents the number of bits in the network ID. In CIDR terminology, the forward slash with the number of bits used for the network ID—for example, /24—is known as a CIDR block. You'll learn how to calculate subnets and their various subnet masks in a later module.

DHCP (Dynamic Host Configuration Protocol)

Recall that static IP addresses are manually assigned by the network administrator, whereas dynamic IP addresses are automatically assigned by a DHCP server each time a computer connects to the network. Because it can become unmanageable to keep up with static IP address assignments, most network administrators choose to use dynamic IP addressing by running a DHCP server. Let's see what decisions must be made when configuring DHCP on a network.

Applying Concepts 3-3: Configure a DHCP Server

While each type of DHCP server software is configured differently, they offer many options in common. Generally, you define a range of IP addresses, called a **DHCP scope** or DHCP pool, to be assigned to clients when they request an address. For example, Figure 3-9 shows a screen provided by the firmware utility for a home router, which is also a DHCP server.

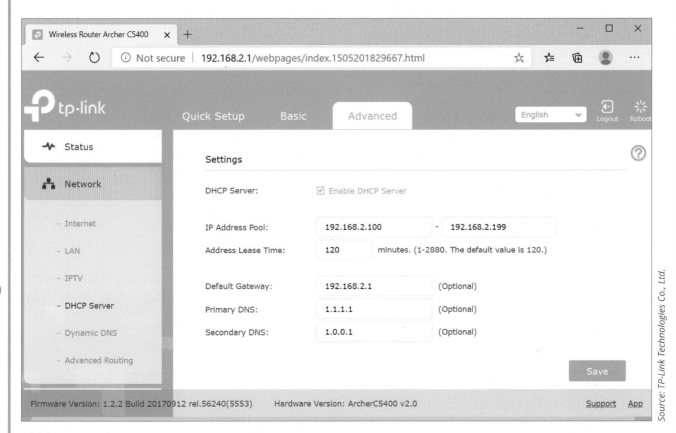

Figure 3-9   Set a range of IP addresses on a DHCP server

Using this screen, you set the starting IP address (192.168.2.100 in the figure) and the ending IP address (192.168.2.199 in the figure) of the DHCP scope. The scope includes the following additional information, called **scope options**:

- A time limit, called a **lease time**, which restricts the amount of time a network host can keep the IP address before it must request a renewal. When the lease time expires without renewal, the DHCP server returns the IP address to the available address pool.
- The default gateway's IP address, which each client must know to send messages to hosts on other networks. The default gateway is typically a router or firewall.
- The primary and secondary DNS server addresses, which clients use to match computer names with IP addresses. DNS servers might be internal to the local network or external and accessed through the default gateway, like you saw in the *On the Job* story at the beginning of this module.

When other nodes on the network frequently need to know the IP address of a particular client, you can have DHCP offer that client the same IP address every time it requests one. The DHCP server recognizes this client based on its MAC address, so this reserved IP address is called a variety of names: **MAC reservation**, **IP reservation**, or

DHCP reservation. For example, a network printer should consistently use the same IP address so that computers on the network can always find it. In Figure 3-10, which shows the management interface for a TP-Link SOHO router, an OKI Data network printer has a reserved IP address of 192.168.2.200.

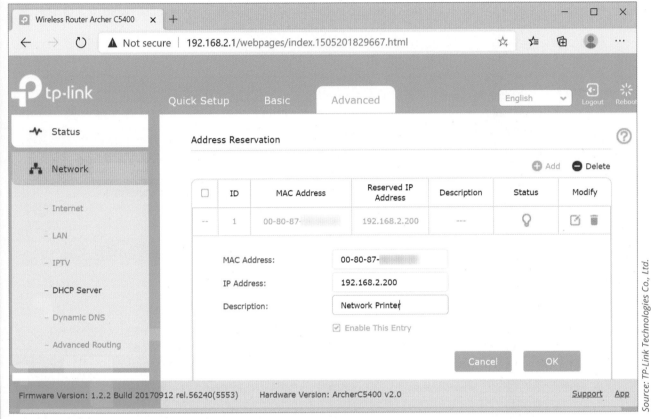

Figure 3-10   Reserve an IP address for one or more network clients, such as a network printer

Source: TP-Link Technologies Co., Ltd.

NOTE 3-8

A reserved IP address is not quite the same thing as a static IP address. A reserved IP address is offered to the client by DHCP when the client requests an IP address. A static IP address is configured on the client itself so that the client never requests an IP address from DHCP in the first place. If you have one or more clients on the network with static IP addresses, you need to configure an IP **exclusion range** on the DHCP server. This excludes one or more IP addresses from the IP address pool so the server doesn't offer those IP addresses to other clients.

In Linux systems, you configure the DHCP software by editing a configuration file in a text editor. For example, the configuration file for one Linux distro's DHCP server is dhcpd.conf (notice the .conf file extension), which is stored in the /etc/dhcp directory. Figure 3-11 shows the configuration file as it appears in vim, which is a Linux text editor. A hash symbol (#) at the beginning of a line identifies the line as a comment line (a line that is not executed). The range of IP addresses that will be assigned to clients in Figure 3-11 is 10.254.239.10 to 10.254.239.20, which consists of 11 IP addresses.

```
# If this DHCP server is the official DHCP server for the local
# network, the authoritative directive should be uncommented.
authoritative;

# Use this to send dhcp log messages to a different log file (you also
# have to hack syslog.conf to complete the redirection).
log-facility local7;

# No service will be given on this subnet, but declaring it helps the
# DHCP server to understand the network topology.

#subnet 10.152.187.0 netmask 255.255.255.0 {
#}

# This is a very basic subnet declaration.

subnet 10.254.239.0 netmask 255.255.255.224 {
  range 10.254.239.10 10.254.239.20;
  option routers rtr-239-0-1.example.org, rtr-239-0-2.example.org;
}

# This declaration allows BOOTP clients to get dynamic addresses,
# which we don't really recommend.

#subnet 10.254.239.32 netmask 255.255.255.224 {
#  range dynamic-bootp 10.254.239.40 10.254.239.60;
#  option broadcast-address 10.254.239.31;
#  option routers rtr-239-32-1.example.org;
#}
```

DHCP range of IP addresses

Source: Canonical Group Limited

Figure 3-11   Edit a configuration file in a text editor to set an IP address range for a Linux-based DHCP server

Address Translation

Recall that most devices on a network are assigned a private IP address, while only a few, representative devices (such as a router) receive a public IP address for communicating directly on the Internet. When private devices need access to other networks or the Internet, a public-facing gateway (such as a router or firewall) substitutes the private IP addresses used by computers on the private network with its own public IP address. This process is called **NAT (Network Address Translation)**. Besides requiring only a single public IP address for the entire private network, another advantage of NAT is security; the gateway hides the private network's hosts behind this one address.

How does the gateway keep track of which local host is to receive a response from a web server on the Internet? **PAT (Port Address Translation)** assigns a separate TCP port to each session between a local host and an Internet host. See Figure 3-12. When the Internet host responds to the local host, the gateway uses PAT to determine which local host is the intended recipient.

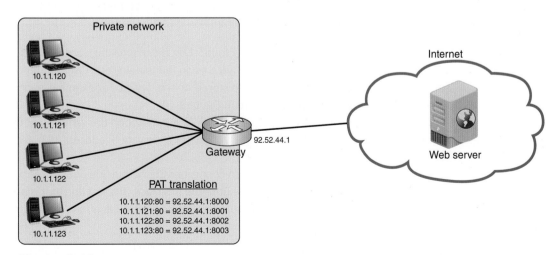

Figure 3-12   PAT (Port Address Translation)

This discussion of ports edges into transport layer addressing, which you'll read about shortly. For now, let's get back to NAT. Two variations of NAT you need to be aware of include the following:

- **SNAT**—Using SNAT (Source Network Address Translation), the gateway assigns the same public IP address to a host each time it makes a request to access the Internet. Small home networks with only a single public IP address provided by its ISP use SNAT.
- **DNAT**—Using DNAT (Destination Network Address Translation), hosts outside the network address a computer inside the network (such as a web server or an email server) by a predefined public IP address. When a message sent to the public IP address reaches the router managing DNAT, the destination IP address is changed to the private IP address of the host inside the network. The router must maintain a translation table of public IP addresses mapped to various hosts inside the network.

Figure 3-13 contrasts SNAT and DNAT. SNAT changes the *source* IP addresses of *outgoing* messages and is used to reduce the number of public IP addresses needed by a network. DNAT changes the *destination* IP address of *incoming* messages and is often used by organizations that provide services to the Internet. The various servers can use private IP addresses for security and also to allow network administrators more freedom to manage these servers. For example, they can switch a web server to a backup computer while doing maintenance on the primary server by simply making a change in the router's DNAT settings, redirecting a public IP address to the backup computer.

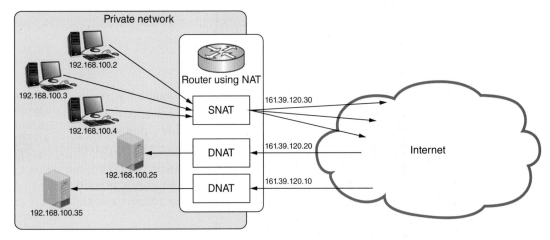

Figure 3-13 SNAT for outgoing messages, and DNAT for incoming messages

Applying Concepts 3-4: Configure Address Translation Using NAT

For simple default gateways such as a home router, configuring address translation means making sure NAT is turned on. That's about all you can do. However, for more advanced gateways, such as an industrial-grade Cisco router or Linux server, you configure the NAT software by editing NAT translation tables stored on the device. For example, suppose your network supports a web server available to the Internet, as shown in Figure 3-14.

On the web, the website is known by the public IP address 69.32.208.74. Figure 3-15 shows the sample text file required to set up the translation tables for DNAT to direct traffic to the web server at private IP address 192.168.10.7. Note that any line beginning with an exclamation mark (!) is a comment.

The first section of code defines the router's outside interface, which connects with the outside network and is called the serial interface. The second section defines the router's inside Ethernet interface. The last line that is not a comment line says that, when clients from the Internet send a request to IP address 69.32.208.74, the request is translated to the IP address 192.168.10.7.

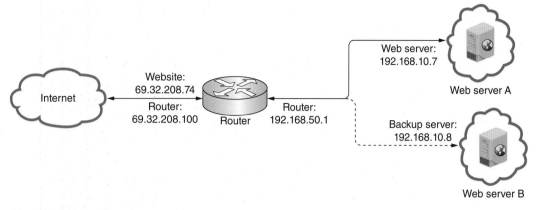

Figure 3-14 Messages to the website are being routed to web server A

```
interface serial 0/0
  ip address 69.32.208.100 255.255.255.0
  ip nat outside

!--- Defines the serial 0/0 interface as the router's NAT outside interface
!--- with an IP address of 69.32.208.100

interface ethernet 1/1
  ip address 192.168.50.1 255.255.255.0
  ip nat inside

!--- Defines the Ethernet 1/1 interface as the router's NAT inside interface
!--- with an IP address of 192.168.50.1


ip nat inside source static 192.168.10.7 69.32.208.74

!--- States that source information about the inside host will be translated
!--- so the host's private IP address (192.168.10.7) will appear as the
!--- public IP address (69.32.208.74). Both ingoing and outgoing traffic
!--- exchanged with the public IP address will be routed to the host at the
!--- private IP address.
```

Figure 3-15 NAT translation table entry in Linux

At the end of this module, you'll create your own NAT translation table entry using this example as a template. To help you better understand where the IP addresses in a translation table entry come from, answer the following questions about the information in Figures 3-14 and Figure 3-15:

1. What is the router's outside interface IP address?
2. What is the router's inside interface IP address?
3. What is the website's public IP address?
4. What is the private IP address of the active web server?

IPv6 Addresses

As IPv4 address supplies started running low, the IPv6 standards were developed to allow for more public IP addresses on the Internet. IPv6 designers also worked to improve routing capabilities and speed of communication over the established IPv4 standards. Let's begin this discussion by looking at how IPv6 addresses are written, as follows:

- Recall that an IPv6 address has 128 bits that are written as eight blocks (also called quartets) of hexadecimal numbers separated by colons, like this: 2001:0000:0B80:0000:0000:00D3:9C5A:00CC
- Each block is 16 bits long. For example, the first block in the preceding IP address is the hexadecimal number 2001, which can be written as 0010 0000 0000 0001 in binary.

7 Application
6 Presentation
5 Session
4 Transport
▶ 3 Network
2 Data Link
1 Physical

- Because IPv6 addresses are so long, shorthand notation helps to make these addresses easier to read and write. For example, leading zeroes in a four-character hex block can be eliminated. This means the sample IP address can be written as 2001:0000:B80:0000:0000:D3:9C5A:CC.
- If blocks contain all zeroes, they can be eliminated and replaced by double colons (::). To avoid confusion, only one set of double colons is used in an IPv6 address. This means the sample IP address can be written two ways:
  - 2001::B80:0000:0000:D3:9C5A:CC
  - 2001:0000:B80::D3:9C5A:CC

  In this example, the preferred method is the second one (2001:0000:B80::D3:9C5A:CC) because this way, the address contains the fewest zeroes.

The way computers communicate using IPv6 has changed the terminology used to describe TCP/IP communication. Here are a few terms used in the IPv6 standards:

- A link, sometimes called the local link, is any LAN bounded by routers. Neighbors are two or more nodes on the same link.
- When a network is configured to use both IPv4 and IPv6 protocols, the network is said to be dual stacked. However, if packets on this network must traverse other networks where dual stacking is not used, the solution is to use tunneling, which is a method of transporting IPv6 packets over an IPv4 network.
- The last 64 bits, or four blocks, of an IPv6 address identify the interface and are called the interface ID or interface identifier. These 64 bits uniquely identify an interface on the local link.

Types of IPv6 Addresses

IPv6 classifies IP addresses differently than IPv4 does. IPv6 supports these three types of IP addresses, classified by how the address is used, as follows:

- Unicast address—Specifies a single node on a network. Figure 3-16 diagrams three types of unicast addresses, including the following:

Global address

3 bits	45 bits	16 bits	64 bits
001	Global routing prefix	Subnet ID	Interface ID

Link local address

64 bits	64 bits
1111 1110 1000 0000 0000 0000 0000 .... 0000 FE80::/64	Interface ID

Loopback address

127 bits	1 bit
0000 0000 0000 0000 000	1

Figure 3-16 Three types of IPv6 addresses

  - Global address—Can be routed on the Internet and is similar to public IPv4 addresses. Most begin with the prefix 2000::/3, although other prefixes are being released. The /3 indicates that the first three bits are fixed and are always 001. Looking at Figure 3-16, notice the 16 bits reserved for the subnet ID, which can be used to identify a segment of a large corporate network.
  - Link local address—Can be used for communicating with nodes in the same link and is similar to an autoconfigured APIPA address in IPv4. It begins with FE80::/10. The first 10 bits (indicated by /10) of the reserved prefix are fixed (1111 1110 10), and the remaining 54 bits in the 64-bit prefix are all zeroes. Therefore, a link local address prefix is sometimes written as FE80::/64, as shown in Figure 3-16. Link local addresses are not allowed past the local link or on the Internet.
  - Loopback address—Similar to the IPv4 loopback address, can be used to test that an interface and supporting protocol stack are functioning properly. Consists of 127 zeros followed by a 1 and is written ::1/128.

- **Multicast address**—Delivers packets to all nodes in a targeted, multicast group.
- **Anycast address**—Identifies multiple destinations, with packets delivered to the closest destination. For example, a DNS server might send a DNS request to a group of DNS servers that have all been assigned the same anycast address. A router handling the request examines routes to all the DNS servers in the group and routes the request to the closest server.

Recall that with IPv4 broadcasting, messages are sent to every node on a network. However, IPv6 reduces network traffic by eliminating broadcasting. The concepts of broadcasting, multicasting, anycasting, and unicasting are depicted in Figure 3-17 for easy comparison. In the figure, each pink circle is the sending node. The yellow squares are the intended recipients. The blue triangles are other nodes on the network and do not receive the transmission.

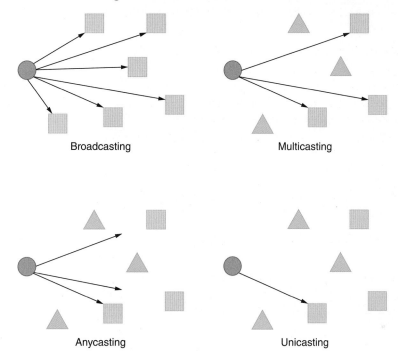

Figure 3-17   Concepts of broadcasting, multicasting, anycasting, and unicasting

Interestingly, due to the way switches learn MAC addresses of connected devices, multicasting can cause traffic congestion problems called **multicast flooding**. The multicast group is assigned a single IP address, which means no particular MAC address can be associated with that IP address. Instead, when the switch receives a multicast message, it must flood all its interfaces with the transmission, which defeats the purpose of multicasting.

To fix this problem, a switch that must handle multicast traffic should have IGMP snooping enabled on it. IGMP (Internet Group Management Protocol) is a network-layer protocol used to manage multicast group memberships and direct multicast traffic to the correct devices. However, because switches are layer 2 devices, they miss out on the IGMP information that identifies group members. IGMP snooping, then, gives switches the ability to detect IGMP messages on the network and gather information from those messages to add accurate entries in their MAC address tables.

Table 3-3 lists some currently used address prefixes for IPv6 addresses. Notice in the table the unique local unicast addresses, which work on local links and are similar to IPv4 private IP addresses. You can expect more prefixes to be assigned as they are needed.

Table 3-3   Address prefixes for types of IPv6 addresses

IP address type	Address prefix	Notes
Global unicast	2000::/3	First 3 bits are always 001
Link local unicast	FE80::/10 (also written as FE80::/64)	First 10 bits are always 1111 1110 10 followed by 54 zeroes
Unique local unicast	FC00::/7	First 7 bits are always 1111 110
	FD00::/8	First 8 bits are always 1111 1101
Multicast	FF00::/8	First 8 bits are always 1111 1111

You can use the `ipconfig` command to view IPv4 and IPv6 addresses assigned to all network connections on a computer. For example, in Figure 3-18, four IP addresses have been assigned to the physical and virtual connections on this computer.

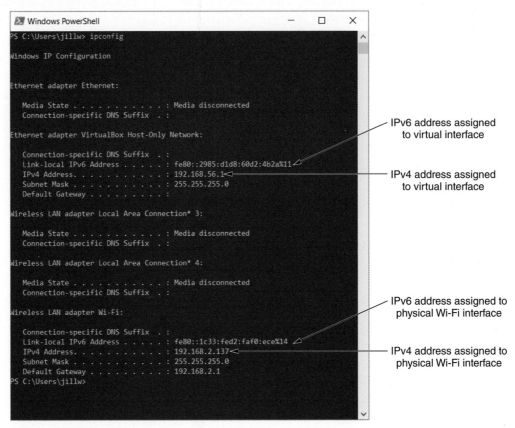

Figure 3-18   The `ipconfig` command shows IPv4 and IPv6 addresses assigned to this computer

IPv6 Autoconfiguration

IPv6 addressing is designed so that a computer can autoconfigure its own link local IP address without the help of a DHCPv6 server. This process is called **SLAAC (stateless address autoconfiguration)** and is similar to how IPv4 uses an APIPA address but results in an address the computer can continue to use on the network. The following SLAAC steps describe how a computer using IPv6 makes a network connection:

Step 1—The computer creates its IPv6 address. It uses FE80::/64 as the first 64 bits, called the prefix. Depending on how the OS is configured, the last 64 bits (called the interface ID) can be generated in one of two ways:

- **The 64 bits are randomly generated**—In this case, the IP address is called a temporary address and is never registered in DNS or used to generate global addresses for use on the Internet. The IP address changes often to help prevent hackers from discovering the computer. This is the default method used by Windows 10.

- **The 64 bits are generated from the network adapter's MAC address**—MAC addresses consist of 48 bits (formally called EUI-48) and must be converted to the 64-bit standard, called the **EUI-64 (Extended Unique Identifier-64)** standard. To generate the interface ID, the OS takes the 48 bits of the device's MAC address, inserts a fixed 16-bit value in the middle of the 48 bits, and inverts the value of the seventh bit.

Step 2—The computer checks to make sure its IP address is unique on the network. It does this by sending a message to the IP address and, if there's a reply, then the address is a duplicate and the computer tries again with a different address.

Step 3—The computer asks if a router on the network can provide configuration information. This message is called an **RS (router solicitation)** message. If a router responds with DHCP information in what's called an

RA (router advertisement) message, the computer uses whatever information this might be, such as the IP addresses of DNS servers or the network prefix. The process is called prefix discovery; the computer then uses the prefix to generate its own link local or global IPv6 address by appending its interface ID to the prefix.

Because a computer can generate its own link local or global IP address, a DHCPv6 server usually serves up only global IPv6 addresses to hosts that require static address assignments. For example, web servers and DNS servers can receive their static IPv6 addresses from a DHCPv6 server.

NOTE 3-9

On larger networks, IP address infrastructure can quickly become overwhelming. An **IPAM (IP address management)** system, whether as a standalone product or embedded in another product such as Windows Server, provides a way to plan, deploy, and monitor a network's IP address space. IPAM tools can automatically detect IP address ranges, assignments, reservations, and exclusions, integrate this information with data from DNS records, and provide constant monitoring for growth, security, and troubleshooting purposes. In a project at the end of this module, you'll use an IP scanning tool similar in concept to Nmap that can identify information about all devices connected to a network.

Now you're ready to take another step up the OSI model to layer 4, where ports are used to identify an application when it receives communication from a remote host.

REMEMBER THIS...

- Describe the role of a default gateway.
- Memorize the IP ranges of the IPv4 classes.
- Distinguish between RFC1918 addresses and public IP addresses.
- Describe the role of DHCP and various scope options.
- Explain the NAT process.
- Identify types of IPv4 and IPv6 addresses, including multicast, unicast, anycast, broadcast, link local, and loopback.
- Explain key IPv6 concepts, including tunneling, dual stack, shorthand notation, router advertisement, and SLAAC.

SELF-CHECK

3. What command shows you a computer's TCP/IP configuration?
   a. `ping`
   b. `ipconfig`
   c. `ssh`
   d. `nmap`
4. Which of the following IPv4 addresses is a public IP address?
   a. 10.0.2.14
   b. 172.16.156.254
   c. 192.168.72.73
   d. 64.233.177.189
5. Which IPv6 prefix can be routed on the Internet?
   a. 2000::/3
   b. FE80::/10
   c. ::1/128
   d. FC00::/7

Check your answers at the end of this module.

You're Ready

You're now ready to complete **Project 3-1: Create a NAT Translation Table Entry**, or you can wait until you've finished reading this module.

You're Ready

You're now ready to complete **Project 3-2: Change IPv6 Autoconfiguration Settings**, or you can wait until you've finished reading this module.

PORTS AND SOCKETS

✔ CERTIFICATION

1.5 Explain common ports and protocols, their application, and encrypted alternatives.

1.6 Explain the use and purpose of network services.

2.1 Compare and contrast various devices, their features, and their appropriate placement on the network.

Average reading time: 10 minutes

7 Application
6 Presentation
5 Session
▶ 4 Transport
▶ 3 Network
2 Data Link
1 Physical

A port is a number assigned to a **process**, such as an application or a service, that can receive data. Whereas an IP address is used to find a computer, a port is used to find a process running on that computer. TCP and UDP ports ensure that data is transmitted to the correct process among multiple processes running on a single device. If you compare network addressing with the addressing system used by the postal service, and you equate a host's IP address to the address of a building, then a port is similar to an apartment number within that building.

A **socket** consists of both a host's IP address and a process's TCP or UDP port, with a colon separating the two values. For example, the standard port for the Telnet service is TCP 23. If a host has an IP address of 10.43.3.87, the socket for Telnet running on that host is 10.43.3.87:23.

When the host receives a request to communicate on TCP port 23, it establishes or opens a **session**, which is an ongoing conversation, with the Telnet service. At that point, the socket is said to be open. When the TCP session is complete, the socket is closed or dissolved. You can think of a socket as a virtual conversation or circuit between a server and client (see Figure 3-19).

Port numbers range from 0 to 65535 and are categorized by IANA into three types:

- **Well-known ports**—Range from 0 to 1023 and are assigned by IANA to widely used and well-known utilities and applications, such as Telnet, FTP, and HTTP. Table 3-4 lists some of the most common well-known ports and registered ports used by TCP and/or UDP.
- **Registered ports**—Range from 1024 to 49151 and can be used temporarily by processes for nonstandard assignments to increase security. Default assignments of these registered ports must be registered with IANA.

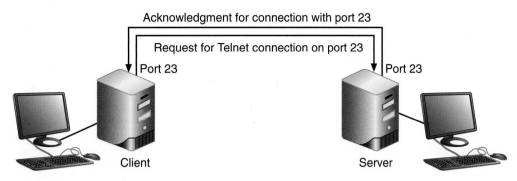

Figure 3-19 A virtual connection for the Telnet service

- **Dynamic and private ports**—Range from 49152 to 65535 and are open for use without restriction.
  - **Dynamic port**—Number assigned by a client or server as the need arises. For example, if a client application has several open sockets with multiple servers, it can use a different dynamic port number for each socket.
  - **Private port**—Number assigned by a network administrator that is different from the well-known port number for that service. For example, the administrator might assign a private port number other than the standard port 80 to a web server on the Internet so that several people can test the site before it's made available to the public. To reach the web server, a tester must enter the private port number in the browser address box along with the web server's IP address.

Table 3-4 Common well-known and registered TCP and UDP ports

Port	Process name	Protocol used	Used for:
20	FTP-DATA	TCP	File transfer—data
21	FTP	TCP	File transfer—control (an FTP server listens at port 21 and sends/receives data at port 20)
22	SSH	TCP	Secure communications between Linux computers or, if installed, between Windows computers
22	SFTP	TCP	Encrypted file transfer using SSH
23	TELNET	TCP	Unencrypted control of remote computers
25	SMTP	TCP	Outgoing email messages
53	DNS	TCP or UDP	Name resolution
67	DHCP	UDP	Distribution of IP addresses on a network—client to server messages
68	DHCP	UDP	Distribution of IP addresses on a network—server to client messages
69	TFTP	UDP	Simple file transfer
80	HTTP	TCP or UDP	Requests between web servers and web clients
110	POP3	TCP	Incoming email messages (downloaded messages)
123	NTP	UDP	Network time synchronization
143	IMAP4	TCP	Incoming email messages (messages stored on server)

(continues)

Table 3-4   Common well-known and registered TCP and UDP ports *(continued)*

Port	Process name	Protocol used	Used for:
161	SNMP	TCP or UDP	Messages sent to managed network devices from SNMP manager
162	SNMP	Typically UDP	Responses or unsolicited information sent from network devices to manager
389	LDAP	TCP or UDP	Access to network-based directories
443	HTTPS	TCP	Secure implementation of HTTP over SSL or TLS
445	SMB	TCP	Network file sharing
514	Syslog	UDP	Manages and stores information about system events
587	SMTP TLS	TCP	SMTP encrypted by TLS
636	LDAPS	TCP or UDP	Secure access to network-based directories
993	IMAP4 over SSL	TCP or UDP	IMAP4 encrypted by SSL or TLS
995	POP3 over SSL	TCP or UDP	POP3 encrypted by SSL or TLS
1433	SQL Server	TCP	Connections to installation of Microsoft SQL Server from other databases or applications
1521	SQLnet, also called Oracle Net Services	TCP	Connections to installation of Oracle Database from other databases or applications
3306	MySQL		Connections to installation of MySQL Server from other databases or applications
3389	RDP	TCP	Encrypted control of remote Windows computers
5060	SIP	UDP	Creation of unencrypted connections for multimedia session
5061	SIP	UDP	Creation of encrypted connections for multimedia session

EXAM TIP   To prepare for the CompTIA Network+ exam, you need to memorize all the well-known and registered ports listed in Table 3-4. Some of these protocols are discussed in detail in later modules. They're collected in Table 3-4 for easy reference and last-minute review before taking your exam. Pay close attention to secure alternatives for common protocols. For example, what is the secure port for SMTP? If you answered 25, that is incorrect. SMTP over TLS is encrypted and runs on port 587. The Network+ exam is known to test on this type of distinction.

In Module 1, you learned about most of the protocols listed in Table 3-4. A few of them have already been covered in this module. Here's a brief description of the ones not yet covered:

- **TFTP (Trivial File Transfer Protocol)**—Most commonly used by computers (without user intervention) as they are booting up to request configuration files from another computer on the local network. TFTP uses UDP, whereas normal FTP uses TCP.
- **NTP (Network Time Protocol)**—A simple protocol used to synchronize clocks on computers throughout a network. The genius of NTP is how it can almost completely account for the variable delays across a network, even on the open Internet. It does this through a hierarchy of time servers where stratum-1 servers communicate directly with a primary time source, such as GPS (Global Positioning System) or Galileo (Europe's version of GPS). These servers track UTC (Coordinated Universal Time) and provide this information to lower

strata servers. Each hop between NTP servers increases the **stratum** number by 1 up to 16. NTP servers at any stratum can then convert the provided UTC into its local time zone. Not every network has its own time server, but those that do can maintain accuracy for its NTP clients to within a millisecond of each other and are closely synced to the UTC.

- **LDAP (Lightweight Directory Access Protocol)**—A standard protocol for accessing network-based directories. **LDAPS (Lightweight Directory Access Protocol over SSL)** uses SSL to encrypt its communications. You'll learn more about LDAP and LDAPS in a later module.
- **SMB (Server Message Block)**—First used by earlier Windows OSs for file sharing on a network. UNIX uses a version of SMB in its Samba software, which can share files with other operating systems, including Windows systems.
- **Syslog (system log)**—A Linux or UNIX standard for generating, storing, and processing messages about events on a system. It describes methods for detecting and reporting events and specifies the format and contents of messages. The syslog utility does not alert a user to problems—it only keeps a history of messages issued by the system.
- **SQLnet**, also known as Oracle Net Services—Used by Oracle Database to communicate with other Oracle Databases or with database clients. This interconnection allows applications and databases to be distributed across different machines and still communicate as if they were on the same machine.

Which port a protocol communicates over becomes especially relevant when configuring firewalls. Recall that a firewall is a dedicated device or software on a computer that selectively filters or blocks traffic between networks. It works by blocking traffic on all ports and between all IP addresses except those that are specifically approved by the network admin. You will learn more about firewalls in later modules. For now, note that all firewalls are porous to some degree in that they always let *some* traffic through; the question is what kind of traffic they allow—some of this filtering is accomplished by opening or closing ports. For example, if you have a SQL Server database that provides data to clients throughout your network, you'll need to allow port 1433 (and a few others) on the firewall protecting that database.

REMEMBER THIS...

- Explain how a port (as part of a socket) identifies a running process.
- Memorize the given list of well-known ports.
- Choose secure ports when possible.

SELF-CHECK

6. When hosting a secure email server for access from the Internet, which port should be open on the corporate firewall?
   a. 25
   b. 110
   c. 443
   d. 587

7. Which port should be open so you can remote into the corporate office's Linux Server from a branch office?
   a. 22
   b. 23
   c. 1433
   d. 3389

Check your answers at the end of this module.

DOMAIN NAMES AND DNS

CERTIFICATION

1.6 Explain the use and purpose of network services.

Average reading time: 25 minutes

7 Application
6 Presentation
5 Session
4 Transport
③ Network
2 Data Link
1 Physical

When is the last time you entered a website's IP address into your browser's address bar so you could go to that website? For that matter, do you know the IP address for any website you visit frequently? Probably not. Instead, you type in a website address, such as *cengage.com*. Your browser adds some more information, such as *https://www.cengage.com*, which is called a URL. A **URL (uniform resource locator)** is an application layer addressing scheme that identifies where to find a particular resource on a network or across networks. Application layer addressing was created because character-based names are easier for humans to remember than numeric IP addresses. The first part of the URL, https, identifies the protocol to be used, in this case, HTTPS. The next part is the FQDN. Recall that an FQDN is a host name and a domain name together, as shown in Figure 3-20 and described next:

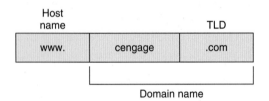

Figure 3-20   A fully qualified domain name

- The host name is determined by the website developer or administrator.
- Domain names must be registered with an Internet naming authority that works on behalf of ICANN.
- The last part of an FQDN (*com* in this example) is called the **TLD (top-level domain)**.

Table 3-5 lists some well-known ICANN-approved TLDs. No restrictions exist on the use of the .com, .org, and .net TLDs, and ICANN restricts what type of hosts can be associated with the .arpa, .mil, .edu, and .gov TLDs. Other TLDs are dedicated to hosts in specific countries, such as .us, .eu (for countries in the European Union), .ca (Canada), and .au (Australia). Companies can also register their own TLD, although this is not cheap. A complete list of current TLDs can be found at *iana.org/domains/root/db/*.

While FQDNs are convenient for humans, a computer must convert the FQDN to an IP address before it can find the referenced computer. Suppose you type an FQDN into a browser address bar; how does your computer figure out the IP address for that web server? To answer this question, you need to learn about **name resolution**, which is an application layer process of discovering the IP address of a host when its FQDN is known.

Table 3-5   Some well-known top-level domains

Domain suffix	Type of organization
ARPA	Reverse lookup domain (special Internet function)
COM	Commercial
EDU	Educational
GOV	Government
ORG	Noncommercial organization (such as a nonprofit agency)
NET	Network (such as an ISP)
MIL	United States military organization
BIZ	Businesses
INFO	Unrestricted use

In the mid-1980s, DNS (Domain Name System) was designed to associate computer names with IP addresses. DNS is an application layer client-server system of computers and databases made up of these elements:

- **Namespace**—The entire collection of computer names and their associated IP addresses stored in databases on DNS name servers around the globe
- **Name servers**—Computers that hold these databases, organized in a hierarchical structure
- **Resolvers**—A DNS client that requests information from DNS name servers

Let's take a closer look at each of these components.

Namespace Databases

DNS namespace databases are stored on thousands of servers around the world, rather than being centralized on a single server or group of servers. In other words, DNS doesn't follow a centralized database model, but rather a distributed database model. Because data is distributed over thousands of servers, DNS will not fail catastrophically if one or a handful of servers experiences errors.

Each organization that provides host services (for example, websites or email) on the public Internet is responsible for providing and maintaining its own DNS authoritative servers for public access, or they can use a third-party or cloud-hosted DNS server. An authoritative name server is the authority on computer names and their IP addresses for computers in their domains. The domains (for example, *cengage.com*) that the organization is responsible for managing are collectively called a DNS zone. A large organization can keep all its domains in a single zone, or it can subdivide its domains into multiple zones to make each zone easier to manage.

Name Servers

An organization might have these four common types of DNS servers:

- **Primary DNS server**—The authoritative name server for the organization, which holds the authoritative DNS database for the organization's zones. This server is contacted by clients, both local and over the Internet, to resolve DNS queries for the organization's domains.
- **Secondary DNS server**—The backup authoritative name server for the organization. When a secondary DNS server needs to update its database, it makes the request to the primary server for the update; this update process is called a zone transfer.
- **Caching DNS server**—A server that accesses public DNS data and caches the DNS information it collects. This server receives DNS queries from local network clients and works to resolve them by contacting other DNS servers for information. Caching DNS servers do not store zone files (which is why they must rely on their caches and resolution efforts), and, therefore, do not participate in zone transfers, which further helps to reduce network traffic on the intranet.
- **Forwarding DNS server**—An optional server that receives queries from local clients but doesn't work to resolve the queries. Typically, a forwarding server will maintain its own DNS cache from previous queries, and so it might already have the information the client needs. If not, the forwarding server forwards the query to another server to resolve. Several forwarding servers might be strategically placed throughout the organization's network to reduce network traffic on slow links.

Any of these DNS server types can coexist on the same machine, depending on the needs of the network. For example, a primary DNS server for one zone might be a secondary DNS server for a different zone within the organization. A primary DNS server might also serve as a caching server for its local network clients (although for security purposes, this is not recommended). A caching server might also rely on forwarding for certain clients or certain types of traffic.

NOTE 3-10

A registry, also known as a domain name registry operator, is an organization or country that is responsible for one or more TLDs and that maintains a database or registry of TLD information. A domain name registrar such as GoDaddy (*godaddy.com*) is an organization accredited by registries and ICANN to lease domain names to companies or individuals, following the guidelines of the TLD registry operators.

NOTE 3-11

The primary and secondary DNS servers listed in a client's IP configuration, like what you saw in Applying Concepts 3-2, are not the same thing as an organization's primary and secondary authoritative DNS servers. The client's configuration is referring to the network's caching or forwarding servers.

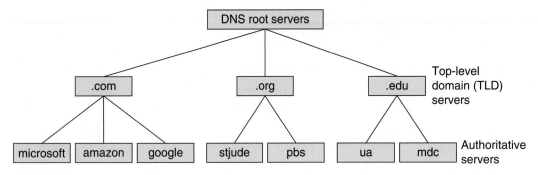

Figure 3-21   Hierarchy of name servers

NOTE 3-12

Recall that an application uses an API call to request the operating system perform a service or task.

NOTE 3-13

DNS messages are application layer messages that use UDP at the transport layer. Communication with DNS servers occur through port 53.

DNS name servers are organized in a global hierarchical structure shown in Figure 3-21. At the root level, 13 clusters of **root DNS servers** hold information used to locate the TLD (top-level domain) servers. These TLD servers hold information about the authoritative name servers owned by various organizations and how to find them.

To understand how these servers interact, let's look at an example. Suppose an employee at Cengage, using a computer in the *cengage.com* domain, enters *www.mdc .edu* in their web browser address box. The browser makes an API call to the DNS resolver, a TCP/IP component in the OS, for the IP address of the *www.mdc.edu* host.

Here are the steps to resolve the name, which are also illustrated in Figure 3-22:

Step 1—The resolver on the client computer first searches its DNS cache, a database stored on the local computer, for the match. If it can't find the information there, the resolver sends a DNS message or query to its local DNS server. In this example, let's assume this caching server doesn't yet know the IP address of the *www.mdc.edu* host.

Steps 2 and 3—The local name server queries a root server with the request. The root server responds to the local name server with a list of IP addresses of TLD name servers responsible for the .edu suffix.

Steps 4 and 5—The local name server makes the same request to one of the TLD name servers responsible for the .edu suffix. The TLD name server responds with the IP address of the *mdc.edu* authoritative server.

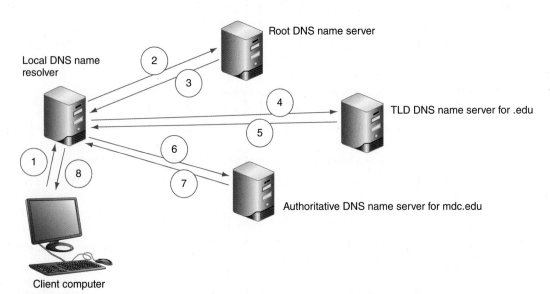

Figure 3-22   Queries for name resolution of *www.mdc.edu*

Steps 6 and 7—The local name server makes the request to the authoritative name server at Miami Dade Community College, which responds to the Cengage name server with the IP address of the *www. mdc.edu* host.

Step 8—The local name server responds to the client resolver with the requested IP address. Both the Cengage name server and the Cengage client computer store the information in their DNS caches, and, therefore, don't need to ask again until that information expires.

Requests sometimes involve additional name servers. Following are a few ways the process can get more complex:

- A client's local caching server typically is not the same machine as the authoritative name server for the organization's domain. Instead, the caching server exists only to resolve names for its own local clients.
- Name servers within a company might not have access to root servers. The local name server might forward the query to the name server at the company's ISP, which might forward the query to a name server elsewhere on the Internet. This name server might query a root server; however, if any name server in the process has the requested information, it responds without the involvement of a root server, TLD name server, or authoritative name server.
- A TLD name server might be aware of an intermediate name server rather than the authoritative name server. When the local name server queries this intermediate name server, it might respond with the IP address of the authoritative name server.

Notice in these steps, the local name server kept working until the FQDN resolution was made, but other servers only aided in the process. As you can see, there are two types of DNS requests:

- **Recursive lookup**—A query that demands a resolution or the answer "It can't be found." For example, the initial request the resolver makes to the local server is a recursive query. The local server must provide the information requested by the resolver, as in "The buck stops here." If the local server doesn't have that information already, it reaches out to other servers to find the information or determine the information is not available.
- **Iterative lookup**—A query that does not demand resolution. For example, when the local server issues queries to other servers, the other servers only provide information if they have it.

Resource Records in a DNS Database

If you've ever worked with a database, you're already familiar with some typical database components such as records and fields. DNS information, being a database, is similarly organized. Namespace databases are stored in DNS zone files, which are simple text files consisting of **resource records** that each store specific kinds of information about the zone. These records consist of fields specific to the kind of information that record type should hold, such as the zone name, class (these days, that's always Internet class), and record type. Other fields in each record vary according to the purpose of that record. A DNS administrator (including network administrators and website administrators) needs to be familiar with these record types. The following list describes some of the most common DNS record types found in a zone file:

- **SOA (start of authority) record**—Listed at the beginning of the zone file and gives important information about the zone, such as a contact email address, when the zone was last updated, how long the zone information is valid until it should be refreshed, and necessary information for how to perform a zone transfer.
- **A (address) record**—Stores the name-to-address mapping for a host. This resource record provides the primary function of DNS, which is to match a given FQDN to its IPv4 address in response to a **forward lookup** request.
- **AAAA (address) record** (called a "quad-A record")—Holds the name-to-address mapping for IPv6 addresses.
- **CNAME (canonical name) record**—Holds alternative names for a host, such as *blog.mycompany.com* or *shop. mycompany.com*. These names can be used in place of the **canonical name**, which is the complete and properly formatted name, such as *www.mycompany.com*. The web server at *www.mycompany.com* can then detect the request for the Blog or Shop page and direct the client to the appropriate page on the website.
- **PTR (pointer) record**—Used for a **reverse lookup**, also called **rDNS (reverse DNS)**, which provides a host name when you know its IP address. PTR records are usually created by ISPs and stored in a specially formatted

reverse lookup zone file, or reverse zone. Reverse zones differ from a typical forward lookup zone file, or forward zone, that holds A records. In a reverse zone, the IP addresses must instead be stored in reverse—with the last octet listed first—plus the domain *.in-addr.arpa*. For example, the IP address 1.2.3.4 would be stored in a PTR record as *4.3.2.1.in-addr.arpa*.

- **NS (name server) record**—Indicates the authoritative name server for a domain. It's mostly used for delegating subdomains to other name servers.
- **MX (mail exchanger) record**—Identifies an email server and is used for email traffic.
- **SRV (service) record**—Identifies the hostname and port of a computer that hosts a specific network service besides email, such as FTP or SIP.
- **TXT (text) record**—Holds any type of free-form text. It might contain text designed to be read by humans regarding network, server, or accounting issues. Most often it's used by the following:

  - **SPF (Sender Policy Framework)**—A validation system that helps fight spam by identifying the email servers allowed to send email on behalf of a domain.
  - **DKIM (DomainKeys Identified Mail)**—An authentication method that uses encryption to verify the domain name of an email's sender.

 EXAM TIP   While there are more than 100 types of DNS resource records, the CompTIA Network+ exam expects you to know about the nine types in the preceding list. Make sure you can explain the basic purpose of each DNS record type listed. Study the examples given in Table 3-6 to help you better understand each record type.

Table 3-6 lists some sample zone file entries. Each line, or record, contains the text *IN*, which refers to the class and indicates the record can be used by DNS servers on the Internet.

An actual DNS zone file begins with a **TTL (Time to Live)** directive that identifies how long the information in the file should be saved in a cache on a server. Administrators can set the TTL based on how frequently they expect the IP addresses to change. TTL information is included in zone transfers.

Table 3-6   Records in a DNS zone file

Record	Description
www.example.com IN SOA admin.example.com 2022052403 86400 7200 3600000	Lists email contact information, date of latest revision, and time specifications indicating how long the information is valid; notice the @ symbol in the email is not allowed and so a period is used instead
www.example.com IN A 92.100.80.40	Maps the server named www in the *example.com* domain to the IP address 92.100.80.40
www.example.com IN AAAA 2001:db8:cafe:f9::d3	Maps a name to an IPv6 address
demo.example.com IN CNAME www.example.com	Says that the *www.example.com* host can also be addressed by its alias name *demo.example.com*
40.80.100.92.in-addr-arpa IN PTR www.example.com	Used for reverse lookup—that is, to find the name when you know the IP address; note the IP address is reversed and *in-addr-arpa* is appended to it
www.example.com IN NS ns1.otherdns.com	Directs DNS queries to a third-party, authoritative DNS server
example.com IN MX 10 mail.us.example.com example.com IN MX 20 mail2.us.example.com	Tells email servers the preferred routes to take, ordered by best route, when sending email to the *example.com* domain

Table 3-6 Records in a DNS zone file *(continued)*

Record	Description
_sip._udp.example.com IN SRV 0 75 5060 fastsip.example.com _sip._udp.example.com IN SRV 0 25 5060 slowsip.example.com	Directs SIP traffic (_sip.) to two SIP servers (*fastsip.example.com* and *slowsip.example.com*) using UDP (_udp.) at the transport layer and the registered SIP port (5060); while the priority for both is 0 (the highest priority), the traffic load is distributed more heavily on the faster server (75) and more lightly on the slower server (25)
example.com IN TXT v=spf1 include:outlook.com ~all	Adds the outlook.com email server as an approved sender for the example.com domain; the phrase v=spf1 defines the SPF version

DNS Server Software

By far, the most popular DNS server software is BIND (Berkeley Internet Name Domain), which is free, open-source software that runs on Linux, UNIX, and Windows platforms. You can download the BIND software from *isc.org*. Most Linux and UNIX distributions include BIND in the distribution.

Many other DNS server software products exist. For example, Windows Server has a built-in DNS service called DNS Server, which partners closely with AD (Active Directory) services. This server role enables AD clients to find the domain controller for initial authentication and, later, to find other computers that are identified by name on the network. DNS Server can even be configured to provide different information to external clients, who are typically accessing network resources over the Internet. Previously, it was necessary to run two different DNS servers, one for internal clients and one for external clients. Today, Windows Server is capable of more nuanced configuration, called split-brain or split-horizon deployment, to handle these two populations differently. For example, consider a fictional website, *careers.example.com*, that lists internal job postings for employees and different job postings and information posted to the public. DNS policies differentiate between internal and external clients, sending their requests for name resolution on the same FQDN to different IP addresses and, therefore, different information on the website.

Applying Concepts 3-5: Change DNS Servers

In Applying Concepts 3-2, you practiced finding TCP/IP settings on a Windows 10 computer using the Settings app and the CLI. You might have noticed that, in the Settings app, you could only change the DNS settings if you turned off DHCP. While it's possible to set preferred DNS servers without disabling DHCP, you must do so in Control Panel. It's a bit of a challenge to find Control Panel in Windows 10. Here are a few options:

- In the Search box, start typing **control** and press **Enter** when the Control Panel app appears.
- Press **Win+R**, type **control**, and press **Enter**.
- Click **Start**, scroll down and click **Windows System**, and then click **Control Panel**.

You can pin Control Panel to the Start menu or to your taskbar at the bottom of your screen to make it more accessible in the future. With Control Panel open, right-click its icon in the taskbar, and click **Pin to taskbar**.

When Control Panel is used for projects in this course, steps are written for the Large icons view unless stated otherwise. This generally makes the most important items to technicians easier to access. To change the view in Control Panel, click the **View by** drop-down menu in the top right corner of the window. Windows will usually remember the last view you used the next time you open Control Panel.

As for DNS servers, in most cases, your computer is probably using the DNS servers your ISP provides. For various reasons (such as performance improvements, filter options, or outage problems), you might want to change your DNS servers to third-party options such as Google Public DNS, OpenDNS, Cloudflare, or Verisign DNS. You can search online for these DNS servers' IP addresses. Then complete the following steps to configure your Windows 10 computer to refer to one of these DNS providers instead:

1. In Control Panel, click **Network and Sharing Center**. In the left pane, click **Change adapter settings**.
2. Right-click the active network connection and click **Properties**. In the connection's properties dialog box, click **Internet Protocol Version 4 (TCP/IPv4)**, and then click **Properties**. See Figure 3-23.
3. Select *Use the following DNS server addresses* to manually assign DNS server addresses. For example, if you want to use Cloudflare's DNS servers, you would enter 1.1.1.1 as the Preferred DNS server and 1.0.0.1 as the Alternate DNS server. Then click **OK**. Which DNS servers did you decide to use?

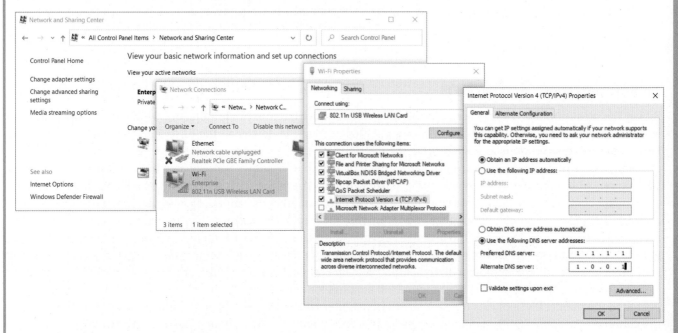

Figure 3-23   Configure TCP/IP for a network interface by using static or dynamic IP addressing

REMEMBER THIS…

- Describe DNS's global hierarchy of servers.
- Identify lookup types, including forward lookup, reverse lookup, recursive lookup, and iterative lookup.
- Explain the purpose of each DNS resource record type, including SOA, A, AAAA, CNAME, PTR, NS, MX, SRV, and TXT.

SELF-CHECK

8. When your computer requests a DNS lookup, which DNS server holds the most reliable information for that DNS record?
   a. Caching DNS server
   b. Forwarding DNS server
   c. Primary DNS server
   d. Root DNS server

9. Which DNS record type is listed first in a zone file?
   a. A
   b. AAAA
   c. CNAME
   d. SOA

10. Which DNS record type is used to find an FQDN from a given IP address?
    a. A
    b. CNAME
    c. PTR
    d. MX

Check your answers at the end of this module.

You're Ready

You're now ready to complete **Project 3-3: Manage a DNS Cache**, or you can wait until you've finished reading this module.

TROUBLESHOOTING ADDRESS PROBLEMS

✅ CERTIFICATION

1.5 Explain common ports and protocols, their application, and encrypted alternatives.

5.3 Given a scenario, use the appropriate network software tools and commands.

5.5 Given a scenario, troubleshoot general networking issues.

Average reading time: 30 minutes

Now that you are familiar with the basics of network addressing, you can learn how to solve problems with network connections. Event Viewer is one of the first places to start looking for clues when something goes wrong with a computer. It can provide valuable information about the problems the computer is experiencing, and it might even make suggestions for what to do next. For example, consider the printer error shown in Figure 3-24.

When Event Viewer doesn't give the information you need, move on to the TCP/IP troubleshooting commands discussed next.

Troubleshooting Tools

Command-line tools are a great way to get a look "under the hood" when something is going wrong on your network. Some of the most helpful tools are `ping`, `ipconfig` (Windows only), `ip` and `ifconfig` (Linux only), `nslookup`, and `dig` (Linux only). Let's see what each of these tools can do. As you read, consider practicing the commands at a Windows command prompt or Linux shell prompt.

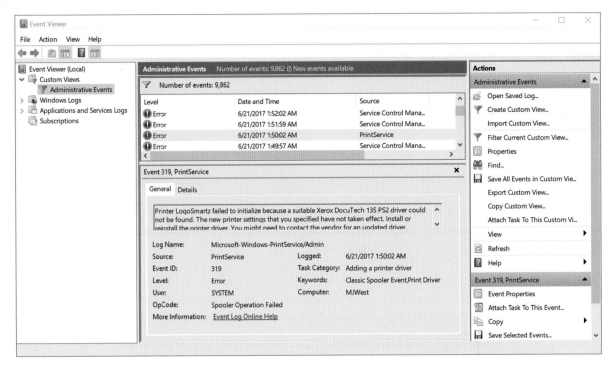

Figure 3-24   Event Viewer provided the diagnosis of a printer problem and recommended steps to fix the problem

NOTE 3-14

You've already seen some basics of how to work with PowerShell or Command Prompt in Windows. As a network professional, you'll also need to know how to work with Linux commands—you'll get some practice with Linux in projects later in this course. When working on a Linux system, you'll need to open a shell prompt. The steps for accessing a shell prompt vary depending on the Linux distribution that you're using. For Ubuntu Desktop, use any of the following options to open Terminal:

- Click **Activities** at the top of the left sidebar, type **terminal**, and click **Terminal** (see Figure 3-25).
- Click the **Show Applications** icon in the bottom left corner and click **Terminal** (see Figure 3-25).
- Press **Ctrl+Alt+T** on your keyboard.

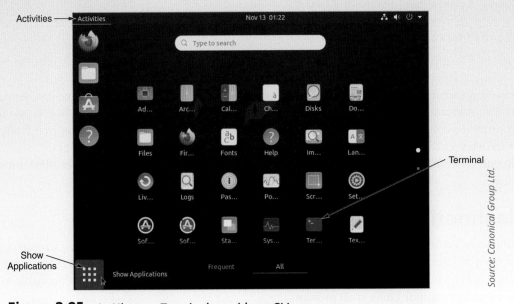

Source: Canonical Group Ltd.

Figure 3-25   In Ubuntu, Terminal provides a CLI

To close the shell prompt, click the red **X** icon or enter the **exit** command.

ping

The **ping (Packet Internet Groper)** utility is used to verify that TCP/IP is installed, bound to the NIC, configured correctly, and communicating with the network. Think about how a whale sends out a signal and listens for the echo. The nature of the echo can tell the whale a lot of information about the object the original signal bumped into. The ping utility starts by sending out a signal called an echo request to another computer, which is simply a request for a response. The other computer then responds to the request in the form of an echo reply. The protocol used by the echo request and echo reply is **ICMP (Internet Control Message Protocol)**, a lightweight protocol used to carry error messages and information about a network.

NOTE 3-15

When looking at command options, brackets indicate parameters you can add. Italics indicate information you would fill in with specific data, such as the target computer's actual IP address.

Generally, the first tool you should use to test basic connectivity to the network, Internet, and specific hosts is ping. The `ping` command has several options, called parameters or switches. Table 3-7 gives some examples of how these parameters can be used. A few of them are listed below:

`ping [-a] [-t] [-n] [-?] [IP address] [host name] [/?]`

IPv6 networks use a version of ICMP called ICMPv6. Here are two variations of ping for different operating systems, which can be used with IPv6 addresses:

- `ping6`—On Linux computers running IPv6, use `ping6` to verify whether an IPv6 host is available. When you ping a multicast address with `ping6`, you get responses from all IPv6 hosts on that subnet.
- `ping -6`—On Windows computers, use `ping` with the `-6` parameter. The `ping -6` command verifies connectivity on IPv6 networks.

Table 3-7   Options for the `ping` command

Sample `ping` commands	Description
`ping google.com`	Ping a host using its host name to verify you have Internet access and name resolution. *Google.com* is a reliable site to use for testing.
`ping 8.8.8.8`	Ping an IP address on the Internet to verify you have basic Internet access without involving name resolution. The address 8.8.8.8, which is easy to remember, points to Google's public DNS servers.
`ping -a 8.8.8.8`	Test for name resolution and display the host name to verify DNS is working.
`ping 92.10.11.200`	In this example, 92.10.11.200 is the address of a host on another subnet in your corporate network. This `ping` shows if you can reach that subnet.
`ping 192.168.1.1`	In this example, 192.168.1.1 is the address of your default gateway. This `ping` shows if you can reach it.
`ping 127.0.0.1`	Ping the loopback address, 127.0.0.1, to determine whether your workstation's TCP/IP services are running.
`ping localhost`	This is another way of pinging your loopback address.
`ping -? or ping /?`	Display the help text for the `ping` command, including its syntax and a full list of parameters.
`ping -t 192.168.1.1`	Continue pinging until interrupted. To display statistics while the `ping` continues running, press CTRL+Break (the Break key is usually paired with the Pause key). To stop pinging, press CTRL+C. Checking statistics while pinging a target outside your local network can provide insightful information on how well your Internet connection is performing. For example, you might ping one of Google's public DNS servers at 8.8.8.8. Figure 3-26 shows a `ping` to this IP address with the `-t` parameter where statistics were displayed during the `ping` and again after the `ping` was cancelled.
`ping -n 2 192.168.1.1`	Define the number of echo requests to send. By default, `ping` sends four echo requests. This example limits that number to two, or you could increase the number of requests.

NOTE 3-16

In Windows, the `-6` parameter is not necessary when pinging an IPv6 address (as opposed to pinging a host name) because the format of the address itself specifies that an IPv6 host is being pinged.

For the `ping6` and `ping -6` commands to work over the Internet, you must have access to the IPv6 Internet. Your ISP might provide native IPv6 connectivity, or you might be able to use an IPv6 tunnel provided by an IPv6 tunnel broker service, such as IPv6 Tunnel Broker (*tunnelbroker.net*), offered by Hurricane Electric, or SixXS (Six Access at *sixxs.net/main*).

Try pinging Google's IPv6 DNS server, as follows:

```
ping -6 2001:4860:4860::8888
```

Figure 3-27 shows the results on a computer with an ISP that does provide access to the IPv6 Internet; the IPv6 ping was successful after a short delay.

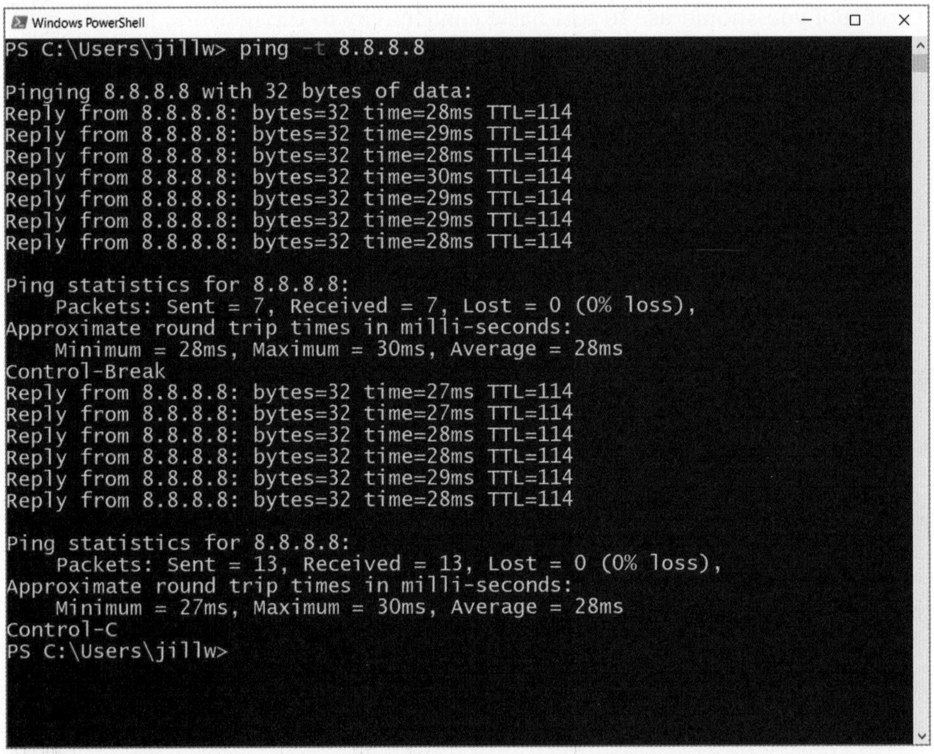
Windows PowerShell
PS C:\Users\jillw> ping -t 8.8.8.8
Pinging 8.8.8.8 with 32 bytes of data:
Reply from 8.8.8.8: bytes=32 time=28ms TTL=114
Reply from 8.8.8.8: bytes=32 time=29ms TTL=114
Reply from 8.8.8.8: bytes=32 time=28ms TTL=114
Reply from 8.8.8.8: bytes=32 time=30ms TTL=114
Reply from 8.8.8.8: bytes=32 time=29ms TTL=114
Reply from 8.8.8.8: bytes=32 time=29ms TTL=114
Reply from 8.8.8.8: bytes=32 time=28ms TTL=114
Ping statistics for 8.8.8.8:
Packets: Sent = 7, Received = 7, Lost = 0 (0% loss),
Approximate round trip times in milli-seconds:
Minimum = 28ms, Maximum = 30ms, Average = 28ms
Control-Break
Reply from 8.8.8.8: bytes=32 time=27ms TTL=114
Reply from 8.8.8.8: bytes=32 time=27ms TTL=114
Reply from 8.8.8.8: bytes=32 time=28ms TTL=114
Reply from 8.8.8.8: bytes=32 time=28ms TTL=114
Reply from 8.8.8.8: bytes=32 time=29ms TTL=114
Reply from 8.8.8.8: bytes=32 time=28ms TTL=114
Ping statistics for 8.8.8.8:
Packets: Sent = 13, Received = 13, Lost = 0 (0% loss),
Approximate round trip times in milli-seconds:
Minimum = 27ms, Maximum = 30ms, Average = 28ms
Control-C
PS C:\Users\jillw>

Figure 3-26 Results of a successful `ping -t` showing statistics while the `ping` is running and again after it's complete

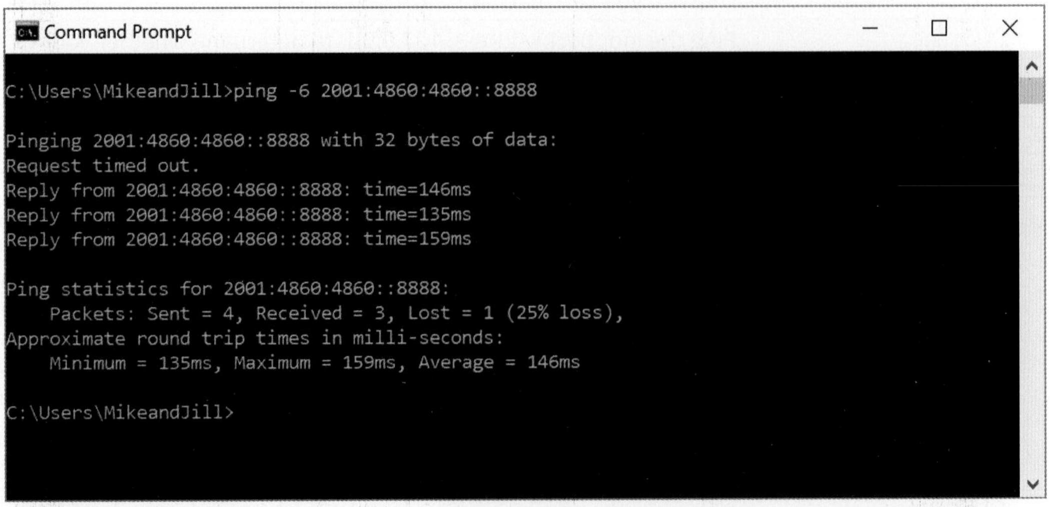
Command Prompt
C:\Users\MikeandJill>ping -6 2001:4860:4860::8888
Pinging 2001:4860:4860::8888 with 32 bytes of data:
Request timed out.
Reply from 2001:4860:4860::8888: time=146ms
Reply from 2001:4860:4860::8888: time=135ms
Reply from 2001:4860:4860::8888: time=159ms
Ping statistics for 2001:4860:4860::8888:
Packets: Sent = 4, Received = 3, Lost = 1 (25% loss),
Approximate round trip times in milli-seconds:
Minimum = 135ms, Maximum = 159ms, Average = 146ms
C:\Users\MikeandJill>

Figure 3-27 After an initial delay, the `ping -6` was successful

ipconfig

The ipconfig command shows current TCP/IP addressing and domain name information on a Windows computer. You can also use ipconfig to change some of these settings. Here are two ways to use ipconfig:

- In a PowerShell or Command Prompt window, enter **ipconfig** to view IP configuration information (see Figure 3-28). Notice which local connections are available on your computer and which ones are currently connected. Also locate your active connection's IPv4 or IPv6 address, subnet mask, and default gateway.

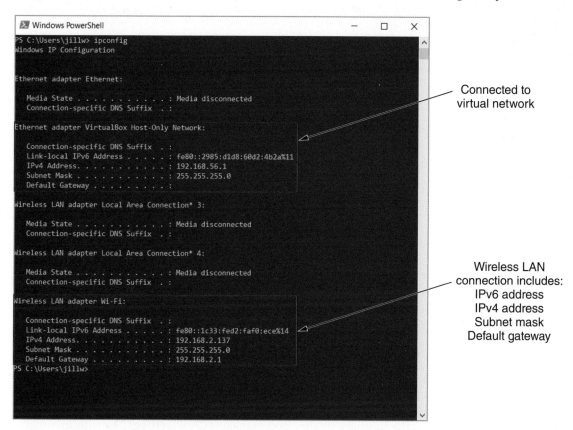

Figure 3-28 This computer is connected to two different network interfaces, one of which is a virtual network from VirtualBox

- The ipconfig command shows an abbreviated summary of configuration information. To see a more complete summary, enter the command **ipconfig /all**. See Figure 3-29 for an example.

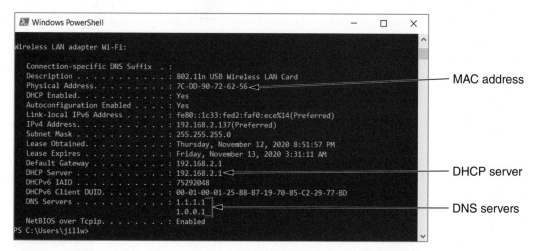

Figure 3-29 ipconfig /all gives more information than ipconfig by itself

Table 3-8 describes some helpful parameters for the `ipconfig` command. Notice that, with the `ipconfig` command, you need to type a forward slash (/) before a parameter, rather than the hyphen you use with the `ping` command.

Table 3-8 Examples of the `ipconfig` command

`ipconfig` command	Description
`ipconfig /?` or `ipconfig -?`	Display the help text for the `ipconfig` command, including its syntax and a full list of parameters.
`ipconfig /all`	Display TCP/IP configuration information for each network adapter.
`ipconfig /release`	Release the IP address when dynamic IP addressing is being used. Releasing the IP address effectively disables the computer's communications with the network until a new IP address is assigned.
`ipconfig /release6`	Release an IPv6 IP address.

`ipconfig /renew`	Lease a new IP address (often the same one you just released) from a DHCP server. To solve problems with duplicate IP addresses, misconfigured DHCP, or misconfigured DNS, reset the TCP/IP connection by consecutively entering these two commands:
	
	`ipconfig /release`
	
	`ipconfig /renew`

`ipconfig /renew6`	Lease a new IPv6 address from a DHCPv6 server.
`ipconfig /displaydns`	Display information about name resolutions that Windows currently holds in the DNS resolver cache.
`ipconfig /flushdns`	Flush—or clear—the name resolver cache, which might solve a problem when the browser cannot find a host on the Internet or when a misconfigured DNS server has sent wrong information to the resolver cache.

ip

On UNIX and Linux systems, use the **ip** utility to view and manage TCP/IP settings. As with ipconfig on Windows systems, you can use ip to view and modify TCP/IP settings and to release and renew the DHCP configuration. The ip command is built in the following format, where options define variations of an action; objects can refer to a link, address, route, rule, etc.; and command defines what to do to the object.

`ip [options] object {command | help}`

When entering `ip` commands, you can abbreviate to save time. For example, the command `ip link` can be abbreviated `ip l`. The full spellout of a command is sometimes written inside brackets to show which part of the command is optional: `ip l[ink]`.

NOTE 3-17

Remember that Linux and UNIX commands are case sensitive. Be sure to type ip and not Ip.

Any `ip` commands that change the state of a link require elevated privileges. In Linux and UNIX systems, this is accomplished by logging in as the root user or by temporarily elevating the current user's privileges with the `sudo` (superuser do) command. Also, any changes to link configurations are not saved by default—they will be lost upon the next restart unless the configuration changes are added to a startup script or edits are made to underlying configuration files.

If your Linux or UNIX system provides a GUI (graphical user interface), first open a shell prompt from the desktop. At the shell prompt, you can use the `ip` commands listed in Table 3-9.

Table 3-9 Some `ip` commands

`ip` command	Description
`ip link show`	Display basic data link layer information, including the MAC address of the NIC, as shown in Figure 3-30.
`sudo ip link set eth0 up`	Bring the eth0 interface to an "up" state. Notice that elevated privileges and a password are required to execute this command.
`sudo ip link set eth0 down`	Bring the eth0 interface to a "down" state. Notice that elevated privileges and a password are required to execute this command.
`ip address show`	Display all IP addresses associated with a device.
`sudo ip address delete` `192.168.201.191/24 device eth0`	Remove an existing class C IP address from the device's eth0 interface. Notice that elevated privileges and a password are required to execute this command.
`sudo ip address add` `192.168.201.191/24 device eth0`	Add a static class C IP address to the device's eth0 interface. Notice that elevated privileges and a password are required to execute this command.
`ip help`	Display the full list of available objects and commands.
`ip link help`	Display options specific to the `ip link` command.

Figure 3-30 Basic link information available through `ip link show`

Source: The Linux Foundation

ifconfig

Similar to ip, the **ifconfig** utility allows you to view and manage TCP/IP settings on UNIX and Linux systems. As with ipconfig on Windows systems and ip on UNIX/Linux systems, you can use ifconfig to view and modify TCP/IP settings; however, ifconfig is older and more limited than ip. Note that ifconfig has been deprecated in many Linux distributions, including Ubuntu. This means it's not installed by default, and users are intended to use the `ip` command instead. However, you can install ifconfig by running the command `sudo apt install net-tools`.

If your Linux or UNIX system provides a GUI (graphical user interface), first open a shell prompt from the desktop. At the shell prompt, you can use the `ifconfig` commands listed in Table 3-10.

Table 3-10   Some `ifconfig` commands

`ifconfig` command	Description
`ifconfig`	Display basic TCP/IP information and network information, including the MAC address of the NIC.
`ifconfig -a`	Display TCP/IP information associated with every interface on a Linux device; can be used with other parameters. See Figure 3-31.
`sudo ifconfig eth0 down`	Mark the eth0 interface, or network connection, as unavailable to the network. Notice that elevated privileges and a password are required to execute this command.
`sudo ifconfig eth0 up`	Reinitialize the eth0 interface after it has been taken down (via the `ifconfig eth0 down` command), so that it is once again available to the network. Notice that elevated privileges and a password are required to execute this command.
`ifconfig eth0 netmask 255.255.255.224`	Change the eth0 interface's subnet mask to 255.255.255.224.
`man ifconfig`	Display the manual pages, called man pages, for the `ifconfig` command, which tells you how to use the command and about command parameters (similar to the `ipconfig /?` command in Windows).

Source: The Linux Foundation

Figure 3-31   Detailed information available through `ifconfig -a`

NOTE 3-18

Other `ifconfig` parameters, such as those that apply to DHCP settings, vary according to the type and version of the UNIX or Linux system you use.

hostname

The **hostname** utility offers very basic commands used to display a device's host name, either in Windows, UNIX, or Linux systems. In Windows, hostname has no additional parameters. In UNIX or Linux, hostname offers a few more options including the ability to change the computer's name, as shown in Figure 3-32. Table 3-11 explains some of the options.

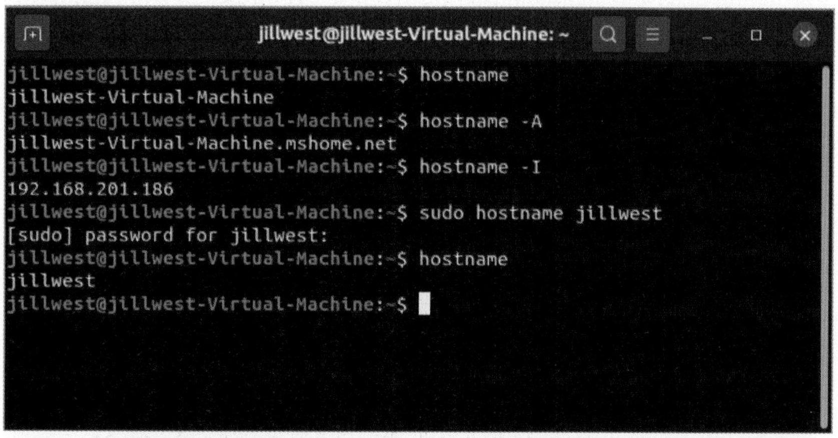

Figure 3-32 Use `hostname` to view or change a device's host name

Table 3-11 Some `hostname` commands

hostname **command**	Description
hostname	Display a device's hostname.
hostname -A	Display a device's FQDN.
hostname -I	Resolve a device's hostname with its IP address on the network.
sudo hostname jillwest	Set a new hostname on a device. Notice that elevated privileges and a password are required to execute this command.

nslookup

The **nslookup (name space lookup)** utility allows you to query the DNS database from any computer on the network and find the host name of a device by specifying its IP address, or vice versa. This is useful for verifying that a host is configured correctly or for troubleshooting DNS resolution problems. For example, if you want to find out whether the host named *cengage.com* is operational, enter the command `nslookup cengage.com`.

Figure 3-33 shows the result of running a simple `nslookup` command. Notice that the command provides the target host's IP address as well as the name and address of the primary DNS server that provided the information.

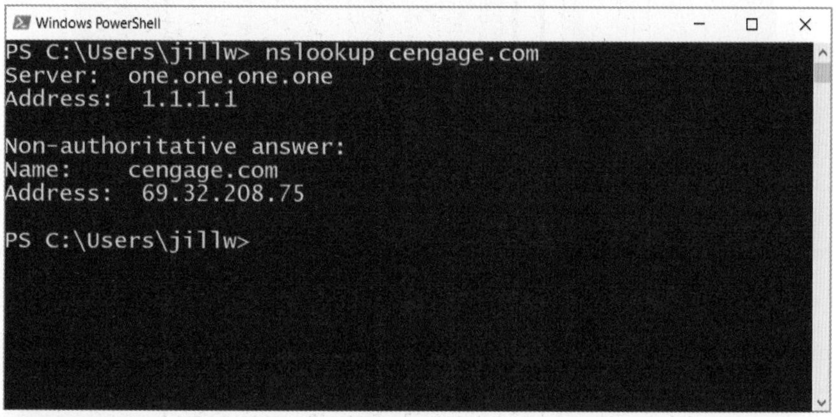

Figure 3-33 `nslookup` shows DNS server and web host information

To find the host name of a device whose IP address you know, you need to perform a reverse DNS lookup: `nslookup 69.32.208.74`. In this case, the response would include the FQDN of the target host and the name and address of the primary DNS server that made the response.

The nslookup utility is available in two modes: interactive and noninteractive. Nslookup in noninteractive mode gives a response for a single `nslookup` command. This is fine when you're investigating only one server, or when you're retrieving single items of information at a time. To test multiple DNS servers at one time, use the nslookup utility in interactive mode, which makes available more of the utility's options. To launch interactive mode, enter the **nslookup** command without any parameters.

As shown in Figure 3-34, after you enter this command, the command prompt changes to a greater-than symbol (>). You can then use additional commands to find out more about the contents of the DNS database. For example, on a computer running UNIX, you could view a list of all the host name and IP address correlations on a particular DNS server by entering the command `ls`.

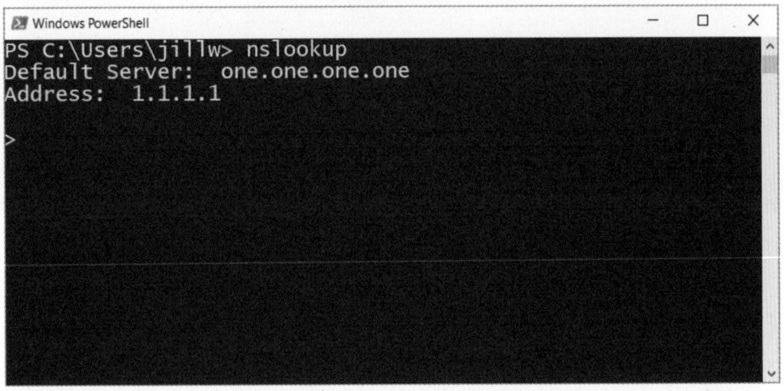

Figure 3-34 Interactive mode of the nslookup utility

You can change DNS servers from within interactive mode with the `server` subcommand and specifying the IP address of the new DNS server. Assign a new DNS server, such as Google's public DNS server, with the command: `server 8.8.8.8` (see Figure 3-35).

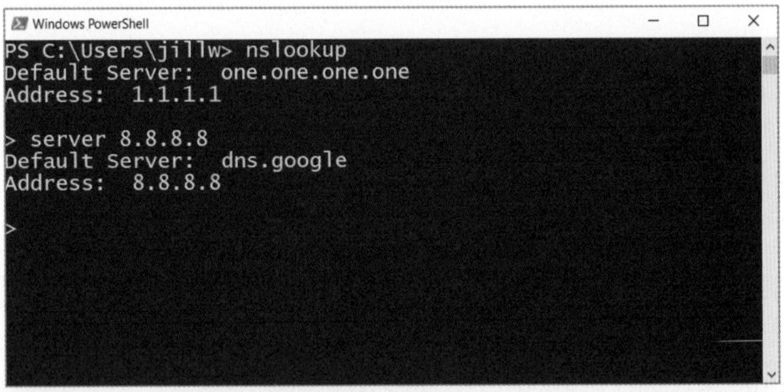

Figure 3-35 The `server` subcommand can be used to change DNS servers

To exit nslookup interactive mode and return to the normal command prompt, enter `exit`.

Many other nslookup options exist. To see these options on a UNIX or Linux system, use the `man nslookup` command. On a Windows-based system, use the `nslookup /?` command.

dig

The **dig (domain information groper)** utility is available on Linux and macOS and provides more detailed domain information than nslookup. It's installed by default in Ubuntu. You can install dig on other distributions with the command `apt-get install dnsutils`. Use dig to query DNS nameservers for information about host addresses and other DNS records. The dig utility is newer than nslookup; it uses more reliable sources of information to output its results and makes more advanced options available for complex queries. For a time, nslookup in Linux was deprecated in favor of dig (and a related command, `host`), but has since been resurrected because it's considered easier to use than dig. Some sample `dig` commands are covered in Table 3-12.

Table 3-12 Sample `dig` commands

Sample `dig` commands	Description
`dig google.com`	Perform a DNS lookup on a domain name.
`dig @8.8.8.8 google.com`	Specify a name server (found at 8.8.8.8) to resolve the *google.com* domain.
`dig @8.8.8.8 google.com MX`	Request a list of all MX records in the *google.com* domain using a specific name server (found at 8.8.8.8).
`dig google.com ANY`	Request a list of all record types in the *google.com* domain.
`dig -x 74.125.21.102`	Perform a reverse lookup on a Google IP address.
`man dig`	Display the man page for the `dig` command.

IP Scanner

While not a command-line tool, an **IP scanner** can be used to gather information about all devices connected to a network, including host names, manufacturer names, operating systems, IP addresses, MAC addresses, interfaces used, and open ports with running services. You already practiced using Nmap in an earlier module, and you're learning to use ipconfig in this module. While Nmap and ipconfig are powerful tools, they can lack efficiency in a large, corporate environment. More sophisticated IP scanners can help detect and manage large numbers of devices throughout a complex network.

Common Network Issues

At this point, you already understand a great deal about how a network works and what resources it needs to function well. Let's look at some common network problems to see how these concepts start to come together.

Incorrect Time

When a single computer keeps showing the wrong time after powering on, a good IT technician first suspects a dead CMOS battery. When several devices in a domain consistently sync to the wrong time, technicians start wondering from where those devices are getting their time information. Recall that NTP relies on a time server, either on the local network or on the Internet, to sync time settings across devices. This only works when the time source is reliable, NTP packets are being successfully received and processed, and the time settings are not configured for a manual time setting. To resolve NTP issues, try the following:

- Check to make sure the NTP port 123 is open on any relevant firewalls.
- Confirm the system is configured to set its time from a valid NTP server.
- Try changing to a different NTP server in case there's a network bottleneck slowing down NTP messages from the original NTP server.

You can check a domain computer's time source from a PowerShell or Command Prompt window. Enter the command `w32tm /query /source`. If your computer is not a member of a domain, you can determine and adjust the time server your computer syncs to when it connects to the Internet with the following steps:

1. Right-click the time and date in the system tray and click **Adjust date/time**. Make sure *Set time automatically* is turned **On**.
2. Look a little further down at the *Synchronize your clock* section. The time server your computer is using should be listed here (see Figure 3-36).

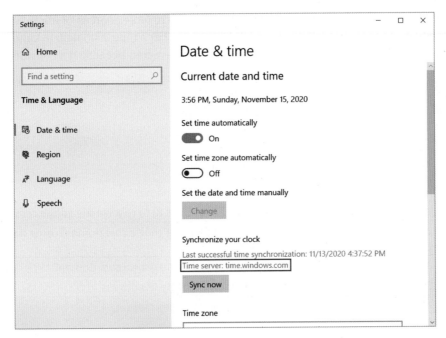

Figure 3-36 This computer is syncing with the Windows time server

3. Scroll down and click **Date, time, & regional formatting**. Next, click **Additional date, time, & regional settings** to see options in Control Panel's Clock and Region window.

4. Click **Set the time and date**, click the **Internet Time** tab, and click **Change settings**. The Internet Time Settings dialog box opens, as shown in Figure 3-37.

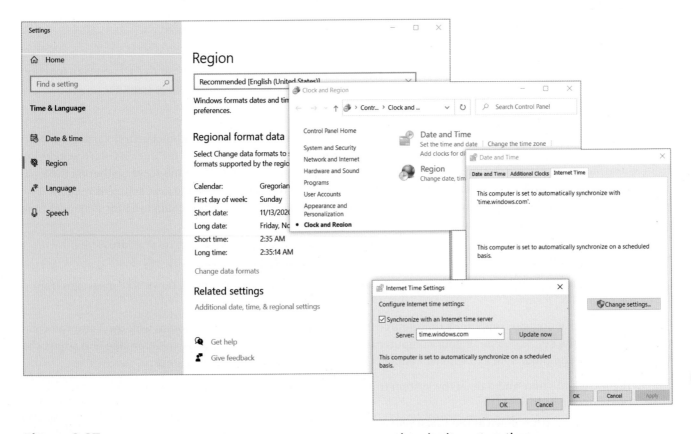

Figure 3-37 Change the time server your computer uses to synchronize its system time

5. Click the drop-down arrow to select a different time server, preferably one that is close to you geographically. Click **Update now**, and then click **OK**.

DHCP Issues

When a DHCP server gives a client an IP address, it sets a time limit, or lease time, on the IP address. At the end of the lease, the IP address assignment expires. By default, this time limit is usually anywhere from 120 minutes to eight days, depending on the device and software used. Because DHCP has a limited scope from which to draw IP addresses, the limited lease helps ensure that IP addresses are available to new clients when needed. If the lease is set too long, the network tends to suffer from DHCP scope exhaustion, meaning the available IP addresses get used up and no new clients can connect to the network. If the lease is set too short, clients' IP addresses expire quickly and new leases must be negotiated, which increases network traffic and disrupts network availability to clients.

If you're getting DHCP errors, or if multiple clients are having trouble connecting to the network, check the settings on your DHCP server. Make sure the DHCP scope is large enough to account for the number of clients the network must support, including clients that aren't active but still have an IP address leased out. A stable network with little client turnover, such as in a small office, can handle a longer lease time—perhaps months—even with a limited DHCP scope. On larger networks, especially those where many client devices log on and off frequently (such as in a popular coffee shop, a school cafeteria, or a busy sales office), a shorter lease time will increase the available IP addresses at any given moment.

Network Connection Configuration Issues

An IP address alone is not enough to get a computer connected to a network. When a computer is struggling to establish a network connection, check its TCP/IP configuration settings. You learned how to do this earlier in the module. For convenience, here are the steps again to access this information:

1. Open the Network and Sharing Center and click **Change adapter settings**.

2. Right-click the active network connection and click **Properties**.

3. Click **Internet Protocol Version 4 (TCP/IPv4)** and click **Properties**.

If the computer is not obtaining an IP address and related information from a DHCP server, the static settings might be using the wrong information. Try switching to DHCP, at least temporarily. If a static assignment is necessary, you can check a working computer on the network to determine the correct subnet mask and default gateway address. Here are some common IP setting issues you might encounter:

- **Incorrect IP address**—Pinging the wrong IP address, or making a typo when configuring a device with the incorrect IP address, is an easy mistake to make and can cause connection issues. Double check yourself as you make configuration changes and always document every single change you make on a device or network so you can access current records later when you need them.
- **Duplicate IP address**—This error message indicates that two devices on the same network are trying to use the same IP address. Usually this happens when at least one node is configured with a static IP address, and (1) another node is configured with the same static IP address, or (2) this IP address was not reserved in DHCP and the server is attempting to assign the IP address to another node.
- **Incorrect subnet mask**—A computer needs a subnet mask to identify which bits in its IP address identify the network portion and which bits identify its own host ID. An incorrect subnet mask will result in a failed or extremely limited connection to the network. Depending on the exact misconfiguration, the computer might have outgoing connectivity with other network devices and even with the Internet. But most other network devices won't be able to find the misconfigured node for purposes of normal network communication.
- **Incorrect gateway**—An incorrect IP address for the default gateway can have the opposite effect: The incorrectly configured client might be able to communicate directly with devices on its network, but it will not be able to communicate with any devices outside the local network, including public DNS servers like what was described in this module's *On the Job* story.
- **Incorrect DNS or DNS issues**—Suppose you have a static IP address, subnet mask, and default gateway all configured correctly, you open a browser to check the connection, and you can't get to a web page. You open a PowerShell window, ping the gateway, and ping Google's public DNS server, and everything is working. But

you still can't navigate to websites. Most likely, you're experiencing a DNS problem. Trying to use a DNS server that is unreachable or doesn't exist will cause name resolution issues. If pinging an IP address works but pinging a hostname or trying to connect to a website from your browser doesn't work, this indicates a possible name resolution problem. It could be the DNS server doesn't exist, is unreachable, or is currently experiencing an outage, or it could be a DNS configuration issue on your end, for example, if you entered the wrong DNS IP addresses or failed to enter DNS server information at all. When you set a static IP address, you also must set addresses for the primary and backup DNS servers. This is an easy detail to overlook. On the other hand, if you're using DHCP and still experiencing problems with names not resolving, your default DNS servers might be down. Consider changing to a public, cloud-hosted DNS server. Many public DNS servers are available free online, such as the following:

a. Google (*developers.google.com/speed/public-dns*): 8.8.8.8 and 8.8.4.4

b. OpenDNS Home (*opendns.com*): 208.67.222.222 and 208.67.220.220

c. CloudFlare (*cloudflare.com/dns*): 1.1.1.1 and 1.0.0.1

Some of these DNS servers also block known malware, adult content, and advertisements.

REMEMBER THIS...

- Describe ICMP's role when running a `ping`.
- Use common tools for solving connection problems, such as `ping`, `ipconfig`, `ip`, `ifconfig`, `dig`, `nslookup`, `hostname`, and an IP scanner.
- Explain how to troubleshoot common network issues, such as DHCP scope exhaustion, DNS issues, and IP settings issues (incorrect IP address, duplicate IP address, incorrect subnet mask, incorrect gateway, and incorrect DNS).

SELF-CHECK

11. What protocol does ping use?
  a. HTTP
  b. ICMP
  c. DHCP
  d. FTP

12. Which command disables a computer's connection to the network?
  a. `sudo ip link set eth0 up`
  b. `sudo hostname testVM`
  c. `ipconfig /release`
  d. `ping localhost`

13. What problem will `ping google.com` check for that `ping 8.8.8.8` will not?
  a. Default gateway configuration
  b. Incorrect DNS server
  c. DHCP scope exhaustion
  d. Name resolution issues

Check your answers at the end of this module.

You're Ready

You're now ready to complete **Project 3-4: Download and Use an IP Scanner**, or you can wait until you've finished the Review Questions for this module.

You're Ready

After you finish the Hands-On Projects, you're ready to complete the **Module 3 Capstone Projects**.

MODULE SUMMARY

Addressing Overview

- Addressing methods operate at the data link, network, transport, and application layers of the OSI model.
- A MAC address is embedded on every NIC on the globe and is assumed to be unique to that NIC.
- An IP address is assigned to nearly every interface and can be used to find any computer in the world if the IP address is public on the Internet.
- A port is a number used by the transport layer to identify one application among several that might be running on a host.
- Every host on a network is assigned a unique character-based name called the FQDN (fully qualified domain name), consisting of a host name and a domain name.
- MAC addresses contain two parts, are 48 bits long, and are written as hexadecimal numbers separated by colons. The first 24 bits (six hex characters) are known as the OUI (Organizationally Unique Identifier), which identifies the NIC's manufacturer. The last 24 bits make up the extension identifier or device ID and identify the device itself.

IP Addresses

- You can permanently assign a static IP address to a device, or you can configure the device to request and receive (or lease) a dynamic IP address from a DHCP server each time it connects to the network. A DHCP (Dynamic Host Configuration Protocol) server manages the dynamic distribution of IP addresses to devices on a network.
- Network technicians need to be comfortable with the CLI (command line interface) because it is quicker and often more powerful and flexible than a GUI (graphical user interface).
- A subnet mask indicates what portion of an IP address is the network portion, called the network ID or network address, and what part is the host portion, called the host ID or node ID.
- When using classful addressing, which is an older method of managing IP address ranges, the dividing line between the network and host portions is determined by the numerical range the IP address falls in. In contrast to classful addressing, classless addressing allows the dividing line between network and host portions to fall anywhere along the string of binary bits in an IP address. Moving this dividing line allows for segmenting networks within networks in a process called subnetting.
- Class A (1.x.y.z to 126.x.y.z), class B (128.0.x.y to 191.255.x.y), and class C (192.0.0.x to 223.255.255.x) addresses, for the most part, can be used to connect to and access Internet resources. Class D (begins with octets 224 through 239) and class E (begins with 240 through 254) IP addresses are not available for general use.
- To conserve its public IP addresses, a company can instead use private IP addresses for devices on its private networks—that is, devices that do not directly connect to the Internet but instead communicate through a representative device such as a router. These addresses were set aside for private use by IANA's RFC1918 (Request for Comment 1918) document, released in 1996.
- A broadcast message is read by every node on the network. A LAN, which consists of all the nodes a broadcast reaches, can be referred to as a broadcast domain. Routers don't forward broadcast messages, thus creating a boundary for a LAN.

- A DHCP scope, or DHCP pool, defines a range of IP addresses to be assigned to clients when they request an address. Other scope options include limiting the lease time and identifying the default gateway and DNS servers.
- When private devices need access to other networks or the Internet, a public-facing gateway (such as a router or firewall) substitutes the private IP addresses used by computers on the private network with its own public IP address. This process is called NAT (Network Address Translation). Besides requiring only a single public IP address for the entire private network, another advantage of NAT is security; the gateway hides the entire private network behind this one address.
- IPv6 offers a lot more public IP addresses than does IPv4 and also provides improvements to routing capabilities and speed of communication. In IPv6, a link, sometimes called the local link, is any LAN bounded by routers. Neighbors are two or more nodes on the same link.
- IPv6 supports three types of IP addresses, classified by how the address is used: unicast address (including global address, link local address, and loopback address), multicast address, and anycast address. IPv6 reduces network traffic by eliminating broadcasting.
- IPv6 addressing uses a process called SLAAC (stateless address autoconfiguration) so that a computer can autoconfigure its own link local IP address without the help of a DHCPv6 server. After generating an IPv6 address and confirming the address is unique on the network, the computer asks if a router on the network can provide configuration information. This message is called an RS (router solicitation) message. If a router responds with DHCP information in what's called an RA (router advertisement) message, the computer uses whatever information this might be, such as the IP addresses of DNS servers or the network prefix.

Ports and Sockets

- A port is a number assigned to a process, such as an application or a service, that can receive data. Whereas an IP address is used to find a computer, a port is used to find a process running on that computer. A socket consists of both a host's IP address and a process's TCP or UDP port, with a colon separating the two values.
- Well-known ports range from 0 to 1023 and are assigned by IANA to widely used and well-known utilities and applications. Registered ports range from 1024 to 49151 and can be used temporarily by processes for non-standard assignments to increase security. Dynamic and private ports range from 49152 to 65535 and are open for use without restriction.
- Which port a protocol communicates over becomes especially relevant when configuring firewalls. A firewall works by blocking traffic on all ports except those that are specifically approved by the network admin.

Domain Names and DNS

- Name resolution is the process of discovering the IP address of a host when its FQDN is known. An authoritative name server is the authority on computer names and their IP addresses for computers in their domains. The domains an organization is responsible for managing are called a DNS zone. DNS (Domain Name System) associates computer names with IP addresses. DNS namespace databases are stored on thousands of servers around the world, rather than being centralized on a single server or group of servers.
- The primary DNS server holds the authoritative DNS database for the organization's zones. When a secondary DNS server needs to update its database, it makes the request to the primary server for the update; this update process is called a zone transfer.
- A caching DNS server accesses public DNS data and caches the DNS information it collects. This server receives DNS queries from local network clients and works to resolve them by contacting other DNS servers for information. Caching DNS servers do not store zone files, which is why they must rely on their caches and resolution efforts.

- DNS name servers are organized in a global hierarchical structure. At the root level, 13 clusters of root DNS servers hold information used to locate the TLD (top-level domain) servers. These TLD servers hold information about the authoritative servers owned by various organizations.
- There are two types of DNS requests: recursive lookups, which demand a resolution or the answer that the information can't be found, and iterative lookups, which do not demand resolution and only provide information if the server already has it.
- Namespace databases are stored in DNS zone files, which are simple text files consisting of resource records that each store specific kinds of information about the zone. These records consist of fields specific to the kind of information that record type should hold, such as the zone name, class (these days, that's always Internet class), and record type. Other fields in each record vary according to the purpose of that record.

Troubleshooting Address Problems

- The ping (Packet Internet Groper) utility is used to verify that TCP/IP is installed, bound to the NIC, configured correctly, and communicating with the network. The ping utility starts by sending out a signal called an echo request to another computer, which is simply a request for a response. The other computer then responds to the request in the form of an echo reply. The protocol used by the echo request and echo reply is ICMP (Internet Control Message Protocol), a lightweight protocol used to carry error messages and information about a network.
- The `ipconfig` command shows current TCP/IP addressing and domain name information on a Windows computer. You can also use `ipconfig` to change some of these settings.
- On UNIX and Linux systems, use the ip utility to view and manage TCP/IP settings. As with ipconfig on Windows systems, you can use ip to view and modify TCP/IP settings and to release and renew the DHCP configuration. Any `ip` commands that change the state of a link require elevated privileges. In Linux and UNIX systems, this is accomplished by logging in as the root user or by temporarily elevating the current user's privileges with the `sudo` (superuser do) command. Also, any changes to link configurations are not saved by default—they will be lost upon the next restart unless the configuration changes are added to a startup script or edits are made to underlying configuration files.
- Similar to ip, use the ifconfig utility to view and manage TCP/IP settings on UNIX and Linux systems. The ifconfig utility has been deprecated in many Linux distributions, including Ubuntu. This means it's not installed by default, and users are intended to use the `ip` command instead. However, you can install it by running the command `sudo apt install net-tools`.
- The hostname utility offers very basic commands used to display a device's host name, either in Windows, UNIX, or Linux system. In Windows, hostname has no additional parameters. In UNIX or Linux, hostname offers a few more options including the ability to change the computer's name.
- The nslookup (name space lookup) utility allows you to query the DNS database from any computer on the network and find the host name of a device by specifying its IP address, or vice versa. This is useful for verifying that a host is configured correctly or for troubleshooting DNS resolution problems.
- The dig (domain information groper) utility is available on Linux and macOS and provides more detailed domain information than nslookup. It's installed by default in Ubuntu. You can install dig on other distributions with the command `apt-get install dnsutils`. Use dig to query DNS nameservers for information about host addresses and other DNS records.
- While not a command-line tool, an IP scanner can be used to gather information about all devices connected to a network, including host names, manufacturer names, operating systems, IP addresses, MAC addresses, interfaces used, and open ports with running services. Sophisticated IP scanners can help detect and manage large numbers of devices throughout a complex network.

Key Terms

For definitions of key terms, see the Glossary.

A (address) record
AAAA (address) record
anycast address
APIPA (Automatic Private IP Addressing)
authoritative name server
broadcast
broadcast domain
caching DNS server
canonical name
CIDR (Classless Interdomain Routing) notation
classful addressing
classless addressing
CNAME (canonical name) record
default gateway
device ID
DHCP (Dynamic Host Configuration Protocol)
DHCP reservation
DHCP scope
DHCP scope exhaustion
dig (domain information groper)
DNS zone
domain name
dual stacked
dynamic IP address
EUI-64 (Extended Unique Identifier-64)
exclusion range
extension identifier
forward lookup
forwarding DNS server
FQDN (fully qualified domain name)
gateway
global address
host ID
host name
hostname
IANA (Internet Assigned Numbers Authority)

ICANN (Internet Corporation for Assigned Names and Numbers)
ICMP (Internet Control Message Protocol)
ifconfig
interface
interface ID
ip
IP reservation
IP scanner
IPAM (IP address management)
ipconfig
IPv4 (Internet Protocol version 4)
IPv6 (Internet Protocol version 6)
iterative lookup
LDAP (Lightweight Directory Access Protocol)
LDAPS (Lightweight Directory Access Protocol over SSL)
lease time
link
link local address
loopback address
MAC address table
MAC reservation
multicast
multicast address
multicast flooding
MX (mail exchanger) record
name resolution
NAT (Network Address Translation)
neighbor
network ID
node ID
NS (name server) record
nslookup (name space lookup)
NTP (Network Time Protocol)
octet
OUI (Organizationally Unique Identifier)
PAT (Port Address Translation)
ping (Packet Internet Groper)

primary DNS server
private IP address
process
PTR (pointer) record
public IP address
RA (router advertisement)
rDNS (reverse DNS)
recursive lookup
registered port
resource record
reverse lookup
RFC1918 (Request for Comment 1918)
root DNS server
RS (router solicitation)
scope option
secondary DNS server
session
SLAAC (stateless address autoconfiguration)
SMB (Server Message Block)
SOA (start of authority) record
socket
SQLnet
SRV (service) record
static IP address
stratum
subnet
subnet ID
subnet mask
subnetting
syslog (system log)
TFTP (Trivial File Transfer Protocol)
TLD (top-level domain)
TTL (Time to Live)
tunneling
TXT (text) record
unicast address
URL (uniform resource locator)
well-known port
zone transfer

Review Questions

1. Which part of a MAC address is unique to each manufacturer?
   a. The network identifier
   b. The OUI
   c. The device identifier
   d. The physical address

2. What type of device does a computer turn to when attempting to connect with a host with a known IP address on another network?
   a. Default gateway
   b. DNS server
   c. Root server
   d. DHCP server

3. What decimal number corresponds to the binary number 11111111?
   a. 255
   b. 256
   c. 127
   d. 11,111,111

4. Suppose you send data to the 11111111 11111111 11111111 11111111 IP address on an IPv4 network. To which device(s) are you transmitting?
   a. All devices on the Internet
   b. All devices on your local network
   c. The one device that is configured with this IP address
   d. No devices

5. When your computer first joins an IPv6 LAN, what is the prefix of the IPv6 address the computer first configures for itself?
   a. FF00::/8
   b. ::1/128
   c. 2000::/3
   d. FE80::/64

6. If you are connected to a network that uses DHCP, and you need to terminate your Windows workstation's DHCP lease, which command would you use?
   a. `ipconfig /release`
   b. `ipconfig /renew`
   c. `ifconfig /release`
   d. `ifconfig /renew`

7. Which of these commands has no parameters in Windows?
   a. `ping`
   b. `ipconfig`
   c. `hostname`
   d. `nslookup`

8. Which DNS server offers the most current resolution to a DNS query?
   a. Primary DNS server
   b. Root DNS server
   c. Caching DNS server
   d. TLD DNS server

9. You have just brought online a new secondary DNS server and notice your network-monitoring software reports a significant increase in network traffic. Which two hosts on your network are likely to be causing the increased traffic and why?
   a. The caching and primary DNS servers because the caching server is requesting zone transfers from the primary server
   b. The secondary and primary DNS servers because the secondary server is requesting zone transfers from the primary server
   c. The root and primary DNS servers because the primary server is requesting zone transfers from the root server
   d. The web server and primary DNS server because the web server is requesting zone transfers from the primary DNS server

10. Which type of DNS record identifies an email server?
   a. AAAA record
   b. CNAME record
   c. MX record
   d. PTR record

11. What is the range of addresses that might be assigned by APIPA?

12. You are the network manager for a computer training center that allows students to bring their own laptops to class for learning and taking notes. Students need access to the Internet, so you have configured your network's DHCP server to issue IP addresses automatically. Which DHCP option should you modify to make sure you are not wasting addresses used by students who have left for the day?

13. You have decided to use SNAT and PAT on your small office network. At minimum, how many IP addresses must you obtain from your ISP for all five clients in your office to be able to access servers on the Internet?

14. Explain how the bits of an IPv6 address are organized and describe IPv6 shorthand notation.

15. FTP sometimes uses a random port for data transfer, but an FTP server always, unless programmed otherwise, listens to the same port for session requests from clients. What port does an FTP server listen on?

16. You issue a transmission from your workstation to the following socket on your LAN: 10.1.1.145:53. Assuming your network uses standard port designations, what application layer protocol handles your transmission?

17. Suppose you want to change the default port for RDP as a security precaution. What port does RDP use by default, and from what range of numbers should you select a private port number?

18. You have just set up a new wireless network at your house, and you want to determine whether your Linux laptop has connected to it and obtained a valid IP address. What command will give you the information you need?

19. While troubleshooting a network connection problem for a coworker, you discover the computer is querying a nonexistent DNS server. What command-line utility can you use to assign the correct DNS server IP address?

20. When running a scan on your computer, you find that a session has been established with a host at the address 208.85.40.44:443. Which application layer protocol is in use for this session? What command-line utility might you use to determine the domain name of the other computer?

Hands-On Projects

NOTE 3-19

Websites and applications change often. While the instructions given in these projects were accurate at the time of writing, you might need to adjust the steps or options according to later changes.

Note to Instructors and Students: A rubric is provided for evaluating student performance on these projects. Please see Appendix D.

Project 3-1: Create a NAT Translation Table Entry

Estimated Time: 20 minutes
Objective: Given a scenario, configure a subnet and use appropriate IP addressing schemes. (Obj. 1.4)
Resources:
- No special resources required

Context: Your corporation hosts a website at the static public IP address 92.110.30.123. A router directs this traffic to a web server at the private IP address 192.168.11.100. However, the web server needs a hardware upgrade and will be down for two days. Your network administrator has asked you to configure the router so that requests to the IP address 92.110.30.123 are redirected to the backup server for the website, which has the private IP address 192.168.11.110. The router's inside Ethernet interface uses IP address 192.168.11.254, and its outside interface uses the IP address 92.110.30.65. Answer the following questions about the new static route you'll be creating:

1. What is the router's outside interface IP address?
2. What is the router's inside interface IP address?
3. What is the website's public IP address?

Use the example given in Figure 3-15 earlier in the module as a template to create the NAT translation table entries for the address translation. For the subnet masks, use the default subnet mask for a Class C IP address license. Include appropriate comment lines in your table. **Take a screenshot of your NAT translation table**; submit this visual with your answers to this project's questions.

Project 3-2: Change IPv6 Autoconfiguration Settings

Estimated Time: 20 minutes (+15 minutes for group work, if assigned)
Objective: Given a scenario, configure a subnet and use appropriate IP addressing schemes. (Obj. 1.4)
Group Work: This project includes enhancements when assigned as a group project.
Resources:

- Windows 10 computer with administrative access
- Internet access

Context: By default, when configuring an IPv6 address, Windows 10 generates a random number to fill out the bits needed for the NIC portion of the IPv6 address. This security measure helps conceal your device's MAC address, and it further protects your privacy by generating a new number every so often. There may be times, however, when you need your system to maintain a static IPv6 address. To do this, you can disable IPv6 autoconfiguration using the netsh utility in an elevated PowerShell or Command Prompt window. Forcing the computer to use SLAAC to generate its IPv6 address will result in the same IPv6 address every time. Complete the following steps:

1. In this project, you'll use the netsh utility. Do some research online about this tool and answer the following questions:
   a. What is netsh used for?
   b. What is the role of a netsh context?
   c. What netsh command access the interface context for managing network connections?
2. Open an elevated PowerShell or Command Prompt window.
3. Enter `ipconfig /all` and find the TCP/IP information for the active network connection. **Take a screenshot** of this information; submit this visual with your answers to this project's questions. What is your computer's current IPv6 address and MAC address? Carefully compare the two addresses. Are they in any way numerically related?
4. To disable the random IP address generation feature, enter the command:
   `netsh interface ipv6 set global randomizeidentifiers=disabled`
5. To instruct Windows to use the EUI-64 standard instead of the default settings, enter the command:
   `netsh interface ipv6 set privacy state=disabled`
   Figure 3-38 shows where both commands were entered and accepted.

```
Administrator: Windows PowerShell                                    —    □    ×

Wireless LAN adapter Wi-Fi:

    Connection-specific DNS Suffix  . :
    Description . . . . . . . . . . . : 802.11n USB Wireless LAN Card
    Physical Address. . . . . . . . . : 7C-DD-90-72-62-56
    DHCP Enabled. . . . . . . . . . . : Yes
    Autoconfiguration Enabled . . . . : Yes
    Link-local IPv6 Address . . . . . : fe80::1c33:fed2:faf0:ece%14(Preferred)
    IPv4 Address. . . . . . . . . . . : 192.168.2.137(Preferred)
    Subnet Mask . . . . . . . . . . . : 255.255.255.0
    Lease Obtained. . . . . . . . . . : Friday, November 13, 2020 1:40:08 PM
    Lease Expires . . . . . . . . . . : Friday, November 13, 2020 3:40:07 PM
    Default Gateway . . . . . . . . . : 192.168.2.1
    DHCP Server . . . . . . . . . . . : 192.168.2.1
    DHCPv6 IAID . . . . . . . . . . . : 75292048
    DHCPv6 Client DUID. . . . . . . . : 00-01-00-01-25-88-B7-19-70-85-C2-29-77-BD
    DNS Servers . . . . . . . . . . . : 1.1.1.1
                                        1.0.0.1
    NetBIOS over Tcpip. . . . . . . . : Enabled
PS C:\WINDOWS\system32> netsh interface ipv6 set global randomizeidentifiers=disabled
Ok.

PS C:\WINDOWS\system32> netsh interface ipv6 set privacy state=disabled
Ok.

PS C:\WINDOWS\system32>
```

Figure 3-38   PowerShell outputs a confirmation for each `netsh` command entered

6. Enter `ipconfig /all` again. What is your computer's new IPv6 address? How closely does this number resemble the MAC address? Notice after *FE80::* that the fixed value FF FE has been inserted halfway through the MAC address values. The host portion of the IPv6 address might use a slightly different value than the OUI in the MAC address because the seventh bit of the MAC address is inverted.

7. **For group assignments:** Complete the following steps:
   a. Attempt to ping each other's devices using ping -6 and IPv6 addresses. What response did you get?
   b. Attempt to ping Google's IPv6 DNS address on the Internet: 2001:4860:4860::8888. What response did you get?
   c. There are many reasons why pinging an IPv6 address on your local network might not work even if the network and its devices are functioning properly. For example, your LAN might not support IPv6. In some cases, you might have successfully pinged an IPv6 address on your local network but not on the Internet. If one or both of your pings did not work, spend a few moments with your group doing some investigating and troubleshooting to see if you can determine where the IPv6 ping is failing and what you would need to do to fix it. What possibilities did you come up with?

8. Re-enable random IPv6 address generation with these two commands:

```
netsh interface ipv6 set global randomizeidentifiers=enabled
netsh interface ipv6 set privacy state=enabled
```

Project 3-3: Manage a DNS Cache

Estimated Time: 10 minutes
Objective: Explain the use and purpose of network services. (Obj. 1.6)
Resources:

- Windows 10 computer with administrative access
- Internet access

Context: You have learned that clients as well as name servers store DNS information to associate names with IP addresses. In this project, you view the contents of a local DNS cache, clear it, and view it again after performing some DNS lookups. Then you change DNS servers and view the DNS cache once again. Complete the following steps:

1. To view the DNS cache, open an elevated PowerShell or Command Prompt window and enter the following command: `ipconfig /displaydns`

2. If this computer has been used to resolve host names with IP addresses—for example, if it has been used to retrieve email or browse the web—a list of locally cached resource records appears. Read the file to see what kinds of records have been saved, using the scroll bar if necessary. What is the most common record type in this list?

3. Clear the DNS cache with this command: `ipconfig /flushdns`
   The operating system confirms that the DNS resolver cache has been flushed. One circumstance in which you might want to empty a client's DNS cache is if the client needs to reach a host whose IP address has changed (for example, a website whose server was moved to a different hosting company). If the DNS information is locally cached, the client will continue to look for the host at the old location. Clearing the cache allows the client to retrieve the new IP address for the host.

4. View the DNS cache again with the command: `ipconfig /displaydns`

5. Open a browser window and navigate to three websites you have not recently visited, such as **howstuffworks.com**, **nautil.us**, and **mapcrunch.com**.

6. Return to the PowerShell or Command Prompt window and view the DNS cache containing the new list of resource records. **Take a screenshot** of one of these records that was collected in response to your browser activity; submit this visual with your answers to this project's questions.

 EXAM TIP The Network+ exam includes two types of questions: performance-based questions (called PBQs) and multiple-choice questions. You're already familiar with multiple-choice questions. PBQs give you a scenario of some kind and require you to interact with tools such as a network diagram, user interface, or command-line interface to complete tasks related to the scenario. A common performance-based question on the Network+ exam requires you to know how to manage DNS from a CLI using ipconfig. You might also see a multiple-choice question that covers similar information.

Project 3-4: Download and Use an IP Scanner

Estimated Time: 20 minutes

Objective: Given a scenario, use the appropriate network software tools and commands. (Obj. 5.3)

Group Work: This project includes enhancements when assigned as a group project.

Resources:

- Windows 10 computer with administrative access
- Internet access

Context: You've already seen the kind of information you can detect about your network devices using Nmap. In this project, you will use a free, popular tool called Advanced IP Scanner to detect devices on your network and determine what additional information an IP scanner can collect. Complete the following steps:

> ⓘ **CAUTION** Take note that scanning a network you don't own or don't have permission to scan is illegal. Do not use an IP scanner on public Wi-Fi networks at all. Also don't use an IP scanner on any network you don't own unless you have written permission from the owner to scan the network.

1. Go to **advanced-ip-scanner.com**. Download and install the free application Advanced IP Scanner. When the installation is finished, run Advanced IP Scanner.
2. In the user interface, notice you have two options for the scan: Scan the local machine's subnet or scan a class C subnet. Depending on your network configuration, there might be no difference between these two options. If there is, choose the option that is most appropriate for your network. Also, if you are using the computer on which you installed your VMs from earlier Capstone Projects, the scan might target two IP ranges. What IP range(s) will you be scanning?
3. When you're ready, click **Scan**. Give the scanner a few minutes to complete the scan.
4. When the scan is complete, **take a screenshot** of the results. Blur out any private information and submit this visual with your answers to this project's questions. Figure 3-39 shows the results of one network scan. Even some devices that do not have names were identifiable by manufacturer, such as the Roku device.

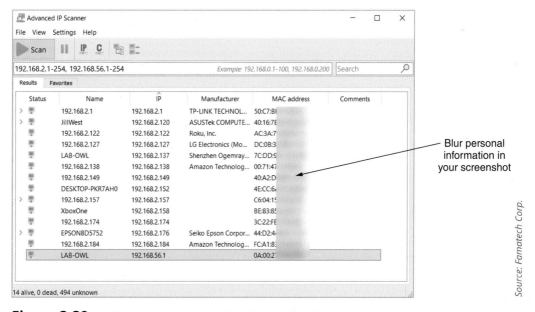

Figure 3-39 Advanced IP Scanner found and identified several devices on this LAN

Source: Famatech Corp.

5. What surprises you about the results of your scan? Are there any devices you can't identify that you need to research further? Keep in mind that it's important to track which devices are connected to your network to ensure no one is using your network without permission and to ensure no devices are leaking sensitive information to the Internet or being maliciously controlled over the Internet.
6. Depending on the device, Advanced IP Scanner offers some remote-control options. For example, right-click one of the devices in your scan results and explore the options in the pop-up menu. Some of these tools require Radmin, which is a free remote access application. You can experiment with this tool if you want to. You also

have some command-line tools in Advanced IP Scanner. Use the Ping tool to check the connection with one of the devices on your network. How does this ping function differently than the pings you've run in other projects? When you're ready, press **Ctrl+C** to stop the ping.

7. **For group assignments:** One option for remotely accessing a computer through Advanced IP Scanner is RDP for Windows computers. Find another group member's computer in your scan results, right-click, point to **Tools**, and click **RDP**. The other person will need to enter their user account credentials. Alternatively, each group member can create a guest account and share those credentials with group members to use with RDP from Advanced IP Scanner.

8. In your wiki, add a new page titled **Applications:AdvancedIPScanner**. Indicate the module and project number for this installation, the computer you used for this project, a brief description of what you learned, and any other information you might find helpful when using Advanced IP Scanner later.

Capstone Projects

NOTE 3-20

Websites and applications change often. While the instructions given in these projects were accurate at the time of writing, you might need to adjust the steps or options according to later changes.

Note to Instructors and Students: A rubric is provided for evaluating student performance on these projects. Please see Appendix D.

Capstone Project 3-1: Set Up an Ubuntu Server in a VM

Estimated Time: 45 minutes
Objective: Given a scenario, use the appropriate network software tools and commands. (Obj. 5.3)
Resources:
- Access to the same computer used to complete Capstone Project 1-1 or Capstone Project 1-2
- Internet access
- If desired, instructor can provide Ubuntu Server image file

Context: In the Module 1 Capstone Projects, you created a virtual machine using Oracle VirtualBox or Windows 10 Client Hyper-V. In Capstone Project 2-1, you added a second VM, this one running Ubuntu Desktop. In this Capstone Project, you create a third VM and install Ubuntu Server in the VM. You also learn how to use some Linux commands. Using the same computer that you used in Capstone Project 1-1 or 1-2 (which should have Oracle VirtualBox or Client Hyper-V installed and activated), complete the following steps:

1. Go to **ubuntu.com/server** and download the Ubuntu Server OS to your hard drive using **Option 3: Manual install**. If you're given the choice of multiple versions, choose the latest version. The file that downloads is an ISO file.
2. Open the Oracle VM VirtualBox Manager or Hyper-V Manager. Refer back to the directions in the Module 1 Capstone Projects if needed, and give the VM an informative name. Note that if you're using Hyper-V Manager and you use the Quick Create option, click *Local installation source*, deselect *This virtual machine will run Windows (enables Windows Secure Boot)*, and then click *Change installation source*. In VirtualBox, mount the ISO file that contains the Ubuntu Server download to a virtual DVD in your VM.

NOTE 3-21

Ubuntu Server is only available as a 64-bit OS. To install a 64-bit guest OS in a VM, the host OS must also be 64-bit.

3. Start the VM and install Ubuntu Server, accepting all default settings. Be sure to record your Ubuntu hostname, username, and password in your LastPass vault. When given the option, decline to install any extra software bundled with the OS other than standard system utilities.

4. After you restart the VM, Ubuntu Server launches, which does not have a GUI interface. Enter your username and password to log in. You should now see the shell prompt, as shown in Figure 3-40.

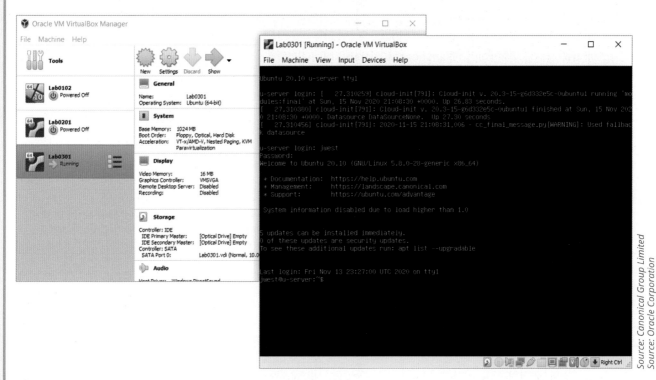

Figure 3-40   Ubuntu Server is installed in a VM in VirtualBox

Source: Canonical Group Limited
Source: Oracle Corporation

5. Practice using Ubuntu Server by entering, in order, each of the commands listed in Table 3-13. As you do so, you'll examine the directory structure, create a new directory, and put a blank file in it.

Table 3-13   Practice Linux commands in Ubuntu Server

Step	Command	Description
1	`pwd`	Displays the full path to the current directory. When you first log in to a system, that directory is /home/*username*.
2	`mkdir mydir`	Creates a directory named mydir. The directory is created in the current directory. You must have permission to edit the current directory.
3	`dir`	Lists files and directories in the current directory. In Linux, a directory is treated more like a file than a Windows folder.
4	`cd mydir`	Goes to the directory you just created in the /home/*username* directory. What is your new shell prompt?
5	`touch myfile`	Creates a blank file named myfile in the current directory
6	`ls`	Similar to dir, lists current directory contents

(continues)

Table 3-13 Practice Linux commands in Ubuntu Server *(continued)*

Step	Command	Description
7	`cd ..`	Moves up one level in the directory tree. **Take a screenshot** of the commands you've entered so far and their output; submit this visual with your answers to this project's questions.
8	`cd /etc`	Changes directory to the /etc directory, where text files are kept for configuring installed programs. What is your new shell prompt?
9	`ls`	Examines the contents of the /etc directory
10	`cd /home`	Changes directory to the /home directory
11	`ping 127.0.0.1`	Pings the loopback address. Pinging continues until you stop it by pressing CTRL+C.
12	**CTRL+C**	Breaks out of a command or process; use it to recover after entering a wrong command or to stop a command that requires you manually halt the output.
13	`ifconfig`	Displays basic TCP/IP information and network information, including the MAC address of the NIC
14	`ip address show`	Displays IP and MAC addresses. Notice the difference in output for `ifconfig` compared to `ip address show`. What is your VM's IPv4 address? Note that Linux calls this address inet. (Be careful you don't answer with the loopback address! Most likely, the active network connection is on the eth0 interface.)
15	`ip help`	Displays available objects and options for the `ip` command
16	`dig google.com`	Performs a DNS lookup on the *google.com* domain name
17	`df`	Displays the amount of free space on your hard drive. In this case, the VM is reporting on its virtual hard drive.
18	`exit`	Logs out; the login shell prompt appears, where you can log in again. Enter your username and password to log in again.
19	`sudo poweroff`	Elevates privilege to shut down the VM. You'll need to enter your password, and then the system shuts down.

6. Add the new VM's information to your VMclients page in your wiki. On the Virtualization:VMclients page, click **Edit** at the bottom of the page and add the new VM to your list. Include the module number, hypervisor used, VM computer name, and VM operating system. Also note any additional information that you might find helpful when you return to this VM in the future such as how to view the Linux Manual or how to shut down the system. When you're finished, click **Save**.

7. **Take a screenshot** of the edited wiki page; submit this visual with your answers to this project's questions.

Capstone Project 3-2: Build a MAC Address Table in Packet Tracer

Estimated Time: 45 minutes

Objective: Given a scenario, configure and deploy common Ethernet switching features. (Obj. 2.3)

Resources:
- Computer with Cisco Packet Tracer installed
- Internet access

Context: In Capstone Project 2-2, you installed Packet Tracer and practiced interacting with the user interface. Earlier in this module, you learned about MAC address tables that switches use to track which device is connected to each of a switch's ports. In this Capstone Project, you build a small network in Packet Tracer and observe changes to a switch's MAC address table. Complete the following steps:

1. Open Packet Tracer and, if necessary, sign in with your Networking Academy account.

2. In the Devices pane, click **Network Devices** category and then click **Switches**. Add a **PT-Switch** to your workspace. Give the switch a moment to boot.

3. Click **Switch0** to open its configuration window. Click the **CLI** tab. This takes you to the CLI for this switch where you can enter commands to interact with the switch. While Packet Tracer offers some options for configuring devices through their GUIs, the tasks in this project can only be completed from the CLI.

4. Click at the bottom of the IOS Command Line Interface pane in the empty space below "Press RETURN to get started!" Press **Enter** to activate the CLI. By default, you begin in user EXEC command mode, which has the lowest level of privileges in a Cisco device. You can see what mode you're in by looking at the prompt—user EXEC mode shows the prompt *Switch>*. To enter privileged EXEC mode, enter `enable`. The prompt changes to *Switch#*.

5. Now that you're in privileged EXEC mode, you can check the switch's current MAC address table. Enter `show mac address-table`. What entries are listed?

6. From the **End Devices** group in the Devices pane, add two **PCs** to your workspace.

7. Click **PC0**. In PC0's configuration window, click the **Desktop** tab and then click **IP Configuration**. In this project and most Packet Tracer projects in this course, you'll set static IP addresses. Enter the following information and then close the configuration window (the information saves automatically):

   IP address: **192.168.0.2**
   Subnet mask: **255.255.255.0**

8. Repeat Step 7 for PC1 and enter the following information for PC1:

   IP address: **192.168.0.3**
   Subnet mask: **255.255.255.0**

9. It's important to get in the habit of keeping good documentation as you work. In the toolbar above your workspace, click the **Place Note (N)** tool. Click under each PC and document that device's IP address and subnet mask, as shown in Figure 3-41.

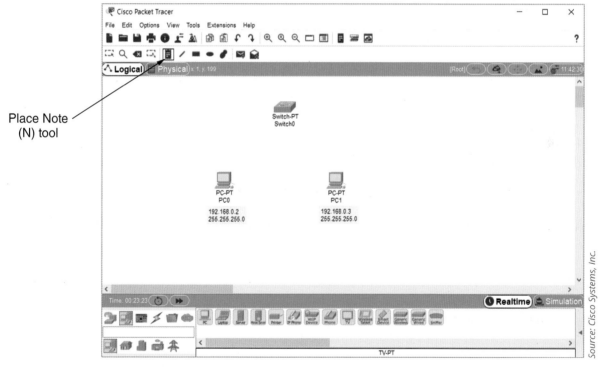

Figure 3-41   Use notes to document your network configurations

10. Now you're ready to connect your PCs to your switch. In the Devices pane, click **Connections** and then click the **Copper Straight-Through** cable, which is a thick, black line. Click **PC0** and select its **FastEthernet0** interface. Then click **Switch0** and select its **FastEthernet0/1** interface. Repeat this process for PC1, connecting PC1's **FastEthernet0** interface to Switch0's **FastEthernet1/1** interface. Wait for all indicator lights to turn into green triangles.

11. Access Switch0's CLI again. Click at the bottom of the CLI pane and press **Enter**. Check Switch0's MAC address table. What entries are listed?

Recall that the switch must see traffic crossing its interfaces to collect MAC addresses for connected devices. To generate traffic, run a ping from PC0 to PC1. Complete the following steps:

12. Click **PC0** and click the **Desktop** tab. Click **Command Prompt**. At the C:\> prompt, enter `ping 192.168.0.3` and wait for the ping to complete.

13. Return to Switch0's CLI and check its MAC address table again. **Take a screenshot** of the output; submit this visual with your answers to this project's questions.

A switch can only see network traffic that crosses its interfaces. It's possible for traffic from multiple devices to enter a switch at a single switch port. In this case, the switch will record multiple MAC addresses for a single interface. Complete the following steps:

14. Add a second **PT-Switch** and a third **PC**.

15. Configure PC2 with the following information and create a note to document this configuration:
    IP address: **192.168.0.4**
    Subnet mask: **255.255.255.0**

16. In the **Connections** group, click the **Fiber** cable, which is the solid orange line. Click **Switch0** and select its **FastEthernet4/1** interface. Then click **Switch1** and select its **FastEthernet4/1** interface.

17. Use a **Copper Straight-Through** cable to connect PC2's **FastEthernet0** interface to Switch1's **FastEthernet0/1** interface. Wait for all indicator lights to turn into green triangles.

18. Check Switch0's MAC address table again. What entries are listed? Given this information, which connected device is Switch0 currently aware of?

19. Sending a ping between PC2 and PC0 will inform Switch0 of three devices' MAC addresses. Which devices do you expect Switch0 to know about after the ping?

20. From PC2, ping PC0. Did the ping work?

21. Return to Switch0's CLI and check its MAC address table again. **Take a screenshot** of the output; submit this visual with your answers to this project's questions.

22. Examine the three devices listed in Switch0's MAC address table and answer the following questions:
    a. How many devices is Switch0 currently aware of?
    b. Which device is connected to Switch0's Fa0/1 interface? How can you confirm which device matches this MAC address?
    c. Which two devices communicated across Switch0's Fa4/1 interface?

23. Currently, PC1 is not showing in Switch0's MAC address table. What can you do to make Switch0 aware of PC1?

24. You do not need to save this Packet Tracer network for future projects. However, before closing the network, take some notes in your Wikidot website about your work in this project, commands that you learned, and new insights you have about how Packet Tracer works.

Note to Instructors: A Packet Tracer solution file is provided for each Packet Tracer project through the Instructors site.

Solutions to Self-Check Questions

Addressing Overview

1. What numbering system do humans use to write MAC addresses?

   Answer: d. Hexadecimal

   Explanation: A MAC address is 48 bits, written as six **hexadecimal** numbers separated by colons, as in 00:60:8C:00:54:99. A hexadecimal number (also called a hex number) is a number written in the base-16 number system, which uses the 16 numerals 0, 1, 2, 3, 4, 5, 6, 7, 8, 9, A, B, C, D, E, and F. IPv4 addresses are written as four decimal numbers called octets, for example, 92.106.50.200. Each octet, when written in binary, consists of exactly 8 bits. A binary number is a number written in the base-2 number system, which uses only the numerals 0 and 1.

2. What Windows command outputs a computer's MAC address?

Answer: c. `ipconfig /all`

Explanation: In a PowerShell or Command Prompt window, you can enter **`ipconfig /all`** to identify your NIC's MAC address. The `ipconfig` command without the `/all` parameter will not show the MAC address. The `ping` command is used to check connectivity between two devices. Oui-lookup is not a standard Windows command.

IP Addresses

3. What command shows you a computer's TCP/IP configuration?

Answer: b. `ipconfig`

Explanation: You can find TCP/IP configuration information and more using the **`ipconfig`** command. The `ping` command is used to check connectivity between two devices. The `ssh` command creates an encrypted channel or tunnel between two computers. Nmap is a simple and popular command-line utility used to detect network devices.

4. Which of the following IPv4 addresses is a public IP address?

Answer: d. 64.233.177.189

Explanation: IP addresses within the ranges 10.0.0.0 through 10.255.255.255, 172.16.0.0 through 172.31.255.255, and 192.168.0.0 through 192.168.255.255 are RFC1918, or private, IP addresses. The address **64.233.177.189** is a public IP address and goes to one of Google's servers.

5. Which IPv6 prefix can be routed on the Internet?

Answer: a. 2000::/3

Explanation: Global IPv6 addresses that can be routed on the Internet often begin with the prefix **2000::/3**, although other prefixes are being released. Link local addresses begin with FE80::/10. The loopback address is written ::1/128. Many unique local unicast addresses begin with FC00::/7.

Ports and Sockets

6. When hosting a secure email server for access from the Internet, which port should be open on the corporate firewall?

Answer: d. 587

Explanation: SMTP (Simple Mail Transfer Protocol) is used to send email messages to and between email servers. The old port for SMTP is 25, but encrypted transmissions to an SMTP server use port **587**. Port 110 is the non-secure port for POP3, which is another email protocol. Port 443 is the secure port for encrypted HTTP.

7. Which port should be open so you can remote into the corporate office's Linux Server from a branch office?

Answer: a. 22

Explanation: In Linux operating systems, SSH (Secure Shell) provides secure, encrypted remote access and works over port **22**. Port 3389 serves RDP (Remote Desktop Protocol) on Windows systems. Port 23 supports the unsecure Telnet. Port 1433 supports communications with Microsoft SQL Server.

Domain Names and DNS

8. When your computer requests a DNS lookup, which DNS server holds the most reliable information for that DNS record?

Answer: c. Primary DNS server

Explanation: The **primary DNS server** is the authoritative name server for the organization, which holds the authoritative DNS database for the organization's zones. The caching DNS server and forwarding DNS server might contain needed DNS information in their cache, but this information could potentially be outdated. Root

DNS servers play a role in DNS resolution by holding information used to locate the TLD (top-level domain) servers. These TLD servers hold information about the authoritative servers owned by various organizations.

9. Which DNS record type is listed first in a zone file?

Answer: d. SOA

Explanation: An **SOA (start of authority)** record is listed at the beginning of the zone file and gives important information about the zone, such as a contact email address, when the zone was last updated, how long the zone information is valid until it should be refreshed, and necessary information for how to perform a zone transfer. A (address) records, AAAA (address for IPv6) records, and CNAME (canonical name) records are placed later in the zone file and provide mapping information.

10. Which DNS record type is used to find an FQDN from a given IP address?

Answer: c. PTR

Explanation: A **PTR (pointer)** record is used for reverse lookups to provide a host name when you know an IP address. A (address) records find IPv4 addresses when the host name is known. CNAME (canonical name) records hold alternative names for a host. An MX (mail exchange) record identifies an email server.

Troubleshooting Address Problems

11. What protocol does ping use?

Answer: b. ICMP

Explanation: The protocol used by the ping echo request and echo reply is **ICMP (Internet Control Message Protocol)**, a lightweight protocol used to carry error messages and information about a network. HTTP is used for communications with web servers. DHCP is used to dynamically assign IP addresses on a network. FTP is a file transfer protocol.

12. Which command disables a computer's connection to the network?

Answer: c. `ipconfig /release`

Explanation: The `ipconfig /release` command releases the IP address when dynamic IP addressing is being used. Releasing the IP address effectively disables the computer's communications with the network until a new IP address is assigned. The `sudo ip link set eth0 up` command brings the eth0 interface to an "up" state. The `sudo hostname testVM` command sets a new hostname on a device. The `ping localhost` command pings the loopback address on a device.

13. What problem will `ping google.com` check for that `ping 8.8.8.8` will not?

Answer: d. Name resolution issues

Explanation: Pinging a host using its host name can verify you have Internet access and functioning **name resolution (DNS) services** because the host name must first be resolved before the host can be located and pinged. Pinging any device outside your network will check default gateway configuration, even if you ping its IP address instead of its host name. Pinging a target's host name or IP address will not determine whether you're using the correct DNS server. DHCP scope exhaustion is not determined with the `ping` command.

PROTOCOLS

After reading this module and completing the exercises, you should be able to:

1. Describe the functions of core TCP/IP protocols
2. Identify how each protocol's information is formatted in a TCP/IP message
3. Secure network connections using encryption protocols
4. Configure remote access connections between devices
5. Employ various TCP/IP utilities for network discovery and troubleshooting

On the Job

Intermittent errors (those that come and go) are among the most difficult to solve, so keeping careful logs of errors is often an essential troubleshooting technique. As an independent contractor for a large telecommunications company, I served on the third and final tier of a help desk that supported an application used by internal customers (company employees) over several wide area networks. The application functioned on more than 100 dedicated circuits that all terminated to feed a large database at corporate headquarters.

Transactions managed by the application were scanned for errors before they were posted to the database. Over time we were able to identify the source of most of these errors as bugs in the application. As we requested fixes from the application developer, we happily saw drastic reductions in the number of errors. However, a few intermittent errors proved to be most difficult to troubleshoot. After eliminating application bugs as the source of the problem, we began to suspect hardware. We carefully logged each error and searched for patterns of consistency: a particular circuit, client computer, branch office, type of transaction, currency, amount of transaction, time of day, and even day of the week. After weeks of logging and searching, we could not uncover a pattern and yet still intermittent errors persisted. Finally, it occurred to us to search for patterns of *no* errors. We went back through our logs and identified about 15 circuits that consistently yielded no errors since we had been keeping logs.

As we worked with the hardware teams, it came to light that these 15 or so circuits all had couplers installed and *none* of the other circuits used couplers. We all felt we had uncovered a significant clue, but still the problem wasn't solved. My team decided to request a network analyzer to monitor problematic circuits. Before we had the analyzer in place, the application developer was finally able to reproduce the problem in the lab by using progressively faster circuits. The application required a buffer on the receiving end, which held incoming data before it was processed by the application. Faster circuits produced a buffer overflow, resulting in corrupted transactions. The mystery was solved. The couplers had managed to slightly reduce performance of the circuits, which allowed the application buffer to keep up with these slightly slower circuits. After weeks of troubleshooting, the solution was a simple programmer fix: Increase the application buffer size.

Jean Andrews
Author and Independent Contractor

In Module 1, you learned that a protocol is a rule that governs how computers on a network exchange data and instructions, and then in Module 2, you learned about network infrastructure equipment. In Module 3, you learned how the data link, network, transport, and application layer protocols navigate that infrastructure with various types of addresses as they determine where to send transmitted application data and instructions. You've also learned about the tasks associated with each layer of the OSI model, such as formatting, addressing, and error correction. All these tasks are governed by protocols.

This module focuses on how an application's data and instructions make the trip from one host to another at the transport, network, and data link layers. To better understand these processes, you'll learn how protocol messages are constructed at each of these layers. You'll then explore other kinds of protocols that offer security through encryption or network access over remote connections. You'll round out the module learning about some more troubleshooting tools and common network problems.

TCP/IP CORE PROTOCOLS

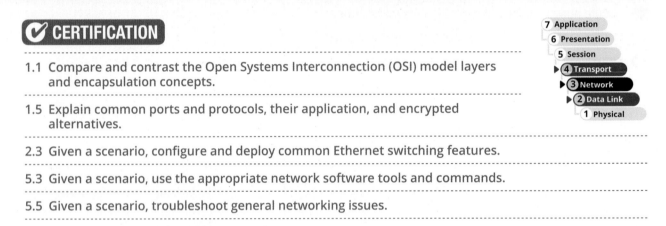

CERTIFICATION

1.1 Compare and contrast the Open Systems Interconnection (OSI) model layers and encapsulation concepts.

1.5 Explain common ports and protocols, their application, and encrypted alternatives.

2.3 Given a scenario, configure and deploy common Ethernet switching features.

5.3 Given a scenario, use the appropriate network software tools and commands.

5.5 Given a scenario, troubleshoot general networking issues.

Average reading time: 54 minutes

TCP/IP is a suite of protocols, or standards, that includes TCP, IP (IPv4 and IPv6), UDP, ARP, and many others. In this part of the module, you'll learn about message headers used at the transport layer. You'll then work your way down the layers of the OSI model, examining each layer's headers (and layer 2's trailer) along the way. First, let's summarize what you've learned so far about headers and trailers as illustrated in Figure 4-1 and described in the following list:

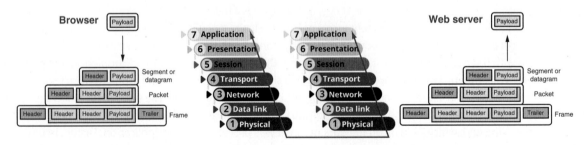

Figure 4-1 Each layer adds its own data and addresses its transmission to the corresponding layer in the destination device

- **Layers 7, 6, and 5**—Data and instructions, known as the payload, are generated by an application running on the source host. For example, in Figure 4-1, the payload is created by the browser as data passes from the highest layer of the OSI model, down on through the next two highest layers.

- **Layer 4**—In the process of encapsulation, a transport layer protocol, usually either TCP or UDP, adds a header in front of the payload. This header includes a port to identify the receiving application on the destination host. The entire message then becomes a segment (when using TCP) or datagram (when using UDP).
- **Layer 3**—The network layer adds its own header in front of the passed-down segment or datagram. This header identifies the IP address of the destination host and the message is called a packet.
- **Layer 2**—The packet is passed to the data link layer on the NIC, which encapsulates this data with its own header and trailer, creating a frame. This layer's frame includes a physical address used to find a node on the local network.
- **Layer 1**—The physical layer on the NIC receives the frame and places the actual transmission on the network.

The receiving host decapsulates the message at each layer in reverse order and then presents the payload to the receiving application. As you saw in the *On the Job* story at the beginning of this module, it's important to understand how the various OSI layers work together when you're troubleshooting a difficult-to-diagnose problem. What appears to be a problem at one layer might actually be caused by a process at a different layer.

In transit, the transmission might pass through any number of connectivity devices, such as switches and routers. Connectivity devices, also called networking devices, are specialized devices that allow two or more networks or multiple parts of one network to connect and exchange data. Each device is known by the innermost OSI layer header it reads and processes, as shown in Figure 4-2. For example, if a switch reads and processes the data link layer header but passes the message along without reading higher-layer headers, it is known as a layer 2 switch. In contrast, a router that reads and processes the network layer header and leaves alone the transport layer header is known as a layer 3 device. A layer 4 firewall will dig deep enough to read the transport layer header to check which port a message is directed to, and a layer 7 firewall might read through the entire message to check for signs of malware.

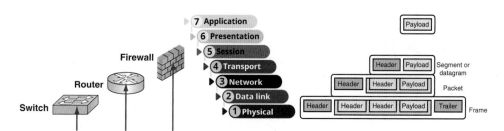

Figure 4-2   Connectivity devices are known by the highest OSI layer they read and process

With this quick review in hand, let's examine the details of the core TCP/IP protocols, beginning with TCP.

TCP (Transmission Control Protocol)

Recall that TCP operates in the transport layer of the OSI model and provides reliable data delivery services. It's helpful to compare TCP to making a phone call as you look at three characteristics of TCP in its role as a reliable delivery protocol:

- **Connection-oriented**—Before TCP transmits data, it ensures that a connection or session is established, similar to making sure someone is listening on the other end of a phone call before you start talking. TCP uses a three-step process called a **three-way handshake** to establish a TCP connection. This process is described in detail later in this section. Only after TCP establishes this connection does it transmit the actual data, such as an HTTP request for a web page.

- **Sequencing and checksums**—In the analogy of a phone call, you might ask the other person if they can hear you clearly, and repeat a sentence as necessary. In the same vein, TCP sends a character string called a checksum; TCP on the destination host then generates a similar string. If the two checksums fail to match, the destination host asks the source to retransmit the data. In addition, because messages don't always arrive in the same order they were created, TCP attaches a chronological sequence number to each segment so the destination host can, if necessary, reorder segments as they arrive.
- **Flow control**—You might slow down your talking over the phone if the other person needs a slower pace to hear every word and understand your message. Similarly, flow control is the process of gauging the appropriate rate of transmission based on how quickly the recipient can accept data. For example, suppose a receiver indicates its buffer can handle up to 4000 bytes. The sender will issue up to 4000 bytes in one or many small packets and then pause, waiting for an acknowledgment before sending more data.

TCP manages all these elements—the three-way handshake, checksums, sequencing, and flow control—by posting data to fields in the TCP header at the beginning of a TCP segment.

Fields in a TCP Segment

Figure 4-3 lists the items, called fields, included in a TCP segment. Each block shown in the figure represents a series of bits with each row representing 32 bits. If you were to string the rows alongside each other, in order from top to bottom, you would create one, long series of bits. This is a TCP segment. All the fields except the last one, the data field, are part of the TCP header. The content of the data field is the entire message passed down from the layer above the transport layer.

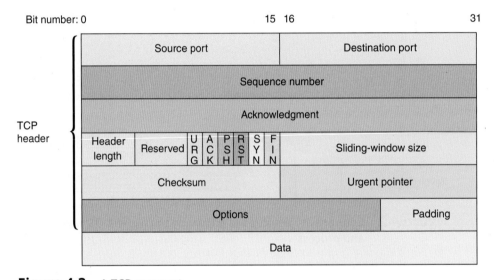

Figure 4-3 A TCP segment

NOTE 4-1

Headers are constructed in groups of 32 bits called words. Each word consists of 4 bytes, called blocks, of 8 bits each. This explains why diagrams of headers, such as the one in Figure 4-3, are depicted in 32-bit groups.

The fields shown in Figure 4-3 are defined in Table 4-1. Remember, the data field in the bottom row is not part of the TCP header. When the TCP segment is sent down to the network layer (layer 3), the entire segment becomes the data portion of an IP message. This payload is then encapsulated in an IP packet.

Table 4-1   Fields in a TCP segment

Field	Length	Function
Source port	16 bits	Indicates the port at the source host. Recall that a port is the number that identifies a process on a host. The port allows a process to be available for incoming or outgoing data.
Destination port	16 bits	Indicates the port at the destination host.
Sequence number	32 bits	Identifies the data segment's position in the stream of data segments being sent.
Acknowledgment number	32 bits	Confirms receipt of data via a return message to the sender.
TCP header length	4 bits	Indicates the length of the TCP header in bytes. The header can be a minimum of 20 bytes to a maximum of 60 bytes in 4-byte increments. It's also called the Data offset field because it indicates the offset from the beginning of the segment until the start of the data carried by the segment.
Reserved	6 bits	Indicates a field reserved for later use.
Flags	6 bits	Identifies a collection of six 1-bit fields or flags that signal special conditions about other fields in the header. The following flags are available to the sender: • **URG**—If set to *1*, the Urgent pointer field later in the segment contains information for the receiver. If set to *0*, the receiver will ignore the Urgent pointer field. • **ACK**—If set to *1*, the Acknowledgment field earlier in the segment contains information for the receiver. If set to *0*, the receiver will ignore the Acknowledgment field. • **PSH**—If set to *1*, data should be sent to an application without buffering. • **RST**—If set to *1*, the sender is requesting that the connection be reset. • **SYN**—If set to *1*, the sender is requesting a synchronization of the sequence numbers between the two nodes. This code indicates that no payload is included in the segment, and the acknowledgment number should be increased by 1 in response. • **FIN**—If set to *1*, the segment is the last in a sequence and the connection should be closed.
Sliding-window size (or window)	16 bits	Indicates how many bytes the sender can issue to a receiver before acknowledgment is received. This field performs flow control, preventing the receiver's buffer from being deluged with bytes.
Checksum	16 bits	Allows the receiving node to determine whether the TCP segment became corrupted during transmission.
Urgent pointer	16 bits	Indicates a location in the data field where urgent data resides.
Options	0–32 bits	Specifies special options, such as the maximum segment size a network can handle.
Padding	Variable	Contains filler bits to ensure that the size of the TCP header is a multiple of 32 bits.
Data	Variable	Contains data sent by the source host. The data field is not part of the TCP header—it is encapsulated by the TCP header. The size of the data field depends on how much data needs to be transmitted, the constraints on the TCP segment size imposed by the network type, and the limitation that the segment must fit within an IP packet at the next layer.

Now let's see how the fields in the TCP header are used to perform a three-way handshake to establish a TCP session.

TCP Three-Way Handshake

The TCP three-way handshake establishes a session before TCP transmits the actual data, such as an HTTP request for a web page. Think about how a handshake works when meeting a new acquaintance. You reach out your hand, not knowing how the other person will respond. If the person offers their hand in return, the two of you grasp hands, and you can then proceed with the conversation. Figure 4-4 shows the three transmissions in a TCP handshake, which are summarized in the following list:

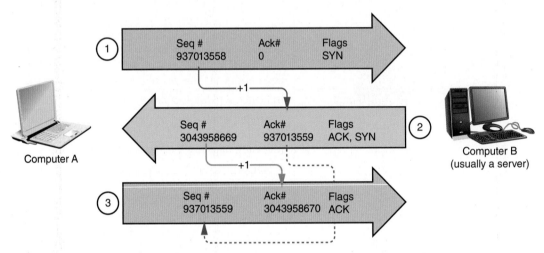

Figure 4-4   The three-way handshake process establishes a TCP session

Step 1, SYN (request for a connection)—Computer A issues a message to computer B with the following information:

- In its Sequence number field, computer A selects and sends a seemingly random number that will be used to synchronize communication. In Figure 4-4, for example, this number is 937013558.
- Its SYN bit is set to 1, which means the SYN flag is activated. This indicates the desire to communicate and synchronize sequence numbers. It's as if computer A is offering a hand to computer B to see if there will be a response.
- The ACK bit is usually set to 0 for this first transmission because there is no information yet from computer B to acknowledge.

Step 2, SYN/ACK (response to the request)—When computer B receives this message, it responds with a segment containing the following information:

- The ACK and SYN bits are both set to 1, essentially saying, "Yes, I'm here *and* I'm listening."
- The Acknowledgment number field contains a number that equals the sequence number computer A originally sent, plus 1. As Figure 4-4 illustrates, computer B sends the number 937013559. In this manner, computer B signals to computer A that it has received the request for communication and further, it expects computer A to respond again with the sequence number 937013559.
- In its Sequence number field, computer B sends its own seemingly random number (in Figure 4-4, this number is 3043958669).

Step 3, ACK (connection established)—Computer A issues a segment with the following information:

- The sequence number is 937013559 because this is what computer B indicated it expects to receive.
- The Acknowledgment number field equals the sequence number that computer B sent, plus 1. In the example, this number is 3043958670.
- The ACK bit is set to 1.

The connection has now been established, and in the next message, computer A will begin data transmission.

Up until this point, no payload has been included in any of the three initial messages, and the sequence numbers have increased by exactly 1 in each acknowledgment. After these three transmissions, the payload or data is sent. This can be done in a single message for a small amount of data, such as a web page request, or fragmented over several messages, such as the data for the web page itself.

At this point, the sequence numbers will each be increased by the number of bits included in each received segment as confirmation that the correct length of message was received. In the example shown in Figure 4-4, computer A will send the next message, which will include the payload (such as an HTTP request) from a higher OSI layer. Suppose that computer A's web page request message, the fourth message in this session, is 725 bits long. Computer B will receive this message, count the bits, and add 725 to the sequence number (937013559) of the received message. This new number, 937014284, becomes the acknowledgment number for the return message (which would be the fifth message in the session).

The two hosts continue communicating in this manner until computer A issues a segment whose FIN bit is set to 1, indicating the end of the transmission.

NOTE 4-2

The ISN (Initial Sequence Number) of the first SYN message in the three-way handshake appears to be random, but in reality, it is calculated by a specific, clock-based algorithm, which varies by operating system. The existence of these algorithms and their predictability is actually a security loophole that hackers can use to undermine a host's availability for connections.

Applying Concepts 4-1: Examine a Sample TCP Header

In Project 2-4, you captured and filtered to a TCP stream using Wireshark. Now that you know the function of each TCP segment field, you can interpret a segment's header contents. Let's practice with an example. Figure 4-5 shows a sample TCP header.

```
Transmission Control Protocol, Src Port: http (80), Dst Port: 1958 (1958), Seq: 3043958669, Ack: 937013559, Len: 0
     Source port : http (80)
     Destination port: 1958 (1958)
     Sequence number: 3043958669
     Acknowledgment number: 937013559
     Header length: 24 bytes
 ⊟ Flags:_ 0xx0012 (SYN, ACK)
        0... .... = Congestion Window Reduced (CWR): Not set
        .0.. .... = ECN-Echo: Not set
        ..0. .... = Urgent: Not set
        ...1 .... = Acknowledgment: Set
        .... 0... = Push: Not set
        .... .0.. = Reset: Not set
        .... ..1. = Syn: Set
        .... ...0 = Fin: not set
     window size: 5840
     Checksum: 0x206a (correct)
 ⊟ Options: (4bytes)
        Maximum segment size: 1460 bytes
```

Figure 4-5   TCP segment header

Suppose the segment in Figure 4-5 was sent from computer B to computer A. Table 4-2 interprets the rows shown in Figure 4-5, beginning with the row labeled "Source port."

Table 4-2 Translation of TCP field data

Field name	TCP header data
Source port	The segment was issued from computer B's port 80, the port assigned to HTTP by default.
Destination port	The segment is addressed to port 1958 on computer A.
Sequence number	The segment is identified by sequence number 3043958669.
Acknowledgment number	By containing a value other than zero, this field informs computer A that its last communication was received. Computer B is indicating that the next segment it receives from computer A should have the sequence number of 937013559, which is the same as this segment's acknowledgment number.
Header length	The TCP header is 24 bytes long—4 bytes larger than its minimum size, which means that some of the available options were specified or the padding space was used.
Flags: Congestion Window Reduced (CWR) and ECN-Echo	These optional flags can be used to help TCP react to and reduce traffic congestion. They are only available when TCP is establishing a connection. However, in this segment, they are not activated.
Flags: Acknowledgment and Syn	Of all the possible flags in the Figure 4-5 segment, only the ACK and SYN flags are set. This means that computer B is acknowledging the last segment it received from computer A, and it's also negotiating a synchronization scheme for sequencing.
Window size	The window size is 5840, meaning that computer B can accept 5840 bytes of data from computer A before computer A should expect an acknowledgment.
Checksum	The valid outcome of the error-checking algorithm used to verify the segment's header is 0x206a. When computer A receives this segment, it will perform the same calculation, and if the result matches, it will know the TCP header arrived without damage.
Maximum segment size	The maximum TCP segment size for this session is 1460 bytes.

NOTE 4-3

A computer doesn't "see" the TCP segment as it's organized and formatted in Figure 4-5. The information in Figure 4-5 was generated by a **protocol analyzer** (in this case, Wireshark), which is an application that collects and examines network messages. Wireshark translates each message into a user-friendly format. From the computer's standpoint, the TCP segment arrives as a series of bits: 0s and 1s. The computer relies on TCP standards to determine how to interpret each bit in the segment based on its location and value. You'll use the Wireshark protocol analyzer again in a later module.

TCP is not the only core protocol at the transport layer. A similar but less complex protocol, UDP, is discussed next.

UDP (User Datagram Protocol)

UDP (User Datagram Protocol) is an unreliable, connectionless protocol. The term *unreliable* does not mean that UDP can't be used reliably. Instead, it means that UDP does not guarantee delivery of data, and no connection is established by UDP before data is transmitted. By default, UDP provides no handshake to establish a connection, acknowledgment of transmissions received, error checking, sequencing, or flow control and is, therefore, more efficient and faster than TCP. Instead of conversing with someone on a phone call, this would be more like talking on a radio show where you send out your signal whether anyone is listening or not. UDP is useful when a great volume of data must be transferred quickly, such as live audio or video transmissions over the Internet. It's also used for small requests, such as DNS, or in situations when the data changes often and speed is more important than complete accuracy, such as when gaming over a network.

7 Application
6 Presentation
5 Session
▶ 4 Transport
3 Network
2 Data Link
1 Physical

In contrast to a TCP header's 10 fields, the UDP header contains only four fields: Source port, Destination port, Length, and Checksum. Use of the UDP Checksum field is optional on IPv4 networks but required for IPv6 transmissions. Figure 4-6 depicts a UDP datagram. Contrast its header with the much larger TCP segment header shown earlier in Figure 4-3.

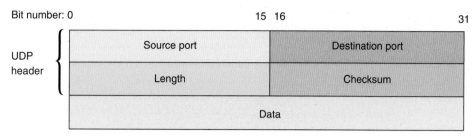

Figure 4-6   A UDP datagram

NOTE 4-4

Application layer protocols can work in conjunction with UDP to emulate some of the reliability normally provided by TCP. For example, RTP (Real-time Transport Protocol), which is used to transmit audio and video on the web, operates at the application layer of the OSI model and relies on UDP at the transport layer. RTP applies its own sequence numbers to indicate the order in which messages should be assembled at their destination. These sequence numbers also help to indicate whether messages were lost during transmission.

Now that you understand the functions of and differences between TCP and UDP at layer 4, you're ready to step down a layer and learn more about IP (Internet Protocol) at layer 3. TCP segments and UDP datagrams are often passed down to IP for further encapsulation at the network layer.

IP (Internet Protocol)

IP (Internet Protocol) belongs to the network layer of the OSI model. It specifies where data should be delivered, identifying the data's source and destination IP addresses. IP is the protocol that enables TCP/IP to internetwork—that is, to traverse more than one LAN segment and more than one type of network through a router. As you know, at the network layer of the OSI model, data is organized in packets. The IP packet acts as an addressed envelope for data and contains information necessary for routers to transfer data between different LAN segments, getting data where it needs to go.

IP is a connectionless protocol, meaning IP does not establish a session to send its packets. Each IP packet travels separately from all other packets in its series, where some messages might take a different route than others even if they're going to the same place. Once IP delivers the message to the correct host, it depends on TCP to ensure the messages are reassembled in the right order, if that's necessary. It also relies on either TCP or UDP to ensure each message reaches the correct application on the receiving host.

As you already know, two versions of IP are used on networks today. IPv4, which was introduced to the public in 1981, is still the standard on most networks. IPv6 was released in 1998 and offers better security, better prioritization provisions, more automatic IP address configurations, and additional IP addresses. Most new applications, servers, clients, and network devices support IPv6. However, due to the cost of upgrading infrastructure, many organizations have hesitated to transition their networks from IPv4. As a network support technician, you need to know how to support both versions of IP. Let's first see how IPv4 packets are constructed, and then you'll look at how IPv6 packets differ.

IPv4 Packets

Figure 4-7 depicts an IPv4 packet. Its fields are explained in Table 4-3. Note that the data field in the bottom row of the table does not belong to the IPv4 header.

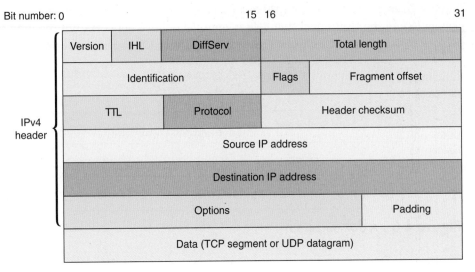

Figure 4-7   An IPv4 packet

Table 4-3   Fields in an IPv4 packet

Field	Length	Function
Version	4 bits	Identifies the version number of the protocol—for example, IPv4 or IPv6. The receiving workstation looks at this field first to determine whether it can read the incoming data. If it cannot, it will reject the packet.
IHL (Internet header length)	4 bits	Indicates the length of the IP header in bytes. The header can be a minimum of 20 bytes to a maximum of 60 bytes in 4-byte increments. It's also called the Data offset field because it indicates the offset from the beginning of the packet until the start of the data carried by the packet.
DiffServ (Differentiated services)	8 bits	Informs routers the level of precedence they should apply when processing the incoming packet. Differentiated services allows up to 64 values and a wide range of priority-handling options.
Total length	16 bits	Identifies the total length of the IP packet, including the header and data, in bytes. An IP packet, including its header and data, cannot exceed 65,535 bytes.
Identification	16 bits	Identifies the message to which a packet belongs and enables the receiving host to reassemble fragmented messages. This field and the following two fields, Flags and Fragment offset, assist in reassembly of fragmented packets. IP packets that are larger than what the network allows are fragmented into smaller packets for transmission and then reassembled by the receiver.
Flags	3 bits	Indicates whether a message is fragmented and, if it is fragmented, whether this packet is the last fragment. The first bit is reserved for future use. When the second bit is set, it prevents the packet from being fragmented. A value of 1 in the third bit indicates more fragments are on the way.
Fragment offset	13 bits	Identifies where the packet fragment belongs in the series of incoming fragments.

Field	Length	Function
TTL (Time to Live)	8 bits	Indicates the maximum duration that the packet can remain on the network before it is discarded. Although this field was originally meant to represent units of time, on modern networks it represents the maximum number of router **hops** it has remaining, which is the number of times a packet can still be forwarded by a router to another router. The TTL for packets varies and can be configured; it is usually set at 32 or 64. Each time a packet passes through a router, its TTL is reduced by 1. When a router receives a packet with a TTL equal to 0, it discards that packet and sends a *TTL expired* message via ICMP back to the source host.
Protocol	8 bits	Identifies the type of protocol contained in the payload of the packet (for example, TCP, UDP, or ICMP).
Header checksum	16 bits	Allows the receiving host to calculate whether the IP header has been corrupted during transmission. If the checksum accompanying the message does not match the calculated checksum when the packet is received, the packet is presumed to be corrupt and is discarded.
Source IP address	32 bits	Indicates the IPv4 address of the source host.
Destination IP address	32 bits	Indicates the IPv4 address of the destination host.
Options	Variable	May contain optional routing and timing information.
Padding	Variable	Contains filler bits to ensure that the header is a multiple of 32 bits.
Data	Variable	Includes the data originally sent by the source host, plus any headers from higher layers. The data field is not part of the IP header—it is encapsulated by the IP header.

Applying Concepts 4-2: Examine a Sample IPv4 Header

Let's examine the IPv4 header shown in the Wireshark capture in Figure 4-8. The fields are explained in Table 4-4, beginning with the Version field.

```
☐Internet Protocol, Src Addr: 140.147.249.7 (140.147.249.7), Dst Addr: 10.11.11.51 (10.11.11.51)
       Version: 4
       Header length: 20 bytes
    ⊞ Differentiated Services Field: 0x00 (DSCP 0x00: Default; ECN 0x00)
       Total Length: 44
       Identification: 0x0000 (0)
    ☐Flags: 0x04
          .1.. = Don't fragment: Set
          ..0. = More fragments: Not set
       Fragment offset: 0
       Time to live: 64
       Protocol: TCP (0x06)
       Header checksum: 0x9ff3 (correct)
       Source: 140.147.249.7 (140.147.249.7)
       Destination: 10.11.11.51 (10.11.11.51)
```

Figure 4-8   IPv4 packet header

Table 4-4   Explanation of IPv4 header fields listed in Figure 4-8

Field name	IPv4 header data
Version	The transmission relies on version 4 of the Internet Protocol.
Header length	The packet has a header length of 20 bytes. Because this is the minimum size for an IP header, you can deduce that the packet contains no options or padding.
Differentiated Services Field	No options for priority handling are set, which is not unusual in routine data exchanges such as requesting a web page.
Total Length	The total length of the packet is 44 bytes. This makes sense when you consider that its header is 20 bytes and the TCP segment that it encapsulates is 24 bytes. Considering that the maximum size of an IP packet is 65,535 bytes, this is a very small packet.
Identification	This field uniquely identifies the packet. This packet, the first one issued from computer B to computer A in the TCP connection exchange, is identified in hexadecimal notation as 0x0000 or simply 0.
Flag: Don't fragment and Fragment offset	The Don't fragment option is set to 1, indicating this packet is not fragmented. And because it's not fragmented, the Fragment offset field does not apply and is set to 0.
Time to live	This packet's TTL is set to 64. If the packet were to keep traversing networks, it would be allowed 64 more hops before it was discarded.
Protocol	This field indicates that a TCP segment is encapsulated within the packet. TCP is always indicated by the hexadecimal string of 0x06.
Header checksum	This field provides the correct header checksum answer, which is used by the recipient of this packet to determine whether the header was damaged in transit.
Source and Destination	These last two fields show the IPv4 addresses for the packet's source and destination, respectively.

IPv6 Packets

Due to the added information it carries, IPv6 uses a different packet format than IPv4. The fields in an IPv6 packet header are shown in Figure 4-9 and described in Table 4-5. Remember that the data field in the bottom row does not belong to the IPv6 header.

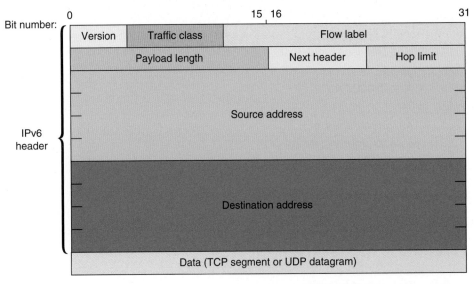

Figure 4-9   An IPv6 packet

Table 4-5 Fields in an IPv6 packet

Field	Length	Function
Version	4 bits	Indicates which IP version the packet uses.
Traffic class	8 bits	Identifies the packet's priority. It is similar to, but not the same as, the DiffServ field in IPv4 packets.
Flow label	20 bits	Indicates which flow, or sequence of packets from one source to one or multiple destinations, the packet belongs to. Routers interpret flow information to ensure that packets belonging to the same transmission arrive together. Flow information may also help with traffic prioritization.
Payload length	16 bits	Indicates the size of the payload, or data, carried by the packet. Unlike the Total length field in IPv4 packets, the Payload length in IPv6 packets does not refer to the size of the whole packet.
Next header	8 bits	Identifies the type of header that immediately follows the IPv6 packet header, usually TCP or UDP.
Hop limit	8 bits	Indicates the number of times the packet can be forwarded by routers on the network, similar to the TTL field in IPv4 packets. When the hop limit reaches 0, the packet is discarded.
Source address	128 bits	Indicates the full IPv6 address of the source host.
Destination address	128 bits	Indicates the full IPv6 address of the destination host.
Data	Variable	Includes the data originally sent by the source host, plus any headers from higher layers. The data field is not part of the IPv6 header—it is encapsulated by the IPv6 header.

If you compare the fields and functions listed in Table 4-5 with those listed for the IPv4 packet in Table 4-3, you'll notice some similarities and some differences. For example, both packets begin with a 4-bit Version field. Other fields, such as the TTL in IPv4 and the hop limit in IPv6, are similar, but slightly different. One striking difference between the two versions is that IPv6 packets accommodate the much longer IPv6 addresses. Also, there is no Fragment offset field in IPv6 packets. This is because IPv6 hosts adjust their packet sizes to fit the requirements of the network before sending IPv6 messages.

Applying Concepts 4-3: Examine a Sample IPv6 Header

Figure 4-10 shows the contents of an IPv6 packet header captured by Wireshark, and Table 4-6 breaks down what it all means. This packet formed part of a message issued by ping.

```
⊟ Internet Protocol Version 6, Src: 2001:470:1f10:1a6::2 (2001:470:1f10:1a6::2), Dst: 2001:470
  ⊞ 0110 .... = Version: 6
  ⊞ .... 0000 0000 .... .... .... .... .... = Traffic class: 0x00000000
    .... .... .... 0000 0000 0000 0000 0000 = Flowlabel: 0x00000000
    Payload length: 64
    Next header: ICMPv6 (0x3a)
    Hop limit: 64
    Source: 2001:470:1f10:1a6::2 (2001:470:1f10:1a6::2)
    Destination: 2001:470:1f10:1a6::1 (2001:470:1f10:1a6::1)
```

Figure 4-10 IPv6 packet header

Table 4-6   Explanation of IPv6 header fields listed in Figure 4-10

Field name	IPv6 header data
Version	Version 6 of the Internet Protocol is used, expressed in binary format as 0110.
Traffic class and Flowlabel	Both these fields are set to 0x00000000, which means neither field has a specified value. Routers receiving a packet that lacks Traffic class or Flow label information will not prioritize the packet or make any guarantees that it will reach its destination at the same time as any other packets. For many types of traffic, this is perfectly acceptable.
Payload length	This packet carries 64 bits of data. Considering that IPv6 packets can carry payloads as large as 64 KB, this is a very small packet.
Next header	The data in this packet's payload belongs to an ICMPv6 transmission.
Hop limit	This packet can be forwarded by routers up to 64 times before it is discarded.
Source and Destination	These last two fields show the IPv6 addresses for the packet's source and destination hosts, respectively.

IP is the primary network layer protocol, but another layer 3 protocol, ICMP, also plays a significant role on both IPv4 and IPv6 networks. Let's see how ICMP works, and then you'll round out your list of protocols with ARP, NDP, and Ethernet at layer 2.

ICMP (Internet Control Message Protocol)

Whereas IP helps direct data to its correct destination, ICMP (Internet Control Message Protocol) is a core network layer protocol that reports on the success or failure of data delivery. It can indicate when part of a network is congested, when data fails to reach its destination, and when data has been discarded because the allotted Time to Live has expired (that is, when the data has traveled its allotted number of hops without reaching its destination). ICMP announces these transmission failures to the sender, but it does not correct errors it detects—those functions are left to higher-layer protocols, such as TCP. Instead, ICMP's announcements provide critical information for troubleshooting network problems. ICMP messages are generated automatically by network devices, such as routers, and by utilities, such as ping.

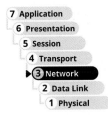

Because it operates at layer 3 alongside IP, ICMP messages contain both an IP header and an ICMP header. Figure 4-11 depicts an ICMP header that is inserted after the ICMP message's IP header. The fields are explained in Table 4-7. Note that the data field in the bottom row of the table does not belong to the ICMP header.

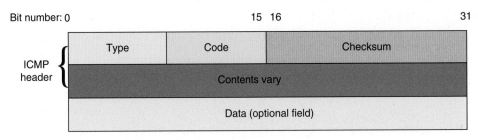

Figure 4-11   An ICMP packet

Table 4-7   An ICMP packet

Field	Length	Function
Type	8 bits	Indicates the type of ICMP message, such as Destination Unreachable.
Code	8 bits	Indicates the subtype of the message, such as Destination host unknown.
Checksum	16 bits	Allows the receiving node to determine whether the ICMP packet became corrupted during transmission.
Rest of header	32 bits	Varies depending on message type and subtype.
Data	Variable	Usually contains the IP header and first 8 bytes of the data portion of the IP packet that triggered the ICMP message.

IPv6 relies on ICMPv6 (Internet Control Message Protocol for use with IPv6) to perform the functions that ICMPv4 and ARP perform in IPv4 networks. This includes detecting and reporting data transmission errors, discovering other nodes on a network, and managing multicasting. To understand the different purposes of ICMPv4 and ICMPv6, let's first take a closer look at ARP at layer 2 on IPv4 networks.

ARP (Address Resolution Protocol) on IPv4 Networks

ARP (Address Resolution Protocol) works in conjunction with IPv4 to discover the MAC address of a node on the local network and to maintain a database that maps local IPv4 addresses to MAC addresses. ARP is a layer 2 protocol that works with IPv4 in layer 3. It's sometimes said to function at layer 2.5 because it touches information (IP addresses and MAC addresses) at both layers. However, it operates only within its local network bound by routers.

| 7 Application |
| 6 Presentation |
| 5 Session |
| 4 Transport |
| 3 Network |
| ▶ 2 Data Link |
| 1 Physical |

ARP relies on broadcasting, which transmits simultaneously to all nodes on a particular network segment. For example, if one node needs to know the MAC address of another node on the same network, the first node issues a broadcast message to the network, using ARP, that essentially says, "Will the computer with the IP address 1.2.3.4 please send me its MAC address?" The node with the IP address 1.2.3.4 then transmits a reply containing its physical address.

The database of IP-to-MAC address mappings is called an **ARP table** or ARP cache, and it is kept on a computer's hard drive. Each OS can use its own format for the ARP table. A sample ARP table is shown in Figure 4-12.

```
IP Address           Hardware Address      Type

123.45.67.80         60:23:A6:F1:C4:D2     Static
123.45.67.89         20:00:3D:21:E0:11     Dynamic
123.45.67.73         A0:BB:77:C2:25:FA     Dynamic
```

Figure 4-12   Sample ARP table

ARP tables might contain two types of entries:

- **Dynamic ARP table entries** are created when a client makes an ARP request for information that could not be satisfied by data already in the ARP table; once received, the new information is recorded in the table for future reference.
- **Static ARP table entries** are those that someone has entered manually using the ARP utility. This ARP utility, accessed via the `arp` command in both Windows and Linux, provides a way of obtaining information from and manipulating a device's ARP table.

To view a Windows workstation's ARP table, open a PowerShell or Command Prompt window and enter the command `arp -a`. Figure 4-13 shows sample results of this command run on a computer connected to a home network and to a virtual network in VirtualBox. The first line of each set of records contains the interface IP address, which is the local computer's address on that network. The columns and rows below it contain the addresses of other nodes on the network, along with their physical addresses (MAC addresses) and record types.

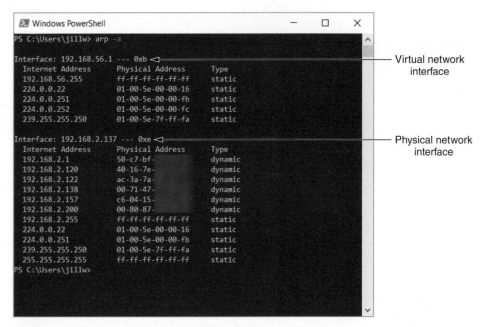

Figure 4-13 The `arp -a` command lists devices on the network

The `arp` command can be used on IPv4 devices to diagnose and repair problems with ARP tables, as described next:

- If you notice inconsistent connectivity issues related to certain addresses, you might need to flush the ARP table on any device experiencing the problem with the command `arp -d`. This forces the device to repopulate its ARP table and correct any errors. You can also list a specific IP address to delete only that one record from the ARP table: `arp -d 192.168.1.15`. After deleting an entry, you can run a ping to repopulate the ARP table with the target device's information.
- The command `arp -s` can be used to add a static entry to the ARP table. For example, the following command run with elevated permissions would add a mapping of the listed IP address with the listed MAC address: `arp -s 192.168.1.15 00-11-22-AA-BB-CC`

NDP (Neighbor Discovery Protocol)

On IPv4 networks, neighbor discovery is managed by ARP with help from ICMP. However, IPv6 devices learn about other devices on their networks through a process called neighbor discovery. **NDP (Neighbor Discovery Protocol)** information carried in ICMPv6 messages automatically detects neighboring devices and automatically adjusts when neighboring nodes fail or are removed from the network. NDP eliminates the need for ARP and some ICMP functions in IPv6 networks, and it's much more resistant to hacking attempts than ARP.

The SLAAC process you learned about earlier is managed by NDP, as are router and network prefix discovery and neighbor discovery. NDP offers several ICMPv6 message types to perform these tasks, as follows:

- **RA (router advertisement)**—A router periodically sends an RA message out each of its configured interfaces to provide information about the network prefix, link MTU, and hop limits. The router might also advertise itself as the default router.
- **RS (router solicitation)**—To avoid waiting for the next scheduled RA message, a newly connected IPv6 host can send an RS message to request information from the router right away.
- **Redirect**—A router might send this type of message to inform hosts on the network that another router is a better gateway for a particular destination network.

- **NS (neighbor solicitation)**—IPv6 devices send NS messages to request the MAC address of a neighboring node (in IPv6, the MAC address is called the link-layer address). These messages are used to ensure no two devices are using the same IPv6 address and to verify a neighbor's reachability.
- **NA (neighbor advertisement)**—IPv6 devices send NA messages in response to NS messages to inform other network devices of their MAC address information.

Ethernet

The most important data link layer standard, Ethernet, is adaptable, capable of running on a variety of network media, and offers excellent throughput at a reasonable cost. Because of its many advantages, Ethernet is, by far, the most popular network technology used on modern LANs. Ethernet II is the current Ethernet standard and was developed by DEC, Intel, and Xerox (abbreviated as DIX) before IEEE began to standardize Ethernet.

Other Ethernet standards exist, such as Ethernet 802.3. However, those standards tend to be used only for backward compatibility or to meet the needs of specific situations or vendor-specific devices. Other Ethernet standards add more fields to the header, which allows for more nuanced control of messages (even establishing a session similar to what TCP does at the transport layer). The tradeoff is that less space is allotted for data when using additional fields from other Ethernet standards. Interestingly, the data link layer can be divided into two sublayers, as follows:

- **LLC (logical link control) sublayer**—The upper portion of the data link layer that identifies the type of message (the only LLC sublayer function in an Ethernet II frame) and handles multiplexing, flow and error control, and reliability (requires other types of Ethernet frames).
- **MAC sublayer**—The lower portion of the data link layer that identifies the destination and source MAC addresses, includes the message, and provides the checksum in the frame's trailer.

Unlike higher-layer protocols, Ethernet adds both a header and a trailer to the payload it inherits from the layer above it. This creates a frame around the payload. Figure 4-14 depicts an Ethernet II frame, and the details of the Ethernet II frame fields are listed in Table 4-8.

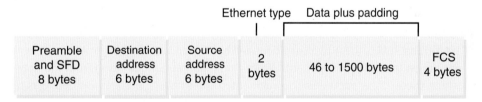

Figure 4-14 Ethernet II frame

Table 4-8 Fields of an Ethernet II frame

Field name	Length	Description
Preamble	7 bytes	Synchronizes the recipient's receiver clock.*
SFD (start frame delimiter)	1 byte	Indicates the frame is about to begin.*
Destination address	6 bytes	Provides the recipient's MAC address.
Source address	6 bytes	Provides the sender's MAC address.
Type field	2 bytes	Specifies the upper-layer protocol carried in the frame. For example, an IP packet has 0x0800 in the Type field. In an Ethernet II frame, this field is the only component of the LLC sublayer.
Data	46 bytes to 1500 bytes	If the data is not at least 46 bytes, padding is added to meet the minimum.
FCS (frame check sequence)	4 bytes	Ensures that the data at the destination exactly matches the data issued from the source using the CRC (cyclic redundancy check) algorithm.

*Not included when calculating a frame's total size

Notice in Table 4-8 that the preamble and SFD fields are not included when calculating a frame's size. Most protocol analyzers such as Wireshark can't capture these first two fields (and sometimes not even the FCS), as this data is removed from incoming transmissions by the hardware before it becomes visible to any but the most sophisticated capture tools.

Together, the header and the FCS make up the 18-byte "frame" around the data. The data portion of an Ethernet frame may contain from 46 to 1500 bytes of information. Therefore, you can calculate the minimum and maximum frame sizes:

- 18-byte frame + 46 bytes minimum data size = 64 bytes minimum frame size
- 18-byte frame + 1500 bytes maximum data size = 1518 bytes maximum frame size

MTU (maximum transmission unit) is the largest size, in bytes, that routers in a message's path will allow at the network layer. Therefore, this defines the maximum payload size that a layer 2 frame can encapsulate. For Ethernet, the default MTU is 1500 bytes, a value that is generally considered the Internet standard. However, other layer 2 technologies might allow higher MTUs or require lower MTUs. Because of the overhead present in each frame and the time it takes for the NIC to manage a frame, the use of larger frame sizes on a network generally results in faster throughput.

There are a couple of notable exceptions to Ethernet frame size limitations:

- Ethernet frames on a VLAN (virtual LAN) can have an extra 4-byte field between the Source address field and the Type field, which is used to manage VLAN traffic. If this field exists, the maximum frame size is 1522 bytes. You'll learn more about VLANs later.
- Some special-purpose networks use a proprietary version of Ethernet that allows for a **jumbo frame**, in which the MTU can be set above 9,000 bytes, depending on the type of Ethernet architecture used.

NOTE 4-5

You might have noticed that the maximum size of an IP packet is 65,535 bytes, while the maximum size of a network layer packet being transmitted over an Ethernet network is only 1500 bytes. Why the discrepancy?

Fragmentation is the process of dividing packets that are too large for a network's hardware into smaller packets that can safely traverse the network. In an IPv4 network, routers examine incoming packets to determine if the packet size is larger than the outgoing interface's MTU (that is, if the packet is larger than 1500 bytes) and if the packet is allowed to be fragmented. A packet that meets these two conditions will be divided into smaller packets, each with its own header that indicates its position in the series of fragments. While the IP packet handed down from the network layer can be thousands of bytes long, these longer packets will be fragmented into smaller messages for framing at the data link layer.

Fragmentation slows down network communications, so ideally, MTUs are set at a level that works for all devices along the message's path. TCP also helps avoid fragmentation by negotiating at the beginning of a session an MSS (maximum segment size), which defines the maximum size of the transport layer message.

Legacy Networking: Collisions and CSMA/CD

When IEEE released its first 802.3 standard in the early 1980s, it was officially called IEEE 802.3 CSMA/CD (Carrier Sense Multiple Access with Collision Detection), and was unofficially called Ethernet after the similar DIX standard that was published a few years earlier. As you've already learned, a CSMA/CD frame uses a slightly different layout than the Ethernet II frame layout. The IEEE frame is called an 802.3 frame, and the Ethernet II frame is called a DIX frame.

CSMA/CD networks often used a hub at the physical layer of the OSI model. All nodes connected to a hub compete for access to the network. The MAC (media access control) method used by nodes for arbitration on the network is **CSMA/CD (Carrier Sense Multiple Access with Collision Detection)**. Take a minute to think about the full name *Carrier Sense Multiple Access with Collision Detection*:

- *Carrier Sense* refers to an Ethernet NIC listening and waiting until no other nodes are transmitting data.
- *Multiple Access* refers to several nodes accessing the same network media.
- *Collision Detection* refers to what happens when two nodes attempt a transmission at the same time.

When the transmissions of two nodes interfere with each other, a **collision** happens. After a collision, each node waits a random amount of time and then resends the transmission. A **collision domain** is the portion of a network in which collisions can occur. Hubs connecting multiple computers in a star-bus topology resulted in massive collisions.

Recall that structured cabling guidelines provide detailed recommendations on the maximum distances cable segments can run between nodes. It's interesting to note that these maximum cable lengths are partly determined by CSMA/CD. If a cable is too long, the entire message can be transmitted before a collision can be detected. In this case, the node does not know to resend the corrupted transmission.

To ensure that any collisions are detected, frames are made large enough to fill the entire cable during transmission. It might seem odd to think about a transmission "filling a cable," but think about water going through a water hose. You can turn on the spigot and run the water for a very short time. The water runs through the hose to the other end but the hose isn't filled all at the same time. Only if you leave the water running long enough, will water start coming out the other end while it's still entering the hose at the spigot. With a long enough transmission, a similar thing happens on a cable—the beginning of the message starts arriving at its destination before the end of the message has been completely transmitted.

Today's networks still use DIX and 802.3 frames. However, you're unlikely to encounter a hub on a modern network. Instead, each connection to a switch consists of its own collision domain, and this connection can support communication in two directions at the same time. Therefore, the CSMA/CD process rarely plays a significant role because collisions are nearly impossible on today's wired networks.

 EXAM TIP The CompTIA Network+ exam expects you to understand how CSMA/CD works and how to troubleshoot problems from collisions.

REMEMBER THIS...

- Explain the differences between TCP and UDP at the transport layer.
- Identify similarities and differences in headers for TCP, UDP, IP, ICMP, and Ethernet.
- Use `arp -a` to view a device's ARP table.

SELF-CHECK

1. Which protocol's header includes the source MAC address?
   a. Ethernet
   b. UDP
   c. IP
   d. TCP

2. Which of these protocols does *not* include some kind of integrity check field in its header?
   a. TCP
   b. ICMP
   c. IPv6
   d. IPv4

3. An ARP table maps MAC addresses to what information?
   a. IPv6 addresses
   b. Physical interfaces
   c. TCP or UDP ports
   d. IPv4 addresses

Check your answers at the end of this module.

You're Ready

You're now ready to complete **Project 4-1: Install and Use WSL (Windows Subsystem for Linux)**, or you can wait until you've finished reading this module.

ENCRYPTION PROTOCOLS

 **CERTIFICATION**

1.5 Explain common ports and protocols, their application, and encrypted alternatives.

4.1 Explain common security concepts.

5.5 Given a scenario, troubleshoot general networking issues.

Average reading time: 19 minutes

So far in this module, you've seen how protocols package data to move it across a network. What protocols help to keep that data safe? In terms of security, data exists generally in three states:

- **At rest**—Data is most secure when it's stored on a device that is protected by a firewall, anti-malware software, and physical security (such as being inside a locked room). However, these protections are no guarantee. Additional protections include storing portions of the data in separate locations so that no single portion is meaningful on its own.
- **In use**—For data to be used, it must be accessible, which brings inherent risk. Tightly controlling access to the data and reliable authentication of users help reduce these risks. You'll learn more about access control and authentication methods later.
- **In motion**—This is when data is most vulnerable. Especially when data must leave your own, trusted network, it's exposed to a multitude of potential gaps, intrusions, and weak links. Wireless transmissions, especially, are susceptible to interception. And wired transmissions also risk exposure. The number of devices, organizations, and transmission methods involved in sending a single email across the Internet highlights the need for a layer of security that travels with the data.

Encryption is the last layer of defense against data theft. In other words, if an intruder has bypassed all other methods of security, including physical security (for instance, they have broken into the data center) and network design security (for instance, they have defied a firewall's packet-filtering techniques or removed encapsulated frames from transmissions), data in motion or at rest may still be safe if it is encrypted. **Encryption** protocols use a mathematical code, called a cipher, to scramble data into a format that can be read only by reversing the cipher—that is, by deciphering, or decrypting, the data. The purpose of encryption is to keep information private. Many forms of encryption exist, with some being more secure than others. Even as new forms of encryption are developed, new ways of cracking their codes emerge, too.

To protect data at rest, in use, and in motion, encryption methods are primarily evaluated by three benchmarks:

- **Confidentiality**—Data can only be viewed by its intended recipient or at its intended destination.
- **Integrity**—Data is not modified in the time after the sender transmits it and before the receiver picks it up.
- **Availability**—Data is available and accessible to the intended recipient when needed, meaning the sender is accountable for successful delivery of the data.

Together, these three principles form the standard security model called the **CIA (confidentiality, integrity, and availability) triad.** Encryption can happen at various layers of the OSI model. Let's first begin with a brief description of what key encryption is, and then you'll learn about some of the most common encryption protocols used to protect data stored on or traveling across networks.

Key Encryption

The most popular kind of encryption encodes the original data's bits using a key, or a random string of characters, to scramble the data—sometimes several times in different sequences—and generates a unique and consistently sized data block called ciphertext. The key is created according to a specific set of rules, or algorithms. Key encryption can be separated into two categories, as illustrated in Figure 4-15 and described next:

- Private key encryption—Data is encrypted using a single key that only the sender and the receiver know. Private key encryption is also known as symmetric encryption because the same key is used during both

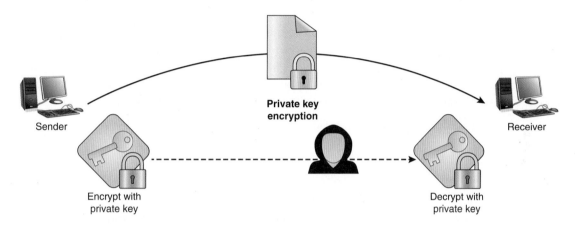

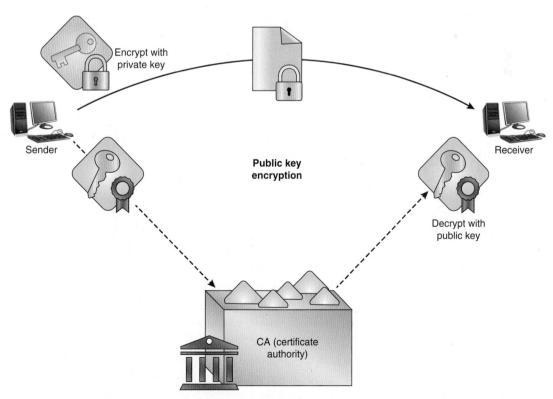

Figure 4-15   Private key encryption uses only one key, which must be securely communicated between sender and receiver, while public key encryption relies on a second, public key that can safely be obtained by anyone

the encryption and decryption of the data. A potential problem with private key encryption is that the sender must somehow share the key with the recipient without it being intercepted.

- **Public key encryption**—Data is encrypted with a private key known only to the user, and it's decrypted with a mathematically related public key that can be made available through a third-party source, such as a public key server. This ensures data integrity, as the sender's public key will only work if the data has not been tampered with. Alternatively, data can be encrypted with the public key, and then can only be decrypted with the matching private key. This ensures data confidentiality, as only the intended recipient (the owner of the keys) can decrypt the data. A public key server is a publicly accessible host, such as a server on the Internet, that freely provides a list of users' public keys, much as a telephone book provides a list of peoples' phone numbers. The combination of a public key and a private key is known as a key pair. Because public key encryption requires the use of two different keys, one to encrypt and the other to decrypt, it is also known as **asymmetric encryption**.

With the abundance of private and public keys, not to mention the number of places where each may be kept, users need simple and secure key management. One answer to this problem is to use digital certificates. A person or a business can request a **digital certificate**, which is a small file containing that user's verified identification information and the user's public key. The digital certificate is issued, maintained, and validated by an organization called a **CA (certificate authority)**. The use of certificate authorities to associate public keys with certain users is known as **PKI (public-key infrastructure)**.

NOTE 4-6

Digital certificates are primarily used to certify and secure websites where financial and other sensitive information is exchanged, but they're also used for other types of websites and to secure email communications, to authenticate client devices in a domain, or to authenticate users to a network. **Authentication** involves a process of ensuring that a user, device, or application is who they say they are. When surfing the web, at some point you might have gotten an error that said the website's SSL certificate was untrusted. Certificate issues like this might mean the website's digital certificate used by the encryption protocol SSL/TLS (which is used to secure HTTP) was not signed by a trusted CA, the certificate has expired, or it wasn't associated with a trusted root certificate. The browser alerts you that the website you're about to visit might not be the website you think it is.

The next two sections detail specific protocols, including SSL and TLS, that are used to encrypt data as it is transmitted over a network. The first encryption protocol in the list, IPsec, operates at the network layer.

IPsec (Internet Protocol Security)

IPsec (Internet Protocol Security) is an encryption protocol suite that defines a set of rules for encryption, authentication, and key management for TCP/IP transmissions. It is an enhancement to IPv4 and is native to IPv6. IPsec works at the network layer of the OSI model—it adds security information to the headers of IP packets and encrypts the data payload. IPsec creates secure connections in five steps, as follows:

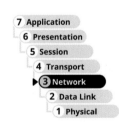

7 Application
6 Presentation
5 Session
4 Transport
▶ 3 Network
2 Data Link
1 Physical

1. **IPsec initiation**—Noteworthy traffic, as defined by a security policy, triggers the initiation of the IPsec encryption process.
2. **Key management**—Through a key management process, two nodes agree on common parameters for the keys they will use. This phase primarily includes two services:
   - **IKE (Internet Key Exchange)**—Negotiates the exchange of keys, including authentication of the keys; the current version is IKEv2, which you'll see again in the discussion on VPNs (virtual private networks) later in this module.
   - **ISAKMP (Internet Security Association and Key Management Protocol)**—Works within the IKE process to establish policies for managing the keys.

3. **Security negotiations**—IKE continues to establish security parameters and associations that will serve to protect data while in transit.

4. **Data transfer**—After parameters and encryption techniques are agreed upon, a secure channel is created, which can be used for secure transmissions until the channel is broken. Data is encrypted and then transmitted. Either **AH (authentication header)** encryption or **ESP (Encapsulating Security Payload)** encryption may be used. Both types of encryption provide authentication of the IP packet's data payload through public key techniques. In addition, ESP encrypts the entire IP packet for added security.

5. **Termination**—IPsec requires regular reestablishment of a connection to minimize the opportunity for interference. To maintain communication, the connection can be renegotiated and reestablished before the current session times out.

IPsec can be used with any type of TCP/IP transmission and operates in two modes:

- **Transport mode**—Connects two hosts.
- **Tunnel mode**—Runs on routers or other connectivity devices in the context of VPNs.

SSL (Secure Sockets Layer) and TLS (Transport Layer Security)

SSL (Secure Sockets Layer) and TLS (Transport Layer Security) are both methods of encrypting TCP/IP transmissions—including web pages and data entered into web forms—en route between the client and server using public key encryption technology. The two protocols can work side by side and are widely known as SSL/TLS or TLS/SSL. All browsers today (for example, Google Chrome, Mozilla Firefox, Apple Safari, Microsoft Edge, and Internet Explorer) support SSL/TLS to secure HTTP transmissions.

7 Application
6 Presentation
5 Session
▶ 4 Transport
3 Network
2 Data Link
1 Physical

SSL was originally developed by Netscape and operates in the application layer. Since that time, the IETF (Internet Engineering Task Force), which is an organization of volunteers who help develop Internet standards, has standardized the similar TLS protocol. TLS operates in the transport layer and uses slightly different encryption algorithms than SSL, but otherwise is essentially the updated version of SSL. SSL has now been deprecated and should be disabled whenever possible, leaving the more secure TLS to provide protection. In reality, you'll often see them both enabled for backward compatibility. You'll also often see the terms used interchangeably—many times, even when someone says SSL, they're referring to TLS.

As you recall, HTTP uses TCP port 80, whereas HTTPS (HTTP Secure) uses SSL/TLS encryption and TCP port 443 rather than port 80. Other protocols you've studied that offer SSL/TLS encrypted alternatives include SMTP TLS, LDAP over SSL, IMAP over SSL, and POP3 over SSL. Each time a client and server establish an SSL/TLS connection, they establish a unique session, which is an association between the client and server that is defined by an agreement on a specific set of encryption techniques. The session allows the client and server to continue to exchange data securely as long as the client is still connected to the server. A session is created by a handshake protocol, one of several protocols within SSL/TLS, and perhaps the most significant. As its name implies, the handshake protocol allows the client and server to introduce themselves to each other and establishes terms for how they will securely exchange data.

This handshake conversation is similar to the TCP three-way handshake you learned about earlier in this module. Given the scenario of a browser accessing a secure website, the SSL/TLS handshake works as follows:

Step 1—The browser, representing the client computer in this scenario, sends a client hello message to the web server, which contains information about what level of security the browser is capable of accepting and what type of encryption the browser can decipher. The client hello message also establishes a randomly generated number that uniquely identifies the client and another number that identifies the session.

Step 2—The server responds with a server hello message that confirms the information it received from the browser and agrees to certain terms of encryption based on the options supplied by the browser. Depending on the web server's preferred encryption method, the server might choose to issue to the browser a public key or a digital certificate.

Step 3—If the server requests a certificate from the browser, the browser sends it. Any data the browser sends to the server is encrypted using the server's public key. Session keys used only for this one session are also established. After the browser and server have agreed on the terms of encryption, the secure channel is in place and they begin exchanging data.

The certificate and key exchange process can add more steps, requiring up to 10 steps for a TLS 1.2 handshake. Recall that public key encryption is more secure than private key encryption but also takes longer. During a TLS 1.2 handshake, public key encryption is used to establish a secure session. To save time going forward, part of the handshake process is negotiating the exchange of a private key so the conversation can continue at a faster pace using private key encryption. However, this requires three round-trip messages. The newest version, TLS 1.3, reduces the number of steps and requires only one round-trip sequence. In some cases, TLS 1.3 can avoid the handshake process altogether in what's called 0-RTT (zero round-trip time).

NOTE 4-7

Transmissions over secure connections, such as when using HTTPS websites, might be intercepted but cannot be read. For example, suppose you are using unsecured Wi-Fi at a coffee shop and log on to Twitter from your laptop browser. Without TLS protecting your logon information, anyone lounging nearby can hack into, read, and steal your unencrypted wireless transmissions.

Some online activities, however, such as online banking, should never be performed on unsecure Wi-Fi hotspots. Despite the security provided by these encryption techniques, other steps of the process can break down. One example might include browsing an insecure portion of a website (HTTP) for part of the browsing session, which provides a brief opportunity for your browser to be hijacked by a hacker and sent to what looks like the official logon page, but really is not.

Applying Concepts 4-4: Browser Security

You can change the settings in your browser to make sure you're using the latest version of TLS. On a Windows machine, changes you make to one browser for these settings will affect other browsers installed on your computer. Complete the following steps:

1. In the Settings app, search for **Internet options**, and then click **Internet Options** in the search results.
2. On the **Advanced** tab, scroll down to the Security section. Which SSL/TLS options are currently enabled?
3. Disable **SSL 3.0**, **TLS 1.0**, and **TLS 1.1**. Make sure **TLS 1.2** and **TLS 1.3** are enabled. While TLS 1.3 might be labeled experimental, it was finalized in 2018 and provides better security at faster speeds and is already widely used by websites. Also, if you regularly use an unsecured wireless network like at a coffee shop or a restaurant, also select **Warn if changing between secure and not secure mode** so you'll be notified when interacting with an unsecured website. See Figure 4-16. Click **OK**.

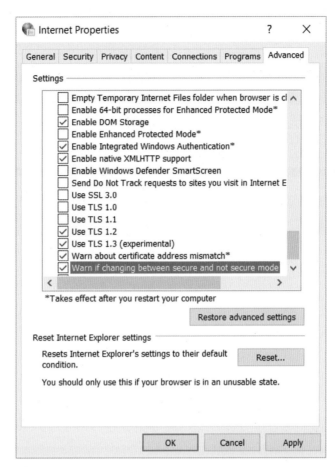

Figure 4-16   TLS 1.2 and TLS 1.3 provide the best
security for surfing online

Some browsers will prevent navigation to unsecured websites when the warning option is checked as previously instructed. This is a good thing if you're using a questionable network. But if you have trouble navigating to unsecured sites you feel comfortable with, you'll need to go back and uncheck this option in Internet options.

 **CAUTION**   When visiting secure websites, it's important to notice if you have a secure connection with a trusted website before entering personal information on that site. Edge, for example, shows a padlock icon when the site's certificate has been identified and confirmed. This visual is still no guarantee, however, as scammers are now figuring out how to impersonate HTTPS websites' credentials.

4. In your browser, navigate to **paypal.com**. What is the exact address shown in the address box after the page loads in the browser?
5. Click the padlock icon and then click the certificate listed. What CA verified the legitimacy of the website?

Now that you understand a little about encryption and related security concerns, you're ready to dive into remote connection protocols that require encryption for security.

REMEMBER THIS...

- Explain how private key encryption and public key encryption work.
- Compare the roles of AH encryption and ESP encryption in IPsec.
- Describe the security provided by SSL/TLS for HTTP, SMTP, LDAP, IMAP, and POP3.

SELF-CHECK

4. Which two components of the CIA triad are ensured by adequate encryption methods? Choose *two*.
   a. Confidentiality
   b. Availability
   c. Accountability
   d. Integrity

5. Which IPsec encryption type encrypts the IP header?
   a. IKE
   b. ESP
   c. ISAKMP
   d. AH

Check your answers at the end of this module.

REMOTE ACCESS PROTOCOLS

✓ CERTIFICATION

1.2 Explain the characteristics of network topologies and network types.

1.5 Explain common ports and protocols, their application, and encrypted alternatives.

2.1 Compare and contrast various devices, their features, and their appropriate placement on the network.

3.2 Explain the purpose of organization documents and policies.

4.2 Compare and contrast common types of attacks.

4.4 Compare and contrast remote access methods and security implications.

5.3 Given a scenario, use the appropriate network software tools and commands.

Average reading time: 34 minutes

As a remote user, you can connect to a network and its resources via **remote access**, which is a service that allows a client to connect with and log on to a server, LAN, or WAN in a different geographical location (or just across the room). After connecting, a remote client can access files, applications, and other shared resources, such as printers, like any other client on the server, LAN, or WAN. To communicate via remote access, the client and host need a transmission path plus the appropriate software to complete the connection and exchange data.

7 Application
6 Presentation
5 Session
4 Transport
3 Network
2 Data Link
1 Physical

All types of remote access techniques connecting to a network require some type of **RAS (remote access server)** software to accept a remote connection and grant it privileges to the network's resources. Also, software must be installed on both the remote client and the remote access server to negotiate and maintain this connection. There are two types of remote access servers:

- **Dedicated devices**—Devices such as Digi's Connect IT 48 remote access server are dedicated solely as an RAS to run software that, in conjunction with their operating system, performs authentication for clients. Authentication involves a process of comparing and matching a client's credentials with the credentials in a client database to enable the client to log on to the network or other resource. An ISP might use a dedicated device to authenticate client computers or home routers to access the ISP resources and the Internet. See Figure 4-17.

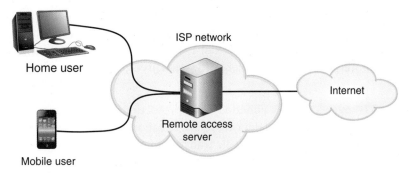

Figure 4-17 An ISP uses a remote access server to authenticate subscribers to its services, including access to the Internet

- **Software running on a server**—The remote access service might run under a network operating system to allow remote logon to a corporate network. For example, DirectAccess is a service first introduced in Windows Server 2008 R2 that can automatically authenticate remote users and computers to the Windows domain and its corporate network resources. A similar service, Always On VPN, has been available since Windows Server 2012 R2 and is expected to replace DirectAccess. Both work on similar principles, as shown in Figure 4-18.

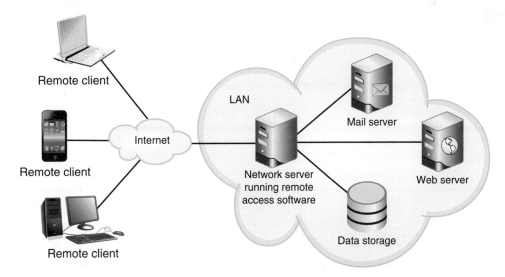

Figure 4-18 Always On VPN authenticates users to the Windows domain

Several types of remote access methods exist. Three of the most common, which you'll explore in greater depth throughout this section, include the following:

- Remote file access, which allows a remote client to upload and download data files and configuration files.
- Terminal emulation, also called remote virtual computing, which allows a remote client to take over and command a host computer. Examples of terminal emulation software are Telnet, SSH, Remote Desktop, and VNC (Virtual Network Computing). You'll read more details on these shortly.

- **VPN (virtual private network)**, which is a virtual connection that remotely accesses resources between a client and a network, two networks, or two hosts over the Internet or other types of networks.

Security and privacy are of utmost concern when managing and using remote access connections. To this end, data is often encrypted before it is transmitted over the remote connection. Some remote access protocols natively include encryption functionality, whereas other remote access methods must be paired with a specific encryption protocol, such as the ones you learned about earlier in this module. As you read, pay close attention to which protocols offer encryption and how reliable that encryption is believed to be.

Remote File Access

FTP (File Transfer Protocol) is commonly used to provide remote file access. Now that you understand more about how encryption can secure transmissions, you're ready to learn about some remote file access options related to FTP. Recall that FTP is a utility that can transfer files to and from a host computer running FTP server software. Three related technologies include the following:

- **FTPS (FTP Secure or FTP over SSL)**—An added layer of protection for FTP using SSL/TLS that can encrypt both the control and data channels. Recall that FTP listens at port 21, which is the command channel. Data is usually transferred over port 20, which is the data channel. FTPS is typically configured to listen at port 21, like FTP, but requires two data channels. By default, those data channels are at ports 989 and 990. However, FTPS can also be configured to negotiate its data ports within a predefined range each time it makes a connection. FTPS can be difficult to configure through a firewall.
- **SFTP (Secure FTP)**—A file-transfer version of SSH that includes encryption and authentication, and it's sometimes inaccurately called FTP over SSH or SSH FTP. Note that SFTP is an extension of the SSH protocol, not of FTP. Unlike FTP or FTPS, which use a control channel and one or two data channels, SFTP uses only a single connection—both inbound and outbound communications are usually configured to cross SSH's port 22. SFTP and FTPS are incompatible with each other.
- **TFTP (Trivial FTP)**—A simple protocol similar to FTP except that it includes no authentication or security for transferring files and uses UDP at the transport layer (unlike FTP, which relies on TCP at the transport layer). TFTP requires very little memory and is most often used by machines behind the scenes to transfer boot files or configuration files. It's not safe for communication over the Internet, is not capable of giving users access to directory information, and limits file transfers to 4 GB. TFTP listens at port 69 and negotiates a data channel for each connection. A **TFTP server** is often used to remotely boot devices that don't have their own hard drives, to collect log files, or to back up and update network device configuration files.

 EXAM TIP The Network+ exam might give you a scenario that requires you know how to use a TFTP server. In Capstone Project 4-1 at the end of this module, you'll work with a TFTP server in Packet Tracer to back up and restore a router.

Terminal Emulation

A **terminal emulator** is software that allows a user on one computer, called the client, to control another computer, called the host or server, across a network connection. Examples of command-line software that can provide terminal emulation include Telnet and SSH. Some GUI-based software examples are Remote Desktop for Windows, join.me, VNC (virtual network computing), and TeamViewer. You'll explore these options further in a moment. For now, understand that a host may allow clients a variety of privileges, from merely viewing the screen to running applications and modifying data files on the host's hard disk. After connecting, if the remote user has sufficient privileges, they can send keystrokes and mouse clicks to the host and receive screen output in return. In other words, to the remote user, it appears as if they're working on the LAN- or WAN-connected host itself.

For example, a traveling salesperson can use a laptop to "remote in" to a desktop computer at corporate headquarters. This way, they can remotely update a workbook file stored on the desktop computer using Excel, an application that is also installed on the desktop. Another example is when a student needs to use Windows-only software that is not compatible with their MacBook. Instead, the student can remote into a Windows lab computer at their school from their MacBook and work with the Windows software remotely, as shown in Figure 4-19.

Local computer's macOS desktop

Remote virtual Windows desktop

Source: Apple Inc.

Figure 4-19   VDI connection to a Windows computer from a MacBook

Telnet

As you've learned, the Telnet protocol is a terminal emulation utility used by Telnet client/server applications that allow an administrator or other user to control a computer remotely. For example, if you were a network administrator working at one building on your school's campus and had to modify the configuration on a router in another building, you could use Telnet to access the router and run commands to change configuration settings. However, Telnet provides little security for establishing a connection (poor authentication) and no security for transmitting data (no encryption).

While Telnet is typically installed by default in most popular OSs, often it must first be enabled. A Telnet connection is created from the client computer's CLI using the `telnet` command. For example, the command `telnet 192.168.2.1` will connect to a device on the network at the IP address listed (such as a router), and `telnet lab-owl` will connect to a computer on the network named lab-owl (such as a server). In both cases, you must enter a password to complete the connection. You could then interact with the host's CLI using your local computer's CLI. For example, you might want to configure the remote device's interfaces. To close a telnet session, access the telnet prompt again with the keyboard shortcut Ctrl+] (that's the Ctrl key with the close-bracket key) and enter the command `quit`, or just close the CLI window.

SSH (Secure Shell)

SSH (Secure Shell) is a collection of protocols that performs both authentication and encryption. With SSH, you can securely log on to a host, execute commands on that host, and copy files to or from the host. SSH encrypts data exchanged throughout the session. It guards against several security threats, including the following:

- Unauthorized access to a host
- Interception of data in transit, even if the data must be transferred via intermediate nodes
- IP **spoofing**, in which an attacker attempts to hide their identity or impersonate another device by modifying the IP header
- DNS spoofing, in which a hacker forges name server records to falsify their host's identity

Depending on the version, SSH may use Triple DES, AES, Blowfish, or other, less-common encryption schemes or techniques.

EXAM TIP

After completing your Network+ certification, you might consider studying for the Security+ certification. CompTIA's Security+ exam covers a broad range of foundational topics in IT security, including the encryption techniques listed here for SSH. This essential understanding of security concerns, techniques, and concepts will serve you well no matter which area of IT you choose to specialize in.

SSH was developed by SSH Communications Security, and use of their SSH implementation requires paying for a license. However, open source versions of the protocol suite, such as OpenSSH, are available for most computer platforms.

To form a secure connection, SSH must be running on both the client and server. Like Telnet, the SSH client is a utility that can be run at the shell prompt on a UNIX or Linux system or at a CLI on a Windows-based system. Other versions of the program come with a graphical interface. The SSH suite of protocols is included with all modern UNIX and Linux distributions and with macOS client operating systems. For Windows-based computers, you need to download a freeware SSH client, such as PuTTY (*putty.org*). You can see in Figure 4-20 that PuTTY supports several connection types, including both SSH and Telnet. PuTTY can also be run from the command line. In a later module, you'll practice using PuTTY to remotely connect to a VM in the cloud.

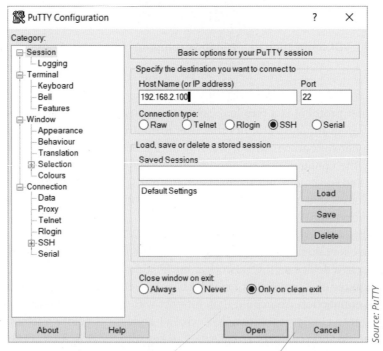

Figure 4-20 On a Windows computer, use an app like PuTTY to create an SSH connection to another computer

SSH allows for password authentication or authentication using public and private keys. The following steps describe how to authenticate using keys:

Step 1—Generate a public key and a private key on your client workstation by running the `ssh-keygen` command (or by choosing the correct menu options in a graphical SSH program). The keys are saved in two different, encrypted files on your hard disk.

Step 2—Transfer the public key to an authorization file on the host to which you want to connect.

Step 3—When you connect to the host via SSH, the client and host exchange public keys. If both can be authenticated, the connection is completed.

SSH listens at port 22 and is highly configurable. For example, you can choose among several encryption methods. At the end of this module in Capstone Project 4-2, you'll practice using SSH in Ubuntu.

RDP (Remote Desktop Protocol)

Recall that RDP (Remote Desktop Protocol) is a Microsoft proprietary protocol used by Windows Remote Desktop and Remote Assistance client/server utilities to connect to and control a remote computer. RDP provides a remote desktop connection so that you see on your local computer's screen what you would see if you were sitting in front of the remote computer instead. It's not just a CLI like what you get with SSH and Telnet. It's a GUI desktop with windows, icons, shortcut keys, menus, and sound. You can even run a hypervisor on the remote desktop so that, from your local computer, you can control the remote host and all its VMs.

Figure 4-21 shows a local computer's Windows desktop, a remote desktop connection with another Windows computer, and an Ubuntu VM running on the remote computer. At the end of this module, you'll practice using RDP to connect two computers.

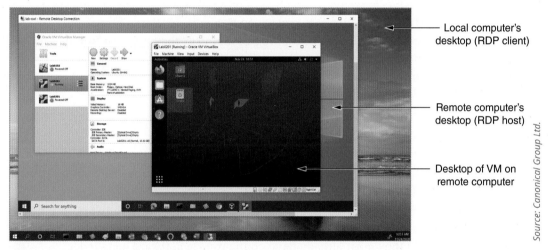

Local computer's desktop (RDP client)

Remote computer's desktop (RDP host)

Desktop of VM on remote computer

Source: Canonical Group Ltd.

Figure 4-21   From one keyboard, interact with the local desktop, the remote desktop, and the VM's desktop

For larger corporate networks, a simple RDP connection might not suffice. For example, if you have several remote workers connecting to their office desktops at the same time, you might run out of your available public IP addresses and then have to manage connections through a process called port forwarding. Instead, a remote desktop gateway run from a single Windows server can manage all these RDP connections to the network's computers through a single public IP address. The remote desktop gateway can also link to Active Directory's authentication services, manage user authorization to control which users can access which network resources once logged in, and audit activity through all hosted RDP connections. Additionally, the remote desktop gateway incorporates SSL/TLS to provide secure connections to all users so there's no need for additional encryption through a VPN.

NOTE 4-8

Authentication and authorization are two different processes. Authentication is the sign-in process that allows a user to access a resource such as a network if they provide the correct credentials, such as username and password. Authorization determines what the user can do once they get into the resource. For example, any employee might be allowed to sign into the network (authentication), but only an administrator has permission to edit user accounts (authorization). A remote desktop gateway can manage both these processes independently for all network resources rather than for only a single desktop.

Suppose you have many remote users, such as salespeople for a company or students at a school, who regularly need access to a desktop managed by your company. You want to offer a consistent desktop experience with installed applications that your users commonly need. However, you don't want to purchase dozens of physical computers for these users to connect to. Instead, you can offer virtual desktops running in VMs that the system creates, or "spins up," only when needed. This implementation is called **VDI (Virtual Desktop Infrastructure)**. It differs from a traditional RDP connection in that the VDI connection targets only VMs. However, VDI can use RDP to create the connection to each VM. VDI also offers greater flexibility with options to access VMs running many different OSs or many different configurations of installed applications. VDI can also provide either persistent or non-persistent instances. With a persistent instance, when the user remotes back into the desktop, any changes they made will still be there including files they saved. With a non-persistent instance, the desktop is reset each time someone signs in.

In contrast, **RDS (Remote Desktop Services)** uses RDP to allow multiple users to access the same virtual or physical Windows Server system at one time. RDS can provide access to the entire Server OS or just to a single application using RemoteApp. RDS is cheaper to support than VDI; however, RDS is more difficult to manage and more limited in customization options.

VNC (Virtual Network Computing)

VNC (Virtual Network Computing) is similar in concept to RDP but uses the cross-platform protocol RFB (remote frame buffer) to remotely control a workstation or server. VNC is slower than Remote Desktop and requires more network bandwidth. However, because VNC is open source, many companies have developed their own software that can

- Run OSs on client computers
- Remotely access computers, tablets, and smartphones
- Remotely control media equipment and surveillance systems

Out-of-Band Management

Telnet, SSH, RDP, and VNC all rely on the existing network infrastructure for a network administrator to remotely control the device. Before the devices can be configured, they must already be booted up, and they must already have configuration software installed. This is called **in-band management**, and it inherently limits troubleshooting capabilities. **Out-of-band management**, however, relies on a dedicated connection (either wired or wireless) between the network administrator's computer and each critical network device, such as routers, firewalls, servers, power supplies, applications, and security cameras. These dedicated connections allow network administrators to remotely

- Power up a device
- Change firmware settings
- Reinstall operating systems
- Monitor hardware sensors
- Troubleshoot boot problems
- Limit network users' access to management functions
- Manage devices even when other parts of the network are down

Out-of-band management solutions come in an array of options, from basic reboot abilities to full-scale device management. A remote management card is attached to the network device's console port, or sometimes the remote management card is built into the device. A dial-in modem—either through a wired phone line or through a cellular connection—might be attached to the device to provide backup CLI access in the event of a catastrophic network shutdown. A single device, such as a console server or console router, provides centralized management of all linked devices.

VPNs (Virtual Private Networks)

A VPN (virtual private network) is a network connection encrypted from end to end that creates a private connection to a remote network. A VPN is sometimes referred to as a tunnel. For example, a national insurance provider uses VPNs to securely connect its agent offices across the country with its databases at the national headquarters. By relying on the public transmission networks already in place (that is, the Internet), VPNs avoid the expense of having to lease private point-to-point connections between each office and the national headquarters.

The software or hardware required to establish VPNs is typically inexpensive, and in some cases, is included in the OS or a networking device's hardware. Many routers and firewalls include embedded VPN solutions. A router-based VPN is the most common implementation of VPNs on UNIX-based networks, as opposed to the server-based VPNs that Windows networks often use. Third-party solutions also work with Windows, UNIX, and Linux network operating systems.

Based on the kinds of endpoints they connect, VPNs can be loosely classified according to three models:

- **Site-to-site VPN**—Tunnels connect multiple sites on a WAN, as shown in Figure 4-22. At each site, a VPN gateway on the edge of the LAN establishes the secure connection. Each gateway is a router, firewall, or remote access server with VPN software installed, and it encrypts and encapsulates data to exchange over the tunnel. Meanwhile, clients, servers, and other hosts on the protected LANs communicate through the VPN gateways as if they were all on the same, private network without needing to run VPN software themselves. Site-to-site VPNs require that each location have a static public IP address.

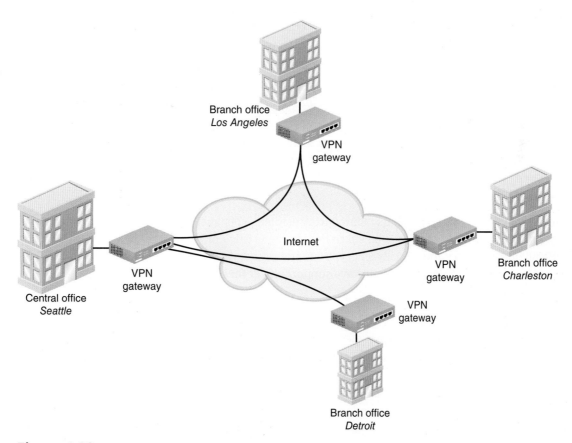

Figure 4-22   A VPN gateway connects each site to one or more other sites

- **Client-to-site VPN**, also called host-to-site VPN—Remote clients, servers, and other hosts establish tunnels with a private network through a VPN gateway (called the **VPN headend**) at the edge of the LAN, as shown in Figure 4-23. The tunnel created between the client and the headend encrypts and encapsulates data. This is the type of VPN typically associated with remote access. To establish a client-to-site VPN, only the VPN headend needs a static public IP address. As with site-to-site VPNs, clients and hosts on the protected LAN communicate with remote clients by way of the VPN headend and are not required to run VPN software. However, each remote client on a client-to-site VPN must either run VPN software to connect to the VPN headend or establish a more limited, web-based, **clientless VPN** connection, which uses a browser and is secured by SSL/TLS.

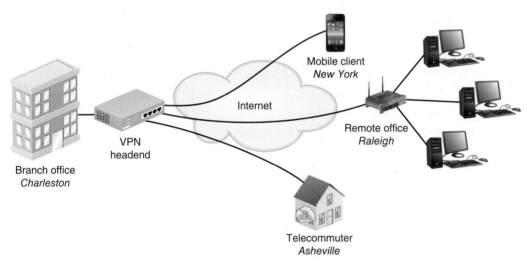

Figure 4-23   Remote clients connect to the LAN through the VPN headend

- **Host-to-host VPN**—Two computers create a VPN tunnel directly between them. Both computers must have the appropriate software installed, and they don't serve as a gateway to other hosts or resources on their respective networks. In a host-to-host VPN, usually the site that receives the VPN connection (such as a home network) needs a static public IP address. Another option, however, is to subscribe to a service such as Dynamic DNS by Oracle (*dyn.com/dns*), which automatically tracks dynamic IP address information for subscriber locations.

The beauty of VPNs is that they can be tailored to a customer's distance, user, and bandwidth needs, so, of course, every configuration is unique. However, all share the characteristics of privacy achieved over public transmission facilities using encapsulation and, usually, encryption. The primary encryption techniques used by VPNs today are IPsec, OpenSSL, and SSL/TLS. Most VPN gateways support any of these standards.

VPN Protocols

To ensure a VPN can carry all types of data in a private manner over any kind of connection, special VPN protocols encapsulate higher-layer protocols in a process known as tunneling. Recall that IPv6 hosts can tunnel through an IPv4 network and vice versa. A similar process is used by VPN protocols to create a virtual connection, or tunnel, between two VPN endpoints.

To understand how a VPN tunnel works, imagine a truck being transported across a river on a ferry. The truck is carefully loaded, tethered, and covered, and then it's carried across the water to its destination. At its destination, the cover and tethers are removed, and the cargo is unloaded. The truck can then drive on down the road as it was originally designed to function. Similarly, with VPN tunneling protocols, complete frames are encrypted, encapsulated, and transported inside normal IP packets and data link layer frames. In other words, the inner frame travels across the network as the payload inside another frame. Once the inner frame is released on the other side of the tunnel, it acts as it would have on the network where it originated, allowing users to access network resources as if they were locally logged onto the network.

Two common approaches to VPN tunneling either require all network traffic to traverse the VPN tunnel or only some of that traffic. Consider the following comparison, as illustrated in Figure 4-24:

- **Full tunnel VPN**—Captures all network traffic, whether destined for the Internet or for the corporate network. The client has no access to its local network and is assigned an IP address from the remote network.
- **Split tunnel VPN**—Only captures traffic destined for the corporate network. The client can communicate with local network resources directly and with Internet resources, such as Google or Zoom, through a local Internet connection. The client is assigned an IP address from the local network.

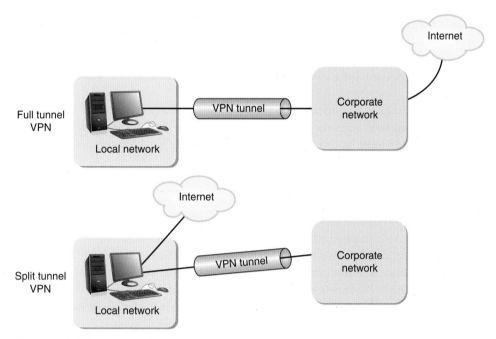

Figure 4-24   A full tunnel VPN protects all traffic, while a split tunnel VPN only captures traffic destined for the corporate network

While security must be handled differently with a split tunnel VPN where the computer can still communicate with local resources, the primary benefit is that a split tunnel VPN reduces the amount of traffic routed through the corporate network, thereby increasing the user's privacy and decreasing latency. This is especially helpful if the remote user needs access to the Internet for personal reasons, such as streaming music or video, making online purchases, or performing online banking.

Many VPN tunneling protocols operate at the data link layer to encapsulate the VPN frame inside a network layer packet. Some VPN tunneling protocols work instead at layer 3, which enables additional features and options, especially for site-to-site VPN traffic. Most tunneling protocols rely on an additional encryption protocol to provide data security. Figure 4-25 shows an Ethernet frame encapsulated in a VPN frame that is encrypted by IPsec.

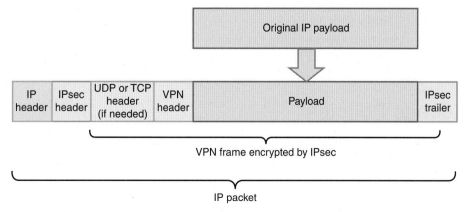

Figure 4-25   The VPN frame, such as GRE or L2TP, is encapsulated inside the network layer packet

Some common VPN tunneling protocols are described in the following list:

- L2TP (Layer 2 Tunneling Protocol) is a VPN tunneling protocol based on technology developed by Cisco and standardized by the IETF. L2TP is a standard accepted and used by multiple vendors, so it can connect a VPN that uses a mix of equipment types—for example, a Juniper router and a Cisco router. Also, L2TP can connect two routers, a router and a remote access server, or a client and a remote access server. Typically, L2TP is implemented with IPsec for security, and this L2TP/IPsec combination is considered secure and acceptable for most situations.
- GRE (Generic Routing Encapsulation), developed by Cisco, is a layer 3 protocol used to transmit IP and other kinds of messages through a tunnel. Like L2TP, GRE is used in conjunction with IPsec to increase the security of the transmissions.
- OpenVPN is an open source VPN protocol that uses a custom security protocol called OpenSSL for encryption. OpenVPN can cross many firewalls where IPsec might be blocked. It is both highly secure and highly configurable.
- IKEv2, as you learned earlier, is a component of the IPsec protocol suite and offers fast throughput and good stability when moving between wireless hotspots. It's compatible with a wide variety of devices and is often recommended by VPN providers as the most secure option among the VPN protocols they support.

Multipoint VPNs

While IPsec itself can be used as a tunneling protocol, it often provides encryption for another tunneling protocol. This pairing offers more flexibility and other features that IPsec can't offer alone. For example, what if you have several branch offices that all need tunnels to each other? In this case, an enterprise-wide VPN can include elements of both the client-to-site and site-to-site models. This multipoint VPN configuration is achieved through creative adaptation and use of VPN tunneling protocols. For example, GRE is a versatile tunneling protocol used to create tunnels for many other protocols (including IPv6 tunnels over an IPv4 network) and can be used to support VPN tunnels. It can be paired with IPsec for greater security. However, GRE is designed to connect a single point to a single point. If you want to connect multiple branch offices to the main office and to each other, you must configure multiple GRE tunnels.

To work around this limitation, Cisco developed a proprietary protocol called mGRE (multipoint GRE). This protocol allows the configuration of multiple tunnel destinations on a single interface. mGRE employs a second layer of routing information to track both the underlay network (the Internet that actually moves packets from location to location) and the overlay network (the VPN connections that logically connect each location). In this configuration, as shown in Figure 4-26, a hub router sits at the headquarters location, and each remote office has a spoke router. Usually, when hosting enterprise VPN connections, the involved gateways all need static IP addresses from the ISP. With mGRE, however, only the hub router needs a static public IP address. The process requires spoke routers at branch locations to communicate with the hub router at the headquarters to announce and collect updated IP address information for other spoke routers.

This type of enterprise VPN using Cisco devices is called DMVPN (Dynamic Multipoint VPN). It dynamically creates VPN tunnels between branch locations as needed rather than requiring constant, static tunnels for site-to-site connections. The spoke routers can communicate with the hub router to create VPN tunnels as needed, even from a spoke router to a spoke router. This technology is much more scalable for networks that need to connect several remote sites across the Internet.

Remote Access Policies

A good remote access policy protects a company's data, network, and liability, no matter what type of remote access is involved. Here are some common requirements:

- Devices used for remote access must be kept up to date with patches, anti-malware software, and a firewall.

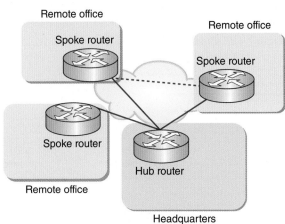

Figure 4-26   VPN tunnels are automatically created as needed, even between spoke routers

- Device access must be controlled by a strong password and biometric measures, such as fingerprint, retina, or face recognition. The device should lock down automatically after only a few minutes of inactivity.
- Passwords must be strong and must be changed periodically. Password best practices are discussed further in later modules.
- Passwords cannot be shared, even with a family member.
- The device's internal and external storage devices must be encrypted. Note that some countries require that encrypted storage devices be decrypted or that encryption keys be filed with authorities. Employees who travel abroad should account for this when deciding what data to transport.
- Company and customer data that is accessed, transferred, stored, or printed must be kept secure.
- The loss or theft of any devices used for remote access or to process remotely accessed data (such as a printer) must be reported to the company immediately (or within a reasonable time frame, such as 72 hours).
- Encrypted VPN software must be used to remotely access company network resources. Typically, these options are clearly defined in the policy.
- While remotely connected to the company network, the device must not be connected to the open Internet or any other network not fully owned and controlled by the employee. This restriction is usually built into full tunnel VPN solutions.
- Remote sessions must be terminated when not in use. In most cases, remote sessions should be configured to time out automatically as a precaution.

REMEMBER THIS...

- Compare FTP, FTPS, SFTP, and TFTP.
- Given a scenario, choose the appropriate remote access tool: Telnet, SSH, RDP, VNC, or a VPN.
- Practice using Telnet, SSH, and Remote Desktop.
- Describe how a VPN works.

SELF-CHECK

6. Which remote file access protocol uses port 22?
   a. FTPS
   b. TFTP
   c. FTP
   d. SFTP

7. You need to remote into a Linux server in another building on your network. Which of the following protocols should you use?
   a. RDP
   b. SSH
   c. SFTP
   d. VPN

8. You're working from home and need to access a file server at the office while working in an application from your work desktop. At the same time, you often stream music in your browser. Which VPN type will be most efficient while still meeting your needs?
   a. Full tunnel VPN
   b. Host-to-host VPN
   c. Site-to-site VPN
   d. Split tunnel VPN

Check your answers at the end of this module.

You're Ready

You're now ready to complete **Project 4-2: Use Remote Desktop**, or you can wait until you've finished reading this module.

TROUBLESHOOTING NETWORK ISSUES

✅ CERTIFICATION

4.2 Compare and contrast common types of attacks.

5.3 Given a scenario, use the appropriate network software tools and commands.

5.5 Given a scenario, troubleshoot general networking issues.

Average reading time: 22 minutes

As with any type of communication, many potential points of failure exist in the TCP/IP transmission process. The number of points increases with the size of the network and the distance of the transmission. Fortunately, TCP/IP comes with a complete set of utilities that can help you track down most TCP/IP-related problems without using expensive software or hardware to analyze network traffic. You should be familiar with the purposes of the following tools and their parameters, not only because the CompTIA Network+ certification exam covers them, but also because you will regularly need these tools in your work with TCP/IP networks.

Troubleshooting Tools

You've already learned about eight very important TCP/IP utilities—ping, ipconfig, ip, ifconfig, hostname, nslookup, dig, telnet, and arp. The following sections present additional TCP/IP utilities that can help you discover information about nodes on your network. The module then concludes with a summary of all these utilities along with a few troubleshooting scenarios.

netstat

The **netstat** utility displays TCP/IP statistics and details about TCP/IP components and connections on a host. Information that can be obtained from the `netstat` command includes the following:

- The port on which a TCP/IP service is running
- Which network connections are currently established for a client
- How many messages have been handled by a network interface since it was activated
- How many data errors have occurred on a particular network interface

EXAM TIP
The netstat utility has been deprecated in most Linux distributions, although it's still often included in the distribution by default. While the versatile ss (socket statistics) utility is designed to replace netstat, the CompTIA Network+ exam still expects you to know how to use netstat. Both utilities use many of the same parameters.

To better understand what netstat can do, consider this example. Suppose you are a network administrator in charge of maintaining file, print, and web servers for an organization. You discover that your web server, which has multiple processors, sufficient hard disk space, and multiple NICs, is suddenly taking twice as long to respond to HTTP requests. Besides checking the server's memory resources and its software for indications of problems, you can use netstat to determine the characteristics of traffic going into and out of each NIC. Perhaps you discover that one NIC is consistently handling 80 percent of the traffic instead of only half. You might run hardware diagnostics on the other NIC and discover that its onboard processor is failing, making it much slower than the first NIC.

Table 4-9 shows some parameters you can use with `netstat` in Windows. You can also use `netstat` on Linux machines with a different set of parameters.

Table 4-9 `netstat` command options

`netstat` **command**	Description
`netstat`	List all active TCP/IP connections on the local machine, including the transport layer protocol used (usually just TCP), messages sent and received, IP address, and state of those connections.
`netstat -n`	List current connections, including IP addresses and ports.
`netstat -f`	List current connections, including IP addresses, ports, and FQDNs.
`netstat -a`	List all current TCP connections and all listening TCP and UDP ports.
`netstat -e`	Display statistics about messages sent over a network interface, including errors and discards.
`netstat -s`	Display statistics about each message transmitted by a host, separated according to protocol type (TCP, UDP, IP, or ICMP).
`netstat -r`	Display routing table information.
`netstat -o`	List the PID (process identifier) for each process using a connection and information about the connection.
`netstat -b`	List the name of each process using a connection and information about the connection. Requires elevated permissions.

tracert or traceroute

The Windows **tracert** utility uses ICMP echo requests to trace the path from one networked node to another, identifying all intermediate hops between the two nodes. Linux, UNIX, and macOS systems use UDP datagrams or, possibly, TCP SYN messages, for their **traceroute** utility, but the concept is still the same.

Both traceroute and tracert utilities employ a trial-and-error approach to discover the nodes at each hop from the source to the destination, as described here:

- Tracert sends an ICMP echo request to the destination node and listens for an ICMP echo reply from that node.
- Traceroute sends UDP messages to a random, unused port on the destination node, and listens for an ICMP "Port Unreachable" error message in response from that node.
- Both utilities limit the TTL of these repeated trial messages, called **probes**, thereby triggering routers along the route to return specific information about the route being traversed. In fact, by default, they send three probes with each iteration so averages can be calculated from the three responses at each step.

Study Figure 4-27 to see how a trace works with traceroute. The steps are also described next:

Step 1— The first three UDP datagrams transmitted have their TTL set to 1. Because the TTL determines how many more network hops a datagram can make, datagrams with a TTL of 1 expire as they hit the first router. When they expire, an ICMP error message is returned to the source—in this case, the node that began the trace.

Step 2—Using the return messages, the trace now knows the identity of the first router. It then transmits a series of datagrams with a TTL of 2 to determine the identity of the second router.

Step 3—The process continues for the next router in the path, and then the fourth, fifth, and so on, until the destination node is reached. The trace also returns the amount of time it took for the datagrams to reach each router in the path.

NOTE 4-9

Command parameters can be combined into a single command. For example, entering the command `netstat -an` will display the IP addresses and ports of active TCP connections and also listening TCP and UDP ports.

NOTE 4-10

Traceroute can be configured to use TCP or ICMP messages. See the traceroute man pages to learn how to configure this and many other options.

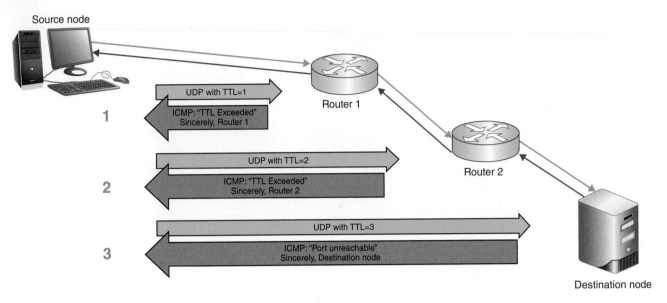

Figure 4-27   The traceroute utility uses error messages from routers to map nodes on a route

This process is identical for tracert in Windows except for two modifications. First, the probes sent from the source are ICMP echo request messages; each message is still limited by the specific TTL restrictions. Second, the final reply from the destination node is an ICMP echo reply rather than an ICMP port unreachable error message.

Applying Concepts 4-5: Trace the Route to Google.com

You can perform a trace using an IP address or a host name. On a UNIX or Linux system, the command syntax would be the following:

`traceroute 8.8.8.8` or `traceroute google.com`

Because tracert is installed by default on Windows, use a Windows machine for this exercise instead:

1. On a Windows system, perform a trace on one of Google's public DNS servers with the command `tracert 8.8.8.8`. How many hops were traced? What is the IP address of the final hop?
2. Use tracert to perform a trace on Google's web server with the command `tracert` *google.com*. How many hops were traced this time? What is the IP address of the final hop? Why is this IP address different than the IP address of the final hop in the previous step?

The `traceroute` or `tracert` command has several available parameters. Table 4-10 describes some of the more popular ones.

Table 4-10   `traceroute` and `tracert` command options

Command	Description

`traceroute -n google.com`
 	
or
 	
`tracert -d google.com`
	Instruct the command to not resolve IP addresses to host names.

`traceroute -m 12 google.com`
 	
or
 	
`tracert -h 12 google.com`
	Specify the maximum number of hops when attempting to reach a host; this parameter must be followed by a specific number. Without this parameter, the command defaults to 30.

Command	Description

`traceroute -w 2 google.com`
 	
or
 	
`tracert -w 2000 google.com`
	Identify a timeout period for responses; this parameter must be followed by a variable to indicate the number of seconds (in Linux) or milliseconds (in Windows) that the utility should wait for a response. The default time is usually between 3 and 5 seconds for Linux and 4000 milliseconds (4 seconds) for Windows.

`traceroute -f 3 google.com`	Set the first TTL value and must be followed by a variable to indicate the number of hops for the first probe. The default value is 1, which begins the trace at the first router on the route. Beginning at later hops in the route can more quickly narrow down the location of a network problem. `tracert` does not have a corresponding parameter for this function.
`traceroute -I google.com`	Instruct the command to use ICMP echo requests instead of UDP datagrams.
`traceroute -T google.com`	Instruct the command to use TCP SYN probes instead of UDP datagrams.

`traceroute -4 google.com`
 	
or
 	
`tracert -4 google.com`
	Force the command to use IPv4 packets only.

`traceroute -6 google.com`
 	
or
 	
`tracert -6 google.com`
	Force the command to use IPv6 packets instead of IPv4. The other parameters can be added to these IPv6 commands and function essentially the same as they do in IPv4.

Note that a trace test might stop before reaching the destination. This usually happens for one of three reasons: (1) The device the trace is attempting to reach is down, (2) the target device is too busy to process lower-priority messages such as UDP or ICMP, or (3) a firewall blocks UDP and ICMP transmissions, especially if it receives several in a short period of time. If you are trying to trace a route to a host situated behind a firewall, you can try using TCP in traceroute. Otherwise, your efforts might be thwarted. (Because ping uses ICMP transmissions, the same limitations exist for that utility.)

One possible work-around for firewall-imposed limitations on multiple UDP or ICMP probes in a short period of time is to add more of a delay between the probe repetitions. This can be done with the `-z` parameter followed by the number of seconds (up to 10) for the minimum wait time between probes. This option, like many others, is only available for traceroute, not tracert.

A trace cannot detect router configuration problems or predict variations of routes over time. Therefore, a trace is best used on a network with which you are already familiar. The traceroute or tracert utility can help you diagnose network congestion or network failures. You can then use your judgment and experience to compare the actual test results with what you anticipate the results should be.

NOTE 4-11

Many Linux distributions, like Ubuntu, do not include the traceroute utility by default. You will have to install traceroute to use it on those systems. You might find in its place a simpler utility called tracepath. The `tracepath` command does not provide as many options as `traceroute`. However, it is based on the same principles, and it might be sufficient to save you the time of installing the traceroute package.

tcpdump

The **tcpdump** utility is a free, command-line packet sniffer that runs on Linux and other UNIX operating systems. You've already learned about the protocol analyzer Wireshark where you captured a packet and examined the information provided at various OSI layers, and the *On the Job* story at the beginning of this module showed how a network analyzer was used to identify the source of a difficult-to-diagnose problem with some applications. A **packet sniffer** is very similar and many people use the terms interchangeably. In essence, the difference between a packet sniffer and a protocol analyzer is the level of interpretation and analysis the tool provides for the data captured from the network interface.

Like Wireshark, tcpdump captures traffic that crosses a computer's network interface. The output can be saved to a file that you can filter or play back. Because of its robust configuration options and straightforward, command-line interface, it's a popular tool among security professionals and hackers alike. When used on a network device, such as a router or switch, tcpdump can become a very powerful tool indeed.

You must either use the `sudo` command or log in as root to access tcpdump. To do this, either enter `sudo` before each `tcpdump` command, or at the shell prompt, enter `sudo su root`, which changes you over to the root account. Table 4-11 gives some `tcpdump` examples.

Table 4-11   `tcpdump` command options

tcpdump command	Description
`tcpdump not port 22` or `tcpdump not port 23`	Filter out SSH or Telnet packets, which is helpful when running tcpdump on a remotely accessed network device.
`tcpdump -n`	Instruct the command to not resolve IP addresses to host names.
`tcpdump -c 50`	Limit the number of captured packets to 50.
`tcpdump -i any`	Listen to all network interfaces on a device.
`tcpdump -D`	List all interfaces available for capture.
`tcpdump port http`	Filter out all traffic except HTTP.
`tcpdump -w capture.cap`	Write the file output to a file named capture.cap.
`tcpdump -r capture.cap`	Read the file capture.cap and output the data in the terminal window. This file can also be read by applications like Wireshark.

Solving Common Network Problems

You can use the tools presented in this module to troubleshoot and solve several common problems on your network. Table 4-12 gives a brief summary of all the command-line utilities you've covered so far in this course and how they can help you.

Table 4-12   Command-line utilities

Command	Common uses
`arp`	Provide a way to obtain information from and manipulate a device's ARP table.
`dig`	Query DNS servers with more advanced options than nslookup.
`ipconfig`, `ip`, or `ifconfig`	Provide information about TCP/IP network connections and the ability to manage some of those settings.
`netstat`	Display TCP/IP statistics and details about TCP/IP components and connections on a host.
`nmap`	Detect, identify, and monitor devices on a network.
`nslookup`	Query DNS servers and provide the ability to manage the settings for accessing those servers.
`ping`	Verify connectivity between two nodes on a network.
`ssh`	Establish a secured connection with a remote host for executing commands from the remote device's CLI.
`telnet`	Establish an unsecured connection with a remote host for executing commands from the remote device's CLI.
`tcpdump`	Capture traffic that crosses a computer's network interface.
`traceroute` or `tracert`	Trace the path from one networked node to another, identifying all intermediate routers between the two nodes.

Using what you've learned, let's explore a few common network problems and how to solve them.

Duplicate MAC Addresses

Devices on separate networks can have the same MAC address without causing any problems. Even if duplicate MAC addresses need to communicate with each other across separate networks, the fact that MAC addresses exist at layer 2 means the MAC addresses themselves are not transmitted outside of their local network. However, two devices on the *same* network with the same MAC address *is* a problem.

Because MAC addresses are assigned statically by the manufacturer, you might wonder how two devices could possibly have the same MAC address. Sometimes manufacturers (by accident or by neglect) reuse the same MAC address for two or more devices. Additionally, a MAC address can be impersonated, which is a security risk called **MAC spoofing**. On a network where access is limited to certain devices based on their MAC address (see Figure 4-28), an attacker can spoof an approved device's MAC address and gain access to the network. This is a relatively easy attack to carry out, which is why MAC address filtering is not considered a reliable way to control access to a network.

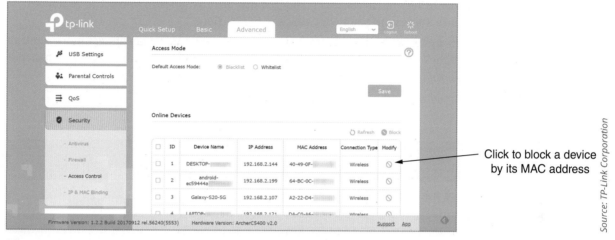

Figure 4-28 This home router can block, or blacklist, a device based on its MAC address

Most of the time, though, duplicate MAC addresses only cause intermittent connectivity issues for the computers involved in the duplication. Here's how the situation develops:

Step 1—Each computer regularly broadcasts its IP address and the duplicated MAC address so devices on the network can update their ARP tables.

Step 2—Those other devices, in response, update their records to point toward one computer, and then the other computer, and then back to the first one, and so on, depending upon the latest transmission they received.

Step 3—Sometimes devices will send communications to the correct computer, and sometimes their records will be wrong.

Thankfully, duplicate MAC addresses are a relatively rare problem. It happens most often when managing multiple virtual devices on a large network, and in those cases, it's typically due to human error. Most switches will detect the problem and produce helpful error messages of some kind. Then it's a matter of tracking down which virtual devices have the same MAC address and updating each device's configuration.

Applying Concepts 4-6: Change a MAC address

It only takes a few, short steps to change a Windows computer's MAC address. Complete the following steps:

1. Open Network and Sharing Center, and click **Change adapter settings**.
2. Right-click any wired network adapter and click **Properties**. Then click **Configure**.
3. On the Advanced tab, click **Network Address** (on a VM, this field is called Locally Administered Address). Select the **Value** radio button, and then enter a 12-digit value with no hyphens or colons, and click **OK**. Close all windows and restart the computer.
4. Run `ipconfig /all` to confirm the new MAC address is active.
5. To return to the default MAC address, repeat the earlier steps but select **Not Present** on the Advanced tab.

Hardware Failure

When a router, switch, NIC, or other hardware goes down, your job as a network technician includes identifying the location of the hardware failure. Even on smaller networks, it can be a challenge to determine exactly which device is causing problems. Though you could manually check each device on your network for errors, you might be able to shorten your list with a little detective work first. Here's how:

1. Use tracert or traceroute (depending on your OS) to track down malfunctioning routers and other devices on larger networks. Because ICMP messages are considered low priority, be sure to run the command multiple times and compare the results before drawing any conclusions.

2. Keep in mind that routers are designed to route traffic to other destinations. You might get more accurate tracert or traceroute feedback on a questionable router if you target a node on the other side of that router rather than aiming for the router itself.

3. As you home in on the troublesome device, use ping to test for network connectivity.

REMEMBER THIS...

- Practice using netstat, tracert, traceroute, tcpdump, and Wireshark.
- Explain how to solve problems related to duplicate MAC addresses or hardware failure.

SELF-CHECK

9. You need to determine which device on your network is sending excessive messages to your Ubuntu Server. Which utility will give you this information?
   a. traceroute
   b. tcpdump
   c. netstat
   d. arp

10. What protocol must be allowed through a firewall for tracert to work correctly?
   a. SSH
   b. NDP
   c. ICMP
   d. TLS

Check your answers at the end of this module.

You're Ready

You're now ready to complete **Project 4-3: Redirect Command Output to a Text File**, or you can wait until you've finished the Review Questions for this module.

You're Ready

You're now ready to complete **Project 4-4: Repair a Duplicate IP Address**, or you can wait until you've finished the Review Questions for this module.

You're Ready

After you finish the Hands-On Projects, you're ready to complete the **Module 4 Capstone Projects**.

MODULE SUMMARY

TCP/IP Core Protocols

- Data and instructions, known as the payload, are generated by an application running on the source host. In a process called encapsulation, a transport layer protocol (usually either TCP or UDP) adds a header to the payload. The network layer adds its own header to the passed-down segment or datagram. The packet is passed to the data link layer on the NIC, which encapsulates this data with its own header and trailer, creating a frame. The physical layer places the actual transmission on the network. The receiving host decapsulates the message at each layer in reverse order and then presents the payload to the receiving application.
- Each device is known by the innermost OSI layer header it reads and processes.
- Before TCP transmits data, it ensures that a connection or session is established. TCP also sends a character string called a checksum; TCP on the destination host then generates a similar string. If the two checksums fail to match, the destination host asks the source to retransmit the data. TCP also supports flow control, which is the process of gauging the appropriate rate of transmission based on how quickly the recipient can accept data.
- The TCP header includes several important fields, including Source port, Destination port, Sequence number, Acknowledgment number, TCP header length, several flags, Sliding-window size, and an Urgent pointer. TCP uses the sequence number and acknowledgment number fields to orchestrate a three-way handshake that establishes a session.
- UDP (User Datagram Protocol) is an unreliable, connectionless protocol, which means that UDP does not guarantee delivery of data, and no connection is established by UDP before data is transmitted. The UDP header contains only four fields: Source port, Destination port, Length, and Checksum.
- IP (Internet Protocol) belongs to the network layer of the OSI model and specifies where data should be delivered, identifying the data's source and destination IP addresses. IP is the protocol that enables TCP/IP to internetwork—that is, to traverse more than one LAN segment and more than one type of network through a router. The first field of an IP header indicates the IP version. Additional information in the header relates to fragmentation, TTL (Time to Live), identification of the encapsulated protocol, and source and destination IP addresses.
- Whereas IP helps direct data to its correct destination, ICMP (Internet Control Message Protocol) is a core network layer protocol that reports on the success or failure of data delivery. It can indicate when part of a network is congested, when data fails to reach its destination, and when data has been discarded because the allotted Time to Live has expired (that is, when the data has traveled its allotted number of hops). ICMP

announces these transmission failures to the sender, but it does not correct errors it detects—those functions are left to higher-layer protocols, such as TCP.

- ARP (Address Resolution Protocol) works in conjunction with IPv4 to discover the MAC address of a node on the local network and to maintain a database that maps local IP addresses to MAC addresses. ARP is a layer 2 protocol that works with IPv4 in layer 3. It's sometimes said to function at layer 2.5 because it touches information (IP addresses and MAC addresses) at both layers. However, it operates only within its local network bound by routers. To view a Windows workstation's ARP table, open a PowerShell or Command Prompt window and enter the command `arp -a`.
- The most important data link layer standard, Ethernet, is adaptable, capable of running on a variety of network media, and offers excellent throughput at a reasonable cost. Unlike higher-layer protocols, Ethernet adds both a header and a trailer to the payload it inherits from the layer above it. This creates a frame around the payload. Included in the Ethernet frame is information about the destination and source MAC addresses, the encapsulated protocol, and the FCS (frame check sequence) to ensure the data at the destination exactly matches the data issued from the source.

Encryption Protocols

- In terms of security, data exists generally in three states: at rest, in use, and in motion. Encryption is the last layer of defense against data theft. Encryption protocols use a mathematical code, called a cipher, to scramble data into a format that can be read only by reversing the cipher—that is, by deciphering, or decrypting, the data.
- To protect data at rest, in use, and in motion, encryption methods are primarily evaluated by three benchmarks: confidentiality, integrity, and availability. These three principles form the standard security model called the CIA (confidentiality, integrity, and availability) triad.
- With private key encryption, data is encrypted using a single key that only the sender and the receiver know. A potential problem with private key encryption is that the sender must somehow share the key with the recipient without it being intercepted.
- With public key encryption, data is encrypted with a private key known only to the user, and it's decrypted with a mathematically related public key that can be made available through a third-party source, such as a public key server. This ensures data integrity, as the sender's public key will only work if the data has not been tampered with. Alternatively, data can be encrypted with the public key, and then it can only be decrypted with the matching private key. This ensures data confidentiality, as only the intended recipient (the owner of the keys) can decrypt the data.
- IPsec (Internet Protocol Security) is an encryption protocol suite that defines a set of rules for encryption, authentication, and key management for TCP/IP transmissions. IPsec works at the network layer of the OSI model—it adds security information to the headers of IP packets and encrypts the data payload. Either AH (authentication header) encryption or ESP (Encapsulating Security Payload) encryption may be used. Both types of encryption provide authentication of the IP packet's data payload through public key techniques. In addition, ESP encrypts the entire IP packet for added security.
- SSL (Secure Sockets Layer) and TLS (Transport Layer Security) are both methods of encrypting TCP/IP transmissions en route between the client and server using public key encryption technology. SSL operates in the application layer. TLS operates in the transport layer and uses slightly different encryption algorithms than SSL, but otherwise is essentially the updated version of SSL.
- HTTP uses TCP port 80, whereas HTTPS (HTTP Secure) uses SSL/TLS encryption and TCP port 443. Other protocols that offer SSL/TLS encrypted alternatives include SMTP TLS, LDAP over SSL, IMAP over SSL, and POP3 over SSL. Each time a client and server establish an SSL/TLS connection, they establish a unique session, or an association between the client and server that is defined by an agreement on a specific set of encryption techniques. The session allows the client and server to continue to exchange data securely as long as the client is still connected to the server.

Remote Access Protocols

- FTPS (FTP Security or FTP Secure) is an added layer of protection for FTP using SSL/TLS that can encrypt both the control and data channels. SFTP (Secure FTP) is a file-transfer version of SSH that includes encryption and authentication, and it's sometimes inaccurately called FTP over SSH or SSH FTP. Note that SFTP is an extension of the SSH protocol, not of FTP. TFTP (Trivial FTP) is a simple version of FTP that includes no authentication or security for transferring files and uses UDP at the transport layer (unlike FTP, which relies on TCP at the transport layer). TFTP requires very little memory and is most often used by machines behind the scenes to transfer boot files or configuration files.
- Terminal emulation, also called remote virtual computing, allows a remote client to take over and command a host computer. Examples of terminal emulation software are Telnet, SSH, Remote Desktop, and VNC (Virtual Network Computing).
- Examples of command-line software that can provide terminal emulation include Telnet and SSH. Some GUI-based software examples are Remote Desktop for Windows, join.me, VNC (virtual network computing), and TeamViewer. A host may allow clients a variety of privileges, from merely viewing the screen to running programs and modifying data files on the host's hard disk.
- SSH allows for password authentication or authentication using public and private keys. First, generate a public key and a private key on your client workstation by running the `ssh-keygen` command (or by choosing the correct menu options in a graphical SSH program). Then transfer the public key to an authorization file on the host to which you want to connect. When you connect to the host via SSH, the client and host exchange public keys. If both can be authenticated, the connection is completed.
- RDP (Remote Desktop Protocol) is a Microsoft proprietary protocol used by Windows Remote Desktop and Remote Assistance client/server utilities to connect to and control a remote computer. Similarly, VNC (Virtual Network Computing) uses the cross-platform protocol RFB (remote frame buffer) to remotely control a workstation or server. VNC is slower than Remote Desktop and requires more network bandwidth. However, because VNC is open source, many companies have developed their own software using VNC.
- Telnet, SSH, RDP, and VNC all rely on the existing network infrastructure for a network administrator to remotely control the device. Before the devices can be configured, they must already be booted up, and they must already have configuration software installed. This is called in-band management, and it inherently limits troubleshooting capabilities. Out-of-band management, however, relies on a dedicated connection (either wired or wireless) between the network administrator's computer and each critical network device.
- A VPN (virtual private network) is a virtual connection that remotely accesses resources between a client and a network (client-to-site VPN), two networks (site-to-site VPN), or two hosts over the Internet or other types of networks (host-to-host VPN).
- To ensure a VPN can carry all types of data in a private manner over any kind of connection, special VPN protocols encapsulate higher-layer protocols in a process known as tunneling. Two common approaches to VPN tunneling either require all network traffic to traverse the VPN tunnel or only some of that traffic. While IPsec itself can be used as a tunneling protocol, it often provides encryption for another tunneling protocol. This pairing offers more flexibility and other features that IPsec can't offer alone.

Troubleshooting Network Issues

- The netstat utility displays TCP/IP statistics and details about TCP/IP components and connections on a host. The `netstat` command can be used to obtain information about the port on which a TCP/IP service is running, which network connections are currently established for a client, how many messages have been handled by a network interface since it was activated, and how many data errors have occurred on a particular network interface.
- The Windows tracert utility uses ICMP echo requests to trace the path from one networked node to another, identifying all intermediate hops between the two nodes. Linux, UNIX, and macOS systems use UDP datagrams or, possibly, TCP SYN messages, for their traceroute utility, but the concept is still the same.

- The tcpdump utility is a free, command-line packet sniffer that runs on Linux and other UNIX operating systems. Like Wireshark, tcpdump captures traffic that crosses a computer's network interface. Because of its robust configuration options and straightforward, command-line interface, it's a popular tool among security professionals and hackers alike. You must either use the `sudo` command or log in as root to access tcpdump.
- Devices on separate networks can have the same MAC address without causing any problems. However, two devices on the *same* network with the same MAC address *is* a problem. Most of the time duplicate MAC addresses only cause intermittent connectivity issues for the computers involved in the duplication. It happens most often when managing multiple virtual devices on a large network, and in those cases, it's typically due to human error.
- When a router, switch, NIC, or other hardware goes down, a network technician's job is to identify the location of the hardware failure. Various tools help to narrow down the possibilities, including using tracert or traceroute to track down malfunctioning routers and other devices on larger networks, targeting a node on the other side of a suspected router problem rather than aiming for the router itself, and using ping to test for network connectivity.

Key Terms

For definitions of key terms, see the Glossary.

AH (authentication header)
ARP (Address Resolution Protocol)
ARP table
asymmetric encryption
authentication
CA (certificate authority)
checksum
CIA (confidentiality, integrity, and availability) triad
clientless VPN
client-to-site VPN
collision
collision domain
CSMA/CD (Carrier Sense Multiple Access with Collision Detection)
digital certificate
DMVPN (Dynamic Multipoint VPN)
dynamic ARP table entry
encryption
ESP (Encapsulating Security Payload)
Ethernet II
FTPS (FTP Secure or FTP over SSL)

full tunnel VPN
GRE (Generic Routing Encapsulation)
hop
in-band management
IPsec (Internet Protocol Security)
jumbo frame
key
link-layer address
LLC (logical link control) sublayer
MAC spoofing
MAC sublayer
mGRE (multipoint GRE)
MTU (maximum transmission unit)
NDP (Neighbor Discovery Protocol)
netstat
out-of-band management
packet sniffer
PKI (public-key infrastructure)
private key encryption
probe
protocol analyzer
public key encryption

RAS (remote access server)
RDS (Remote Desktop Services)
remote access
remote desktop connection
remote desktop gateway
site-to-site VPN
split tunnel VPN
spoofing
static ARP table entry
symmetric encryption
tcpdump
terminal emulator
TFTP server
three-way handshake
traceroute
tracert
VDI (Virtual Desktop Infrastructure)
VNC (Virtual Network Computing)
VPN (virtual private network)
VPN headend

Review Questions

1. Which protocol's header would a layer 4 device read and process?
   a. IP
   b. TCP
   c. ARP
   d. HTTP

2. What field in a TCP segment is used to determine if an arriving data unit exactly matches the data unit sent by the source?
   a. Source port
   b. Acknowledgment number
   c. DiffServ
   d. Checksum

3. At which OSI layer does IP operate?
   a. Application layer
   b. Transport layer
   c. Network layer
   d. Data link layer

4. What is the Internet standard MTU?
   a. 65,535 bytes
   b. 1,522 bytes
   c. 1,500 bytes
   d. 9,198 bytes

5. Which two protocols manage neighbor discovery processes on IPv4 networks?
   a. ICMP and ARP
   b. IPv4 and IPv6
   c. TCP and UDP
   d. NDP and Ethernet

6. You're getting a duplicate IP address error on your computer and need to figure out what other device on your network is using the IP address 192.168.1.56. What command will show you which MAC address is mapped to that IP address?
   a. `telnet 192.168.1.56`
   b. `tracert 192.168.1.56`
   c. `arp -a`
   d. `netstat -n`

7. What is one advantage offered by VDI over RDS and VNC?
   a. Offers access to multiple OSs in VMs
   b. Supports remote access to mobile devices
   c. Allows multiple users to sign in at once
   d. Provides open source flexibility

8. Which encryption protocol does GRE use to increase the security of its transmissions?
   a. SSL
   b. SFTP
   c. IPsec
   d. SSH

9. Which encryption benchmark ensures data is not modified after it's transmitted and before it's received?
   a. Confidentiality
   b. Integrity
   c. Availability
   d. Symmetric

10. Which remote file access protocol is an extension of SSH?
    a. SFTP
    b. TFTP
    c. FTPS
    d. HTTPS

11. What three characteristics about TCP distinguish it from UDP?

12. What process is used to establish a TCP connection?

13. What is the difference between dynamic ARP table entries and static ARP table entries?

14. Which two fields in an Ethernet frame help synchronize device communications but are not counted toward the frame's size?

15. Explain the key difference between how symmetric encryption works and how asymmetric encryption works.

16. Which secured tunneling protocol might be able to cross firewalls where IPsec is blocked?

17. When surfing online, you get some strange data on an apparently secure website, and you realize you need to check the legitimacy of the site. What kind of organization issues digital certificates for websites?

18. What `tcpdump` command will capture data on the eth0 interface and redirect output to a text file named checkme.txt for further analysis?

19. Which terminal emulation protocol is similar to RDP but is open source?

20. Which port must be open for RDP traffic to cross a firewall?

Hands-On Projects

NOTE 4-12

Websites and applications change often. While the instructions given in these projects were accurate at the time of writing, you might need to adjust the steps or options according to later changes.

Note to Instructors and Students: A rubric is provided for evaluating student performance on these projects. Please see Appendix D.

Project 4-1: Install and Use WSL (Windows Subsystem for Linux)

Estimated Time: 45 minutes
Objective: Given a scenario, use the appropriate network software tools and commands. (Obj. 5.3)
Resources:
- Windows 10 computer with administrative access
- Internet access

Context: WSL (Windows Subsystem for Linux) is a Linux shell for Windows that allows users to interact with underlying Windows functions and system files. It's not a VM, and it's not a fully separate operating system. It runs on any 64-bit Windows 10 system with the Anniversary Update (version 1607) or later. To use it, you must first turn on Developer Mode, and then enable the Windows Subsystem for Linux feature. To enable Windows Subsystem for Linux and install an Ubuntu Terminal on a Windows 10 system, complete the following steps:

1. First, turn on Developer Mode.
   a. Open the **Settings** app and click **Update & Security**. In the left pane, scroll down and click **For developers**.
   b. Select **Developer mode**, as shown in Figure 4-29. Click **Yes** to turn on Developer Mode and close the Settings app.

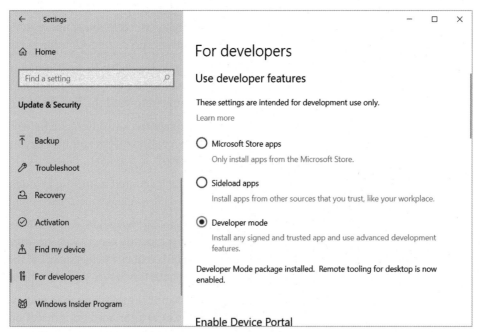

Figure 4-29   Turn on Developer Mode from the Settings app

2. Enable Windows Subsystem for Linux.

   a. Open **Control Panel** and click **Programs and Features**. In the left pane, click **Turn Windows features on or off**.
   b. Scroll down and click **Windows Subsystem for Linux**, as shown in Figure 4-30. Click **OK**.

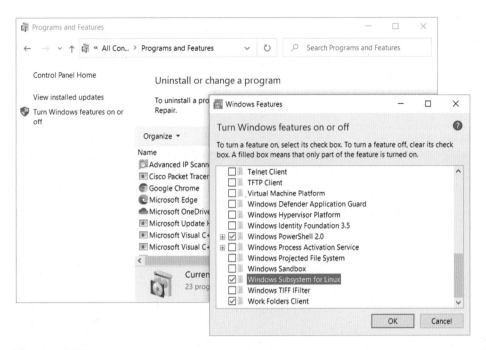

Figure 4-30   Turn on the Windows Subsystem for Linux feature

---

NOTE 4-13

To open Turn Windows features on or off directly, you can also click Start, begin typing **turn Windows**, then click **Turn Windows features on or off**.

---

   c. Restart the computer when the changes are complete to finish enabling Windows Subsystem for Linux.

Now that you have enabled Windows Subsystem for Linux, you can install a distribution of Linux designed to run on Windows. To install and run Ubuntu on Windows, do the following:

3. Open the **Microsoft Store** app and search for **Ubuntu**. Install the latest, free Ubuntu on Windows app, as shown in Figure 4-31.

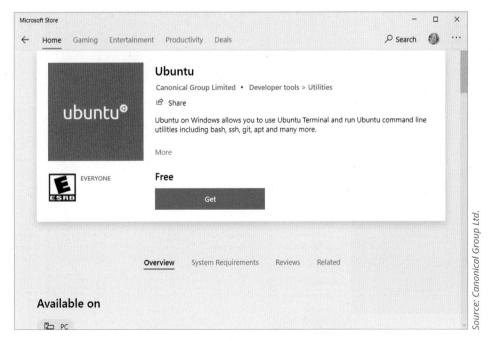

Source: Canonical Group Ltd.

Figure 4-31   Install the Ubuntu on Windows app from the Microsoft Store

4. After the installation is complete, launch the app. Enter a new UNIX username at the prompt. This username can be different from your Windows username.
5. Enter a password at the next prompt. The cursor will not move as you type the password. Re-enter the password at the next prompt. Add this information as a Secure Note in your LastPass vault.
6. After the installation is complete, you'll see the Ubuntu Terminal, as shown in Figure 4-32. What is the Ubuntu prompt on your computer? Include all symbols in your answer.

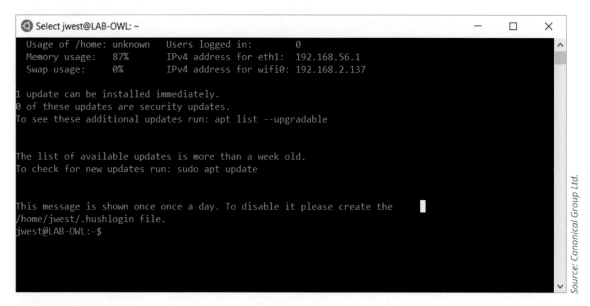

Figure 4-32   Ubuntu on Windows is installed and provides an Ubuntu Terminal

At this point, many of the Linux commands you have become familiar with will work as usual at the Ubuntu shell prompt. The commands interact with the underlying Windows system files, and changes to those files can be monitored through other Windows tools.

7. Enter the commend **pwd** to show your current working directory (recall the Linux calls folders *directories*). What is the current directory?
8. To open a File Explorer window showing this directory, enter the command **explorer.exe.** (Notice the extra space and period after the explorer.exe portion.) Figure 4-33 shows the command entered in the Ubuntu Terminal window and the File Explorer window showing Ubuntu's home directory.

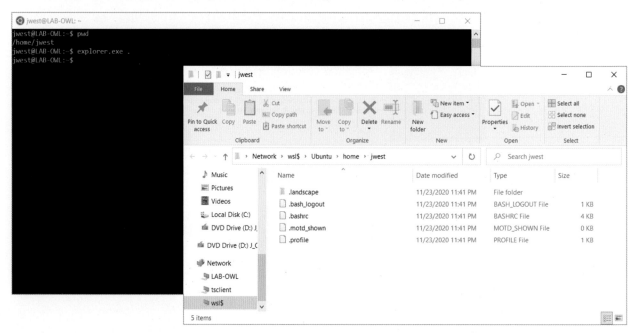

Figure 4-33   You can see Ubuntu's home directory in File Explorer

9. To create a new directory, enter the command **mkdir mydir**. Refresh the File Explorer window. Do you see your new directory listed?

10. To navigate to that directory in Ubuntu, enter the command **cd mydir**. To create a new file in that directory, enter the command **touch myfile.txt**. In File Explorer, open the **mydir** folder. What items do you see listed here?

11. Choose three other Linux commands and practice using them. For each one, **take a screenshot** of the Ubuntu Terminal window showing the command and its output. Submit this visual with your answers to this project's questions.

12. In your wiki, add a new page titled **Applications:WSL-Ubuntu**. Indicate the module and project number for this installation, the computer you used for this project, a brief description of what you learned, and any other information you might find helpful when using Ubuntu on Windows later.

Project 4-2: Use Remote Desktop

Estimated Time: 45 minutes

Objective: Compare and contrast remote access methods and security implications. (Obj. 4.4)

Group Work: This project can be completed by an individual working alone or, if desired, in cooperation with a team of two or three classmates. In some cases, working as a group could provide beneficial insights when troubleshooting challenging steps and brainstorming solutions. Check with your instructor for details specific to your class.

Resources:

- Two Windows computers (with administrative access) on the same network
  - These two computers can be both physical, both virtual, or one of each.
  - One of these systems must have Windows 10 Professional, Education, or Enterprise installed, and the other can have any edition of Windows 7, 8, 8.1, or 10.
  - If you're using a VM as one computer and the VM's physical host as the second computer, the VM must serve as the RDP host and must have Windows 10 Professional, Education, or Enterprise installed. You might need to create a new Windows VM to meet these requirements if you previously installed Windows 10 Home on your VM. If you do create a new VM, be sure to record credentials in your LastPass vault. The physical computer will be the RDP client.
  - If you're using a VirtualBox VM as one computer and a physical machine as the second computer, the VM's network adapter must be configured in the bridged mode. Before starting the VM, open the VM's **Settings** window, click **Network**, and change the *Attached to* field to **Bridged Adapter**. Click **OK**. You can now start the VM.
- Internet access or a Windows ISO file if a new VM is needed

Context: The host or server computer is the remote computer that serves up Remote Desktop to your local client computer. Note that a Windows Home computer cannot serve as an RDP host, although it can connect as a client to another RDP host. To prepare your host computer, you need to get its name and configure the Remote Desktop service. Complete the following steps on a Windows 10 (Professional, Education, or Enterprise) machine:

1. Right-click the **Start** button and click **System**. Under Device specifications, find the device's name and copy it to a text file using Notepad for future reference in this project. What is the RDP host's device name?

2. To enable the Remote Desktop service on the host computer, in the left pane of the Settings window, scroll down and click **Remote Desktop**. Click the slider to **Enable Remote Desktop**. In the warning box, click **Confirm**.

3. Make sure you know the sign-in credentials for a user on this system. Users who have administrative privileges are allowed to use Remote Desktop by default, but other users need to be added. If you need to add a user, click **Select users that can remotely access this PC** and follow the directions on-screen.

4. Verify that Windows Firewall is set to allow Remote Desktop activity to this computer. To do this, in the Settings app, search for **firewall**, click **Firewall & network protection** and then click **Allow an app through firewall**.

5. The Allowed apps window appears. Scroll down to Remote Desktop. If the changes don't match the settings in Figure 4-34, click **Change settings** and make any needed adjustments. Click **OK** to apply any changes. Close the Windows Defender Firewall and Settings windows. You will learn more about Windows Defender Firewall later.

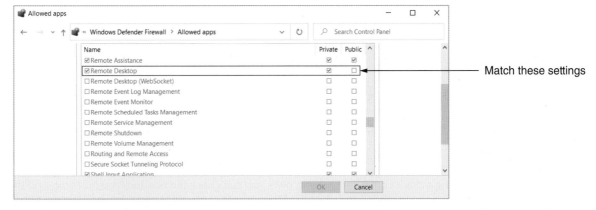

Figure 4-34   Allow Remote Desktop communication on a private network through Windows Defender Firewall

You are now ready to test Remote Desktop by accessing the host computer (physical or virtual) from another computer (physical or virtual) on your local network. Note that any edition of Windows 7, 8.1, or 10 can serve as a client computer (the computer viewing the host computer's desktop) for a Remote Desktop connection. The following steps are written specifically for Windows 10.

Follow these steps on the client computer (any edition of Windows 7, 8, 8.1, or 10) to create a Remote Desktop connection to the host computer:

6. First, confirm the two computers can communicate on the network. In a PowerShell or Command Prompt window, ping the RDP host computer from the RDP client computer. If the `ping` works, continue to Step 7. If it does not work, you'll need to do some troubleshooting. Here are some possible solutions:

    a. Make sure both computers are connected to the same network and subnet. In most cases, the first three octets of each computer's IP address should be identical to each other.

    b. Make sure both computers can communicate successfully with other resources on the network. For example, try pinging the default gateway.

    c. Make sure both computers are connected to the network in Private mode. To check this, click the network connection's icon on the right side of the taskbar near the clock, and then click **Network & Internet settings**. The connection should be labeled "Private network" on both computers. If it is not, click **Change connection properties** and choose the **Private** option. Note that if you're working on a physical machine connected to a Hyper-V virtual switch, the network status will show *vEthernet* and you will not have the option to change between Public and Private network modes because the computer should already be in Private network mode.

    d. If the `ping` still won't work, enabling File and Printer Sharing on Windows Defender Firewall sometimes solves the problem. To do this, open Network and Sharing Center and click **Change advanced sharing settings**. Select **Turn on file and printer sharing** for private networks on both computers.

7. Press **Win+R**, type **mstsc** in the search box, and press **Enter**. This is easier to remember if you know that Remote Desktop Services was formerly called Microsoft Terminal Services; mstsc (Microsoft Terminal Services Client) is the client portion. Alternately, you can click **Start**, scroll down and click **Windows Accessories**, and then click **Remote Desktop Connection**.

8. Enter the host name of the computer to which you want to connect. To be able to transfer files from one computer to the other, click **Show Options** and then click the **Local Resources** tab, as shown in the left side of Figure 4-35. Under *Local devices and resources*, click **More**. The dialog box on the right side of Figure 4-35 appears.

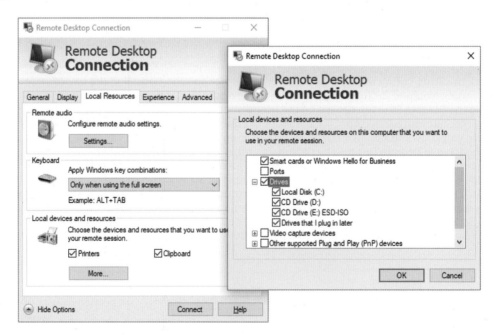

Figure 4-35   Allow drives to be shared using the Remote Desktop Connection

9. Check **Drives**, click **OK**, and then click **Connect** to make the connection. If a warning box appears, check the box for *Don't ask me again for connections to this computer* and then click **Connect** again.

10. Enter a password for the remote computer. If you need to sign in with a different account than the one you're using on the client computer, click **More choices**, click **Use a different account**, and enter the account credentials. If you're using a client computer that you own, you can check the box for *Remember me*, and then click **OK**. If a warning box appears saying the identity of the remote computer cannot be verified, you can check the box for *Don't ask me again for connections to this computer*. Click **Yes** to continue with the connection.

NOTE 4-14

Even though Windows normally allows more than one user to be logged on at the same time, Remote Desktop does not. When a Remote Desktop session is opened, all local users on the host computer are logged off.

11. The desktop of the remote computer appears in a maximized window that covers your entire screen. Float your cursor at the top of your screen to find the RDP controls. From here, you can reduce the size of the RDP window so you can see both your local computer's desktop and the remote computer's desktop, as shown in Figure 4-36. When you click inside the RDP window, you can work with the remote computer just as if you were sitting in front of it, except the response time will be slower. To move files back and forth between computers, use File Explorer on the remote computer. Files on your local computer and on the remote computer will appear in File Explorer on the remote computer's screen in the This PC group.

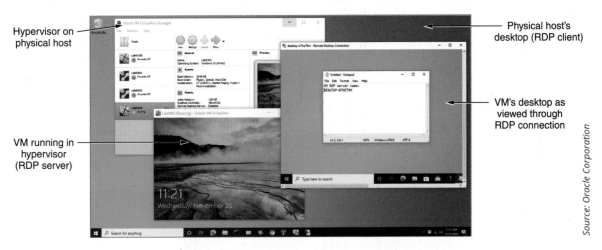

Hypervisor on physical host

Physical host's desktop (RDP client)

VM's desktop as viewed through RDP connection

VM running in hypervisor (RDP server)

Source: Oracle Corporation

Figure 4-36   **Physical host (RDP client) connected by RDP to VM (RDP server)**

12. Position File Explorer on the remote computer's desktop so that you can see both the server's and the client's hard drives listed in the left pane. **Take a screenshot**; submit this visual with your answers to this project's questions.
13. To close the connection to the remote computer, shut down or sign out of the remote computer or close the Remote Desktop Connection window.
14. In your wiki, add a new page titled **Applications:RDP**. Indicate the module and project number for this activity, the computers you used for this project, a brief description of what you learned, and any other information you might find helpful when using RDP later.
15. If you created a new VM for this project, add the new VM's information to your VMclients page in your wiki. Include the module number, hypervisor used, VM computer name, and VM operating system. Also note any additional information that you might find helpful when you return to this VM in the future.

Project 4-3: Redirect Command Output to a Text File

Estimated Time: 15 minutes
Objective: Given a scenario, use the appropriate network software tools and commands. (Obj. 5.3)
Resources:
  • Internet access
Context: Sometimes when you're using a command such as tcpdump, the sheer volume of output can be daunting to work with. There's no way to search through the output for specific information, and you can only expand the PowerShell or Command Prompt window so far. One solution to this problem is to redirect the command output to a text file where you can search the text, copy and paste text, and save the output for future reference. To accomplish this feat, you'll need to add a redirection operator to the command whose output you want to export to a text file. Complete the following steps:

1. First, try this simple command in PowerShell or Command Prompt:

```
ipconfig > ipconfigtest.txt
```

This runs the ipconfig command and redirects the output to a text file named ipconfigtest.txt. By default, the file is saved to the current default folder, for example, C:\Users\JillWest. Use File Explorer to find the file. **Take a screenshot** showing the file and its file path; submit this visual with your answers to this project's questions.

2. To specify the location of the file when you create it, add the path to the file in the command line. For example, to save the file to the desktop, use the following command (substitute the correct file path to your desktop). What command and file path did you enter?

```
ipconfig > C:\Users\Username\Desktop\ipconfigtest.txt
```

NOTE 4-15

If you're not sure what the file path is to your Desktop, you can find it in File Explorer. In the navigation pane on the left, right-click the **Desktop** link and click **Properties**. The file path is shown in the Location field. Note that your desktop might be showing your OneDrive Desktop, which would be located at the following path:

C:\Users\Username\OneDrive\Desktop

In this case, you might not be able to send command output to your OneDrive desktop. Save your files for this project to a folder on your hard drive instead.

3. If you already have a file on the desktop by that name, the file will be overwritten with the new data. What if you would rather append data to an existing file? In this case, use the >> operator. Enter this command (substitute the correct file path to your desktop):

```
ipconfig >> C:\Users\Username\Desktop\ipconfigtest.txt
```

Now the new output will appear at the end of the existing file, and all the data is preserved within this single file. This option is useful when collecting data from repeated tests or from multiple computers, where you want all the data to converge into a single file for future analysis.

NOTE 4-16

When reusing an earlier command or portions of an earlier command, you can press the up arrow on your keyboard to recall earlier commands. Then use the side arrows to place your cursor to make edits.

4. Where do command parameters fit when redirecting output? Let's use the `netstat` command to show the IP address and port of each TCP and UDP connection on the computer. In the following command, substitute the correct file path to your desktop to output the data to a new file. Notice that any parameters you want to use should be inserted after the command itself and before the redirection operator.

```
netstat -an > C:\Users\Username\Desktop\connections.txt
```

Open the file you just created. How many TCP ports are in the ESTABLISHED state?
5. Open your browser and visit two or three websites in different tabs. With your browser still open, run the netstat command again and append the new data to your existing file. What command did you run? How many TCP ports are in the ESTABLISHED state now?
6. You can include a space in the filename by putting quotation marks around the entire filename *and* location. Enter the following command:

```
ping 8.8.8.8 > "C:\Users\Username\Desktop\find google.txt"
```

7. **Take a screenshot** of your File Explorer window showing the files you created in this project from Step 2 through Step 6; submit this visual with your answers to this project's questions.

Project 4-4: Repair a Duplicate IP Address

Estimated Time: 15 minutes (+5 minutes for group work, if assigned)
Objective: Given a scenario, troubleshoot general networking issues. (Obj. 5.5)
Group Work: This project includes enhancements when assigned as a group project.
Resources:
- Windows 10 computer with administrative access

Context: ARP can be a valuable troubleshooting tool for discovering the identity of a machine whose IP address you know, or for identifying two machines assigned the same IP address. Let's see what happens when two devices on the network are assigned the same IP address. First you change the IP address of a local Windows machine to match an IP address of another device—in other words, you "break" the computer. Then you see how the `arp` command helps you diagnose the problem. Complete the following steps:

1. Open a PowerShell or Command Prompt window and enter the command `arp -a`. Your device's IP address is listed as the Interface address at the top of the list. Write down this IP address and the address of another device on the network.
2. Open the Network and Sharing Center, click **Change adapter settings**, right-click the active network connection, and click **Properties**. If necessary, enter an administrator password in the UAC box and click **Yes**.
3. Select Internet Protocol Version 4 (TCP/IPv4) and click **Properties**. Set the IP address to match the other device's IP address that you wrote down in Step 1. The system automatically assigns the Subnet mask, as shown in Figure 4-37. Also assign the Cloudflare public DNS servers: 1.1.1.1 and 1.0.0.1. Click **OK** and then click **Close**.

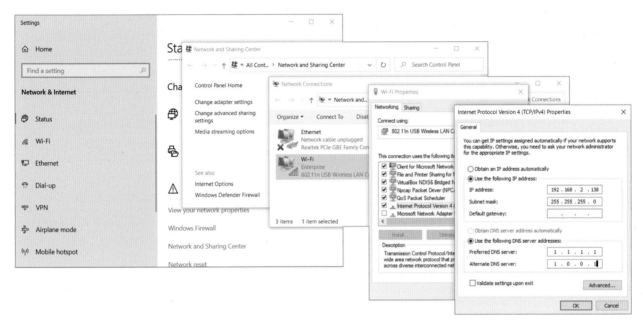

Figure 4-37 The subnet mask is assigned automatically

4. Back at the CLI, enter `ipconfig /all`.
5. Find the appropriate network connection and identify your computer's current IPv4 address. Answer the following questions:
    a. Has your computer identified the duplicate IP address problem yet? How do you know?
    b. Your computer might also have autoconfigured another IP address. If so, what address did your computer resort to?
    c. **Take a screenshot** of your TCP/IP configuration information; submit this visual with your answers to this project's questions.
6. In the window on the left side of Figure 4-38, you can see a warning that the IP address is a duplicate. The system also shows a preferred IPv4 address of 169.254.143.79, which is an APIPA address. How can you tell this is an APIPA address?

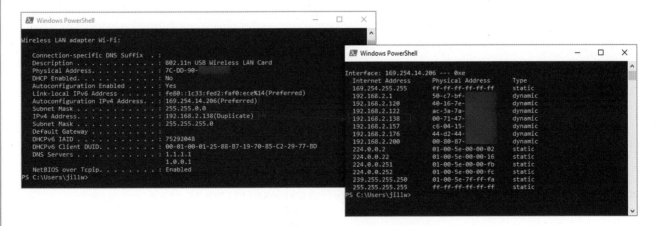

Figure 4-38 The computer automatically configured an APIPA address

7. To confirm the duplication of IP addresses, enter the command `arp -a`. You can see in Figure 4-38 that the local computer's IPv4 address listed on the left matches another IP address in the ARP table on the right, and again you see the APIPA address assigned to the local interface. What are two ways to solve this problem?

8. **For group assignments:** Run the `arp -a` command in your CLI window and answer the following questions:
   a. How many other APIPA addresses appear in the output?
   b. Which ones belong to your group members?
   c. How many digits in these APIPA addresses are the same for all group members?

9. Open the Internet Protocol Version 4 (TCP/IPv4) Properties dialog box again and select the options **Obtain an IP address automatically** and **Obtain DNS server address automatically** and then click **OK.** Close all active windows except your CLI.

10. Run the `ipconfig` command or the `arp -a` command to confirm that a unique IP address has been assigned to your local device's active network interface. What is the new IP address?

11. Close the PowerShell or Command Prompt window.

Capstone Projects

NOTE 4-17

Websites and applications change often. While the instructions given in these projects were accurate at the time of writing, you might need to adjust the steps or options according to later changes.

Note to Instructors and Students: A rubric is provided for evaluating student performance on these projects. Please see Appendix D.

Capstone Project 4-1: Set Up and Use a TFTP Server in Packet Tracer

Estimated Time: 30 minutes
Objective: Given a scenario, use the appropriate network software tools and commands. (Obj. 5.3)
Resources:

- Computer with Cisco Packet Tracer installed

Context: In Capstone Project 2-2, you installed Packet Tracer, and you used it again in Capstone Project 3-2. Earlier in this module, you learned about TFTP servers that can be used to back up and configure network devices. In this Capstone Project, you configure a router, back up the router configuration on a TFTP server, and then create a replacement router from the backup file. Note that Cisco devices keep active configuration settings in a file called running-config. There are actually two files: The startup-config file provides initial settings when the device boots, and the running-config file maintains those settings in the device's memory while it is powered on. When you make changes to the running-config file, that does not change the startup-config file, which means your settings are lost on the device's next power cycle. You can copy the running-config file contents to the startup-config file for later access. In this project, you'll focus on working with the running-config file. Complete the following steps:

1. Open Packet Tracer and, if necessary, sign in with your Networking Academy account.

2. In the Devices pane, click **Network Devices** category and then click **Routers**. Add a **PT-Router** to your workspace. Below the router's icon in the workspace, change the router's display name to **RtrGiraffe**. Add a note to indicate the router's IP address: **192.168.2.1/24**

3. Click the router to open its configuration window. Click the **Config** tab. Change the hostname to **RtrGiraffe**. As you make this change, notice the commands scrolling in the Equivalent IOS Commands pane at the bottom of the window.

4. Under INTERFACE, click **FastEthernet0/0**. Set the router's IP address to **192.168.2.1**. The subnet mask field should automatically populate with 255.255.255.0. Check the **On** box to activate the port.

5. In the Devices pane, click **End Devices** category. Add a **Server** to your workspace. Below the server's icon in the workspace, change the server's display name to **TFTPserver**. Add a note to indicate the server's IP address: **192.168.2.100/24**

6. Click the server to open its configuration window. Click the **Config** tab and click **FastEthernet0**. Set the server's IP address to **192.168.2.100**. The subnet mask field should automatically populate with 255.255.255.0.

7. In the Devices pane, click **Connections** category. Because you're connecting a server directly to a router, you need a crossover cable, which you'll learn more about later in this course. Click the straight, dashed line for the **Copper Cross-Over** cable and connect the **FastEthernet0/0** interface on the router with the **FastEthernet0** interface on the server.

8. In the server's configuration window, click the **Desktop** tab and click **Command Prompt**. Ping the router to confirm the connection works. What command did you use?

The server's TFTP service is on by default, so you're now ready to back up the router's running-config file to the server. You'll need to perform this task from the router's CLI. Complete the following steps:

9. In the router's configuration window, click the **CLI** tab. Click inside the IOS Command Line Interface pane and press **Enter**. The prompt should show `RtrGiraffe (config-if)#`. This prompt gives you some helpful information:
    a. The router's hostname is RtrGiraffe.
    b. The router's CLI is currently in the interface configuration mode, which is what you used to configure the FastEthernet0/0 interface. To exit this mode, enter `exit`.

10. Your router is now in global configuration mode, indicated by the `(config)#` portion of the prompt. You need to step down one more mode level, so enter `exit` again and then press **Enter**.

11. Your router is now in privileged EXEC mode, which is what you need to copy the running-config file to the TFTP server. Enter the command `copy running-config tftp`, which instructs the router to copy its running-config file to the TFTP server. You'll need to provide a little more information:
    a. Enter the server's IP address: **192.168.2.100**
    b. Enter the name of the file to be saved on the server: **Giraffe**

Now you're ready to check the logs on the TFTP server to confirm the file was copied successfully. Complete the following steps:

12. In the server's configuration window, click the **Services** tab and then click **TFTP** in the left pane. **Take a screenshot** of the logs, which should show the Giraffe entry at the top. Submit this visual with your answers to this project's questions.

Suppose your existing router fails, and you need to replace it with a new router. In the real world, you likely would have made many more configuration changes than simply the router's hostname and IP address. It would be time consuming and risky to attempt to copy this configuration manually to a new router. But you are prepared and have a backup configuration file! You're now ready to create a new router and copy the configuration file to this router. Complete the following steps:

13. From the Devices pane, add a new **PT-Router** to your workspace. Give this router the display name and hostname **RtrZebra** and set the FastEthernet0/0 interface to the same IP address as the first router: **192.168.2.1**. Be sure to make these changes to the documentation in your workspace *and* to the router's configuration settings. The workspace documentation is for your benefit, but the router only knows about changes made within its configuration window.

14. Grab RtrGiraffe's end of the cable and drag it to RtrZebra, connecting the cable to the **FastEthernet0/0** interface, as shown in Figure 4-39. From the server, ping the new router to confirm the connection works. What command did you use?

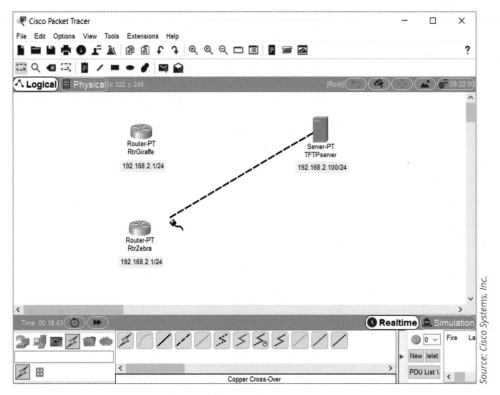

Source: Cisco Systems, Inc.

Figure 4-39 Move the cable from the old router to the new router

15. In RtrZebra's configuration window, click the **CLI** tab. Click inside the IOS Command Line Interface pane and press **Enter**. What is this router's hostname, as indicated by the prompt?

16. Enter the `exit` command twice and press **Enter** again to get to privileged EXEC mode.

17. To copy the old router's running-config file from the TFTP server to the new router, enter the command `copy tftp running-config`. Provide the TFTP server's IP address and the filename to be copied (**Giraffe**). Press **Enter** twice. What is the new router's hostname now, as indicated by the prompt? Why do you think this is?

18. At this point, if you were to power cycle the new router, it would lose all these settings. To save the running-config data to the startup-config file so the changes persist, enter the command `copy running-config startup-config`

19. You do not need to save this Packet Tracer network for future projects. Before closing the network, take some notes in your Wikidot website about your work in this project, commands that you learned, and new insights you have about how Packet Tracer works.

Note to Instructors: A Packet Tracer solution file is provided for each Packet Tracer project through the Instructors site.

Capstone Project 4-2: Use SSH in Ubuntu

Estimated Time: 30 minutes (+5 minutes for group work, if assigned)
Objective: Compare and contrast remote access methods and security implications. (Obj. 4.4)
Group Work: This project includes enhancements when assigned as a group project.
Resources:
- Access to the same computer used to complete Capstone Project 1-1 or Capstone Project 1-2
- Internet access

Context: In this project, you will learn to use SSH in Ubuntu. Using the Ubuntu VMs you created in Capstone Projects 2-1 and 3-1, follow these steps to create an SSH connection.

NOTE 4-18

If you're using VirtualBox, you first need to check the Network settings for this VM. Select the VM, click **Settings**, and click **Network**. If necessary, change the *Attached to* setting to **Bridged Adapter**. Click OK.

On the Ubuntu Server VM, do the following:

1. Start the VM and log on. Refer to your LastPass vault if you don't remember your logon information.
2. SSH is included in Ubuntu Server but is not installed. Enter this command to install and start SSH: `sudo apt-get install ssh` (You'll have to enter your password, and you'll have to give permission to install the software.)
3. Enter the command `ip address show` and write down the IP address of the Ubuntu Server VM. Leave this VM running.

On the Ubuntu Desktop VM, do the following:

4. Start the VM and log on. Refer to your LastPass vault if you don't remember your logon information.
5. Open a shell prompt and enter the command `ip address show`. Note the IP address of the Ubuntu Desktop VM.
6. Enter the `ssh` command with the IP address of the Ubuntu Server VM. For example, if the server IP address is 192.168.1.147, enter this command:

   `ssh 192.168.1.147`

   If your username on the Ubuntu Server machine is not the same as your username on the Ubuntu Desktop machine, you'll need to add a bit more information to this command to remote into the server. Try this command instead:

   `ssh server_username@server_ipaddress`

   For example, if the server IP address is 192.168.1.147 and the server username is jillwest, you would enter this command:

   `ssh jillwest@192.168.1.147`

7. Enter your password on the server to log on to the server using SSH. You now have an SSH session established between the Ubuntu Desktop VM and the Ubuntu Server VM.
8. Enter the `dir` command. What directory is listed? Recall that you created this directory in Capstone Project 3-1.
9. Enter the `ip address show` command. Which IP address is displayed in the command output: the Ubuntu Desktop VM's address or the Ubuntu Server VM's address?
10. **Take a screenshot** of your Ubuntu Desktop VM's Terminal window showing your commands run on the SSH session with the Ubuntu Server VM; submit this visual with your answers to this project's questions.
11. When you're finished using the SSH session, enter the `exit` command to break the session.
12. **For group assignments:** Establish an SSH session with another group member's Ubuntu VM, either their Desktop VM or their Server VM. The VM's owner will need to enter their credentials to authenticate the connection. What command did you use to establish the connection? (Note that this should work from a Hyper-V VM to a VirtualBox VM but might not work in reverse.)
13. To shut down each VM, enter the `sudo poweroff` command in each VM.
14. Add some notes to your Wikidot website about the SSH installation on the Ubuntu Server VM.

Solutions to Self-Check Questions

TCP/IP Core Protocols

1. Which protocol's header includes the source MAC address?

   Answer: a. Ethernet

   Explanation: **Ethernet** encapsulates data with a header and trailer, creating a frame. This frame includes the MAC address of the sender. A header for TCP and UDP at the transport layer includes a port to identify the communicating application on the source host. IP identifies the IP address of the source host.

2. Which of these protocols does *not* include some kind of integrity check field in its header?

Answer: c. IPv6

Explanation: **IPv6** does not include its own checksum field. Instead, IPv6 requires that the transport layer header (TCP or UDP) include a checksum field. IPv4 and ICMP both include a checksum field as well, either for the header or for the entire packet.

3. An ARP table maps MAC addresses to what information?

Answer: d. IPv4 addresses

Explanation: ARP (Address Resolution Protocol) works in conjunction with IPv4 to discover the MAC address of a node on the local network and to maintain a database that maps local **IPv4 addresses** to MAC addresses. A MAC address table maps MAC addresses to physical interfaces on a switch. IPv6 relies on ICMPv6 to discover other nodes on a network. Gateways such as routers track TCP and UDP ports for address translation.

Encryption Protocols

4. Which two components of the CIA triad are ensured by adequate encryption methods? Choose *two*.

Answer: a. Confidentiality and d. Integrity

Explanation: With public key encryption, data is encrypted with a private key known only to the user, and it's decrypted with a mathematically related public key that can be made available through a third-party source. This ensures data **integrity**, as the sender's public key will only work if the data has not been tampered with. Alternatively, data can be encrypted with the public key, and then can only be decrypted with the matching private key. This ensures data **confidentiality**, as only the intended recipient (the owner of the keys) can decrypt the data. Availability refers to the data being available to the intended recipient when needed, meaning the sender is accountable for successful delivery of the data.

5. Which IPsec encryption type encrypts the IP header?

Answer: b. ESP

Explanation: Either AH (authentication header) encryption or ESP (Encapsulating Security Payload) encryption may be used in IPsec. Both types of encryption provide authentication of the IP packet's data payload through public key techniques. In addition, **ESP** encrypts the entire IP packet, including the IP header. IKE (Internet Key Exchange) negotiates the exchange of keys, including authentication of the keys. ISAKMP (Internet Security Association and Key Management Protocol) works within the IKE process to establish policies for managing the keys.

Remote Access Protocols

6. Which remote file access protocol uses port 22?

Answer: d. SFTP

Explanation: Unlike FTP (File Transfer Protocol) or FTPS (FTP Secure), which use a control channel on port 21 and one or two data channels on port 20, **SFTP (Secure FTP)** uses only a single connection—both inbound and outbound communications are usually configured to cross SSH's port 22. TFTP (Trivial FTP) listens at port 69.

7. You need to remote into a Linux server in another building on your network. Which of the following protocols should you use?

Answer: b. SSH

Explanation: The **SSH (Secure Shell)** suite of protocols is included with all modern UNIX and Linux distributions and with macOS client operating systems. RDP (Remote Desktop Protocol) is a Microsoft proprietary protocol used by Windows. SFTP (Secure FTP) is a file-transfer version of SSH that includes encryption and authentication. A VPN (virtual private network) is a network connection encrypted from end to end that creates a private connection to a remote network.

8. You're working from home and need to access a file server at the office while working in an application from your work desktop. At the same time, you often stream music in your browser. Which VPN type will be most efficient while still meeting your needs?

Answer: d. Split tunnel VPN

Explanation: A **split tunnel VPN** will only capture traffic destined for the corporate network, such as communication with the file server and the work desktop, and the client can use local network resources to stream music from the Internet, which will result in lower latency and will use fewer corporate network resources. A full tunnel VPN captures all network traffic, whether destined for the Internet or for the corporate network. A host-to-host VPN creates a VPN tunnel directly between two devices and would not provide access to other resources, such as music streaming. A site-to-site VPN connects multiple sites across a WAN and requires more expensive equipment than a client-to-site VPN for the split tunnel configuration.

Troubleshooting Network Issues

9. You need to determine which device on your network is sending excessive messages to your Ubuntu Server. Which utility will give you this information?

Answer: b. tcpdump

Explanation: The **tcpdump** utility captures traffic that crosses a computer's network interface, which can then be analyzed to determine which devices are transmitting traffic across each interface. The traceroute utility traces the path from one networked node to another, identifying all intermediate hops between the two nodes. The netstat utility displays TCP/IP statistics and details about TCP/IP components and connections on a host. This ARP utility, accessed via the `arp` command in both Windows and Linux, provides a way of obtaining information from and manipulating a device's ARP table.

10. What protocol must be allowed through a firewall for tracert to work correctly?

Answer: c. ICMP

Explanation: The Windows tracert utility sends an **ICMP (Internet Control Message Protocol)** echo request to the destination node and listens for an ICMP echo reply from that node. SSH (Secure Shell) is a collection of protocols that performs both authentication and encryption. NDP (Neighbor Discovery Protocol) information carried in ICMPv6 messages automatically detect neighboring devices and automatically adjust when neighboring nodes fail or are removed from the network. TLS (Transport Layer Security) is a method of encrypting TCP/IP transmissions en route between the client and server using public key encryption technology.

CABLING

After reading this module and completing the exercises, you should be able to:

1 Explain basic data transmission concepts, including frequency, bandwidth, throughput, multiplexing, and common transmission flaws

2 Describe the physical characteristics of and official standards for coaxial cable, twinaxial cable, twisted-pair cable, fiber-optic cable, and their related connectors

3 Compare the benefits and limitations of various networking media

4 Select and use the appropriate tool to troubleshoot common cable problems

On the Job

I was asked to consult on a network problem concerning slow speeds and dead network jacks. The business was located in a building that was configured for two rental spaces with a single entrance. After entering the front door, I encountered a door to one set of offices on the right and the same on the left. Straight ahead was a door to the mechanical rooms.

When I removed the wall plates, I found that the installer had untwisted the pairs by at least one inch on all the jacks. On some of the nonfunctional wall jacks, the pairs were untwisted three inches or more and stuffed haphazardly into the wall box.

The next mystery was the single 12-port switch, which didn't make sense because I was now able to achieve link on 19 wall sockets. This meant that it was time to start removing ceiling tiles and following wires. Fortunately, all the wires came together in a bundle that exited into the ceiling above the entryway. From there, most of the bundle turned and went toward the mechanical room, where the fiber-modem and 12-port switch were located. Unfortunately, a few of the wires went toward the other rental space. The other set of offices was not currently rented, and so was not accessible without contacting the landlord. The landlord was hesitant to give access to the other space. He insisted that the problem could not have anything to do with the wiring in that part of the building because his nephew, who was an electrician, had done all the network cabling in the building. Instead, the landlord insisted that the tenants must have messed up the wall jacks on their side.

After tracing cable after cable above the suspended ceiling, I finally found another network switch hiding on top of one of the ceiling tiles. All the cable terminations had around two inches of the pairs untwisted to make it easier to install the RJ-45 terminals.

I reconnected all the wall jacks and replaced all the terminals on the cables at the hidden switch. All the client's wall jacks were now able to achieve link and connect, transferring at 100 Mbps full-duplex.

Todd Fisher Wallin
Operations Coordinator
Driftless Community Radio

Just as highways and streets provide the foundation for automobile travel, networking media provides the physical foundation for data transmission. Networking media are the physical or atmospheric paths that signals follow. The first networks used thick coaxial cables. Today's local area networks use copper or fiber cabling or wireless transmissions. This module focuses on wired networks. Wireless networking is covered in a later module.

Networking media technologies change rapidly because networks are always evolving to meet the demand for greater speed, versatility, and reliability. Understanding the characteristics of various networking media is critical to designing and troubleshooting networks. You also need to know how data is transmitted over these various media types. This module discusses the details of data transmission and physical networking media. You'll learn what it takes to make data transmission dependable and how to correct some common transmission problems.

TRANSMISSION BASICS

☑ CERTIFICATION

1.3: Summarize the types of cables and connectors and explain which is the appropriate type for a solution.

2.1: Compare and contrast various devices, their features, and their appropriate placement on the network.

2.3: Given a scenario, configure and deploy common Ethernet switching features.

3.1: Given a scenario, use the appropriate statistics and sensors to ensure network availability.

5.2: Given a scenario, troubleshoot common cable connectivity issues and select the appropriate tools.

Average reading time: 21 minutes

7 Application
6 Presentation
5 Session
4 Transport
3 Network
2 Data Link
▶ 1 Physical

The transmission techniques used on today's networks are complex and varied. Through minor tweaks and major renovations, network administrators constantly seek ways to maximize the efficiency of their networks. In this section, you'll first look at what measurements indicate network efficiency, and then you'll explore obstacles to good network performance. Optimizing network performance is a more complex topic and is covered in later modules.

Frequency, Bandwidth, and Throughput

In networking and similar technologies, it's common for one term to be used to refer to multiple concepts and principles. Often such terms are used incorrectly or inconsistently, even by corporations and professionals. As a networking professional, it's important to understand both the technical meanings of essential terms and the more informal, common usages. These can be two very different things.

For example, the terms *bandwidth* and *throughput* are often confused. A networking professional needs to measure or make decisions based on these two transmission characteristics. People commonly think bandwidth and throughput are identical, but they are fundamentally different. To make things more complicated, the term *bandwidth* has additional meanings in relation to frequencies, electric circuits, radar, or other technologies. Let's take a closer look at each of the terms needed for your work in networking, their definitions, and the various ways they're used:

- **Frequency** for today's network cabling is typically measured in MHz (megahertz) or GHz (gigahertz), which indicates the number of times in a second that an electrical signal can change states (for example, change from a positive to a negative charge or vice versa). This is similar to the frequencies used in wireless networking, but it's not quite the same. Wireless signals such as FM radio or Wi-Fi, where frequency is also measured in MHz or GHz, must be contained within a specific range of the electromagnetic spectrum to prevent the signal from interfering with other signals using nearby frequencies. By contrast, wired signals don't have to be so tightly contained because the cable itself mostly limits the dispersion of the signal. Instead, a wired signal covers a wide spectrum of electromagnetic frequencies, and it's rated for efficiency up to a specified maximum frequency. A cable's maximum frequency is important to know because it affects how quickly you can transfer data over that cable. Imagine you are a traffic engineer overseeing traffic flowing onto a freeway via a system of green lights—one car per each green light, as shown in Figure 5-1. The current system flashes one green light a minute, therefore releasing one car per minute. If you want to release more cars onto the freeway in a shorter period of time, you could increase the number of green lights per minute. The number of light cycles per minute is an example of frequency. You'll see maximum frequencies identified for different categories of copper cabling. Sometimes this maximum frequency is also called bandwidth to indicate the *possible range* of frequencies up to that maximum. In this case, bandwidth refers to a frequency in MHz or GHz. However, bandwidth can also refer to the transfer of data, as described next.

- **Bandwidth** for today's networks is measured in Mbps (megabits per second) or Gbps (gigabits per second). The term refers to the amount of data you could theoretically transmit during a given period of time, taking into consideration factors such as frequency, distance, and SNR (signal-to-noise ratio). In the freeway analogy,

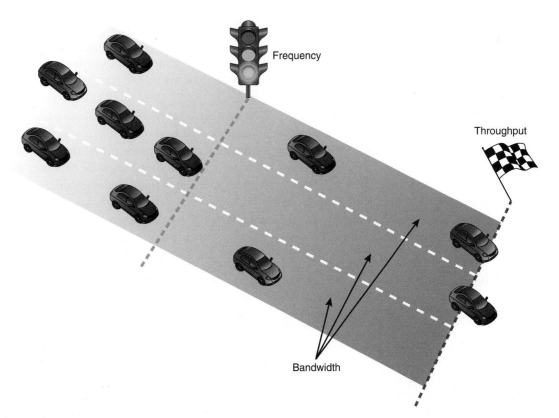

Figure 5-1 Freeway analogy for frequency, bandwidth, and throughput

bandwidth refers to the number of lanes on a freeway. You can increase bandwidth by adding more lanes to the freeway, which allows you to release more cars per green light—for example, three lanes on the freeway allows you to release three cars for every green light instead of just one. At the same time, consider that adding too many lanes for anticipated traffic, so that some lanes are never used, would be a waste of resources. Essentially, bandwidth refers to the number of lanes available for data transfer or, to use a different analogy, the size of the pipe through which water is pumped.

- **Throughput** (also called payload rate or effective data rate) for today's networks is also measured in Mbps (megabits per second) or Gbps (gigabits per second). The term refers to the number of data bits (0s and 1s) that are actually received across a connection each second. Throughput takes into consideration the reality of a network environment, including delays to cross interfaces, noise affecting signals, errors that result in lost data, and more. In the freeway analogy, throughput would measure the number of people who arrive at their destination per minute. This number might be different than the maximum number the freeway could possibly support and takes into account problems such as weather, traffic congestion, red lights at intersections, and different driving styles.

It helps to think of the term *bandwidth* as a range of possibilities, or as a definition of the maximum possible. When discussing frequencies, bandwidth identifies the full range of available frequencies (the width of the band) for a specific application. When discussing data rates, bandwidth identifies the theoretical maximum number of bits per second. You might even use bandwidth to identify how much work you can handle in a day or how much stress you can tolerate before you must make some scheduling or lifestyle changes. Be aware that many sources use these terms—frequency, bandwidth, and throughput—interchangeably in some contexts. This is why you'll often see bandwidth measured in two ways: in MHz/GHz or in Mbps/Gbps.

At one time, the terms frequency, throughput, and bandwidth were directly related mathematically—a cable with a maximum frequency of 100 MHz could transmit a maximum of 100 Mbps: 100 MHz correlated with 100 Mbps. Today, however, additional layers of technology complicate the mathematical relationship between these measurements. For example, now you can find cables with a maximum frequency of 250 MHz rated for a maximum throughput of 1000 Mbps, which is a 400 percent increase in possible throughput.

New technologies such as modulation and encoding offer innovative methods for increasing theoretical bandwidth and effective data throughput given the same maximum frequency. For example, if you want to transport more people on a freeway during a given period of time, you can use larger vehicles like double-decker buses, which carry a lot more people per vehicle than small cars do. Using the same three lanes of traffic and the same green light frequency, you can now transport dozens more people per minute per lane of traffic. Similarly, using **modulation** (sending data over an analog signal) and **encoding** (converting data into a digital signal for transmission), you can pack a lot more bits of data into each signal's state change.

Usually, a low-cost residential broadband Internet connection that is rated for a maximum bandwidth of 3 Mbps has an actual throughput that is lower than the advertised maximum, perhaps even much lower. This explains why providers often advertise "*up to* 3 Mbps." For a network connection to achieve an actual throughput of 1 Gbps, it might require a transmission rate of 1.25 Gbps or more because of the overhead used by Ethernet frames, delays crossing interfaces, noise in the environment, and other factors. Applications that require significant throughput like this include videoconferencing, telephone signaling, and multimedia streaming. By contrast, instant messaging and email, for example, require much less bandwidth. Table 5-1 summarizes the terminology and abbreviations used when discussing different throughput rates.

Table 5-1   Throughput measures

Quantity	Prefix	Abbreviation
1 bit per second	n/a	1 bps = 1 bit per second
1000 bits per second	kilo	1 Kbps = 1 kilobit per second
1,000,000 bits per second	mega	1 Mbps = 1 megabit per second
1,000,000,000 bits per second	giga	1 Gbps = 1 gigabit per second
1,000,000,000,000 bits per second	tera	1 Tbps = 1 terabit per second

NOTE 5-1

Be careful not to confuse bits and bytes when discussing throughput and bandwidth:

- Data *storage* quantities are typically expressed in multiples of bytes.

- Data *transmission* quantities (in other words, throughput) are more commonly expressed in multiples of bits per second.

When representing different data quantities, a small *b* represents bits, while a capital *B* represents bytes. To put this into context, a fast Internet connection might transmit data at 1 Gbps (gigabit per second), while an SD movie file might be 1–2 GB (gigabytes) in size.

Another difference between data storage and data throughput measures is that, with data storage, the prefix *kilo* means 2 to the 10th power (written as 2^{10}), or 1024. With data throughput, *kilo* means 10 to the 3rd power (written as 10^3), or 1000. In other words, data storage measurements use powers of 2 while data throughput measurements use powers of 10.

Transmission Flaws

On a busy network, why is actual throughput less than the potential bandwidth of the network? Three factors that can degrade network performance are noise, attenuation, and latency.

Noise

Noise, or interference, can degrade or distort a signal and, on a network, is measured in **dB (decibel) loss**. A decibel is a relative measure of signal loss (a negative number) or gain (a positive number). In other words, the loss or gain is measured as a comparison between the signal's strength at transmission versus its strength when it arrives at its destination. The signal might get weaker due to noise (interference), or it might get stronger with help from an amplifier.

So how much power change is indicated by each dB up or down? As a general rule, a loss of 3 dB between the transmitter and receiver indicates the signal has lost half its power. But again, dB loss or gain is a relative measure. Therefore, a loss of 3 dB on a 10-watt signal means the signal arrives at 5 watts. But a loss of 3 dB on a 1000-watt signal means the signal arrives at 500 watts. A 1000-watt signal with a 6-dB loss arrives at 250 watts (half of half the original signal strength, or one quarter). That's a big loss! You can see why noise on the network can be problematic.

Two common sources of noise are the following:

- **EMI (electromagnetic interference)**—Caused by motors, power lines, televisions, copiers, fluorescent lights, microwave ovens, manufacturing machinery, and other sources of electrical activity (including a severe thunderstorm). One type of EMI is RFI (radio frequency interference), or electromagnetic interference caused by radio waves. (Often, you'll see EMI referred to as EMI/RFI.) Strong broadcast signals from radio or TV antennas can generate RFI.
- **Crosstalk**—Occurs when a signal traveling on one wire or cable infringes on the signal traveling over an adjacent wire or cable, as shown in Figure 5-2. The resulting noise, or crosstalk, is equal to a portion of the second line's signal. If you've ever been on a traditional, landline phone and heard the conversation on a second line in the background, you have heard the effects of crosstalk.

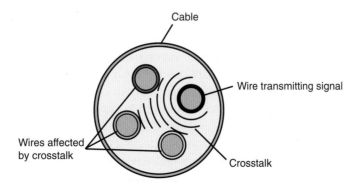

Figure 5-2   Crosstalk between wires in a cable

In data networks, crosstalk can be extreme enough to prevent the accurate delivery of data. Three common types are the following:

- **Alien crosstalk**—Crosstalk that occurs between two cables
- **NEXT (near end crosstalk)**—Crosstalk that occurs between wire pairs near the source of a signal
- **FEXT (far end crosstalk)**—Crosstalk measured at the far end of the cable from the signal source

In every signal, a certain amount of noise is unavoidable. However, engineers have devised several ways to limit the potential for noise to degrade a signal. One way is simply to ensure that the strength of the signal exceeds the strength of the noise. Proper cable design and installation are also critical for protecting against noise effects.

Attenuation

Another transmission flaw is attenuation, or the loss of a signal's strength as it travels away from its source. Just as your voice becomes fainter as it travels farther, so do signals fade with distance. To compensate for attenuation, signals are boosted en route using a repeater, which regenerates a digital signal in its original form without the noise it might have previously accumulated. Figure 5-3 shows a digital signal distorted by noise and then regenerated by a repeater. A switch on an Ethernet network works as a multiport repeater, as the bits transmitted "start over" at each port on the switch.

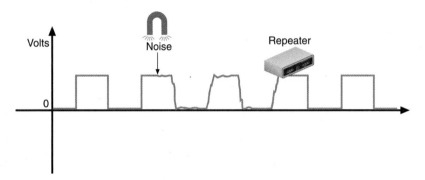

Figure 5-3   A digital signal distorted by noise and then repeated

Latency

Although electrons travel rapidly, they still must travel, and a brief delay takes place between the instant when data leaves the source and when it arrives at its destination. This delay is called latency.

The length of the cable affects latency, as does the existence of any intervening connectivity device, such as a router. Different devices affect latency to different degrees. For example, modems convert, or modulate, both incoming and outgoing signals for transmission over a network. Thus, they increase a connection's latency far more than switches, which simply repeat a signal. Other factors can also increase latency, such as cable limitations, number of transfers between devices, noise in the network, traffic congestion overwhelming network devices, processing delays (such as analysis by intervening firewalls or DNS resolution), collisions with other messages, and conversion from one type of transmission to another (such as converting from wired to wireless transmission). The most common way to measure latency on data networks is by calculating a packet's RTT (round trip time), or the length of time it takes for a packet to go from sender to receiver and then back from receiver to sender. RTT is usually measured in milliseconds.

Latency causes problems when a receiving node is expecting some type of communication, such as the rest of a data stream it has begun to accept. If packets experience varying amounts of delay, they can arrive out of order—a problem commonly called jitter, or more precisely, PDV (packet delay variation). This might cause streaming video or voice transmissions to pause repeatedly, jump around, or stall out completely. Another latency-related problem occurs if the node does not receive the rest of the data stream within a given time, and it, therefore, assumes no more data is coming. In this case, transmission errors are returned to the sender.

While noise, attenuation, and latency degrade a network's efficiency, there are some changes you can make to the network to increase efficiency. First, let's consider settings on a device's NIC.

Duplex, Half-Duplex, and Simplex

Network connections perform best when network devices are properly configured. Two important NIC settings include the direction in which signals travel over the media and the number of signals that can traverse the media at any given time. These two settings are combined to create different methods of communication as follows:

- **Full-duplex**, also called **duplex**—Signals are free to travel in both directions over a medium simultaneously. As an analogy, talking on the telephone is a full-duplex transmission because both parties in the conversation can speak at the same time. Modern NICs use a full-duplex configuration by default.
- **Half-duplex**—Signals may travel in both directions over a medium but in only one direction at a time. For example, an apartment building's intercom system might be half-duplex if only one person can speak at a time.
- **Simplex**—Signals may travel in only one direction, and this is sometimes called one-way, or unidirectional, communication. Broadcast radio and garage door openers are examples of simplex transmissions.

In Windows, you can use Device Manager to configure a NIC, including speed and duplex settings. For example, notice in Figure 5-4 that you can choose Full Duplex, Half Duplex, or Auto Negotiation, which allows the NIC to select the best link speed and duplex that is also supported by a neighboring device. However, if you specify a particular speed and duplex that's not supported by the neighboring device, the result is a **speed and duplex mismatch** and, therefore, slow or failed transmission.

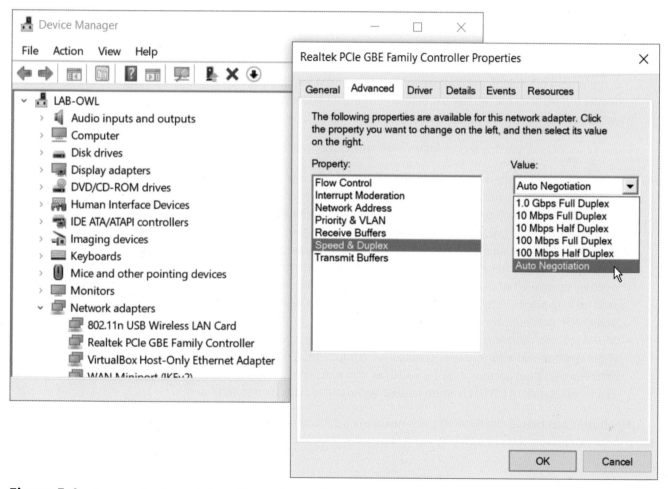

Figure 5-4   A network adapter's Speed & Duplex configuration can be changed

Multiplexing

Duplexing allows a signal to travel in both directions in a cable at one time. This might be achieved by pairing two wires together inside the cable, where one wire transmits and the other receives. Or it might be accomplished by transmitting two or more signals on the same wire. A form of transmission that allows multiple signals to travel simultaneously over one medium is known as multiplexing.

Networks rely on multiplexing to increase the amount of data that can be transmitted in a given timespan over a given bandwidth. To carry multiple signals, the medium's channel is logically separated into multiple smaller channels, or subchannels. Many different types of multiplexing are available, and the type used in a situation depends on what the media, transmission, and reception equipment can handle. For each type of multiplexing, a device that can combine many signals on a channel, a multiplexer (mux), is required at the transmitting end of the channel. At the receiving end, a demultiplexer (demux) separates the combined signals.

Different types of multiplexing manipulate signals in different ways. Three common types of multiplexing used on copper lines are the following:

- TDM (time division multiplexing)—Divides a channel into multiple intervals of time, or time slots. Time slots are reserved for their designated nodes regardless of whether the node has data to transmit. This can be inefficient if some nodes on the network rarely send data.
- STDM (statistical time division multiplexing)—Assigns time slots to nodes (similar to TDM), but it then adjusts these slots according to priority and need. This approach uses all slots rather than leaving some unused, which provides improved efficiency in using available bandwidth on a network. Still, neither TDM nor STDM allows multiple signals on a line at the exact same time.
- FDM (frequency division multiplexing)—Assigns different frequencies to create multiple frequency bands, each used by a subchannel, so that multiple signals can transmit on the line at one time. Signals are modulated into different frequencies, then multiplexed to simultaneously travel over a single channel, and demultiplexed at the other end. Telephone companies once used FDM for all phone lines and still multiplex signals on residential phone lines for the last leg before entering a residence. (The last leg is sometimes referred to as the last mile even though it's not necessarily a mile long.)

Three types of multiplexing technologies used with fiber-optic cable include the following:

- WDM (wavelength division multiplexing)—Works with any fiber-optic cable to carry multiple light signals simultaneously by dividing a light beam into different wavelengths, or colors, on a single fiber. The technology works similar to how a prism spreads white light into various colors. Original WDM provided only two wavelengths or channels per strand of fiber in only one direction at a time. Newer bidirectional WDM supports full-duplex light transmissions in both directions at the same time.
- DWDM (dense wavelength division multiplexing or dense WDM)—Increases the number of channels provided by normal WDM to between 80 and 320 channels. Dense WDM can be amplified en route and is typically used on high-bandwidth or long-distance WAN links, such as the connection between a large ISP and its (even larger) NSP (network service provider).
- CWDM (coarse wavelength division multiplexing or coarse WDM)—Lowers cost by spacing frequency bands wider apart to allow for cheaper transceiver equipment. CWDM multiplexers typically can support several channels per fiber, such as 4, 8, 16, or 18, as you can see on this manufacturer's website in Figure 5-5. The effective distance of CWDM is more limited because the signal is not amplified.

Monitoring and optimizing network performance is a substantial part of network administration. You'll revisit this topic more extensively later.

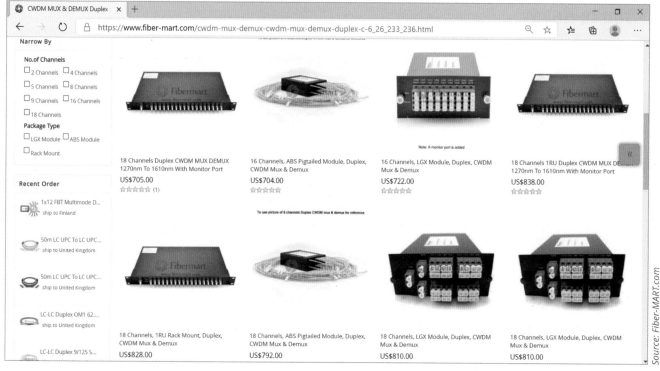

Figure 5-5 CWDM multiplexers available in 16-channel, 18-channel, and other varieties

Source: Fiber-MART.com

REMEMBER THIS...

- Compare frequency, bandwidth, and throughput.
- Describe how to minimize noise, attenuation, and latency problems.
- Configure speed and duplex settings on a NIC.
- Explain how WDM, bidirectional WDM, DWDM, and CWDM work.

SELF-CHECK

1. When you measure the amount of data coming into your home network, what metric are you identifying?
   a. Duplex
   b. Bandwidth
   c. Noise
   d. Throughput
2. Which of the following improves overall network performance?
   a. Jitter
   b. Multiplexing
   c. Attenuation
   d. Latency

Check your answers at the end of this module.

You're Ready

You're now ready to complete **Project 5-1: Latency around the World**, or you can wait until you've finished reading this module.

COPPER CABLE

 CERTIFICATION

1.3: Summarize the types of cables and connectors and explain which is the appropriate type for a solution.

2.3: Given a scenario, configure and deploy common Ethernet switching features.

5.2: Given a scenario, troubleshoot common cable connectivity issues and select the appropriate tools.

Average reading time: 44 minutes

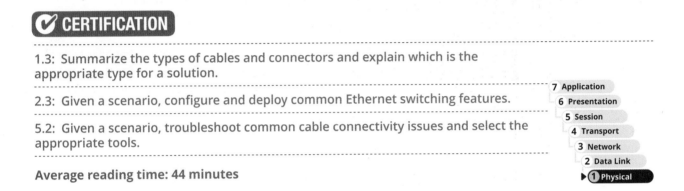

7 Application
6 Presentation
5 Session
4 Transport
3 Network
2 Data Link
▶ 1 Physical

Now that you understand some of the basics of data transmission on a network, you're ready to learn about different types of transmission media. Let's begin with a relatively simple cable type, coaxial cable, and then you'll explore how newer media improve upon this older technology.

EXAM TIP The CompTIA Network+ exam expects you to know the characteristics and limitations of each type of media covered here, how to install and design a network with each type, how to troubleshoot networking media problems, and how to provide for future network growth with each option.

Coaxial Cable and Twinaxial Cable

Coaxial cable and twinaxial cable are good examples of how solid technology continues to find its niche in modern networks even as the network itself transforms through the years. Let's look at what role each of these cable types plays in a modern network.

Coaxial Cable

Coaxial cable, called "coax" for short, was the foundation for Ethernet networks in the 1980s. You'll most likely never see a coaxial cable network for computers, as coax has been replaced by newer media types; however, a form of coax is still used for cable Internet, cable TV, and some multimedia connection types.

Coaxial cable has a central metal core (often copper) surrounded by an insulator, a braided metal shielding, and an outer cover, called the sheath or jacket (see Figure 5-6). The core can have a solid metal wire or several thin strands of metal wire and carries the electromagnetic signal. The shielding protects the signal against noise and is a ground for the signal. The plastic insulator can be PVC (polyvinyl chloride) or Teflon and protects the core from the metal shielding because if the two made contact, the wire would short-circuit. The sheath protects the cable from physical damage and might be PVC or a more expensive fire-resistant plastic.

Coaxial cabling comes in hundreds of specifications, which are all assigned an RG specification number. RG stands for *radio guide,* which is appropriate because coaxial cabling can be used by radio frequencies in broadband transmission. The RG ratings measure the materials used for shielding and conducting cores, which in turn influence their transmission characteristics, such as attenuation, throughput, and impedance (a measure of the opposition to a current's flow through a cable, as expressed in ohms).

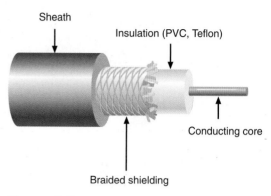

Figure 5-6   Coaxial cable

Each type of coax is suited to a different purpose. A cable's AWG (American Wire Gauge) refers inversely to the size of the conducting core. In other words, the larger the AWG, the smaller the diameter of the core wire. Coax cable is also categorized according to its impedance rating, meaning, its efficiency at transferring power and data over a distance. Lower impedance results in better power transfer, and higher impedance yields less attenuation of the data signal over a distance. An impedance of 50 ohms was determined to be a good compromise in these factors for computer networks and CB (citizens band) or ham radio connections where the effectiveness of the cable is more focused on a device's ability to *transmit* a signal. In contrast, 75 ohms better sustains the strength of a signal and, therefore, yields better performance for *receiving* devices, such as satellite and cable TV receiver boxes, televisions, radio receivers, police scanners, and audio connections in a home theater system. Table 5-2 lists the two most common coaxial cable specifications still in use today.

Table 5-2   Coaxial cable specifications

Type	Impedance	Core	Uses
RG-59	50 ohms or 75 ohms	20 or 22 AWG core, usually made of braided copper	Still used for relatively short connections, for example, when distributing video signals from a central receiver to multiple monitors within a building. RG-59 is less expensive than the more common RG-6 but suffers from greater attenuation.
RG-6	50 ohms or 75 ohms	18 AWG conducting core, usually made of solid copper	Used to deliver broadband cable Internet service and cable TV, particularly in the last stretch to the consumer's location; also widely used for inexpensive cabling in AV systems. Cable Internet service entering a home is RG-6.

EXAM TIP   The CompTIA Network+ exam expects you to know about RG-6 cables and F-connectors.

These two coaxial cable types, RG-6 and RG-59, can terminate with one of two connector types:

- An F-connector attaches to coaxial cable so that the core in the center of the cable extends into the center of the connector. After being attached to the cable by crimping or compression, connectors are threaded and screwed together like a nut-and-bolt assembly. A male F-connector, or plug, attached to coax is shown in Figure 5-7. A corresponding female F-connector, or jack, would be coupled with the male connector. F-connectors are most often used with RG-6 cables.
- A BNC connector is crimped, compressed, or twisted onto a coaxial cable. BNC stands for *Bayonet Neill-Concelman,* a term that refers to both an older style of connection and its two inventors. (Sometimes the term *British Naval Connector* is also used.) A BNC connector connects to another BNC connector via a turn-and-lock mechanism—this

Figure 5-7 F-connector

is the bayonet coupling referenced in its name. Unlike an F-connector, a male BNC connector provides its own conducting pin. BNC connectors are used with RG-59 coaxial cables, and less commonly, with RG-6. Figure 5-8 shows a BNC connector.

NOTE 5-2

When sourcing connectors for coaxial cable, you need to specify the type of cable you are using. For instance, when working with RG-6 coax, choose an F-connector made specifically for RG-6 cables. That way, you'll be certain that the connectors and cable share the same impedance rating. If impedance ratings don't match, data errors will occur and transmission performance will suffer.

Twinaxial Cable

Twinaxial cable, called "twinax" for short, looks very similar to coax cable except that there are two cores, or conductors, inside the cable. The two cores cooperate in a half-duplex fashion to transmit data, and so twinax is capable of supporting much higher throughput than coax. More recent twinax cables contain multiple pairs of these cores to carry even more data (see Figure 5-9). In fact, given the right circumstances, twinax might be a better choice than fiber to carry 10-Gigabit signals or higher over very short distances. This makes twinax an inexpensive option for short, high-speed connections, such as when connecting switches to routers or servers in a data center. For this reason, twinax is also called a DAC (direct attach copper) cable, which is a copper cable designed to handle very high-speed connections at very short distances. While limited in distance, installing twinax is significantly cheaper than installing fiber, consumes less power, and provides excellent protection from possible sources of interference. Because it's made from 26 or 28 AWG copper, twinax is also particularly resistant to damage from rough handling.

Figure 5-8 BNC connector

Eight core pairs

Braided shielding

Foil shielding

Two cores within a pair

Figure 5-9 Twinax cable contains two cores in each pair

The type of twinax cable determines its maximum supported distances, as described next:

- **Passive**—Does not contain internal electrical components and is sufficient for the shortest distances of less than about 5 or 7 meters.
- **Active**—Contains internal electrical components to strengthen signals over slightly longer distances, up to 10 meters.

Twinax is factory terminated (see Figure 5-10), usually with some of the same kinds of modular transceivers as what fiber terminations use, which you'll learn more about later in this module. This means twinax cable lengths are fixed with a preinstalled transceiver on each end. Depending on the connector type, twinax can support throughput up to 100 Gbps. However, the higher data rates require even shorter distance limitations.

Figure 5-10 Twinax cable is factory terminated with transceivers; each core pair is welded to a circuit board inside the transceiver

Next, you'll learn about a medium you're more likely to find throughout a modern computer network: twisted-pair cable.

Twisted-Pair Cable

Twisted-pair cable consists of color-coded pairs of insulated copper wires, each with a diameter of 0.4 to 0.8 mm (approximately the diameter of a sewing pin). Every two wires are twisted around each other to form pairs, and all the pairs are encased in a plastic sheath, as shown in Figure 5-11.

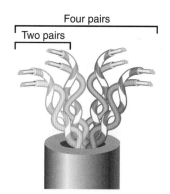

Figure 5-11 Twisted-pair cable

NOTE 5-3

The terms *wire* and *cable* are often used synonymously. Strictly speaking, *wire* is a subset of *cabling* because the *cabling* category also includes fiber-optic cable, which is almost never called *wire*. The exact meaning of the term *wire* depends on context. For example, if you said, in a somewhat casual way, "We had 6 gigs of data go over the wire last night," you would be referring to whatever transmission media helped carry the data—whether fiber cable, radio waves, or copper cable.

Twisted-pair cabling in Ethernet networks contains four wire pairs. On **Fast Ethernet** networks, which have a maximum data rate of 100 Mbps, one pair sends data, another pair receives data, and the other two pairs are not used for data transmission. Networks using **Gigabit Ethernet** and higher standards, with a data rate of 1000 Mbps or more, use all four pairs for both sending and receiving. You'll learn more about Ethernet standards later in this module.

NOTE 5-4

The more twists per foot in a pair of wires, the more resistant the pair will be to crosstalk or noise. Higher-quality, more-expensive twisted-pair cable contains more twists per foot. The number of twists per meter or foot is known as the **twist ratio**. Because twisting the wire pairs more tightly requires more cable, however, a high twist ratio can result in greater attenuation. For optimal performance, cable manufacturers must strike a balance between minimizing crosstalk and reducing attenuation. Interestingly, there are no imposed standards for twist ratio. What matters in qualifying a manufacturer's cable for a particular standard is its effective throughput (no matter how that effect is achieved), not specifically the number of twists in the wires.

In 1991, the TIA/EIA organizations finalized their specifications for twisted-pair wiring in a standard called "TIA/EIA-568." The TIA/EIA 568 standard divides twisted-pair wiring into several categories. The categories you might see on a computer network are Cat (category) 3, 5, 5e, 6, 6a, 7, 7a, and 8, all of which are described in Table 5-3. (Cat 4 cabling exists, too, but it is rarely used.) Modern LANs use Cat 5e or higher wiring, which is the minimum required to support Gigabit Ethernet. Cat 6 and above are certified for multigigabit transmissions, although Cat 6 cable has shorter distance limitations when supporting 10 Gbps. While Cat 7/7a cables never gained significant popularity, Cat 8 cables are already widely available even for home networks.

Table 5-3   Twisted-pair cabling standards

Standard	Maximum supported bandwidth	Maximum rated frequency	Description
Cat 3 (Category 3)	10 Mbps	Up to 16 MHz	Used more commonly for wired telephone connections and should never be used for a modern computer network.
Cat 5 (Category 5)	100 Mbps (Fast Ethernet)	100 MHz	Required minimum standard for Fast Ethernet.
Cat 5e (Enhanced Category 5)	1000 Mbps (1 Gbps, Gigabit Ethernet)	350 MHz	A higher-grade version of Cat 5 wiring that contains high-quality copper, offers a higher twist ratio, and uses slightly more advanced methods for reducing crosstalk.
Cat 6 (Category 6)	1 Gbps or, at shorter distances, 10 Gbps	250 MHz	Includes a plastic core to prevent crosstalk between twisted pairs in the cable. Can also contain foil insulation covering each bundle of wire pairs and a fire-resistant plastic sheath.
Cat 6a (Augmented Category 6)	10 Gbps	500 MHz	Reduces attenuation and crosstalk and allows for potentially exceeding traditional network segment length limits. Can reliably transmit data at multigigabit per second rates. Backward-compatible with Cat 5, Cat 5e, and Cat 6 cabling, which means that it can replace lower-level cabling without requiring connector or equipment changes.

(continues)

Table 5-3   Twisted-pair cabling standards *(continued)*

Standard	Maximum supported bandwidth	Maximum rated frequency	Description
Cat 7 (Category 7) Not included in TIA/EIA standards	10 Gbps or, at shorter distances, up to 100 Gbps	600 MHz	Supports higher frequencies because each wire pair is wrapped in its own shielding, then packaged in additional shielding beneath the sheath. To reach its fullest potential, it requires more sophisticated connectors, either GG45, which is backward-compatible with RJ-45, or TERA, which is not. It's thicker and less flexible than earlier versions and is also less common.
Cat 7a (Augmented Category 7) Not included in TIA/EIA standards	40–100 Gbps at very short distances	1000 MHz	Uses increased bandwidth to offer higher data rates than Cat 7 but still requires specialized connectors to reach full potential.
Cat 8 (Category 8) Class I (Cat 8.1) and Class II (Cat 8.2)	25 Gbps and 40 Gbps at longer distances than Cat 7	2 GHz	Already widely available for purchase by consumers for home networks. Relies on further improved and extensive shielding. Optimized for short-distance backbone connections within the data center and supports up to 40 Gbps over 30 meters (98 feet), which rivals fiber-optic cables at these distances. Cat 8 Class I offers the advantage of using connectors that are backward-compatible with Cat 5e and Cat 6 standards, which reduces the cost and complexity of installation. Cat 8 Class II cables are backward-compatible with Cat 7/7a specialty connectors.

In Figure 5-12, notice the reference on the cable to UTP. All twisted-pair cable falls into one of two classifications: STP (shielded twisted pair) or UTP (unshielded twisted pair). Let's look at characteristics of each type.

STP (Shielded Twisted Pair)

Recall that STP (shielded twisted pair) cable consists of twisted-pair wires that are not only individually insulated but might also be surrounded by a shielding made of a metallic substance such as a foil. Some STP cables use a braided copper shielding. The shielding acts as a barrier to external electromagnetic forces, thus preventing them from affecting the signals traveling over the wire inside the shielding. It also contains the electrical energy of the signals inside. The shielding must be grounded to enhance its protective effects and prevent reflection issues. The effectiveness of STP's shield depends on these characteristics:

- Level and type of environmental noise
- Thickness and material used for the shield
- Grounding mechanism
- Symmetry and consistency of the shielding

NOTE 5-5

To identify the category of a twisted-pair cable, check for information stamped on the jacket, as shown in Figure 5-12.

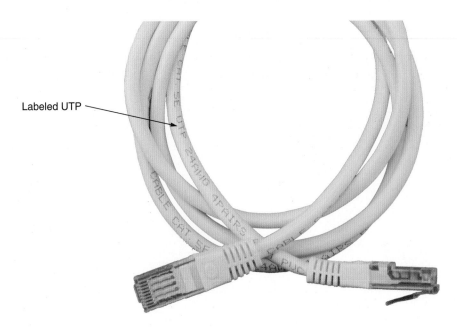

Labeled UTP

Figure 5-12   A Cat 5e data cable

Figure 5-13 depicts an STP cable.

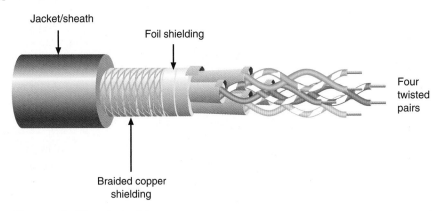

Jacket/sheath

Foil shielding

Four
twisted
pairs

Braided copper
shielding

Figure 5-13   STP cable

Newer types of cables, such as Cat 8, incorporate more sophisticated shielding materials, more tightly twisted wires, and higher bandwidths to offer data rates rivaling fiber-optic cable at short distances. Figure 5-14 shows a consumer-grade Cat 8 cable cut open so you can see the layers of shielding. Notice the braided shielding under the jacket, the foil shielding around all four twisted pairs, and the individual foil shielding around each twisted pair.

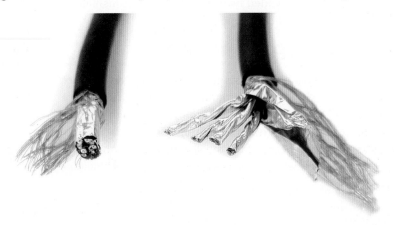

Figure 5-14   The insides of a Cat 8 cable

UTP (Unshielded Twisted Pair)

UTP cabling consists of one or more insulated wire pairs encased in a plastic sheath. As its name implies, UTP does not contain additional shielding for the twisted pairs. As a result, UTP is both less expensive and less resistant to noise than STP. Historically, UTP was more popular than STP due to its lower price. However, modern cable prices have dropped low enough that it might only cost a few pennies more per foot for high quality shielding. Figure 5-15 depicts three types of UTP cable: PVC-grade Cat 5e, plenum-grade Cat 5e, Cat 6 with its plastic core, and a UTP cable with an RJ-45 connector attached. Recall that a plenum-grade cable's jacket is flame-resistant, while the PVC cable's coating is toxic when burned.

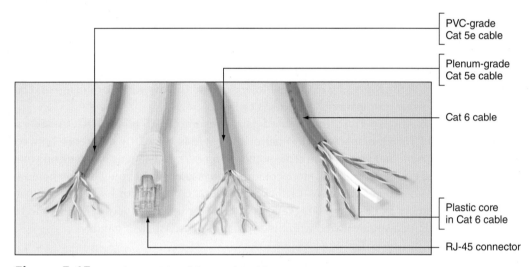

Figure 5-15   Various UTP cables and RJ-45 connector

NOTE 5-6

More specifically, **plenum-grade cable** is designed to withstand high temperatures, such as would be experienced in an attic space; it offers a highly fire-retardant jacket to reduce the spread of flames in areas with air circulation; and it burns with less smoke that is nontoxic. A similar cable type, **riser-rated cable**, is also coated with a fire-retardant jacket and is a thicker cable to make it easier to push or pull through risers in buildings or between floors. A riser is a vertical space in a building that is *not* designed for managing airflow, such as elevators, pipes, conduits, or ducts intended for pipes and cables. These are two similar cable types that are best suited to different circumstances.

Comparing STP and UTP

STP and UTP share several characteristics. The following list highlights their similarities and differences:

- **Throughput**—STP and UTP can both transmit data at 10 Mbps, 100 Mbps, 1 Gbps, and 10 Gbps, depending on the grade of cabling and the transmission method in use. Only STP can transmit at rates faster than 10 Gbps. Note that the *speed of the signal* crossing the cable isn't the point. Electrical signals travel at a speed supported by the conductor material, such as copper, and can approach the speed of light. However, shielding, data transmission methods, signal frequencies, number of wires used, errors, and other factors can affect the *rate of data transfer* across a cable's length. This characteristic might be referred to as bandwidth, throughput, data rate, bit rate, data transfer speed, or simply "speed."
- **Cost**—STP and UTP vary in cost, depending on the grade of copper used, the category rating, and any enhancements. Typically, STP is more expensive than UTP because it contains more materials. It also requires grounding, which can lead to more expensive installation. High-grade UTP can be expensive, too, however.
- **Connector**—STP and UTP use **RJ-45 (registered jack 45)** modular connectors and data jacks, which look similar to analog telephone connectors and jacks, only larger. However, telephone connections follow the **RJ-11 (registered jack 11)** standard. Figure 5-16 shows

Figure 5-16   RJ-45 and RJ-11 connectors

a close-up of an RJ-45 connector for a cable containing four wire pairs. For comparison, this figure also shows a traditional RJ-11 phone line connector. Most types of Ethernet that rely on twisted-pair cabling use RJ-45 connectors.

- **Noise immunity**—Because of its shielding, STP is more noise resistant than UTP. On the other hand, noise on UTP cable can be reduced with filtering and balancing techniques.

- **Size and scalability**—The maximum segment length for both STP and UTP is 100 meters, or 328 feet, on Ethernet networks that support data rates from 1 Mbps to 10 Gbps. Some categories of STP require shorter segment lengths to achieve maximum throughput.

Cable Pinouts

Proper cable termination is a basic requirement for two nodes on a network to communicate. Poor terminations, as you read in the *On the Job* story at the beginning of this module, can lead to power loss or noise—and consequently, errors—in a signal. Closely following termination standards is critical.

TIA/EIA has specified two methods of inserting twisted-pair wires into RJ-45 plugs: TIA/EIA-568A and TIA/EIA-568B (also known as T568A and T568B, respectively). Functionally, there is very little difference between these two standards. You only must be certain that you use the same standard on every RJ-45 plug and jack on your network so data is transmitted and received correctly. T568B is more common and is likely what you'll find on home and business networks. However, the federal government requires T568A on all federal contracts for backward-compatibility.

Figure 5-17 depicts pin numbers and assignments (called pinouts) for both standards. *Tx* refers to transmit, and *Rx* refers to receive. Standard pinouts are designed with the avoidance of crosstalk in mind.

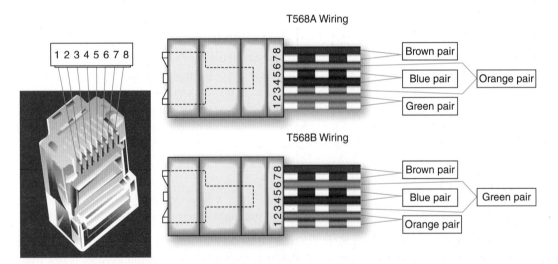

Pin #	T568A Color	T568B Color	Fast Ethernet function	Gigabit Ethernet function
1	White/green	White/orange	Tx+	Bidirectional+
2	Green	Orange	Tx−	Bidirectional−
3	White/orange	White/green	Rx+	Bidirectional+
4	Blue	Blue	*Unused*	Bidirectional+
5	White/blue	White/blue	*Unused*	Bidirectional−
6	Orange	Green	Rx−	Bidirectional−
7	White/brown	White/brown	*Unused*	Bidirectional+
8	Brown	Brown	*Unused*	Bidirectional−

Figure 5-17 T568A and T568B standard terminations for Fast Ethernet and Gigabit Ethernet

With Fast Ethernet, only the orange and green pairs are used: One pair transmits and one pair receives. The difference between pinouts in T568A and T568B is that these two pairs are reversed. For Gigabit Ethernet, all four pairs are used for transmitting and receiving. This more efficient use of wires helps account for the higher bandwidth of Gigabit connections.

The most common type of networking cable is a **straight-through cable**, also called a **patch cable**. To create one, terminate the RJ-45 plugs at both ends of the cable identically, following one of the TIA/EIA-568 standards. It's called a straight-through cable because it allows signals to pass "straight through" from one end to the other.

These straight-through cables are designed for most connections you'll need in a network, such as connecting a workstation to a switch or a switch to a router. Computers and routers are intended to send and receive signals on the wires as identified in Figure 5-17; this port configuration is called **MDI (medium dependent interface)**. In contrast, switches use an alternate port configuration called **MDI-X (MDI crossover)**, which ensures that switches are listening on the MDI transmit wires and transmitting on the MDI receive wires. For typical network connections, this works well—most workstations and servers connect to switches, and most switches connect to routers. However, to connect like devices (MDI to MDI or MDI-X to MDI-X) requires a different kind of cable called a crossover cable, which you'll learn about shortly. Newer devices, however, typically have **auto-MDI-X** ports, which automatically negotiate the transmit and receive wires between devices, even if you're not using the correct cable for the application. While using the wrong cable can still cause problems or increased crosstalk, the connection will work.

NOTE 5-7

A **loopback adapter** attaches to a port, such as an RJ-45 port, or a cable connector. It crosses the transmit line with the receive line to create a closed loop, tricking a host into thinking it's connected to a network as it "hears" its own data transmission. This is one way to test a port or cable for connectivity. See Figure 5-18. Inserting a loopback plug directly into a port will test for a bad port. Inserting a cable connector into a loopback jack will additionally test the cable for continuity (but not performance).

You'll create your own loopback plug and jack in projects at the end of this module.

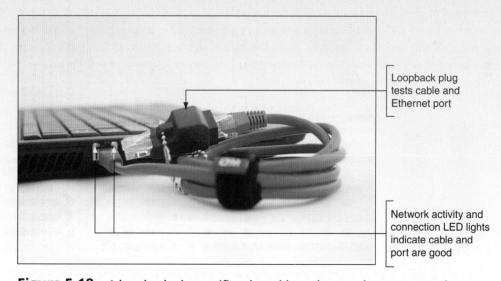

Loopback plug
tests cable and
Ethernet port

Network activity and
connection LED lights
indicate cable and
port are good

Figure 5-18   A loopback plug verifies the cable and network port are good

Legacy Networking: Crossover Cable

With older networking devices that did not support Gigabit Ethernet, each wire could only be used to either transmit or receive, not both. A straight-through cable was always used to connect two unlike devices—for example, to connect a server transmitting on the wire a switch received on, or a switch transmitting on the wire a router received on. When you needed to connect two like devices (for example, a switch to a switch), a problem occurred because the two switches were both transmitting on the same wire and both listening to receive on the same wire. The solution was to use a crossover cable. A **crossover cable** has the transmit and receive wires reversed and was used to connect a computer to a computer or a switch to a switch. See Figure 5-19. Notice in the figure a crossover cable was also needed to connect a computer to a router because legacy routers are expected to connect only to switches. As you read earlier, modern devices have an autosense function that enables them to detect the way wires are terminated in a plug and then adapt their transmit and receive signaling accordingly. This means crossover cables are now largely obsolete, except when they are needed to support older devices.

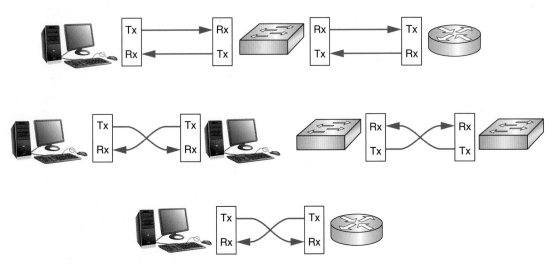

Figure 5-19   On legacy networks, straight-through cables connect unlike devices and crossover cables connect like devices

In a straight-through cable, each wire connects to the same pin on each end. For example, the orange/white wire goes *straight through* from pin 1 to pin 1. In a crossover cable, the transmit and receive wires are reversed, as shown in Figure 5-20. The diagram on the left in Figure 5-20 has the orange and green pairs reversed and will work with Fast Ethernet because this Ethernet standard requires only two pairs. The diagram on the right in Figure 5-20 has all four pairs reversed (blue, orange, green, and brown pairs) and will work with Gigabit Ethernet because Gigabit Ethernet transmits on four pairs. (However, Gigabit Ethernet devices almost never need a crossover cable.)

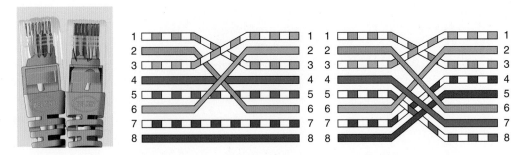

Figure 5-20   Two crossed pairs in a crossover cable are compatible with Fast Ethernet; four crossed pairs are compatible with Gigabit Ethernet

 EXAM TIP   One potential cause of NEXT (near end crosstalk) is an improper termination—for example, one in which wire insulation has been damaged, where wire pairs have been untwisted too far, or where straight-through or crossover standards have been mismatched on older devices. This last problem can happen when the TX (transmission) and RX (receive) wires are crossed, which, on the CompTIA Network+ exam, is called a **TX/RX reverse**.

Rollover Cable

Whereas a crossover cable reverses the transmit and receive wire pairs, a rollover cable reverses all the wires without regard to how they are paired. With a rollover cable, it's as if the cable terminations are a mirror image of each other, as shown in Figure 5-21. **Rollover cables**, also called **console cables**, are used to connect a computer to the console port of a router. Routers generally have two different kinds of ports: Ethernet ports and the console port. Ethernet ports allow for network communications and are the type of port used to create LANs through the router. A router's console port is used to communicate with the router itself, such as when making configuration changes to the device.

Figure 5-21   RJ-45 terminations on a rollover cable

EXAM TIP   The CompTIA Network+ exam expects you to be able to choose the correct cable type (straight-through, crossover, rollover, or console) for a given cable application.

Applying Concepts 5-1: Terminate Twisted-Pair Cable

It's likely that at some point in your career, you will have to replace an RJ-45 connector on an existing cable, such as when a wire inside the cable is damaged or if pins in the connector are bent. This section describes how to terminate twisted-pair cable. The tools you'll need—a wire cutter or snips, cable stripper, and cable crimper—are pictured in Figures 5-22, 5-23, and 5-24, respectively. Alternatively, you can use a single device that contains all three of these tools. A **wire cutter** is a pliers-shaped tool, and **snips** are more like heavy-duty scissors; both can make a clean cut through a cable. A **cable stripper** pulls off the protective covering without damaging the wires inside. A **cable crimper** pushes

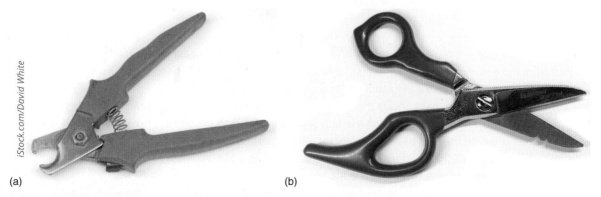

iStock.com/David White

(a)   (b)

Figure 5-22   (a) Wire cutter and (b) snips

Francesco Ocello/Shutterstock.com

Figure 5-23 Cable stripper

on the pins inside an RJ-45 connector so they pierce the wire's insulation, thus creating contact between the two conductors. You'll also need an RJ-45 connector, which might come with a boot. A boot is a plastic cover to protect the wires where they enter the connector.

Following are the steps to create a straight-through patch cable using Cat 5e twisted-pair cabling. To create a crossover cable or rollover cable, you would simply reorder the wires in Step 4 to match Figure 5-20 or Figure 5-21, respectively. The process of fixing wires inside the connector is called crimping, and it is a skill that requires practice—so don't be discouraged if the first cable you create doesn't

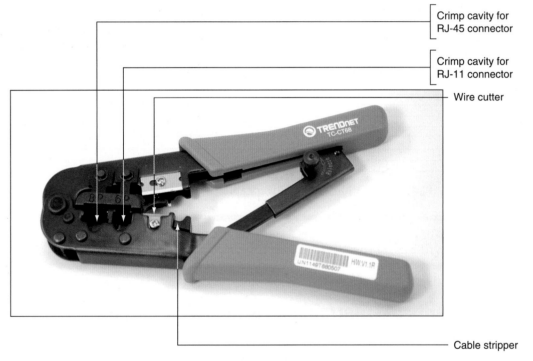

Crimp cavity for RJ-45 connector

Crimp cavity for RJ-11 connector

Wire cutter

Cable stripper

Figure 5-24 This cable crimper can crimp RJ-45 and RJ-11 connectors

reliably transmit and receive data. You'll get more practice terminating cables in two Hands-On projects at the end of this module. To create a straight-through patch cable using Cat 5e twisted-pair cabling, complete the following steps:

1. Using the wire cutter or snips, make a clean cut at both ends of the twisted-pair cable. Cut the cable the length you want the final cable to be, plus a few extra inches. If you're using a boot, slide one onto each end of the cable with the smaller opening facing the length of the cable and the larger opening facing the cut end that you're terminating.

2. Using the cable stripper, remove the sheath off one end of the twisted-pair cable, beginning at approximately 1 inch from the end. This is easier if you first score the sheath with a pair of scissors or a small knife. Be careful to neither damage nor remove the insulation that's on the twisted-pair wires inside.

3. In addition to the four wire pairs, inside the sheath you'll find a string. This string, known as a rip cord, is included to make it possible to remove an additional length of the outer sheath beyond the point where your cutting tool might have nicked the wire pairs. Use a pocketknife, cable cutters, or snips to start a new cut at the edge of the sheath and then pull the string through the cut to expose an additional inch of the inner wires, as shown in Figure 5-25. Cut off the excess string and sheath.

4. Carefully untwist each pair and straighten each wire. Make a clean cut evenly across the wires about an inch from the opening in the sheath.

Nick in wire

Figure 5-25 Pull back the sheath an inch beyond any damage to the inner wires, then cut off the extra sheath and string

5. To make a straight-through cable, align all eight wires on a flat surface, one next to the other, ordered according to their colors and positions listed earlier in Figure 5-17. It might be helpful first to groom—or pull steadily across the length of—the unwound section of each wire to straighten it out and help it stay in place. Which T568 standard are you using? In what order will you need to place each wire in the connector?

6. Measure 1/2 inch from the end of the wires and cleanly cut the wires straight across at this length. As you can see in Figure 5-26, it might help to hold the RJ-45 connector next to the wires to determine how short to cut the wires.

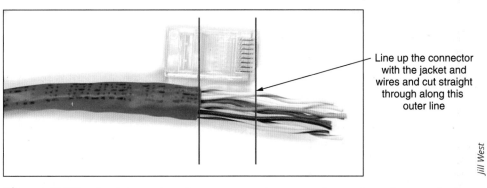

Line up the connector with the jacket and wires and cut straight through along this outer line

Figure 5-26 Straighten the wires, arrange them in order, and cut them to the appropriate length

7. Keeping the wires in line and in order, gently slide them into their positions in the RJ-45 plug. The plug should be positioned with the flat side facing toward you and the pin side facing away from you, so the appropriate wires enter the correct slots for the wiring standard. The sheath should extend into the plug about 3/8 of an inch.

8. After the wires are fully inserted, place the RJ-45 plug in the crimping tool and press firmly to crimp the wires into place. Be careful not to rotate your hand or the wires as you do this, otherwise only some of the wires will be properly terminated.

9. Remove the RJ-45 connector from the crimping tool. Look through the clear plastic connector to make sure each wire appears to be in contact with its pin (see Figure 5-27). It might be difficult to tell simply by looking at the connector. To test the connection, try to pull the plug off the wire. If it comes out, start over. However, the real test is whether your cable will successfully transmit and receive signals. If the connection appears solid, slide the boot over the connector so it fits snugly over the clip.

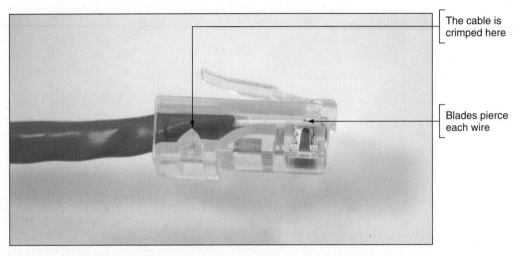

Figure 5-27   Blades in the connector pierce the insulation of each individual copper wire

10. Repeat Steps 2 through 9 for the other end of the cable. After completing Step 9 for the other end, use a cable tester to test the signal through the cable, or connect a computer to a switch and see if they can successfully communicate. You'll learn more about cable testers later in this module. If the cable transmits on all wires as expected, you will have created a straight-through patch cable.

PoE (Power over Ethernet)

In 2003, IEEE released its 802.3af standard, which specifies a method for supplying electrical power over twisted-pair Ethernet connections, also known as PoE (Power over Ethernet). Although the standard is relatively new, the concept is not. In fact, home telephones have long received power from the telephone company over the line that enters a residence. This power is necessary for dial tone and ringing.

On an Ethernet network, carrying power over network connections can be useful for nodes that are located far from traditional power receptacles or that need a constant, reliable power source, such as security cameras placed on exterior walls. The amount of power provided is relatively small—15.4 watts for standard PoE devices and 25.5 watts for the newer PoE+ devices, defined by the 802.3at standard. But that's enough to power a wireless access point, an IP telephone, or a security camera mounted high on a wall.

The PoE standard specifies two types of devices:

- **PSE (power sourcing equipment)**—The device that supplies the power
- **PDs (powered devices)**—Devices that receive power from the PSE

PoE requires Cat 5 or better copper cable. Inside the cable, electric current may run over an unused pair of wires or over the pair of wires used for data transmission. The standard allows for both approaches; however, on a single network, the choice of current-carrying pairs should be consistent between all PSE and PDs.

A switch or router that is expected to provide power over Ethernet must support the technology. The switch shown in Figure 5-28 indicates PoE is available on all 8 of its ports.

Also, the end node must be capable of receiving PoE. The PSE device first determines whether a node is PoE-capable before attempting to supply it with power. While the security camera in Figure 5-29 includes an optional power adapter connector, its Ethernet connector is designed to optionally receive PoE instead.

Let's look at how these devices might be arranged on a network. The top part of Figure 5-30 shows a PoE-capable switch providing power and data connections to a PoE-capable security camera.

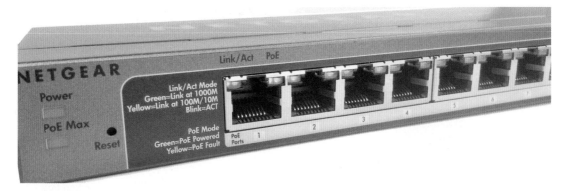

Figure 5-28 PoE-capable switch

Figure 5-29 PoE-capable security camera

On networks that demand PoE but don't have PoE-capable equipment, you can add PoE adapters, like the one shown in Figure 5-31. One type of adapter, called an injector or midspan and shown in the bottom left of Figure 5-30, connects to a non-PoE switch or router to inject power onto the network. Another type of adapter, called a splitter and shown in the bottom right of Figure 5-30, attaches to a non-PoE client, such as an outdoor camera, to receive power over the Ethernet connection. Use one or both, depending on the needs of the devices being installed.

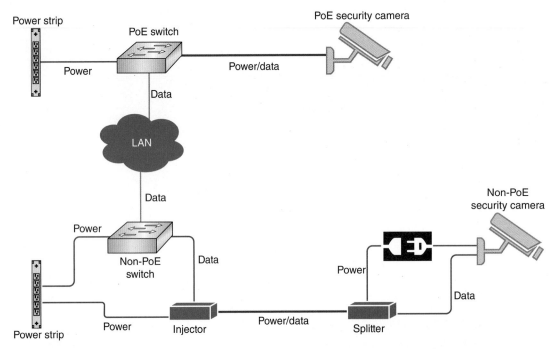

Figure 5-30 PoE adapters can add PoE functionality to non-PoE devices on a network

Source: D-Link North America

Figure 5-31 Power and data separately enter this PoE injector through ports shown on the right and exit together through the port shown on the left

You've now explored copper cabling at the physical layer, but the data link layer is also affected by the physical media that make up a network. Let's see how this works.

Ethernet Standards for Twisted-Pair Cable

A cable's category (such as Cat 5e or Cat 6) determines the fastest network speed it can support. This is a layer 1 characteristic. A device's NIC is also rated for maximum network speeds, which are defined by various **Ethernet standards**. Although Ethernet is generally thought of as a layer 2 protocol, it also has layer 1 functions that determine a transmission's frequency and other electrical characteristics. Other familiar layer 2 technologies, such as USB and Wi-Fi, also include physical layer components. Part of the function of this layer is to provide signaling between two nodes as they negotiate a common language by which to communicate. As for Ethernet, most LANs today use devices and NICs that can support Fast Ethernet and Gigabit Ethernet. When they first connect, devices auto-negotiate for the fastest standard they have in common. However, the network must be wired with cabling that is capable of supporting those speeds. Table 5-4 lists the various Ethernet standards supported by the different categories of twisted-pair cabling.

7 Application
6 Presentation
5 Session
4 Transport
3 Network
▶ 2 Data Link
▶ 1 Physical

Table 5-4   Ethernet standards used with twisted-pair cabling

Standard	Maximum transmission throughput (Mbps)	Maximum distance per segment (m)	Physical media	Pairs of wires used for transmission
10BASE-T	10	100	Cat 3 or better UTP	2 pair
100BASE-T or 100BASE-TX (*Fast Ethernet*)	100	100	100BASE-T: Cat 5 or better 100BASE-TX: Cat 6 or better	2 pair
1000BASE-T (*Gigabit Ethernet*)	1000	100	Cat 5 or better (Cat 5e is preferred)	4 pair
10GBASE-T (*10-Gigabit Ethernet*)	10,000	100	Cat 6a or Cat 7 (Cat 7 is preferred)	4 pair
40GBASE-T	40,000	30	Cat 8	4 pair

EXAM TIP   Memorize every detail in Table 5-4. You'll need them to pass the exam.

NOTE 5-8

Two new standards were recently ratified by IEEE:

2.5GBASE-T—2500 Mbps, requires Cat 5e or better

5GBASE-T—5000 Mbps, requires Cat 6 or better

These new standards provide intermediate steps between Gigabit Ethernet and 10-Gigabit Ethernet. A network can support a variety of Ethernet standards at once. When matched with the proper twisted-pair category of cable, it's possible to progressively upgrade a network, one device or NIC at a time.

The fastest Ethernet standard currently is 100GBASE-T, which achieves dramatic transmission rates on twisted-pair cabling that is comparable to fiber-optic cabling and is less expensive than fiber-optic. Still, as with other twisted-pair Ethernet standards, the maximum segment length for 100GBASE-T is 100 meters. This limitation means that 100GBASE-T is not appropriate for long-distance WANs, but could easily support the use of converged services, such as video and voice, at every desktop in a LAN.

Now that you've learned about the capabilities of copper wires to conduct signals, let's explore the possibilities when light signals are transmitted over glass fibers.

REMEMBER THIS...

- Identify RG-6 coaxial cable, F-connectors, and twinaxial cable.
- Compare the categories of twisted pair cable: Cat 5, Cat 5e, Cat 6, Cat 6a, Cat 7, and Cat 8.
- Memorize the T568A and T568B pinouts.
- Given a scenario, choose the correct cable: straight-through, crossover, rollover, and console.
- Explain the primary Ethernet standards for copper cabling: 10BASE-T, 100BASE-TX, 1000BASE-T, 10GBASE-T, and 40GBASE-T.
- Describe how to incorporate PoE and PoE+ devices in a network.
- Use common network cabling tools: cable crimper, loopback adapter, snips/cutters, and cable stripper.

SELF-CHECK

3. What is the minimum twisted-pair category required for 10-Gigabit Ethernet at 100 meters?
   a. Cat 5e
   b. Cat 6a
   c. Cat 7
   d. Cat 8

4. Pin 1 on one end of a cable is orange and white striped. What color should Pin 1 be on the other end of the cable to create a crossover cable?
   a. Orange and white striped
   b. Solid blue
   c. Solid brown
   d. Green and white striped

5. What is the typical maximum segment length for Ethernet networks?
   a. 10 meters
   b. 100 meters
   c. 1000 meters
   d. 10,000 meters

Check your answers at the end of this module.

You're Ready

You're now ready to complete **Project 5-2: Create a Loopback Plug**, or you can wait until you've finished reading this module.

You're Ready

You're now ready to complete **Project 5-3: Create a Loopback Jack**, or you can wait until you've finished reading this module.

FIBER-OPTIC CABLE

✓ CERTIFICATION

1.3: Summarize the types of cables and connectors and explain which is the appropriate type for a solution.

2.1: Compare and contrast various devices, their features, and their appropriate placement on the network.

5.2: Given a scenario, troubleshoot common cable connectivity issues and select the appropriate tools.

5.5: Given a scenario, troubleshoot general networking issues.

Average reading time: 27 minutes

7 Application
6 Presentation
5 Session
4 Transport
3 Network
2 Data Link
▶ 1 Physical

Fiber-optic cable, or simply *fiber,* contains one or several glass or plastic fibers at its center, or core. Data is transmitted through the central fibers via pulsing light typically sent from one of two possible sources:

- **Laser**—An intense, focused light that can travel extremely long distances with very high data throughput
- **LED (light-emitting diode)**—A cool-burning, long-lasting technology used on shorter fiber-optic connections, such as between floors in a building or between a switch and a router

Surrounding the fibers is a layer of glass or plastic called cladding. The cladding is less dense than the glass or plastic in the strands and so reflects light back to the core in patterns that vary depending on the transmission mode. This reflection allows the fiber to bend around corners without diminishing the integrity of the light-based signal (although bend radius limitations do apply).

Outside the cladding, a plastic buffer protects the cladding and core. Because the buffer is opaque, it also absorbs any light that might escape. To prevent the cable from stretching, and to protect the inner core further, strands of Kevlar (a polymeric fiber) surround the plastic buffer. Finally, a plastic sheath covers the strands of Kevlar. Figure 5-32 shows a fiber-optic cable with multiple, insulated fibers. The clear strands you see protruding from each line are not the actual cores—these are the visible cladding around each core. A core itself is microscopic in width.

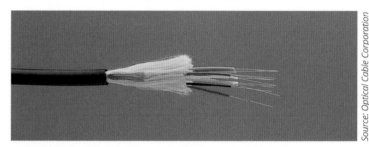

Figure 5-32 A fiber-optic cable

Source: Optical Cable Corporation

Like twisted-pair and coaxial cabling, fiber-optic cabling comes in a number of varieties, depending on its intended use and the manufacturer. For example, fiber-optic cables used to connect the facilities of large telephone and data carriers may contain as many as 1000 fibers and be heavily sheathed to prevent damage from extreme environmental conditions. At the other end of the spectrum, fiber-optic patch cables for use on LANs might contain only two strands of fiber and be pliable enough to wrap around your hand.

Because each strand of glass in a fiber-optic cable usually transmits in one direction only—in simplex fashion—two strands are often needed for full-duplex communication. One solution is to use a zipcord cable, in which two strands are combined side by side in conjoined jackets, as depicted in Figure 5-33. You'll find zipcords where fiber-optic cable spans relatively short distances, such as connecting a server and switch. A zipcord may come with one of many types of connectors on its ends, as described later in this section.

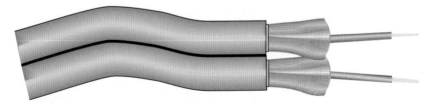

Figure 5-33 Zipcord fiber-optic patch cable

With a zipcord cable, full-duplex communication is achieved by sending data on one port and receiving data through the other. A newer technology allows bidirectional transmission on both ports, which means each fiber cable carries data in both directions. It uses the newer bidirectional WDM technology to separate the data traveling in each direction on different wavelengths of light, or colors. To work, it requires special equipment on each end of the connection called a BiDi (pronounced *bye-dye*) transceiver, also called a WDM transceiver. BiDi transceivers are more expensive than their standard, duplex cousins, but they reduce by half the amount of fiber cabling needed for the same data throughput, making them more economical.

Fiber-optic cable is the industry standard for high-speed networking and provides the following benefits over copper cabling:

- Extremely high throughput
- Very high resistance to noise

- Excellent (though not perfect) security
- Ability to carry signals for much longer distances before requiring repeaters

While fiber cable itself is not hugely more expensive than comparable copper cable, the most significant drawback to fiber is that it is more expensive to install, and fiber equipment is pricier. Fiber-optic cable requires special equipment for splicing, or joining, which means that quickly repairing a fiber-optic cable in the field (given little time or resources) can be difficult. Fiber's characteristics are summarized in the following list:

- **Throughput**—Fiber has proven reliable in transmitting data at rates that can reach 100 gigabits (or 100,000 megabits) per second per channel. Fiber's amazing throughput is partly due to the physics of light traveling through glass. Unlike electrical pulses traveling over copper, light experiences virtually no resistance. Therefore, light-based signals can be transmitted at faster rates and with fewer errors than electrical pulses. In fact, a pure glass strand can accept up to 1 billion laser light pulses per second. Its high throughput capability makes it suitable for network backbones and for supporting applications that generate a great deal of traffic, such as video or audio conferencing.
- **Cost**—Fiber-optic cable is the most expensive wired transmission medium. Because of its cost, most organizations find it impractical to run fiber to every desktop. Not only is the cable itself more expensive than copper cabling, but fiber-optic transmitters and connectivity equipment can cost as much as five times more than those designed for UTP networks. In addition, hiring skilled fiber-cable installers costs more than hiring twisted-pair cable installers.
- **Noise immunity**—Because fiber does not conduct electrical current to transmit signals, it is unaffected by EMI. Its impressive noise resistance is one reason why fiber can span such long distances.
- **Size and scalability**—Depending on the type of fiber-optic cable used, segment lengths vary from 2 to 40,000 meters. The maximum limit is due primarily to optical loss, or the degradation of the light signal after it travels a certain distance away from its source (just as the light of a flashlight dims after a certain number of feet). Optical loss accrues over long distances and grows with every connection point in the fiber network. Dust or oil in a connection (for example, from people handling the fiber while splicing it) can further exacerbate optical loss.

While the distance a cable can carry light depends partly on the light's wavelength, it also depends on whether the cable is single mode or multimode. Let's see what the primary differences are between these two types of fiber cable.

SMF (Single Mode Fiber)

SMF (single mode fiber) consists of a narrow core of 8 to 10 microns in diameter. Laser-generated light travels a single path over the core, reflecting very little. Because it reflects little, the light does not disperse as the signal travels along the fiber. This continuity allows SMF to accommodate the highest bandwidths and longest distances (without requiring repeaters) of all wired network transmission media. Figure 5-34 depicts a simplified version of how signals travel over single mode fiber.

The Internet backbone depends on single mode fiber. However, because of its relatively high cost, SMF is rarely used for short connections, such as those between a server and switch.

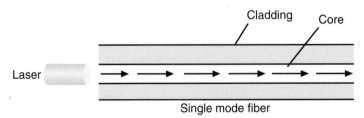

Figure 5-34 Transmission over single mode fiber-optic cable

MMF (Multimode Fiber)

MMF (multimode fiber) contains a core with a larger diameter than SMF, usually 50 or 62.5 microns, over which many pulses of light generated by a laser or LED light source travel at various angles. Signals traveling over multimode fiber experience greater attenuation than those traversing single mode fiber. Therefore, MMF is not suited to distances longer than a few kilometers. On the other hand, MMF is less expensive to install and, therefore, is typically used to connect routers, switches, and servers on the backbone of a network or to connect a desktop workstation to the network. Figure 5-35 depicts a simplified view of how signals travel over multimode fiber.

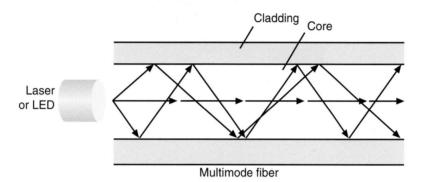

Figure 5-35   Transmission over multimode fiber-optic cable

The transition between SMF and MMF cabling might occur at an FDP (fiber distribution panel), which is usually a case on a rack where fiber cables converge, connect with each other, and connect with fiber-optic terminal equipment from the ISP. Splices at the FDP (or elsewhere on the network) might be accomplished by joining two fiber cables in a permanent bond using a fusion splicer, which melts the tips of two fibers together so light can pass cleanly through the joint, or various connectors might be used to create temporary splices.

NOTE 5-9

Although the process is a bit more sensitive to error than terminating copper cable, you can also terminate fiber-optic cable. A typical fiber termination kit might include the following tools:

- **Fiber stripper**—Strips off the outer layers of a fiber-optic cable

- **Fiber cleaver**—Cuts a clean slice through the fiber strands

   If you don't have this equipment on hand, you can find a few videos on the web that demonstrate the process and tools.

Fiber Connectors

Just as fiber cables are classified by SMF or MMF, fiber-cable connectors are also grouped along these lines. MMF connectors can be classified by the number of fibers they connect, and SMF connectors are classified by the size and shape of the ferrule. The ferrule is the extended tip of a connector that makes contact with the receptacle in the jack or other connector, as you can see in Figure 5-36.

SMF connectors are designed to reduce back reflection, which is the return of the light signal back into the fiber that is transmitting the signal. Back reflection is measured as optical loss in dB (decibels). Shapes and polishes currently used on SMF ferrules to reduce back reflection include the following:

- UPC (ultra-physical contact)—Extensive polishing of the tips creates a rounded surface, which allows the two internal fibers to meet and increases efficiency over older types of connections.
- APC (angled physical contact)—Uses a polished curved surface, but the end faces are placed at an angle to each other; the industry standard for this angle is 8 degrees.

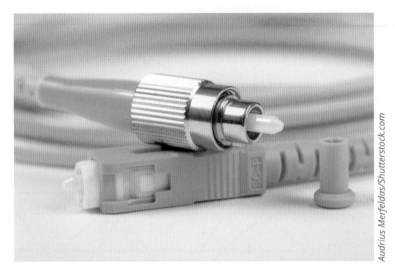

Audrius Merfeldas/Shutterstock.com

Figure 5-36 A cap protects the ferrule when the connector is not in use

NOTE 5-10

UPC adapters and connectors are often blue, and APC adapters and connectors are often green. But not always.

You can see how these two types of ferrule shapes compare in Figure 5-37. The red arrows indicate the back reflection for each connection. Notice how the APC connection reflects any signal loss in a different direction than the source of the signal. Back reflection worsens in UPC connections over time, but APC connections are not as sensitive to degradation from repeatedly disconnecting and reconnecting cables.

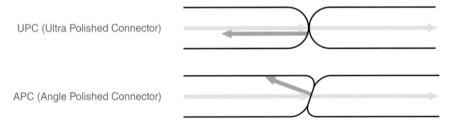

UPC (Ultra Polished Connector)

APC (Angle Polished Connector)

Figure 5-37 Two types of mechanical connections in fiber-optic connectors

Table 5-5 summarizes the fiber connectors you'll need to know for the CompTIA Network+ exam. SMF connectors are typically available with a 1.25-mm ferrule or a 2.5-mm ferrule, though other sizes can be found. The most common 1.25-mm ferrule connector is **LC (local connector)**. Two 2.5-mm ferrules are **SC (subscriber connector or standard connector)** and **ST (straight tip)**. The most common type of MMF connector is **MT-RJ (mechanical transfer-registered jack)**.

Older fiber networks might use ST or SC connectors. However, LC and MT-RJ connectors are now more common because of their smaller sizes, which allows for a higher density of connections at each termination point. The MT-RJ connector is unique in that it contains two strands of fiber in a single ferrule. With two strands per ferrule, a single MT-RJ connector provides full-duplex signaling. SC and LC connectors are also available in full-duplex mode.

Table 5-5 Characteristics of fiber connectors

Photo	Connector	Polish	Ferrule characteristics	Full-duplex?
LC *Source: Senko Advanced Components, Inc.*	LC	UPC, APC	1.25 mm	Yes
ST *Source: Senko Advanced Components, Inc.*	ST	UPC	2.5 mm	No
SC *Source: Senko Advanced Components, Inc.*	SC	UPC, APC	2.5 mm	Can be
MT-RJ *Source: Senko Advanced Components, Inc.*	MT-RJ	N/A	2 fibers	Yes

EXAM TIP You've read about several cable connectors in this module. You can see a list of all the ones you'll need to know for the CompTIA Network+ exam, along with images to help you identify them visually, in Appendix B.

Media Converters

As long as networks contain both copper and fiber media, some kind of conversion must take place. A **media converter** is hardware that enables networks or segments running on different media to interconnect and exchange signals. For example, suppose an Ethernet segment leading from your company's data center uses fiber-optic cable to connect to a workgroup switch that only accepts twisted-pair (copper) cable. In that case, you could use a media converter to interconnect the switch with the fiber-optic cable. The media converter completes the physical connection and also converts the electrical signals from the copper cable to light wave signals that can traverse the fiber-optic cable, and vice versa. Such a media converter is shown in Figure 5-38.

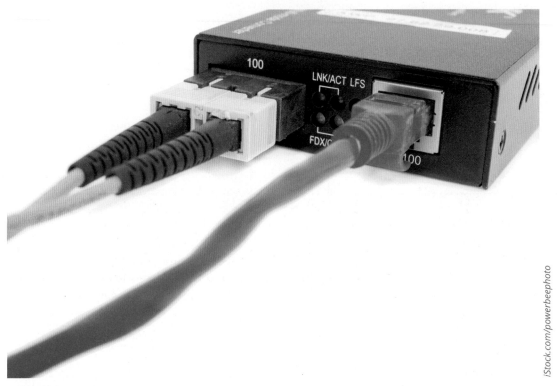

iStock.com/powerbeephoto

Figure 5-38   Copper wire-to-fiber media converter

You must select the correct media converter for the type of fiber being connected, whether it's SMF to copper or MMF to copper. Converters are also needed to connect networks using MMF with networks using SMF. Figure 5-39 shows a converter that connects single mode and multimode portions of a network.

Fiber Transceivers

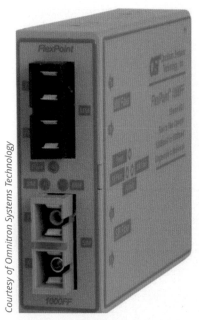

Courtesy of Omnitron Systems Technology

Figure 5-39   Single mode to multimode converter

Suppose you are purchasing a switch that will be part of a network for a new, fast-growing business. The current requirements for the switch might be two fiber-optic connections for the network backbone and 24 RJ-45 Gigabit Ethernet connections for clients and servers. For the future, however, you are considering fiber-optic connectivity to every desktop.

Rather than ordering a switch that contains exactly the currently needed number and type of onboard interfaces, you could order a switch that allows you to change and upgrade its interfaces at any time. These switches contain sockets where one of many types of modular interfaces, called **transceivers**, can be plugged in. Such transceivers are easily inserted into the sockets to connect with its motherboard and upgraded later as technology improves. A hardware component that can be changed in this manner, without disrupting operations, is called **hot-swappable**. Using hot-swappable transceivers means you don't have to purchase a new switch, open the chassis of the existing switch (causing network downtime and risking hardware damage), or even turn off the switch to upgrade the network. Modular interfaces can also be installed on some expansion board NICs and media converters.

GBIC (Gigabit interface converter), pronounced *jee-bick,* was a standard type of transceiver designed in the 1990s for Gigabit Ethernet connections. GBICs might contain RJ-45 ports for copper cables or SC ports for fiber-optic connections. Figure 5-40 shows a GBIC that can be used on a Gigabit Ethernet fiber network.

Newer transceivers that have made the GBIC obsolete include the following:

- **SFP (small form-factor pluggable)**—Provides the same function as GBICs and is more compact, allowing more ports per linear inch. Also known as mini GBICs or SFP GBICs. Typically used for 1 Gbps connections, but theoretically capable of 5 Gbps.

Figure 5-40   GBIC (Gigabit interface converter) with dual SC ports

- **XFP (10 Gigabit small form-factor pluggable)**—Supports up to 10 Gbps and is slightly larger than SFP with lower power consumption than SFP+.
- **SFP+**—Developed later than XFP and is the same module size as SFP; theoretical maximum transmission speed is 16 Gbps. SFP+ transceivers are still widely used today.
- **QSFP (quad small form-factor pluggable)**—Complies with the 802.3ba standard, squeezing four channels in a single transceiver and supporting data rates up to 40 Gbps (4 x 10 Gbps).
- **QSFP+**—Generally the same technology as QSFP while supporting data rates over 40 Gbps. Highest speed format at the time of this writing is QSFP56-DD, which doubles the data lanes to eight and supports a total theoretical maximum data rate of 400 Gbps (8 x 50 Gbps). The twinax cable you saw earlier in Figure 5-10 is terminated with QSFP+ transceivers.
- **CFP (centum form-factor pluggable)**—Intended for 100-Gbps network connections, with each succeeding generation (CFP2, CFP4, CFP8) becoming smaller and more energy-efficient. *Centum* is Latin for 100.

To avoid using the incorrect transceiver, you must pair these devices based on supported speeds and protocols. Also consider the cable connectors you'll be using. Most modern transceivers support LC or, occasionally, RJ-45 connectors.

Figure 5-41 shows two SFPs. The black dust plug on the left side of the bottom transceiver is covering two ports for fiber-optic cable connectors, one for transmitting and another for receiving data. Figure 5-42 shows two transceivers installed in a media converter. The transceiver on the left is an SFP+, and the transceiver on the right is an XFP.

Installing a transceiver of any of these types is simply a matter of sliding it into a compatible socket on the connectivity device. Most transceivers come with a tab or latch system to lock them into place. They are also keyed so that they will slide into the socket only when aligned properly. The switch or router need not be powered down when you add or remove transceivers. However, do not attach cables before inserting a transceiver, and always remove the cables before removing a transceiver. Figure 5-43 illustrates how a fiber-optic SFP+ is installed in a switch.

Some transceivers contain management interfaces separate from the switch's configuration utility. For example, a 16-Gbps SFP+ on a router could have its own IP address. A network administrator could use the Telnet utility to connect to the transceiver and configure its ports for a particular speed or routing protocol without accessing the router's operating system. Earlier in Figure 5-10, if you look closely, you can see a small chip on the circuit board. This chip allows the transceiver to communicate with the device into which it is installed.

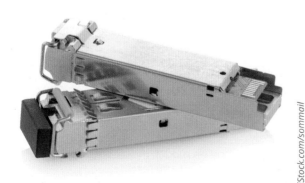

Figure 5-41   These SFPs slide into a switch to add fiber-optic connectivity

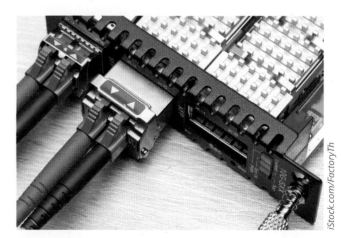

Figure 5-42   This media converter supports both SFP+ and XFP

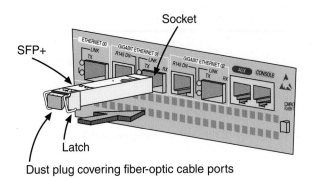

Socket

SFP+

Latch

Dust plug covering fiber-optic cable ports

Figure 5-43   Installing an SFP+ in a switch

NOTE 5-11

A helpful tool when testing a transceiver's functionality or checking for a mismatch is a loopback adapter. Recall from earlier in this module that a loopback adapter can create a closed loop to trick a device into thinking it's connected to a network. A loopback adapter can do much the same thing with a transceiver, although a fiber-optic loopback adapter is specifically needed for use on a fiber connector. Figure 5-44 shows a fiber-optic loopback adapter with two LC fiber-cable connectors.

Figure 5-44   Fiber-optic loopback adapter

Ethernet Standards for Fiber-Optic Cable

Long before IEEE developed a 10GBASE-T standard for twisted-pair cable, it established standards for achieving high data rates over fiber-optic cable. In fact, fiber optic is the best medium for delivering high throughput. Table 5-6 lists various Ethernet standards established by IEEE for fiber-optic cabling and covered in the CompTIA Network+ objectives. Notice in the table there are Ethernet standards for Fast Ethernet, Gigabit Ethernet, and 10-Gigabit Ethernet that all use fiber-optic cables. As you saw when discussing transceivers, even faster Ethernet standards are available, up to 100-Gigabit Ethernet.

7 Application
6 Presentation
5 Session
4 Transport
3 Network
▶ **2** Data Link
▶ **1** Physical

Table 5-6   Ethernet standards using fiber-optic cable

Standard	Maximum transmission bandwidth (Mbps)	Maximum distance per segment (m)	Physical media
100BASE-SX (*Fast Ethernet*)	100	Up to 300, depending on modal bandwidth and fiber core diameter	MMF
100BASE-FX (*Fast Ethernet*)	100	Up to 2000, depending on modal bandwidth and fiber core diameter	MMF
1000BASE-SX (*Gigabit Ethernet*)	1000	Up to 550, depending on modal bandwidth and fiber core diameter	MMF
1000BASE-LX (*Gigabit Ethernet*)	1000	550 for MMF, 5000 for SMF	MMF or SMF
10GBASE-SR (*10-Gigabit Ethernet*)	10,000	Up to 300, depending on modal bandwidth and fiber core diameter	MMF
10GBASE-LR (*10-Gigabit Ethernet*)	10,000	10,000	SMF

For the CompTIA Network+ exam, you need to know these six fiber Ethernet standards. Here are some important details about each:

- 100BASE-SX is a low-cost solution for Fast Ethernet and uses a short 850-nanometer wavelength light signal, hence the *S* in its name *SX*. (A nanometer equals 0.000000001 meters, or about the width of six carbon atoms in a row.) The maximum segment length for 100BASE-SX and other MMF cables depends on two things: the diameter of the fiber and the modal bandwidth used to transmit signals. **Modal bandwidth** is a measure of the highest frequency of signal a multimode fiber can support over a specific distance and is measured in MHz-km. It is related to the distortion that occurs when multiple pulses of light, although issued at the same time, arrive at the end of a fiber at slightly different times. The higher the modal bandwidth, the longer a multimode fiber can carry a signal reliably. Only one repeater may be used between segments. At most, segment lengths for this standard are limited to a short 300-meter distance.
- 100BASE-FX also offers Fast Ethernet speeds (thus the *F* in its name *FX*), uses a longer wavelength of 1300 nanometers, and is rated up to 2 kilometers. 100BASE-FX still uses MMF cable, but similar standards, 100BASE-LX and 100BASE-BX, offer even longer distances (10 kilometers) over SMF instead.
- 1000BASE-SX is a form of Gigabit Ethernet and uses short wavelengths of 850 nanometers. 1000BASE-SX is best suited for short network runs—for example, connecting a data center with a data closet in an office building.
- 1000BASE-LX is the more common fiber version of Gigabit Ethernet and uses long wavelengths (hence the *L* in its name *LX*) of 1300 nanometers. Because of its long segments, it's used for long backbones connecting buildings in a MAN or for connecting an ISP with its telecommunications carrier.
- 10GBASE-SR is the "short range" standard for 10-Gigabit Ethernet. Using 850 nanometer wavelengths and MMF, the maximum supported distances vary according to the type of cabling used and max out around 400 meters.
- 10GBASE-LR uses lasers emitting 1310 nanometer light. This "long range" version of 10-Gigabit Ethernet can extend as far as 10 kilometers.

Common Fiber-Cable Problems

Working with fiber cable presents a set of troubleshooting challenges that don't arise when you are working with copper cables. Problems unique to fiber cable include the following:

7 Application
6 Presentation
5 Session
4 Transport
3 Network
2 Data Link
▶ 1 Physical

- **Fiber type mismatch**—This term is misleading because a fiber type mismatch is actually more of a fiber core mismatch. Connecting an SMF cable to an MMF cable will prevent the transmission from traversing the connection successfully, though some of the signal can get through. However, even same-mode cables can be mismatched if the cores have different widths. A cable with a 50-micron core, for example, should not be connected to a cable with a 62.5-micron core, even though they're both MMF.
- **Wavelength mismatch**—SMF, MMF, and POF (Plastic Optical Fiber) each use different wavelengths for transmissions. A wavelength mismatch occurs when transmissions are optimized for one type of cable but sent over a different type of cable.
- **Dirty connectors**—If fiber connectors get dirty or just a little dusty, signal loss and other errors can start to cause problems. Always keep protectors on fiber connectors and dust covers over fiber jacks when they're not in use.
- **Link loss**—As with most things, networks rarely function in an ideal environment. The power of a light signal emitted at one end of a connection is subjected to many losses along its way to the other end, including losses from distance along the cable, losses from multiplexing, and losses from imperfect connections, patches, or splices. A transceiver must offer a sufficient power budget to overcome all these losses (measured in dB) and still produce a strong-enough signal at the receiving end. This calculation is called an **optical link budget**, and it considers all anticipated losses along the length of the connection. A low optical link budget results in link loss issues, including reduced transmission efficiency and downtime.

REMEMBER THIS...

- Explain the differences between SMF and MMF fiber cable.
- Identify common fiber connectors and ferrule types: LC, ST, SC, MT-RJ, APC, and UPC.
- Compare fiber transceiver types: SFP, SFP+, QSFP, and QSFP+.
- Explain common fiber Ethernet standards: 100BASE-SX, 100BASE-FX, 1000BASE-SX, 1000BASE-LX, 10GBASE-SR, and 10GBASE-LR.

SELF-CHECK

6. Which of the following statements is *not* true?
   a. SMF has a thinner core than MMF.
   b. SMF supports lower bandwidths than MMF.
   c. MMF is better suited than SMF to backbone connections within the data center.
   d. MMF signals experience greater reflection within the core than SMF signals.

7. Which fiber connector does *not* support full-duplex transmissions?
   a. LC
   b. MT-RJ
   c. SC
   d. ST

8. What is the earliest transceiver type to support four channels on a single transceiver to increase throughput?
   a. QSFP
   b. SFP+
   c. SFP
   d. QSFP+

Check your answers at the end of this module.

CABLE TROUBLESHOOTING TOOLS

 **CERTIFICATION**

5.2: Given a scenario, troubleshoot common cable connectivity issues and select the appropriate tools.

- -

Average reading time: 14 minutes

7 Application
6 Presentation
5 Session
4 Transport
3 Network
2 Data Link
▶ 1 Physical

Symptoms of cabling problems can be as elusive as occasional lost packets or as obvious as a break in network connectivity. You can start troubleshooting a network connection problem by checking the network connection LED status indicator lights on the network ports of the devices involved. A steady light indicates connectivity, and a blinking light indicates activity. A red or amber light, as shown in Figure 5-45, might indicate a problem. Check the device NICs and make sure cable connections are solid.

If all the devices check out and you suspect a cabling issue, you need to know which tools are designed to analyze and isolate problems related to particular types of network media. Several tools are available, ranging from simple continuity testers that indicate whether a cable is faulty, to sophisticated cable performance testers that graphically

Figure 5-45   Status indicator lights for an onboard
network port

depict a cable's attenuation and crosstalk characteristics over the length of the cable. Knowing the specific tool to use for a particular troubleshooting scenario can help you quickly zero in on the problem and the solution. The following sections describe a variety of cable troubleshooting tools, their functions, and their relative costs.

Toner and Probe Kit

Ideally, you and your networking colleagues would label each port and wire termination in a data room so that problems and changes can be easily managed. However, because of personnel changes and time constraints, a data room might be disorganized and poorly documented. If this is the case where you work, a tone generator and a tone locator can help you determine where a wire, possibly out of hundreds, terminates:

- **Tone generator (or toner)**—A small, electronic device that issues a signal on a wire
- **Tone locator (or probe)**—A device that emits an audible tone when it detects electrical activity on a wire

They are sold together as a set, often called a toner and probe kit or just toner probe (see Figure 5-46).

Figure 5-46   A toner and probe kit by Fluke Corporation

Place the tone generator at one end of a wire using the appropriate connector. Swipe the tone locator over each of the terminations you suspect to be the other end of that wire. You can verify the location of the wire's termination when you hear the tone.

Figure 5-47 depicts the use of a tone generator and a tone locator. Work by trial and error, guessing which termination corresponds to the wire over which you've generated a signal until the tone locator indicates the correct choice.

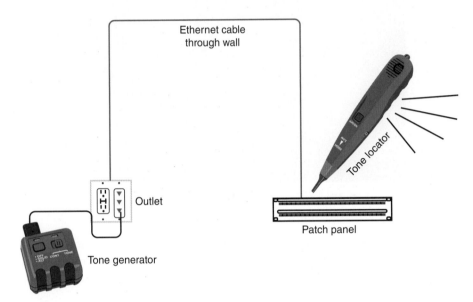

Figure 5-47   A toner and probe kit locates the termination of a wire

Tone generators and tone locators cannot be used to determine any characteristics about a wire, such as whether it's defective or whether its length exceeds IEEE standards for a certain type of network. They are only used to determine where a wire terminates.

> **⚠ CAUTION**   A tone generator should never be used on a wire that's connected to a device's port or network adapter. Because a tone generator transmits electricity over the wire, it could damage the device or network adapter.

Multimeter

A **multimeter** is a simple instrument that can measure many characteristics of an electric circuit, including its resistance, voltage, and impedance (see Figure 5-48). Although you could use separate instruments for measuring impedance on an AC (alternating current) circuit, resistance (opposition to electrical current) on a DC (direct current) circuit, and voltage on an AC or DC circuit, it is more convenient to have one instrument that accomplishes all these functions.

Recall that impedance is a measure of the opposition to a current's flow through a cable and is expressed in ohms. Lower impedance results in better power transfer, and higher impedance yields less attenuation of the data signal over a distance. Impedance is the telltale factor for ascertaining where faults in a cable lie. A certain amount of impedance is required for a signal to be properly transmitted and interpreted. However, very high or low levels of impedance can signify a damaged wire, incorrect pairing, or a termination point. In other words, changes in impedance can indicate where current is stopped or inhibited.

As a network professional, you might use a multimeter to do the following:

- Measure voltage to verify that a cable is properly conducting electricity—that is, whether its signal can travel unimpeded from one node on the network to another.

Figure 5-48   A multimeter

- Check for the presence of noise on a wire (by detecting extraneous voltage).
- Test for short or open circuits in the wire (by detecting unexpected resistance or loss of voltage).
  - A **short circuit** is an unwanted connection, such as when exposed wires touch each other.
  - An **open circuit** is one where needed connections are missing, such as when a wire breaks.

Cable Continuity Tester

In troubleshooting a physical layer problem, you might find the cause of a problem by simply testing a cable's continuity—that is, whether it is carrying a signal to its destination. Tools used to test the continuity of the cable might be called cable checkers, **continuity testers**, or cable testers. The term **cable tester**, however, is a general term that might also refer to more sophisticated tools that measure cable performance.

A cable continuity tester (see Figure 5-49) is battery operated and has two parts:

- The base unit connects to one end of the cable and generates voltage.
- The remote unit connects to the other end of the cable and detects the voltage.

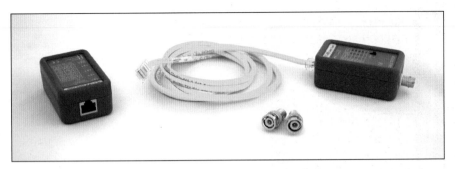

Figure 5-49 Use a cable tester pair to determine the type of cable and if the cable is good

Most cable testers provide a series of lights that signal pass/fail or other information, and some units also emit an audible tone. Here are some additional characteristics to consider when selecting a cable tester:

- Some continuity testers will verify that the wires in a UTP or STP cable are paired correctly following TIA/EIA 568 standards and that they are not shorted, exposed, or crossed. This is called a **wire map test**, and it indicates that each pin on one end is paired with the appropriate pin on the other end. It might seem like mixing colors wouldn't matter on a cable so long as both ends of the cable match. However, an incorrect pinout can cause excessive crosstalk issues, voltage spikes, reduced performance, and problematic connections, especially with older devices. Make sure that the cable tester you purchase can test the type of network you use—for example, 1000BASE-T or 10GBASE-T Ethernet. Common problems a wire map test can detect are illustrated in Figure 5-50 and include the following:
  - **Reversed pair**—The wires of one pair (for example, the orange pair) are reversed with each other when they shouldn't be. For example, perhaps the solid orange wire is inserted into the pin where the striped orange wire should go, and the striped orange wire is inserted where the solid orange wire should go.

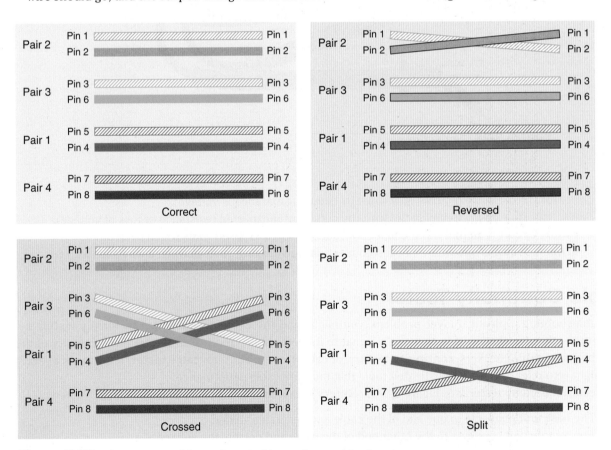

Figure 5-50 Common problems detected by a wire map test

○ **Crossed pair**—Two pairs are reversed with each other when they shouldn't be. For example, perhaps the wires of the green pair are inserted where the wires of the blue pair should go, and vice versa.

○ **Split pair**—One wire from each of two pairs are reversed with each other when they shouldn't be. For example, perhaps the solid blue wire from the blue pair is inserted where the striped brown wire from the brown pair should go, and vice versa. This is one of the most difficult wire map issues to detect as this wiring could still pass a simple continuity test.

- Continuity testers for fiber-optic cables issue light pulses on the fiber and determine whether they reach the other end of the fiber. Some continuity testers offer the ability to test both copper and fiber-optic cables.
- Most continuity testers are portable and lightweight, and typically use one 9-volt battery. A continuity tester can cost between $10 and $300 and can save many hours of work. Popular manufacturers of these cable testing devices include Belkin, Fluke, and Greenlee.

> **⊘ CAUTION** Do not use a continuity tester on a live network cable. Disconnect the cable from the network and then test its continuity.

Cable Performance Tester

Whereas continuity testers can determine whether a single cable is carrying current, more sophisticated equipment is needed to measure the overall performance of a cabling structure. A device used for this sophisticated testing is called a **cable performance tester**, line tester, certifier, or network tester. It allows you to perform the same continuity and fault tests as a continuity tester, but can also be used to:

- Measure the distance to a connectivity device, termination point, or damage in a cable
- Measure attenuation along a cable
- Measure NEXT (near end crosstalk) between wires as well as alien crosstalk
- Measure termination resistance and impedance
- Issue pass/fail ratings for various categories of cabling standards
- Store and print cable testing results or directly save data to a computer database
- Graphically depict a cable's attenuation and crosstalk characteristics over the length of the cable

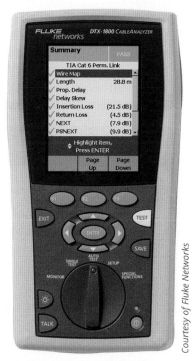

A sophisticated performance tester will include a **TDR (time domain reflectometer)**. A TDR issues a signal on a cable and then measures the way the signal bounces back (or reflects) to the TDR. Bad connectors, crimps, bends, short circuits, cable mismatches, bad wiring, or other defects modify the signal's amplitude before it returns to the TDR, thus changing the way it reflects. The TDR analyzes the return signal and, based on its condition and the amount of time the signal took to return, determines cable imperfections.

Performance testers for fiber-optic connections use **OTDRs (optical time domain reflectometers)**. Rather than issue an electrical signal over the cable as twisted-pair cable testers do, an OTDR transmits light-based signals of different wavelengths over the fiber. Based on the type of return light signal, the OTDR can do the following:

- Accurately measure the length of the fiber
- Determine the location of faulty splices, breaks, bad or mismatched connectors, or bends
- Measure attenuation over the cable

Because of their sophistication, performance testers for both copper and fiber-optic cables cost significantly more than continuity testers. A high-end kit could cost up to $50,000, while a very low-end unit could sell for a few hundred dollars. Figure 5-51 shows an example of a high-end cable performance tester that can measure the characteristics of both copper and fiber-optic cables.

Figure 5-51 The DTX-1800 device by Fluke Networks is a high-end cable performance tester designed to certify structured cabling

Courtesy of Fluke Networks

OPM (Optical Power Meter)

An **OPM (optical power meter)**, also called a **fiber light meter**, measures the amount of light power transmitted on a fiber-optic line. The device must be calibrated precisely, following highly accurate optical power standards set by the NIST (National Institute of Standards and Technology), which is a nonregulatory agency of the U.S. Department of Commerce. However, the surrounding room temperature, connection type, and skill of the technician conducting the test all affect the accuracy of the final test results. A simple light meter is pictured in Figure 5-52. More sophisticated and accurate meters are available at much higher price points.

As you conclude your exploration of various cable testing tools, consider that the time it takes to test a cable before installation could save many hours of troubleshooting after the network is in place. Recall the *On the Job* story at the beginning of this module where the consultant spent many unpleasant hours tracing poorly installed cables and devices. Whether you make your own cables or purchase cabling from a reputable vendor, test the cable to ensure that it meets your network's required standards. Just because a cable is labeled "Cat 6a," for example, does not necessarily mean that it will live up to that standard.

Figure 5-52 This optical power meter measures light power transmitted on a fiber-optic line

REMEMBER THIS...

- Describe the purpose of common troubleshooting tools: toner and probe kit, multimeter, cable tester, cable performance tester (including an OTDR), and a fiber light meter.
- Explain how to troubleshoot common cabling issues, such as incorrect pinout and open or short circuits.

SELF-CHECK

9. Which tool could you use to determine if a laptop's power cable is working properly?
   a. Continuity tester
   b. Cable performance tester
   c. Toner and probe kit
   d. Multimeter

10. Which tool could you use to test a twisted-pair cable's pinout?
    a. OTDR
    b. Toner probe
    c. OPM
    d. Continuity tester

Check your answers at the end of this module.

You're Ready

You're now ready to complete **Project 5-4: Test a LAN's Speed and Throughput**, or you can wait until you've finished the Review Questions for this module.

You're Ready

After you finish the Hands-On Projects, you're ready to complete the **Module 5 Capstone Projects**.

MODULE SUMMARY

Transmission Basics

- Frequency is typically measured in MHz (megahertz) or GHz (gigahertz), which indicates the number of times in a second that an electrical signal can change states (for example, change from a positive to a negative charge or vice versa). You'll see maximum frequencies identified for different categories of copper cabling, but sometimes this maximum frequency is also called bandwidth to indicate the possible range of frequencies up to that maximum. Bandwidth is measured in Mbps (megabits per second) or Gbps (gigabits per second) and refers to the amount of data you could theoretically transmit during a given period of time, taking into consideration factors such as frequency, distance, and SNR (signal-to-noise ratio). Throughput (also called payload rate or effective data rate) is also measured in Mbps (megabits per second) or Gbps (gigabits per second) and refers to the number of data bits (0s and 1s) that are actually received across a connection each second. Throughput takes into consideration the reality of a network environment.
- Noise, or interference, can degrade or distort a signal and, on a network, is measured in dB (decibel) loss. EMI (electromagnetic interference) is caused by motors, power lines, televisions, copiers, fluorescent lights, microwave ovens, manufacturing machinery, and other sources of electrical activity (including a severe thunderstorm). Crosstalk occurs when a signal traveling on one wire or cable infringes on the signal traveling over an adjacent wire or cable.
- Attenuation is the loss of a signal's strength as it travels away from its source. To compensate for attenuation, signals are boosted en route using a repeater, which regenerates a digital signal in its original form without the noise it might have previously accumulated.
- Latency is the brief delay between the instant when data leaves the source and when it arrives at its destination. The most common way to measure latency on data networks is by calculating a packet's RTT (round trip time), or the length of time it takes for a packet to go from sender to receiver, then back from receiver to sender. RTT is usually measured in milliseconds. If packets experience varying amounts of delay, they can arrive out of order—a problem commonly called jitter, or more precisely, PDV (packet delay variation).
- Two important NIC settings include the direction in which signals travel over the media (duplex) and the number of signals that can traverse the media at any given time (multiplexing). To carry multiple signals, the medium's channel is logically separated into multiple smaller channels, or subchannels. FDM (frequency division multiplexing) on copper cables assigns different frequencies to create multiple frequency bands, each used by a subchannel.
- Fiber-optic cables typically use WDM (wavelength division multiplexing), which divides a light beam into different wavelengths, DWDM (dense WDM), which increases the number of channels provided by normal WDM, and CWDM (coarse WDM), which lowers cost by spacing frequency bands wider apart to allow for cheaper transceiver equipment.

Copper Cable

- Coaxial cable, called "coax" for short, was the foundation for Ethernet networks in the 1980s. Coax has been replaced by twisted-pair cable and fiber; however, RG-6 coax is still used for cable Internet, cable TV, and some multimedia connection types. An F-connector attaches to coaxial cable so that the pin in the center of the cable extends into the center of the connector. A BNC connector connects to another BNC connector via a turn-and-lock mechanism.

- Twinaxial cable, called "twinax" for short, looks very similar to coax cable except that there are two cores, or conductors, inside the cable. More recent twinax cables contain multiple pairs of these cores to carry even more data. Twinax is an inexpensive option for short, high-speed connections, such as when connecting switches to routers or servers in a data center. For this reason, twinax is also called a DAC (direct attach copper) cable. Twinax is factory terminated, usually with some of the same kinds of modular transceivers as what fiber terminations use. Depending on the connector type, twinax can support throughput up to 100 Gbps. However, the higher data rates require even shorter distance limitations in the range of 5–10 meters.

- Twisted-pair cabling in Ethernet networks contains four wire pairs. On Fast Ethernet networks, which have a maximum speed of 100 Mbps, one pair sends data, another pair receives data, and the other two pairs are not used for data transmission. Networks using Gigabit Ethernet and higher standards, with a speed of at least 1000 Mbps, use all four pairs for both sending and receiving.

- The TIA/EIA 568 standard divides twisted-pair wiring into several categories: Cat (category) 3, 5, 5e, 6, 6a, 7, 7a, and 8. Modern LANs use Cat 5e or higher wiring, which is the minimum required to support Gigabit Ethernet. Cat 6 and above are certified for multigigabit transmissions, although Cat 6 cable has shorter distance limitations when supporting 10 Gbps. While Cat 7/7a cables never gained significant popularity, Cat 8 cables are already widely available even for consumers and their home networks.

- STP (shielded twisted pair) cable consists of twisted-pair wires that are not only individually insulated, but might also be surrounded by a shielding made of a metallic substance such as a foil. The shielding acts as a barrier to external electromagnetic forces, thus preventing them from affecting the signals traveling over the wire inside the shielding. UTP cabling consists of one or more insulated wire pairs encased in a plastic sheath. As its name implies, UTP does not contain additional shielding for the twisted pairs. As a result, UTP is both less expensive and less resistant to noise than STP.

- TIA/EIA has specified two methods of inserting twisted-pair wires into RJ-45 plugs: TIA/EIA-568A and TIA/EIA-568B (also known as T568A and T568B, respectively). Functionally, there is very little difference between these two standards. You only must be certain that you use the same standard on every RJ-45 plug and jack on your network so data is transmitted and received correctly. T568B is more common and is likely what you'll find on home and business networks. However, the federal government requires T568A on all federal contracts.

- The most common type of networking cable is a straight-through cable, also called a patch cable. To create one, terminate the RJ-45 plugs at both ends of the cable identically, following one of the TIA/EIA-568 standards. A crossover cable has the transmit and receive wires reversed and was used to connect a PC to a PC or a switch to a switch. Rollover cables, also called console cables, are used to connect a computer to the console port of a router.

- PoE (Power over Ethernet) is a method for supplying electrical power over twisted-pair Ethernet connections. The amount of power provided is relatively small—15.4 watts for standard PoE devices and 25.5 watts for the newer PoE+ devices. The PoE standard specifies two types of devices: PSE (power sourcing equipment) and PDs (powered devices). A switch or router that is expected to provide power over Ethernet must support the technology. Also, the end node must be capable of receiving PoE. On networks that demand PoE but don't have PoE-capable equipment, you can add PoE adapters.

- A device's NIC is rated for maximum network speeds, which are defined by various Ethernet standards. When two devices first connect, they auto-negotiate for the fastest standard they have in common, such as 10BASE-T, 100BASE-TX, 1000BASE-T, or 10GBASE-T.

Fiber-Optic Cable

- Fiber-optic cable, or simply "fiber," contains one or several glass or plastic fibers at its center, or core. Data is transmitted through the central fibers via pulsing light typically sent from a laser or an LED (light-emitting diode). SMF (single mode fiber) consists of a narrow core of 8 to 10 microns in diameter. Laser-generated light travels a single path over the core, reflecting very little. Because it reflects little, the light does not disperse as the signal travels along the fiber. This continuity allows SMF to accommodate the highest bandwidths and longest distances (without requiring repeaters) of all network transmission media.

- MMF (multimode fiber) contains a core with a larger diameter than SMF, usually 50 or 62.5 microns, over which many pulses of light generated by a laser or LED light source travel at various angles. Signals traveling over multimode fiber experience greater attenuation than those traversing single mode fiber. Therefore, MMF is not suited to distances longer than a few kilometers. On the other hand, MMF is less expensive to install and, therefore, typically used to connect routers, switches, and servers on the backbone of a network or to connect a desktop workstation to the network.

- The transition between SMF and MMF cabling might occur at an FDP (fiber distribution panel), which is usually a case on a rack where fiber cables converge, connect with each other, and connect with fiber-optic terminal equipment from the ISP. Splices at the FDP (or elsewhere on the network) might be accomplished by joining two fiber cables in a permanent bond using a fusion splicer, which melts the tips of two fibers together so light can pass cleanly through the joint, or various connectors might be used to create temporary splices.

- SMF connectors are designed to reduce back reflection, which is the return of the light signal back into the fiber that is transmitting the signal. Shapes and polishes currently used on SMF ferrules to reduce back reflection include UPC (ultra-physical contact) and APC (angled physical contact).

- SMF connectors are typically available with a 1.25-mm ferrule or a 2.5-mm ferrule, though other sizes can be found. The most common 1.25-mm ferrule connector is LC (local connector). Two 2.5-mm ferrules are SC (subscriber connector or standard connector) and ST (straight tip). The most common type of MMF connector is MT-RJ (mechanical transfer-registered jack).

- Common fiber transceivers include SFP (small form-factor pluggable), SFP+, QSFP (quad small form-factor pluggable), and QSFP+. SFP was the first to offer Gigabit Ethernet speeds with SFP+ improving on those speeds. QSFP was the first to squeeze four channels in a single transceiver to support significantly higher data rates. QSFP+ improved on this technology to offer even higher data rates.

- Long before IEEE developed a 10GBASE-T standard for twisted-pair cable, it had established standards for achieving high data rates over fiber-optic cable, which is the best medium for delivering high throughput. Common fiber Ethernet standards include 100BASE-FX, 100BASE-SX, 1000BASE-LX, 1000BASE-SX, 10GBASE-SR, and 10GBASE-LR.

Cable Troubleshooting Tools

- You can start troubleshooting a network connection problem by checking the network connection LED status indicator lights on the network ports of the devices involved. A steady light indicates connectivity, and a blinking light indicates activity. A red or amber light might indicate a problem.

- A toner and probe kit can help determine where a wire, possibly out of hundreds, terminates. Tone generators and tone locators cannot be used to determine any characteristics about a wire, such as whether it's defective or whether its length exceeds IEEE standards for a certain type of network. They are only used to determine where a wire terminates.

- A multimeter is a simple instrument that can measure many characteristics of an electric circuit, including its resistance, voltage, and impedance. You might use a multimeter to measure voltage to verify that a cable is properly conducting electricity, to check for the presence of noise on a wire, or to test for short or open circuits in the wire.

- A continuity tester determines whether a cable is carrying a data signal to its destination. Some continuity testers will verify that the wires in a UTP or STP cable are paired correctly following TIA/EIA 568 standards and that they are not shorted, exposed, or crossed. Continuity testers for fiber-optic cables issue light pulses on the fiber and determine whether they reach the other end of the fiber.

- A sophisticated cable performance tester measures the overall performance of a cabling structure. It allows you to perform the same continuity and fault tests as a continuity tester, but it can also be used to measure the distance to a connectivity device, termination point, or damage in a cable; measure attenuation along a cable; measure NEXT (near end crosstalk) between wires as well as alien crosstalk; measure termination resistance and impedance; issue pass/fail ratings for various categories of cabling standards; store and print cable testing results or directly save data to a computer database; and graphically depict a cable's attenuation and crosstalk characteristics over the length of the cable.

- A sophisticated performance tester will include a TDR (time domain reflectometer). A TDR issues a signal on a cable and then measures the way the signal bounces back (or reflects) to the TDR. Performance testers for fiber-optic connections use OTDRs (optical time domain reflectometers). Rather than issue an electrical signal over the cable as twisted-pair cable testers do, an OTDR transmits light-based signals of different wavelengths over the fiber.

- An OPM (optical power meter), also called a fiber light meter, measures the amount of light power transmitted on a fiber-optic line. The device must be calibrated precisely, following highly accurate optical power standards set by the NIST. However, the surrounding room temperature, connection type, and skill of the technician conducting the test all affect the accuracy of the final test results.

Key Terms

For definitions of key terms, see the Glossary.

1000BASE-LX
1000BASE-SX
1000BASE-T
100BASE-FX
100BASE-SX
100BASE-T
100BASE-TX
10BASE-T
10GBASE-LR
10GBASE-SR
10GBASE-T
40GBASE-T
APC (angled physical contact)
attenuation
auto-MDI-X
back reflection
bandwidth
bidirectional WDM
BNC connector
cable crimper
cable performance tester
cable stripper
cable tester
Cat 5 (Category 5)
Cat 5e (Enhanced Category 5)
Cat 6 (Category 6)
Cat 6a (Augmented Category 6)
Cat 7 (Category 7)
Cat 7a (Augmented Category 7)
Cat 8 (Category 8)
CFP (centum form-factor pluggable)
cladding
coaxial cable
console cable
continuity
continuity tester
crossover cable
CWDM (coarse wavelength division multiplexing or coarse WDM)
dB (decibel) loss
duplex
DWDM (dense wavelength division multiplexing or dense WDM)

encoding
Ethernet standards
Fast Ethernet
F-connector
FDM (frequency division multiplexing)
FDP (fiber distribution panel)
ferrule
fiber light meter
frequency
full-duplex
fusion splicer
Gigabit Ethernet
hot-swappable
impedance
jitter
latency
LC (local connector)
LED (light-emitting diode)
loopback adapter
MDI (medium dependent interface)
MDI-X (MDI crossover)
media converter
MMF (multimode fiber)
modal bandwidth
modulation
MT-RJ (mechanical transfer-registered jack)
multimeter
multiplexing
open circuit
OPM (optical power meter)
optical link budget
optical loss
OTDR (optical time domain reflectometer)
patch cable
pinout
plenum-grade cable
PoE (Power over Ethernet)
PoE+

QSFP (quad small form-factor pluggable)
QSFP+
repeater
RG-6
riser-rated cable
RJ-11 (registered jack 11)
RJ-45 (registered jack 45)
rollover cable
RTT (round trip time)
SC (subscriber connector or standard connector)
SFP (small form-factor pluggable)
SFP+
short circuit
SMF (single mode fiber)
snips
speed and duplex mismatch
ST (straight tip)
STDM (statistical time division multiplexing)
straight-through cable
TDM (time division multiplexing)
TDR (time domain reflectometer)
throughput
TIA/EIA-568A
TIA/EIA-568B
tone generator (or toner)
tone locator (or probe)
transceiver
twinaxial cable
twist ratio
twisted-pair
TX/RX reverse
UPC (ultra-physical contact)
WDM (wavelength division multiplexing)
wire cutter
wire map test
XFP (10 Gigabit small form-factor pluggable)

Review Questions

1. Which transmission characteristic is never fully achieved?
   a. Latency
   b. Throughput
   c. Bit rate
   d. Bandwidth

2. Which kind of crosstalk occurs between wire pairs near the source of the signal?
   a. Alien
   b. TX/RX reverse
   c. FEXT
   d. NEXT

3. Which kind of multiplexing assigns slots to nodes according to priority and need?
   a. WDM (wavelength division multiplexing)
   b. STDM (statistical time division multiplexing)
   c. TDM (time division multiplexing)
   d. CWDM (coarse wavelength division multiplexing)

4. Which cable is best suited for ultra-high-speed connections between a router and a switch on the same rack?
   a. RG-6 coaxial cable
   b. Cat 5e twisted-pair cable
   c. Cat 6 twisted-pair cable
   d. Passive twinaxial cable

5. Which of these categories of twisted-pair cable can support Gigabit Ethernet?
   a. Cat 5, cat 6, cat 7
   b. Cat 5e, cat 6, cat 3
   c. Cat 5e, cat 6a, cat 7
   d. Cat 6, cat 7a, cat 5

6. Suppose you're creating patch cables to be used in a government office. What color wire goes in the first pin?
   a. White/orange
   b. White/green
   c. Brown
   d. Blue

7. What is the earliest twisted-pair cabling standard that meets the minimum requirements for 10GBASE-T transmissions at 100 meters?
   a. Cat 5e
   b. Cat 6
   c. Cat 6a
   d. Cat 7

8. What type of fiber-cable problem is caused when pairing a 50-micron core cable with a 62.5-micron core cable?
   a. Dirty connectors
   b. Wavelength mismatch
   c. Fiber type mismatch
   d. TX/RX reverse

9. Which part of a toner and probe kit emits an audible tone when it detects electrical activity on a wire pair?
   a. TDR
   b. Tone generator
   c. Tone locator
   d. Toner

10. Which fiber connector contains two strands of fiber in each ferrule?
    a. MT-RJ
    b. SC
    c. ST
    d. LC

11. How is latency measured, and in what unit?

12. What is a twist ratio, and why is it important?

13. What fiber is used in fiber-optic cabling to protect the inner core and prevent the cable from stretching?

14. What characteristic of optical transmission is primarily responsible for the distance limitations of fiber-optic cabling?

15. Why is SMF more efficient over long distances than MMF?

16. Why do APC ferrules create less back reflection than UPC ferrules?

17. Which fiber transceiver is the same size as SFP transceivers, but can support network speeds over 10 Gbps?

18. Suppose you're assisting with a cable installation using fiber-optic cabling that will support Gigabit Ethernet. You're approved to install segments up to 4000 m in length. What mode of fiber cable are you using?

19. What is the difference between short circuits and open circuits?

20. What kind of tool can measure the distance to the location of damage in a cable?

Hands-On Projects

NOTE 5-12

Websites and applications change often. While the instructions given in these projects were accurate at the time of writing, you might need to adjust the steps or options according to later changes.

Note to Instructors and Students: A rubric is provided for evaluating student performance on these projects. Please see Appendix D.

Project 5-1: Latency around the World

Estimated Time: 20 minutes (+5 minutes for group work, if assigned)
Objective: Given a scenario, use the appropriate network software tools and commands. (Obj. 5.3)
Group Work: This project includes enhancements when assigned as a group project.
Resources:

- Internet access

Context: In Module 4, you learned that IP tracks the number of times a message jumps or hops from one router to another on its way to its destination. Each of these hops requires a tiny bit of time—the more routers a message must traverse, the longer it will take to reach its destination. In this module, you learned that latency is the delay caused by the time it takes messages to travel over network media from one place to another. This concept is easy to see in the real world, where it takes longer, for example, for you to travel across the country than it does to go down the street to the grocery store. Even though network messages travel much faster than a car or a jet plane, it still takes time for them to get from one place to another. And then the response must also travel across a similar number of hops, resulting in a longer RTT (round trip time). To see how distance affects a message's RTT, complete the following steps:

1. **For group assignments:** Open a PowerShell or Command Prompt window and run `tracert` on the IP address of one of your group members. If your group member is on the same LAN as you are, use their private IP address. If your group member is on a different network than you are, run `tracert` on their network's public IP address. You and they both can discover your respective network's public IP address using an IP address lookup tool online. Go to **google.com** and search for **What is my IP address**. The search results will list your network's public IP address at the top. Now that you know your public IP address, share that information with your group member and get their public IP address as well. How many hops did it take for your `tracert` messages to reach your group member's computer or network?

NOTE 5-13

For an Ubuntu or other Linux installation, use `traceroute` rather than `tracert` for this project. You might need to first install the traceroute utility. On Ubuntu, run this command:

```
sudo apt-get install traceroute
```

2. In a PowerShell or Command Prompt window, run `tracert` on a website whose servers are located on a different continent from your location—across one ocean. For example, if you're located in the Midwest or Eastern United States, you can run the command **tracert london.edu** (London Business School). If you are on the West Coast, however, you might get more useful results for this step by targeting a server across the Pacific Ocean, such as **tracert www.tiu.ac.jp** (Tokyo International University). What command did you use?
3. Examine the output and find the point in the route when messages started jumping across the ocean. By what percentage does the RTT increase after the jump compared with before it? You can see an example in Figure 5-53.

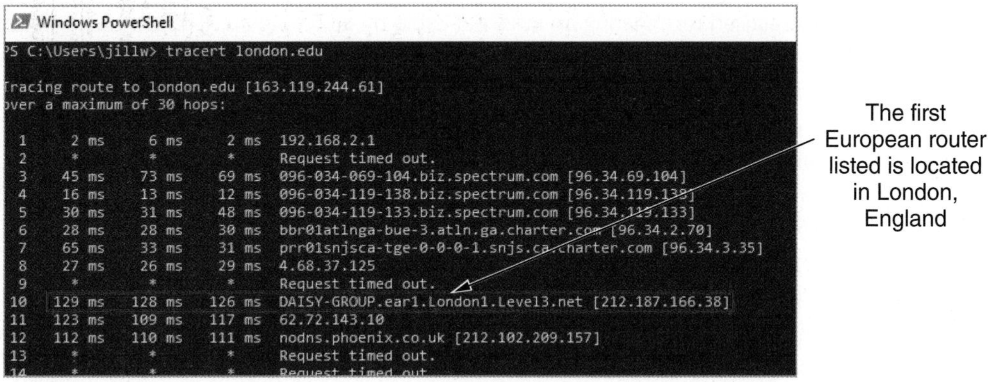

```
Windows PowerShell
PS C:\Users\jillw> tracert london.edu

Tracing route to london.edu [163.119.244.61]
over a maximum of 30 hops:

  1     2 ms     6 ms     2 ms  192.168.2.1
  2      *        *        *    Request timed out.
  3    45 ms    73 ms    69 ms  096-034-069-104.biz.spectrum.com [96.34.69.104]
  4    16 ms    13 ms    12 ms  096-034-119-138.biz.spectrum.com [96.34.119.138]
  5    30 ms    31 ms    48 ms  096-034-119-133.biz.spectrum.com [96.34.119.133]
  6    28 ms    28 ms    30 ms  bbr01atlnga-bue-3.atln.ga.charter.com [96.34.2.70]
  7    65 ms    33 ms    31 ms  prr01snjsca-tge-0-0-0-1.snjs.ca.charter.com [96.34.3.35]
  8    27 ms    26 ms    29 ms  4.68.37.125
  9      *        *        *    Request timed out.
 10   129 ms   128 ms   126 ms  DAISY-GROUP.ear1.London1.Level3.net [212.187.166.38]
 11   123 ms   109 ms   117 ms  62.72.143.10
 12   112 ms   110 ms   111 ms  nodns.phoenix.co.uk [212.102.209.157]
 13      *        *        *    Request timed out.
 14      *        *        *    Request timed out.
```

The first European router listed is located in London, England

Figure 5-53 The latency time increases significantly as messages start to cross the ocean

To calculate the percentage for this jump, select a time from just after the jump (129, for example) and divide it by a time from just before the jump (such as 27), then multiply by 100 percent: 129/27 × 100% = 478%. In this case, the sample data yields a 478 percent increase. It takes nearly five times as long for a message to go round-trip across the Atlantic from the United States to London, England (the location of this first European router), as it does for a message to travel round trip between two servers that are both located on the U.S. East Coast (this local computer and the last U.S. router in the route).

4. Choose a website whose servers are on a continent even farther away from you. For example, if you are in the United States, you could trace the route to the University of Delhi in India at the address du.ac.in. What command did you use? How many hops did it take until the route crossed an ocean? What other anomalies do you notice about this global route?

5. Choose one more website as close to directly across the globe from you as possible. U.S. locations might want to use the University of Western Australia at uwa.edu.au. What command did you use? How many hops are in the route? Did the route go east or west around the world from your location? How can you tell?

6. Scott Base in Antarctica runs several webcams from various research locations. Run a trace to the Scott Base website at **antarcticanz.govt.nz**. What's the closest router to Scott Base's web server that your trace reached? If you can't tell from the command output where the last response came from, go to **iplocation.net** in your browser. Enter the final hop's IP address to determine that router's location.

7. Think about other locations around the world that might be reached through an interesting geographical route, such as traversing a place you would like to visit or tapping routers in an exotic location. Find a website hosted in that location and trace the route to it. Which website did you target? Where is it located? What are some router locations along the route of your trace? **Take a screenshot** of the output for your trace; submit this visual with your answers to this project's questions.

8. Try the `ping` command on several of these same IP addresses. Did it work? Why do you think this is the case?

Project 5-2: Create a Loopback Plug

Estimated Time: 30 minutes
Objective: Given a scenario, troubleshoot common cable connectivity issues and select the appropriate tools. (Obj. 5.2)
Resources:
- 6-inch length of UTP cabling (Cat 5 or Cat 5e)
- Unused RJ-45 plug
- Wire cutters, snips, or heavy-duty scissors
- Cable crimper

Note: This hardware can be purchased in bulk and distributed to students. Alternatively, students can purchase their own supplies at stores such as Lowe's, Home Depot, Amazon.com, or Newegg.com.

Context: In this module, you practiced terminating an Ethernet cable by attaching an RJ-45 connector. You also learned that a loopback plug crosses the transmit line with the receive line to trick a device into thinking it's connected to a network. You can create your own loopback plug by altering the pinout on the connector and forcing the transmissions to loop back in on themselves. A loopback plug is helpful for determining if a NIC on a workstation or a port on a switch is working or not. Complete the following steps:

1. Cut to loosen the cable's covering, then slide the covering off the cable to separate the wire pairs into four groups. Flatten the wire pairs but do not untwist them. Select one wire pair (one solid and one striped) and lay the other pairs aside because you won't need them. Which wire pair did you choose?
2. Untwist the wires on each end an inch or less and straighten the tips. If needed, give each wire a clean cut to make sure the two wires on each end are even with each other.
3. Insert one end of the twisted pair into the RJ-45 plug, making sure the solid color wire goes into slot 1, and the striped wire goes into slot 2. Push the wires all the way into the slots. Make sure the wire tips touch the plastic surface at the front end inside the plug.
4. Loop the wire pair around and insert the other end into the plug. The solid color wire goes into slot 3, and the striped wire goes into slot 6. (Slots 4, 5, 7, and 8 are not needed unless you'll be testing Gigabit Ethernet equipment.)

NOTE 5-14

If you want to include the other two pins in the adapter so you can test VoIP and similar Gigabit Ethernet equipment, you'll need to use a second twisted pair from your original cable. Before crimping, insert one end of the second pair into the plug. Press the solid color wire into slot 4 and the striped wire into slot 5. Loop the wire around and press the solid color wire into slot 7 and the striped wire into slot 8.

5. Push the wires all the way in and then use the crimper to secure the wires in the plug. If a boot came with the plug, you can insert it over the wire loop and push it all the way through to cover the wire/plug connection, as shown in Figure 5-54. **Take a photo of your loopback plug**; submit this visual with your answers to this project's questions.

Push boot over connector after crimping wires

Figure 5-54 Adding the boot to the loopback plug is optional

6. Insert the loopback plug into a device's Ethernet port that is known to be working correctly and has LED indicator lights. If the port's link indicator lights up (this might take a minute), you've successfully created a loopback plug.
7. Working with the actual hardware can be an enlightening experience as you work to get each wire lined up with the correct pin or realize how much force is required to crimp a cable inside the connector. What was the most difficult part of this project for you? What was the most satisfying part of the project?

Project 5-3: Create a Loopback Jack

Estimated Time: 20 minutes
Objective: Given a scenario, troubleshoot common cable connectivity issues and select the appropriate tools. (Obj. 5.2)
Resources:

- 2-inch length of UTP cabling (Cat 5 or Cat 5e)
- Unused RJ-45 data/phone jack
- Punchdown tool

Note: This hardware can be purchased in bulk and distributed to students. Alternatively, students can purchase their own supplies at home improvement stores such as Lowe's, Home Depot, Amazon.com, or Newegg.com.

Context: A loopback plug can be used to test a port on a switch or a workstation's NIC. A loopback jack, however, can be used to test a cable or to identify which port a cable is connected to. This is especially helpful when the cable is already run through the wall or is tangled up with other cables. Creating a loopback plug is pretty straightforward, and wiring a loopback jack is even easier. Complete the following steps:

1. Cut to loosen the cable's covering, then slide the covering off the cable to separate the wire pairs into four groups. Flatten the wire pairs but do not untwist them. Select one wire pair (one solid and one striped) and lay the other pairs aside because you won't need them. Which wire pair did you choose?
2. Turn the jack so the slots are easily accessible. Take a single wire and press one end into the slot next to the "A–green/white" icon. Press the other end into the slot with the "A–orange/white" icon.

NOTE 5-15

There is some variation in how RJ-45 jacks are designed. If these generic directions don't match the jack you're using, check the documentation that came with the jack.

3. Take the other, single wire, press one end into the slot next to the "A–orange" icon, and press the other end into the slot next to the "A–green" icon. In some cases, depending on the actual jack you use, the two wires will create an "X" shape through the center of the jack between the slots, as shown in Figure 5-55. With other jacks, the wires might cross over each other on one side only. **Take a photo of the pinout for your loopback jack**; submit this visual with your answers to this project's questions.
4. Use the punchdown tool to punch the wires all the way into their respective slots. The punchdown tool will also clip the excess length off the wires. Make sure to orient the punchdown tool so the cutting side will slice the outside length of the wire and not the inside length. If a cover came with the jack, place it over the wires.
5. To test your loopback jack, plug a patch cable you know to be good into a device's Ethernet port that you know works, then plug the jack onto the other end of the cable. Wait up to a minute to give the link sufficient time to be established. If the port's link indicator lights up, you've successfully created a loopback jack.

Figure 5-55   With this jack, the wires cross in the middle

For storage, you can plug your loopback plug into your loopback jack (see Figure 5-56), giving you a handy two-in-one tool for your toolkit.

Project 5-4: Test a LAN's Speed and Throughput

Estimated Time: 45 minutes (+5 minutes for group work, if assigned)
Objective: Given a scenario, use the appropriate statistics and sensors to ensure network availability. (Obj. 3.1)
Resources:

- Windows 10 or macOS computer with administrative access
- Internet access
- A second Windows 10 or macOS computer on the LAN with administrative access and with a shared folder

Figure 5-56   Attach the plug and jack together to protect their connections when storing them

Note: At least one of these two computers should have a wired connection to the network. Optionally, to test a fully wired network connection between two computers, make sure both computers have a wired connection to the network rather than a Wi-Fi connection on one of them.

Note: For the second part of this project, the second device could instead be an Android or iOS mobile device. For students who are working from home and don't have a second computer, they can complete Steps 8-13.

Context: A variety of software and web-based tools are available to help you establish baseline measurements—and later, detect fluctuations and problems—in the efficiency of your network and Internet connections. This project walks you through two different tests you can perform on your school's lab network or at home on your own LAN. Complete the following steps:

1. TotuSoft's LAN Speed Test is a simple, free program that only needs access to a shared folder on the local area network to test throughput speeds on the network. The Public Users folder on another workstation meets this requirement. Check to make sure you have access to a shared folder on another computer on your network. For example, on a Windows 10 computer, open File Explorer and click **Network** in the navigation pane. If you have access to a shared folder, the computer should appear in the list of networked devices. You should be able to navigate into that computer's folders to locate the shared folder. If you don't already have a shared folder on another computer, do some research online for that computer's OS to determine how to share a folder with everyone on the local network.

2. **For group assignments:** Create a folder on your computer for a group member to test against. Share that folder with your group member. Check to make sure you have access to their shared folder.

3. Go to **totusoft.com**. Download and install the latest version of **LAN Speed Test**.

4. Launch LAN Speed Test. Close the screen asking you to register—registration is not required to use the free version. The app will automatically detect your own computer's IP address. Note that if your computer also has a hypervisor installed, you might need to change the MAC field to the physical NIC's MAC address in order to see the computer's IPv4 address on the physical network.

5. Before running the test, answer the following questions:
   a. What network media connects your computer to your network?
   b. If this is a wired connection, what is the cable's category rating? Based on this information, what is the maximum throughput the cable supports?
   c. What network media connects the target computer to your network?
   d. If this is a wired connection, what is the cable's category? Based on this information, what is the maximum throughput the cable supports?

6. Next to the Folder field, click the **Choose Folder/Server to test** to button (which contains three dots), and locate the shared folder on another workstation or server on your network, as shown in Figure 5-57. Select the folder as the target and click **Start Test**.

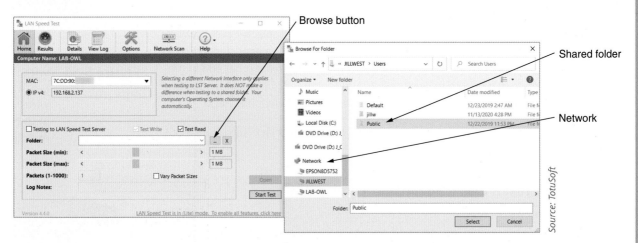

Figure 5-57   Browse to a shared folder on another computer on your network

7. When the test has finished running, answer the following questions:
   a. How do your test results for upload and download speeds compare with the maximum supported throughput for your cables?
   b. If your test results differ from the standards you were expecting, how do you explain these results?

TamoSoft, another security and network monitoring software company, offers a free Throughput Test that works on both wired and wireless LAN connections on computers (Windows and macOS) or mobile devices (Android and iOS). Complete the following steps:

1. Go to **tamos.com** and find the free Throughput Test on the Download page. Download and install it on two devices (computer or mobile device) on the same LAN, accepting default settings in the setup wizard.
2. One device will act as the client and one as the server.
   a. On the server device, click **Start** and, in the Start menu, click **Run Server**. If necessary, click **Yes** in the UAC dialog box.
   b. On the client device, click **Start** and, in the Start menu, click **Run Client**. If necessary, click **Yes** in the UAC dialog box.

NOTE 5-16

If Run Server and Run Client are not visible at the top of the Start menu on a Windows 10 computer, scroll down and click to expand TamoSoft Throughput Test. Then click Run Server or Run Client, respectively.

3. On the device acting as the server, note its IP address, which is reported automatically in the TamoSoft Throughput Test window. Note that if you're running the server software on a computer with Hyper-V activated, you might see two IP addresses: one for the physical network and one for the virtual network. You need the IP address for the physical network for this project. Nothing more is needed on this end of the connection because the server only needs to listen for the client.
4. On the device acting as the client, enter the server's IP address, then click **Connect**. Figure 5-58 shows the server and client consoles side by side. **Take a screenshot** of your client console while the test is running; submit this visual with your answers to this project's questions.

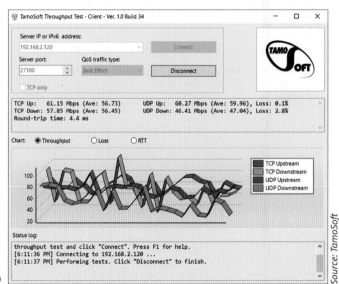

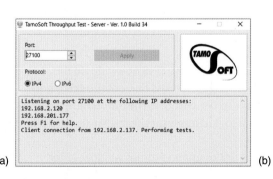

(a)   (b)

Figure 5-58   Server (a) and client (b) consoles for Throughput Test, with results showing on the client side

5. In the Chart pane, TCP and UDP throughput are monitored. Upstream refers to traffic moving from the client device to the server device. Downstream refers to traffic moving from the server device to the client device. Other charts include Loss and RTT. Let the test run for a couple of minutes, then click **Disconnect**. Examine the results and answer the following questions.
   a. On the Throughput chart, what was the highest reading obtained, and what kind of traffic was it?
   b. On the Loss chart, were there any significant loss results, and what kind of traffic was involved? What theories do you have about why this might be? Where would you look next to resolve this problem?
   c. On the RTT (round trip time) chart, were there any spikes? Do you notice any correlation between the timing of the spikes on this chart and the timing of problem indicators on the other two charts?
6. Document both these application installations in your wikidot website.

Capstone Projects

NOTE 5-17

Websites and applications change often. While the instructions given in these projects were accurate at the time of writing, you might need to adjust the steps or options according to later changes.

Note to Instructors and Students: A rubric is provided for evaluating student performance on these projects. Please see Appendix D.

Capstone Project 5-1: Decode a TCP Segment in a Wireshark Capture

Estimated Time: 45 minutes
Objective: Given a scenario, use the appropriate network software tools and commands. (Obj. 5.3)
Resources:

- Windows 10 computer with administrative access and Wireshark installed
- Internet access

Context: In Module 2, you installed Wireshark and examined several messages in your capture. In Module 4, you dissected sample headers captured by Wireshark to interpret the fields included in each header. In this project, you'll pull these concepts together and use Wireshark to capture your own DNS messages, examine TCP headers in a TCP stream, and practice interpreting the information that you find. Complete the following steps:

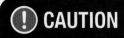 **CAUTION** Scanning a network you don't own or don't have permission to scan is illegal. Do not use Wireshark on public Wi-Fi networks at all. Also don't use Wireshark on any network you don't own unless you have written permission from the owner to do so.

1. Open Wireshark and snap the window to one side of your screen. Open a browser and snap that window to the other side of your screen so you can see both windows.

NOTE 5-18

In Windows, you can quickly snap the active window to one side of your screen by pressing the Win key with the left or right arrow key. Alternatively, you can drag a window to one edge of your screen until it snaps into position.

2. Before starting your capture, clear your browser's DNS cache so you can capture a DNS query. To do this, you need to access the net-internals page for the browser. For example, in Edge's address bar, enter **edge://net-internals/#dns** and then click **Clear host cache**. Similarly, in Chrome, enter **chrome://net-internals/#dns** and click **Clear host cache**. For other browsers, do some research online to find more specific instructions to clear the browser's DNS cache.

3. You'll also need to clear your computer's DNS cache. In a PowerShell or Command Prompt window, enter `ipconfig/flushdns`.

4. Start the Wireshark capture on your active network connection. In the browser, navigate to either **nasa.gov/nasalive** or **explore.org/livecams—if** you've visited one of these sites recently, choose the other one. Once the page loads, stop the Wireshark capture. You'll have fewer messages to sort through if you can do this entire process fairly quickly.

Somewhere in your capture, a DNS message will show the original request to resolve the name **nasa.gov** or **explore.org** to its IP address. A series of TCP messages after that will show the three-way handshake, along with the rest of the data transmission. Because your transmission has to do with DNS and then requesting a secure web page using HTTPS, you need to filter first to DNS and then to TCP port 443. Complete the following steps:

5. Apply the following filter to your capture to expose the messages involved with your DNS request: **dns**

6. The correct DNS messages show DNS in the Protocol field and something to the effect of "Standard query" and "**www.nasa.gov**" or "**explore.org**" in the Info field, as shown in Figure 5-59. Notice that in this capture, the local computer made a DNS query to its primary (1.1.1.1) DNS server to resolve the domain name.

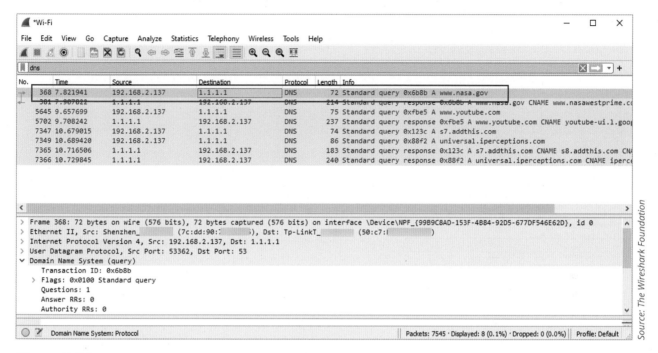

Figure 5-59   This DNS message is a request to resolve the domain name *www.nasa.gov*

Source: The Wireshark Foundation

7. Once you've located the message querying the DNS server, click on it and examine the details of the message in the second pane. Answer the following questions:
   a. What is the OUI of the source's NIC?
   b. Which IP version was used?
   c. If the message used IPv4, what was the TTL? If IPv6, what was the hop limit?
   d. Did the message use TCP or UDP?
   e. What is the source port? The destination port?
   f. What DNS record type is requested?
8. With the DNS message selected, update your filter to **dns or tcp.port eq 443**.
9. Check your filter results for the first [SYN] message after the selected DNS request. Open the TCP segment header in the second pane. Make sure the Sequence Number (relative sequence number) is 0, as shown in Figure 5-60. If it's not, try the next SYN message. When you find the first SYN message after the DNS message and with a Sequence Number (relative sequence number) of 0, check the TCP flags. Which flags are set in the TCP segment?

   Wireshark shows relative sequence numbers and also the raw numbers used in the segments themselves. Relative numbers are easier for humans to keep up with, but they provide no security in that they're very predictable. Random numbers, on the other hand, are more difficult to fake.

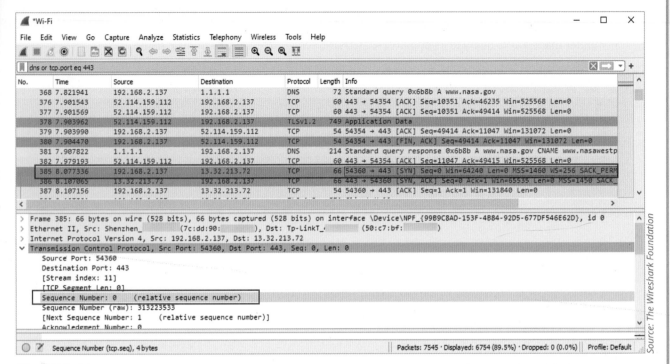

Figure 5-60 A relative sequence number of 0 indicates the beginning of the three-way handshake

10. Apply another filter layer to show only the messages for this TCP conversation. To do this, right-click the **[SYN]** message you selected earlier, point to **Follow**, and click **TCP Stream**. Close the Follow TCP Stream dialog box that opens, as you will be examining data in the actual capture.

11. Immediately after that initial [SYN] message, locate the [SYN, ACK] message and answer the following questions:
    a. What is the source IP address? The destination IP address?
    b. In the TCP header, what is the relative sequence number? The relative acknowledgment number?
    c. Which TCP Flags are set?

12. Locate the third message in this three-way handshake, the [ACK] message, and answer the following questions:
    a. What is the source IP address? The destination IP address?
    b. In the TCP header, what is the relative sequence number? The relative acknowledgment number?
    c. Which flags are set in the TCP segment?

13. The three-way handshake establishes the session, but the conversation continues as the web server begins to respond to your browser's request for the web page. First, the web server redirects the conversation to a secure website using HTTP over SSL/TLS. Look for a series of messages listing TLS in the Protocol field. Locate the Client Hello and Server Hello messages, as shown in Figure 5-61. A few lines below that, locate the Certificate and Server Key Exchange message where the server completes its Hello process or the Change Cipher Spec message where a new set of encryption keys is requested. **Take a screenshot** of your capture showing these messages; submit this visual with your answers to this project's questions.

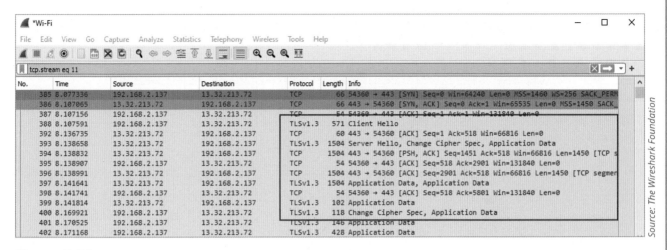

Source: The Wireshark Foundation

Figure 5-61   The web server establishes a secure link with the web client

14. Soon after this key exchange, you'll see several messages using the TLS protocol that are labeled Application Data. Look at the Length field for these messages. What is the size of the longest message listed?

15. Click on one of the longest messages and answer the following questions:
   a. List the types of headers included in this message, in order.
   b. What is the source IP address? The destination IP address?
   c. In the TCP header, which flags are set in the TCP segment?

Capstone Project 5-2: Build a Packet Tracer Network

Estimated Time: 1 hour
Objective: Compare and contrast the Open Systems Interconnection (OSI) model layers and encapsulation concepts. (Obj. 1.1)
Resources:
- Computer with Cisco Packet Tracer installed
- Storage space for Packet Tracer network file to be accessed in later modules

Context: In Capstone Project 2-2 in Module 2, you installed Packet Tracer and completed several modules in the Introduction to Packet Tracer course. In Module 3, you worked with MAC address tables in Packet Tracer. And in Module 4, you set up a TFTP server in Packet Tracer. Look back at your notes on your Wikidot website if you need help remembering details about what you learned in these earlier projects. In this project, you will begin to build a more extensive network, and you'll continue building on this network in future modules. Make sure you're working on a computer where you'll be able to save your Packet Tracer network file for later use, either by working on the same computer every time or by saving your file in the cloud where you can get to it later. The Packet Tracer network you begin building in this project is the starting point for many additions to this network in later modules. To begin building your more extensive Packet Tracer network, complete the following steps:

1. Open **Packet Tracer** and, if necessary, sign in with your Networking Academy account.
2. Add one **PT-Router** to the workspace.
3. Add two **2960 switches** to the workspace.
4. Add two **PCs** to the workspace.
5. Arrange these devices in a pyramid shape, with the workstations at the bottom, the switches in the middle, and the router at the top. See Figure 5-62 to get an idea of the correct layout. Use the **Copper Straight-Through** connection to connect each of these devices as described next:

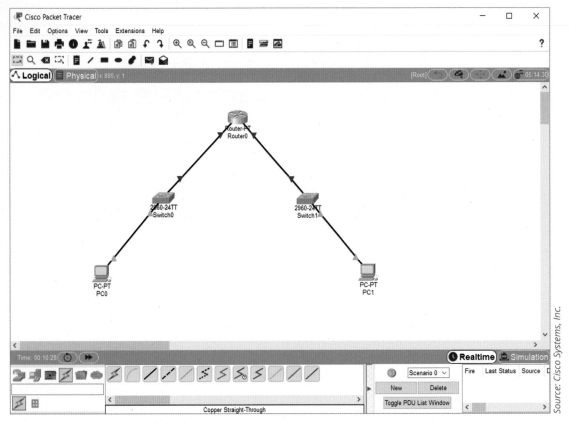

Figure 5-62   Arrange the devices in a pyramid shape

    a. On each workstation, connect the Ethernet cable to the **FastEthernet0** interface.

    b. On each switch, connect the Ethernet cable from the workstation to the **FastEthernet0/1** interface. Connect the Ethernet cable to the router to the **FastEthernet0/2** interface.

    c. On the router, connect Switch0 to the **FastEthernet0/0** interface, and connect Switch1 to the **FastEthernet1/0** interface.

    d. Wait a few minutes for the workstation-to-switch connections to turn to green triangles on both ends of each connection.

The router and the switch must be configured for the connections to come up:

  6. Click **Router0** to open its configuration window. Click the **Config** tab. As you make changes, notice the commands that show up in the Equivalent IOS Commands pane at the bottom of the window.

  7. Click the **FastEthernet0/0** interface. Make the following changes to the interface's configuration:

    IP Address: **192.168.0.1**

    Subnet Mask: **255.255.255.0**

    Port Status: **On**

  8. Click the **FastEthernet1/0** interface. Make the following changes to the interface's configuration:

    IP Address: **172.16.0.1**

    Subnet Mask: **255.255.0.0**

    Port Status: **On**

  9. Close the **Router0** window and wait a few minutes for the switch-to-router connections to turn to green triangles on both ends of each connection.

  10. Click **PC0** to open its configuration window. Click the **Desktop** tab and then click **IP Configuration**. Make the following changes to the workstation's configuration:

    IP Configuration: **Static**

    IP Address: 192.168.0.100

    Subnet Mask: 255.255.255.0

    Default Gateway: 192.168.0.1

11. Close the IP Configuration window by clicking the small, blue **X** near the upper right corner. Then click **Command Prompt**. Enter `ipconfig` to confirm the network configuration is correct.

12. Close **Command Prompt** and close the **PC0** configuration window.

13. Click **PC1** to open its configuration window. Click the **Desktop** tab and then click **IP Configuration**. Make the following changes to the workstation's configuration:

    IP Configuration: **Static**

    IP Address: **172.16.0.100**

    Subnet Mask: **255.255.0.0**

    Default Gateway: **172.16.0.1**

14. Close the IP Configuration window by clicking the small, blue **X** near the upper right corner. Then click **Command Prompt**. Enter `ipconfig` to confirm the network configuration is correct.

15. Enter the command `ping 192.168.0.100`. Was the ping successful? If so, then you have successfully begun building your Packet Tracer network. If not, troubleshoot your network to determine where the problem is and fix it. What problems did you have to fix, if any?

16. In the main Packet Tracer window, open the **Simulation Panel** (click the **Simulation** button in the lower right corner, or press **Shift+S**). In the PC1 configuration window, run the ping again. Move or minimize the PC1 configuration window so you can see the devices in the workspace. In the Simulation Panel, click the **Play** button and watch what happens.

17. When you're ready, click any ICMP message on the network to examine its details and to see an explanation of each step in the process. Click through the various layers and read their explanations. Click the Inbound PDU Details and Outbound PDU Details tabs to examine the headers of each ICMP message. Explore at least three different ICMP messages and answer the following questions for each of the three messages:
    a. Which two devices are exchanging each message (sender and receiver)?
    b. Which OSI layers added headers to each message?

18. When you've explored the ICMP messages, in the Simulation Panel, click the **Reset Simulation** button to stop the simulation. Close the **Simulation Panel**, close **Command Prompt**, and close the **PC1** window.

19. Add a **Note** to each connection that lists its IP address, subnet mask, and default gateway if relevant. Figure 5-63 shows an example for the router, which has two interfaces with IP addresses. After adding all your documentation, **take a screenshot of your Packet Tracer network**; submit this visual with your answers to this project's questions.

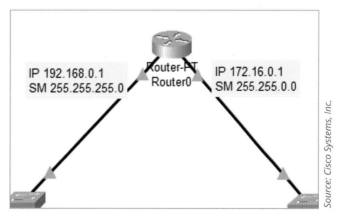

Figure 5-63   Good documentation makes troubleshooting easier

20. Click **File** and **Save**. Give the file an informative name (such as NetPlusPTnetwork), and save your Packet Tracer file in a safe place for future projects. What is the name of your Packet Tracer file?

21. Add the Packet Tracer network file's name and location to the Packet Tracer page on your Wikidot website, along with any notes you think might be helpful to you for the next Packet Tracer project. When you're finished, close Packet Tracer.

Note to Instructors: A Packet Tracer solution file is provided for each Packet Tracer project through the Instructors site. Some Packet Tracer projects build on earlier Packet Tracer networks. If needed for one or more students, you can provide a previous project's solution file as a start file for one of these progression projects.

Solutions to Self-Check Questions

Transmission Basics

1. When you measure the amount of data coming into your home network, what metric are you identifying?

Answer: d. Throughput

Explanation: **Throughput** refers to the number of data bits (0s and 1s) that are actually received across a connection each second. Bandwidth refers to the amount of data you could theoretically transmit during a given period of time. Noise, or interference, degrades or distorts a signal on a network. Duplex indicates if and when a signal can travel in both directions on a medium.

2. Which of the following improves overall network performance?

Answer: b. Multiplexing

Explanation: Networks rely on **multiplexing** to increase the amount of data that can be transmitted in a given timespan over a given bandwidth. Latency is the delay between when data leaves the source and when it arrives at its destination. If packets experience varying amounts of delay, they can arrive out of order—a problem commonly called jitter. Attenuation is the loss of a signal's strength as it travels away from its source.

Copper Cable

3. What is the minimum twisted-pair category required for 10-Gigabit Ethernet at 100 meters?

Answer: b. Cat 6a

Explanation: **Cat (Category) 6a** can support throughput of 1 Gbps or, at shorter distances, 10 Gbps. Cat 5e maxes out at 1 Gbps. Cat 7 and Cat 8 both support throughput of 10 Gbps or higher at the full 100 meters segment length.

4. Pin 1 on one end of a cable is orange and white striped. What color should Pin 1 be on the other end of the cable to create a crossover cable?

Answer: d. Green and white striped

Explanation: A crossover cable reverses the transmit and receive wires. If Pin 1 on one end of a cable is orange and white striped, then the other end of the crossover cable would need to cross the orange and white striped wire to Pin 3. Pin 1, then, would need to receive the **green and white striped wire** from Pin 3 on the first end. If the orange and white striped wire continues to Pin 1 on the second end, the cable is more likely a straight-through cable. The solid blue wire typically stays in the middle at Pin 4 or possibly crosses over to Pin 7. The solid brown wire typically stays on the other end of the connector at Pin 8 or possibly crosses over to Pin 5.

5. What is the typical maximum segment length for Ethernet networks?

Answer: b. 100 meters

Explanation: The maximum segment length for both STP and UTP is **100 meters**, or 328 feet, on Ethernet networks that support data rates from 1 Mbps to 10 Gbps. Some categories of STP require shorter segment lengths to achieve maximum throughput, which can vary from 10 Mbps to 100 Gbps.

Fiber-Optic Cable

6. Which of the following statements is *not* true?

Answer: b. SMF supports lower bandwidths than MMF.

Explanation: Because it reflects little, the light in an SMF (single mode fiber) cable does not disperse as the signal travels along the fiber. This continuity allows SMF to accommodate the highest bandwidths and longest distances (without requiring repeaters) of all network transmission media. Therefore, **it's not true that SMF supports lower bandwidths than MMF (multimode fiber)**. SMF's core is 8 to 10 microns in diameter, which is thinner than MMF's core at 50 to 62.5 microns. MMF is less expensive to install and, therefore, typically used to connect routers, switches, and servers on the backbone of a network; because of its relatively high cost, SMF is rarely used for short connections. Many pulses of light generated by a laser or LED light source travel at various angles through MMF's larger core, bouncing off the interior surfaces of the core and, therefore, suffer from greater attenuation than SMF signals. Inside the SMF core, laser-generated light travels a single path over the core, reflecting very little. Because it reflects little, the light does not disperse as the signal travels along the fiber.

7. Which fiber connector does *not* support full-duplex transmissions?

Answer: d. ST

Explanation: The older **ST (straight tip)** fiber connector does not support full-duplex transmission. The MT-RJ (mechanical transfer-registered jack) connector is unique in that it contains two strands of fiber in a single ferrule. With two strands per ferrule, a single MT-RJ connector provides full-duplex signaling. SC (subscriber connector) and LC (local connector) fiber connectors are also available in full-duplex mode.

8. What is the earliest transceiver type to support four channels on a single transceiver to increase throughput?

Answer: a. QSFP

Explanation: **QSFP (quad small form-factor pluggable)** transceivers squeeze four channels in a single transceiver to support data rates up to 40 Gbps (4 x 10 Gbps). QSFP+ improved on the same technology to support even higher data rates. Older transceivers, such as SFP (small form-factor pluggable) and SFP+ did not support multiple channels per transceiver.

Cable Troubleshooting Tools

9. Which tool could you use to determine if a laptop's power cable is working properly?

Answer: d. Multimeter

Explanation: You might use a **multimeter** to measure voltage to verify that a cable is properly conducting electricity, whether that cable is a data cable on a network or a power cable. A continuity tester determines whether a cable is carrying a data signal to its destination. A toner and probe kit can help determine where a wire, possibly out of hundreds, terminates.

10. Which tool could you use to test a twisted-pair cable's pinout?

Answer: d. Continuity tester

Explanation: Some **continuity testers** will verify that the wires in a UTP or STP cable are paired correctly following TIA/EIA 568 standards. OTDRs and OPMs are used to test fiber-optic cables. A toner probe can help determine where a wire, possibly out of hundreds, terminates.

WIRELESS NETWORKING

After reading this module and completing the exercises, you should be able to:

1. Describe characteristics of wireless transmissions
2. Explain 802.11 standards and innovations
3. Plan a Wi-Fi network
4. Secure a Wi-Fi network
5. Troubleshoot a Wi-Fi network

On the Job

I've installed wireless network equipment for the past 15 years. Our company builds and repairs computers and installs wireless networks and surveillance systems in office buildings, warehouses, and homes. We work with both directional wireless and open-space, broadcast wireless.

When installing a wireless AP, we're always careful to take note of any device specifications, such as the AP's range, and we must consider what obstacles are in the device's line of sight. We evaluate any walls, ceilings, and other obstacles that come in between the source of the wireless signal and the various locations of receiving devices, such as printers, computers, and cell phones.

One installation comes to mind that really baffled us. It was an older home here in Dalton, Georgia, and was built around the early 1900s.

The house wasn't huge, and we installed an AP in the kitchen area. We initially tested the signal in the kitchen and, as expected, received four bars of signal strength. Next, we walked into the living room, which was just on the other side of the wall from the kitchen. In the living room, however, we barely received one bar.

We put in a higher wattage output AP and upon repeating the test, we still just received 1 bar in the living room. As part of our investigation, we went into the attic and discovered that this wall between the kitchen and the living room was built of plaster instead of sheetrock. Further investigation revealed that underneath the plaster was a layer of chicken wire. A little research revealed that in the old days, some walls incorporated chicken wire in the internal structure to hold the plaster against the wall. This wall was like a fortress, blocking our wireless signal.

We installed a second AP in another room to solve the problem. The moral to this story is, when installing wireless, beware of what an impact a single wall can have, especially in older homes.

Scott Merritt, Service Mgr.
Dalton Computer Services, Inc.

For decades, radio and TV stations have transmitted analog signals through the air. Air provides an intangible means of transporting data over networks and is often used in conjunction with wired technologies.

This module first looks at how wireless transmissions work, regardless of the type of wireless technology used. These wireless characteristics apply to satellite, Bluetooth, Wi-Fi, cellular, and other wireless signals. Some of these wireless signals, such as satellite and cellular, can travel long distances and will be discussed in more detail later in this course. This module explores how to set up, manage, secure, and troubleshoot local wireless networks that you might find in an enterprise setting or that you might set up in your own home.

CHARACTERISTICS OF WIRELESS TRANSMISSIONS

✓ CERTIFICATION

1.2 Explain the characteristics of network topologies and network types.

2.1 Compare and contrast various devices, their features, and their appropriate placement on the network.

2.4 Given a scenario, install and configure the appropriate wireless standards and technologies.

5.4 Given a scenario, troubleshoot common wireless connectivity issues.

Average reading time: 30 minutes

In previous modules, you learned about signals that travel over a physical medium, such as a copper or fiber-optic cable. LANs that transmit signals through the air via RF (radio frequency) waves are known as WLANs (wireless local area networks). Wireless transmission media is now common in business and home networks and necessary in some specialized network environments such as IoT (Internet of Things). Wired and wireless signals share many similarities, including use of the same layer 3 and higher protocols, for example. However, the nature of the atmosphere makes wireless transmission vastly different from wired transmission at lower OSI layers. You'll start by looking at what wireless signals are, and then you'll study how they're transmitted.

The Wireless Spectrum

All wireless signals are carried through the air by electromagnetic waves. The **wireless spectrum**, commonly called the airwaves, is the frequency range of electromagnetic waves used for data and voice communication. As defined by the FCC (Federal Communications Commission), which controls its use, the wireless spectrum spans frequency ranges or **bands** between 9 kHz and 300 GHz. (Recall that a Hz or hertz is one cycle per second.) Table 6-1 lists from low to high the frequency ranges commonly used for wireless network connections and data transfer. Many of these technologies are covered in this module or later in this course. Others are briefly described next. Notice in the table that several of the bands cover a frequency range that is further subdivided into channels. Some bands have only a single frequency, called a fixed frequency, for that band.

Table 6-1 Frequency ranges of wireless technologies listed from low to high frequencies

Technologies	Frequency range (band) in kHz, MHz, or GHz	Description
RFID	125 kHz–134.2 kHz	The lowest of several frequency ranges for RFID and approved for global use
NFC	13.56 MHz	Fixed frequency
Z-Wave	90.842 MHz	Fixed frequency

(continues)

Table 6-1   Frequency ranges of wireless technologies listed from low to high frequencies *(continued)*

Technologies	Frequency range (band) in kHz, MHz, or GHz	Description
Cellular	824 MHz–896 MHz	Commonly called the 800 band
RFID	858 MHz–930 MHz	One of several bands assigned to RFID
Cellular	1850 MHz–1990 MHz	Commonly called the 1900 band
Wi-Fi: 802.11b/g/n/ax	2.4 GHz–2.4835 GHz	11 or 14 20-MHz channels
ZigBee	2.4 GHz–2.4835 GHz	16 channels
Bluetooth	2.4 GHz–2.4835 GHz	79 channels
RFID	2.446 GHz–2.454 GHz	Highest frequency range for RFID
ANT+	2.457 GHz	Fixed frequency
Wi-Fi: 802.11a/n/ac/ax	5.1 GHz–5.8 GHz	24 20-MHz channels or *(802.11n and above)* 12 40-MHz channels or *(802.11ac and above)* 6 80-MHz channels or 2 160-MHz channels
Wi-Fi: 802.11ax (Wi-Fi 6E)	5.925 GHz–7.125 GHz	59 20-MHz channels or 29 40-MHz channels or 14 80-MHz channels or 7 160-MHz channels
IR	300 GHz–300,000 GHz	10 channels plus 4 near-infrared channels

The following list gives a brief explanation of the wireless technologies in Table 6-1 that are not covered elsewhere in this course. Most of these technologies are used for various purposes in supporting **IoT (Internet of Things)** networks, which include a wide range of devices not normally considered to be a computing device. Due to the diverse nature of IoT devices and purposes, many kinds of wireless technologies are employed to better serve the needs of these connections:

- **RFID (Radio Frequency Identification)** uses electromagnetic fields to store data on a small chip in an RFID tag, which includes an antenna that can both transmit and receive, and possibly a battery. The tag holds 1–8 KB of data, such as a serial number, credit card information, or medical data, which it can transmit to a nearby reader. RFID is commonly used for inventory management. Because the tag does not need to be precisely positioned close to the reader, an employee can quickly scan a shelf of several items to determine what's in stock and what needs to be re-ordered without having to scan each individual item. An RFID tag might also be embedded in the customer's credit card, allowing for so-called "contactless" payment.

- **NFC (near-field communication)** is a form of RFID and transfers data wirelessly over very short distances (usually 10 cm or less). A tiny antenna embedded in the device sends its radio signal at a fixed frequency of 13.56 MHz. The signal can also be transmitted in one direction by an NFC tag, or smart tag, such as when employees need to access a secure area of a building. Other uses of NFC tags include ticketing, cashless payment, shopping loyalty or membership programs, identification, data sharing, and PC logon capabilities. NFC tags, such as the ones shown in Figure 6-1, require no power source other than the receiving device's power field. The NFC tag collects power from the smartphone or other device by magnetic induction, which is a form of wireless power transmission. Once power is introduced to the NFC tag by the receiving device's proximity, the tag transmits its data. They can be programmed to transmit stored data, launch apps, direct a browser to a web page, or change device settings. This makes them useful even for casual, personal use, such as changing your phone's settings when you pass through your front door at home or when you get into your car.

Figure 6-1   These programmable NFC tags have sticky backs for attaching to a flat surface like a wall, desk, or car dashboard

- **Z-Wave** is a smart home protocol that provides two basic types of functions: signaling to manage wireless connections, and control to transmit data and commands between devices. A Z-Wave network controller, called a hub, receives commands from a smartphone or computer and relays the commands to various smart devices on its network. Devices on the network are identified by a 1-byte Node ID, and the entire network has a 4-byte Network ID. Multiple Z-Wave networks can coexist in the same space because the Network ID prevents communication outside of a device's Z-Wave network. Z-Wave transmissions offer a range of up to 100 m per hop, and they can tolerate up to four hops through repeaters. Z-Wave–controlled devices can serve as repeaters on a Z-Wave mesh network.

- Based on the 802.15.4 standard, **ZigBee** is a low-powered, battery-conserving wireless technology. It is designed to handle small amounts of data and is therefore ideal for use in ISM (industrial, scientific, and medical) sensors. ZigBee is also used in IoT devices for purposes such as building automation, HVAC control, AMR (Automatic Meter Reading), and fleet management. The protocol is known for its relative simplicity and reliability when compared to other technologies such as Bluetooth, and its level of security, which is accomplished using 128-bit AES encryption.

- **Bluetooth**, defined by IEEE 802.15.1 specifications, is named after a medieval king of Denmark named Harald Bluetooth, who fought to merge several Danish tribes under a single government. Like its namesake, Bluetooth technology unites separate entities—such as mobile devices, PCs, and accessories—under a single communications standard. Bluetooth operates in the radio band of 2.4 GHz to 2.4835 GHz and hops between frequencies within that band (up to 1600 hops/sec) to help reduce interference. Most Bluetooth devices require close proximity to form a connection, with the exact distance requirements depending on the class of Bluetooth device.

- **ANT+** (pronounced *ant plus*) technology is based on the ANT protocol, which is an ad hoc wireless protocol operating at about 2.4 GHz. This is one less acronym to learn, as the term ANT simply refers to the insect, which is small in size and a tenacious worker. The ANT protocol was originally developed in 2004 by ANT Wireless, a division of Dynastream Innovations. The company is currently owned by Garmin. While ANT+ is a proprietary protocol, it is also open source and therefore used by many manufacturers in addition to Garmin. ANT+ gathers and tracks information from sensors that are typically embedded in heart rate monitors, GPS devices, and other activity monitoring devices. Garmin's smartwatches, for example, track an athlete's activity levels and geographic movement, and then wirelessly sync this data to the person's smartphone, computer, and web-based accounts such as Strava (a social media site for athletic activities) or Facebook. Unlike Bluetooth, ANT+ can also sync data from multiple devices for the same activity, such as a smartwatch, smartphone, bicycle computer (like the one shown in Figure 6-2), or fitness equipment such as a treadmill.

iStock.com/piola666

Figure 6-2 A cycling computer can track location, speed, elevation, and more

- **IR (infrared)** technology has found new life in the world of IoT, where it's used primarily to collect data through various sensors. IR is also commonly used in remote controls such as the one that comes with the projector shown in Figure 6-3. Infrared standards are defined by the IrDA (Infrared Data Association) at the website *irda.org*. IR exists just below the spectrum that is visible to the human eye, with longer wavelengths than red light. Because it's a form of light, IR requires a nearly unobstructed **LOS (line of sight)** between the transmitter and receiver—some devices use a scatter mode that reflects IR signals off nearby surfaces in order to circumvent some obstacles, but IR cannot pass through these obstacles. This limitation can actually be used to increase the security of IR transmissions. An LED in a device creates the invisible radiation, which is then detected by a sensor's semiconductor material that converts the signals into electrical current. IR sensors are used to collect information such as the following:
  - Presence or level of liquid, based on the quality of a reflection
  - Variations in reflections from skin caused by variations in blood flow, which can be used to monitor heart rate
  - Proximity to the device, which can trigger an action such as steering a vehicle away from an obstacle
  - Commands from a control device, such as a game or TV remote control

Figure 6-3 This remote control contains an IR transceiver to communicate with the projector

Figure 6-4 shows where these bands fit in the wireless spectrum. Frequency bands used for AM, FM, and satellite communications are included in Figure 6-4 for comparison and to show where potential overlap of signals might occur.

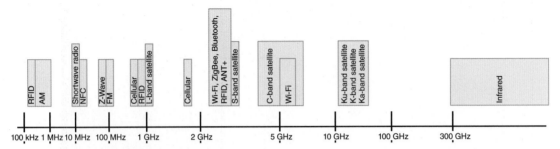

Figure 6-4   The wireless spectrum

Notice in Figure 6-4 that Wi-Fi, Bluetooth, ZigBee, ANT+, as well as some satellite signals share the frequency ranges around 2.4 GHz. How do these technologies share these airwaves without one signal interfering with another? Let's explore how channels are managed to reduce interference caused by overlapping channels.

NOTE 6-1

The airwaves are considered a natural resource. In the United States, the FCC grants organizations in different locations exclusive rights to use each frequency and specifies which frequency ranges can be used for what purposes. Other countries have similar regulatory agencies to manage the impact of transmitted signals on airwave availability for public, private, and government use. The ITU (International Telecommunication Union) is a United Nations agency that sets standards for international telecommunications including wireless frequency allocations and satellite orbits. Some bands can only be used with a license (for example, a band devoted to television, FM, AM, or ham radio). Others, such as Wi-Fi bands and CB (citizens band) radio, are available for public use without a license so long as radios using these bands conform to restrictions on the signal transmission strength. In the case of Wi-Fi, this means you can own and use a consumer-grade Wi-Fi device without acquiring a license granted by the FCC to use the band.

Channel Management

A band used by a wireless device is defined by its overall frequency range. To allow multiple devices to share the same band, the band is subdivided into channels, and channels are further subdivided into narrowband channels. Most wireless devices implement one of two technologies to take advantage of the frequencies within its band to avoid interference:

- **FHSS (frequency hopping spread spectrum)**—A short burst of data is transmitted on a particular frequency within the band, and the next burst goes to the next frequency in the sequence. Frequency hopping can happen hundreds of times a second. FHSS is cheaper to implement than DSSS and performs better than DSSS in crowded, indoor environments.
- **DSSS (direct sequence spread spectrum)**—Data streams are divided and encoded into small chunks, called chips, which are spread over all available frequencies within one of three wide channels, all at the same time. The process of dividing and encoding the data is called chipping, and the spreading ratio used to transform the data is called the chipping code, which is unique to each device. DSSS uses the available bandwidth more efficiently than FHSS and tends to have a higher throughput.

Here's a breakdown of how each wireless standard in the 2.4 GHz range uses its allotted band; you'll learn more about each of these standards later in this module:

- Wi-Fi, commonly used for wireless Internet access, uses DSSS. In the United States, the FCC has defined 11 channels within the 2.4-GHz band for Wi-Fi and 24 channels in the 5-GHz band. (Other countries might have 14 Wi-Fi channels for the 2.4-GHz band.) In the United States, each channel is 20 MHz wide. A Wi-Fi **AP (access point)**, which is the central connectivity device for Wi-Fi clients on a network, is manually configured to use a selected group of channels. Wi-Fi client devices scan the entire band for active channels.

- Bluetooth, commonly used to connect wireless personal devices, uses FHSS to take advantage of the 79 channels allocated to the Bluetooth band. In a network of Bluetooth devices (called a piconet), one device is designated the master and provides a clock the other devices use to coordinate their channel hopping. Because Bluetooth transmissions are constantly hopping channels, interference and collisions are less likely to cause significant problems.

- ZigBee, commonly used in ISM (industrial, scientific, and medical) devices, uses DSSS and 16 channels.

Even with the frequency spread of FHSS or DSSS to avoid interference, collisions can still happen. Each technology has a procedure to follow when it senses a collision. For example, when a Bluetooth device senses a collision with a Wi-Fi channel, it backs off using the frequencies in that Wi-Fi channel for a short time, giving Wi-Fi the opportunity to finish its transmission, as shown in Figure 6-5. Wi-Fi devices use a "listen before transmit" strategy to find a silent channel. More details about how Wi-Fi handles collisions are covered later in the module.

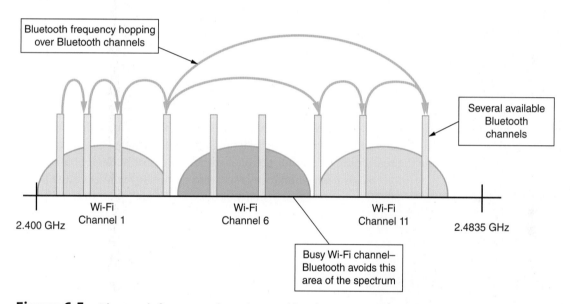

Figure 6-5   Bluetooth frequency hopping avoids a busy Wi-Fi channel

Antennas

The air provides no fixed path for signals to follow, so signals travel without guidance. Contrast this to wired media, such as STP or fiber-optic cable, which do provide a fixed signal path. The lack of a fixed path requires wireless signals to be transmitted, received, controlled, and corrected differently than wired signals. Part of this work is done at a hardware level.

Just as with wired signals, wireless signals originate from electrical current traveling along a conductor. The electrical signal travels from the transmitter to an antenna, which then emits the signal as a series of electromagnetic waves into the atmosphere. The signal moves through the air and eventually reaches (or rather, passes) its destination. At the destination, another antenna detects the signal going by, and a receiver converts it back to current. Figure 6-6 illustrates this process.

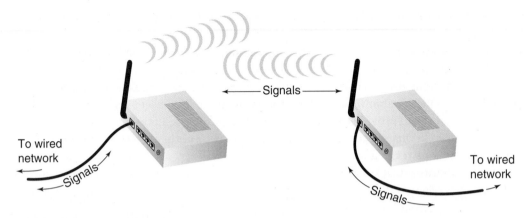

Figure 6-6 Wireless transmission and reception

Notice that antennas are used for both the transmission and reception of wireless signals. As you might expect, to exchange information, two antennas must be tuned to the same frequency so they can communicate on the same channel. Thus, each type of wireless service requires an antenna specifically designed for that service. The service's specifications determine the antenna's power output, frequency, and radiation pattern. An antenna's **radiation pattern** describes the relative strength over a three-dimensional area of all the electromagnetic energy the antenna sends or receives. Radiation patterns can be used to classify antennas into two basic categories:

- **Directional antenna** (also called a unidirectional antenna)—Issues wireless signals along a single direction. This type is used when the source needs to communicate with one destination, as in a point-to-point link or in a specific area. A satellite downlink (for example, the kind used to receive digital TV signals) uses directional antennas.
- **Omnidirectional antenna**—Issues and receives wireless signals with (somewhat) equal strength and clarity in all directions, although in the real world, an omnidirectional antenna is never perfectly balanced. This type is used when many receivers or mobile receivers must be able to pick up the signal in many directions. TV and radio stations use omnidirectional antennas, as do most towers that transmit cellular signals and most mobile devices.

The geographical area that an antenna or wireless system can reach is known as its **range**. Receivers must be located within a transmitter's range to receive accurate signals consistently. Even within an antenna's range, however, signals may be hampered by obstacles and rendered unintelligible. Choosing the correct type of antenna for the application can help solve the problem.

Typical users might not put much thought into a wireless device's antenna, as the antenna is usually attached directly to the device or even embedded within it (such as with a smartphone or laptop). However, network technicians need to be more aware of what antennas devices have, and they also need some basic knowledge on other types of antennas and how to work with them.

Consider a situation where you need to transmit high volumes of data wirelessly between two segments of your network. In addition to connecting multiple nodes within a LAN, wireless technology can be used to connect two different parts of a LAN or two separate LANs. Such connections might use a fixed link with directional antennas between two access points, as shown in Figure 6-7.

Because point-to-point links must transmit in only one general direction, they can apply more energy to signal propagation through a unidirectional antenna. This allows them to achieve a greater transmission

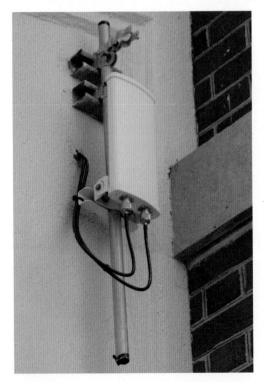

Figure 6-7 An outdoor unidirectional antenna that transmits across a nearby football field

distance than mobile wireless links can offer. For example, access points connecting two WLANs could be located up to 1000 feet apart.

When using a separate antenna, such as the one you see in Figure 6-7, keep in mind that you must use cabling to connect the antenna to the network, and in many cases, antennas use coax cable. However, Wi-Fi and similar wireless signals will rapidly degrade over even a few feet of coax cable. This attenuation, or signal loss, over the antenna cable typically necessitates placing a network access point in close vicinity to the antenna.

You can determine the gain or loss of an access point attached to an external antenna by considering initial power output of the AP, signal loss along the antenna cable (attenuation), and signal gain from the antenna itself—which is measured in dBi (decibels relative to isotrope) and is a theoretical ratio used to measure antenna performance. This overall calculation is referred to as **EIRP (effective isotropic radiated power)** and is measured in dBm (decibels relative to one milliwatt). Now that you understand the components, you can see that the formula for this calculation is simple addition and subtraction:

EIRP = transmission power (dBm) − cable loss (dB) + antenna gain (dBi)

Of course, the AP's and antenna's performance aren't the only factors that determine the quality of the signal received by the client. The wireless client's own antenna, distance to the wireless client, and noise in the environment all affect the power of the received signal. **RSSI (received signal strength indicator)** measures in dBm the power of the signal on the receiver's end. The scale used for this measurement varies by manufacturer, but typically, because RSSI is shown as negative numbers, closer to 0 is better. Table 6-2 shows relative RSSI levels commonly used.

Table 6-2   RSSI levels

RSSI (dBm)	Rating	Effect
−30 dBm	Excellent	Typically only achieved when the client is very close to the AP.
−50 dBm	Good	Provides reliable delivery of time-sensitive data, such as with VoIP or streaming video.
−70 dBm	Acceptable	Minimum required for reliable data delivery.
−80 dBm	Not good	Minimum required for basic connectivity.
−90 dBm	Unusable	Will experience difficulty establishing a connection.

In a project at the end of this module, you'll have the opportunity to measure RSSI for Wi-Fi networks in your area. For now, let's see what kinds of environmental factors can affect the drop in power between transmission and reception.

Signal Propagation

Propagation refers to the way in which a wave travels from one point to another. Ideally, a wireless signal would travel directly in a straight line from its transmitter to its intended receiver. This straight-line propagation, known as LOS (line of sight), maximizes distance for energy used and results in reception of the clearest possible signal. However, because the atmosphere is an unguided medium and the path between a transmitter and a receiver is not always clear of obstacles, wireless signals do not usually follow a straight line.

When an obstacle stands in a signal's way, the signal might pass through the object, it might be absorbed by the object, or it might be subject to any of the following phenomena, depending upon the object's geometry and its constituent materials:

- **Attenuation**—As with wired signals, wireless signals also experience attenuation. After a signal is transmitted, the farther it moves away from the transmission source, the more it weakens. Similar to wired transmission, wireless signals can be amplified by increasing the power of the transmission or extended by repeating the signal from a closer broadcast point using a repeater (also called a **wireless range extender**), such as the one designed for a home network shown in Figure 6-8.

NOTE 6-2

Satellite and infrared transmissions require a clear line of sight. However, some signals might be blocked in what appears to be a clear line of sight. For example, many energy-efficient windows are covered with a film that filters out certain layers of sunlight. Even though you can see through the window, a satellite signal, such as an XM radio satellite signal, might not be able to get through.

Jill West

Figure 6-8 Wi-Fi range extender

- **Fading**—As a signal runs into various obstacles, its energy will gradually fade, which causes the strength of the signal that reaches the receiver to be lower than the transmitted signal's strength. Excessive fading can cause dropped connections or slow data transmission.
- **Interference**—Electromagnetic waves in the atmosphere can interfere with wireless communications similar to how EMI (electromagnetic interference) affects wired transmissions. Because wireless signals cannot depend on a conduit or shielding to protect them from extraneous EMI, they are more vulnerable to noise than wired transmissions are. The proportion of noise to the strength of a signal is called the **SNR (signal-to-noise ratio)**. Signals traveling through areas in which many wireless communications systems are in use—for example, the center of a metropolitan area—are the most apt to suffer from interference and, therefore, will exhibit a lower SNR than signals traveling through a relatively clear environment.
- **Refraction**—As a wave travels into and through a different transmission medium, such as when traveling through glass or other solids, the wave's direction, speed, and wavelength are altered, or refracted. Imagine how light waves are altered when entering the water in a pool. If you're underwater looking back at the surface, the image you see is distorted.
- **Reflection**—The wave encounters an obstacle and reflects, or bounces back, toward its source. A wireless signal will bounce off objects whose surface dimensions are large compared with the signal's average **wavelength** (the distance from the crest of one wave to the crest of the next wave). In the context of a wireless LAN, whose wavelengths are approximately 12 cm, such objects include walls, floors, ceilings, and the Earth—anything with a large, flat surface. In addition, signals reflect more readily off conductive materials, such as metal, than off insulators, such as concrete.
- **Scattering**—When a wireless signal encounters an object that has small surface dimensions compared with the signal's wavelength, it's diffused or scattered in multiple directions. Scattering is also related to the roughness of the surface a wireless signal encounters. The rougher the surface, the more likely a signal is to scatter when it hits that surface. In an office building, objects such as chairs, books, plants, and computers cause scattering of wireless LAN signals. For signals traveling outdoors, precipitation such as rain and mist also cause scattering.

- **Diffraction**—A wireless signal is diffracted, or split into secondary waves, when it encounters an obstruction. The secondary waves continue to propagate generally in the direction in which they were split. If you could see wireless signals being diffracted, they would appear to be bending around the obstacle. Objects with sharp edges—including the corners of walls and desks—cause diffraction.

Wireless signals follow many different paths to their destination. Such signals are known as multipath signals. Figure 6-9 illustrates multipath signals caused by reflection, scattering, and diffraction.

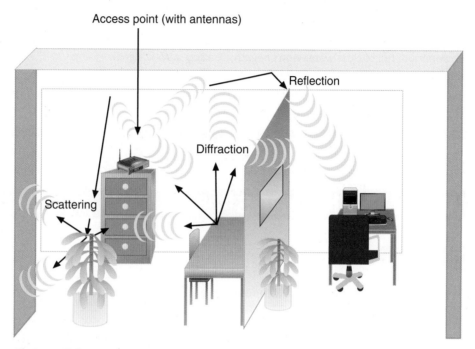

Figure 6-9   Multipath signal propagation

The multipath nature of wireless signals is both a blessing and a curse. On one hand, because signals bounce off obstacles, they have a better chance of reaching their destination. The downside to multipath signaling is that, because of their various paths, multipath signals travel different distances between their transmitter and a receiver. Thus, multiple instances of the same signal can arrive at a receiver at different times. This might cause signals to be misinterpreted, resulting in data errors. Error-correction algorithms detect the errors, and sometimes the sender must retransmit the signal. The more errors that occur, the slower the throughput.

Many standards have been developed to account for—and even take advantage of—the various characteristics of wireless transmissions. The best known is IEEE's 802.11 standards, also known as Wi-Fi. Let's look more closely at these core standards for wireless networks.

REMEMBER THIS...

- Explain what a WLAN is.
- Describe regulatory impacts of wireless bands and channels.
- Compare directional and omnidirectional antennas.
- Explain EIRP and RSSI.

SELF-CHECK

1. Which of the following statements is false?
   a. Each Wi-Fi channel contains multiple frequency bands.
   b. Wi-Fi functions on two different frequency bands.
   c. Each Wi-Fi channel contains multiple frequencies.
   d. Wi-Fi spreads its data across all available frequencies within a wide channel.

2. Which of the following statements is true?
   a. A satellite dish receives signals equally from any direction.
   b. A fish aquarium full of clear water won't negatively affect a Wi-Fi signal.
   c. A Wi-Fi client connects to a range extender that connects to an AP.
   d. A smartphone always directs its signal toward the closest cell tower.

Check your answers at the end of this module.

802.11 WLAN STANDARDS

✓ CERTIFICATION

1.2 Explain the characteristics of network topologies and network types.

2.1 Compare and contrast various devices, their features, and their appropriate placement on the network.

2.4 Given a scenario, install and configure the appropriate wireless standards and technologies.

4.2 Compare and contrast common types of attacks.

Average reading time: 29 minutes

WLANs define operations at OSI layers 1 and 2. Just like wired LANs, they support the same TCP/IP higher-layer OSI protocols (such as IP, TCP, and UDP) you're already familiar with. This compatibility ensures that wireless and wired transmission methods can be integrated on the same network.

The most popular OSI physical and data link layer standards used by WLANs are popularly referred to as Wi-Fi. **Wi-Fi (wireless fidelity)** is a collection of wireless standards and their amendments, extensions, and corrections developed by IEEE's 802.11 committee. Notable wireless standards developed by the IEEE 802.11 committee and its task groups are 802.11b, 802.11a, 802.11g, 802.11n, 802.11ac, and 802.11ax.

The 802.11 standards employ various technologies at the physical layer. In addition, 802.11n and later standards modify the way frames are used at the MAC sublayer, which, as you've already read, is the lower portion of the data link layer that is specifically involved with managing MAC addresses in message frames. Recall that layer 2's other sublayer is the LLC sublayer, which is primarily concerned with multiplexing, flow and error control, and reliability.

Table 6-3 summarizes the technical details of the 802.11 standards. The following list gives a more detailed description of each standard.

Table 6-3   Technical details for 802.11 wireless standards

Standard	Frequency band	Maximum theoretical throughput	Geographic range
802.11b (Wi-Fi 1)	2.4 GHz	11 Mbps	100 m
802.11a (Wi-Fi 2)	5 GHz	54 Mbps	50 m
802.11g (Wi-Fi 3)	2.4 GHz	54 Mbps	100 m
802.11n (Wi-Fi 4)	2.4 GHz or 5 GHz	600 Mbps	Indoor: 70 m Outdoor: 250 m
802.11ac (Wi-Fi 5)	5 GHz	Wave 1 (3 data streams): 1.3 Gbps Wave 2 (4 data streams): 3.47 Gbps Wave 3 (8 data streams): 6.93 Gbps	Indoor: 70 m Outdoor: 250 m
802.11ax (Wi-Fi 6 and Wi-Fi 6E)	2.4 GHz or 5 GHz or (Wi-Fi 6E only) 6 GHz	9.6 Gbps	Indoor: 70 m Outdoor: 250 m

EXAM TIP   In preparation for the CompTIA Network+ exam, memorize every detail shown in Table 6-3.

- **802.11b**—In 1999, the IEEE released its 802.11b standard, which separates the 2.4-GHz band into 22-MHz channels. Among all the 802.11 standards, 802.11b was the first to take hold and has been retroactively dubbed Wi-Fi 1. It is also the least expensive of all the 802.11 WLAN technologies. However, most network administrators have replaced 802.11b with faster standards.

- **802.11a**—Although the 802.11a task group began its standards work before the 802.11b group, 802.11a (now called Wi-Fi 2) was released *after* 802.11b. The higher throughput of 802.11a, as compared with 802.11b, is attributable to its use of higher frequencies, its unique method of modulating data, and more available bandwidth. Perhaps most significant is that the 5-GHz band is not as congested as the 2.4-GHz band. Thus, 802.11a signals are less likely to suffer interference. However, higher-frequency signals require more power to transmit, and they travel shorter distances than lower-frequency signals. As a result, 802.11a networks require a greater density of access points to cover the same distance that 802.11b networks cover. The additional access points, as well as the nature of 802.11a equipment, make this standard more expensive than either 802.11b or 802.11g. For this and other reasons, 802.11a is rarely preferred.

- **802.11g**—IEEE's 802.11g WLAN standard, now referred to as Wi-Fi 3, was designed to be just as affordable as 802.11b while increasing its maximum theoretical throughput with different data modulation techniques. In addition, 802.11g benefits from being compatible with 802.11b networks. This was a significant advantage at the time when network administrators were upgrading their wireless access points to the 802.11g technology while still needing to offer wireless access to older computers.

- **802.11n**—In 2009, IEEE ratified the 802.11n standard, which is now named Wi-Fi 4. However, it was in development for years before that, and as early as mid-2007, manufacturers were selling 802.11n-compatible transceivers in their networking equipment. The primary goal of IEEE's 802.11n committee was to create a wireless standard that provided much higher effective throughput than the earlier 802.11 standards, and they succeeded. 802.11n boasts a maximum throughput of 600 Mbps, making it a realistic platform for telephone and video signals. IEEE also specified that the 802.11n standard must be backward-compatible with the 802.11a, b, and g standards. This is made possible because 802.11n uses both the 2.4-GHz and the 5-GHz frequency bands.

- **802.11ac**—Officially approved in early 2014, 802.11ac (Wi-Fi 5) operates on the 5-GHz band and exceeds benchmarks set by earlier standards by increasing its useful bandwidth and amplitude. 802.11ac is the first Wi-Fi standard to approach Gigabit Ethernet capabilities, providing better support for more wireless clients at a time. In fact, 802.11ac access points function more like a switch than a hub in that they can handle multiple transmissions at one time over the same frequency spectrum. This standard was deployed in three waves, with each successive release offering higher speeds by using more data streams.

- **802.11ax**—The most current Wi-Fi standard at the time of this writing is 802.11ax, commonly called **Wi-Fi 6**, which operates in both the 2.4 GHz and 5 GHz frequency ranges. Improvements include further development of modulation and multiuser technologies, which you'll read about shortly, to increase data speeds and transmission distances. An interesting technique called BSS coloring also reduces interference from neighboring Wi-Fi networks. While theoretical maximum speeds for 802.11ax reach near 10 Gbps, actual speeds are expected to run only about 30–60 percent faster than actual Wi-Fi 5 speeds. More significantly, however, Wi-Fi 6 can support higher speeds for more network clients at the same time, which is particularly important for smart home environments with potentially dozens of IoT devices, or for a stadium or conference center environment with hundreds or thousands of Wi-Fi clients.
- **Wi-Fi 6E**—Building on improvements of 802.11ax, Wi-Fi 6E will use the currently unlicensed 6 GHz frequency range. At a total of 1200 MHz, this range is wider than either the 2.4 GHz (70 MHz wide) or 5 GHz (500 MHz wide) ranges, allowing far more available channels and much higher speed transmissions but at shorter distances.

NOTE 6-3

The actual geographic range of any wireless technology depends on several factors, including the power of the antenna, physical barriers or obstacles between sending and receiving nodes, and interference in the environment. Therefore, although a technology is rated for a certain average geographic range, it might actually transmit signals in a shorter or longer range at various times under various conditions.

A more relevant measure of an AP's performance in a particular environment is how well it saturates its range with a strong, fast signal. This is one of the primary advantages of 802.11ac and 802.11ax over 802.11n: The newer standards do a better job of providing faster transmissions throughout their geographic range. So, for example, at 75 m, the signal from an 802.11ac AP will be more effective than the signal from an 802.11n AP under the same conditions.

Regardless of the standard followed, all 802.11 networks share many features and innovations in common. For example, all 802.11 networks follow the same access method, as described in the following section. In addition, some newer innovations give the later standards a significant performance boost over earlier standards.

802.11 Innovations

Although some of their physical layer services vary, all the 802.11 standards use half-duplex signaling. In other words, an antenna on a wireless node using one of the 802.11 techniques can either transmit or receive, but it cannot do both simultaneously unless the node has more than one transceiver installed. Some wireless access points can simulate full-duplex signaling by using multiple frequencies. But the transmission for each antenna is still only half-duplex.

Despite this physical limitation, beginning with 802.11n, several innovations have been implemented that contribute to making later 802.11 standards much faster and much more reliable:

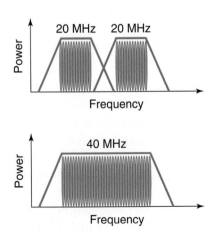

Figure 6-10   Channel bonding

- **Channel bonding**—Beginning with 802.11n, two adjacent 20-MHz channels can be combined, or bonded, to make a 40-MHz channel, as shown in Figure 6-10. In fact, bonding two 20-MHz channels more than doubles the bandwidth available in a single 20-MHz channel. That's because the small amount of bandwidth normally reserved as buffers against interference at the top and bottom of the 20-MHz channels can be assigned to carry data instead. Because the 5-GHz band contains more channels and is less crowded (at least, for now), it's better suited to channel bonding than the 2.4-GHz band. The newer standards take channel bonding to a higher level by supporting 20-, 40-, and 80-MHz channels, with optional use of 160-MHz channels.
- **MIMO (multiple input-multiple output)**—First available in 802.11n, multiple antennas on the access point and on a client device process incoming or outgoing data simultaneously. Figure 6-11 shows an 802.11n/802.11ac dual-band SOHO router with three antennas. There

are some multiantenna 802.11g devices available, but these antennas take turns processing the data stream. 802.11n/ac devices, however, simultaneously process data through two or more antennas. As you learned earlier, wireless signals propagate in a multipath fashion. Therefore, multiple signals cannot be expected to arrive at the same receiver in concert. MIMO uses this phenomenon to its advantage by adjusting either the phase or amplitude of signals from each antenna. This improves the transmission in two ways:

Figure 6-11   Dual-band SOHO router with three antennas

Source: Amazon.com

○ **Signal quality and range**—Spatial diversity of the different antennas eliminates noise in the transmission, which also increases the distance it can effectively travel. Each antenna receives a slightly different version of the signal, and the strengths of each signal are summed.

○ **Signal capacity**—Spatial multiplexing adds a new data stream between each additional pair of antennas, thereby increasing the amount of data being transmitted and received. This effect increases linearly with the addition of each pair of antennas.

- **MU-MIMO (multiuser MIMO)**—Related to MIMO, MU-MIMO is an even newer technology implemented by 802.11ac Wave 2 and newer products that allows multiple antennas to service multiple clients simultaneously. The antennas use different spatial streams that rely on clients being positioned relatively far apart from one another. This feature reduces congestion and thereby contributes to even faster data transmission. As with MIMO, however, a MU-MIMO access point can only be used at full capacity when the involved client devices also support MU-MIMO technology. In reality, MU-MIMO is currently only available for downstream (AP to client) transmissions and is rarely implemented in indoor environments where clients are located in close proximity to each other.

- **OFDMA (Orthogonal Frequency Division Multiple Access)**—Improving upon an earlier technology called OFDM, OFDMA supports more efficient multiuser functionality for 802.11ax devices. In essence, OFDMA allows the 802.11ax AP to subdivide each channel into smaller frequency allocations for each client, such as 2 MHz or 4 MHz of each 20-MHz channel. The AP can then transmit multiple small frames to multiple clients at one time using parts of the channel.

- **Frame aggregation**—Beginning with 802.11n, networks can use one of two techniques for combining multiple data frames into one larger frame: A-MSDU (Aggregated Mac Service Data Unit) or A-MPDU (Aggregated Mac Protocol Data Unit). Both approaches combine multiple frames to reduce overhead. 802.11ac uses A-MPDU for all transmissions by default. 802.11ax continues to use A-MPDU but with additional enhancements that allow for more flexibility in choosing which frames can be aggregated. To understand how frame aggregation works, suppose three small data frames are combined into one larger frame. Each larger frame will have only one copy of the same addressing information that would appear in the smaller frames. Proportionally, the header fields take up less of the aggregated frame's space. In addition, replacing four small frames with one large frame means an access point and client will have to exchange one-quarter the number of messages to negotiate media access and error control.

Figure 6-12 illustrates the lowered overhead accomplished by both A-MSDU and A-MPDU. The advantage of A-MSDU over A-MPDU is that more of the frame's information is combined with other frames transmitted at the same time. The potential disadvantage to using larger frames is the increased probability of errors when transmitting larger blocks of data. Therefore, the advantage of A-MPDU is that each frame added to the mix retains some of its error checking data, resulting in greater reliability.

Figure 6-12 A-MSDU and A-MPDU aggregated frames

Note that not all the techniques listed here are used in every 802.11 implementation. Further, reaching maximum throughput depends on the number and type of these strategies used. It also depends on the band the network uses, environmental factors, and capabilities of wireless clients. Considering these factors, an 802.11 network's actual throughputs vary considerably.

Access Method

You've learned that the data link layer, specifically the MAC sublayer, is responsible for appending physical addresses to a data frame and for governing multiple nodes' access to a single medium. Like 802.3 (Ethernet), 802.11 appends 48-bit physical addresses to a frame to identify its source and destination. The use of the same physical addressing scheme allows 802.11 networks to easily blend with other IEEE 802 networks, including Ethernet (802.3) networks. However, 802.11 networks use a different access method than Ethernet networks do.

Wireless devices are not designed to transmit and receive simultaneously and so cannot prevent collisions. Instead, 802.11 standards specify the use of **CSMA/CA (Carrier Sense Multiple Access with Collision Avoidance)** procedures to access a shared medium. Compared with CSMA/CD (Carrier Sense Multiple Access with Collision Detection), CSMA/CA minimizes the potential for collisions, but cannot detect the occurrence of a collision and so cannot take steps to recover from the collisions that do occur. Figure 6-13 illustrates the basic process. The steps are as follows:

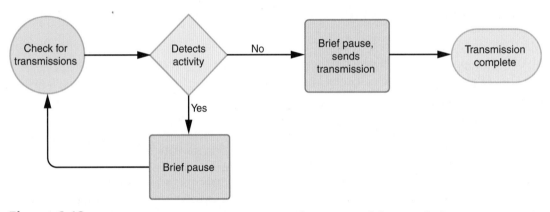

Figure 6-13 CSMA/CA uses ACK messages to confirm successful transmission

Step 1: Using CSMA/CA, a node on an 802.11 network checks for existing wireless transmissions (the green circle in Figure 6-13) before it begins to send data.

- If the source node detects no transmission activity on the network, it waits a brief, random amount of time and then sends its transmission.
- If the source does detect activity, it waits a brief period before checking the channel again.

Step 2: The destination node receives the transmission and, after verifying its accuracy, issues an ACK (acknowledgment) packet to the source.

- If the source receives this acknowledgment, it assumes the transmission was properly completed.
- Interference or other transmissions on the network could impede this exchange. If, after transmitting a message, the source node fails to receive acknowledgment from the destination node, it assumes its transmission did not arrive properly, and it begins the CSMA/CA process anew.

The use of ACK packets to verify every transmission means that 802.11 networks require more overhead than 802.3 networks. A wireless network with a theoretical maximum throughput of 1 Gbps will, in fact, transmit less data per second than a wired Ethernet network with the same theoretical maximum throughput.

Nodes that are physically located far apart from each other on a wireless network present a particular challenge in that they are too far apart to collaborate in preventing collisions. This is called the hidden node problem, where a node is not visible to other nodes on the other side of the coverage area. One way to ensure that packets are not inhibited by other transmissions is to reserve the medium for one node's use. In 802.11, this can be accomplished through the optional **RTS/CTS (Request to Send/Clear to Send)** protocol. Figure 6-14 illustrates the CSMA/CA process when using RTS/CTS.

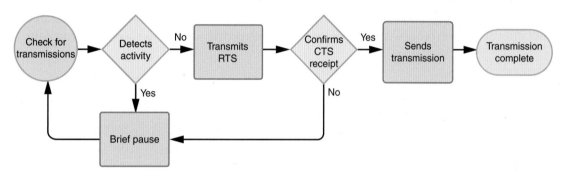

Figure 6-14   CSMA/CA with the optional RTS/CTS protocol

When using RTS/CTS, a source node issues an RTS signal to the access point requesting the exclusive opportunity to transmit. If the access point agrees by responding with a CTS signal, the access point temporarily suspends communication with all nodes in its range and waits for the source node to complete its transmission. When used, RTS/CTS decreases network efficiency. However, it can be worthwhile when transmitting large packets.

Association and Wireless Topologies

Suppose you bring your laptop to a local café, turn it on, and soon your laptop prompts you to log on to the café's wireless network to gain access to the Internet through its hotspot. This seemingly simple process, known as **association**, involves a number of packet exchanges between the café's access point and your computer. Association is another function of the MAC sublayer described in the 802.11 standard.

While a wireless device is on and has its wireless protocols running, it periodically surveys its surroundings for evidence of an access point, a task known as **scanning**. A device can use either active scanning or passive scanning:

- **Active scanning**—The wireless client takes the initiative:
  - The device transmits a special frame, known as a **probe**, on all available channels within its frequency range.
  - An AP detects the probe frame and issues a probe response containing all the information a device needs to associate with the AP, including a status code and node ID, or station ID, for that device.
  - The device can agree to associate with that AP. The final decision to associate with an AP, at least for the first time, usually requires the consent of the user.
  - The two nodes begin communicating over the frequency channel specified by the AP.
- **Passive scanning**—The AP takes the initiative:
  - A wireless-enabled device listens on all channels within its frequency range for a special signal, known as a beacon frame, issued periodically from an AP. The beacon frame contains information that a wireless node requires to associate itself with the AP, including the network's transmission rate and the **SSID (service set identifier)**, a character string used to identify an access point.
  - The device—usually with the consent of the user—can choose to associate with the AP.
  - The two nodes agree on a frequency channel and begin communicating.

When setting up a WLAN, most network administrators use the AP's configuration utility to assign a custom SSID, rather than the default SSID provided by the manufacturer. The default SSID often contains the name of the manufacturer and perhaps even the model number of the access point, which can give hackers a head-start on cracking into the network. Changing the SSID contributes to better security and easier network management, though you should keep the following tips in mind:

- Disguise the nature of the network identified by the SSID to avoid giving hackers more information than necessary. For example, it's probably not a good idea to name the Accounting Department's access point "Acctg."
- Minimize confusion for employees by using easily recognized—though uncommon—SSIDs. The point of this is to increase security on client devices as they travel to other areas, so they don't inadvertently attempt to connect to networks with an identical name.

IEEE terminology includes a couple of notable variations to the standard service set configuration. These terms reflect the most common wireless topologies as well:

- **IBSS (independent basic service set)** using an **ad hoc topology**—A small number of nodes closely positioned transmit directly to each other without an intervening connectivity device, as shown in Figure 6-15.

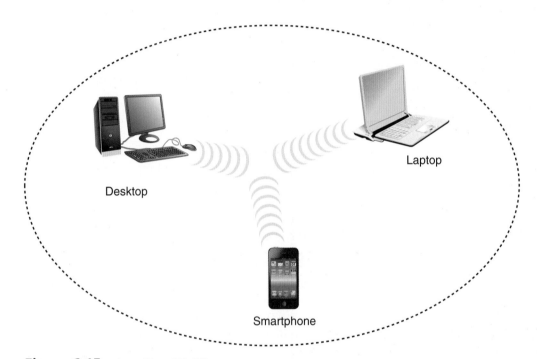

Desktop

Laptop

Smartphone

Figure 6-15   An ad hoc WLAN

- **BSS (basic service set)** using an **infrastructure topology**—A group of nodes share an access point, as shown in Figure 6-16. The AP accepts wireless signals from multiple nodes and retransmits them, usually on a wired connection, to the rest of the network. To cover its intended range, an access point must have sufficient power and must be strategically placed so that all connected nodes can communicate with it. The identifier for this group of nodes is known as a **BSSID (basic service set identifier)**.
- **ESS (extended service set)** using a mesh topology—Several access points work as peer devices on the same network, as illustrated in Figure 6-17, where the AP devices cooperate to provide more fault-tolerant network access to clients across a larger geographical range. These APs are configured and managed by a **wireless LAN controller**, which might be used only initially to configure the APs, or the APs might remain connected to the wireless controller for continued management. Clients that belong to the same ESS share a special identifier called an **ESSID (extended service set identifier)**. In practice, many networking professionals don't distinguish between the terms *SSID* and *ESSID*. They simply configure every access point in a group or LAN with the same SSID.

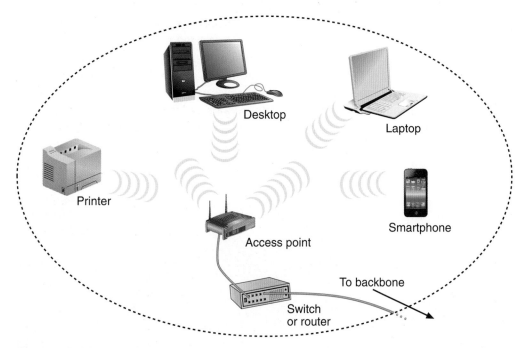

Figure 6-16   An infrastructure WLAN

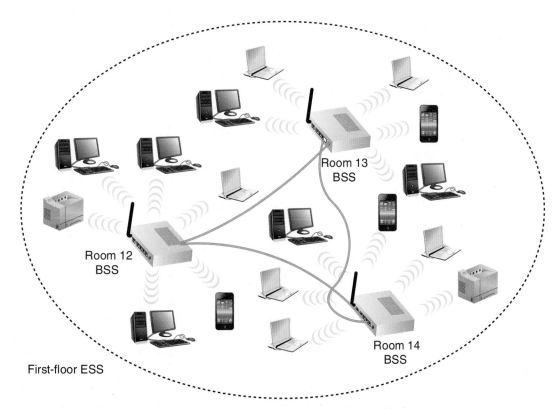

Figure 6-17   A network with multiple BSSs form an ESS—devices can be moved from one room to the next without losing network connectivity

A wireless controller might be a physical device installed locally, such as the one shown in Figure 6-18, or it might be cloud-based, VM-based, or embedded in one of the APs. Centralized wireless management is made possible by a lightweight wireless protocol, such as Cisco's proprietary LWAPP (Lightweight Access Point Protocol) or Cisco's newer CAPWAP (Control and Provisioning of Wireless Access Points), both of which direct all wireless frames to the controller by adding extra headers to the frames. The wireless controller can provide centralized authentication for wireless clients, load balancing, and channel management so that neighboring APs don't try to use overlapping channels. The controller manages AP redundancy by directing wireless traffic to alternate APs when an AP fails. Wireless controllers can also detect the presence of unauthorized APs, called **rogue access points**, by recognizing when an unauthorized AP attempts to connect to the network.

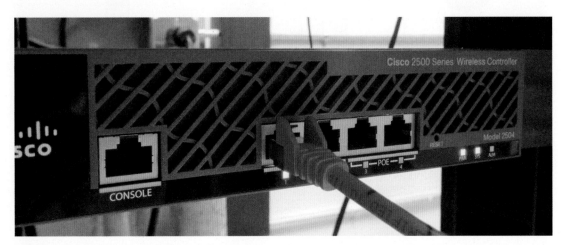

Figure 6-18   Use a wireless controller to configure, deploy, and manage APs

Within an ESS, a client can associate with any one of many APs that use the same ESSID. This allows users to **roam**, or change from AP to AP, without losing wireless network service. As devices roam between APs within a single ESS, connecting to a different AP requires **reassociation**. This is an automatic process that occurs when:

- A mobile device moves out of one AP's range and into the range of another.
- The initial AP is experiencing a high rate of errors. On a network with multiple APs, network managers can take advantage of the nodes' scanning feature to automatically balance transmission loads between access points.

IEEE 802.11 Frames

You have learned about some types of overhead required to manage access to the 802.11 wireless networks—for example, ACKs, probes, and beacons. For each of these functions, the 802.11 standard specifies a frame type at the MAC sublayer. These frame types are divided into three groups:

- **Management frames**—Involved in association and reassociation; examples of this type of frame include probe and beacon frames.
- **Control frames**—Related to medium access and data delivery; examples of this type of frame include ACK and RTS/CTS frames.
- **Data frames**—Responsible for carrying data between nodes. An 802.11 data frame is illustrated in Figure 6-19. Compare the 802.11 data frame with the Ethernet II data frame also shown in Figure 6-19. As you can see in the figure, the 802.11 data frame carries significant overhead—that is, it includes a large quantity of fields in addition to the data field.

The 802.11 data frame's fields are summarized in Table 6-4.

802.11 data frame:

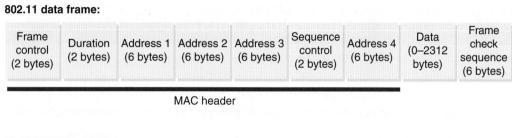

MAC header

802.3 (Ethernet II) frame:

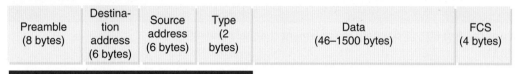

MAC header

Figure 6-19   Basic 802.11 data frame compared with an 802.3 Ethernet II frame

Table 6-4   Fields in an 802.11 data frame

Field name	Length	Description
Beginning of header: Frame control	2 bytes	Holds information about the protocol in use; the type of frame being transmitted; whether the frame is part of a larger, fragmented packet; whether the frame is one that was reissued after an unverified delivery attempt; the type of security the frame uses; and more.
Duration	2 bytes	Indicates how long the field's transmission will take so other nodes know when the channel will be available again.
Address 1	6 bytes	Source address.
Address 2	6 bytes	Transmitter address.
Address 3	6 bytes	Receiver address.
Sequence control	2 bytes	Indicates how a large packet is fragmented.
Address 4	6 bytes	Destination address.
Data	0–2312 bytes	Includes the data originally sent by the source host, plus headers from higher layers. The Data field is not part of the frame header or trailer—it is encapsulated by the frame.
Trailer: Frame check sequence	6 bytes	Uses a cyclical code to check for errors in the transmission.

Notice that the 802.11 data frame contains four address fields; by contrast, the 802.3 (Ethernet II) frame has only two. The transmitter and receiver addresses refer to the access point or another intermediary device (if used) on the wireless network.

Another unique characteristic of the 802.11 data frame is its Sequence Control field. This field is used to indicate how a large packet is fragmented—that is, how it is subdivided into smaller packets for more reliable delivery. Recall that on wired TCP/IP networks, error checking occurs at the transport layer of the OSI model and packet fragmentation, if necessary, occurs at the network layer. However, in 802.11 networks, error checking and packet fragmentation are handled at the MAC sublayer of the data link layer. By handling fragmentation at a lower layer, 802.11 makes its transmission—which is less efficient and more error-prone—transparent to higher layers. This means 802.11 nodes are more easily integrated with 802.3 networks and prevent the 802.11 conversations of an integrated network from slowing down the 802.3 conversations.

REMEMBER THIS...

- Compare 802.11 standards and their frequencies and ranges.
- Explain channel bonding.
- Describe how to configure IBSS, BSS, and ESS wireless networks.

SELF-CHECK

3. What was the first 802.11 standard to implement channel bonding?
   a. 802.11n
   b. 802.11ax
   c. 802.11g
   d. 802.11ac

4. Which type of identifier allows wireless clients to roam freely from AP to AP?
   a. BSSID
   b. IP address
   c. ESSID
   d. Transmitter address

Check your answers at the end of this module.

IMPLEMENTING A WI-FI NETWORK

 **CERTIFICATION**

2.1 Compare and contrast various devices, their features, and their appropriate placement on the network.

3.2 Explain the purpose of organization documents and policies.

Average reading time: 22 minutes

Now that you understand how wireless signals are exchanged, what can hinder them, and which physical and data link layer standards they follow, you are ready to put these ideas into practice. This section first describes the WLAN topologies and how to design small WLANs, which are the types you might use at home or in a small office. Then you'll walk through the process of installing and configuring access points and clients on larger wireless networks.

7 Application
6 Presentation
5 Session
4 Transport
3 Network
▶ ② Data Link
▶ ① Physical

Determine the Design

The design of a wireless network, the networking devices used, and the wireless technologies implemented are all affected by the network's environment, the number and expectations of users, and the networked devices that will need to be supported. Let's consider several forms of wireless networks you might work with.

SOHO Networks

A home or small office network, called a SOHO network, generally requires only one central AP and possibly some range extenders. The AP device often combines switching, routing, and other network functions as well. In this case, the device is more accurately called a wireless router or SOHO router, and it connects wireless clients to the LAN in addition to serving as their gateway to the Internet. Figure 6-20 illustrates the typical arrangement of a home or small office WLAN and is described next.

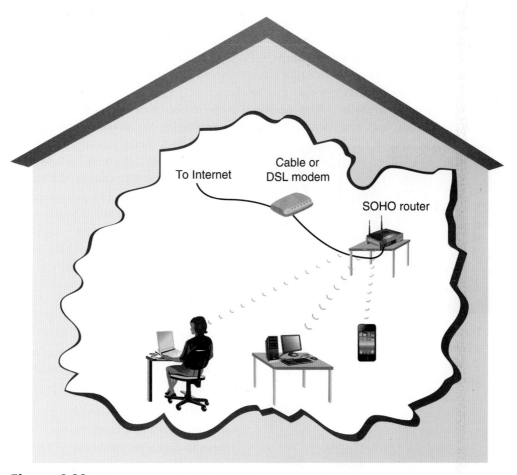

Figure 6-20   Home or small office WLAN arrangement

- The ISP's signal comes into the premises through a cable or DSL modem.
- The modem connects to the SOHO router using an RJ-45 cable. This cable is inserted into the SOHO router's WAN port, which is set apart from the other data ports and might be labeled "Internet" or remain unlabeled. Notice the yellow port on the SOHO router in Figure 6-21.

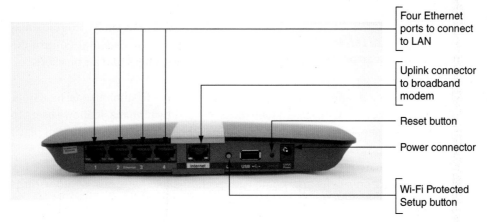

Figure 6-21   Connectors and ports on the back of a Cisco SOHO router

- The additional ports allow for wired access to the router, which contains switch hardware inside the device to manage connected devices. An AP that does not include routing or switching functions would lack these extra ports and act much like a wireless hub.

Many home or office networks include IoT devices and even expandable IoT networks. Today, networking is no longer limited to computing devices. All sorts of things can be connected to a network, from toasters, refrigerators, bathroom scales, and garage doors to watches, lamps, cars, thermostats, doorbells, and even the kitchen sink. This IoT (Internet of Things) is made up of any device that can be connected to the Internet—that is, any sensor, computer, or wearable device that talks to other devices over a network.

One of the fastest-growing areas of IoT is personal monitoring devices, such as health monitors, exercise equipment, GPS locators, and smartwatches. Another exploding IoT market interconnects smart home devices. You might already be familiar with Amazon Echo, Apple HomePod, or Google Home. These voice-controlled **smart speakers** and their embedded personal assistant apps (such as Alexa, Siri, and Google Assistant) can interlink a plethora of devices, from locks and lights to security cameras and coffee pots. You can control these devices through voice commands while interacting with a smart speaker, or you can control IoT devices through an app on your smartphone (see Figure 6-22). All these connected devices within a home create a type of LAN called a HAN (home area network).

iStock.com/RyanKing999

Figure 6-22 This engineer team is designing app screens for a voice-controlled speaker that can manage many smart home devices

Let's briefly look at what some of these smart home devices might offer to better understand how the network should be designed to support them:

iStock.com/monkeybusinessimages

Figure 6-23 A smart thermostat can be controlled by voice or by a smartphone app or smartwatch app

- **Smart thermostat**—More sophisticated than programmable thermostats, a smart thermostat allows users to adjust temperature settings based on daily schedules, shifting activity levels inside the home, current weather conditions outside, and in response to voice commands. You can control your home's temperature remotely from a smartphone (see Figure 6-23), such as when the outdoor temperature drops unexpectedly while you're away from home. Further, the thermostat itself will monitor activity levels to automatically adjust its schedule for optimized energy savings and offer tips to save even more on utility bills. Some smart thermostats can be linked with other environmental control devices, such as smart humidifiers and air purifiers.

- **Smart doorbell**—This device monitors an entryway for movement. To minimize false alarms from animals, you can set it up to filter out everything except movement caused by humans. It allows users to communicate with visitors remotely by video, even while away from home. Some smart doorbells can play a pre-recorded message, and a few offer AI-powered facial recognition to identify familiar faces. The video feed can be stored locally on the device's onboard storage drive (such as a microSD card), on a hub device inside the house, or to the cloud. Many smart doorbells now come with rechargeable batteries, so no wiring is required for installation.

- **Security camera**—These devices come with rechargeable batteries, wireless capability, and significant weather proofing to maximize installation options. Some cameras can also be connected to a solar panel so they don't need to be taken down to recharge. Many of these cameras can be installed almost anywhere, even on a tree trunk, for optimal perspective on a monitored area (see Figure 6-24). The camera sends alerts and video feeds through Wi-Fi to a smartphone app where the user can remotely monitor covered areas, such as entryways and parking areas. Most of today's cameras include some type of night vision capability, and many include two-way audio similar to a smart doorbell.

- **Smart refrigerator**—Also called a smart fridge, this device uses RFID or barcode tracking to detect items stored in the refrigerator, and it alerts users when essential items are running low or have expired. Many smart fridges also include interior cameras so you can see what's inside it from the store. Unfortunately, smart fridges are still much more expensive than so-called dumb fridges and are wracked with problems in terms of dropped services from the manufacturer or quickly outdated smart technology.

Now that you have a better understanding of the diversity of devices your wireless network might need to support, consider these factors when deciding where to install a SOHO WLAN's access point:

- **Distance**—Consider typical distances between the AP and its clients, and distance restrictions for the 802.11 standard your AP is using. If your home or small office spans three floors, and clients are evenly distributed among the floors, you might choose to situate the AP on the second floor.
- **Type and number of obstacles**—Consider the type and number of obstacles between the AP and its clients. If your three-story building is constructed like a bunker with massive concrete floors, you might consider installing a separate AP on each floor. If a building or office space is long and narrow, you might need two APs on the same floor—one at each end of the building. Remember from the *On the Job* story at the beginning of this module, sometimes obstacles can be more consequential than they at first appear.

Figure 6-24 This wireless security camera distinguishes between humans and animals to send more useful alerts and reduce false positives

- **Coverage**—Place the AP in a high spot, such as on a shelf or rack or in a drop ceiling.
- **Interference**—Make sure the AP is not close to potential sources of interference, including cordless phones, fluorescent lights, or microwave ovens.

Corporate Network

Larger wireless networks warrant a more systematic approach to access point placement. Before placing APs in every data room, it's wise to conduct a site survey. A **site survey** assesses client requirements, facility characteristics, and coverage areas; the resulting site survey report will help you determine an AP arrangement that will ensure reliable wireless connectivity within a given area.

Suppose you are the network manager for a large organization whose wireless clients are distributed over six floors of a building. On two floors, your organization takes up 2000 square feet of office space, but on the other four floors, your offices are limited to only 200 square feet. In addition, clients move between floors regularly, and the lobby-level floor has less wireless traffic than the others. Other building occupants are also running wireless networks. Let's see what activities might contribute to developing a thorough site survey report in this situation:

- Study building blueprints to identify potential obstacles, clarify the distances your network needs to span on each floor, and anticipate wireless demand from devices that tend to occupy each floor during the course of business.
- Consider whether any Wi-Fi access points will be used as a **wireless bridge** to connect two networks or two remote portions of one network, as shown in Figure 6-25. The throughput demands of a wireless bridge connected to another AP can be significantly higher than typical Wi-Fi clients.

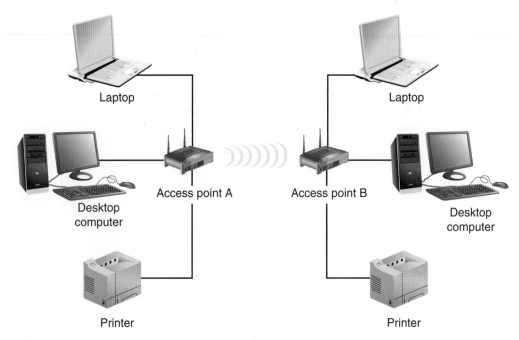

Figure 6-25 A wireless bridge provides remote wired access

- Determine whether certain floors require multiple APs. Visually inspecting the floors will also help determine coverage areas and best AP locations.
- Measure the signal coverage and strength from other WLANs to inform your decision about the optimal strength and frequency for your wireless signals.
- Test proposed access-point locations. In testing, a "dummy" AP is carried from location to location while a wireless client connects to it and measures its range and throughput. (Some companies sell software specially designed to conduct such testing.)
- Test wireless access from the farthest corners of your space. This testing will reveal unforeseen obstacles, such as EMI issued from lights or heavy machinery.
- Consider the materials used in objects that aren't always present in the environment, such as stocked inventory in a warehouse.
- Consider how the wireless portions of the network will integrate with the wired portions. Access points connect these two portions of your overall network.

The site survey can be completed more efficiently with the use of wireless survey tools such as site survey software. Popular examples include NetSpot, VisiWave, the iBwave Wi-Fi Suite, and inSSIDer by MetaGeek. After the initial setup, you can use these programs to monitor wireless network performance and possible interference or intrusion by other wireless signals in the area. Many of these programs, for example, offer a heat map feature that maps Wi-Fi signals and other noise in your location. An accurate heat map can also pinpoint gaps in Wi-Fi coverage, called dead zones, throughout the building to ensure that employee productivity isn't adversely affected by dropped Wi-Fi connections or unnecessarily slow connections.

After a site survey has identified and verified the optimal quantity and location of access points, you are ready to install them. Recall that to ensure seamless connectivity from one coverage area to another, all APs must belong to the same ESS and share an ESSID. Configuring APs, including assigning ESSIDs, is described in the next section. In preparation, Figure 6-26 shows an example of an enterprise wireless network.

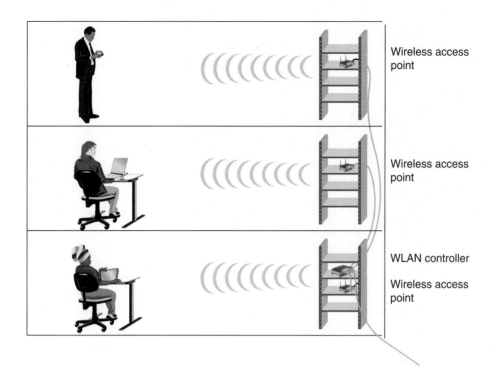

Figure 6-26   An enterprise-scale wireless network

Configure Wi-Fi Connectivity Devices

You have learned that access points provide wireless connectivity for mobile clients on an infrastructure WLAN. APs vary in which wireless standards they support, their antenna strength, and other features, such as support for voice signals or the latest security measures. You can buy a small AP or SOHO router for less than $50. More sophisticated or specialized APs cost much more—for example, those designed for outdoor use, as on city streets or at train platforms. However, as wireless networking has become commonplace, even the least expensive devices are increasingly sophisticated.

The setup process for a SOHO router is similar regardless of the manufacturer or model. The variables you will set during installation include the following:

- Administrator password (which is different than the Wi-Fi password used by Wi-Fi clients to associate with the AP)
- SSID (and determine whether it's broadcast)
- Security options such as type and credentials needed to associate with the AP
- Whether or not DHCP and related options are used, note that most network administrators do not configure their wireless access point as a DHCP server and, in fact, doing so when another DHCP server is already designated will cause addressing problems on the network

In the Hands-On Projects at the end of this module, you will practice installing and configuring a SOHO router. If something goes awry during your SOHO router configuration, you can force a reset of all the variables you changed. Wireless routers feature a reset button on their back panel. The following steps describe how to reset a SOHO router:

1. Disconnect all data cables and unplug the power cable.
2. Using the end of a paper clip, depress the reset button while you plug the power cable back in.
3. Continue holding down the button for at least 30 seconds (the required duration varies among manufacturers; check your router's documentation for the duration yours requires).
4. Release the button; at this point, the router's values should be reset to the manufacturer's defaults.

After successfully configuring your SOHO router, you are ready to introduce it to the network. In the case of a small office or home WLAN, this means using a patch cable to connect the device's WAN port to your modem's LAN port. Afterward, clients should be able to associate with the access point and gain Internet access. The following section describes how to configure clients to connect to your WLAN.

Configure Wi-Fi Clients

Wireless access configuration varies from one type of client to another. A gaming or media device will require a slightly different process than a laptop or tablet, and an IoT device such as a smart plug or a smart lock will differ yet again. The specific steps vary by device type and manufacturer. In general, as long as an AP is broadcasting its SSID, clients in its vicinity will detect it and offer the user the option to associate with it. If the AP uses encryption, you will need to provide the right credentials to associate with it successfully. Later in this module, you'll have the chance to change some of the security settings on a wireless Windows client.

In an enterprise environment, configuring clients for wireless access to the network can entail a much more involved, two-part process:

- **Onboarding**—Users or network technicians install a specific app, called an agent, on a user's device, whether the device is a smartphone, laptop, or tablet. This gives the device trusted access to certain portions of the network. Access to email services, file-sharing services, and certain network administrative features might all be controlled by the device's permission levels enabled by on-boarding that device. The agent might also scan the device for any needed OS or security updates, required security settings (such as timeouts or sign-in requirements), and any existing malware.
- **Offboarding**—The reverse procedure involves removing the agent. For security purposes, network administrators need a feature that allows them to do this remotely in case a device is lost or stolen. This feature, called a **remote wipe**, clears a device of important information, permissions, and apps without having physical access to the device. It might even allow you to completely disable the device, making any network or data access impossible.

Onboarding and offboarding policies are especially critical in a **BYOD (bring your own device)** environment where IT staff must ensure the safety of the network while allowing access by a wide range of employee-owned devices using network resources. These policies might specify a minimum version OS and a requirement to keep the OS updated, certain access restrictions such as minimum password length and an automatic timeout, and permissions to monitor device activity or to wipe data from the device with or without further notice.

Applying Concepts 6-1: Explore a Linux Wireless Interface

As with Windows operating systems, most Linux and UNIX clients provide a graphical interface for configuring their wireless interfaces. Because each version differs somewhat from the others, describing the steps required for each graphical interface is beyond the scope of this course. However, iwconfig, a command-line utility for viewing and setting wireless interface parameters, is common to nearly all versions of Linux and UNIX. The following steps, which can be performed on a Linux machine or a Linux VM, provide a basic primer for using the iwconfig command:

1. Make sure your wireless NIC is installed and that your Linux or UNIX workstation or host machine is within range of a working AP. You must also be logged into Linux or UNIX as root or a user with root-equivalent privileges. (Recall that the root user on UNIX or Linux systems is comparable to an administrative user on Windows systems.)
2. Open Terminal and enter `iwconfig`. The output should look similar to that shown in Figure 6-27.

```
% iwconfig

lo         no wireless extensions.


eth0       no wireless extensions.


eth1       IEEE 802.11abgn   ESSID:"CLASS_1"

           Mode:Managed   Frequency:2.412 GHz   Access Point: 00:0F:66:8E:19:89

           Bit Rate:54 Mb/s     Tx-Power:14 dBm

           Retry long limit:7   RTS thr:off     Fragment thr:off

           Power Management:on

           Link Quality=60/70   Signal level=-50 dBm

           Rx invalid nwid:0   Rx invalid crypt:0   Rx invalid frag:0

           Tx excessive retries:0   Invalid misc:747   Missed beacon:0
```

Figure 6-27   Output from the `iwconfig` command

3. Here's a brief description of the output:
   - `lo` indicates the loopback interface.
   - `eth0` represents an interface that is not wireless (that is, a wired NIC).
   - `eth1` represents the wireless interface; on your computer, the wireless NIC might have a different designation.
   - `iwconfig` also reveals characteristics of the AP's signal, including its frequency, power, and signal level.
4. For more detailed information about this command, enter **`man iwconfig`**. Using the `iwconfig` command, you can modify the SSID of the access point you choose to associate with, as well as many other variables. Some examples are detailed in Table 6-5. The syntax of the following examples assumes your workstation has labeled your wireless NIC eth1.

Table 6-5   Sample `iwconfig` commands

Command	Description
`iwconfig eth1 essid CLASS_1`	Instructs the wireless interface to associate with an AP whose SSID (or ESSID, as shown in this command) is CLASS_1.
`iwconfig eth1 mode Managed`	Instructs the wireless interface to operate in infrastructure mode (as opposed to ad hoc mode).
`iwconfig eth1 channel auto`	Instructs the wireless interface to automatically select the best channel for wireless data exchange.
`iwconfig eth1 freq 2.422G`	Instructs the wireless interface to communicate on the 2.422 GHz frequency.
`iwconfig eth1 key 6e225e3931`	Instructs the wireless interface to use the hexadecimal number 6e225e3931 as its key for secure authentication with the AP. (The number 6e225e3931 is only an example; on your network, you will choose your own key.)

In this and the previous section, you have learned how to configure wireless clients and access points. Optimized configurations help increase network efficiency as well as securing network resources from damage or intrusion. The following section explains some key points about securing a wireless network.

REMEMBER THIS...

- Describe IoT devices, including refrigerators, smart speakers, smart thermostats, and smart doorbells.
- Identify information generated by a site survey.
- Explain the primary points of onboarding and offboarding policies.

SELF-CHECK

5. Which device on the network will require the greatest throughput capacity?
   a. Smart speaker
   b. Wireless LAN controller
   c. Wireless bridge
   d. Smart thermostat
6. Which off-boarding policy can protect proprietary corporate information if a smartphone is lost?
   a. Remote wipe
   b. Trusted access
   c. OS update requirements
   d. Site survey

Check your answers at the end of this module.

You're Ready

You're now ready to complete **Project 6-1: Configure a SOHO Router**, or you can wait until you've finished reading this module.

You're Ready

You're now ready to complete **Project 6-2: Modify SOHO Router Wireless Settings**, or you can wait until you've finished reading this module.

WI-FI NETWORK SECURITY

✔ CERTIFICATION

2.4 Given a scenario, install and configure the appropriate wireless standards and technologies.

4.1 Explain common security concepts.

4.2 Compare and contrast common types of attacks.

4.3 Given a scenario, apply network hardening techniques.

5.4 Given a scenario, troubleshoot common wireless connectivity issues.

Average reading time: 26 minutes

As you have learned, most organizations use one or more of the 802.11 protocol standards on their WLANs. By default, the 802.11 standard does not by itself offer any security. The client only needs to know the access point's SSID, which many access points broadcast. Network administrators may prevent their access points from broadcasting the SSIDs, making them harder to detect. However, this does not provide true security. Two solutions to this problem are authentication and encryption:

- **Authentication**—Allows a wireless client to log on to the network, either by providing the correct password for the SSID or by providing user credentials that might be processed by an authentication server. The authentication process can be somewhat strengthened with **MAC filtering**, or MAC address filtering, which prevents the AP from authenticating any device whose MAC address is not listed by the network administrator. (MAC filtering can also be instituted on a switch.) But it can be time consuming to maintain a current list of all approved MAC addresses, and, as you've seen, MAC addresses are easily impersonated.
- **Encryption algorithms**—Scramble data transmitted over the airwaves into a format that cannot easily be interpreted if the signal is intercepted. The purpose of encryption is to keep information private. Many forms of wireless encryption exist, with some being more secure than others.

Let's explore some of the available techniques for securing wireless networks with authentication and encryption, beginning with an outdated technology called WEP.

Legacy Networking: WEP (Wired Equivalent Privacy)

For some measure of security, 802.11 allows for optional encryption using the **WEP (Wired Equivalent Privacy)** standard. In fact, WEP offered two forms of authentication, neither of which is secure:

- **OSA (Open System Authentication)**—No key is used at all. The wireless access client, knowing only the access point's SSID, requests authentication. The AP generates a single-use code for that session only, and the computer accepts the code. However, no encrypted data can be sent over this temporary connection, and any device can be authenticated. In fact, no real authentication occurs.
- **SKA (Shared Key Authentication)**—All wireless access clients use the same key, which can then be used to encrypt transmissions. When configuring WEP, you establish a character string that is required to associate with the access point, also known as the network key. The user must provide the correct key before the client can gain access to the network via the access point. The network key can be saved as part of the client's wireless connection's properties. WEP uses the same key both to authenticate network clients and to encrypt data in transit. However, the key can be cracked, compromising the security of all clients on the network.

The first implementation of WEP allowed for 64-bit network keys, and current versions of WEP allow for more secure 128-bit or even 256-bit network keys. However, one of the most significant disadvantages of WEP is that it uses a shared encryption key for all clients and the key might never change. WEP's use of the shared key for authenticating all users and for encrypting data makes it more susceptible to discovery than a dynamically generated, random, or single-use key. Even 128-bit network keys can be cracked in a matter of minutes. Moreover, WEP does not offer end-to-end data transmission security.

WEP was replaced with a quick-fix improvement called WPA when IEEE devised a new wireless security standard called 802.11i that included the subset standard WPA. The following sections explore the progressive improvements made to the 802.11i standard, eventually resulting in the development of the more secure and reliable WPA2.

WPA (Wi-Fi Protected Access)

A significant disadvantage to WEP is that it uses the same network key for all clients and the key is static, which means it won't change without manual intervention. Due to this inherent insecurity, a replacement security technology was developed, called **WPA (Wi-Fi Protected Access)**, which dynamically assigns every transmission its own key. 802.11i incorporates an encryption key generation and management scheme known as **TKIP (Temporal Key Integrity Protocol)**, pronounced *tee-kip*, to improve security for legacy WEP-based devices. TKIP accomplished three significant improvements:

- **Message integrity**—Uses a message integrity code, called Michael, that ensures incoming packets are, in fact, coming from their declared source. This is also called packet authentication.
- **Key distribution**—Assigns every transmission its own key.
- **Encryption**—Includes encryption originally provided by **RC4 (Rivest Cipher 4)**, a now insecure encryption cipher that is still widely used.

In reality, TKIP was a quick fix, designed more as an integrity check for WEP transmissions than as a sophisticated encryption protocol. WPA's TKIP uses the same encryption mechanism as WEP but with improved algorithms to wrap the older WEP transmissions in a more securely encrypted transmission. However, you'll still find modern wireless network devices offering TKIP to provide compatibility with older wireless clients.

WPA2 (Wi-Fi Protected Access, Version 2)

The data confidentiality methods used in WPA were replaced by stronger technologies for the updated version, **WPA2**, which can be enabled on most consumer-grade APs today. **CCMP**, which is short for **Counter Mode with CBC (Cipher Block Chaining) MAC (Message Authentication Code) Protocol**, improves wireless security for newer devices that can use WPA2. Acronyms within acronyms are only the beginning of what makes this protocol so interesting. Whereas TKIP was meant to be backward-compatible as much as possible, CCMP is more future-focused. CCMP helps ensure data confidentiality with both encryption and packet authentication by providing the following:

<table>
<tr>
<td>

NOTE 6-4

Two similar types of cipher algorithms are stream ciphers and block ciphers. The essential difference is that stream ciphers encrypt one byte (or possibly one bit) at a time, while block ciphers encrypt much larger chunks, or blocks, in each calculation.

</td>
<td>

- **Message integrity**—CCMP includes CBC-MAC, which ensures incoming packets are, in fact, coming from their declared source, and does so using the block cipher algorithm AES, described next.
- **Encryption**—CCMP also uses **AES (Advanced Encryption Standard)**, which provides faster and more secure encryption than TKIP for wireless transmissions. AES relies on a more sophisticated family of ciphers along with multiple stages of data transformation.

The Wi-Fi Alliance (*wi-fi.org*) released the next iteration, WPA3, in 2018 and has begun to certify WPA3 devices. Some touted features of the new standard include disallowing legacy protocols, ability of users to choose their own passwords, more advanced encryption and authentication methods, and better protection of data in

</td>
</tr>
</table>

transit. In particular, WPA3's new handshake design was intended to close a security vulnerability in WPA2's hand-shake that leaves the hash of the password vulnerable during the initial association process. However, researchers are already identifying flaws in the design and security of WPA3 and believe that another round of security enhancements will be necessary.

Personal and Enterprise

On many wireless routers and access points, you might have noticed options for WPA-Personal and WPA-Enterprise, or WPA2-Personal and WPA2-Enterprise. The Personal versions of WPA and WPA2 are sometimes referred to as WPA-PSK or WPA2-PSK, where **PSK** stands for **Pre-Shared Key**. This is the common configuration on home wireless networks in which you need to enter a passphrase for your device to authenticate to the network. The passphrase and the SSID characters are then used to calculate a unique encryption key for each device.

The most secure Wi-Fi communication is made possible by combining a RADIUS authentication server with WPA or WPA2, known as WPA-Enterprise or WPA2-Enterprise, respectively. While you'll learn more about RADIUS later, for now, understand that **RADIUS (Remote Authentication Dial-In User Service)** is an open source authentication and authorization service. A RADIUS server can be used to offer a central authentication point for wireless, mobile, and remote users. In the context of Wi-Fi, a RADIUS server is used in cooperation with an authentication mechanism called EAP.

EAP (Extensible Authentication Protocol) differs from other authentication protocols in that it only provides the framework for authenticating clients and servers. It does not perform encryption or authentication on its own. Instead, it works with other encryption and authentication schemes to verify the credentials of users and devices. One of EAP's advantages is its flexibility. It is supported by nearly all modern operating systems and can be used with many different authentication methods. For example, although the typical network authentication involves a user ID and password, EAP also works with biometric methods, such as retina or hand-scanning.

EAP functions alongside RADIUS by organizing communications with the network client devices, while RADIUS handles the actual authentication on the server. In this case, EAP messages are encapsulated inside RADIUS messages between the network device, such as a switch or access point, and the RADIUS server. Figure 6-28 shows how EAP and RADIUS handle different portions of the interaction.

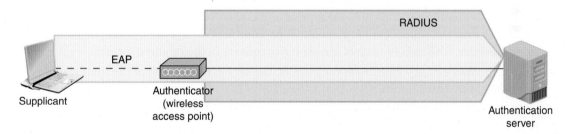

Figure 6-28   EAP messages are encapsulated in RADIUS messages

The three main EAP entities, as shown in Figure 6-28, are the following:

- **Supplicant**—The device requesting authentication, such as a smartphone or laptop
- **Authenticator**—The network device that initiates the authentication process, such as a wireless access point
- **Authentication server**—The server that performs the authentication

The conversation between these entities looks something like the diagram shown in Figure 6-29. The steps are described next:

Step 0:   The wireless device associates with the access point, usually with WPA2. The process begins with Step 0 here because association is an essential precursor to the authentication process, but it's not part of that process.

Step 1:   The supplicant requests authentication, and the authenticator initiates the authentication process by asking a newly connected supplicant to verify itself.

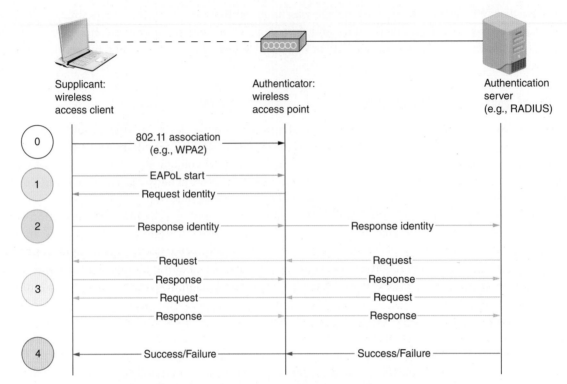

Figure 6-29 If a RADIUS server is used here, EAP communications between the authenticator and the RADIUS server are encapsulated in RADIUS messages

Step 2: After the supplicant responds, the authenticator forwards that information to the authentication server, such as a RADIUS server.

Step 3: The server usually sends more than one request in response. In its first request, it asks the supplicant's identity and indicates the type of authentication to use. In subsequent requests, the server asks the supplicant for authentication information to prove the supplicant's identity. The supplicant responds to each of the server's requests in the required format.

Step 4: If the responses match what the server expects, the server authenticates the supplicant. Otherwise, authentication fails.

EAP is adaptable to new technology. It was originally designed to work only on point-to-point connections, usually on a WAN. However, it was adapted to work on both wired and wireless LANs in the **802.1X** standard, dubbed **EAPoL (EAP over LAN)**. In this case, EAP is carried by Ethernet messages. To accomplish this, 802.1X allows only EAPoL traffic over any switch or AP port connected to a wired or wireless client until that client has authenticated with the authentication server. This is called PNAC (port-based network access control), or sometimes port-based authentication. Today, 802.1X is primarily used on wireless LANs.

Several versions and adaptations of EAP exist. Some of the most common versions include the following:

- **EAP-TLS**—Similar to how HTTPS uses SSL/TLS encryption to secure HTTP transmissions, EAP-TLS uses TLS encryption to protect communications. EAP-TLS also uses PKI (public-key infrastructure) certificates to exchange public keys and authenticate both the supplicant and the server through mutual authentication. While these certificates can be a challenge to set up, the resulting authentication strength is often worth the trade-off in convenience. Figure 6-30 shows the addition of a CA (Certificate Authority) to the network to help manage the certificates needed by EAP-TLS.

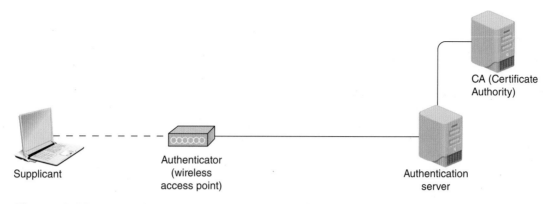

Figure 6-30   EAP-TLS requires a Certificate Authority

- **PEAP (Protected EAP)**—While EAP-TLS is certificate-based, PEAP and EAP-FAST are tunnel-based. PEAP (Protected EAP) creates an encrypted TLS tunnel between the supplicant and the server before proceeding with the usual EAP process. As shown in Figure 6-31, PEAP is called the outer method. Then another form of EAP is used for the inner method, which is the process that occurs inside the protected tunnel. The most common inner method is EAP-MSCHAPv2, which runs a session inside the tunnel, perhaps to a RADIUS server and beyond to Active Directory.

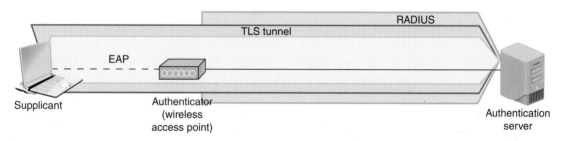

Figure 6-31   PEAP creates an encrypted TLS tunnel

- **EAP-FAST (EAP-Flexible Authentication via Secure Tunneling)**—Also a form of tunneled EAP, this technology was developed by Cisco and works similarly to PEAP, except faster. The most important difference with EAP-FAST is that it uses PACs (Protected Access Credentials), which are somewhat similar to cookies that websites store on a user's computer to track their activities. A PAC is stored on the supplicant device for speedier establishment of the TLS tunnel in future sessions.

Other Security Configurations

Some additional security options you might want to enable on your wireless network include the following:

- **AP and antenna placement**—It might seem like a simple thing but it's important to think about where you place your AP in your home or business area. Placing the AP near an outside wall might result in a weak signal on the far side of your building but leave a strong signal vulnerable to attack from someone parked nearby. Positioning the AP in the center of its intended range increases the strength of the signal for approved users while reducing the likelihood that anyone outside of that area can get a strong enough signal to connect to the network. Also, some APs have antennas that can be positioned to optimize signal reach. Consider what antenna placement will give the best signal where you want it and reduce the strength of the signal outside your building or other intended range. Similarly, experiment with various power levels to determine the needed transmission power to reach your intended range while not overly extending your range outside the area you manage.

- **Geofencing**—This more sophisticated security technique detects a Wi-Fi client's geographical position and activates resources or access according to that location. For example, a shopping mall or store might use geofencing to offer customers Internet access and targeted marketing information (such as coupons) while not making these resources available to people outside a defined area. Deploying a mesh network of APs makes it possible to track a Wi-Fi client device's physical movement throughout the network.

- **Guest network**—Many establishments—and homeowners, for that matter—create an isolated guest network through their Wi-Fi router/access point. The guest network has a separate SSID and passphrase and can be managed with different rules or time restrictions. This is a smart security precaution, as it gives guests access to Internet service through an open network without opening the doors to the entire LAN on that router. Parents, also, might want to give their children use of an SSID with more limited network access to enforce household rules regarding Internet use.

- **Wireless client isolation**—This technique is similar to a guest network but simpler. Wireless client isolation allows a wireless client onto the network but imposes firewall rules to restrict that client's ability to communicate with only the default gateway, not other devices on the network. Like with a guest network, wireless clients are able to communicate with the Internet but have no access to other network resources.

- **Captive portal**—If you do provide a guest network, either at home or at a business, be sure to set up a captive portal. This is the first page a new client sees in the browser when connecting to the guest network, and it usually requires the user to agree to a set of terms and conditions before gaining further access to the guest network. The captive portal should remind users of the following details:
  - They are connecting to a network that does not provide user authentication or data encryption. This means data is not secure when transmitted over this connection.
  - They should be careful about what data they transmit, even over email, while using the guest network.
  - They should take extra care to avoid engaging in any illegal activity through the network connection, as that activity could be traced back to your public IP address.

NOTE 6-5

Captive portals can cause issues of their own. For example, if you've configured custom DNS servers for your network, you might find that clients trying to associate with your network will sometimes get stuck on the captive portal page or not be able to pull it up at all. Firewalls or pop-up blockers in the browser can block the captive portal, and browsers configured with autofill options might also fail to properly load a captive portal page. In some cases, the browser cannot successfully open the captive portal page because the browser was first trying to reach a secure website using HTTPS, and HTTPS doesn't cooperate with the interference of the captive portal. You can get around this limitation by having the wireless client first navigate to a nonsecure web page, such as *neverssl.com*, and that can trigger the captive portal to open successfully.

- **IoT access considerations**—Think about how best to give network access to your IoT devices. Hardening your IoT network starts with changing default device names, usernames, and passwords for those devices, creating strong passwords, and using the strongest encryption settings the devices offer. Where possible, use two-factor authentication so you not only provide a password to access device settings, but you also get a one-time code sent to your smartphone for authentication. Many cybersecurity experts recommend creating an entirely separate Wi-Fi network for all IoT devices, such as a guest network (and use a strong password on the guest network). Disable features you're not using, and update software and firmware when those updates become available. Finally, don't access your IoT software and devices when using a public network, such as at a coffee shop.

Security Threats to Wi-Fi Networks

Wireless transmissions are particularly susceptible to eavesdropping. Several additional security threats to wireless networks are discussed in the following list:

- **War driving**—A hacker searches for unprotected wireless networks by driving around with a laptop or smartphone configured to receive and capture wireless data transmissions. (The term is derived from the term *war dialing*, which is a similar tactic involving old, dial-up modems.) War driving is surprisingly effective for obtaining private information. Years ago, the hacker community publicized the vulnerabilities of a well-known store chain, which were discovered while war driving. The retailer used wireless cash registers to help customers make purchases when the regular, wired cash registers were busy. However, the wireless cash registers transmitted purchase information, including credit card numbers and customer names, to network APs in cleartext (in other words, unencrypted). By chance, a person in the parking lot who was running a protocol analyzer program on his laptop obtained several credit card numbers in a very short time. The person alerted the retailer to the security risk (rather than exploiting the information he gathered). Needless to say, after the retailer discovered its error, it abandoned the use of wireless cash registers until a thorough evaluation of its data security could be conducted.

- **War chalking**—Once hackers discover vulnerable access points, they make this information public by drawing symbols with chalk on the sidewalk or a wall within range of a wireless network. The symbols, patterned after marks that hobos devised to indicate hospitable places for food or rest, indicate the access point's SSID and whether it's secured. Alternatively, many websites offer maps of these open networks, as reported by war drivers.

- **Evil twin**—Clients running Linux, macOS, or a modern version of Windows will first attempt to associate with a known access point. This feature can result in network devices connecting to rogue access points, or access points offering a connection to the Internet without the authorization of the area's network administrator. One type of rogue access point, an evil twin, can be used to trick a device into connecting to the wrong network by broadcasting the same SSID as the authorized network or another SSID that appears just as legitimate to the user. Suppose another user brings their own AP to a café and its signal is twice as strong as the café's AP. Your laptop will automatically recognize the other user's stronger AP as the best option. If the user has configured their AP with the same SSID as the café's, and if you've configured your laptop to trust that SSID, your laptop might complete association to this evil twin AP without your knowledge. The person controlling the evil twin could then steal your data or gain access to another network that trusts your system. Note that a user can create a rogue access point inadvertently, too—for example, by bringing an AP to work, using software to turn a workstation into an AP, or creating a hotspot with a smartphone. As a network technician, you should check regularly for evil twins or other rogue access points within your network's geographical area. Especially be on the lookout for access points that show a stronger signal than your corporate AP because Windows lists SSIDs by signal strength, and users are accustomed to selecting the SSID at the top of the list.

- **WPA attack**—These attacks, also called WPA cracking, involve an interception of the network keys communicated between clients and access points.

- **WPS attack**—WPS (Wi-Fi Protected Setup) is a user-friendly—but not very secure—security setting available on some consumer-grade APs. Part of the security involves requiring a PIN (personal identification number) to access the AP's settings or to associate a new device with the network. The problem is that the PIN can be easily cracked through a brute force attack, which means simply trying numerous possible character combinations to find the correct combination. This gives the attacker access to the network's WPA2 key. The PIN feature in WPS should be disabled if possible.

⚠ CAUTION

Not all wireless threats are related to Wi-Fi. The prevalence of RFID chips in credit cards has contributed to the upsurge of a type of fraud called skimming. The culprit installs a card reader, or skimmer, on a payment terminal, such as a gas pump or ATM. The skimmer collects data stored on the magnetic strips or on RFID chips in cards used at that terminal. Physical contact is required to collect data from a magnetic strip, but the RFID chip can transmit data to a skimmer several inches away. The criminal returns later to collect the device along with the stolen data it has accumulated.

Always examine a payment terminal for signs of tampering. If it looks different than nearby terminals, a skimmer might be cleverly disguised right in front of you, such as the one shown in Figure 6-32. The skimmer is designed to detach easily so the thief can retrieve it quickly, so pull on the payment terminal a little to see if anything budges. Consider googling for images of credit card skimmers, ATM skimmers, and gas pump skimmers. The more familiar you are with what to look for, the safer you'll be. If you see something suspicious, call the police and don't use that terminal.

Skimmer

Figure 6-32 Skimmers on payment terminals can be surprisingly difficult to spot

In a similar scam, thieves steal information from your credit card while it sits snugly in your wallet. A thief can swipe an RFID reader near the victim's pocket or bag and collect information from enclosed RFID credit cards, which is called electronic pickpocketing. Many manufacturers sell RFID-blocking wallets of varying quality and effectiveness. You can also wrap your wallet or cards in a layer of aluminum foil. In all circumstances, pay close attention to the people who stand near you in checkout lines, shopping areas, restaurants, and other public spaces.

Most newer credit cards contain a different kind of chip called an EMV (Europay, Mastercard, and Visa) chip that generates a unique transaction number each time it's activated. However, some EMV credit cards also include RFID technology for contactless payments, which can still transmit your credit card information to a snooping thief.

Applying Concepts 6-2: Examine Wireless Security Settings

Now that you understand some of the security options available for a wireless network connection, let's explore how to check the current settings on your AP and change them if necessary. Using a Windows 10 computer that is connected to a local network via Wi-Fi, complete the following steps:

1. Open the Network and Sharing Center. Under *View your active networks*, click the Wi-Fi connection and then click **Wireless Properties**.
2. In the Wireless Network Properties dialog box, look for the following information on both the Connection and the Security tabs.
   a. What are the network's Name and SSID?
   b. Is the connection configured to connect automatically when the wireless network is in range?
   c. What are the network's Security and Encryption types?

REMEMBER THIS...

- Compare Wi-Fi encryption standards: WPA/WPA2 Personal and WPA/WPA2 Enterprise.
- Explain the roles of AES and TKIP in Wi-Fi encryption.
- Describe Wi-Fi authentication technologies: RADIUS, EAP, and 802.1X.
- Apply Wi-Fi security practices: MAC filtering, antenna placement, power levels, guest network isolation, geofencing, and captive portals.

SELF-CHECK

7. Which Wi-Fi encryption standard was designed to use AES encryption?
   a. WPA
   b. WPA2
   c. WEP
   d. WEP2

8. Which standard adapted EAP to WLANs?
   a. 802.11g
   b. 802.11i
   c. 802.1X
   d. 802.3

Check your answers at the end of this module.

You're Ready

You're now ready to complete **Project 6-3: Optimize Wireless Security on a SOHO Router**, or you can wait until you've finished reading this module.

TROUBLESHOOTING WI-FI NETWORKS

✓ CERTIFICATION

5.2 Given a scenario, troubleshoot common cable connectivity issues and select the appropriate tools.

5.3 Given a scenario, use the appropriate network software tools and commands.

5.4 Given a scenario, troubleshoot common wireless connectivity issues.

Average reading time: 22 minutes

You've already learned about several tools used to test copper and fiber-optic cables in Ethernet networks. Cable continuity and performance testers, of course, will tell you nothing about the wireless connections, nodes, or access points on a network. For that, you need tools that contain wireless NICs and run wireless protocols. As you learned earlier in the module, you can start gathering information about a wireless environment by viewing the wireless network connection properties on your workstation. However, this tells you only a little about your wireless environment—and it only applies to one workstation. To get the full picture of your wireless environment, you need to use more advanced wireless network tools, as described in the following section.

Wi-Fi Network Tools

Many applications can scan for wireless signals over a certain geographical range and discover all the access points and wireless nodes transmitting in the area. This is useful for determining whether an access point is functioning properly, whether it is positioned correctly so that all the nodes it serves are within its range, whether nodes and access points are communicating over the proper channels within a frequency band, and whether wireless signals are present that shouldn't be. Here are two tools you need in your toolkit:

- **Spectrum analyzer**—A device that can assess the quality of a wireless signal by scanning a band of frequencies for signals and noise. A spectrum analysis is useful, for example, to ascertain where interference is greatest.
- **Wi-Fi analyzer**—Software that can evaluate Wi-Fi network availability as well as help optimize Wi-Fi signal settings or help identify Wi-Fi security threats. Identifying the wireless channels being used nearby helps you optimize wireless channel utilization in your vicinity.

Software tools that can perform wireless network assessment are often available for free and might be provided by the access point's manufacturer. Following is a list of specific capabilities common to wireless network testing tools:

- Identify transmitting APs, nodes, and the channels over which they are communicating
- Measure signal strength from and determine the range of an AP
- Indicate the effects of attenuation, signal loss, and noise
- Interpret signal strength information to rate potential AP locations
- Ensure proper association and reassociation when moving between APs
- Capture and interpret traffic exchanged between APs and nodes
- Measure throughput and assess data transmission errors
- Analyze the characteristics of each channel within a frequency band to indicate the clearest channels

A Wi-Fi analyzer can help you identify the channels being used by area wireless networks. Wireless networks perform best when using channels not used by nearby networks. For this reason, it's best to program the network for channels at the beginning, center, and end of the channel bandwidth. For example, recall that 2.4 GHz-band devices offer up to 14 channels, although most only offer 11 channels in the United States. In the United States, then, neighboring Wi-Fi networks typically use channels 1, 6, and 11 to minimize overlap. When all 14 channels are available, such as in many parts of Europe, the channel spread might still be 1-6-11 to maximize compatibility with devices from other areas of the world, or it might instead be 1-5-9-13 to maximize use of the available bandwidth.

If your wireless network is programmed for the same channel as your neighbor's wireless network, you will get better performance by changing your network's channel to part of the band not currently in use in your vicinity. In reality, many home routers are configured to automatically seek the least crowded channel.

Avoid Pitfalls

NOTE 6-6

In a project at the end of this module, you'll have the opportunity to practice using a Wi-Fi analyzer app on your smartphone.

You might have had the frustrating experience of not being able to log on to a network, even though you were sure you'd typed in your username and password correctly. Maybe it turned out that your Caps Lock key was on, changing your case-sensitive password. Or maybe you were trying to log on to the wrong server. On every type of network, many variables must be accurately set on clients, servers, and connectivity devices for communication to succeed. Wireless networks add a few more variables. Following are some wireless configuration pitfalls to avoid, according to the problem you're facing.

No Connection

When you can't get the Wi-Fi client to connect to the AP at all, consider the following common issues:

- **Wrong SSID**—Your wireless client must select the correct SSID. As you have learned, you may instruct clients to search for any available access point (or clients might be configured to do this by default). However, if the access point does not broadcast its SSID, or if your workstation is not configured to look for access points, you will have to enter the SSID during client configuration. Also, bear in mind that SSIDs are case sensitive. That is, *MYHOUSE* does not equal *MyHouse*.

- **Encryption protocol mismatch**—Your wireless client must be able to use and must be configured to allow the same encryption protocols that your access point offers. Most of the time, this is negotiated automatically between the AP and the client. To configure the security type manually on a Windows 10 client, open the Network and Sharing Center, click Change adapter settings, right-click the active connection and click Status, and then open the connection's Properties dialog box. Click the Security tab to change the security type, encryption type, or network security key, as shown in Figure 6-33.

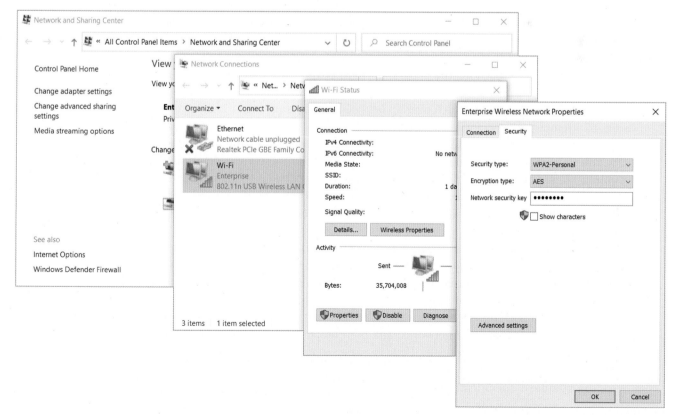

Figure 6-33   Adjust a network connection's security settings

- **Incorrect passphrase**—Similarly, you must use a security key, or passphrase, that matches that of the access point. If incorrect, your client cannot authenticate with the access point.
- **Static channel utilization**—You have learned that the access point establishes the channel and frequency over which it will communicate with clients. Clients, then, automatically sense the correct channel and frequency. However, if you have instructed your client to use only a channel or frequency different from the one your access point uses, association will fail to occur.
- **Mismatched RF band**—Some wireless devices are designed to use only one Wi-Fi band. For example, when purchasing wireless security cameras, these devices might be limited to work only in the 2.4 GHz band. In that case, you'll need an AP that offers a Wi-Fi standard on that band.
- **Mismatched standards (802.11 b/a/g/n/ac/ax)**—If your access point is set to communicate only via 802.11ac, even if the documentation says it supports 802.11n and 802.11ac, clients must also follow the 802.11ac standard. Clients might also be able to detect and match the correct type of 802.11 standard. However, if they are configured to follow only one standard, they won't find an access point broadcasting via a different standard.
- **Long AP association time**—Sometimes a Wi-Fi client gets stuck waiting for the association process to complete. While this problem can be caused by many factors (for example, confirm the passphrase is correct), some of the most common issues are users trying to connect at the edge of the network's covered range or moving throughout the network where the device must frequently reassociate with a nearby AP. A client trying to connect with a Wi-Fi network must be able to receive a strong enough signal from the AP in order to complete the association process because, if packets are missed due to a weak signal, the association will not complete.

Slow Connections

When dealing with slow Wi-Fi connections, consider the following common issues:

- **Insufficient wireless coverage**—On a network, many factors can cause data errors and a resulting decrease in performance. Be sure to check the recommended geographic range for your AP, and keep clients well within that distance. If a client is too far from an AP or if there are too many obstacles between the two nodes, communication might occur, but data errors become more probable and slow down communication. You can confirm whether this is the problem by checking the RSSI level at the client's location. Also remember to place your AP in a high spot for best signal transmission to clients.
- **RF attenuation/signal loss**—Each access point's power level, or the strength of the signal the access point emits, should be optimized for the geographic area covered by that AP. Power levels that are too low will result in dropped signals as clients roam to the peripheral areas of the AP's range. However, maxed out power levels will result in too much overlap between AP coverage areas, causing clients from other coverage areas to attempt to connect with APs that are farther away but transmitting the stronger signal. Begin with a 50 percent power setting, and make incremental changes as needed to optimize the amount of overlap between APs. You can use site survey information and a Wi-Fi analyzer to help you determine where dead spots might require a boost in transmission power or perhaps a range extender to fill in those areas with a strong signal. Also keep in mind that even if a client can receive a signal from a high-powered AP installed on the other end of the building, the return signal from the client might not be reliably strong enough to reach the AP, which is called a near–far effect.
- **Interference**—If intermittent and difficult-to-diagnose wireless communication errors occur, interference might be the culprit. Check for sources of EMI, such as fluorescent lights, heavy machinery, cordless phones, and microwaves in the data transmission path.
- **Channel overlap**—Using channels or frequencies that are too close to each other on the frequency spectrum can interfere with each other's transmissions. You can use a Wi-Fi analyzer to determine which channels are being used by nearby wireless networks, and then utilize a less crowded channel. Most home routers are programmed to do this automatically. However, keep in mind that you might need to switch bands for your device to find a relatively clear channel.
- **Wireless standard specifications**—Each Wi-Fi standard (802.11 b/a/g/n/ac/ax) is restrained by specific throughput, speed, and distance limitations. Choosing the correct standard for a specific network's needs can make a significant difference in the effectiveness of the signal. For example, a small home network might

function fine with an older Wi-Fi standard if the homeowner only uses a few devices for checking email or surfing the web. However, consider a business that relies on VoIP for communicating with customers all day long, a homeowner who frequently streams movies online or spends a lot of time gaming, or a large warehouse where devices must communicate with the network from anywhere within the building. In all these cases, a newer Wi-Fi standard will offer more appropriate throughput rates and more reliable coverage distances.

- **Simultaneous wired and wireless connections**—A workstation is designed to transmit either via a wired or a wireless connection, but not both at the same time. When troubleshooting connection issues, consider whether the computer is making conflicting attempts to communicate with the network through both types of connections. You can resolve the issue by disabling the Wi-Fi adapter or by unplugging the Ethernet cable.

- **Problems with firmware updates**—Updates to a NIC or access point's firmware can help patch vulnerabilities and increase functionality. The flip side of this issue, however, is that updates should be tested before being rolled out system wide.

- **Incorrect antenna type**—You might think that omnidirectional antennas would nearly always be the best choice when setting up Wi-Fi coverage. The idea is to place the AP in the center of its coverage area and then send the signal out in all directions. However, in many situations, installing unidirectional antennas instead will enhance a signal's availability, directing the signal right where you need it while not wasting a signal in areas where you don't. For example, suppose a company installs an omnidirectional antenna near a factory's 30-foot-high ceiling. Because the antenna's signal is broadcast in all directions from its location, distributing its signal strength in a spherical shape, the best possible signal would only be available to workers who could walk on the ceiling—obviously, that's not a viable situation. To be useful, the signal needs to be directed down to the floor. A unidirectional antenna, in this case, can be positioned up high and pointed down to create a dome-shaped coverage that spreads out as it nears the plant floor, as shown in Figure 6-34.

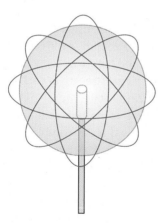

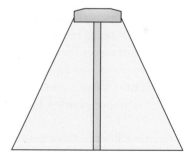

An omnidirectional antenna placed high near a ceiling broadcasts a signal in all directions, but the signal is mostly inaccessible to workers on the floor

A unidirectional antenna can be positioned near the ceiling, but aimed at the floor, giving workers substantial access to its signal

Figure 6-34   A unidirectional antenna provides more efficient signal coverage in this situation

- **Mismatched antenna polarization**—Radio waves radiating from an antenna emanate from the antenna either along the antenna's vertical axis or along its horizontal axis. This is called the antenna's polarization, and it's important to know so you can position the antenna for maximum coverage through the intended range. Most Wi-Fi antennas are vertically polarized, meaning the antenna should point straight up to get the best coverage. However, some devices with multiple antennas might be intended to have antennas pointing in different directions, such as one diagonally to the left, another diagonally to the right, and a center antenna pointing straight up. But this is not always the case when a home router has multiple antennas—sometimes all the antennas should be pointed straight up. It's important to check manufacturer recommendations for antenna orientation to optimize the signal's reach.

NOTE 6-7

Consider that Wi-Fi clients also have antennas with polarization limitations. For example, in most laptops, the Wi-Fi antenna is wrapped around the screen just inside the outer edge of the top lid. If you tip the laptop on its side, or if the laptop's lid is oriented at an unusual angle, you'll likely experience significantly decreased performance on its Wi-Fi connection. The better aligned the AP's and client's antennas are to each other, the better quality connection.

- **Client saturation or overcapacity**—APs vary in the number of device connections they can handle at any given time. A SOHO network's AP might take 10–15 devices before becoming overwhelmed, whereas a high-powered, commercial AP can handle a much larger client load without exceeding its bandwidth saturation limitations. The Wi-Fi 5 and Wi-Fi 6 standards also provide the advantage of expanding available bandwidth while also managing that bandwidth more efficiently to support more clients. When shopping for a new AP, keep in mind that the actual, effective capacity in the real world will be significantly less than the AP's advertised capacity.
- **Client disassociation issues**—If your Wi-Fi client device is frequently disassociating from the AP, confirm the AP is not using an overly crowded Wi-Fi channel and consider using a narrower channel (such as 20 MHz or 40 MHz) rather than a larger, bonded channel. Also check for interference in the area that could be degrading the signal and breaking the communication between AP and client.

Applying Concepts 6-3: Snail-Speed Wi-Fi

Your company recently rented new office space across town to make room for expansion in the Accounting Department, and part of your responsibility with the new acquisition was to install three new 802.11ac APs. You carefully planned and then installed each AP throughout the building to optimize wireless coverage and minimize dead zones. Each AP overlaps somewhat with one or both the other APs, and they're all set with the same ESSID and channel so clients can roam freely. You've checked and double-checked the signal strength at each workstation and in all common work areas, such as meeting rooms, lobby, and even the lunchroom.

You completed the job just before the weekend, at the same time as the 19 accounting employees finished setting up their file cabinets and reception area furniture. Some of your fellow IT technicians completed workstation setup that same day; most of the workstations are connected to the network via Wi-Fi due to restrictions imposed by your company's contract with the property owner. Today, Monday, the accounting personnel report for work at the new building.

At first, the new remote office's network seems to be working fine. The local network is communicating well with the home office's network, and everyone has access to all the files they need on the file servers. As everyone gets settled in for the day and starts their Monday duties, however, the network slows to a snail's pace. It's not long before you start to get complaints about emails being delayed, files not being accessible, and print jobs to network printers getting lost. You make a beeline across town to figure out what's wrong.

During your investigation, you find that all the hosts on the local network are accessible. However, you find it odd that even though your ping tests are usually successful, sometimes they aren't. You know the APs are all new devices, and you double-check their configurations to try to determine a common source for all the problems you've noted. Here's a summary of the results you've gathered:

- All three APs are active and communicating successfully with your laptop.
- All three APs are configured with identical ESSIDs and other settings.
- For good measure, you also walk around the office space with your wireless analyzer to confirm again there are no significant dead zones or interference.

Why are wireless transmissions being lost in transit? Below are several possible resolutions. Select the best one and explain your reasoning:

- **a.** One of the APs is faulty and not processing transmissions. It should be removed and replaced.
- **b.** The NICs in the employees' workstations were damaged during the move. Probably several just need to be reseated while some might need to be replaced.

c. The increased interference from people moving around in the office space is interfering with the Wi-Fi signals. Power levels on the APs needs to be increased.

d. The APs should not have the same ESSID. Rename each AP so their ESSIDs don't match.

e. Three APs are insufficient for the wireless load of the Accounting Department. More APs should be added.

f. The APs are all part of the same LAN and should be separated into isolated LANs.

g. The workstation computers are programmed to search for and connect with the wrong ESSID, or the network keys are entered wrong. Every workstation's wireless interface settings should be checked.

h. The APs are all programmed to use the same channel. They should be programmed for different channels.

REMEMBER THIS...

- Use a spectrum analyzer or Wi-Fi analyzer to evaluate a Wi-Fi network's signals.
- Explain the specifications and limitations of various Wi-Fi standards.
- Consider antennas, channels, AP settings, and information from a site survey in troubleshooting Wi-Fi problems.
- Describe how to diagnose and resolve common Wi-Fi issues, such as interference, channel overlap, SSID and passphrase problems, encryption protocol mismatch, insufficient wireless coverage, or client disassociation issues.

SELF-CHECK

9. Which device will let you determine all frequencies within a scanned range that are present in a specific environment, not just Wi-Fi?

   a. Wi-Fi analyzer

   b. Captive portal

   c. Wireless LAN controller

   d. Spectrum analyzer

10. Which problem would a low RSSI level indicate?

   a. Mismatched standards

   b. Insufficient wireless coverage

   c. Incorrect passphrase

   d. Encryption protocol mismatch

Check your answers at the end of this module.

You're Ready

You're now ready to complete **Project 6-4: Use a Wi-Fi Analyzer App on Your Smartphone**, or you can wait until you've finished the Review Questions for this module.

You're Ready

After you finish the Hands-On Projects, you're ready to complete the **Module 6 Capstone Projects**.

MODULE SUMMARY

Characteristics of Wireless Transmissions

- All wireless signals are carried through the air by electromagnetic waves. The wireless spectrum, commonly called the airwaves, is the frequency range of electromagnetic waves used for data and voice communication. As defined by the FCC (Federal Communications Commission), which controls its use, the wireless spectrum spans frequency ranges or bands between 9 kHz and 300 GHz. Recall that a Hz or hertz is one cycle per second.

- Due to the diverse nature of IoT (Internet of Things) devices and purposes, many kinds of wireless technologies are employed to better serve the needs of these connections, including RFID (Radio Frequency Identification), NFC (near-field communication), Z-Wave, ZigBee, Bluetooth, ANT+, and IR (infrared).

- Most wireless devices implement one of two technologies to take advantage of the frequencies within its band to avoid interference. FHSS (frequency hopping spread spectrum) consists of short bursts of data transmitted on a particular frequency within the band, and the next burst goes to the next frequency in the sequence. DSSS (direct sequence spread spectrum) creates data streams that are divided and encoded into small chunks, called chips, which are spread over all available frequencies within one of three, wide channels, all at the same time.

- An antenna's radiation pattern describes the relative strength over a three-dimensional area of all the electromagnetic energy the antenna sends or receives. A directional antenna issues wireless signals along a single direction. This type is used when the source needs to communicate with one destination, as in a point-to-point link or in a specific area. An omnidirectional antenna issues and receives wireless signals with (somewhat) equal strength and clarity in all directions, although in the real world, an omnidirectional antenna is never perfectly balanced. This type is used when many receivers or mobile receivers must be able to pick up the signal in many directions.

- You can determine the gain or loss of an access point attached to an external antenna by considering initial power output of the AP, signal loss along the antenna cable (attenuation), and signal gain from the antenna itself. This overall calculation is referred to as EIRP (effective isotropic radiated power) and is measured in dBm (decibels relative to one milliwatt). In contrast, RSSI (received signal strength indicator) measures in dBm the power of the signal on the receiver's end. The wireless client's own antenna, distance to the wireless client, and noise in the environment all affect the power of the received signal.

- When an obstacle stands in a signal's way, the signal might pass through the object, it might be absorbed by the object, or it might be subject to some other phenomena, depending upon the object's geometry and its constituent materials. The multipath nature of wireless signals gives them a better chance of reaching their destination. However, multiple instances of the same signal can arrive at a receiver at different times. This might cause signals to be misinterpreted, resulting in data errors.

802.11 WLAN Standards

- Wi-Fi (wireless fidelity) is a collection of wireless standards and their amendments, extensions, and corrections developed by IEEE's 802.11 committee. Notable wireless standards developed by the IEEE 802.11 committee and its task groups are 802.11b, 802.11a, 802.11g, 802.11n, 802.11ac, and 802.11ax.

- Beginning with 802.11n, several innovations have been implemented that contribute to making later 802.11 standards much faster and much more reliable: channel bonding, MIMO (multiple input-multiple output), MU-MIMO (multiuser MIMO), OFDMA (Orthogonal Frequency Division Multiple Access), and frame aggregation.

- 802.11 standards specify the use of CSMA/CA (Carrier Sense Multiple Access with Collision Avoidance) procedures to access a shared medium. Compared with CSMA/CD (Carrier Sense Multiple Access with Collision Detection), CSMA/CA minimizes the potential for collisions, but it cannot detect the occurrence of a collision and so cannot take steps to recover from the collisions that do occur.

- IEEE terminology includes a couple of notable variations to the standard service set configuration, including IBSS (independent basic service set) using an ad hoc topology, BSS (basic service set) using an infrastructure topology, and ESS (extended service set) using a mesh topology.
- The 802.11 data frame contains four address fields; by contrast, the 802.3 (Ethernet II) frame has only two. The transmitter and receiver addresses refer to the access point or another intermediary device (if used) on the wireless network. Another unique characteristic of the 802.11 data frame is its Sequence Control field. This field is used to indicate how a large packet is fragmented—that is, how it is subdivided into smaller packets for more reliable delivery.

Implementing a Wi-Fi Network

- Many home or office networks include IoT devices and even expandable IoT networks. Today, networking is no longer limited to computing devices. All sorts of things can be connected to a network, from toasters, refrigerators, bathroom scales, and garage doors to watches, lamps, cars, thermostats, doorbells, and even the kitchen sink. The IoT is made up of any device that can be connected to the Internet—that is, any sensor, computer, or wearable device that talks to other devices over a network.
- Larger wireless networks warrant a more systematic approach to access point placement. Before placing APs in every data room, it's wise to conduct a site survey. A site survey assesses client requirements, facility characteristics, and coverage areas; the resulting site survey report will help you determine an AP arrangement that will ensure reliable wireless connectivity within a given area.
- The setup process for a SOHO router is similar regardless of the manufacturer or model. The variables you will set during installation include administrator password, SSID, security options and credentials, and DHCP options.
- In an enterprise environment, configuring clients for wireless access to the network can entail a much more involved, two-part process: onboarding, which gives the device trusted access to certain portions of the network, and offboarding, which might include permissions to perform a remote wipe to clear a device of important information, permissions, and apps without having physical access to the device.

Wi-Fi Network Security

- Authentication allows a wireless client to log on to the network, either by providing the correct password for the SSID or by providing user credentials that might be processed by an authentication server. Encryption algorithms can scramble data transmitted over the airwaves into a format that cannot easily be interpreted if the signal is intercepted. The purpose of encryption is to keep information private.
- WEP offered two forms of authentication, neither of which is secure: OSA (Open System Authentication) and SKA (Shared Key Authentication).
- WPA (Wi-Fi Protected Access) dynamically assigns every transmission its own key. 802.11i incorporates an encryption key generation and management scheme known as TKIP (Temporal Key Integrity Protocol), pronounced *tee-kip*, to improve security for legacy WEP-based devices. TKIP accomplished three significant improvements: message integrity, key distribution, and encryption.
- WPA2 uses CCMP, which is short for Counter Mode with CBC (Cipher Block Chaining) MAC (Message Authentication Code) Protocol and improves wireless security for newer devices that can use WPA2. Whereas TKIP was meant to be backward-compatible as much as possible, CCMP helps ensure data confidentiality with both encryption and packet authentication.
- The Personal versions of WPA and WPA2 are sometimes referred to as WPA-PSK or WPA2-PSK, where PSK stands for Pre-Shared Key. This is the common configuration on home wireless networks in which you need to enter a passphrase for your device to authenticate to the network. The passphrase and the SSID characters are then used to calculate a unique encryption key for each device.

- The most secure Wi-Fi communication is made possible by combining a RADIUS authentication server with WPA or WPA2, known as WPA-Enterprise or WPA2-Enterprise, respectively. RADIUS (Remote Authentication Dial-In User Service) is an open source authentication and authorization service. A RADIUS server can be used to offer a central authentication point for wireless, mobile, and remote users.
- Additional Wi-Fi security configuration options include central AP and antenna placement, geofencing, guest network, wireless client isolation, and captive portal. Also think about how best to give network access to your IoT devices. Hardening your IoT network starts with changing default device names, usernames, and passwords for those devices, creating strong passwords, and using the strongest encryption settings the devices offer. Where possible, use two-factor authentication. Many cybersecurity experts recommend creating an entirely separate Wi-Fi network for all IoT devices, such as a guest network. Disable features you're not using, and update software and firmware when those updates become available. Finally, don't access your IoT software and devices when using a public network, such as at a coffee shop.

Troubleshooting Wi-Fi Networks

- A spectrum analyzer can assess the quality of a wireless signal by scanning a band of frequencies for signals and noise. A spectrum analysis is useful, for example, to ascertain where interference is greatest. A Wi-Fi analyzer can evaluate Wi-Fi network availability as well as help optimize Wi-Fi signal settings or help identify Wi-Fi security threats. Identifying the wireless channels being used nearby helps you optimize wireless channel utilization in your vicinity.
- Common problems that can prevent a wireless client from connecting with an AP include wrong SSID, encryption protocol mismatch, incorrect passphrase, static channel utilization, mismatched RF band, mismatched Wi-Fi standards, and stalled AP association. Common issues that can cause slow Wi-Fi connections include insufficient wireless coverage, RF attenuation, interference, channel overlap, insufficient wireless standards, simultaneous wired and wireless connections, problems with firmware updates, incorrect antenna type, mismatched antenna polarization, client saturation or overcapacity, and client disassociation issues.

Key Terms

For definitions of key terms, see the Glossary.

802.11a
802.11ac
802.11ax
802.11b
802.11g
802.11n
802.1X
ad hoc topology
AES (Advanced Encryption Standard)
ANT+
AP (access point)
association
band
Bluetooth
brute force attack
BSS (basic service set)
BSSID (basic service set identifier)
BYOD (bring your own device)
captive portal

CCMP (Counter Mode with CBC [Cipher Block Chaining] MAC [Message Authentication Code] Protocol)
channel bonding
CSMA/CA (Carrier Sense Multiple Access with Collision Avoidance)
diffraction
directional antenna
DSSS (direct sequence spread spectrum)
EAP (Extensible Authentication Protocol)
EAPoL (EAP over LAN)
EIRP (effective isotropic radiated power)
ESS (extended service set)
ESSID (extended service set identifier)
evil twin

fading
FHSS (frequency hopping spread spectrum)
geofencing
guest network
IBSS (independent basic server set)
infrastructure topology
interference
IoT (Internet of Things)
IR (infrared)
LOS (line of sight)
MAC filtering
MIMO (multiple input-multiple output)
MU-MIMO (multiuser MIMO)
NFC (near-field communication)
OFDMA (Orthogonal Frequency Division Multiple Access)
offboarding

omnidirectional antenna
onboarding
polarization
probe
propagation
PSK (Pre-Shared Key)
radiation pattern
RADIUS (Remote Authentication
 Dial-In User Service)
range
RC4 (Rivest Cipher 4)
reassociation
reflection
refraction
remote wipe
RFID (Radio Frequency
 Identification)
roam

rogue access point
RSSI (received signal strength
 indicator)
RTS/CTS (Request to Send/Clear to
 Send)
scanning
scattering
security camera
site survey
smart doorbell
smart refrigerator
smart speaker
smart thermostat
SNR (signal-to-noise ratio)
spectrum analyzer
SSID (service set identifier)
TKIP (Temporal Key Integrity
 Protocol)

wavelength
WEP (Wired Equivalent
 Privacy)
Wi-Fi (wireless fidelity)
Wi-Fi 4
Wi-Fi 5
Wi-Fi 6
Wi-Fi 6E
Wi-Fi analyzer
wireless bridge
wireless client isolation
wireless LAN controller
wireless range extender
wireless spectrum
WPA (Wi-Fi Protected Access)
WPA2
ZigBee
Z-Wave

Review Questions

1. What is the lowest layer of the OSI model at which wired and wireless transmissions share the same protocols?
   a. Layer 4
   b. Layer 3
   c. Layer 2
   d. Layer 1

2. As you're troubleshooting a dead zone in your office, which measurement will help you determine the edges of the dead zone?
   a. RSSI
   b. Channel
   c. EIRP
   d. Band

3. Which one of the following wireless transmission types requires a clear LOS to function?
   a. Bluetooth
   b. NFC
   c. IR
   d. Wi-Fi

4. Which of the following wireless technologies does *not* use the 2.4 GHz band?
   a. Z-Wave
   b. Bluetooth
   c. ZigBee
   d. Wi-Fi

5. Which function of WPA/WPA2 security ensures data cannot be read in transit?
   a. Message integrity
   b. Authentication
   c. Encryption
   d. Key distribution

6. Which protocol replaced TKIP for WPA2?
   a. CCMP
   b. WEP
   c. RADIUS
   d. RC4

7. Which 802.11 standard functions in both the 2.4-GHz and 5-GHz bands?
   a. 802.11g
   b. 802.11ac
   c. 802.11b
   d. 802.11ax

8. Which Carrier Sense technology is used on wireless networks to reduce collisions?
   a. CSMA/CD
   b. EAPoL
   c. CSMA/CA
   d. SSID

9. You've just completed a survey of the wireless signals traversing the airspace in your company's vicinity, and you've found an unauthorized AP with a very strong signal near the middle of the 100-acre campus. Its SSID is broadcasting the name of a smartphone model. What kind of threat do you need to report to your boss?
   a. Rogue AP
   b. War driving
   c. Evil twin
   d. Hidden node

10. You just settled in for some study time at the local coffee shop, and you pause long enough to connect your smartphone to the Wi-Fi so you can listen to some music while you study. As you're about to sign in, you realize that you clicked on an SSID called "Free Coffee and Internet." What kind of security trap did you almost fall for?
    a. Guest network
    b. Captive portal
    c. Evil twin
    d. Brute force attack

11. To exchange information, two antennas must be tuned to the same _____.

12. What addresses does an 802.11 frame contain that an 802.3 frame does not?

13. When a wireless signal encounters a large obstacle with wide, smooth surfaces, what happens to the signal?

14. Signals traveling through areas in which many wireless communications systems are in use will exhibit a lower _____ due to the higher proportion of noise.

15. What is the primary difference between how WPA2-Personal and WPA2-Enterprise are implemented on a network?

16. Why do wireless networks generally experience a greater reduction in throughput compared with wired networks?

17. What size bonded channels do 802.11ac and 802.11ax support?

18. What feature of a site survey maps the Wi-Fi signals in your location?

19. You're setting up a home network for your neighbor, who is a music teacher. She has students visiting her home regularly for lessons and wants to provide Internet access for their parents while they're waiting on the children. However, she's concerned about keeping her own data private. What wireless feature can you configure on her AP to meet her requests?

20. Which 802.11X authentication protocol is often used by WLANs?

Hands-On Projects

NOTE 6-8

Websites and applications change often. While the instructions given in these projects were accurate at the time of writing, you might need to adjust the steps or options according to later changes.

Note to Instructors and Students: A rubric is provided for evaluating student performance on these projects. Please see Appendix D.

Project 6-1: Configure a SOHO Router

Estimated Time: 30 minutes
Objective: Compare and contrast various devices, their features, and their appropriate placement on the network. (Obj. 2.1)
Resources:

- New or reset router
  Note: To reset the router manually, use the end of a paper clip or pen to press and hold the reset button on the back of the router for up to 30 seconds.

- Router's default IP address, admin username, and admin password
  Note: To find this information, look in the router's documentation, look for a sticker on the router itself, or search online for your model and brand of router.
- Patch cable
- Wired connection to the Internet through a modem or similar device
- Windows 10 computer with administrative access

NOTE 6-9

If you don't have a physical router to practice on, you can instead use a simulated router online. Many router manufacturers offer router simulators on their websites so you can explore menu and configuration options. When you make changes in the simulated interface, those changes are not saved. However, you'll still have the chance to see where to find the options and practice making these changes. Consider practicing on one or more of the following simulators:

TP-Link (use **admin** for both the username and password)

https://emulator.tp-link.com/EMULATOR_wr810nv2_eu/userRpm/LoginRpm.htm

LinkSys

http://ui.linksys.com/WRT54G/v8/8.00.0/basic.htm

D-Link

http://support.dlink.ca/emulators/wbr2310/lan.htm

Context: In this project, you configure a SOHO router, which includes routing, switching, wireless access functions, and other network services in a single device. Configuration steps on various SOHO wireless connectivity devices differ, but they involve a similar process and require you to modify the same variables. Always follow the manufacturer's directions rather than the general directions given here. Complete the following steps:

1. Connect the computer to the router with a patch cable plugged into a network (Ethernet) port on the router (see Figure 6-35). Then plug the router into a power outlet and turn it on.

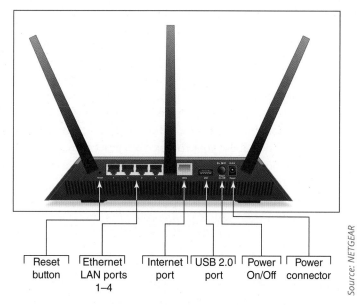

Source: NETGEAR

Reset	Ethernet	Internet	USB 2.0	Power	Power
button	LAN ports	port	port	On/Off	connector
	1–4				

Figure 6-35   Connections and ports on the back of a NETGEAR router

2. Connect the ISP modem or other device to the router's Internet port.

3. Optional: Connect any other devices on the network that require a wired connection.

4. Firmware on the router (which can be flashed for updates) contains a configuration program that you can access using a web browser from anywhere on the network. In your browser address box, enter the IP address of the router (for many routers, this address is **192.168.1.1**). Sign in using the default admin username and password. For the example router, the default username and password are both **admin**, although yours might be different. What is the IP address and sign-in information for your router?

5. The main setup page appears. The setup program will take you through the process of configuring the router. After you've configured the router, you might have to turn your cable or DSL modem off and then turn it back on so that it correctly syncs up with the router. Figure 6-36 shows the main page for a router that has already been configured. For most situations, the default settings on this and other pages should work without any changes. What basic steps did the setup program have you follow to configure the router?

Figure 6-36   Main page for router firmware setup

6. In Figure 6-36, the BASIC tab is selected. Most of the settings you would want to adjust on this router are on the ADVANCED tab. Find a screen or menu on your router—like an Advanced tab—that shows the most options for changing the router's network configuration, operation mode, guest network configuration, parental controls, and security settings. **Take a screenshot** showing these options; submit this visual with your answers to this project's questions.

7. It's extremely important to protect access to your network and prevent others from hijacking your router. If you have not already done so, change the default admin password so that others cannot change your router setup. To change the password on the router shown in the figure, you click **ADVANCED**, **Administration**, and **Set Password**. What are the steps for your router? Record your new router password in your LastPass vault along with any other helpful information about your router, such as its management IP address.

8. Spend some time examining the various features of your router. If you make any changes that you want to keep, be sure to save them. Answer the following questions:
   a. What is the public IP address of the router on the ISP network?
   b. Why is it necessary for the router to have two IP addresses?

9. When finished, you can sign out now or stay signed in for the next project.

Project 6-2: Modify SOHO Router Wireless Settings

Estimated Time: 20 minutes (+ 10 minutes for group work, if assigned)

Objective: Given a scenario, install and configure the appropriate wireless standards and technologies. (Obj. 2.4)

Group Work: This project includes enhancements when assigned as a group project.

Resources:

- Router used in Project 6-1
- Computer used in Project 6-1 connected to one of the router's data ports

Context: Now that you have installed your new SOHO router, you're ready to modify its wireless network configuration through the administrator interface. This project picks up where Project 6-1 left off. Complete the following steps:

1. Sign into your router's administrative interface. Refer to your LastPass vault if you need help remembering this information.
2. Access the wireless settings page. Review the settings that appear on this page, including the SSID. You might have assigned an SSID in Project 6-1 during the initial setup. If not, assign an SSID and security key now. Record this information in your LastPass vault.
3. Answer the following questions:
   a. Which 802.11 standards does this router use to communicate with wireless clients? You might need to look on the router itself or in its documentation to determine this information.
   b. Which bands are enabled on the router?
   c. Is the SSID set to broadcast or not?
   d. What would happen if you disabled the broadcast?
   e. Would clients still be able to communicate with the router?
4. Disconnect the patch cable between your computer and the router.
5. Click the **Network** icon in your taskbar. Windows displays a list of wireless networks that are broadcasting availability. **Take a screenshot** of the available networks and indicate which one is yours; submit this visual with your answers to this project's questions.
6. Select the name of your wireless network. If you are comfortable with automatically connecting to this network in the future, check **Connect automatically** and then click **Connect**. Because you are attempting to connect to a secured network, Windows will prompt you for the security key. Refer to your notes in LastPass if you need help remembering this information.
7. After connecting, open a browser and navigate to **speedtest.net** or a similar speed test website. Run a speed test to determine your connection's download and upload speeds, respectively. What are your test results?
8. **For group projects:** Set up a guest network on your router with a separate SSID and a unique password. Share that information with one of your group members. Each group member should attempt to sign into their teammate's guest network and then run a new speed test. Share your speed test results with the owner of the network. How do the speed test results for your guest network compare to the speed test results you collected yourself?

Project 6-3: Optimize Wireless Security on a SOHO Router

Estimated Time: 30 minutes
Objective: Given a scenario, apply network hardening techniques. (Obj. 4.3)
Resources:
- Home network with administrative access to the SOHO router; alternatively, continue working with the router used in Projects 6-1 and 6-2
- Computer connected to the SOHO network through either a wired or wireless connection

Context: Properly securing a wireless access point is not the kind of chore most home users think to do. Some IT students have even created businesses securing home networks for their neighbors, friends, and family. In this project, you work with AP settings that increase a home wireless network's security. These steps are specific to a Linksys router, but they can easily be adapted for other consumer-grade brands. Complete the following steps:

1. On your (or a friend's, with their permission) home network, sign into the router's configuration console. If no factory settings have been changed yet, you can use the default access credentials provided by the manufacturer.
2. As you make changes, be sure to write down access information for the network owner. Provide instructions on how to keep this information safe, such as locked up in a safe or stored at a separate location. Ideally, you would walk the network owner through the process of setting up a password manager using a tool such as LastPass, KeePass, or another secure password manager.

3. On the wireless settings page, change the SSID to a name that is unique and completely unrelated to the brand or type of router being used or to the names of the residents.

4. Whether the SSID is broadcast or not is a personal preference. It's more convenient to broadcast the SSID and does not seriously affect the network's security. Save your changes. Note that, if your computer is connected to the router through a wireless connection, the connection might temporarily be lost. You'll need to re-establish the connection after the router resets its wireless network and sign in again. What changes did you make to the wireless network settings?

5. On the wireless security page, check the security mode. Select **WPA Auto** if available, otherwise select **WPA2**. The encryption type should be **AES** unless older devices are in use, in which case you'll have to resort to the **TKIP or AES** setting.

6. Change the security key for the wireless network to a nondictionary code that includes both letters and numbers, and at least 10 digits. The more digits, the more secure the key. A long security key is more secure than a completely random but short one, so consider using a line from a favorite song with a couple of numbers and symbols thrown in. Save your changes.

7. **Take a screenshot** showing the encryption and security settings for the wireless network—blur the password if that information is visible. Submit this visual with your answers to this project's questions.

8. On the administration page, set the admin password to a phrase that, again, includes both letters and numbers, the longer the better. Make sure the network owner is given this information and the information is stored in a safe place. Also disable Remote Management. Save your changes.

9. Go to each device that is used regularly on the network and force each device to "forget" the network so the previous settings will be removed from the device. Reconnect each device to the network with the new settings.

Project 6-4: Use a Wi-Fi Analyzer App on Your Smartphone

Estimated Time: 20 minutes (+5 minutes for group work, if assigned)
Objective: Given a scenario, use the appropriate network software tools and commands. (Obj. 5.3)
Group Work: This project includes enhancements when assigned as a group project.
Resources:
- Smartphone (Android or iOS) and the ability to install an app on the device
- Access to a wireless network broadcasting in the area

Context: You can turn your smartphone into a Wi-Fi analyzer tool by installing a free or inexpensive app through your phone's app store. These days, such apps are easy to find, easy to use, and provide useful information without much hassle. In this project, you install a Wi-Fi analyzer app on your phone and try it out on your home or school Wi-Fi network. While these instructions are specific to an Android smartphone installing the Wifi Analyzer app, you can adjust the steps to work for other smartphones and different apps. Complete the following steps or adapt as needed for your device:

1. Connect your smartphone to a nearby Wi-Fi network.

2. Go to your phone's app store and search for the app called **Wifi Analyzer**. The Android app used in this specific example was created by farproc, but you can choose a different app if you want to.

3. Install the app and open it. You can look at the Online Help page at this time, or you can wait until later. You can also choose to try any experimental features, such as channel width information, or you can wait until later.

4. At the time of this writing, Wifi Analyzer is programmed to automatically start scanning for Wi-Fi signals. It provides a live feed of signal strength and channel coverage for the wireless networks in its reach. You can see in Figure 6-37 that several home networks were available at the time of the scan, with several of these using various overlapping channels. The local networks provided the strongest signals. Notice the scale on the left side of Figure 6-37 showing Signal Strength (which is another name for RSSI) measured in dBm.
Assuming −70 dBm is the cutoff for reliable data delivery, how many networks on your scan could provide a reliable Wi-Fi connection?

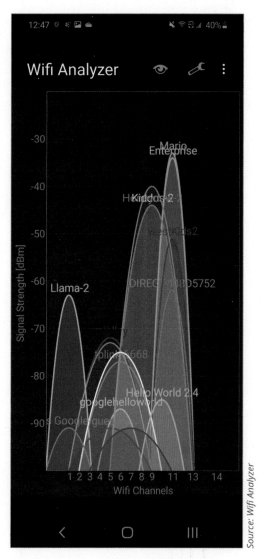

Figure 6-37   The Wifi Analyzer app detected several home networks nearby

5. **Take a screenshot** of the scan information showing in your app; submit this visual with your answers to this project's questions. The button combination needed to take a screenshot varies by device. For example, for some Android smartphones, you press the Power button and the Volume Down button together to take a screenshot. For some iPhones, you press the Side Button and the Volume Up button together, the Home Button and the Power Button together, or the Side Button and the Home Button together. Check online if you need more help for your device. To move the file to your computer so you can submit the file to your instructor, you can save the screenshot to a cloud service, such as Drive or iCloud, or you can email the image to yourself.

6. Find your own wireless network in the scan results. What channel is your network using?

The Wifi Analyzer app provides some interesting features, including a signal meter, as shown on the left side of Figure 6-38, and a list of detailed information for each hotspot, as shown on the right side of Figure 6-38. Notice in the list of hotspots that device MAC addresses and manufacturers are listed, as are each hotspot's channel, frequency, and security method (such as WEP or WPA2).

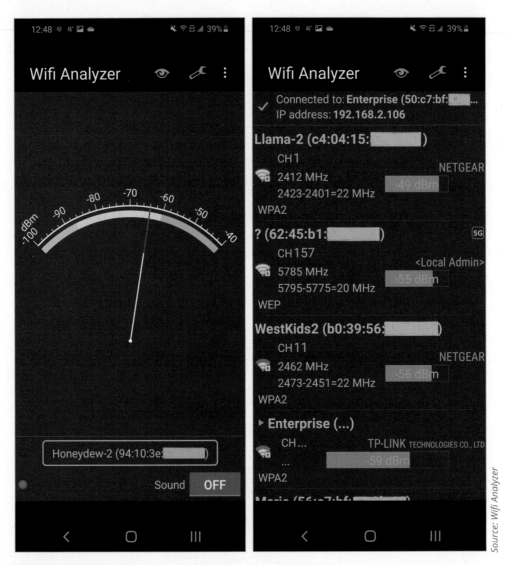

Source: Wifi Analyzer

Figure 6-38　Readings from the Wifi Analyzer app

7. Take a few minutes to explore your Wi-Fi analyzer app's features and answer the following questions:
   a. What features and information did you find?
   b. What changes might you want to make to your Wi-Fi network's settings to increase its performance or security?

8. **For group projects:** Have one group member activate a Wi-Fi hotspot on their phone. Then other group members run a new scan on their Wi-Fi analyzer apps and find the phone's hotspot in the results. How do these results vary from the information you saw with other Wi-Fi networks in your scans? Try moving around to different rooms. How quickly does the strength of the signal shift?

9. Document this app installation in your Wikidot website, including the name of the app, the device on which you installed it, and notes about what the app does and how to use it.

Capstone Projects

Note to Instructors and Students: A rubric is provided for evaluating student performance on these projects. Please see Appendix D.

Capstone Project 6-1: Create and Secure a Basic Wireless Network in Packet Tracer

Estimated Time: 30 minutes

Objective: Given a scenario, troubleshoot common wireless connectivity issues. (Obj. 5.4)

Resources:

- Computer with Cisco Packet Tracer installed

Context: In Module 5, Capstone Project 5-2, you began building a wired Packet Tracer network that you will continue to expand throughout several modules. That network is designed to help you explore several networking concepts you'll encounter in a corporate network. This project, however, focuses on concepts for a SOHO network. Do *not* use your existing Packet Tracer network from Module 5 for this project—you'll come back to that network later. In this project, start with a new Packet Tracer file to create a SOHO wireless network in Packet Tracer. You'll use this network for both Capstone Projects in this module, and you will *not* need to save this network for future modules. Complete the following steps:

1. Open Packet Tracer—make sure you're starting from a new file, not an existing network. From the **Network Devices > Wireless Devices** menu, insert a **WRT300N** wireless router.
2. On the wireless router's **Config** tab, set its LAN-facing IP address to **192.168.5.1** and subnet mask to **255.255.255.0**.
3. From the **End Devices** menu, insert a **Laptop**.
4. On the laptop's **Physical** tab, replace the Ethernet network module with a wireless module:
   a. Click the laptop's power button to turn off the laptop.
   b. Drag the PT-LAPTOP-NM-1CFE card from the laptop to the MODULES pane. Zoom in if necessary. The card is labeled **FAST ETH 0**.
   c. Drag the **WPC300N** module from the MODULES pane to empty slot on the laptop, as shown in Figure 6-39.

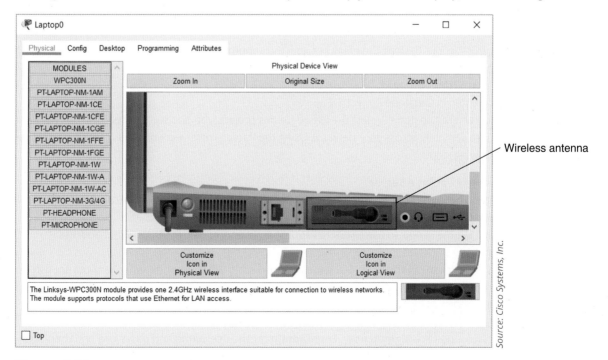

Source: Cisco Systems, Inc.

Figure 6-39 The laptop now has a wireless module

    d. Turn the laptop back on.

    e. Within a few seconds, a wireless connection is automatically created between the wireless router and the laptop. If not, troubleshoot the problem.

5. Now you need to set up some security parameters on the wireless router:

    a. On the wireless router's **Config** tab on the **Wireless** page, select **WPA2-PSK** authentication. This option will use a passphrase instead of a RADIUS server, which is less secure but is more likely what you would use on a small SOHO network.

    b. Set the PSK Pass Phrase to **networkplus**.

    c. Make sure the encryption type is **AES**, which is more secure than TKIP.

    d. What has happened to your wireless network connection? Why do you think this is?

6. To solve this problem, you need to give the client the proper credentials:

    a. On the laptop's **Config** tab, enter the correct authentication information.

    b. If the connection does not re-establish, troubleshoot the problem.

    c. **Take a screenshot** of the information you entered on the wireless interface's configuration menu to establish successful authentication; submit this visual with your answers to this project's questions.

The wireless router offers many of the same GUI-based options you might see on a home router's user interface. To explore some of the security options, complete the following steps:

7. On the wireless router's **GUI** tab, what is the current DHCP pool? What is the client lease time?

8. On the **Wireless** > **Basic Wireless Settings** page, change the default SSID to **HappyVintage**. Scroll to the bottom of the screen and click **Save Settings**.

9. On the **Wireless** > **Wireless Security** page, WPA2 Personal is already selected. What other security mode options do you have? Which of these security modes is the most secure?

10. AES encryption is selected. What other encryption option do you have? Which of these encryption options is most secure?

11. Close the wireless router's configuration window. What changed on your network? Why do you think this is?

12. On the laptop's **Config** tab, on the **Wireless0** page, correct the SSID. What happens on your network?

13. Save your project for use in Capstone Project 6-2 or continue with that project now.

14. Make some notes on your Wikidot website about your activities in Packet Tracer for this project.

Note to Instructors: A Packet Tracer solution file is provided for each Packet Tracer project through the Instructors site. Some Packet Tracer projects build on earlier Packet Tracer networks. If needed for one or more students, you can provide a previous project's solution file as a start file for one of these progression projects.

Capstone Project 6-2: Add IoT Devices to a Basic Wireless Network in Packet Tracer

Estimated Time: 45 minutes

Objective: Compare and contrast various devices, their features, and their appropriate placement on the network. (Obj. 2.1)

Resources:

- Computer with Cisco Packet Tracer installed
- Packet Tracer network created in Capstone Project 6-2

Context: This project picks up where Capstone Project 6-1 left off. In this project, you add some wireless IoT devices and configure them to be controlled remotely across your network. Using the Packet Tracer network you created in Capstone Project 6-1, complete the following steps:

1. From the **End Devices** menu, insert a **Server**.

2. Using a **Copper Straight-Through** cable, connect Server0's **FastEthernet0** port to the wireless router's **Ethernet 1** port. Wait for the router-to-server connection to turn to green triangles on both ends.

3. On Server0's **Config** tab, set the server to use DHCP to request an IP address assignment. What address is assigned to the server?

4. On Server0's **Services** tab, click **IoT** in the SERVICES pane and turn it on. What other network services are listed in this pane that you recognize?

5. On Server0's **Desktop** tab, click **IoT Monitor**. Enter Server0's IP address that you noted in Step 3 and then click **Login**. You'll get an error message that you used the wrong username or password—this is because you have not yet created a user account. Click **Sign up now**. Enter **admin** for the username and password and then click **Create**. You are now logged into the IoT server.

6. From the **End Devices** > **Home** menu, add the **Light**.

7. This light currently has a wired Ethernet port and not a wireless interface. To change this, at the bottom of the light's configuration window, click **Advanced**. On the **I/O Config** tab, change the Network Adapter to **PT-IOT-NM-1W**.

8. On the light's **Config** tab on the **Wireless0** page, enter the correct authentication information for the light to automatically connect wirelessly to your network, as shown in Figure 6-40. If the connection does not establish automatically, troubleshoot the problem. What authentication information did the light need to connect to the wireless router?

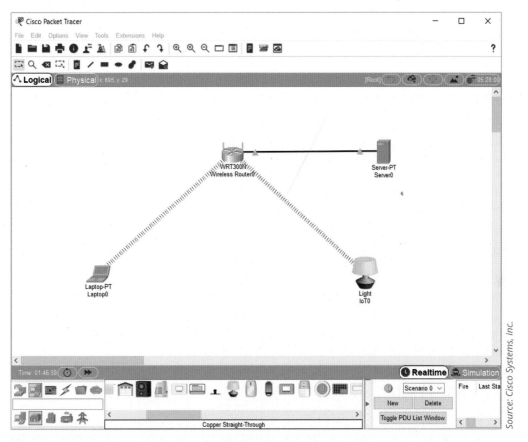

Figure 6-40 The IoT light connects wirelessly to the network

Source: Cisco Systems, Inc.

9. The light is connected to the network but is not yet talking to the IoT server. To fix this, click **Settings** in the left pane. Scroll down to the IoT Server section. Select **Remote Server**, and then enter the server's address, username, and password. Click **Connect**.

10. On the server's IoT Monitor page, the light should now be listed under IoT Server – Devices. Position the server's configuration window so you can see the light in your workspace. In the server's configuration window, click the **IoT0** entry to open the remote controls. Change the light's status. What happens to the light in your network?

11. Add a second IoT device of your choice. Make the needed changes to this device to connect it wirelessly to the network if possible or with a wired connection if necessary. Then register your new IoT device with the IoT server. Confirm that you can remotely control it from the server's IoT Monitor page.

12. Position the network devices and the IoT Monitor page so you can see all devices on the network and both IoT devices listed on the IoT Monitor page. **Take a screenshot** showing all this information; submit this visual with your answers to this project's questions.

13. You can save your project for future reference and experimentation; however, you will not need this network for future projects in this course.

14. Make some notes on your Wikidot website about your activities in Packet Tracer for this project.

Note to Instructors: A Packet Tracer solution file is provided for each Packet Tracer project through the Instructors site. Some Packet Tracer projects build on earlier Packet Tracer networks. If needed for one or more students, you can provide a previous project's solution file as a start file for one of these progression projects.

Solutions to Self-Check Questions

Characteristics of Wireless Transmissions

1. Which of the following statements is false?

Answer: a. Each Wi-Fi channel contains multiple frequency bands.

Explanation: A band covers a frequency range that is further subdivided into channels; therefore, a **Wi-Fi channel cannot contain multiple frequency bands**. In the United States, the FCC has defined 11 channels within the 2.4-GHz band for Wi-Fi and 24 channels in the 5-GHz band. Wi-Fi uses DSSS, which means its data streams are spread over all available frequencies within one of three, wide channels, all at the same time.

2. Which of the following statements is true?

Answer: c. A Wi-Fi client connects to a range extender, which connects to an AP.

Explanation: **A Wi-Fi client can connect to a wireless range extender, which can connect to an AP (access point)** to further extend the WLAN range. Satellite dishes are shaped to receive directional signals from one direction. Water in a fish aquarium and the glass around it will both refract waves as they travel into and through these different mediums. Cellular towers and cellular devices use omnidirectional antennas to improve mobility of cellular client devices.

802.11 WLAN Standards

3. What was the first 802.11 standard to implement channel bonding?

Answer: a. 802.11n

Explanation: Beginning with **802.11n**, two adjacent 20-MHz channels can be combined, or bonded, to make a 40-MHz channel. Because the 5-GHz band contains more channels and is less crowded (at least, for now), it's better suited to channel bonding than the 2.4-GHz band. The newer standards take channel bonding to a higher level by supporting 20-, 40-, and 80-MHz channels, with optional use of 160-MHz channels.

4. Which type of identifier allows wireless clients to roam freely from AP to AP?

Answer: c. ESSID

Explanation: Within an ESS (extended service set), a client can associate with any one of many APs that use the same **ESSID (ESS identifier)**. This allows users to roam, or change from AP to AP, without losing wireless network service. The identifier for a group of nodes using only one AP is a BSSID (basic service set identifier). The transmitter address field in an 802.11 header identifies the MAC address of the device transmitting a Wi-Fi message. IP addresses function at layer 3 and are not part of the Wi-Fi header.

Implementing a Wi-Fi Network

5. Which device on the network will require the greatest throughput capacity?

Answer: c. Wireless bridge

Explanation: A **wireless bridge** connects two networks or two remote portions of one network; the throughput demands of a wireless bridge connected to another AP can be significantly higher than typical Wi-Fi clients. IoT devices, such as a smart speaker and a smart thermostat, generally only need sufficient throughput to process commands, send updated sensor data, or possibly stream music or video—however, even streaming video will require less throughput than a bridge that supports multiple wireless clients. A wireless LAN controller might be used only initially to configure the APs, or the APs might remain connected to the wireless controller for continued management—however, management communication does not require much throughput capabilities.

6. Which off-boarding policy can protect proprietary corporate information if a smartphone is lost?

Answer: a. Remote wipe

Explanation: The ability to perform a **remote wipe** is part of an off-boarding policy that clears a device of important information, permissions, and apps without having physical access to the device. On-boarding gives the device trusted access to certain portions of the network. An on-boarding agent might also scan the device for any needed OS or security updates, required security settings (such as timeouts or sign-in requirements), and any existing malware. A site survey assesses client requirements, facility characteristics, and coverage areas when determining the best placement for APs in a wireless network.

Wi-Fi Network Security

7. Which Wi-Fi encryption standard was designed to use AES encryption?

Answer: b. WPA2

Explanation: CCMP, which is short for Counter Mode with CBC (Cipher Block Chaining) MAC (Message Authentication Code) Protocol, improves wireless security for newer devices that can use **WPA2 (Wi-Fi Protected Access, version 2)**. CCMP uses AES (Advanced Encryption Standard) to provide faster and more secure encryption than TKIP for wireless transmissions. WPA incorporates an encryption key generation and management scheme known as TKIP (Temporal Key Integrity Protocol) to improve security for legacy WEP-based devices. WEP (Wired Equivalent Privacy) offered two forms of authentication, neither of which is secure: OSA (Open System Authentication) and SKA (Shared Key Authentication). WEP2 does not exist.

8. Which standard adapted EAP to WLANs?

Answer: c. 802.1X

Explanation: EAP (Extensible Authentication Protocol) was originally designed to work only on point-to-point connections, usually on a WAN. However, it was adapted to work on both wired and wireless LANs in the **802.1X** standard, dubbed EAPoL (EAP over LAN). 802.11g is an early Wi-Fi standard. 802.11i was designed as a new wireless security standard to replace WEP and included the subset standard WPA. 802.3 is an Ethernet standard for wired networks.

Troubleshooting Wi-Fi Networks

9. Which device will let you determine all frequencies within a scanned range that are present in a specific environment, not just Wi-Fi?

Answer: d. Spectrum analyzer

Explanation: A **spectrum analyzer** can assess the quality of a wireless signal by scanning a band of frequencies for signals and noise. A Wi-Fi analyzer can evaluate Wi-Fi network availability as well as help optimize Wi-Fi signal settings or help identify Wi-Fi security threats. A captive portal is the first page a new client sees in the browser when connecting to the guest network, and usually requires the user to agree to a set of terms and conditions before gaining further access to the guest network. A wireless LAN controller is used to configure and manage APs in a mesh network.

10. Which problem would a low RSSI level indicate?

Answer: b. Insufficient wireless coverage

Explanation: You can confirm whether **insufficient wireless coverage** is the problem by checking the RSSI (received signal strength indicator) level at the client's location. Mismatched standards will prevent a client from detecting an AP's broadcast. An incorrect passphrase or encryption protocol mismatch will prevent the completion of a client's authentication process.

NETWORK ARCHITECTURE

After reading this module and completing the exercises, you should be able to:

① Explain types of abstraction in the design of physical network architecture

② Describe and explain virtualization technologies on a network

③ Summarize cloud characteristics, models, and connectivity options

④ Identify methods to increase network availability

On the Job

A small-business client of our IT consulting firm approached us about upgrading their three servers. They wanted to upgrade to more advanced technology and were also concerned about reducing their energy consumption. The three servers performed three very different functions. One was dedicated to handling the domain, user logins, file and print sharing, and related services. Another hosted a company-wide sales application, which included a large database. The last was dedicated to backing up the database and other important data.

Upon investigating the client's current systems, we identified a few interesting characteristics. First, average utilization levels for all three servers were well below 50 percent. Moreover, the peak utilization times for the three servers were staggered. The domain server was busiest first thing in the morning, when users first logged into the network, with another small spike after lunchtime. The application server had consistent utilization throughout the day, with the largest peak time at the end of the workday as sales staff input sales for the day. The backup server peaked during off-work hours, as it copied data from the database and other storage while they were not in use.

These findings meant that we could use a hypervisor to run all three servers as virtual machines on a single host server device. This allowed each virtual server to utilize the host's hardware resources when they were needed the most and, during times of lower utilization, free up those resources for other virtual servers. Not only did this result in a more acceptable level of average server utilization, but it actually decreased power utilization overall, allowing our client to enjoy a lower electric bill.

Brent M. Ferns, Sr., M.B.A., M.S.A.
Associate Dean of Business and Computer Science
Palm Beach State College

Through the past several modules, you've learned about the hardware found on a network, the cabling and radio waves that connect this hardware, the way devices on a network are addressed, and the core protocols that make networks work. These concepts cover the basics of how a simple network functions. However, businesses—especially very large businesses—need networking technology that constantly improves to ensure ever faster performance and more reliable service and security.

Consider the progression of telephone technology. In the beginning, the telephone existed to carry a voice conversation between two people. It required manual switching (Figure 7-1) and the quality of the sound wasn't all that great. Telephones eventually got better but were still wired to a single location. Then telephones became mobile. Next, they gained the ability to do other things, like texting, taking pictures and video, browsing the web, and playing games. The idea of "phoning someone" became less about having a voice conversation and more about being able to connect to others in a variety of ways, through text, photos, video calls, email, visiting websites, and using social media apps. You might say that today's smartphones abstracted the idea of "connection" from early telephone conversations and thereby expanded the possibilities of how people connect today.

Figure 7-1   A mid-twentieth century telephone switchboard

Abstraction is a critical concept in this module and in modern networking. The process of networking isn't just about bits running along a cable or through the air. Networking also involves decision-making devices that are configured to:

- Prioritize some traffic over other traffic
- Direct traffic to different locations
- Filter traffic for security
- Correct problems with messages that experience errors

This decision making doesn't always happen directly on the hardware routers and switches—it can be abstracted to another device or even to software running in a VM (virtual machine). You've already learned that a network's physical topology might be configured very differently than its logical topology. Network abstraction—that is, the separation of decision making from hardware—takes this idea further. Examples of network abstraction include the following:

- Networking devices might be controlled remotely by another device.
- Networking devices might exist as virtual devices like a VM.
- Networking devices might only exist as logical constructs that govern traffic in a virtual environment.

You'll begin this module with a discussion of how to manage physical switches and some of the configuration and organizational considerations for switches in a network design. This overall network design—the devices involved, how they're configured, the services implemented to support the network, and the way devices are connected to the network—is called a network's **architecture**. You'll first read about physical network architecture, such as switch hierarchy and special storage networks. You'll then explore how virtual devices expand network design parameters while strengthening network availability and security. And then you'll see how the concept of virtualization in the cloud has further broadened the possibilities for network architecture beyond the walls of the on-site data center. Get ready to think "outside the box" as you learn how network architecture has expanded beyond the confines of physical space.

PHYSICAL ARCHITECTURE

 **CERTIFICATION**

1.2 Explain the characteristics of network topologies and network types.

1.7 Explain basic corporate and datacenter network architecture.

2.1 Compare and contrast various devices, their features, and their appropriate placement on the network.

2.3 Given a scenario, configure and deploy common Ethernet switching features.

3.3 Explain high availability and disaster recovery concepts and summarize which is the best solution.

4.1 Explain common security concepts.

4.3 Given a scenario, apply network hardening techniques.

5.5 Given a scenario, troubleshoot general networking issues.

Average reading time: 45 minutes

At this point, you've gotten a little experience working with switches in Packet Tracer and perhaps in your school's lab. You've connected devices to switches, and you know how to ensure devices on the same switch can communicate with each other. The responsibility of switch management extends well beyond the tasks associated with connecting devices. As networks rely increasingly on switch-based technologies, managed switches and layer 3 switches (which you'll learn about shortly) play a much more critical role in an enterprise environment. At the same time, switch security becomes a more important—and more complex—factor in protecting a network's resources.

Let's first look at some of the variety of switch types available. Then you'll learn about some of the configuration changes you can make to these switches to better manage paths between them.

The Cisco switches you've worked with in Packet Tracer run a basic operating system called IOS (Internetwork Operating System). Recall from Capstone Project 3-2 in Module 3, you used a command from Cisco's IOS for switches, `show mac address-table`. However, there are many other brands of networking devices available, including Huawei, Arista, and Juniper. In this module, as you study commands used to configure switches, you'll start learning some of the variations of commands used on other vendors' devices.

Managed Switches

An **unmanaged switch** provides plug-and-play simplicity with minimal configuration options and has no IP address assigned to it. Unmanaged switches are not very expensive, but their capabilities are limited. **Managed switches**, on the other hand, can be configured via a command-line interface or a web-based management GUI, and sometimes can be configured in groups. Sometimes, they are also assigned IP addresses for the purpose of continued management.

Recall that switches are layer 2 devices. However, higher-layer switches also exist:

7	Application
6	Presentation
5	Session
4	Transport
3	Network
▶ ②	Data Link
▶ ①	Physical

- **Layer 3 switch**—Capable of interpreting layer 3 data and can work much like a router, supporting the same routing protocols and making routing decisions. Layer 3 switches are less expensive than routers and are designed to work on large LANs, providing faster layer 3 traffic management within the confines of a known network architecture. The primary difference is the way the hardware is built, but, in fact, it's often difficult to distinguish between a layer 3 switch and a router. In some cases, the difference comes down to what the manufacturer has decided to call the device to improve sales.
- **Layer 4 switch**—Capable of interpreting layer 4 data. They operate anywhere from layer 4 to layer 7, and they're also known as content switches or application switches. Among other things, the ability to interpret higher-layer data enables switches to perform advanced filtering, keep statistics, and provide security functions.

The features of layer 3 and layer 4 switches vary widely depending on the manufacturer and price point, and they can cost significantly more than layer 2 switches. This variability is exacerbated by the fact that key players in the networking trade have not agreed on standards for these switches. They are typically used as part of a network's backbone and are not appropriate on a single LAN. What they all have in common is that they're optimized for fast layer 2 data handling.

In this section, you'll first learn how paths between switches are managed, and you'll learn about some innovative ways to organize switches for optimized traffic management. Then you'll examine switch security concerns and some ways switches are used to optimize server performance.

Switch Path Management

Figure 7-2 shows where a typical layer 2 switch is positioned on a basic network. This switch manages all network traffic on the LAN unless a host on the network wants to communicate with a host on another network, and then that traffic goes through the router.

7	Application
6	Presentation
5	Session
4	Transport
▶ ③	Network
▶ ②	Data Link
1	Physical

Suppose you design a larger network with several interconnected switches. To make the network more fault tolerant, you install multiple, or redundant, switches at critical junctures. **Redundancy** allows data the option of traveling through more than one switch toward its destination and makes your network less vulnerable to hardware malfunctions. For example,

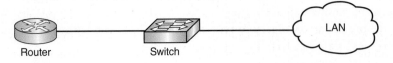

Figure 7-2   A switch connecting end devices to a router

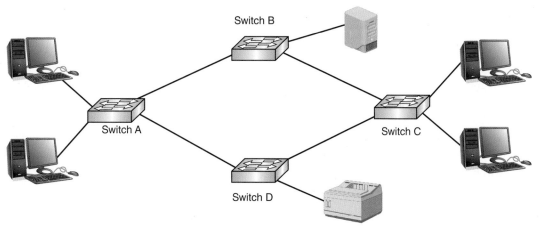

Figure 7-3 Network of switches

if one switch suffers a power supply failure, traffic can reroute through a second switch. Your network might look something like the one pictured in Figure 7-3, where several switches work together to connect hosts in several areas of your building. (In reality, of course, many more hosts would connect to each switch.)

A potential problem with the network shown in Figure 7-3 has to do with traffic loops. What if a server attached to switch B issues a broadcast frame? Switch B then reissues the broadcast to all its ports except the port to which the server is attached. In that case, switch B will issue the broadcast frame to switches A and C, which will both reissue the broadcast frame to switch D, which then reissues the received broadcast frame from each direction back to both switches A and C, and so on around the loop. If not limited in some way, these redundant broadcast transmissions will flood the network (called a broadcast storm), and the high traffic volume will severely impair network performance or possibly disable the network entirely.

Many Huawei, Arista, Juniper, Cisco, and similar devices offer a type of flood guard known as storm control that protects against flooding attacks from broadcast and multicast traffic. Storm control monitors network traffic at one-second intervals to determine if the traffic levels are within acceptable thresholds. Any time traffic exceeds the predefined threshold, all traffic is dropped for the remainder of the time interval. This feature is managed on three of these vendors' devices using the `storm-control` command (without the hyphen on Huawei devices: `storm control`). However, eliminating—or otherwise controlling—switching loops can greatly reduce the potential for a broadcast storm.

To eliminate the possibility of this and other types of traffic loops, STP (Spanning Tree Protocol) was developed by Radia Perlman at Digital Equipment Corporation in 1985 and then adopted by the IEEE in 1990.

The first iteration of STP, defined in IEEE standard 802.1D, functions at the data link layer. It prevents traffic loops, also called switching loops, by calculating paths that avoid potential loops and by artificially blocking the links that would complete a loop. In addition, STP can adapt to changes in the network. For instance, if a switch is removed, STP will recalculate the best loop-free data paths between the remaining switches.

So how does STP select and enforce switching paths on a network? Consider the following process:

> **NOTE 7-2**
>
> In the following explanation, you can substitute *switch* wherever the word *bridge* is used. As you have learned, a switch is really just a glorified bridge. STP terminology refers to a layer 2 device as a *bridge* because STP was designed and created before switches existed.

Step 1: STP selects a root bridge that will provide the basis for all subsequent path calculations. Only one root bridge exists on a network. From this root bridge, a series of logical branches, or data paths, emanate like branches on a tree. STP selects the root bridge based on its BID (Bridge ID). The BID is a combination of a 2-byte priority field (which can be set by a network admin) and the bridge's MAC address. To begin with, all bridges on the network share the same priority number, and so the bridge with the lowest MAC address becomes the root bridge by default.

Step 2: STP examines the possible paths between all other bridges and the root bridge. It chooses the most efficient of these paths, called the least cost path, for each of the bridges. To enforce this path, STP stipulates that each bridge can have only one root port, which is the bridge's port that is closest to and forwards frames to the root bridge. closest to the root bridge, can forward frames toward the root bridge.

Step 3: STP disables links that are not part of a shortest path. To do this, it enables only the lowest-cost port on each link between two bridges to *transmit* network traffic. This port is called the designated port. All ports can, however, continue to *receive* STP information in case updates are later needed.

Figure 7-4 illustrates a switched network with certain paths selected and one blocked by STP. In this drawing, root ports pointing upstream toward the root bridge are labeled *RP*. Designated ports pointing downstream from the root bridge are labeled *DP*. For example, traffic from the root bridge (switch D) going to switch B would be forwarded through switch C. Even though switch B is also connected to switch A, STP has limited the logical pathway so messages destined for switch B will only go through switch C. Now suppose switch C were to fail. STP would automatically adapt by choosing a different logical pathway for frames destined for switch B. This way, redundancy is maintained while avoiding switching loops.

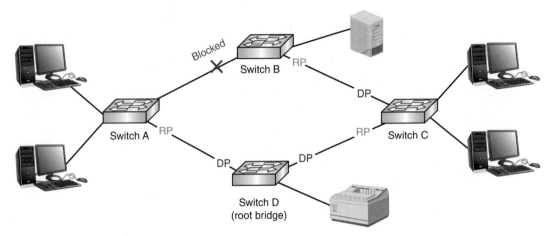

Figure 7-4 *DP* indicates downstream designated ports, and *RP* indicates upstream root ports

STP information is transmitted between switches via **BPDUs (Bridge Protocol Data Units)**. To protect the integrity of STP paths and the information transmitted by these BPDUs, some security precautions that must be configured on STP-enabled interfaces include the following:

- **BPDU guard**—Blocks BPDUs on any port serving network hosts, such as workstations and servers, and thereby ensures these devices aren't considered as possible paths. BPDU guards also enhance security by preventing a rogue switch or computer connected to one of these ports from hijacking the network's STP paths.
- **BPDU filter**—Disables STP on specific ports. For example, you might use a BPDU filter on the demarc, where the ISP's service connects with a business's network, to prevent the ISP's WAN topology from mixing with the corporate network's topology for the purpose of plotting STP paths.
- **Root guard**—Prevents switches beyond the configured port from becoming the root bridge. For example, an ISP might configure a root guard on an interface facing a customer's network to ensure that none of the customer's switches becomes the ISP's root bridge.

Network developers have repeatedly modified STP to improve and customize its functioning. The original STP is considered too slow for today's networks. For instance, it could take up to two minutes to detect and account for a link failure. With that kind of lag time, older versions of STP would bog down network transmissions, especially where high-volume, speed-dependent traffic, like telephone or video signals, is involved. Newer technologies to improve on or replace STP include the following:

- RSTP (Rapid Spanning Tree Protocol), defined in IEEE's 802.1w standard, and MSTP (Multiple Spanning Tree Protocol), originally defined by the 802.1s standard, can detect and correct for link failures in milliseconds.
- TRILL (Transparent Interconnection of Lots of Links) is a multipath, link-state protocol developed by the IETF.
- SPB (Shortest Path Bridging) is a descendent of STP and is defined in IEEE's 802.1aq standard. SPB differs from earlier iterations of STP in that it keeps all potential paths active while managing the flow of data across those paths to prevent loops. By utilizing all network paths, SPB greatly improves network performance.
- Some switch manufacturers, such as Cisco and Extreme Networks, have designed proprietary versions of STP that are optimized to work most efficiently on their equipment. One popular example is Rapid PVST+ (Per

VLAN Spanning Tree Plus) by Cisco. A VLAN (virtual LAN) is similar in concept to subnets, but it functions at OSI layer 2 instead of OSI layer 3. You'll learn more about VLANs later in this course.

Protocols designed to replace STP, such as SPB, operate at layer 3 instead of or in addition to layer 2, making them more compatible with various types of technologies like the connection protocols used on storage networks, which you'll learn more about shortly.

When installing switches on your network, you don't need to enable or configure STP (or the more current version that came with your switch). It will come with the switch's operating software and should function smoothly by default and without intervention. However, if you want to designate preferred paths between bridges or choose a special root bridge, for example, STP and its relatives allow you to alter default prioritizations.

Switch Port Security

Switches are designed to offer lots of ports through which devices can access a network by sending and receiving messages. Ideally, you want approved devices connected to a switch's ports, and no unapproved devices transmitting on those ports. This might seem like a simple goal until you consider how easy it is to unplug an Ethernet cable from an approved computer and plug it into an unapproved laptop. Depending on how the switch's port, or interface, is configured, this simple vulnerability could give an attacker easy and trusted access to your entire network!

One type of attack (intentional or not) that could be conducted with this kind of unauthorized network access is the broadcast storm you read about as you studied Spanning Tree. For example, if someone connects a hub to two unsecured switch ports, the hub creates a loop that generates a broadcast storm. Another example is connecting both ports on a VoIP phone to the network, or possibly connecting a computer through both a wired and wireless network connection. Controlling who can connect what device to a switch's port can help prevent this type of attack.

As a first layer of defense, unused physical and virtual ports on switches and other network devices should be disabled until needed. You can do this on Cisco, Huawei, and Arista routers and switches with the `shutdown` command. To enable them again, use the `no shutdown` command on Cisco or Arista devices, and use `undo shutdown` on Huawei devices. On a Juniper device, the corresponding commands are `disable` and `enable`, respectively. This will prevent an attacker from plugging into an unused port to conduct their attack. However, what about ports that are being used by legitimate devices?

Another Cisco command (which is also used on Arista devices) to secure switch access ports is `switchport port-security` (or just `port-security` on Huawei switches). This is essentially a MAC filtering function that also protects against MAC flooding, which makes it a type of flood guard. Acceptable MAC addresses are stored in a MAC address table. This table can be configured manually or dynamically. By default, the table allows only one MAC address to be active on the port; however, a network administrator can allow more MAC addresses per port. (On a Juniper switch, the `mac-limit` command restricts the number of MAC addresses allowed in the MAC address table. Approved MAC addresses are configured with the `allowed-mac` command.) Once the MAC address table is full, a security violation occurs if another device attempts to connect to the port. By default, the switch will shut down the port, or it can be configured to restrict data from the rogue device. Either way, the switch generates a notification to the network administrator. At the end of this module, you'll have the opportunity to practice securing switch ports on a switch in Packet Tracer, and then you'll see what happens when a hacker attempts to take over that port.

This type of switch port security is only one layer of defense—more of a deterrent, really. As you already know, MAC spoofing is not difficult to accomplish. The biggest challenge in this attack is learning the port's approved MAC address so that an attacker can spoof that address. As you'll learn through the rest of this course and throughout your career in IT, security should always be implemented in layers, which is a strategy called **defense in depth**.

Hierarchical Design

The network shown earlier in Figure 7-3 shows only four switches operating at the data link layer. While this example is larger than the typical home network, it hardly qualifies as a corporate network. Enterprise-grade networks might contain dozens or hundreds of switches (many of which also function at higher OSI layers) in addition to many routers, servers, and firewalls to increase performance and to better protect the network from problems if one or more devices fail. In the interest of increased redundancy, often you'll find teams or clusters of these devices working together to support higher volumes of traffic, such as when a cluster of web servers all work together to support a single website. A **load balancer** helps to evenly distribute traffic to each device in a cluster so every device carries a portion of the load.

With all these devices on a network, network engineers must take a more organized approach to designing the network to ensure that every device can function at its best without being swamped with too many kinds of tasks. To this end, Cisco and other manufacturers have developed a hierarchical design for switches on a network. In general, you can think of this hierarchy as having three tiers—that is, a **three-tiered architecture**, as illustrated in Figure 7-5 and described next:

- The **access layer**, or **edge layer**, consists of workgroup switches connected directly to hosts such as servers, printers, and workstations. Ideally, hosts connect *only* to access switches and never to switches at the other layers, although this is not always the case in the real world. Access switches typically organize traffic according to OSI layer 2 technologies.
- The **distribution layer**, or **aggregation layer**, is a highly redundant mesh of connections between multilayer switches or routers. It provides routing within the corporate network as well as traffic filtering and the network's connection to one or more WANs, such as a WAN connection to your **branch offices** at other locations or to the Internet. Other network blocks might also connect to this layer, such as a server network or a storage area network. Ideally, distribution switches manage traffic according to OSI layer 3 technologies; however, this isn't always possible due to limitations of certain applications needed on the network.
- The **core layer** consists of highly efficient multilayer switches or routers that support the network's backbone traffic. Typically, no filtering or routing is performed at this layer so as to minimize the processing required of these switches. Surprisingly, this layer is considered the simplest layer and doesn't need switches with lots of ports. These switches simply need to pass traffic in and out of a few backbone ports as quickly as possible. These switches nearly always function primarily at OSI layer 3.

In Figure 7-5, notice the multiple switches at each layer, and the multiple connections between switches. This mesh topology provides redundancy to protect the network from device or connection failure. For example, if a distribution switch's connection with one of the core switches fails, the distribution switch has a redundant connection with the other core switch.

The diagram in Figure 7-5 is simplified so you can see the relationship between the layers of this three-tiered architecture and the necessity for redundant connections. Figure 7-6 lays out the network devices a little more realistically. This figure shows you why the core layer is considered the center, or backbone, of the network. You can also see where hosts connect to the access layer, and other network blocks connect to the distribution layer.

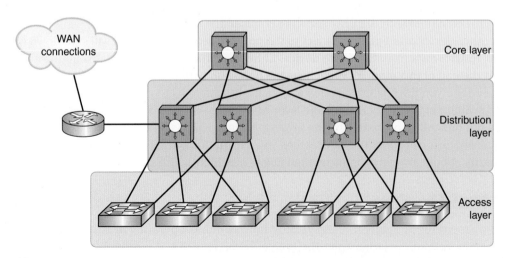

Figure 7-5   In a three-tiered architecture, switches at each layer are optimized to perform different functions

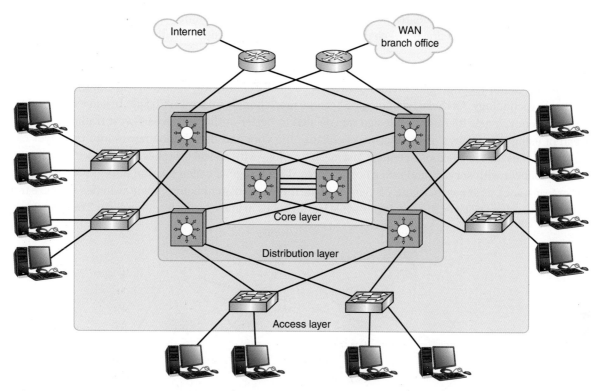

Figure 7-6 The distribution layer serves as the interface between the core and access layers and also connects other network blocks to the network

One of the advantages of this three-tier design is that traffic destined for nearby nodes can be handled differently and more efficiently than traffic that must traverse longer paths to its destination. The flow of traffic between peers within a network segment is called **east-west traffic**, and messages that must leave the local segment to reach their destinations are called **north-south traffic**. For example, as illustrated in Figure 7-7, traffic from web clients on the Internet requesting information from a web server in the data center is north-south traffic. Traffic from the web server requesting information from a database server within the same data center is east-west traffic. This east-west traffic

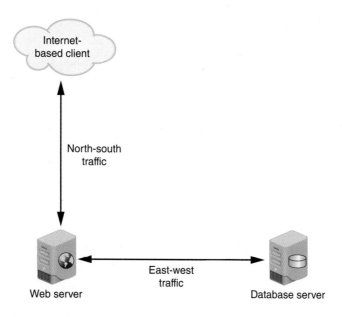

Figure 7-7 Messages from outside the network create a north-south traffic flow, while messages between peers within the network generate an east-west traffic flow

between servers in the same data center never leaves the access or distribution layers (depending on the network design). However, north-south traffic between the web server and the Internet flows through more switches throughout all layers in the design hierarchy.

Years ago, the traffic type that needed the most optimization was north-south traffic. However, you'll soon learn about newer data center technologies, including virtualization, SDN (software-defined networking), cloud computing, and new server technology. As these technologies became more popular, east-west traffic began experiencing significantly worse latency. A new hierarchical design was needed to better optimize this east-west traffic.

Instead of using three layers, newer networks collapse the core and distribution layers into one layer called the spine. Spine switches on the backbone connect in a mesh topology with all leaf switches (but not with each other), and leaf switches connect with servers and other host devices. This design is called a **spine-and-leaf architecture** (also spine-leaf or leaf-spine), as shown in Figure 7-8. Similar to the three-tiered architecture, spine switches organize traffic and network segments using OSI layer 3 technologies while leaf switches manage traffic by either layer 2 or layer 3 principles.

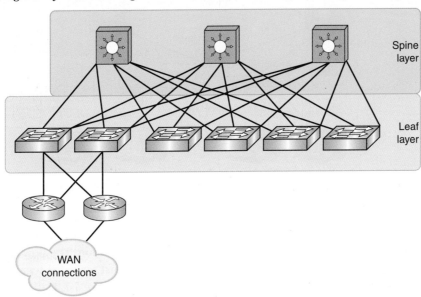

Figure 7-8 Two architecture layers provide more efficient access between any two network resources

Leaf switches often reside in the same rack as the servers they support. Two rack architectures include the following:

- **ToR (top of rack) switching**—While ToR switches are not necessarily positioned at the top of the rack, the top location in the rack often provides the best accessibility and cable management. The ToR switch connects all other devices in the rack to the rest of the network, as shown in Figure 7-9.
- **EoR (end of row) switching**—Where ToR is a vertically oriented arrangement, EoR is more horizontal in orientation. Instead of placing a switch at the top of each rack, EoR switching places several leaf switches in a rack at the end of each row of racks or in the middle of each row—called MoR (middle of row) switching. This approach requires fewer switches (and, therefore, fewer hops for much of the network's traffic) and less rack space, but more cabling and more work at cable management.

Each of these switch architectures offers benefits such as a reduced need for cabling and lower latency. Keeping the bulk of a network's cabling within the rack for very short connections means the network requires less cabling overall and provides increased flexibility in the network design. Very short cable runs make very high-speed cables—supporting 10 GbE (Gigabit Ethernet) or even 40 GbE or 100 GbE—an affordable option to connect leaf switches to spine switches.

The spine-and-leaf design also provides many benefits over the older, three-tiered architecture:

- **Improved redundancy**—Every leaf switch is connected to multiple (or perhaps all) spine switches in a full mesh topology, which provides redundant connections in case one link fails.
- **Decreased latency**—Because each leaf switch is connected to every spine switch, messages must traverse fewer hops to reach their destination.

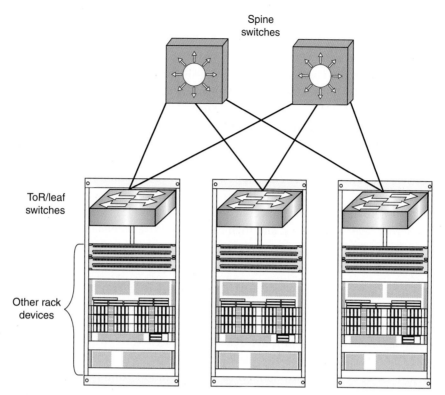

Figure 7-9   Leaf switches often server as the ToR switch in a rack

- **Increased performance**—A spine-and-leaf network can replace the older, error-laden STP with newer path management technologies such as TRILL and SPB. These technologies take advantage of the redundant links to increase performance and redundancy without creating problematic switching loops.
- **Improved scalability**—The number of available and usable paths for messages across a network improves scalability. This means a network can support larger numbers of host devices without overwhelming network pathways.
- **Increased security**—Traffic at all layers can be more easily inspected and monitored. With the traditional three-layer hierarchy, typically north-south traffic was filtered through a firewall as it entered the network. However, after that point, traffic was considered trustworthy and was rarely inspected. A spine-and-leaf architecture allows for security inspections of all traffic, including east-west traffic flows. This permutation of security priorities will come up again when you study security in network design later in this course.
- **Reduced expense**—Surprisingly, the hardware needed to build a spine-and-leaf architecture is typically less expensive than the switches needed for a three-tiered architecture.

The improvements offered by spine-and-leaf architecture were partly needed due to modern technologies such as SDN (software-defined networking). Let's look at what SDN is and why it's a favored approach to networking today.

Software-Defined Networking (SDN)

As network infrastructures became more complex, configuring all these networking devices to create and manage the network infrastructure presented a growing challenge. SDN (software-defined networking) is a centralized approach to networking that removes most of the decision-making power from network devices and instead handles that responsibility at a software level. Let's break that definition down with an analogy.

Suppose you're planning a neighborhood party and need everyone to bring a dish to share. You could take the so-called "pot-luck" approach where everyone brings whatever food they want based on what they like best. In that case, you might end up with a table full of desserts and no salad or veggies (not a terrible thing, but in the end, not well balanced). Instead, suppose you group your neighbors by floor in the building or by street in the neighborhood. You ask one group to bring a main course, another group to bring a side dish or casseroles, and a third group to bring desserts. This coordinated effort results in a more balanced meal that everyone (regardless of diet restrictions) can enjoy.

SDN relies on a similar concept—centralize control of network devices so networking rules (such as switching paths) are applied in a more coordinated manner. You give one device, called the SDN controller, a bird's eye view of the entire network so it can make more informed decisions on how to direct messages through the network. This **SDN controller** integrates configuration and management control of all network devices, both physical and virtual, into one cohesive system that is overseen by the network administrator through a single dashboard. Instead of reconfiguring each network device individually, the SDN controller can be used to reconfigure groups of network devices all at one time. It can even make configuration changes automatically in response to changing network conditions.

SDN relies on a form of abstraction called disaggregation, which basically means separating into pieces all the functions of a system so each piece can be handled by separate devices. This is kind of like when each person in an assembly line specializes in one type of task. For example, instead of each person performing all the steps to assemble a car, each person specializes in doing a small part of the work. In the end, this division of labor produces higher quality products at a faster rate. SDN creates the same kind of benefit for networks. Essentially, SDN abstracts the functions of network devices into different layers, or planes, and then relocates those planes in ways that make network management more effective (see Figure 7-10).

Consider the following explanation of each of these planes.

- **Infrastructure plane** (also called **data plane**)—This plane is made up of the physical or virtual devices (switches, routers, firewalls, and load balancers) that receive and send network messages on their way to their destinations. This is the plane where bits cross interfaces. This is also the plane where messages are decapsulated to examine layers of headers, MAC addresses are matched to switch ports, addresses are changed for NAT processing, and messages are re-encapsulated for the jump to the next device. The primary function of the infrastructure plane is to forward data on to its destination. Think of the infrastructure plane as the network's brawn (physical strength).

- **Control plane**—Think of the control plane as the network's brain (intelligence)—it handles the decision-making processes. Traditionally, the infrastructure plane and the control plane co-exist on the same device. With SDN, the control plane is abstracted to an SDN controller, which remotely manages networking devices. For example, consider the processing power that goes into building a switch's MAC address table, or the time and effort STP requires to optimize switching paths. All this work can be done by the SDN controller, which then downloads to network devices the required MAC address tables and other policies. This way, the switch doesn't have to think about what the network looks like or what devices are connected where. The switch simply compares each incoming message to its list of rules from the controller, and it sends the message on its way. If a message doesn't match one of the switch's preconfigured rules, the switch can send the message to the SDN controller for further analysis. This level of insight allows the SDN controller to create more nuanced rules specific to its network's needs. The SDN controller communicates with the infrastructure plane using APIs defined by an SDN protocol such as the popular and open source OpenFlow. Recall that APIs (application programming interfaces) are access points into available processes to generate a response of some kind. Several vendors offer SDN controller software, including VMware, Cisco, HP, IBM, and Juniper. Open source SDN controllers include ODL (OpenDayLight), ONOS (Open Network Operating System), and OpenKilda.

- **Application plane**—The SDN controller also communicates with network applications using APIs. Applications the SDN might need to communicate with include web browsers, VoIP software, network services like DNS, and

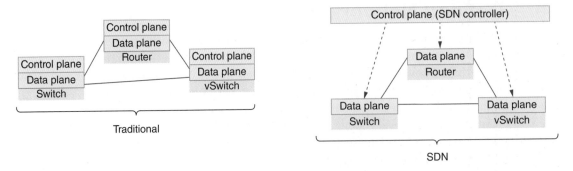

Figure 7-10   Distributed control planes in a traditional network versus a centralized control plane in an SDN network

apps specific to SDN. For example, you might install an analytics application that monitors network traffic for signs of a security breach. The application plane corresponds to OSI's application layer.

- **Management plane**—While not a typical layer for network communication, this plane could be considered a part of the control plane. It allows network administrators to remotely manage network devices, monitor those devices, and analyze data collected about the devices. Protocols in this plane include SSH, Telnet, SNMP (Simple Network Management Protocol), and even HTTP for web-based user interfaces.

In a traditional network, these planes co-exist within each device and are distributed across the network, as illustrated in Figure 7-11.

In an SDN network, the control plane (and, to a degree, the management plane) is moved to the SDN controller so devices can be centrally managed in conjunction with information from network applications, as shown in Figure 7-12.

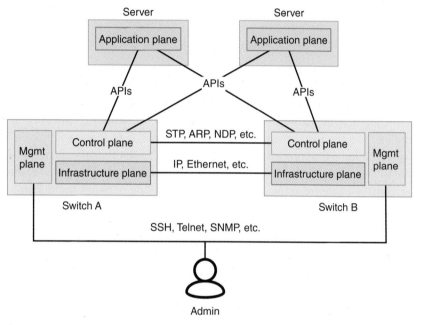

Figure 7-11 Each plane has its own functions and methods of communication

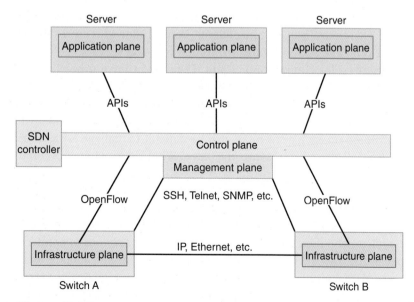

Figure 7-12 SDN centralizes the control plane to an SDN controller

Notice the SDN controller serves as the middleman between network applications and network hardware to ensure the network can best support the needs of those applications. Communication between the SDN controller and network devices is called an SBI (southbound interface). Communication between the SDN controller and applications through APIs is called an NBI (northbound interface).

SDN controller design varies by manufacturer. One of the possible variations is the degree to which the control plane is centralized to the SDN controller. Cisco, for example, achieves an unusual balance so that some of the control plane is centralized while some of it remains distributed to the underlying hardware devices. Other key differences between SDN controllers include the following:

- The level of support for network virtualization tools
- The number of switches the SDN controller can support
- Its ability to function across a WAN connection
- The way the SDN solution scales as your network grows
- The types of security filtering offered
- The ability to provide centralized monitoring of all physical and virtual portions of the network

While SDN does increase complexity, it also increases performance and efficiency. SDN can often be used to manage network devices from multiple manufacturers, obtaining consistent management techniques on the network. Physical and virtual devices can all be managed from a central interface. SDN also creates the potential to implement more sophisticated network functions while using less-expensive devices. Networking hardware in an SDN architecture is significantly less expensive than their more sophisticated counterparts. In the marketplace, these low intelligence, brandless devices are often called white box switches. The SDN controller can also generate more complex rules for managing traffic, such as tables within tables or condition-dependent rules. As you can see, one of the primary advantages to separating the control plane from the data plane is to provide network technicians with more centralized control of network settings and management.

In recent years, the concept of SDN architecture has expanded to include management of fully virtualized network resources and resources that are hosted in places other than an organization's own network (such as the cloud). All these resources can be centrally managed by a network's administrator through the framework of modern SDN software. Later in this module, you'll explore virtualization technologies, which is a significant step of abstraction away from physical devices. Further, virtualization lays the groundwork for a burgeoning IT industry: cloud computing. This module also covers the basics to get you started in the cloud. But first, let's look at a special kind of network that abstracts physical storage away from network servers.

Storage Area Network (SAN)

As you read about SDN, you learned that the control function of switches can be abstracted away from the switches and handled by a controller. This centralized, or consolidated, control allows for more flexible and responsive network path management. A similar principle can be applied to storage space on servers.

Server devices are optimized for compute functions. They might have powerful CPUs and loads of memory resources for fast data processing. Traditionally, each server contains its own storage space, which might include one or more storage drives called DAS (direct-attached storage). Making space on every server device to maximize its storage is not only bulky in your space-limited racks, but it's also difficult to manage when you have dozens of servers. Controlling access to data stored on each server can also be difficult to manage for a large data center. What if you could consolidate storage from all those servers into one place? What kinds of benefits could that kind of architecture offer your data center?

Large enterprises that require fast access to data and large amounts of storage often have a specialized storage area network connected to their corporate network. A SAN (storage area network) is a distinct network of storage devices that communicate directly with each other and with other portions of the network. Essentially, a SAN abstracts storage services from compute services, and then provides high-speed network services to connect them.

In a typical SAN, specialized SAN devices contain multiple storage drives and are designed to make data available to a network of servers. With multiple connections and clusters of storage devices arranged in RAID (Redundant Array of Independent Disks) arrays, this type of architecture is as fault tolerant as reasonably possible. If one storage device within a SAN suffers a fault, data is automatically retrieved from elsewhere in the SAN. If one connection in a

SAN suffers a failure, another connection is already in place to handle network traffic, which is called multipathing. Multipathing techniques can also provide load balancing to help ensure that the demand on storage is spread evenly across all storage devices in the SAN.

SANs are not only extremely fault tolerant, but they are also extremely fast. Consider how quickly your computer's CPU needs to access data stored on your computer's storage drive. That data travels a very short distance, probably over a SATA (Serial Advanced Technology Attachment) cable, between your computer's hard drive and its CPU. In a SAN, storage drives are located in one or more separate devices, possibly even in a different rack or a different room. The network connections between servers and SAN devices must support extremely high data throughput. To maximize throughput, SANs rely on one of these networking technologies:

- **FC (Fibre Channel)** is a storage networking architecture that runs separately from Ethernet networks to maximize speed of data storage and access. Although FC can run over copper cables, fiber-optic cable is much more commonly used. Fibre Channel requires special hardware, which makes it an expensive storage connection technology. Specialized FC switches connect SAN storage devices with each other and with the outside network. Instead of NICs, FC devices connect with the network through HBAs (host bus adapters). At the time of this writing, FC networks can achieve speeds as high as 128 GFC (Gigabit Fibre Channel) over a single lane or approaching 512 GFC on quad lanes using QSFP technology. Specifications are in development to reach speeds up to 1 TFC (Terabit Fibre Channel) as soon as 2024. Figure 7-13 shows a Fibre Channel SAN connected to a traditional Ethernet network. Besides being expensive, Fibre Channel requires extensive training for IT personnel to support it.
- **FCoE (Fibre Channel over Ethernet)** is a newer technology that allows FC to travel over Ethernet hardware and connections. To do this, the FC frame is encapsulated inside an FCoE frame, which is then encapsulated inside an Ethernet frame, as illustrated in Figure 7-14. This preserves much of the higher speed capabilities of FC, along with the convenience and cost-efficiency of using existing Ethernet network equipment, as shown

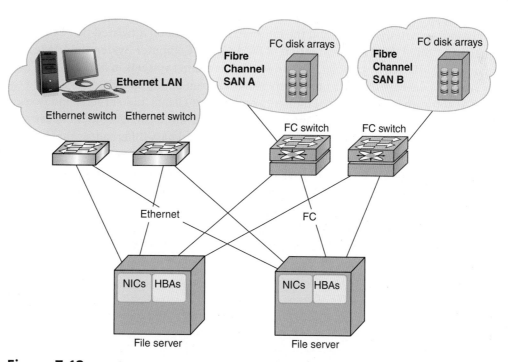

Figure 7-13 A Fibre Channel SAN connected to an Ethernet LAN

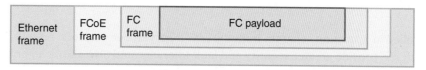

Figure 7-14 FCoE encapsulation

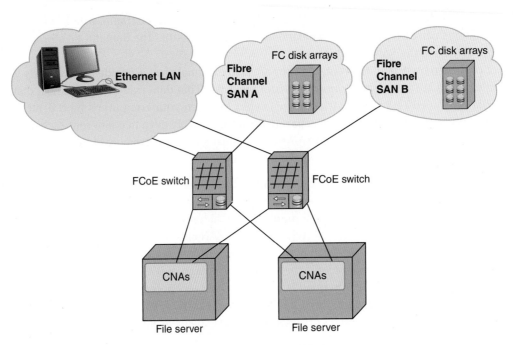

Figure 7-15   A SAN using FCoE to connect to a LAN

in Figure 7-15. With the installation of CNAs (converged network adapters), FCoE switches can connect to network servers and to switches for both the LAN and the SAN.

- **iSCSI (Internet SCSI)**, pronounced "i-scuzzy," is a transport layer protocol that runs on top of TCP to allow fast transmissions over LANs, WANs, and the Internet. It can work on a twisted-pair Ethernet network with ordinary Ethernet NICs. iSCSI is an evolution of SCSI (Small Computer System Interface), which is a fast transmission standard used by internal hard drives and operating systems in file servers. The advantages of iSCSI over Fibre Channel are that it is not as expensive, can run on the already established Ethernet LAN by installing iSCSI software (called an iSCSI initiator) on network clients and servers, and does not require as much special training for IT personnel. Some network administrators configure iSCSI to use jumbo frames on the Ethernet LAN. iSCSI architecture is very similar to FC. The primary difference is that Ethernet equipment and interfaces can be used throughout the storage network. In fact, this is the primary advantage of iSCSI over other options, making it relatively straightforward to implement. iSCSI doesn't offer nearly the same performance benchmarks, however, and currently maxes out around 10 Gbps with 40 Gbps speeds on the horizon.
- **IB (InfiniBand)**, like FC, requires specialized network hardware. Although it's very fast, InfiniBand tends to serve a few niche markets rather than being widely available. IB falls on the difficult end of the installation and configuration spectrum, and it runs on the expensive side as well.

NOTE 7-3

You can get updated information about Fibre Channel and its related technology, FCoE (Fibre Channel over Ethernet), at *fibrechannel.org*.

A SAN can be installed in a location separate from the LAN it serves. For example, remote SANs can be kept in an ISP's data center, which can provide greater security and fault tolerance and also allows an organization to outsource the management of its SAN.

SANs are highly scalable and have a very high fault tolerance, massive storage capabilities, and fast data access. SANs are best suited to environments with huge quantities of data that must always be quickly available. For example, consider the storage volumes used by VMs. Hosting large numbers of VMs is a prime use case for a SAN. Let's look more closely at virtualization technology and how various components of that system take yet another step up in the progression of network abstraction.

REMEMBER THIS...

- Explain how STP works.
- Compare three-tiered architecture with spine-and-leaf architecture.
- Explain the planes of SDN.
- Use common port security best practices.
- Describe SAN technologies, including FC, FCoE, and iSCSI.

SELF-CHECK

1. Which STP bridge serves as the basis for all path calculations?
   a. Designated bridge
   b. Header bridge
   c. Spanning bridge
   d. Root bridge

2. Which type of switch is best used for connections to web servers?
   a. Edge switch
   b. Core switch
   c. Spine switch
   d. Aggregation switch

3. Which SDN plane moves traffic from switch port to switch port?
   a. Control plane
   b. Management plane
   c. Application plane
   d. Infrastructure plane

4. Which SAN connection technology can run over ordinary Ethernet NICs without any special equipment needed?
   a. FC
   b. iSCSI
   c. SATA
   d. IB

Check your answers at the end of this module.

You're Ready

You're now ready to complete **Capstone Project 7-1: Secure Switch Ports in Packet Tracer**, or you can wait until you've finished reading this module.

VIRTUAL ARCHITECTURE

 **CERTIFICATION**

1.2: Explain the characteristics of network topologies and network types.

Average reading time: 30 minutes

Beginning with the first module in this course, you've created and worked with a variety of virtual machines, or VMs, in several of the Capstone Projects. You've used Hyper-V or VirtualBox to create workstation and server VMs, and you installed both Windows and Linux operating systems on those VMs. By this point, you've had the opportunity to become familiar with the process and some of the terms involved in working with virtualization technology. Now you're ready for a more thorough examination of what you've been accomplishing in these projects.

Virtualization is a virtual, or logical, version of something rather than the actual, or physical, version. For example, when you create an Ubuntu server VM on a Windows PC, the Windows machine is the physical computer, or **host**, and the Ubuntu machine is a logical computer, or **guest**, that is hosted by the physical computer. The Ubuntu operating system acts as if it is installed on a separate, physical machine and is generally not aware of its physical host. In essence, virtualization has abstracted the computer system from the computer hardware so that multiple systems can exist on the same hardware. How is this possible?

The key to this feat is a type of software known as a hypervisor. A **hypervisor** creates and manages a VM, and it allocates hardware resources for the host and any of its guest VMs. Together, all the virtual devices on a single computer share the same CPU, hard disks, memory, and physical network interfaces. Yet each VM can be configured to use a different operating system and can emulate a different type of CPU, storage drive, or NIC, than the physical computer it resides on. Meanwhile, to users, a VM appears and acts essentially the same as a physical computer running the same software. Figure 7-16 illustrates some of the elements of virtualization.

There are two types of hypervisors: Type 1 and Type 2. The differences are diagrammed in Figure 7-17 and explained next.

- **Type 1 hypervisor**—Installs on a computer before any OS and is, therefore, erroneously called a "bare-metal" hypervisor. In reality, a type 1 hypervisor is itself a minimal operating system, many of which are built on a Linux kernel. Like any OS, the hypervisor relies on firmware to enable communication with the underlying hardware. It partitions the hardware computing power to multiple VMs, each with their own OS. Popular examples include Citrix Hypervisor, ESXi by VMware, and Hyper-V by Microsoft.

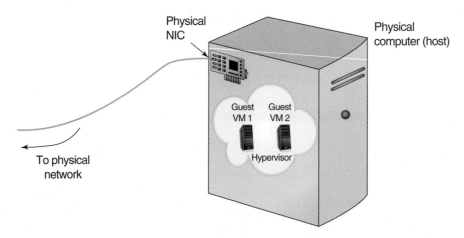

Figure 7-16 Elements of virtualization

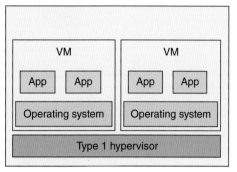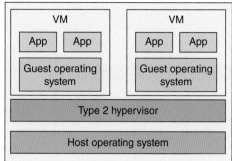

Figure 7-17   Type 1 and Type 2 hypervisors

- **Type 2 hypervisor**—Installs in a host OS as an application and is called a hosted hypervisor. VirtualBox, which you've seen in the Capstone Projects, is an example of a type 2 hypervisor, as is the popular VMware Player. A type 2 hypervisor is not as powerful as a type 1 hypervisor because it is dependent on the host OS to allot its computing power. VMs hosted by a type 2 hypervisor also are not as secure or as fast as a type 1 hypervisor's VMs.

Hyper-V has elements of both categories. Hyper-V is embedded in Windows Server 2008 and beyond, and in Windows 10 (sometimes called Client Hyper-V), which you might have worked with in the Capstone Projects. Hyper-V Manager appears to run as an application and, therefore, looks more like a type 2 hypervisor. In reality, when Hyper-V is enabled in Windows, it creates a virtualization layer underneath the existing OS installation, thereby establishing its role as a type 1 hypervisor. This arrangement is unusual, however, in that the existing Windows OS continues to be given privileged access through the virtualization layer to the underlying hardware, while guest VMs are not given this level of access.

Another hypervisor, KVM (Kernel-based Virtual Machine), is native to Linux OSs and also has elements of both a type 1 and type 2 hypervisor. When installed, KVM effectively converts the existing Linux OS to a type 1 hypervisor. However, the original OS is still accessible and can still host other applications.

A VM's software and hardware characteristics are assigned when it is created in the hypervisor. As you have learned, these characteristics can differ completely from those of the host machine. Keep in mind that a VM is entirely a logical entity—it's not confined to the features of the local hardware in the same way that a physical machine is. You can customize the VM with a guest operating system, amount of memory, hard disk size, and processor type, to name just a few options. Figure 7-18 shows a screen from VMware Player's VM creation wizard that allows you to specify the amount of memory allocated to a VM. Notice in the figure you could click on other devices in the hardware list, such as processors, optical disc drives, and the network adapter, to make changes to those specifications as well.

While there are limits imposed by the physical hardware, such as total available RAM or storage space, the hypervisor makes it possible for a VM guest to function differently than the host machine or other guest machines. As you learn more about virtualization, train yourself to notice how logical functions operate on a different layer, or plane, than what might be implied by the physical hardware. To help you understand the difference between physical systems and virtual systems, consider the following analogy.

Think about the foundation of a house. In many cases, a foundation is made of cement blocks or poured concrete, it usually reaches deep into the ground, and it defines the outline of the house to be built above it. Looking only at the foundation, however, would not necessarily indicate how many floors the house will have, what colors the walls will be, or what materials will be used on the inside or the outside. On a single foundation, you might even build two townhouses or four apartments. Similarly, the physical hardware of a computer defines some outer limits of capabilities, such as how much RAM is available to all running VMs or how much storage space is available for all VM-associated data. However, within those limits, you can create many virtual machines with a variety of characteristics. These VMs are managed by the hypervisor without being directly defined by the hardware supporting it all.

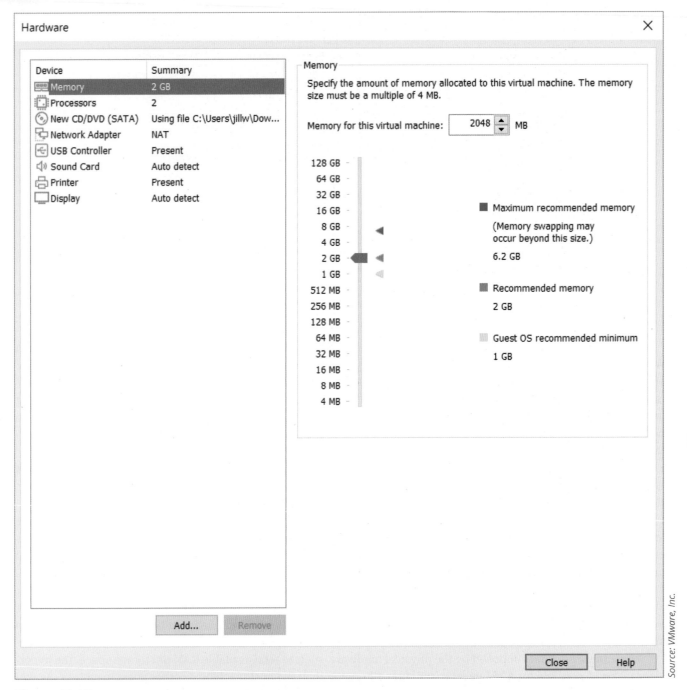

Figure 7-18   Specifying a VM's memory in VMware

Network Connection Types

In Module 4's Project 4-2, you used Remote Desktop to connect two computers. You had the opportunity to use a VM for one or both of the computers. And if you were using the VirtualBox hypervisor, you had to ensure the VM's network adapter was set to Bridged mode. Now you're ready to learn what that setting means.

Every VM has its own virtual network adapter, or **vNIC (virtual NIC)**, that can connect the VM to a network, either virtual or physical. Just like a physical NIC, a vNIC operates at the data link layer and provides the computer with network access. Each VM can have several vNICs, no matter how many NICs the host machine has. The maximum number of vNICs on a VM depends on the limits imposed by the hypervisor. For example, VirtualBox allows up to eight vNICs per VM. Upon creation, each vNIC is automatically assigned a MAC address.

Figure 7-19 shows a dialog box from the VMware Player wizard that allows you to customize properties of a virtual workstation's vNIC. One of many options you can configure for each vNIC is its inbound and outbound transmission speeds. For example, you could select transmission speeds that simulate a DSL or cable broadband connection, which you'll learn more about later.

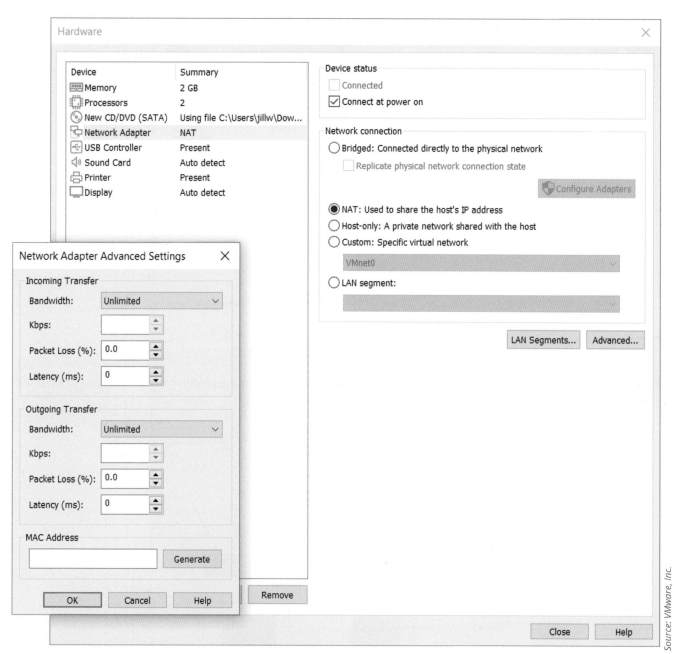

Figure 7-19   Customizing vNIC properties in VMware

As soon as the virtual machine's vNIC is selected, the hypervisor creates a connection between that VM and the host. Depending on the hypervisor, this connection might be called a bridge or a switch. This **vSwitch (virtual switch)** or bridge is a logically defined device that operates at the data link layer to pass frames between nodes. Thus, it can allow VMs to communicate with each other and with nodes on a physical LAN. In a type 1 hypervisor, such as Hyper-V, the host and its guests all use the vSwitch (see Figure 7-20). In a type 2 hypervisor, such as VirtualBox, the guests rely on the vSwitch while the host remains connected directly to the physical network.

One host can support multiple virtual switches, which are controlled by the hypervisor. Figure 7-21 illustrates a host machine with two physical NICs that support several virtual machines and their vNICs. A virtual switch connects the vNICs to the network.

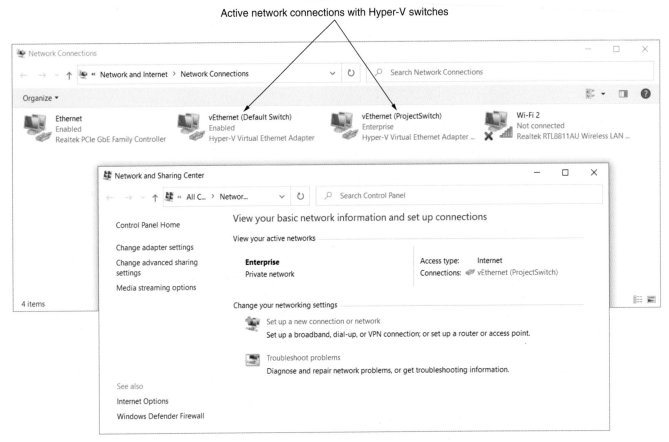

Figure 7-20 The OS of a host computer running Hyper-V is connected to the physical network through Hyper-V's vSwitch

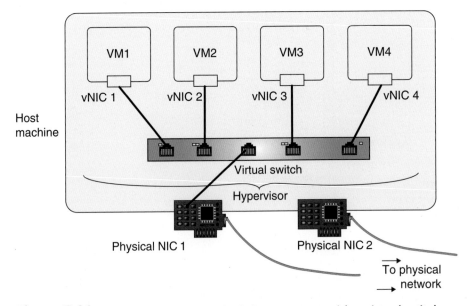

Figure 7-21 Virtual servers on a single host connect with a virtual switch

VMs can go through a virtual switch on the host computer to reach the physical network and can communicate with physical or virtual routers, other network devices, and other hosts on the local or another network. For example, in Figure 7-22, a VM on Host A can communicate with a VM on Host B.

The way a vNIC is configured determines whether the VM is joined to a virtual network or attempts to join the physical LAN that the host machine is connected to. These various configurations are called networking modes, the

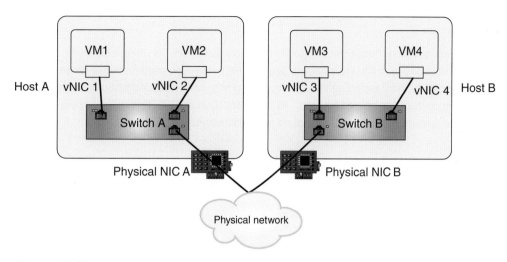

Figure 7-22   Virtual switches exchange traffic across the physical network

most common of which are bridged, NAT, and host-only, as described next. These descriptions are specific to the type 2 hypervisors you've been using in your projects. However, type 1 hypervisors offer these and other network configurations as well.

Bridged Mode

In **bridged mode**, a vNIC accesses a physical network using the host machine's NIC, as shown in Figure 7-23. In other words, the virtual interface and the physical interface are bridged. If your host machine contains multiple physical adapters—for example, a wireless NIC and a wired NIC—you can choose which physical adapter to use as the bridge when you configure the virtual adapter.

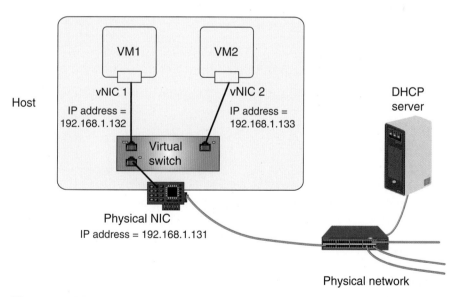

Figure 7-23   This vNIC accesses the physical network directly in bridged mode

Although a bridged vNIC communicates through the host's adapter, it obtains its own IP address, default gateway, and subnet mask from a DHCP server on the physical LAN. For example, suppose your DHCP server is configured to assign addresses in the range of 192.168.1.100 through 192.168.1.254 to nodes on your LAN. The router might assign your host machine's physical NIC an IP address of 192.168.1.131. A guest on your host might obtain an IP address of 192.168.1.132. A second guest on that host might obtain an IP address of 192.168.1.133, and so on.

When connected using bridged mode, a VM appears to other nodes as just another client or server on the network. Other nodes communicate directly with the VM without realizing it is virtual.

NOTE 7-4

In VMware and VirtualBox, you can choose the bridged connection type when you create or configure the virtual adapter. In KVM, you create a bridge between the VM and your physical NIC when you modify the vNIC's settings. In Hyper-V, you create a bridged connection type by assigning VMs to an external network switch. Additionally, bridged mode is the most common networking mode for VMs hosted by type 1 hypervisors such as ESXi. Figure 7-24 shows the bridging options for a virtual machine in VMware Player with the Bridged network connection type selected.

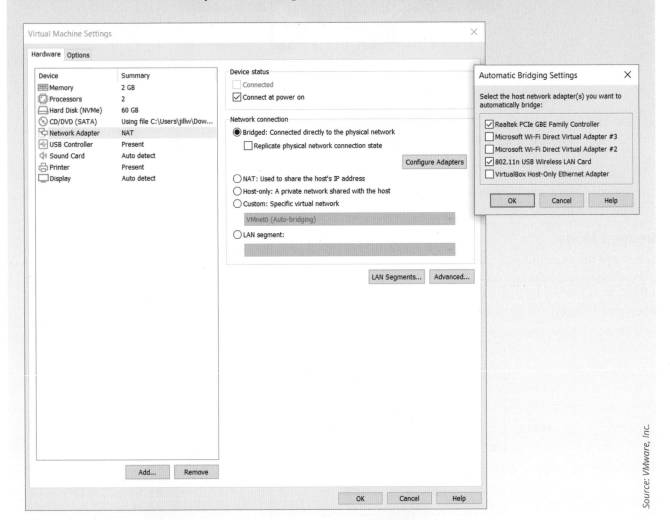

Figure 7-24 Selecting the Bridged option for a vNIC in VMware Player

VMs that must be available at a static IP address, such as mail servers or web servers, should be assigned bridged network connections. However, VMs that other nodes do not need to access directly can be configured to use the NAT networking mode.

NAT Mode

In **NAT mode**, a vNIC relies on the host machine to act as a NAT (network address translation) device. In other words, the VM obtains IP addressing information from its host rather than from a server or router on the physical network. To accomplish this, the hypervisor acts as a DHCP server. A vNIC operating in NAT mode can still communicate with other nodes on the network and vice versa. However, other nodes communicate with the host machine's IP address to reach the VM; the VM itself is invisible to nodes on the physical network. Figure 7-25 illustrates a VM operating in NAT mode.

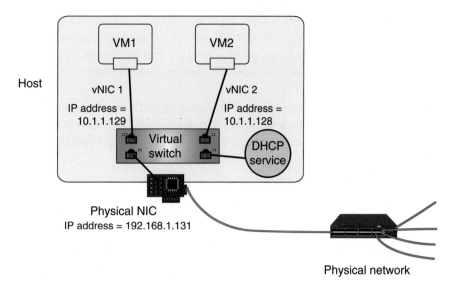

Figure 7-25   The vNIC accesses the physical network via NAT in NAT mode

NOTE 7-5

NAT is the default network connection type selected when you create a VM in VMware Player, VirtualBox, or KVM. In Hyper-V, the NAT connection type is created by assigning VMs to an internal network run on a virtual switch. Figure 7-26 shows the default switch in Hyper-V, which hosts an internal network type using NAT. Notice all other options are grayed out. The only way to change these other options is to create a new virtual network switch in the Hyper-V Virtual Switch Manager.

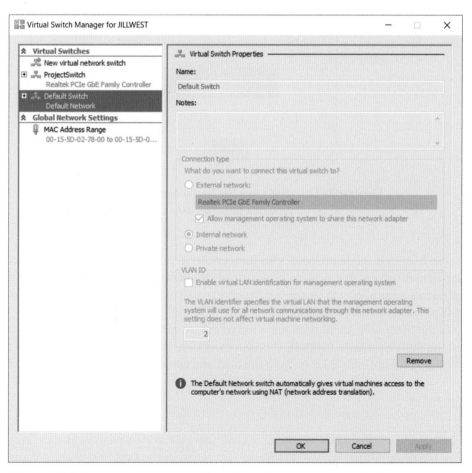

Figure 7-26   The default switch in Hyper-V gives VMs access to the host's network using NAT

Once you have selected the NAT configuration type, you can configure the pool of IP addresses available to the VMs on a host. For example, suppose, as shown in Figure 7-25, your host machine has an IP address of 192.168.1.131. You might configure your host's DHCP service to assign IP addresses in the range of 10.1.1.120 through 10.1.1.254 to the VMs you create on that host. Because these addresses will never be evident beyond the host, you have flexibility in choosing their IP address range.

The NAT network connection type is appropriate for VMs that do not need to be accessed at a known address by other network nodes. For example, virtual workstations that are mainly used to run stand-alone applications, or that serve as test beds to test applications or operating system installations, are good candidates for NAT network connections.

Host-Only Mode

In **host-only mode**, VMs on one host can exchange data with each other and with their host, but they cannot communicate with any nodes beyond the host. In other words, the vNICs never receive or transmit data via the host machine's physical NIC. In host-only mode, as in NAT mode, VMs use the DHCP service in the host's virtualization software to obtain IP address assignments.

Figure 7-27 illustrates how the host-only option creates an isolated virtual network. Host-only mode is appropriate for test networks or if you simply need to install a different operating system on your workstation to use an application that is incompatible with your host's operating system. For example, suppose a project requires you to create diagrams in Microsoft Visio and your workstation runs Red Hat Linux. You could install a Windows 10 VM solely for the purpose of installing and running Visio.

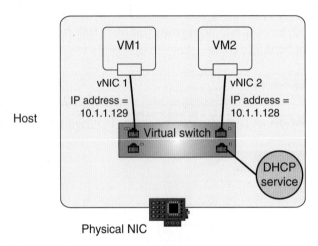

Figure 7-27   vNICs in a host-only network can only talk to other VMs running on that host

Obviously, because host-only mode prevents VMs from exchanging data with a physical network, this configuration cannot work for virtual servers that need to be accessed by clients across a LAN. Nor can it be used for virtual workstations that need to access LAN or WAN services, such as email or web pages. Host-only networking is less commonly used than NAT or bridged mode networking.

Figure 7-28 shows the "Host-only Adapter" mode selected in VirtualBox. Notice a similar mode called Internal Network. In VirtualBox, the difference is that with Host-only networking, VMs can communicate with the physical host. With Internal networking, VMs are isolated even from the host and can only communicate with each other.

NOTE 7-6

You can choose host-only networking when you create or configure a VM in VMware or VirtualBox. In Hyper-V, the host-only connection type is created by assigning VMs to a private virtual network. In KVM, host-only is not a predefined option, but can be assigned to a vNIC via the command-line interface.

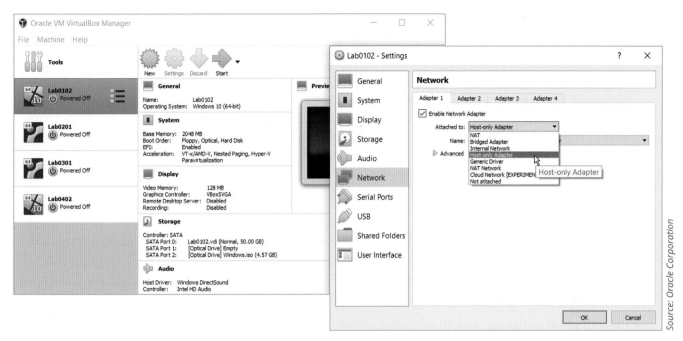

Figure 7-28 VirtualBox offers both Host-only mode and Internal mode

Source: Oracle Corporation

Virtualization software gives you the flexibility of creating several networking types on one host machine. For example, on one host you could create a host-only network to test multiple versions of Linux. On the same host, you could create a group of Windows Server machines that are connected to your physical LAN using the bridged connection type. Or, rather than specifying one of the networking connection types described previously, you could also create a VM that is not connected to any nodes, whether virtual or physical. Preventing the VM from communicating with other nodes keeps it completely isolated. This might be desirable when testing unpredictable software or an image of untrusted origin.

Pros and Cons of Virtualization

Virtualization has become the de facto standard for many resources on enterprise networks worldwide. It's unlikely you'll work with a business-grade network that does not incorporate virtualization in some way. Virtualization offers several advantages, including the following:

- **Efficient use of resources**—Physical clients or servers devoted to one function typically use only a fraction of their capacity. Without virtualization, a company might purchase five computers to run five different services—for example, an email server, a file server, two web servers, and a database server. The *On the Job* story at the beginning of this module gave an example of a company running three different servers for various tasks. Each server needs its own, dedicated system, resulting in a lot of waste because each service might demand only 10–20 percent of its computer's processing power and memory. With virtualization, a single, powerful computer can support all five services. This creates a significant single point of failure, however, if this one server goes down for any reason. Therefore, in actual practice, most of these network services are also duplicated across multiple physical servers.

- **Cost and energy savings**—With virtualization, organizations save money by purchasing fewer and less-expensive physical machines. They also save electricity because there are fewer and more efficient computers drawing power and less demand for air conditioning in the computer room, as you saw in this module's *On the Job* story. Some institutions with thousands of users, such as Stanford University, are using virtualization to conserve energy and are promoting it as part of campus-wide sustainability efforts. Thin clients, for example, are very small, energy-efficient computers that can be used to populate large computer labs on a college campus. Thin clients connect to a central server to perform most of their processing functions. When a user signs into a domain account on the thin client, the thin client then contacts the server for all other functions.

The server hosts the thin client's software, including the operating system and most or all applications. In other words, the thin client's entire desktop is virtualized and hosted by the server.

- **Fault and threat isolation**—In a virtual environment, the isolation of each guest system means that a problem with one guest does not affect the others. For example, an instructor might create multiple instances of an operating system and applications on a single computer that's shared by several classes. This allows each student to work on their own instance of the OS environment. Any configuration errors or changes they make on their guest machine will not affect other students. In another example, a network administrator who wants to try a beta version of an application might install that application on a guest machine rather than on the host, in case the untested software causes problems. Furthermore, because a VM is granted limited access to hardware resources, security attacks on a guest pose less risk to a host or the physical network to which it's connected.

- **Simple backups, recovery, and replication**—Virtualization software enables network administrators to save backup images of a guest machine. The images can later be used to recreate that machine on another host or on the same host. This feature allows for simple backups and quick recovery. It also makes it easy to create multiple, identical copies of one VM, called clones. Some virtualization software allows you to save image files of VMs that can be imported into a competitor's virtualization software.

Not every type of client or server is a good candidate for virtualization, however. Potential disadvantages to creating multiple guests on a single host machine include the following:

- **Compromised performance**—When multiple VMs contend for finite physical resources, one VM could monopolize those resources and impair the performance of others on the same computer. In theory, careful management and resource allocation should prevent this. In practice, however, it is unwise to force a critical application—for example, a hospital's emergency medical systems or a factory's real-time control systems—to share resources and take that risk. Imagine a brewery that uses computers to measure and control tank levels, pressure, flow, and temperature of liquid ingredients during processing. These functions are vital for product quality and safety. In this example, where specialty software demands real-time, error-free performance, it makes sense to devote all a computer's resources to this set of functions, rather than share that computer with, for example, the brewery's human resources database server. In addition to multiple guest systems vying for limited physical resources, a hypervisor also requires some overhead.

- **Increased complexity**—Although virtualization reduces the number of physical machines to manage, it increases complexity and administrative burden in other ways. For instance, a network administrator who uses virtual servers and switches must thoroughly understand virtualization software. In addition, managing addressing and switching for multiple VMs is more complex than doing so for physical machines. Finally, because VMs are so easy to set up, they might be created capriciously or as part of experimentation, and then forgotten. As a result, extra VMs might litter a server's hard disk, consume resources, and unnecessarily complicate network management. By contrast, abandoned physical servers might only take up rack space.

- **Increased licensing costs**—Because every instance of commercial software requires its own license, every VM that uses such software comes with added cost. In some cases, the added cost brings little return. For example, a software developer might want to create four instances of Windows Server on a single computer to test new software using four testing procedures on four different OS installation configurations. To comply with Microsoft's licensing restrictions, the developer will have to purchase four licenses for Windows Server. Depending on the developer's intentions, it might make more sense, instead, to share one installation of Windows Server and separate the four testing procedures by using four different logon IDs. Alternatively, the developer could save the initial VM image and start over fresh for each test.

- **Single point of failure**—If a host machine fails, all its guest machines will fail, too. As mentioned earlier, an organization that creates VMs for its email server, file server, web servers, and database server on a single physical computer would lose all those services if the one, physical computer went down. Wise network administrators implement measures such as clustering and automatic failover to prevent that from happening.

Most of the potential disadvantages in this list can be mitigated through thoughtful design and virtualization control. Similarly, the same advantages and disadvantages of client virtualization apply to virtualizing other network devices. Next, let's look at what can be accomplished when virtualization technology is used elsewhere on the network.

NFV (Network Functions Virtualization)

You've seen how a single workstation can host many VM workstations or servers, each with its own network connection, operating system, and applications. Networking devices can also be virtualized. For example, instead of purchasing an expensive hardware firewall to protect a LAN, suppose you were to install a firewall's operating system in a VM on an inexpensive server. Suppose you also install a router VM on that server instead of purchasing an expensive hardware router. You've now provided your network with two sophisticated, virtualized devices—a virtual firewall and a virtual router—on one, inexpensive server instead of paying for two, expensive, dedicated devices.

NOTE 7-7

To clarify, a software firewall is merely an application, like Windows Firewall. It's very limited in scope and features, and only services a single client. A dedicated firewall device, such as those made by Fortinet, Cisco, or Palo Alto Networks, serves an entire network (or portion of a network). It has many more features than a firewall app and runs its own OS.

A virtual firewall emulates a hardware firewall, and it's hosted in a virtualized environment. Examples include the pfSense virtual firewall by Netgate and Barracuda's CloudGen firewall, which can also provide protection for cloud-based portions of the network. There must be a hypervisor present (usually type 1) to host a virtual firewall.

These distinctions apply to other devices as well, such as routers, switches, and load balancers.

Now replicate these savings over dozens of devices for a large network, and you can begin to see some of the advantage of virtualizing network functions. Other advantages include the following:

- Virtual devices can be quickly and sometimes automatically migrated, or moved, from one server to another in the event of a hardware failure or maintenance.
- Resources, such as hardware, energy usage, and physical space, are utilized more efficiently.
- Services can be easily scaled to meet the changing needs of a network.

Merging physical and virtual network architecture is called **NFV (Network Functions Virtualization)**. NFV provides flexible, cost-saving options for many types of network devices, including virtual servers, data storage, load balancers, and firewalls. However, there are a few caveats and considerations to keep in mind:

- You'll need licenses for each of the virtualized devices as well as for the type 1 hypervisor that will host them. Fortunately, the cost of these licenses amounts to a fraction of the cost of similarly featured hardware devices.
- The interaction between physical and virtual devices introduces a small degree of latency as data passes through the hypervisor and its connections. Usually, this delay is negligible. However, it might be a relevant consideration in some cases.
- Even some of the most die-hard virtualization fans are uncomfortable using a virtual firewall to protect the entire network. The server hosting a virtual firewall occasionally needs to be restarted in the course of regular maintenance or some kind of failure, and in that event, the hosted firewall goes down with the server. Instead, many network admins believe that virtual firewalls are only appropriate for securing virtual-only portions of the network, or for serving as a backup to physical firewall devices.

REMEMBER THIS...

- Compare type 1 and type 2 hypervisors.
- Describe virtual network devices, such as a vSwitch and a vNIC.
- Explain the role of NFV in optimizing network architecture.

SELF-CHECK

5. Which virtual network connection type assigns a VM its IP address from the physical network?
   a. NAT
   b. Bridged
   c. Private
   d. Host-only

6. Which network architecture technique are you using when you run a virtual router on a network?
   a. STP
   b. SAN
   c. NFV
   d. SDN

Check your answers at the end of this module.

You're Ready

You're now ready to complete **Capstone Project 7-2: Explore Virtual Network Configuration Options in Hyper-V** or **Capstone Project 7-3: Explore Virtual Network Configuration Options in VirtualBox**, depending on which hypervisor you've been using throughout this course. Or you can wait until you've finished reading this module.

CLOUD ARCHITECTURE

 **CERTIFICATION**

1.7 Explain basic corporate and datacenter network architecture.

1.8 Summarize cloud concepts and connectivity options.

3.1 Given a scenario, use the appropriate statistics and sensors to ensure network availability.

Average reading time: 26 minutes

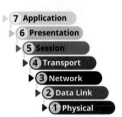

On network diagrams, the Internet is frequently drawn as a cloud allowing access to information stored on web servers around the world. When it was first introduced, the image captured something essential about modern networking, so now the term **cloud computing**, or simply cloud, refers to the flexible provision of data storage, applications, or services to clients over the Internet. You might already be familiar with cloud storage services such as Dropbox, OneDrive, and Google Drive, which let you store your own data on web-based servers. Web-based email is another example of cloud computing. Most cloud service providers use virtualization software to supply multiple platforms to users. For example, industry leaders Rackspace (in its private, public, or hybrid cloud products) and Amazon (in its Elastic Compute Cloud, or EC2, service) use Xen virtualization software by Citrix to create virtual environments for their customers.

Cloud computing covers a broad range of services, from hosting websites and database servers to providing virtual servers for collaboration or software development. You can think of the cloud as an abstraction of IT from the data center. That's not entirely accurate, as you can run your cloud in your own data center. However, a cloud architecture gives you a lot more flexibility in choosing and configuring your resources. Let's look at this distinction a little more closely. All cloud services have the following features in common, according to NIST (National Institute of Standards and Technology):

- **On-demand self-service**—Services, applications, and storage in a cloud are available to users at any time, upon the user's request.
- **Broad network access**—Client devices of all types, including smartphones, laptops, desktops, thin clients, and tablet computers, can access services, applications, and storage in a cloud, no matter what operating system they run or where they are located, if they have an Internet connection.
- **Resource pooling**—Host computers in the cloud provide multiple services or resources such as disk space, applications, and services that are pooled, or consolidated. For example, a single cloud provider can host hundreds of websites for hundreds of different customers on just a few servers. This is called multitenancy where several customers (tenants) pay for resources running on the same hardware.
- **Measured service**—Everything offered by a cloud provider, including applications, desktops, storage, and other services, is measured. A provider might limit or charge by the amount of bandwidth, processing power, storage space, or client connections available to customers.
- **Rapid elasticity**—Services and storage capacity can be scaled up or down without negatively affecting the efficiency and effectiveness of the workload, which is called scalability. The fact these resources can be changed quickly and dynamically—even automatically—in response to changing demands, refers to elasticity. For example, if your website suddenly receives a burst of traffic following a major marketing campaign, scalability ensures you can increase the cloud resources the website needs without disrupting your web services, while elasticity refers to your web servers' ability to scale up quickly and automatically as soon as the increased traffic is detected.

Let's consider a scenario where cloud enables a company to partner with people who are scattered across the globe. Suppose an organization that develops graphic design software employs dozens of creative and highly skilled developers on a project. These developers, half of them working from home, are located in six different countries. How can these employees, located so far away from the central office and from each other, collaborate successfully?

The company contracts with a CSP (cloud services provider) to host its servers, making the company's test platforms easily accessible to any of its employees via the Internet. The company's developers can load any kind of software on the servers, test it from afar, and share this content with distant members of the team. If additional storage space is needed, that resource can be dynamically allocated. This means the storage space reserved for the software can be increased automatically as the need arises. Later, when it's no longer needed, that space can be freed up again for other developers. In addition, the CSP ensures the underlying hardware servers hosting the cloud resources are secure and regularly backed up. Cloud removes from the company's IT personnel the burden of managing the underlying hardware so they can focus on other priorities. Figure 7-29 illustrates some of the benefits of cloud for this organization.

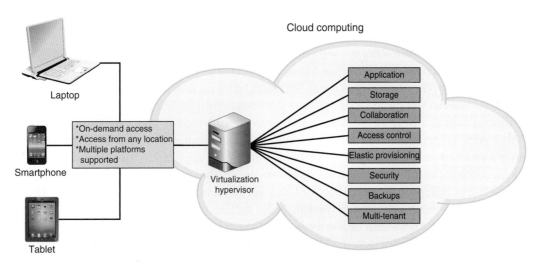

Figure 7-29 Characteristics of cloud services

Cloud Service Models

As you can see, managing cloud resources involves shared responsibilities—the ISP has some responsibility, and the cloud customer has other responsibilities. The dividing line between those groups of responsibilities varies according to the service being used. It's important for a cloud customer to understand exactly what they're responsible for and exactly what they can count on the CSP to provide for each service the customer uses. Most of the time, this dividing line is consistent for services within certain service models.

Cloud service models are categorized by the types of services they provide. NIST has developed a standard definition for each category, which varies by the division of labor implemented. For example, as shown in Figure 7-30, an organization is entirely responsible for their own network, top to bottom. In this traditional arrangement for an **on-premises data center**, which is the physical location of the customer and the hardware they own, the organization maintains its own network infrastructure devices, manages its own network services and data storage, and purchases licenses for its own applications. Three of the many cloud service models are also illustrated in Figure 7-30. These common service models incrementally increase the amount of management responsibilities outsourced to cloud vendors.

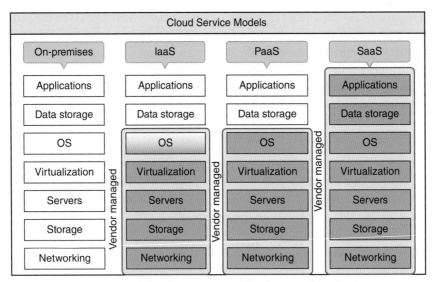

Figure 7-30 At each progressive level of these cloud service models, the vendor takes over more computing responsibility for the organization

To understand the various service models, it's helpful to compare them to the many ways to acquire a pizza for dinner. On the traditional end of the scale, you can make the pizza yourself. On the other end of the scale, you can have someone else make it and serve it to you. Check out each service model in Figure 7-30, and explore their differences using a pizza analogy:

- **On-premises**—All the hardware, software, and everything else is located and managed at your location. This would be like making your own pizza from scratch at home. You provide all the ingredients, bake it in your own oven, and eat it at your own table. For example, you install Microsoft Office on your laptop and keep all your documents on your hard drive. You can work with Office and your documents without being connected to the Internet.
- **IaaS (Infrastructure as a Service)**—Hardware services are provided virtually, including network infrastructure devices such as virtual servers and DNS services. These services rely on the network infrastructure at the vendor's site, but customers are responsible for their own application installations, data management and backup, and possibly operating systems. For example, customers might use the vendor's servers to store data, host websites, and provide email, DNS, or DHCP services, but must provide their own NOS licenses and productivity software, such as customer tracking, sales management, and an office suite.

  In the pizza analogy, this would be like a take-and-bake restaurant. You decide the type of crust you want and the toppings; the restaurant puts it all together for you. Then you take the unbaked pizza home, bake it yourself, and eat it at your own table. AWS (Amazon Web Services) provides many IaaS services, such as EC2 (Elastic Compute Cloud), which allows you to create and run your own VMs in the cloud. AWS provides the

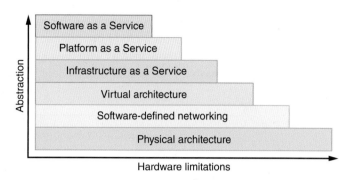

Figure 7-31   Abstraction levels of cloud service models

processing power, storage space, and deployment services. You create VMs and choose OSs to install on them. You load applications, databases, etc., and run Internet and other network services on them. You can think of IaaS as the least abstracted of the cloud service models, as shown in Figure 7-31.

- **PaaS (Platform as a Service)**—Developers often require access to multiple platforms during the development process. A platform in this context includes the operating system, the runtime libraries or modules the OS provides to applications, and the hardware on which the OS runs. Rather than purchasing and maintaining a separate device for each platform, another option is to subscribe to PaaS services. Developers can build and test their applications within these virtual, online environments, which are tailored to the specific needs of the project. Many new cloud technologies have emerged over recent years in relation to the PaaS category, including **containers**, which are essentially micro-versions of servers that provide only the resources needed to run an application, and **serverless compute**, which are services that allow customers to run their code directly in the cloud without having to manage a server environment at all. Alternatively, an organization's entire network might be built on platform services provided by a vendor. Any platform managed by a vendor resides on the vendor's hardware and relies on their uptime and accessibility to meet performance parameters. However, the customers are responsible for their own applications and/or data storage, including maintaining backups of the data.

  In the pizza analogy, this is the delivery option. You decide on the crust and toppings, the restaurant bakes it for you, and then they bring it to your front door within 30 minutes. You provide your own table and do the cleanup after dinner. GCP (Google Cloud Platform at *cloud.google.com*) specializes in PaaS where you can run code directly in the cloud without needing to create a server environment. Similarly, Alexa (Amazon's personal assistant app) runs code in a PaaS or FaaS (Function as a Service) called Lambda—when you talk to Alexa, you're talking to AWS's cloud.

- **SaaS (Software as a Service)**—Applications are provided through an online user interface and are compatible with a variety of devices and operating systems. Online email services such as Gmail and Yahoo! are good examples of SaaS, as are CRM (customer relationship management) apps, such as Salesforce and Zoho, and online office productivity tools such as Microsoft's Office 365 and Google Docs. Except for the interface itself (the device and whatever browser software is required to access the website), the vendor provides every level of support from network infrastructure through data storage and application implementation.

  Here you see the full capability of pizza provider services. The restaurant provides the crust and all the ingredients, bakes it for you, and serves it directly to the table in the restaurant they have provided. You had to get yourself to the restaurant, but you didn't need to bring anything to make it all work (except your payment, of course), and they do the cleanup after you leave. This is similar to applications you run online, like email, office productivity apps, or CRM software.

- **XaaS (Anything as a Service)**—In this broader model, the "X" represents an unknown, just as it does in algebra. (And you thought you would never again use algebra.) Here, the cloud can provide any combination of functions depending on a client's exact needs. This includes monitoring, storage, applications, and virtual desktops. For example, **DaaS (Desktop as a Service)** is a type of SaaS where you can access a virtual desktop through your browser. The virtual desktop will include an OS and a range of installed applications, depending on how you have the service configured, what licenses you bring to the table, and how much you're willing to pay. Recall that VDI is based on the same concept—DaaS uses the same technology except the CSP hosts the back end of the VDI deployment.

Consider the service models as they're shown in Figure 7-32. The smaller, upper end of the pyramid indicates how little a SaaS customer needs to understand and interact with a cloud provider's infrastructure for the customer to perform their work. In contrast, an IaaS customer interacts more heavily with their service provider's infrastructure for every aspect of their cloud needs. IaaS is more pervasively integrated with a client's computer network than is SaaS.

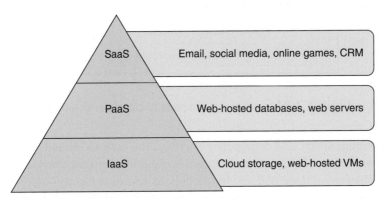

Figure 7-32   IaaS customers must understand more about a cloud provider's platform and services than SaaS customers

At the same time, consider how accessible each type of cloud service is to end users. In Figure 7-33, the triangle is upside-down. End users, the largest group of cloud computing consumers, can easily access and use SaaS products without much setup, whereas IaaS products require extensive preparation by a much smaller group of more skilled network architects and administrators, who provide systems for their users. In the middle of this pyramid is PaaS, which is often used by application developers, both professionals and laypersons, for testing their products. Customers at the lower layers of this pyramid build products that support customers at the higher layers, such as when a company subscribes to an IaaS product, on which it offers its own PaaS products to its own unique market of customers.

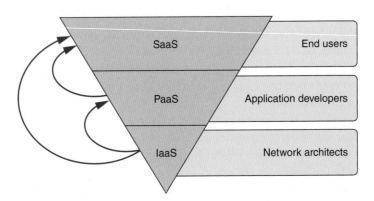

Figure 7-33   SaaS are more immediately accessible to a wide market of end users than other categories of cloud services

Cloud Deployment Models

Cloud services are delivered in a variety of deployment models, depending on who manages the underlying hardware and who has access to it. The main deployment models you are likely to encounter are the following:

- **Public cloud**—Service provided over public transmission lines, such as the Internet. Most of the examples discussed in this part of the module operate in public clouds.
- **Private cloud**—Service established on an organization's own servers in its own data center, or established virtually for a single organization's private use and made available to users over a WAN connection through

some type of remote access. If hosted internally, this arrangement allows an organization to use existing hardware and connectivity, potentially saving money. If hosted virtually, the organization benefits from the usual advantages of virtual services, such as scalability and accessibility.

- **Community cloud**—Service shared between multiple organizations, but not available publicly. Organizations with common interests, such as regulatory requirements, performance requirements, or data access, might share resources in this way. For example, a medical database might be made accessible to all hospitals in a geographic area. In that case, the community cloud could be hosted internally by one or more of the organizations involved or hosted by a third-party provider. But it would not be made available to the public.

- **Hybrid cloud**—A combination of public and private cloud resources. In the real world, the hybrid cloud infrastructure is a common result of transitory solutions. (In IT, "solution" refers to a product, service, or combination of products and services, and often includes extra features such as ongoing customer service.) An example of a hybrid cloud by design might arise when a company stores data in a private cloud but uses a public cloud email service.

- **Multicloud**—A combination of the other service models in a single deployment, and probably the most common service model in use. In the real world, multicloud infrastructure is a common result of "best in class" selections of available cloud services. A company might choose the best cloud service for their databases from one CSP, the best cloud service for their web servers from another CSP, and the best cloud service for their CRM software from another CSP. The challenge here is finding ways to link the various cloud services in productive ways. This is becoming easier, especially as third-party providers such as Aviatrix develop products designed to support a multicloud environment.

Orchestration and Automation

As you read about in the virtualization section, one potential drawback of working in a virtualized or cloud environment is that it's easy to spin up, or create, virtual resources (such as a cloud-based VM) and then forget about them as they continue to accrue charges. Another, related challenge in the cloud is creating identical resources over time and tracking what changes are made to the cloud infrastructure and when. As companies rely more heavily on cloud services and give more privileged access to more employees, it can be difficult to track who makes what changes and how those changes affect other resources.

In some projects at the end of this module, you'll use AWS's management console, a web-based GUI, to spin up cloud resources. However, cloud resources can also be managed through a CLI. In fact, CLI-based management provides a more traceable and consistent method of making changes in the cloud. For example, suppose you want to create an EC2 instance using the t2.micro instance type, as you'll be doing in Project 7-2. Instead of clicking through the GUI, you could enter the following command at the AWS CLI:

```
aws ec2 run-instances --image-id ami-0ff8a91507f77f867 --count 1 --instance-type t2.micro
--key-name MyKeyPair --security-groups MySG
```

While this command might seem overwhelming, once you have it built with the proper parameters, it's a simple matter of copy-and-paste to run it again and again. Suppose, instead of entering this command at a CLI, you built a series of commands in a script that you could feed the cloud platform. This process of using text-based commands in a computer-readable configuration file to create and manage cloud resources is called **IaC (infrastructure as code)**. IaC allows you to log changes made to your cloud resources—you can track who made the changes, when changes were made, and what was the state of your cloud resources before and after each change. You can even use this information to revert to an earlier state if needed.

As you've already read, many cloud resources can be scaled up or down automatically. Sensibly, a programmed, computer-generated response to a specific event is referred to as **automation**. However, automation is limited to specific, single events. As you convert more of your cloud maintenance and security tasks into code that can be run from scripts, you can automate many tasks to work together in a complex and lengthy workflow, which is called **orchestration**. A robust and well-designed cloud deployment is almost fully orchestrated to minimize hands-on time required by cloud admins and to reduce the chances of human error when changes need to be made.

Connectivity and Security

While cloud offers many significant advantages and opportunities for expansion, there are some drawbacks worth considering. Dependence on the Internet means dependence on your network's connection to the ISP and reliance on other third parties as well. Potential risks to your cloud's availability and security include the following:

- ISP outages
- ISP-imposed bandwidth limitations in response to increased demand on its network
- Cloud provider outages
- Failure of the cloud provider's backup and security systems
- Misconfiguration that exposes one client's data to another client
- Unauthorized access to data by cloud provider employees or by illegitimate users
- Breaches of confidentiality agreements when data is stored online
- Failure to properly comply with data security regulations (such as for healthcare, financial, or government entities)
- Questions over ownership of intellectual property stored in the cloud (for example, photos or comments made on social media websites, or files saved in online storage accounts)
- Questions over data maintenance if a payment is not made on time
- Risks to the network, proprietary data, or customer information caused by BYOC (bring your own cloud) services on users' personal devices
- Reduced consumer confidence, fines, lawsuits, and possibly criminal charges when cloud breaches occur

One way to reduce the inherent risks of cloud computing is to use encryption. Another way is to carefully choose the method by which your network connects to your cloud resources. Business requirements, risk management, and cost all factor into this decision. Cloud providers will often offer attractive SLAs (service-level agreements) based upon their own technology's availability. However, the WAN connection that links their resources with your network is just as important. To this end, organizations generally have an array of options:

- **Internet**—Provides the simplest and cheapest option, but with high and unpredictable latency as well as significant security concerns.
- **VPN (virtual private network)**—Relies on the same VPN technologies used to connect on-premises networks with branch offices and remote workers.
- **Remote access connections**—Uses tunneling or terminal emulation technologies to increase security, including SSH and RDP.
- **Leased line**—Relies on private WAN options to reserve a dedicated amount of bandwidth between the cloud provider and the customer's premises. Depending on the respective locations of provider and customer, this might require the cooperation of multiple ISPs to reach the cloud provider's servers. Hybrid pay-per-use models are available where the customer reserves a portion of anticipated bandwidth needs, and then is invoiced for additional bandwidth used during the pay period. Works in conjunction with a private or dedicated direct connection.
- **Private or dedicated direct connection**—Maximizes predictability and minimizes latency, and of course comes with a high price tag. Some of the larger cloud service providers maintain multiple PoPs (Points of Presence) around the world. This means the provider rents space at a data center facility, called a colocation facility, that is shared by a variety of providers. In many cases, ISPs can provide dedicated access from a customer's premises to a cloud provider's PoP. This is more cost effective when an organization subscribes to multiple cloud providers who all use the same colocation. Amazon's Direct Connect and Microsoft's Azure ExpressRoute both offer dedicated connection services.

As you can see, the cloud offers some significant advantages over conventional, on-prem networks while also offering the ability to integrate with on-prem resources in a hybrid deployment. However, the cloud presents many concerns that will be familiar to those who work with physical networks, such as performance and availability. CSPs have integrated many cloud services that address performance concerns. For example, in a project at the end of this module, you'll practice working with AWS's CloudWatch service to set up an alarm to track expenses in your account. CloudWatch can be used to monitor performance metrics for cloud resources, such as CPU (central processing unit) and memory usage in a cloud VM, and alert admins if a resource encounters problems. Other techniques can also be used to monitor and manage cloud resource availability. Many of the same availability principles for the on-prem network can be applied to the cloud environment. Let's look at what these principles are and examine strategies for maximizing network availability.

REMEMBER THIS...

- Identify the defining characteristics of cloud services.
- Compare the primary cloud service models: IaaS, PaaS, and SaaS.
- Describe popular cloud deployment models, including public, private, community, multicloud, and hybrid.
- Explain the benefits of IaC.
- Compare automation and orchestration.

SELF-CHECK

7. Which cloud characteristic ensures you can manage cloud resources from an iPad?
   a. Rapid elasticity
   b. Resource pooling
   c. Multitenancy
   d. Broad network access

8. When you set private IP address ranges for servers in your cloud, what service model are you using?
   a. IaaS
   b. SaaS
   c. DaaS
   d. PaaS

Check your answers at the end of this module.

You're Ready

You're now ready to complete **Project 7-1: Create a CloudWatch Alarm in AWS**, or you can wait until you've finished reading this module.

You're Ready

You're now ready to complete **Project 7-2: Create an EC2 Instance in AWS**, or you can wait until you've finished reading this module.

You're Ready

You're now ready to complete **Project 7-3: Remote into a Cloud VM Instance in AWS**, or you can wait until you've finished reading this module.

NETWORK AVAILABILITY

✅ CERTIFICATION

1.4: Given a scenario, configure a subnet and use appropriate IP addressing schemes.

2.1: Compare and contrast various devices, their features, and their appropriate placement on the network.

2.3: Given a scenario, configure and deploy common Ethernet switching features.

3.1: Given a scenario, use the appropriate statistics and sensors to ensure network availability.

3.3: Explain high availability and disaster recovery concepts and summarize which is the best solution.

7 Application
6 Presentation
5 Session
4 Transport
3 Network
2 Data Link
1 Physical

Average reading time: 24 minutes

In the world of networking, the term **availability** refers to how consistently and reliably a connection, system, or other network resource can be accessed by authorized personnel. It's often expressed as a percentage, such as 98% or 99.5%. The term **HA (high availability)** refers to a system that functions reliably nearly all the time. For example, a server that allows staff to log on and use its programs and data 99.999 percent of the time is considered highly available, whereas one that is functional only 99.9 percent of the time is significantly less available. In fact, the number of 9s in a system's availability rating is sometimes referred to colloquially as "four 9s" (99.99 percent) or "three 9s" (99.9 percent) availability. You might hear a network manager use the term in a statement such as, "We're a four 9s shop." This could be an impressive track record for a small ISP or a school's LMS (learning management system). For a hospital network, however, where lives are at stake, four nines likely wouldn't be enough.

NOTE 7-8

Various cloud services and ISPs offer three nines, four nines, five nines, or better availability, depending on what's defined in their SLAs (service-level agreements). When shopping for cloud services, examine the SLA carefully so you'll know what aspects of a service are guaranteed available.

However, be aware there's a difference between availability (the ability to access a resource) and **durability** (the resource's ongoing existence). For example, AWS lists its storage service, S3, at 99.999999999% durability (that's 11 nines!), but S3's *availability* is 99.99% for its Standard storage class. Why the discrepancy?

That 11 nines durability means you could store 10,000,000 objects in S3 and expect to lose one of those objects every 10,000 years on average (okay, not bad). This is because S3 stores each object on multiple devices in multiple, physical data centers. The four nines availability means that, each year on average, there should only be 52.6 minutes when you can't get to your objects in S3—this is also pretty good, considering you can relax in knowing that your stored data isn't lost during that 52 minutes, even if you can't get to it for a bit.

Similar terms include **reliability**, which refers to how well a resource functions without errors, and **resiliency**, which refers to a resource's ability to recover from errors even if it becomes unavailable during the outage.

One way to consider availability is by measuring a system or network's **uptime**, which is the duration or percentage of time it functions normally between failures. As shown in Table 7-1, a system that experiences 99.999 percent uptime is *unavailable*, on average, only 5 minutes and 15 seconds per year.

On a computer running Linux or UNIX, you can view the length of time your system has been running with the command `uptime`. On a Windows 10 system, uptime information is found in Task Manager.

Table 7-1   Availability and downtime equivalents

Availability	Downtime per day	Downtime per month	Downtime per year
99%	14 minutes, 23 seconds	7 hours, 18 minutes, 17 seconds	87 hours, 39 minutes, 29 seconds
99.9%	1 minute, 26 seconds	43 minutes, 49 seconds	8 hours, 45 minutes, 56 seconds
99.99%	8 seconds	4 minutes, 22 seconds	52 minutes, 35 seconds
99.999%	0.4 seconds	26 seconds	5 minutes, 15 seconds

Applying Concepts 7-1: Windows Task Manager

Windows 10 provides uptime data, along with a great deal of additional performance information, in Task Manager. Complete the following steps to view this information on a Windows 10 computer:

1. Right-click **Start** and click **Task Manager**.
2. On the **Performance** tab, examine the CPU and Memory utilization statistics. What is the current uptime?
3. Click **Open Resource Monitor** to view additional performance data and graphs.

Fault Tolerance

A key factor in maintaining the availability of network resources is **fault tolerance**, or the capacity of a system to continue performing despite an unexpected hardware or software malfunction. The key to fault tolerance in network design is supplying multiple paths that data can use to travel from any one point to another. Therefore, if one connection or component fails, data can be rerouted over an alternate path.

To better understand the issues related to fault tolerance, it helps to know the difference between failures and faults as they apply to networks, as described next:

- **Failure**—A deviation from a specified level of system performance for a given period of time. In other words, a failure occurs when something doesn't work as promised or as planned. For example, if your car breaks down on the highway, you can consider the breakdown to be a failure.
- **Fault**—A malfunction of one component of a system. A fault can result in a failure. For example, the fault that caused your car to break down might be a leaking water pump. The goal of fault-tolerant systems is to prevent faults from progressing to failures.

Fault tolerance can be realized in varying degrees; the optimal level of fault tolerance for a system depends on how critical its services and files are to productivity. At the highest level of fault tolerance, a system remains unaffected by even the most drastic problem, such as a regional power outage. In this case, a backup power source, such as an electrical generator, is necessary to ensure fault tolerance. However, less dramatic faults, such as a malfunctioning NIC on a router, can still cause network outages, and you should guard against them.

Redundancy

Devices on a network typically have a calculated **MTBF (mean time between failures)**. This is the average amount of time that will pass for devices exactly like this one before the next failure is expected to occur. While any single device might experience a failure much sooner or later, vendors and technicians budget for repairs or replacement of devices based on the advertised MTBF. Once a device fails, there is an average amount of time required to repair the device. This is called **MTTR (mean time to repair)**, and this cost must also be considered. Figure 7-34 shows how these concepts are related.

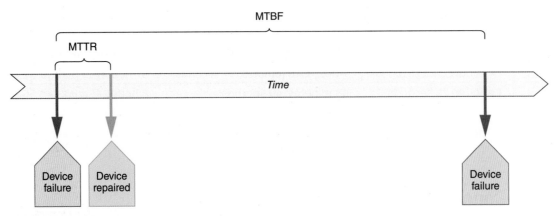

Figure 7-34   Every device eventually fails, it's just a question of when

MTBF, MTTR, and related concepts can all apply to services or systems as well. An ISP service might have an advertised MTBF and MTTR that are defined in the SLA. For example, any time your WAN connection goes down, the ISP might guarantee that it will be back up within two to four hours. Of course, these numbers vary according to provider, connection type, and subscription level, and should be taken into account when selecting WAN service options. You'll learn more about WAN technologies later.

To help protect against faults and failures, networks are often designed with two or more of the same item, service, or connection filling the same role on the network. If one part, service, or connection fails, the other takes over. Recall this is called redundancy and refers to an implementation in which more than one component is installed and ready to use for storing, processing, or transporting data. Redundancy is intended to eliminate single points of failure. To maintain high availability, you should ensure that critical network elements, such as your connection to the Internet or your file server's hard disk, are redundant. Some types of redundancy—for example, redundant sources of electrical power for a building—require large investments, so your organization should weigh the risks of losing connectivity or data against the cost of adding duplicate (or triplicate) components.

As you can see, the main disadvantage of redundancy is its cost. Redundancy is like a homeowner's insurance policy: You might never need to use it, but if you don't get it, the cost when you do need it can be much higher than your premiums. Redundant ISP services, for example, can be costly. Compared to the cost to a business of not having Internet access if a trunk line is severed, however, the additional WAN interface might make sense. As a rule, you should invest in connection redundancies for any connection that is absolutely necessary.

Even when dedicated links and VPN connections remain sound, a faulty device or interface in the data path can affect service for a user, a whole segment, or the whole network. To understand how to increase the fault tolerance of a connection from end to end, consider a typical link to the Internet. Figure 7-35 provides a representation of this arrangement.

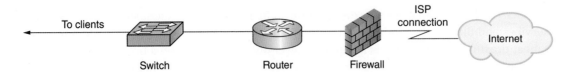

Figure 7-35   Single Internet link connectivity

Notice the many single points of failure in the arrangement depicted in Figure 7-35. In addition to the ISP link failing—for example, if a backhoe accidentally cuts a cable during road construction—any of the critical nodes in the diagram (firewall, router, or switch) could suffer a fault or failure and impair connectivity or performance. Figure 7-36 illustrates a network design that ensures full redundancy for all the components linking two locations to an ISP.

To achieve the utmost fault tolerance, each critical device requires redundant NICs, power supplies, cooling fans, and processors, all of which should, ideally, be able to immediately assume the duties of an identical component, a capability known as **automatic failover**. If one NIC in a router fails, for example, automatic failover ensures that the router's other NIC can automatically handle the first NIC's responsibilities.

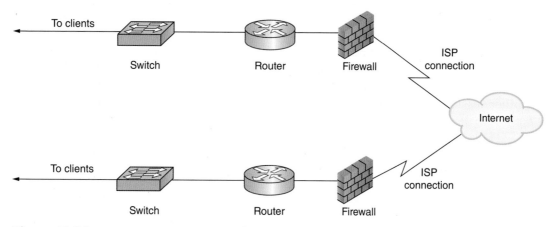

Figure 7-36 Fully redundant ISP connectivity

In cases where failover-capable components are impractical, you can provide some level of fault tolerance by using hot-swappable parts. Recall that hot-swappable refers to identical components that can be changed (or swapped) while a machine is still running (hot). There are two approaches to this:

- **Hot spare**—A duplicate component that is already installed in a device and can immediately assume the original component's functions in case that component fails.
- **Cold spare**—A duplicate component that is not installed but that can be installed in case of a failure. Relying on a cold spare results in an interruption of service.

When you purchase switches or routers to support critical links, look for those that contain failover capable or hot-swappable components. As with other redundancy provisions, these features add to the cost of your device.

Redundant Links

Besides using redundant devices, you can also use redundant connections, or links, between devices. **Link aggregation** is the seamless combination of multiple network interfaces or ports to act as one logical interface, and it can help solve problems like network bottlenecks. This implementation is also known by a variety of other terms, such as **port aggregation** on Cisco devices, **NIC teaming** on Windows devices, and a variety of others such as bonding, bundling, or Cisco's EtherChannel. Regardless of the terms used, link aggregation causes two or more NICs to work in tandem handling traffic between two or more devices (usually switches and servers). All the physical links involved in creating the one logical link are called a LAG (link aggregation group), bundle, or team, as shown in Figure 7-37. This configuration allows for three major advantages:

- Increased total throughput
- Automatic failover between the aggregated NICs
- **Load balancing**, which is a distribution of traffic over multiple components or links to optimize performance and fault tolerance

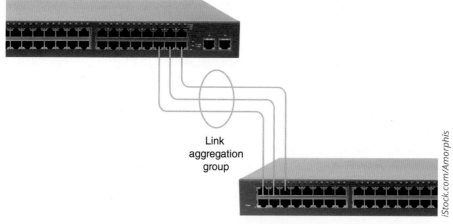

iStock.com/Amorphis

Figure 7-37 Two switches treat these three physical links as one logical link

Link aggregation isn't about speed of network traffic so much as bandwidth, or total potential to handle more network traffic at one time. Because packets and sessions generally aren't separated between the duplicate connections, the benefits of link aggregation are primarily noticed on busy networks. For example, if a single session is all handled on only one of the aggregated connections, that session doesn't reach its destination any faster. However, if two sessions are being transmitted at the same time, one session can traverse one of the aggregated links, and the other session can traverse the other link at the same time. Neither session must wait on the other (see Figure 7-38).

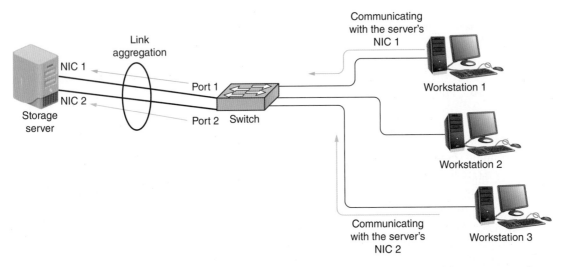

Figure 7-38 Link aggregation allows two workstations to communicate with a server at the same time

For multiple NICs or ports to use link aggregation, they must be properly configured in each device's operating system. For example, all involved interfaces must be configured for full duplex, and have the same speed, VLAN, and MTU settings. Many manufacturers now use **LACP (Link Aggregation Control Protocol)**, which was initially defined by IEEE's 802.3ad standard and currently defined by the 802.1AX standard (notice the change in working group from 802.3 to 802.1). LACP dynamically coordinates communications between hosts on aggregated connections, kind of like what DHCP does for IP addressing. Most of these devices offer similar configuration options, such as the following:

- **Static configuration**—Both hosts are manually configured to handle the division of labor between the redundant links according to particular rules without the ability to compensate for errors.
- **Passive mode**—The port passively listens for LACP-defined link aggregation requests, but it will not initiate the request.
- **Active mode**—The port is set to automatically and actively negotiate for link aggregation using LACP. This allows for fault tolerance should one or more links fail, as LACP will automatically reconfigure active links to compensate. In reality, this is the most common configuration for all ports involved in link aggregation, and it provides the most protection against link misconfigurations or failures.

Figure 7-39 shows the link aggregation options on a SOHO router. Here, you can aggregate two or more of the router's four LAN ports, depending on which ones are currently connected to another device.

More sophisticated load balancing for all types of servers can be achieved using a load balancer which, as you've already read, is a device dedicated to the task of distributing traffic intelligently among multiple computers. It can determine which among a pool of servers is experiencing the most traffic before forwarding the request to a server with lower utilization. This server pool might be configured as a cluster. **Clustering** refers to the technique of grouping redundant resources such as servers so they appear as a single device to the rest of the network. Clustering can be configured with groups of servers, routers, or applications. Although it usually accompanies load balancing, it doesn't have to.

Source: TP-Link Technologies Co., Ltd.

Figure 7-39   Aggregate LAN3 and LAN4 to a network server

Let's look at an example of how clustering and load balancing might work. Suppose you have two web servers that, together, host a single website (see Figure 7-40). To access the website, web clients direct requests to a single **VIP (virtual IP address)** that represents the entire cluster. To the client, the cluster looks like a single web server. On the back end, though, a load balancer directs traffic evenly between the web servers, and both servers have access to all the data needed to respond to any web page requests from clients. The clients, however, are not aware that two physical machines are at work. As far as a client is concerned, it's talking with a single server.

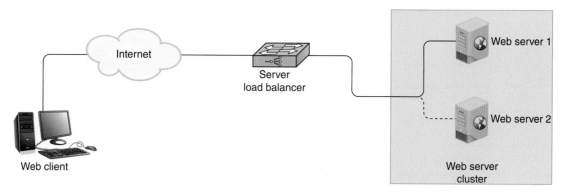

Figure 7-40   Two web servers work together in a cluster to host a single website

In this way, a popular website can respond more quickly to the high number of visitors interacting with the site at any one time. Each web server also serves as a backup to the other one. Should one server fail, the other can take over the full load until the malfunctioning server can be fixed or replaced. In the cloud or other virtualized environments, web server VMs or containers can be configured to automatically scale up to handle higher volumes of traffic. These autoscaling groups typically run a minimum number of servers at all times and then add more servers to the cluster only as needed. When the traffic subsides, the extra servers are removed so the website owner is not charged for unneeded server resources.

Applying Concepts 7-2: Add a Virtual IP Address to Windows 10

You can add multiple, virtual IP addresses to a Windows computer. This is not the same use case as previously described with load balancing. Instead, it might be used to assign a different IP address to multiple instances of the same service running on a single machine. For example, you might have three different websites running on one machine, and each website would need its own IP address. To see how to add multiple IP addresses to one network adapter on a Windows computer, complete the following steps:

1. Use PowerShell or Command Prompt to determine your computer's current IP address, subnet mask, default gateway, and DNS servers. What command did you use? What information did you find?
2. Open the **Network and Sharing Center**. Click **Change adapter settings**.
3. Open the properties box for the active network connection. Open the properties box for TCP/IPv4.
4. Configure a static IP address using the information you gathered in Step 1. Do *not* click OK. Instead, click **Advanced**.
5. On the IP Settings tab, under IP addresses, click **Add**, as shown in Figure 7-41. Enter a second IP address in the same subnet as the original IP address and using the same default gateway. For example, if your first IP address is 192.168.2.123, you might add a second IP address at 192.168.2.124. Click **Add**.

Figure 7-41 Add multiple, virtual IP addresses to a single, physical network connection

6. Click **OK** two more times, and close all open windows except PowerShell or Command Prompt. Run `ipconfig` again to determine your current IP addresses, subnet mask, and default gateway. What information is reported this time?
7. Ping your VIP (the second IP address you added). Was it successful?
8. If you have another computer on this subnet, ping each of the first computer's two IP addresses from the other computer. Are the pings successful? Why do you think this is?
9. On the second computer, run the command `arp -a`. What is significant about the MAC addresses listed for the first computer's two IP addresses?
10. What steps do you need to take to return your computer to the IP configuration it had when you started? If desired, do this now.

In some cases, you might have a set of IP addresses to share among multiple hosts. For example, if you have multiple routers that support multiple interfaces, and you want to interlace those routers as a fault-tolerant cluster, you would have a list of several IP addresses pointing to the cluster as a group. This is accomplished with **CARP (Common Address Redundancy Protocol)**, which allows a pool of computers or interfaces to share one or more IP addresses. This pool is known as a group of redundancy or redundancy group. When using CARP, one device, acting as the group master, receives requests for an IP address, then parcels out the requests to one of several devices in the group.

EXAM TIP CARP is a free alternative to **VRRP (Virtual Router Redundancy Protocol)**, or Cisco's propriety version called **HSRP (Hot Standby Routing Protocol)**. Although VRRP and HSRP function somewhat differently than CARP and are used solely for routers, the general idea is the same.

Clustering servers is used in many different ways to pool resources on a network and provide redundancy for fault tolerance. Another scenario is when pooling servers that host VMs. In a server cluster, the VMs are configured with varying amounts of redundancy to provide fault tolerance if one server fails. This can also allow for—and, in fact, necessitates—more efficient networking solutions between the VMs. Recall that VMs connect to a network via a vSwitch that exists in the host's hypervisor. In a server cluster, a single, distributed vSwitch can service VMs across multiple hosts, as illustrated in Figure 7-42. This is called distributed switching. It centralizes control of the VMs, simplifies network operations, and minimizes the chances for configuration errors. To do this, an agent is installed on each physical host and is then controlled by a supervisor module in the distributed switch. Examples of distributed switch products are VMware's VDS (vSphere Distributed Switch) that is native to its vSphere platform and a variety of third-party products, including Cisco's Nexus 1000v series.

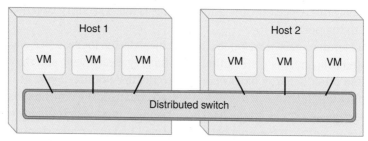

Figure 7-42   Distributed switching centralizes management of VM network connections

REMEMBER THIS...

- Compare MTTR and MTBF.
- Explain key redundancy concepts, including load balancing, NIC teaming, link aggregation, and port aggregation.
- Configure a VIP.

SELF-CHECK

9. Which is longer for a reliable device?
   a. MTBF
   b. MTTR

10. Which protocol balances traffic across multiple links?
    a. CARP
    b. LACP
    c. VIP
    d. VRRP

Check your answers at the end of this module.

MODULE SUMMARY

Physical Architecture

- The overall network design—the devices involved, how they're configured, the services implemented to support the network, and the way devices are connected to the network—is called a network's architecture.
- An unmanaged switch provides plug-and-play simplicity with minimal configuration options and has no IP address assigned to it. Unmanaged switches are not very expensive, but their capabilities are limited. Managed switches, on the other hand, can be configured via a command-line interface or a web-based management GUI, and sometimes can be configured in groups.
- Redundancy allows data the option of traveling through more than one switch toward its destination, and it makes your network less vulnerable to hardware malfunctions. A potential problem with redundancy has to do with traffic loops. STP (Spanning Tree Protocol) and similar technologies eliminate or otherwise control switching loops to greatly reduce the potential for a broadcast storm.
- The Cisco command (which is also used on Arista devices) to secure switch access ports is `switchport port-security` (or just `port-security` on Huawei switches). This is essentially a MAC filtering function that also protects against MAC flooding, which makes it a type of flood guard. Acceptable MAC addresses are stored in a MAC address table. Once the MAC address table is full, a security violation occurs if another device attempts to connect to the port.
- Cisco and other manufacturers have developed a hierarchical design for switches on a network. The three tiers are the access layer (edge layer), the distribution layer (aggregation layer), and the core layer. Hosts connect to the access layer, and other network blocks connect to the distribution layer.
- A spine-and-leaf architecture (also spine-leaf or leaf-spine) collapses the core and distribution layers into one layer called the spine. Spine switches on the backbone connect in a mesh topology with all leaf switches (but not with each other), and leaf switches connect with servers and other host devices.
- SDN (software-defined networking) is a centralized approach to networking that removes most of the decision-making power from network devices and instead handles that responsibility at a software level. This SDN controller integrates configuration and management control of all network devices, both physical and virtual, into one cohesive system that is overseen by the network administrator through a single dashboard. To do this, SDN separates into pieces all the functions of a system into three layers, or planes: infrastructure plane (data plane), control plane, and application plane. While not a typical layer for network communication, the management plane could be considered a part of the control plane. It allows network administrators to remotely manage network devices, monitor those devices, and analyze data collected about the devices.
- A SAN (storage area network) is a distinct network of storage devices that communicate directly with each other and with other portions of the network. Essentially, a SAN abstracts storage services from compute services and then provides high-speed network services to connect them. The network connections between servers and SAN devices must support extremely high data throughput. To maximize throughput, SANs often rely on one of these networking technologies: FC (Fibre Channel), FCoE (Fibre Channel over Ethernet), iSCSI (Internet SCSI), and IB (InfiniBand).

Virtual Architecture

- Virtualization is a virtual, or logical, version of something rather than the actual, or physical, version. A hypervisor creates and manages a VM, and it allocates hardware resources for the host and any of its guest VMs. Together, all the virtual devices on a single computer share the same CPU, hard disks, memory, and physical network interfaces. A type 1 hypervisor installs on a computer before any OS and is, therefore, erroneously called a "bare-metal" hypervisor. A type 2 hypervisor installs in a host OS as an application and is called a hosted hypervisor.
- The way a vNIC is configured determines whether the VM is joined to a virtual network or attempts to join the physical LAN that the host machine is connected to. These various configurations are called networking modes, the most common of which are bridged, NAT, and host-only.

- Virtualization offers several advantages, including efficient use of resources; cost and energy savings; fault and threat isolation; and simple backups, recovery, and replication. Potential disadvantages to creating multiple guests on a single host machine include compromised performance, increased complexity, increased licensing costs, and a single point of failure.
- Merging physical and virtual network architecture is called NFV (Network Functions Virtualization). NFV provides flexible, cost-saving options for many types of network devices, including virtual servers, data storage, load balancers, and firewalls.

Cloud Architecture

- Cloud computing refers to the flexible provision of data storage, applications, or services to clients over the Internet. All cloud services have the following features in common, according to NIST (National Institute of Standards and Technology): on-demand self-service, broad network access, resource pooling, measured service, and rapid elasticity.
- Cloud service models incrementally increase the amount of management responsibilities outsourced to cloud vendors. Common cloud service models include IaaS (Infrastructure as a Service), PaaS (Platform as a Service), SaaS (Software as a Service), and XaaS (Anything as a Service).
- Cloud services are delivered in a variety of deployment models, depending on who manages the underlying hardware and who has access to it. The main deployment models you are likely to encounter are public cloud, private cloud, community cloud, hybrid cloud, and multicloud.
- The process of using text-based commands in a computer-readable configuration file to create and manage cloud resources is called IaC (infrastructure as code). A programmed, computer-generated response to a specific event is referred to as automation. However, automation is limited to specific, single events. Many cloud management tasks can be automated to work together in a complex and lengthy workflow, which is called orchestration.
- The WAN connection that links cloud resources with the local network is critical. Connectivity options include Internet, VPN, remote access connections, leased line, and private or dedicated direct connection.

Network Availability

- In the world of networking, the term availability refers to how consistently and reliably a connection, system, or other network resource can be accessed by authorized personnel. It's often expressed as a percentage, such as 98% or 99.5%. There's a difference between availability (the ability to access a resource) and durability (the resource's ongoing existence). Similar terms include reliability, which refers to how well a resource functions without errors, and resiliency, which refers to a resource's ability to recover from errors even if it becomes unavailable during the outage.
- A key factor in maintaining the availability of network resources is fault tolerance, or the capacity of a system to continue performing despite an unexpected hardware or software malfunction. The key to fault tolerance in network design is supplying multiple paths that data can use to travel from any one point to another.
- Devices on a network typically have a calculated MTBF (mean time between failures). This is the average amount of time that will pass for devices exactly like this one before the next failure is expected to occur. Once a device fails, there is an average amount of time required to repair the device. This is called MTTR (mean time to repair), and this cost must also be considered.
- Link aggregation is the seamless combination of multiple network interfaces or ports to act as one logical interface, and it can help solve problems like network bottlenecks. This implementation is also known by a variety of other terms, such as port aggregation on Cisco devices, NIC teaming on Windows devices, and a variety of others such as bonding, bundling, or Cisco's EtherChannel. Regardless of the terms used, link aggregation causes two or more NICs to work in tandem handling traffic between two or more devices (usually switches and servers).

Key Terms

For definitions of key terms, see the Glossary.

access layer
aggregation layer
application plane
architecture
automatic failover
automation
availability
BPDU (Bridge Protocol
  Data Unit)
branch office
bridged mode
broadcast storm
CARP (Common Address
  Redundancy Protocol)
cloud computing
cloud service model
clustering
colocation facility
community cloud
container
control plane
core layer
CSP (cloud services provider)
DaaS (Desktop as a Service)
data plane
defense in depth
distributed switching
distribution layer
durability
east-west traffic
edge layer
elasticity
EoR (end of row) switching
failure
fault

fault tolerance
FC (Fibre Channel)
FCoE (Fibre Channel over Ethernet)
guest
HA (high availability)
host
host-only mode
HSRP (Hot Standby Routing
  Protocol)
hybrid cloud
hypervisor
IaaS (Infrastructure as a Service)
IaC (infrastructure as code)
IB (InfiniBand)
infrastructure plane
iSCSI (Internet SCSI)
LACP (Link Aggregation Control
  Protocol)
layer 3 switch
layer 4 switch
least cost path
link aggregation
load balancer
load balancing
managed switch
management plane
MTBF (mean time between
  failures)
MTTR (mean time to repair)
multicloud
multipathing
multitenancy
NAT mode
NFV (Network Functions
  Virtualization)

NIC teaming
north-south traffic
on-premises data center
orchestration
PaaS (Platform as a Service)
PoP (Point of Presence)
port aggregation
private cloud
public cloud
redundancy
reliability
resiliency
root bridge
root port
SaaS (Software as a Service)
SDN (software-defined
  networking)
SDN controller
serverless compute
spine-and-leaf architecture
STP (Spanning Tree
  Protocol)
three-tiered architecture
ToR (top of rack) switching
type 1 hypervisor
type 2 hypervisor
unmanaged switch
uptime
VIP (virtual IP address)
virtualization
vNIC (virtual NIC)
VRRP (Virtual Router Redundancy
  Protocol)
vSwitch (virtual switch)
XaaS (Anything as a Service)

Review Questions

1. What software allows you to define VMs and
   manage resource allocation and sharing among
   VMs on a host computer?
   a. Hypervisor
   b. NFV (Network Functions Virtualization)
   c. SDN (software-defined networking)
   d. Terminal emulation

2. What virtual, logically defined device operates
   primarily at the data link layer to pass frames
   between nodes?
   a. Virtual firewall
   b. Virtual switch
   c. Virtual router
   d. Virtual load balancer

3. Which device can manage traffic to multiple servers in a cluster so all servers equally share the traffic?
   a. Router
   b. Firewall
   c. Switch
   d. Load balancer

4. With which network connection type does the VM obtain IP addressing information from its host?
   a. Bridged mode
   b. Managed mode
   c. NAT mode
   d. Isolation mode

5. Which type of switch connects all devices in a rack to the rest of the network?
   a. ToR switch
   b. Spine switch
   c. EoR switch
   d. Core switch

6. Which cloud service model gives software developers access to multiple platforms for testing code?
   a. IaaS
   b. PaaS
   c. SaaS
   d. XaaS

7. When shopping for a new router, what does the MTBF tell you?
   a. How long until that device fails
   b. How much it will cost to repair that device
   c. How long devices like this one will last on average until the next failure
   d. How long it will usually take to repair that device

8. What information does the `switchport port-security` command use to restrict access to a switch's interface?
   a. MAC address
   b. Port number
   c. IP address
   d. Broadcast address

9. Which of the following features of a network connection between a switch and server is *not* improved by link aggregation?
   a. Bandwidth
   b. Fault tolerance
   c. Speed
   d. Availability

10. Which cloud management technique executes a series of tasks in a workflow?
    a. Automation
    b. IaC
    c. SLA
    d. Orchestration

11. List two advantages to using virtualization on a network.

12. List available options for connecting to cloud resources.

13. How does a vNIC get a MAC address without manual intervention?

14. What type of adapters are required on servers in an FCoE storage network?

15. What are two use cases for a VIP (virtual IP address)?

16. Which type of hypervisor is installed directly on top of the server's firmware?

17. Only one _____ exists on a network using STP.

18. What protocol is most often used to bond ports between a switch and a busy server?

19. How is licensing an important concern when using virtualization?

20. What kind of device can be used to configure and manage physical and virtual networking devices across the network?

Hands-On Projects

NOTE 7-9

Websites and applications change often. While the instructions given in these projects were accurate at the time of writing, you might need to adjust the steps or options according to later changes.

Note to Instructors and Students: A rubric is provided for evaluating student performance on these projects. Please see Appendix D.

Project 7-1: Create a CloudWatch Alarm in AWS

Estimated Time: 45 minutes
Objective: Given a scenario, use the appropriate statistics and sensors to ensure network availability. (Obj. 3.1)
Resources:
- AWS account (instructions for free accounts and free credits are included below)
- Internet access

Context:

NOTE 7-10

To Instructors: AWS Educate offers a plethora of helpful and free resources for schools, instructors, and students. At the time of this writing, students can only join AWS Educate when you post an invitation link in your LMS (learning management system) or when you send an email invite from the AWS Educate classroom, which provides students with free credits and tools for you to help them with their work in AWS. You can allocate free credits to your students for every class, and it does not count against their free credits in their own accounts. Creating an instructor's AWS Educate account is easy and free. Creating a classroom in AWS Educate is even easier, and you can allocate free AWS credits for your students. For more information, visit **aws.amazon.com/education/awseducate/**. If you have questions or need assistance, contact AWS Educate staff or email the author at *jillwestauthor@gmail.com*.

The Hands-on Projects in this module use the AWS (Amazon Web Services) public cloud platform. The steps below can help you create an AWS account if you don't have one already. In this project, you'll create a CloudWatch alarm. Often, CloudWatch alarms are used to monitor availability and performance of cloud resources. In this case, you'll use CloudWatch to alert you if your cloud resources accumulate charges beyond a set maximum. While this shouldn't be necessary if you follow all steps and properly delete all resources after you're finished with them, the alarm serves as a backup measure to help protect your liability.

If you're using an AWS Educate account for this project, you'll be able to complete most of the steps and create the alarm; however, the alarm will not trigger because of a permissions limitation in AWS Educate. If you're using a standard AWS account, this alarm will help protect your liability for costs in AWS. Complete the following steps:

1. If you don't already have an AWS account, you'll need to create one. Choose one of the following options:
   a. Your instructor might have an AWS Educate classroom for you. In this case, your instructor should send you an invitation email to join the classroom, or your instructor might post a link in your LMS (learning management system). Follow the steps given in the email. No credit card is required.
   b. Alternatively, you can create a standard, free account with AWS directly. When you first create an AWS account, you get some Always Free services and 12 months Free Tier services that allow you to test-drive some services within predefined limits. The AWS projects in this course can be completed within the limits of Free Tier services at the time of this writing, although that could change. Be sure to read and understand the terms and conditions of Free Tier services, which services are included, and what are the defined limits. To sign up, go to **aws.amazon.com/free/**. A credit card *is* required for this option.
2. After creating your AWS account, regardless of the approach you used, save your sign-in information in your LastPass vault.

3. Sign into your AWS management console. If you're using an AWS Educate classroom, you'll need to access your AWS management console through your AWS Educate classroom. If you're using a standard AWS account, sign in directly at **aws.amazon.com**.

Steps 4, 5, and 6 can only be completed using a standard AWS account. If you're using an account through AWS Educate, skip to Step 7. If you're using a standard AWS account, make sure you're signed in as the root user or as an IAM user with permission to view billing information, and then complete the following steps:

4. At the top of the console, make sure the **US East (N. Virginia)** region is selected.
5. At the top of the console, click the name of your account, and then click **My Billing Dashboard**.
6. In the navigation pane on the left, click **Billing preferences**. Select **Receive Billing Alerts**. Click **Save preferences**.

Regardless of the account type you're using, complete the following steps to create a billing alarm in CloudWatch:

7. At the top of the console, click **Services**. Services are grouped according to the kinds of resources they create. In the Management & Governance group, click **CloudWatch**.
8. In the navigation pane on the left, click **Alarms**. Click **Create alarm**. A CloudWatch alarm is a free resource in the CloudWatch service.
9. Click **Select metric**. Note that you can float your cursor just above the tabs to find a resize tool so you can adjust the size of each section on this page. On the All metrics tab, click **Billing**. Click **Total Estimated Charge**. Check **USD**. Click **Select metric**.
10. By default, the Statistic field is set to Maximum, and the Period field is set to 6 hours. In the Conditions section, the Threshold type is set to Static, and the *Whenever EstimatedCharge is. . .* field is set to Greater. Scroll to the bottom of the page to the *than. . .* field. Under *Define the threshold value*, enter **5**. This metric will trigger the alarm if charges exceed $5 once within six hours. Click **Next**.

In AWS, an alarm is an event that is triggered when certain conditions are met (similar to a smoke detector identifying smoke in the air). In contrast, a topic handles any notifications that should be sent if the alarm is triggered (such as the noise a smoke detector emits when smoke is detected). Basically, an alarm identifies that something occurred, and the topic is the programmed response(s) to that alarm. In AWS, that response might be an email or text message sent to an admin, among other possibilities. As you're setting up your alarm, you also need to set up a topic, as follows:

11. Under *Select an SNS topic*, select **Create new topic**. In the Email endpoints field, enter your email address (an account you monitor regularly—this email does *not* have to be the same address you use to access your AWS console). Click **Create topic**. Scroll down and click **Next**.
12. Give the alarm an informative name and description. What name and description did you use? Click **Next**.
13. Study the information on the Preview and create page to make sure you understand the alarm you're creating. In your own words, give an example of what could trigger this alarm.
14. Click **Create alarm**.

Your email address was listed as a subscription to the topic, meaning a message should be sent to your address if the alarm is triggered. However, to reduce spamming, you must confirm your email subscription before you'll receive notices:

15. To confirm your email subscription to the topic you created, go to your email account, open the email from AWS Notifications, and click **Confirm subscription**.
16. Return to your AWS console. What is the initial state of the alarm?
17. Wait a couple minutes until the alarm state changes. What is the new state of the alarm?
18. Click the alarm to see more information about it. **Take a screenshot** of the Details section of your alarm; submit this visual with your answers to this project's questions.
19. Currently, only your email address is subscribed to the alarm's topic. To see all current subscriptions in SNS (Simple Notification Service), click **Services**. In the Application Integration group, click **Simple Notification Service**. In the navigation pane, click **Topics**. Click the topic that is listed here. What is the status of your email subscription? If there are any problems indicated for the email subscription, troubleshoot those now.

You can also subscribe to the topic with your phone number to receive a text notification if the alarm is triggered. This step is optional:

20. **Optional:** Click **Create subscription**. The topic for your alarm should already be selected, as shown in Figure 7-43. Choose the **SMS** protocol, which is the protocol used to send text messages to phones. Enter your phone number (a number where you can receive text messages) in the Endpoint field—be sure to put a **1** in front of your 10-digit phone number and don't use spaces, dots, or dashes between the numbers. Click **Create subscription**.

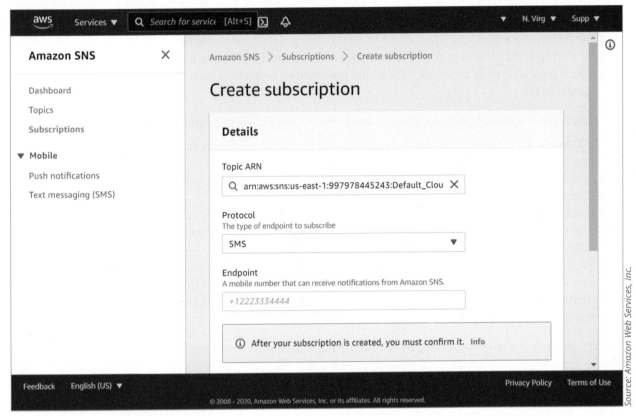

Figure 7-43   This new subscription will send a text message if the topic receives an alert from the CloudWatch alarm

21. On your Wikidot site, create a new page titled **Cloud:AWS**. Add notes about the CloudWatch alarm you just created, including details for the threshold that triggers the alarm, the topic that responds to the alarm, and any subscriptions to your email address and (optionally) your phone number.

Project 7-2: Create an EC2 Instance in AWS

Estimated Time: 45 minutes
Objective: Summarize cloud concepts and connectivity options. (Obj. 1.8)
Resources:
- AWS account created in Project 7-1
- Internet access

Context: This project picks up where Project 7-1 left off. In this project, you will create an EC2 instance, which is a VM in the cloud.

 **CAUTION**   Depending on the status of your account and the selections you make during this project, an EC2 instance and its supporting resources (such as storage) can deplete your credits or accrue charges. Make sure to follow these steps carefully and delete all created resources at the end of the AWS projects in this module.

Complete the following steps:

1. Sign into your AWS management console. If you're using an AWS Educate classroom, you'll need to access your AWS management console through your AWS Educate classroom. If you're using a standard AWS account, sign in directly at **aws.amazon.com**.

2. Most AWS resources reside in a specific geographical region in the world. Regular AWS accounts have access to nearly all these regions. However, AWS Educate accounts are limited. The region is listed in the top right corner of your console. Click the drop arrow to see all the available regions. What region is currently selected in your account?

3. At the top of the console, click **Services**. In the Compute group, click **EC2**. EC2 (Elastic Compute Cloud) is one of the oldest and most used AWS services. The EC2 dashboard shows you how many of each EC2 resource type you have in your account, which should currently be 0 across the board except for one security group. Scroll down and click the orange **Launch instance** button and then click **Launch instance** from the list.

4. Step 1 of creating an EC2 instance is to choose an AMI (Amazon Machine Image). This image determines the OS your instance will run. Notice that many of the AMIs are labeled as Free tier eligible. List three different OSs included in Free tier eligible AMIs.

5. Amazon has optimized a Linux AMI for use in the AWS environment. Next to the Amazon Linux AMI, click **Select**.

6. Step 2 is to choose an instance type. The instance type determines the virtualized hardware resources available to the instance. For example, the t2.micro type has 1 vCPU, 1 GiB (gibibyte) of memory, and low to moderate network performance. A more robust instance type, c5.large, has 2 vCPUs, 4 GiB of memory, and up to 10 Gigabit network performance. Select **t2.micro** and click **Next: Configure Instance Details**.

NOTE 7-11

A gibibyte is similar to a gigabyte, but mathematically they are not the same. A gigabyte (GB) is typically calculated as a power of 10 (10^9 or 1,000,000,000 bytes). A gibibyte (GiB) is calculated as a power of 2 (2^{30} or 1,073,741,824 bytes). Many cloud platforms use GiB for certain metrics.

7. Step 3 gives you the opportunity to set several specific configurations for your instance. What options here stand out to you and why?

8. Keep all default settings for Step 3 and click **Next: Add Storage**.

9. By default, the instance is assigned one root volume, which is where the OS will be installed. What type of volume is your root volume? Click **Next: Add Tags**.

10. Tags give you the option to define your own key-value pairs to further identify your instance and other resources. For example, you might want a key called "Name" so you can name all your instances. Or you might want a key called "Department" so you can track billing for each department at your company. Click **Add Tag**. Under Key, type **Name**. Under Value, give your instance an informative name. What did you name your instance? Click **Next: Configure Security Group**.

11. By default, your instance will be placed in a new security group with port 22 open for SSH (Secure Shell) access. The Source (0.0.0.0/0) is a wildcard that indicates the SSH connection could come from any IP address. Normally, this would not be a secure option. Because you're just practicing for now, you can leave all these default settings as is. Click **Review and Launch**.

12. Review your instance configuration and click **Launch**. You'll need a key pair for Project 7-3 where you'll remote into this instance. In the first field, select **Create a new key pair**. In the second field, give the key pair an informative name. What did you name your key pair? Click **Download Key Pair**, and save the file in a place where you can find it easily in the next project. Then click **Launch Instances**.

NOTE 7-12

Students sometimes get an error at this point, possibly related to the restrictions placed on using AWS through the classroom account. If you do get an error, retry the process of launching an instance. Sometimes it takes a couple attempts.

13. Scroll down and click **View Instances**. At first, the instance is listed as Running and Initializing. Select the instance and scroll down to see additional details about the instance. Your instance was automatically assigned a Public IP address. If you had a web server running on the instance, this is the IP address you would assign to your URL. In Project 7-3, you'll use the instance's DNS information to remote into your instance. **Take a screenshot** of the Instance summary information section that shows the Public IPv4 address; submit this visual with your answers to this project's questions.

14. You'll need this EC2 instance for Project 7-3, "Remote into a Cloud VM Instance." Depending on your account status and the options you chose while creating your EC2 instance, this instance and its related resources (such as storage) could accrue charges or deplete your available credit. If you're not able to complete Project 7-3 soon, you might consider deleting this instance now and creating a new one again later when you're ready for Project 7-3. Now that you know the steps, creating a new instance doesn't take very long. *If* you need to delete the instance now, click **Instance state** and **Terminate instance**. Otherwise, leave the instance running and continue with Project 7-3.

Project 7-3: Remote into a Cloud VM Instance

Estimated Time: 45 minutes
Objective: Summarize cloud concepts and connectivity options. (Obj. 1.8)
Resources:

- Windows computer with administrative privileges or with PuTTY already installed
- AWS account from Project 7-1
- EC2 instance created in Project 7-2
- Access to the key pair file downloaded in Project 7-2
- Internet access

Context: This project picks up where Project 7-2 left off. In this project, you SSH into the EC2 instance you created in your AWS account. To do this, you'll need a SSH client. In this project, you'll use PuTTY, which is a free and open source terminal emulator.

 **CAUTION** Depending on the status of your account and the selections you make during this project, an EC2 instance and its supporting resources (such as storage) can deplete your credits or accrue charges. Make sure to follow these steps carefully and delete all created resources at the end of the AWS projects in this module.

To begin, you'll need to install PuTTY:

1. Go to **putty.org**. Download and install PuTTY. Be sure to choose the correct installer for your computer.

Now you need to convert the key pair to a file type that PuTTY can use:

2. Click **Start**, type **puttygen**, and press **Enter**.
3. With **RSA** selected under Parameters, click **Load**. Change the file type to **All Files (*.*)**.
4. Select the key pair you downloaded in Project 7-2 and click **Open**. Click **OK**.
5. Click **Save private key** and then click **Yes**.
6. Give the file an informative name. What did you name your private key file? Make sure the **.ppk** file type is selected and click **Save**. Close the PuTTY Key Generator window.

Now you're ready to collect some information about your EC2 instance:

7. Sign into your AWS management console. If you're using an AWS Educate classroom, you'll need to access your AWS management console through your AWS Educate classroom. If you're using a standard AWS account, sign in directly at **aws.amazon.com**.

8. At the top of the console, click **Services**. In the Compute group, click **EC2**. On the EC2 Dashboard, click **Instances (running)**.

9. Here you should have one instance running. Select the instance. Click **Actions** and click **Connect**. Click **SSH client** for detailed information about your instance.

10. Under Example, select and copy the portion of the text from the username (ec2-user) through the URL (amazonaws.com), as shown in Figure 7-44. What is the information you copied?

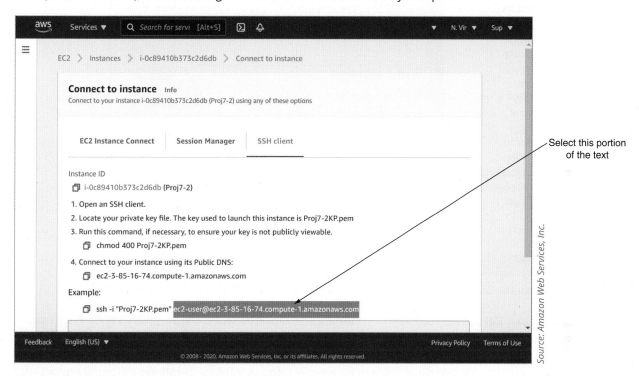

Figure 7-44   Select the sign-in information from the username through the URL

You now have the information you need to remote into your EC2 instance using PuTTY:

11. On your local computer, open **PuTTY**.

12. Paste the information you copied from your AWS console into the Host Name field. Make sure the Port field lists **22**, and make sure **SSH** is selected for the Connection type, as shown in Figure 7-45.

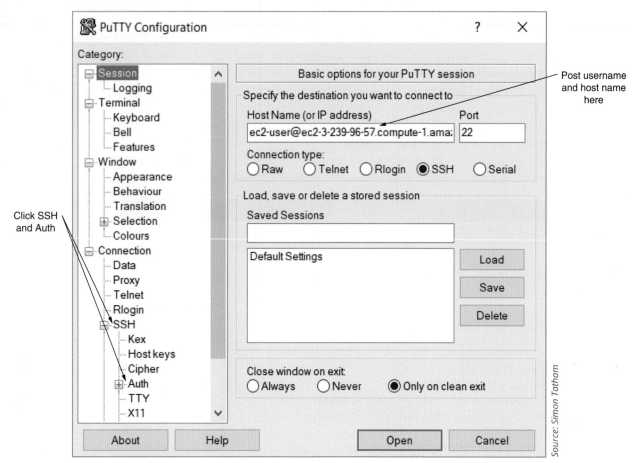

Click SSH and Auth

Post username and host name here

Source: Simon Tatham

Figure 7-45 Paste the username and host name information from AWS in the Host Name field

13. In the left pane, click **SSH** and then click **Auth**. On the right side, click **Browse** and find the private key file you created earlier in Step 6. Click **Open**. In the security alert dialog box, click **Yes** to add your private key to PuTTY's cache.

14. When the SSH connection is established, interact with your Linux VM's apps, utilities, or other resources using at least three of the Linux networking commands you learned in earlier modules. What commands did you practice using?

15. Create a directory named mydir and create a new file in the directory. Enter the command `ls -R` to show the directory and file you created.

16. **Take a screenshot** of the output; submit this visual with your answers to this project's questions.

When you're finished working with your instance, you're ready to power down the machine and delete it:

17. In your AWS console, click **Instances** so you can see your instance's state listed.

18. Position your management console window and your PuTTY window so you can see both windows on your screen at the same time.

19. To shut down the machine, enter the command `sudo poweroff`. The connection is severed. Close your PuTTY window. Refresh the data in your console. What state is your instance in now?

20. Turning the instance off does not delete any resources in your AWS cloud. In some cases, you continue to be charged for resources even if they're turned off. To delete your instance, select the instance, click **Instance state**, and click **Terminate instance**. Click **Terminate**. What is the instance state now?

 **CAUTION** Depending on the status of your account and the selections you made during the AWS projects, your EC2 instance and its supporting resources (such as storage) can deplete your credits or accrue charges. Double-check to make sure you've terminated all resources you created in the AWS projects.

Capstone Projects

NOTE 7-13

Websites and applications change often. While the instructions given in these projects were accurate at the time of writing, you might need to adjust the steps or options according to later changes.

Note to Instructors and Students: A rubric is provided for evaluating student performance on these projects. Please see Appendix D.

Capstone Project 7-1: Secure Switch Ports in Packet Tracer

Estimated Time: 30 minutes
Objective: Given a scenario, apply network hardening techniques. (Obj. 4.3)
Resources:
- Computer with Cisco Packet Tracer installed
- Access to the Packet Tracer network created in Capstone Project 5-2
- Storage space for Packet Tracer network file to be accessed in later modules

Context: In Capstone Project 5-2, you created the initial version of a network in Packet Tracer that you will continue to build on throughout other modules. In this project, you'll add another PC to this network and explore options for securing a switch's port. Be sure to save your network at the end of this project for use in future projects. Complete the following steps:

1. Add a new PC to your network, as shown in Figure 7-46. Create the needed connection with a Copper Straight-Through cable, connecting PC2 to Switch1's FastEthernet0/20 interface. The link between the switch and the PC should come up automatically.

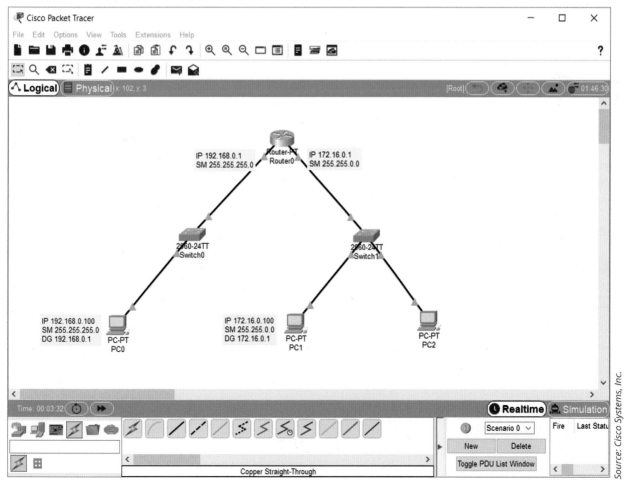

Figure 7-46   Add a new PC to your Packet Tracer network

2. Configure the PC with the following static IP addresses:
   a. IPv4 address: 172.16.0.110
   b. Subnet mask: 255.255.0.0
   c. Default gateway: 172.16.0.1
3. You can use the `switchport` command to explore the options available for port security on the switch's port that faces PC2. On the switch's CLI tab, click in the IOS Command Line Interface box, press **Enter** and then enter the commands from Table 7-2. In Step 4, there are questions for you to answer as you work through the commands in Table 7-2, so be sure to look ahead at those questions as you work through the commands in the table.

Table 7-2   Explore port security options on a switch

Command	Purpose
`enable`	Enters privileged EXEC mode
`configure terminal`	Enters global configuration mode
`interface fastethernet0/20`	Enters interface configuration mode for FastEthernet0/20
`switchport port-security ?`	Shows options for the `switchport port-security` command
`switchport port-security mac-address ?`	Shows options for the `switchport port-security mac-address` command
`switchport port-security maximum ?`	Shows options for the `switchport port-security maximum` command
`switchport port-security violation ?`	Shows options for the `switchport port-security violation` command

4. Answer the following questions:
   a. What are the four options listed for the `switchport port-security` command?
   b. What are the two configuration options for the `switchport port-security mac-address` command?
   c. How many MAC addresses can be allowed using the `switchport port-security maximum` command?
   d. What are the three configuration options for the `switchport port-security violation` command?

NOTE 7-14

When reentering the same or similar commands repeatedly at the IOS CLI, you can press the up arrow on your keyboard to recall recent commands. Then make edits to a recalled command before entering it.

5. Now you're ready to configure port security on the switch's port that faces PC2. But first, you must configure the port for access mode. This indicates to the switch the port will be connected to an endpoint rather than to another switch. On the switch's CLI tab, enter the commands from Table 7-3.

Table 7-3   Configure port security on a switch

Command	Purpose
`switchport mode access`	Sets access mode for this port
`switchport access vlan 1`	Assigns this port to VLAN 1 (you'll learn more about VLANs later)
`switchport port-security`	Enables port security on the port
`switchport port-security maximum 1`	Sets the maximum number of MAC addresses allowed on this port (default value is 1)
`switchport port-security violation shutdown`	Requires the port to shut down if port-security is violated (default is shutdown)
`switchport port-security mac-address sticky`	Instructs the port to dynamically learn the MAC addresses of connected devices until the maximum number is reached, and to statically remember those MAC addresses, that is, to make them "stick"
`exit`	Returns to global configuration mode
`exit` and press **Enter**	Returns to privileged EXEC mode
`copy run start` and press **Enter**	Saves the current settings

6. Now that you've secured the port and instructed the switch to automatically learn and remember the MAC address of the connected computer, you're ready to check the MAC address table. Enter the command `show mac-address-table`. What MAC address information is listed?

7. The switch has not yet seen any packets from PC2 to learn its MAC address. So you need to send some packets across the interface from which the switch can collect MAC address information. From PC2, ping PC1. What command did you use?

8. On Switch1, rerun the `show mac-address-table` command and answer the following questions:
   a. Now what information is listed?
   b. What is the type of each entry?
   c. Why do you think this is?

9. Pretend a hacker gains physical access to the Ethernet cable connected to PC2. They remove the cable from PC2 and connect it to their own laptop. What will happen when they try to access the network? To find out, do the following:
   a. Delete the cable connecting PC2 to the switch as follows: Click anywhere in the workspace to deselect any objects, click the **Delete (Del)** button in the Common tools bar, click the cable leading to PC2, and then press **Esc** to exit Delete mode. What information is reported on the switch's CLI tab?
   b. Add a laptop to the workspace. Set its static IP address information to the following:
      - IPv4 address: 172.16.0.110
      - Subnet mask: 255.255.0.0
      - Default gateway: 172.16.0.1
   c. Add a Copper Straight-Through connection from the laptop to the switch's FastEthernet0/20 port. Wait for the link to come up. What information is reported on the switch's CLI tab now?

10. The connection is successfully established, but can the hacker do anything on the network? After both ends of the new connection turn to green triangles, go to the laptop's Command Prompt interface. Position the laptop's configuration window off to the side of the workspace so you can see the network and enter commands at the same time. Ping PC1, watch the effect, and then answer the following questions:
    a. What happened when you attempted the ping?
    b. What information is reported on the switch's CLI tab?
    c. What do you think "administratively down" means?

11. The switch has automatically shut down the port in response to the security violation. **Take a screenshot** of your network showing the administratively down link; submit this visual with your answers to this project's questions.

12. Now try to reconnect the legitimate computer. Delete the laptop and its connection to the switch and add a new connection between PC2 and the switch's FastEthernet0/20 port. What happens?

13. Try to ping PC1 from PC2. What happens?

14. To reenable the connection from PC2, go to the switch's CLI tab. Position the switch's configuration window off to the side of the workspace so you can see the network and enter commands at the same time. Press **Enter** to return to the command prompt and then enter the commands from Table 7-4. What happens to the connection?

Table 7-4 Restart a switch's port

Command	Purpose
`configure terminal`	Enters global configuration mode
`interface fastethernet0/20`	Enters interface configuration mode for FastEthernet0/20
`shutdown`	Disables the port
`no shutdown` and press **Enter**	Enables the port

15. After both ends of the new connection turn to green triangles, ping PC1 from PC2 to confirm the connection is restored. Save your project in a safe place for future projects.

16. Make some notes on your Wikidot website about your activities in Packet Tracer for this project.

Note to instructors: A Packet Tracer solution file is provided for each Packet Tracer project through the Instructors site. Some Packet Tracer projects build on earlier Packet Tracer networks. If needed for one or more students, you can provide a previous project's solution file as a start file for one of these progression projects.

Capstone Project 7-2: Explore Virtual Network Configuration Options in Hyper-V

Estimated Time: 45 minutes (+10 minutes for group work, if assigned)

Objective: Explain the characteristics of network topologies and network types. (Obj. 1.2)

Group Work: This project includes enhancements when assigned as a group project.

Resources:
- Access to the same computer used to complete Capstone Project 1-1
- Internet access

NOTE 7-15

This project is designed for students who completed Capstone Project 1-1, "Set Up a Windows Virtual Machine Using Hyper-V." If you complete this project, your instructor might not require you to complete Capstone Project 7-3, "Explore Virtual Network Configuration Options in VirtualBox."

Context: In the Module 1 Capstone Projects, you created a virtual machine using Oracle VirtualBox or Windows 10 Client Hyper-V. In this project, you will explore the network settings for your VM in Hyper-V, practice communicating between the VM and the host machine, and practice communicating between the VM and a host on the Internet. The host computer, which is the physical computer, should be connected to the Internet. Complete the following steps:

1. Open **Hyper-V Manager**.
2. In Capstone Project 1-1, you created a new, external switch. To confirm this switch is using the correct configuration, click **Virtual Switch Manager**. What switches are listed in the Virtual Switches section?
3. Hyper-V automatically creates a Default Switch. Click the **Default Switch** and read the note at the bottom of the Virtual Switch Properties pane. What networking mode does this default switch use?
4. To ensure everyone starts this project from the same configuration, click your other virtual switch (in Figure 7-47, this switch is called ProjectSwitch). Confirm the switch is configured to use the **External network** connection type, as shown in Figure 7-47. If you made any changes, click **OK**. Close the Virtual Switch Manager window.

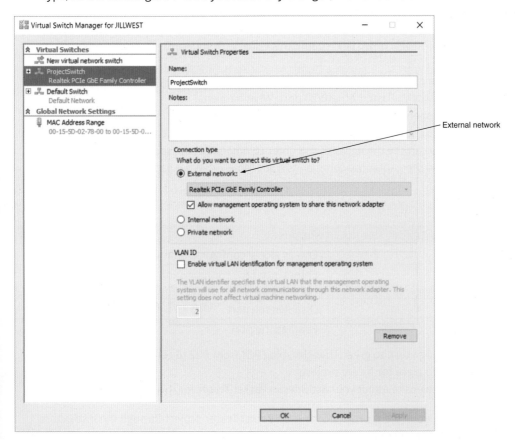

Figure 7-47   The switch you created earlier should use the External network connection type

5. Connect to and start your Windows 10 VM. In the VM, open a PowerShell or Command Prompt window and enter `ipconfig`.

6. **Take a screenshot** of the command output; submit this visual with your answers to this project's questions.

7. Check the VM's connection to the Internet by pinging one of Google's DNS servers with the command `ping 8.8.8.8`. Was the ping successful?

8. Open a PowerShell or Command Prompt window on the host computer, the physical PC hosting the VirtualBox VM. Enter `ipconfig` and answer the following questions:
   a. Which active network connections are listed?
   b. What does this tell you about the physical host machine's physical and virtual network connections?
   c. Which of these network connections is using the virtual switch you created in Capstone Project 1-1?
   d. What are the host machine's IPv4 address, subnet mask, and default gateway for this network connection?

9. Compare the host computer's address information on this connection with the VM's information. Both computers should have a subnet mask of 255.255.255.0, which means both computers use the first three octets to identify the network ID. Look at the first three octets of each computer's IPv4 address, and answer the following questions:
   a. Do both network IDs match? If so, they're on the same subnet. If not, the computers are on different subnets.
   b. Are these two computers on the same subnet? Why do you think this is?
   c. If possible, check the IP address of a third, physical device on your network and compare that information with the IP addressing information for your physical host and guest VM. Based on the three networking modes you learned about in the module, which networking mode corresponds to a virtual switch using the External network connection type?
   d. Ping the host PC from the guest VM. Does it work?

NOTE 7-16

If you're completing this project in a school lab, your computer might be using a different subnet mask. In that case, the subnet mask could be 255.0.0.0 or 255.255.0.0. For 255.0.0.0, look at the *first* octet only to determine whether the VM and its host are on the same subnet. For 255.255.0.0, look at the first *two* octets to determine whether the VM and its host are on the same subnet. Continue with these parameters for the following steps.

10. Return to the Hyper-V Manager window. In the right pane under the name of your VM, click **Settings**. In the Settings window, click **Network Adapter**. Change the Virtual switch to **Default Switch** and click **OK**.

11. Return to the VM's window. You might see a message indicating that the VM has detected a network change, and it's requesting permission to find PCs and other devices and content on the network. If so, click **Yes**.

12. Repeat the `ipconfig` command and answer the following questions:
    a. What are the IPv4 address, subnet mask, and default gateway now?
    b. Which network connection on the host PC is now using the same virtual switch as the guest VM?
    c. How does the VM's IP information compare with the host PC's information?
    d. Are the two computers on the same subnet?
    e. Ping the host PC's IP address on the Default Switch from the guest VM. Does it work?
    f. Ping the host PC's IP address on the *other* virtual switch from the guest VM. Does it work?

13. On the VM, ping Google's DNS server again. Was the ping successful?

14. Based on the three networking modes you learned about in the module, which networking mode is the Default Switch using?

15. On the Hyper-V Manager window, click Virtual Switch Manager. In the left pane, make sure **New virtual network switch** is selected. In the right pane, click **Private** and then click **Create Virtual Switch**. Give the switch a name and click **OK**. In your wikidot website, add a note on your Virtualization:VMclients page about the virtual switch you just created.

16. Return to the VM's **Settings**, **Network Adapter** menu, click the **Virtual switch** down arrow, click the private switch you just created, and then click **OK**.

17. On the VM, repeat `ipconfig`, ping both the host PC's IPv4 addresses (one for each virtual switch), and ping Google's DNS server again. What changed?

18. Change the VM's *Virtual switch* setting back to the switch you created in Capstone Project 1-1 and click **OK**. On the VM, repeat `ipconfig`, ping the host PC's IP address on the same switch, and ping Google's DNS server again. What changed?

19. Close all windows on the VM, shut down the VM, and close all windows on the host machine.

20. **For group assignments:** Partner with someone using VirtualBox in Capstone Project 7-3, "Explore Virtual Network Configuration Options in VirtualBox." Take turns explaining to each other what you learned about the way virtual network connections work in the hypervisor you used. If necessary, show your partner how to configure the networking modes in Hyper-V, and ask your partner to demonstrate these same tasks in VirtualBox. What are the primary differences between Hyper-V and VirtualBox for how to configure various networking modes? What are the similarities in how virtual networking works in these hypervisors?

Capstone Project 7-3: Explore Virtual Network Configuration Options in VirtualBox

Estimated Time: 45 minutes (+10 minutes for group work, if assigned)
Objective: Explain the characteristics of network topologies and network types. (Obj. 1.2)
Group Work: This project includes enhancements when assigned as a group project.
Resources:

- Access to the same computer used to complete Capstone Project 1-2
- Internet access

NOTE 7-17

This project is designed for students who completed Capstone Project 1-2, "Set Up a Windows Virtual Machine Using Oracle VirtualBox." If you complete this project, your instructor might not require you to complete Capstone Project 7-2, "Explore Virtual Network Configuration Options in Hyper-V."

Context: In the Module 1 Capstone Projects, you created a virtual machine using Oracle VirtualBox or Windows 10 Client Hyper-V. In this project, you will explore the network settings for your VM in VirtualBox, practice communicating between the VM and the host machine, and practice communicating between the VM and a host on the Internet. The host computer, which is the physical computer, should be connected to the Internet. Complete the following steps:

1. Open **VirtualBox**. To ensure everyone starts this project from the same configuration, select your Windows 10 VM and click **Settings**. In the left pane, click **Network**. Make sure the Adapter 1 tab is selected, as shown in Figure 7-48. If necessary, change the *Attached to* option to **NAT**. Click **OK**. Start your **Windows 10 VM**.

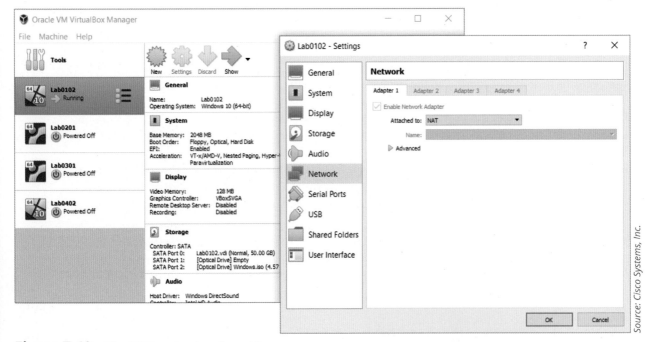

Figure 7-48   The NAT option is selected here

2. In the VM, open a PowerShell or Command Prompt window and enter `ipconfig`.
3. **Take a screenshot** of the command output; submit this visual with your answers to this project's questions.
4. Check the VM's connection to the Internet by pinging one of Google's DNS servers with the command `ping 8.8.8.8`. Was the ping successful?
5. Open a PowerShell or Command Prompt window on the host computer, the physical PC hosting the VirtualBox VM. Enter `ipconfig`. What are the host machine's IPv4 address, subnet mask, and default gateway for the active, physical network connection (either Ethernet or Wi-Fi)?
6. Compare the host computer's address information with the VM's information. Both computers should have a subnet mask of 255.255.255.0, which means both computers use the first three octets to identify the network ID. Look at the first three octets of each computer's IPv4 address and answer the following questions:
   a. Do both network IDs match? If so, they're on the same subnet. If not, the computers are on different subnets.
   b. Are these two computers on the same subnet? Why do you think this is?
   c. Ping the host PC from the guest VM. Does it work?

NOTE 7-18

If you're completing this project in a school lab, your computer might be using a different subnet mask. In that case, the subnet mask could be 255.0.0.0 or 255.255.0.0. For 255.0.0.0, look at the *first* octet only to determine whether the VM and its host are on the same subnet. For 255.255.0.0, look at the first *two* octets to determine whether the VM and its host are on the same subnet. Continue with these parameters for the following steps.

7. Return to the Oracle VM VirtualBox Manager window and open the VM's **Settings** window. In the Settings window, click **Network** and make sure the **Adapter 1** tab is selected.
8. Click the **Attached to** down arrow, click **Bridged Adapter**, and then click **OK**.
9. Return to the VM's window. You might see a message indicating that the VM has detected a network change, and it's requesting permission to find PCs and other devices and content on the network. If so, click **Yes**.
10. Repeat the `ipconfig` command and answer the following questions:
    a. What are the IPv4 address, subnet mask, and default gateway now?
    b. How does this information compare with the host PC's information?
    c. Are the two computers on the same subnet now?
    d. Ping the host PC from the guest VM. Does it work?
11. On the VM, ping Google's DNS server again. Was the ping successful?
12. On the Oracle VM VirtualBox Manager window, return to the VM's **Settings**, **Network** menu, click the **Attached to** down arrow, click **Host-only Adapter**, and then click **OK**.
13. On the VM, repeat `ipconfig`, ping the host PC, and ping Google's DNS server again. What changed?
14. On the host PC, run `ipconfig` again and answer the following questions:
    a. Which adapter on the host PC's output has an IPv4 address on the same subnet as the VM?
    b. What does this tell you about the host machine's physical and virtual network connections?
    c. Try pinging the host's VirtualBox adapter. Does the ping work?
15. Change the VM's *Attached to* setting to **NAT** and click **OK**. On the VM, repeat `ipconfig`, ping the host PC's physical adapter, and ping Google's DNS server again. What changed?
16. Close all windows on the VM, shut down the VM, and close all windows on the host machine.
17. **For group assignments:** Partner with someone using Hyper-V in Capstone Project 7-2, "Explore Virtual Network Configuration Options in Hyper-V." Take turns explaining to each other what you learned about the way virtual network connections work in the hypervisor you used. If necessary, show your partner how to configure the networking modes in VirtualBox and ask your partner to demonstrate these same tasks in Hyper-V. What are the primary differences between Hyper-V and VirtualBox for how to configure various networking modes? What are the similarities in how virtual networking works in these hypervisors?

Solutions to Self-Check Questions

Physical Architecture

1. Which STP bridge serves as the basis for all path calculations?

Answer: d. Root bridge

Explanation: The **root bridge**, or master bridge, provides the basis for all path calculations. Only one root bridge exists on a network. From this root bridge, a series of logical branches, or data paths, emanate like branches on a tree.

2. Which type of switch is best used for connections to web servers?

Answer: a. Edge switch

Explanation: In a three-tiered architecture, **edge switches** connect directly to hosts such as servers, printers, and workstations. Ideally, hosts connect *only* to edge (also called access) switches and never to switches at the other layers, although this is not always the case in the real world. Aggregation switches, or distribution switches, provide a highly redundant mesh of connections that route traffic within the corporate network as well as providing traffic filtering and the network's connection to a WAN. The core layer consists of highly efficient multilayer switches or routers that support the network's backbone traffic. In a two-tiered spine-and-leaf architecture, spine switches on the backbone connect in a mesh topology with all leaf switches, which in turn connect with servers and other host devices.

3. Which SDN plane moves traffic from switch port to switch port?

Answer: d. Infrastructure plane

Explanation: The **infrastructure plane** is made up of the physical or virtual devices that handle actual transmissions on the network, moving traffic from each port on a switch to other ports. The control plane handles the decision-making processes performed by network protocols. The application plane includes applications running on the network, such as DNS or VoIP. The management plane could be considered a part of the control plane and allows network administrators to remotely manage network devices, monitor those devices, and analyze data collected about the devices.

4. Which SAN connection technology can run over ordinary Ethernet NICs without any special equipment needed?

Answer: b. iSCSI

Explanation: **iSCSI (Internet SCSI)** can work on a twisted-pair Ethernet network with ordinary Ethernet NICs. FC (Fibre Channel) requires special hardware: specialized FC switches connect servers with each other and with the outside network. Instead of NICs, FC devices communicate through HBAs (host bus adapters). SATA (Serial Advanced Technology Attachment) cables connect a computer's hard drive to its motherboard. IB (InfiniBand), like FC, requires specialized network hardware.

Virtual Architecture

5. Which virtual network connection type assigns a VM its IP address from the physical network?

Answer: b. Bridged

Explanation: Although a **bridged** vNIC communicates through the host's adapter, it obtains its own IP address, default gateway, and subnet mask from a DHCP server on the physical LAN. In NAT mode, the VM obtains IP addressing information from its host rather than from a server or router on the physical network. In host-only mode, VMs use the DHCP service in the host's virtualization software to obtain IP address assignments. In Hyper-V, the host-only connection type is created by assigning VMs to a private virtual network.

6. Which network architecture technique are you using when you run a virtual router on a network?

Answer: c. NFV

Explanation: **NFV (Network Functions Virtualization)** is a network architecture that merges physical and virtual network devices. STP (Spanning Tree Protocol) is a switching protocol defined by the IEEE standard 802.1D that prevents traffic loops by artificially blocking the links that would complete a loop. A SAN (storage area network) is a distinct network of storage devices that communicate directly with each other and with other portions of the network. SDN (software-defined networking) is a centralized approach to networking that removes most of the decision-making power from network devices and instead handles that responsibility at a software level.

Cloud Architecture

7. Which cloud characteristic ensures you can manage cloud resources from an iPad?

Answer: d. Broad network access

Explanation: **Broad network access** means client devices of all types can access services, applications, and storage in a cloud, no matter what operating system they run or where they are located, if they have an Internet connection. Rapid elasticity means resources can be changed quickly and dynamically—even automatically—in response to changing demands. Resource pooling refers to the fact that host computers in the cloud provide multiple services or resources such as disk space, applications, and services that are pooled, or consolidated, usually among multiple tenants, which is multitenancy.

8. When you set private IP address ranges for servers in your cloud, what service model are you using?

Answer: a. IaaS

Explanation: **IaaS (Infrastructure as a Service)** provides virtual hardware services, including network infrastructure devices such as virtual servers and DNS services. PaaS (Platform as a Service) provides a platform on which to test or run code without having to manage the underlying server. SaaS (Software as a Service) consists of applications provided through an online user interface that are compatible with a variety of devices and operating systems. DaaS (Desktop as a Service) is a type of SaaS where you can access a virtual desktop through your browser.

Network Availability

9. Which is longer for a reliable device?

Answer: a. MTBF

Explanation: The **MTBF (mean time between failures)** is the average amount of time that will pass for devices before the next failure is expected to occur. This should be significantly longer than the MTTR (mean time to repair), which is the average amount of time required to repair a device once it fails.

10. Which protocol balances traffic across multiple links?

Answer: b. LACP

Explanation: **LACP (Link Aggregation Control Protocol)** dynamically coordinates communications between hosts on aggregated connections. A VIP (virtual IP address) is a single IP address that can represent multiple devices in a cluster. CARP (Common Address Redundancy Protocol) allows a pool of computers or interfaces to share one or more IP addresses. CARP is a free alternative to VRRP (Virtual Router Redundancy Protocol), which functions differently than CARP but is used for the same purpose.

SEGMENTATION

After reading this module and completing the exercises, you should be able to:

1 Explain the purposes of network segmentation

2 Describe how subnetting works

3 Calculate subnets

4 Configure VLANs

On the Job

I recently provided the technical expertise to build a new FM radio station in rural Wisconsin. In addition to specifying and installing microphones, speakers, and sound boards, I also designed and created the station's network. Within the station's building, the network connects studios, office computers, and a VoIP (Voice over IP) telephone system. Beyond the building, the network sends the station's broadcast signal to its antenna.

When I set up the radio station network, I decided to separate different kinds of network traffic. To do this, I chose to create VLANs, rather than creating multiple physical networks, for several reasons, not the least of which is the cost of acquiring and maintaining multiple network switches. Managing multiple subnets on a single device has simplified deployment and long-term maintenance.

The VLANs are set up as follows:

- VLAN 101 (IP address subnet 10.10.1.0/24) is the transmitter network.
- VLAN 201 (IP address subnet 10.20.1.0/24) is the studio network.
- VLAN 301 (IP address subnet 10.30.1.0/24) is the office network.
- VLAN 401 (IP address subnet 10.40.1.0/24) is the telephone network.

Using VLANs allows the station to keep general Internet traffic off the latency-sensitive studio subnet. The systems on the studio subnet include the audio automation players and the analog-to-digital audio encoders. These computers receive and send digital audio over the network and demand timely delivery of packets. Further, these computers do not need to access Internet resources. We chose to isolate these systems from the others using VLANs (and access lists) to help guarantee the timely delivery of audio data.

Meanwhile, placing our VoIP telephones on a separate VLAN prevents studio audio traffic, as well as the general office and Internet traffic, from interfering with the telephone system traffic.

David Klann
WDRT 91.9FM

Network segmentation takes the divide-and-conquer approach to network management. When done well, it increases both performance and security on a network. A network can be segmented physically by creating multiple LANs or logically using VLANs (virtual LANs). Either way, the larger broadcast domain is divided into smaller segments, and the IP address space is subdivided as well.

In this module, you'll learn about two important concepts that enable and support network segmentation: subnets and VLANs. Fundamentally, a subnet is a group of IP addresses, and a VLAN is a group of ports on one or more switches. Subnets and VLANs usually work together, but you'll learn about each of them separately first.

Before you dig into how subnetting works, you'll take a brief look at why you might want to segment a network using either multiple LANs or multiple VLANs. Then you'll explore the important role subnetting plays in network segmentation. And finally, you'll see how VLANs work and the unique flexibility they offer.

NETWORK SEGMENTATION

✔ CERTIFICATION

4.1 Explain common security concepts.

Average reading time: 8 minutes

7 Application
6 Presentation
5 Session
4 Transport
▶ ③ Network
▶ ② Data Link
▶ ① Physical

When a network is segmented into multiple smaller networks, traffic on one network is separated from another network's traffic and each network is its own broadcast domain. A network administrator might separate a network's traffic into smaller portions to accomplish the following goals:

- **Enhance security**—Transmissions in broadcast domains are limited to each network so there's less possibility of hackers or malware reaching remote, protected networks in the enterprise domain. At the same time, other devices, such as a web server, can be made more accessible from the open Internet than the rest of the network is. For example, a **screened subnet** (formerly called a DMZ, or demilitarized zone) can provide an area of the network with less stringent security policies that allow traffic from website visitors, while other portions of the network cannot be accessed from the Internet. Enforcing network segmentation is one layer of security in a solid defense-in-depth strategy because it secures sensitive network traffic separately from other traffic.
- **Improve performance**—Segmenting limits broadcast traffic by decreasing the size of each broadcast domain. The more efficient use of bandwidth results in better overall network performance. The *On the Job* story at the beginning of this module gave an excellent example of how this applies in a real-world situation where time-sensitive studio traffic was isolated and prioritized differently than general office and Internet traffic.
- **Simplify troubleshooting**—When troubleshooting, rather than examining the whole network for errors or bottlenecks, the network administrator can narrow down the problem area to a smaller network segment. For example, suppose a network is subdivided with separate smaller networks for Accounting, Human Resources, and IT. One day there's trouble transmitting data only to a certain group of users—those on the Accounting network. This fact gives the network administrator some significant insight into the nature of the problem.

Networks are commonly segmented according to one of the following groupings:

- **Geographic locations**—For example, the floors of a building connected by a LAN, or the buildings connected by a WAN
- **Departmental boundaries**—For example, the Accounting, Human Resources, and Sales departments
- **Device types**—For example, printers, desktops, and IP phones

As you explore options for network segmentation throughout this module, keep in mind there are a variety of ways to go about separating broadcast domains on a network. Each segmentation method addresses different needs, offering varying capabilities and limitations. The OSI model also plays a part in network segmentation. You can use physical devices such as routers to create separate LANs. At layer 2, you can create virtual LANs, which you'll learn more about later in this module. At layer 3, you can use subnetting to organize devices within the available IP address space, whether the LANs are defined physically or virtually. Figure 8-1 can help you visualize the relationship between these various concepts.

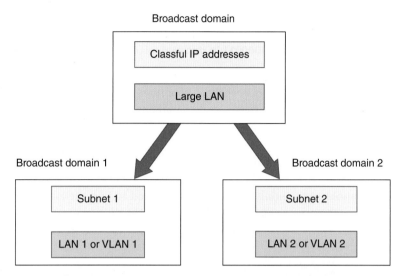

Figure 8-1 Network segmentation divides a large broadcast domain into smaller broadcast domains

Applying Concepts 8-1: Binary Calculations

For calculations used with this module's learning objectives, you'll need to become comfortable with converting decimal numbers to binary and back, especially for a few, commonly used values. You won't be allowed to use a calculator during the CompTIA Network+ exam, but when calculating conversions on the job, using a calculator can make the task much simpler. Take, for example, the decimal number 131. Complete the following steps to convert it to a binary number using the Windows 10 Calculator:

1. Open the Calculator app. Click the menu icon, and then click **Programmer**. Verify that the **DEC** option is selected (it should show a blue bar to the left of the option).

2. Type **131**. Other formats of this number are listed automatically. The binary equivalent of the decimal number 131, which is 1000 0011, appears next to the BIN option.

3. Select the **BIN** option, as shown in Figure 8-2. Type any 8-digit binary number to convert it to a decimal number. What binary number did you enter? What decimal number does it convert to?

If you're connected to the Internet and using a web browser, you can quickly convert binary and decimal numbers using Google calculator:

Figure 8-2 Use the Windows Calculator app to convert between decimal and binary

4. Go to **google.com**, and then type the number you want to convert along with the desired format in the search text box. For example, to convert the decimal number 131 into binary form, enter **131 in binary**. You see the following result: 131 = 0b10000011. The prefix "0b" (that's a zero, not the letter *O*) indicates that the following number is in binary format. Notice that Google assumes a number is in decimal form unless stated otherwise.

5. To convert a binary number into decimal form, type 0b (again, that's the number zero, not the letter *O*) before the binary number. For example, entering **0b10000011 in decimal** returns the decimal number 131.

To best prepare yourself for the CompTIA Network+ exam, consider manually performing the calculations in this module and use the calculator only to check your results. If your manual calculations don't match the calculator's computations, make sure you investigate carefully to see where you made a mistake. Repeat until your calculations are consistently correct.

Regardless of how you go about segmenting a network, you'll need to find the right balance between separating and connecting devices within each network portion. Let's begin with a discussion of how subnetting complements physical or virtual segmentation.

REMEMBER THIS...

- List advantages of network segmentation.
- Explain how segmentation increases network security.

SELF-CHECK

1. Which of the following techniques does *not* break up a large broadcast domain into smaller broadcast domains?
   a. Adding more routers to a network
   b. Adding more layer 2 switches to a network
   c. Adding more VLANs to a network

2. What is the binary number 1111 1111 in decimal?
   a. 255
   b. 100
   c. 8
   d. 192

Check your answers at the end of this module.

SUBNET MASKS

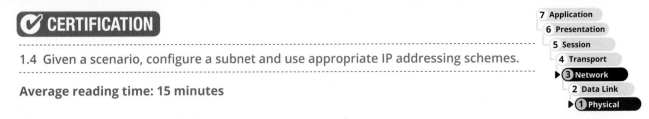

✔ **CERTIFICATION**

1.4 Given a scenario, configure a subnet and use appropriate IP addressing schemes.

Average reading time: 15 minutes

7 Application
6 Presentation
5 Session
4 Transport
▶ ③ Network
2 Data Link
▶ ① Physical

Suppose your company's network is expanding from 20 or 30 computers and other devices to more than a hundred devices. The network began as a single LAN with workstations and printers connected by a few layer 2 switches, one switch connected to a router, and then on to the ISP. See Figure 8-3. Because there is only a single LAN (broadcast domain), any node on the network can communicate directly with any other node, and the one router serves as the default gateway for the whole network. The entire LAN has one pool of IP addresses, for example, 192.168.89.0/24, with a subnet mask of 255.255.255.0.

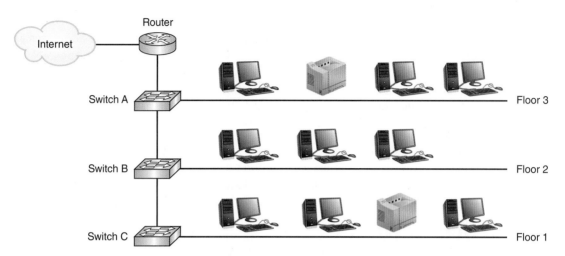

Figure 8-3   A single LAN with some switches and a router

As the network grows, you'll need to better manage network traffic by segmenting the network so that each floor contains a separate LAN, or broadcast domain. One way to accomplish this is to connect each switch separately to the router so each switch is using its own router interface, as illustrated in Figure 8-4.

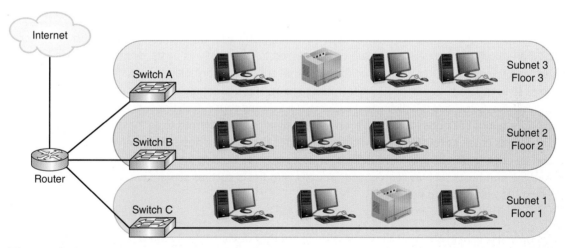

Figure 8-4   A separate subnet for each floor

A router doesn't forward broadcast traffic between its interfaces (see Figure 8-5), and so this configuration will break up the one, large broadcast domain into three smaller broadcast domains. You can think of a router as a broadcast boundary, and fundamentally, routers are tools you can use to divide and conquer network traffic. However, you also need to manage the IP address space at the logical layer. To do this, you need to configure (either manually or through the DHCP server) the clients on each subnet so they know which devices are on their own subnet and which devices are not. And you need to configure the router so it can forward traffic between the LANs as necessary.

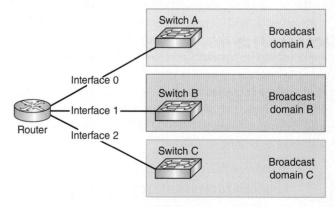

Figure 8-5   A router divides broadcast domains between its interfaces

At this point, you have three separate and smaller LANs, or subnets, within the larger network. However, a device on Subnet 2, for example, doesn't yet know that devices on Subnet 3 aren't still sharing the same LAN. How do you divide the pool of IP addresses so that a computer on Subnet 2 knows to send transmissions for devices on other subnets to the default gateway instead of trying to communicate with them directly? The solution is to divide your pool of IP addresses into three groups, or subnets, one for each LAN or floor of the building. This technique is called subnetting.

Subnetting helps solve the fundamental problem with classful addressing: too many node addresses assigned to each classful network. For example, a single class B network has 65,536 IP addresses all on the one LAN. Imagine the challenges involved in managing such a highly populated LAN, not to mention the poor performance that would result. Subnetting helps manage IP address space more efficiently. Also, though it might not be obvious at this point, using well-chosen subnets provides the following benefits:

- Network documentation is easier to manage.
- Problems are easier to locate and resolve.
- Routers can more easily manage IP address spaces that don't overlap.
- Routing is more efficient on larger networks when IP address spaces are mathematically related at a binary level.

How Subnet Masks Work

A device uses a subnet mask to determine which subnet or network it belongs to. To review a little of what you've already learned regarding IP addresses and subnet masks, recall that an IPv4 address has 32 bits and is divided into two parts: the network portion, which identifies the network and is called the network ID, and the node portion, which identifies the node and is called the node ID or host ID. You can know where the dividing line is between the portions of bits by looking at the subnet mask, or by checking the CIDR block (such as /24).

NOTE 8-1

You might sometimes find the term *network ID* used interchangeably with the terms *network number* or *network prefix*.

Also, when calculating subnets, nodes are often referred to generically as hosts, even if that node is a networking device such as a firewall or router. The reason for this is that subnetting formulas must distinguish between network ID bits (referred to as "n") and node or host ID bits (referred to as "h"). This course uses a similar approach and refers to all subnet nodes as hosts to make this distinction easier to track during your calculations. As you work, keep in mind that all hosts are nodes but not all nodes are hosts, even though all nodes are referred to as "hosts" when calculating subnets. *Networking* devices (such as routers and switches) are nodes that are not hosts. They serve a fundamentally different purpose on a network than do *networked* devices, or hosts, such as servers, workstations, and printers. However, each node (including non-hosts such as routers and firewalls, and hosts such as servers and printers) receives one of the available host IDs within the subnet.

When a computer is ready to send a transmission to another device, it first compares the bits in its own network ID to the bits in the network ID of the destination device. If the bits match, the other device is on the sending computer's own network, and it sends the transmission directly to that device. If the bits don't match, the destination is on another network, and the computer sends the transmission to the default gateway on its network. The gateway is responsible for sending the transmission toward the correct network.

How does a computer use a subnet mask to determine how many bits of its IP address is the network ID? Recall that an IPv4 subnet mask is 32 bits long. The number of 1s in the subnet mask's bits determines the number of bits in the IP address that belong to the network ID. For example, suppose a computer has an IP address of 192.168.123.132 and its subnet mask in decimal is 255.255.255.0. To identify the bits that make up the network ID, first convert these numbers to binary, as follows:

- IP address 192.168.123.132 in binary:

  11000000.10101000.01111011.10000100
- Subnet mask 255.255.255.0 in binary:

  11111111.11111111.11111111.00000000

NOTE 8-2

In this example and in many others in this module, a **bold red font** is used for the network ID portion of an IP address.

A subnet mask is always a series of 1s followed by a series of 0s. The 1s mark the network portion of an IP address and the 0s mark the host portion. Therefore, the network ID portion of the IP address in the example is 24 bits, or the first three octets: **192.168.123**. The host portion is the last octet: 132. Putting these two pieces together and using bold red for the network ID, this IP address is written as **192.168.123**.132.

By convention, you'll see 0s used to complete the four octets when referring to the network ID and the host portion of an IP address separately, like this:

- Network ID: **192.168.123**.0
- Host portion: 0.0.0.132

Now suppose this computer needs to communicate with a host at **192.168.30**.140. Because the network IDs don't match (that is, **192.168.123** does not match **192.168.30**), the computer knows the remote host is not on its own network and sends the transmission directly to its default gateway.

Applying Concepts 8-2: Use the Logical ANDing Function to Calculate a Network ID

To calculate a host's network ID given its IPv4 address and subnet mask, computers follow a logical process of combining bits known as **ANDing**. In ANDing, a bit with a value of 1 combined, or ANDed, with another bit with a value of 1 results in a 1. A bit with a value of 0 ANDed with any other bit results in a 0. If you think of 1 as "true" and 0 as "false," the logic of ANDing makes sense: ANDing a true statement to a true statement still results in a true statement. But ANDing a true statement to a false statement results in a false statement.

ANDing logic is demonstrated in Table 8-1, which provides every possible combination of having a 1 or 0 bit in an IPv4 address or subnet mask.

Table 8-1   ANDing

IP address bit	1	1	0	0
Subnet mask bit	1	0	1	0
Resulting bit	**1**	**0**	**0**	**0**

A sample IPv4 host address, its default subnet mask, and its network ID are shown in Figure 8-6 in both binary and dotted decimal notation. Notice that the address's fourth octet could have been composed of any combination of 1s and 0s, and the network ID's fourth octet would still result in all 0s.

	IP address:	11000000	00100010	01011001	01111111	192.	34.	89.	127
AND	Subnet mask:	11111111	11111111	11111111	00000000	255.	255.	255.	0
Equals	Network ID:	11000000	00100010	01011001	00000000	192.	34.	89.	0

Figure 8-6   Example of ANDing a host's network ID

Figure 8-6 shows how ANDing logic is applied to an IPv4 address plus a default subnet mask. It works the same way for networks that are subnetted with classless subnet masks, discussed later in this module.

Legacy Networking: Classful Addressing in IPv4

Recall that every IPv4 address can be associated with a network class—A, B, C, D, or E (though class D and E addresses are reserved for special purposes). Classful addressing is the simplest type of subnetting and uses only whole octets for the network ID and host portions. In the earlier example of **192.168.123**.132, the network ID consists of three octets, and is, therefore, an example of classful addressing. Table 8-2 lists how the 32 bits are allocated with classful addressing for classes A, B, and C.

Table 8-2   Classful addressing uses whole octets for the network ID

Class	Network portion in bold red: n = network ID bit h = host address bit	Bits in network ID	Bits in host portion
A	**nnnnnnnn**.hhhhhhhh.hhhhhhhh.hhhhhhhh	8	24
B	**nnnnnnnn.nnnnnnnn**.hhhhhhhh.hhhhhhhh	16	16
C	**nnnnnnnn.nnnnnnnn.nnnnnnnn**.hhhhhhhh	24	8

There are a couple of interesting mathematical patterns to notice about classful IPv4 addressing:

- The last octet of a classful network ID is always equal to 0 (and may have preceding octets equal to 0). For example, the network ID for a class A network might be **92**.0.0.0, and the network ID for a class B network might be **147.12**.0.0.
- A host cannot be assigned the same address as the network ID, which explains why the last octet of a host's IP address is almost never 0.
- Each octet can range in value from 0 to 255—you'll never use a number greater than 255 in any octet for any reason.

Although classful addressing rules no longer restrict addressing options on modern networks, you can still use the classes as a starting point for IPv4 subnet calculations.

Each network class is associated with a default subnet mask, as shown in Table 8-3. For example, by default, a class A address's first octet (or 8 bits) represents network information. This means that if you work on a network whose hosts are configured with a subnet mask of **11111111** 00000000 00000000 00000000, or 255.0.0.0, you know that the network is likely using class A addresses (though not necessarily). What if you were to "borrow" some host bits to make more subnets on your network? This is where classless addressing—and the need for calculating subnets—comes in. The next section describes how to calculate IPv4 subnets and how to determine the range of usable host addresses on a subnet (that is, addresses used for networked and networking devices), as well as the subnet masks the host addresses use. Later in the section, you will learn how subnetting differs in IPv6.

Table 8-3   Default IPv4 subnet masks

Network class	Default subnet mask (binary)	Number of bits used for network information	Default subnet mask (dotted decimal notation)
A	11111111 00000000 00000000 00000000	8	**255**.0.0.0
B	11111111 11111111 00000000 00000000	16	**255.255**.0.0
C	11111111 11111111 11111111 00000000	24	**255.255.255**.0

REMEMBER THIS...

- List reasons for creating subnets on a network.
- Explain how subnet masks work.
- Memorize the default subnet masks for class A, B, and C networks.

SELF-CHECK

3. Which of the following is *not* a benefit of subnetting?
  a. Problems are easier to locate and resolve.
  b. Available IP address space is managed more efficiently.
  c. Network documentation is easier to manage.
  d. Routers more easily manage IP address spaces that overlap.

4. What is the network ID of the IP address 192.168.72.149/16?
  a. 0.0.0.149
  b. 192.168.0.0
  c. 0.0.72.149
  d. 192.168.72.0

Check your answers at the end of this module.

You're Ready

You're now ready to complete **Project 8-1: Test Subnet Boundaries in Packet Tracer**, or you can wait until you've finished reading this module.

CALCULATING SUBNETS

✔ **CERTIFICATION**

1.4 Given a scenario, configure a subnet and use appropriate IP addressing schemes.

1.6 Explain the use and purpose of network services.

Average reading time: 49 minutes

7 Application
6 Presentation
5 Session
4 Transport
▶ ③ Network
2 Data Link
▶ ① Physical

Subnetting, which alters the rules of classful IPv4 addressing, is called classless addressing. To subnet a network, you borrow bits that *would* represent host information in classful addressing and use those bits instead to represent network information. By doing so, you increase the number of bits available for the network ID, and you also reduce the number of bits available for identifying hosts. Consequently, you increase the number of networks and reduce the number of usable host addresses in each network or subnet. The more bits you borrow for network information, the more subnets you can have, but the fewer hosts each subnet will contain. In many cases, this is actually the goal of subnetting.

Consider the following example of a network that initially has only a single class C subnet and all its hosts (up to 254) are on the same subnet. By borrowing only one bit from the host ID, you can have two subnets with up to 126 hosts (a more manageable number) per subnet. Let's see how this works.

IPv4 Subnet Calculation in Binary

Suppose you have a network with one router and a switch connected to one interface on the router with your devices connected to that one switch. You then add a second switch to a different interface on the router to divide your local network into two LANs—you can then redistribute your network devices so some of them stay connected to the LAN on the first switch, and others are moved to the new LAN on the second switch.

NOTE 8-3

It's not the addition of the second switch that creates the second LAN—it's the use of the second interface on the router. If you instead daisy-chained the second switch off the first switch so that both switches were using the same router interface, you would still have only one LAN. In a project at the end of this module, you experiment with the boundaries of subnets and broadcast domains to see how this works.

The network ID of the original network is 192.168.89.0, and its subnet mask is 255.255.255.0. Let's create two subnets of IP addresses, one for each LAN. The results of each of the following steps are shown later in Table 8-4:

1. **Borrow from host bits**—Currently, the network ID is 24 bits. First convert the network ID to binary:
   - Network ID 192.168.89 in binary:

     11000000.10101000.01011001

   Borrow one bit from the host portion to give to the network ID, which will then have 25 bits (notice one additional red bit in the fourth octet). Here, the borrowed bit (underlined) is an "x" to show it can have a value of 0 or 1:
   - **11000000.10101000.01011001.x**

   How many subnets do you have now? The underlined red bit can be either a 0 or a 1, which gives you the possibility of two subnets:
   - **11000000.10101000.01011001.0**
   - **11000000.10101000.01011001.1**

2. **Determine the subnet mask**—Recall that the subnet mask marks the bits in an IP address that belong to the network ID. Therefore, the subnet mask for both subnets is as follows:
   - 11111111.11111111.11111111.10000000 or decimal 255.255.255.128

   To calculate that last octet, you convert binary 10000000 to decimal, which is 128. You can use a calculator to do the conversion, manually calculate it, or memorize this and a handful of other common binary-to-decimal conversions.

3. **Determine the network IDs**—Recall that in the network ID, the underlined red bit can be a 0 or 1. Therefore, the network ID for each subnet is as follows:
   - Subnet 1: **11000000.10101000.01011001.0**0000000 or decimal 192.168.89.0
   - Subnet 2: **11000000.10101000.01011001.1**0000000 or decimal 192.168.89.128

   In CIDR notation, the network ID for each subnet is the following:
   - Subnet 1: 192.168.89.0/25
   - Subnet 2: 192.168.89.128/25

4. **Determine the ranges of IP addresses for hosts in the subnet**—Start with the range of available IP addresses for subnet A. For host addresses, use the last seven bits in the last octet. (The first bit for this octet is always 0 and belongs to the network ID.) Start counting in binary and convert to decimal:
   - **0**0000000 is not used because it's the network ID for this subnet
   - **0**0000001 or decimal 1
   - **0**0000010 or decimal 2
   - **0**0000011 or decimal 3
   - …

- **0**1111110 or decimal 126
- **0**1111111 or decimal 127, which is reserved for broadcasting within the subnet and cannot be used as a host address

The range of possible IP addresses is 192.168.89.0 through 192.168.89.127 (which is 128 possibilities). However, the first and last addresses cannot be used. Therefore, the range of host IP addresses for subnet A is 192.168.89.1 through 192.168.89.126 (that's 128-2, yielding 126 possibilities).

For subnet B, the first bit of the last octet is 1 and the range of host addresses is as follows:

- **1**0000000 is not used because it's the network ID for this subnet
- **1**0000001 in decimal: 129
- **1**0000010 in decimal: 130
- **1**0000011 in decimal: 131
- ...
- **1**1111110 in decimal: 254
- **1**1111111 in decimal: 255 is not used because it's reserved for broadcasting

Therefore, the range of host IP addresses for subnet B is 192.168.89.129 through 192.168.89.254 (another 126 possibilities).

Table 8-4 Steps to divide IP addresses for network ID 192.168.89.0 into two subnets

Step 1: Borrow from host bits.				
Network ID	**192**	**168**	**89**	0
In binary	**11000000**	**10101000**	**01011001**	00000000
Borrow 1 bit	**11000000**	**10101000**	**01011001**	x0000000

Step 2: Determine the subnet mask.				
In binary	**11111111**	**11111111**	**11111111**	10000000
In decimal	**255**	**255**	**255**	128

Step 3: Determine the network IDs.				
Network ID 1	**11000000**	**10101000**	**01011001**	00000000
In decimal	**192**	**168**	**89**	0
In CIDR notation	192.168.89.0/25			
Network ID 2	**11000000**	**10101000**	**01011001**	10000000
In decimal	**192**	**168**	**89**	128
In CIDR notation	192.168.89.128/25			

Step 4: Determine range of host IP addresses.				
Subnet 1:				
First host, binary	**11000000**	**10101000**	**01011001**	000000001
First host, decimal	192	168	89	1
Last host, binary	**11000000**	**10101000**	**01011001**	01111110
Last host, decimal	192	168	89	126
Subnet 2:				
First host, binary	**11000000**	**10101000**	**01011001**	10000001
First host, decimal	192	168	89	129
Last host, binary	**11000000**	**10101000**	**01011001**	11111110
Last host, decimal	192	168	89	254

Notice that you gained a network (the larger network became two smaller subnets), but you lost some host addresses (each subnet offers a possible 126 host addresses for a total of 252 hosts, which is two fewer than the original network's possible 254 hosts). The difference is because each subnet needs its own network ID and broadcast address. Instead of the original network's one network ID and one broadcast address, you now have two network IDs and two broadcast addresses, which reduces the total number of available host addresses. Subnetting offers many advantages, but one disadvantage is that you lose possible host addresses each time you divide a network into more subnets.

IPv4 Subnet Calculations Using Formulas

Now you're ready to move on to a more complicated example, performing calculations using formulas and without so much binary involved. Suppose you want to divide your local network, which has a network ID of 192.168.89.0, into six subnets to correspond to your building's six floors. The following steps walk you through the process:

1. **Decide how many bits to borrow**—How many bits must you borrow from the host portion of the IP addresses to get six subnets? Use this formula to determine the number of bits:

$$2^n = Y$$

   - n equals the number of bits that must be switched from the host address to the network ID.
   - Y equals the number of subnets that result.

   You want six separate subnets (meaning that Y, in this case, should be equal to or greater than 6). Experiment with different values for n until you find a value large enough to give you at least the number of subnets you need. For example, you know that $2^2 = 4$; however, 4 is not high enough. Instead consider that $2^3 = 8$; this will give you enough subnets to meet your current needs and allow room for future growth. Now that n equals 3, you know that three bits in the host addresses of your class C network must become network ID bits. You also know that three bits in your subnet mask must change from 0 to 1.

2. **Determine the subnet mask**—As you know, the default subnet mask for a class C network is **255.255.255.**0, or **11111111 11111111 11111111** 00000000. In this default subnet mask, the first 24 bits indicate the position of network information.

   Changing three of the default subnet mask's bits from host to network information gives you the subnet mask **11111111 11111111 11111111 111**00000. In this modified subnet mask, the first 27 bits indicate the bits for the network ID. For the original class C network whose network ID is 192.168.89.0, the slash notation for its first subnet would now be 192.168.89.0/27 because 27 bits of the subnet's address are used to provide network information.

   Converting from binary to the more familiar dotted decimal notation, this subnet mask becomes 255.255.255.224 because 11100000 in binary is 224 in decimal for the final octet. When you configure the TCP/IP properties of clients on your network, as shown in Figure 8-7, you'll specify this new subnet mask.

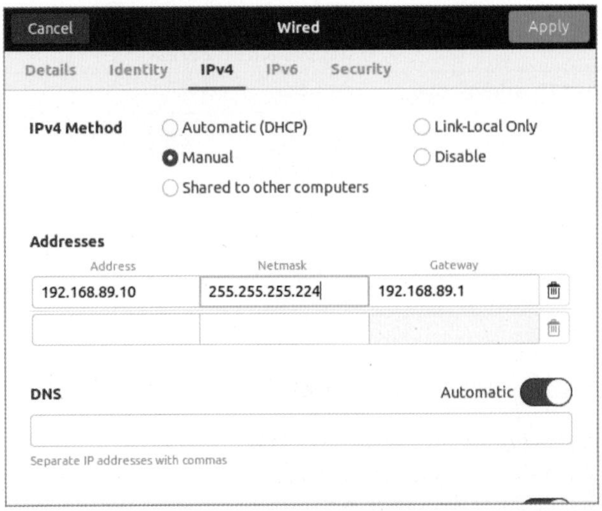

Cancel	Wired	Apply

Details   Identity   **IPv4**   IPv6   Security

IPv4 Method   ○ Automatic (DHCP)   ○ Link-Local Only
                  ● Manual   ○ Disable
                  ○ Shared to other computers

Addresses
Address	Netmask	Gateway
192.168.89.10	255.255.255.224	192.168.89.1	🗑
			🗑

DNS   Automatic ⬤

Separate IP addresses with commas

Source: Canonical Group Limited

Figure 8-7   IPv4 client configuration for a subnet in Ubuntu Desktop

NOTE 8-4

When examining the subnet mask for a network, if any octet is not 255 or 0, you know that this network is a subnet and classful addressing is not used. The unusual number (224 in the example) is often called the *interesting octet*. Subtract the interesting octet value from 256 and you get what is called the **magic number**. In this example, the magic number is 256 − 224 = 32. This magic number can be used to calculate the network IDs in all the subnets of the larger network, which you'll see next.

3. **Calculate the network ID for each subnet**—The first three octets of the network ID for the original class C network (192.168.89) are the same for all eight possible subnets. The network IDs differ in the last octet. Use the magic number to calculate each subnet's network ID as follows:

- **Subnet 1**: **192.168.89.0**
- **Subnet 2**: 192.168.89.0 + 32 yields **192.168.89.32**
- **Subnet 3**: 192.168.89.32 + 32 yields **192.168.89.64**
- **Subnet 4**: 192.168.89.64 + 32 yields **192.168.89.96**
- **Subnet 5**: 192.168.89.96 + 32 yields **192.168.89.128**
- **Subnet 6**: 192.168.89.128 + 32 yields **192.168.89.160**
- **Subnet 7**: 192.168.89.160 + 32 yields **192.168.89.192**
- **Subnet 8**: 192.168.89.192 + 32 yields **192.168.89.224**

This method of adding on the same number over and over is called skip-counting. You probably learned this technique in elementary school. For example, skip-counting by twos gives you 0, 2, 4, 6, 8, 10, etc. Skip-counting by threes gives 0, 3, 6, 9, 12, etc. In the last octet, you can skip-count by 32 to get all eight subnets' final octets: 0, 32, 64, 96, 128, 160, 192, and 224.

4. **Determine the IP address range for hosts in each subnet**—Recall that you have borrowed three bits from what used to be host information in the IP address. That leaves five bits instead of eight available in the last octet of your class C addresses to identify hosts. To calculate the number of possible addresses, keep in mind that each of the five bits has two possible values, a 0 or a 1. Therefore, the number of possible addresses is $2^5 = 2 \times 2 \times 2 \times 2 \times 2 = 32$. But you can't use two of these addresses for hosts because one is used for the network ID (the one where all five bits are 0 in binary) and one for the broadcast address (the one where all five bits are 1 in binary). That leaves you 30 host addresses in each subnet. As a shortcut to calculating the number of hosts, you can use the following formula:

$$2^h - 2 = Z$$

- h equals the number of bits remaining in the host portion.
- Z equals the number of hosts available in each subnet.

In summary, $2^5 - 2$ yields 30 possible hosts per subnet.

In this example, you can have a maximum of 8 (number of subnets) × 30 (number of hosts per subnet), or 240, unique host addresses on the entire, larger network. Recall that each time you subnet a network, you lose two possible host addresses with each subnet. This overhead is the price you pay for subnetting a network, in exchange for the advantages you gain.

When calculating subnets, you'll work with the following information, some of which is initially known and some of which must be calculated:

- Number of subnets
- Number of host addresses per subnet
- Network ID for each subnet
- Broadcast address for each subnet
- Range of possible host addresses within each subnet

In this example, you've already calculated the number of subnets, number of host addresses, and each subnet's network ID. Once you know the network ID of the subnets, calculating the address range of hosts and each subnet's broadcast address is relatively simple. For example, take subnet 5. The network ID is 192.168.89.128. The broadcast address is the last address before the next subnet's network ID. In this case, that's 192.168.89.160 − 1, which is 192.168.89.159.

For the host addresses in this subnet, start back at the network ID. You won't use the network ID for a host address, so you start with the next value and keep going until you reach the broadcast address for the subnet. Therefore, the available host address range for subnet 5 includes 192.168.89.129 through 192.168.89.158, yielding for this particular subnet a total of 30 available host addresses.

Table 8-5 lists the network ID, broadcast address, and the range of usable host addresses for each of the eight subnets in this subnetted class C network. Together, the existing network ID plus the additional bits used for subnet information are sometimes called the extended network prefix.

Table 8-5   Subnet information for eight subnets in a sample IPv4 class C network

Subnet number	Network ID (extended network prefix)	Range of host addresses	Broadcast address
1	192.168.89.0 or **11000000 10101000 01011001 00000000**	192.168.89.1-30	192.168.89.31 or **11000000 10101000 01011001 00011111**
2	192.168.89.32 or **11000000 10101000 01011001 00100000**	192.168.89.33-62	192.168.89.63 or **11000000 10101000 01011001 00111111**
3	192.168.89.64 or **11000000 10101000 01011001 01000000**	192.168.89.65-94	192.168.89.95 or **11000000 10101000 01011001 01011111**
4	192.168.89.96 or **11000000 10101000 01011001 01100000**	192.168.89.97-126	192.168.89.127 or **11000000 10101000 01011001 01111111**
5	192.168.89.128 or **11000000 10101000 01011001 10000000**	192.168.89.129-158	192.168.89.159 or **11000000 10101000 01011001 10011111**
6	192.168.89.160 or **11000000 10101000 01011001 10100000**	192.168.89.161-190	192.168.89.191 or **11000000 10101000 01011001 10111111**
7	192.168.89.192 or **11000000 10101000 01011001 11000000**	192.168.89.193-222	192.168.89.223 or **11000000 10101000 01011001 11011111**
8	192.168.89.224 or **11000000 10101000 01011001 11100000**	192.168.89.225-254	192.168.89.255 or **11000000 10101000 01011001 11111111**

NOTE 8-5

You can also calculate the magic number by raising 2 to the power of the number of bits in the host portion of the subnet mask's interesting octet. Use this formula:

$$2^h = \text{magic number}$$

In this example, the host portion has five bits, meaning h equals 5. Therefore, the magic number is $2^5 = 32$. You can then use this number to determine the subnets' network IDs.

Several websites provide excellent tools that can help you calculate subnet information or to check your calculations after performing them manually. Two such sites are *subnetmask.info* and *cidr.xyz*. Other websites and apps can give you practice calculating subnets in preparation for your certification exams. Check out the website *subnettingquestions.com* in your browser or the Subnetting Practice app with the "/24" icon on both Android and iPhone.

Subnet Mask Tables

Class A, class B, and class C networks can all be subnetted. But because each class reserves a different number of bits for network information, each class has a different number of host information bits that can be used for subnet information. The number of hosts and subnets on your network will vary depending on your network class and the way you use subnetting.

Table 8-6 lists the numbers of subnets and hosts that can be created by subnetting a class B network. Notice the available subnet masks that can be used instead of the default class B subnet mask of 255.255.0.0. Also compare the listed numbers of hosts per subnet to the 65,534 hosts available on a class B network that is not subnetted.

Table 8-6 IPv4 class B subnet masks

Subnet mask	CIDR block	Number of subnets on network	Number of hosts per subnet
255.255.128.0 or 11111111 11111111 10000000 00000000	/17	2	32,766
255.255.192.0 or 11111111 11111111 11000000 00000000	/18	4	16,382
255.255.224.0 or 11111111 11111111 11100000 00000000	/19	8	8190
255.255.240.0 or 11111111 11111111 11110000 00000000	/20	16	4094
255.255.248.0 or 11111111 11111111 11111000 00000000	/21	32	2046
255.255.252.0 or 11111111 11111111 11111100 00000000	/22	64	1022
255.255.254.0 or 11111111 11111111 11111110 00000000	/23	128	510
255.255.255.0 or 11111111 11111111 11111111 00000000	/24	256	254
255.255.255.128 or 11111111 11111111 11111111 10000000	/25	512	126
255.255.255.192 or 11111111 11111111 11111111 11000000	/26	1024	62
255.255.255.224 or 11111111 11111111 11111111 11100000	/27	2048	30
255.255.255.240 or 11111111 11111111 11111111 11110000	/28	4096	14
255.255.255.248 or 11111111 11111111 11111111 11111000	/29	8192	6
255.255.255.252 or 11111111 11111111 11111111 11111100	/30	16,384	2

Table 8-7 lists the numbers of subnets and hosts that can be created by subnetting a class C network. Notice that a class C network allows for fewer subnets than a class B network. This is because class C addresses have fewer host information bits that can be borrowed for network information. In addition, fewer bits are left over for host information, which leads to a lower number of hosts per subnet than the number available to class B subnets.

Subnetting Questions on Exams

Although it's impossible to know for sure, you're likely to encounter two types of subnet calculation problems on the CompTIA Network+ exam:

- Given certain network requirements (such as required number of hosts or required number of subnets), calculate possible subnets and host IP address ranges.
- Given an IP address, determine its subnet's network ID, broadcast address, and first/last host addresses.

You've already seen steps for solving the first type of problem using a class C network ID. Now you're ready to work through another example of the same type of problem, but this time you'll begin with a class B network ID. Then you'll work through an example of the second type of subnetting problem.

Table 8-7   IPv4 class C subnet masks

Subnet mask	CIDR block	Number of subnets on network	Number of hosts per subnet
255.255.255.128 or 11111111 11111111 11111111 10000000	/25	2	126
255.255.255.192 or 11111111 11111111 11111111 11000000	/26	4	62
255.255.255.224 or 11111111 11111111 11111111 11100000	/27	8	30
255.255.255.240 or 11111111 11111111 11111111 11110000	/28	16	14
255.255.255.248 or 11111111 11111111 11111111 11111000	/29	32	6
255.255.255.252 or 11111111 11111111 11111111 11111100	/30	64	2

Applying Concepts 8-3: Calculate IPv4 Subnets and Host IP Address Ranges

Suppose your organization uses the class B network ID of 172.20.0.0 for its entire network and wants to create 15 subnets. Complete the following steps, answering the questions as you go:

1. You first need to decide how many bits to borrow from the host address bits. Recall that you can use the formula $2^n = Y$. To get at least 15 new subnets (without creating more subnets than necessary), how many bits must be borrowed from the host address portion? How many bits total will be used for identifying a host's subnet?

2. You can now calculate the subnet mask. The default subnet mask for a class B network is 255.255.0.0, and so the third octet is the one that will change. What is the subnet mask for these subnets, written in dotted decimal notation?

3. The magic number will tell you by what amount to skip-count when you're listing the subnets' network IDs. There are two ways to calculate the magic number: Subtract the interesting octet's value from 256, or use the formula 2^h where h equals the number of host bits in the interesting octet. What is the magic number you can use to calculate the network IDs?

4. Now you can calculate the network IDs for each subnet. Begin with the original network ID. Then in the third octet, count up by the magic number with each iteration. The last subnet's network ID will be equal to 256 minus the magic number, because you can't use 256 itself in any IP address. What is the CIDR notation for the first subnet's network ID? For the second subnet's network ID? For the last subnet's network ID?

5. If 20 bits are used to identify the network and subnet, that leaves 12 bits to identify each host. Using the formula $2^h - 2 = Z$ where h equals the total number of host bits, how many host addresses are possible in each subnet? (You might need a calculator for this step, such as the Windows 10 Calculator app in Scientific mode. Note that it's unusual to see an exam question where you're working with bits in the third octet because you can't use a calculator during the exam.)

6. The range of available host addresses consists of all the possible IP addresses between the network ID and the broadcast address (which is one below the network ID for the next subnet). What is the range of host addresses for the first subnet? For the second subnet? For the last subnet?

Now you're ready to work through the other type of subnetting problem that you'll likely see on your CompTIA Network+ exam: calculating a host's network information.

Applying Concepts 8-4: Calculate an IPv4 Host's Network Information

This time, you'll work backwards in your calculations by starting with one host's IP address information. Suppose a server on your network displays the following IPv4 network configuration:

IPv4 address: 192.168.89.130
Subnet mask: 255.255.255.224

Your task is to determine the network ID of the subnet this server is located on, the broadcast address, and the range of available host addresses on this subnet. Complete the following steps, answering the questions as you go:

1. You don't necessarily need to use binary for these calculations. Find the magic number and go from there. As with your earlier calculations, you need to subtract the interesting octet's value from 256 to get the magic number. What is the magic number?

2. If the interesting octet is located at the end of the subnet mask, you can assume the first three octets of the IP address identify the classful network ID before this network was subnetted. This network ID also serves as the network ID for the first subnet. What is the network ID of the first subnet?

3. You can now use the magic number to calculate the remaining subnets' network IDs. What is the second subnet's network ID? What is the final subnet's network ID?

4. To narrow this down to your server's subnet, either skip-count up from a lower numbered subnet or skip-count down from a higher numbered subnet. Either way will work. You're looking for a network ID that is as close to the server's IP address as possible without going over. What is the network ID of the server's subnet?

5. You can look at the next higher subnet's network ID and subtract 1 to determine the broadcast address of the server's subnet. What is the broadcast address?

6. Finally, any IP address between the subnet's network ID and its broadcast address is the range of available host IP addresses. What is this range?

EXAM TIP If these calculation processes seem overwhelming, you're not alone. Many people have developed a variety of handy shortcuts for calculating subnets. In a Hands-On Project at the end of this module, you'll see how to use a shortcut to answer each of the two primary types of subnetting exam questions. If these shortcuts don't resonate with you, you can search online to find a shortcut that does click. There are many options, and sometimes it's just a matter of finding the approach that is easiest for you to remember and work with.

Implementing Subnets on a Network

Now that you've calculated the subnets for the scenarios presented earlier in the module, how do you implement them? Figure 8-8 shows the subnets assigned to the three LANs you saw earlier in Figure 8-4. Also in Figure 8-8, you can see the IP address of the default gateway for each LAN, which is the IP address assigned to the router's interface on that LAN. Note that only three of the eight possible subnets listed earlier in Table 8-5 are used.

Figure 8-9 illustrates another scenario in which an enterprise network uses the same class C range of private addresses that begin with 192.168.89. The network administrator has subnetted this class C network into six (of eight possible) smaller networks.

The administrator must program each interface on the router with its IP address and subnet mask for its subnet. Though tedious on larger networks, static IP addressing can also be used on network hosts. Figure 8-10a shows the TCP/IPv4 properties dialog box of an Ubuntu workstation on the first subnet. Figure 8-10b shows the static configuration for a Windows workstation on the second subnet. As shown in the figure, the first IP address in the range of host addresses for the subnet is assigned to the router's interface on the subnet, which serves the subnet as its default gateway. This convention varies between organizations, though. Some network admins prefer to use the *last* available host address in a range for the default gateway.

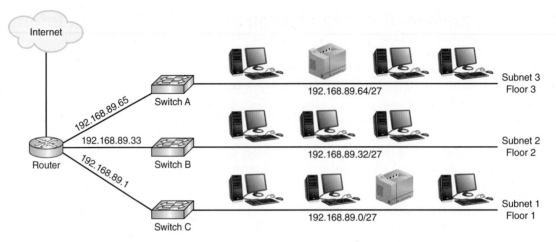

Figure 8-8 Subnets 1, 2, and 3 and their respective default gateways

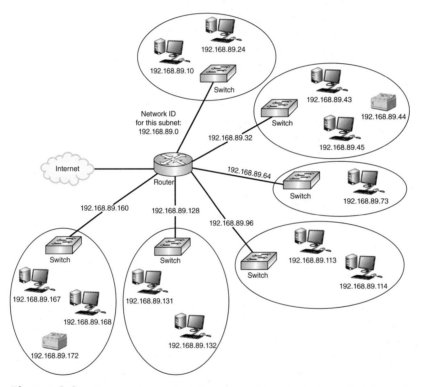

Figure 8-9 One router connecting several LANs, each assigned a subnet

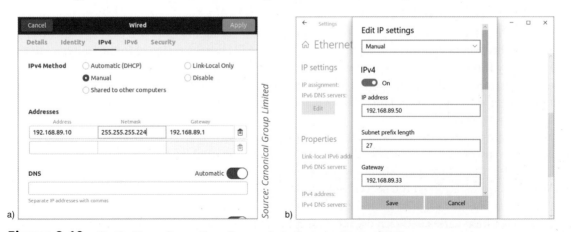

Figure 8-10 Static IP configurations for workstations on two subnets

For dynamic IP addressing, the administrator programs each subnet's DHCP server with the network ID, subnet mask, range of IP addresses, and default gateway for the subnet. In many cases, however, it's cost prohibitive to create a separate DHCP server for each subnet. Recall that DHCP relies on broadcast transmissions to function properly, and broadcast messages are bound by routers. However, there are times you want some types of broadcast traffic, such as DHCP messages, to travel beyond each broadcast domain. This allows hosts in various subnets to access centralized network services. Recall that DHCP relies on UDP at the transport layer. Other centralized network services also use UDP traffic, including TFTP, NTP, and DNS. Configuring **UDP forwarding** on your network allows routers, firewalls, or layer 3 switches to forward this UDP traffic across broadcast domains, which enables centralization of key network services. How does this work?

As illustrated in Figure 8-11, a LAN device sends a broadcast message on the local subnet intended for a local network server (such as DHCP). When the switch broadcasts this message to all its interfaces, a **relay agent**—a router, firewall, or layer 3 switch configured to support UDP forwarding—detects the message according to a list of services that are enabled for forwarding (which might include DHCP, DNS, and NTP, for example). Forwarded network services are identified by port, such as port 67 for DHCP or port 123 for NTP. When one of these broadcast messages is detected on the local subnet, the relay agent forwards those messages to a designated **IP helper address** on another network. This IP helper address might point specifically to a single server, such as when only DHCP traffic is forwarded. Or it might be the broadcast address for the other subnet so several network servers can monitor traffic for messages, such as when you have DHCP, NTP, and DNS all forwarded to a centralized network services subnet. The intended network server detects the message, collects the needed information from the request, and responds to the request as configured. The relay agent then routes the response back to the client in the original subnet.

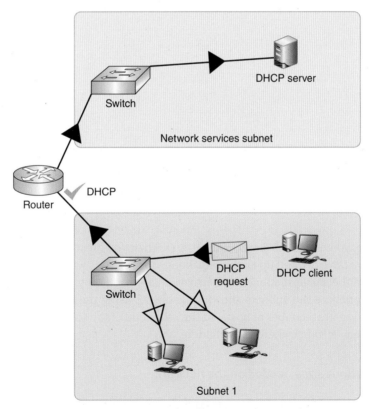

Figure 8-11   The router detects the DHCP broadcast message and forwards the message to the DHCP server on a different subnet

For example, consider the scenario where a centrally managed DHCP server provides DHCP assignments to multiple subnets (and VLANs). The following steps describe this process:

Step 1:   A DHCP relay agent programmed to support UDP forwarding on port 67 receives the DHCP request from a client in one of its local broadcast domains.

Step2: The relay agent repackages the message with the IP helper information and routes this transmission to its new destination in a different broadcast domain.

Step3: The DHCP server notes the relay agent's source interface IP address and assigns the DHCP client an IP address on the same subnet.

Variable Length Subnet Mask (VLSM)

Hosting your centralized network services, such as DHCP, within a single subnet that is accessed by all other subnets is one way to simplify network management and reduce management overhead. As you can imagine, however, this subnet of centralized network servers will have a lot fewer hosts than a subnet of a few dozen (or a few hundred) employees. Traditional subnetting results in multiple subnets that are all the same size, and this uniformity in subnet size can be inefficient in complex networks. **VLSM (Variable Length Subnet Mask)** allows subnets to be further subdivided into smaller and smaller groupings until each subnet is about the same size as the necessary IP address space. This is often referred to as "subnetting a subnet."

To understand how this works, consider a pizza being shared by members of a young family. Dad might need a very large slice of the pizza, while Mom prefers a medium slice, and the children each need smaller slices. Similarly, with VLSM, some subnets can have larger "slices" of the network, while other subnets (such as a two-point connection between two routers) can be limited to only a few host addresses. See Figure 8-12.

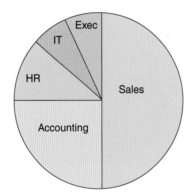

Figure 8-12 VLSM creates subnets of various sizes

To create VLSM subnets, you create the largest subnet first. Then you create the next largest subnet, and then the next one, and so on, until you have divided up all the remaining space. In this way, you ensure that the largest subnets get the space they need, and the smallest subnets are also sized appropriately. Let's work through an example.

Suppose you need to configure the subnets shown in Table 8-8 using the 192.168.10.0/24 IP address space. The Sales department needs the greatest number of hosts. At the other end of the spectrum, your WAN links only need two hosts each. The other subnets fall somewhere in the middle.

Table 8-8 Subnets of various sizes needed on the network

Subnet	Included hosts	Number of hosts	CIDR notation (as calculated next)
1	Sales	120	192.168.10.0 /25
2	Accounting	58	192.168.10.128 /26
3	HR	25	192.168.10.192 /27
4	IT	6	192.168.10.224 /29
5	Executives	5	192.168.10.232 /29
6	WAN link	2	192.168.10.240 /30
7	WAN link	2	192.168.10.244 /30

Step 1: Determine the appropriate subnet mask and other network information for the largest subnet. By borrowing one bit from the host bits, you get the following available subnets:

- Subnet 1: 192.168.10.0 /25 assigned to Sales
- Subnet 2: 192.168.10.128 /25 for smaller subnets

You assign the first of these subnets to the Sales department. Now you can use the second subnet for further calculations.

Step 2: Determine the appropriate subnet mask and other network information for the next largest subnet. By borrowing one more bit from the host bits, you get the following available subnets:

- Subnet 2: 192.168.10.128 /26 assigned to Accounting
- Subnet 3: 192.168.10.192 /26 for smaller subnets

You assign the first of these subnets to the Accounting department. Now you can use the remaining subnet for further calculations.

Step 3: Determine the appropriate subnet mask and other network information for the next largest subnet. By borrowing one more bit from the host bits, you get the following available subnets:

- Subnet 3: 192.168.10.192 /27 assigned to HR
- Subnet 4: 192.168.10.224 /27 for smaller subnets

You assign the first of these subnets to the Human Resources department. Now you can use the other subnet for further calculations.

Step 4: The next two departments are about the same size, and they'll each fit within a /29 subnet. By borrowing two more bits from the host bits this time, you get the following available subnets:

- Subnet 4: 192.168.10.224 /29 assigned to IT
- Subnet 5: 192.168.10.232 /29 assigned to Executives
- Subnet 6: 192.168.10.240 /29 for smaller subnets
- Subnet 7: 192.168.10.248 /29 for future use

You assign the first two of these subnets to the IT department and the Executive suite. Now you can use one of the other subnets for further calculations.

Step 5: The last two required subnets only need two host addresses each, and they'll each fit within a /30 subnet. By borrowing one more bit from the host bits to further subdivide Subnet 6, and renumbering the remaining space to be Subnet 8 (which will be reserved for future use on your network), you get the following available subnets:

- Subnet 6: 192.168.10.240 /30 assigned to WAN link
- Subnet 7: 192.168.10.244 /30 assigned to WAN link
- Subnet 8: 192.168.10.248 /29 for future use

You assign each of these subnets to a WAN link, with the final subnet left over for future use.

Figure 8-13 shows the mathematically determined distribution, with each department allocated the IP address space it needs.

This is an efficient way to define IP address spaces on a network. However, in reality, it's not a good idea to configure subnets so tightly. In this case, for example, there's very little room for future growth. Most companies should allow for significant growth, especially as technology continues to expand the need for IP addresses on a network.

One way to prepare for this growth is to begin with a larger IP address space. For example, you might start with a /23 or even a /22 network. Then subdivide from there, giving each subnet significantly more host addresses than it currently needs. This works for private IP addresses, but not so much for public IP addresses. Another way to

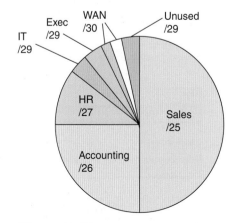

Figure 8-13 Actual subnet allocations

account for future growth is to convert the network to IPv6 addressing instead of IPv4. Let's look at how IPv6 subnetting works.

Subnets in IPv6

Recall that IPv6 addresses are composed of 128 bits, compared with IPv4's 32-bit addresses. That means many more addresses are available in IPv6, compared with IPv4's available addresses. Given so many addresses, an ISP can offer each of its customers an entire IPv6 subnet, or thousands of addresses, rather than a handful of IPv4 addresses that must be shared among all the company's nodes. In this case, subnetting helps network administrators manage the enormous volume of IPv6 addresses.

Subnetting in IPv6 is simpler than subnetting in IPv4, and it differs from IPv4 in substantial ways:

- IPv6 addressing uses no classes. There are no IPv6 equivalents to IPv4's class A, class B, or class C networks. Every IPv6 address is classless.
- IPv6 does not use subnet masks.
- A single IPv6 subnet can supply 18,446,744,073,709,551,616 IPv6 addresses.

Let's see how these numbers pan out. Recall that a unicast address is an address assigned to a single interface on the network. Also recall that every unicast address can be represented in binary form, but it's more commonly written as eight blocks of four hexadecimal characters separated by colons. For example, 2608:FE10:1:AA:002:50FF:FE2B:E708 is a valid IPv6 address. As shown in Figure 8-14, let's divide that address into parts:

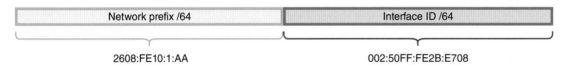

Figure 8-14 Network prefix and interface ID in an IPv6 address

- The last four blocks, which equate to the last 64 bits, identify the interface. (On many IPv6 networks, those 64 bits are based on the interface's EUI-64 version of each device's MAC address.)
- The first four blocks or 64 bits normally identify the network and serve as the network prefix, also called the **site prefix** or **global routing prefix**. In the IPv6 address **2608:FE10:1:AA**:002:50FF:FE2B:E708, the site prefix is **2608:FE10:1:AA** and the interface ID is 002:50FF:FE2B:E708. You might see site prefixes represented as, for example, 2608:FE10:1:AA::/64, where the number of bits that identify the network follow a slash.
- The fourth hexadecimal block in the site prefix can be altered to create subnets within a site. Let's take a closer look at how that block fits into the big picture.

As shown in Figure 8-15, an RIR (regional Internet registry) might assign an ISP a block of addresses that share a 32-bit routing prefix, such as 2608:FE10::/32. That ISP, in turn, might assign a very large organization a block of addresses that share the same 48-bit site prefix, such as 2608:FE10:1::/48, and smaller business customers might receive a 56-bit site prefix, such as 2608:FE10:1:AA::/56, or a 64-bit site prefix, such as 2608:FE10:1:AA::/64.

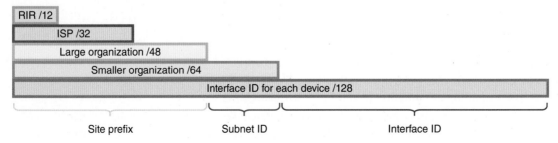

Figure 8-15 Hierarchy of IPv6 routes and subnets

The subnet ID is one block long, which is four hexadecimal characters, or 16 bits in binary. An organization with a /48 site prefix can use all 16 bits to create up to 65,536 subnets. A /56 site prefix can create up to 256 subnets, and a /64 site prefix has only the single subnet, which contains over 18 quintillion possible host addresses (this is more than twice the estimated number of grains of sand in all the beaches and deserts of the earth). As you can see, IPv6 allows for a huge number of potential hosts on a single network.

Consider your sample network with a site prefix of 2608:FE10:1/48 and see what happens with the next block of bits at a binary level. In binary, that fourth block, the Subnet ID, could be all zeroes:

0000 0000 0000 0000

Or it could be all 1s:

1111 1111 1111 1111

And then there's every possible combination in between:

0000 0000 0000 0001
0000 0000 0000 0010
0000 0000 0000 0011
0000 0000 0000 0100
...
1111 1111 1111 1100
1111 1111 1111 1101
1111 1111 1111 1110

That's 65,536 possible subnets. A sample network with a site prefix of 2608:FE10:1:AA/56 can work with eight of those bits to create 256 possible subnets:

0000 0000
0000 0001
0000 0010
...
1111 1101
1111 1110
1111 1111

Sometimes organizations further subdivide this block into site, sub-site, and subnet IDs. For example, consider Figure 8-16, where the Subnet ID block is managed at two levels: the first half for subsites (such as offices in different states or different cities) and the second half for subnets within each site (such as floors in a building or departments located at each site).

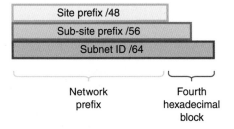

Figure 8-16   The Subnet ID block can be used to identify subsites within an organization

Calculating subnets can feel overwhelming when you're first learning how to work with these numbers. The key here is practice. Find a subnet calculation system that works for you, and then practice often. Rest assured that you don't have to be a "math" person to learn these skills.

Now that you have learned how subnets manage IP address spaces at the network layer, you're ready to explore network segmentation at the data link layer: VLANs.

REMEMBER THIS...

- Calculate IPv4 subnets.
- Explain how to implement VLSM.
- Use CIDR notation.
- Describe UDP forwarding, IP helper addresses, and DHCP relay.

SELF-CHECK

5. If a server has a subnet mask of 255.255.255.224, how many bits in its IP address identify the host?
   a. 27 bits
   b. 8 bits
   c. 30 bits
   d. 5 bits

6. What is the minimum number of bits that should be borrowed to create 14 subnets?
   a. 4 bits
   b. 2 bits
   c. 16 bits
   d. 8 bits

7. Suppose you're calculating the range of host IP addresses for a subnet (the targeted subnet). If the *next* subnet's network ID is 192.168.42.128, what is the *targeted* subnet's broadcast address?
   a. 192.168.42.96
   b. 192.168.42.0
   c. 192.168.42.127
   d. 192.168.42.255

Check your answers at the end of this module.

You're Ready

You're now ready to complete **Project 8-2: Calculate Subnets**, or you can wait until you've finished reading this module.

You're Ready

You're now ready to complete **Project 8-3: Shortcuts to Subnet Calculations**, or you can wait until you've finished reading this module.

VIRTUAL LANS (VLANs)

✔ CERTIFICATION

1.4 Given a scenario, configure a subnet and use appropriate IP addressing schemes.

2.3 Given a scenario, configure and deploy common Ethernet switching features.

4.1 Explain common security concepts.

4.2 Compare and contrast common types of attacks.

4.3 Given a scenario, apply network hardening techniques.

5.5 Given a scenario, troubleshoot general networking issues.

7 Application
6 Presentation
5 Session
4 Transport
3 Network
▶ 2 Data Link
1 Physical

Average reading time: 28 minutes

Let's begin with a discussion about the similarities and differences between subnets and VLANs. As you've learned, a subnet groups IP addresses so that clients on a large network can be logically organized into smaller networks. As you've also seen, this is often accomplished by using multiple ports on a router, which creates multiple broadcast domains within the larger network with subnets organizing the available IP address space.

By contrast, a **VLAN (virtual local area network or virtual LAN)** groups ports on one or more switches so that some of the local traffic on each switch is forced to go through a router, thereby limiting the traffic to a smaller broadcast domain. As virtual LANs, VLANs abstract the broadcast domain from the networking hardware. This is similar to how VMs abstract computing functions from a computer's hardware. When using VLANs, the boundaries of the broadcast domain can be virtually defined anywhere within a single physical LAN.

Recall the example given earlier in this module of a large network on three floors of a building, as shown earlier in Figure 8-3. Rather than running each switch's connection all the way to the router so you can connect each switch to a different router interface, you could instead use managed switches and VLANs to segment the network. For example, suppose you segment the network by department in the company rather than by floors in the building, as shown in Figure 8-17.

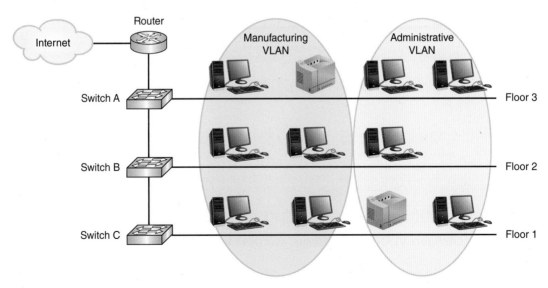

Figure 8-17 A simple VLAN design

To do this, you might need to install managed switches to replace the original switches; however, most modern switches have built-in VLAN functionality. You'll then assign each host to a specific VLAN by configuring the switch port each host is connected to. Essentially, you'll tell the switch to "tag" traffic from that port as belonging to a specific

VLAN. Once the tag is added to the host's transmissions, all other switches in the network treat that tagged traffic as belonging only to the one VLAN.

Although you can add router interfaces to separate a large LAN into manageable smaller LANs, reasons for using VLANs to do the job instead include the following:

- Identify groups of devices whose data should be given priority handling, such as executive client devices or an ICS (industrial control system) that manages a refrigeration system or a gas pipeline.
- Isolate connections with heavy or unpredictable traffic patterns, such as when separating heavy VoIP traffic from other network activities.
- Isolate groups of devices that rely on legacy protocols incompatible with the majority of the network's traffic, such as a legacy SCADA (supervisory control and data acquisition) system monitoring an oil refinery.
- Separate groups of users who need special or limited security or network functions, such as when setting up a guest network.
- Configure temporary networks, such as when making specific network resources available to a short-term project team.
- Reduce the cost of networking equipment, such as when upgrading a network design to include additional departments or new types of network traffic.

Switch Port Configuration

Recall that managed switches can be configured via a CLI or a web-based management GUI (see Figure 8-18). VLANs can only be implemented through managed switches, whose ports can be partitioned into groups.

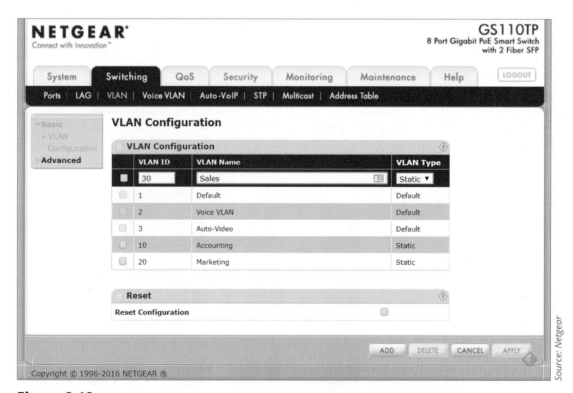

Figure 8-18   Configure VLANs on a managed switch's management interface

Figure 8-19 shows how the switch's physical ports are grouped by VLAN, according to some of the VLANs listed in Figure 8-18. Notice that, for this switch, VLANs 1, 2, and 3 are default VLANs and cannot be deleted.

Recall that switches are primarily layer 2 devices (although, of course, you've learned about switches functioning at other layers to perform functions in addition to switching). By sorting traffic based on layer 2 information, VLANs create two or more broadcast domains from a single broadcast domain, which is also a layer 2 construct. Let's look at some illustrations to see how this works.

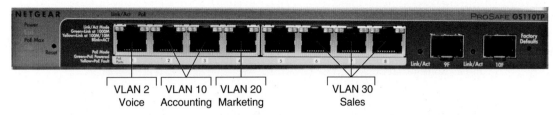

Figure 8-19   Each port on a managed switch might be configured for a different VLAN

Figure 8-20 shows a basic network with one broadcast domain. The switch manages all network traffic on the LAN unless a host on the network wants to communicate with a host on another network, and then that traffic goes through the router. For example, if Computer A on the LAN sends a message to Computer B on the same LAN, the switch handles the message without involving the router.

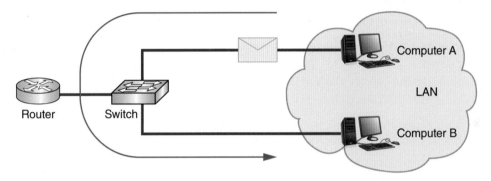

Figure 8-20   A switch connecting devices within a LAN to each other and to a router

Figure 8-21 shows what happens when ports on a managed switch are partitioned into two VLANs. Traffic *within* each VLAN still goes through the switch as normal to reach other devices on the *same* VLAN. Traffic to hosts on other networks still goes through the router. However, traffic between hosts on VLAN 1 and VLAN 2 must now *also* go through the router, which is called inter-VLAN routing. This simple VLAN configuration, where one router connects to a switch that supports multiple VLANs, is sometimes called a "router-on-a-stick."

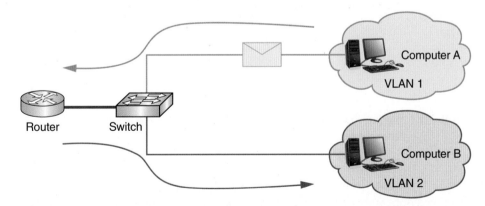

Figure 8-21   A managed switch with its ports partitioned into two groups, each belonging to a different VLAN

To visualize what happens at the hardware level, look at Figure 8-22. Here you can see that several ports on the switch are assigned to VLAN 1 or VLAN 2. The ports for a VLAN don't have to be located next to each other—each port is individually configured to belong to a specific VLAN. Any device that is connected to a VLAN-configured port is automatically considered to be part of that VLAN. All transmissions coming from the connected host will be associated with the VLAN on that switch's port.

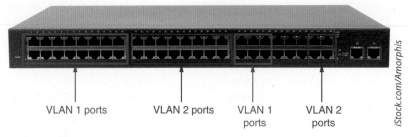

Figure 8-22 Each port on a switch can be assigned to a different VLAN

To identify the transmissions that belong to each VLAN, the switch adds a small field called a **tag** to the Ethernet header that identifies the port through which messages arrive at the switch (see Figure 8-23). The tag travels with the transmission until it reaches one of the following:

- The switch port connected to the destination device, if the destination device is connected to the same switch as the sending device
- A router for routing to the correct VLAN, if the destination device is connected to a different switch

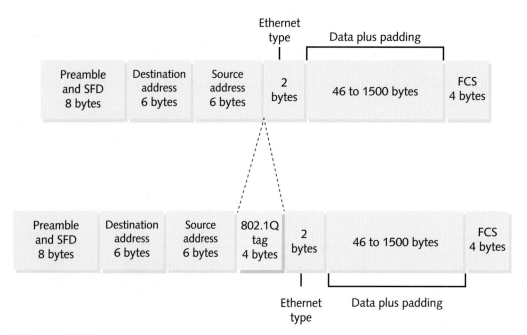

Figure 8-23 The 802.1Q VLAN tag is inserted after the Source address field in an Ethernet frame

At that point, the tag is stripped from the frame. If the frame is being routed to a new VLAN, the router adds a new tag, which is then removed once the frame reaches its final switch port. In most cases, neither the sending device nor the receiving device is aware of the VLAN infrastructure.

Port tagging is specified in the IEEE **802.1Q** standard, which defines how VLAN information appears in frames and how switches interpret that information. Note that the 802.1Q standard is sometimes referred to simply as "dot1q," which will be easy to remember when you start working with VLAN commands in a Packet Tracer project at the end of this module.

You've seen that a switch can support more than one VLAN. Similarly, a VLAN can include ports from more than one switch. Suppose you add a couple more switches to the LAN, as in Figure 8-24. Switch B's ports in this example network can be configured with the same or different VLANs as the ports on Switch A.

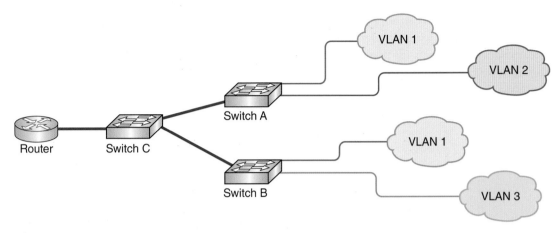

Figure 8-24 Three switches on a LAN with multiple VLANs

Consider the following scenarios:

- Traffic from a device on VLAN 1 connected to Switch A can travel to another device on VLAN 1 connected to Switch B as if it were local traffic (that is, same broadcast domain and won't cross the router interface) because these two devices are in the same VLAN.
- Devices on separate VLANs—even if they're connected to the same switch—can't talk to each other without their traffic going through the router. Therefore, transmissions from a device on VLAN 1 connected to Switch B must go through the router to reach a device on VLAN 3, even though both devices are plugged into the same switch.

VLAN Trunks

Notice in Figure 8-24 that Switch A is connected to devices on two VLANs, and it's also connected to Switch C. These are two very different types of connections. Ports connected to endpoint devices (hosts) are usually configured to support traffic for only one VLAN. However, the port that connects to Switch C (which is a node but not a host) must be able to carry traffic for multiple VLANs. Therefore, each port on a switch that supports VLANs is configured as one of two types of VLAN ports:

- **Access port**—Connects the switch to a host, such as a workstation, server, or printer. The device connected to an access port does not know which VLAN it belongs to, nor can it recognize other VLANs on the same switch. An access port typically carries traffic for only one VLAN.
- **Trunk port**—Connects the switch to a networking device such as a router or another switch (or possibly a server). This interface manages traffic from multiple VLANs, as shown in Figure 8-25. A trunk line (or just "trunk") is a link between two trunk ports.

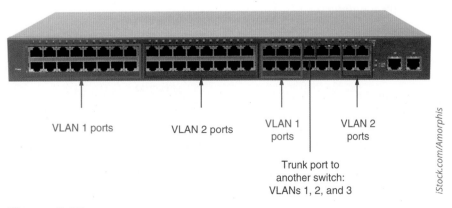

Figure 8-25 A trunk port supports traffic from multiple VLANs

With **trunking**, a single switch can support traffic belonging to several VLANs across the network. The term *trunk* originated in the telephony field, where it refers to an aggregation of logical connections over one physical connection. For example, a trunk carries signals for many residential telephone lines in the same neighborhood over one cable. Similarly, in the context of switching, a trunk is a single physical connection between networking devices through which many logical VLANs can transmit and receive data. Figure 8-26 shows the relative location of access ports, trunk ports, and trunk lines on the sample network.

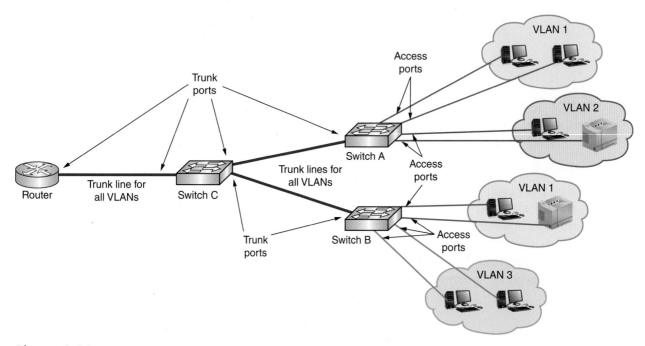

Figure 8-26   Each trunk line carries traffic for multiple VLANs

Trunking protocols assign and interpret the VLAN tags in Ethernet frames, thereby managing the distribution of VLAN frames through a trunk. The most popular protocol for exchanging VLAN information over trunks is Cisco's VTP (VLAN Trunk Protocol). VTP allows changes to a VLAN database on one switch, called the stack master, to be communicated to all other switches in the network. This provides network administrators with the ability to centrally manage all VLANs by making changes to a single switch. Other switches besides the stack master in the same VTP domain can also communicate VLAN updates, such as the addition of a new VLAN.

VLANs and Subnets

In most situations, each VLAN is assigned its own subnet of IP addresses. This means that a particular subnet, working at layer 3, includes the same group of hosts as a specific VLAN, working at layer 2. For example, the sample network (shown earlier in Figure 8-24 and again here in Figure 8-27) is divided into three subnets where VLAN 1 = Subnet 1, VLAN 2 = Subnet 2, and VLAN 3 = Subnet 3.

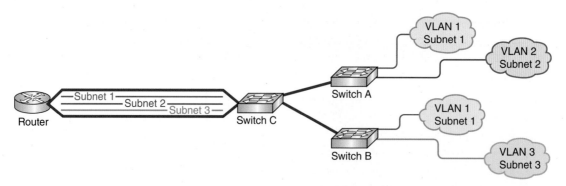

Figure 8-27   Three subnets are connected to a single router interface

As traffic from each VLAN reaches the router, the router sees three logical LANs connected to a single router port, as you can see in Figure 8-28. Each of these logical interfaces on the one physical interface is called a subinterface.

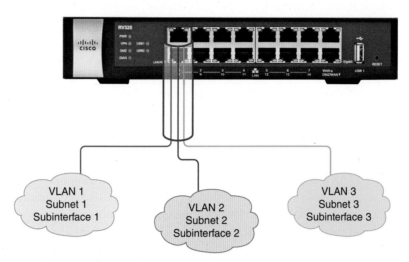

Figure 8-28   One router interface is configured to support three different subnets

For example, if these three VLANs are connected to the router's fastethernet0/0 interface, they might be configured to use the following subinterfaces using decimal numbers at the end of each interface's name:

- `fastethernet0/0.1` for Subnet 1 and VLAN 1
- `fastethernet0/0.2` for Subnet 2 and VLAN 2
- `fastethernet0/0.3` for Subnet 3 and VLAN 3

Also, each VLAN and subnet combination acts as a single broadcast domain. Keep in mind, though, that VLANs and subnets serve two different segmentation purposes: Subnets organize IP addressing space at layer 3, while VLANs segment network traffic at layer 2. Additionally, you won't necessarily see a 1:1 relationship between subnets and VLANs on every network—for example, you might see multiple subnets assigned to a single VLAN. Although it is possible to do otherwise, network administrators find life much easier when they adhere to the following rule:

1 broadcast domain = 1 VLAN = 1 subnet

So how do VLAN clients receive the appropriate IP address assignments from the subnet's range of addresses portioned to each VLAN? One way to do this is to run a DHCP server for the entire network and use a DHCP relay agent to help sort DHCP requests by subnet, as described earlier in this module. Instead, the router can provide DHCP services with each subinterface configured with its own, subnetted range of IP addresses. In a project at the end of this module, you get practice doing exactly this using a router in Packet Tracer.

Types of VLANs

You already know that different types of IP addresses serve different purposes (such as private, public, loopback, and APIPA IP addresses). The same is true of VLANs. Here are common VLAN types you'll likely encounter when managing a network:

- **Default VLAN**—Typically preconfigured on a switch and initially includes all the switch's ports. Other VLANs might be preconfigured as well, depending on the device and manufacturer (such as the voice and video VLANs shown earlier in Figure 8-18). The default VLAN cannot be renamed or deleted; however, ports in the default VLAN can be reassigned to other VLANs.
- **Native VLAN**—Receives all untagged frames from untagged ports. By default, this is the same as the default VLAN. However, this configuration poses a security risk when untagged traffic can travel in a VLAN-managed network. To protect the network from unauthorized traffic, the native VLAN should be changed to an unused VLAN so that untagged traffic essentially runs into a dead-end. To do this on a Cisco switch, for example, use

the command `switchport trunk native vlan`. On a Juniper switch, the native VLAN is configured with the command `set port-mode trunk` followed by `set native-vlan-id`. Each switch port can be configured for a different native VLAN using these commands. However, switch ports on each end of a trunk should agree on the native VLAN assignment. A native VLAN mismatch (or just VLAN mismatch) is a configuration error that occurs when ports don't agree.

- **Data VLAN** (or user **VLAN**)—Carries user-generated traffic, such as email, web browsing, or database updates.
- **Management VLAN**—Can be used to provide administrative access to a switch. By default, this might be the same as the default VLAN; however, this poses a security risk and should be changed.
- **Voice VLAN**—Supports VoIP traffic, which requires high bandwidths, priority over other traffic, flexible routing, and minimized latency.
- **Private VLAN**—Partitions a VLAN broadcast domain into subdomains. Within a private VLAN is a single primary VLAN that defines the entire private VLAN's domain, plus one or more secondary VLANs that each occupy a portion of the VLAN's domain, as shown in Figure 8-29. Hosts assigned to a secondary VLAN cannot communicate outside their own subdomain within the private VLAN, which provides options for isolated VLAN traffic. However, a server or load balancer might instead be connected to a **promiscuous port** within the primary VLAN so it can communicate with hosts inside all the secondary VLANs. Two types of secondary VLANs are illustrated in Figure 8-29 and are described next:
  - **Isolated VLAN**—The host on each switch port is completely isolated from hosts in the same and other secondary VLANs within the primary VLAN. A host in an isolated VLAN might or might not be allowed to communicate on a trunk line with the larger network (such as the Internet). This is commonly used when you want to isolate traffic within the VLAN but still allow each host to connect with the larger network or the Internet. For example, you might host an email server or a database server within an isolated VLAN.
  - **Community VLAN**—Hosts within the same community VLAN can communicate with each other but not with hosts in other secondary VLANs. Hosts in a community VLAN might or might not be allowed to communicate on a trunk line with the larger network and on to the Internet. You might use a community VLAN to group workstations within a department or host devices serving a specific customer (such as a tenant in a small office building).

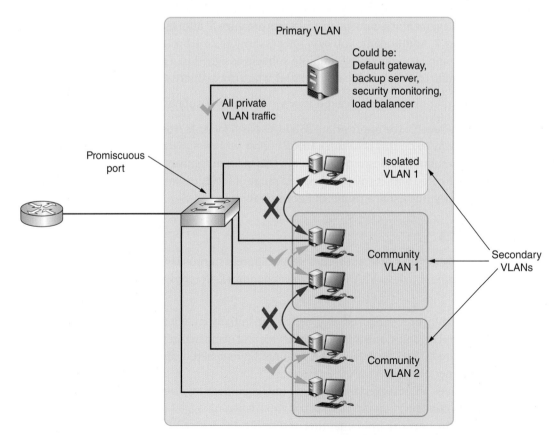

Figure 8-29 A private VLAN restricts communication between members of the VLAN

In addition to defining the types of traffic handled by a VLAN, you can also specify security parameters, filtering instructions (for example, if the switch should not forward any frames from a certain VLAN), performance requirements for certain ports, and network addressing and management options. Options vary according to the switch manufacturer and model. In a Capstone Project at the end of this module, you will have the opportunity to create and configure VLANs on a switch in your Packet Tracer network.

View Configured VLANs

Once you create a VLAN, you also maintain it via the switch's software. Figure 8-30 illustrates the output of a show vlan command on a Cisco switch on a large, enterprise network. The show vlan command is used to list the current VLANs recognized by a switch. The OSs on other manufacturers' switches include similar maintenance commands.

```
VLAN   Name                            Status     Ports
----   --------------------------      ---------  -------------------------------
1      default                         active     Te1/1, Te1/2, Gi1/5, Gi1/6
                                                  Te2/1, Te2/2, Gi2/5, Gi2/6
                                                  Gi4/3, Gi5/12, Gi6/12, Gi6/19
                                                  Gi8/11, Gi8/19, Gi9/4
5      VLAN0005                        active
13     VLAN0013                        active     Gi3/2, Gi3/3, Gi3/4, Gi8/12
14     VLAN0014                        active     Gi4/1, Gi4/2, Gi4/4, Gi9/12
16     VLAN0016                        active     Gi5/8
18     VLAN0018                        active     Gi1/3, Gi2/3
19     VLAN0019                        active     Gi5/11, Gi6/11
104    VLAN0104                        active     Gi1/4, Gi2/4, Gi3/5, Gi3/6
                                                  Gi4/5, Gi4/6, Gi5/1, Gi5/2
                                                  Gi5/3, Gi5/4, Gi5/5, Gi5/6
                                                  Gi5/7, Gi5/9, Gi5/10, Gi5/13
                                                  Gi5/14, Gi5/15, Gi5/16, Gi5/17
                                                  Gi5/18, Gi5/19, Gi5/20, Gi5/21
                                                  Gi5/22, Gi5/23, Gi5/24, Gi6/1
                                                  Gi6/2, Gi6/3, Gi6/4, Gi6/5
                                                  Gi6/6, Gi6/7, Gi6/9, Gi6/10
                                                  Gi6/13, Gi6/14, Gi6/15, Gi6/16
                                                  Gi6/17, Gi6/18, Gi6/20, Gi6/21
                                                  Gi6/22, Gi6/23, Gi6/24, Gi7/6
                                                  Gi7/8, Gi7/11, Gi7/12, Gi7/19
                                                  Gi8/8, Gi8/24, Gi9/1, Gi9/2
                                                  Gi9/3, Gi9/13
105    VLAN0105                        active     Gi7/24, Gi9/5, Gi9/6, Gi9/7
                                                  Gi9/8, Gi9/10, Gi9/11, Gi9/14
                                                  Gi9/16, Gi9/18, Gi9/19, Gi9/20
                                                  Gi9/21, Gi9/22, Gi9/23, Gi9/24
                                                  Gi10/1, Gi10/2, Gi10/4, Gi10/5
                                                  Gi10/6, Gi10/8, Gi10/9, Gi10/10
                                                  Gi10/11, Gi10/12, Gi10/13
                                                  Gi10/14, Gi10/15, Gi10/16
                                                  Gi10/17, Gi10/18, Gi10/19
                                                  Gi10/20, Gi10/21, Gi10/22
                                                  Gi10/23, Gi10/24
106    VLAN0106                        active     Gi6/8
107    VLAN0107                        active     Gi7/1, Gi7/2, Gi7/3, Gi7/4
                                                  Gi7/5, Gi7/7, Gi7/9, Gi7/10
                                                  Gi7/13, Gi7/14, Gi7/16, Gi7/17
                                                  Gi7/18, Gi7/21, Gi7/22, Gi8/1
                                                  Gi8/2, Gi8/3, Gi8/4, Gi8/5
                                                  Gi8/6, Gi8/7, Gi8/9, Gi8/10
                                                  Gi8/13, Gi8/14, Gi8/16, Gi8/17
                                                  Gi8/18, Gi8/21, Gi8/22
108    VLAN0108                        active     Gi7/15, Gi7/20, Gi7/23, Gi8/15
                                                  Gi8/20, Gi8/23
109    VLAN0109                        active
601    VLAN0601                        active
1002   fddi-default                    act/unsup
1003   token-ring-default              act/unsup
1004   fddinet-default                 act/unsup
1005   trnet-default                   act/unsup

VLAN   Type   SAID       MTU    Parent  RingNo  BridgeNo  Stp   BrdgMode  Trans1  Trans2
----   -----  ---------- -----  ------  ------  --------  ----  --------  ------  ------
1      enet   100001     1500   -       -       -         -     -         0       0
5      enet   100005     1500   -       -       -         -     -         0       0
13     enet   100013     1500   -       -       -         -     -         0       0
14     enet   100014     1500   -       -       -         -     -         0       0
16     enet   100016     1500   -       -       -         -     -         0       0
18     enet   100018     1500   -       -       -         -     -         0       0
19     enet   100019     1500   -       -       -         -     -         0       0
104    enet   100104     1500   -       -       -         -     -         0       0
105    enet   100105     1500   -       -       -         -     -         0       0
106    enet   100106     1500   -       -       -         -     -         0       0
107    enet   100107     1500   -       -       -         -     -         0       0
108    enet   100108     1500   -       -       -         -     -         0       0
109    enet   100109     1500   -       -       -         -     -         0       0
601    enet   100601     1500   -       -       -         -     -         0       0
1002   fddi   101002     1500   -       -       -         -     -         0       0
1003   tr     101003     1500   -       -       -         -     -         0       0
1004   fdnet  101004     1500   -       -       -         ieee  -         0       0
1005   trnet  101005     1500   -       -       -         ibm   -         v       0
```

Figure 8-30   Output of the show vlan command on a Cisco switch

Figure 8-30 lists 18 VLANs configured on the network. The following list analyzes this output:

- The first half of the command output shows each VLAN's number, name, status, and which ports belong to it. For example, VLAN number 18, which is named "VLAN0018," is active and contains the ports "Gi1/3" and "Gi2/3." A port called "Gi1/3," in this case, refers to the third port on the first Gigabit Ethernet module of this switch.
- VLAN number 1 and VLANs 1002 through 1005 are defaults pre-established on the Cisco switch. Other than VLAN 1, these default VLANs are not currently in use.
- The second half of the command output provides additional information about each VLAN, including the type of network it operates on. In this example, all VLANs that are active and not pre-established defaults use Ethernet, which is indicated by the *enet* type.
- Each VLAN is assigned a different SAID (security association identifier), which indicates to other connectivity devices which VLAN a transmission belongs to. By default, Cisco switches assign a VLAN the SAID of 100,000 plus the VLAN number.
- In this example, each VLAN is configured to transmit and receive frames with an MTU (maximum transmission unit) of 1500 bytes, which is the default selection. Rarely do network administrators change this variable.

Dynamic VLAN Assignment

You've read how devices can be assigned to a VLAN based on the switch port the device is connected to. This is called a static VLAN assignment. A device might instead receive a dynamic VLAN assignment according to other criteria, such as the following:

- Client device information, such as MAC address or location, can be used to group devices by VLAN when they first join the network.
- Authentication processes in cooperation with a RADIUS server can be used to further distinguish which traffic should be assigned to which VLANs, such as when an IT employee signs in on a workstation compared to when a sales employee signs in on the same device. You'll learn more about RADIUS when studying authentication and security through network design.
- Devices that have not yet authenticated to the network or whose authentication failed can be placed in a quarantine VLAN for basic Internet access and for communications required to attempt authentication.
- All WLAN traffic might be grouped within the same VLAN. Alternatively, authentication methods might be used to further segment wireless traffic, or VLAN traffic can be tagged according to the SSID the device is connected to.

Troubleshoot and Secure VLANs

Configuration errors are a common cause of VLAN problems. The show vlan command discussed earlier yields information that can help you identify misconfigurations. Start by checking the configuration against your documentation and then check physical connections. If that doesn't work, consider these common configuration errors:

- **Incorrect VLAN assignment**—This can happen due to a variety of situations, including plugging a device into the wrong switch port or misconfigurations of the client authentication process in which a VLAN is assigned to a device before the authentication process is complete. If devices are not able to communicate with network services as expected, checking VLAN assignment and other configuration options should be an early step in the troubleshooting process.
- **Incorrect port mode**—Switch ports connected to endpoints, such as workstations and servers, should nearly always use access mode. Switch ports connected to other network devices should be configured in trunk mode only if that connection must support multiple VLANs.
- **VLAN isolation**—By grouping certain nodes into a VLAN, you are not merely including those nodes—you are also excluding other groups of nodes. This means you can potentially cut off an entire group of nodes from the rest of the network. VLANs must be connected to and configured on a router or layer 3 switch to allow different VLANs to exchange data outside their own broadcast domain.

Hackers sometimes take advantage of the way VLANs are tagged to implement an attack called **VLAN hopping**. The attacker generates transmissions that appear, to the switch, to belong to a protected VLAN, then crosses VLANs to access sensitive data or inject harmful software. There are two approaches to VLAN hopping:

- **Double tagging**—The hacker stacks VLAN tags in Ethernet frames. When the first, legitimate tag is removed by a switch, the second, illegitimate tag is revealed, tricking a switch into forwarding the transmission on to a restricted VLAN.
- **Switch spoofing**—An attacker connects to a switch and then makes the connection look to the switch as if it's a trunk line. The switch might auto-configure its port into trunk mode when it detects trunk mode on the other end of the connection. A hacker can then feed their own VLAN traffic into that port and access VLANs throughout the network.

The following mitigation efforts will reduce the risk of VLAN hopping and further help enforce network segmentation:

- Don't use the default VLAN.
- Change the native VLAN to an unused VLAN ID.
- Disable auto-trunking on switches that don't need to support traffic from multiple VLANs.
- On switches that do carry traffic from multiple VLANs, configure all ports as access ports unless they're used as trunk ports.
- Specify which VLANs are supported on each trunk instead of accepting a range of all VLANs.
- Use physical security methods such as door locks to restrict access to network equipment.

REMEMBER THIS...

- Explain how port tagging supports VLANs.
- Configure subinterfaces on a router.
- Compare common types of VLANs, including default VLAN, data VLAN, voice VLAN, and private VLAN.
- Describe options for dynamic VLAN assignments.
- List common VLAN problems, including incorrect VLAN, incorrect port mode, and VLAN isolation.
- Explain the threat posed by VLAN hopping.

SELF-CHECK

8. At what OSI layer do VLANs function?
- **a.** Network layer
- **b.** Transport layer
- **c.** Physical layer
- **d.** Data link layer

9. Suppose you have a small network with one router, one switch, and a few computers that are grouped into three VLANs. Which of the following statements is *false*?
- **a.** Traffic between computers on the same VLAN must go through the router.
- **b.** Traffic from any computer to another network must go through the router.
- **c.** Traffic between computers on different VLANs must go through the router.

10. Which VLAN on a switch cannot be renamed or deleted?
- **a.** Native VLAN
- **b.** Management VLAN
- **c.** Default VLAN
- **d.** Data VLAN

Check your answers at the end of this module.

You're Ready

You're now ready to complete **Project 8-4: Configure VLANs Using a Switch's GUI**, or you can wait until you've finished the Review Questions for this module.

You're Ready

After you finish the Hands-On Projects, you're ready to complete the **Module 8 Capstone Projects**.

MODULE SUMMARY

Network Segmentation

- A network administrator might separate a network's traffic into smaller portions to enhance security, improve network performance, and simplify troubleshooting.
- Networks are commonly segmented according to geographic locations, departmental boundaries, or device types.
- You can use physical devices such as routers to create separate LANs. At layer 2, you can create virtual LANs. At layer 3, you can use subnetting to organize devices within the available IP address space, whether the LANs are defined physically or virtually.

Subnet Masks

- Connecting each switch to a different router interface will segment network traffic. A router doesn't forward broadcast traffic between its interfaces, and so this configuration will break up the one, large broadcast domain into three smaller broadcast domains. You can think of a router as a broadcast boundary, and fundamentally, routers are tools you can use to divide and conquer network traffic.
- Managing the IP address space at the logical layer helps clients know which devices are on their own subnet and which devices are on other networks. Subnetting helps solve the fundamental problem with classful addressing: too many node addresses assigned to each classful network. Well-chosen subnets make network documentation easier to manage, helps to locate and resolve network problems, and makes routing more efficient.
- A device uses a subnet mask to determine which subnet or network it belongs to. When a computer is ready to send a transmission to another device, it first compares the bits in its own network ID to the bits in the network ID of the destination device. If the bits match, the other device is on the sending computer's own network, and it sends the transmission directly to that device. If the bits don't match, the destination is on another network, and the computer sends the transmission to the default gateway on its network.
- In classful addressing, each network class is associated with a default subnet mask. In contrast, classless addressing allows the network to "borrow" host bits to identify subnets within the network.

Calculating Subnets

- Subnetting, or classless addressing, alters the rules of classful IPv4 addressing. To subnet a network, you borrow bits that *would* represent host information in classful addressing and use those bits instead to represent network information. By doing so, you increase the number of bits available for the network ID, and you also reduce the number of bits available for identifying hosts. Consequently, you increase the number of networks and reduce the number of usable host addresses in each network or subnet. The more bits you borrow for network information, the more subnets you can have, but the fewer hosts each subnet will contain.
- To calculate subnets on a network, you first determine how many host bits to borrow, then calculate the subnet mask, determine the network ID for each subnet, and identify the range of IP addresses for hosts on each subnet.
- Common formulas used in calculating subnet information include $2^n = Y$, 256 – the interesting octet, and $2^h - 2 = Z$. You can also use subnet mask tables to look up common calculations.
- There are two common types of subnetting questions on certification exams:
  - Given certain network requirements (such as required number of hosts or required number of subnets), calculate possible subnets and host IP address ranges.
  - Given an IP address, determine its subnet's network ID, broadcast address, and first/last host addresses.
- The administrator must program each interface on the router with its IP address and subnet mask for its subnet. Though tedious on larger networks, static IP addressing can also be used on network hosts. For dynamic IP addressing, the administrator programs each subnet's DHCP server with the network ID, subnet mask, range of IP addresses, and default gateway for the subnet.
- Allowing some types of broadcast traffic, such as DHCP messages, to travel beyond each broadcast domain lets hosts in various subnets access centralized network services. DHCP and other centralized network services use UDP traffic, including TFTP, NTP, and DNS. Configuring UDP forwarding on the network allows routers, firewalls, or layer 3 switches to forward this UDP traffic across broadcast domains, which enables centralization of key network services.
- Traditional subnetting results in multiple subnets that are all the same size, and this uniformity in subnet size can be inefficient in complex networks. VLSM (Variable Length Subnet Mask) allows subnets to be further subdivided into smaller and smaller groupings until each subnet is about the same size as the necessary IP address space.
- IPv6 addressing uses no classes and does not use subnet masks. A single IPv6 subnet can supply 18,446,744,073,709,551,616 IPv6 addresses. The fourth hexadecimal block in the site prefix can be altered to create subnets within a site.

Virtual LANs (VLANs)

- A VLAN (virtual local area network or virtual LAN) groups ports on one or more switches so that some of the local traffic on the switch is forced to go through a router, thereby limiting the traffic to a smaller broadcast domain. As virtual LANs, VLANs abstract the broadcast domain from the networking hardware. When using VLANs, the boundaries of the broadcast domain can be virtually defined anywhere within a single physical LAN.
- VLANs can only be implemented through managed switches, whose ports can be partitioned into groups. When ports on a managed switch are partitioned into VLANs, traffic *within* each VLAN still goes through the switch as normal to reach other devices on the *same* VLAN. Traffic to hosts on other networks still goes through the router. However, traffic between hosts on VLAN 1 and VLAN 2 must now *also* go through the router, which is called inter-VLAN routing.
- Two types of VLAN ports include access ports, which connect the switch to hosts and typically carries traffic for only one VLAN, and trunk ports, which connect a switch to another networking device such as a router or another switch and manages traffic from multiple VLANs.
- In most situations, each VLAN is assigned its own subnet of IP addresses. This means that a particular subnet, working at layer 3, includes the same group of hosts as a specific VLAN, working at layer 2.

- Common VLAN types include default VLANs, a native VLAN, data VLANs, the management VLAN, a voice VLAN, and a private VLAN, which contains secondary VLANs.
- On Cisco devices, use the `show vlan` command to view a list of the current VLANs configured on a switch. The OSs on other manufacturers' switches include similar maintenance commands.
- Devices can be assigned to a VLAN based on the switch port the device is connected to. This is called a static VLAN assignment. A device might instead receive a dynamic VLAN assignment according to other criteria, including client device information, results of authentication processes, the lack of completed authentication, or WLAN association.
- Common VLAN problems include incorrect VLAN assignment, incorrect port mode, or unintended isolation of devices on a VLAN. VLAN hopping is an attack type specific to the VLAN configurations.

Key Terms

For definitions of key terms, see the Glossary.

802.1Q	magic number	trunk port
access port	private VLAN	trunking
ANDing	promiscuous port	UDP forwarding
data VLAN	relay agent	VLAN (virtual local area network
default VLAN	screened subnet	or virtual LAN)
dynamic VLAN	site prefix	VLAN hopping
assignment	static VLAN assignment	VLSM (Variable Length Subnet
global routing prefix	subinterface	Mask)
IP helper address	tag	voice VLAN

Review Questions

1. How many bits of a class A IP address are used for host information?
   a. 8 bits
   b. 16 bits
   c. 24 bits
   d. 32 bits

2. What is the formula for determining the number of possible hosts on a network?
   a. $2^n = Y$
   b. $2^n - 2 = Y$
   c. $2^h = Z$
   d. $2^h - 2 = Z$

3. Which of the following is *not* a good reason to segment a network?
   a. To limit access to broadcast domains
   b. To reduce the demand on bandwidth
   c. To increase the number of networking devices on a network
   d. To narrow down the location of problems on a network

4. What is the greatest number of bits you could borrow from the host portion of a class B subnet mask and still have at least 130 hosts per subnet?
   a. 0 bits
   b. 8 bits
   c. 9 bits
   d. 10 bits

5. What do well-chosen subnets accomplish?
   a. IP address spaces overlap for easier management.
   b. Network documentation is easier to manage.
   c. Routing efficiency is decreased by ensuring IP address spaces are not mathematically related.
   d. Problems affect the entire network, making them more difficult to pin down.

6. Which formulas can be used to calculate the magic number? Choose two.
   a. 256 – the interesting octet
   b. $2^h - 2$
   c. 2^n
   d. 2^h

7. Which hexadecimal block in an IPv6 address is used for the Subnet ID?
   a. The first one
   b. The third one
   c. The fourth one
   d. The eighth one

8. Which assignment technique requires a RADIUS server?
   a. Dynamic VLAN assignment
   b. Dynamic IP address assignment
   c. Static IP address assignment
   d. Static VLAN assignment

9. Which port mode on a switch enables that port to manage traffic for multiple VLANs?
   a. Private
   b. Community
   c. Access
   d. Trunk

10. Which IEEE standard determines how VLANs work on a network?
    a. 802.1X
    b. 802.11
    c. 802.3af
    d. 802.1Q

11. What is the network ID with CIDR notation for the IP address 172.16.32.108 whose subnet mask is 255.255.255.0?

12. Suppose your company has leased one class C license, 120.10.10.0, and wants to sublease the first half of these IP addresses to another company. What is the CIDR notation for the subnet to be subleased? What is the subnet mask for this network?

13. Subnetting operates at the _____ layer while VLANs function at the _____ layer.

14. Which VLAN on a switch manages untagged frames?

15. An attacker configures a VLAN frame with two tags instead of just one. The first tag directs the frame to the authorized VLAN. After the frame enters the first VLAN, the switch appropriately removes the tag, then discovers the next tag, and sends the frame along to a protected VLAN, which the attacker is not authorized to access. What kind of attack is this?

16. What area of a network can provide less stringent security so a web server is more accessible from the open Internet?

17. On which networking device do you configure VLANs?

18. Which IP addressing technique subnets a subnet to create subnets of various sizes?

19. Which VLAN type would be the best fit for a company's web servers that need to be accessible from the Internet but should not be able to communicate with each other?

20. Which Cisco command lists configured VLANs on a switch?

Hands-On Projects

NOTE 8-6

Websites and applications change often. While the instructions given in these projects were accurate at the time of writing, you might need to adjust the steps or options according to later changes.

Note to Instructors and Students: A rubric is provided for evaluating student performance on these projects. Please see Appendix D.

Project 8-1: Test Subnet Boundaries in Packet Tracer

Estimated Time: 45 minutes
Objective: Given a scenario, configure a subnet and use appropriate IP addressing schemes. (Obj. 1.4)
Resources:
- Packet Tracer

Context: This Packet Tracer project starts with a new network and is *not* intended to build on your Packet Tracer network for the Capstone Projects. In this project, you will experiment with various devices and configurations to explore the boundaries of subnets and broadcast domains. For this project, do *not* use your existing Packet Tracer network (most recently worked on in Module 7)—you'll come back to that network file in this module's Capstone Projects. In this project, start with a new Packet Tracer file to experiment with router and switch behaviors. You will *not* need to save this network for future projects or modules. Complete the following steps:

1. Open Packet Tracer—make sure you're starting from a new file, not an existing network.
2. Add a **PT-Router**, a **PT-Switch**, and two **PC**s. Configure these devices with the following information:
   a. Router0's FastEthernet0/0 interface:
      - IP Address: **192.168.2.1**
      - Subnet Mask: **255.255.255.0**
      - Port Status: **On**
   b. PC0's FastEthernet0 interface:
      - IP Address: **192.168.2.100**
      - Subnet Mask: **255.255.255.0**
      - Default Gateway: **192.168.2.1**
   c. PC1's FastEthernet0 interface:
      - IP Address: **192.168.3.100**
      - Subnet Mask: **255.255.255.0**
      - Default Gateway: **192.168.2.1**
3. Use **Copper Straight-Through** cables to connect the PCs to the switch and the switch to the router using the interfaces configured above (see Figure 8-31). Wait for all connections to show green triangles on both ends.

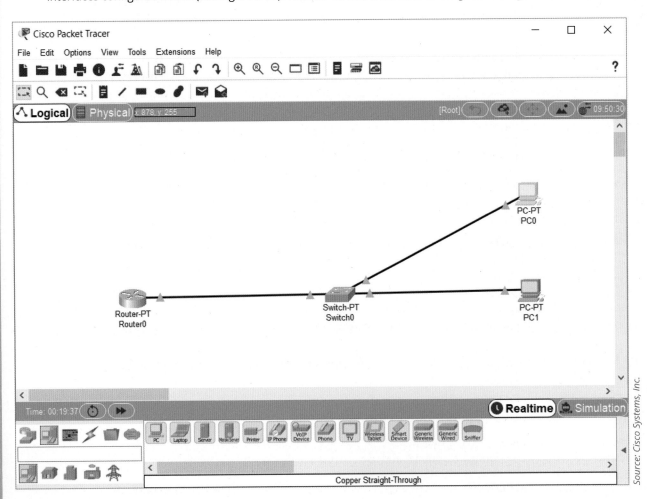

Figure 8-31 One router, one switch, and two PCs

4. Ping the following connections to determine whether they work:
   a. From PC0, ping the router. What command did you use? Did it work? Why or why not?
   b. From PC0, ping PC1. What command did you use? Did it work? Why or why not?
   c. From Router0, ping PC0. What command did you use? Did it work? Why or why not?
   d. From Router0, ping PC1. What command did you use? Did it work? Why or why not?

As you can see, only devices within the router's own subnet can communicate with the router. However, can devices on a different subnet from the router but connected to the same switch communicate with *each other*? To find out, complete the following steps:

5. Add a new **PC** to the workspace and configure it with the following information:
   a. PC2's FastEthernet0 interface:
      - IP Address: **192.168.3.150**
      - Subnet Mask: **255.255.255.0**
      - Default Gateway: **192.168.2.1**
6. Use a **Copper Straight-Through** cable to connect PC2 to the switch. Wait for the connection to show green triangles on both ends.
7. Ping the following connections to determine whether they work:
   a. From PC2, ping PC0. What command did you use? Did it work? Why or why not?
   b. From PC2, ping PC1. What command did you use? Did it work? Why or why not?
   c. From PC2, ping the router. What command did you use? Did it work? Why or why not?

Based on these results, you can see that a switch might successfully send messages between devices within various subnets if those messages can rely on broadcasts (such as ping). However, all devices on a router's interface must be configured to use the same subnet as the router in order to reach that router and send messages outside the LAN. What happens when you daisy-chain multiple switches on a single router interface? To find out, complete the following steps:

8. Delete the connection between PC2 and Switch0 (but do not delete the PC or the switch).
9. Add a new **PT-Switch** to the workspace. Use a **Copper Cross-Over** cable to connect the two switches. Use a **Copper Straight-Through** cable to connect PC2 to Switch1. Wait for the connections to show green triangles on both ends.
10. Ping the following connections to determine whether they work:
    a. From PC0, ping PC2. What command did you use? Did it work? Why or why not?
    b. From PC1, ping PC2. What command did you use? Did it work? Why or why not?

Even with multiple switches, the same limitations apply: Only devices within the same subnet can communicate with each other. What happens if you move one switch to a different router interface? Will devices on the same subnet across both switches continue to be able to communicate with each other? To find out, complete the following steps:

11. Delete the connection between the two switches. Configure the router with the following information:
    a. Router0's FastEthernet1/0 interface:
       - IP Address: **192.168.3.1**
       - Subnet Mask: **255.255.255.0**
       - Port Status: **On**
12. Use a **Copper Straight-Through** cable to connect Switch1 to the router's FastEthernet1/0 interface. Wait for the connections to show green triangles on both ends.
13. On the router's CLI tab, enter the **exit** command twice and then enter the command **show ip route**. Which two networks is the router aware of?
14. Ping the following connections to determine whether they work:
    a. From PC2, ping the router's FastEthernet1/0 interface. What command did you use? Did it work? Why or why not?
    b. From PC2, ping PC0. What command did you use? Did it work? Why or why not?
    c. From PC2, ping PC1. What command did you use? Did it work? Why or why not?

Remember that the router can only "see" one subnet per router interface. PC1 is hidden in an unreachable subnet on the other side of Router0's FastEthernet0/0 interface. Successful communication between devices on the rogue subnet on Switch0 relies on broadcast message rules. To see the broadcast process in action, complete the following steps:

15. Add a new **PC** to the workspace and configure it with the following information:
    a. PC3's FastEthernet0 interface:
       - IP Address: **192.168.3.200**
       - Subnet Mask: **255.255.255.0**
       - Default Gateway: **192.168.2.1**
16. Use a **Copper Straight-Through** cable to connect PC3 to Switch0 (see Figure 8-32). Wait for the connection to show green triangles on both ends before continuing with the next step.

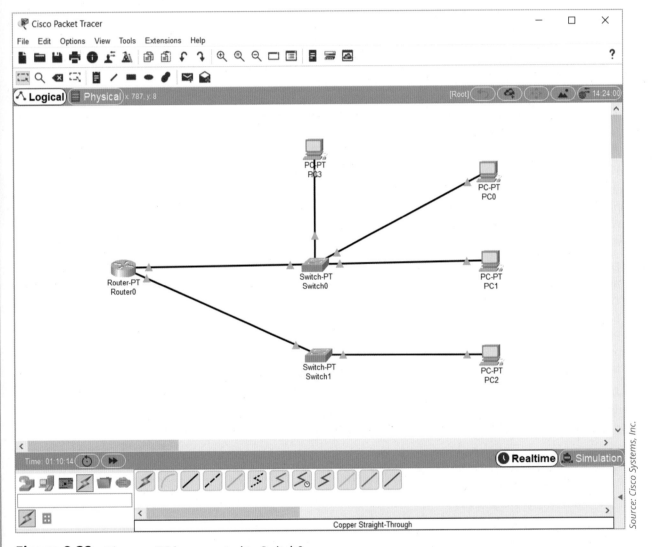

Figure 8-32   The new PC is connected to Switch0

17. In the lower right corner, click **Simulation**.
18. From PC1, ping PC3. In the Simulation Panel, click the **Play (Alt + P)** button. After the first message passes through the switch, click the **Play (Alt + P)** button again to pause the simulation. What did the switch do with the ping request? Continue the ping simulation to see that PC3 is able to respond to the ping because subnets alone do not limit broadcast domains.

As you can see, a switch broadcasts messages such as a ping request to all its interfaces for any MAC address it doesn't know. That's why the ping can work between subnets on a switch. Notice that subnetting (division of IP address ranges) does *not* limit the broadcast domain—the message is broadcast to all the switch's interfaces, not just the interfaces connected to devices on a single subnet. However, routers *don't* forward broadcast messages, so the router serves as a boundary for the broadcast domain.

19. **Take a screenshot** of your Packet Tracer network; submit this visual with your answers to this project's questions. You can save your project for future reference and experimentation; however, you will not need this network file for future projects in this course.

20. Make some notes on your Wikidot website about your activities in Packet Tracer for this project.

Note to instructors: A Packet Tracer solution file is provided for each Packet Tracer project through the Instructors site.

Project 8-2: Calculate Subnets

Estimated Time: 30 minutes (+30 minutes for group work, if assigned)
Objective: Given a scenario, configure a subnet and use appropriate IP addressing schemes. (Obj. 1.4)
Group Work: This project includes enhancements when assigned as a group project.
Resources:

- Access to word processing or spreadsheet software, such as Docs, Word, or Excel
- Internet access if group work is assigned

Context: In this module, you saw how to calculate subnets for both class B and class C networks. In this project, you work with a class B private network. Complete the steps as follows:

1. Your employer is opening a new location, and the IT director has assigned you the task of calculating subnets for the new network. You've determined that you need 50 subnets for the class B network beginning with the network ID 172.20.0.0. How many host bits will you need to use for network information in the new subnets?

2. After the subnetting is complete, how many unused subnets will be waiting on hold for future expansion? How many possible hosts can each subnet support?

3. What is the new subnet mask?

4. Recreate Table 8-9 in a spreadsheet or document, and then fill in the blanks. (*Hint:* Look for patterns in the numbers to help you complete the missing pieces.) When you're finished, **take a screenshot of your completed table**; submit this visual with your answers to this project's questions.

Table 8-9 Calculate subnets

Subnet	Network ID	Range of host addresses	Broadcast address
1	172.20.0.0	172.20.0.1 through 172.20.3.254	
2	172.20.4.0	_____ through 172.20.7.254	
3		172.20.8.1 through _____	172.20.11.255
4			
5			
...	...	...	...
50			

5. What is the CIDR block for this network?

6. What is the broadcast address of the subnet for the host at 172.20.6.139?

7. Is the host at 172.20.11.250 on the same subnet as the host at 172.20.12.3? How do you know?

8. **For group assignments:** Create your own subnetting scenario starting with a class C network. For example, choose a required number of subnets (between 2 and 64) or a required number of hosts (between 2 and 126) per subnet, and select a starting IP address (where the last octet is 0). Trade your scenario with a group

member and work through the calculations required by your teammate's scenario to determine the following information:

- Number of network bits and number of host bits
- Subnet mask
- Number of available subnets
- Number of available host addresses per subnet

Give your calculations back to your teammate. Check your teammate's calculations on a website such as **cidr.xyz** or **subnettingquestions.com**. How well did your teammate do with your subnetting scenario? How well did you do with your teammate's scenario? What resource was most helpful to you in solving the subnetting problem you were given by your teammate?

Project 8-3: Shortcuts to Subnet Calculations

Estimated Time: 30 minutes (+20 minutes for group work, if assigned)
Objective: Given a scenario, configure a subnet and use appropriate IP addressing schemes. (Obj. 1.4)
Group Work: This project includes enhancements when assigned as a group project.
Resources:
- Access to word processing or spreadsheet software, such as Docs, Word, or Excel
- Internet access

Context: There are many handy shortcuts you can find online for calculating subnets quickly and easily. On the job, it would probably be best to use a subnet calculator, such as the one at *subnet-calculator.com*, to better ensure you don't make any time-consuming mistakes in your calculations. However, on CompTIA's Network+ certification exam, subnetting shortcuts can help you get to an answer without wasting much of your limited time.

NOTE 8-7

At the time of this writing, you are allowed to use a dry-erase board for calculations during the exam if you take the test at a testing center. However, if you take the exam remotely from home, you are not allowed to use any writing instruments at all.

To use this shortcut method, you'll first draw a series of numbers. This might look confusing at first, but hang in there. It should make sense by the end. Complete the following steps:

1. Write one row of eight numbers from right to left, starting with 1 on the right, then 2, then 4, and so on, doubling each number as you move left. See the top row in Figure 8-33.

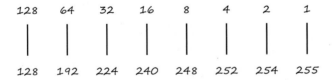

Figure 8-33   Write these numbers and connect the two numbers in each column

2. Below this first row, write another row of eight numbers from right to left, this time starting with 255 on the right. Subtract the number directly above 255 to get the next number, 254. Subtract the number directly above 254 to get 252, and so on. You know you've done it correctly if the left-most number in both rows is 128. (After you've done this a few times, you'll likely have these numbers memorized.) When you're finished, draw a line connecting the corresponding numbers in each row, as shown in Figure 8-33.
3. Above the top row, write another row of eight numbers, but this time work left to right. Start with 2 on the left and double each number as you move to the right. See the top row in Figure 8-34.

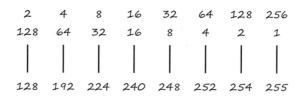

Figure 8-34   If you have trouble memorizing these numbers, just memorize the pattern of how to get them and where to write them

You're now ready to use your shortcut to calculate subnets. Let's start with the class C network at 192.168.15.0 and create as many subnets as possible with at least 10 hosts each, as follows:

4. On the second row (the row immediately above the vertical lines), find the smallest number that covers the needed hosts and circle it, as shown in Figure 8-35. This is your magic number. In Figure 8-35, the magic number is 16, which is the smallest number that will provide at least 10 hosts as required by the scenario.

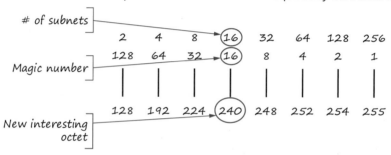

Figure 8-35   Circle the magic number, the number of subnets, and the new subnet octet

5. Circle the number directly above the magic number, as shown in Figure 8-35. This tells you how many subnets you'll be creating.

6. Circle the number directly below the magic number, as shown in Figure 8-35. This is the new interesting octet in the subnet mask. What is the subnet mask for the subnets in this scenario?

7. Recreate Table 8-10 in a spreadsheet or document. To calculate the subnets' network IDs, start with the original network IP address 192.168.15.0 for the first subnet, as shown in Table 8-10. In the fourth octet, skip-count by the magic number as high as you can go without going over 255. Add this information to Table 8-10 in the Network ID column. The second subnet is done for you.

Table 8-10   Subnetting practice

Network ID	Host IP range	Broadcast address
192.168.15.0	192.168.15.1 – 192.168.15.14	192.168.15.15
192.168.15.16	192.168.15.17 – 192.168.15.30	192.168.15.31

8. Fill in the rest of Table 8-10. Recall that you can subtract 1 from a network ID to get the previous subnet's broadcast address. The host IP address range consists of all numbers between the network ID and the broadcast address. When you're finished, **take a screenshot of your completed table**; submit this visual with your answers to this project's questions.

With one minor modification, you can also use this shortcut diagram to help you solve the other type of subnetting problem you learned about in this module: finding network information when given a single host's IP address and subnet mask. Note that this system only works as described here for IP addresses using more than 24 bits in the network ID portion.

Let's practice one. Suppose you're told that 192.168.89.130/27 is a host's CIDR notation. How do you find the host's network ID, broadcast address, and the range of host addresses in the same subnet? Complete the following steps:

9. Write the number 24 to the left of the second row, as shown in Figure 8-36.

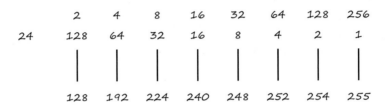

Figure 8-36 Write the number 24 to the left of the second row

10. The CIDR block in this scenario is /27. Point at the number 24 you just wrote and say "24." Count up by 1 with each jump that you make from left to right along the second row. Stop when you reach the CIDR number for this host. Follow along in Figure 8-37 for this example: Point to the number 24 and say "24." Say "25" when you jump to 128 in the second row. Say "26" when you jump to 64 in the second row. Say "27" when you jump to 32 in the second row. Because 27 is the CIDR number for the host address, this is where you stop. Circle the number you stopped on, which in this case is 32. This is the magic number.

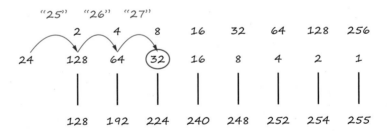

Figure 8-37 Count up by 1 with each jump along the second row

If more than eight bits were used for the host portion, this method would not work. However, because less than eight bits are used for the host portion, you can assume that the starting network ID for these subnets is the first three octets of the host's IP address (192.168.89) with 0 in the final octet. This means you can now fill in enough information about this host's subnet and the surrounding subnets to find the information you need.

11. Recreate Table 8-11 in a spreadsheet or document. Complete only the needed portions of the table. To simplify things, the table only includes enough subnets to allow you to work one subnet beyond the host's subnet so you can find the host's broadcast address. When you're finished, **take a screenshot of your completed table**; submit this visual with your answers to this project's questions.

Table 8-11   More subnetting practice

Network ID	Host IP range	Broadcast address
192.168.89.0	xxxxxxx	xxxxxxx
	xxxxxxx	xxxxxxx
	xxxxxxx	xxxxxxx
	xxxxxxx	xxxxxxx
	xxxxxxx	xxxxxxx

How well did these shortcuts help you? If it clicked for you, great! Keep practicing with these methods and you might even learn it well enough to do most of it in your head. If it didn't work for you, do a Google search for *subnetting shortcuts* and find a method that does work for you.

Several good websites and apps can give you a variety of practice subnet questions so you can become especially comfortable with calculating subnets. Do a Google search for *subnetting practice*, or try an app on your phone, such as Subnetting Practice (with the /24 icon), available on both Android and iPhone. A good subnetting practice app like Subnetting Practice (with the /24 icon) will give you options on the types of problems to work with (see Figure 8-38a), will tell you the correct answer (see Figure 8-38b), and will explain why that answer is correct.

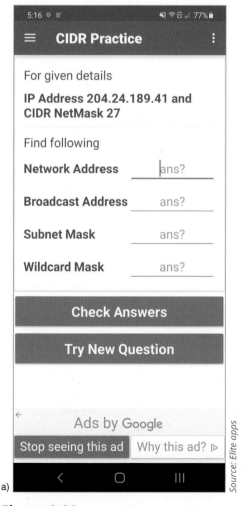

a)

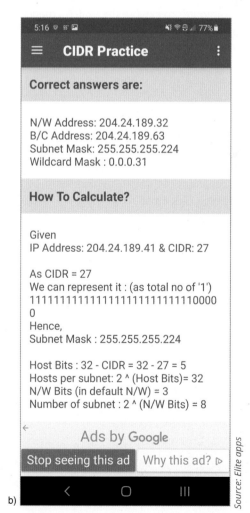

b)

Figure 8-38   Practice subnetting problems on your smartphone

12. **For group assignments:** Share with your group the subnetting shortcut method that makes the most sense to you. As you listen to your other group members explaining their shortcut methods, take notes of any formulas, shorthand calculations, or memorized facts required for each of their methods. Give a short description of each method according to what information must be memorized, what formulas are used, and any other significant details required to make that method work in a testing environment where no calculators are allowed.

Project 8-4: Configure VLANs Using a Switch's GUI

Estimated Time: 15 minutes
Objective: Given a scenario, configure and deploy common Ethernet switching features. (Obj. 2.3)
Resources:
  • Internet access
Context: As you saw in the module, some switches allow you to configure VLANs through a graphical user interface instead of through a command-line interface. In this project, you use an online switch simulator to practice configuring VLANs on a Linksys switch. Complete the following steps:

1. In your browser, go to **ui.linksys.com**. Scroll down to find the **LGS528P** switch and click on it. At the time of this writing, the web address is **ui.linksys.com/LGS528P/**. If you can't find this switch, look for another enterprise-grade switch.
2. Click the latest version available for this switch. At the time of this writing, the version is **V1.0.1.4**.
3. Click **Log In**. You do not need a username or password.
4. Take a few minutes to explore the switch's management interface, especially the **Configuration** tab. Answer the following questions:
   a. How many ports does it have?
   b. What is the switch's current IPv4 address? Why does this switch have an IP address at all?
   c. How many VLANs are currently configured on the switch? Which one is the default VLAN?
5. If you're not already there, click the **Configuration** tab and then click **VLAN Management**.
6. Click the **Edit** button. Select **VLAN 2** and name it **Accounting**. Click **Apply**, and then click **Close**. Because this is a simulator, the changes are not saved. However, what information would you expect to see in the VLAN list had your configuration change saved?
7. Click the **Add** button. Make sure **Single VLAN** is selected. Create your own VLAN with an ID number and name. **Take a screenshot** of this information; submit this visual with your answers to this project's questions. Click **Apply** and then click **Close**.
8. In the left pane under VLAN Management, click **Interfaces**. Note that all interfaces are currently configured for trunk mode. At the bottom of the list, click **Edit**. Select a port, make sure **Access** mode is selected, click **Apply**, and then click **Close**. What change would this configuration effect on the switch's port and the traffic it will carry?

Although none of the changes you make in this simulator are saved, it's still a good way to help you visualize what kinds of changes this switch can support. Other manufacturers also offer simulators for some of their devices.

Capstone Projects

Note to Instructors and Students: A rubric is provided for evaluating student performance on these projects. Please see Appendix D.

Capstone Project 8-1: Add Subnets to Your Packet Tracer Network

Estimated Time: 1 hour
Objective: Given a scenario, configure a subnet and use appropriate IP addressing schemes. (Obj. 1.4)
Resources:

- Computer with Cisco Packet Tracer installed
- Access to the Packet Tracer network created in Capstone Project 7-1
- Storage space for Packet Tracer network file to be accessed in later projects and modules

Context: In earlier Capstone Projects, you've installed Packet Tracer and experimented with MAC address tables, a TFTP server, and IoT devices. In Module 5, Capstone Project 5-2, you began building a Packet Tracer network, which you added to in Module 7, Capstone Project 7-1. In this project, you will calculate subnet information for nine subnets, which you will then configure on your network in Packet Tracer. Later in Capstone Project 8-2, you will configure VLANs on the Packet Tracer network. Begin by adding a few more devices to your network. Complete the following steps:

1. In Packet Tracer, open your Packet Tracer file from Capstone Project 7-1.
2. Add the following new devices:
   a. Three new **PT-Routers**
   b. Four new **2960 switches**
   c. Four new **PCs**

   Arrange the devices as shown in Figure 8-39. You might need to shift the original devices around so you can see the entire network. Don't worry about configuring any of the devices yet.

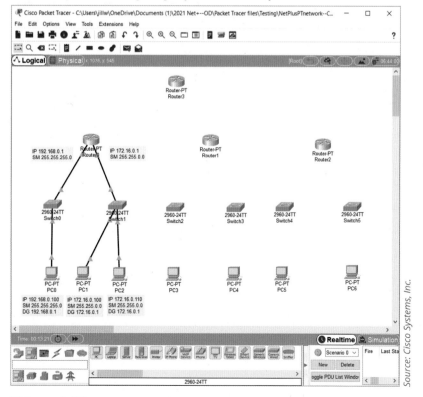

Figure 8-39 Add more devices to your Packet Tracer network

Source: Cisco Systems, Inc.

3. Connect the new devices to each other using **Copper Straight-Through** cables as described next:
   a. On each PC, connect the Ethernet cable to the **FastEthernet0** interface.
   b. On each switch, connect the Ethernet cable from the workstation to the **FastEthernet0/1** interface. Connect the Ethernet cable from the switch to its router to the switch's **FastEthernet0/2** interface.
   c. On Router1, connect Switch2 to the **FastEthernet0/0** interface and connect Switch3 to the **FastEthernet1/0** interface.
   d. On Router2, connect Switch4 to the **FastEthernet0/0** interface and connect Switch5 to the **FastEthernet1/0** interface.
   e. Wait a few minutes for the workstation-to-switch connections to turn to green triangles on both ends of each connection.
4. Use a **Fiber** cable to connect Router0 (**FastEthernet4/0**) to Router3 (**FastEthernet4/0**). Repeat with Router1 (**FastEthernet4/0**) to Router3 (**FastEthernet5/0**). Note that any connection to a router will remain red until the ports are configured. Also notice that you've now used up the existing fiber connections available on Router3, so you need to add a new interface module.
5. Click **Router3**. On the Physical tab, scroll to the right and click the power switch to turn the router off. Drag and drop a **PT-ROUTER-NM-1FFE MODULE** to an open slot in the Physical Device View, as shown in Figure 8-40. Turn the power back on. Close the Router3 window.

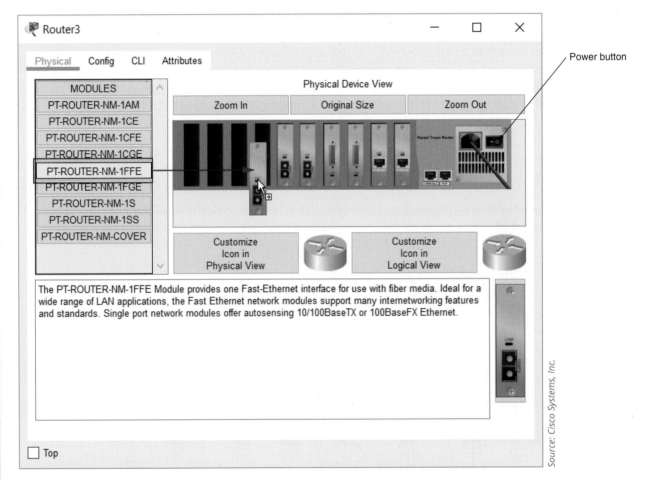

Figure 8-40 Add a new Fast-Ethernet interface for fiber media to the router

6. Use a **Fiber** cable to connect Router2 (**FastEthernet4/0**) to Router3 (**FastEthernet6/0**).

Now you're ready to calculate the subnets you'll use in your Packet Tracer network. Answer the following questions:

7. You'll need a different subnet for each connection to a router or each connection between routers. How many subnets will you need altogether?

8. Using the formula $2^n = Y$, how many bits will you need to borrow from the host portion of the IP address?
9. What will your new subnet mask be?
10. What is the magic number for these calculations?
11. How many possible hosts can each subnet have?
12. Recreate Table 8-12 in a spreadsheet or document. Fill in the Network ID column in the table with the first several subnets for this network. The first one is filled in for you. The table only covers the subnets you'll need for this project.

Table 8-12   Subnet information for Packet Tracer network

Subnet number	Network ID	Range of host addresses	Broadcast address
1	192.168.43.0		
2			
3			
4			
5			
6			
7			
8			
9			

13. Fill in the Broadcast address column in Table 8-12.
14. Fill in the Range of host addresses column in Table 8-12. When you're finished, **take a screenshot of your completed table**; submit this visual with your answers to this project's questions.

Three of these subnets only need two host addresses, because they connect only two routers. Take the first subnet here and divide it again into three additional, smaller subnets. Answer the following questions:

15. If you borrow one more bit from the host portion of the IP address in Subnet 1, how many smaller subnets will this create? Is this enough?
16. If you borrow two more bits from the host portion of the IP address in Subnet 1, how many smaller subnets will this create? Is this enough?
17. What's the new subnet mask for these smaller subnets?
18. How many hosts can each of these smaller subnets have?
19. Recreate Table 8-13 in a spreadsheet or document. Fill in the table with the smaller subnets' information. The first one is filled in for you. When you're finished, **take a screenshot of your completed table**; submit this visual with your answers to this project's questions.

Table 8-13   Smaller subnets for router-to-router connections

Subnet number	Network ID	Range of host addresses	Broadcast address
1A	192.168.43.0	192.168.43.1 – 192.168.43.2	192.168.43.3
1B			
1C			
1D			

Let's look at where each of these subnet assignments belong on your network in Packet Tracer. Complete the following steps:

20. Each of the four smaller subnets in Table 8-13 will be assigned to a connection between two routers. Each router interface will be assigned a host IP address within that smaller subnet. Notice in Table 8-14 how the IP addresses

for these smaller subnets are assigned to each router's interfaces (Fa4/0 for Routers 0, 1, and 2, and all three interfaces for Router3). Recreate Table 8-14 in a spreadsheet or document and fill in the subnet masks for the router interfaces.

Table 8-14 IP address assignments for device interfaces

Device	Interface	IP address	Subnet mask	Default gateway
Router0	Fa0/0	192.168.43.17		N/A
	Fa1/0	192.168.43.33		N/A
	Fa4/0	192.168.43.1		N/A
Router1	Fa0/0	192.168.43.49		N/A
	Fa1/0	192.168.43.65		N/A
	Fa4/0	192.168.43.5		N/A
Router2	Fa0/0	192.168.43.81		N/A
	Fa1/0	192.168.43.97		N/A
	Fa4/0	192.168.43.9		N/A
Router3	Fa4/0	192.168.43.2		N/A
	Fa5/0	192.168.43.6		N/A
	Fa6/0	192.168.43.10		N/A
PC0	Fa0	192.168.43.30	255.255.255.240	192.168.43.17
PC1	Fa0			
PC2	Fa0			
PC3	Fa0			
PC4	Fa0			
PC5	Fa0			
PC6	Fa0			

21. Subnet 2 (192.168.43.16) is assigned to PC0's subnet. Notice in Table 8-14 that PC0's default gateway (192.168.43.17) is the first usable host address in the subnet, and PC0's interface (192.168.43.30) has the last usable host address in the subnet. Also, PC0's default gateway address is the IP address of Router0's interface (Fa0/0) on that subnet.

22. Repeat this pattern and assign the following subnets to each PC, filling in the relevant information for that workstation and its router in Table 8-14. You'll update configurations for PCs 0, 1, and 2 in a later step.
    a. Subnet 3 is assigned to PC1 (192.168.43.45) and PC2 (192.168.43.46).
    b. Subnet 4 is assigned to PC3.
    c. Subnet 5 is assigned to PC4.
    d. Subnet 6 is assigned to PC5.
    e. Subnet 7 is assigned to PC6.
    When you're finished, **take a screenshot of your completed table**; submit this visual with your answers to this project's questions.
Now you're ready to configure these subnets on your network in Packet Tracer. Complete the following steps:

23. Click **Router0** and click the **Config** tab. Configure each of the three connected interfaces with the information listed for Router0 in Table 8-14. Turn on any connected ports that are not already on. Update the on-screen notes to reflect these changes and make new notes as needed.

24. Repeat Step 23 for each of the other three routers. Make sure to update your on-screen documentation for every router interface.

25. Click **PC0**, click the **Desktop** tab, and click **IP Configuration**. Configure the IP Address, Subnet Mask, and Default Gateway information listed for PC0 in Table 8-14. Update the on-screen notes to reflect these changes and make new notes as needed.

26. Repeat Step 25 for each of the other PCs.
27. If any link does not turn green triangles, troubleshoot the configuration to find the problem. Most of the time, the problem is a typo or forgetting to turn on a port.
28. After all the links turn to green triangles, test the following connections:
    a. From PC1, ping PC2. Does it work? Why or why not?
    b. From PC1, ping PC0. Does it work? Why or why not?
    c. From PC1, ping each of Router0's interfaces. Do these work? Why or why not?
    d. From PC1, ping PC6. Does it work?
    e. From Router0, ping Router3's Fa4/0 interface (192.168.43.2). Does it work?
    f. From Router0, ping Router3's Fa6/0 interface (192.168.43.10). Does it work?
    g. What theory do you have about why traffic is not crossing the routers?

NOTE 8-9

If at any point you need to check which interface a particular connection is using on a device, in the workspace, float your cursor over the connection. Packet Tracer will show the interface in use on each end.

Currently, devices within a single router's networks should be able to ping each other. For example, PC0 can ping PC2, and PC3 can ping PC4. However, the routers do not yet have any configurations to help them find each other or to help them know where various networks are located. This is a function of routing protocols, which you'll learn about in the WAN module. You'll make more changes to this network later to configure routing. For now, complete the following steps to save your Packet Tracer file:

29. Save this Packet Tracer file in a safe place for future projects.
30. Make some notes on your Wikidot website about your activities in Packet Tracer for this project. When you're finished, close **Packet Tracer** or continue to Capstone Project 8-2.

Note to instructors: A Packet Tracer solution file is provided for each Packet Tracer project through the Instructors site. Some Packet Tracer projects build on earlier Packet Tracer networks. If needed for one or more students, you can provide a previous project's solution file as a start file for one of these progression projects.

Capstone Project 8-2: Add VLANs to Your Packet Tracer Network

Estimated Time: 30 minutes
Objective: Given a scenario, configure and deploy common Ethernet switching features. (Obj. 2.3)
Resources:
- Computer with Cisco Packet Tracer installed
- Access to the Packet Tracer network created in Capstone Project 8-1
- Storage space for Packet Tracer network file to be accessed in later projects and modules

Context: This Capstone Project picks up where Capstone Project 8-1 left off. In this project, you'll create VLANs on switches in your Packet Tracer network, and you'll test the connections to see which devices can communicate with each other at each successive configuration. Feel free to experiment beyond the tests suggested here. You might even want to create copies of your Packet Tracer file along the way so you can experiment more extensively, or create your own, unique network with different configurations.

Let's begin by creating a pair of simple VLANs on Switch0. After completing Capstone Project 8-1, complete the following steps:

1. In Packet Tracer, open your Packet Tracer file from Capstone Project 8-1.
2. On the far-left side of the workspace, add three more PCs as shown in Figure 8-41. If you need to create more space on that side of the workspace, use the **Select** tool from the Common tools bar. Press and hold the mouse button and drag the mouse pointer to select all items on the screen, release the mouse button, and then press and drag on any selected object to move the entire group.

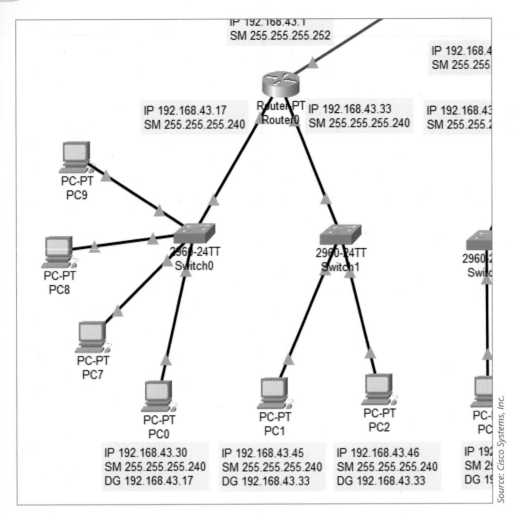

Figure 8-41   Four workstations for two VLANs on one switch

3. Connect each of these PCs to the switch using **Copper Straight-Through** cables and the following interfaces:
   - PC7 to FastEthernet0/3
   - PC8 to FastEthernet0/4
   - PC9 to FastEthernet0/5

Now you're ready to configure two VLANs on the switch. As you make configuration changes, remember to watch the commands in the Equivalent IOS Commands pane that Packet Tracer automatically generates for you. Complete the following steps:

4. Click **Switch0** and then click the **Config** tab. In the left pane, click **VLAN Database**.
5. Create two VLANs: one for Accounting and one for Sales. Recall that VLAN 1 already exists as the default VLAN, so be sure to start with VLAN 2. Enter the following information for the first new VLAN and then click **Add**:

   VLAN Number: **2**

   VLAN Name: **Accounting**

6. Enter the following information for the second new VLAN and then click **Add**:

   VLAN Number: **3**

   VLAN Name: **Sales**

7. Confirm that both new VLANs appear in the middle pane. **Take a screenshot** showing the list of VLANs, their numbers, and their names; submit this visual with your answers to this project's questions.
8. Now that you've created the two new VLANs, you need to configure ports for each VLAN. In the left pane, click **FastEthernet0/1**. What mode and VLAN is this port already configured for?

9. Make sure **Access** is selected and then change the VLAN to **2:Accounting**. What command did Packet Tracer use to configure this interface for VLAN 2?

10. Repeat this process for the other three PCs connected to Switch0. Use the following information:

    FastEthernet0/3 (connected to PC7): **Access** mode, VLAN **2**

    FastEthernet0/4 (connected to PC8): **Access** mode, VLAN **3**

    FastEthernet0/5 (connected to PC9): **Access** mode, VLAN **3**

11. To confirm your configurations are correct, click the **CLI** tab. The current prompt should be `Switch (config-if)#`. This says you're configuring a switch and you're in interface configuration mode. Enter the command **exit** to return to global configuration mode. The prompt should now be `Switch (config)#`. Enter the command **do show vlan**. The output should look like Figure 8-42. If it doesn't, troubleshoot the steps you've taken so far to see what needs to be changed. Press **Tab** to return to the prompt.

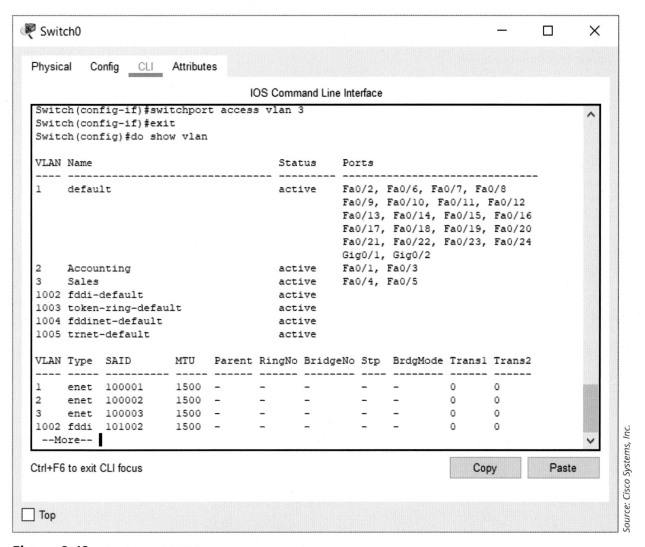

Figure 8-42 Two new VLANS have two ports each

12. Now that you've configured each of the access ports connected to the PCs, you need to configure the port connected to the router for trunk mode. Back on the **Config** tab, click **FastEthernet0/2**, which is the interface connected to the router. Change the mode to **Trunk** and wait for the connection to re-establish. Back on the **CLI** tab, enter **do show interfaces trunk** to see the new trunk port configuration on your switch.

13. Before you leave the switch to work on the PCs, you need to save the configurations you've completed so far. To do this, on the CLI tab, enter the command **exit** twice and press **Enter** again to leave global configuration mode and use privileged EXEC mode instead. Enter the command **copy run start** and then press **Enter** again. Close the Switch0 window.

VLANs are configured on a switch; however, you still need to configure IP addresses on the PCs. Complete the following steps:

14. For this step, you'll initially leave all four PCs on the same subnet even though they're on different VLANs. Use **192.168.43.17** as the default gateway for all three PCs and add the following information:

    PC7: **192.168.43.29 255.255.255.240**

    PC8: **192.168.43.20 255.255.255.240**

    PC9: **192.168.43.19 255.255.255.240**

15. First, test the communication between two PCs that are on the same VLAN and on the same subnet. From PC0, ping PC7 (192.168.43.29). Does it work? Why or why not?

16. Now ping PCs across VLANs, which in this case, are still on the same subnet. From PC0, ping PC8 (192.168.43.20). Does it work? Why or why not?

Now you need to configure the router to send traffic between VLANs. To do this, you must configure a subinterface on the router for each VLAN. Recall this means you're dividing the one physical interface into two logical interfaces. But first, you must remove the IP address configuration on the physical interface so you can use this IP address space for the subinterfaces. Complete the following steps:

17. Click **Router0** and then click the **Config** tab. In the left pane, click **FastEthernet0/0**. Delete the IP address and subnet mask information.

18. Now click the **CLI** tab. Enter the commands listed in Table 8-15 to configure a subinterface for each VLAN using two subnets of the original subnet configured for this network.

19. Now, because you've adjusted the subnetting for these devices, go back to each of the four PCs and update their IP configuration information to reflect the correct subnet and the correct default gateway, as needed. What information did you change? Also update your notes for all involved devices as needed.

Table 8-15   Create subinterfaces on the router's physical interface

Command	Purpose
interface fastethernet0/0.2 and press **Enter** again	Creates the subinterface and enters interface configuration mode for the subinterface
encapsulation dot1Q 2	Sets encapsulation for VLAN 2
ip address 192.168.43.25 255.255.255.248	Assigns network information to the subinterface
exit	Returns to global configuration mode
interface fastethernet0/0.3 and press **Enter** again	Creates the subinterface and enters interface configuration mode for the subinterface
encapsulation dot1Q 3	Sets encapsulation for VLAN 3
ip address 192.168.43.17 255.255.255.248	Assigns network information to the subinterface
exit	Returns to global configuration mode
exit and press **Enter**	Returns to privileged EXEC mode
show ip interface brief	Displays IP configuration information—confirm your configurations are listed as expected
copy run start and press **Enter**	Saves the current settings

20. From PC0, ping PC8 (192.168.43.20). Does it work now? Why or why not?
21. Make sure all your router and PC interfaces are properly documented. **Take a screenshot** of your entire Packet Tracer network; submit this visual with your answers to this project's questions.
22. Save this Packet Tracer file in a safe place for future projects.
23. Make some notes on your Wikidot website about your activities in Packet Tracer for this project. When you're finished, close **Packet Tracer**.

Note to instructors: A Packet Tracer solution file is provided for each Packet Tracer project through the Instructors site. Some Packet Tracer projects build on earlier Packet Tracer networks. If needed for one or more students, you can provide a previous project's solution file as a start file for one of these progression projects.

Solutions to Self-Check Questions

Network Segmentation

1. Which of the following techniques does *not* break up a large broadcast domain into smaller broadcast domains?

   Answer: b. Adding more switches to a network

   Explanation: **Adding more switches to a network** expands the broadcast domain. You can use physical devices like routers to create separate LANs and, therefore, separate broadcast domains. At layer 2, you can create virtual LANs to break up the broadcast domain.

2. What is the binary number 1111 1111 in decimal?

   Answer: a. 255

   Explanation: An 8-bit binary number of all 1s is equal to **255** in decimal. This is a good conversion to memorize.

Subnet Masks

3. Which of the following is *not* a benefit of subnetting?

   Answer: d. Routers more easily manage IP address spaces that overlap.

   Explanation: It's not true that **routers more easily manage IP address spaces that overlap**—If IP address ranges connected to a router's own interfaces overlap, the router will not be able to route messages accurately between the LANs. Benefits of subnetting include efficiently managing available IP address space, easier management of network documentation, and easier location and resolution of network problems.

4. What is the network ID of the IP address 192.168.72.149/16?

   Answer: b. 192.168.0.0

   Explanation: The CIDR notation of /16 indicates the first 16 bits, or two octets, of the IP address identify the network ID: 192.168. By convention, 0s can be used to complete the four octets when referring to the network ID: **192.168.0.0**. The host ID is 0.0.72.149. For 192.168.72.0 to be the network ID and 0.0.0.149 to be the host ID, the CIDR notation would have had to be /24.

Calculating Subnets

5. If a server has a subnet mask of 255.255.255.224, how many bits in its IP address identify the host?

   Answer: d. 5

   Explanation: The interesting octet, 224, converts to 11100000. This shows that three bits were borrowed for the network ID, leaving **five bits** for the host ID.

6. What is the minimum number of bits that should be borrowed to create 14 subnets?

Answer: a. Four bits

Explanation: Use the formula $2^n = Y$ to determine how many bits to borrow to create a desired number of subnets, where n is the number of bits to borrow and Y is the number of subnets that many borrowed bits will create. 2^3 equals 8, which is not enough subnets for the targeted 14 subnets. 2^4 equals 16, which is sufficient for the targeted 14 subnets. Therefore, **four bits** should be borrowed from the host portion for the network portion.

7. Suppose you're calculating the range of host IP addresses for a subnet (the targeted subnet). If the *next* subnet's network ID is 192.168.42.128, what is the *targeted* subnet's broadcast address?

Answer: c. 192.168.42.127

Explanation: The broadcast address is always 1 below the network ID for the next subnet. Therefore, 192.168.42.(128 – 1) yields **192.168.42.127**.

Virtual LANs (VLANs)

8. At what OSI layer do VLANs function?

Answer: d. Data link layer

Explanation: By sorting traffic based on **data link layer** information, VLANs create two or more broadcast domains from a single broadcast domain, which is also a layer 2 construct.

9. Suppose you have a small network with one router, one switch, and a few computers that are grouped into three VLANs. Which of the following statements is false?

Answer: a. Traffic between computers on the same VLAN must go through the router.

Explanation: **Traffic between computers on the same VLAN goes through the switch** to reach other devices on the *same* VLAN; this traffic does *not* need to go through the router. Traffic to hosts on other networks goes through the router. Traffic between hosts on different VLANs must also go through the router, which is called inter-VLAN routing

10. Which VLANs on a switch cannot be renamed or deleted?

Answer: c. Default VLAN

Explanation: A **default VLAN** is typically preconfigured on a switch, initially includes all the switch's ports, and cannot be renamed or deleted. However, ports in the default VLAN can be reassigned to other VLANs. The native VLAN receives all untagged frames from untagged ports; by default, this is the same as the default VLAN but should be changed to an unused VLAN. The management VLAN can be used to provide administrative access to a switch; by default, this might be the same as the default VLAN and should be changed. Data VLANs carry user-generated traffic, such as email, web browsing, or database updates; you might have many data VLANs on a network.

WIDE AREA NETWORKING

After reading this module and completing the exercises, you should be able to:

1 Identify the fundamental elements of WAN service options

2 Explain how routers manage internetwork communications

3 Compare and contrast WAN connectivity technologies

4 Explain the most common wireless WAN technologies

5 Troubleshoot common connection problems

On the Job

The European "cooperative" public Internet Exchange model has come to the United States in the last few years, changing WAN internetworking considerations related to cloud service access. These days, WAN networking is as much about connecting to cloud services as to far-away offices. A public IX (Internet Exchange) is a less-expensive, cooperative way to directly or near-directly peer with other companies' networks, rather than paying an ISP for expensive Internet bandwidth. In this model, for small fees associated with running the cooperative network at a few data centers in a metropolitan area, we can peer directly with content partners' networks. This requires no ISP in the middle and makes it possible to route directly to our peers.

Last year, one of our SaaS security software delivery teams advocated for hosting their application at data centers directly connected to a public IX in the United States rather than at our traditional data centers. The SaaS application is very sensitive to Internet latency, and more than 50 percent of its traffic is exchanged with just a few content providers, including Microsoft, Amazon hosting services, and Google.

At first, I couldn't understand the rationale for adding *more* data center locations when we already had quite a few. Then the SaaS security team showed me traffic tests. I also ran my own. I learned that the other traffic providers were a hop or two closer when tested from the IX location. More importantly, when connected to the IX network's peering, we saw much faster effective transport speeds with all of our big content partners. Because a peering network allows less expensive Internet transit, some companies might prefer IX routes to routes over the Internet, resulting in better results than the hops saved would suggest.

In a couple of locations, we looked at extending an IX network to our nearby facilities via WAN circuits. But when we compared the cost of the extension to just renting data center space at the IX, it made more sense to host at the location where the IX was already connected, even after buying more network gear.

Public "cooperative" IX examples include the following:

- AMS-IX (Bay Area Internet Exchange)
- SFMIX (San Francisco Metro Internet Exchange)
- FL-IX (Florida Internet Exchange)
- NYIIX (New York International Internet Exchange)

The United States also has some older Internet Exchange providers, but usually their hosting fees are higher, making total cost potentially much higher than in this newer model.

Brooke Noelke
Cloud Service Architect
McAfee

In previous modules, you have learned about basic transmission media, network models, and networking hardware associated with LANs. This module focuses on WANs (wide area networks), which, as you know, are networks that connect two or more geographically distinct LANs. WANs are of significant concern for organizations attempting to meet the needs of telecommuting workers, global business partners, and Internet-based commerce.

The distance requirements of WANs affect their entire infrastructure, and, as a result, WANs differ from LANs in many respects. To understand the fundamental difference between a LAN and a WAN, think of the hallways and stairs of your house or school as LAN pathways. These interior passages allow you to go from room to room. To reach destinations outside the building, however, you need to use sidewalks and streets. These public thoroughfares are analogous to WAN pathways—except that WAN pathways are not necessarily public.

This module discusses WAN topologies and various technologies used by WANs. It also notes some potential pitfalls in establishing and maintaining WAN connections.

WAN ESSENTIALS

 **CERTIFICATION**

1.2 Explain the characteristics of network topologies and network types.

Average reading time: 11 minutes

A WAN traverses a significant distance and usually supports very high data throughput. Each of the following scenarios demonstrates a need for a WAN:

- A bank with offices around the state needs to connect those offices with each other to gather transaction and account information into a central database. Furthermore, it needs to connect with global financial clearinghouses to, for example, conduct transactions with other institutions.
- Regional sales representatives for a national pharmaceutical company need to submit their sales figures to a file server at the company's headquarters and receive email from the company's mail server.
- An automobile manufacturer in Detroit contracts its plastic parts manufacturing to a Delaware-based company. Through WAN links, the auto manufacturer can video conference with the plastics manufacturer, exchange specification data, and even examine the parts for quality from a remote location.
- A clothing manufacturer sells its products over the Internet to customers worldwide.

Although all these businesses need WANs, they might not need the same kinds of WANs. Depending on the traffic load, budget, geographical breadth, and commercially available technology, each might implement a different transmission method. For every business need, a few WAN connection types might be capable of meeting that need. At the same time, many WAN technologies can coexist on the same network to meet different needs.

The following list summarizes the major characteristics of WANs and explains how a WAN differs from a LAN:

- LANs connect nodes, such as workstations, servers, printers, and other devices, in a small geographical area on a single organization's network, whereas WANs use networking devices, such as routers and modems, to connect networks spread over a wide geographical area.
- LANs and WANs may differ at layers 1 and 2 of the OSI model in access methods, topologies, and, sometimes, transmission media. For example, the way DSL transmits bits over a WAN differs from the way Ethernet transmits bits over a LAN.
- Both LANs and WANs use the same protocols from OSI layers 3 and above. Recall that layer 3 protocols are responsible for directing data between LANs.
- LANs are mostly owned and operated by the companies that use them. On the other hand, WANs are usually owned and operated by telcos (telecommunications carriers), also known as NSPs (network service providers), such as AT&T, Verizon, Spectrum, and Comcast. Corporations lease WAN connections from these carriers, often with payments based on the amount of bandwidth used or reserved. Alternatively, as you read about in the *On the Job* story at the beginning of this module, corporations might connect directly to an IX (Internet Exchange), sometimes called an IXP (Internet Exchange point). This is similar to the difference between buying merchandise at retail prices versus buying products wholesale through a purchasing cooperative. IXs are where the networks of ISPs and other telecommunications providers intersect. By connecting directly into an IX, companies are able to cut out some of the "middleman" expense of WAN connections.

As you can see, WANs are used to connect LANs. Recall that CANs (campus area networks) and MANs (metropolitan area networks) also connect LANs. Typically, a CAN is a collection of LANs within a single property or nearby properties, such as buildings belonging to a school where all the buildings and most or all the network media spanning those connections are confined within land owned by the school. With a CAN, it's likely that a single organization (or group of organizations) owns all the connected LANs and most or all the networking media connecting those LANs.

Similarly, a MAN is a collection of LANs within a limited geographical area, such as a downtown area or even a city, county, or province. With MANs, many customers might own one or more of the connected LANs, and a single, third-party provider leases use of the networking media connecting these LANs. These connections often must be made across property not owned by either the MAN provider or the MAN customers. MAN connections might be made available to the general public (such as when a city makes high-speed Internet access available to all downtown area residents), or it might be restricted to a single customer (such as when a hospital is connected to its satellite medical offices). The following list gives examples where MANs can be useful:

- Connecting a city's police stations
- Connecting a hospital with its regional medical centers
- Connecting a home office with its branch offices and a warehouse location

The reason to make these distinctions between WANs, MANs, CANs, and LANs is because different technologies and protocols have been developed to best serve each of these markets. Networking technology that works well for a long-haul connection across hundreds of miles to support the Internet backbone isn't well suited for network connections between two buildings situated next door to each other, even though both these networks might connect multiple LANs. Throughout this module, you'll learn more about the nuances of when to use various technologies, depending on distances, networking media, and types of communications needed on the network. Figure 9-1 illustrates this fundamental difference between WAN and LAN connectivity.

The individual geographic locations or endpoints connected by a WAN are known as WAN sites. A WAN link is a connection between one WAN site (or endpoint) and another site (or endpoint). WAN links can be point-to-point (connects one site to only one other site) or multipoint (connects one site to two or more other sites).

Entry Point Equipment

If you have DSL or cable Internet service, you connect your home router to a modem. A modem is a modulation/demodulation device that converts between digital and analog signals. The customer's endpoint device on a WAN is called the DTE (data terminal equipment), and the carrier's endpoint device for the WAN is called the DCE (data

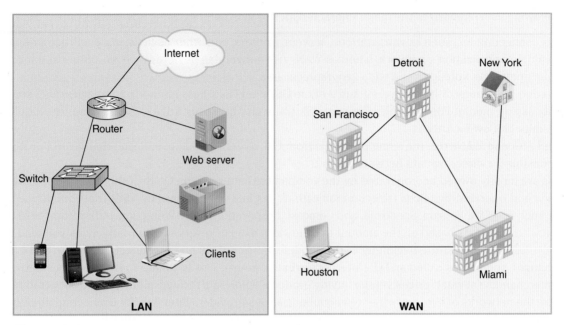

Figure 9-1   Differences in scale between LAN and WAN

circuit-terminating equipment). In this case, the router is the DTE, usually owned by the customer, and the modem is the DCE, usually owned by the ISP. Figure 9-2 shows this setup, with a router and modem at the customer's site defining the dividing line between each network.

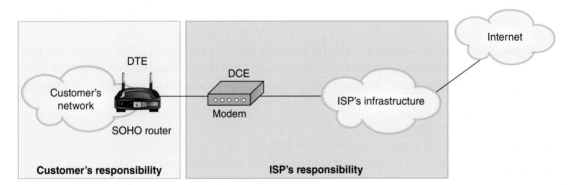

Figure 9-2   A router and a modem define the endpoints where a LAN connects to a WAN

Generally, the DTE is the responsibility of the customer and the DCE is the responsibility of the ISP. The DTE communicates on the LAN, and the DCE communicates on the WAN. Sometimes the DTE and DCE are combined in the same device. For example, a router might have one WAN network adapter, or WIC (WAN interface connector), that connects to a fiber-optic WAN and one LAN network adapter that connects to an Ethernet, twisted-pair LAN.

When working with your network's connection to your ISP at the service-related entry point, you need to know the difference between equipment that belongs to the ISP and equipment that belongs to the subscriber. Equipment located on the customer's premises, regardless of who owns it and who is responsible for it, is called CPE (customer premises equipment). Equipment belonging to the ISP, despite its location on the customer's premises, should only be serviced by the ISP's technicians even if it is located on the customer's side of the demarc (demarcation point). Equipment owned by the customer is the responsibility of the customer and will not be serviced by the ISP. The following list describes devices commonly found at or near the demarc:

- **NIU (network interface unit)**—The NIU, also called NID (network interface device), at the demarc connects the ISP's local loop to the customer's network. A more intelligent version of an NIU is a **smartjack**, or INID (Intelligent NID), which can provide diagnostic information about the interface. For example, a smartjack might include loopback capabilities. Just like the loopback adapter you use to test a port or cable on your computer, the smartjack can loop the ISP's signal back to the CO (central office) for testing. The ISP is responsible for all wiring leading up to the NIU and for the NIU itself. The customer is responsible for everything past the NIU unless the equipment is owned by the ISP, such as with a line driver, CSU/DSU, or set-top box.

- **Line driver**—Essentially a repeater, a line driver can be installed either on copper lines (in which case, it is called a copper line driver) or fiber lines (in which case, it is called a fiber line driver) to boost the signal across greater distances. The device might be placed on either side of the demarc and, if located on the customer's side, might be owned by either party.
- **CSU/DSU (channel service unit/data service unit)**—This device serves as the endpoint for a dedicated connection between an ISP and a customer. Like line drivers, these devices can be owned by either party, depending upon who is responsible for providing this device according to the terms of service. However, the CSU/DSU is typically placed on the customer's side of the demarc between the demarc and the first router.

Now that you understand the basic components that differentiate WANs from LANs, you're ready to learn about specific technologies and types.

> **EXAM TIP** The CompTIA Network+ exam expects you to know about a variety of ISP connection types and to be able to identify the networking environments best suited to each. For wired WANs and related technologies, you need to know about leased lines, DSL, cable broadband, metro-optical networks, MPLS, SD-WAN, and cloud connectivity options. Wireless WANs covered later in this module include satellite and cellular technologies.

REMEMBER THIS...

- Compare LANs, CANs, MANs, and WANs.
- Explain the purpose of a smartjack.

SELF-CHECK

1. Which network type supports long-haul connections between ISPs?
   a. WAN
   b. CAN
   c. MAN
   d. LAN

Check your answers at the end of this module.

ROUTING PROTOCOLS

 CERTIFICATION

1.1 Compare and contrast the Open Systems Interconnection (OSI) model layers and encapsulation concepts.

2.2 Compare and contrast routing technologies and bandwidth management concepts.

3.3 Explain high availability and disaster recovery concepts and summarize which is the best solution.

5.3 Given a scenario, use the appropriate network software tools and commands.

Average reading time: 33 minutes

7 Application
6 Presentation
5 Session
4 Transport
▶ ③ Network
2 Data Link
1 Physical

You've spent a lot of time over the past few modules learning how switches work, both at layer 2 and layer 3, within a corporate network. As you know, routers serve as gateways to connect networks. To study WAN technologies, you must learn more about how routers work. A router joins two or more networks and passes packets from one network to another. Routers are responsible for determining the next network to which a packet should be forwarded on its way to its destination. A typical router consists of an internal processor, an operating system, memory, input and output jacks for different types of network connectors (depending on the network type), and, usually, a management console interface. Three examples of routers are shown in Figure 9-3, with the most complex on the left and the simplest on the right. High-powered, multiprotocol routers may have several slot bays to accommodate multiple network interfaces. At the other end of the scale are simple, inexpensive routers often used in small offices and homes, and they require little configuration.

Courtesy of Juniper Networks, Inc
Courtesy of NETGEAR

Figure 9-3   ISP, business, and consumer routers

A router's strength lies in its intelligence—that is, its ability to interact with transmissions and make decisions. Although any one router can be specialized for a variety of tasks, all routers can do the following:

- Connect dissimilar networks, such as a LAN and a WAN, which use different types of protocols.
- Interpret layer 3 and often layer 4 addressing and other information contained in these headers.
- Determine the best path for data to travel from point A to point B. The **best path** is the most efficient route to the message's destination calculated by the router, based upon the information the router has available to it.
- Reroute traffic if the path of first choice is down but another path is available.

In addition to performing these basic functions, routers may perform any of the following optional functions:

- Filter broadcast transmissions to alleviate network congestion.
- Acting as a simple firewall, prevent certain types of traffic from getting to a network, enabling customized segregation and security.
- Support simultaneous local and remote connectivity.
- Provide high network fault tolerance through redundant components such as power supplies or network interfaces.
- Monitor network traffic and report statistics.
- Diagnose internal or other connectivity problems and trigger alarms.

Routers are often categorized according to their location on a network or the Internet and the routing protocols they use. The various categories are described in the following list and diagrammed in Figure 9-4:

- **Core routers**, also called **interior routers**, are located inside networks within the same autonomous system. An **AS (autonomous system)** is a group of networks, often on the same domain, that are operated by the same organization. For example, Cengage might have several LANs that all fall under its domain with each LAN

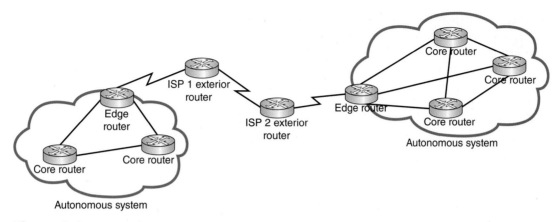

Figure 9-4   Core, edge, and exterior routers

connected to the others by core routers. An AS is sometimes referred to as a trusted network because the entire domain is under the organization's control. Core routers communicate only with routers within the same AS.

- **Edge routers**, or **border routers**, connect an autonomous system with an outside network, also called an untrusted network. For example, the router that connects a business with its ISP is an edge router.
- **Exterior router** refers to any router outside the organization's AS, such as a router on the Internet backbone. Sometimes a technician might refer to their own edge router as an exterior router because it communicates with routers outside the AS. But keep in mind that every router communicating over the Internet is a trusted edge router for some organization's AS, even if that organization is a large telecommunications company managing a portion of the Internet backbone.

On small office or home office LANs, routers are simple to install: Plug in the network cable from the cable modem connected to your ISP on one port and connect your computer(s) to your LAN through another port or by a wireless connection. Turn on the router and computer and use a web-based utility program on the router to set it up.

However, high-powered, multiprotocol routers can be a challenge to install on sizable networks. Typically, an engineer must be very familiar with routing technology to figure out how to place and configure a router to the best advantage. If you plan to specialize in network design, engineering, or management, you should research router types and their capabilities further. As you learn more about how routers work, keep in mind that layer 3 and layer 4 switches can perform the same functions.

Routing Tables

A **routing table** is a database that holds information about where hosts are located and the most efficient way to reach them. As you know, a router has two or more network ports, or interfaces, and each port connects to a different network. Each network connection is assigned an interface ID, and logically, the router belongs to every network it connects to. A router relies on its routing table to identify which network a host belongs to and which of the router's interfaces points toward the best next hop to reach that network.

For example, in Figure 9-5, suppose a workstation in LAN A wants to print to the network printer in LAN D. The following steps describe how routing tables would be used in this transmission:

Step 1:   Workstation 1 issues a print command to a network printer. IP on the workstation recognizes that the IP address of the printer is on a different LAN than the workstation and forwards the transmission through switch A to its default gateway, router A.

Step 2:   Router A examines the destination IP address in the packet's header and searches its routing table to determine which of its interfaces the message should go to. Table 9-1 shows how a routing table is designed, with each entry explained in plain English instead of using IP addresses and other data. Each row in the routing table describes one route, including a destination network and how to get there. The first two columns provide information used to match messages to a route. The next two columns provide forwarding information for the route. Routing metrics are route ratings used as tie breakers when needed.

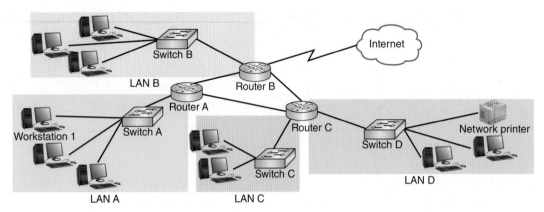

Figure 9-5 Routers rely on routing tables to locate destination hosts

Here's a breakdown of how the route-search process uses information in Table 9-1:

- Router A examines all rows in its routing table. In each row, it uses information in the first two columns—the destination network's IP address and netmask—to calculate the range of IP addresses included in that network.

- If the message's destination IP address fits in the calculated range for a route, the router then reads the IP address of the gateway in the third column. This gateway is the next hop router. It also reads in the fourth column the interface it will use to send the message out.

- If it finds more than one possible route, the router uses **routing metrics** (information about each route) in the last column to determine which route is most efficient. The smaller the metrics number, the better the route. Notice in Figure 9-5 and in Table 9-1 that two routes can reach the network printer on LAN D. Of these two routes, the router would select the one with the lower metrics value. You'll learn more about routing metrics later in this module.

- If it doesn't find a matching entry, the router looks for 0.0.0.0 in the first column. This route is the **default route**—the route to use if no other route is a match. In most cases, the routing table must

Table 9-1 Portions of router A's routing table in plain English

Destination network ID	Netmask	Gateway	Interface	Routing metrics (tie breaker)
LAN A's IP address	LAN A's netmask	None (This is router A's own LAN.)	Port that points toward switch A	1
LAN B's IP address	LAN B's netmask	Router B's IP address	Port that points toward router B	4
LAN C's IP address	LAN C's netmask	Router C's IP address	Port that points toward router C	5
LAN D's IP address	LAN D's netmask	Router B's IP address	Port that points toward router B	10
LAN D's IP address	LAN D's netmask	Router C's IP address	Port that points toward router C	5
IP address on the Internet	That host's netmask	Router B's IP address	Port that points toward router B	23
0.0.0.0 (wildcard entry for any network)*	0 (wildcard entry for any netmask)	Router B's IP address**	Port that points toward router B	3

*This row is the default route.

**This router is router A's gateway of last resort.

contain a default route so it can handle traffic with no predefined route, such as DNS messages. The gateway in the third column of this route is called the gateway of last resort, which is the router that accepts unrouteable messages from other routers.

- If no default route is defined, the router will drop the message.

In this scenario, router A finds two matches with LAN D's network information and chooses the best of these two options based on their respective routing metrics. Router A then determines that it should send the message out the port that faces router C.

Step 3: Before it forwards the message, router A decreases the number of hops tallied in the TTL (time to live) field of the packet header. It then sends the message to router C.

Step 4: Router C decreases the packet's hop count by 1, reads the packet's destination IP address, searches its routing table for matching network information, and determines the message is destined for its own LAN D. It sends the message to switch D on LAN D.

Step 5: Using its ARP table, switch D matches the destination IP address with the printer's MAC address. If switch D didn't have a matching entry in its ARP table for the network printer's IP address, it would use an ARP broadcast to request the printer's MAC address. Switch D then delivers the transmission to the printer, which picks up the message and begins printing.

NOTE 9-1

What's the difference between a default gateway, a default route, and a gateway of last resort?

- Most hosts have a default gateway—a router or layer 3 switch—where they send all routable messages. Hosts can't communicate with other networks without a default gateway.

- Most routers have a default route as a backup route when no other route can be determined.

- The default route points to a gateway of last resort. A router's gateway of last resort is where it sends messages addressed to networks the router can't find in its routing table.

Routing Path Types

Routing paths are determined in one of two ways as described next:

- **Static routes**—A network administrator configures a routing table to direct messages along specific paths between networks. For example, it's not uncommon to see a static route between a small business and its ISP. However, static routes can't adapt to network congestion, failed connections, or device relocations, and they require human intervention to configure or adjust.

- **Dynamic routes**—A router automatically calculates the best path between two networks and accumulates this information in its routing table. If congestion or failures affect the network, a router using dynamic routing can detect the problems and reroute messages through a different path. When a router is added to a network, dynamic routing ensures that the new router's routing tables are updated.

route

The **route** utility allows you to view a host's routing table. The `route` command can also be used to add or delete static routes, which you'll practice doing in a project at the end of this module. Here are some variations of the `route` command for different operating systems:

- **Linux or UNIX**—Enter `route` at a shell prompt.
- **Windows**—Enter `route print` in a CLI.
- **Cisco's IOS**—Enter `show ip route` at the CLI using privileged EXEC mode.

Routing tables on workstations typically contain no more than a few, unique entries, including the default gateway and loopback address. However, routing tables on Internet backbone routers, such as those operated by ISPs, maintain hundreds of thousands of entries.

Routing Metrics

Finding the best route or best path for messages to take across networks is one of the most valued and sophisticated functions performed by a router. Some examples of routing metrics used to determine the best path include the following:

- Hop count, which is the number of network segments crossed
- Theoretical bandwidth and actual throughput on a potential path
- Delay, or latency, on a potential path, which decreases performance
- Load, which is the traffic or processing burden sustained by a router in the path
- MTU (maximum transmission unit), which is the largest IP packet size in bytes allowed by routers in the path without fragmentation (excludes the frame used by the local network)
- Routing cost, which is a value assigned to a particular route as judged by the network administrator; the more desirable the path, the lower its cost
- Reliability of a potential path, based on historical performance
- A network's topology

Routing Protocols to Determine Best Paths

To determine the best path, routers communicate with each other through routing protocols. Routing protocol messages, similar to scouting parties exploring unknown terrain, go forth to collect data about current network status and contribute to the selection of best paths. Routers use this data to create their routing tables. Keep in mind that *routing* protocols are not the same as *routable* protocols such as IP (which can be routed across networks). However, routing protocols might piggyback on IP to reach their destinations. Also, the various routing protocols operate at different layers of the OSI model—usually layer 3, layer 4, or layer 7. However, this discussion is primarily concerned with the effects that routing protocols have on layer 3 routing activities.

Routers rate the reliability and priority of a routing protocol's data based on these criteria:

- AD (administrative distance)—Each routing protocol is assigned a default AD, which is a number indicating the protocol's reliability, with lower values being given higher priority. This assignment can be changed by a network administrator when one protocol should take precedence over a previously higher-rated protocol on that network.
- Convergence time—Routing protocols are also rated on the time it takes to recognize a best path in the event of a change or network outage. Some routing protocols are more efficient than others at communicating topology changes across the network.
- Overhead—A routing protocol is rated on its overhead, or the burden placed on the underlying network to support the protocol. The difference here is related to how much processing power each routing protocol requires of routers and how much information must be transferred between routers and how often.

The most common routing protocols are summarized in Table 9-2 and are described in more detail in the following sections. Other routing protocols exist, but their descriptions exceed the scope of this course.

Table 9-2 Summary of common routing protocols

Routing protocol	Type	Algorithm used
RIP (Routing Information Protocol)	IGP	Distance-vector
RIPv2 (Routing Information Protocol, version 2)	IGP	Distance-vector
OSPF (Open Shortest Path First)	IGP	Link-state
IS-IS (Intermediate System to Intermediate System)	IGP	Link-state
EIGRP (Enhanced Interior Gateway Routing Protocol)	IGP	Advanced distance-vector
BGP (Border Gateway Protocol)*	EGP	Advanced distance-vector or path vector

*CompTIA classifies BGP as a "hybrid routing protocol."

EXAM TIP Table 9-2 provides an overview of the routing protocols covered in this module. For the CompTIA Network+ exam, it's important to know which routing protocols function within an autonomous system and which of these protocols communicate between these systems. You'll also want to know the classification of protocols, especially distance-vector versus link-state.

Interior and Exterior Gateway Protocols

As you examine Table 9-2, you can see that a routing protocol is classified as either an IGP or an EGP. Here's an explanation of the two types, which are diagrammed in Figure 9-6:

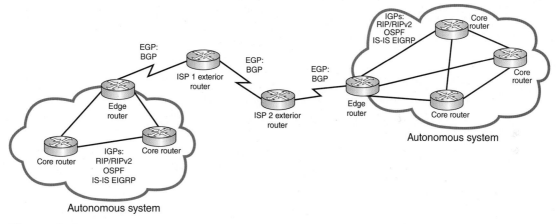

Figure 9-6 BGP is the only routing protocol that communicates across the Internet

- **IGPs (interior gateway protocols)** are routing protocols used by core routers and edge routers within autonomous systems. IGPs are often grouped according to the algorithms they use to calculate best paths, as follows:
  - **Distance-vector routing protocols** calculate the best path to a destination based on the distance to that destination. Some distance-vector routing protocols factor only the number of hops to the destination, whereas others consider route latency and other network traffic characteristics. Distance-vector routing protocols periodically exchange their entire routing tables with neighboring routers even if there's not been a change to a route, which requires the transfer of large amounts of data simply to keep routing tables updated. Also, routers relying on this type of routing protocol must accept the data they receive from their neighbors and cannot independently assess network conditions two or more hops away. This limitation is sometimes called "routing by rumor," and it results in slow convergence and higher likelihood of persistent errors when network conditions change. RIP and RIPv2 are distance-vector routing protocols.
  - **Link-state routing protocols** focus less on the number of hops between routers and more on the state of a connection. These protocols collect information about all their connected links and send that information to other routers on the network. Other routers, then, can use this information about links throughout the network to build their own routing tables, independently mapping the network and determining the best path between itself and a message's destination node. These protocols tend to adapt more quickly to changes in the network, but they can also be more complex to configure and troubleshoot. They also require more processing power to incorporate information from throughout the network to build each device's routing table. Part of this resource demand is offset by the fact link-state routing protocols only send information when something changes. OSPF and IS-IS are link-state routing protocols, and they're highly scalable for very large networks.
  - **Hybrid routing protocols** exhibit characteristics of both distance-vector and link-state routing protocols. For example, Cisco's EIGRP functions primarily as a distance-vector routing protocol but incorporates elements of link-state routing, for example, by syncing link information across the network only when something changes.
- **EGPs (exterior gateway protocols)** are routing protocols used by edge routers and exterior routers to distribute data outside of autonomous systems. The one EGP protocol you need to know for the Network+ exam is the only EGP currently in use, BGP.

NOTE 9-2

An older routing protocol named Exterior Gateway Protocol is obsolete. However, the generic term *exterior gateway protocol* now refers to any routing protocol that routes information between autonomous systems.

Let's look at the details of these routing protocols, beginning with RIP and RIPv2, which are both outdated but still in use on many networks because of their simplicity and compatibility with older routers.

Legacy Networking: RIP (Routing Information Protocol)

RIP (Routing Information Protocol), a distance-vector routing protocol, is the oldest routing protocol. Here are some notable considerations when using RIP on a network.

Advantages:

- **Simplicity**—Quick and easy configuration.
- **Stability**—Prevents routing loops from continuing indefinitely by limiting the number of hops a message can take between its source and its destination to 15. If the number of hops in a path exceeds 15, the network destination is considered unreachable.

Disadvantages:

- **Limited metrics**—Only considers the number of hops between nodes when determining the best path rather than other, more complex factors.
- **Excessive overhead**—Broadcasts routing tables every 30 seconds to other routers, regardless of whether the tables have changed.
- **Poor convergence time**—Might take several minutes for new information to propagate to the far reaches of the network.
- **Limited network size**—Does not work well in very large network environments where data might have to travel through more than 15 routers to reach its destination (for example, on a metro network).
- **Slower and less secure**—Outdated by newer routing protocols.

Developers have improved RIP since its release in 1988 and informally renamed the original RIP as RIPv1 (Routing Information Protocol, version 1). The next version of RIP was published in 1994 and standardized by the IETF in 1998. RIPv2 (Routing Information Protocol, version 2) generates less broadcast traffic and functions more securely than RIPv1. An extension to RIPv2 that was first proposed in 1997 is RIPng (RIP next generation), which extends RIP support to IPv6. Still, RIPv2 and RIPng cannot exceed 15 hops, and they are also considered outdated routing protocols.

NOTE 9-3

When discussing limitations of routing protocols, the 15-hop limit is specific to RIP and its later versions. This is an identifying factor you can use to distinguish RIP from other routing protocols.

OSPF (Open Shortest Path First)

OSPF (Open Shortest Path First) is an IGP and a link-state routing protocol used on core or edge routers. It was introduced as an improvement to RIP and can coexist with RIP or RIPv2 on a network. Characteristics include the following:

- **Supports large networks**—Imposes no hop limits on a transmission path.
- **Complex algorithms**—Calculates more efficient best paths than RIP. Under optimal network conditions, the best path is the most direct path between two points. If excessive traffic levels or an outage prevent data from following the most direct path, a router might determine that the most efficient path actually goes through additional routers.

- **Shared data**—Maintains a database of the other routers' links. If OSPF learns of the failure of a given link, the router can rapidly compute an alternate path.
- **Low overhead, fast convergence**—Demands more memory and CPU power for calculations, but keeps network bandwidth to a minimum with a very fast convergence time, often invisible to users.
- **Stability**—Uses algorithms that prevent routing loops.
- **Multi-vendor routers**—Supported by all modern routers. It is commonly used on autonomous systems that rely on a mix of routers from different manufacturers.

IS-IS (Intermediate System to Intermediate System)

Another IGP, which is also a link-state routing protocol, is IS-IS (Intermediate System to Intermediate System). IS-IS uses a best-path algorithm similar to OSPF's. It was originally codified by ISO, which referred to routers as "intermediate systems," thus the protocol's name. Unlike OSPF, however, IS-IS is designed for use on core routers only. Also, IS-IS is not handcuffed to IPv4 like OSPF is, so it's easy to adapt to IPv6. Service providers generally prefer to use IS-IS in their own networks because it's more scalable than OSPF, but OSPF is still more common.

EIGRP (Enhanced Interior Gateway Routing Protocol)

EIGRP (Enhanced Interior Gateway Routing Protocol), an IGP, was developed in the mid-1980s by Cisco Systems. It is an advanced distance-vector protocol that combines some of the features of a link-state protocol and so is sometimes referred to as a hybrid protocol. With a fast convergence time and low network overhead, it's easier to configure and less CPU-intensive than OSPF. EIGRP also offers the benefits of supporting multiple protocols and limiting unnecessary network traffic between routers.

Originally, EIGRP was proprietary to Cisco routers. In 2013, parts of the EIGRP standard were released to the public so that networks running routers from other vendors can now use EIGRP. It accommodates very large and heterogeneous networks, but it is still optimized for Cisco routers and not many manufacturers have made the transition. On LANs that use Cisco routers exclusively, EIGRP is generally preferred over OSPF.

BGP (Border Gateway Protocol)

The only current EGP is BGP (Border Gateway Protocol), which has been dubbed the "protocol of the Internet." Whereas OSPF and IS-IS scouting parties only scout out their home territory, a BGP scouting party can go cross-country. BGP spans multiple autonomous systems and is used by edge and exterior routers on the Internet. Here are some special characteristics of BGP:

- **Path-vector routing protocol**—Communicates via BGP-specific messages that travel between routers over TCP sessions.
- **Efficient**—Determines best paths based on many factors.
- **Customizable**—Can be configured to follow policies that might, for example, avoid a certain router, or instruct a group of routers to prefer one route over other available routes.

BGP is the most complex of the routing protocols mentioned in this module. If you maintain networks for an ISP or large telecommunications company, you will need to understand BGP in depth.

Routing Redundancy

Recall that fault tolerance on a network is accomplished through using redundant hardware, connections, services, and copies of data. For example, if one router fails, another router can take over. You might even have a cluster of routers so your network could tolerate the failure of multiple devices without losing service. On a small network, having two or three ISP connections with one or two routers for each might provide sufficient redundancy. Larger networks should also have multiple ISP connections with each using geographically separate hardware and network media. For example, you might want one ISP connection to enter your property from one direction and another ISP connection to enter from the other side of your building or campus (see Figure 9-7). These diverse paths increase your network's fault tolerance should the proverbial backhoe damage underground lines from one ISP, or in case of flooding, fire, power outage, or other damage that is restricted to a relatively small area.

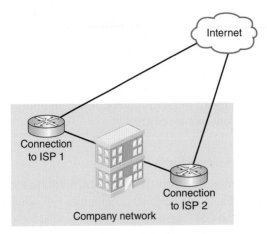

Figure 9-7 Redundant ISP connections to the Internet

If you're paying for two or more ISP connections, should you use both of them all the time, or should one be kept only as a backup when the first one fails? This question highlights the key difference between two contrasting redundancy techniques, as described next:

- **Active-active redundancy**—All redundant resources are active at all times, and work is distributed among them. For example, you might load balance your Internet traffic between two ISP connections, but either ISP service could take over if the other one fails. This arrangement can provide increased performance during normal operation, as all your available resources are actively working. You might have the load distributed evenly among all resources, or you might have one or more redundant resources running a reduced load.
- **Active-passive redundancy**—Only one or a few redundant resources are active at any time with the backup devices on standby ready to fill in if they're needed. For example, you might run all your Internet traffic over a single ISP service, but you have a second one on standby in case it's needed.

So how do you make this happen when you're running two routers in a network? For example, you know you can only configure one default gateway on your computer. Do you configure half your network hosts to use one default gateway and half to use the other? Is there a way to make them automatically failover if one gateway fails?

Instead of managing redundancy manually, you can configure an **FHRP (First Hop Redundancy Protocol)** on a router or layer 3 switch to provide a single VIP (Virtual IP) address as the default gateway that, in turn, potentially points to multiple routers. Two popular FHRPs you learned about in an earlier module and a third FHRP that is gaining in popularity are described next:

- **VRRP (Virtual Router Redundancy Protocol)**—Industry standard across vendors. The VIP points to the primary, active router, and all other routers stand by as potential backups. Configurations are made using the `vrrp` command.
- **HSRP (Hot Standby Routing Protocol)**—Proprietary to Cisco. The VIP points to the active router, a standby router is configured for auto failover, and other routers listen for indications the active and standby routers have both failed. Configurations are made using the `standby` command.
- **GLBP (Gateway Load Balancing Protocol)**—Also proprietary to Cisco devices. GLBP gateways are weighted according to priority, and traffic is load balanced among all gateways. Configurations are made using the `glbp` command.

REMEMBER THIS...

- Identify the primary differences between the routing protocols RIP, RIPv2, OSPF, EIGRP, and BGP.
- Compare link-state, distance-vector, and hybrid routing protocol characteristics.
- Explain how to configure router redundancy using common FHRPs.
- Use the `route` command to view routing tables in various OSs.

SELF-CHECK

2. Which routing protocol runs between your network's edge router and your ISP's edge router?
   a. EIGRP
   b. RIPv2
   c. OSPF
   d. BGP

3. Which command will output your Windows computer's routing table?
   a. `show ip route`
   b. `route print`
   c. `route`

4. Which routing protocol is limited to 15 hops?
   a. EIGRP
   b. OSPF
   c. BGP
   d. RIPv2

Check your answers at the end of this module.

You're Ready

You're now ready to complete **Project 9-1: Create a Routing Table Entry in Windows**, or you can wait until you've finished reading this module.

You're Ready

You're now ready to complete **Project 9-2: Create a Path MTU Black Hole**, or you can wait until you've finished reading this module.

WAN CONNECTIVITY

✓ CERTIFICATION

1.2 Explain the characteristics of network topologies and network types.

1.8 Summarize cloud concepts and connectivity options.

2.1 Compare and contrast various devices, their features, and their appropriate placement on the network.

2.2 Compare and contrast routing technologies and bandwidth management concepts.

5.3 Given a scenario, use the appropriate network software tools and commands.

Average reading time: 42 minutes

7 Application
6 Presentation
5 Session
4 Transport
▶ 3 Network
▶ 2 Data Link
▶ 1 Physical

Connecting your network to other networks plays an integral role in building and managing a network. However, the tools you'll use to connect networks vary greatly according to the size of your network, your network's bandwidth needs, and the relative locations of your network's segments. Imagine you're starting a new company. Initially, you're working from home and the only employee is you. Your WAN requirements consist entirely of connecting your home network to the Internet. However, as your company grows, you'll need other kinds of WAN connections. Throughout this section, you'll read about WAN connectivity options that will serve your company as it expands from your basement into a global entity. Notice the ways your WAN needs shift over time and what technologies are available to meet those needs.

Some of these service options are called by common names that you might recognize if you've ever shopped around for home or business Internet service or if you've noticed commercials or billboards advertising Internet subscription options. Many of these connections use existing telephone lines, the existing cable TV infrastructure, or specialized copper or fiber cables. Later in this module, you'll also learn about WAN services provided wirelessly, including cellular and satellite connections.

As you compare options for WAN services, keep in mind a significant difference between technologies—whether the connection is shared among many customers or dedicated to one customer. The following list explains these two options:

- **Broadband**—Especially well-suited for residential customers, the cables (whether telephone, coaxial, or fiber) and available bandwidth are shared between multiple customers. The ISP makes a "best effort" attempt to provide *up to* the advertised bandwidth, and actual performance varies considerably during busy usage. Bandwidth is also **asymmetrical**, or asynchronous, meaning download speeds (data traveling from the carrier's switching facility to the customer) are faster than upload speeds (data traveling from the customer to the carrier's switching facility). For a higher premium, businesses can get faster broadband speeds and possibly one or more static IP addresses included in the package. However, uptime, service, and bandwidth are still not guaranteed.

- **DIA (dedicated Internet access)**—The cable itself or a portion of its available bandwidth is dedicated to a single customer; this is more common for business customers and comes with an SLA-defined (service-level agreement) guarantee of minimum uptime percentages and maximum recovery times if the service goes down. Bandwidth is **symmetrical**, or synchronous, meaning download and upload speeds are about the same. This is especially important for businesses that back up large amounts of data online. The subscription will also often include a certain number of static IP addresses.

Applying Concepts 9-1: Test Your Internet Connection's Speed

You can test your own Internet connection to see what the current upload and download speeds are using a **bandwidth speed tester**, or a speed test website. During the test, data will be sent to your computer and then requested from your computer to measure download and upload speeds, respectively. Complete the following steps:

1. In your browser, go to **speedtest.net**. At the time of this writing, you start the test by clicking **GO**. The test begins, as shown in Figure 9-8.
2. Wait for the test to complete and then write down your speed test results. What are your current download and upload speeds?
3. Try a different site and compare results. Go to **verizon.com/speedtest**, click **Get started** and wait for the test to complete (see Figure 9-9). What are the results this time? How do they compare to your first results? Why do you think this is?

While these websites are designed to test throughput between your network and a host on the Internet, you can also use throughput testing software, such as Lakehorn's Network Speed Tester, to check the performance of your local network. Recall from Hands-On Project 5-4 that you also used the TotuSoft LAN Speed Test application and the TamoSoft Throughput Test application.

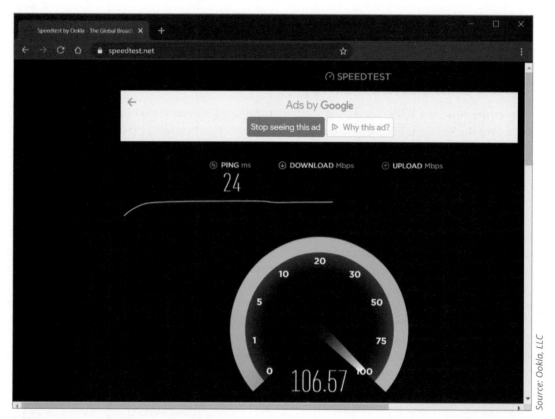

Figure 9-8   Speed test in progress

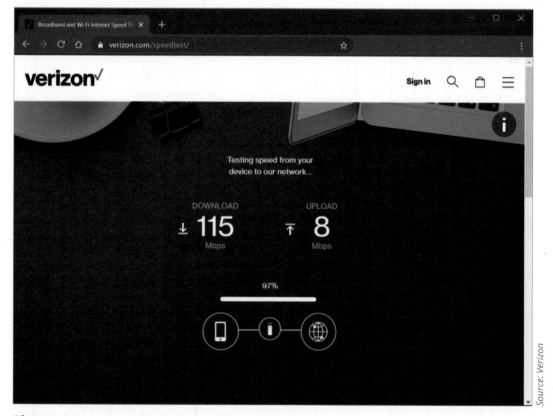

Figure 9-9   Another speed test for comparison

These first three WAN connectivity options cover broadband ISP services you might use for your home office: DSL, cable, and fiber Internet. Then you'll learn about high-speed WAN service options more commonly used by businesses.

DSL (Digital Subscriber Line)

DSL (digital subscriber line) is a WAN connection method introduced by researchers at Bell Laboratories in the mid-1990s. It operates over the PSTN (public switched telephone network), also called POTS (plain old telephone service), which is a network of lines and carrier equipment that provide landline telephone service to homes and businesses. Originally, the PSTN carried only analog traffic. All its lines were copper wires, and switching was handled by operators who manually connected calls upon request. Today, switching is computer controlled, and nearly all the PSTN uses digital transmission and fiber for backbone connections. Signals may deliver voice, video, or data traffic and travel over fiber-optic or twisted-pair copper cable connections.

The telephone company terminates lines and switches calls between different locations at the CO (central office). The portion of the PSTN that connects any residence or business to the nearest CO is known as the local loop, or the "last mile" (though it is not necessarily a mile long), as illustrated in Figure 9-10. It's the part of the PSTN most likely to still use copper wire and carry analog signals. That's because extending fiber-optic cable to every residence and business is costly. However, fully digital connections are increasingly common, especially for businesses that rely heavily on WAN connections. No matter what kind of media is used, the end of the local loop—and the end of the carrier's responsibility for the network—is the customer's demarcation point where wires terminate at the NIU.

DSL can support multiple data and voice channels over a single line, but it can span only limited distances without the help of repeaters. Also, the distance between the customer and the central office affects the actual throughput a customer experiences. Close to the central office, DSL achieves its highest maximum throughput. The farther away the customer's premises, the lower the throughput.

To understand how DSL and voice signals can share the same line, it's helpful to note that telephone lines carry voice signals over a very small range of frequencies between 300 and 3300 Hz. This leaves higher, inaudible frequencies unused and available for carrying data. DSL uses data modulation techniques at the physical layer of the OSI model to achieve extraordinary data throughput over regular telephone lines. Recall that modulation techniques can allow a single channel to carry more data per cycle of a signal. Depending on its version, a DSL connection might use a modulation

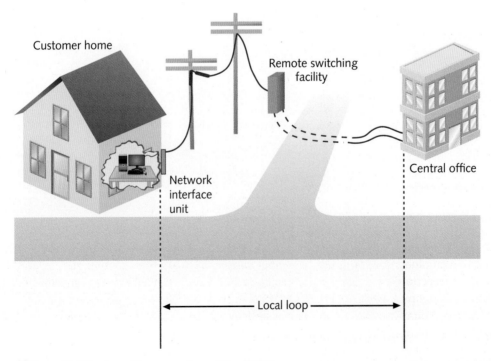

Figure 9-10   Local loop portion of the PSTN

technique based on amplitude or phase modulation to alter the waves at higher frequencies to carry data. The types of modulation used by different DSL versions affect their throughput and the distance their signals can travel before requiring a repeater. Modulation is performed by a DSL modem. A **DSL modem**, such as the one shown in Figure 9-11, contains ports to connect both to your incoming telephone line and to your computer or network connectivity device.

Figure 9-11   A DSL modem

Types of DSL

The types of DSL vary according to their throughput rates, data modulation techniques, capacity, and distance limitations, as well as how they use the PSTN. The term xDSL (extended DSL) refers to all DSL varieties. In each case, the *x* in *xDSL* is replaced by the variety's name (there's that algebra again). The better-known DSL varieties include the following:

- **ADSL (asymmetric DSL)**—Faster download speeds than upload speeds and is the most common form of DSL. Asymmetrical communication is well suited to users who receive more information from the network than they send to it—for example, people watching movies online or people surfing the web. ADSL and VDSL (discussed next) create multiple narrow channels in the higher frequency range to carry more data. For these versions, a splitter must be installed at the carrier and at the customer's premises to separate the data signal from the voice signal before it reaches the terminal equipment (for example, the phone or the computer). The latest version of ADSL is ADSL2+, which extends the reach of DSL to within two kilometers of the provider's location. It also provides a maximum theoretical throughput of 24 Mbps downstream and a maximum of 3.3 Mbps upstream (depending on how close it is to its source). The reason upstream and downstream bandwidth are different on a DSL line is because of the way the bandwidth is broken up for different purposes. Figure 9-12 shows the distribution of bandwidth for voice, upstream, and downstream communications.

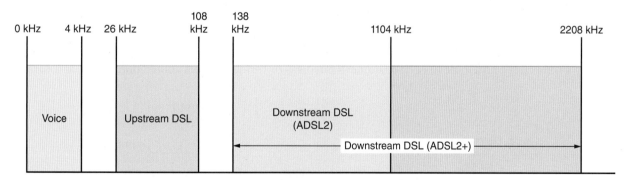

Figure 9-12   More bandwidth allocated for downstream than upstream

- **VDSL (very high bit rate DSL or variable DSL)**—Faster than ADSL and is also asymmetric, with faster download speeds than upload speeds. A VDSL line that carries up to 52 Mbps in one direction and up to 16 Mbps in the opposite direction can extend only a maximum of 1.6 km before dropping to speeds similar to ADSL2+. VDSL2 offers throughput speeds nearing 100 Mbps in both directions but drops off quickly at even shorter distances. These limitations might suit businesses located close to a telephone company's CO (for example, in the middle of a metropolitan area), but it won't work for most individuals.
- **SDSL (symmetric DSL)**—Equal download and upload speeds maxing out around 2 Mbps. Symmetrical transmission is suited to users who both upload and download significant amounts of data—for example, a bank's

branch office that sends large volumes of account information to the central server at the bank's headquarters and, in turn, receives large amounts of account information from the central server at the bank's headquarters. SDSL cannot use the same wire pair that is used for voice signals. Instead, this type of DSL uses the extra pair of wires contained in a telephone cable (which are otherwise typically unused).

NOTE 9-4

Published distance limitations and throughput can vary from one service provider to another, depending on how far the provider is willing to guarantee a particular level of service. In addition, service providers may limit each user's maximum throughput based on terms of the service agreement. For example, in 2011, AT&T capped the total amount of data transfer allowed for each of its DSL subscribers to 150 GB per month. The company instituted the new policy in response to a dramatic spike in downstream bandwidth usage due to Netflix streaming. In fact, in 2010, Netflix accounted for nearly 30 percent of all downstream Internet traffic requested by fixed users in the United States. Today, many providers cap a subscriber's high-speed data usage, although typically the caps are higher now than the one in this example.

Telecommunications carriers and related vendors have positioned DSL as a competitor for cable broadband and leased line services. The installation, hardware, and monthly access costs for DSL are significantly less than the cost for other options, but the cost in comparison with cable broadband varies widely by location. At the time of this writing, DSL home Internet service costs approximately $35 per month in the United States, though prices vary by speed and location. Generally speaking, DSL throughput rates, especially upstream, are lower than cable broadband, which is its main competition among residential customers.

Cable Broadband

While local and long-distance phone companies strive to make DSL the preferred method of Internet access for consumers, cable companies are pushing their own connectivity option. **Cable broadband** (also called cable Internet or cable modem access) is based on the coaxial cable wiring used for TV signals, although in reality, much of the coaxial infrastructure has been replaced with fiber. Cable broadband was standardized by an international, cooperative effort orchestrated by CableLabs that yielded a suite of specifications called **DOCSIS (Data Over Cable Service Interface Specifications)**. Cable broadband service is typically offered at asymmetric speeds, such as up to 70 Mbps download and 7 Mbps upload. The newest DOCSIS standard, 4.0, theoretically allows for symmetric multi-gigabit speeds up to 10 Gbps downstream and 6 Gbps upstream, thus rivaling some fiber-optic Internet service options once experienced speeds start to approach the standard's defined maximums.

In fact, many cable companies employ fiber cabling for a significant portion of their physical infrastructure. As illustrated in Figure 9-13, **HFC (hybrid fiber coaxial)** networks use fiber-optic cabling to connect the cable company's distribution center, or headend, to distribution hubs and then to optical nodes near customers. Either fiber-optic or coaxial cable then connects a node to each customer's business or residence via a connection known as a cable drop.

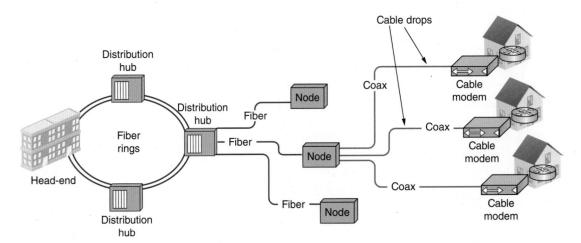

Figure 9-13 HFC infrastructure

Cable broadband connections require that the customer use a special cable modem, a device that modulates and demodulates signals for transmission and reception via cable wiring (see Figure 9-14). The cable modem must conform to the correct version of DOCSIS supported by the ISP. Most newer cable modems use DOCSIS 3.1 with 4.0 becoming available, but ISPs might charge extra when later modem models are used. Table 9-3 presents the versions of DOCSIS along with their specifications.

Like DSL modems, cable modems operate at the physical and data link layers of the OSI model, and, therefore, do not manipulate higher-layer protocols like IP. The cable modem connects to a customer's PC via the NIC's RJ-45, USB, or wireless interface. Alternatively, the cable modem could connect to a networking device, such as a switch or router, thereby supplying bandwidth to a LAN rather than to just one computer. It's also possible to use a device that combines cable modem functionality with a SOHO router to share available bandwidth on an entire network.

Source: Zoom Telephonics, Inc.

Figure 9-14   A cable modem

Table 9-3   DOCSIS versions and specifications

Version	Maximum upstream throughput	Maximum downstream throughput	Description
DOCSIS 1.x (1.0 and 1.1)	10 Mbps	40 Mbps	Outdated; single channel; throughput was shared among customers
DOCSIS 2.x (2.0 and 2.0 + IPv6)	30 Mbps	40 Mbps	Outdated; single channel; reduces disparity between upstream and downstream throughputs
DOCSIS 3.0	100 Mbps	1000 Mbps	Multiple channels: minimum of 4, no maximum
DOCSIS 3.1	1–2 Gbps	10 Gbps	In 2017, CableLabs published Full Duplex DOCSIS 3.1, which offers symmetrical Gigabit upload and download speeds.
DOCSIS 4.0	6 Gbps	10 Gbps	Expanding upon DOCSIS 3.1 standards, CableLabs added RF bandwidth options for upstream speeds to support full-duplex, multigigabit throughput.

Applying Concepts 9-2: Determine a Cable Modem's DOCSIS Version

You can determine the DOCSIS version of a cable modem on a SOHO network with a little detective work. This activity requires a SOHO network serviced by cable broadband and a computer (Windows, Linux, or Mac) connected to the network. Alternatively, you can find a cable modem for sale online and use the posted information and photos for parts of this activity. Complete the following steps to identify the DOCSIS version of a cable modem:

1. Examine the labels on the cable modem to determine the device's manufacturer and model number. In some cases, the DOCSIS version might be printed on one of these labels. If you're looking at a cable modem online, examine the posted specifications for this information. If the DOCSIS version isn't labeled or posted, continue with the following steps.
2. Research the manufacturer and model number information online. You might find the DOCSIS information while conducting your research. If not, the minimum information you need is the cable modem's default internal IP address (such as 192.168.0.1 or 192.168.100.1) and admin username and password (if there is one).

3. Choose one of the following options:
   a. If you're researching a cable modem listed online, check the manufacturer's website for an emulator to interact with the cable modem's user interface. Alternatively, you can choose a TP-Link cable modem emulator at **tp-link.com/us/support/emulator/**.
   b. If you're working with a cable modem on your own network, enter the default internal IP address in a web browser and log on if necessary.
4. Explore the user interface to locate the cable modem's hardware information. Figure 9-15 shows the hardware information for a cable modem made by ARRIS. What is the DOCSIS version of your cable modem?

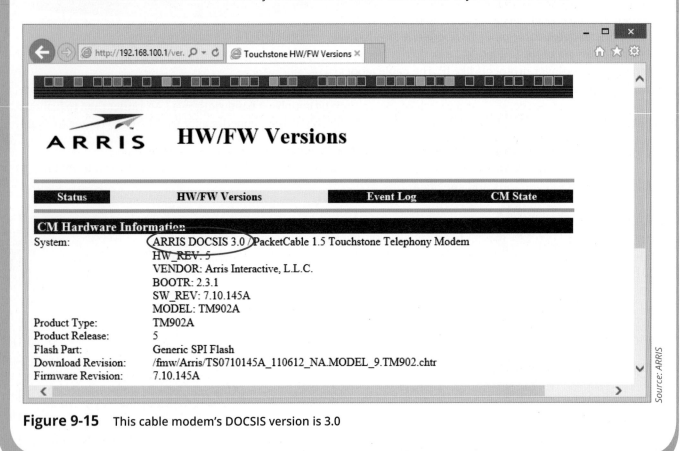

Figure 9-15   This cable modem's DOCSIS version is 3.0

Source: ARRIS

Like DSL, cable broadband provides a dedicated and always-up, or continuous, connection that does not require dialing up a service provider to create the connection. Unlike DSL, cable broadband requires many subscribers to share the same local line, thus raising concerns about security and actual (versus theoretical) throughput. For example, if your cable company supplied you and five of your neighbors with cable broadband services, one of your neighbors could, with some technical prowess, capture the data that you transmit to the Internet. (Modern cable networks provide encryption for data traveling to and from customer premises; however, these encryption schemes can be thwarted.)

Moreover, the throughput of a cable line is fixed. As with any fixed resource, the more one person uses, the less that is left for others. In other words, the greater the number of users sharing a single line, the less throughput available to each individual user. Cable companies counter this perceived disadvantage by rightly claiming that at some point (for example, at a remote switching facility), a telephone company's DSL bandwidth is also fixed and shared among a group of customers.

In the United States, cable broadband access costs approximately $30–$60 per month when bundled with cable TV and/or digital voice services. Cable broadband is less often used in businesses than DSL, primarily because most office buildings do not contain an existing coaxial cable infrastructure.

Fiber

The fact is, most of the Internet backbone already runs on fiber. Even if you connect your new home office to the Internet via an old-school dial-up connection, most of the distance your data travels on the Internet will run over fiber cables. It's that last mile to your location that really slows your data down. While DSL and cable broadband offer significantly faster speeds than dial-up, they're still very slow by modern standards.

A growing trend in ISP offerings for WAN connection services is to offer FTTN (fiber-to-the-node), FTTH (fiber-to-the-home), or similar arrangements. In these scenarios, the ISP runs a fiber connection to one of a few nearby locations, as illustrated in Figure 9-16 and described next:

- **FTTN (fiber-to-the-node** or **fiber-to-the-neighborhood)**—A nearby service junction that serves a few hundred customers
- **FTTC (fiber-to-the-curb)**—A nearby pole or equipment cabinet that serves a few customers
- **FTTB (fiber-to-the-building)** or **FTTH (fiber-to-the-home)**—The junction box at the demarc to your building

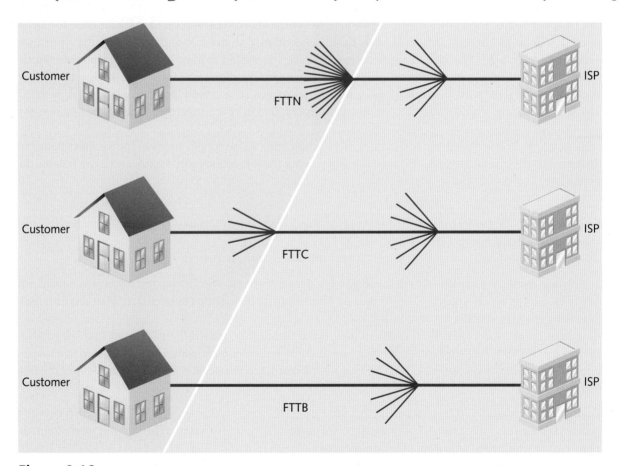

Figure 9-16 Getting fiber closer to your own network increases your Internet speeds

As you can see, each progressive scenario brings the fiber closer to your own network. The closest options cost more but also reduce the distance over which your data must traverse copper cabling.

While this option has limited availability in many market areas, those who can choose fiber often do. Fiber's higher speeds, with symmetric speeds often reaching as high as 1–2 Gbps for home or small business fiber services, offset the increased cost of up to $100 monthly. Additionally, so long as the ISP can provide you with a fiber connection, your distance from their offices won't negatively affect your experienced speeds.

Fiber technology and availability to business customers—and even to residential customers—continues to improve. Rising market demand for last-mile fiber service is causing increased investments by ISPs into their access-level fiber infrastructure. Traditionally, fiber investment focused on long-haul connections across hundreds and thousands of miles. In contrast, MONs (metropolitan optical networks) bring fiber to the customer. This dense, localized grid of junctions and fiber cables attempts to make direct fiber connections available to as many customers as possible while balancing the significant expense of replacing existing telephone and coaxial cable infrastructure with fiber equipment and fiber-optimized technologies.

You've already learned about some of the technologies that handle multiple signals on each fiber connection, such as DWDM (dense wavelength division multiplexing). However, DWDM does not easily lend itself to handling the high numbers of communications channels and the wide variety of network protocols needed within a metro network environment. This mismatch between what pre-existing fiber technology was designed to do and what is needed in the metro market is sometimes referred to as the "metro gap." In response to these emerging needs, newer technology has been developed or adapted to support MONs and the expectations of customers in these markets. With 100 Gbps speeds already available on long-haul connections, the industry is now aiming for similar speeds for MONs on the ISP's end of broadband fiber connections.

Leased Lines

When you first established your imaginary company at the beginning of this section, broadband access to the Internet from your basement office was sufficient. Perhaps you began with cable or DSL and then, as you started to earn profits, you moved to a fiber connection. Excitingly, your business continued to grow. Within a few months, your basement was no longer large enough to hold all your inventory. Initially, you rented storage space in a small warehouse while you continued to work from home. But soon you realized you were spending several hours a week at the storage unit and out of touch with your customers and small group of employees. You moved into a larger warehouse rental that included office space, and you decided to open two storefronts, one in your hometown and another in a neighboring city.

At this point, you realize your broadband Internet connection can no longer provide the support your business needs. Instead of basic Internet access, you need to connect your three locations with higher and more reliable throughput speeds to support the following activities:

- VoIP calls with customers and vendors
- E-commerce traffic to your website
- Sales activity from physical storefronts
- Upload and download traffic to exchange large graphic files with customers

You call your local ISP asking how to get dedicated WAN connections. The ISP suggests that you consider leased lines for each location, which would provide dedicated bandwidth on fiber optic connections. What are the advantages and disadvantages of this option for your business?

Where fiber broadband offers the benefits of fiber optic technology, leased fiber takes all that speed boost and pools the bandwidth for a single customer. While a leased line's dedicated bandwidth might be listed at a lower speed than the maximum theoretical speeds advertised for fiber broadband services, a dedicated line offers the following advantages:

- **Dedicated bandwidth**—The customer pays for a specific bandwidth (such as 2 Gbps) and reserves that bandwidth for their sole use without having to share it with other customers. Throughput won't fluctuate in response to traffic demands from other customers.
- **Symmetrical bandwidth**—Leased line speeds are typically symmetrical, meaning upload and download speeds will be the same.
- **SLA-backed guarantee**—Performance is backed by SLA-enforced uptime, repair time, and possibly backup options (such as having a broadband connection available during an outage). If bandwidth falls below a defined threshold, the customer has options for recourse to protect their business activities during the outage.

When subscribing to a leased line, existing fiber optic cabling can be configured for the leased line, or a dedicated fiber optic cable must be installed to connect the customer to the nearest ISP exchange, or PoP (Point of Presence).

Some of this installation cost is covered by the ISP, but certain expenses might be charged back to the customer. Alternatively, new cables can be installed to directly connect a business's own locations. For example, each branch office might have a direct line to the company's own headquarters.

Ongoing monthly costs of a leased line vary greatly depending on many factors, including required bandwidth and the distance to the ISP's exchange or between the company's own locations. Typical costs will range between $300 and $1000 monthly. This can get especially expensive for multiple leased lines, as shown in Figure 9-17. However, this particular arrangement gives each location allotted bandwidth directly to the ISP and on to the Internet. From the ISP's central office, communications between your locations (such as between the warehouse and a storefront) traverse the ISP's high-speed backbone network to connect the two leased lines. Further, more locations can easily be added to the company's leased line network by subscribing to a new leased line for each new location. Alternatively, sometimes what's needed is a point-to-point leased line between two customer locations. In this case, the ISP cannot provide supportive services, such as monitoring uptime or optimizing VoIP traffic.

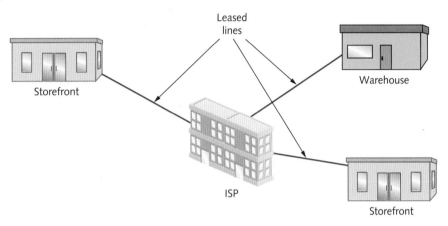

Figure 9-17 Each location needs its own leased line

MPLS (Multiprotocol Label Switching)

Your leased lines serve the company well for nearly two years. Both storefronts quickly gain a loyal customer following, and you're able to optimize your logistics at the warehouse to efficiently service both storefronts and all website customers. As the word spreads and business continues to boom, you decide over the next year to open three more storefronts throughout your region. You also recognize your warehouse space is no longer sufficient, and your employees are tightly cramped in the existing office space. These growing pains lead to the decision to move to a standalone warehouse space and to open a headquarters office in a separate location. With all these new locations to network, managing so many leased lines is becoming unfeasible. Further, you're told by your IT staff that leased lines don't offer the level of nuanced control they need for handling the different types of applications on your network. Their suggested solution: MPLS.

MPLS (multiprotocol label switching) was introduced by the IETF (Internet Engineering Task Force) in 1999. As its name implies, MPLS enables multiple types of layer 3 protocols to travel over any one of several connection-oriented layer 2 protocols. Essentially, MPLS allows you to use any connectivity option for each site that makes sense while centrally managing bandwidth between each site. For example, in Figure 9-18, you might have your warehouse connected to the ISP using DSL while your storefronts use fiber broadband and your central office has a leased line.

Despite the various service levels of each location's connection to the ISP, you can manage segmentation and QoS for different types of traffic across your entire network, even if your locations are spread hundreds or thousands of miles apart. These advantages are explained next:

- **QoS (quality of service)** refers to a group of techniques for adjusting the priority assigned to various types of traffic. For example, you might want to prioritize VoIP traffic over email traffic. One of the characteristics that sets MPLS apart from other WAN technologies is its ability to support QoS traffic shaping across WAN connections.

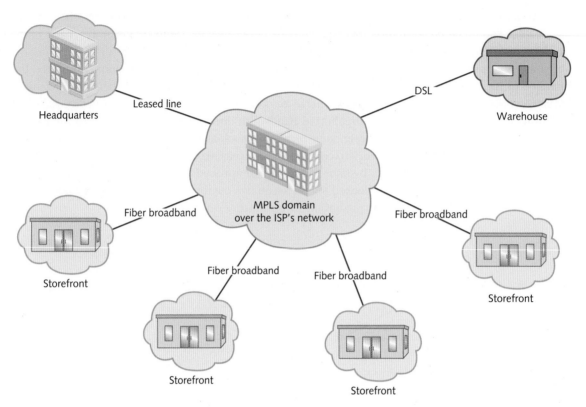

Figure 9-18 MPLS provides cohesive WAN management for multiple connection types

- Additionally, you can set routes for traffic between sites so the ISP's routers don't have to stop and think with each packet where that packet should go next. Essentially, MPLS lets routers function more like switches, working with information in layer 2 headers instead of having to dig to layer 3 and process routing information. This saves time and reduces latency.

With MPLS, the first ISP router (the provider's edge router, also called the MPLS ingress router) receives a message in a data stream and adds one or more labels to the layer 3 packet. These MPLS labels together are sometimes called a shim because of their placement between layer 3 and layer 2 information. For this reason, MPLS is sometimes said to belong to "layer 2.5." Next, the network's layer 2 protocol header is added, as shown in Figure 9-19.

These MPLS labels include information about where the router should forward the message next and, sometimes, prioritization information. Each router in the data stream's path (see Figure 9-20) revises the label to indicate the packet's next hop. In this manner, routers on a network can take into consideration network congestion, QoS indicators assigned to the messages, plus other criteria; however, these transit routers, called LSRs (label switching routers), don't have to take time to map a path for the messages. Network engineers maintain significant control in setting these paths. Consequently, MPLS offers potentially faster transmission than traditionally routed networks.

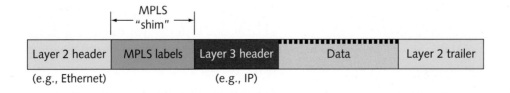

Figure 9-19 MPLS shim within a frame

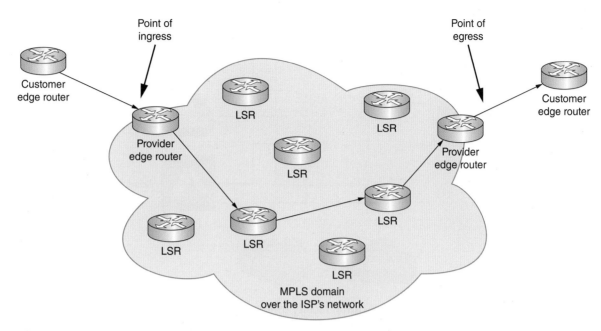

Figure 9-20   Label switching routers simply forward the message without calculating routes

While MPLS does offer decreased latency, this benefit is not quite as noticeable today as it was when MPLS first became available. The primary benefits of MPLS today include the following:

- MPLS connections are highly scalable for businesses, which means a business can add more and longer connections for less cost than similarly scaled leased lines.
- Customers can prioritize their own traffic across the WAN according to QoS attributes, such as giving VoIP traffic higher priority over email traffic.
- The ability to label traffic offers more reliability, predictability, and security (when properly implemented) than when using cheaper connections over the open Internet.

Cloud Connectivity Options

Over the next few months, as you're working through the growing pains of adding new storefronts and moving offices, your IT team suggests some additional improvements to your network configurations that will better serve your company into the next phase. Primarily, they suggest that you migrate many of your network resources to the cloud. For example, you don't need to host your own email servers, and running your website from the cloud will allow that resource to scale as needed without having to purchase new hardware in the future. You give your team the green light to begin the migration of a few servers with the intent of a larger scale migration when the transition to your new offices is scheduled to be completed.

During the initial migration, your team sets up a group of VPN (virtual private network) connections to your cloud resources from each of your company locations. This process requires the installation of a VPN device at each location. The VPNs travel over each location's Internet connection, giving employees direct and secure access to your first few cloud resources like email and, eventually, to a lot more resources like the customer database and HR tools.

At first, the VPNs work well enough. Later in the year, as the cloud migration nears completion, it becomes obvious that a VPN will not be sufficient for the home office. Instead, your cloud provider recommends a **private-direct connection**, or **interconnection**, to their cloud infrastructure. In this scenario, you lease a dedicated line from your ISP to one of your cloud provider's PoPs, or colocation facilities (see Figure 9-21). From there, you pay for the connection to the cloud provider's physical infrastructure and, usually, some kind of data transfer fees (such as $.02 per GB transferred out of the cloud provider's network).

As you research your cloud provider's available PoP locations, you realize the colocation you've chosen also offers private-direct connections with another cloud provider your team has been considering for a multicloud deployment. The cost efficiency of leasing a single direct line to this colocation will more than pay for itself over time now that you can use the same physical line for multiple purposes. This benefit also opens additional opportunities to host more resources in your hybrid cloud, including virtual desktops for your home office.

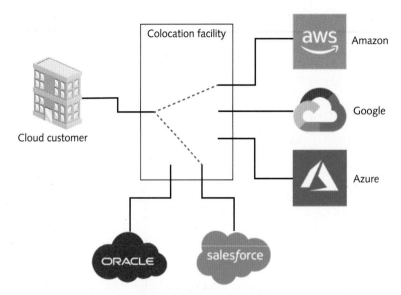

Figure 9-21 A colocation facility offers connections to multiple cloud platforms

Software-defined WAN (SD-WAN)

Over the next couple of years, you settle into your new offices. All your stores and your website continue to thrive. Customers are happy, and so are your employees. Suddenly, a random social media video featuring some of your products goes viral on the Internet, and you start getting a rapid increase in website traffic. Interestingly, much of that traffic originates from three Asian countries. Order volumes to these countries spike. You're sure it won't last long, but six months later, these sales numbers have only increased. As you further investigate your popularity explosion in these countries, you make some connections with new business associates in those areas. Casual chit-chat turns into some serious discussion about expanding your company into India and Thailand. You're committed to hiring locals to provide everything from order management and HR to customer support. At the same time, this expansion will require a significant investment in new overseas locations for storefronts, offices, and a warehouse, which also means needing new WAN connections.

As you discuss the pending expenditure in these other countries with your IT team, you realize the need for centralized management of company network resources. MPLS connections all the way to Asia won't suffice to meet your company's needs over the coming years. Instead, your team suggests a newer solution called SD-WAN.

Similar to its SDN cousin, **SD-WAN (software-defined wide area network)** relies on abstracted, centralized control of networking devices to manage network functions across a diverse infrastructure. SD-WAN offers the following benefits:

- **Transport agnostic**—As shown in Figure 9-22, an SD-WAN controller can manage network configurations at multiple locations throughout the world, regardless of the type of connection each segment uses to reach the SD-WAN (such as broadband, leased line, MPLS, cellular, and others).
- **Active-active load balancing and automatic failover**—An SD-WAN managed network offers active-active load balancing where it can choose the best physical WAN connection for different types of traffic according to traffic prioritization and current network conditions. For example, suppose a branch office has three Internet connections as shown in Figure 9-23: an MPLS connection, a broadband connection, and a 5G wireless connection. SD-WAN can route traffic over each of these connections according to each data stream's configured priority. If one WAN connection goes down, the SD-WAN controller can switch traffic to another WAN connection.
- **Intent-based management**—A network admin can indicate in the controller's GUI their intent for traffic, such as limiting bandwidth for a specific application, and the SD-WAN controller institutes all configuration changes needed on all affected network devices.
- **Zero-touch provisioning**—An SD-WAN edge device can be shipped to a branch location where a non-technical person can plug in the device without any configuration needed on-site. The device then finds and checks

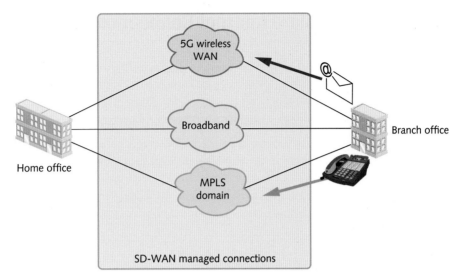

Figure 9-22   SD-WAN supports many underlying WAN connectivity technologies

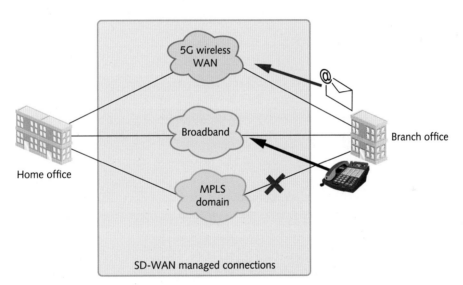

Figure 9-23   The SD-WAN controller can direct traffic through the optimal path for that traffic at a given time

in with the remote SD-WAN controller for further instructions. Trained technicians at the home office can remotely finish deploying the SD-WAN configurations at the branch office without any additional assistance from on-site personnel.

- **Reduced cost**—Because SD-WAN solutions can be deployed over any kind of underlying WAN connection (such as cable, DSL, fiber broadband, or 5G), expensive leased lines and MPLS connections can be abandoned in favor of SD-WAN management for many of a company's connections. While the company might not replace all their MPLS or leased line connections, SD-WAN can be used to optimally manage all available WAN connections and minimize the need for more expensive WAN services.

Improvements to SD-WAN technologies are still needed surrounding security when traffic traverses the Internet, costs for underlying WAN connections (such as MPLS), and flexibility for cloud and mobile users. Still, the advantages offered by SD-WAN are causing an industry shift away from older, more traditional WAN connectivity options.

Your fictional company has used a wide variety of wired WAN technologies through its journey from your basement to its global presence. Similar to LANs, WANs utilize multiple wireless technologies as well. You'll read about two of the most common of these in the next section.

Applying Concepts 9-3: Explore Internet Connection Options in Your Area

Selecting a particular WAN solution because its theoretical maximum speed is faster than another solution's theoretical maximum speed won't help much if your local carrier doesn't actually offer service at that speed. Selecting a WAN solution for a corporation requires familiarity with the options available in your area and their actual performance levels relative to each other. Complete the following steps to evaluate the ISP options available to a business in your area:

1. Compile a list of ISPs in your town or city. If you live in a rural area with few options, select a nearby city with more options so that you'll be able to include some of the private WAN technologies in addition to residential WAN offerings.

2. Check the website for each ISP to determine what broadband and dedicated services they offer in your area, both for residential customers and corporate customers. Include both wired and wireless options. Answer the following questions:
   a. What are their advertised speeds?
   b. How much does each solution cost on a monthly basis?
   c. What installation fees are there, if any?
   d. How far away are you located from their CO? (If you're researching another city besides your own, use a fictional location in that same city.)
   e. What effect will this distance likely have on the actual speeds of each service option?

3. Search online for consumer reviews of each ISP in your list. What kinds of ratings does each ISP receive online?

REMEMBER THIS...

- Explain various WAN services, including DSL, cable, MONs, leased lines, MPLS, cloud connectivity options, and SD-WAN.
- Use a bandwidth speed tester to check a WAN connection's speed.

SELF-CHECK

5. You just moved into a rural office space that has telephone service but no cable. Which WAN service could you use without needing to install new wiring to your location?
   a. Fiber broadband
   b. DSL
   c. Leased fiber
   d. Cable broadband

6. Which of these WAN services is backed by an SLA?
   a. DSL
   b. Leased line
   c. Fiber broadband
   d. Cable broadband

7. Which WAN service offers active-active load balancing?
   a. Cable broadband
   b. DSL
   c. SD-WAN
   d. Fiber broadband

Check your answers at the end of this module.

You're Ready

You're now ready to complete **Project 9-3: Create WAN Links in Packet Tracer**, or you can wait until you've finished reading this module.

WIRELESS WANS

✓ **CERTIFICATION**

1.2 Explain the characteristics of network topologies and network types.

2.4 Given a scenario, install and configure the appropriate wireless standards and technologies.

Average reading time: 16 minutes

The best 802.11ac signal can travel approximately a quarter of a mile. But other types of wireless networks can connect stations over much longer distances. For example, in large cities, dozens of surveillance cameras trained on municipal buildings and parks beam video images to central public safety headquarters. Meanwhile, in developing countries, wireless signals deliver lectures and training videos to students in remote, mountainous regions. In rural areas of the United States, elderly patients at home wear medical monitoring devices, such as blood pressure sensors and blood glucose meters, which use wireless networks to convey information to their doctors hundreds of miles away. Such networks can even alert paramedics in case of an emergency. All of these are examples of wireless WANs. Unlike wireless LANs, wireless WANs are designed for high-throughput, long-distance digital data exchange. The following sections describe a variety of ways wireless clients can communicate across a city or state.

Cellular

Cellular networks were initially designed to provide analog phone service. However, since the first mobile phones became available to consumers in the 1970s, cellular services have changed dramatically. In addition to voice signals, cellular networks now deliver text messages, web pages, music, and videos to smartphones and other handheld devices. Cellular networking is a complex topic, with rapidly evolving encoding and access methods, changing standards, and innovative vendors vying to dominate the market. This module does not detail the various encoding and access methods used on cellular networks. To prepare you for the CompTIA Network+ exam, this section describes current cellular data technology and explains the role it plays in wide area networking.

Although their access methods and features might differ, all cellular networks share a similar infrastructure in which coverage areas are divided into cells. Each cell is served by an antenna array and its base station, together called a **cell site**. The tower—the tall part you can easily see from a distance—is often owned by a third-party entity similar to how owners of office buildings or malls lease out portions of their property to other businesses. Cellular providers lease space on the towers for their antenna arrays, as shown in Figure 9-24, and space on the ground for base station equipment.

At the base station, a controller assigns frequencies to mobile clients and manages communication with them. In network diagrams, cells are depicted as hexagons. Multiple cells share borders to form a network in a honeycomb pattern, as shown in Figure 9-25. Antennas are positioned at three corners of each cell, radiating their signals and providing coverage over three equidistant lobes. When a client passes from one coverage area to another, the mobile

Antenna array

Tower

Mike West

Figure 9-24   This tower offers space for several antenna arrays

device begins communicating with a different antenna. Its communication might change frequencies or even carriers between cells. The transition, which normally happens without the user's awareness, is known as a handoff.

Cell sizes vary from roughly 1000 feet to 12 miles in diameter. The size of a cell depends on the network's access method and the region's topology, population, and amount of cellular traffic. An urban area with dense population and high volume of data and voice traffic might use cells with a diameter of only 2000 feet, their antennas mounted on tall buildings (see Figure 9-26a) or disguised to look like landscaping (see Figure 9-26b). In sparsely populated rural areas, with antennas mounted on isolated hilltop towers, cells might span more than 10 miles. In theory, the division of a network into cells provides thorough coverage over any given area. In reality, cells are misshapen due to terrain, EMI, and antenna radiation patterns. Some edges overlap and others don't meet up, leaving gaps in coverage.

As shown earlier in Figure 9-25, each base station is connected to an MSC (mobile switching center), also called an MTSO (mobile telecommunications switching office), by a wireless link or fiber-optic cabling. The MSC might be located inside a telephone company's central office or it might stand alone and connect to the central office via another

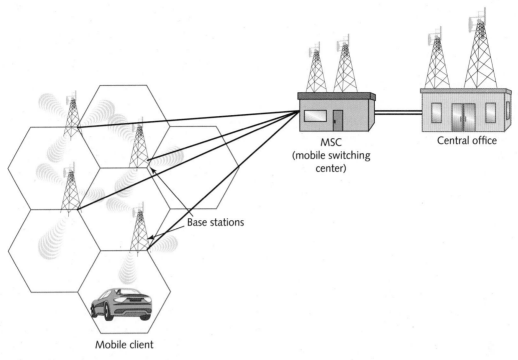

Figure 9-25 Cellular network

Figure 9-26 a) Cellular antennas on a tall building; b) A concealed tower

fiber-optic cable or a microwave link. At the MSC, the mobile network intersects with the wider wired network. Equipment at an MSC manages mobile clients, monitoring their location and usage patterns, and switches cellular calls. It also assigns each mobile client an IP address. From the switching center, packets sent from cellular networks are routed to wired data networks through backbones using WAN technologies you learned about earlier in this module.

To put today's services in context, it's useful to understand that each leap in cellular technology has been described as a new generation. Each successive generation has brought a greater range of services, better quality, and higher throughputs, as described in the following list:

- 1G (first generation) services from the 1970s and 1980s were analog.
- 2G (second generation) services in the 1990s used digital transmission and paved the way for texting and media downloads on mobile devices. Data transmission on 2G systems didn't exceed 240 Kbps.
- **3G (third generation)** services were released in the early 2000s. Data rates rose to 384 Kbps. To switch to fully digital transmissions, two competing 2G technologies emerged as market leaders for 3G, as follows:
  - ○ **GSM (Global System for Mobile Communications)** is an open standard that is accepted and used worldwide. Digital communication of data is separated by timeslots on a channel using **TDMA (time division multiple access)**, which is similar to TDM (time division multiplexing). The primary difference is that multiplexed

TDM signals all come from the same source (such as a router), while multiplexed TDMA signals come from several sources (such as several smartphones in the same vicinity). First introduced with the release of 2G devices, GSM initially only provided voice communications but added data services with the evolution of GPRS (General Packet Radio Services) and EGPRS (Enhanced GPRS), also called EDGE (Enhanced Data rates for GSM Evolution). GSM networks require that a cellular device have a SIM (Subscriber Identity Module) card containing a microchip to hold data about the subscription a user has with the cellular carrier.

○ CDMA (Code Division Multiple Access) differs from GSM in that it spreads a signal over a wider bandwidth so multiple users occupy the same channel, a technology called spread-spectrum. Codes on the packets keep the various calls separated. CDMA networks do not require a SIM card in a cellular device because devices are compared against a whitelist, which is a database of subscribers that contains information on their subscriptions with the provider. However, CDMA networks (such as Verizon's) still require SIM cards to use their LTE (Long Term Evolution) features. While CDMA and GSM co-exist in the United States, globally GSM is by far the more popular technology.

- **4G (fourth generation)** services are characterized by an all-IP network for both data and voice transmission. 4G standards, released in 2008, specify minimum throughputs of 100 Mbps with the goal of supporting 1 Gbps speeds. Variations of 4G include the following:

○ LTE (Long-Term Evolution) is essentially the result of a marketing debacle. 4G standards were released ahead of their time, that is, before available hardware was capable of providing the required speeds to qualify as 4G. However, the new 4G protocols and techniques that did work supported better speeds than 3G, and cellular providers had already begun marketing new 4G networks and devices. So LTE became an ambiguous marketing term that meant "faster than 3G but not really 4G." As hardware has improved, so have LTE speeds. Typical speeds now for LTE connections might reach 100 Mbps download and up to 75 Mbps upload.

○ LTE-A (LTE-Advanced) can more realistically approach 4G standards. Sometimes misleadingly called 5G E (5G Evolution), LTE-A is basically true 4G as defined back in 2008 but only recently emerging in real-world networks.

- **5G (fifth generation)** services require minimum speeds of 1 Gbps and max out at 20 Gbps download and 10 Gbps upload; however, actual speeds vary greatly. The 5G standards were initially released in 2016; cellular companies began deploying 5G infrastructure and devices in 2019. Note that the term 5G is completely unrelated to the 5-GHz band used by Wi-Fi. The following technologies contribute to 5G improvements:

○ **Bands**—One factor in experienced speeds is the band used. Some 5G providers (such as T-Mobile) have focused on building out widely available 5G infrastructure using the same lower bands that 4G uses, resulting in only moderately improved speeds. Other 5G providers (such as Verizon) are focusing instead on higher-density but less widely available infrastructure that uses new and smaller millimeter-wave frequencies in a newly available higher band. These dense but weaker frequencies provide high speeds for short distances while offering much lower resilience across long distances or when crossing obstacles such as walls and landscaping. When you are standing near a cell site, you could experience a strong 5G signal (with speeds easily exceeding 1 Gbps). But that speed could plummet to closer to 4G speeds at 200–300 Mbps if you walk around the corner of a nearby building or stand behind a tree.

○ **Cell density**—To reach a reasonable level of availability and effectiveness, many small 5G antennas must be installed in close proximity to each other so 5G clients can receive a close and strong signal throughout the coverage area.

○ **Channels**—5G works to increase speeds by using wider channels, similar to how Wi-Fi's 5-GHz band can be bonded into larger channels. Where 4G uses up to seven 20-MHz channels, 5G can use up to eight 100-MHz channels in the high band, which ranges from 20 to 100 GHz. Low band 5G (narrow but long-reaching frequencies) uses the same channels as 4G under 2 GHz. Mid band 5G (in the range of 2–10 GHz) offers two 100-MHz channels with the ability to stack low-band 20-MHz channels.

○ **Client volume**—While 5G cells must be placed closer together so millimeter-wave frequencies can reach clients, each cell site can support more clients. This will work well for sensor networks and IoT devices.

Satellite

In 1945, Arthur C. Clarke (the author of *2001: A Space Odyssey*) wrote an article in which he described the possibility of communication between manned space stations that continually orbited the Earth. Other scientists recognized the value of using satellites to convey signals from one location on Earth to another. By the 1960s, the United States was using satellites to transmit telephone and television signals across the Atlantic Ocean. Since then, the proliferation of this technology and reductions in its cost have made satellite transmission appropriate and available for transmitting consumer voice, video, music, and data.

Satellite Orbits

Most satellites circle the Earth 22,300 miles above the equator in a geosynchronous orbit. GEO (geosynchronous earth orbit) satellites orbit the Earth at the same rate as the Earth turns. A special case of geosynchronous orbit, called geostationary orbit (because it appears stationary from Earth), stays directly above the equator. This is especially common with communications satellites. Consequently, at every point in their orbit, the satellites maintain a constant distance from a specific point on the Earth's equator.

Satellites are generally used to relay information from one point on Earth to another. Information must first be transmitted to the satellite from Earth in an uplink from an Earth-based transmitter. Often, the uplink signal information is scrambled (in other words, its signal is encoded) before transmission to prevent unauthorized interception. At the satellite, a transponder receives the uplink signal, then transmits it to an Earth-based receiver in a downlink. Each satellite uses unique frequencies for its downlink. These frequencies, as well as the satellite's orbit location, are assigned and regulated by the FCC. Back on Earth, the downlink is picked up by a dish-shaped antenna. The dish shape concentrates the signal so that it can be interpreted by a receiver. Figure 9-27 provides a simplified view of satellite communication.

Geosynchronous earth orbiting satellites are the type used by the most popular satellite data service providers. This technology is well established, and it's the least expensive of all satellite technology. Also, because many of these satellites remain in a fixed position relative to the Earth's surface, stationary receiving dishes on Earth can be counted on to receive satellite signals reliably, weather permitting.

Satellite Internet Services

A handful of companies offer high-bandwidth Internet access via GEO satellite links. Each subscriber uses a small satellite antenna and receiver, or satellite modem, to exchange signals with the service provider's satellite network. Clients may be fixed, such as rural residents who are too remote for DSL, or mobile subscribers, such as travelers on ocean-going yachts.

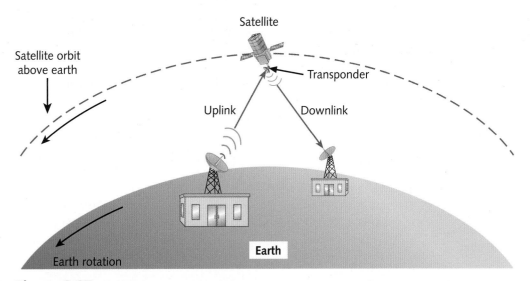

Figure 9-27 Satellite communication

Clients can exchange signals with satellites as long as they have a line-of-sight path from an unobstructed view of the sky. To establish a satellite Internet connection, each subscriber must have a fixed dish antenna, which is approximately 2 feet high by 3 feet wide (see Figure 9-28). In North America, these dish antennas are pointed toward the Southern Hemisphere (because many geosynchronous satellites travel over the equator). The dish antenna's receiver is connected via cable to a modem. This modem typically uses an Ethernet interface to connect with the subscriber's router or computer.

Andrey_Popov/Shutterstock.com

Figure 9-28   A small satellite dish provides Internet connection

As with several other wireless WAN technologies, satellite services are typically asymmetrical, and bandwidth is shared among many subscribers. Throughputs vary and are controlled by the service provider. Downlink speeds might reach 100 Mbps, while uplink rates are much slower. Compared with other wireless WAN options, satellite services are slower and suffer more latency. In addition, the inconsistent latency causes jitter problems, degrading signal quality. Given these drawbacks, satellite data service is preferred only in circumstances that allow few alternatives or in cases where satellite receiving equipment is already installed.

REMEMBER THIS...

- Explain cellular and satellite Internet options.
- Compare cellular technologies, including 3G, 4G, 5G, LTE, CDMA, and GSM.

SELF-CHECK

8. Which cellular generation was the first to offer speeds up to 1 Gbps?
   a. 2G
   b. 3G
   c. 4G-LTE
   d. 4G

9. Which wired WAN service offers speeds most comparable to the highest satellite Internet speeds in a similar price range?
   a. DSL
   b. Cable broadband
   c. Fiber broadband
   d. Leased fiber

Check your answers at the end of this module.

TROUBLESHOOTING CONNECTIONS

 **CERTIFICATION**

3.1 Given a scenario, use the appropriate statistics and sensors to ensure network availability.

5.3 Given a scenario, use the appropriate network software tools and commands.

5.5 Given a scenario, troubleshoot general networking issues.

Average reading time: 21 minutes

As a network administrator, one of your primary responsibilities is to keep connections within and between networks working well. With this in mind, there are steps you can take to troubleshoot a problem with a WAN connection before contacting your ISP, and there are preventive measures you can perform to avoid having the problem in the first place.

Internet Connectivity Issues

When you lose Internet connectivity, a little troubleshooting can help determine the location of the problem and the party responsible for repairing the connection. The following list presents some common issues to look for on your own equipment:

- **Interference**—Obviously, interference can cause problems with a wireless connection, and you have already learned that interference can wreak havoc with wired connections as well. Intermittent problems or problems that affect unrelated portions of a network are common indicators of interference issues.
- **DNS issues**—Correct DNS server information and a functioning DNS server are critical requirements for enabling Internet access. Computers can be programmed to use DNS servers on a corporate network or the ISP's DNS servers, or alternatively, they can be pointed to public DNS servers such as those run by Google or Cloudflare.
- **Router misconfiguration**—Routing tables with incorrect routes can result in dropped messages with no error feedback. Other router configuration issues to consider when Internet connectivity fails might include blocked ports that should be open, speed or duplex mismatches, incorrect IP address range or subnet mask, or an incorrect default gateway. Similarly, attackers can take advantage of some types of router misconfigurations that result in network failure due to an attack. You'll learn more about router security later in this course.
- **Interface error**—Misconfigured interfaces, such as an incorrect default gateway or missing DNS server addresses, can result in interface errors. One possible evaluation technique for bypassing an interface error, which will help confirm that the interface misconfiguration is the issue, is to switch to a different interface on the same device. For example, if your computer's wired connection is having problems, try connecting to the network using the computer's wireless interface.

Interface Problems

Interface problems can be challenging to track down. Several commands provide insights into device and interface performance, vulnerabilities, and misconfigurations that might be causing problems. A thorough device configuration review can often locate problems that don't necessarily generate symptoms pointing directly to their cause. On routers and switches, this requires checking overall device configuration as well as individual interface configurations. The following discussion focuses on Cisco devices so you can practice using these commands in Packet

Tracer. However, most other networking brands, such as Juniper and Huawei, use similar commands and modes to accomplish similar tasks.

With Cisco devices, recall that different commands are available depending on the mode you're in. For example, when you first start working with a router, you begin in the user EXEC mode. To step up to the privileged EXEC mode, you enter `enable`, which can also be abbreviated as simply `en`. Table 9-4 explains the most used modes on Cisco routers and switches.

Table 9-4   Cisco CLI modes

Mode	Default prompt on a router	Command to enter mode	Description
User EXEC	`Router>`	Login to device	Offers limited commands to evaluate current configurations without making changes to the configuration.
Privileged EXEC	`Router#`	`enable` or `en`	Typically requires a password and offers access to all EXEC commands, which provide tools for testing and helpful information about the current configurations. You can also run EXEC commands from other modes by prefacing the EXEC command with the `do` command.
Global configuration	`Router(config)#`	`configure terminal` or `conf t`	Allows device configuration changes and gives access to more specific configuration modes.
Interface configuration	`Router(config-if)#`	`interface` or `int`	Allows configuration changes to an interface. Specific configuration modes for features or protocols allow changes to configurations such as interfaces, DHCP, and routing. Configuration submodes and subsubmodes dig deeper into configuration options.

To take one step down from a higher mode into a lower mode, enter the `exit` command. From any higher mode, enter the `end` command or press Ctrl+Z to return to privileged EXEC mode.

show config

As you've seen in the Capstone Projects, when making a configuration change to a Cisco device, those changes are held in the running configuration file. You can see the device's running-config file with the command `show running-config` (or `sh run`). The output is likely several pages long. Use the following keys to navigate the output:

- Press Enter to move down one line at a time.
- Press the spacebar to move down one page at a time.
- Press Tab or the down arrow to exit the output.

The temporary running-config file is held in the device's RAM and is, therefore, reset when the device is restarted. To make your changes persist beyond a device's power cycle, you must copy the running-config file to the startup-config file with the command `copy running-config startup-config` (or `copy run start`).

The startup-config file is not stored in RAM but instead is stored in NVRAM, which persists through a power cycle. To see the device's stored startup-config file, enter the command `show startup-config` (or `sh start`).

show interface

Interface configuration, status, and statistics can all provide helpful information in troubleshooting a network connection problem. To get an overview of all the device's interfaces, enter the command `show interface` (or `sh int`). Figure 9-29 shows output for a Cisco router's interface that is connected to two VLANs on a switch.

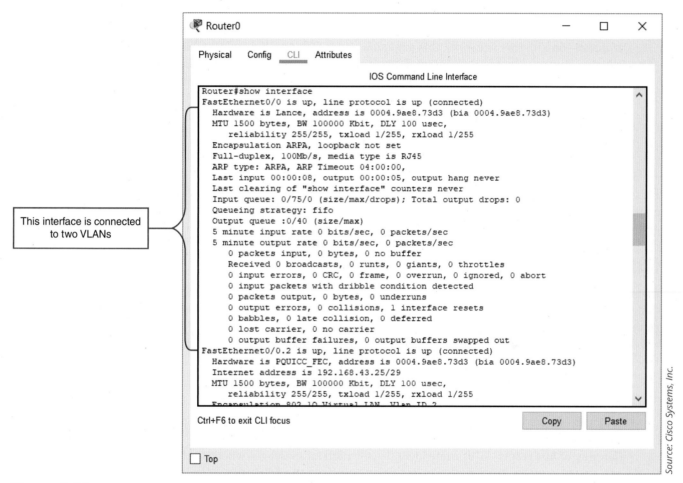

This interface is connected to two VLANs

Figure 9-29 A router's interface information

Notice the following information in this output:

- **Link state**—Indicates whether the interface is up or down. The first portion, FastEthernet0/0, refers to the physical layer: Is a physical cable connected to the interface? The second portion, line protocol, refers to the data link layer: Are basic protocols functioning properly across the link, such as clocking and framing? If the interface is "administratively down," it has been shut down using the `shutdown` command or has encountered a configured limitation, such as a security breach. Bring it back up using the `no shutdown` (or `no shut`) command.
- **MTU**—Indicates the maximum network-layer packet size the interface can support. The Ethernet standard MTU is 1500 bytes.
- **BW (bandwidth)**—Indicates the link's supported bandwidth, which is used by routing protocols to calculate best paths. The rest of the information on this line is also used for routing metrics, including delay, reliability, and load.

- **Encapsulation**—For Ethernet networks, the encapsulation value is always set to ARPA. The statement "loopback not set" does not refer to the loopback interface but to the interface's current mode. Loopback mode is sometimes used for testing.
- **Duplex and speed**—Indicates if the link is operating in full-duplex mode, the link's bandwidth (such as 100 Mbps), and the physical connection type (such as RJ-45).
- **Send and receive traffic statistics**—Interface statistics are tracked over time and can be cleared. Information here will indicate when the statistics were most recently reset. The next several lines indicate statistics that have been gathered since the most recent reset and include number of packets dropped due to queue overflow, average input and output rates, total number of packets and bytes received or sent by the system, and number of broadcast frames, runts, and giants received. **Runts** are messages that are too small and were dropped—on Ethernet networks, this minimum size is 64 bytes. Excessive collisions on a network can result in high numbers of runts being reported. **Giants** are frames that are too large, and these are also dropped. On Ethernet networks, this maximum frame size is usually 1518 bytes, although jumbo frames over this size might be supported. Excessive giants being reported is usually a result of misconfigurations. Additional statistics indicate the number of CRC errors. CRC (Cyclic Redundancy Checksum) confirms the data in a message has not been corrupted. A **CRC error** indicates messages are being damaged in transit, such as when there's a cable problem or a damaged NIC.

While the `show interface` command displays OSI layer 1 and 2 information, the `show ip interface` (or `sh ip int`) command focuses on detailed layer 3 information, such as IP addressing, helper address, accounting, compression, NAT, and many other settings. For a more concise list of interfaces, IP addresses, and interface status, enter the command `show ip interface brief` (or `sh ip int br`).

Routing Issues

Just as interfaces must be properly configured for network connections to work as expected, misconfigured routing tables also can cause problems for network connections. On a Cisco router, the `show ip route` command lists the router's routing table information, as shown in Figure 9-30.

The routing table lists several types of routes and other information about the routes. Some of the most used route types and information are described next:

- **C (connected)**—Networks directly connected to the router's own interfaces are classified as C (connected).
- **S (static)**—Static routes are manually configured by a network admin.
- **Protocol**—Codes identify the routing protocol used to configure the route, such as R (RIP), B (BGP), D (EIGRP), and O (OSPF).
- **Gateway of last resort**—This route identifies the path for messages when another route doesn't apply.

Common routing issues include the following:

- **Missing route**—If no matching route exists for a message, the message will be dropped. For this reason, a gateway of last resort should be configured to handle messages with no matching route. You can add a gateway of last resort using one of the following commands: `ip default-gateway` (used when no routing is configured on the router), `ip default-network` (requires that routing is configured on the router and chooses a classful default route from existing routes), or `ip route 0.0.0.0 0.0.0.0` (sets a default route for messages with no matching route in the routing table and requires that routing is configured on the router). A similar problem is caused when existing routes are not being advertised through routing protocols. As you'll see in a project at the end of this module, you need to identify which of its connected routes you want each router to advertise.
- **Routing loop**—Routing protocols can sometimes route messages continuously through the same paths without the message ever reaching its destination, which can negatively impact network performance. Making too many topology changes too quickly can cause this problem, as routers need time to adjust to each change. Distance-vector routing protocols reach convergence more slowly than other types of routing protocols. A conservative TTL (time-to-live) can ensure these stray packets are dropped after so many hops. Limitations can also be placed on the routers' ability to share their routing tables with neighbors so this sharing moves

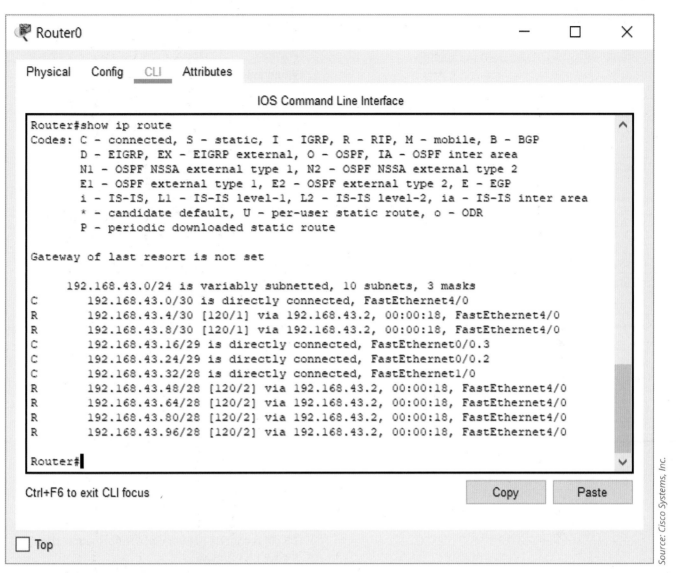

```
Router0                                                      —   □   ✕

 Physical   Config   CLI   Attributes

                        IOS Command Line Interface

Router#show ip route
Codes: C - connected, S - static, I - IGRP, R - RIP, M - mobile, B - BGP
       D - EIGRP, EX - EIGRP external, O - OSPF, IA - OSPF inter area
       N1 - OSPF NSSA external type 1, N2 - OSPF NSSA external type 2
       E1 - OSPF external type 1, E2 - OSPF external type 2, E - EGP
       i - IS-IS, L1 - IS-IS level-1, L2 - IS-IS level-2, ia - IS-IS inter area
       * - candidate default, U - per-user static route, o - ODR
       P - periodic downloaded static route

Gateway of last resort is not set

     192.168.43.0/24 is variably subnetted, 10 subnets, 3 masks
C       192.168.43.0/30 is directly connected, FastEthernet4/0
R       192.168.43.4/30 [120/1] via 192.168.43.2, 00:00:18, FastEthernet4/0
R       192.168.43.8/30 [120/1] via 192.168.43.2, 00:00:18, FastEthernet4/0
C       192.168.43.16/29 is directly connected, FastEthernet0/0.3
C       192.168.43.24/29 is directly connected, FastEthernet0/0.2
C       192.168.43.32/28 is directly connected, FastEthernet1/0
R       192.168.43.48/28 [120/2] via 192.168.43.2, 00:00:18, FastEthernet4/0
R       192.168.43.64/28 [120/2] via 192.168.43.2, 00:00:18, FastEthernet4/0
R       192.168.43.80/28 [120/2] via 192.168.43.2, 00:00:18, FastEthernet4/0
R       192.168.43.96/28 [120/2] via 192.168.43.2, 00:00:18, FastEthernet4/0

Router#

 Ctrl+F6 to exit CLI focus                          Copy        Paste

 □ Top
```

Source: Cisco Systems, Inc.

Figure 9-30   A router's routing table

outward from each router without old information looping back on itself—this is called a split horizon. Similarly, a routing timer ensures that all the routers in the system share their routing tables at the same time. This way, there's no question as to which routing table entry is the most recent when something has changed on the network.

- **Asymmetrical routing**—This is caused when messages going in one direction in a conversation (such as from a web server to a client) travel a different path than messages going in the other direction (such as from client to web server). While this is typically unavoidable (especially when using BGP on the Internet) and is not a problem, it can cause issues for NAT and for firewalls that need to see traffic in both directions of a conversation to properly apply filtering rules. Firewalls often rely on TCP sessions to approve outgoing traffic in response to approved incoming traffic. If some incoming traffic hits a different firewall than the one a server is configured to use for its outgoing messages, the firewall might incorrectly reject outgoing traffic that should have been approved. For organizations using multiple firewalls, thoughtful configuration of traffic flow and internal routing can be used to avoid problems with asymmetrical routing.

Table 9-5 summarizes commonly used Cisco commands for routers and switches, many of which you've used in the Packet Tracer projects in this course.

Table 9-5   Common Cisco commands

Command	Mode	Purpose
`?`	Any	When entered alone, outputs a list of available commands in the current mode. When entered after portions of a command, outputs a list of available parameters for that command. When entered after one or a few letters, outputs a list of commands beginning with those letters.
`show running-config` or `sh run`	Privileged EXEC	Displays the running-config file.
`copy running-config startup-config` or `copy run start`	Privileged EXEC	Copies the running configuration to the startup-config file.
`show mac address-table`	Privileged EXEC	Displays MAC address table on a switch.
`show vlan brief` or `sh vlan br`	Privileged EXEC	Displays a concise list of VLAN assignment information on a switch.
`show ip route` or `sh ip ro`	EXEC	Displays a router's routing table. Add parameters to specify types of routes, such as `show ip route rip`. Delete a route from the routing table with the command `clear ip route x.x.x.x` (where the last part lists the IP address of the target network you want to clear from the routing table).
`show ip protocol database`	Any	Displays a routing protocol's routing database on a router, such as `show ip rip database`.
`ip route destinationaddress subnetmask nexthopaddress`	Global configuration	Sets a static route on a router.
`show interface` or `sh int`	EXEC	Displays physical and data link layer information about a device's interfaces.
`show ip interface brief` or `sh ip int br`	EXEC	Displays concise network layer information about a device's interfaces.
`show interface trunk` or `sh int tr`	EXEC	Displays trunks configured on a switch.
`show interface switchport` or `sh int sw`	EXEC	Displays detailed VLAN configurations for each of a switch's interfaces.
`interface fastethernet0/0` or `int fa0/0`	Global configuration	Enters interface configuration mode for specified interface.
`ip address address subnet` or `ip addr address subnet`	Interface configuration	Sets IP information for an interface.
`no shutdown` or `no shut`	Interface configuration	Enables an interface. Similarly, `shutdown` will disable an interface.
`ip name-server dns1address dns2address`	Global configuration	Sets DNS server addresses.
`hostname`	Global configuration	Changes the device's name.

Applying Concepts 9-4: Internet Down

One evening, you're up late working to meet a fast-approaching deadline when suddenly your Internet connection fails. Much of your work requires Internet access for research, but you belay the panic for a few moments to evaluate the situation:

- You try a couple different websites in your browser, then open a different browser application and try a couple websites again. None of the sites will load.
- You check all the cable connections between your computer and your network's demarc. Everything looks normal.
- You power cycle the modem and router by unplugging both devices from the electrical outlet, waiting a few minutes, plugging in the modem, waiting for it to establish a connection with the ISP, and then plugging in the router.
- You check the Network Connections status on your computer and confirm that you have a functioning connection with your network.
- You try again to navigate to a website in your browser, but the page still won't load.
- You open a PowerShell window and ping one of Google's servers at 8.8.8.8. The ping works.
- You ping Google's website at *google.com*, but this time it doesn't work.
- You pull up an outage reporting website for your ISP on your smartphone and find that a few hundred other people have reported an outage in your area.

With a quick adjustment, you get your Internet service functioning again and continue with your work. Which of the following did you do and why?

a. You switched out the Ethernet cable connecting your modem to your router because the cable was damaged.

b. You used `ipconfig` to release the IP address on your computer and get a new one from your network's DHCP service because your computer had a duplicate IP address.

c. You changed the DNS settings on your router to point to Google's DNS servers instead of the DNS servers of your ISP because the ISP's DNS servers are down.

d. You switched to a different ISP because the former ISP's service was unreliable.

e. You replaced the router with a new router you had ready to go, knowing that the old router had already exceeded its life expectancy and had finally ceased to function.

f. You created an ad hoc network with another computer on your network and used that computer's access to the Internet to continue your research because the Wi-Fi radio on your computer had died and will need to be replaced.

g. You performed a factory reset on your modem so it would reinitiate a connection with the ISP.

h. You updated the default gateway on your computer because it was unable to communicate with the router.

i. You restarted your computer because Windows had updates that needed to be installed.

REMEMBER THIS...

- Use basic network platform commands, including show interface, show config, and show route.
- Analyze connection problems using interface information, including link state, speed/duplex, and traffic statistics.
- Troubleshoot common routing issues, including missing route, routing loop, and asymmetrical routing.

SELF-CHECK

10. Where is a router's hostname stored when you first change the name?
   a. Routing table
   b. Startup-config file
   c. Whitelist
   d. Running-config file

11. Which problem is most likely caused by a damaged cable?
   a. Routing loop
   b. CRC error
   c. Asymmetrical route
   d. Excessive giants

Check your answers at the end of this module.

You're Ready

You're now ready to complete **Project 9-4: Explore IOS Command Modes in Packet Tracer**, or you can wait until you've finished the Review Questions for this module.

You're Ready

After you finish the Hands-On Projects, you're ready to complete the **Module 9 Capstone Projects**.

MODULE SUMMARY

WAN Essentials

- A WAN traverses a significant distance and usually supports very high data throughput. Although many types of businesses need WANs, they might not need the same kinds of WANs.
- Typically, a CAN is a collection of LANs within a single property or nearby properties, such as buildings belonging to a school where all the buildings and most or all the network media spanning those connections are confined within land owned by the school. With a CAN, it's likely that a single organization (or group of organizations) owns all the connected LANs and most or all the networking media connecting those LANs.
- A MAN is a collection of LANs within a limited geographical area, such as a downtown area or even a city, county, or province. With MANs, many customers might own one or more of the connected LANs, and a single, third-party provider leases use of the networking media connecting these LANs. These connections often must be made across property not owned by either the MAN provider or the MAN customers. MAN connections might be made available to the general public, or it might be restricted to a single customer.
- A modem is a modulation/demodulation device that converts between digital and analog signals. The customer's endpoint device on a WAN is called the DTE (data terminal equipment), and the carrier's endpoint

device for the WAN is called the DCE (data circuit-terminating equipment). The NIU, also called NID (network interface device), at the demarc connects the ISP's local loop to the customer's network. A more intelligent version of an NIU is a smartjack, or INID (Intelligent NID), which can provide diagnostic information about the interface.

Routing Protocols

- A router joins two or more networks and passes packets from one network to another. Routers are responsible for determining the next network to which a packet should be forwarded on its way to its destination. Routers are often categorized according to their location on a network or the Internet and the routing protocols they use. The various categories include core routers, edge routers, and exterior routers.
- A routing table is a database that holds information about where hosts are located and the most efficient way to reach them. A router relies on its routing table to identify which network a host belongs to and which of the router's interfaces points toward the best next hop to reach that network. Routing paths are determined by static routes or dynamic routes, which are listed in the routing table. The route utility allows you to view a host's routing table.
- To determine the best path, routers communicate with each other through routing protocols. Routers rate the reliability and priority of a routing protocol's data based on AD (administrative distance), convergence time, and overhead.
- IGPs (interior gateway protocols) are routing protocols used by core routers and edge routers within autonomous systems. IGPs are often grouped according to the algorithms they use to calculate best paths, including distance-vector routing protocols, link-state routing protocols, and hybrid routing protocols. EGPs (exterior gateway protocols) are routing protocols used by edge routers and exterior routers to distribute data outside of autonomous systems. The only EGP protocol currently in use is BGP.
- The most popular routing protocols in use today include RIP (Routing Information Protocol) and RIPv2 (Routing Information Protocol, version 2), which are legacy protocols, and the link-state routing protocol OSPF (Open Shortest Path First), the similar IS-IS (Intermediate System to Intermediate System), Cisco's hybrid protocol EIGRP (Enhanced Interior Gateway Routing Protocol), and the Internet protocol BGP (Border Gateway Protocol).
- Three popular FHRPs (First Hop Redundancy Protocol) used by routers and layer 3 switches to provide a single VIP (Virtual IP) address as the default gateway to a network are VRRP (Virtual Router Redundancy Protocol), HSRP (Hot Standby Routing Protocol), and GLBP (Gateway Load Balancing Protocol).

WAN Connectivity

- Two categories of WAN connectivity services are broadband, where the cables (whether telephone, coaxial, or fiber) and available bandwidth are shared between multiple customers, and DIA (dedicated Internet access), where the cable or a portion of its available bandwidth is dedicated to a single customer.
- DSL (digital subscriber line) is a WAN connection method that operates over the PSTN (public switched telephone network), which is a network of lines and carrier equipment that provide landline telephone service to homes and businesses.
- Cable broadband (also called cable Internet or cable modem access) is based on the coaxial cable wiring used for TV signals, although in reality, much of the coaxial infrastructure has been replaced with fiber.
- To reduce the distance signals must travel over copper cables to reach customers, many ISPs use MONs (metropolitan optical networks) to offer FTTN (fiber-to-the-node), FTTH (fiber-to-the-home), or similar arrangements. A MON is a dense, localized grid of junctions and fiber cables that attempts to make direct fiber connections available to as many customers as possible while balancing the significant expense of replacing existing telephone and coaxial cable infrastructure with fiber equipment and fiber-optimized technologies.

- Leased lines provide dedicated bandwidth on fiber optic connections. The customer pays for a specific bandwidth (such as 2 Gbps) and reserves that bandwidth for their sole use without having to share it with other customers. Throughput won't fluctuate in response to traffic demands from other customers.
- MPLS (multiprotocol label switching) enables multiple types of layer 3 protocols to travel over any one of several connection-oriented layer 2 protocols. One of the characteristics that sets MPLS apart from other WAN technologies is its ability to support QoS traffic shaping across WAN connections.
- With a private-direct connection, or interconnection, to the cloud, you lease a dedicated line from your ISP to one of your cloud provider's PoPs, or colocation facilities. From there, you pay for the connection to the cloud provider's physical infrastructure and, usually, some kind of data transfer fees.
- SD-WAN (software-defined wide area network) relies on abstracted, centralized control of networking devices to manage network functions across a diverse infrastructure. SD-WAN offers the following benefits: transport agnostic, active-active load balancing, automatic failover, intent-based management, zero-touch provisioning, and reduced cost compared to services such as leased lines and MPLS.

Wireless WANs

- With 3G (third generation) cellular services, data rates rose to 384 Kbps. To switch to fully digital transmissions, two competing 2G technologies emerged as market leaders for 3G: GSM (Global System for Mobile Communications) and CDMA (Code Division Multiple Access).
- 4G (fourth generation) services are characterized by an all-IP network for both data and voice transmission. 4G standards, released in 2008, specify minimum throughputs of 100 Mbps with the goal of supporting 1 Gbps speeds. LTE (Long-Term Evolution) became an ambiguous marketing term that meant "faster than 3G but not really 4G." As hardware has improved, so have LTE speeds. Typical speeds now for LTE connections might reach 100 Mbps download and up to 75 Mbps upload. LTE-A (LTE-Advanced) can more realistically approach 4G standards. Sometimes misleadingly called 5G E (5G Evolution), LTE-A is basically true 4G as defined back in 2008 but only recently emerging in real-world networks.
- 5G (fifth generation) services require minimum speeds of 1 Gbps and max out at 20 Gbps download and 10 Gbps upload, however, actual speeds vary greatly. 5G relies on three frequency bands called low band, mid-band, and high band.
- Satellite Internet clients can exchange signals with satellites as long as they have a line-of-sight path from an unobstructed view of the sky. To establish a satellite Internet connection, each subscriber must have a fixed dish antenna pointed toward the sky over the equator. The dish antenna's receiver is connected via cable to a modem. As with several other wireless WAN technologies, satellite services are typically asymmetrical, and bandwidth is shared among many subscribers. Throughputs vary and are controlled by the service provider. Downlink speeds might reach 100 Mbps, while uplink rates are much slower.

Troubleshooting Connections

- When making a configuration change to a Cisco device, those changes are held in the running configuration file. You can see the device's running-config file with the command `show running-config` (or `sh run`).
- Interface configuration, status, and statistics can all provide helpful information in troubleshooting a network connection problem. To get an overview of all the device's interfaces, enter the command `show interface` (or `sh int`).
- Just as interfaces must be properly configured for network connections to work as expected, misconfigured routing tables also can cause problems for network connections. On a Cisco router, the `show ip route` command lists the router's routing table information.

Key Terms

For definitions of key terms, see the Glossary.

3G (third generation)
4G (fourth generation)
5G (fifth generation)
active-active redundancy
active-passive redundancy
AD (administrative distance)
AS (autonomous system)
asymmetrical
asymmetrical routing
bandwidth speed tester
best path
BGP (Border Gateway Protocol)
border router
broadband
cable broadband
cable modem
CDMA (Code Division Multiple Access)
cell site
convergence time
core router
CRC error
default route
DIA (dedicated Internet access)
distance-vector routing protocol
DOCSIS (Data Over Cable Service Interface Specifications)
DSL (digital subscriber line)
DSL modem

dynamic route
edge router
EGP (exterior gateway protocol)
EIGRP (Enhanced Interior Gateway Routing Protocol)
exterior router
FHRP (First Hop Redundancy Protocol)
gateway of last resort
giant
GSM (Global System for Mobile Communications)
HFC (hybrid fiber coaxial)
hybrid routing protocol
IGP (interior gateway protocol)
interconnection
interior router
IS-IS (Intermediate System to Intermediate System)
leased line
link-state routing protocol
local loop
long-haul connection
LTE (Long-Term Evolution)
LTE-A (LTE-Advanced)
modem
MON (metropolitan optical network)

MPLS (multiprotocol label switching)
OSPF (Open Shortest Path First)
overhead
private-direct connection
PSTN (public switched telephone network)
QoS (quality of service)
RIP (Routing Information Protocol)
RIPv2 (Routing Information Protocol, version 2)
route
routing cost
routing loop
routing metric
routing protocol
routing table
runt
SD-WAN (software-defined wide area network)
SIM (Subscriber Identity Module) card
smartjack
static route
symmetrical
TDMA (time division multiple access)

Review Questions

1. Which OSI layer is responsible for directing data from one LAN to another?
   a. Transport layer
   b. Network layer
   c. Data link layer
   d. Physical layer

2. What kind of route is created when a network administrator configures a router to use a specific path between nodes?
   a. Trace route
   b. Static route
   c. Default route
   d. Dynamic route

3. When a router can't determine a path to a message's destination, where does it send the message?
   a. Default gateway
   b. Routing table
   c. Administrative distance
   d. Gateway of last resort

4. A routing protocol's reliability and priority are rated by what measurement?
   a. Routing table
   b. MTU
   c. Latency
   d. AD

5. Which routing protocol does an edge router use to collect data to build its routing tables for paths across the Internet?
   a. RIPv2
   b. BGP
   c. OSPF
   d. IP

6. What is the lowest layer of the OSI model at which LANs and WANs support the same protocols?
   a. Layer 2
   b. Layer 3
   c. Layer 4
   d. Layer 5

7. What kind of device can monitor a connection at the demarc but cannot interpret data?
   a. Line driver
   b. CSU/DSU
   c. DTE
   d. Smartjack

8. What specifications define the standards for cable broadband?
   a. PSTN
   b. HFC
   c. FTTC
   d. DOCSIS

9. What method does a GSM network use to separate data on a channel?
   a. SIM
   b. CDMA
   c. TDMA
   d. TDM

10. Which of these cellular technologies offers the fastest speeds?
    a. 4G-LTE
    b. LTE-A
    c. CDMA
    d. GSM

11. Where is an MPLS label inserted into a message's headers?

12. What four functions do all routers perform?

13. What database does a router consult before determining the most efficient path for delivering a message?

14. Give three examples of routing metrics used by routers to determine the best of various available routing paths.

15. List three IGPs (interior gateway protocols).

16. How can you create a private and secure connection with your cloud network over the Internet?

17. List three transport methods that can be used to support an SD-WAN.

18. When you list a router's routing table, one of the routes is labeled with an S. Which routing protocol was used to create this route?

19. What command will ensure the configuration changes you made to a switch will persist after you restart the switch?

20. What device must be installed on a DSL network to protect the sound quality of phone calls?

Hands-On Projects

NOTE 9-5

Websites and applications change often. While the instructions given in these projects were accurate at the time of writing, you might need to adjust the steps or options according to later changes.

Note to Instructors and Students: A rubric is provided for evaluating student performance on these projects. Please see Appendix D.

Project 9-1: Create a Routing Table Entry in Windows

Estimated Time: 15 minutes

Objective: Given a scenario, use the appropriate network software tools and commands. (Obj. 5.3)

Resources:
- Windows computer with administrative access

Context: A computer's routing table can be viewed and modified using the `route` command in an elevated PowerShell or Command Prompt window. Complete the following steps:

1. On a Windows computer, you could use either `route print` or `netstat -r` to view the routing table. Because you'll need the `route` command to modify the routing table, open an elevated PowerShell or Command Prompt window and enter the **route print** command to view the routing table.

2. The list of interfaces on your computer should look familiar—you've seen this information before when you've run `ipconfig`. Several of the IPv4 routes on your routing table should look familiar as well. 127.0.0.1 is your loopback address, and the surrounding 127.x.y.z routes refer to reserved addresses in that domain. In Figure 9-31, you can see that this computer's IP address is 192.168.2.123. You can also see surrounding reserved addresses for that private domain, including the network ID and the broadcast address. This computer is also hosting a virtual network in VirtualBox with the network ID 192.168.56.0. 224.0.0.0 is reserved for multicasting, and 255.255.255.255 for certain broadcast messages. **Take a screenshot** of your computer's IPv4 Route Table and identify the local network connections in the output; submit this visual with your answers to this project's questions.

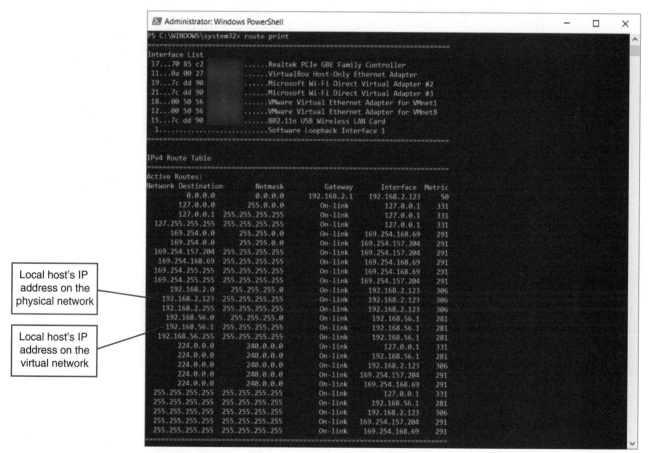

Figure 9-31   Several of the active routes on this computer involve its own IP addresses

In the IPv6 section on your route table, ::1/128 is the loopback address. FE80::/64 is the link local address, and an FE80::/128 address is the IPv6 address assigned to your computer. FF00::/8 is the multicast address.

Now you're ready to add an entry to the routing table. This route will send messages destined for the private network 172.16.50.0/24 to the private IP address 192.168.10.8. Complete the following steps:

3. Enter the following command:

   ```
   route add 172.16.50.0 mask 255.255.255.0 192.168.10.8
   ```

4. Now all messages generated by this routing table's local host and addressed to an IP address in the network 172.16.50.0/24 will instead be routed to a host at 192.168.10.8. You can see in Figure 9-32 where this new entry has been inserted in the IPv4 Route Table. Run **route print** again on your computer to confirm your entry was recorded. What metric was assigned to your static route?

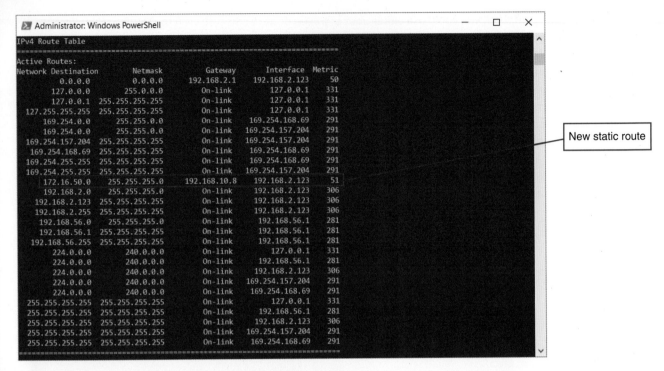

Figure 9-32   The static route has been successfully added

Windows resets its routing table during reboot, which means that if you restart your computer now, your static route will be lost. To make the static route persist beyond reboot, you would need to add the −p parameter after the word route in the command from Step 2 (see Figure 9-33). Instead, you can delete this route:

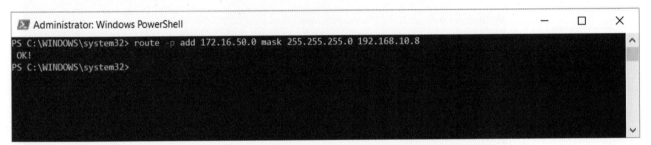

Figure 9-33   The -p parameter will ensure this route persists through reboot

5. Enter the following command:

```
route delete 172.16.50.0
```

Project 9-2: Create a Path MTU Black Hole

Estimated Time: 15 minutes
Objective: Compare and contrast the Open Systems Interconnection (OSI) model layers and encapsulation concepts. (Obj. 1.1)
Resources:
- Internet access

Context: When a router receives a message that is too large for the next segment's MTU, the router is supposed to respond with an ICMP error message to the sender. Sometimes, though, these error messages are not returned correctly. This can result in an MTU black hole along the path, where messages are being lost for no apparent reason.

You can use the `ping` command to determine the largest size message that can successfully traverse a path to its destination by adjusting the buffer size of the ICMP echo message. Using too large of a buffer will prevent the messages from returning in response to your ping. Start with a smaller buffer and work your way up to determine the largest MTU the route can handle. The ping parameters needed in Windows are –f (do not fragment the IP packet) and –l (packet length or buffer size is specified following the lowercase L).

What is the largest packet that can reach the *cengage.com* host from your computer without creating an MTU black hole? To find out, complete the following steps:

1. Ping *cengage.com* using an IP packet size of 1024. What is the ping command you used? Did it work?
2. Keep increasing the packet size until the packet does not return. Do not allow the packet to be fragmented. **Take a screenshot** showing your progression of attempts until you find the largest packet that successfully gets through; post this visual with your answers to this project's questions. What is the MTU for your route to the Cengage web servers?
3. What error message appears when an MTU error occurs?

Project 9-3: Create WAN Links in Packet Tracer

Estimated Time: 30 minutes

Objective: Compare and contrast various devices, their features, and their appropriate placement on the network. (Obj. 2.1)

Resources:

- Packet Tracer

Context: This Packet Tracer project starts with a new network and is *not* intended to build on your Packet Tracer network for the Capstone Projects. For this project, do *not* use your existing Packet Tracer network (most recently worked on in Module 8)—you'll come back to that network file in this module's Capstone Projects. In this project, start with a new Packet Tracer file to experiment with WAN links. You will *not* need to save this network for future projects or modules.

You can create several kinds of WAN connections in Packet Tracer. In this project, you'll keep the topology simple so you can see the process instead of getting mired in the details. You'll create DSL connections between two networks and a web server, which will host your own web page. Complete the following steps:

1. Open Packet Tracer and add the following devices to your workspace, as shown in Figure 9-34:
   a. Two **PCs**
   b. One **Server**
   c. Two **PT-Switches**
   d. Two **DSL Modems** (from the Network Devices > WAN Emulation group)
   e. One **PT-Cloud** (from the Network Devices > WAN Emulation group)
2. Configure the Server with the following information:
   a. Static IP address: **192.168.2.10/24**
   b. Default Gateway: **192.168.2.1**
   c. DNS server: **192.168.2.10**
3. Configure the services you need on the Server. On the **Services** tab, click **DHCP**. Add the following information:
   a. DNS server: **192.168.2.10**
   b. Start IP address: **192.168.2.100**
   c. Subnet mask: **255.255.255.0**
   d. Maximum Number of Users: **50**
4. Click **Save** and then turn the DHCP service **On**.
5. Click **DNS**, configure the following information, click **Add** to create the new A record, and then turn **On** the DNS service:
   a. Name: **www.cengage.com**
   b. Address: **192.168.2.10**

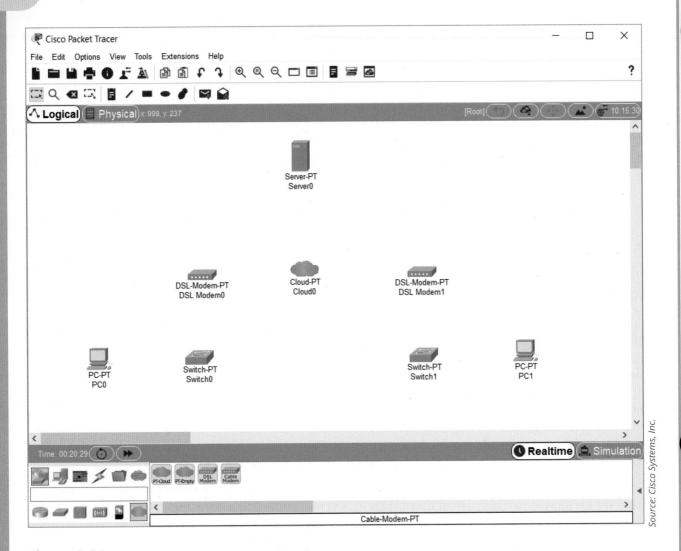

Source: Cisco Systems, Inc.

Figure 9-34   Add these devices to your network

6. Click **HTTP**. Next to the index.html file, click **(edit)**. As shown in Figure 9-35, delete the line that says *Welcome to Cisco Packet Tracer. Opening doors to new opportunities. Mind Wide Open*. Replace that text with your own message, such as **Welcome to Jill West's web page!!** (using your own name, of course). Click **Save** and then click **Yes**. Close the Server's configuration window.

7. Add and configure interfaces on the cloud. Click the **Cloud**. Turn off the physical device (scroll to the right to view the Power button if necessary). Drag one **PT-CLOUD-NM-1CFE** module to an available slot. Turn the physical device back on.

8. Click the **Config** tab and click **DSL**. At the top under DSL, make sure **Modem4** and **FastEthernet8** are selected for the ports and click **Add**. Then select **Modem5** and **FastEthernet8** and click **Add** again. Close the Cloud's configuration window.

9. Configure each PC to use **DHCP**.

10. Connect each PC to its Switch using a **Copper Straight-Through** cable.

11. Connect each Switch to its DSL Modem using a **Copper Cross-Over** cable. Use **FastEthernet** ports on the Switches, and **Port 1** on each Modem.

12. Connect each Modem to the Cloud using a **Phone** cable. On the Cloud, connect to the **Modem** ports.

13. Connect the Cloud to the Server using a **Copper Straight-Through** cable.

14. Once all ports are up, wait a couple of minutes and then confirm that each PC received an IP address. What IP address did PC0 get? What about PC1?

15. On each PC, ping the Server. What command did you use? Does it work? If not, troubleshoot the problem.

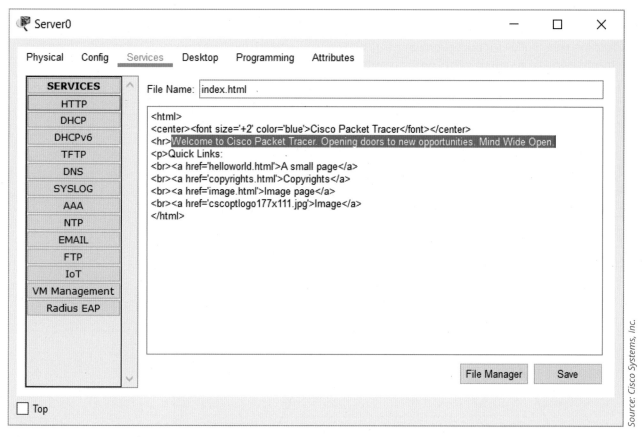

Figure 9-35   Replace this text with your own

16. On one PC, ping **www.cengage.com**. What command did you use? Does it work? If not, troubleshoot the problem.
17. On one PC, open a web browser and navigate to **www.cengage.com**.
18. **Take a screenshot** of the web page showing your custom text; submit this visual with your answers to this project's questions.
19. Save your Packet Tracer network for future reference if desired. Make some notes on your Wikidot website about your activities in this project.

Note to instructors: A Packet Tracer solution file is provided for each Packet Tracer project through the Instructors site.

Project 9-4: Explore IOS Command Modes in Packet Tracer

Estimated Time: 45 minutes
Objective: Given a scenario, use the appropriate network software tools and commands. (Obj. 5.3)
Resources:
- Packet Tracer

Context: This Packet Tracer project starts with a new network and is *not* intended to build on your Packet Tracer network for the Capstone Projects. For this project, do *not* use your existing Packet Tracer network (most recently worked on in Module 8)—you'll come back to that network file in this module's Capstone Projects. In this project, start with a new Packet Tracer file to experiment with IOS command modes. You will *not* need to save this network for future projects or modules.

The command modes in Cisco's IOS (Internetwork Operating System) provide structure to types of commands you can use as well as offering the opportunity to define hierarchical access to networking devices. For example, you might want to give a new technician the ability to see routes on a router but not to make configuration changes to the router. With command modes, you can configure different passwords at different levels to manage this access (which you'll do in a later module). It can be confusing at first to remember which modes allow which commands. To explore commands available in various modes on Cisco switches and routers, complete the following steps:

1. Open Packet Tracer and add the following devices to your workspace, as shown in Figure 9-36:
   a. Two **PCs**
   b. Two **PT-Switches**
   c. Two **PT-Routers**

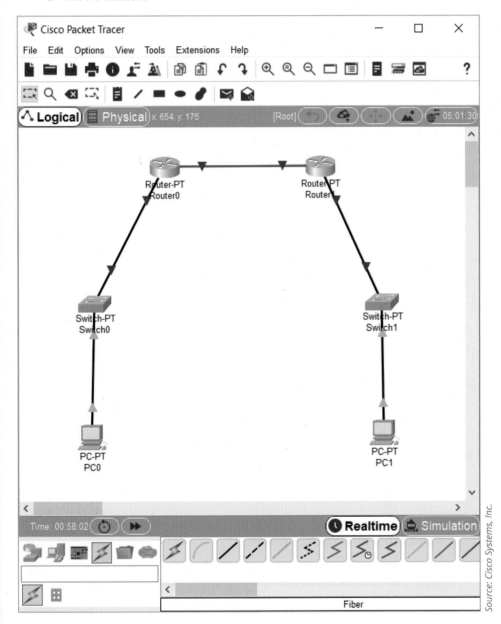

Figure 9-36 Network for exploring IOS modes

2. Connect all the devices as shown in Figure 9-36.
3. Configure static IP addresses on the routers and PCs. Place each PC in its router's LAN with the router's interface as the default gateway.
4. Document your configurations in your workspace. When you're finished, **take a screenshot** of your network with its IP addressing documentation; submit this visual with your answers to this project's questions.

5. Confirm that each PC can ping its default gateway. If they can't, troubleshoot and fix the problem. What corrections did you have to make?

6. Access Switch0's CLI. What mode are you in when you first access the CLI? How do you know?

7. Enter **?** to see more information. What commands can you enter in this mode?

8. Enter **enable**. What does the prompt look like now? What mode is this?

9. View the running configuration. What command did you enter?

10. Notice the switch's current hostname in the output. Change the hostname to a name of your choice. What commands did you enter? What does the prompt look like now?

11. What mode are you in now? How do you know?

12. Without changing modes, enter a command to list the switch's physical and data link interface information. What command did you enter?

13. Scan through the command's output. Which two interfaces are up?

14. Enter interface configuration mode for one of those interfaces. What command did you enter?

15. What does the prompt look like now? What mode are you in?

Currently, your PCs cannot ping each other because there are no routes configured on your routers. Complete the following steps:

16. Enter Router0's CLI. Enter the command **show ip route**. What routes are currently configured on this router? Does this router know about the second LAN?

17. You can give each router a static route so it can find the other router's LAN. What mode do you need to access to do this?

18. Enter **enable** and then enter **configure terminal**.

19. To add the static route, enter the command **ip route** *destinationaddress netmask nexthopaddress*. For example, if your second LAN's network address is 192.168.10.0/24 and your Router0 is connected to Router1's interface at 172.16.20.3/24 (as shown in Figure 9-37), you would enter the command **ip route 192.168.10.0 255.255.255.0 172.16.20.3**.

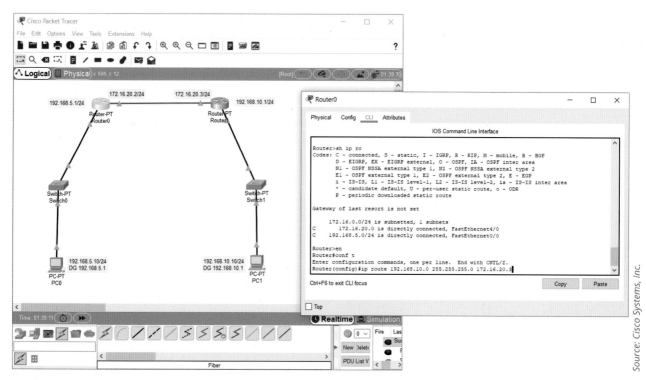

Figure 9-37   Each static route will point one router to the other router's LAN

Source: Cisco Systems, Inc.

20. Check your routing table again to ensure the new route was added. **Take a screenshot of the output**; submit this visual with your answers to this project's questions.
21. You'll also need a static route on Router1 to Switch0's LAN. Repeat Steps 18 and 19 on Router1.
22. Ping from PC0 to PC1. Does it work? If not, troubleshoot the problem and fix it. What corrections did you have to make?
23. Save your Packet Tracer network for future reference if desired. Make some notes on your Wikidot website about your activities in this project.

Note to instructors: A Packet Tracer solution file is provided for each Packet Tracer project through the Instructors site.

Capstone Projects

NOTE 9-6

Websites and applications change often. While the instructions given in these projects were accurate at the time of writing, you might need to adjust the steps or options according to later changes.

Note to Instructors and Students: A rubric is provided for evaluating student performance on these projects. Please see Appendix D.

Capstone Project 9-1: Configure RIP on Routers in Packet Tracer

Estimated Time: 30 minutes
Objective: Compare and contrast routing technologies and bandwidth management concepts. (Obj. 2.2)
Resources:
- Computer with Cisco Packet Tracer installed
- Access to the Packet Tracer network created in Capstone Project 8-2
- Storage space for Packet Tracer network file to be accessed in later projects and modules

Context: This Capstone Project picks up where Capstone Project 8-2 left off. In this project, you'll configure dynamic routing across your network using RIPv2. Currently, your PCs can't communicate beyond their own LAN. A routing protocol will enable connections across multiple LANs. Complete the following steps:

1. Determine which PCs can talk to each other. Test the following pings:
   a. From PC0, ping PC1. Does it work?
   b. From PC0, ping any of Router3's interfaces. Does it work?
   c. From PC0, ping any of Router2's interfaces. Does it work?
   d. From PC0, ping PC6. Does it work?
2. **Take a screenshot** of your Packet Tracer network and mark all the devices PC0 can successfully ping; submit this visual with your answers to this project's questions.
3. Click **Router0**. In Router0's CLI, enter the commands listed in Table 9-6.

Table 9-6   Configure RIPv2 on each router

Command	Purpose
`enable`	Enters privileged EXEC mode
`configure terminal`	Enters global configuration mode
`router rip`	Enables RIP
`version 2`	Specifies RIPv2, which is required to support classless routing
`network 192.168.43.0`	Specifies connected network to advertise—all networks directly connected to the router must be listed to be included in RIPv2 routing tables
`network 192.168.43.16`	Specifies connected network to advertise
`network 192.168.43.24`	Specifies connected network to advertise
`network 192.168.43.32`	Specifies connected network to advertise
`exit`	Returns to global configuration mode
`exit` and press **Enter**	Returns to privileged EXEC mode
`show ip route rip`	Displays routing table entries learned through RIP
`copy run start` and press **Enter**	Saves the current settings

4. Repeat the commands listed in Table 9-6 for each of the routers, substituting the network addresses directly connected to each router. For example, for Router1, you'll list the network addresses 192.168.43.4, 192.168.43.48, and 192.168.43.64.

5. As RIP is enabled on each router, the router learns of the routes connected to it. To see the routes learned by Router3, enter the command `show ip route rip`. How many routes has Router3 learned through RIP?

6. Determine which PCs can talk to each other. Test the following pings:
   a. From PC0, ping PC1. Does it work?
   b. From PC0, ping any of Router3's interfaces. Does it work?
   c. From PC0, ping any of Router2's interfaces. Does it work?
   d. From PC0, ping PC6. Does it work?

7. **Take a screenshot** of your Packet Tracer network and mark all the devices PC0 can successfully ping; submit this visual with your answers to this project's questions.

8. Save this Packet Tracer file in a safe place for future projects.

9. Make some notes on your Wikidot website about your activities in **Packet Tracer** for this project. When you're finished, close Packet Tracer or continue to Capstone Project 9-2.

Note to instructors: A Packet Tracer solution file is provided for each Packet Tracer project through the Instructors site. Some Packet Tracer projects build on earlier Packet Tracer networks. If needed for one or more students, you can provide a previous project's solution file as a start file for one of these progression projects.

Capstone Project 9-2: Sabotage and Repair Interfaces in Your Packet Tracer Network

Estimated Time: 45 minutes (+20 minutes for group work, if assigned)

Objective: Given a scenario, troubleshoot general networking issues. (Obj. 5.5)

Group Work: This project includes enhancements when assigned as a group project.

Resources:

- Computer with Cisco Packet Tracer installed
- Access to the Packet Tracer network created in Capstone Project 9-1
- Storage space for Packet Tracer network file to be accessed in later projects and modules

Context: This Capstone Project picks up where Capstone Project 9-1 left off. In this project, you'll experiment with commands covered in this module to troubleshoot network problems. The commands covered in this module are intended to help you identify and correct device configuration problems. To do this, you'll need to remember what commands are available to you and understand how and when to use them. Complete the following steps:

1. In Packet Tracer, open your Packet Tracer file from Capstone Project 9-1. Take a few moments to document your current configurations. For example, make sure that all your notes in your workspace match the actual configurations of your switches, routers, and PCs. Test your pings and make sure everything works.
2. Save a copy of your Packet Tracer file so you'll have a master file you can check as changes are made to your test file. What is the name of your master file?
3. Table 9-7 lists a variety of ways you might create a problem on your network. For each problem listed, complete the change to sabotage your network.

Table 9-7   Network problems and solutions

Problem	Symptoms	Test	Solution
Change IP address			
Change subnet mask			
Change default gateway			
Change VLAN			
Change port mode (i.e., access or trunk)			
Delete VLAN			
Shut down port			
Require DHCP with no DHCP server			
Disable RIP			
Move cable to wrong port			
Remove physical module			
Power down device			

4. Experiment to see how you might experience the problem on the network (such as a disabled connection, poor network performance, or failed ping). What symptoms might users of the network notice and report? Complete the Symptoms column in Table 9-7 for this problem.
5. Identify what test would diagnose the source of that problem. For example, the `show vlan` command would help you identify a missing or misconfigured VLAN, and the `show ip route` command would help you identify a missing or misconfigured route. What test successfully identified the problem? Complete the Test column in Table 9-7 for this problem.
6. Repair the problem and confirm the network is functioning as expected. How did you repair the problem? Complete the Solution column in the table for this problem.
7. Repeat Steps 3 through 6 for each problem listed in Table 9-7. Fill in the table as you go. When you're finished, **take a screenshot of your completed table**; submit this visual with your answers to this project's questions.
8. **For group assignments:** Trade computers with a team member. Using Table 9-7 as a reference, choose a problem and sabotage your teammate's network. Then go back to your own network and identify the problem your teammate instituted. Document the symptoms and the tests you used to identify the problem and then fix the problem. What problem did you find and how did you fix it? Repeat this process for two more problems.
9. Retest your network to ensure all PCs can ping each other. Confirm all devices are configured correctly. As needed, refer to your notes from Step 1.
10. Save this Packet Tracer file in a safe place for future projects.
11. Make some notes on your Wikidot website about your activities in Packet Tracer for this project. When you're finished, close **Packet Tracer**.

Note to instructors: A Packet Tracer solution file is provided for each Packet Tracer project through the Instructors site. Some Packet Tracer projects build on earlier Packet Tracer networks. If needed for one or more students, you can provide a previous project's solution file as a start file for one of these progression projects.

Solutions to Self-Check Questions

WAN Essentials

1. Which network type supports long-haul connections between ISPs?

Answer: a. WAN

Explanation: A **WAN (wide area network)** traverses a significant distance and usually supports very high data throughput, such as the long-haul connections between ISPs across hundreds of miles to support the Internet backbone. LANs (local area networks) connect nodes, such as workstations, servers, printers, and other devices, in a small geographical area on a single organization's network. CANs (campus area networks) and MANs (metropolitan area networks) also connect LANs. Typically, a CAN is a collection of LANs within a single property or nearby properties. Similarly, a MAN is a collection of LANs within a limited geographical area where a single, third-party provider leases use of the networking media connecting these LANs.

Routing Protocols

2. Which routing protocol runs between your network's edge router and your ISP's edge router?

Answer: d. BGP

Explanation: **BGP (Border Gateway Protocol)** spans multiple autonomous systems and is used by edge and exterior routers on the Internet.

3. Which command will output your Windows computer's routing table?

Answer: b. `route print`

Explanation: The `route print` command can be used to view a Windows computer's routing table and to add or delete static routes. On Linux or UNIX systems, use the command `route`. On a Cisco device, use the command `show ip route`.

4. Which routing protocol is limited to 15 hops?

Answer: d. RIPv2

Explanation: The 15-hop limit is specific to RIP and **RIPv2**. This is an identifying factor you can use to distinguish RIP from other routing protocols, such as BGP, OSPF, and EIGRP.

WAN Connectivity

5. You just moved into a rural office space that has telephone service but no cable. Which WAN service could you use without needing to install new wiring to your location?

Answer: b. DSL

Explanation: **DSL (digital subscriber line)** operates over the PSTN (public switched telephone network), which is a network of lines and carrier equipment that provide landline telephone service to homes and businesses. Cable broadband uses the coaxial cable wiring used for TV signals. Fiber broadband and leased fiber both require fiber cables, although it's possible there could be a fiber broadband service that reaches a nearby node, which then runs over the phone lines for the final stretch to the office's location.

6. Which of these WAN services is backed by an SLA?

Answer: b. Leased line

Explanation: **Leased line** performance is backed by SLA-enforced uptime, repair time, and possibly backup options. DSL, cable, and fiber broadband all rely on a "best-effort" service level to provide *up to* the advertised bandwidth, and actual performance varies considerably during busy usage.

7. Which WAN service offers active-active load balancing?

Answer: c. SD-WAN

Explanation: An **SD-WAN (software-defined wide area network)** managed network offers active-active load balancing where it can choose the best physical WAN connection for different types of traffic according to traffic prioritization and current network conditions. DSL, cable, and fiber broadband all offer "best-effort" service over a single connection to the ISP.

Wireless WANs

8. Which cellular generation was the first to offer speeds up to 1 Gbps?

Answer: d. 4G

Explanation: **4G** standards, released in 2008, specify minimum throughputs of 100 Mbps with the goal of supporting 1 Gbps speeds. Typical speeds for 4G-LTE connections might reach 100 Mbps download and up to 75 Mbps upload, with 2G and 3G running even slower.

9. Which wired WAN service offers speeds most comparable to the highest satellite Internet speeds in a similar price range?

Answer: b. Cable broadband

Explanation: **Cable broadband** service is typically offered at asymmetric speeds, such as up to 70 Mbps download and 7 Mbps upload, although later DOCSIS standards are capable of higher speeds. This is similar to satellite Internet's advertised speeds reaching up to 100 Mbps. DSL is significantly slower, maxing out around 52 Mbps. Fiber broadband and leased fiber both offer speeds well over 1 Gbps.

Troubleshooting Connections

10. Where is a router's hostname stored when you first change the name?

Answer: d. Running-config file

Explanation: When making a configuration change to a Cisco device such as changing its hostname, those changes are held in the **running-config file**. To make your changes persist beyond a device's power cycle, you must copy the running-config file to the startup-config file. A routing table is a database that holds information about where hosts are located and the most efficient way to reach them. CDMA networks do not require a SIM card in a cellular device because devices are compared against a whitelist, which is a database of subscribers that contains information on their subscriptions with the provider.

11. Which problem is most likely caused by a damaged cable?

Answer: b. CRC error

Explanation: A **CRC (Cyclic Redundancy Checksum) error** indicates messages are being damaged in transit, such as when there's a cable problem or a damaged NIC. A routing loop can be caused by making too many topology changes too quickly. Asymmetrical routing is caused when messages going in one direction in a conversation (such as from a web server to a client) travel a different path than messages going in the other direction (such as from client to web server). Giants are frames that are too large and they are dropped; excessive giants being reported is usually a result of misconfigurations.

RISK MANAGEMENT

After reading this module and completing the exercises, you should be able to:

1. Identify people, technology, and malware security risks to a network
2. Increase network security through risk assessment and management
3. Use physical security to prevent and detect intrusions
4. Implement device hardening techniques
5. Explain how security policies guide users' activities on a network

On the Job

Security often involves synthesizing tidbits of information from many disparate sources to form an accurate picture of what has happened. My team once responded to a report that desktop computers at a biomedical corporation were crashing. Their hard drives had been erased, apparently, by a virus that circumvented the company's antivirus protections.

While examining an affected PC, we noticed that a few processes were still running—thanks to the fact that the operating system generally won't allow the deletion of files that are in use. Among these processes were several instances of svchost.exe. Closer examination revealed that one of these had the same name as the legitimate Windows executable, but was in fact an impostor: A saboteur was at work.

Using a disassembler, we determined that the Trojan checked a folder on a server every minute for the presence of a command file. It would then execute the contents of the command file. We built a program to monitor that directory and archive copies of any files that appeared; our program also recorded the user account that put the file there and the name of the system from which this was done.

The account had domain administrator privileges, and this led us to examine the domain's logon scripts, where we found the code that installed the Trojan on users' workstations. We wrote a second program to record the MAC address of the system when it registered its name with the DHCP server and inspect the ARP tables from the network's switches to find the physical port to which it was connected. Then, with a building wiring diagram, we were able to track the culprit to a specific cubicle.

Finding the source of this problem involved knowledge about network infrastructure, operating systems, administration techniques, programming, and reverse engineering. This is an extreme example, to be sure, but real-world security problems seldom confine themselves to a single technical area of specialization.

Peyton Engel
Technical Architect, CDW Corporation

In the early days of computing, when secured mainframes acted as central hosts and data repositories were accessed only by dumb terminals with limited rights, network security was all but unassailable. As networks have become more geographically distributed and heterogeneous, however, the risk of their misuse has increased astronomically. Consider the largest, most heterogeneous network in existence: the Internet. Because it contains billions of points of entry, millions of servers, and billions of miles of transmission paths, it leads to millions of attacks on private networks every day. The threat of an outsider accessing an organization's network via the Internet, and then stealing or destroying data, is very real.

In this module, you will learn about numerous threats to your network's data and infrastructure, how to manage those vulnerabilities, and, perhaps most important, how to convey the importance of network security to the rest of your organization through an effective security policy. Later, you'll continue your study of network security and go behind the scenes with ways to secure network access and activity. If you choose to specialize in network security, consider attaining CompTIA's Security+ certification, which requires deeper knowledge of the topics covered in this course.

SECURITY RISKS

✓ CERTIFICATION

3.2 Explain the purpose of organization documents and policies.

4.1 Explain common security concepts.

4.2 Compare and contrast common types of attacks.

4.5 Explain the importance of physical security.

Average reading time: 36 minutes

The exact nature of security risks varies widely for different types of organizations. For example, if you work for a large savings and loan institution that allows its clients to view their current loan status online, you must consider risks associated with data and access. If someone obtains unauthorized access to your network, all your customers' personal financial data could be vulnerable. On the other hand, if you work for a local car wash that uses its internal LAN only to track assets and sales, you may be less concerned if someone gains access to your network because the implications of unauthorized access or use of sensitive data, called a **data breach**, are less dire. When considering security risks, the fundamental questions are "What is at risk?" and "What do I stand to lose if it is stolen, damaged, or eradicated?"

To understand how to manage network security, you first need to know how to identify threats to your network. And to do that, you must be familiar with the terms coined by network security experts to help in identifying specific risks and protective measures. A **hacker**, in the original sense of the word, is someone who masters the inner workings of computer hardware and software to better understand them. To be called a hacker used to be a compliment, reflecting extraordinary computer skills. Today, *hacker* is used more generally to describe individuals who gain unauthorized access to systems or networks with or without malicious intent. Hacking might also refer to finding a creative way around a problem, increasing functionality of a device or program, or otherwise manipulating resources beyond their original design, and has even come to be used in reference to noncomputer-related scenarios, such as *life hacking* or *guitar hacks*.

Hackers are categorized according to their intent and the prior approval of the organizations whose networks they're hacking. Consider the following categories:

- **White hat hacker**—These IT security experts are hired by organizations to assess the company's security and risks. They're sometimes called ethical hackers because their goal is to identify security vulnerabilities the organization needs to resolve for its own protection. The scope of this hacking is usually clearly defined in a written contract before testing begins, and hacking activities are limited by existing laws and restrictions. At no point is private data compromised outside of that trusted relationship.

- **Black hat hacker**—These groups or individuals use their skills to bypass security systems with the intent to cause damage, steal data, or compromise privacy. They're not concerned with legal restrictions, and their goal is to achieve personal gain or execute a personal agenda against an individual or organization. Some black hat hackers and groups are also available for hire to serve someone else's agenda.

- **Gray hat hacker**—These hackers abide by a code of ethics all their own. Although they might engage in illegal activity, their intent is to educate and assist. For example, a computer hobbyist who hacks a local business's weak Wi-Fi password—and then reports that weakness to the business owners without damaging or stealing the company's data—has engaged in gray hat hacking. Gray hats are vulnerable to legal prosecution and, therefore, often go to great lengths to remain anonymous.

As you can see, while hackers' motivations can vary from malicious to beneficial, the goal of hacking is to find weaknesses in the security system. A weakness of a system, process, or architecture that could lead to compromised information or unauthorized access is known as a **vulnerability**. The act of taking advantage of a vulnerability is known as an **exploit**. For example, Figure 10-1 shows an intruder climbing over a low fence. The low fence is a vulnerability. The act of breaching that fence is an exploit and is also a crime. For a more technical example, recall that an unauthorized access point can act as an evil twin. Once unsuspecting clients associate with such access points, the hacker can steal data in transit or access information on the client's system. The evil twin masquerades as a valid access point, using the same SSID (service set identifier) and potentially other identical settings. In other words, the evil twin is an *exploit* that takes advantage of a *vulnerability* inherent in wireless communications in which SSIDs are openly broadcast and Wi-Fi clients scan for connections.

PK Studio/Shutterstock.com

Figure 10-1   Vulnerability versus exploit

Cybersecurity vulnerabilities are often made public, in which case they are tracked by The MITRE Corporation in the **CVE (Common Vulnerabilities and Exposures)** dictionary. This project is funded by the U.S. Department of Homeland Security. The list is free to access, use, and analyze, but only MITRE can make changes to it. While the CVE doesn't contain details of the vulnerabilities themselves, it does provide a tracking system that is used by vulnerability databases. Each vulnerability receives a standardized identifying number, which makes it easier to track vulnerabilities across systems. You can learn more about the CVE and download your own copy at *cve.mitre.org*.

A **zero-day exploit**, or zero-day attack, is one that takes advantage of a software vulnerability that hasn't yet or has only very recently become public. Zero-day exploits are particularly dangerous because the vulnerability is exploited before the software developer can provide a solution for it or before the user applies the published solution. For example, Microsoft schedules regular security updates to Windows on the second (and sometimes fourth) Tuesday of each month, called Patch Tuesday (see Figure 10-2). Hackers can use this information to identify recently announced vulnerabilities in Windows and then immediately proceed to attack unpatched machines. Due to the quick timing of these attacks, the day after Patch Tuesday is informally dubbed Exploit Wednesday. Most current vulnerabilities, however, are well known. Throughout this module, you will learn about several kinds of exploits and how to prevent or counteract security threats.

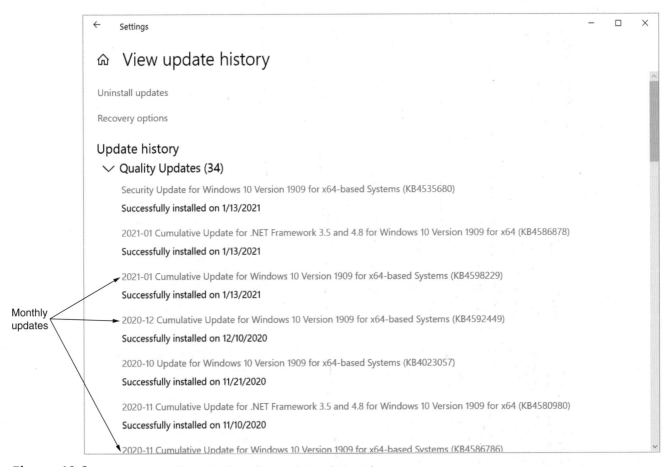

Figure 10-2   Updates installed the day after each Patch Tuesday

As you read about each vulnerability, think about whether it applies to your network (and if so, how damaging it might be), how an exploit of the vulnerability could be prevented, and how it relates to other security threats. Keep in mind that malicious and determined intruders may use one technique, which then allows them to use a second technique, which then supports a third technique, and so on. For example, a hacker might discover someone's username by watching them log on to the network. The hacker might then use a password-cracking program to access the network and plant a small program file. This code, when activated, generates an extraordinary volume of traffic that overwhelms and disables the network. None of the risks discussed in this module stand alone. Any risk can open the door to further exploitation.

People Risks

By some estimates, human error, ignorance, and omission cause more than half of all security breaches sustained by networks. Human error alone accounts for so many security breaches because taking advantage of people is often an easy way to circumvent network security. End-user awareness and training can be a monumental task that requires regular attention and due diligence. Ultimately, it is the company's responsibility to ensure that its employees adhere to applicable standards and policies. An uninformed employee's inadvertent missteps that cause a data breach can result in extreme litigation expenses for a company.

One of the most common methods by which an intruder gains access to a network is to simply ask users for their passwords. As bold as this might sound, it's not uncommon for an intruder to pose as a technical support analyst who needs to know a user's password to troubleshoot a problem. This strategy is called social engineering because it involves manipulating social relationships to gain access. Common types of social engineering include the following:

- Phishing—Communication that appears to come from a legitimate source and requests access or authentication information. For example, a hacker might send an email asking you to submit your username and password to a website whose link is provided in the message, claiming that it's necessary to verify your account, a purchase, or other account information. Phishing emails are extremely effective, especially the more sophisticated ones. When well-executed, these emails can trick even a savvy IT security professional. For example, the phishing email shown in Figure 10-3 appears to come from Chase, a credit card company. If the victim has a Chase card, they might decide they at least need to read the email to find out if it's real. The email creates a sense of urgency by saying the receiver's credit card might have been compromised. The logo and formatting give the email a sense of formality, which implies authority. The seeming detail in the alleged charge gives a sense of credibility to build trust. However, further investigation reveals this email to be a scam. Notice the cursor in the figure is floating over the red button, revealing the button's target address in the lower left corner of the image. If you clicked the button, this is the address the link would go to. Even though the link lists a transaction ID, which might be convincing, the link itself does not go to the Chase website. Scrolling to the bottom of the email, the fine print shown in Figure 10-4 is even more revealing—the email claims to come from Chase, but the company listed in the fine print is Capital One, a completely different company. Once you know what you're looking for, it can be fun to pick apart a phishing email to discover its flaws.

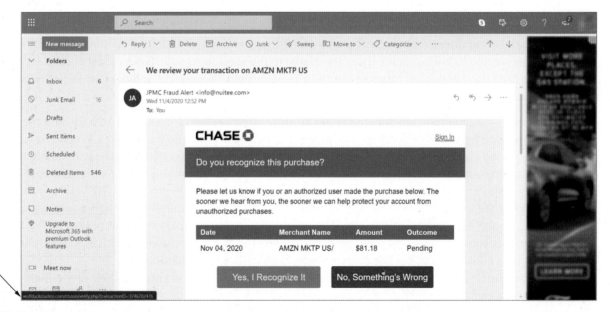

Button's actual link

Figure 10-3   Phishing emails often include legitimate-looking logos, buttons, instructions, and fine print

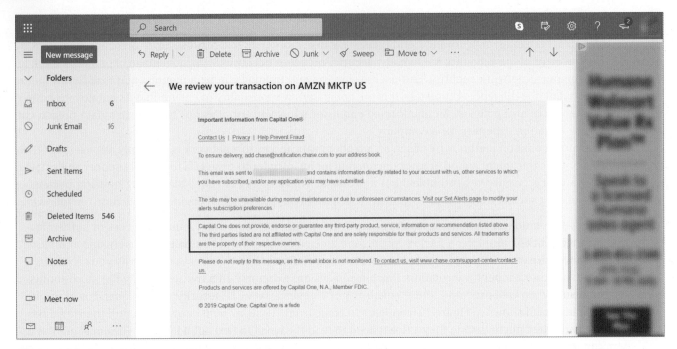

Figure 10-4 Careful investigation reveals clues the email is fake

- **Baiting**—A malware-infected file, such as a free music download, or a malware-infested device, such as a USB flash drive, is seemingly left unguarded for someone to take and attempt to use on their own computer. The malware then infects the computer and gives the attacker access to the victim's computer, data, or online accounts. Leaving malware-infested flash drives lying in a parking lot or other obvious location is a favorite tactic among many hackers. This is especially common at hacking conventions, where attendees should know better than to plug an unknown flash drive into their computer, and yet still many take the bait.
- **Quid pro quo**—A free gift or service is offered in exchange for private information or "temporary" access to the user's computer system. This tactic is surprisingly effective with people who have not been adequately trained to detect social engineering attempts.

Social engineering doesn't necessarily require lengthy processes of building relationships with victims. More transient in nature, the following attack types are related to the ways foot traffic flows in and out of a building or other space. With a little good acting, an attacker can "hide in plain sight," appearing to belong while acting with malicious intent. Consider the following examples:

- **Tailgating**—An unauthorized person follows an authorized person into a secure area without the authorized person's knowledge or cooperation. For example, you might punch in a code on a keypad to enter a gated neighborhood and drive off, unaware that another car has followed you through the gate before it closed.
- **Piggybacking**—A person uses deception to follow an authorized employee into a restricted area. For example, someone who appears to be a delivery person and is carrying a large box might ask you to "hold the door," which gives the attacker access through an otherwise secure door. Similarly, a friendly sounding conversation with an employee as they walk into a building might get an intruder past the front desk security. It might feel rude to deny someone's request for assistance in holding open a secure door or to chat politely when someone strikes up a conversation, but not everyone who is nice has good intentions.
- **Shoulder surfing**—A person secretly observes an authorized person entering their credentials to access a secure area and then uses that information later. You should always be aware of who is around you and what they can see. For example, when entering a code into a keypad on a secured door, cover the keypad with your hand so no one can see your code.

Increasing environmental awareness, or situational awareness, is key to protecting secure spaces from unauthorized access. For example, teach employees that they can and should hold firm boundaries with people they don't know when entering through a secure door or gate. Management should support employees who enforce access policies, even when it results in a legitimate customer becoming angry.

Hackers use psychological insights to develop and refine their techniques. The more you understand their processes—and teach your coworkers about these techniques—the more effectively you can defend against them. Figure 10-5 shows the typical social engineering attack cycle. Phase 1, research, is the most important, and it often requires the most time investment. Attackers build familiarity by initially asking for seemingly benign information. As they gather more data, they use these tidbits to build trust and gain access to more private information. This is Phase 2, building trust.

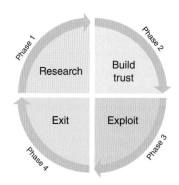

Figure 10-5   This cycle might happen quickly over a few seconds, or take much longer, even several years

Phase 3, exploit, is the point of action on the part of the victim that gives the attacker the access they desire. This might be as simple as holding the door open, or it might be more involved, such as divulging trade secrets with someone the victim believes to be a colleague. Finally, in Phase 4, exit, the attacker executes an exit strategy in such a way that does not leave evidence or raise suspicion. The attacker might then repeat the cycle, gaining deeper access until the objective is achieved.

The most important defense against social engineering is employee training, along with frequent reminders and tips regarding the latest scams. Employee training programs might be regularly scheduled throughout the year with required compliance and pass rates (see Figure 10-6). This technique follows the "use it or lose it" principle so employees are regularly exposed to cybersecurity concepts and best practices. It's easy to forget this information for those who don't work in IT, and frequent review can help employees more consistently apply these practices.

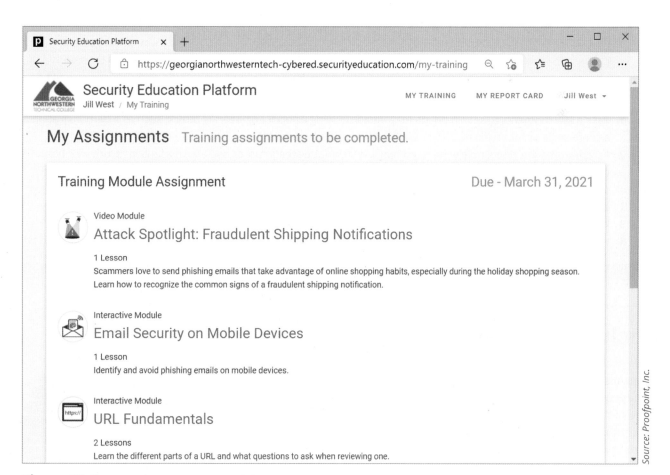

Source: Proofpoint, Inc.

Figure 10-6   Security awareness training

Less predictably, IT security staff can provide updates on current threats and the measures the company is taking to protect everyone. This helps build a sense of urgency and vigilance as employees recognize the importance of their role in protecting company data and other IT resources. Updates and training programs should be mindfully designed and written with professionalism to encourage users to engage with the information. Further, organizations can build a sense of accountability by occasionally conducting practice runs. These simulations can identify weaknesses in employee understanding of their cybersecurity responsibilities. You'll learn more about this technique later in this module.

Employee training helps protect a company from external threats. However, it doesn't address internal threats from insiders. An insider is someone who is or was trusted by an organization, such as an employee, former employee, contractor, or other associate. When a trusted person has or develops malicious intent, this presents an **insider threat**. These attackers pose a particularly high risk to an organization due to their knowledge of the company's systems, procedures, and layers of security.

Whether people-related risks come from malicious insiders or naïve, trusted users, companies can take measures to reduce these risks, such as the following:

- Perform background checks for new hires and, where relevant, for contractors.
- Enforce the **principle of least privilege**, meaning employees and contractors are only given enough access and privileges to do their jobs, and these privileges are terminated as soon as the person no longer needs them.
- Design checks and balances on employee behavior, such as scheduled access, mandatory vacations, and job rotations.
- Deploy a **DLP (data loss prevention)** solution that identifies sensitive data on the network and prevents it from being copied (such as downloading to a flash drive) or transmitted off the network (such as emailing or posting to cloud storage).

Applying Concepts 10-1: Social Engineering in Action

One of the most eye-opening experiences in learning to protect against social engineering is to see an attack in action. Complete the following steps:

1. Take a few moments to search online for a video showing a social engineering attack, such as a demonstration at a conference or for research. What's the link to the video you found?
2. As you watch the video, notice the psychological techniques the attacker uses, such as mixing truth with lies, creating a sense of urgency or scarcity, implying authority, playing on emotions, intimidation, generalizing to cover for unknown details, feigning familiarity, appealing to empathy, or offering favors to create a sense of owing a favor in return. What tactics did you identify in the video?
3. What technical expertise (if any) was required to complete the attack?
4. What advice could you give coworkers, friends, or family members to protect themselves from this kind of attack?

Technology Risks

This section describes security risks inherent in all seven layers of the OSI model. Attacks on transmission media, NICs, network access methods (for example, Ethernet), switches, routers, access points, and gateways require more technical sophistication than those that take advantage of human errors. For instance, to eavesdrop on transmissions passing through a switch, an intruder must use a device such as a protocol analyzer (like Wireshark) connected to one of the switch's ports. Because a router connects one type of network to another, an intruder

might take advantage of the router's security flaws by sending a flood of TCP/IP transmissions to the router, thereby disabling it from carrying legitimate traffic.

A **DoS (denial-of-service) attack** occurs when legitimate users are unable to access normal network resources, such as a web server, because of an attacker's intervention. Most often, this type of attack is achieved by flooding a system with so many requests for services that it can't respond to any of them, as shown in Figure 10-7. As a result, all data transmissions are disrupted.

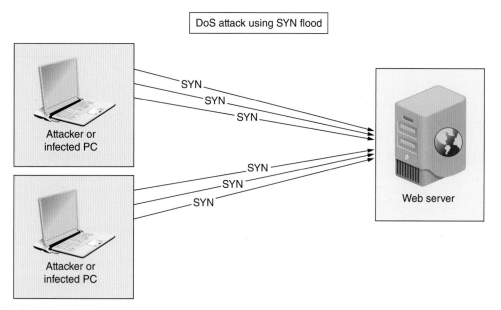

Figure 10-7   A simple DoS attack flooding a web server with SYN requests

This incursion is a relatively simple attack to launch (for example, a hacker could create a looping program that sends thousands of email messages to your system per minute). DoS attacks can also result from malfunctioning software. Because DoS attacks are so common, let's look at several DoS subtypes:

- **DDoS (distributed DoS) attack**—Whereas a DoS attack comes from one or a few sources owned by the attacker, DDoS attacks are orchestrated through many sources, as shown in Figure 10-8. Most of these machines are zombies, which means the owners are unaware that their computers are being used in the coordinated attack. A type of malware called a bot is installed on each machine and gives the bot herder, or central controller, remote control of the computer. Many people believe their computers are not at high risk of security compromise if they don't keep valuable information on the computer. They don't realize their computing resources are also a target. Computers can be requisitioned as part of a botnet, also called a zombie army, in coordinated DDoS attacks without the owners' knowledge or consent. These botnets are sometimes made available for hire on the black market. The traffic spike caused by so many attackers is much more difficult to defend against than an attack from a single source. Effective firewalls can greatly reduce the chances of a computer being drafted into illegal botnets.
- **DRDoS (distributed reflection DoS) attack**—A DRDoS attack is a type of DDoS attack that is bounced off uninfected computers, called reflectors, before being directed at the target. This is achieved by spoofing the source IP address in the attack to make it look like all the requests for response are being sent by the target. As a result, all the reflectors send their responses to the target, thereby flooding the target with traffic, as shown in Figure 10-9.

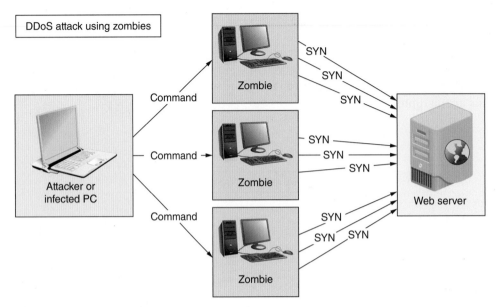

Figure 10-8 A SYN flood coordinated through several malware-infected, zombie computers

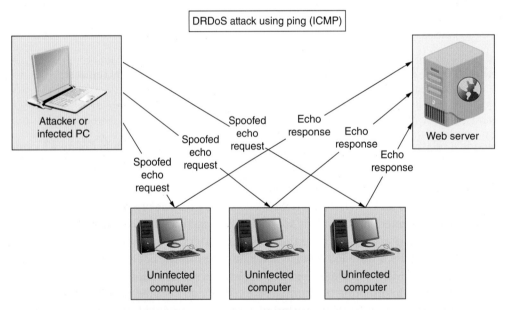

Figure 10-9 Spoofed ICMP echo requests appear to come from the victim computer

- **Amplified DRDoS attack**—A DRDoS attack can be amplified when conducted using small, simple requests that trigger very large responses from the target, as shown in Figure 10-10. Several protocols lend themselves to being used in these kinds of attacks, including DNS, NTP, ICMP, SNMP, and LDAP.
- **PDoS (permanent DoS) attack**—A PDoS attack damages a device's firmware beyond repair. This is called "bricking" the device because it effectively turns the device into a brick. PDoS attacks usually target routers or switches.

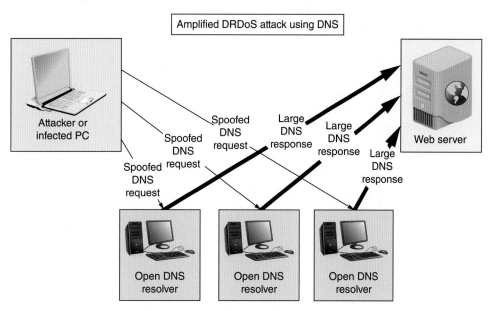

Figure 10-10   Spoofed DNS requests prompt large responses sent to the victim

- **Friendly DoS attack**—An unintentional DoS attack, or friendly attack, is not done with malicious intent. An example might be when a website is flooded with an unexpectedly high amount of shopping traffic during a flash sale, or when a significant event is reported on the news and people flood to certain, related websites, especially if a specific website was mentioned in news reports.

Other technology risks are related to weaknesses of wireless transmissions, authentication vulnerabilities, lack of encryption, or flaws in software design. Consider the following types of attacks and vulnerabilities:

- **On-path attack**—An on-path attack, previously called a MitM (man-in-the-middle) attack, relies on intercepted transmissions and can take several forms. In all these forms, the attacker redirects and captures secure transmissions as they occur. For example, in the case of an evil twin attack (a type of on-path attack), a hacker could intercept transmissions between clients and a rogue access point. Through these captured transmissions, the attacker can learn users' passwords or even supply users with a phony website that looks valid but presents clickable options capable of harming their systems.
- **Deauth (deauthentication) attack**—When a Wi-Fi client is legitimately connected to a wireless access point, the AP or the client can send a deauthentication frame to tell the other device that the authentication session is being terminated. A valid deauth frame could come from the wireless client or AP for any number of legitimate reasons, including inactivity, the client is leaving the area, the AP is overwhelmed with too many clients, or an unspecified reason. These frames are unencrypted and are easily spoofed. In a deauth (deauthentication) attack, the attacker sends faked deauthentication frames to the AP, the client, or both (or as a broadcast to the whole wireless network) to trigger the deauthentication process and knock one or more clients off the wireless network. This is essentially a Wi-Fi DoS attack in that valid users are prevented from having normal access to the network. At minimum, it can be a frustrating experience for users. In the hands of a skilled attacker, further information can be collected for more destructive attacks, such as an on-path attack.
- **Insecure protocols and services**—Certain TCP/IP protocols are inherently insecure. For example, IP addresses can be falsified, checksums can be thwarted, UDP requires no authentication, and TCP requires only weak authentication. FTP is notorious for its vulnerabilities. In a well-known exploit called **FTP bounce**, hackers take advantage of this insecure protocol. When a client running an FTP utility requests data from an FTP server, the client normally specifies its own IP address and FTP's default port number. However, it is possible for the client to specify any port on any host's IP address. By commanding the FTP server to connect to a different computer, a hacker can scan the ports on other hosts and transmit malicious code. To thwart FTP bounce attacks, most modern FTP servers will not issue data to hosts other than the client that originated the request.

Other insecure protocols include HTTP (use HTTPS with SSL/TLS instead), Telnet (use along with IPsec), SNMPv1, and SNMPv2 (use SNMPv3 instead). You'll learn more about SNMP later in this course.

- **DNS poisoning or DNS spoofing**—By altering DNS records on a DNS server, an attacker can redirect Internet traffic from a legitimate web server to a phishing website, which is called DNS poisoning or DNS spoofing. Because of the way DNS servers share their cached entries, poisoned DNS records can spread rapidly to other DNS servers, ISPs, home and business networks, and individual computers. In fact, intentional DNS spoofing is one way China maintains its so-called "Great Firewall," which blocks its citizens from accessing websites such as YouTube, Pinterest, and Facebook. However, in 2010, China's DNS records somehow leaked into neighboring countries' DNS root servers. The altered DNS records started spreading around the world, blocking Internet traffic in other countries from accessing popular websites and redirecting that traffic to Chinese servers.

- **Back doors**—Software might contain back doors, which are security flaws that allow unauthorized users to gain access to the system. Unless the network administrator performs regular updates, a hacker might exploit these flaws. Legacy systems are particularly notorious for leaving these kinds of gaps in a network's overall security net.

Malware Risks

Malware (malicious software) refers to any program or piece of code designed to intrude upon or harm a system or its resources. Included in this category are viruses, Trojan horses, worms, bots, and ransomware. You can find lists and maps online of recent outbreaks of malware, intrusions, and attacks. Figure 10-11 shows Kaspersky's interactive world map (*cybermap.kaspersky.com/*) where you can explore attack statistics by country based on data gathered by Kasperky's security tools. Figure 10-12 shows where further statistics analysis is available to compare countries and detection types.

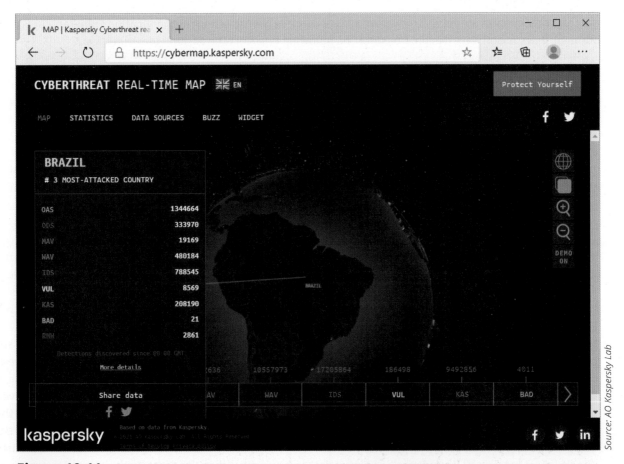

Source: AO Kaspersky Lab

Figure 10-11 Security professionals track the emergence of new threats

Figure 10-12 Cyberattack statistics grouped by detection type

Other companies provide similar maps and reporting dashboards. For example, Figure 10-13 shows a map and statistics streamed by SonicWall (*securitycenter.sonicwall.com/m/page/worldwide-attacks*). Digging deeper, you can find additional statistics and threat metrics on the SonicWall site (see Figure 10-14). Notice the breakdown of attack types, including malware, ransomware, spam volume, cryptojacking, and IoT malware. Statistics on this site report that IoT malware has risen by more than 350 percent over the previous year with a particularly noticeable spike in October of 2019.

These cyberattack maps break down statistics according to attack types, such as malware, spam, phishing, and more. Malware is a generalized term that refers to many kinds of malicious software, as described in the following list:

- **Virus**—A program that replicates itself with the intent to infect more computers, either through network connections when it piggybacks on other files or through the exchange of external storage devices. A virus might damage files or systems, or it might simply annoy users by, for example, flashing messages or pictures on the screen.

- **Trojan horse (or Trojan)**—A program that disguises itself as something useful but actually harms your system; named after the famous wooden horse in which soldiers were hidden. Because Trojan horses do not replicate themselves, they are not considered viruses. An example of a Trojan horse is an executable file that someone sends you over the Internet, promising that the executable will install a great new game, when in fact it erases data on your hard disk or mails spam to all the users in your email app's address book.

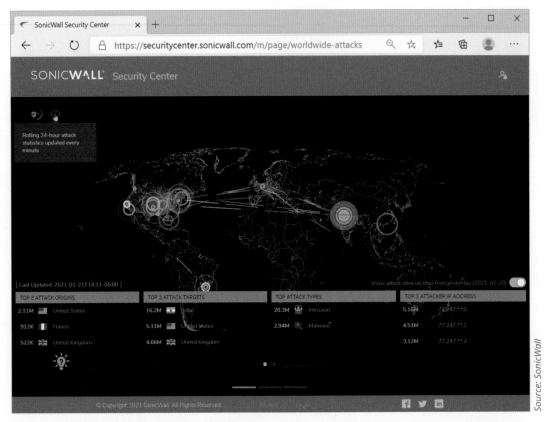

Figure 10-13   World map showing top three attack origins and top three attack targets according to SonicWall data

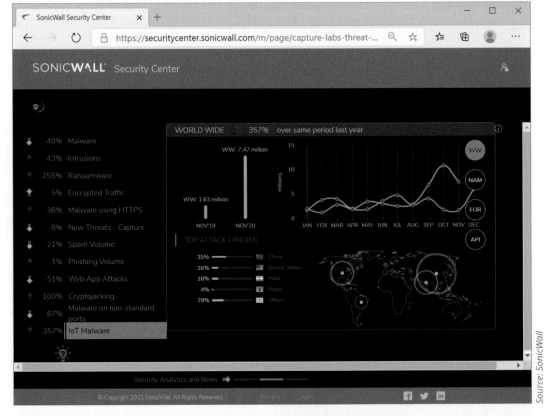

Figure 10-14   Statistics showing change in attack volumes over time

- **Worm**—A program that runs independently of other software and travels between computers and across networks. They may be transmitted by any type of file transfer, including email attachments. Worms do not alter other programs in the same way that viruses do, but they can carry viruses. Because they can transport and hide viruses, you should be concerned about picking up worms when you exchange files on the Internet, via email, or on flash drives.

- **Bot** (short for robot)—A process that runs automatically, without requiring a person to start or stop it. Bots can be beneficial or malicious. Especially when used for ill intent, it does not require user interaction to run or propagate itself. Instead, it connects to a central server called a **C&C (command-and-control) server**, which then commands an entire **botnet** of similarly infected devices. Bots can be used to damage or destroy a computer's data or system files, issue objectionable content, launch DoS attacks, or open back doors for further infestation. Bots are especially difficult to contain because of their fast, surreptitious, and distributed dissemination.

- **Ransomware**—A program that locks a user's data or computer system until a ransom is paid. In most cases, the infection encrypts data on the computer and can also encrypt data on backup devices, removable storage devices, and even cloud storage accounts connected to the computer, such as Dropbox or OneDrive. The victim receives a message, such as the one shown in Figure 10-15, with the demand for payment and instructions on how to make the payment, usually through untraceable online payment systems. The amount of ransom varies, and for large organizations, has reached well into the millions of dollars. To add a sense of urgency, some ransomware starts deleting data at certain time increments, showing a countdown clock to the next scheduled deletion. Even if victims pay the ransom, they don't always get their data back. Currently, the only mostly reliable defense is to make manual backups of data on a regular basis *and* disconnect the backup media from the computer between backups. However, some ransomware threatens to send the user's files to email contacts stored on the computer or to post stolen data online. Researchers are finding that ransomware victims are increasingly paying the ransom in exchange for keeping their data private, even if they have sufficient backups in place.

Source: New Jersey Cybersecurity & Communications Integration Cell

Figure 10-15   This version of the Jigsaw ransomware threatens to send all the user's data to all contacts collected from the computer

Certain characteristics can make malware harder to detect and eliminate. Some of these characteristics, which can be found in any type of malware, include the following:

- **Encryption**—Some malware is encrypted to prevent detection. Most anti-malware software searches files for a recognizable string of characters that identifies the virus. However, encryption can thwart the anti-malware program's attempts to detect it.
- **Stealth**—Some malware disguises itself as legitimate programs or replaces part of a legitimate program's code with destructive code.
- **Polymorphism**—Polymorphic malware changes its characteristics (such as the arrangement of bytes, size, and internal instructions) every time it's transferred to a new system, making it harder to identify.
- **Time dependence**—Some malware is programmed to activate on a particular date. This type of malware can remain dormant and harmless until its activation date arrives. One example of time-dependent malware is a logic bomb, which is code (or a bug in code) that will start when certain conditions are met. (Logic bombs can also activate when other types of conditions, such as a specific change to a file, are met, and they are not always malicious.)

Malware can exhibit more than one of the preceding characteristics. The Natas virus, for example, combines polymorphism and stealth techniques to create a very destructive virus. Hundreds of new viruses, worms, Trojan horses, bots, and ransomware are unleashed on the world's computers each month. Although it is impossible to keep abreast of every virus in circulation, you should at least know where you can find out more information about malware. An excellent resource for learning about new malware, their characteristics, and ways to get rid of them is the McAfee Threat Center at *mcafee.com/enterprise/en-us/threat-center.html*.

REMEMBER THIS...

- Compare internal versus external threats.
- Explain the CVE and zero-day attacks.
- Compare technology-based attacks, including DoS, DDoS, botnets, on-path attacks, ransomware, deathentication, and malware.
- Compare human and environmental attacks, including phishing, tailgating, piggybacking, and shoulder surfing.
- Discuss strategies for employee training.

SELF-CHECK

1. The ability to insert code into a database field labeled "Name" is an example of a(n) _____.
   a. attack.
   b. vulnerability.
   c. breach.
   d. exploit.
2. Which of the following social engineering attack types most likely requires that the attacker have existing knowledge about the victim?
   a. Tailgating
   b. Shoulder surfing
   c. Piggybacking
   d. Phishing

3. You're playing a game on your Xbox when you suddenly get bumped off your Wi-Fi network. You reconnect and start playing, then get bumped off again. What type of attack is most likely the cause?

   a. On-path attack

   b. FTP bounce

   c. Deauth attack

   d. DDoS

Check your answers at the end of this module.

You're Ready

You're now ready to complete **Project 10-1: Play with Windows Sandbox**, or you can wait until you've finished reading this module.

RISK ASSESSMENT AND MANAGEMENT

✅ CERTIFICATION

3.2 Explain the purpose of organization documents and policies.

4.1 Explain common security concepts.

5.3 Given a scenario, use the appropriate network software tools and commands.

Average reading time: 17 minutes

Before spending time and money changing your network security, first identify and examine your network's current security risks. Consider the effect that a loss or breach of data, applications, or access would have on your network. The more serious the potential consequences, the more attention you need to pay to security. To accurately evaluate your risk and vulnerabilities, you'll need to conduct several security assessments.

Effective risk management happens at two layers, as follows:

- A **security risk assessment** evaluates threats to and vulnerabilities of the network.
- A **business risk assessment** evaluates the impact of potential threats on business processes.

To determine these risks to the business, you must first have a good understanding of the various processes the business relies on. A **business process** is a series of steps that accomplishes a defined goal. For example, the series of steps involved in receiving an order from a customer, delivering a product or service, and billing the customer is an operations business process. The steps needed to assemble a product is a manufacturing business process. Business professionals use techniques to identify, define, evaluate, and analyze these various business processes. From the IT perspective, then, a **process assessment** ensures that you and others responsible for network security understand your company's business processes, which will help you minimize the impact of security threats on those processes.

Similarly, a **vendor risk assessment** (also called a third-party risk assessment) evaluates security and compliance risks related to suppliers and vendors a company does business with. Not all security threats are directly implemented against your own company—sometimes, the attack is routed through a business partner of some kind. During a vendor risk assessment, you'll need to get the answers to several important questions: Is the vendor trustworthy? Are they financially stable? Do they maintain compliance standards? Is their IT security reliable? These and many other questions should be explored and answered before beginning a formal relationship with a vendor and periodically (perhaps annually) during the relationship. This assessment might require the cooperation of people from many departments to cover all vendors. For example, a compromised HVAC vendor could result in a network-wide data breach. It's critical to evaluate all possible avenues of compromise to your network, considering not just technical vulnerabilities but also security gaps caused by business processes and relationships.

Every organization should assess its network's security risks by conducting a **posture assessment**, which is a thorough examination of each aspect of the network to determine how it might be compromised. One component of a posture assessment might include a **threat assessment**, which identifies specific security threats to the network and related risk factors. A threat's consequences might be severe, potentially resulting in a network outage or the dispersal of top-secret information, or it might be mild, potentially resulting in a lack of access for one user or the dispersal of a relatively insignificant piece of corporate data. The more devastating a threat's effects and the more likely it is to happen, the more rigorously your security measures should address it. An assessment process might include the following steps:

1. Identify threats and risk factors.
2. Determine which resources (people, equipment, data, etc.) might be harmed by each threat.
3. Develop plans for responding to threats if they occur and, in the meantime, for reducing identified risks.
4. Document findings and next steps.

Posture assessments should be performed at least annually and preferably quarterly. They should also be performed after making any significant changes to the network. If your IT Department has sufficient skills and time for routine posture assessments, they can be performed in-house. A qualified consulting company can also assess the security of your network. If the company is accredited by an agency that sets network security standards, the assessment qualifies as a **security audit**, also called an IT audit.

Certain customers—for example, a military agency—might require your company to pass an accredited security audit before they'll do business with you. Regulators require some types of companies, such as accounting firms, to host periodic security audits. But even if an audit is optional, the advantage of having an objective third party analyze your network is that they might find risks you overlooked because of your familiarity with your environment. Security audits might seem expensive, but if your network hosts confidential and critical data, they are well worth the cost. Beyond meeting requirements imposed by business partners, an audit and assessment report can help you deeply evaluate your organization's security posture and close vulnerabilities.

In addition, you can set auditing policies on your network's devices and servers to constantly monitor activities that might need attention. For example, Figure 10-16 shows Event Viewer in Windows Server, which logs security events such as changing user accounts. You'll learn more about log management later in this course.

In this section of the module, you'll first learn about attack simulations and various scanning tools used for posture assessments and security audits. Then you'll see how you can bait hackers so you can learn more about their activities.

Attack Simulations

To ensure that your security efforts are thorough, it helps to think like a hacker. During a posture assessment, for example, you might use some of the same methods a hacker uses to identify cracks in your security architecture. In fact, security experts often conduct simulated attacks on a network to determine its weaknesses. Let's look at three types of attack simulations.

Vulnerability Assessment

A **vulnerability assessment** is used to identify vulnerabilities in a network. It's often performed by a company's own employees and does not attempt to exploit any vulnerabilities. A vulnerability assessment might also be the first step in other attack simulations or in a real attack. During attack simulations, there are two types of vulnerability assessments:

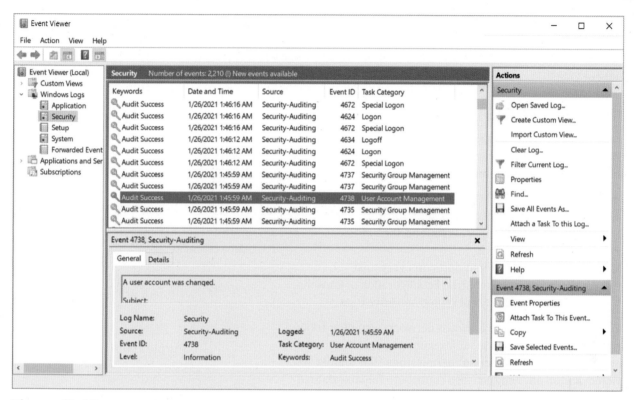

Figure 10-16 Audit logs in Event Viewer

- **Authenticated**—In this case, the attacker is given the same access to the network as a trusted user would have, such as an employee or an intruder who has somehow hacked into a user's account.
- **Unauthenticated**—In this case, the attacker begins on the perimeter of the network, looking for vulnerabilities that do not require trusted user privileges.

Penetration Testing

Pen (penetration) testing takes advantage of ethical hacking techniques to identify weaknesses and the extent of those weaknesses. This attack simulation begins with a vulnerability assessment using various tools and then attempts to exploit those vulnerabilities. A penetration test might be something as simple as a network admin clicking around through the network to see what vulnerabilities surface, such as discovering that the default credentials for a networked HVAC system were never changed. Or it might consist of a much more robust process, relying on a professional pen testing organization to conduct a thorough examination of the company's network and resulting in a lengthy report recommending important, critical, and urgent changes to make to the network.

You've already used or read about many pen testing tools, including Wireshark and Nmap. Other pen testing tools might include the following:

- SimplyEmail to gather information posted online related to an email address
- Hashcat or John the Ripper to crack passwords
- Aircrack-ng to monitor and manipulate wireless transmissions
- Metasploit for vulnerability scanning
- PowerShell scripts to perform multiple tasks at a time

Red Team–Blue Team Exercise

During a **red team–blue team exercise**, the red team conducts the attack, and the blue team attempts to defend the network, as illustrated in Figure 10-17. Usually, the red team is a hired attacker, such as a consultant or security organization, and the blue team is the company's own IT, security, and other staff. In some cases, the blue team has no warning of the impending attack to better evaluate day-to-day defenses. The red team relies heavily on social engineering to attempt to access the company's private data, accounts, or systems without getting caught. In this case, the company's detection and response to the attack is the primary focus, rather than the technical vulnerabilities of the network itself.

Scanning Tools

Scanning tools provide hackers—and you—with a simple and reliable way to discover crucial information about your network, including but not limited to the following:

- Every available host
- Each host's running services and software, including operating systems, applications, and their versions
- Software configurations
- Open, closed, and filtered ports on every host
- Existence, type, placement, and configuration of firewalls
- Unencrypted or poorly encrypted sensitive data

Used intentionally on your own network, scanning tools improve security by pointing out insecure ports, software and firmware that must be patched, permissions that should be restricted, and so on. They can also contribute valuable data to asset management and audit reports. Let's look at three popular scanning tools you can use:

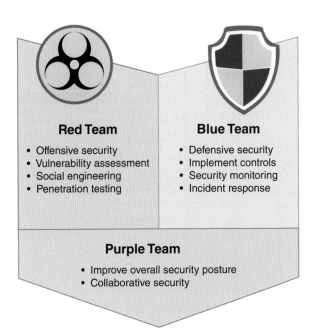

Figure 10-17 Working against each other, the red team and the blue team collaboratively improve the organization's security posture

- **Nmap**—The scanning tool Nmap and its GUI version, Zenmap, are designed to scan large networks quickly and provide information about a network and its hosts. (You used both of these in an earlier module.) Nmap began as a simple **port scanner**, which is an application that searches a device for open ports indicating which insecure service might be used to craft an attack. For example, if a server's port 23 is open, Telnet can be used to remote into the target device and take control of it. Developers later expanded Nmap's capabilities to include gathering information about hosts and their software. When running Nmap, you can choose what type of information to discover, thereby customizing your scan results. In a project at the end of this module, you'll use another app, Advanced Port Scanner, to find open protocol ports on your network.
- **Nessus**—Developed by Tenable Security (*tenable.com*), Nessus performs even more sophisticated vulnerability scans than Nmap. Among other things, Nessus can identify unencrypted, sensitive data (such as credit card numbers) saved on your network's hosts. The program can run on your network or from off-site servers continuously maintained and updated by the developer.
- **Metasploit**—This popular penetration testing tool combines known scanning and exploit techniques to explore potentially new attack routes. For example, Figure 10-18 shows a Metasploit scan using HTTP, SMTP, and SMB probes; the application also employs Nmap, Telnet, FTP, and UDP probes. Notice that the scan successfully identified the administrative username and password transmitted in plaintext for this home network's SOHO router. You can download an open source version of the Metasploit framework from their website at *metasploit.com*.

As you can see, these tools can provide useful insights into your network's weaknesses that need attention. Used by hackers—or more likely, by bots—these tools can instead lead to compromised security. In other words, each of these tools can be used for legitimate purposes as well as illegal ones. However, even if the scanning tools are used against you, you can learn from them. For example, a properly configured firewall will collect information about scanning

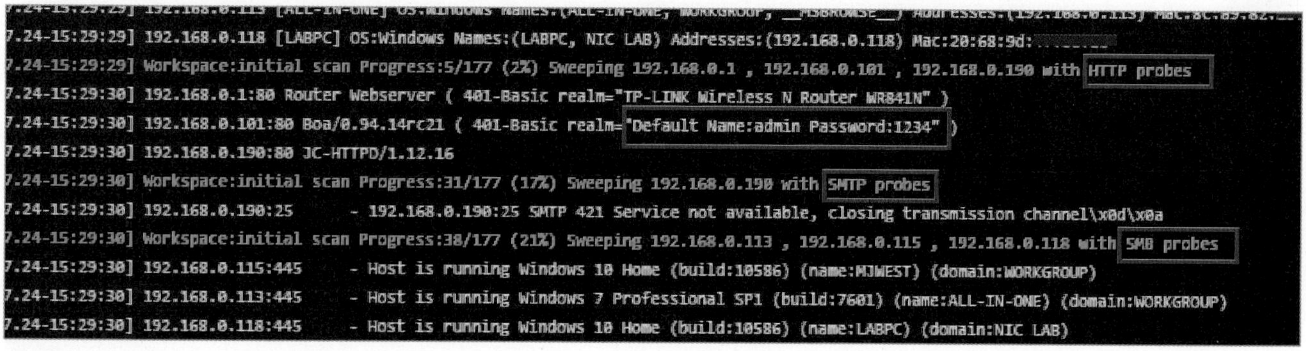

```
7.24-15:29:29] 192.168.0.113 [ALL-IN-ONE] OS:Windows Names:(ALL-IN-ONE, WORKGROUP, __MSBROWSE__) Addresses:(192.168.0.113) Mac:8c:89:82:...
7.24-15:29:29] 192.168.0.118 [LABPC] OS:Windows Names:(LABPC, NIC LAB) Addresses:(192.168.0.118) Mac:20:68:9d:...
7.24-15:29:29] Workspace:initial scan Progress:5/177 (2%) Sweeping 192.168.0.1 , 192.168.0.101 , 192.168.0.190 with HTTP probes
7.24-15:29:30] 192.168.0.1:80 Router Webserver ( 401-Basic realm="TP-LINK Wireless N Router WR841N" )
7.24-15:29:30] 192.168.0.101:80 Boa/0.94.14rc21 ( 401-Basic realm="Default Name:admin Password:1234" )
7.24-15:29:30] 192.168.0.190:80 JC-HTTPD/1.12.16
7.24-15:29:30] Workspace:initial scan Progress:31/177 (17%) Sweeping 192.168.0.190 with SMTP probes
7.24-15:29:30] 192.168.0.190:25      - 192.168.0.190:25 SMTP 421 Service not available, closing transmission channel\x0d\x0a
7.24-15:29:30] Workspace:initial scan Progress:38/177 (21%) Sweeping 192.168.0.113 , 192.168.0.115 , 192.168.0.118 with SMB probes
7.24-15:29:30] 192.168.0.115:445     - Host is running Windows 10 Home (build:10586) (name:MJWEST) (domain:WORKGROUP)
7.24-15:29:30] 192.168.0.113:445     - Host is running Windows 7 Professional SP1 (build:7601) (name:ALL-IN-ONE) (domain:WORKGROUP)
7.24-15:29:30] 192.168.0.118:445     - Host is running Windows 10 Home (build:10586) (name:LABPC) (domain:NIC LAB)
```
Source: Rapid7 LLC

Figure 10-18   Metasploit detected a SOHO router's administrative username and password

attempts in its log. By reviewing the log, you will discover what kinds of exploits could be—or have been—attempted against your network. Therefore, another way to learn about hackers is to lure them to your network on purpose, as described next.

Honeypots and Honeynets

Staying a step ahead of hackers and constantly evolving exploits requires vigilance. Those who want to learn more about hacking techniques or nab a hacker in the act might create a **honeypot**, which is a decoy system that is purposely vulnerable and filled with what appears to be sensitive (though false) content, such as financial data. To lure hackers, the system might be given an enticing name, for example, one that indicates a DNS name server or a storage location for confidential data. Once hackers access the honeypot, a network administrator can use monitoring software and logs to track the intruder's moves. In this way, the network administrator might learn about new vulnerabilities that must be addressed on real networked hosts.

To fool hackers and gain useful information, honeypots should not appear too blatantly insecure, and tracking mechanisms must be well hidden. Hackers know honeypots exist and are often skilled at detecting them. In addition, a honeypot must be isolated from secure systems to prevent a savvy hacker from using it as an intermediate host for other attacks. In more elaborate setups, several honeypots might be connected to form a **honeynet**. Honeypot software options include KFSensor (*keyfocus.net*), Thinkst Canary (*canary.tools*), and Honeyd (*honeyd.org*).

Honeypots and honeynets can provide unique information about hacking behavior and, if configured well, are low maintenance sources of information with few false positives. But in practice, security researchers or those merely curious about hacking trends are more likely than overworked network administrators to establish and monitor these decoy systems.

Now that you understand the variety of risks facing networks and several ways of identifying these risks on a specific network, you're ready to learn about techniques for securing the network's physical devices, beginning with physical security.

REMEMBER THIS...

- Explain common assessment types, including business risk assessments (process assessment and vendor risk assessment), and security risk assessments (posture assessment and threat assessment).
- Compare common attack simulations, including vulnerability assessment, penetration testing, and red team–blue team exercises.
- Use a port scanner.

SELF-CHECK

4. What is the first step in improving network security?
   a. Document next steps.
   b. Identify risks.
   c. Determine which resources might be harmed.
   d. Develop plans for responding to threats.

5. Which assessment type would most likely discover a security risk related to employee on-boarding?
   a. Vendor risk assessment
   b. Process assessment
   c. Threat assessment
   d. Posture assessment

6. Which team might ask a user for a password?
   a. Red team
   b. Blue team

Check your answers at the end of this module.

You're Ready

You're now ready to complete **Project 10-2: Scan a Network with Advanced Port Scanner**, or you can wait until you've finished reading this module.

PHYSICAL SECURITY

✓ CERTIFICATION

2.1 Compare and contrast various devices, their features, and their appropriate placement on the network.

4.5 Explain the importance of physical security.

Average reading time: 13 minutes

Physical access to a network's critical components must be restricted and controlled. Consider the damage that could be done if an intruder were able to steal devices, directly connect their own computer to unprotected console ports, damage or destroy expensive equipment, or simply reset these devices by pressing the physical reset button. Only trusted networking staff should have access to secure computer rooms, data rooms, network closets, storage rooms, entrance facilities, and locked equipment cabinets. Furthermore, only authorized staff should have access to the premises, such as offices and data centers, where these rooms are located.

Preventative measures such as locked doors can make it more difficult for unauthorized people to get into these areas. However, it's also important to have good detection measures in place for those times when someone is able to breach a secured perimeter. Let's look at physical security methods you can use for both prevention and detection.

Prevention Methods

If computer rooms are not locked, intruders may steal equipment or sabotage software or hardware. For example, a malicious visitor could slip into an unsecured computer room and take control of a server where an administrator is logged on, then steal data or reformat the server's hard drive. Although a security policy defines who has access to the computer room, locking the locations that house networking equipment is necessary to keep unauthorized individuals out. Physical access control devices can minimize unauthorized access to secured areas and devices. Access control hardware ranges from a simple deadbolt to more sophisticated options and can manage access to buildings, rooms, or storage spaces. Consider the following access control technologies:

- **Keypad, or cipher lock**—Requires the entry of a code to open the door, which can reduce the inherent risk of lost keys. Changing the cipher lock's code regularly can also help increase security. Cipher locks are not designed solely for physical security, such as on an outside door, so much as for the purpose of controlling access to an area, such as an indoor data room. The cipher lock can be used to log who comes and goes, enable or disable unescorted entry, schedule open access times, and even respond to access made under duress (with a special hostage code that trips an alarm when entered). Figure 10-19 shows one example of a cipher lock.

Figure 10-19   A cipher lock can document who enters an area and when

- **Access badge**—Identifies the person by name and perhaps includes a photo, title, and other information. Additionally, many organizations provide electronic access badges, or **smart cards**. When the smart card is swiped through a **badge reader**, the door unlocks and the person's access to the secured area is time stamped and logged in a database. These badges can be programmed to allow their owner access to some, but not all, rooms in a building. Some badges, such as the one in Figure 10-20, are proximity cards (also called prox

Figure 10-20   A proximity card does not require physical contact with a proximity reader

cards), which do not require direct contact with a proximity reader to be detected. In fact, the reader can be concealed inside a wall or other enclosure and requires very little maintenance. With a typical range of about 5–10 cm, the card can be detected even while it's inside a wallet or purse. Figure 10-21 depicts a typical badge access security system.

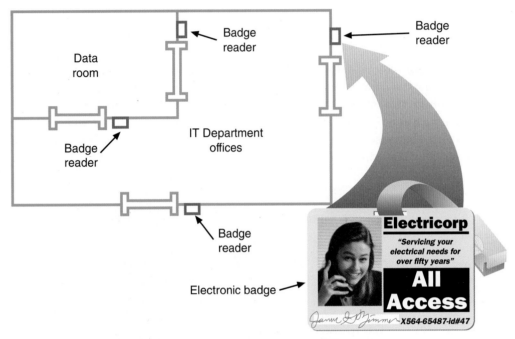

Figure 10-21   Badge access security system

- **Biometrics**—Involves biorecognition access in which a device scans an individual's unique physical characteristics (called biometrics) such as iris color patterns or hand geometry to verify the person's identity. Organizations might use biometric devices to regulate entrance through gates or other physical barriers to their campuses. See Figure 10-22.
- **Access control vestibule**—Previously known as a mantrap, creates a confined space between two locking doors where one door must lock closed before the other can open.
- **Locking rack** and **locking cabinet**—Provides a final layer of physical defense should an attacker gain access to a data room or some other controlled space. Locking racks restrict physical access to servers, routers, switches, and firewalls installed on the rack to prevent an intruder from making configuration changes to these devices. Locking cabinets might be used to store hardware not in use, such as spare devices, radio equipment, or tools.
- **Smart locker**—Allows controlled access to equipment, computers, packages, hardware in need of repair, or even to written account credentials stored for emergency access. To open a locker, the user must provide more sophisticated authentication, such as a barcode on their phone, so specific users are logged as having accessed the locker and when. This way, equipment can be checked out for temporary use and only by specific people. The smart locker can also generate an alert if equipment is not returned by a specific time.

Figure 10-22   Fingerprint scanner

iStock.com/tongo51

Temporary credentials can be issued as needed, such as for packages arriving at a public smart locker. In Figure 10-23, this Amazon Hub Locker on a college campus allows students to receive Amazon packages without needing to visit the mail center, thus saving time for students and employees. When a package arrives, the student receives an email on their smartphone with a bar code. As shown in Figure 10-24, the bar code is scanned at the locker's authentication panel to open the appropriate slot containing the student's package.

Figure 10-23   Amazon Locker on a college campus

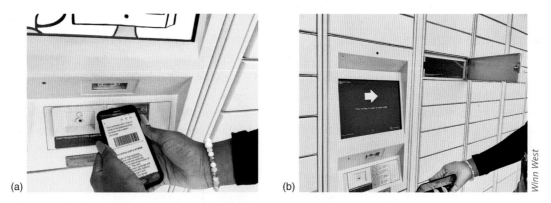

(a)   (b)

Figure 10-24   Scan the barcode from an email to access the package

> **⚠ CAUTION**   A door might not be the only way to enter a room containing sensitive equipment. Drop ceilings, also called suspended ceilings, can provide easy access to someone determined to get around a locked door. Secured rooms should be completely surrounded by impenetrable walls, ceilings, and floors. If a data room does have a drop ceiling, make sure the walls extend all the way up to the true ceiling beyond the drop ceiling grid.

Detection Methods

Despite all precautions, sometimes breaches do occur. The key to protecting sensitive data and systems is to detect intrusions as quickly as possible and be prepared to respond appropriately. Beyond detecting the presence of an intruder, however, security detection technologies can detect other types of events as well. For example, the temperature of vaccines in transit, the movement of delivery and transportation vehicles, and the expiration of food items can all be monitored for the safety and security of the people who use these items. The following list explores some methods of detecting physical intrusions and other kinds of events:

- **Motion detection**—Triggers an alarm when it detects movement within its field of view. Sensors like the one in Figure 10-25 are often found in home security systems. To reduce false alarms, AI-powered motion detectors can discern between different types of movement, such as small animals passing by, plants or trees blowing in the wind, or humans approaching a door. Motion sensors might be configured to simply record the date and time of motion detection or to trigger lights, alarms, or video cameras.

Figure 10-25   Motion detectors trigger an alarm when movement is detected

- **Cameras**—Placed in data centers, computer rooms, data rooms, and data storage areas, as well as facility entrances. The camera feeds are centrally managed through a video surveillance system, called **CCTV (closed-circuit TV)**, to monitor activity in these secure areas (see Figure 10-26). Security cameras might run continuously, or they might be equipped with motion detectors to start recording when movement occurs within their viewing area.

Figure 10-26   Security professionals monitor CCTV cameras

IT technicians might be called upon to install and service a video surveillance system for the entire company (see Figure 10-27). The video footage generated from these cameras is contained within a secure segment of the network, and it's usually saved for a period of time in case it's needed later in a security breach investigation or prosecution procedures.

Figure 10-27   IT personnel might be responsible for the installation and maintenance of a CCTV network

- **Tamper detection**—Identifies physical penetration, temperature extremes, input voltage variations, input frequency variations, or certain kinds of radiation. Many devices that need protection can't be kept within a secure area. For example, utility meters, parking meters, entry doors, ATMs, network cables, and even security cameras are potential targets. Tamper detection sensors might trigger defensive measures such as an alarm or shutdown, or it might activate a video camera or other security system. Another tamper detection option is a sticker or latch, as shown in Figure 10-28. Any damage to the sticker or latch tells you the device was tampered with.

Figure 10-28   A single-use, plastic security seal

- **Asset tags**—Monitor the movement and condition of equipment, inventory, and people. Whether a simple barcode or a wireless-enabled transmitter, such as the RFID label on the box in Figure 10-29, asset tracking enables constant or periodic collection of information. This data is then reported to a central management

Figure 10-29 The RFID label on this box allows the delivery service to track its progress

iStock.com/nullplus

application for monitoring, logging, and reporting. As wireless technologies have improved, these asset tracking systems have grown beyond Wi-Fi-dependent systems, which tend to be expensive and require frequent battery replacement for each asset being tracked. Today, these systems often use Bluetooth, RFID (such as NFC), cellular, and GPS wireless technologies. These technologies are sometimes combined with cloud technology to provide deeper insights through data analytics and with IoT technology to increase the security of IoT networks.

As with other security measures, the most important way to ensure physical security is to plan for it. You can begin your planning by asking questions related to physical security checks in your security audit. Consider the following questions:

- Which rooms contain critical systems or data and must be secured?
- Through what means might intruders gain access to the facility, computer room, data room, network closet, or data storage areas (including doors, windows, adjacent rooms, ceilings, large vents, temporary walls, hallways, and so on)?
- How and to what extent are authorized personnel granted entry? Do they undergo background or reference checks? Is their need for access clearly justified? Can their hours of access be restricted? Who ensures that lost keys or ID badges are reported?
- Are employees instructed on how to ensure security as they enter or leave secured areas (for example, by not propping open doors)?
- Are authentication methods (such as ID badges) difficult to forge or circumvent?
- Do supervisors or security personnel make periodic physical security checks?
- Are all combinations, codes, or other access means to computer facilities protected at all times, and are these combinations changed frequently?
- What is the plan for documenting and responding to physical security breaches?

REMEMBER THIS...

- Explain common detection methods, including cameras, motion detection, asset tags, and tamper detection.
- Explain common prevention methods, including badge readers, biometrics, locking racks, locking cabinets, access control vestibule, and smart lockers.

DEVICE HARDENING

✅ CERTIFICATION

3.2 Explain the purpose of organization documents and policies.

4.1 Explain common security concepts.

4.3 Given a scenario, apply network hardening techniques.

4.5 Explain the importance of physical security.

5.5 Given a scenario, troubleshoot general networking issues.

Average reading time: 31 minutes

Besides securing network devices from external tampering, you can take many steps to secure the device from network- or software-supported attacks as well. These practices are called device hardening. There are many layers of defense you can implement, although the options vary from one device to another. In this section, you'll learn about device hardening practices that apply generically to many types of devices. Later you'll explore device hardening techniques that are more specific to networking devices and require a deeper understanding of a network's design.

Updates and Security Patches

Updates to applications, operating systems, and device firmware address several issues, including fixing bugs, adding new features, and closing security gaps. The content in this module is primarily concerned with security issues. Because of the urgency of protecting networks and data from being compromised, security gaps are often addressed in smaller, more frequent updates called patches. Consider a situation where a single, failed patch compromised the personal identification information of more than 100 million people.

In September 2017, Equifax (one of the three major consumer credit reporting agencies) announced a major data breach where hackers accessed confidential information repeatedly from mid-May through July of that year. Names, Social Security numbers, birthdates, addresses, and, in some cases, driver's license numbers for approximately 143 million people, mostly U.S. residents, were compromised. That's nearly half the U.S. population. For about 209,000 of those people, credit card numbers were also stolen. How did this happen?

According to reports, a web server bug had been discovered months earlier in an open source software package used by Equifax. The bug allowed extensive back-door access to web servers run by major banking, government, retail, and other organizations. While a patch was issued by the software developer one day after the bug was discovered, security professionals suspect that Equifax either failed to apply the patch or inadequately implemented the patch in their systems before the breach occurred. Further, it appears Equifax had failed to renew a public key certificate that should have allowed Equifax's internal security systems to fully monitor data traversing their network. This means attackers were able to remove high volumes of data without Equifax's knowledge. To learn more about this story, do a search online for "Equifax breach technical details" or something similar. Look for authoritative news sources that specialize in the IT industry, such as *krebsonsecurity.com*, *techradar.com*, or *computerworld.com*, and also look for government websites with official, public notices.

> **CAUTION**
>
> To help protect your personal and financial information, experts recommend that you check your credit report at least once a year. U.S. residents can do this for free at *annualcreditreport. com*, a federal government approved site sponsored by all three major credit reporting agencies (Equifax, Experian, and TransUnion). Type that address directly into your browser's address bar to make sure you don't end up on a spoofed website. You can order a free, annual report from each of the three agencies through this site, either all at once or spaced throughout the year.
>
> If you're concerned about any indications of fraud on your account, you can contact one of these agencies to report the fraud and try to resolve the problem. You can also place a temporary fraud alert on your account for 90 days or more at no charge. A fraud alert notifies potential creditors to take extra security precautions before approving a new line of credit on your account.

The process of properly managing and applying security patches includes the following:

- **Discovery**—In this first phase, you investigate what's on your network so that you can protect it. Good documentation will help indicate whether a newly discovered vulnerability and its patch applies to your network, how extensively the issue affects your systems, how urgent the change is, and what you'll need to do to implement the patch correctly.
- **Standardization**—Updating OS and application versions consistently across the network will simplify the change process for future updates.
- **Defense in depth**—Recall that the term "defense in depth" refers to applying multiple layers of defense. For layered security to be effective, you need to understand how these various solutions interact and look for any gaps in coverage.
- **Vulnerability reporting**—Identifying and prioritizing relevant security issues and patch releases is essential. In some organizations, one or more staff members take primary responsibility for this task. Network administrators can also subscribe to reporting services from vendors, third parties, and government organizations.
- **Implementation**—Implementing patches includes validating, prioritizing, testing, and applying them. Careful implementation is especially important with security patches, which, as you have seen, can serve a critical role in protecting a business's interests. Performing patch rollouts in phases, or tiers, requires formal change management processes.
- **Assessment**—In this phase, you evaluate the success of patch implementation and the overall effectiveness of the patch. Was the patch applied everywhere it was needed? Is it working as expected? Can you detect any further gaps in security?
- **Risk mitigation**—In some cases, it may not be possible to apply a patch where needed. For example, a new patch might not be compatible with legacy software on a server. In this case, the server can't support the patch without compromising the older software. To lessen the resulting risk, you should apply other layers of protection to the affected devices and applications.

NOTE 10-1

Opinions about how to handle firmware updates vary widely. Some network admins take the approach, "If it ain't broke, don't fix it." That is, they don't upgrade firmware unless they see a pressing reason to do so. Others prefer to address firmware upgrades routinely, alongside other regular updates. Customer support technicians often tell clients to update the firmware on their device and then call back if there's still a problem. On the job, be sure to research firmware upgrades thoroughly before deciding whether to implement them. If possible, perform the firmware upgrade locally rather than remotely. And be prepared to troubleshoot unexpected problems after the upgrade.

Administrative Credentials

Most devices that can be configured through a management interface come with a default access account. Often, the username (if there is one) is something like "admin". The password might be "password", "admin", or "1234". Because these default credentials are so commonly used, they're also extremely insecure. Surprisingly, many network administrators—even in large organizations—never take the time to change these credentials to something more difficult to crack. When configuring a device, make it a habit to change the default administrative credentials before you do anything else and record this information in a safe place. When you do so, avoid common usernames and passwords. You'll learn more about how to create secure passwords later in this module.

> **⚠ CAUTION**   Be careful to configure secure usernames and passwords on *all* devices connected to any part of your network, even if the device itself seems to be an insignificant security threat, such as the chiller for an HVAC system or security cameras in a CCTV network. Any access point into the network can be used to compromise the network's data or other resources.

Recall that many devices are managed through remote access connections, the most common of which is SSH. Also recall that SSH keys can be used to authenticate devices making the remote connection. This is especially helpful for power users such as system administrators or when using SSH connections for automated processes such as file transfers, financial transactions, or configuration updates. Over long-distance connections, using SSH keys is more secure than using passwords because a securely encrypted key is more difficult to crack than a password. However, just like usernames and passwords, these authentication credentials should be changed from the provider's default settings. To do this, first remove the existing keys with the `rm` command. Then generate a new key pair with the `ssh-keygen` command. Figure 10-30 shows the PuTTY Key Generator, which can also be used to create SSH key pairs.

Figure 10-30   Use the PuTTY Key Generator to create a public/ private key pair

Many devices offer the option to configure several administrative accounts with varying levels of access. Additionally, user accounts on an enterprise's domain might be capable of accessing different features within a device's management interface. For example, a support technician in a company might be given an admin account with the ability to configure certain features on a single device or on all similar devices within a domain, such as workstations or certain servers. A high-level network administrator might, instead, have a domain admin account, which allows the person to make changes to Active Directory on a server, access private customer information in a database, or recover from a backup after a system failure.

Some user accounts are given **privileged access**, which allows these users to perform more sensitive tasks, such as viewing or changing financial information, making configuration changes, or adjusting access privileges for other users. Figure 10-31 shows some of the rights that can be assigned to users in a Windows Server domain. Security precautions that might be taken for these accounts include the following:

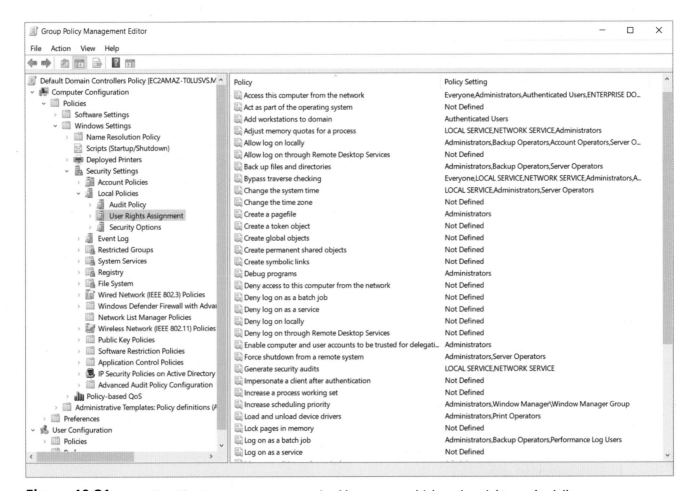

Figure 10-31 In Active Directory, users are organized by groups, which assign rights and privileges

- **Limited use**—These accounts should only be used when those higher privileges are necessary to accomplish a task. Even those employees who have a privileged user account should also have a lower-level account for normal activities. In fact, anyone who has a user account of any kind should be given only the least privilege, or least amount of access, needed to do a specific job.
- **Limited location**—Many companies require the privileged account be accessed only on location so that no one, not even a legitimate network administrator, can access the device remotely and make high-level changes from outside the protected network. One advantage to this restriction is that access credentials for this account will never be cached on a workstation or other end user device.
- **Limited duration**—Privileged accounts should be carefully accounted for and disabled as soon as they're not needed, such as when an employee is terminated.

- **Limited access**—The passwords for these accounts should be especially secure and difficult to crack. Passwords should also be stored securely, and when possible, multi-factor authentication should be required, which you'll learn more about in a later module.
- **Limited privacy**—A privileged account can be used for destructive activity, whether malicious or not. For that reason, every user action in these accounts should be logged and monitored by someone other than the owner of that account. In fact, this logging activity provided key information in troubleshooting the network infiltration described in this module's *On the Job* story. Privileged user monitoring software is available from companies such as Imperva (*imperva.com*), ManageEngine (*manageengine.com*), and Splunk (*splunk.com*).

Services and Protocols

Imagine that a hacker wants to bring a library's database and mail servers to a halt. Suppose also that the library's database is public and can be searched by anyone on the web. The hacker might begin by scanning for ports on the database server to determine which ports are open to certain processes or services. If they found an open port on the server, the hacker might connect to the system and deposit code that would, a few days later, damage operating system files. Or they could launch a heavy stream of traffic that overwhelms the database server and prevents it from functioning. They might also use the newly discovered access to determine the root password on the system, gain access to other systems, and launch a similar attack on the library's mail server, which is attached to the database server. In this way, even a single vulnerability on one server (an unprotected open port) can daisy-chain into destructive access to multiple systems.

Insecure services and protocols, such as Telnet and FTP, should be disabled in a system whenever possible (see Figure 10-32). Leaving these software ports open and services running practically invites an intrusion because it's so easy to crack into a system through these open doors. To protect devices from these threats, follow these guidelines:

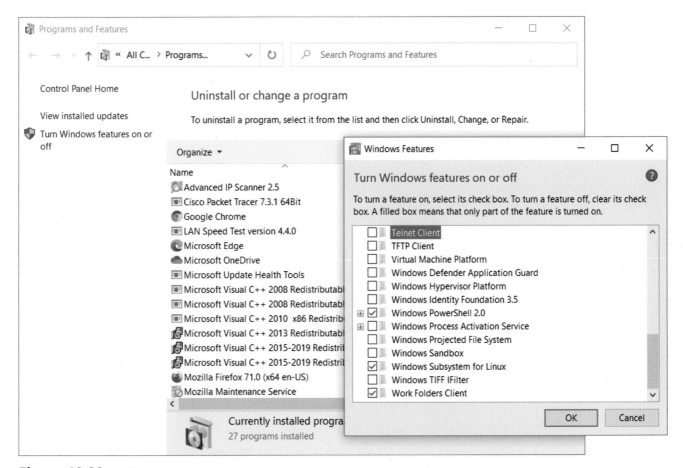

Figure 10-32   Disable Telnet in Windows

- **Reduce access paths**—Disable unneeded connection technologies, such as Bluetooth, Wi-Fi, NFC, and IR.
- **Choose secure protocols**—Use secure protocols, such as SSH and SFTP, instead of insecure protocols, such as Telnet and FTP.
- **Reduce start-up processes**—Minimize the number of start-up programs to include only those apps that you really need.
- **Disable unneeded services**—Stop any running services on a computer or network that are not needed. You can Google your OS and "unneeded services" to determine which services are most likely good candidates for disabling.
- **Declutter software**—Disable or uninstall applications that are no longer needed.
- **Streamline the network**—Remove network segments that are no longer needed.
- **Close unused ports**—Close TCP/IP ports on the local firewall and the network firewall that are not used for ongoing activities. For example, port 22 for SSH should not be open unless you need to remotely access that device. Ports 137-139 for NetBIOS should be closed to prevent legacy access methods that can be exploited by common malware such as WannaCry ransomware. Figure 10-33 shows the results of a port scan that revealed insecure ports open on a lab computer.

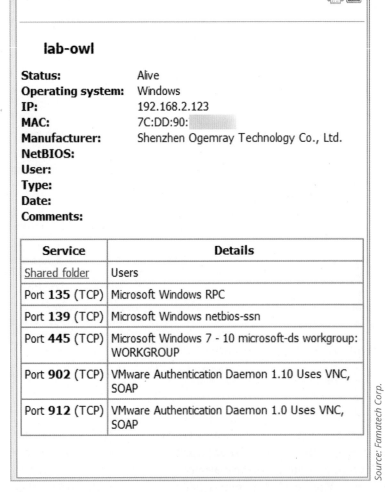

Figure 10-33   Insecure open ports on a lab computer

Passwords

To understand how best to secure passwords, you first need to understand how hashing works. **Hashing** means to transform data through an algorithm that is mathematically irreversible. Hashing is not the same as encryption, though it's often listed as a type of encryption and does, in a similar manner, transform data from one format to another. Encrypted data can be decrypted, but hashed data cannot (see Figure 10-34). Hashing is mostly used to ensure data integrity—that is, to verify the data has not been altered, which is similar to the purpose of a checksum. However, hashes can play a critical role in a good encryption protocol.

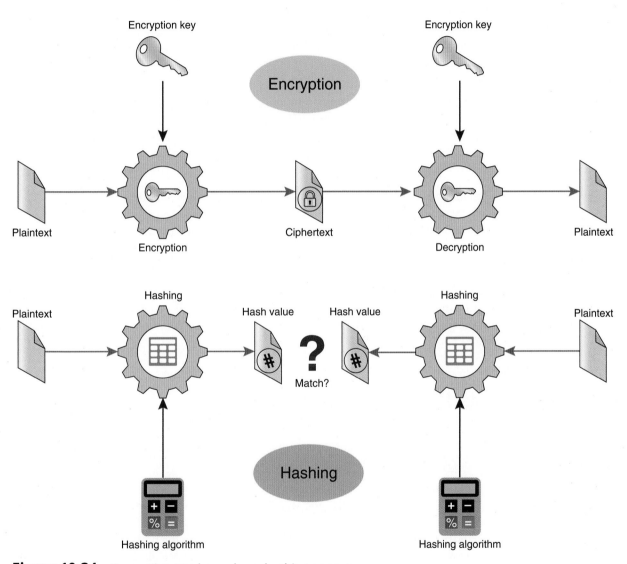

Figure 10-34 Encryption can be undone; hashing cannot

If a secure algorithm is used, hashing is realistically impossible to reverse. Instead, you can take known data, hash it using the same hashing function, and compare the new hash with the stored, hashed data. If the hashes match, this indicates the known data is exactly the same as the original data. If the output does not match, this indicates the data has likely been altered. In fact, this is often the most secure way to store and use passwords.

A well-designed password database does not store passwords in plaintext, but rather, it stores the *hash* of each password. When the user enters their password, the system hashes that password and then compares the hashed password with the stored hash for that password. If the hashes match, the system knows the user entered the correct password. This way, only the hash is transported and examined. Even if hackers access the stored hashes, they can't reverse the hashes to determine the original passwords. And the system won't accept the hash for authentication, only the original password that successfully generates the expected hash.

The most commonly used hashing algorithm today is some form of **SHA (Secure Hash Algorithm)**. You might hear this pronounced "shaw" or "shay." The primary advantage of SHA over older hashing algorithms is its resistance to collisions. A collision is when two different data sources result in the same hash. A prevalence of collisions from a hashing algorithm essentially defeats the purpose of hashing. However, the added security to avoid collisions means the hashing process takes longer than with less secure options. On this note, there are several versions of SHA:

- **SHA-0**—The original version of SHA was developed by the NSA and was later dubbed SHA-0. It used a 160-bit hash function.
- **SHA-1**—The original version was quickly replaced by the next, slightly modified version, SHA-1, due to an undisclosed flaw in SHA-0. SHA-1 has also since been retired in favor of the next two iterations of SHA, although many systems still rely on the easily cracked SHA-1.
- **SHA-2**—Also designed by the NSA, SHA-2 supports a variety of hash sizes, the most popular of which are SHA-256 (with a 256-bit hash) and SHA-512 (with a 512-bit hash). Note that the 2 in SHA-2 refers to the version number, whereas the larger numbers in SHA-256 and SHA-512 refer to the length of the hash functions.
- **SHA-3**—The most recent iteration of SHA, SHA-3, was developed by private designers for a public competition in 2012. SHA-3 is very different in design from SHA-2, even though it uses the same 256- and 512-bit hash lengths.

SHA-2 and SHA-3 are often implemented together for increased security. It's also common for data to be hashed in multiple passes along with encryption passes layered into the process.

What does hashing have to do with device hardening? Consider the following options:

- Passwords are often stored in hashed form to prevent them from being read even if they were to be accessed. Using a highly secure hash algorithm nearly guarantees that stolen passwords will be useless to the thief.
- Entire files can also be hashed. File hashing is accomplished by applying a hash algorithm to all the data in a file. Some sites provide hashes of files you might download from their site. If you hash your downloaded file and the hash matches the provider's hash, then you can be fairly confident your copy of the file has not been infected or corrupted.

Applying Concepts 10-2: Hash a Text String

Several hashing tools are available free online. One website, *onlinemd5.com*, lets you choose between three hashing algorithms: MD5 (an older, outdated hashing algorithm), SHA-1, and SHA-256. Complete the following steps:

1. In your browser, go to **onlinemd5.com**. The first tool shown on this page can hash an entire file, but you'll practice with smaller portions of text. Scroll down to the *MD5 & SHA1 Hash Generator For Text* box (see Figure 10-35).
2. **MD5** should be selected by default. Type a string of text into the box and watch the hash output calculate automatically as you type. What do you notice about the length of the string hash as you enter each additional letter?
3. Copy the final string hash into a text document for later comparison. Windows Notepad works well for this purpose.
4. Select **SHA1** and copy the new string hash into your text document for comparison.
5. Select **SHA-256** and copy the new string hash into your text document for comparison. Which string hash is longer? Why do you think that is?
6. Change exactly one character in your original text. What happens to the string hash?
7. Just a single character change results in a completely different hash. What if your original text is much longer than what you have now? Type a lot more text into the hash generator. What happens to the string hash?

Figure 10-35   Input text to hash

You can also use the command line in Windows PowerShell, macOS Terminal, and Linux Terminal to hash an entire file. Search online for the commands used for each CLI listed in Table 10-1 and write the correct commands in the Command column.

Table 10-1   Hashing commands in Windows, macOS, and Linux

OS	Task	Command
Windows	Hash a file using MD5	
Windows	Hash a file using SHA-1	
Windows	Hash a file using SHA-256 (default)	
macOS	Hash a file using MD5	
macOS	Hash a file using SHA-1 (default)	
macOS	Hash a file using SHA-256	
Linux	Hash a file using MD5	
Linux	Hash a file using SHA-1	
Linux	Hash a file using SHA-256	

Anti-Malware Software

You might think that you can simply install a virus-scanning program on your network and move to the next issue. In fact, protection against harmful code involves more than just installing anti-malware software. It requires choosing the most appropriate anti-malware program for your environment, monitoring the network, continually updating the anti-malware program, and educating users. Anti-malware on devices might consist of software embedded in the OS, such as Microsoft Defender Antivirus (see Figure 10-36), or you might install third-party anti-malware solutions, such as Bitdefender (*bitdefender.com*), Kaspersky (*kaspersky.com*), and Malwarebytes (*malwarebytes.com*), the last of which is especially good for removing malware if it does infect your computer.

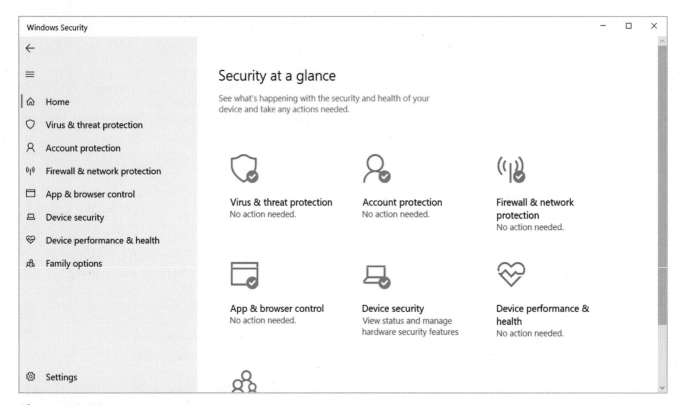

Figure 10-36 Built-in Windows anti-malware

Even if a user doesn't immediately notice malware on their system, the harmful software generally leaves evidence of itself, whether by changing the operation of the machine or by announcing its signature characteristics in the malware code. Although the latter can be detected only via anti-malware software, users can typically detect the operational changes without any special software. For example, you might suspect a virus on your system if any of the following symptoms arise:

- Unexplained increases in file sizes
- Significant, unexplained decline in system or network performance (for example, a program takes much longer than usual to start or to save a file)
- Unusual error messages with no apparent cause
- Significant, unexpected loss of system memory
- Periodic, unexpected rebooting
- Fluctuations in display quality

When implementing anti-malware software on devices and the network, one of your most important decisions is where to install the software. Some scenarios include the following:

- **Host-based**—If you install anti-malware software on every desktop, you have addressed the most likely point of entry but ignored the most important files that might be infected—those on the servers. Host-based anti-malware also provides insufficient coverage when a significant portion of the network is virtualized.

- **Server-based**—If the anti-malware software resides on the servers and checks every file and transaction, you will protect important files but slow your network performance considerably.
- **Network-based**—Securing the network's gateways, where the Internet connects with the interior network, can provide a formidable layer of defense against the primary source of intrusion—the Internet. However, this does nothing to prevent users from putting the network at risk with infected files on flash drives, laptops, or smartphones, and it cannot respond to problems that manage to wriggle through the edge defenses. Network-based firewalls and defenses must be implemented throughout the network, not just on the perimeter. In a later module, you'll learn more about security in network design.
- **Cloud-based**—Many anti-malware solutions already employ cloud-based resources within their programming. And cloud-based anti-malware provides the same kinds of benefits as other cloud-based solutions, such as scalability, cost efficiency, and shared resources. These cloud vendors are still working out bugs, and it can be a challenge to ensure that coverage soaks the entire network with no blind spots. Cloud solutions also increase the amount of Internet traffic to perform their duties, which can increase costs.

To find a balance between sufficient protection and minimal impact on performance, you must examine your network's vulnerabilities and critical performance needs. However, be aware that anti-malware is not a completely reliable form of protection. Other methods of device hardening are more effective, especially when multiple layers of security are put in place.

Asset Disposal

Securing your network devices doesn't stop when you're finished with those devices. You might think it doesn't matter what happens to a device after you throw it in the garbage or drop it off at the recycling center. However, mining data from discarded devices is a lucrative business that can yield significant insights into a company's operations, proprietary systems, and sensitive data. IT assets of all kinds must be carefully tracked both during and after their service time, as your company is legally responsible for the data contained on those devices even after you stop using them. IT devices that must be tracked include workstations, laptops, tablets, smartphones, printers, copiers, fax machines, scanners, servers, firewalls, routers, switches, and any other device or media that stores data (such as flash drives, tape drives, and hard drives).

In many cases, companies will hire professional disposal services that adequately sanitize or destroy devices so no data can be recovered. Reputable vendors provide end-to-end insurance coverage for hardware and data from the moment they take possession of each device. Typically, hard drives are destroyed before devices leave the customer's premises. Devices slated for disposal are then inventoried, tracked (possibly with GPS tracking), transported securely, and treated according to relevant data protection and environmental regulations and laws. The vendor returns certification of the following information:

- Chain of custody, that is, who had possession of each device and when, at what time the device arrived at the disposal facility, and the device's final destination (for example, if it's resold)
- Date and time of sanitization and methods used
- Valuation of any resaleable devices
- Whether each device was resold if reasonable, recycled if possible, or destroyed if necessary

The certificate the disposal service provides, which is called a CEED (Certificate of Electronic Equipment Destruction), serves as legal protection should data later be recovered from your devices. This kind of documentation must be presented during some types of audits.

When not using a disposal service, you take full responsibility to ensure any sensitive data on disposed devices is completely unusable. Recall that many devices, especially mobile devices like smartphones and tablets, are configured to allow a remote wipe of all data should the device be lost or stolen. While a remote wipe or factory reset can clear much of a device's data, often this process only makes the data inaccessible by conventional means. A skilled forensics investigator or hacker could still recover this data. Therefore, when the device is still in your possession, it must be thoroughly sanitized before disposal. To conform to this requirement, make sure all employees know to return aged devices to IT staff for proper disposal.

REMEMBER THIS...

- Describe common hardening and security policies.
- Explain the principle of least privilege and the concept of defense in depth.
- Apply device hardening best practices, including port security, disabling unneeded services, changing default passwords, and patching firmware.
- Properly dispose of IT assets.
- Compare host-based and network-based firewalls.

SELF-CHECK

8. The following ports were listed as open during a recent port scan. Which one is no longer used except by legacy software and should be closed?
   a. 22
   b. 53
   c. 139
   d. 443

9. You sent a coworker a .exe file to install an app on their computer. What information should you send your coworker so they can ensure the file has not been tampered with in transit?
   a. Public encryption key
   b. Hash of the encryption key
   c. Private encryption key
   d. Hash of the file

Check your answers at the end of this module.

You're Ready

You're now ready to complete **Project 10-3: Secure a Workstation**, or you can wait until you've finished reading this module.

SECURITY POLICIES FOR USERS

✔ CERTIFICATION

3.2 Explain the purpose of organization documents and policies.

4.2 Compare and contrast common types of attacks.

4.3 Given a scenario, apply network hardening techniques.

5.5 Given a scenario, troubleshoot general networking issues.

Average reading time: 29 minutes

Most network security breaches begin or continue due to human error. This section describes hardening techniques designed to minimize break-ins by communicating with and effectively managing the users in your organization with well-planned security policies.

A security policy for network users identifies your security goals, risks, levels of authority, designated security coordinator and team members, responsibilities for each team member, and responsibilities for each employee. In addition, it specifies how to address security breaches. It should not state exactly which hardware, software, architecture, or protocols will be used to ensure security, nor how hardware or software will be installed and configured. These details change from time to time and should be shared only with authorized network administrators or managers.

This section discusses written security policies that guide a user's activity on a network. You might also think of the term "security policy" in regard to rules programmed into a computer or other device. A software security policy programmed into an operating system or a firewall defines the conditions that must be met for a device or transmission to be given access to a network or computing resource. For example, you can set a network-wide security policy that prompts users to change their passwords every three months, and it requires a minimum number of characters for those passwords.

This provides two levels of protection. On one hand, there's the written rule, included in an Employee Handbook, specifying that users must comply with password restrictions. On the other hand, there's the security policy configured in Active Directory or a similar directory service. This policy is programmed into the device or network by a network administrator to enforce the rules written in the Employee Handbook. Later in this module, you'll get a chance to practice setting local security policies in Windows.

Security Policy Goals

Before drafting a security policy, you should understand why the security policy is necessary and how it will serve your organization. Typical goals for security policies include the following:

- Ensure that authorized users have appropriate access to the resources they need.
- Prevent unauthorized users from gaining access to the network, systems, applications, or data.
- Protect sensitive data from unauthorized access, both from within and from outside the organization.
- Prevent accidental or intentional damage to hardware or software.
- Create an environment in which the network and systems can withstand and, if necessary, quickly respond to and recover from any type of threat.
- Communicate each employee's responsibilities with respect to maintaining data integrity and system security.
- For each employee, obtain a signed consent to monitoring form, which is a document that ensures employees are made aware that their use of company equipment and accounts can be monitored and reviewed as needed for security purposes.

NOTE 10-2

A company's security policy need not pertain exclusively to computers or networks. For example, it might state that each employee must shred paper files that contain sensitive data or that each employee is responsible for signing in their visitors at the front desk and obtaining a temporary badge for those visitors.

After defining the goals of your security policy, you can devise a strategy to attain them. First, you might form a committee composed of managers and interested parties from a variety of departments in addition to your network administrators. The more decision makers you include, the more effective the policy created by the committee will ultimately be. This committee can assign a security coordinator, who will then drive the creation of the security policy.

To increase the acceptance of your security policy in your organization, tie security measures to business needs and clearly communicate the potential effects of security breaches. For example, if your company sells clothing over the Internet, make sure users and managers understand that a two-hour outage (as could be caused by a hacker who uses IP spoofing to gain control of your systems) could cost the company $100,000 in lost sales. With this understanding, employees are more likely to embrace the security policy.

A security policy must address an organization's specific risks. To understand your risks, you should conduct a posture assessment that identifies vulnerabilities and that rates both the severity of each threat and its likelihood of occurring, as described earlier in this module. After you have identified risks and assigned responsibilities for managing them, you're ready to outline the policy's content, as described in this section. Although compiling all this information might seem daunting, the process ensures that everyone understands the organization's stance on security and the reasons it is so important.

BYOD (Bring Your Own Device)

Recall that BYOD (bring your own device) refers to the practice of allowing people to bring their smartphones, laptops, or other technology into a facility for the purpose of performing work or school responsibilities. Variations on this theme include the following:

- **BYOA (bring your own application)**—Employees or students supply their choice of software on a computer or mobile device.
- **BYOC (bring your own cloud)**—Employees or students supply their choice of cloud application or storage.
- **BYOT (bring your own technology)**—A generic reference that includes the other BYO options.
- **CYOD (choose your own device)**—Employees or students are allowed to choose a device from a limited number of options, usually supplied by the company or school.

These days, BYOD doesn't necessarily refer to "bringing" a device anywhere. As more employees and students work from home, organizations are needing to adopt BYOD-friendly policies more than ever (see Figure 10-37). Employees and students need to keep in touch and complete work on a wide variety of devices, and this can create a security nightmare as companies work through these BYOD challenges.

Organizations offering BYOD options need detailed policies concerning what is allowed and what isn't, what reimbursements or allowances the company might offer, what restrictions will keep the organization's data and networks safe, and what configurations to the device are required to comply with the policies. BYOD practices can be cheaper for organizations to implement and tend to improve efficiency and morale for employees and students. However, security and legal compliance concerns must be sufficiently addressed in clearly defined BYOD policies and protocols.

Part of a BYOD policy might include on-boarding and off-boarding procedures. Recall that the process of configuring wireless clients for network access is called on-boarding. These configurations can be handled automatically by **MDM (mobile device management)** soft-

Figure 10-37 Employees and students are relying more heavily on their own devices for connecting to organizational resources

Bojan Milinkov/Shutterstock.com

ware. MDM works with all common mobile platforms and their service providers, and it can add or remove devices remotely. Examples of MDM software include VMware's Workspace ONE (*vmware.com/products/workspace-one.html*) and Cisco's Meraki Systems Manager (*meraki.cisco.com/products/systems-manager/*).

MDM software can automate enrollment, enforce password policies and other security restrictions, encrypt data on the device, sync data across corporate devices, wipe the device, and monitor the device's location and communications. The best MDM packages include granular control over these options. For example, an administrator might configure the software to remove corporate data from all devices while leaving personal data untouched. A less intrusive option is MAM (mobile application management), which targets specific apps on a device rather than controlling the entire device.

AUP (Acceptable Use Policy)

An **AUP (acceptable use policy)** explains to users what they can and cannot do while accessing a network's resources. It also explains penalties for violations and might describe how these measures protect the network's security. For example, Figure 10-38 shows one school's AUP for all faculty, staff, students, and guests who use the campus computer labs and other technology resources. This AUP details what kind of information is protected, how to protect it, whose responsibility it is to keep each user account secure, what the computers can be used for, what kinds of activities are prohibited, and much more. The AUP also includes details explaining why these measures are helpful for everyone who needs these resources for school and work.

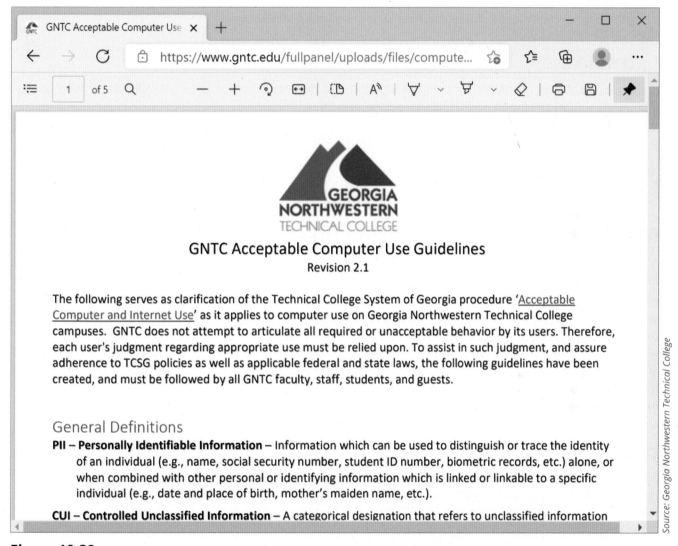

Source: Georgia Northwestern Technical College

Figure 10-38   A good AUP gives some explanation on the importance of included rules and restrictions

Employers should never assume that employees inherently know what is acceptable use of company IT resources and what is not. Detailing this information clarifies expectations for everyone. Some of the restrictions might include the following:

- Use company resources to fulfill job obligations and not for personal tasks that should be performed outside of business hours using the employee's own resources.
- Be aware that activities on the network can be and are monitored and may be formally audited.
- Immediately report any suspected compromise of confidential data or customer privacy.
- Always sign off or lock a device when not in use.
- Don't do anything illegal using company devices or other resources.
- Don't try to circumvent network security restrictions.

- Don't market products or services to other network users.
- Don't forward spam email.
- Don't violate the rights of any person or organization.
- Don't violate copyright, trade secret, patent, intellectual property, or other regulations. This includes but is not limited to the following:
  - Don't install, use, or distribute pirated materials.
  - Don't copy, digitize, or distribute copyrighted materials.
- Don't export software, technical information, or encryption technology.

NOTE 10-3

International and regional export controls limit what software, data, technology, and devices can cross certain political boundaries. For example, you might need an export license to travel internationally with encrypted data, and some countries might require that you decrypt data before entering the country. In some countries, authorities might confiscate devices temporarily or permanently. For this reason, you should never carry confidential data about patients, clients, or customers internationally.

NDA (Non-Disclosure Agreement)

A security policy should also define what *confidential* and *private* mean to the organization. This is often done in an NDA (non-disclosure agreement). In general, information is confidential if it could be used by other parties to impair an organization's functioning, decrease customers' confidence, cause a financial loss, damage an organization's status, or give a significant advantage to a competitor. However, if you work in an environment such as a hospital, where most data is sensitive or confidential, your security policy should classify information in degrees of sensitivity that correspond to how strictly its access is regulated. For example, top-secret data may be accessible only by the organization's CEO and vice presidents, whereas confidential data may be accessible only to those who must modify or create it to do their jobs (for example, doctors or hospital accountants).

NOTE 10-4

Any information covered by an NDA might also be protected from international export.

Password Policy

Choosing a secure password is one of the easiest and least expensive ways to help guard against unauthorized access. Unfortunately, too many people prefer to use an easy-to-remember password. If your password is obvious to you, however, it might also be easy for a hacker to figure out. An organization can enforce password policies to require that all users create passwords conforming to certain restrictions. Figure 10-39 shows password policies that can be configured for all of an organization's IAM (Identity and Access Management) users to require that they create secure passwords on AWS's cloud platform.

The following guidelines for creating passwords should be part of your organization's security policy. It is especially important for network administrators to choose well designed passwords, and also to keep passwords confidential and change them frequently. Tips for making and keeping passwords secure include the following:

- **Change default passwords**—Always change system default passwords after installing new software or equipment. For example, after installing a router, the default administrator's password on the router might be set by the manufacturer to *password*, with this information printed on a sticker on the bottom of the device. Change administrative credentials before making any other configuration changes.
- **Avoid personal information**—Do not use familiar information, such as your name, nickname, birth date, anniversary, pet's name, child's name, spouse's name, user ID, phone number, address, favorite color, favorite hobby, or any other words or numbers that others might associate with you.
- **Avoid real words**—Do not rely solely on words that might appear in a dictionary, even an "urban" or "slang" dictionary. Hackers can use programs that try a combination of your user ID and every word in a dictionary

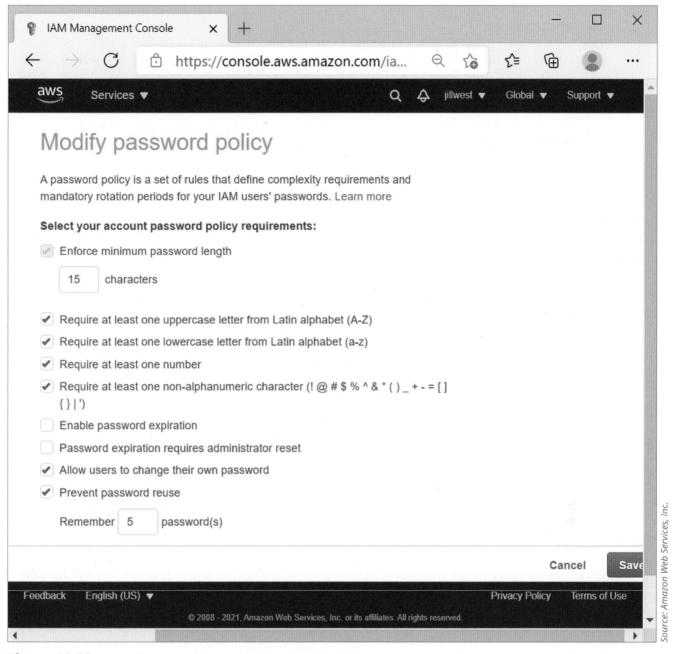

Figure 10-39 Set minimum password configuration policies

to gain access to the network. This is known as a **dictionary attack**, and it is typically the first technique a hacker uses when trying to guess a password (besides asking the user for their password). A dictionary attack will take into account typical user behavior regarding passwords, such as starting with short possibilities, checking words commonly used for passwords, and making common symbol substitutions for letters (such as using @ for the letter a). Other kinds of password attacks include the following:

- **Rainbow table attack**—This more technically challenging attack involves matching known passwords with hashes in a database of hashed passwords to identify as many passwords as possible. For example, you can determine that the word "password"—when hashed with MD5—is *5f4dcc3b5aa765d61d8327deb882cf99*. Then you check through the hacked password database and find all the hashes that list this particular hash. You then know which of the passwords, in their original plaintext, are "password". To defend against this type of attack, organizations will salt passwords, which means to add some extraneous characters that only the organization knows about.

- ○ **Brute-force attack**—Recall that, in a brute-force attack, a hacker attempts numerous possible character combinations until the correct combination is found. Many hackers using this approach will start with common passwords (such as "password", "123456", or "qwerty") and then alter one character at a time until finding a successful combination (such as "p@ssword"). The primary defenses against a brute-force attack are using a long password and using two-factor authentication, which you'll learn more about later.
- **Long is strong**—Make the password longer than eight characters—the longer, the better. Statistically speaking, a shorter password is more vulnerable to a brute-force attack than a longer one is. Current recommendations suggest that passwords should consist of at least 15 characters if the application or website allows that length. Remember this mantra: "Long is strong."
- **Increase complexity**—A well-designed password benefits from both length and complexity characteristics. Consider the following tips:
  - ○ Choose a combination of letters, numbers, and symbols. However, don't use common replacements of certain numbers or symbols for certain letters as hackers already know to look for these, and they're harder for you to remember.
  - ○ Use a combination of uppercase and lowercase letters, preferably in a random pattern instead of starting with a capital letter at the beginning of the password.
  - ○ Add special characters, such as exclamation marks or hyphens, if allowed.
  - ○ Do not repeat words or number sequences.
  - ○ Do not use a single letter, number, or symbol more than twice in succession (such as "passworddddddddddd").
  - ○ Do not use easily recognized phrases such as a line from a famous song, poem, or movie.

NOTE 10-5

Current research indicates that a long, random string of words, such as *correcthorsebatterystaple*, is easier to remember, more secure, and takes longer to crack than a seemingly randomized series of letters, numbers, and symbols that is short enough for a human to remember. The idea is to combine length with randomness in a way that works well for human memory and is statistically challenging for computers to crack. You can then add some complexity by inserting numbers and symbols and by intentionally misspelling one or more words in the series, such as *correct12HORSbatery!@STAPL*.

- **Don't use sticky notes**—Do not write down your password or share it with others, including coworkers or family members. Never store passwords in an unencrypted spreadsheet or document or in a web browser. Many browsers store these passwords in plaintext and can be easily hacked.
- **Update passwords**—Change your password at least every 60 days or more frequently. If you are a network administrator, establish controls through directory services that force users to change their passwords every 60 days.
- **Don't reuse passwords**—Do not allow passwords to be reused for the same account after they have expired. And use different passwords for different applications, accounts, and websites. For example, choose separate passwords for your email account, online banking, VPN connection, and so on. That way, if someone learns one of your passwords, they won't be able to use the same information to access all your secured accounts.
- **Use a password manager**—Make it easier to keep a secure record of long, random passwords by installing and using password management software such as LastPass (*lastpass.com*), KeePass (*keepass.info*), or 1Password (*1password.com*). These applications can generate unique strings of random letters, numbers, and symbols for each password, and store them securely in an encrypted database which is accessible from multiple devices through a single, master password. This way, users only need to remember one, well-formed password that is sufficiently long and random to help maximize security of their password database.

Password guidelines should be clearly communicated to everyone in your organization through your security policy. Although users might grumble about designing memorable but secure, long, random passwords and changing their passwords frequently, you can assure them that the company's financial, proprietary, and personnel data is safer as a result.

NOTE 10-6

Even if data is encrypted, at some point data is accessed, stored, or otherwise manipulated in its unencrypted form, and this is when vulnerability is greatest. This threat is called endpoint vulnerability because data is exposed in its unencrypted form at an endpoint of use, such as when a password is entered on a user's smartphone. For example, suppose a user has taken all precautions to create a long, complex password for their online bank account. The bank's website stores the account access information in a securely encrypted database. However, if the user then writes the password on a sticky note and hides it under the keyboard on their desk, this highly secured bank account is still extremely vulnerable to thieves.

Privileged User Agreement

A PUA (privileged user agreement), or privileged access agreement, addresses the specific concerns related to privileged access given to administrators and certain support staff. For example, doctors who have access to HIPAA-protected patient information must sign a privileged user agreement that defines what they can and can't do with that patient data and what special precautions they must take to protect the patient's privacy. Certain checks and balances must also be maintained and defined in the PUA. For example, the person who can authorize vendor payments should not be the same person who creates vendor accounts.

The privileged user agreement outlines guidelines, rules, restrictions, and consequences of violations, all of which help minimize the risk involved in allowing privileged access to some users. When accessing a privileged account, the user is advised to stay signed into the account only as long as necessary to perform the needed tasks, and then sign off, not relying on the time-out feature to sign them out. Privileged users need more frequent training and reminders to avoid falling for social engineering attacks of various types. And in many cases, activity in privileged accounts will be specially monitored through a PAM (privileged account management) tool, such as BeyondTrust's (*beyondtrust.com*) PAM products or CyberArk's (*cyberark.com*) solutions on-premises or in the cloud.

Anti-Malware Policy

Anti-malware software alone will not keep your network safe from malicious code. Because most malware infections can be prevented by applying a little technology and forethought, it's important that all network users understand how to prevent the spread of malware. An anti-malware policy provides rules for using anti-malware software and policies for installing programs, sharing files, and using external storage such as flash drives. To be most effective, an anti-malware policy should be authorized and supported by the organization's management staff. Suggestions for anti-malware policy guidelines include the following:

- Every computer in an organization should be equipped with malware detection and cleaning software that regularly scans for malware. This software should be centrally distributed and updated to stay current with newly released malware.
- Users should not be allowed to alter or disable the anti-malware software.
- Users should know what to do in case their anti-malware program detects malware. For example, you might recommend that the user stop working on their computer and instead call the help desk to receive assistance in disinfecting the system.
- An anti-malware team should be appointed to focus on maintaining the anti-malware measures. This team would be responsible for choosing anti-malware software, keeping the software updated, educating users, and responding in case of a significant malware outbreak.
- Users should be prohibited from installing any unauthorized software on their systems. This edict might seem extreme, but in fact, users downloading programs (especially games) from the Internet is a common source of malware. If your organization permits game playing, you might institute a policy in which every game must first be checked for malware and then installed on a user's system by a technician.
- System-wide alerts should be issued to network users notifying them of a serious malware threat and advising them how to prevent infection, even if the malware hasn't been detected on your network yet.

When drafting an anti-malware policy, bear in mind that these measures are not meant to restrict users' freedom, but rather to protect the network from damage and downtime. Explain to users that the anti-malware policy protects their own data as well as critical system files. If possible, automate the anti-malware software installation and operation so users barely notice its presence. Do not rely on users to run their anti-malware software each time they insert a USB drive or open an email attachment because they will quickly forget to do so.

Applying Concepts 10-3: Has Your Email Been Hacked?

How can you know if one of your accounts has been hacked if you can still get to the account and you don't yet notice any changes? Perhaps your username and password have been posted for sale as part of a hacked password database, waiting for the highest bidder to exploit your compromised credentials. Perhaps your email is posted publicly on the dark web for hackers to peruse at their pleasure. How can you know?

Troy Hunt (*troyhunt.com*) has developed a website called Have I Been Pwned, pronounced "powned" as a play on the words "owned" and "pawned" (as in chess). Troy analyzes user credentials after a breach to determine patterns in passwords that are easily hacked. While no one has a list of all successful hacks, the HIBP (Have I Been Pwned) website provides an in-depth resource to identify emails posted publicly in hacking databases.

To determine whether your email address is included in a published hack, complete the following steps:

1. In your browser, go to **haveibeenpwned.com**. Go to the FAQs page and answer the following questions:
   a. How does the website owner choose which data breaches to include in his site?
   b. How does the website protect the privacy of those whose data is included in the reported data breaches?
   c. What does the website do with information you submit in checking if your accounts have been included in a data breach?
   d. What can you conclude if your email address is not found in the site's database?
2. Return to the home page. Enter your email address (you can choose any of your email addresses) to see if that address has been pwned. What results did you get?
3. Based on these results, what steps do you need to take to further secure your accounts?

REMEMBER THIS...

- Explain the roles of password policies, AUPs, BYOD policies, and NDAs in network security.
- Compare various password attack types, including brute-force and dictionary attacks.
- Use good password management techniques.

SELF-CHECK

10. What kind of software can be used to secure employee-owned devices?
    a. PUA
    b. NDA
    c. MDM
    d. BYOD

11. Which of the following is the most secure password?
   a. p@$$w0rd
   b. yellowMonthMagneficant
   c. $t@rw@r$
   d. 09181973

12. An attacker guesses an executive's password ("M@nd@lori@n") to a sensitive database after chatting for a while at a club. What kind of password attack did the hacker use?
   a. Dictionary attack
   b. Brute-force attack
   c. Zero-day attack
   d. Rainbow table attack

Check your answers at the end of this module.

You're Ready

You're now ready to complete **Project 10-4: Create a Secure Master Password in LastPass**, or you can wait until you've finished the Review Questions for this module.

You're Ready

After you finish the Hands-On Projects, you're ready to complete the **Module 10 Capstone Projects**.

MODULE SUMMARY

Security Risks

- A weakness of a system, process, or architecture that could lead to compromised information or unauthorized access is known as a vulnerability. The act of taking advantage of a vulnerability is known as an exploit.
- Social engineering involves manipulating social relationships to gain access. Common types of social engineering include phishing, baiting, quid pro quo, tailgating, piggybacking, and shoulder surfing.
- A DoS (denial-of-service) attack occurs when legitimate users are unable to access normal network resources, such as a web server, because of an attacker's intervention. Several DoS subtypes include DDoS (distributed DoS) attack, DRDoS (distributed reflection DoS) attack, amplified DRDoS attack, PDoS (permanent DoS) attack, and friendly DoS attack.
- Common technology-based attacks and vulnerabilities include on-path attacks, deauth (deauthentication) attacks, insecure ports and protocols, FTP bounce, and back doors.
- Malware is a generalized term that refers to many kinds of malicious software, including virus, Trojan, worm, bot, and ransomware.

Risk Assessment and Management

- Effective risk management happens at two layers: the network layer and the business layer. A security risk assessment evaluates threats to and vulnerabilities of the network. A business risk assessment evaluates the impact of potential threats on business processes.
- Every organization should assess its security risks by conducting a posture assessment, which is a thorough examination of each aspect of the network to determine how it might be compromised. One component of a posture assessment might include a threat assessment, which identifies specific security threats to the network and related risk factors. If the company performing the posture assessment is accredited by an agency that sets network security standards, the assessment qualifies as a security audit, also called an IT audit.
- A vulnerability assessment is used to identify vulnerabilities in a network. Pen (penetration) testing takes advantage of ethical hacking to identify weaknesses and the extent of those weaknesses. This attack simulation begins with a vulnerability assessment using various tools and then attempts to exploit those vulnerabilities. During a red team–blue team exercise, the red team conducts the attack, and the blue team attempts to defend the network.
- Scanning tools—such as Nmap, Nessus, and Metasploit—can provide useful insights into your network's weaknesses that need attention. Used by hackers (or more likely, by bots) these tools can instead lead to compromised security.
- A honeypot is a decoy system that is purposely vulnerable and filled with what appears to be sensitive (though false) content. In more elaborate setups, several honeypots might be connected to form a honeynet.

Physical Security

- Access control hardware ranges from a simple deadbolt to more sophisticated options and can manage access to buildings, rooms, or storage spaces. Physical access control technologies include a keypad or cipher lock, an access badge system, biometrics, an access control vestibule, locking racks and locking cabinets, and smart lockers.
- Despite all precautions, sometimes breaches do occur. The key to protecting sensitive data and systems is to detect intrusions as quickly as possible and be prepared to respond appropriately. Methods of detecting physical intrusions and other kinds of events include motion detection, security cameras, tamper detection, and asset tags.

Device Hardening

- Besides securing network devices from external tampering, you can take many steps to secure the device from network- or software-supported attacks as well. These practices are called device hardening. There are many layers of defense you can implement, although the options vary from one device to another.
- Updates to applications, operating systems, and device firmware address several issues, including fixing bugs, adding new features, and closing security gaps. Because of the urgency of protecting networks and data from being compromised, security gaps are often addressed in smaller, more frequent updates called patches.
- Because default credentials are so commonly used, they're also extremely insecure. When configuring a device, make it a habit to change the default administrative credentials before you do anything else and record this information in a safe place. When you do so, avoid common usernames and passwords.
- Insecure services and protocols, such as Telnet and FTP, should be disabled in a system whenever possible. Leaving these software ports open and services running practically invites an intrusion because it's so easy to crack into a system through these open doors.
- Passwords are often stored in hashed form to prevent them from being read even if they were to be accessed. Using a highly secure hash algorithm nearly guarantees that stolen passwords will be useless to the thief.
- When implementing anti-malware software on devices and the network, one of your most important decisions is where to install the software. Some scenarios include host-based, server-based, network-based, or cloud-based.

- IT assets of all kinds must be carefully tracked both during and after their service time, as your company is legally responsible for the data contained on those devices even after you stop using them. IT devices that must be tracked include workstations, laptops, tablets, smartphones, printers, copiers, fax machines, scanners, servers, firewalls, routers, switches, and any other device or media that stores data (such as flash drives, tape drives, and hard drives). Disposal services provide a CEED (Certificate of Electronic Equipment Destruction), which serves as legal protection should data later be recovered from your devices. This kind of documentation must be presented during some types of audits.

Security Policies for Users

- A security policy for network users identifies your security goals, risks, levels of authority, designated security coordinator and team members, responsibilities for each team member, and responsibilities for each employee. In addition, it specifies how to address security breaches. It should not state exactly which hardware, software, architecture, or protocols will be used to ensure security, nor how hardware or software will be installed and configured. These details change from time to time and should be shared only with authorized network administrators or managers.
- To increase the acceptance of your security policy in your organization, tie security measures to business needs and clearly communicate the potential effects of security breaches.
- Organizations offering BYOD options need detailed policies concerning what is allowed and what isn't, what reimbursements or allowances the company might offer, what restrictions will keep the organization's data and networks safe, and what configurations to the device are required to comply with the policies. BYOD practices can be cheaper for organizations to implement and tend to improve efficiency and morale for employees and students. However, security and legal compliance concerns must be sufficiently addressed in clearly defined BYOD policies and protocols.
- An AUP (acceptable use policy) explains to users what they can and cannot do while accessing a network's resources. It also explains penalties for violations and might describe how these measures protect the network's security.
- A security policy should also define what *confidential* and *private* mean to the organization. This is often done in an NDA (non-disclosure agreement).
- An organization's security policy should include guidelines for creating secure passwords. It is especially important for network administrators to choose well designed passwords, and also to keep passwords confidential and change them frequently. Tips for making and keeping passwords secure include the following: Change default passwords, avoid personal information, avoid real words, use long passwords, increase complexity, don't use sticky notes, update passwords, don't reuse passwords, and use a password manager.
- A PUA (privileged user agreement), or privileged access agreement, addresses the specific concerns related to privileged access given to administrators and certain support staff.
- An anti-malware policy provides rules for using anti-malware software and policies for installing programs, sharing files, and using external storage such as flash drives. To be most effective, an anti-malware policy should be authorized and supported by the organization's management staff.

Key Terms

For definitions of key terms, see the Glossary.

access badge	botnet	CEED (Certificate of Electronic
access control vestibule	business process	Equipment Destruction)
asset tag	business risk assessment	CVE (Common Vulnerabilities and
AUP (acceptable use policy)	C&C (command-and-control)	Exposures)
badge reader	server	data breach
biometrics	CCTV (closed-circuit TV)	DDoS (distributed DoS) attack

deauth (deauthentication) attack
device hardening
dictionary attack
DLP (data loss prevention)
DNS poisoning
DoS (denial-of-service) attack
exploit
FTP bounce
hacker
hashing
honeynet
honeypot
insider threat
locking cabinet
locking rack
logic bomb

malware (malicious software)
MDM (mobile device management)
motion detection
NDA (non-disclosure agreement)
on-path attack
pen (penetration) testing
phishing
piggybacking
port scanner
posture assessment
principle of least privilege
privileged access
process assessment
PUA (privileged user agreement)
ransomware
red team–blue team exercise

security audit
security policy
security risk assessment
SHA (Secure Hash Algorithm)
shoulder surfing
smart card
smart locker
social engineering
tailgating
tamper detection
threat assessment
vendor risk assessment
vulnerability
vulnerability assessment
zero-day exploit

Review Questions

1. Your organization has just approved a special budget for a network security upgrade. What procedure should you conduct to develop your recommendations for the upgrade priorities?
   a. Data breach
   b. Security audit
   c. Exploit
   d. Posture assessment

2. Which type of DoS attack orchestrates an attack bounced off uninfected computers?
   a. FTP bounce
   b. Ransomware
   c. DRDoS attack
   d. PDoS attack

3. A company accidentally sends a newsletter with a mistyped website address. The address points to a website that has been spoofed by hackers to collect information from people who make the same typo. What kind of attack is this?
   a. Phishing
   b. Tailgating
   c. Quid pro quo
   d. Baiting

4. A former employee discovers six months after he starts work at a new company that his account credentials still give him access to his old company's servers. He demonstrates his access to several friends to brag about his cleverness and talk badly about the company. What kind of attack is this?
   a. Principle of least privilege
   b. Insider threat
   c. Vulnerability
   d. Denial of service

5. What type of attack relies on spoofing?
   a. Deauth attack
   b. Friendly DoS attack
   c. Tailgating
   d. Pen testing

6. You need to securely store handheld radios for your network technicians to take with them when they're troubleshooting problems around your campus network. What's the best way to store these radios so all your techs can get to them and so you can track who has the radios?
   a. Locking rack
   b. Smart locker
   c. Locking cabinet
   d. Access control vestibule

7. Leading up to the year 2000, many people expected computer systems the world over to fail when clocks turned the date to January 1, 2000. What type of threat was this?
   a. Ransomware
   b. Logic bomb
   c. Virus
   d. Worm

8. Which of the following attack simulations detect vulnerabilities and attempt to exploit them? Choose two.
   a. Red team–blue team exercise
   b. Vulnerability assessment
   c. Security audit
   d. Pen testing

9. Which of the following is considered a secure protocol?
   a. FTP
   b. SSH
   c. Telnet
   d. HTTP

10. A company wants to have its employees sign a document that details some project-related information that should not be discussed outside the project's team members. What type of document should they use?
    a. AUP
    b. NDA
    c. MDM
    d. BYOD

11. What is the difference between a vulnerability and an exploit?

12. What are the four phases in the social engineering attack cycle?

13. List five subtypes of DoS attacks.

14. What type of scan process might identify that Telnet is running on a server?

15. Give an example of biometric detection.

16. What unique characteristic of zero-day exploits makes them so dangerous?

17. What steps should your company take to protect data on discarded devices?

18. A neighbor hacks into your secured wireless network on a regular basis, but you didn't give her the password. What loophole was most likely left open?

19. Which form of SHA was developed by private designers?

20. Why might organizations be willing to take on the risk of BYOD?

Hands-On Projects

NOTE 10-7

Websites and applications change often. While the instructions given in these projects were accurate at the time of writing, you might need to adjust the steps or options according to later changes.

Note to Instructors and Students: A rubric is provided for evaluating student performance on these projects. Please see Appendix D.

Project 10-1: Play with Windows Sandbox

Estimated Time: 30 minutes (+5 minutes for group work, if assigned)
Objective: Compare and contrast common types of attacks. (Obj. 4.2)
Group Work: This project includes enhancements when assigned as a group project.
Resources:
- Windows 10 Pro, Enterprise, or Education 64-bit computer (either physical or virtual machine) with administrative access

Note: If your physical computer has Windows 10 Home, your Windows VM that you created in Module 1 might have Windows 10 Pro, Enterprise, or Education on it already. If not, recall that you created a Windows 10 Pro VM for Hands-on Project 4-2: Use Remote Desktop. However, you will need to enable nested virtualization for the VM. This information only applies to VirtualBox, as Hyper-V can only be run on Windows 10 Pro, Enterprise, or Education. If you're running Hyper-V, you can use your physical machine for this Windows Sandbox project. If you're running VirtualBox on a Windows 10 Home physical machine, go to the VM's **Settings** window and click **System**. Click the **Processor** tab. Select **Enable Nested VT-x/AMD-v** and click **OK**. Note that not all host computers support this feature.

- Virtualization support enabled in UEFI/BIOS
- Internet access

Context: A sandbox provides an isolated space on your computer to run questionable software or multiple instances of the same software or to access websites that might present a threat to your computer's system. Web browsers themselves act as simple sandboxes, but you can create a safer environment with dedicated sandbox software. As of the May 2019 update, Windows 10 Pro, Enterprise, and Education offer a built-in Sandbox app. This app runs on the same principles as Hyper-V in that it spins up a barebones VM where you can access websites through a browser or run applications. The sandboxed environment restricts these processes from accessing any other system resources in case something goes wrong. Windows Sandbox can run alongside Hyper-V or other hypervisors on the same computer. In this project, you enable Windows Sandbox and explore some of its features. Complete the following steps:

1. Using an administrator account on a Windows machine, go to **Programs and Features** in Control Panel and click **Turn Windows features on or off** (see Figure 10-40). Select the Windows Sandbox checkbox and click **OK**. Wait for the changes to complete and click **Restart now**.

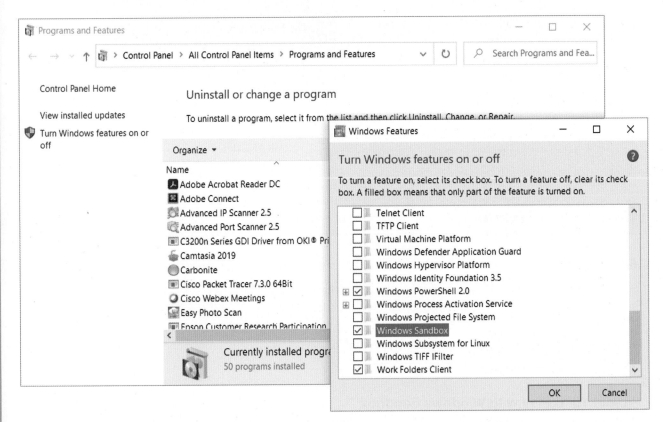

Figure 10-40   Enable Windows Sandbox

2. After reboot, from the Start menu, launch **Windows Sandbox** and click **Yes** on the UAC dialog box. A lightweight VM opens as an app. Figure 10-41 shows the host computer's desktop and the Sandbox desktop. In the Sandbox VM, the Start menu shows available applications.

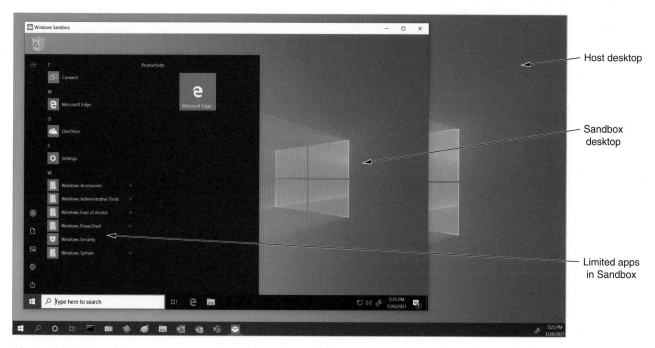

Figure 10-41   The Sandbox VM offers limited apps

3. Open **File Explorer** in the Sandbox. **Take a screenshot** showing your host's desktop, your Sandbox, and File Explorer open inside the Sandbox. Submit this visual with your answers to this project's questions.

4. Depending on the computer you used for your host system, answer the relevant questions in the following list:

   a. If the host computer is your personal computer, what do you notice about the differences between the folders listed in the Sandbox compared to the folders you have on your host computer?

   b. If the host computer is a generic computer created only for your labs, you might not have any personal folders stored on the host. In the host's File Explorer, create a new folder inside the Documents folder. Can you access this folder from your Sandbox's File Explorer?

   c. Click the Sandbox's local disk drive (probably drive C:). How much storage space is allocated to this Sandbox?

5. Close the Sandbox **File Explorer** window and open **Edge** in the Sandbox. Try navigating to **cengage.com**. Does it work?

6. Search for, download, and install the Chrome browser in the Sandbox. Does it work? Can you use the Sandbox's Chrome to surf the web?

7. Right-click **Start** and click **Windows PowerShell**. What prompt is shown?

8. Enter the command `ipconfig /all`. How does the Sandbox IP configuration compare with the host's IP configuration?

9. From the host, ping the Sandbox. Does it work?

10. **For groups assignments:** Attempt to ping a group member's Sandbox on the local network. Does it work?

11. In the host's Start menu, find **Windows Sandbox** and click to open a second instance. Does it work?

12. Leave the current windows open in the Sandbox and close the Sandbox. Wait a moment and open Windows Sandbox again. Are the same windows open? Is Chrome still installed? Why do you think this is?

13. List three kinds of vulnerabilities or attacks for which using Sandbox can provide protection.

14. Close Sandbox. Add a page to your Wikidot website and make some notes about this application.

Project 10-2: Scan a Network with Advanced Port Scanner

Estimated Time: 30 minutes
Objective: Given a scenario, use the appropriate network software tools and commands. (Obj. 5.3)
Resources:

- Windows 10 computer with administrative access
- Connection to a network with permission to scan the connected devices
- Internet access

Context: In this module, you learned that one way to secure a device is to close unneeded software ports in the operating system. Advanced Port Scanner is a free tool that scans a network for open ports and reports on the applications using those ports. In this project, you will download and use Advanced Port Scanner.

 **CAUTION**   Scanning a network you don't own or don't have permission to scan is illegal. Do not use Advanced Port Scanner on public Wi-Fi networks at all. Also don't use Advanced Port Scanner on any network you don't own unless you have written permission from the owner to do so.

Complete the following steps:

1. In your browser, go to **advanced-port-scanner.com**, download the app's software, and then install it using the default settings. Run Advanced Port Scanner when the installation is complete.
2. When Advanced Port Scanner opens, the IP address range for your network should be listed automatically. If not, you can check your computer's current IP address and use that information to insert the correct IP address range yourself. When you're ready, click **Scan**. The results of a scan on a home network and a connected virtual network are shown in Figure 10-42.

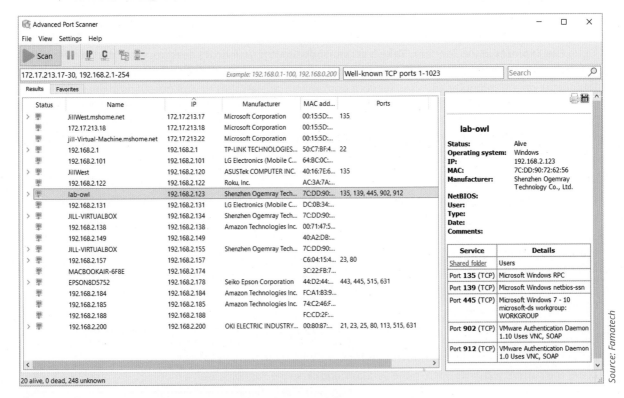

Figure 10-42   Open ports found by Advanced Port Scanner

3. When the scan is complete, look at the ports reported for each device. Which ports for insecure protocols are listed, such as port 21 for FTP? Are there any ports that stand out to you as being open unnecessarily? Use the information pane on the right for any selected device to help you identify the purpose of each open port, and research online for more information as needed.

4. **Take a screenshot** showing at least one device with open, insecure ports or with open ports that aren't being used. Be sure to blur any private information. Submit this visual with your answers to this project's questions.

5. Select another computer on the network besides your local device. Right-click the device name, point to **Tools**, and click **Ping**. What happens? How can you stop this process?

6. Attempt to shut down a device that you know won't be harmed if you succeed. Which device did you attempt to shut down? Were you able to force the device to shut down?

7. On the toolbar, click **Expand all**. How many devices on your network have printers, files, or folders shared to the network? What information here surprises you?

8. Choose a folder or file shared by a device other than your own and double-click it to open it in File Explorer. Can you find a file or folder on your network that should not be shared?

9. Why might it be important for you to scan your own network from time to time?

10. Add a page to your Wikidot website and make some notes about this installation.

Project 10-3: Secure a Workstation

Estimated Time: 20 minutes

Objective: Explain the purpose of organization documents and policies. (Obj. 3.2)

Resources:
- Windows 10 computer
- Internet access

Context: Securing a workstation is one of the most important tasks you will perform when setting up security for an organization or individual. A few simple tweaks to a computer's security configuration will greatly improve its resistance to attack. Follow these steps to require that a user press Ctrl+Alt+Del to log on:

1. Press **Win+R**, and in the Search box, enter **netplwiz**. Write down the usernames displayed in the section labeled *Users for this computer*.

2. Click the **Advanced** tab. Under Secure sign-in, check **Require users to press Ctrl+Alt+Delete**. Research this technique online. Why does this setting help increase the workstation's security?

3. Apply the changes and restart the computer to confirm the change.

Follow these steps to secure the computer using a screen saver and sleep mode:

4. Open **Settings**, click **Accounts**, and click **Sign-in options**. Under Require sign-in, select **When PC wakes up from sleep**.

5. Return to Settings **Home**, click **System**, and click **Power & sleep**. Set the Screen timeouts and Sleep timeouts as desired. **Take a screenshot** of these settings; submit this visual with your answers to this project's questions.

6. Return to Settings **Home**, click **Personalization**, and click **Lock screen**. Scroll down and click **Screen saver settings**. Select a screen saver to activate the screen saver function.

7. Set a wait time. For optimal security, this should be a low number. Check **On resume, display logon screen**. Click **OK** and close all windows.

Follow these steps to require that all users have a password:

8. Press **Win+R**, and in the Search box, enter **gpedit.msc**. The Local Group Policy Editor window opens.

9. Navigate to **Computer Configuration**, **Windows Settings**, **Security Settings**, **Account Policies**, **Password Policy**.

10. Change the Minimum password length policy to a value higher than zero. How many characters did you require? What was your reasoning in choosing the number?

Project 10-4: Create a Secure Master Password in LastPass

Estimated Time: 20 minutes

Objective: Given a scenario, apply network hardening techniques. (Obj. 4.3)

Resources:

- Internet access

Context: In Module 1, you created a LastPass account, which you have continued to use for several projects throughout this course. Recall that in Module 1, you were advised to create a long master password using a line from a song or movie to make it easier to remember. Although this is a quick way to encourage someone to design a more secure password than what most users create, for a password manager's master password or for any kind of privileged user or administrative account, you can certainly do better. It's now time to create a more secure master password for your LastPass account. Complete the following steps:

1. Review the list of tips in this module for creating a secure password. How does your current master password compare to the advice described in these steps?

2. In your browser, go to the website **security.org/how-secure-is-my-password/**.

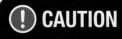 **CAUTION** Be sure to type the *security.org/how-secure-is-my-password/* address directly into your browser's address bar. Do not click on a link to this website from another website, from search engine results, or from a navigation suggestion. The official How Secure Is My Password tool at Security.org is safe to use because the password you type into the calculator is never transmitted off your local computer. The calculations are all performed locally in your browser. To be certain of this, you can navigate to the website, disconnect your computer from the Internet, and then enter your passwords to check their security level. However, many phishing websites spoof the How Secure Is My Password tool and are designed specifically to trick you into typing your most secure passwords into their web pages. As an added precaution, you could type a password that is *similar to* but not *the same as* your actual master password.

3. Enter your current master password (or a very similar password) to see how long it would take a hacker to crack your password based on its length. What time frame does the site report?

4. Considering the tips listed earlier for creating a secure password, make some changes to your current master password. Enter the new password (or a similar password) into the **How Secure Is My Password?** tool at Security.org. Keep making changes and testing your changes until you get calculation results showing at least one million years to crack the password and you've used as many of the other password guidelines as you can. Make sure you use a combination of letters, numbers, and symbols that you can remember without keeping a written copy of the password with you. What time frame does the site report for your new password? **Take a screenshot** of the results; submit this visual with your answers to this project's questions.

5. Change your master password in LastPass to your new, secure password.

6. Determine one or two safe locations where you can keep a recorded copy of your master password, such as written on a note that you keep in a locked box or safe deposit box, or in an encrypted file on your computer. Record your master password in this safe place for your reference if you later forget your master password. Be sure to always keep this note or file secure—do not leave it sitting out for any length of time thinking you'll put it away "later" because "later" might not happen soon enough.

7. Consider who might need access to your passwords should you become incapacitated. Would your parents or siblings need access to this information, or perhaps a spouse, partner, or older child? In LastPass, set up Emergency Access for this trusted person using their email address. Decide what period of time this person should have to wait from the point when access is requested until LastPass approves access. During this wait time, if you are not actually incapacitated, you can decline their request to access your vault.

Capstone Projects

NOTE 10-8

Websites and applications change often. While the instructions given in these projects were accurate at the time of writing, you might need to adjust the steps or options according to later changes.

Note to Instructors and Students: A rubric is provided for evaluating student performance on these projects. Please see Appendix D.

Capstone Project 10-1: Configure Router Passwords in Packet Tracer

Estimated Time: 45 minutes

Objective: Given a scenario, apply network hardening techniques. (Obj. 4.3)

Resources:

- Computer with Cisco Packet Tracer installed
- Access to the Packet Tracer network created in Capstone Project 9-2
- Storage space for Packet Tracer network file to be accessed in later projects and modules

Context: This Capstone Project picks up where Capstone Project 9-2 left off. When configuring a networking device, one of the very first tasks should be to change the default administrative credentials. In this project, you will use the CLI to configure user accounts and passwords for a router in your Packet Tracer network. Complete the following steps:

1. In Packet Tracer, open your Packet Tracer file from Capstone Project 9-2.
2. Click **Router3** and click the **CLI** tab. In the IOS CLI pane, press **Enter** to continue.
3. Enter the commands listed in Table 10-2 to change the router's default name.

Table 10-2   Change a router's hostname

Command	Purpose
`enable`	Enables privileged EXEC mode
`configure terminal`	Enters global configuration mode
`hostname R3`	Renames the router from the default to R3. Notice the prompt change.

4. What prompt do you see now?
5. Now you're ready to create a username and password, which will be required to sign into the router's management interface. Enter the commands listed in Table 10-3.

Table 10-3   Set a username and password and check the configuration

Command	Purpose
`username wrigley` `password cengage`	Creates the user account *wrigley* and requires the password *cengage* for that account
`line console 0`	Accesses the console port configuration interface (that is, the port you might connect a laptop to using a console cable to configure the router)
`login local`	Configures the router to require a locally configured username and password to log into the router's management interface

(continues)

Table 10-3   Set a username and password and check the configuration *(continued)*

Command	Purpose
`end`	Returns to privileged EXEC mode
`logout`	Logs out of the router's interface
Press **Enter** and then log in using the following credentials: Username: **wrigley** Password: **cengage**	Logs back into the router's interface using the new username and password

6. Check the configured username and password in the running-config file. Enter the commands listed in Table 10-4.

Table 10-4   View configurations in the running-config file

Command	Purpose
`enable`	Enables privileged EXEC mode
`show running-config`	Lists the configurations in the running-config file

NOTE 10-9

Press **Enter** to advance one line at a time in the running-config file.
Press the **Spacebar** to advance one page at a time.
When you're finished, press **Tab** to exit the running-config file.

7. What username and password information are shown in the running-config file? Why is this a problem?
8. Passwords should never be stored in plaintext. There's another way to create a password so the password will be stored more securely. Enter the commands listed in Table 10-5.

Table 10-5   Set a username and secret password and confirm configurations

Command	Purpose
`configure terminal`	Enters global configuration mode
`username maya secret cengage`	Creates the user account *maya* and requires the secret password *cengage* for that account
`do show running-config`	Lists the configurations in the running-config file

9. **Take a screenshot** of the usernames and passwords shown in the running-config file this time; submit this visual with your answers to this project's questions. The password for both accounts is *cengage*. Why do these passwords look different in the running-config file?
10. While you're at it, set two more passwords. Either one of these passwords could be required to enable privileged EXEC mode (although in reality, only the last enable password will continue to work). The difference is that one password will be stored in plaintext and the other will be hashed. Enter the commands listed in Table 10-6.

Table 10-6   Set a password and a secret password that can enable privileged EXEC mode

Command	Purpose
`enable password networkplus`	Requires the password *networkplus* to enable privileged EXEC mode
`enable secret comptia`	Requires the password *comptia* to enable privileged EXEC mode
`do show running-config`	Lists the configurations in the running-config file

11. **Take a screenshot** of the enable passwords shown in the running-config file; submit this visual with your answers to this project's questions.
12. You can encrypt existing passwords on a router, rather than having to go back and reconfigure each insecure password. Enter the commands listed in Table 10-7.

Table 10-7   Encrypt existing passwords

Command	Purpose
`service password-encryption`	Encrypts any plaintext passwords
`do show running-config`	Lists the configurations in the running-config file

13. What do you notice now about the two enable passwords? What about the two user account passwords?
14. Compare the complexity of the encryption for the passwords that were originally stored in plaintext with the passwords that were originally hashed. The secret passwords show a much more complex code. Notice the 5 in front of the secret passwords, which indicates the MD5 hash was used. Also notice the 7 in front of the other passwords. These Type 7 passwords use a weak encryption algorithm that is easily cracked. In your browser, go to **packetlife.net/toolbox** and click **Type 7 Reverser**. Copy and paste the Type 7 password string for each of the Type 7 passwords in Packet Tracer into the Type 7 hash box on the website. Note that you will need to select and then right-click each string instead of using the Ctrl + C shortcut to copy each string into your Clipboard. After pasting each string into the hash box, click **Reverse**. Do the values match your original plaintext passwords?
15. What happens when you paste a Type 5 password string into the hash box?
16. To save these configurations, enter the command `copy run start`, and then press **Enter** again to accept the default filename.
17. Make some notes on your Wikidot website about your activities in Packet Tracer for this project.

Note to instructors: A Packet Tracer solution file is provided for each Packet Tracer project through the Instructors site. Some Packet Tracer projects build on earlier Packet Tracer networks. If needed for one or more students, you can provide a previous project's solution file as a start file for one of these progression projects.

Capstone Project 10-2: Install Kali Linux in a VM

Estimated Time: 60 minutes
Objective: Given a scenario, use the appropriate network software tools and commands. (Obj. 5.3)
Resources:
- Access to the same computer used to complete Capstone Project 1-1 or Capstone Project 1-2

Note: The Windows 10 VM created in Module 1 and the Kali Linux VM created in this project will be used together in a later module. Both VMs need to be hosted on the same physical computer.

- Internet access

Context: Kali Linux is a unique distribution of Linux in that it is designed specifically for enhancing the security of a network. The operating system can be run from a flash drive or CD, and it includes an impressive array of security tools. In this project, you research the features of Kali Linux and then you download and install Kali Linux in a VM.

> 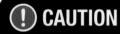 **CAUTION** It's highly illegal to perform penetration testing procedures on a network that you do not own or have specific permission to test. If you choose to use the penetration testing tools included in Kali Linux, this is best done on your own, home network where you own the networking equipment and pay the bill yourself.
>
> If you use a network that you do not own, be sure to obtain explicit permission from the network owner, preferably in writing, signed, and dated. If you practice using the pen testing tools in a school lab, be sure to follow your instructor's directions carefully.
>
> Penetration testing a network you don't own without the owner's permission can incur multiple federal felony charges, even if the network owner is a relative or friend. Please be absolutely certain you have permission *in writing* before using the Kali Linux pen testing tools.

Complete the following steps:

1. Spend some time researching Kali Linux to answer the following questions:
   a. What company maintains Kali Linux? What distribution was the predecessor to Kali Linux?
   b. What is the main purpose(s) of the Kali Linux distribution?
   c. What are the installation options for Kali Linux? For example, can you use a USB flash drive?
   d. Can you dual-boot Kali Linux next to other operating systems? If so, which ones?
   e. For which hypervisors does Kali Linux offer custom images?
   f. On the Downloads page, which hashing algorithm does the website use to confirm the validity of the Kali download files?
2. In your browser, go to **kali.org**. Find the downloads for the Kali Linux Images. Download the appropriate Kali image for the hypervisor you're using for this project.
   a. If you're using VirtualBox, follow instructions on the screen for downloading the appropriate Kali Linux VirtualBox image for your system (32-bit or 64-bit).
   b. If you're using Hyper-V, download the Kali Linux Installer image that is appropriate for your system (32-bit or 64-bit).
3. Import the Kali Linux image into your hypervisor with the following steps, which differ from the way you've created VMs previously:
   - In VirtualBox, click **File**, **Import Appliance**. Locate the downloaded image and click **Open**. Accept the default settings and click **Import** to complete the process. You might need to disable USB 2.0 support to start the VM in VirtualBox. If so, open the VM's Settings window, click **USB**, and select the **USB 1.1 (OHCI) Controller**, as shown in Figure 10-43. Click **OK**.
   - In Hyper-V, click **Quick Create**, and then click **Local installation source**. Deselect the box for *This virtual machine will run Windows*. Click **Change installation source** and then locate and select your ISO file. Click **Create Virtual Machine**. When it's ready, click **Connect** and **Start**. Select **Graphical Install** and press **Enter**. Complete the full installation steps. Be sure to give this VM a name after it's created.
4. Start and sign into the Kali Linux VM. At the time of this writing, the hypervisor virtual images of Kali Linux are all configured with the default username **kali** and password **kali**. If you installed Kali Linux using the Installer file, you created your own username and password. Note that the username should be entered in lowercase, even if you created it using one or more capital letters. Be sure to record this information in your LastPass account.
5. Take a quick tour around the Kali Linux desktop, as shown in Figure 10-44. You can explore the tools on your own if you want to. Make sure that you own the network you're penetration testing, or make sure you have detailed *written, signed, and dated* permission from the network owner before using any of the tools provided in Kali Linux.

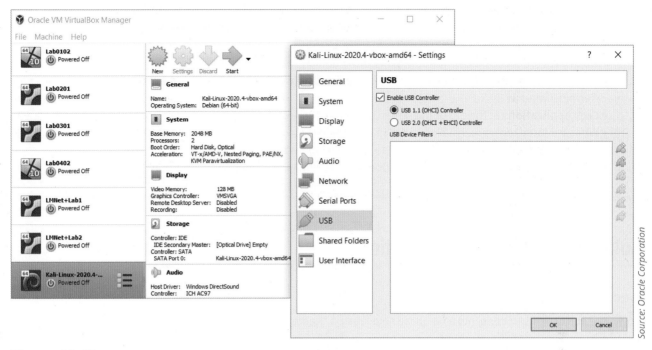

Figure 10-43 In VirtualBox, select the USB 1.1 controller

Figure 10-44 The Kali Linux desktop in a VirtualBox VM

Answer the following questions:

- Open the File System window. When you click **kali** in the left pane, what folders are listed? Close the File System window.
- Open the Terminal Emulator window. What is the default command prompt?
- Ping Google's public DNS server (8.8.8.8). Is the ping successful? Press **Ctrl+C** to stop the output. Close the Terminal window.
- Click **Applications** at the top of the screen. Which categories of tools are available?
- What are three tools pre-installed in Kali that you've used in earlier labs or read about in this course?
- Click **Log Out** at the top of the screen and click **Shut Down** to power down the VM.

6. Add some notes to your Wikidot website about the new VM installation.

Solutions to Self-Check Questions

Security Risks

1. The ability to insert code into a database field labeled "Name" is an example of a(n):

   Answer: b. vulnerability

   Explanation: A weakness of a system, process, or architecture that could lead to compromised information or unauthorized access is known as a **vulnerability**. The act of taking advantage of a vulnerability is known as an exploit or attack. Unauthorized access or use of sensitive data is called a data breach.

2. Which of the following social engineering attack types requires the attacker to spend the most time with the victim?

   Answer: d. Phishing

   Explanation: **Phishing** is communication that appears to come from a legitimate source and requests access or authentication information; to be effective, phishing must build on pre-existing knowledge about the victim, such as knowing the victim's name, the name of their boss, companies they do business with, or similar information. Tailgating, piggybacking, and shoulder surfing are more transient in nature and don't require any existing knowledge about the victim to be successful.

3. You're playing a game on your Xbox when you suddenly get bumped off your Wi-Fi network. You reconnect and start playing, then get bumped off again. What type of attack is most likely the cause?

   Answer: c. Deauth attack

   Explanation: In a **deauth (deauthentication) attack**, the attacker sends faked deauthentication frames to the AP, the client, or both (or as a broadcast to the whole wireless network) to trigger the deauthentication process and knock one or more clients off the wireless network. An on-path attack, previously called a MitM (man-in-the-middle) attack, relies on intercepted transmissions. In a well-known exploit called FTP bounce, hackers take advantage of the insecure FTP protocol. DDoS (distributed DoS) attacks are orchestrated through many sources to prevent legitimate users from accessing normal network resources.

Risk Assessment and Management

4. What is the first step in improving network security?

   Answer: b. Identify risks.

   Explanation: Before spending time and money changing your network security, first **identify your network's current security risks**. The next steps include determining which resources might be harmed if each risk were exploited, developing plans to respond to threats, and documenting next steps.

5. Which assessment type would most likely discover a security risk related to employee on-boarding?

Answer: b. Process assessment

Explanation: A **process assessment** is used to identify business processes and evaluate risks related to those processes, such as a security risk in an existing employee on-boarding process. A vendor risk assessment (also called a third-party risk assessment) evaluates security and compliance risks related to suppliers and vendors a company does business with. A threat assessment identifies specific security threats to the network and related risk factors. A posture assessment is a thorough examination of each aspect of the network to determine how it might be compromised.

6. Which team might ask a user for a password?

Answer: a. Red team

Explanation: During a red team–blue team exercise, the red team conducts the attack, and the blue team attempts to defend the network. The **red team** relies heavily on social engineering, such as asking users for their passwords to determine if users are adequately trained to resist social engineering tactics.

Physical Security

7. Which physical security device works through wireless transmission?

Answer: a. Badge reader

Explanation: Some badges are proximity cards, which do not require direct contact with a **badge reader** to be detected. Previously known as a mantrap, an access control vestibule creates a confined space between two locking doors where one door must lock closed before the other can open. A keypad, or cipher lock, requires the entry of a code to open the door. Biorecognition access in which a device scans an individual's unique physical characteristics is called biometrics.

Device Hardening

8. The following ports were listed as open during a recent port scan. Which one is no longer used except by legacy software and should be closed?

Answer: c. 139

Explanation: **Ports 137-139** for NetBIOS should be closed to prevent legacy access methods that can be exploited by common malware such as WannaCry ransomware. Port 22 is used by SSH and should be open only if it's needed. Port 53 is used by DNS and must be left open for network connections to work. Port 443 is used by HTTPS and must be left open for web browsing to work.

9. You sent a coworker a .exe file to install an app on their computer. What information should you send your coworker so they can ensure the file has not been tampered with in transit?

Answer: d. Hash of the file

Explanation: Hashing is mostly used to ensure data integrity—that is, to verify the data has not been altered. With hashing, your coworker can hash the file and compare the new hash with the expected **hash of the file** that you send. If the hashes match, this indicates the file is exactly the same as the original file. If the output does not match, this indicates the file has likely been altered.

Security Policies for Users

10. What kind of software can be used to secure employee-owned devices?

Answer: c. MDM

Explanation: Mobile device configurations can be handled automatically by **MDM (mobile device management)** software, which increases BYOD (bring your own device) security by ensuring that employee-owned devices conform to company-defined security policies. An NDA (non-disclosure agreement) defines what information an organization identifies as confidential and private and how that information should be protected. A PUA (privileged user agreement), or privileged access agreement, addresses the specific concerns related to privileged access given to administrators and certain support staff.

11. Which of the following is the most secure password?

    Answer: b. yellowMonthMagneficant

    Explanation: The password **yellowMonthMagneficant** is 22 characters long and uses an incorrect spelling of at least one of the words. Statistically speaking, a shorter password is more vulnerable to a brute-force attack than a longer one is. A well-designed password benefits from both length and complexity characteristics.

12. An attacker guesses an executive's password ("M@nd@lori@n") to a sensitive database after chatting for a while at a club. What kind of password attack did the hacker use?

    Answer: b. Brute-force attack

    Explanation: In a **brute-force attack**, a hacker attempts numerous possible character combinations until the correct combination is found. In this case, the attacker used social engineering to identify special interests of the target and then employed a brute-force attack to determine the exact combination of characters used for the password. A dictionary attack tries various words found in a dictionary that are commonly used for passwords. A rainbow table attack matches known hashes to hashes in a database of hashed passwords. A zero-day attack takes advantage of a software vulnerability that hasn't yet or has only recently become public.

SECURITY IN NETWORK DESIGN

After reading this module and completing the exercises, you should be able to:

1. Incorporate security into the design of a network
2. Describe the functions and features of various network security devices
3. Explain how authentication, authorization, and accounting work together to help secure a network
4. Compare authentication technologies

On the Job

I was the network administrator and entire IT department for a mortgage company owned by a bank, which I'll call Bank A. Much of my job focused on certain legal and financial processes that had to run at different intervals, ranging from daily to quarterly. To facilitate these processes, I created static routes that allowed for the direct encrypted transfer of files from the mortgage company's servers to Bank A's servers.

Eventually, our company was purchased by another bank, which I'll call Bank B. Naturally, many of our legal and financial processes had to change. This in turn necessitated numerous changes to the network. Working with Bank B's IT department, I began updating Access Control Lists, and providing detailed information to our third-party Intrusion Prevention Service to make sure legitimate business was not accidently blocked. We tested firewalls, ACLs, VPNs, batch processes, static routes, and were confident that everything had been implemented successfully. It took coordination from three teams of people working over two weeks and weekends, but we got everything ready by the time the acquisition was announced. Everything went smoothly. The people at the mortgage company saw no changes to their work. The people at Bank B received all the files that they needed in the correct formats.

Fast-forward two months. I was working off-site, and my phone starts ringing nonstop. Some files needed to be transferred to a federal agency within hours or the mortgage company would be fined hundreds of thousands of dollars. No person at the mortgage company had permission or knowledge to investigate the issue. I had to pull off the interstate, find a coffee shop with Internet access, and get to work solving the problem.

Eventually we figured out the issue was a static route associated with a quarterly process that we had overlooked. I started by calling the people at Bank A to ask if they could detect any network traffic trying to reach a specific IP address. After some digging around, they found traffic from the mortgage company's network being refused by a decommissioned server. To fix the problem, I configured new static routes and the files made it in on time by less than an hour.

Johnathan Yerby, Ph.D.
Middle Georgia State University

In the previous module, you began your study of network security with an exploration of threats to the network, physical security, and security policies for users. A non-technical network user will likely be exposed to all these things at some point in a non-IT career. In this module, you'll see what security precautions IT professionals need to implement behind-the-scenes on a network to help keep it secure.

Let's begin with a discussion of how to implement security into the very design of a network. Then you'll read about network security devices, which is a category that includes far more than just firewalls. You'll then explore the complementary processes of network access control and dig into various authentication protocols that validate the identity of people, services, and devices on your network.

NETWORK HARDENING BY DESIGN

✅ CERTIFICATION

4.1 Explain common security concepts.	7 Application
	6 Presentation
	5 Session
4.2 Compare and contrast common types of attacks.	4 Transport
	▶ ③ Network
4.3 Given a scenario, apply network hardening techniques.	▶ ② Data Link
	1 Physical
5.5 Given a scenario, troubleshoot general networking issues.	

Average reading time: 21 minutes

Throughout this course, you've learned about many security features and techniques used to secure software, devices, data, and traffic on a network. It's easy to feel like your network is safe once you've implemented some of these strategies and created a secure perimeter around your valuable resources. However, network security professionals today can't afford to be naïve. Attackers continue to develop their tactics and techniques to infiltrate networks, steal data, and damage resources. What's outside the network has never been trusted, but now, what's inside the network also can't be trusted. This is called a **zero trust** security model where everything in the network is considered untrustworthy until proven otherwise. Not only do routers at the edge of the network need firewall protection. Routers, switches, servers, and every other device inside the network are also at risk from malware, malicious users, intruders, bots, and even unintentional errors, misconfigurations, or failures. For these and many other reasons, security must be implemented in many, seemingly redundant layers that permeate the network and protect resources from every angle. As you've read in earlier modules, this strategy is called defense in depth.

Router and Switch Security Configurations

Networking devices such as routers and switches are designed to pass traffic through the network as quickly and efficiently as possible. However, opening these devices to unlimited traffic can cause problems, either for the devices themselves, for targets on the network, or for the network as a whole. Networking devices offer built-in features to help protect them from attacks and traffic spikes. In this section, you'll read about security features configured on both routers and switches. In the next section, you'll learn about security features specific to switches.

Access Control Lists (ACLs)

Before a hacker can gain access to files on your network's server, they must traverse one or more switches and routers. Although devices such as firewalls, described later in this module, provide more tailored security, manipulating switch and router configurations affords a small degree of security, especially when these devices sit on or near the edge of a network where they can control access to the network. This section describes a fundamental way to control traffic through routers, switches, and firewalls with the conversation focusing primarily on routers.

A router's main function is to examine packets and determine where to direct them based on their network layer addressing information. Thanks to a router's **ACL (access control list)**, or access list, routers can also decline to forward certain packets depending on their content. An ACL acts like a filter to instruct the router to permit or deny traffic according to one or more of the following variables:

- Network layer protocol (for example, IP or ICMP)
- Transport layer protocol (for example, TCP or UDP)
- Source IP address
- Destination IP address (which can restrict or allow certain websites)
- TCP or UDP port number

Each time a router receives a packet, it examines the packet and refers to its ACL to determine whether the packet meets criteria for permitting or denying travel on the network. See Figure 11-1. Each statement or test in the ACL specifies either a permit or deny flag. The router starts at the top of the list and makes a test based on the first statement. If a packet's characteristics match a permit statement, the packet is released toward its destination. If the packet's characteristics match a deny statement, the packet is immediately discarded. If the packet's characteristics don't match the first statement, the router moves down the list to the next statement in the ACL. If the packet does not match any criteria given in the statements in the ACL, the packet is dropped (as shown by the last "No" value in Figure 11-1). This last decision is called the **implicit deny** rule, which ensures that any traffic the ACL does not explicitly permit is denied by default.

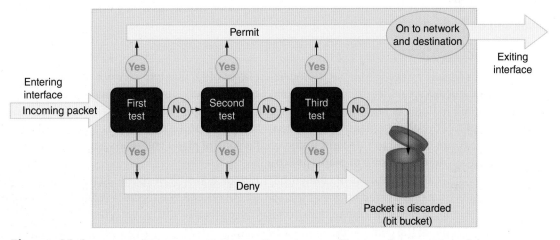

Figure 11-1 A router uses an ACL to permit or deny traffic to or from a network it protects

On most routers, each interface must be assigned a separate ACL, and different ACLs may be associated with inbound and outbound traffic. When ACLs are installed on routers, each ACL is assigned a number or name.

The `access-list` command is used to assign a statement to an ACL on Cisco routers and similar routers. The command must identify the ACL and include a permit or deny argument. Here are a few sample commands used to create statements in the ACL named acl_2, which controls incoming traffic to a router:

- To permit ICMP traffic from any IP address or network to any IP address or network:

```
access-list acl_2 permit icmp any any
```

- To deny ICMP traffic from any IP address or network to any IP address or network:

```
access-list acl_2 deny icmp any any
```

- To permit TCP traffic from 2.2.2.2 host machine to 5.5.5.5 host machine:

```
access-list acl_2 permit tcp host 2.2.2.2 host 5.5.5.5
```

- To permit TCP traffic from 2.2.2.2 host machine to 3.3.3.3 host machine to destination web port 80 (the "eq" parameter says "equal to" and "www" is a keyword that stands for port 80):

```
access-list acl_2 permit tcp host 2.2.2.2 host 3.3.3.3 eq www
```

Statements can also specify network segments (groups of IP addresses) by using a network address for the segment and a wildcard mask. The bits in a wildcard mask work opposite of how bits in a subnet mask work. The 0s in the wildcard mask say to match the IP address bits to the network address given, and the 1s say you don't care what the value of those bits are. For example, a wildcard mask of 0.0.0.255 can be written as 00000000.00000000.00000000.11111111, which says the first three octets of an IP address must match the given network address and the last octet can be any value. For example, the following command permits TCP traffic to pass through when the first three octets of an IP address are 10.1.1 and the last octet can be any value:

```
access-list acl_2 permit tcp 10.1.1.0 0.0.0.255
```

NOTE 11-1

In ACL statements, any is equivalent to using a wildcard mask of 255.255.255.255, which allows all IP addresses to pass through.

An access list is not automatically installed on a router. If you don't configure an ACL, the router allows all traffic through. Once you create an ACL and assign it to an interface, you have explicitly permitted or denied certain types of traffic. Naturally, the more statements or tests a router must scan (in other words, the longer the ACL), the more time it takes a router to act and, therefore, the slower the router's overall performance.

When troubleshooting a problematic connection between two hosts, or between some applications or ports on two hosts, consider that the problem might be a misconfigured ACL blocking needed services, ports, or addresses. For example, suppose you can successfully ping a host, but Telnet and tracert attempts cannot connect with the same host. You can use a process of elimination on the device's various ACLs to identify the incorrect ACL settings and correct the problem. Common errors include listing the ACL statements in the wrong order, using the wrong criteria when defining a rule, or constructing a rule incorrectly.

Control Plane Policing (CoPP)

As you know, the control plane refers to the decision-making layer of connected networking devices. For example, a router's control plane manages routing protocols to build and constantly update routing tables. This functionality can become overwhelmed in times of high traffic or during an attack. While ACLs filter traffic into and out of router interfaces on the data plane, the control plane needs a separate layer of protection. In this case, an adaptation of QoS (quality of service) filters can be used to rate-limit traffic on the control plane and management plane of routers and switches using a feature called CoPP (control plane policing).

The following steps describe the process of configuring CoPP on a switch or router. In this scenario, ICMP traffic is permitted with no limits from one trusted device at 192.168.2.2. All other ICMP traffic is limited and, when exceeding that limit, is dropped. You might have the opportunity to test these steps in the lab on a real router. However, Packet Tracer does not support some of the commands required here.

Begin by defining an ACL that will identify which traffic is relevant to your CoPP policies. For example, the following commands, entered in global configuration mode, create an ACL numbered 100 that defines the relevant ICMP traffic:

```
access-list 100 permit icmp any any
access-list 100 deny icmp host 192.168.2.2 any
```

Next, you need to create a class map, which will classify traffic according to defined criteria such as an ACL. Use the following command to create a class map named limit-icmp and to enter class-map configuration mode (which is similar in concept to the interface configuration mode you've used in some of your projects):

```
class-map limit-icmp
```

Now you can match the class to your identified traffic with the following command:

```
match access-group 100
```

Exit class-map configuration mode with the exit command. You now need a policy map, which will apply policies to the traffic identified by the class map. Use the following command to create a policy map named copp-test and to enter pmap configuration mode:

```
policy-map copp-test
```

The `class` command entered in pmap configuration mode will pair the class map you created earlier to your new policy map, as follows:

```
class limit-icmp
```

This command also takes you into the pmap-class configuration mode, as shown in Figure 11-2.

```
Press RETURN to get started!



Router>en
Router#conf t
Enter configuration commands, one per line.  End with CNTL/Z.
Router(config)#int gig0/0
Router(config-if)#ip add 192.168.2.1 255.255.255.0
Router(config-if)#no shut

Router(config-if)#
%LINK-5-CHANGED: Interface GigabitEthernet0/0, changed state to up

Router(config-if)#exit
Router(config)#access-list 100 permit icmp any any
Router(config)#access-list 100 deny icmp host 192.168.2.2 any
Router(config)#class-map limit-icmp
Router(config-cmap)#match access-group 100
Router(config-cmap)#exit
Router(config)#policy-map copp-test
Router(config-pmap)#class limit-icmp
Router(config-pmap-c)#
```

Source: Cisco Systems, Inc.

Figure 11-2 Pmap-class configuration mode

Next, the `police` command will define actions to perform when these criteria are met. For example, if the bps (bits per second) rate stays below the threshold of 8000, the identified messages will be transmitted. However, if the rate exceeds 8000 bps, packets are dropped. The following command in pmap configuration mode defines this scenario:

```
police 8000 conform-action transmit exceed-action drop
```

You now need to shift to control plane configuration mode. From global configuration mode, enter the following command:

```
control-plane
```

Finally, apply the QoS service policy you created earlier to the control plane on the device with the following command:

```
service-policy input copp-test
```

After all that work, you can test your configuration by running a lot of large pings from a trusted source and from an untrusted source to compare the outcomes. If you did it all correctly, the untrusted source's pings will sometimes be dropped to enforce the defined maximum ICMP bits per second on the router's control plane, while the trusted source's pings will not be limited.

Switch Security Configurations

Some security features, such as CoPP, work on both routers and switches. Some features, however, are specific to switches due to the types of traffic switches manage. Consider the following security features on switches.

Router Advertisement (RA) Guard

Default trust relationships between one network device and another might allow a hacker to access the entire network because of a single flaw. For example, recall from earlier in this course you learned how IPv6 clients receive RA (router advertisement) messages to determine network information, such as IP addresses of DNS servers and the default gateway as well as the network prefix. One weakness of this system is that IPv6 clients are a bit gullible—if several devices send RA messages, clients don't know which advertisements to believe (see Figure 11-3). Clients have no way of authenticating RA messages to know which of these messages come from legitimate sources and which might come from a network attacker. This creates two vulnerabilities:

- Malicious RA messages can be used to misconfigure network clients, thus hijacking network traffic.
- High volumes of RA messages can create a network DoS attack, slowing or disabling the network. In a project at the end of this module, you'll practice using RA messages to flood and disable a virtual network.

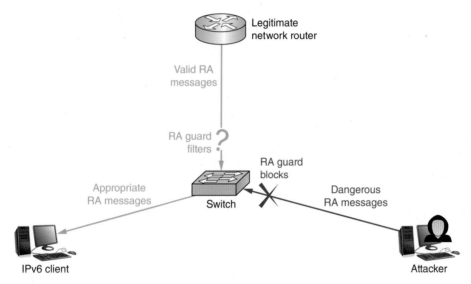

Figure 11-3   An attacker sends illegitimate RA messages

The solution to this problem is to configure RA guards on network switches. The **RA guard** feature filters RA messages so these messages can only come from specific interfaces on the switch. Additionally, RA guard offers other criteria that can filter RA messages on valid interfaces according to source MAC or IP address, router priority, or other options.

RA guard is configured on Cisco switches using the `raguard` command, which accesses the RA guard policy configuration mode (similar to other configuration modes you've used or read about here). You might create one RA guard policy for hosts attached to the switch, and this policy might be named something like HOSTS. The HOSTS policy blocks all RA messages for interfaces with that policy applied. You might create a second RA guard policy for routers attached to the switch, and this policy might be named something like ROUTERS. The ROUTERS policy might filter RA messages to ensure they're coming from a trusted router.

DHCP Snooping

Similar to RA messages, by default, DHCP messages are allowed to flow freely through ports on switches so that clients can request and receive DHCP assignments. A **rogue DHCP server** running on a client device, however, could be used to implement an on-path attack by configuring the attacker's IP address as the victim computers' default gateway. Alternatively, the attacker could give their IP address as the DNS server and then spoof websites.

DHCP messages should be monitored by enabling **DHCP snooping** on a switch. This way, switch ports connected to clients won't be allowed to transmit DHCP responses that should only come from a trusted DHCP server. In Figure 11-4, you can see the layer 3 switch trusts the DHCP offer made by the DHCP server, and this offer can be forwarded to the workgroup switches. A DHCP offer from the attacking computer on the bottom right of the figure, however, will not be trusted.

DHCP snooping is configured on a Cisco switch using the `ip dhcp snooping` command. When enabled, the switch snoops, or listens to, DHCP messages exchanged between the network's DHCP server and its clients. The switch then gathers legitimate IP-to-MAC address pairings as assigned by DHCP and collects this information in a

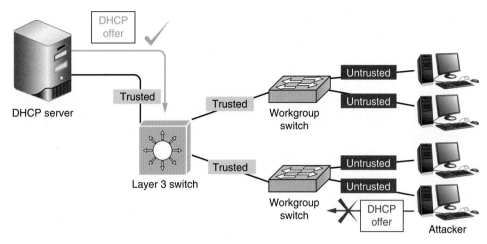

Figure 11-4   DHCP offer messages can only enter a trusted port on a switch, not an untrusted port

DHCP snooping binding database. Figure 11-5 shows a sample database from a switch where two PCs have received DHCP assignments from a legitimate DHCP server. The switch can use this information for other layers of security, as you'll read about next. In a project at the end of this module, you'll attack a network with a rogue DHCP server and then defend the network using DHCP snooping.

```
Switch#show ip dhcp snooping binding
MacAddress          IpAddress        Lease(sec)   Type            VLAN   Interface
-----------------   --------------   ----------   -------------   ----   ----------------
00:01:96:3E:24:CC   192.168.2.2      86400        dhcp-snooping   1      FastEthernet0/1
00:D0:58:A6:48:8D   192.168.2.3      86400        dhcp-snooping   1      FastEthernet0/2
Total number of bindings: 2
Switch#
```

Source: Cisco Systems, Inc.

Figure 11-5   This switch collected IP-to-MAC address pairing information from eavesdropping on DHCP messages

Dynamic ARP Inspection (DAI)

You learned in an earlier module that an attacker can redirect Internet or other network traffic from a legitimate server by altering DNS records in clients' and servers' caches. Similar to DNS caches, ARP tables can also be altered. Recall that ARP works in conjunction with IPv4 to discover the MAC address of a node on the local network. This information is stored in the ARP table or ARP cache, which maps IP addresses to MAC addresses on the LAN. However, ARP performs no authentication, and so, it is highly vulnerable to attack. As a result, attackers can use **ARP spoofing**, also called ARP poisoning or ARP cache poisoning, to send faked ARP replies that alter ARP tables in the network.

ARP vulnerabilities contribute to the feasibility of several other exploits, including DoS attacks, on-path attacks, and MAC flooding. MAC flooding is when an attacker floods a switch with fictitious MAC addresses. The switch accepts these fake MAC addresses and fills its MAC address table, which means it then must remove valid MAC addresses to keep processing the incoming information. Once its MAC address table is full of illegitimate information, legitimate network clients can no longer communicate except through broadcast transmissions, further slowing the network. Similar to the way you protect against a broadcast storm, port security on switches can reduce or eliminate the risks of MAC flooding. But what about other types of ARP spoofing?

DAI (dynamic ARP inspection) can be configured on a switch to protect against ARP spoofing attacks. When DAI is enabled, the switch compares incoming messages with its DHCP snooping binding table to determine whether the message's source IP address is appropriately matched with its source MAC address according to DHCP assignments on the network. DAI and DHCP snooping work together on network switches.

Applying Concepts 11-1: Explore Computer Forensics Investigations

Now that you understand a bit more about security in network design, you're ready to learn about how computer crimes are committed and discovered. As a network technician, you'll be better prepared to spot security issues if you're already familiar with breaches that have affected other networks in the past. In this activity, you research three computer forensics investigations. Use complete sentences, good grammar, and correct spelling in your answers. Complete the following steps:

1. Using a search engine, find articles, blogs, or videos discussing three different computer forensics cases. Identifying information might have been changed to protect privacy, but be sure the cases are actual cases, not just theoretical ones. Document your source or sources for each case.
2. Answer the following questions for each case:
   - How was the problem discovered?
   - What clues initiated the investigation?
   - What crime was committed or suspected?
   - What evidence was collected using computer forensics?
   - Were there any significant mistakes made in collecting this evidence?
   - What was the final outcome of each case?

REMEMBER THIS...

- Explain zero trust and defense in depth security concepts.
- Compare technology-based attacks, including ARP spoofing and rogue DHCP.
- Apply common security best practices, including ACLs, control plane policing, RA guard, DHCP snooping, and DAI.

SELF-CHECK

1. Which ACL rule will prevent pings from a host at 192.168.2.100?
   a. `access-list acl_2 permit icmp any host 192.168.2.100`
   b. `access-list acl_2 deny icmp host 192.168.2.100 any`
   c. `access-list acl_2 deny tcp host 192.168.2.100 host 192.168.2.1`
   d. `access-list acl_2 deny icmp any host 192.168.2.100`

2. Which two features on a switch or router are integrated into CoPP? *Choose two.*
   a. ICMP
   b. DHCP
   c. QoS
   d. ACLs

3. Which of the following defenses addresses a weakness of IPv6?
   a. DHCP snooping
   b. CoPP
   c. DAI
   d. RA guard

Check your answers at the end of this module.

You're Ready

You're now ready to complete **Project 11-1: Configure ACLs in Packet Tracer**, or you can wait until you've finished reading this module.

You're Ready

You're now ready to complete **Project 11-2: Configure DHCP Snooping in Packet Tracer**, or you can wait until you've finished reading this module.

NETWORK SECURITY TECHNOLOGIES

✓ CERTIFICATION

1.8 Summarize cloud concepts and connectivity options.

2.1 Compare and contrast various devices, their features, and their appropriate placement on the network.

2.3 Given a scenario, configure and deploy common Ethernet switching features.

3.3 Explain high availability and disaster recovery concepts and summarize which is the best solution.

4.1 Explain common security concepts.

4.3 Given a scenario, apply network hardening techniques.

5.2 Given a scenario, troubleshoot common cable connectivity issues and select the appropriate tools.

5.5 Given a scenario, troubleshoot general networking issues.

Average reading time: 34 minutes

Many devices on a network serve non-security purposes and yet are outfitted with significant security features and abilities. Others are designed specifically with network security in mind. In this section, you'll read about many devices that work together to build a secure net around and throughout a network. Using multiple options for network security results in layered security, or defense in depth, as you saw in the *On the Job* story at the beginning of this module. This approach provides more protection than any one type of device or defense can provide on its own. Let's look at how each of these components contributes to security in network design.

Proxy Servers

One technique for enhancing network security is adding a proxy server. A **proxy server**, or proxy, acts as an intermediary between the external and internal networks, screening all incoming and outgoing traffic. Proxy servers manage security at the application layer of the OSI model. Although proxy servers only provide low-grade security relative to other security devices, they can help prevent an attack on internal network resources such as web servers and web clients.

7 Application
6 Presentation
5 Session
4 Transport
3 Network
2 Data Link
1 Physical

To understand how proxies work, think of the secure data on a server as the president and the proxy server as the secretary of state. Rather than have the president risk his safety by leaving the country, the secretary of state travels abroad, speaks for the president, and gathers information on the president's behalf. In fact, foreign leaders may never actually meet the president. Instead, the secretary of state acts as the president's proxy. In a similar way, a proxy server represents a private network to another network (usually the Internet).

Although a proxy server appears to the outside world as an internal network server, in reality it is merely another filtering device for the internal LAN. One of its most important functions is preventing the outside world from discovering addresses on the internal network. For example, suppose your LAN uses a proxy server, and you want to send an email message from your workstation inside the LAN to a colleague via the Internet. The following steps describe the process:

Step 1:   Your message goes to the proxy server. Depending on the configuration of your network, you might or might not have to log on separately to the proxy server first.

Step 2:   The proxy server repackages the data frames that make up the message so that, rather than your workstation's IP address being the source, the proxy server inserts its own IP address as the source.

Step 3:   The proxy server passes your repackaged data to a packet-filtering firewall, which you'll learn more about later in this module.

Step 4:   The firewall verifies that the source IP address in your packets is valid (that it came from the proxy server) and then sends your message to the Internet.

Proxies are often used by enterprise networks to protect internal network clients. However, individuals sometimes rely on proxy servers to mask their Internet activities. In this case, users might want to circumvent traffic restrictions (such as accessing resources in a different political domain) or they might want to maintain anonymity. Examples of proxy server software include Smartproxy (*smartproxy.com*), Luminati (*luminati.io*), Squid (*squid-cache.org*), and, for Windows only, WinGate by Qbik (*wingate.com*), which includes firewall features as well. Figure 11-6 depicts how a proxy server might fit into a corporate network design.

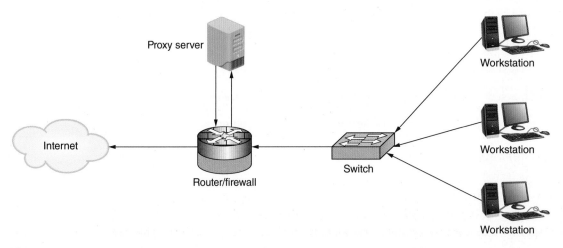

Figure 11-6   A proxy server is used to connect to the Internet

Although proxies might sound similar to VPNs, there are critical differences. For example, a VPN encrypts traffic, while a proxy does not. You also might have noticed that proxy services sound suspiciously similar to NAT, which you learned about earlier. However, they differ significantly. You've already learned that proxy servers can provide some content filtering, which is possible because they function at the application layer rather than at the lower, network layer. Proxy servers can also improve performance for users accessing resources external to their network by caching files. For example, a proxy server situated between a LAN and an external web server can be configured to save recently viewed web pages. The next time a user on the LAN wants to view one of the saved web pages, content is provided by the proxy server. This eliminates the time required to travel over a WAN connection and retrieve the same content multiple times from the external web server. Essentially, the difference is that NAT is an addressing construct to better manage IP addressing schemes, while proxies are security devices to mediate traffic between servers and clients.

Whereas proxy servers access resources on the Internet for a client, a reverse proxy provides services to Internet clients from servers on its own network. In this case, the reverse proxy provides identity protection for the server rather than the client, as well as some amount of application layer firewall protection. Reverse proxies are particularly useful when multiple web servers are accessed through the same public IP address.

NOTE 11-2

Often, firewall and proxy server features are combined in one device. In other words, you might purchase a firewall that can block certain types of traffic from entering your network (a firewall function) and also modify the addresses in the packets leaving your network (a proxy function).

Firewalls

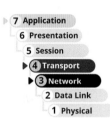

A firewall is a specialized device or software that selectively filters or blocks traffic between networks. A firewall protects a network by blocking certain traffic from traversing the firewall's position, similar to a bouncer checking IDs at the entrance to a private club. While firewalls include filtering from ACLs, they also offer a wide variety of other methods to evaluate, filter, and control network traffic.

A firewall might be placed internally, residing between two interconnected private networks. More commonly, the firewall is placed on the edge of the private network, monitoring the connection between a private network and a public network (such as the Internet), as shown in Figure 11-7. This is an example of a **network-based firewall**, so named because it protects an entire private network. Figure 11-8 shows dedicated firewall appliances that might be purchased for a medium-sized or large corporation's network. You'll also see firewall features integrated into routers, switches, and other network devices.

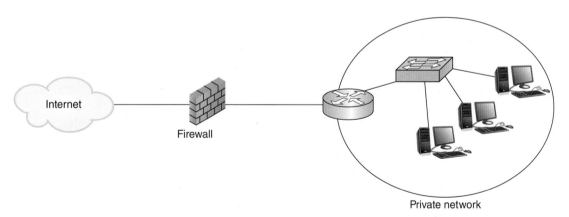

Figure 11-7   Placement of a firewall between a private network and the Internet

In contrast, **host-based firewall** software only protects the computer on which it's installed. These firewalls can be configured more specifically for each server or workstation, whereas network firewalls must be configured for all the traffic allowed on a network. For example, a network firewall might allow SSH on port 22 because several devices on the network must support remote access. In contrast, the firewall on a server that should never be accessed remotely should not allow traffic on port 22. Network firewalls offer the ability to configure much more complex rules and filters, while host firewalls offer protection specific to a single device.

The simplest form of a firewall is a **packet-filtering firewall**, which is a network device or application that examines the header of every packet of data it receives on any of its interfaces (called inbound traffic), as shown in

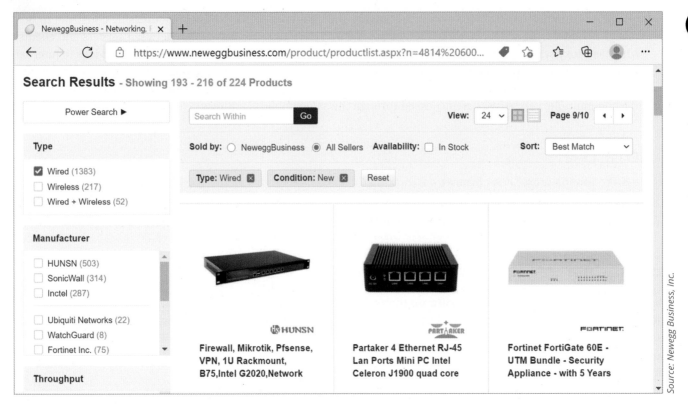

Figure 11-8 Dedicated firewall devices

Source: Newegg Business, Inc.

Figure 11-9. The firewall refers to its ACL to determine whether that type of packet is authorized to continue to its destination, regardless of whether that destination is on the internal LAN or on an external network. If a packet does not meet the filtering criteria, the firewall blocks the packet from continuing. However, if a packet does meet filtering criteria, the firewall allows that packet to pass through to the network the firewall protects. This is a common feature of SOHO routers, and in fact, nearly all routers can be configured to act as packet-filtering firewalls via ACLs.

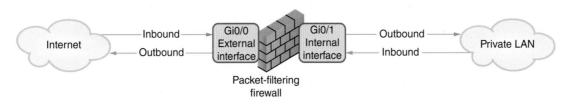

Figure 11-9 Arrows pointing toward the firewall are inbound for that device

Figure 11-9 shows the firewall filtering traffic that comes into the LAN from the Internet, and it also filters traffic that goes out of the LAN to the Internet. One possible reason for blocking Internet-bound traffic is to stop worms from spreading. For example, if you're running a web server, which in most cases only needs to respond to incoming requests and does not need to initiate outgoing requests, you could configure a packet-filtering firewall to block certain types of outgoing transmissions initiated by the web server. In this way, you help prevent spreading worms that are designed to attach themselves to web servers and propagate themselves to other computers on the Internet.

Often, firewalls ship with a default configuration designed to block the most common types of security threats. In other words, the firewall may be preconfigured to accept or deny certain types of traffic. However, many network administrators choose to customize the firewall settings, for example, blocking additional ports or adding criteria for the type of traffic that may travel into or out of ports. Some common criteria by which a packet-filtering firewall might accept or deny traffic include the following:

- Source and destination IP addresses
- Source and destination ports (for example, ports that supply TCP/UDP connections, FTP, Telnet, ARP, ICMP, and so on)
- Flags set in the TCP header (for example, SYN or ACK)
- Transmissions that use the UDP or ICMP protocols
- A packet's status as the first packet in a new data stream or a subsequent packet
- A packet's status as inbound to or outbound from your private network

Based on these options, a network administrator might configure a firewall to prevent any IP address that does not begin with *10.121*, the network ID of the addresses on the local network, from accessing the network's router and servers. Furthermore, the admin might disable—or block—certain well-known ports, such as the insecure NetBIOS ports (137, 138, and 139). Blocking ports prevents *any* user from connecting to and completing a transmission through those ports. This technique is useful to further guard against unauthorized access to the network. In other words, even if a hacker could spoof an IP address that began with *10.121*, they could not access NetBIOS ports (which are notoriously insecure) on the other side of the firewall.

NOTE 11-3

Ports can be blocked not only on firewalls, but also on routers, servers, or any device that uses ports. For example, if you established a web server for testing but did not want anyone in your organization to connect to your test web pages through a browser, you could block port 80 on that server. Be careful, however, when opening or blocking ports used by multiple protocols or types of connections, such as SSH's port 22. An incorrectly configured firewall is an easy thing to overlook when, for example, troubleshooting a newly installed application on a host.

For greater security, you can choose a firewall that performs more complex functions than simply filtering packets. When shopping for firewalls (or other devices), be sure to consider which features are included for the licenses you plan to purchase, as this can affect which features you can actually use. Among the factors to consider when making your decision are the following:

- Does the firewall support encryption?
- Does the firewall support user authentication?
- Does the firewall allow you to manage it centrally and through a standard interface?
- How easily can you establish rules for access to and from the firewall?
- Does the firewall provide internal network logging and auditing capabilities, such as IDS or IPS? IDS and IPS are described later in this module.
- Does the firewall protect the identity of your internal LAN's addresses from the outside world?
- Can the firewall monitor packets according to existing traffic streams? A **stateful firewall** can inspect each incoming packet to determine whether it belongs to a currently active connection (called a stateful inspection) and is, therefore, a legitimate packet. A **stateless firewall** manages each incoming packet as a stand-alone entity without regard to currently active connections. Stateless firewalls are faster than stateful firewalls but are not as sophisticated.
- Does the firewall support filtering at the highest layers of the OSI model, not just at the network and transport layers? **Application layer firewalls** can block designated types of traffic based on application data contained within packets. For example, a school might configure its firewall to prevent responses from a website with questionable content from reaching the client that requested the site. To do this, the firewall must examine the payloads of messages to determine whether these messages are attempting to communicate with a blacklisted website. An application layer firewall can also examine words, phrases, or code contained within that payload, which allows the network to monitor internal traffic for signs of infiltration, malware, or data theft. This capability supports a zero trust environment where messages inside the network aren't automatically trusted simply because they're inside the network.

A SOHO wireless router typically acts as a firewall and includes packet-filtering options. At the other end of the spectrum, devices made by Cisco or Fortinet for enterprise-wide security are known as security appliances and can perform several functions, such as encryption, load balancing, and IPS, in addition to packet filtering. Examples of software that enable a computer to act as a packet-filtering firewall include iptables (a command-line firewall utility for Linux systems), ZoneAlarm (*zonealarm.com*), and Comodo Firewall (*comodo.com*). Some operating systems, such as Windows 10, include firewall software. You'll explore Windows Firewall in the next section. In a project at the end of this module, you'll practice using iptables in Ubuntu Server.

Applying Concepts 11-2: Windows Defender Firewall

Follow these steps to find out how to configure Windows Defender Firewall on a Windows 10 computer:

1. From the search box, search for **Firewall & network protection** and open it in the Settings app. Notice in Figure 11-10 that the firewall is turned on for all three listed network types.

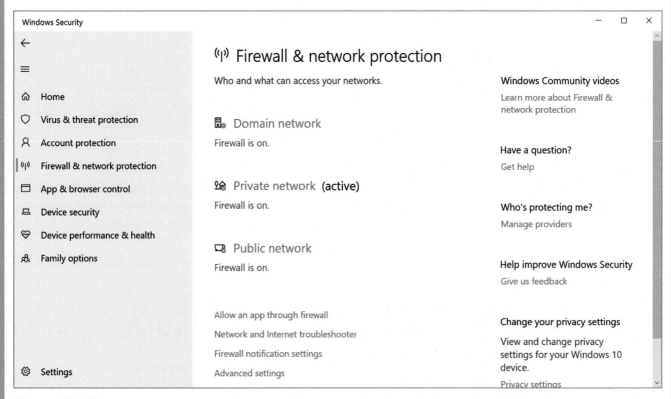

Figure 11-10   Windows Defender Firewall shows the computer is currently connected to a private network

2. To control firewall settings for each type of network location, click that network type. Use the slider to turn the firewall on or off for that network type (see Figure 11-11).
3. If you needed to allow no exceptions through the firewall on a network type, you would check **Blocks all incoming connections, including those in the list of allowed apps**. In the left pane, click **Firewall & network protection** to return to the firewall's main page.
4. To change the apps and programs allowed through the firewall, click **Allow an app through firewall**. The Allowed apps window appears (see Figure 11-12). Click **Change settings**.
5. Scroll down to find the app you want to allow to initiate a connection from a remote computer to this computer and then, in the right side of the window, click the **Private** check box and/or the **Public** check box to indicate which type of network location the app is allowed to use. If you don't see your app in the list, near the bottom of the

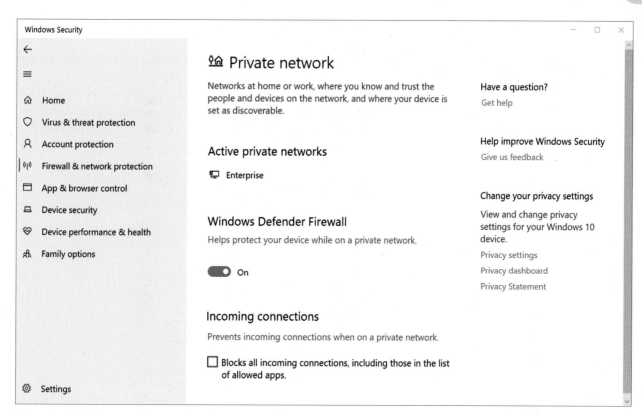

Figure 11-11   Customize settings for a private or public network

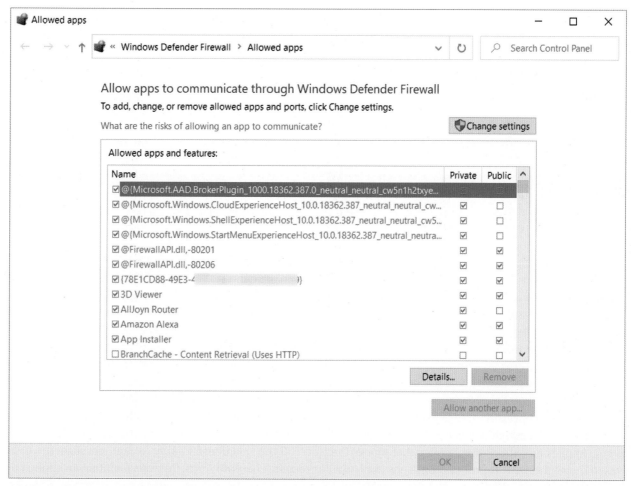

Figure 11-12   Allow apps to communicate through the firewall

window click **Allow another app...** to see more apps or to add your own. When you are finished making changes, click **OK** to return to the Firewall & network protection window.

6. For even more control over firewall settings, in the Firewall & network protection window, click **Advanced settings** and click **Yes** on the UAC page. The Windows Defender Firewall with Advanced Security window opens.

7. In the left pane, select **Inbound Rules** or **Outbound Rules**. A list of apps appears in the middle pane. Right-click an app and select **Properties** from the shortcut menu. The Properties dialog box gives full control of how exceptions get through the firewall, including which users, protocols, ports, and remote computers can use each opening (see Figure 11-13).

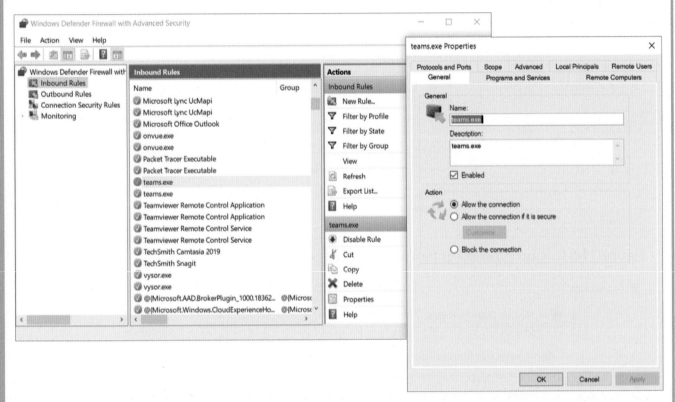

Figure 11-13 Use advanced settings to control exactly how an app can get through Windows Defender Firewall

Firewall Rules

Firewall rules function similarly to ACL rules that you read about earlier in this module. An ACL on a router can filter traffic according to its IP address or port number and can be used to sculpt traffic flows according to internal network needs (such as routing between VLANs). However, ACLs function on a single interface at a time, aren't intended to manage a long list of rules, and can't match rules to multiple streams of traffic within a single conversation (in other words, ACLs are stateless). Firewall rules provide more granular control of filters to secure traffic as it enters, exits, and traverses the network.

When a message crosses a firewall (physical or virtual), the firewall checks its rules to determine whether the message is allowed to pass. Earlier, you learned that routes are applied to a message according to which route in a route table most closely matches the message's destination. With firewalls, however, rules are usually applied in order of priority. The highest-priority rule is checked first. If the message is allowed or denied according to that rule, no further rules are checked. A matching *allow* rule applies an explicit allow policy that lets the traffic through, while a matching *deny* rule applies an explicit deny policy that blocks the traffic. If the rule doesn't apply to that message, the firewall moves to the next rule. This process continues until no rules remain. Like with ACLs, firewalls maintain an implicit deny policy for any messages that don't match a specific rule. Figure 11-14 shows a diagram for how this process plays out.

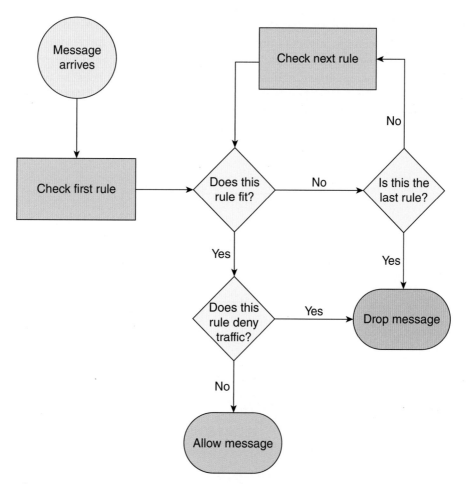

Figure 11-14   Firewall rules are checked in order of priority to determine whether a message is allowed to pass

These rules check for information such as port, protocol, and IP address or CIDR range. If the information matches, the message is allowed or denied according to the matched rule. Firewall rules are configured differently for inbound and outbound traffic. In other words, there's a different list of rules for inbound traffic, which is typically more restricted, than there is for outbound traffic.

However, firewalls can also alter their rules. For example, suppose the firewall is configured to deny incoming ICMP messages so Internet devices cannot ping your web server. At the same time, you've allowed outgoing ICMP messages so your server can ping other devices on the Internet. For your ping to work, however, ICMP responses must be able to enter your network through your firewall. A stateful firewall can acknowledge incoming ICMP responses that match your outgoing ICMP request, and the firewall will allow the return messages. In a Capstone Project at the end of this module, you'll allow ICMP through a Windows firewall so you can ping a Windows VM from another VM.

Troubleshooting Firewalls

The most common cause of firewall problems is firewall misconfiguration. Blocked services, ports, or addresses on a firewall can cause a frustrating failure of service until you locate the specific firewall rule blocking your traffic. At the same time, a misconfigured firewall might allow risky traffic into your network that no one notices until it's too late. Configuring an enterprise-level firewall can take weeks to achieve the best results. The configuration must not be so strict that it prevents authorized users from transmitting and receiving necessary data, yet not so lenient that you unnecessarily risk security breaches.

Further complicating the matter is that you might need to create exceptions to the rules. For example, suppose that your HR manager is working from a conference center in Salt Lake City while recruiting new employees, and they need to access the Denver server that stores payroll information. In this instance, the Denver network administrator might create an exception to allow transmissions from the HR manager's workstation's IP address to reach that server. In the networking industry, creating an exception to the filtering rules is called "punching a hole" in the firewall.

Less commonly, you might experience a full-scale firewall failure. While expensive, adding one or more redundant firewalls to your network can lessen the impact of this type of problem. You can help justify the expense of multiple firewalls by configuring load balancing and active-active failover so all firewalls contribute to increased performance, and any firewall can fail without losing service. In this arrangement, traffic is split between two (or more) firewalls, as shown in Figure 11-15a. Alternatively, redundant firewalls might be arranged in a serial fashion to provide enhanced protection for the internal network (see Figure 11-15b) and more nuanced protection for different network segments (see Figure 11-15c).

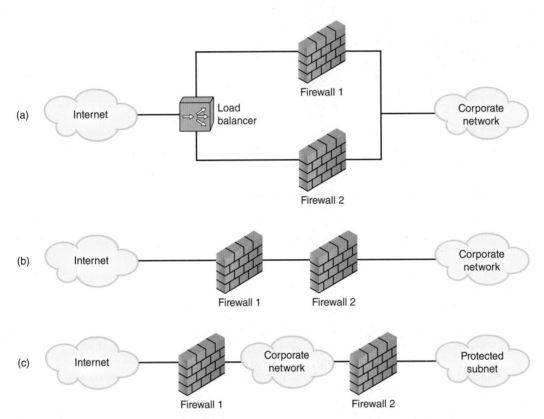

(a) Internet — Load balancer — Firewall 1 / Firewall 2 — Corporate network

(b) Internet — Firewall 1 — Firewall 2 — Corporate network

(c) Internet — Firewall 1 — Corporate network — Firewall 2 — Protected subnet

Figure 11-15 (a) Two load-balanced firewalls; (b) Enhanced security for the internal network; (c) Optimized security for a protected subnet

IDS (Intrusion Detection System)

An **IDS (intrusion detection system)** is a stand-alone device, an application, or a built-in feature running on a workstation, server, switch, router, or firewall. It monitors network traffic, generating alerts about suspicious activity (see the right side of Figure 11-16). Whereas a router's ACL or a firewall acts like a bouncer at a private club who checks everyone's ID and ensures that only club members enter through the door, an IDS is generally installed to provide security monitoring inside the network, similar to security personnel sitting in a private room monitoring closed-circuit cameras in the club and alerting other security personnel when they see suspicious activity.

An IDS uses two primary methods for detecting threats on the network:

- **Statistical anomaly detection**—Compares network traffic samples to a predetermined baseline to detect anomalies beyond certain parameters.
- **Signature-based detection**—Looks for identifiable patterns, or **signatures**, of code that are known to indicate specific vulnerabilities, exploits, or other undesirable traffic on the organization's network (such as games). To maintain effectiveness, these signatures must be regularly updated in a process called

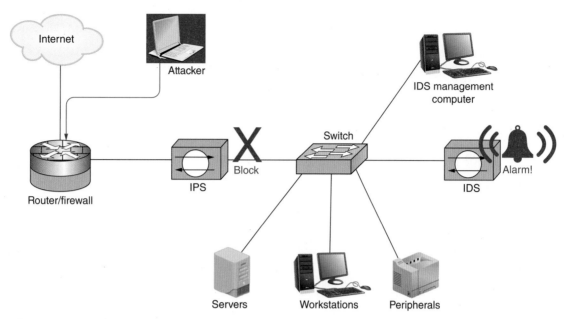

Figure 11-16   An IDS detects traffic patterns, while an IPS can intercept traffic that might threaten a corporate network

signature management. This also includes retiring irrelevant signatures and selecting the signatures most relevant to a specific network's needs to most efficiently use memory and processing resources when scanning network traffic.

The most thorough security employs both IDS implementations listed as follows to detect a wider scope of threats and provide multiple levels of defense:

- An **HIDS (host-based intrusion detection system)** runs on a single computer to detect attacks to that one host. For example, an HIDS might detect an attempt to exploit an insecure application running on a server or repeated attempts to log on to the server. An HIDS solution might also include **FIM (file integrity monitoring)**, which alerts the system of any changes made to files that shouldn't change, such as operating system files. FIM works by generating a baseline checksum of the monitored files and then recalculating the checksum at regular intervals to determine if anything has changed.
- An **NIDS (network-based intrusion detection system)** protects a network or portion of a network and is usually situated at the edge of the network or in a network's protective perimeter, known as a screened subnet (formerly called a DMZ, or demilitarized zone). Here, it can detect many types of suspicious traffic patterns, such as those typical of DoS attacks.

An NIDS sits off to the side of network traffic and is sent duplicates of packets traversing the network. One technique that an NIDS might use to monitor traffic carried by a switch is port mirroring. In **port mirroring**, also called SPAN (switched port analyzer), one port on a switch is configured to send a copy of all the switch's traffic to the device connected to that port. The device runs a monitoring program, which can now see much of the traffic the switch receives. This configuration is managed using the `monitoring session` command on Cisco switches and consists of identifying the source interface (the port to be monitored) and the destination interface (the port where copied messages are sent).

Similarly, an NIDS monitoring device might be connected to a **TAP (test access point)**, which can capture all traffic traversing a network connection, not just some of it (see Figure 11-17). For example, the TAP might be inserted between a switch and a router. Depending on the volume of traffic, the TAP might feed this traffic to multiple monitoring devices.

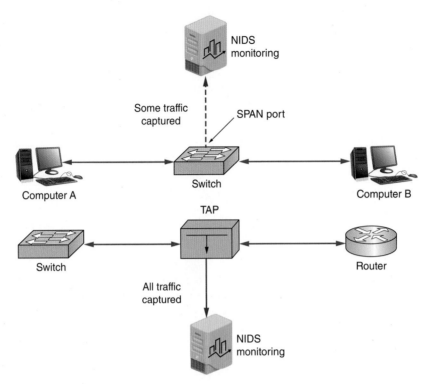

Figure 11-17 SPAN captures some traffic crossing a switch, but a TAP can capture all traffic between two devices

One drawback to using an IDS is the number of false positives it can generate. A false positive is an alert indicating a problem that isn't actually a problem. To understand this term, it might help to compare the possible scenarios for each event or alert on a system. Consider the diagram in Figure 11-18. A true positive is an alert sent for an actual problem. A true negative is when no alert is sent and there is no problem. Either of these situations means the IDS is functioning well. However, if you get an alert when there's no problem (a false positive) or you don't get an alert when there is a problem (a false negative), this can result in extra work for no reason or, worse, missed problems.

	Reality	
	Problem	**No problem**
Alert	True positive	False positive
No alert	False negative	True negative

(row label on left: **Alerts**)

Figure 11-18 A false positive occurs when there is an alert but no real problem

An example of a false positive would be when multiple logon attempts of a legitimate user who forgot their password are interpreted as a security threat. Suppose the IDS is configured to alert the network manager each time such an event occurs. The network manager might get overwhelmed by an endless stream of warnings and eventually ignore all the IDS's messages. As you can see, it's important to take the time to customize IDS software thoughtfully. Also, make sure to update it regularly and remember to reevaluate the rules of detection to ensure the software continues to guard against new threats.

Major vendors of networking hardware, such as Cisco, Juniper Networks, and Palo Alto, sell IDS-equipped devices. However, most IDS solutions these days are software-based and can be installed on a variety of network-connected machines. Examples of popular, open-source IDS software include Suricata (*suricata-ids.org*) and the very popular Snort (*snort.org*).

IPS (Intrusion Prevention System)

Although an IDS can only detect and log suspicious activity, an IPS (intrusion prevention system) stands in-line between the attacker and the targeted network or host where it can prevent traffic from reaching that network or host (see the left side of Figure 11-16). If an IDS is similar to security personnel using closed-circuit cameras to monitor a private club, an IPS would be similar to security personnel walking around in the club available to escort unruly patrons to the exit door. IPSs were originally designed as a more comprehensive traffic analysis and protection tool than firewalls. However, firewalls have evolved, and as a result, the differences between a firewall and an IPS have diminished.

Because an IPS stands in-line with network traffic, it can stop that traffic. For example, if an IPS detects a hacker's attempt to flood the network with traffic, it can prevent that traffic from proceeding to the network. Thereafter, the IPS might quarantine that malicious user based on the sending device's IP address. At the same time, the IPS continues to allow valid traffic to pass.

As with IDS, an NIPS (network-based intrusion prevention system) can protect entire networks while an HIPS (host-based intrusion prevention system) protects a specific host. Using NIPS and HIPS together increases the network's security. For example, an HIPS running on a file server might accept a hacker's attempt to log on if the hacker is posing as a legitimate client. With the proper NIPS, however, such a hacker would likely never get to the server. Like an IDS, an IPS requires careful configuration to avoid an abundance of false alarms.

Both an IDS and IPS can be placed inside a network or on the network perimeter. Notice in Figure 11-19 one NIPS is used to monitor and protect traffic in the DMZ. A second NIPS is positioned inside the private network on the perimeter of segment A to monitor and protect traffic on this one network segment. In the figure, you can see that HIPS software is also running on a server.

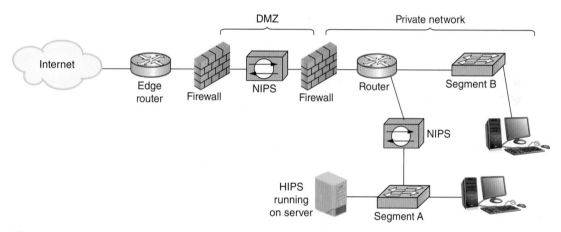

Figure 11-19   Placement of IPS devices and software on a network

Cloud Security Technologies

The security devices you've read about so far can be virtualized and run in the cloud. However, cloud platforms often embed security technologies within their services to protect against security challenges unique to the cloud. In response to these changing needs, many technologies have emerged to protect cloud resources from external attacks. If you think about cloud resources in layers—platform, network, instances, applications, and data—you can see where defense-in-depth strategies can be applied at each of these layers.

While there are some interesting variations in how each security tool functions from platform to platform, most include the following:

- **Granularity**—Some of these security appliances are designed specifically to hold a secure perimeter around individual resources (similar to a host-based firewall). For example, an AWS security group filters traffic into and out of a single EC2 instance or other resource. In contrast, an AWS NACL (network ACL, pronounced *nackle*) filters traffic to an entire VPC (virtual private cloud), similar to a network-based firewall.
- **Awareness**—Some cloud security technologies are stateless and don't map incoming and outgoing traffic streams to each other, while other technologies are stateful and maintain an awareness of how traffic streams

are related to each other. For example, Google's virtual firewall rules are stateful, meaning that traffic allowed in one direction automatically allows traffic in the other direction for an active connection. In contrast, AWS's NACLs are stateless.

- **Default configuration**—Each tool comes with a default configuration that either allows everything or denies everything so admins know what to expect when the tool is initially deployed and can plan for needed configuration changes. For example, you've seen how AWS security groups automatically allow SSH traffic over port 22 if you're creating a Linux EC2 instance. Similarly, Azure's NSG (Network Security Group) tool contains six default rules that cannot be changed or deleted but can be overridden by changing their priority ratings.

Cloud platforms include many other built-in security configurations that help prevent common security mistakes. For example, AWS's S3 (Simple Storage Service) buckets are automatically configured to deny any sort of access from the Internet. In fact, you must perform several configuration steps in S3 to allow Internet access to an S3 bucket, with multiple confirmation steps along the way.

Cloud security works according to the **shared responsibility model**, meaning that the cloud provider is partially responsible for your cloud's security and you're responsible for the rest of it. Figure 11-20 shows how this shared responsibility breaks down according to the type of cloud deployment.

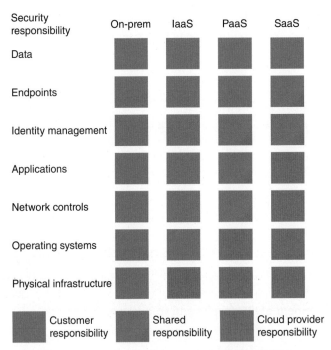

Figure 11-20   The customer's responsibility for security shifts with different cloud deployment structures

REMEMBER THIS...

- Compare and contrast network security devices, including proxy servers, firewalls, IDS, and IPS devices.
- Manage firewalls and firewall rules.
- Troubleshoot firewall settings.
- Compare SPAN and TAP.
- Summarize security implications of cloud computing.

SELF-CHECK

4. Which device can be used to increase network performance by caching websites?
   a. Firewall
   b. Proxy server
   c. IDS
   d. Security group

5. Which firewall type can protect a home network from adult content not suitable for the family's children?
   a. Packet-filtering firewall
   b. Host-based firewall
   c. Stateless firewall
   d. Application layer firewall

6. Which security device relies on a TAP or port mirroring?
   a. NIDS
   b. HIPS
   c. FIM
   d. HIDS

Check your answers at the end of this module.

You're Ready

You're now ready to complete **Project 11-3: Configure Cloud Security in AWS**, or you can wait until you've finished reading this module.

AUTHENTICATION, AUTHORIZATION, AND ACCOUNTING (AAA)

✓ CERTIFICATION

4.1: Explain common security concepts.

4.3: Given a scenario, apply network hardening techniques.

4.4: Compare and contrast remote access methods and security implications.

Average reading time: 24 minutes

As you've seen throughout this course, IT security permeates a network in many ways. Monitoring traffic entering, exiting, and traversing your network is handled by devices such as firewalls and IDS or IPS. You also need to manage which devices and users can access your network and how they prove their identity before being given access. This process is called **access control**. Physical access control, as you've already learned, might include locked doors, badges, or a locked rack. But you also need to implement information access control to limit the users and devices that can get to your data and other network resources.

Controlling access to a network and its resources consists of three major elements: authentication, authorization, and accounting. Together, this framework is abbreviated as AAA (authentication, authorization, and accounting) and is pronounced *triple-A*. Occasionally you'll see the acronym AAAA (authentication, authorization, accounting, and auditing) to further emphasize monitoring and security standards involved in these processes; however, most IT security professionals wrap auditing into accounting and so use the AAA acronym. The components required to manage access control to a network and its resources are described next:

- **Authentication**—As you know, authentication (in this case, user authentication) is the process of verifying a user's credentials (typically a username and password) to grant the user access to secured resources on a system or network. In other words, authentication asks the question, "Who are you?"
- **Authorization**—Once a user has access to the network, the authorization process determines what the user can and cannot do with network resources. In other words, authorization asks the question, "What are you allowed to do?" Authorization restrictions affect layer 2 segmentation, layer 3 filtering, and layer 7 entitlements. For example, what VLAN are you assigned to? What servers or databases can you access? What commands can you run on a device?
- **Accounting**—The accounting system logs users' access and activities on the network. In other words, accounting asks, "What did you do?" The records that are kept in these logs are later audited, either internally or by an outside entity, to ensure compliance with existing organizational rules or external laws and requirements.
- **Auditing**—As you already know, a network security audit consists of a posture assessment that analyzes network configurations for vulnerabilities and might be performed in the context of legal compliance requirements, such as for HIPAA compliance. In the context of AAA, auditing refers to checking user configurations for problems, searching for signs of account misuse, and monitoring a network for compromised accounts. Normally, this is considered a part of network accounting functions and is not listed separately.

Let's look at each of the elements of AAA in more detail, beginning with authentication.

Authentication

The identity of any user or device attempting to access a network, data, or device must be accurately verified before being given access to these resources. This is the role of authentication. Notice that a user can be authenticated to a single device and its local resources or to the network and its resources, which might be local in the on-prem data center or might be distributed across many data centers. When authenticating to a single device using that device's own resources, the process is called local authentication. For example, a user can sign into Windows using a local user account. With network authentication, they can sign into the network using a network user account that is stored in an authentication database, such as Active Directory on a Windows domain. Consider the following explanations.

Local Authentication

Local authentication processes are performed on the local device. Usernames and passwords are stored locally, which has both advantages and disadvantages, as follows:

- **Low security**—Most end user devices are less secure than network servers. A hacker can attempt a brute force attack or other workarounds to access a single device. If those same credentials are used on other devices, then all these devices are compromised. Also, local authentication does not allow for remotely locking down a user account.
- **Convenience varies**—For only a handful of devices, managing local accounts can be done a lot more easily than setting up a Windows domain, directory services, and all the supporting configurations. However, once you surpass about a dozen devices, the convenience of local authentication declines considerably.
- **Reliable backup access**—In the case of a network failure or server failure, the only workable option is local authentication. For this reason, networking devices and servers should be configured with a local privileged account that is only used when authentication services on the network are unavailable, and of course this account should have very secure credentials.

Applying Concepts 11-3: Apply Local Security Policies

With local authentication, you can set security policies to require all local users to have passwords and to rename default user accounts. The **Group Policy** (gpedit.msc) utility is a Windows console that controls what users can do and how the system can be used. Group Policy works by making entries in the Registry; applying scripts to Windows start-up, shutdown, and logon processes; and adjusting security settings. Policies can be applied to the computer or to the user.

Follow these steps to set a few important security policies on a Windows 10 Professional, Enterprise, or Education computer (Windows 10 Home does not include Group Policy):

1. Sign into Windows using an administrator account. Press **Win+R** on your keyboard and then enter **gpedit.msc** to open the Local Group Policy Editor window.
2. To change a policy, first use the left pane to select the appropriate policy group and then use the right pane to view and edit a policy. Consider making the following important security policy adjustments:
   a. ***Change default usernames***—A hacker is less likely to hack into the built-in Administrator account or Guest account if you change the names of these default accounts. To change the name of the Administrator account, select the Security Options group in the left pane as follows: **Computer Configuration**, **Windows Settings**, **Security Settings**, **Local Policies**, **Security Options**. See the left side of Figure 11-21. In the right pane, double-click **Accounts: Rename administrator account**. In the Properties dialog box for this policy (see the right side of Figure 11-21), change the name and click **OK**. To change the name of the Guest account, use the policy **Accounts: Rename guest account.**

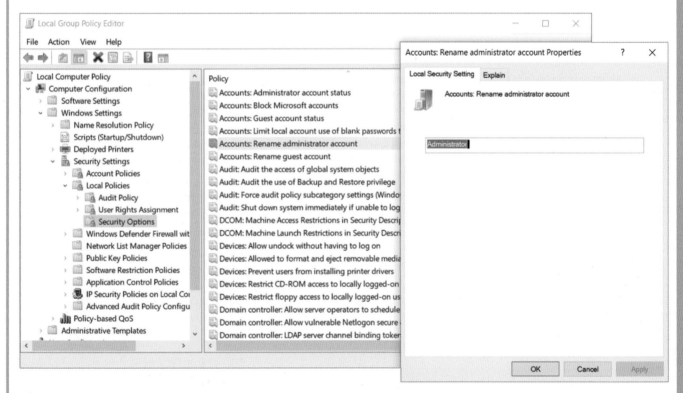

Figure 11-21   Change default usernames in the Local Group Policy Editor

   b. ***Require user passwords***—The **password policy** is probably the most important policy used to secure a system. To require that all user accounts have passwords, select the Password Policy group in the left pane as follows: **Computer Configuration**, **Windows Settings**, **Security Settings**, **Account Policies**, **Password Policy**. See the left side of Figure 11-22. Use the **Minimum password length** policy and set the minimum length to 12 characters or more (see the right side of Figure 11-22).

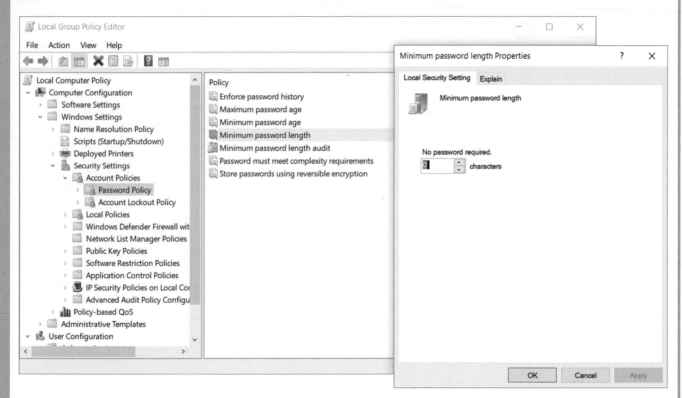

Figure 11-22 Require user passwords

    c. ***Allow only a single logon***—By default, Windows allows fast user switching, which means multiple users can log on to Windows at the same time. By disabling this feature, you require a user to save their work and log off the computer for another user to sign into it. This frees up computer resources and protects user data. To disable access to the fast user switching feature and allow only a single logon, select the Logon group in the left pane as follows: **Computer Configuration**, **Administrative Templates**, **System**, **Logon**. Double-click the **Hide entry points for Fast User Switching** policy. Enable this policy so that the *Switch user* option is dimmed and not available on the sign-in screen, the Start menu, and Task Manager.

3. When you finish setting your local security policies, close the Local Group Policy Editor window. To implement your changes, reboot the system or enter the command `gpupdate.exe` in a PowerShell or Command Prompt window.

NOTE 11-4

Sometimes policies overlap or conflict. To see the current policies for a particular computer or user, you can use the `gpresult` command in a PowerShell or Command Prompt window. To learn about the appropriate parameters for this command, search the *docs.microsoft.com* website.

With local authentication, every computer (workstation or server) on the network is responsible for securing its own resources. If several users need access to a file server, for example, each user must have a local user account on the file server. This local account and password must match the user account and password that the account holder used to sign into Windows at their workstation. As a network grows, keeping all these local accounts straight can become an administrative nightmare. The time will come when you will want to move on to a Windows domain.

    In Windows, you can switch from local authentication to network authentication on the domain using the System Properties dialog box. To make the switch, in the System Properties dialog box (see Figure 11-23), click **Network ID** and

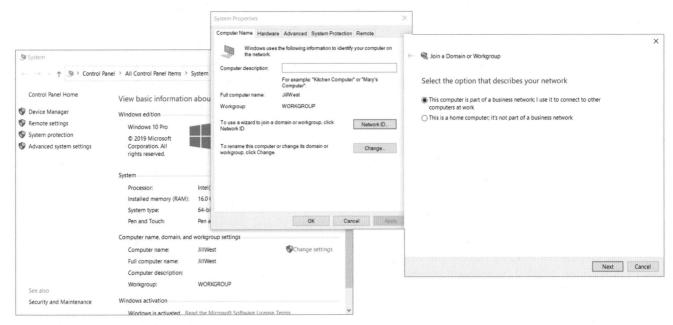

Figure 11-23   Switch from local authentication to authentication on a Windows domain

then select **This computer is part of a business network; I use it to connect to other computers at work**. Click **Next** and select **My company uses a network with a domain**. When you click **Next**, you are given the opportunity to enter your username, password, name of the Windows domain, and the name of your computer on the Windows domain. All this information is stored in Active Directory by Windows Server. When you complete the process, the next time you sign into Windows, you will use the network username to sign into the Windows domain. Active Directory then controls the access you have to resources on the network.

Network Authentication and Logon Restrictions

Network authentication might be performed locally, such as when a student signs into a lab computer, or remotely, such as when a remote employee uses a VPN to access network resources. Regardless of the user's physical location or network connection type, you can harden your network by requiring secure passwords and implementing other authentication restrictions. The following is a list of additional authentication restrictions that strengthen network security:

- **Time of day**—Some user accounts may be active only during specific hours, for example, between 8:00 a.m. and 5:00 p.m. Specifying valid hours for an account can increase security by preventing any account from being used by unauthorized personnel after hours.
- **Total time logged on**—Some user accounts may be restricted to a specific number of hours per day of logged-on time. Restricting total hours in this way can increase security of temporary user accounts. For example, suppose that your organization offers an Adobe Photoshop training class to a group of high school students one afternoon, and the Photoshop program and training files reside on your staff server. You might create accounts that could log on for only four hours on that day.
- **Source address**—You can specify that user accounts may log on only from certain workstations or certain areas of the network (that is, domains or segments). This restriction can prevent unauthorized use of accounts from workstations outside the network.
- **Unsuccessful logon attempts**—Hackers might repeatedly attempt to log on under a valid username for which they do not know the password. As the network administrator, you can set a limit on how many consecutive, unsuccessful logon attempts from a single user ID the server will accept before blocking that ID from even attempting to log on.
- **Geographic location**—Recall that geofencing determines a client's geographic location to enforce a virtual security perimeter. In other words, the client must be located within a certain area to gain access to the network. With geofencing, GPS (global positioning system) or RFID (radio frequency identification) data can be sent to the authentication server to report the location of the device attempting to authenticate to the network.

NOTE 11-5

A special kind of DoS attack called an authentication attack floods a AAA server with authentication requests that must all be processed and responded to. This can force the server to shut down. By default, a floodguard feature might be configured on the AAA server to reclaim compromised resources. Floodguard settings can be changed with the `floodguard` command.

Authorization

Even the best authentication techniques—including encryption, computer room door locks, security policies, and password rules—make no difference if you give users access to resources they shouldn't see. Once a user is given access to your network, that doesn't mean they should have access to everything, such as sensitive data or critical network configurations. Controlling what a user can do once inside your network is the job of authorization. For example, you might have employees working from home who use a VPN to remote into your network. Can those employees print files to the printers? Can they access the customer database? Which applications can they run? What changes can they make to their own data or to data managed by other employees?

User access to network resources typically falls into one of these two categories: 1) the privilege or right to run, install, and uninstall software; and 2) permission to read, modify, create, or delete data files and folders. The way user privileges and permissions are managed vary depending on who determines these privileges and permissions and how users are matched to privileges and permissions.

The most popular authorization method is RBAC (role-based access control). With RBAC, a network administrator receives from a user's supervisor a detailed description of the roles or jobs the user performs for the organization. The administrator is responsible for assigning the privileges and permissions necessary for the user to perform only these roles. In addition, all users might require access to certain public resources on the network, for example, a portion of the company website available to all employees. In most cases, these public rights are very limited.

With role-based access control, a network administrator creates user groups associated with these roles and assigns privileges and permissions to each user group. Each user is assigned to a user group that matches a requirement for their job. In most cases, a user can belong to more than one user group. In some situations, however, a checks and balances safety net is enforced by implementing role separation; this means each user can only be a member of a single group in order to perform any tasks at all. If a user is listed in more than one group, all privileges and permissions are locked down for that user.

For Windows, Figure 11-24 shows the Computer Management window where you can see several built-in user groups and the option to create your own, new groups. For example, the IT Department at a large university will most likely need more than one person who can create new user IDs and passwords for students and faculty. Naturally, the staff in charge of creating these credentials need the correct privileges to perform this task. You could assign the appropriate rights to each staff member individually, but a more efficient approach is to create an identity management *group*, and put all the IT personnel in that group. Later, when someone leaves the IT Department or joins the department, you can easily remove users from or add users to the group.

Windows provides the option to create local groups on individual workstations. Active Directory gives additional options for creating domain local groups, which are centrally managed for the entire network.

Accounting

An important concept in accounting (whether that's the field of accounting or the AAA component of accounting in IT security) is SoD (separation of duties), which refers to a division of labor that ensures no one person can singlehandedly compromise the security of data, finances, or other resources. To accomplish this goal, sensitive privileges and responsibilities are distributed to multiple people. A classic example in the field of accounting is having one person responsible for writing checks and a different person responsible for balancing the financial records. (While this scenario is not the origin of the phrase "checks and balances," it is a good illustration of the concept.)

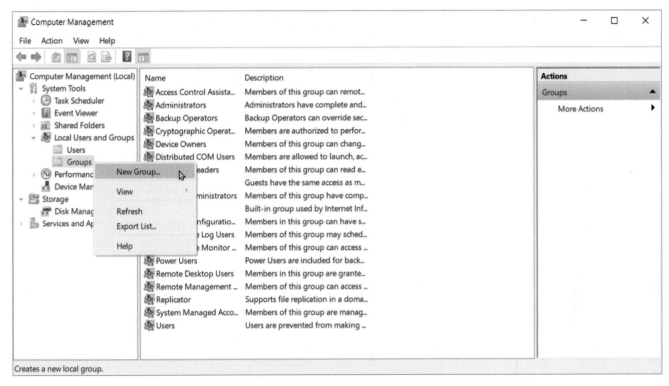

Figure 11-24 Windows allows you to create new groups and add users to these groups

NOTE 11-6

Two other popular methods of access control in addition to RBAC are DAC and MAC. The least secure of these options is **DAC (discretionary access control)**. This is where users decide for themselves who has access to that user's resources. The most restrictive is **MAC (mandatory access control)**. In this case, resources are organized into hierarchical classifications, such as "confidential" or "top secret." This is a vertical organization. Resources are also grouped into categories, perhaps by department, which is a horizontal organization (see Figure 11-25). Users, then, are also classified and categorized. If a user's classification and category match those of a resource, then the user is given access.

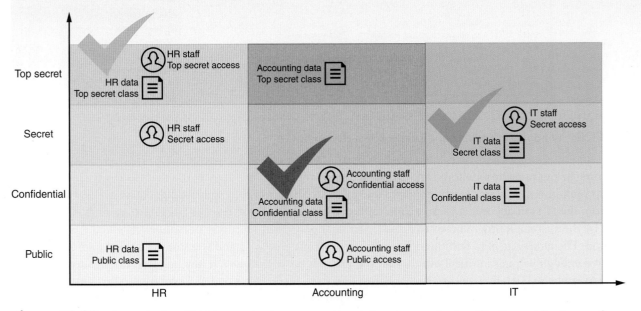

Figure 11-25 A user's classification and category must match a resource's classification and category for the user to have access to that resource

Essentially, SoD ensures that no single person is given sufficient power in a system to commit fraud or otherwise deeply compromise the system's integrity. In the context of AAA's accounting and auditing components, SoD requires that no one is responsible for monitoring and reporting on themselves, which would create a conflict of interest for that person. Accounting and auditing activities should be sufficiently spread across multiple job roles to reduce the company's vulnerability to fraud (intentional damage) or mistakes (unintentional damage).

As actions are performed on data and other resources, all this activity is logged for further analysis. This logging and the follow-up audit of the information is part of AAA's accounting component. Throughout this course, you have been learning about the many logs that systems generate so that an administrator can troubleshoot and audit these systems. With a Linux NOS, most logs are generated as text files. These text files can get quite long, and a network administrator is responsible for making sure they don't hog server storage space. In addition, you can install a log file viewer to make it easier to monitor log files for interesting or suspicious events.

NOTE 11-7

Check out Linux commands `tail`, `head`, `grep`, `sed`, and `awk`, which are useful for searching very long log files.

In Windows, you can use Event Viewer to view Windows logs. For example, in Figure 11-26, you can see an Audit Failure event related to an account that failed to log on. As you can see in the figure, Audit events appear in the Windows Logs, Security group of Event Viewer. Also, before these logon events are logged, you must use Group Policy to turn on the feature.

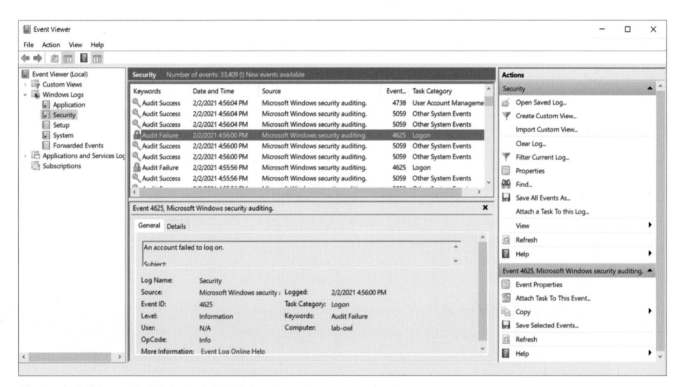

Figure 11-26 Windows Event Viewer displays a security audit event

Data stored in logs must be monitored and analyzed to be of particular use in real time. **SIEM (Security Information and Event Management)** systems can be configured to evaluate all this data, looking for significant events that require attention from the IT staff according to predefined rules. When one of these rules is triggered, an alert is generated and logged by the system. If programmed to do so, a notification is then sent to IT personnel via email, text, or some other method. The challenge is to find the right balance between sensitivity and workload. For example, a SIEM that isn't sensitive enough will miss critical events that require response. However, a few hundred notifications per day will quickly overwhelm IT staff; they can't possibly respond to so many alerts and will eventually start ignoring them.

A SIEM's effectiveness is partly determined by how much storage space is allocated for the generated data and by the number of events it processes per second. As for data storage space, consider all the devices (including switches, routers, servers, and security systems) that will feed data to the SIEM, and allow for future growth of this traffic as well.

The network administrator can fine-tune a SIEM's rules for the specific needs of a particular network by defining which events should trigger which responses. The SIEM system can also be configured to monitor particular indicators of anticipated problems or issues. These rules should be reevaluated periodically. Also, network technicians should review the raw data on a regular basis to ensure that no glaring indicators are being missed by existing rules. Examples of SIEM software include AlienVault OSSIM (Open Source SIEM), IBM Security QRadar, SolarWinds Security Event Manager, and Splunk Enterprise Security.

REMEMBER THIS...

- Explain common network access control concepts, including defense in depth, separation of duties, role-based access, and local authentication.
- Describe the components of AAA: authentication, authorization, and accounting.

SELF-CHECK

7. Which access control technique is responsible for detection of an intruder who succeeds in accessing a network?

    a. Authentication

    b. Accounting

    c. Geofencing

    d. Separation of duties

8. Which authorization method will allow Nancy, a custodian, to access the company's email application but not its accounting system?

    a. RBAC

    b. Auditing

    c. DAC

    d. Local authentication

Check your answers at the end of this module.

AUTHENTICATION TECHNOLOGIES

 **CERTIFICATION**

1.5 Explain common ports and protocols, their application, and encrypted alternatives.

4.1 Explain common security concepts.

Average reading time: 24 minutes

Of the three AAA processes, authentication tends to be the most complicated. Let's look more closely at the building blocks that make authentication happen. Authentication protocols are the processes that require users, devices, and services to prove their identity before being allowed access to the network or other resources. Several types of authentication services and protocols exist, and some also incorporate authorization and auditing components. These technologies vary according to which encryption schemes they rely on and the steps they take to verify credentials.

Directory Services

For clients to authenticate to network resources (as opposed to individual devices), some sort of directory server on the network must maintain a database of account information, such as usernames, passwords, and any other authentication credentials. Often this is accomplished in AD (Active Directory) or something more Linux-focused like OpenLDAP (*openldap.org*) or 389 Directory Server (*directory.fedoraproject.org*).

All these options are built to be LDAP-compliant. LDAP was briefly defined when you studied network protocols in an earlier module. As you read then, LDAP (Lightweight Directory Access Protocol) is a standard protocol for accessing an existing directory. For example, consider the process you use to withdraw money from your bank account. Perhaps you go into the bank and present a cash withdrawal slip. You hand the form to the teller, and they ask for your ID. Alternatively, you might present your bank card at an ATM. The ATM responds by requesting your PIN, and then it asks you how much money you want to withdraw. Either way, you must complete a process that proves you are who you say you are and provides all the information requested by the bank. LDAP works much the same way. It defines the rules for how you communicate with an authentication directory so you can prove you are who you say you are (see Figure 11-27). LDAP provides the rules and structure for the process of authentication, while the authentication directory (such as AD) provides the stored credentials and other relevant data.

The mechanisms of LDAP dictate some basic requirements for any directory it accesses, and so there is a lot of commonality in how directory servers are configured regardless of the software used. LDAP can query the database, which means to draw information out of the database. It can also be used to add new information or edit existing data.

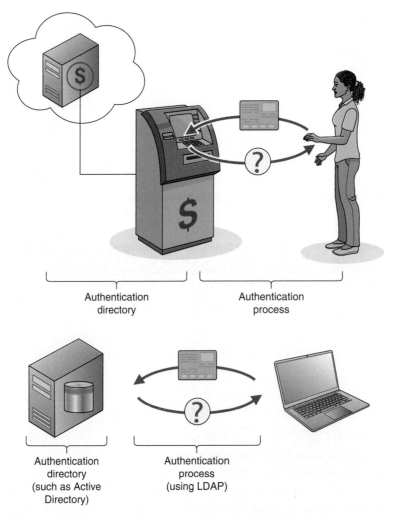

Figure 11-27 The data and process of authentication

One weakness of LDAP is that it transmits user credentials in plaintext. Previously, when local networks defined the perimeter of a trusted environment, this wasn't so bad. But these days, you can't assume that your network is a safe place to transmit passwords and other sensitive data without encryption. Instead, today's on-prem authentication processes should use the more secure LDAPS (LDAP over SSL/TLS), which communicates over port 636 instead of the insecure LDAP ports 389 or 2889.

By default, AD is configured to use the Kerberos protocol, which you'll learn about shortly. However, AD can use LDAP instead or use both side by side. When supporting AD together, Kerberos provides authentication with the database, and then LDAP provides authorization by determining what the user can do while they're on the network. Let's take a closer look at Kerberos.

Applying Concepts 11-4: Compare Windows Server AD to Azure AD

AD DS (Active Directory Domain Services) is the component of Active Directory that is responsible for storing user account information. AD has been around since Windows 2000 Server and took a significant leap forward with Windows Server 2008. However, AD (as it's most commonly called) was not designed to integrate cloud services within its domain. Microsoft's answer to this problem was to introduce Windows Azure Active Directory (AD). Azure AD is not intended as a replacement for AD, but rather as a supplement. Many of the concepts you've learned about in this course, such as cloud computing and security in network design, have built a solid foundation for you to now begin exploring Azure AD. Complete the following steps:

1. Many employers, when interviewing technicians for job openings, will ask the job applicant what they know about Active Directory. Just like you need to be familiar with the user interface for Windows, Linux, and macOS, you also should know your way around AD. Spend some time researching online about how AD works and what it does. Watch some videos for basic functions, such as configuring users and user groups.
2. Write a paragraph or two describing what you've learned. As practice for business-quality communications, carefully edit your writing. Use complete sentences, good grammar, and correct spelling.

NOTE 11-8

Some people have a hard time "hearing" their own writing. They use incomplete sentences or poorly constructed sentences without realizing it, and yet they don't make these kinds of mistakes when speaking. If you struggle to write well, consider having someone else read your paragraph back to you out loud so you can hear your own mistakes. You might also copy and paste the text into Google Translate (*translate.google.com*), which can read it back to you. Listen for statements that don't make sense, that didn't say what you intended them to say, or that could be interpreted in many different ways.

3. Spend some time researching Azure AD and comparing it to Active Directory. What services does Azure AD offer that are the same as AD? What services does Azure AD offer that are different? Which protocols does Azure AD rely on? What AD limitations does Azure AD address? Also watch some videos showing how to use Azure AD.
4. Write two paragraphs describing what you've learned. As practice for business-quality communications, carefully edit your writing. Use complete sentences, good grammar, and correct spelling. Consider drawing a diagram or two to illustrate the information you're sharing.

Kerberos

Recall that Kerberos is the authentication protocol configured by default on Active Directory that works in partnership with LDAP. **Kerberos** is a cross-platform authentication protocol that uses key encryption to verify the identity of clients and to securely exchange information after a client logs on to a system. It is an example of a private key encryption service and is considered especially secure. Let's see how this works.

Kerberos does not automatically trust clients. Instead, it requires clients to prove their identities through a third party. This is similar to what happens when you apply for a passport. The government does not simply believe that you are, for example, "Peter Parker," but instead requires you to present proof, such as your birth certificate. In addition to checking the validity of a client, Kerberos communications are encrypted and unlikely to be deciphered by any device on the network other than the intended client.

To understand specifically how Kerberos authenticates a client, you need to understand some of the terms used when discussing this protocol:

- **Principal**—A Kerberos client or user
- **KDC (Key Distribution Center)**—The server that issues keys to clients during initial authentication
- **Ticket**—A temporary set of credentials a client presents to network servers to prove its identity has been validated

NOTE 11-9

A Kerberos ticket is not the same as a Kerberos key. Using a key is similar to using your credit card to pay for entrance into a carnival or county fair. Your entrance fee includes a time-limited wristband that you can use to obtain a separate ticket for each game, ride, or beverage that you consume during the event. As long as you're at the event for that evening, you can get more tickets by showing your wristband, and each ticket is exchanged for another game, ride, or beverage. However, when you come back the next night, you must start over by using your credit card to purchase a new wristband. Keys, like credit cards, belong to the user or server and initially validate the user's and server's identity to each other during the authentication process to create a session. A ticket, like a carnival ticket, is used to gain access to another network service, such as email, an internal payroll site, a printer, or a file server.

A Kerberos server runs two services:

- **AS (authentication service)**—Initially validates a client. In the carnival analogy, this would be the box office at the entrance gate.
- **TGS (ticket-granting service)**—Issues tickets to an authenticated client for access to services on the network. This would be the ticket booth inside the fairgrounds, where you show your wristband to get more tickets.

Now that you have learned the basic terms used by Kerberos, you can follow the process it requires for client-server communication. Bear in mind that the purpose of Kerberos is to connect a valid user with a network *service* the user wants to access, such as email, printing, file storage, databases, or web applications. To accomplish this, both the user and the service must register their own keys with the AS ahead of time.

Figure 11-28 shows how TGS works. Suppose the principal (the client) is Jamal. The following steps describe the Kerberos authentication process:

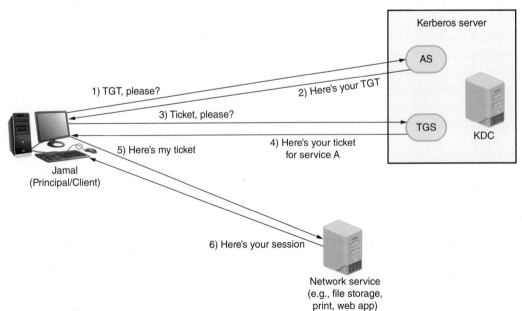

Figure 11-28 The Ticket-Granting Service offers a client a ticket for each network service it needs to access

Step 1: When Jamal first logs on to the network, his computer sends an authentication request to the AS (see Figure 11-29). This request contains Jamal's username, but not his password. However, the time stamp on the request is encrypted with Jamal's password.

Step 2: The AS on the KDC first confirms that Jamal is listed in its database and uses his password (retrieved from its database) to decrypt the timestamp. If all goes well, the AS generates a session key, which is used for encryption and decryption for future communication. It encrypts this key with the user's password (see Figure 11-30). The AS also generates a TGT (Ticket-Granting Ticket), which will expire within a specified amount of time (by default, this limit is 10 hours). The TGT is like the wristband in the carnival analogy. To prevent counterfeiting, the TGT is encrypted with a secret KDC key so that only the KDC can read it and confirm its legitimacy.

Step 3: After receiving the TGT, the principal decrypts the session key using the user's password. If the correct password is used and decryption is successful, the principal can then submit a ticket request to the TGS for access to a network service (see Figure 11-31). The request includes the user's name and a time stamp that are both encrypted using the session key. It also includes the fully encrypted TGT, which the principal never decrypted.

Step 4: The TGS validates the TGT and the rest of the request message's contents and then creates a ticket that allows Jamal to use the network service. This ticket (see Figure 11-32) includes the service's name, a time stamp, and the service's session key, all encrypted using the session key issued to the principal earlier. It also includes information the service will need to confirm the request is valid, including the principal's session key. This part is encrypted using a secret key that the service knows, but the principal does not.

Step 5: Jamal's computer decrypts the information it needs using the session key. It then creates a service request (see Figure 11-33) that contains the encrypted information from the TGS, plus a time stamp encrypted with the session key.

Step 6: The service decrypts the ticket using its own secret key, finds the principal's session key included in the ticket, and then decrypts the remainder of the message to confirm its validity. Finally, the service verifies that the principal requesting its use is truly Jamal as the KDC indicated and then allows access.

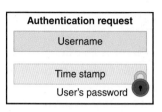

Figure 11-29   Step 1: Authentication request

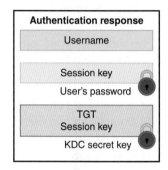

Figure 11-30   Step 2: Authentication response

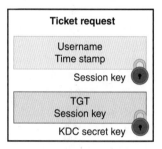

Figure 11-31   Step 3: Ticket request

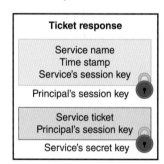

Figure 11-32   Step 4: Ticket response

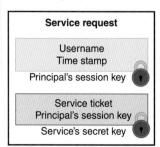

Figure 11-33   Step 5: Service request

NOTE 11-10

Kerberos, which was designed at MIT (Massachusetts Institute of Technology), is named after the three-headed dog in Greek mythology who guarded the gates of Hades. The three heads of the Kerberos authentication protocol are the principal, the network server providing a service, and the KDC. MIT still provides free copies of the Kerberos code. In addition, many software vendors have developed their own versions of Kerberos.

SSO (Single Sign-On)

Kerberos is an example of SSO (single sign-on), a form of authentication in which a client signs on one time to access multiple systems or resources. The primary advantage of single sign-on is convenience. Users don't have to remember several passwords, and network administrators can limit the time they devote to password management. The biggest disadvantage to single sign-on authentication is that once the obstacle of authentication is cleared, the user has access to numerous resources. A hacker needs fewer credentials to gain access to potentially many files or connections.

For greater security, some systems—especially those using SSO—require clients to supply two or more pieces of information to verify their identity. In a 2FA (two-factor authentication) scenario, a user must provide something and know something. For example, they might have to provide a fingerprint scan as well as know and enter a password.

An authentication process that requires two or more pieces of information is known as MFA (multifactor authentication). The following list gives the five most common categories of authentication factors, along with some examples of each:

- **Something you know**—A password, PIN, or biographical data
- **Something you have**—An ATM card, smart card, or key
- **Something you are**—Your fingerprint, facial pattern, or iris pattern
- **Somewhere you are**—Your location in a specific building or secured closet
- **Something you do**—The specific way you type, speak, or walk

Multifactor authentication requires at least one authentication method from at least two different categories. For example, logging into a network might require a password, a fingerprint scan, plus a piece of information generated from a security token. A security token is a device or application that stores or generates information (such as a series of numbers or letters) known only to its authorized user.

On the left side of Figure 11-34, a smartphone app requests a website-generated QR code to set up a user's account, such as Facebook, for 2FA. Once established, a random code is generated every 30 seconds that must be entered in addition to the user's password to access the account. An example of a hardware-based token is the popular RSA SecurID keychain fob from RSA Security, as shown on the right side of Figure 11-34. The RSA SecurID device generates a password that changes every 60 seconds. When logging on, a user provides the number that currently appears on the fob. Before the user is allowed access to secured resources, the network checks with RSA Security's service to verify the number is correct. Similarly, Google Authenticator, Google's number generator service, provides free, software-based security tokens.

Source for (a): Twilio, Inc.
Source for (b): Courtesy of RSA Security LLC

Figure 11-34   (a) A smartphone 2FA app;
(b) A SecurID fob

RADIUS (Remote Authentication Dial-In User Service)

While Active Directory offers powerful authentication and other services, it's limited to working with Windows or Linux clients, and it can't directly support authentication through wireless access points. An alternative to Active Directory is the cross-platform RADIUS (Remote Authentication Dial-In User Service), which is an open-source standard developed by Livingston Enterprises in 1991 and later standardized by the IETF. It runs in the application layer; and in the transport layer, it can use either UDP or, as of 2012, TCP. RADIUS treats authentication and authorization as a single process, meaning that the same type of packet is used for both functions, while accounting is a separate process. Due to its origins as a remote authentication service, RADIUS specializes in supporting clients not directly wired into the network, such as clients of wireless access points or VPN-based clients.

RADIUS can operate as a software application on a remote access server or on a computer dedicated to this type of authentication, called a RADIUS server. Because RADIUS servers are highly scalable, many ISPs use RADIUS as a central authentication point for wireless, mobile, and remote users. RADIUS services are often combined with other network services on a single machine. For example, an organization might combine a DHCP server with a RADIUS server to manage allocation of addresses and privileges assigned to each address on the network.

Figure 11-35 illustrates a RADIUS server managing network access for local and remote users. RADIUS can run on almost all modern OSs. In fact, there are some scenarios where you might want to implement RADIUS alongside Active Directory, as illustrated in Figure 11-36. While RADIUS includes some very sophisticated accounting features, it also only encrypts the password in transmission, and so is not as secure as TACACS+, discussed next.

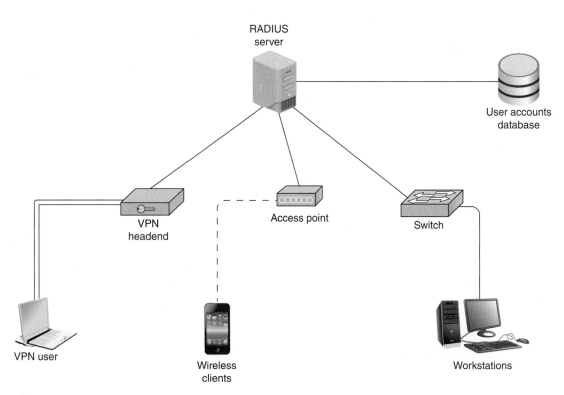

Figure 11-35   A RADIUS server on a network servicing various types of users

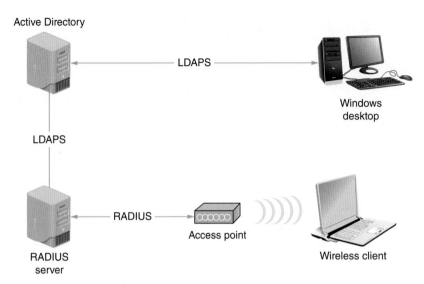

Figure 11-36   RADIUS and Active Directory can work together to support different types of clients

NOTE 11-11

A newer protocol called Diameter was developed in 1998 to replace RADIUS. In geometry, the diameter of a circle is twice its radius; the implication is that the Diameter protocol is twice as good as the RADIUS protocol. While many vendors offer Diameter options on their systems, for the most part, RADIUS is still more widely used.

TACACS+ (Terminal Access Controller Access Control System Plus)

Another AAA protocol, **TACACS+ (Terminal Access Controller Access Control System Plus)**, offers network administrators the option of separating the authentication, authorization, and auditing capabilities. For instance, TACACS+ might provide access and accounting functions, but use another technique, such as Kerberos (discussed earlier in this module), to authenticate users. TACACS+ differs from RADIUS in that it does the following:

- Relies on TCP, not UDP, at the transport layer
- Was developed by Cisco Systems, Inc., for proprietary use
- Is typically used to authenticate to network devices such as routers and switches rather than workstations or servers
- Is most often used for device administration access control for technicians, although it can be used for network resource access control for users
- Encrypts all information transmitted for AAA (RADIUS only encrypts the password)

Applying Concepts 11-5: Protocol Synopsis

Each of the protocols covered in this and previous modules plays an important role in securing transmissions between devices and locations. It's important to have the big picture in mind regarding how these protocols interact with each other and the roles they play in various parts of the system when troubleshooting connectivity and security issues.

In this activity, you synthesize the major characteristics of each protocol into a single reference table. You can create the following Table 11-1 in a word-processing program or a spreadsheet program. Then refer to earlier modules to fill in the missing pieces. Protocol types include encryption, connection, authentication, tunneling, trunking, hashing, and AAA. Some of the listed protocols are included in more than one of these categories.

Table 11-1   Notable encryption and authentication methods

Security method	Type	Primary use(s)	Notes
IPsec	Encryption	TCP/IP transmissions	
SSL		TCP/IP transmissions	
TLS			Secure transmission of HTTP sessions
SSH	Connection, authentication, encryption		
RDP		Remote access	
VNC	Connection		
L2TP	Tunneling	VPN	
GRE		VPN	
OpenVPN		VPN	
IKEv2		VPN	
VTP	Trunking		
SHA		Data integrity	
LDAP	Authentication	Directory access	
Kerberos		Client validation	Verify the identity of clients and securely exchange information after a client logs on to a system
RADIUS			Central authentication point for network users, including wireless, mobile, and remote users
TACACS+	AAA (authentication, authorization, and accounting)	Client validation and monitoring	
EAP		Client verification	
802.1X	Authentication		
AES		Wi-Fi and other uses	

REMEMBER THIS...

- Explain common authentication protocols, including LDAP, LDAPS, RADIUS, TACACS+, and Kerberos.
- Compare authentication methods, including multifactor authentication and SSO.

SELF-CHECK

9. Which authentication protocol is optimized for wireless clients?
  a. RADIUS
  b. Active Directory
  c. TACACS+
  d. Kerberos

10. What does a client present to a network server to access a resource on that server?
  a. Key
  b. Principal
  c. Ticket
  d. Ticket-Granting Ticket

Check your answers at the end of this module.

You're Ready

You're now ready to complete **Project 11-4: Configure RADIUS in Packet Tracer**, or you can wait until you've finished the Review Questions for this module.

You're Ready

After you finish the Hands-On Projects, you're ready to complete the **Module 11 Capstone Projects**.

MODULE SUMMARY

Network Hardening by Design

- A zero trust security model considers everything untrustworthy until proven otherwise. Security must be implemented in many, seemingly redundant layers that permeate the network and protect resources from every angle, which is a strategy called defense in depth.
- A router's main function is to examine packets and determine where to direct them based on their network layer addressing information. Thanks to a router's ACL (access control list), or access list, routers can also decline to forward certain packets depending on their content.
- While ACLs filter traffic into and out of router interfaces on the data plane, the control plane needs a separate layer of protection. In this case, an adaptation of QoS (quality of service) filters can be used to rate-limit traffic on the control plane and management plane of routers and switches using a feature called CoPP (control plane policing).
- IPv6 clients have no way of authenticating RA messages to know which of these messages come from legitimate sources and which might come from a network attacker. The solution to this problem is to configure RA

guards on network switches. The RA guard feature filters RA messages so these messages can only come from specific interfaces on the switch.

- A rogue DHCP server running on a client device could be used to implement an on-path attack by configuring the attacker's IP address as the victim computers' default gateway. Alternatively, the attacker could give their IP address as the DNS server and then spoof websites. DHCP messages should be monitored by enabling DHCP snooping on a switch.
- ARP performs no authentication, and so it is highly vulnerable to attack. As a result, attackers can use ARP spoofing, also called ARP poisoning or ARP cache poisoning, to send faked ARP replies that alter ARP tables in the network. DAI (dynamic ARP inspection) can be configured on a switch to protect against ARP spoofing attacks. When DAI is enabled, the switch compares incoming messages with its DHCP snooping binding table to determine whether the message's source IP address is appropriately matched with its source MAC address according to DHCP assignments on the network.

Network Security Technologies

- A proxy server, or proxy, acts as an intermediary between the external and internal networks, screening all incoming and outgoing traffic. Although proxy servers only provide low-grade security relative to other security devices, they can help prevent an attack on internal network resources such as web servers and web clients.
- A firewall is a specialized device or software that selectively filters or blocks traffic between networks. A firewall might be placed internally, residing between two interconnected private networks. More commonly, the firewall is placed on the edge of the private network, monitoring the connection between a private network and a public network, such as the Internet.
- An IDS (intrusion detection system) is a stand-alone device, an application, or a built-in feature running on a workstation, server, switch, router, or firewall. It monitors network traffic, generating alerts about suspicious activity.
- Although an IDS can only detect and log suspicious activity, an IPS (intrusion prevention system) stands in-line between the attacker and the targeted network or host where it can prevent traffic from reaching that network or host.
- Cloud security works according to the shared responsibility model, meaning that the cloud provider is partially responsible for your cloud's security and you're responsible for the rest of it.

Authentication, Authorization, and Accounting (AAA)

- Controlling access to a network and its resources consists of three major elements: authentication, authorization, and accounting. Together, this framework is abbreviated as AAA (authentication, authorization, and accounting) and is pronounced *triple-A*. Occasionally you'll see the acronym AAAA (authentication, authorization, accounting, and auditing) to further emphasize monitoring and security standards involved in these processes; however, most IT security professionals wrap auditing into accounting and so use the AAA acronym.
- The identity of any user or device attempting to access a network, data, or device must be accurately verified before being given access to these resources. This is the role of authentication.
- Even the best authentication techniques—including encryption, computer room door locks, security policies, and password rules—make no difference if you give users access to resources they shouldn't see. Once a user is given access to your network, that doesn't mean they should have access to everything, such as sensitive data or critical network configurations. Controlling what a user can do once inside your network is the job of authorization.
- An important concept in accounting (whether that's the field of accounting or the AAA component of accounting in IT security) is SoD (separation of duties), which refers to a division of labor that ensures no one person can singlehandedly compromise the security of data, finances, or other resources. In the context of AAA's accounting and auditing components, SoD requires that no one is responsible for monitoring and reporting on themselves, which would create a conflict of interest for that person. Accounting and auditing activities should be sufficiently spread across multiple job roles to reduce the company's vulnerability to fraud (intentional damage) or mistakes (unintentional damage).

Authentication Technologies

- For clients to authenticate to network resources (as opposed to individual devices), some sort of directory server on the network must maintain a database of account information, such as usernames, passwords, and any other authentication credentials. Often this is accomplished in AD (Active Directory) or something more Linux-focused like OpenLDAP or 389 Directory Server.
- The mechanisms of LDAP dictate some basic requirements for any directory it accesses, and so, there is a lot of commonality in how directory servers are configured regardless of the software used. LDAP can query the database, which means to draw information out of the database. One weakness of LDAP is that it transmits user credentials in plaintext. Today's on-prem authentication processes should use the more secure LDAPS (LDAP over SSL/TLS), which communicates over port 636 instead of the insecure LDAP ports 389 or 2889.
- Recall that Kerberos is the authentication protocol configured by default on Active Directory, and it works in partnership with LDAP. Kerberos is a cross-platform authentication protocol that uses key encryption to verify the identity of clients and to securely exchange information after a client logs on to a system.
- Kerberos is an example of SSO (single sign-on), a form of authentication in which a client signs on one time to access multiple systems or resources. The primary advantage of single sign-on is convenience.
- An alternative to Active Directory is the cross-platform RADIUS (Remote Authentication Dial-In User Service), which treats authentication and authorization as a single process, meaning that the same type of packet is used for both functions, while accounting is a separate process. Due to its origins as a remote authentication service, RADIUS specializes in supporting clients not directly wired into the network, such as clients of wireless access points or VPN-based clients.
- Another AAA protocol, TACACS+ (Terminal Access Controller Access Control System Plus), offers network administrators the option of separating the authentication, authorization, and auditing capabilities. It's most often used for device administration access control for technicians, although it can be used for network resource access control for users.

Key Terms

For definitions of key terms, see the Glossary.

2FA (two-factor authentication)
AAA (authentication, authorization, and accounting)
AAAA (authentication, authorization, accounting, and auditing)
access control
accounting
ACL (access control list)
application layer firewall
ARP spoofing
authorization
CoPP (control plane policing)
DAC (discretionary access control)
DAI (dynamic ARP inspection)
DHCP snooping
FIM (file integrity monitoring)
Group Policy
HIDS (host-based intrusion detection system)

HIPS (host-based intrusion prevention system)
host-based firewall
IDS (intrusion detection system)
implicit deny
IPS (intrusion prevention system)
KDC (Key Distribution Center)
Kerberos
MAC (mandatory access control)
MFA (multifactor authentication)
network-based firewall
NIDS (network-based intrusion detection system)
NIPS (network-based intrusion prevention system)
packet-filtering firewall
port mirroring
principal
proxy server

RA guard
RBAC (role-based access control)
rogue DHCP server
security token
shared responsibility model
SIEM (Security Information and Event Management)
signature
signature management
SoD (separation of duties)
SSO (single sign-on)
stateful firewall
stateless firewall
TACACS+ (Terminal Access Controller Access Control System Plus)
TAP (test access point)
ticket
zero trust

Review Questions

1. At what layer of the OSI model do proxy servers operate?
   a. Layer 3
   b. Layer 2
   c. Layer 7
   d. Layer 4

2. Which of the following ACL commands would permit web-browsing traffic from any IP address to any IP address?
   a. `access-list acl_2 deny tcp any any`
   b. `access-list acl_2 permit https any any`
   c. `access-list acl_2 deny tcp host 2.2.2.2 host 3.3.3.3 eq www`
   d. `access-list acl_2 permit icmp any any`

3. Which of the following criteria can a packet-filtering firewall *not* use to determine whether to accept or deny traffic?
   a. Destination IP address
   b. SYN flags
   c. Application data
   d. ICMP message

4. What information in a transmitted message might an IDS use to identify network threats?
   a. Signature
   b. FIM
   c. Port mirroring
   d. ACL

5. Which principle ensures auditing processes are managed by someone other than the employees whose activities are being audited?
   a. Separation of duties
   b. Principle of least privilege
   c. Shared responsibility model
   d. Defense in depth

6. Who is responsible for the security of hardware on which a public cloud runs?
   a. The cloud customer
   b. It depends
   c. Both the cloud customer and the cloud provider
   d. The cloud provider

7. Which of the following is *not* one of the AAA services provided by RADIUS and TACACS+?
   a. Authentication
   b. Authorization
   c. Administration
   d. Accounting

8. Which device would allow an attacker to make network clients use an illegitimate default gateway?
   a. RA guard
   b. DHCP server
   c. Proxy server
   d. Network-based firewall

9. Which policy ensures messages are discarded when they don't match a specific firewall rule?
   a. Implicit allow
   b. Explicit deny
   c. Explicit allow
   d. Implicit deny

10. Active Directory and 389 Directory Server are both compatible with which directory access protocol?
    a. LDAP
    b. RADIUS
    c. Kerberos
    d. AD DS

11. What are the two primary features that give proxy servers an advantage over NAT?

12. What kinds of issues might indicate a misconfigured ACL?

13. Any traffic that is not explicitly permitted in the ACL is _____, which is called the _____.

14. What kind of ticket is held by Kerberos's TGS?

15. What's the essential difference between an IPS and an IDS?

16. What causes most firewall failures?

17. What is the purpose of an ACL when configuring CoPP?

18. Why do network administrators create domain groups to manage user security privileges?

19. What characteristic of ARP makes it particularly vulnerable to being used in a DoS attack?

20. Why would you need separate RA guard policies for network hosts and routers attached to a switch?

Hands-On Projects

NOTE 11-12

Websites and applications change often. While the instructions given in these projects were accurate at the time of writing, you might need to adjust the steps or options according to later changes.

Note to Instructors and Students: A rubric is provided for evaluating student performance on these projects. Please see Appendix D.

Project 11-1: Configure ACLs in Packet Tracer

Estimated Time: 30 minutes
Objective: Given a scenario, apply network hardening techniques. (Obj. 4.3)
Resources:
- Packet Tracer

Context: In this project, you will create a new network in Packet Tracer, configure an ACL on the router, and then test the connections between devices. Complete the following steps:

1. Create a Packet Tracer network with one 1941 router, two 2960 switches, and four PCs, and create all the needed connections with Copper Straight-Through cables, as shown in Figure 11-37. Connect the switches to the router using GigabitEthernet connections.

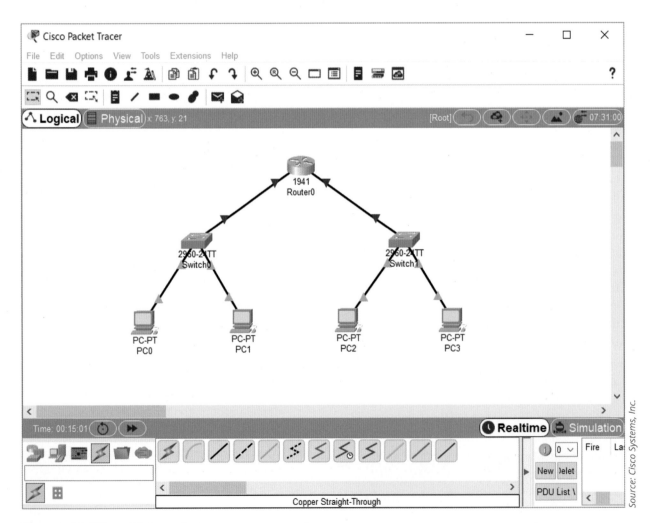

Figure 11-37   Add these devices to your network

2. The links between PCs and switches should come up automatically. On the router's Config tab, configure each GigabitEthernet interface as follows:

   a. Turn the port on.

   b. Assign a Class C IP address with a /24 subnet mask. Make sure these interfaces are on different subnets.

   c. Document this information in your workspace.

3. On each PC, configure an IP address, subnet mask, and default gateway within the appropriate subnet for the router interface it's connected to. For example, if you used 192.168.2.1/24 for Gig0/0 on the router, you could use 192.168.2.10/24 with a default gateway of 192.168.2.1 for one of the PCs on that subnet. As you go, document addressing information in your workspace.

4. Make sure each of the PCs can successfully ping each of the other PCs. **Take a screenshot** of your network, including your addressing documentation notes in your workspace. Submit this visual with your answers to this project's questions.

5. On the router's CLI tab, if your configuration access has timed out, press **Enter**, and then enter the commands from Table 11-2. If you're still in interface configuration mode on the CLI tab, enter `exit` once, and then begin with the `access-list` command in Table 11-2.

Table 11-2   Create an ACL on a router

Command	Purpose
`enable`	Enters privileged EXEC mode
`configure terminal`	Enters global configuration mode
`access-list 1 deny host [PC0's IP address]`	Denies traffic from PC0
`interface gigabitethernet0/0`	Enters interface configuration mode for GigabitEthernet0/0
`ip access-group 1 in`	Applies access-list 1 to incoming traffic on this interface
`end` and press **Enter** again to return to the prompt	Returns to privileged EXEC mode

6. So far, you've blocked traffic coming to the router's GigabitEthernet0/0 interface from PC0. Let's test your work:

   a. From PC0, ping PC1. Does it work? Why do you think this is?

   b. From PC0, ping PC2. Does it work? Why do you think this is?

   c. From PC2, ping PC0. Does it work? Why do you think this is?

   d. From PC2, ping PC1. Does it work? Why do you think this is?

7. Edit the ACL to permit traffic from PC1. On the router's CLI tab, enter the commands from Table 11-3.

Table 11-3   View and edit an ACL on a router

Command	Purpose
`show access-lists`	Shows existing entries in access list 1
`configure terminal`	Enters global configuration mode
`access-list 1 permit host [PC1's IP address]`	Permits traffic from PC1
`exit` and press **Enter** again to return to the prompt	Returns to privileged EXEC mode
`show access-lists`	Shows existing entries in access list 1
`copy run start` and press **Enter** again to use the default filename	Saves the current settings

8. You've now added a new entry to your ACL. Let's test your work:

   a. From PC0, ping PC1. Does it work? Why do you think this is?

   b. From PC0, ping PC2. Does it work? Why do you think this is?

   c. From PC2, ping PC0. Does it work? Why do you think this is?

   d. From PC2, ping PC1. Does it work? Why do you think this is?

9. Save your project for future reference. Make some notes on your Wikidot website about your activities in Packet Tracer for this project.

Note to instructors: A Packet Tracer solution file is provided for each Packet Tracer project through the Instructors site.

Project 11-2: Configure DHCP Snooping in Packet Tracer

Estimated Time: 30 minutes
Objective: Compare and contrast common types of attacks. (Obj. 4.2)
Resources:

- Packet Tracer

Context: In the module, you read about several risks that can come from poorly configured network devices, such as routers and switches. In this project, you'll create a new Packet Tracer network, and then you'll conduct an attack on that network using a rogue DHCP server. You'll then protect the network by configuring DHCP snooping on the switch. Complete the following steps:

1. In Packet Tracer, add a 2960 switch, a 2901 router, and two PCs, as shown in Figure 11-38. Connect the devices to the switch using Copper Straight-Through cables.

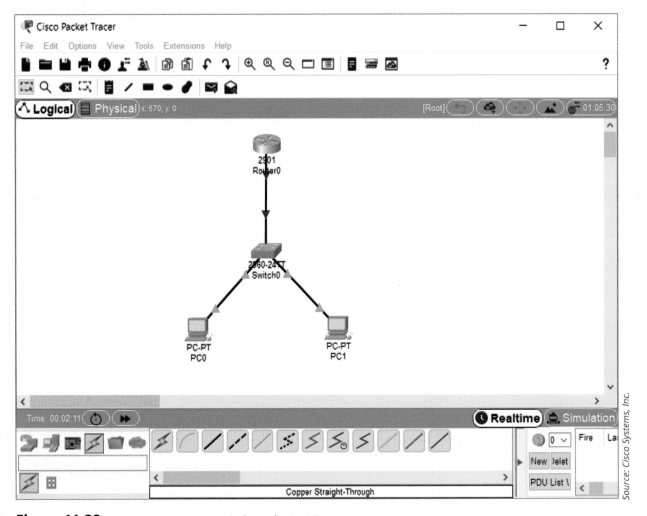

Figure 11-38 Connect a router, switch, and two PCs

2. Enter the commands in Table 11-4 to configure the router's interface and a DHCP pool on the router.

Table 11-4   Configure the router with a DHCP pool

Command	Purpose
`enable`	Enters privileged EXEC mode
`configure terminal`	Enters global configuration mode
`interface gigabit0/0`	Enters interface configuration mode for GigabitEthernet0/0
`ip address 192.168.2.1 255.255.255.0`	Assigns network information to the interface
`no shut` and press **Enter** to return to the prompt	Enables the port
`exit`	Returns to global configuration mode
`ip dhcp pool MyPool`	Creates a DHCP pool named MyPool and enters DHCP configuration mode
`network 192.168.2.0 255.255.255.0`	Assigns network information to the DHCP pool
`default-router 192.168.2.1`	Assigns a default gateway to the DHCP pool
`do show ip dhcp pool`	Displays DHCP pool configuration information
`exit`	Returns to global configuration mode

3. On each PC, request a DHCP assignment. In some cases, it might take a couple of tries for the DHCP assignment to succeed. If it still doesn't work, do some troubleshooting to figure out the problem and fix it. What IP address was assigned to each PC? What is the default gateway address for both PCs?

Suppose an attacker brings their own DHCP server to your network. The attacker configures their device as the default gateway so your PCs start sending their traffic to the wrong device. Complete the following steps:

4. Add a server to your workspace. Do NOT yet connect the attacker's server to your network. Make the following configurations to the server first:
   a. Set the server's static IP address to 192.168.2.20/24.
   b. Turn on the server's DHCP service. Set the pool's default gateway address to 192.168.2.20 and its start IP address to 192.168.2.21/24. Be sure to save these settings.
   c. Use a Copper Straight-Through cable to connect the hacker's server to your switch.
5. After the server's connection with the switch activates, at PC0's Command Prompt, enter the command `ipconfig /release` and then enter the command `ipconfig /renew`. What information does PC0 receive? Which DHCP server did it get its assignment from?

To protect your network, you need to enable DHCP snooping on the switch. This will ensure that DHCP responses can only come from an approved DHCP server. Complete the following steps:

6. Enter the commands in Table 11-5 to configure DHCP snooping on the switch.

Table 11-5   Configure the switch for DHCP snooping

Command	Purpose
`enable`	Enters privileged EXEC mode
`configure terminal`	Enters global configuration mode
`ip dhcp snooping`	Enables DHCP snooping globally on the switch
`ip dhcp snooping vlan 1`	Enables DHCP snooping for VLAN 1
`do show ip dhcp snooping`	Displays current DHCP snooping configuration; confirm DHCP snooping is configured for VLAN 1

7. Now that DHCP snooping is enabled on your switch, no DHCP responses are currently allowed because, by default, all ports on untrusted. To test this, at PC0's Command Prompt, enter the command `ipconfig /release` and then enter the command `ipconfig /renew`. What information does PC0 receive?
8. For the legitimate DHCP server to work on your network, you need to tell the switch which port it should trust for DHCP responses. Enter the commands in Table 11-6 to configure a trusted DHCP port on the switch.

Table 11-6 Configure a trusted port on the switch for DHCP responses

Command	Purpose
`no ip dhcp snooping information option`	Disables the unneeded Option 82 in DHCP snooping
`interface gigabitethernet0/1`	Enters interface configuration mode for GigabitEthernet0/1, which is connected to the router
`ip dhcp snooping trust`	Designates this port as a DHCP trusted port because it is attached to the DHCP server
`exit`	Returns to global configuration mode
`do show ip dhcp snooping`	Displays current DHCP snooping configuration; confirm configuration matches that shown in Figure 11-39
`copy run start` and press **Enter** to accept the default filename	Saves the current settings

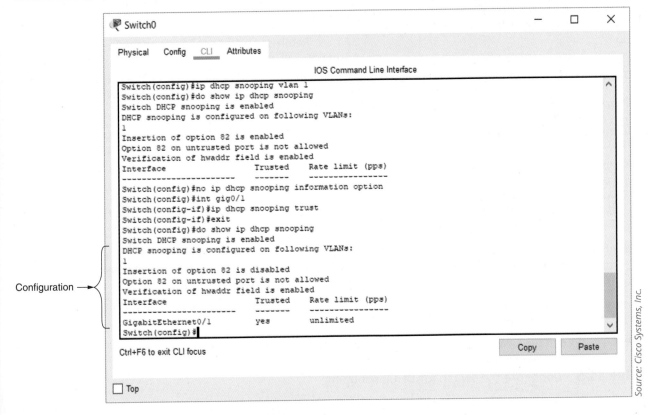

Figure 11-39 Correct DHCP snooping configuration

Source: Cisco Systems, Inc.

9. Now that DHCP snooping is trusted on the correct port on your switch, DHCP responses should be allowed from the legitimate DHCP server. To test this, at PC0's Command Prompt, enter the command `ipconfig /release` and then enter the command `ipconfig /renew`. What information does PC0 receive? Which DHCP server did it get its assignment from? How do you know?

10. Confirm that PC1 can also still receive DHCP information from the legitimate DHCP server. Does it work? How do you know?

11. To see the switch's new records for DHCP assignments on the network, on the switch's CLI in privileged EXEC mode, enter the command `show ip dhcp snooping binding`. How many addresses are listed in the switch's DHCP snooping binding table? Notice the Type for each record is labeled "dhcp-snooping" to indicate the switch learned this information through DHCP snooping.

12. To see which ports the switch trusts for DHCP responses, on the switch's CLI in privileged EXEC mode, enter the command `show ip dhcp snooping`. How many interfaces are listed? How many of these interfaces are trusted?

13. Position your network devices and the switch's CLI console to show your network topology and the output on the switch for Steps 11 and 12. **Take a screenshot**; submit this visual with your answers to this project's questions.
14. Save your project for future reference. Make some notes on your Wikidot website about your activities in Packet Tracer for this project.

Note to instructors: A Packet Tracer solution file is provided for each Packet Tracer project through the Instructors site.

Project 11-3: Configure Cloud Security in AWS

Estimated Time: 30 minutes (+10 minutes for group work, if assigned)
Objective: Given a scenario, apply network hardening techniques. (Obj. 4.3)
Group Work: This project includes enhancements when assigned as a group project.
Resources:
- AWS account created in Hands-on Project 7-1
- Internet access

Context: In Module 7, you created an AWS account of some sort and performed some tasks in the cloud. In this project, you will configure security resources in the cloud, including security groups and NACLS (network ACLs). Use the same AWS account you used in Module 7.

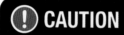 **CAUTION** Depending on the status of your account and the selections you make during this project, an EC2 instance and its supporting resources (such as storage) can deplete your credits or accrue charges. Make sure to follow these steps carefully and delete all created resources at the end of the AWS projects in this module.

Complete the following steps:

1. Sign into your AWS management console. If you're using an AWS Educate classroom, you'll need to access your AWS management console through your AWS Educate classroom. If you're using a standard AWS account, sign in directly at **aws.amazon.com**.
2. Go to the EC2 dashboard and click Launch instance. Click the orange **Launch instance** button and then click **Launch instance** from the list.
3. Select the free tier eligible **Amazon Linux 2 AMI**. Click through the following screens:
   a. Keep the default selection of the free tier eligible t2.micro instance type and click **Next: Configuration Instance Details**.
   b. Keep all default settings and click **Next: Add Storage**.
   c. Keep default settings and click **Next: Add Tags**.
   d. Don't add any tags. Click **Next: Configure Security Group**.

Security groups provide a secure perimeter around each EC2 instance. Each instance can be assigned up to five security groups. A security group blocks all traffic and will only allow traffic that is explicitly allowed. As you can see, EC2 assumes you will want to SSH into your Linux EC2 instance and automatically suggests a rule that will allow SSH from any IP address (0.0.0.0/0) into your EC2 instance through port 22. To explore some of your options here, complete the following steps:

4. Without changing the rule type, what are three other protocols you could choose for rules in your security group?
5. What happens when you change the source to **My IP**? (Be sure to save the displayed information for the group assignment later in this project.)
6. Change the Source back to **Anywhere** and launch your instance. Be sure to use a key pair you have access to—you'll need to connect with your instance shortly. If you still have it, you can use the same key you used for Hands-on Project 7-3. Otherwise, you can refer back to the steps in that project for guidance on how to create a new one.

Now you're ready to connect with your instance:

7. Once it's running, select your instance and click **Connect**. Click **SSH client** for detailed information about your instance. Under Example, select and copy the portion of the text from the username (ec2-user) through the URL (**amazonaws.com**), as shown in Figure 11-40. What is the information you copied?

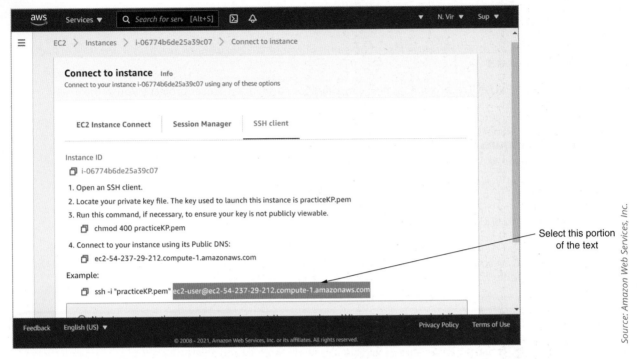

Figure 11-40   Select the sign-in information from the username through the URL

8. Open PuTTY (which you used in Hands-on Project 7-3). Paste the information you copied from your AWS console into the Host Name field. Make sure the Port field lists **22** and make sure **SSH** is selected for the Connection type, as shown in Figure 11-41.

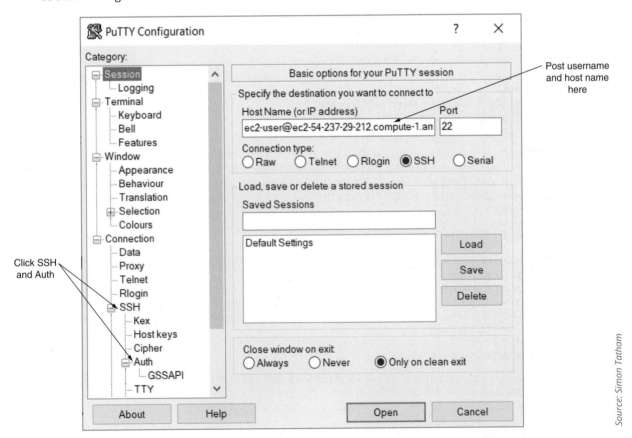

Figure 11-41   Paste the username and host name information from AWS in the Host Name field

9. In the left pane, click **SSH** and then click **Auth**. On the right side, click **Browse** and find the private key file you chose earlier in Step 6. Click **Open**. In the security alert dialog box, click **Yes** to add your private key to PuTTY's cache.

Now that you're connected with your instance, let's see how well the instance's security group works:

10. When the connection is established, try to ping Google's DNS server at 8.8.8.8. Did it work? Why do you think this is?

11. Recall that an EC2 instance's security group is stateful, meaning it will allow returning traffic for a conversation that was initiated by the EC2 instance itself, such as a ping. Check your management console for information about your instance. What is this instance's public IP address?

12. Try pinging this instance from your local computer. Does it work? Why do you think this is?

Let's change this. To add a new rule to your instance's security group, complete the following steps:

13. In your instance's information pane, click the **Security** tab, as shown in Figure 11-42. Scroll down to the list of Security groups and click the security group link.

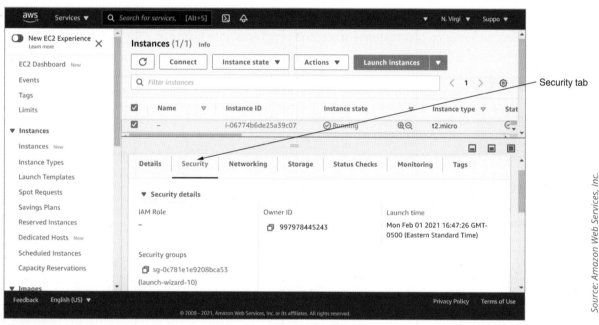

Security tab

Source: Amazon Web Services, Inc.

Figure 11-42   Security groups are listed on the Security tab

14. How many inbound rules are currently listed? What traffic is currently allowed to enter the security group?
15. How many outbound rules are currently listed? What traffic is currently allowed to exit the security group?
16. Click **Edit inbound rules**. Add a new rule that allows **All ICMP – IPv4** traffic from any IPv4 address. (Note that the Google Chrome browser might experience a problem with this step. If so, try Mozilla Firefox.). Save the rules.
17. Try again to ping your EC2 instance from your local computer. Does it work? Why do you think this is?

By default, your VPC's (Virtual Private Cloud) NACL (network ACL) allows all traffic. You can add allow or deny rules to further control traffic into and out of each subnet. Recall that NACL rules are stateless, meaning a protocol's traffic must be allowed in both directions for a conversation such as ping to succeed. Complete the following steps:

18. Return to your instance's information pane and click the **Networking** tab. Locate and click the instance's VPC ID. This takes you to your VPC in the VPC dashboard.
19. Select the VPC listed here (there should just be one). In the VPC's information pane, click the link for the **Main network ACL**. This takes you to the NACL list.
20. Select the NACL listed here (there should just be one). In the NACL's information pane, click the **Inbound rules** tab. What inbound rules are listed here?

Notice that these rules seem contradictory—why would one rule allow all traffic and the next rule deny all traffic? Each rule is assigned a priority. The NACL checks each rule in succession from highest priority to lowest priority. As soon as a rule is found that matches the traffic, that rule is applied. To block ICMP traffic (which is currently allowed by both the NACL and the security group), complete the following steps:

21. Click **Edit inbound rules** and then click **Add new rule**. The new rule will need to be a higher priority than the existing "allow all traffic" rule that is rated at 100. Choose a number below 100 for your new rule. Continue configuring the rule so it will block ICMP – IPv4 traffic from all sources. Be sure to save your changes. **Take a screenshot** of your new NACL inbound rule; submit this visual with your answers to this project's questions.
22. If your goal is only to block outside computers from pinging your EC2 instance, is this NACL inbound rule sufficient to accomplish your goal, or do you also need a corresponding outbound rule? Does it work? Why do you think this is?
23. Try again to ping your EC2 instance from your local computer. Does it work? Why do you think this is?
24. **For group assignments:** Currently, you can't ping your instance from your local computer due to the NACL rule blocking incoming ICMP traffic. This rule applies to all source IP addresses. How can you configure your NACL to allow pings from your computer but still block pings from other computers on the Internet? Each partner should configure a new, higher priority NACL rule that allows ICMP traffic only from their own public IP address. Confirm you can now ping your instance. Then give a partner your instance's public IP addresses and try to ping your partner's instance. Does it work? Why do you think this is?
25. Return to your list of instances in EC2. Recall that turning the instance off does not delete any resources in your AWS cloud. In some cases, you continue to be charged for resources even if they're turned off. To delete your instance, select the instance, click **Instance state**, and click **Terminate instance**. Click **Terminate**. What is the instance state now?

 **CAUTION** Depending on the status of your account and the selections you made during the AWS projects, your EC2 instance and its supporting resources (such as storage) can deplete your credits or accrue charges. Double-check to make sure you've terminated all resources you created in the AWS projects.

Project 11-4: Configure RADIUS in Packet Tracer

Estimated Time: 20 minutes
Objective: Explain common security concepts. (Obj. 4.1)
Resources:
- Packet Tracer

Context: In Capstone Project 6-1, you created and secured a basic wireless network in Packet Tracer. For that project, you secured the wireless network using a pre-shared key. In this project, you'll instead configure a RADIUS server to handle authentication for wireless clients. Complete the following steps:

1. Open Packet Tracer—make sure you're starting from a new file, not an existing network. From the **Network Devices, Wireless Devices** menu, insert a **WRT300N** wireless router.
2. On the wireless router's Config tab, set its LAN-facing IP address to **192.168.5.1/24**.
3. From the **End Devices** menu, insert a **Laptop**.
4. On the laptop's **Physical** tab, replace the Ethernet network module with a **PT-LAPTOP-NM-1W-AC** wireless module. What happens on your network when you turn the laptop back on?
5. Set up some security parameters on the wireless router:
   a. On the wireless router's **Config** tab on the **Wireless** page, select **WPA2** authentication.
   b. Set the RADIUS server's IP address to **192.168.5.2**.
   c. Set the shared secret to **networkplus**.
   d. Make sure the encryption type is **AES**.
   e. What has happened to your network devices? Why do you think this is?
6. To solve this problem, you need to create a RADIUS server:
   a. From the **End Devices** menu, insert a **Server**.
   b. On the server's **Config** tab on the **FastEthernet0** page, set its IP address to **192.168.5.2/24**.
   c. On the server's **Services** tab, on the **AAA** page, turn on the AAA service.
7. In the Network Configuration section, add a new client with the following information:
   a. Client Name: **WRouter0**
   b. Client IP: **192.168.5.1**
   c. Secret: **networkplus**
   d. ServerType: **Radius**
   e. Click **Add**.

8. In the User Setup section, add a new user with the following information:
   a. Username: **User1**
   b. Password: **cengage**
   c. Click **Add**.
9. Using a Copper Straight-Through cable, connect the server to the wireless router. Has the wireless connection with the laptop been reestablished? Why do you think this is?
10. On the laptop's **Config** tab, on the **Wireless0** page, change the following settings:
    a. Authentication: **WPA2**
    b. User ID: **User1**
    c. Password: **cengage**
    d. Close the laptop's configuration window and wait a moment. What happens to the wireless connection?
    e. You didn't configure the laptop's user information on the wireless router. How did the router know to accept the laptop as a wireless client?
11. **Take a screenshot** of your network; submit this visual with your answers to this project's questions.
12. Make some notes on your Wikidot website about your activities in Packet Tracer for this project.

Note to instructors: A Packet Tracer solution file is provided for each Packet Tracer project through the Instructors site.

Capstone Projects

NOTE 11-13

Websites and applications change often. While the instructions given in these projects were accurate at the time of writing, you might need to adjust the steps or options according to later changes.

Note to Instructors and Students: A rubric is provided for evaluating student performance on these projects. Please see Appendix D.

Capstone Project 11-1: Secure Ubuntu Server

Estimated Time: 30 minutes
Objective: Given a scenario, apply network hardening techniques. (Obj. 4.3)
Resources:
- Access to the same computer used to complete Capstone Project 3-1

Context: In Module 3, Capstone Project 3-1, you installed Ubuntu Server in a VM. In this project, you'll perform tasks to secure your Ubuntu Server system. To do this, you will first update your OS and practice working with running services listening on the network. Then you'll learn some basic commands in iptables (Ubuntu Server's default firewall), configure a couple of firewall rules, and save the rules in a file. Complete the following steps:

1. Start your Ubuntu Server VM and log in. Refer to your notes in Wikidot and your account information in LastPass if you need a refresher on where this VM is saved and how to access the user account. You'll need your password several times throughout this project, so keep it handy.
2. First, update your Ubuntu Server OS. To do this, enter the command `sudo apt-get update` and enter your password. After that process completes, enter the command `sudo apt-get upgrade` and enter **y** to continue, which will finish all updates.

Let's install the web server software Nginx so you can practice securing your server. Complete the following steps:

3. Enter `sudo ss -atpu` to see running services on your server. How many services are listed?
4. Enter `sudo apt-get install nginx` and enter **y** to install Nginx.
5. Without any further configuration, Nginx is running on your server. Again enter `sudo ss -atpu`. How many services are running now?

6. Two of these services are Nginx, one for IPv4 and one for IPv6. To see a list of all available services and their current statuses, enter **service --status-all**. What symbol indicates Nginx is running?

7. To stop Nginx, enter **sudo service nginx stop**. How can you confirm Nginx is no longer running on your server?

Now you're ready to configure your iptables firewall. Complete the following steps:

8. Begin by looking at what rules are currently in force. Enter the command **sudo iptables -L** and then enter your password if necessary. The three chains, or lists of rules, are currently empty. What three chains are listed?

Firewall traffic can be set to either accept traffic that doesn't meet a deny rule, which is called implicit allow, or reject traffic that doesn't meet an accept rule, which is called implicit deny. No restrictions are configured by default, so you need to add some. Complete the following steps:

9. Before making other changes, make sure you allow any current connections to continue. Enter the following command, as shown in Figure 11-43:

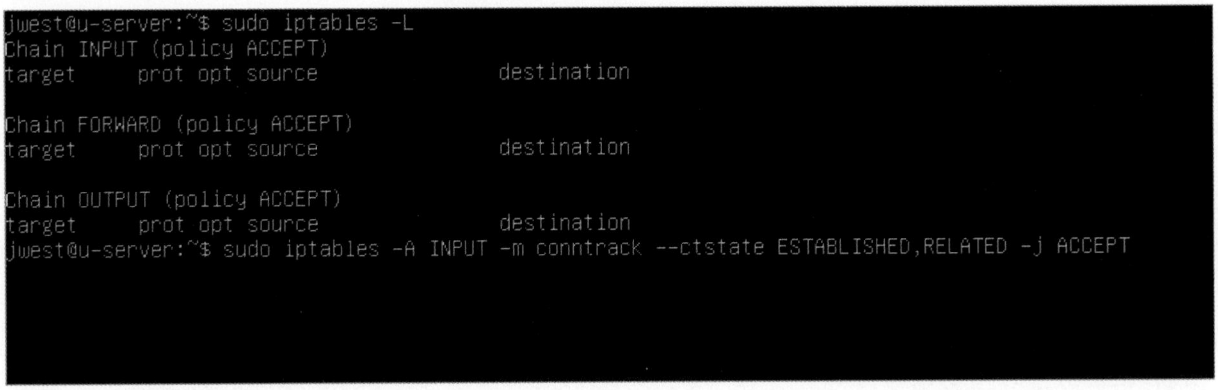

```
jwest@u-server:~$ sudo iptables -L
Chain INPUT (policy ACCEPT)
target     prot opt source               destination

Chain FORWARD (policy ACCEPT)
target     prot opt source               destination

Chain OUTPUT (policy ACCEPT)
target     prot opt source               destination
jwest@u-server:~$ sudo iptables -A INPUT -m conntrack --ctstate ESTABLISHED,RELATED -j ACCEPT
```

Source: Canonical Group Limited

Figure 11-43   Be careful to enter this command exactly as shown on the last line

```
sudo iptables -A INPUT -m conntrack --ctstate ESTABLISHED,RELATED -j ACCEPT
```

10. Enter the **sudo iptables -L** command again to make sure the new rule is listed. Which chain(s) includes the new rule?

11. Next, open port 22 for SSH connections. Enter the following command:

```
sudo iptables -A INPUT -p tcp --dport ssh -j ACCEPT
```

12. The iptables utility automatically knows that SSH runs on port 22 by default, so it opens port 22 when SSH is listed in this command. Sometimes, however, you might want to list the port number itself. Using the command in Step 11 as a guide, what command would you enter to allow HTTPS traffic using the port number instead of the protocol name?

13. Now change the default input policy so it will drop any traffic that doesn't match an accept rule. Enter the following command:

```
sudo iptables -P INPUT DROP
```

14. Enter the **sudo iptables -L** command again to see your changes. Which chain now has a DROP policy? What policy is listed for the other two chains? Using the command in Step 13 as a guide, what command would you enter to change the default forward policy instead?

15. These policies are not persistent, meaning they will be lost the next time you power off the Ubuntu Server VM. To save these rules, you first must export the data to a file. Enter the following command and then enter your password:

```
sudo sh -c "iptables-save > /etc/iptables.rules"
```

16. To confirm your file was saved, change to the /etc directory with the command `cd /etc`. Then, show the directory's contents with the command `ls`.

17. **Take a screenshot** that shows your file in the list; submit this visual with your answers to this project's questions.

18. You won't always have a handy guide to tell you what commands to enter when you want to accomplish a task at the command line. Oftentimes, you must do some research. The iptables utility has the option to automatically restore the rules from the rules file each time you power on the system. Look online and find the command that makes this possible. What did you find? What does this command do?

19. Enter the `sudo poweroff` command to shut down the VM. Make some notes on your Wikidot website about your activities in Ubuntu Server for this project.

Capstone Project 11-2: Defend Against a DoS Attack from Kali Linux

Estimated Time: 1 hour
Objective: Given a scenario, apply network hardening techniques. (Obj. 4.3)
Group Work: This project includes enhancements when assigned as a group project.
Resources:

- Access to the same computer used to complete Capstone Project 1-1 or Capstone Project 1-2 (for a Windows 10 VM), Capstone Project 7-2 (for a private network if using Hyper-V), and Capstone Project 10-2 (for a Kali Linux VM).
- Internet access

Context: In this module, you read about RA messages and a weakness of IPv6 that these messages are not authenticated by the client device. In this project, you'll install a suite of attack tools in your Kali Linux VM that you'll then use to attack a Windows 10 VM on your virtual network. First, you'll install the tools suite in Kali. Then you'll isolate your virtual network so your attack won't affect other devices. Finally, you'll conduct the attack and experiment with the results. Note that the outcome will be different depending on the hypervisor you're using. If possible, partner with a classmate who is using a different hypervisor than you are so you can see how the results will vary.

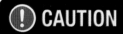

> **⚠ CAUTION**
>
> It's highly illegal to perform penetration testing procedures on a network that you do not own or have specific permission to test. Using the penetration testing tools included in Kali Linux for this project is best done on your own, home network where you own the networking equipment and pay the bill yourself.
>
> If you use a network that you do not own, be sure to obtain explicit permission from the network owner, preferably in writing, signed, and dated. If you practice using the pen testing tools in a school lab, be sure to follow your instructor's directions carefully. Do not use Kali tools on public Wi-Fi networks at all. Make sure you understand what you're doing at each step, and always make sure you've isolated your test network from your physical network. If you follow the steps correctly, the Kali Linux test attack will be contained within your virtual network on a single computer. As a precaution, however, ensure you are using your own network or have the proper permissions in place.
>
> **Penetration testing a network you don't own without the owner's permission can incur multiple federal felony charges, even if the network owner is a relative or friend. Please be absolutely certain you have permission _in writing_ before using the Kali Linux pen testing tools.**

Recall that you created a Kali Linux VM in Capstone Project 10-2. For this project, you'll first need to install the required software while your Kali VM has access to the Internet. Complete the following steps:

1. Start your Kali VM. From Terminal, confirm your Kali VM has an IP address from your local network and can ping your network's gateway and Google's DNS at 8.8.8.8. If not, do some troubleshooting.

2. Once you have an active connection with the Internet, complete the following steps to install the needed software:

   a. Enter `sudo apt update` and enter your password. Source information is updated.

   b. Enter `sudo apt-get install libpcap-dev libssl-dev` and enter **y** when prompted to continue. Supporting software needed for the THC-IPv6 package is installed.

c. Open Firefox and go to **github.com/vanhauser-thc/thc-ipv6**. Click the green **Code** button and click **Download ZIP** to download the zipped folder to your Downloads folder in your VM. When the download is complete, extract the folder contents and save the extracted files to your Downloads folder. Close Firefox.

d. Back in Terminal, enter `cd Downloads` to change your current directory to the Downloads directory.

e. Enter `cd thc-ipv6-master/` to change your current directory to the thc-ipv6-master directory. This is the directory you created when you extracted the THC-IPv6 files.

f. Enter `make`. This consolidates the needed files into a single package for installation.

g. Enter `sudo make install` and enter your password. The software installs.

h. Enter `ls` to display the installed tools included in the THC-IPv6 suite (see Figure 11-44).

i. For this attack, you'll use flood_router26. Do a brief search online. What does this tool do?

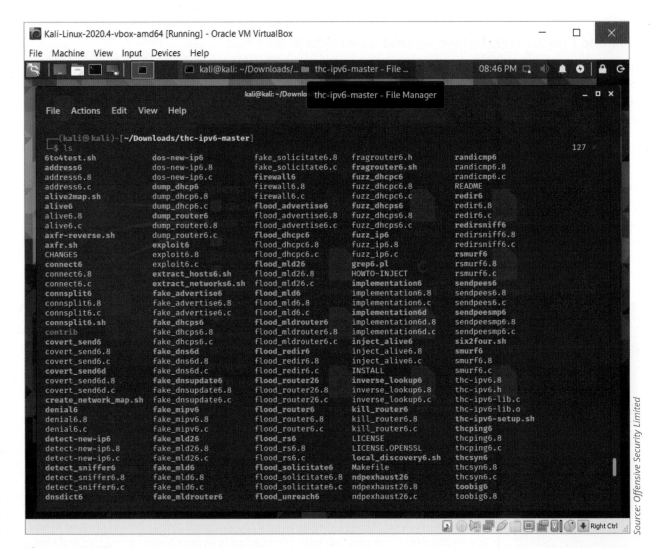

Figure 11-44   Tools in the THC-IPv6 suite

Next, you need to isolate both VMs within an internal network. They'll be able to talk to each other, but not to other devices on your virtual or physical network. This will contain the attack within this isolated network. Complete the following steps:

3. *For Hyper-V users:*

a. You created a private virtual switch in Capstone Project 7-2. To confirm, in the Hyper-V Manager Actions pane, click **Virtual Switch Manager**. In the list of virtual switches, click the switch you created in Capstone Project 7-2. Confirm the virtual switch is connected to a Private network and note the switch's name.

b. Open the Kali VM's Settings box and click **Network Adapter** in the left pane. Change the Virtual switch selection to the private switch and click **OK**.

c. Open the Windows 10 VM's Settings box (this is the VM you created in Capstone Project 1-1) and click **Network Adapter** in the left pane. Change the Virtual switch selection to the private switch and click **OK**. Start your Windows 10 VM so both VMs are running.

4. *For VirtualBox users:*

a. In VirtualBox, set the network adapter for your Kali Linux VM to **Internal Network**. In the Name field, type **AttackNW** and click **OK**.

b. Set the network adapter for your Windows 10 VM to **Internal Network**, choose your newly created **AttackNW** from the dropdown list and then click **OK**. Start your Windows 10 VM so both VMs are running.

Now that your virtual network is isolated, you need to do a little more configuring on the VMs:

5. On the Windows 10 VM, you need to allow ICMP echo requests through the firewall. Open **Windows Defender Firewall** in Control Panel and then click **Advanced settings**. In the left pane, click **Inbound Rules**. Select the **Core Networking Diagnostics – ICMP Echo Request (ICMPv4-In)** rule that is listed for the **Private** network profile and click **Enable Rule**, as shown in Figure 11-45. This will allow ICMP messages through the firewall so the Kali VM can ping the Windows 10 VM. Close the firewall windows.

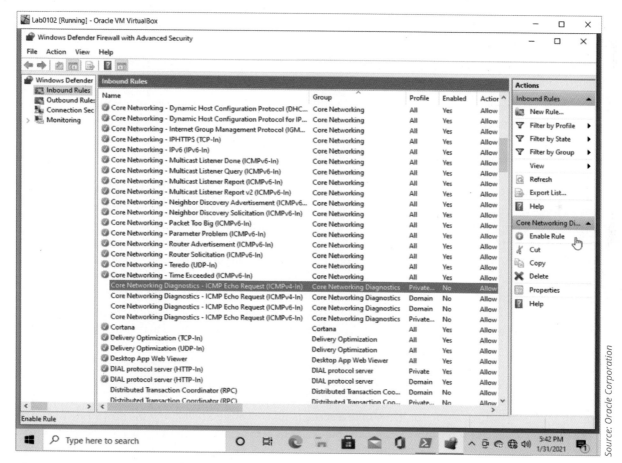

Source: Oracle Corporation

Figure 11-45   Enable ICMPv4 messages to enter the Windows 10 firewall

6. Set a static IP address for each VM as follows:

a. *Windows 10 VM*—Set a static IP address of **192.168.55.10/24** with a default gateway of **192.168.55.1**. Run `ipconfig` to confirm its addressing. If needed, do some troubleshooting to fix the problem. Otherwise, close all windows on the Windows 10 VM except the CLI.

b. *Kali VM*—In Terminal, enter `sudo ip addr flush dev eth0` and then enter your password. This clears all existing IP address configurations.

c. Enter the following commands in Terminal:

- `sudo ip link set eth0 down` to shut down the interface.
- `sudo ip addr add 192.168.55.20/24 dev eth0` to assign a static IP address to the interface.
- `sudo ip link set eth0 up` to turn on the interface.
- `ip a` to confirm the IP address configuration matches that shown in Figure 11-46. If needed, do some troubleshooting to fix the problem. Otherwise, close all windows on the Kali VM except Terminal.

```
  ┌──(jill㉿kali)-[~]
  └─$ ip a
1: lo: <LOOPBACK,UP,LOWER_UP> mtu 65536 qdisc noqueue state UNKNOWN group default qlen 1000
    link/loopback 00:00:00:00:00:00 brd 00:00:00:00:00:00
    inet 127.0.0.1/8 scope host lo
        valid_lft forever preferred_lft forever
    inet6 ::1/128 scope host
        valid_lft forever preferred_lft forever
2: eth0: <BROADCAST,MULTICAST,UP,LOWER_UP> mtu 1500 qdisc mq state UP group default qlen 1000
    link/ether 00:15:5d:02:78:06 brd ff:ff:ff:ff:ff:ff
    inet 192.168.55.20/24 scope global eth0
        valid_lft forever preferred_lft forever
```

Source: Offensive Security Limited

Figure 11-46 The eth0 interface is configured with static IP address 192.168.55.20

7. Perform the following checks:
   a. Ping between the VMs to make sure they can communicate.
   b. Ping Google at 8.8.8.8 to make sure neither VM can communicate with the Internet.
   c. Ping the host and other devices on your network to make sure neither VM can communicate with the rest of your network.

You're now ready to set up your attack from your Kali VM to your internal network, including your Windows 10 VM. Complete the following steps:

8. **For group assignments:** Partner with a classmate who is using a different hypervisor than you are. For example, if you're using VirtualBox, find a partner who is using Hyper-V, and vice versa. As you conduct your attack in the following steps, compare notes on the results.

9. Open your *host* computer's Task Manager, click **More details**, and click the **Performance** tab so you can monitor the host's resources.

10. Position the host's Task Manager window, your Windows 10 VM window, and your Kali VM window so you can see all three windows at the same time. In your Windows 10 VM, open Task Manager, click **More details**, and click the **Performance** tab so you can monitor the VM's resources.

11. On the Windows 10 VM, start a ping to the Kali VM using the -t parameter so the ping will continue until you stop it. What command did you use? How can you stop the ping when you're ready? For now, leave the ping running.

12. In your Kali VM, enter the command **sudo flood_router26 eth0** and, if necessary, enter your password to begin your attack. Each dot on the screen is a burst of RA messages on the local network. What happens to your Windows 10 VM? What happens to your host's resources? In your answers, be sure to mention the hypervisor you're using.

13. In your Kali VM, press **Ctrl+C** on your keyboard to stop the attack. For VirtualBox users, what information now displays in Task Manager for your Windows 10 VM's CPU utilization during the attack? For Hyper-V users, what changes do you notice in your host's CPU utilization?

14. Set up and run the attack again. This time, **take a screenshot** showing both VMs and the host's Task Manager with the attack ongoing; submit this visual with your answers to this project's questions.

Ultimately, the solution to protect network clients from this type of attack is to add RA guard configurations on the switch. Hyper-V includes this type of protection on its virtual switches by default, which is why VMs running on Hyper-V were not affected by the attack. For VirtualBox, an alternative but not long-term solution is to disable IPv6 in the Windows 10 VM to protect it from this attack. If you're using VirtualBox, do the following:

15. In your Windows 10 VM, disable TCP/IPv6 in your network connection's properties box. Run the attack again. What's different this time? When you're ready, stop the attack and the ping.

Once you've completed your testing, do the following:

16. Shut down both VMs. Make some notes on your Wikidot website about your activities with your Windows 10 VM and your Kali Linux VM for this project. Be sure to document network configuration changes so you can reverse these changes later if needed.

Solutions to Self-Check Questions

Network Hardening by Design

1. Which ACL rule will prevent pings from a host at 192.168.2.100?

Answer: b. `access-list acl_2 deny icmp host 192.168.2.100 any`

Explanation: To prevent pings, the ACL must deny ICMP. The scenario requires ICMP be denied from host 192.168.2.100, which should be listed first in the command. Together, these components create the command `access-list acl_2 deny icmp host 192.168.2.100 any`.

2. Which two features on a switch or router are integrated into CoPP? Choose two.

Answer: c. QoS and d. ACLs

Explanation: An adaptation of **QoS (quality of service)** filters can be used to rate-limit traffic on the control plane and management plane of routers and switches using a feature called CoPP (control plane policing). The first step of configuring CoPP is to create an **ACL (access control list)**, which will be used to identify relevant traffic for the CoPP policies. ICMP (Internet Control Message Protocol) is used for ping. DHCP (Dynamic Host Configuration Protocol) is used to dynamically assign IP addresses on a network.

3. Which of the following defenses addresses a weakness of IPv6?

Answer: d. RA guard

Explanation: The **RA (router advertisement) guard** feature filters IPv6 RA messages so these messages can only come from specific interfaces on the switch. DHCP messages should be monitored by enabling DHCP snooping on a switch so that any switch ports connected to clients are not allowed to transmit DHCP responses that should only come from a trusted DHCP server. An adaptation of QoS (quality of service) filters can be used to rate-limit traffic on the control plane and management plane of routers and switches using a feature called CoPP (control plane policing). DAI (dynamic ARP inspection) can be configured on a switch to protect against ARP spoofing attacks.

Network Security Technologies

4. Which device can be used to increase network performance by caching websites?

Answer: b. Proxy server

Explanation: A **proxy server** can improve performance for users accessing resources external to their network by caching files. A firewall is a specialized device or software that selectively filters or blocks traffic between networks. An IDS (intrusion detection system) monitors network traffic, generating alerts about suspicious activity. An AWS security group filters traffic into and out of a single EC2 instance.

5. Which firewall type can protect a home network from adult content not suitable for the family's children?

Answer: d. Application layer firewall

Explanation: **Application layer firewalls** can block designated types of traffic based on application data contained within packets. The simplest form of a firewall is a packet-filtering firewall, which is a network device or application that only examines each message's header. Host-based firewall software only protects the computer on which it's installed. A stateless firewall manages each incoming packet as a stand-alone entity without regard to currently active connections.

6. Which security device relies on a TAP or port mirroring?

Answer: a. NIDS

Explanation: An **NIDS (network-based intrusion detection system)** sits off to the side of network traffic and is sent duplicates of packets traversing the network from a switch configured with port mirroring or from a TAP device. An HIDS (host-based intrusion detection system) runs on a single computer to detect attacks to that one host. An HIDS solution might also include FIM (file integrity monitoring), which alerts the system of any changes made to files that shouldn't change, such as operating system files. Like HIDS, an HIPS (host-based intrusion prevention system) protects a specific host and doesn't need access to all network traffic.

Authentication, Authorization, and Accounting (AAA)

7. Which access control technique is responsible for detection of an intruder who succeeds in accessing a network?

Answer: b. Accounting

Explanation: The **accounting** system logs users' access and activities on the network and can be used to detect illicit activity on a network. In other words, accounting asks, "What did you do?" Authentication is the process of verifying a user's credentials to grant the user access to secured resources on a system or network. Geofencing determines a client's geographic location to enforce a virtual security perimeter. SoD (separation of duties) refers to the division of labor such that no one person can singlehandedly compromise the security of data, finances, or other resources.

8. Which authorization method will allow Nancy, a custodian, to access the company's email application but not its accounting system?

Answer: a. RBAC

Explanation: With **RBAC (role-based access control)**, a network administrator creates user groups associated with these roles and assigns privileges and permissions to each user group. Each user is assigned to a user group that matches a requirement for their job. With DAC (discretionary access control), users decide for themselves who has access to that user's resources. In the context of AAA, auditing refers to checking user configurations for problems, searching for signs of account misuse, and monitoring a network for compromised accounts. Normally, this is considered a part of network accounting functions. Local authentication processes are performed on a single device.

Authentication Technologies

9. Which authentication protocol is optimized for wireless clients?

Answer: a. RADIUS

Explanation: Due to its origins as a remote authentication service, **RADIUS (Remote Authentication Dial-In User Service)** specializes in supporting clients not directly wired into the network, such as clients of wireless access points or VPN-based clients. While Active Directory offers powerful authentication and other services, it's limited to working with Windows or Linux clients, and it can't directly support authentication through wireless access points. TACACS+ (Terminal Access Controller Access Control System Plus) is most often used for device administration access control for technicians. Kerberos is a cross-platform authentication protocol that uses key encryption to verify the identity of clients.

10. What does a client present to a network server to access a resource on that server?

Answer: c. Ticket

Explanation: A **ticket** is a temporary set of credentials a client presents to network servers to prove its identity has been validated. A key belongs to the client or server and is used to initially validate their respective identities to each other during the authentication process to create a session. A principal is a Kerberos client or user. A TGT (Ticket-Granting Ticket) will expire within a specified amount of time and is used to request tickets in order to gain access to network services.

PERFORMANCE AND RECOVERY

After reading this module and completing the exercises, you should be able to:

1. Use appropriate tools to collect data about the network
2. Identify methods to optimize network performance
3. Identify best practices for incident response and disaster recovery

On the Job

Recently, the CISO (Chief Information Security Officer) of an organization determined that there was an increase in network latency, and my team was tasked to root out the culprit. All the usual suspects were tested in our attempt to isolate the problem. Malware scans on the network showed no issues. We looked for employees streaming music or video feeds, but those ideas also proved unfruitful. Finally, we turned on the IDS and used Wireshark to monitor all traffic in and out of the network.

Initially, nothing stood out. But once the daily traffic patterns were laid over our network baseline, there it was staring at us: Rogue devices on the network were consuming a higher than usual amount of bandwidth. These devices were likely employee-owned devices that had been connected to the network without permission. The MAC addresses of these high-consumption devices did not match any of the corporate-owned devices on our inventory list.

As a team we brainstormed ideas to combat the issue. Simply changing the wireless network SSID and password would not suffice, as employees would likely just reconnect their personal devices when they were given the information for their work-owned devices.

Instead, we developed a more complex strategy. First, we blocked all non-company device MAC addresses on the wireless access points. We did this easily enough by consulting the asset inventory list and inputting all corporate-owned devices on a whitelist. We then decided to enable 802.1X on the network switches to ensure only company-owned devices would be able to connect to the wired network, thereby preventing any further issues with rogue devices. We deployed 802.1X utilizing certificate-based credentials that could easily be deployed to all corporate-owned devices. This provided another layer of protection for the wireless network and also allowed us to control wired network access. Finally, we validated the solution by reexamining a network traffic file and confirmed the solution was having the intended effect. Then we just had to answer all the new trouble call tickets about the wireless network no longer working on their personal devices!

Nicholas Pierce
Instructor
Thomas Nelson Community College

Because networks are a vital part of keeping an organization running, you must pay careful attention to measures that keep network resources safe, available, and performing well. Throughout this course, you have learned about building scalable, reliable networks as well as selecting the most appropriate hardware, topologies, and services to operate your network. You have also learned about security measures to guard network access and resources. In this module, you will learn how to optimize networks for today's high bandwidth needs, protect your network's performance from faults and failures, and recover in the event your network experiences a minor outage or a more severe disaster. With proper adjustments, redundancies, and preparations, you can create and maintain a resilient network.

COLLECT NETWORK DATA

✅ CERTIFICATION

1.5 Explain common ports and protocols, their application, and encrypted alternatives.

2.3 Given a scenario, configure and deploy common Ethernet switching features.

3.1 Given a scenario, use the appropriate statistics and sensors to ensure network availability.

4.3 Given a scenario, apply network hardening techniques.

5.3 Given a scenario, use the appropriate network software tools and commands.

Average reading time: 41 minutes

Network management is a general term that means different things to different networking professionals. At its broadest, **network management** refers to the assessment, monitoring, and maintenance of all aspects of a network. It can include controlling user access to network resources, monitoring performance baselines, checking for hardware faults, ensuring optimized QoS (quality of service) for critical applications, maintaining records of network assets and software configurations, and determining what time of day is best for upgrading hardware and software.

Several disciplines fall under the heading of network management. All share the goals of enhancing efficiency and performance while preventing costly downtime or loss. Ideally, network management accomplishes these tasks by helping the administrator predict problems before they occur. For example, a trend in network usage could indicate when a switch will be overwhelmed with traffic. In response, the network administrator could increase the switch's processing capabilities or replace the switch before users begin experiencing slow or dropped connections.

Before you can assess and make predictions about a network's health, however, you must first understand its logical and physical structure and how it functions under typical conditions. And to do that, you must be able to collect data about the network's state, devices, and traffic. Let's begin this discussion with a look at how to monitor the network's physical environment. You'll then learn techniques for monitoring the network itself.

Environmental Monitoring

The best network security and traffic optimization in the world won't do your network any good if the physical environment is not properly maintained. It's essential to monitor the following environmental factors, optimizing for best performance as necessary, to ensure your network functions reliably:

- Device, rack, or room temperature
- Device, rack, or room humidity, dew point, or barometric pressure
- Flooding as sensed by liquid detectors
- Smoke or fire
- Airflow

- Vibration
- Motion as sensed by security cameras
- Room lights on or off
- Room or rack doors open or closed
- Power (main or UPS voltage, battery level, outages, power consumption)

Monitoring sensors in each data room, equipment rack, or device chassis feed information to a physical device or software installed on a server. This data is then presented in an administrative dashboard to network administrators (see Figure 12-1). This dashboard might be accessed over the network or over the Internet, even on a smartphone, allowing network admins to check current environmental data, adjust alarm thresholds, analyze historical data, and respond to alerts. For example, the Room Alert Monitor by AVTECH (*avtech.com*) displays sensor data on a configurable dashboard (see Figure 12-2).

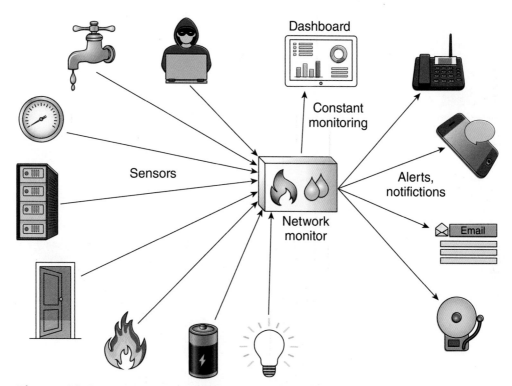

Figure 12-1 Sensors feed data to the network monitor, which outputs information to dashboards and alerts or notifications

Environment monitoring hardware might have dual power connectors for redundancy, a USB console connector for configuration from an attached laptop, a web interface for configuration over the network, additional USB ports for connection to a modem or for saving logs to flash drives, and the ability to maintain wireless connections with sensors. Figure 12-3 shows a diagram of the various connectors on NTI's (Network Technologies Inc.) ENVIROMUX device for medium enterprises. You can see demonstration videos at their website: *networktechinc.com/enviro-monitor.html*.

On the software side, products such as PRTG Network Monitor by Paessler (*paessler.com*) work with ICMP, SNMP, WMI, HTTPS, and others to collect and organize information about monitored devices and sensors. For example, your servers' CPU temperatures and other data can be collected and monitored through the PRTG dashboard (see Figure 12-4). Alerts from monitoring software can be transmitted via email, SMS (Short Message Service, which sends text messages), phone calls, push notifications, audible alerts (such as a siren or voice alert), SNMP traps (you'll learn more about SNMP later in this section), or other options. Monitoring solutions sometimes offer the ability to remotely control some environmental factors, such as adjusting room temperature. In a project at the end of this module, you'll install PRTG in a VM and use the network monitor to detect information about other devices on your network.

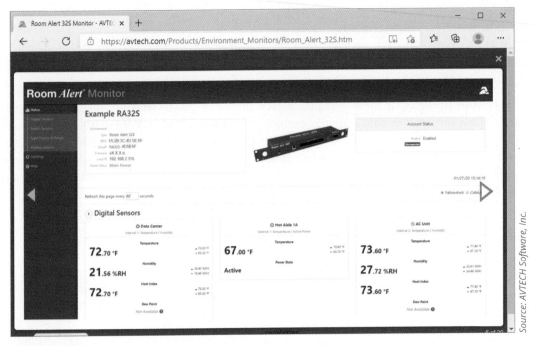

Source: AVTECH Software, Inc.

Figure 12-2 A dashboard provides constant monitoring

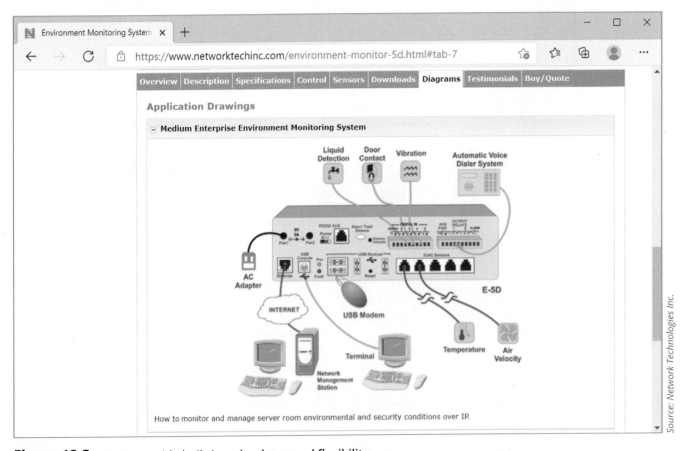

Source: Network Technologies Inc.

Figure 12-3 Ports provide built-in redundancy and flexibility

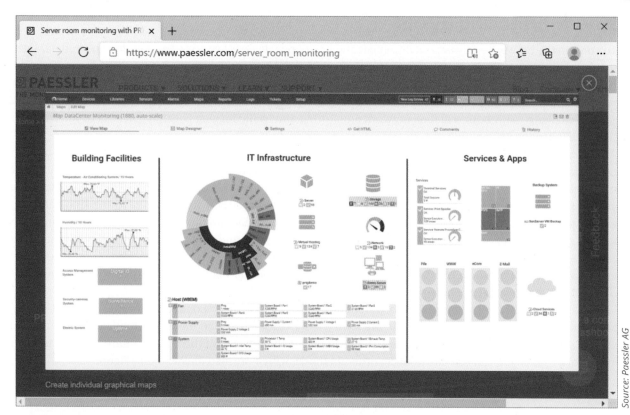

Figure 12-4   Custom dashboards provide insights at a glance

Applying Concepts 12-1: Check Windows 10 Performance Statistics

Much of the data collected by environmental monitoring systems indicates health and status of individual devices on the network, such as a server's CPU usage, demand on memory resources, available storage space, network throughput, and uptime versus downtime. You can see this kind of information for your own Windows 10 computer in Task Manager. Complete the following steps:

1. Press **Ctrl + Alt + Del** and then click **Task Manager**. Click the **Performance** tab.
2. Notice the numbers are changing constantly as you use your computer. Perhaps you're playing some music in the background, or you have a social media site open that is frequently updating. Take a snapshot of each screen as needed to answer the following questions about your computer:
   a. What is your CPU's Utilization and Up time? How many processes are currently running on your CPU?
   b. How much memory is available on your computer? How much of your available memory is in use?
   c. How many storage drives are connected to your computer? What is your primary drive's Read speed and Write speed?
   d. How many network connections does your computer list? What is the maximum possible throughput for the primary network connection?
3. Click **Open Resource Monitor**. Which resources are monitored here?

Traffic Monitoring Tools

As you confirm the network's physical environment and its various devices are operating within expected parameters, you'll also need to monitor the traffic flowing between devices. Some traffic monitoring tools will provide real-time analysis of data with alerts when conditions meet certain thresholds, while other tools are designed to log data for retroactive analysis only as needed. These historical **traffic logs** are primarily used to investigate network performance issues. The challenge with both real-time network monitoring and traffic logging is gaining access to the traffic itself. Consider the following explanation of how network monitors work.

A network monitor is a tool that continually monitors network traffic and might receive data from monitored devices that are configured to report their statistics. A similar tool, a protocol analyzer, can monitor traffic at a specific interface between a server or client and the network. In practice, these two terms—network monitor and protocol analyzer—are often used interchangeably. However, they differ significantly when it comes to the kinds of data you can expect to gather with each tool. Think about the difference between monitoring the traffic that a single device encounters on its connection to the network, versus monitoring devices and traffic patterns throughout the network. For example, Spiceworks is a type of network monitoring software because it can be configured to monitor multiple devices on a network at one time. Wireshark is a type of protocol analyzer because it monitors traffic on the interface between a single device and the network.

Wireshark or other monitoring applications running on a single computer connected to a switch don't see all the traffic on a network—they only see the traffic the switch sends to them, which includes broadcast traffic and traffic specifically addressed to the one computer (see the computer in the red box on the right in Figure 12-5). To track more of the network traffic, you can use one of these other methods, which are also illustrated in Figure 12-5:

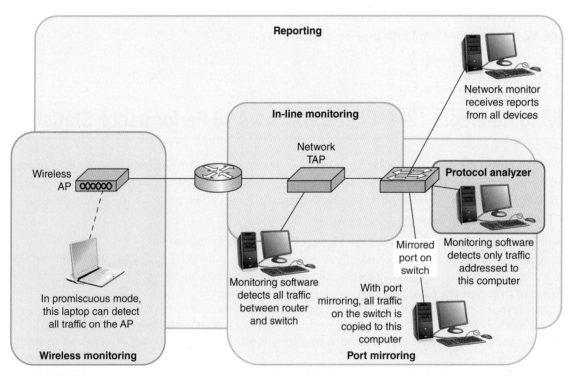

Figure 12-5   Methods to monitor network traffic

- **Wireless monitoring**—Run monitoring software on a computer connected wirelessly to the network (see the computer on the left in Figure 12-5). For the computer to "see" all traffic, its network adapter must support promiscuous mode. In promiscuous mode, a device driver directs the NIC to pass all wireless frames to the operating system and on to the monitoring software, not just those broadcasted or intended for the host. Usually, promiscuous mode is enabled in the monitoring application. Occasionally you'll need to enable the feature through the OS. (For Windows, use the NIC's properties box from Device Manager.)

- **Port mirroring**—Configure a switch to use port mirroring, which ensures that all traffic sent to any port on the switch is also sent to a device connected to the mirrored port, such as the computer in the bottom right of Figure 12-5. Recall you learned about port mirroring (also called SPAN) when you studied NIDS. In a project at the end of this module, you'll configure SPAN on a switch in Packet Tracer. Then you'll monitor traffic through a device connected to the monitored port.
- **In-line monitoring**—Install a device, called a network TAP (test access point) or packet sniffer, in line with network traffic, as shown in the center of Figure 12-5. As you can see in Figure 12-6, a TAP usually has a variety of ports:
  - ○ Two ports send and receive all traffic, usually between a switch and a router.
  - ○ One or two other ports (Ethernet or USB) mirror the traffic, sending it to a computer running monitoring software in promiscuous mode, such as Wireshark.
  - ○ A port on the back is used for device configuration.
- **Reporting**—Many devices can be configured to report their traffic and other statistics to a network monitor, such as the computer in the top right corner of Figure 12-5. These techniques rely on protocols such as syslog and SNMP, which you'll read about shortly.

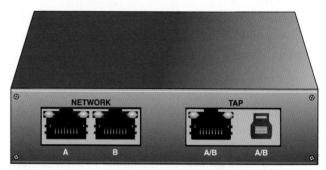

Figure 12-6   Network TAPs are available for both copper and fiber network troubleshooting

Some NOSs come with built-in network monitoring tools. In addition, you can purchase or download free network monitoring tools developed by other software companies. Hundreds of such programs exist. After you have worked with one network monitoring tool, such as Spiceworks, you'll find that other products work in much the same way. Most even use very similar graphical interfaces. All network monitoring tools can perform at least the following functions:

- Set the NIC to run in promiscuous mode so it will pass all traffic it receives to the monitoring software.
- Continuously monitor network traffic on a segment.
- Capture network data transmitted on a segment.
- Capture frames sent to or from a specific node.
- Reproduce network conditions by transmitting a selected amount and type of data.
- Generate statistics about network activity (for example, what percentage of the total frames transmitted on a segment are broadcast frames).

Some network monitoring tools can also perform the following functions:

- Discover all network nodes on a segment.
- Establish a baseline, including performance, utilization rate, and so on.
- Track utilization of network resources (such as bandwidth and storage) and device resources (such as CPU or memory usage), and present this information in the form of graphs, tables, or charts.
- Store traffic data and generate reports.
- Trigger alarms when traffic conditions meet specific thresholds (for example, if usage exceeds 60 percent of capacity).
- Identify usage anomalies, such as top talkers (hosts that send an inordinate amount of data) or top listeners (hosts that receive an inordinate amount of data).

How can capturing data help you solve networking problems? Imagine that traffic on a segment of the network you administer suddenly grinds to a halt one morning at about 8:00 a.m. You no sooner step in the door than everyone from the help desk calls to tell you how slowly the network is running. Nothing has changed on the network since last night when it ran normally, so you can think of no obvious reasons for problems.

At the workstation where you have previously installed a network monitoring tool, you capture all data transmissions for approximately five minutes. You then sort the frames in the network monitoring software, arranging the nodes in order based on the volume of traffic each has generated. You might find that one workstation appears at the top of the list with an excessively high number of bad transmissions. Or you might discover that a server has been compromised by a hacker and is generating a flood of data over the network. Or possibly your current sampling size doesn't yet reveal any problems, and you run a second, longer capture. Once you know the source of the problem, you know where to look for a resolution, as you read about in the *On the Job* story at the beginning of this module.

At the same time, finding the source of the problem requires using the correct tool. A network monitor's data will allow for traffic analysis, which examines the flow of network traffic for patterns and exceptions to those patterns. For example, traffic analysis will identify locations of network bottlenecks, such as an outdated device that should be replaced or a network service that needs more resources. A protocol analyzer, however, will dig into the details of specific packets and perform packet analysis functions, which identify protocols, errors, and misconfigurations. Both approaches can yield insightful information; however, focusing on the most relevant approach will help you locate the source of the problem more quickly.

A network monitor or protocol analyzer can use traffic analysis and packet analysis techniques to identify specific types of data errors and other transmission problems, such as the following:

- **Runts**—Packets that are smaller than the medium's minimum packet size. For instance, any Ethernet packet that is smaller than 64 bytes is considered a runt.
- **Giants**—Packets that exceed the medium's maximum packet size. For example, an Ethernet packet larger than 1518 bytes (or 1522 bytes for VLAN packets) is normally considered a giant.
- **Jabber**—A device that handles electrical signals improperly, usually affecting the rest of the network. A network monitor will detect a jabber as a device that is always retransmitting, effectively bringing the network to a halt. A jabber usually results from a bad NIC. Occasionally, it can be caused by outside electrical interference.
- **Ghosts**—Frames that are not actually data frames, but aberrations caused by a device misinterpreting stray voltage on the wire. Unlike true data frames, ghosts have an invalid pattern at the beginning of the frame pattern.
- **Packet loss**—Packets lost due to an unknown protocol, unrecognized port, network noise, or some other anomaly. Lost packets never arrive at their destination.
- **Discarded packets**—Packets that arrive at their destination beyond their usable time frame and are then discarded, or dropped, by the receiving device. Issues that might cause this include buffer overflow, latency, bottlenecks, or other forms of network congestion. A discarded packet is often referred to as a discard.
- **Interface resets**—Repeated resets of the connection, resulting in lower-quality utilization; typically caused by an interface misconfiguration.

Applying Concepts 12-2: Identify a Process Hogging Network Resources

Suppose you notice a sudden decrease in network performance and suspect malware is hogging network resources. Follow these steps to identify a legitimate process or malware on a Windows machine that is affecting network performance:

1. Every process is assigned a PID (process identifier). To display the PID associated with each network connection, open an elevated PowerShell or Command Prompt window and enter the command `netstat -o`.
2. You can identify the names of the processes for each PID by looking in Task Manager (press **Ctrl + Alt + Del** and then click **Task Manager**). Click **More details**. On the Processes tab, if the PID column is not showing, right-click a column heading and check **PID**.
3. Alternatively, you can have the netstat utility resolve process names. Enter the command `netstat -b`, which will take longer to run. If you don't recognize a process name, do a quick Google search to learn about it.
4. You might need to forcefully stop an out-of-control process. In most cases, you could do this with the Windows Services console (services.msc). To stop a process that refuses to stop by normal means, you can instead use the `taskkill` command with the `/f` parameter and the process's PID. For example, if the PID is 2212, enter the command:

   ```
   taskkill /f /pid:2212
   ```

   If that doesn't work, you might first need to take ownership of the process program file. To do this, enter the command `takeown /f <filename>` using the filename listed for the process when you ran the `netstat -b` command.

Faults and conditions that exceed certain thresholds can trigger alerts, which are messages that indicate some threshold has been met, and those alerts might generate notifications to IT personnel. Depending on the software used, these notifications might be transmitted either by email or text message, also called SMS, or they can automatically prompt support ticket generation. Alerts can also be recorded by system and event logs. Many devices, such as routers, switches, servers, and workstations, include embedded event logging tools of various types and will store logs within their own systems. Other tools collect log entries from devices across the network. Let's look at both possibilities.

Event Viewer in Windows

Virtually every condition recognized by an operating system can be recorded. Records of such activities are kept in a log. For example, each time your computer requests an IP address from the DHCP server and doesn't receive a response, this event is logged. Likewise, a log entry can be added each time a firewall denies a host's attempt to connect to another host on the network that the firewall defends.

Different operating systems log different kinds of events by default, which is called an event log. In addition, network administrators can customize logs by defining conditions under which new entries are created. For example, an engineer might want to know when the relative humidity in a data center exceeds 60 percent. If a device can monitor this information and communicate it in real time to a computer, the results can be written to a log. On Windows-based computers, the event log can be easily viewed with the Event Viewer application, as you will see in the following activity.

Applying Concepts 12-3: Explore Event Viewer in Windows

In this activity, you will use the Event Viewer application to explore the event log on a computer running Windows 10. Ideally, the computer will have been used for a while, so the event log contains several entries. It need not be connected to a network. However, you must be logged on to the computer as a user with administrator privileges. Complete the following steps:

1. Right-click **Start** and click **Event Viewer**.
2. The Event Viewer window opens, with three panes as shown in Figure 12-7. The center pane lists a summary of administrative events. Event Viewer's default screen lists entries for all types of logs kept by the Windows operating system. Notice that events are classified into several types, which might include *Critical, Error, Warning, Information, Audit Success* and, in some cases, *Audit Failure*. The number of events that have been logged in each category is listed to the right of the classification entry. How many Critical and Error events has your workstation logged in the last 24 hours? In the last seven days?
3. If your workstation has logged any critical or error events in the past seven days, click the plus sign next to the event type. A list of events appears. (If you do not have any entries in the Critical or Error categories, click the plus sign next to the event type Warning instead.)
4. Notice that each event log entry is identified by an Event ID, its source, and the type of log on which it's recorded. Scroll through the entries to find one that looks interesting—if possible, one that has occurred more than once in the past seven days. Double-click that entry to read more about it. The Summary page events pane appears in the center of the Event Viewer display (see Figure 12-8).
5. Notice when these errors were recorded. On the General tab in the lower portion of the middle pane, read a detailed description of the error you chose to view. If you were a network manager, would you choose to be alerted whenever this error occurred on a workstation or server? Why or why not?
6. Now click **Windows Logs** in the left pane of Event Viewer to see the different types of logs about Windows events. The Windows Logs listing appears in the center pane, as shown in Figure 12-9.
7. Which of the five logs has recorded the highest number of events? How large is that log file?

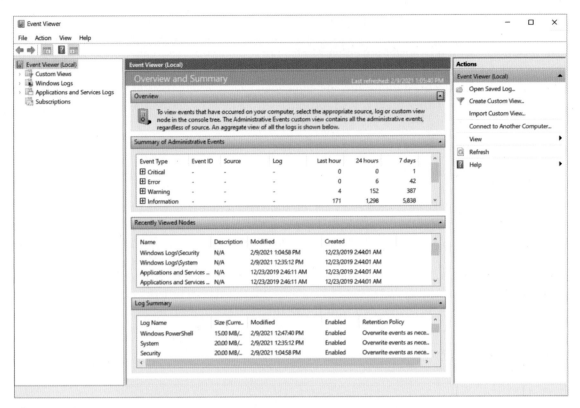

Figure 12-7   Event Viewer logs errors and other activities in Windows

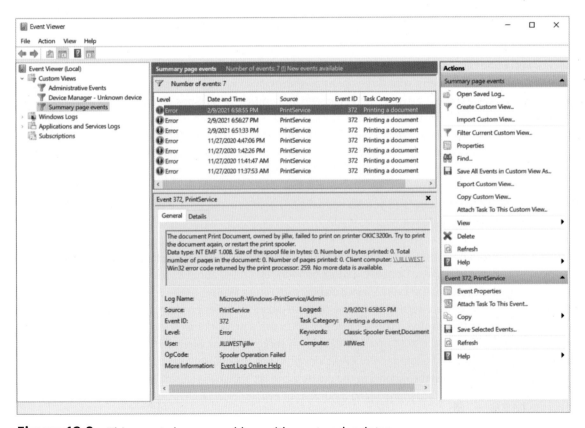

Figure 12-8   This event shows a problem with a network printer

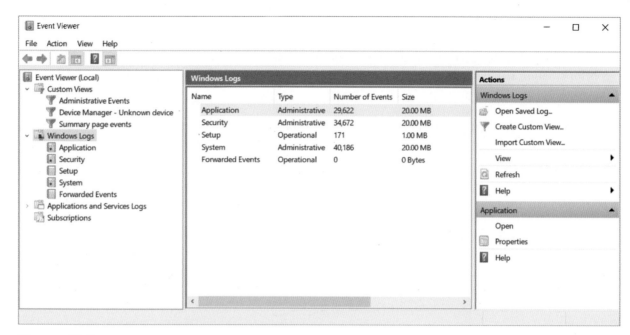

Figure 12-9   Windows Logs listing in Event Viewer

8. Suppose you want to limit the size of the system log. Right-click the **System** log and click **Properties**.
9. The Log Properties - System (Type: Administrative) dialog box opens. Next to the *Maximum log size (KB)* text box, enter **16000** to limit the log file size to 16 MB.
10. Click **OK** to save your change. If you receive a message that indicates your current log's size exceeds the maximum limit you just entered, click **OK** to accept the recommended practice of enforcing the maximum after the log is cleared.

In a project at the end of this module, you'll learn how to work with the data collected in Windows event logs.

Syslog Messages

Event logs and additional information are routinely recorded by many other types of devices. These logs can be centrally collected via the syslog utility. Syslog is a standard for generating, storing, and processing messages about events on many networked systems. It describes methods for detecting and reporting events and specifies the format and contents of messages. The syslog standard addresses three primary components, as described next and illustrated in Figure 12-10:

- **Event message format**—Event messages must be organized and formatted in a specific manner with certain types of information included, although flexibility to this format is built in to allow syslog's use in a wide variety of environments and scenarios.

Event message format   Event message transmission   Event message handling

Figure 12-10   Three components of the syslog standard

- **Event message transmission**—Event messages are transported across the network on port 514. Syslog messages secured by TLS are transported instead over port 6514.
- **Event message handling**—The syslog utility on all monitored devices and on the syslog server follow protocols for creating, handling, analyzing, and storing event messages.

The syslog standard also defines two roles for devices participating in logging events:

- **Generator**—The device that is monitored by a syslog-compatible application and that issues event information
- **Collector**—The server that gathers event messages from generators

You likely don't want to collect every possible event message, as that would generate massive amounts of data to be stored and analyzed. Unless this is necessary for compliance purposes, you'll probably want to limit the types of messages generated, transmitted, and stored. For this purpose, syslog assigns a severity level, also called a logging level or priority value, to each event. For example, "0" indicates an emergency situation, whereas "7" points to specific information that might help in debugging a problem, as shown in Figure 12-11. You configure a filter on the device so that it sends all events from a specific level and above to the syslog server. Further, you can filter syslog messages by the facility, or machine process, which created the event, such as the kernel (facility "0"), users (facility "1"), or security and authorization (facility "4").

Level	State indicated
0	Emergency! System unusable
1	Alert–Immediate action needed
2	Critical–Critical condition
3	Error–Error condition
4	Warning–Warning condition
5	Notification–Normal but significant condition
6	Informational–Informational message only
7	Debugging–Helpful for debugging

Figure 12-11   Syslog severity levels

The filters and other syslog configurations you implement on each device must be carefully considered in situations where you need to conform to regulatory compliance requirements. In some cases, you must be able to track every movement of every user. By referring to information stored in your logs, you should be able to answer the question, "Who did what activity when and in what way?" When tracking this level of information, the collective data is called an audit log, or audit trail. The data in these logs is consistent and thorough enough to retroactively prove compliance and also to defensibly prove user actions (that is, your network logs document user action in a way that is presentable in a court of law). This data is often used in forensics investigations to determine how a particular problem occurred, especially if criminal investigations are involved. Make sure you know exactly what types of actions and other events you must log on your network to meet relevant compliance standards.

NOTE 12-1

Computers running Linux and UNIX record syslog data in a system log, found in the /var/log directory. Configure the types of events to log and what priority to assign each event in the /etc/syslog.conf file (on some systems, this is the /etc/rsyslog.conf file).

Bear in mind that the syslog utility doesn't alert you to any problems, but it does keep a history of messages issued by the system. It's up to you to monitor the system log for issues, review the logs regularly for missed problems, or filter log data to monitor packet flow when troubleshooting a problem or checking for patterns that might indicate developing problems. Most UNIX and Linux desktop operating systems provide a GUI application for easily reviewing and filtering the information in system logs. Other applications are available for sifting through syslog data and generating alerts. In a project at the end of this module, you'll view and sort through data in a system log.

Using the information collected in event logs and system logs for security and fault management requires thoughtful data filtering and sorting. After all, you can't assume that all of the information in these logs points to a problem, even if it is marked with a warning. For example, you might have typed your password incorrectly while trying to log on to your computer, thus generating a log entry. Keep in mind, however, that sometimes seemingly innocuous information turns out to be exactly the data you need to diagnose a problem.

SNMP Communications

You've just learned about logs that are created on individual devices and then collected at a central location on a syslog server. In contrast, organizations often use enterprise-wide network management systems to perform real-time monitoring functions across an entire network. Hundreds of such tools exist. All rely on a similar architecture (see Figure 12-12), in which the following entities work together:

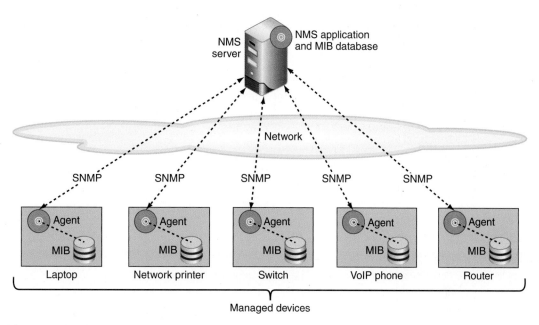

Figure 12-12 Network management architecture

- **NMS (network management system) server**—At least one network management console, which may be a server or workstation, depending on the size of the network, collects data from multiple managed devices at regular intervals in a process called polling.
- **Managed device**—Any network node monitored by the NMS is a managed device. Each managed device may contain several managed objects. This can be any characteristic of the device that is monitored, including components such as a processor, memory, hard disk, or NIC, or intangibles such as performance or utilization. Each managed object is assigned an **OID (object identifier)**, which is standardized across all NMSs.
- **Network management agent**—Each managed device runs a network management agent, which is a software routine that collects information about the device's operation and provides it to the NMS. For example, on a server, an agent can measure how many users are connected to the server or what percentage of the processor's resources are used at any given time. So as not to affect the performance of a device while collecting information, agents demand minimal processing resources.
- **MIB (Management Information Base)**—The list of objects managed by the NMS, as well as the descriptions of these objects, are kept in the MIB (Management Information Base). The MIB also contains data about an object's performance in a database format that can be mined and analyzed. The MIB is designed in a top-down, hierarchical tree structure that supports faster and more efficient analysis.

Agents communicate information about managed devices via any one of several application layer protocols. On modern networks, most agents use SNMP (Simple Network Management Protocol). Recall that SNMP is part of the TCP/IP suite of protocols and typically runs over UDP ports 161 and 162 (though it can be configured to run over TCP ports 10161 and 10162). Port 161 is used to send information from the manager to the installed agents, while port 162 is used for agents to send messages to the manager. One characteristic that sets SNMP apart from syslog is that SNMP can be used to reconfigure managed devices. Additionally, SNMP is used more for real-time network monitoring rather than retroactive analysis.

Three versions of SNMP include the following:

- **SNMPv1 (Simple Network Management Protocol version 1)**—This is the original version, released in 1988. Because of its limited features, it is rarely used on modern networks.
- **SNMPv2 (Simple Network Management Protocol version 2)**—This version improved on SNMPv1 with increased performance and slightly better security, among other features.
- **SNMPv3 (Simple Network Management Protocol version 3)**—This version is similar to SNMPv2 and adds authentication, validation, and encryption for messages exchanged between managed devices and the network management console.

Most, but not all, network management applications support multiple versions of SNMP. SNMPv3 is the most secure version of the protocol. However, some administrators have hesitated to upgrade to SNMPv3 because it requires more complex configuration. Therefore, SNMPv2 is still widely used, despite the many SNMP vulnerabilities listed in the CVE (Common Vulnerabilities and Exposures), one of which is displayed in Figure 12-13. When using older versions of SNMP, it's important to incorporate additional security measures, such as the following:

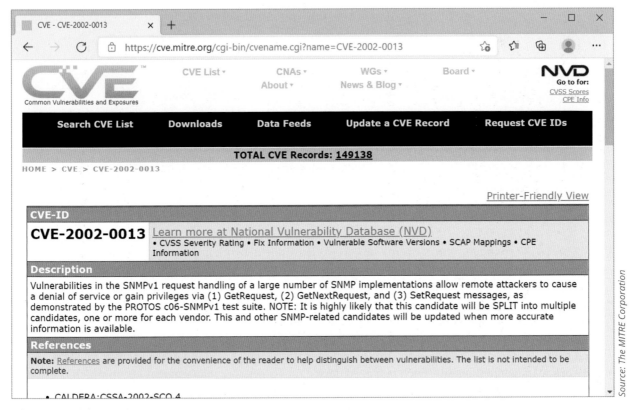

Figure 12-13 One of many SNMP vulnerabilities listed in the CVE

- Disable SNMP on devices where it's not needed.
- Limit approved sources of SNMP messages.
- Require read-only mode so devices can't be reconfigured using SNMP messages.
- Configure strong passwords, called community strings, on SNMP managed devices.
- Use different community strings on different types of devices so, for example, a compromised UPS (which incorporates less secure protections) doesn't result in a compromised router using the same community string.

There are a few, key SNMP messages used to communicate between the NMS and managed devices. As you can see in the following list, most of these conversations are initiated by the NMS:

- **Get Request**—The NMS sends a request for data to the agent on a managed device. See the left side of Figure 12-14.
- **Get Response**—The agent sends a response with the requested information.
- **Get Next**—The NMS might then request the next row of data in the MIB database.
- **Walk**—With this one command, the NMS can issue the equivalent of a sequence of SNMP Get Next messages to walk through sequential rows in the MIB database on a monitored device.
- **Trap**—An agent can be programmed to detect certain abnormal conditions that prompt the generation of Trap messages, where the agent sends the NMS unsolicited data once the specified conditions on the managed

device are met (see the right side of Figure 12-14). For example, on a Cisco server, you could use the command `snmp trap link-status` to instruct the agent to send an alert if or when an interface fails. The trap can later be disabled with the command `no snmp trap link-status`. Trap messages can alert network administrators of unresponsive services or devices, power supply issues, high temperatures, and tripped circuit breakers, which allows technicians to identify and address problems quickly—hopefully before users start to notice the problem. For example, a report of a tripped circuit breaker eliminates the need for further investigation into why a specific device isn't responsive. Or an unresponsive service, such as DHCP, could be restarted remotely.

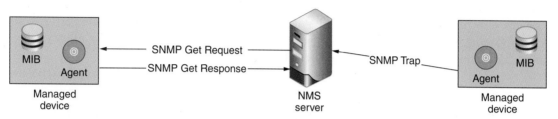

Figure 12-14   Most SNMP conversations are initiated by the NMS server, except when a managed device sends an SNMP Trap message

After data is collected, the network management application can present an administrator with several options to view and analyze the data. For example, a common way to analyze data is by a line graph. Another popular method is a map that shows fully functional links or devices in green, partially (or less than optimally) functioning links or devices in yellow, and failed links or devices in red. An example of the type of map generated by a network performance monitor is shown in Figure 12-15.

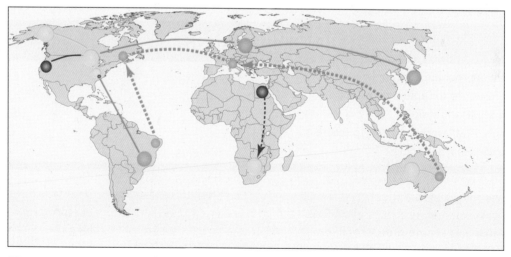

Figure 12-15   Map showing network status

Because of their flexibility, sophisticated network management applications are also challenging to configure and fine-tune. You must be careful to collect only useful data and not an excessive amount of routine information. For example, on a network with dozens of routers, collecting SNMP-generated messages that essentially say "I'm still here" every five seconds would result in massive amounts of insignificant data. A glut of information makes it difficult to ascertain when a router in fact requires attention. Instead, when configuring a network management application to poll a router, you might choose to generate an SNMP-based message only when the router's processor is operating at 75 percent of its capacity or to measure only the amount of traffic passing through a NIC every five minutes.

NetFlow

SNMP provides real-time monitoring of network activities and device states with an emphasis on device health, performance, and configuration. But what if you want to get a comprehensive view of network traffic across all devices? NetFlow is a proprietary traffic monitoring protocol from Cisco that tracks all IP traffic crossing any interface where NetFlow is enabled. From that information, NetFlow creates flow records that show relationships among various traffic types. While SNMP focuses on individual devices, NetFlow focuses on the way network bandwidth is being utilized by identifying how communications from all devices are related to each other.

When NetFlow is enabled on a network device, each unique conversation is collected in a NetFlow cache as a flow record. Additional messages in the same conversation are aggregated into that one flow record. When complete, the flow record is then sent, or exported, to a centralized NetFlow collector for analysis. A NetFlow analyzer, or NetFlow collector, collates flow records from throughout the network to provide insights into traffic patterns, such as why congestion is happening, what changes are occurring, and how those changes are affecting other traffic. A NetFlow analyzer can be hardware-based or software-based, which is more common.

NOTE 12-2

A similar technology, sFlow, is compatible with many platforms and relies on a dedicated hardware chip to avoid placing additional demand on a network device's CPU and memory. While NetFlow is limited to capturing IP traffic, sFlow can sample traffic from all layers 2 through 7.

A significant challenge with NetFlow is determining the optimal balance between tracking all traffic and tracking enough traffic to sufficiently observe network behavior. While NetFlow can provide in-depth access to traffic information, all the data must be transferred from the NetFlow exporter (the router, switch, or other device monitoring its traffic) to the NetFlow analyzer. NetFlow is capable of tracking nearly 100% of messages crossing an interface. However, transferring this volume of flow records to the analyzer will, on its own, negatively impact network performance. The trick is to sample enough traffic to get an accurate picture and catch problems early while not transferring any more flow records than necessary across the network for analysis. Still, NetFlow requires shallower examination of messages on the network and, therefore, fewer resources than other options that capture entire packets. This allows NetFlow to analyze very high volumes of traffic that would overwhelm more traditional approaches.

REMEMBER THIS...

- Implement appropriate environmental monitoring.
- Use port mirroring to capture network traffic.
- Compare SNMP and syslog.
- Explain how SNMP works and how to secure it.
- Compare various types of logs.

SELF-CHECK

1. Which of the following would an environmental monitoring system *not* track?
   a. Liquid detection
   b. User authentication
   c. Data room lights
   d. UPS voltage

2. Which log type would most likely be used first to investigate the cause of high numbers of dropped packets?
   a. Traffic log
   b. System log
   c. Jitter log
   d. Audit log

3. Which of the following is *not* defined by syslog?
   a. Message transmission
   b. Message format
   c. Message handling
   d. Message security

4. Which of the following would be assigned an OID?
   a. An NMS server
   b. A switch's interface
   c. A web server
   d. A UDP port

Check your answers at the end of this module.

You're Ready

You're now ready to complete **Project 12-1: Work with Data in Event Viewer**, or you can wait until you've finished reading this module.

You're Ready

You're now ready to complete **Project 12-2: Configure SPAN and Syslog in Packet Tracer**, or you can wait until you've finished reading this module.

MANAGE NETWORK TRAFFIC

✓ CERTIFICATION

2.2 Compare and contrast routing technologies and bandwidth management concepts.

2.3 Given a scenario, configure and deploy common Ethernet switching features.

3.1 Given a scenario, use the appropriate statistics and sensors to ensure network availability.

5.3 Given a scenario, use the appropriate network software tools and commands.

5.5 Given a scenario, troubleshoot general networking issues.

Average reading time: 26 minutes

After you've begun collecting data on your network's traffic patterns, you're ready to monitor your network's status on an ongoing basis and make changes to best meet the needs of your network's users. This process includes two major factors:

- **Performance management**—Monitoring how well links and devices are keeping up with the demands placed on them
- **Fault management**—Detecting and signaling of device, link, or component faults

To accomplish both fault and performance management, network administrators respond to errors as needed and tweak device and network configurations to optimize performance. To do this effectively, however, you first need to know your starting point, as you'll see next.

Performance Baselines

When it comes to monitoring network performance, data creation is the easy part. The challenge is to identify and efficiently analyze useful and relevant data. To know when there's a problem on the network, you must first know what is normal for that network. A **baseline** is a report of the network's normal state of operation and might include a range of acceptable measurements. Network performance baselines are obtained by analyzing network traffic information and might include information on the utilization rate for your network backbone, number of users logged on per day or per hour, number of protocols that run on your network, statistics about errors (such as runts, jabbers, or giants), frequency with which networked applications are used, or information regarding which users take up the most bandwidth. The graph in Figure 12-16 shows a sample baseline for daily network traffic over a six-week period.

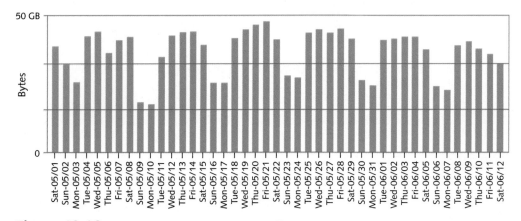

Figure 12-16   Baseline of daily network traffic

Baseline measurements serve as a basis of comparison for future performance increases or decreases caused by network changes or events with past network performance. As you saw in the *On the Job* story at the beginning of this module, a network baseline can provide valuable insights when trying to diagnose a problem or pinpoint an intrusion, over usage, or misconfiguration. Obtaining baseline measurements is the only way to know for certain whether a pattern of usage has changed (and requires attention) or whether a network upgrade made a difference. Each network requires its own approach and a reliable schedule for documenting and reviewing baselines to identify unexpected variations. The elements you measure and monitor depend on which functions are most critical to your network and its users.

For instance, suppose that your network currently serves 500 users, and your backbone traffic exceeds 50 percent capacity at 10:00 a.m. and 2:00 p.m. each business day. That pattern constitutes your baseline. Now suppose that your company decides to add 200 users who perform the same types of functions on the network. This is a 40 percent in users. Therefore, you can estimate that your backbone's capacity should increase by approximately 40 percent to maintain your current service levels.

The more data you gather while establishing your network's baseline, the more accurate your prediction will be. Network traffic patterns can vary considerably over time and must account for two major factors:

- Normal variations throughout the day, week, month, and different seasons. For example, a large retail company will have significantly busier traffic patterns during holiday seasons, and this is completely normal for that network.
- Changes to the network that might be unpredictable in the resulting impact. For instance, the preceding example assumed that all new users would share the same network usage habits as the current users. In fact, however, the new users might generate a lot more (or a lot less) network traffic.

How do you gather baseline data on your network? Several software applications can perform the baselining for you. These applications range from freeware available on the Internet to expensive, customizable hardware and software combination products. Before choosing a network-baselining tool, determine how you will use it. If you manage a small network that provides only one critical application, an inexpensive tool may suffice. For example, you could use the simple CLI-based tool **iPerf** to establish throughput between network hosts, or you could use one of the throughput testing tools you've used in some of your projects in this course, such as TotuSoft's LAN Speed Test or TamoSoft's Throughput Test app. In a project at the end of this module, you'll see how iPerf can test throughput between nearly any two devices on your network. Exploring and documenting this data helps establish a baseline you could reference if (or when) you experience traffic problems in the future.

If you work on a WAN with several critical links, however, investigate purchasing a more comprehensive package. The baseline measurement tool should be capable of collecting the statistics needed. For example, only a sophisticated tool can measure traffic generated by each node on a network, filter traffic according to types of protocols and errors, and simultaneously measure statistics from several network segments.

Once you've gathered this data, analyze the data for typical rates of utilization and failure. Some of the more common network performance KPIs (key performance indicators) include the following:

- **Device availability and performance**—This includes such metrics as CPU and memory usage, temperature, and network connection speed.
- **Interface statistics**—Feedback collated from all network interfaces can provide insights into what's changing on the network and what might be going wrong. For example, a device that regularly shows a low uptime might be repeatedly power cycling.
- **Utilization**—This metric refers to the actual throughput used as a percentage of available bandwidth. No network should be required to operate at maximum capacity. Identify patterns of utilization and ensure that available bandwidth accounts for utilization spikes.
- **Error rate**—Bits can be damaged in transit due to EMI or other interference. The calculated percentage of how often this occurs is the error rate.
- **Packet drops**—Packets that are damaged beyond use, arrive after their expiration, or are not allowed through an interface are dropped. Packet drops result in delayed network communications while devices wait for responses or resend transmissions. Knowing what's normal for your network will help you identify problems when packet drop rates vary.
- **Jitter**—All packets experience some latency. When successive packets experience varying amounts of latency, resulting in their arriving out of order, the user experience is degraded. This is called jitter, a problem that can be addressed through traffic management techniques, which you'll read about next.

Bandwidth Management

As you know, a network's bandwidth is its potential to handle network traffic. This is not just a single number, but a conglomeration of numbers from every link and interface on the network. As you've learned throughout this course, different devices can handle different volumes of traffic, and your overall bandwidth management techniques must take this reality into account. As a subset of performance management, **bandwidth management** refers to a collection of strategies to optimize the volume of traffic a network can support. These techniques might include any of the following technologies:

- **Flow control**—Configure interfaces and protocols to balance permitted traffic volume with a device's capability of handling that traffic.
- **Congestion control**—Adjust the way network devices respond to indications of network performance issues caused by traffic congestion so they don't make the problem worse.
- **QoS (quality of service)**—Prioritize some traffic over other traffic so the most important traffic gets through even during times of congestion.

Let's explore each of these technologies in more detail.

Flow Control

Flow control is a bandwidth management technique configured on a local connection between two devices. The purpose is to ensure the receiver is not overwhelmed with the rate of data transmission. Flow control can be managed either at the data link layer or at the network and transport layers. When managed at the higher layers, rate-based flow control limits the amount of data that can be transmitted but does not provide feedback to the sender when that rate is exceeded. Instead, traffic is lost. In contrast, feedback-based flow control at the data link layer gives the sender some kind of indication when the transmission rate is exceeding the receiver's ability to handle the incoming traffic. Common approaches are the stop-and-wait method and two versions of the sliding window method. Consider the following scenarios:

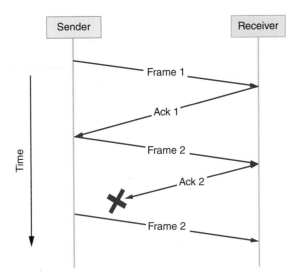

Figure 12-17 Stop-and-wait method

- **Stop-and-wait method**—A sender transmits a frame and then waits for an acknowledgment before transmitting the next frame. See Figure 12-17. If an acknowledgment is not received, the sender retransmits the unacknowledged frame. This way, whether the frame is lost in transit or the acknowledgment is lost, the frame is still resent. At no time is the receiver required to handle more than one incoming frame, and each frame must be acknowledged before sending another frame. This approach is simple and provides high accuracy. However, it's also very slow because only one frame can be sent at a time.

- **Go-back-n sliding window method**—A sender can transmit multiple frames at one time while considering the maximum number of frames the receiver can handle at any time. For example, suppose a receiver can handle up to three incoming frames at any given time, as shown in Figure 12-18. The sender transmits three frames and waits for three acknowledgments. If all three acknowledgments are received, the sender transmits another three frames. If an acknowledgment is missing, the sender retransmits all three frames, even if only one frame was lost.

- **Selective repeat sliding window method**—In this scenario, as shown in Figure 12-19, only the unacknowledged frame is retransmitted. The sender continues sending additional frames as long as space is available in

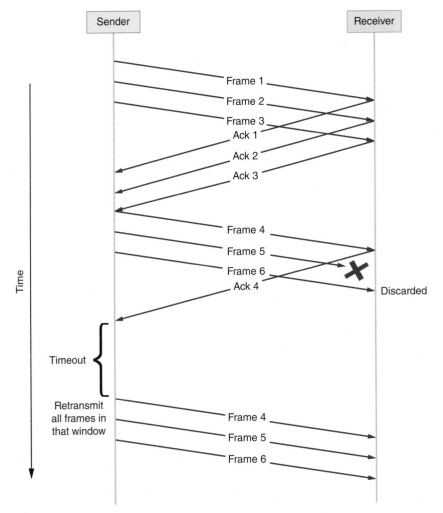

Figure 12-18 Go-back-n sliding window method

the window for new frames. This is a more efficient approach because later frames don't have to wait on as many earlier frames to be acknowledged. However, it's also more complex because the receiver must be able to receive frames out of order and reorganize them, even if a much earlier frame experiences a relatively lengthy delay.

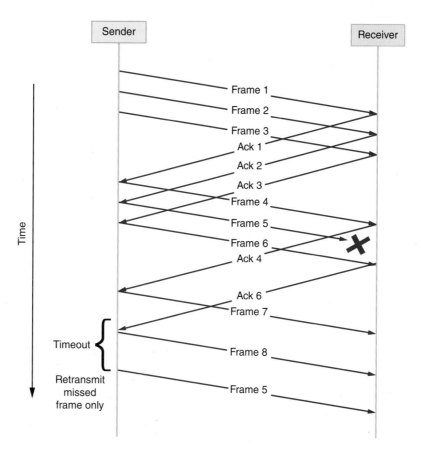

Figure 12-19   Selective repeat sliding window method

Congestion Control

Notice that flow control manages the number of frames transmitted end-to-end between a single sender and a single receiver. Congestion control, however, manages the volume of traffic throughout the network. Think about the perspective of a switch or router when evaluating network traffic performance: Are too many devices trying to send messages at the same time? Is one host sending so much data that it's hogging network resources? These kinds of problems can overwhelm the network as a whole. When the network starts experiencing congestion, messages are corrupted or dropped, and connected devices start resending frames to make up for the loss. This response, then, generates even more traffic, making the congestion even worse.

Congestion control techniques are designed to prevent this congestion before it occurs (called open-loop congestion control) and also to remedy congestion after it starts (called closed-loop congestion control). Open-loop techniques include the following policies:

- **Retransmission policy**—Retransmission timers help reduce increasing congestion caused by devices attempting to resend lost packets too quickly or too often.
- **Window policy**—Senders might be required to use the selective repeat sliding window method to reduce the number of frames that must be resent when errors occur.
- **Acknowledgment policy**—Receivers can be required to send a single ACK message for multiple received frames, thereby reducing acknowledgment traffic on the network.

- **Discarding policy**—Less sensitive frames are discarded so important traffic can survive the congestion.
- **Admission policy**—Routers and switches can temporarily reject new traffic that will contribute to or create congestion rather than admitting that new traffic onto the network.

The closed-loop response to existing congestion includes the following techniques:

- **Implicit signaling**—A sending device detects congestion on the network after experiencing several missed acknowledgment messages.
- **Explicit signaling**—A congested networking device alters existing data packets to indicate to either the sender (this is called backward signaling) or the receiver (this is called forward signaling) that the network is congested.
- **Choke packet**—A router experiencing congestion creates and sends a choke packet to the traffic source, informing it of the congestion so the sender can reduce its rate of transmission.
- **Backpressure**—A node downstream from sender to receiver stops accepting traffic, which transfers the pressure of the congestion upstream toward the source. This technique is limited to specific types of congestion scenarios.

While congestion control manages the entrance of traffic onto the network, other methods allow for more nuanced control of what happens to the traffic once it's on the network. That's where QoS comes in, as you'll read about next.

QoS (Quality of Service) Assurance

You don't want to hear breaks in an online phone conversation or see a buffering message when you watch a movie over the Internet. For that reason, voice and video transmissions are considered delay-sensitive. On the other hand, occasional loss of data (skipping video frames, for example) can be tolerated; for that reason, voice and video transmissions are considered loss-tolerant. Typical web surfing might not present much of a challenge for network bandwidth. However, streaming movies, voice or video calls, and online gaming can all place heavy demands on available bandwidth.

To manage these demands, network administrators must efficiently manage a network's QoS (quality of service) configurations, which is a group of techniques for adjusting the priority a network assigns to various types of transmissions. To do this, network administrators need to be aware of the applications used on a network, including the application protocols they use and the amount of bandwidth they require. For example, variable delays of VoIP packets result in choppy voice quality. A network that handles a lot of VoIP traffic would need to prioritize that traffic to avoid problems with jitter.

From the perspective of a person watching a movie online, optimized QoS translates into an uninterrupted, accurate, and faithful reproduction of audio or visual input. For someone competing in online games, high priority on gaming traffic gives quick and accurate responsiveness to game play in addition to a high-quality audio and visual experience. Network engineers have devised several techniques to address the QoS-related challenges inherent in delivering high-bandwidth network services. The following sections describe some of these techniques.

Traffic Shaping

When a network must handle high volumes of network traffic, users benefit from a bandwidth management and optimization technique known as traffic shaping. Traffic shaping, also called packet shaping, involves manipulating certain characteristics of packets, data streams, or connections to manage the type and amount of traffic traversing a network or interface at any moment. Its goals are to ensure timely delivery of the most important traffic while optimizing performance for all users. Traffic shaping can involve any of the following:

- Delaying less-important traffic, which is called buffering
- Increasing the priority of more-important traffic
- Limiting the volume of traffic flowing into or out of an interface during a specified time period
- Limiting the momentary throughput rate for an interface

The last two techniques belong to a category of traffic shaping known as traffic policing and results in dropped traffic rather than buffered, or delayed, traffic. For example, an ISP might impose a maximum on the capacity it will grant a certain customer. This prevents the customer from tying up more than a certain amount of the WAN's overall capacity. Traffic policing helps the service provider predict how much capacity it must purchase from its network provider. It also holds down costs because the ISP doesn't have to plan for every client using all available throughput at all times (an unlikely scenario).

An ISP that imposes traffic policing might allow customers to choose their preferred maximum daily traffic volume or momentary throughput and pay commensurate fees. A more sophisticated instance of traffic policing is dynamic and considers the network's current traffic patterns. For example, the service provider might allow certain customers to exceed their maximums when few other customers are using the network. Figure 12-20 illustrates how traffic volume might appear on an interface without limits compared with an interface subject to traffic policing.

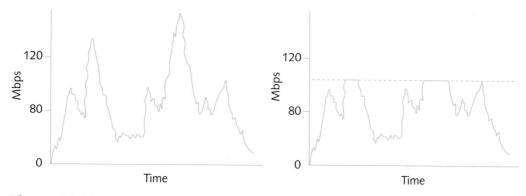

Figure 12-20   Traffic volume before and after applying limits

A controversial example of traffic shaping came to light in 2007. Comcast, one of the largest Internet service providers in the United States, was found to be clandestinely discriminating against certain types of traffic. For users uploading files to P2P (peer-to-peer) networks such as BitTorrent, Comcast was interjecting TCP segments with the RST (reset) field set. These segments were spoofed to appear as if they originated from the accepting site, and they cut the connection as the user attempted to upload files. Soon customers figured out the pattern and used monitoring software such as Wireshark to reveal the forged TCP RST segments. They complained to authorities that Comcast had violated their user agreement. The FCC investigated, upheld the customers' claims, and ordered Comcast to stop this practice. Comcast then chose a different method of traffic shaping. It assigned a lower priority to data from customers who generated a high volume of traffic at times when the network was at risk of congestion.

In the past several years, many ISPs have used traffic throttling to slow down high-bandwidth users. This isn't necessarily a bad thing, so long as all interested parties are aware of what's going on. In fact, some ISPs use traffic shaping to temporarily *increase* a busy user's bandwidth without negatively affecting other users' network activities. To learn more about these practices, search on phrases such as "comcast traffic shaping," "ISP throttling," "net neutrality," and "bandwidth throttling test," which will give you links you can use to test your own Internet connection.

Several types of traffic prioritization exist where more important traffic is treated preferentially. Software running on a router, multilayer switch, gateway, server, or even a client workstation can act as a traffic shaper by prioritizing traffic according to any of the following characteristics:

- Protocol
- IP address
- User group
- DiffServ (Differentiated Services) flag in an IP packet
- VLAN tag in a data link layer frame
- Service or application

Depending on the traffic prioritization software, different types of traffic might be assigned priority classes, such as *high, normal, low,* or *slow;* alternatively, it can be rated on a prioritization scale from 0 (lowest priority) to 7 (highest priority). For example, traffic generated by time-sensitive VoIP applications might be assigned high priority, while online gaming might be assigned low priority (or vice versa, depending on your preferences). Traffic prioritization is needed most when the network is busiest. It ensures that during peak usage times, the most important data gets through quickly, while less-important data waits. When network usage is low, however, prioritization might have no noticeable effects.

Some types of network traffic contribute more significantly to the overall volume of traffic than other types do. When a network is expected to simultaneously support voice, video, and data communications, performance is always a major concern. Let's see what other options are available for addressing these concerns.

DiffServ (Differentiated Services)

DiffServ (Differentiated Services) is a simple technique that addresses QoS issues by prioritizing traffic at layer 3. DiffServ considers all types of network traffic, not just the time-sensitive services such as voice and video. That way, it can assign voice streams a high priority and at the same time assign unessential data streams (for example, employees surfing the Internet on their lunch hour) a low priority. This technique offers more protection for time-sensitive, prioritized services. To prioritize traffic, DiffServ places information in the DiffServ field of an IPv4 packet. The first 6 bits of this 8-bit field are called **DSCP (Differentiated Services Code Point)**. (For a review of the fields in an IP packet, refer to Module 4.) In IPv6 packets, DiffServ uses a similar field known as the Traffic Class field. This information in both IPv4 and IPv6 packets indicates to network routers how the data stream should be forwarded. DiffServ defines two types of forwarding:

- **EF (Expedited Forwarding)**—A data stream is assigned a minimum departure rate from a given node. This technique circumvents delays that slow normal data from reaching its destination on time and in sequence.
- **AF (Assured Forwarding)**—Different levels of router resources can be assigned to data streams. AF prioritizes data handling but provides no guarantee that on a busy network, messages will arrive on time and in sequence.

This description of DiffServ's prioritization mechanisms is oversimplified, but helps you understand some of the many nuanced configurations available for managing network traffic. Because of its simplicity and relatively low overhead, DiffServ is well suited to large, heavily trafficked networks.

CoS (Class of Service)

CoS (Class of Service) is sometimes used synonymously with QoS, but there is an important distinction. The term *QoS* refers to techniques that are performed at various OSI layers via several protocols. By contrast, the term **CoS (Class of Service)** is one method of implementing QoS that refers only to techniques performed at layer 2 on Ethernet frames.

CoS is most often used to more efficiently route Ethernet traffic between VLANs. Frames that have been tagged (addressed to a specific VLAN) contain a 3-bit field in the frame header called the PCP (Priority Code Point). CoS works by setting these bits to one of eight levels ranging from 0 to 7, which indicates to the switch the level of priority the message should be given if the port is receiving more traffic than it can forward at any one time. Waiting messages are cached until the port can get to them, or discarded, depending on the class assignment for that frame.

A network's connectivity devices and clients must support the same set of protocols to achieve their QoS benefits. However, networks can—and often do—combine multiple QoS techniques.

REMEMBER THIS...

- Analyze network and device performance metrics in comparison to performance baselines.
- Compare bandwidth management techniques, including flow control, congestion control, and QoS.
- Explain the various methods of flow control.
- Use iPerf to test throughput between two network devices.

SELF-CHECK

5. Which bandwidth management technique limits traffic specifically between a single sender and a single receiver?

   a. Congestion control

   b. Traffic shaping

   c. Quality of Service

   d. Flow control

6. Which flow control method resends a lost frame along with all frames sent with it?

   a. Selective repeat sliding window

   b. Stop-and-wait

   c. Go-back-n sliding window

   d. Backpressure

7. Which of the following statements is true? Choose *two*.

   a. When streaming a movie, the transmission is sensitive to loss and tolerant of delays.

   b. When sending an email, the transmission is sensitive to delays and tolerant of loss.

   c. When streaming a movie, the transmission is sensitive to delays and tolerant of loss.

   d. When sending an email, the transmission is sensitive to loss and tolerant of delays.

Check your answers at the end of this module.

You're Ready

You're now ready to complete **Project 12-3: Test Network Throughput with iPerf**, or you can wait until you've finished reading this module.

PLAN RESPONSE AND RECOVERY STRATEGIES

 **CERTIFICATION**

3.2 Explain the purpose of organizational documents and policies.

3.3 Explain high availability and disaster recovery concepts and summarize which is the best solution.

Average reading time: 50 minutes

Despite every precaution, disasters and security breaches do happen. Training and preparation can make all the difference in your company's ability to respond and adapt to these situations. This section discusses a spectrum of possible disasters and breaches. As you read about them, think about how you might anticipate your network's and users' needs in various scenarios. First, let's start with some basic terms:

- **Incident**—Any event, large or small, that has adverse effects on a network's availability or resources. This could be a security breach, such as a hacker gaining access to a user's account, an infection, such as a worm or virus, or an environmental issue, such as a fire or flood.
- **Disaster**—An extreme type of incident, involving a network outage that affects more than a single system or limited group of users.

Each of these possibilities requires advance preparation by a team of people and should have plans and procedures in place to reduce the amount of confusion, chaos, and mistakes in handling the event once it occurs. Let's first explore the more general incident response policies and then look at disaster recovery techniques.

Incident Response

An **incident response plan** specifically defines the characteristics of an event that qualifies as a formal incident and the steps that should be followed as a result. Qualifying incidents take into account the full spectrum of possible events, which might include a break-in, fire, weather-related emergency, hacking attack, discovery of illegal content or activity on an employee's computer, malware outbreak, or a full-scale, environmental disaster that shuts down businesses throughout the city or state. The policy is written with the intent of keeping people safe; protecting sensitive data; ensuring network availability and integrity; and collecting data to determine what went wrong, who is responsible, and what actions should be taken in the future to prevent similar damage. An incident response is a six-stage process, which actually begins *before* the incident occurs, as described next:

Step 1: *Preparation*: The response team brainstorms possible incidents and plans procedures for handling them. This includes installing backup systems and compiling all the information required to restore the network, such as passwords, configurations, vendor lists and their SLAs, locations of backup data storage, emergency contact information, and relevant privacy laws.

Step 2: *Detection and identification*: Because security and environmental alarm systems can detect incidents of all kinds, staff not directly involved with incident response planning are educated about what qualifies as an incident and what to do if they notice a potential problem. Any system or staff alerts are routed to assigned personnel to determine whether the event requires escalation—that is, if it should be recognized as something other than a normal problem faced by IT technicians. Each company will have its own criteria for which incidents require escalation, as well as its own chain of command for notification purposes. Make sure you're familiar with your company's requirements.

Step 3: *Containment*: The team works to limit the damage. Affected systems or areas are isolated, and response staff are called in as required by the situation.

Step 4: *Remediation*: The team finds what caused the problem and begins to resolve it so no further damage occurs.

Step 5: *Recovery*: Operations return to normal as affected systems are repaired and put back in operation.

Step 6: *Review*: The team determines what can be learned from the incident and uses this information to make adjustments in preparation for and perhaps prevention of future threats.

The response plan should identify the members of a response team, all of whom should clearly understand the security policy, risks to the network, and security measures that have already been implemented. The responsibilities assigned to each team member should be clearly spelled out, and the team should regularly rehearse their roles by participating in security threat drills. Suggested team roles include the following:

- **Dispatcher**—The person on call who first notices or is alerted to the problem. The dispatcher notifies the lead technical support specialist and then the manager. The dispatcher also creates a record for the incident, detailing the time it began, its symptoms, and any other pertinent information about the situation. The dispatcher remains available to answer calls from clients or employees or to assist the manager.
- **Technical support specialist**—The team member(s) who focuses on only one thing: solving the problem as quickly as possible. After the situation has been resolved, the technical support specialist describes in detail what happened and helps the manager find ways to avoid such an incident in the future. Depending on the size of the organization and the severity of the incident, this role may be filled by more than one person.
- **Manager**—The team member who coordinates the resources necessary to solve the problem. If in-house technicians cannot handle the incident, the manager finds outside assistance. The manager also ensures that the security policy is followed and that everyone within the organization is aware of the situation. As the response ensues, the manager continues to monitor events and communicate with the public relations specialist.

- **Public relations specialist**—If necessary, this team member learns about the situation and the response and then acts as official spokesperson for the organization to the public or other interested parties.

Data Preservation

During some incidents, data will need to be collected in such a way that it can be presented in a court of law for the purpose of prosecuting an instigator of illegal activity. Some of the forensic data available for analysis can be damaged or destroyed if improperly handled. Ideally, one or more first responders would take charge in these cases. **First responders** are the people with training and/or certifications that prepare them to handle evidence in such a way as to preserve its admissibility in court. However, it's critical that every IT technician in a company know how to safeguard sensitive information, logged data, and other legal evidence until the first responder or incident response team can take over the collection of evidence, as described next:

1. **Secure the area**—To prevent contamination of evidence, each device involved must be isolated. This means it should be disconnected from the network (remove the Ethernet cable or disable the Wi-Fi antenna) and secured to ensure that no one else has contact with it until the response team arrives. Ideally, you should leave the device running without closing any applications or files. Different OSs require different shutdown procedures to preserve forensic data, so the shutdown process should be left to incident response experts. However, if a destructive program is running that might be destroying evidence, the fastest and safest solution is to unplug the power cord from the back of the machine (not just from the wall). Treat the entire work area as a crime scene. In some cases, such as with a physical break-in, an entire room or possibly multiple rooms must be secured to protect the evidence.

2. **Document the scene**—Creating a defensible audit trail is one of the highest priorities in the forensics process. An **audit trail** is a system of documentation that makes it possible for a third party to inspect evidence later and understand the flow of events. A *defensible* audit trail is an audit trail that can be justified and defended in a court of law according to specific standards. Document everything you or your team does, noting the time and the reason for each action. For example, if you unplugged the machine because a virus was wiping the hard drive, document the time and describe the symptoms you observed that led you to unplug the machine. Also make a list of everyone found in the area and their access to the computer in question. Make sure no one else enters the area until the response team arrives and don't leave the area unattended even for a few moments.

3. **Monitor evidence and data collection**—Record all items collected for evidence. Take care to preserve all evidence in its original state. Do not attempt to access any files on a computer or server being collected for evidence, as this action alters a file's metadata and could render it inadmissible in court.

4. **Protect the chain of custody**—All collected data must be carefully processed and tracked so it does not leave official hands at any point in the forensics process. Typically, documentation used to track **chain of custody** describes exactly what the evidence is, when it was collected, who collected it, its condition, and how it was secured. If at any point in the process you have custody of evidence, be sure to sign off on a chain of custody document and obtain a signature from the next person in line when you hand over custody of the evidence.

5. **Monitor transport of data and equipment**—Generally, the incident response team is responsible for transporting all evidence to the forensics lab or other authority. Every item should be carefully documented so the exact same configuration can be replicated in the lab. The response team might even have the capability to do a hot seizure and removal, which means they can use specialized devices to transfer a computer from one power source to another without shutting down the computer. This can be especially critical if it's possible the computer or its data will become inaccessible after power is turned off—perhaps because a password is unknown or data is currently in memory.

6. **Create a report**—Be prepared to report on all activities that you observed or participated in during the incident response. It's best to take notes along the way and to write your report in full as soon as possible after the event while it's still fresh on your mind. All this information will likely be included in the final forensics report, so it's important to be thorough and accurate.

Next, let's look at some specifics on handling extreme incidents and recovering from these disasters.

Disaster Recovery Planning

When bad things happen, businesses need a plan to ensure **business continuity**, which is the ability of the company to continue doing business with the least amount of interruption possible. At a high level, a **BCP (business continuity plan)** defines the resources and protocols the business will use to continue providing service to its customers with little or no disruption during a disaster. Considering all possible disasters that could put a company's ability to continue doing business at risk might seem so theoretical as to be impossible to plan for. But if the worst does happen, a plan is essential. Research shows that half of businesses don't survive a major disaster (see Figure 12-21), and many more fail within the first year following a major disaster. By establishing contingency plans ahead of time, a business significantly improves its odds of survival in the face of a natural disaster such as fire, flood, earthquake, hurricane, or tornado, or another catastrophic event such as workplace violence, cyberattack, or industrial sabotage.

wk1003mike/Shutterstock.com

Figure 12-21   A disaster such as a fire can ruin a business

A BCP takes a big-picture approach to preparations, such as identifying critical operations that require significant backups and ensuring core communications channels are available under a variety of possible circumstances. A BCP also includes ways to prevent disasters from affecting the company at all, ways to limit the damage if or when those disasters occur, and processes for restoring operations and limiting downtime.

One part of a BCP, a focused and thorough **disaster recovery plan**, details the processes for restoring critical functionality and data after an outage that affects more than a single system or a limited group of users. A disaster recovery plan accounts for the worst-case scenarios, from a far-reaching hurricane to a military or terrorist attack. It should provide contingency plans for restoring or replacing computer systems, power, telephone systems, and paper-based files. The part of the plan that addresses computer systems should include the following:

- Contact names and phone numbers for emergency coordinators who will execute the disaster recovery response, as well as roles and responsibilities of other staff.

- Details on which data and servers are being backed up, how frequently backups occur, where onsite and offsite backups are kept, and (most importantly) how backed-up data can be recovered in full.
- Details on network topology, redundancy, and agreements with national service carriers, in case local or regional vendors fall prey to the same disaster.
- Regular strategies for testing the disaster recovery plan.
- A plan for managing the crisis, including frequent communications with employees and customers via regular communication modes and via alternative methods in case phone lines or other standard options are unavailable. For example, a terrorist bomb in Nashville, Tennessee, in late 2020 damaged a major cellular provider, cutting cell service throughout the region for days. A widespread natural disaster, such as several tornadoes or a large hurricane, can also knock out all normal communications channels for days or weeks.

Having a comprehensive disaster recovery plan lessens the risk of losing critical data in case of extreme situations. It also makes potential customers and your insurance providers look more favorably on your organization.

Disaster Recovery Contingencies

You've already read about redundancy strategies where, for example, you use multiple servers to run a website or you pay for multiple ISP connections to your network. That way, if one goes down, the other can take over. The same principle applies to your entire data center in disaster recovery planning. An organization can choose from several options for recovering its network infrastructure from a disaster. The options vary by the amount of hardware, software, planning, investment, and employee involvement each requires. These options also vary according to how quickly they will restore network functionality in case a disaster occurs. As you might expect, every contingency plan at this level necessitates a site other than the building where the network's main components normally reside. An organization can maintain its own disaster recovery sites—for example, by renting office space in a different city—or contract with a company that specializes in disaster recovery services to provide the alternate site. Disaster recovery contingencies are commonly divided into three categories, as shown in Figure 12-22 and described next:

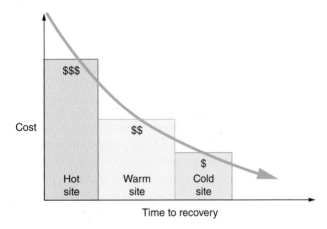

Figure 12-22 The most expensive option also provides the fastest recovery

- **Cold site**—Computers, devices, and connectivity necessary to rebuild a network exist, but they are not appropriately configured, updated, or connected. Therefore, restoring functionality from a cold site could take a long time. For example, suppose your small business network consists of a file and print server, mail server, backup server, Internet gateway, DNS/DHCP server, 25 workstations, four printers, a router, a switch, two access points, and a connection to your local ISP. At your cold site, you might store two server computers on which your company's NOS is not installed, and that do not possess the appropriate configurations and data necessary to operate in your environment. The 25 client machines stored there might be in a similar state. In addition, you might have a router, a switch, and two access points at the cold site, but these might also require configuration to operate in your environment. Finally, the cold site would not necessarily have

Internet connectivity, or at least not the same type your network uses. Supposing you followed good backup practices and stored your backup media at the cold site, you would then need to restore operating systems, applications, and data to your servers and clients; reconfigure your connectivity devices; and arrange with your ISP to have your connectivity restored to the cold site. Even for a small network, this process of rebuilding your network could take weeks.

- **Warm site**—Computers, devices, and connectivity necessary to rebuild a network exist, with some pieces appropriately configured, updated, or connected. For example, a service provider that specializes in disaster recovery might maintain a duplicate of each of your servers in its data center. You might arrange to have the service provider update those duplicate servers with your backed-up data on the first of each month because updating the servers daily is much more expensive. In that case, if a disaster occurs in the middle of the month, you would still need to update your duplicate servers with your latest weekly or daily backups before they could stand in for the downed servers. Recovery using a warm site can take hours or days, compared with the weeks a cold site might require. Maintaining a warm site costs more than maintaining a cold site, but not as much as maintaining a hot site.

- **Hot site**—Computers, devices, and connectivity necessary to rebuild a network are all appropriately configured, updated, and connected to match your network's current state. For example, you might use server mirroring to maintain identical copies of your servers at two WAN locations. In a hot site contingency plan, both locations would also contain identical connectivity devices and configurations, and thus be able to stand in for the other at a moment's notice. With a hot site, your team could drive from your usual location to your hot site, walk in the door, and immediately get back to work. As you can imagine, hot sites are expensive and potentially time consuming to maintain. For organizations that cannot tolerate downtime, however, hot sites provide the best disaster recovery option.

With increasing reliance on the cloud, companies are finding inexpensive and effective disaster recovery solutions that incorporate cloud technologies. **DRaaS (disaster recovery as a service)**, also called a **cloud site**, provides a highly scalable, inexpensive DR option by establishing a cloud configuration that could take over many or most business processes in the event of a disaster. To increase the metaphorical temperature of your cloud site, you might have some cloud resources already configured and running. Other resources, however, can be scripted using IaC (infrastructure as code) and created only when needed after a disaster occurs. Be careful, though, to consider your cloud connectivity needs during a disaster. Some types of disasters might prevent you from accessing the cloud at all, at least for a time.

Power Management

Part of managing a network's availability involves managing the facilities and infrastructure that support the network, such as power connections and power sources during outages or fluctuations. No matter where you live, you have probably experienced a complete loss of power (a blackout) or a temporary dimming of lights (a brownout). Such fluctuations in power are frequently caused by forces of nature, such as hurricanes, tornadoes, or ice storms. They might also occur when a utility company performs maintenance or construction tasks. Power surges, even small ones, can cause serious damage to sensitive computer equipment and can be one of the most frustrating sources of network problems.

Before you learn how to manage power sources to avoid these problems, first arm yourself with an understanding of the nature of an electric circuit and some electrical components that manage electricity.

Applying Concepts 12-4: AC and DC Power and Converters

An electric circuit provides a medium for the transfer of electrical power over a closed loop. If the loop is broken in any way, the circuit won't conduct electricity. In a circuit, DC (direct current) flows at a steady rate in only one direction. By contrast, AC (alternating current) continually switches direction on the circuit.

A flashlight, for example, uses DC. The batteries in a flashlight have positive and negative poles, and the current always flows at a steady rate in the same direction between those poles, as shown on the left side of Figure 12-23. AC, however, travels in compression waves, similar to the coils of a Slinky®, alternating direction on the power line back and forth between the source and destination. Just as waves can travel across a huge body of water, power moving in an AC wave pattern can travel efficiently for long distances, as illustrated on the right side of Figure 12-23. Because AC power can be conducted at very high voltages, the source of the current can be located far away from the point of use, where it is transformed to lower voltages. Consider the power running a typical laptop computer. AC power comes from the power station through the wall outlet to the laptop's power supply, which converts it to DC so the laptop can use it.

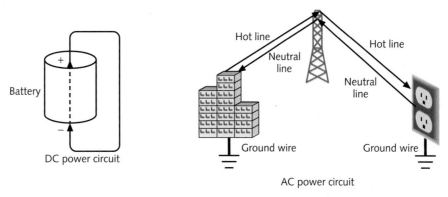

Figure 12-23   DC circuit and AC circuit

NOTE 12-4

For AC power to travel from the electric company to your house, three wires are required. The hot wire carries electricity from the power station to your house. The neutral wire carries unused power from your house back to the power station. A third wire, the ground wire, is used to channel the electric charge in case of a short. These three wires are illustrated and labeled in Figure 12-23.

You're now ready to investigate the types of power fluctuations, or flaws, that network administrators should prepare for. Then you'll learn about devices used to manage the power your network devices need.

Power Flaws

Whatever the cause, power loss or less-than-optimal power cannot be tolerated by networks. The following list describes power flaws that can damage your equipment:

- **Surge**—A momentary increase in voltage due to lightning strikes, solar flares, or electrical problems. Surges might last only a few thousandths of a second, but they can degrade a computer's power supply. Surges are common. You can guard against surges by making sure every computer device is plugged into a **surge protector** (see Figure 12-24), which redirects excess voltage away from the device to a ground, thereby protecting the device from harm. Without surge protectors, systems would be subjected to multiple surges each year.
- **Noise**—Fluctuation in voltage levels caused by other devices on the network or EMI. Some noise is unavoidable on an electrical circuit, but

Figure 12-24   A surge protector

Karen Roach/Shutterstock.com

excessive noise can cause a power supply to malfunction, immediately corrupting application or data files and gradually damaging motherboards and other computer circuits. If you've ever turned on fluorescent lights or a microwave oven and noticed other lights dim at the same time, you have probably introduced noise into the electrical system. Power that is free from noise is called *clean* power. To make sure power is clean, a circuit must pass through an electrical filter.

- **Brownout**—A momentary decrease in voltage; also known as a sag. An overtaxed electrical system can cause brownouts, which you might recognize in your home as a dimming of the lights. Such voltage decreases can cause computers or applications to fail and potentially corrupt data.
- **Blackout**—A complete power loss. A blackout could cause significant damage to your network. For example, if a server loses power while files are open and processes are running, its NOS might be damaged so extensively that the server cannot restart and the NOS must be reinstalled from scratch. A backup power source, however, can provide power long enough for the server to shut down gracefully and avoid harm.

NOTE 12-5

Increasingly, organizations are adding power redundancy—especially for critical servers—by installing dual power supplies in their servers, thereby giving each server at least one backup in case a power supply fails. Each power supply can handle the full power demands of the server if needed. Some companies are also running redundant power circuits to their data centers so if, for example, a circuit breaker trips, the servers can keep running on the other power circuit. Racks often have multiple UPSs installed as well.

Network Power Devices

If you track the journey of power coming into your building all the way to servers, routers, and switches on your data racks, you'll likely encounter several types of devices along the way. Some of these devices are focused on controlling and distributing power, while other devices store or generate power. For example, as you've already read, a surge protector can absorb excess energy from power lines to protect sensitive network equipment from power surges.

A similar device is a **PDU (power distribution unit)**, which might be attached to a nearby wall, the outside of a rack, or within a rack to connect the rack's equipment with a power source. Data rooms aren't designed to provide enough outlets for all its devices to plug directly into the wall. Instead, a PDU acts as a power strip to bring power from outlets, a generator, or a UPS (described next) closer to the devices on the rack, as shown in Figure 12-25. The PDU is specifically designed to handle the high power requirements of a rack full of electronic equipment. Intelligent PDUs can even provide monitoring via SNMP and remote-control features so you can know which devices are consuming the most power, remotely power cycle a device (that is, shut off power to the device and then turn the power back on), and receive alerts or configure alarms to indicate when problems occur.

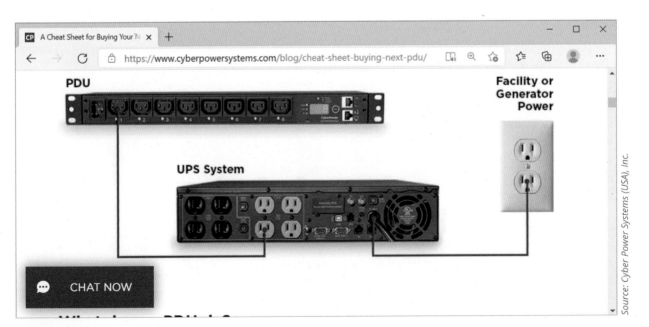

Figure 12-25   Install this PDU on a rack and plug into a UPS

A **UPS (uninterruptible power supply)**, also shown in Figure 12-25, is a battery-operated power source directly attached to one or more devices and to a power supply, such as a wall outlet, that provides a backup power source in the event of a power outage. A UPS can also help prevent undesired fluctuations of the wall outlet's AC power from harming devices. A power supply issue may be long in developing, with on-again/off-again symptoms for some time before the power issue finally solidifies and reveals itself. A good UPS in each data closet or on each rack will help prevent these kinds of problems from affecting the entire network at once. Each critical workstation should also be equipped with a UPS or some other battery backup, which can help to protect the computers themselves. UPSs are classified into two general categories, as follows:

- **Standby UPS, also called an SPS (standby power supply)**—Provides continuous voltage to a device by switching virtually instantaneously to the battery when it detects a loss of power from the wall outlet. Upon restoration of power, the standby UPS switches the device back to AC power (see Figure 12-26a). The problem with standby UPSs is that, in the brief amount of time it takes the UPS to discover that power from the wall outlet has faltered, a device may have already detected the power loss and shut down or restarted. Technically, a standby UPS doesn't provide perfectly continuous power; for this reason, it is sometimes called an offline UPS. Nevertheless, standby UPSs may prove adequate even for critical network devices, such as servers, routers, and gateways. They cost significantly less than online UPSs.

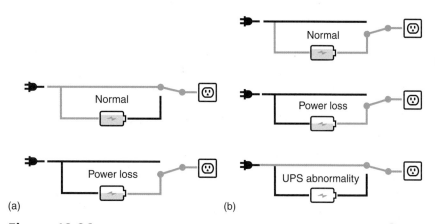

Figure 12-26 Standby UPS vs. online UPS

- **Online UPS**—Uses the AC power from the wall outlet to continuously charge its battery while providing power to a network device through its battery, as illustrated in Figure 12-26b. In other words, a server connected to an online UPS always relies on the UPS battery for its electricity. Because the server never needs to switch from the wall outlet's power to the UPS's battery power, there is no risk of briefly losing service. Also, because the UPS always provides the power, it can handle noise, surges, and sags before the fluctuations reach the attached device. As you can imagine, online UPSs are more expensive than standby UPSs. Figure 12-27 shows some online UPSs installed on a rack in a data room.

UPSs vary widely in the type of power aberrations they can rectify, the length of time they can provide power, and the number of devices they can support. Of course, they also vary widely in price. UPSs intended for home and small office use are designed merely to keep your workstation running long enough for you to properly shut it down in case of a blackout. Other UPSs perform sophisticated operations such

Figure 12-27 Online UPSs installed on a rack

as line filtering or conditioning, power supply monitoring, and error notification. To decide which UPS is right for your network, consider these factors:

- **Amount of power needed**—The more power required by your device, the more powerful the UPS must be. Electrical power is measured in VAs (volt-amperes), also called volt-amps. A VA is the product of the voltage and current (measured in amps) of the electricity on a line. To determine approximately how many VAs your device requires, you can use the following conversion: 1.4 volt-amps = 1 watt (W). A desktop computer, for example, may use a 200 W power supply and, therefore, requires a UPS capable of at least 280 VA to keep the CPU running in case of a blackout. A medium-sized server with a monitor and external tape drive might use 402 W, thus requiring a UPS capable of providing at least 562 VA of power. Determining your power needs can be a challenge. You must account for your existing equipment and consider how you might upgrade the supported device(s) over the next several years. Consider consulting with your equipment manufacturer to obtain recommendations on your power needs.
- **Required time to keep a device running**—The longer you anticipate needing a UPS to power your device, the more powerful your UPS must be. For example, a medium-sized server that relies on a 500 VA UPS to remain functional for 20 minutes might need a 1500 VA UPS to remain functional for 90 minutes. To determine how long your device might require power from a UPS, research the length of typical power outages in your area.
- **Line conditioning**—A UPS should offer surge suppression to protect against surges and line conditioning (a type of filtering) to guard against line noise. A UPS that provides line conditioning includes special noise filters that remove line noise. The manufacturer's technical specifications should indicate the amount of filtration required for each UPS. Noise suppression is expressed in dB levels at a specific frequency (KHz or MHz). The higher the dB level, the greater the protection.
- **Cost**—Prices for good UPSs vary widely, depending on the unit's size and extra features. A relatively small UPS that can power one server for 5 to 10 minutes might cost between $100 and $300. A large UPS that can power a sophisticated router for three hours might cost upwards of $5000. Still larger UPSs, which can power an entire data center for several hours, can cost hundreds of thousands of dollars. On a critical system, you should not try to cut costs by buying an off-brand, potentially unreliable, or weak UPS.

NOTE 12-6

After installing a new UPS, follow the manufacturer's instructions for performing initial tests to verify the UPS's proper functioning. Make it a practice to retest the UPS monthly or quarterly to ensure it will perform as expected in case of a sag or blackout.

As when considering other large purchases, research several UPS manufacturers and their products before selecting a UPS. Make sure the manufacturer provides a warranty and lets you test the UPS with your equipment. Testing UPSs with your equipment is an important part of the decision-making process. Popular UPS manufacturers are APC (*apc.com*), Emerson (*emerson.com*), Falcon (*falconups.com*), and Tripp Lite (*tripplite.com*).

Generators

A generator serves as a backup power source for many devices, providing power redundancy in the event of a total blackout. Generators can be powered by diesel, liquid propane gas, natural gas, or steam. Standard generators provide power that is relatively free from noise and are used in environments that demand consistently reliable service, such as an ISP's or telecommunications carrier's data center. In fact, in those environments, they are typically combined with large UPSs to ensure that clean power is always available. In the event of a power failure, the UPS supplies electricity until the generator starts and reaches its full capacity, typically no more than three minutes. If your organization relies on a generator for backup power, be certain to check fuel levels and quality regularly.

Figure 12-28 illustrates the power infrastructure of a network (such as a data center's) that uses both a generator and dual UPSs. Because a generator produces DC power, it must contain a component to convert the power to AC before the power can be released to the existing AC infrastructure that distributes power in a data center.

Before choosing a generator, calculate your organization's crucial electrical demands to determine the generator's optimal size. Also estimate how long the generator might be required to power your building. Depending on the amount of power draw, a high-capacity generator can supply power for several days. Gas or diesel generators can cost between $10,000 and $3,000,000 (for the largest industrial types). For a company such as an ISP that stands to lose up to $1,000,000 per minute if its data facilities fail completely, a multimillion-dollar investment to ensure available

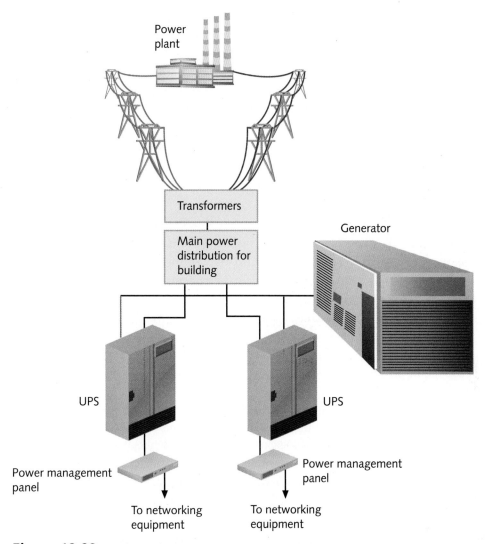

Figure 12-28   UPSs and a generator in a network design

power is a wise choice. Smaller businesses, however, might choose the more economical solution of renting an electrical generator. To find out more about options for renting or purchasing generators in your area, contact your local electrical utility.

Backup Systems

You have probably heard or even spoken the axiom, "If you can't do without it, back it up!" A **backup** is a copy of data or program files created for archiving or safekeeping. Maintaining good backups is essential for providing fault tolerance and reliability. In deciding what to back up, you might be required by certain compliance standards to back up certain types of data for a specified period. For example, HIPAA requires that medical records be saved for at least seven years from the date of the last service to the patient. You might be able to find information about compliance standards relevant to your company in an **audit report**. This is a document generated after an IT audit that evaluates a business's operations, processes, infrastructure, and policies as related to its business goals and relevant laws or other standards. The auditor will identify problems or deficiencies, applicable requirements, how weaknesses or gaps might affect the business, and recommendations to correct the problems. As you design, configure, deploy, and maintain your backup system, keep these points in mind:

Step 1: Decide what to back up. Besides the obvious folders used to hold user and application data, you might also want to back up user profile folders and folders that hold state and configuration files for your applications, services, routers, switches, access points, gateways, and firewalls. Recall in Capstone Project 4-1 you used a TFTP server to back up and restore a router using its startup-config file.

Step 2: Select backup methods. Consider cloud backups, where third-party vendors manage the backup hardware and software. In general, cloud backups are more expensive and reliable than other methods. Because cloud backups are not stored at your local facility, you have the added advantage that backups are protected in case your entire facility is destroyed.

For onsite backups, use only proven and reliable backup software and hardware. For your backup system, now is not the time to experiment with the latest and greatest technology.

- Verify that backup hardware and software are compatible with your existing network hardware and software.
- Make sure your backup software uses data error-checking techniques.
- Verify that your backup storage media or system provides sufficient capacity, with plenty of room to spare, and can also accommodate your network's growth.
- Be aware of how your backup process affects the system, normal network functioning, and your users' computing habits.
- As you make purchasing decisions, make sure you know how much the backup methods and media cost relative to the amount of data they can store.
- Be aware of the degree of manual intervention required to manage backups, such as exchanging backup media on a regular basis or backing up operating systems on servers that run around the clock.
- Make wise choices for storage media, considering advantages and disadvantages of media types. For example, optical media (DVDs and Blu-ray) require more frequent human intervention to exchange disks than exchanging tapes in tape drives or exchanging removable hard drives.
- When storing data to hard drives, recognize that the drives can be installed on computers on the local network, on a WAN, in attached storage devices, or even on a sophisticated SAN.
- Keep your backups secure, including storing backup media offsite in the event of a major disaster such as fire or flooding.

Step 3: Decide what types of backup will be made regularly (see Figure 12-29):

- **Full backup**—Backs up everything every time a backup is done
- **Incremental backup**—Backs up only data that has changed since the last backup
- **Differential backup**—Backs up data that has changed since the last full backup

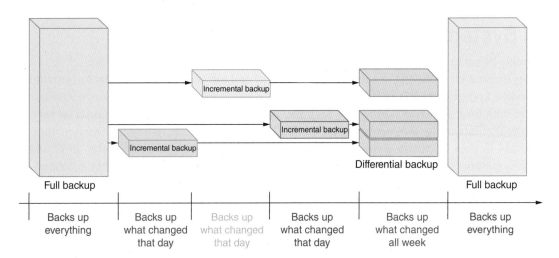

Figure 12-29 Incremental and differential backups demand fewer resources

Step 4: Decide how often backups are needed. In general, you want to back up data after about four hours of actual data entry. Depending on user habits, this might mean you back up daily or weekly, although, by default, Windows 10 performs incremental backups hourly. Many organizations perform at least daily backups, which happen in the middle of the night when there's less network activity.

NOTE 12-7

The OS knows which files to back up for incremental and differential backups because it maintains an archive bit in the attributes for each file.

Step 5: Develop a backup schedule. For example, you might perform a full backup every Thursday night and an incremental backup daily. You might take backup media offsite every Friday and overwrite backups (or destroy or rotate your backup media) every six months. You also must establish policies governing who is responsible for the backups, what information should be recorded in backup logs, and which backup logs are retained and for how long. Be sure to check relevant laws and regulations, as some types of data (such as medical or financial data) must be kept for a number of years.

Step 6: Regularly verify backups are being performed. From time to time, depending on how often your data changes and how critical the information is, you should attempt to recover some critical files from your backup media. Many network administrators attest that the darkest hour of their career was when they were asked to retrieve critical files from a backup and found that no backup data existed because their backup system never worked in the first place!

Data backups provide a way to recover data that is lost. To do this reliably under a wide variety of adverse conditions, the **3-2-1-1 Rule**, as illustrated in Figure 12-30, defines the following backup principles:

NOTE 12-8

When identifying the types of data to back up, remember to include configuration files for devices such as routers, switches, access points, gateways, and firewalls.

- **3**—Keep at least three complete copies of the data.
- **2**—Save backups on at least two different media types, such as hard drive and tape drive, or tape drive and cloud storage.
- **1**—Store at least one backup copy offsite.
- **1**—For greater protection against ransomware, ensure that at least one backup copy is stored offline.

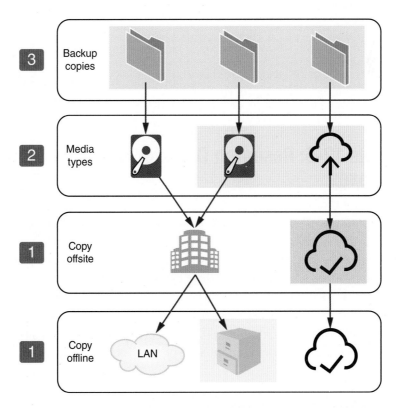

Figure 12-30 The 3-2-1-1 Rule for backups

When designing contingency plans and choosing backup options, factors that will affect your decisions include the following, which are also illustrated in Figure 12-31:

- **RTO (recovery time objective)**—The time your network can reasonably tolerate an outage. RTO shows at what point in the future full functionality will be restored (less any lost data). If you're creating a full backup each month and differential backups each day, you can apply the full backup and one differential backup and you're done. If, however, you're creating an incremental backup each day, then you'll have to apply every incremental backup since the last full backup, which will take more time. While incremental backups take up less space and take less time to create, they require more time to recover and therefore result in more recovery time needed after a loss.
- **RPO (recovery point objective)**—The amount of historical data you'll need to be able to restore from backup in response to an outage. RPO shows at what point in the past data will be recovered from. Data that was created or changed since that point will be lost because data backups were not copying data in real time. For example, relying on a full backup that's created only once a week will result in multiple days' worth of lost data if the disaster happens later in the week. However, if you're also keeping incremental or differential backups each day, your RPO would lose less than a day's worth of data.

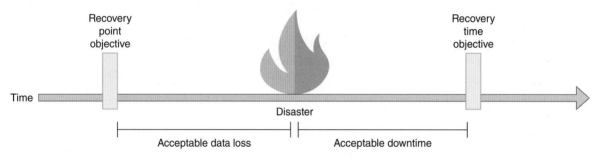

Figure 12-31   RPO defines how much data loss is acceptable while RTO defines how much downtime is acceptable

NOTE 12-9

In both cases, your decisions related to RPO and RTO will likely be somewhat dictated by your company's SLA to your customers or even to other departments within your company.

Applying Concepts 12-5: Research Disaster Recovery Solutions for Small Businesses

Many companies offer DRaaS (disaster recovery as a service) solutions for all types of IT-related problems. These solutions might include basics such as offsite storage and access to virtual servers during recovery or more expensive (but more convenient) options such as customizable backup schedules and single-file recovery, which is the ability to recover a single file at a time rather than an entire drive. In this activity, you will research two different disaster recovery solutions and compare the features, cost, and reviews for each. Use complete sentences, good grammar, and correct spelling in your answers. Complete the following steps:

1. Use a search engine to find companies that provide disaster recovery solutions for small businesses, and select two of these solutions. The more thorough the information provided on the company website, the easier your research will be.

2. For each of your selections, find answers to at least three of the following five questions:
   - What are the key features?
   - Where would the company store your data? In other words, in what geographic areas are their servers located?
   - What kind of encryption does the company use?
   - Which standards are the services compliant with: HIPAA? PCI? SOX? GDPR?
   - Who audits the company and their disaster recovery services? What auditing process is implemented?
3. Find reviews for both solutions. Summarize feedback from at least three customers about these solutions.

REMEMBER THIS...

- Explain the purpose of an incident response plan, a business continuity plan, and a disaster recovery plan.
- Explain the purpose of a PDU, a UPS, and a generator.
- Compare cold site, warm site, hot site, and cloud site.
- Compare RTO and RPO.

SELF-CHECK

8. When repairing a coworker's computer, you find some illegal files. What should you do next?
   a. Shut down the computer and unplug it.
   b. Take screenshots on the computer and save them in your own folder.
   c. Disconnect the computer from the network and leave it running.
   d. Delete the files.

9. Which backup site includes a running server that does not have access to the latest backups?
   a. Warm site
   b. Cold site
   c. Hot site
   d. On site

10. Which power device prevents a critical server from losing power, even for an instant?
    a. Surge protector
    b. Generator
    c. PDU
    d. UPS

Check your answers at the end of this module.

You're Ready

You're now ready to complete **Project 12-4: Organize Your Wikidot Website**, or you can wait until you've finished the Review Questions for this module.

You're Ready

After you finish the Hands-On Projects, you're ready to complete the **Module 12 Capstone Projects**.

MODULE SUMMARY

Collect Network Data

- At its broadest, the term network management refers to the assessment, monitoring, and maintenance of all aspects of a network. It can include controlling user access to network resources, monitoring performance baselines, checking for hardware faults, ensuring optimized QoS (quality of service) for critical applications, maintaining records of network assets and software configurations, and determining what time of day is best for upgrading hardware and software.
- Monitoring sensors in each data room, rack, or device's chassis feed information to a physical device or software installed on a server that presents an administrative dashboard to network administrators.
- Some traffic monitoring tools will provide real-time analysis of data with alerts when conditions meet certain thresholds, while other tools are designed to log data for retroactive analysis only as needed. These historical traffic logs are primarily used to investigate network performance issues. The challenge with both real-time network monitoring and traffic logging is gaining access to the traffic itself.
- Syslog is a standard for generating, storing, and processing messages about events on many networked systems. It describes methods for detecting and reporting events and specifies the format and contents of messages.
- Organizations often use enterprise-wide network management systems to perform real-time monitoring functions across an entire network. These rely on a similar architecture with the following entities: NMS (network management system) server, managed devices, network management agent, and MIB (Management Information Base).
- NetFlow is a proprietary traffic monitoring protocol from Cisco that tracks all IP traffic crossing any interface where NetFlow is enabled. From that information, NetFlow creates flow records that show relationships among various traffic types. While SNMP focuses on individual devices, NetFlow focuses on the way network bandwidth is being utilized by identifying how communications from all devices are related to each other.

Manage Network Traffic

- To know when there's a problem on the network, you must first know what is normal for that network. A baseline is a report of the network's normal state of operation and might include a range of acceptable measurements.
- As a subset of performance management, bandwidth management refers to a collection of strategies to optimize the volume of traffic a network can support. These techniques might include any of the following technologies: flow control, congestion control, and QoS (quality of service).
- Rate-based flow control limits the amount of data that can be transmitted but does not provide feedback to the sender when that rate is exceeded. Instead, traffic is lost. In contrast, feedback-based flow control at the data link layer gives the sender some kind of indication when the transmission rate is exceeding the receiver's ability to handle the incoming traffic.
- Congestion control techniques are designed to prevent this congestion before it occurs (called open-loop congestion control) and also to remedy congestion after it starts (called closed-loop congestion control).
- Network administrators must efficiently manage a network's QoS (quality of service) configurations, which is a group of techniques for adjusting the priority a network assigns to various types of transmissions. To do this, network administrators need to be aware of the applications used on a network, including the application protocols they use and the amount of bandwidth they require.

Plan Response and Recovery Strategies

- An incident response plan specifically defines the characteristics of an event that qualifies as a formal incident and the steps that should be followed as a result. Incident response actually begins *before* the incident occurs.

- During some incidents, data will need to be collected in such a way that it can be presented in a court of law for the purpose of prosecuting an instigator of illegal activity. Some of the forensic data available for analysis can be damaged or destroyed if improperly handled. It's critical that every IT technician in a company know how to safeguard sensitive information, logged data, and other legal evidence until the first responder or incident response team can take over the collection of evidence.

- When bad things happen, businesses need a plan to ensure business continuity, which is the ability of the company to continue doing business with the least amount of interruption possible. At a high level, a BCP (business continuity plan) defines the resources and protocols the business will use to continue providing service to its customers with little or no disruption during a disaster.

- Disaster recovery contingencies are commonly divided into these categories: cold site, warm site, hot site, and (more recently) cloud site. These options vary by the amount of hardware, software, planning, investment, and employee involvement each requires. They also vary according to how quickly they will restore network functionality in case a disaster occurs.

- Part of managing a network's availability involves managing the facilities and infrastructure that support the network, such as power connections and power sources during outages or fluctuations. Some of the devices involved in providing power to a network are focused on controlling and distributing power, while other devices store or generate power.

- You might be able to find information about compliance standards relevant to your company in an audit report. This is a document generated after an IT audit that evaluates a business's operations, processes, infrastructure, and policies as related to its business goals and relevant laws or other standards. The auditor will identify problems or deficiencies, applicable requirements, how weaknesses or gaps might affect the business, and recommendations to correct the problems.

Key Terms

For definitions of key terms, see the Glossary.

3-2-1-1 Rule
alert
audit log
audit report
audit trail
backup
bandwidth management
baseline
BCP (business continuity plan)
buffering
business continuity
chain of custody
cloud site
cold site
congestion control
CoS (Class of Service)
delay-sensitive
differential backup
DiffServ (Differentiated Services)
disaster

disaster recovery plan
DRaaS (disaster recovery as a service)
DSCP (Differentiated Services Code Point)
Event Viewer
first responder
flow control
full backup
hot site
incident
incident response plan
incremental backup
iPerf
log
logging level
loss-tolerant
MIB (Management Information Base)
NetFlow

NetFlow analyzer
network management
NMS (network management system) server
OID (object identifier)
packet analysis
PDU (power distribution unit)
RPO (recovery point objective)
RTO (recovery time objective)
severity level
surge protector
system log
traffic analysis
traffic log
traffic policing
traffic shaping
trap
UPS (uninterruptible power supply)
warm site

Review Questions

1. While troubleshooting a recurring problem on your network, you want to examine the TCP messages being exchanged between a server and a client. Which tool should you use on the server?
   - **a.** Spiceworks
   - **b.** Wireshark
   - **c.** iPerf
   - **d.** NetFlow

2. One of your coworkers downloaded several, very large video files for a special project she's working on for a new client. When you run your network monitor later this afternoon, what list will your coworker's computer likely show up on?
   - **a.** Top talkers
   - **b.** Top listeners
   - **c.** Giants
   - **d.** Jabbers

3. What command requests the next record in an SNMP log?
   - **a.** SNMP Get Request
   - **b.** SNMP Get Next
   - **c.** SNMP Trap
   - **d.** SNMP Get Response

4. What port do SNMP agents listen on?
   - **a.** Port 161
   - **b.** Port 21
   - **c.** Port 162
   - **d.** Port 20

5. Your roommate has been hogging the bandwidth on your router lately. What feature should you configure on the router to limit the amount of bandwidth his computer can utilize at any one time?
   - **a.** Power management
   - **b.** Congestion control
   - **c.** Flow control
   - **d.** Traffic shaping

6. What field in an IPv4 packet is altered to prioritize video streaming traffic over web surfing traffic?
   - **a.** Traffic Class
   - **b.** Priority Code Point
   - **c.** Time to Live
   - **d.** DiffServ

7. Which power backup method will continually provide power to a server if the power goes out during a thunderstorm?
   - **a.** Online UPS
   - **b.** Generator
   - **c.** Dual power supplies
   - **d.** Standby UPS

8. Which type of disaster recovery site contains all the equipment you would need to get up and running again after a disaster, and yet would require several weeks to implement?
   - **a.** Warm site
   - **b.** Standby site
   - **c.** Hot site
   - **d.** Cold site

9. Which log type is used to prove who did what and when?
   - **a.** Traffic log
   - **b.** Audit log
   - **c.** System log
   - **d.** Syslog

10. Which data link layer flow control method offers the most efficient frame transmission when sending large volumes of data?
    - **a.** Go-back-n sliding window
    - **b.** Choke packet
    - **c.** Selective repeat sliding window
    - **d.** Stop-and-wait

11. When you arrive at work one morning, your inbox is full of messages complaining of a network slowdown. You collect a capture from your network monitor. What documentation can help you determine what has changed?

12. What are the primary data link layer flow control methods?

13. What's the difference between an incident and a disaster?

14. Which QoS technique operates at layer 2 to more efficiently route Ethernet traffic between VLANs?

15. What's the difference between a PDU and a UPS?

16. Why might you want to install two power supplies in a critical server?

17. What are the two main categories of UPSs?

18. Which congestion control techniques help to prevent network congestion?

19. What is the primary challenge in properly configuring NetFlow?

20. Which backup type, if performed daily, would offer the lowest RTO and why?

Hands-On Projects

NOTE 12-10

Websites and applications change often. While the instructions given in these projects were accurate at the time of writing, you might need to adjust the steps or options according to later changes.

Note to Instructors and Students: A rubric is provided for evaluating student performance on these projects. Please see Appendix D.

Project 12-1: Work with Data in Event Viewer

Estimated Time: 20 minutes
Objective: Given a scenario, use the appropriate statistics and sensors to ensure network availability. (Obj. 3.1)
Resources:
- Windows 10 computer with administrative privileges

Context: In this module, you learned how to access and view event log information through the Event Viewer application in Windows 10. In this project, you will practice filtering the information contained in the log. As in the "Applying Concepts: Explore Event Viewer in Windows" project, you need a computer running Windows 10. Ideally, it should be a computer that has been used for a while, so that the event log contains several entries. It need not be connected to a network. However, you must be logged on to the computer as a user with administrator privileges. Complete the following steps:

1. Open Event Viewer. In the left pane, click the **Custom Views** arrow and then click **Administrative Events.** A list of Administrative Events appears in the center pane of the Event Viewer window. This log lists Critical, Error, and Warning events.
2. Suppose you want to find out whether your workstation has ever experienced trouble obtaining a DHCP-assigned IP address. In the Actions pane (the pane on the right), in the Administrative Events section, click **Find.** The Find dialog box opens.
3. Type **dhcp** and then click **Find Next.**
4. What is the first DHCP-related event you find? When did it occur? What was the source of this event? Read the description of the event in the General tab to learn more about it. Note: If the computer did not find a DHCP event, first make sure the topmost record is selected before beginning your search to ensure that all the records are searched. If a DHCP event is still not found, search for a different kind of event such as *DNS* or *Service Control Manager*. Otherwise, choose another event at random.
5. Click **Cancel** to close the Find dialog box. Keep the event listing that you found highlighted.
6. Now suppose you want to be notified each time your workstation experiences this error. In the Actions pane, click **Attach Task To This Event.** The Create Basic Task Wizard dialog box opens.
7. In the Name text box, replace the default text with **DHCP_my_computer** or some other text appropriate for the type of event you're saving. Click **Next** to continue.
8. You're prompted to confirm the Log, Source, and Event ID for this error. Click **Next** to continue.
9. You're prompted to indicate the type of action the operating system should take when this error occurs. **Start a program** is the only option not deprecated and should be selected by default. Click **Next** to continue.
10. Now you are asked to provide information about the program you want the system to open. Click the **Browse** button and find the cmd.exe file. The default location for cmd.exe is **C:\Windows\System32\cmd.exe** as shown in Figure 12-32, although your location path might be different. Select the file and click **Open.** Click **Next** to continue.

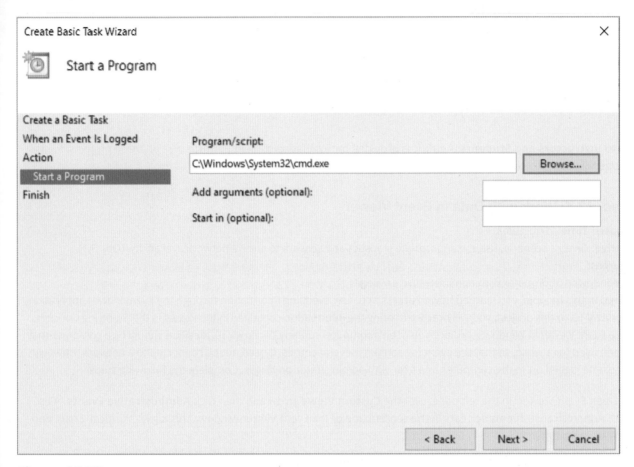

Figure 12-32   Create an action to start Command Prompt

11. A summary of your notification selections appears. **Take a screenshot** of your task configuration; submit this visual with your answers to this project's questions. Click **Finish** to create the task and add it to the actions your operating system will perform.

12. An Event Viewer dialog box opens, alerting you that the task has been created. Click **OK** to confirm.

13. You can see the task you just created by opening Task Scheduler. Press **Win + R** and enter **taskschd.msc**.

14. In the Task Scheduler window, click the down arrow next to **Task Scheduler Library** and then click **Event Viewer Tasks**. Select the task you just created and answer the following questions:

    a. In the lower pane, check the Security options section. Which user account will be used when the task runs?

    b. Click **Run** in the Actions pane. What happens?

    c. What command would keep this task from running without removing it from Task Scheduler?

15. You can now delete this task if you want. Close all open windows.

Project 12-2: Configure SPAN and Syslog in Packet Tracer

Estimated Time: 45 minutes

Objective: Given a scenario, use the appropriate statistics and sensors to ensure network availability. (Obj. 3.1)

Resources:

- Packet Tracer

Context: In this module, you read about various ways to capture network traffic for analysis and monitoring. In this project, you'll experiment with two of these technologies: SPAN on switches and a syslog server. Complete the following steps:

1. Open Packet Tracer. In your Packet Tracer workspace, add a 2960 switch and three PCs.
2. Configure static IP addresses on all three PCs within the same subnet. What IP addresses did you assign each PC?
3. Connect the PCs to the first three switch ports (FastEthernet 0/1 – 0/3). Wait for all connections to come up.
4. In the bottom right corner, click **Simulation**. This opens the Simulation Panel.
5. By default, the simulation will display all messages from all protocols on the network once you start the simulation—you can see a list of applicable filters in the *Event List Filters – Visible Events* section. For this project, you only want to see ICMP messages. At the bottom of the Simulation Panel, click **Show All/None**, which clears all visible event types. Click **Edit Filters**. In the PacketTracer7 filters window, check the box on the IPv4 tab for **ICMP**. Close the PacketTracer7 filters window. Confirm ICMP is the only visible event type listed.
6. When you start the simulation in the next step, you will run pings between PCs on your network, and the results will display in the PDU List Window in the bottom right corner of your Packet Tracer interface. For a more convenient arrangement, in the bottom middle pane, click **Toggle PDU List Window** to move this pane to a larger space in your Packet Tracer interface. If desired, you can also grab the top bar of the Simulation Panel to move this module around on your screen in a separate window.
7. On the common tools bar, click the **Add Simple PDU (P)** button, which looks like a closed envelope. This will create a ping-based conversation between two devices. Click **PC0** as the source device and click **PC1** as the destination device.
8. In the Simulation Panel, click the **Play (Alt + P)** button. As the simulation begins, a PDU leaves PC0 and arrives at the switch. Watch the traffic carefully. To which device does the switch send the first PDU? Why do you think this is?
9. At the bottom of the interface, click the **Delete** button to stop the simulation for this scenario. Click **Realtime** to return to Realtime mode.

Now you're ready to add a sniffer to the network that will monitor all traffic on the switch. Complete the following step:

10. From the End Devices group, add a **Sniffer** to the workspace. Connect the sniffer's Ethernet0 port to the switch's FastEthernet 0/24 port. The sniffer does not need an IP address to do its job.

With these devices connected to your network, you're ready to configure a SPAN monitoring session on the switch. Complete the following steps:

11. On the switch's **CLI** tab, enter the commands in Table 12-1.

Table 12-1 Configure a SPAN monitoring session on a switch

Command	Purpose
`enable`	Enables privileged EXEC mode
`configure terminal`	Enters global configuration mode
`monitor session 1 source int fa0/1 - 3`	Configures source interfaces for the monitoring session
`monitor session 1 destination int fa0/24`	Configures the destination interface for the monitoring session (there can be only one)
`do show monitor`	Displays the monitoring session configuration; confirm your configuration matches that shown in Figure 12-33

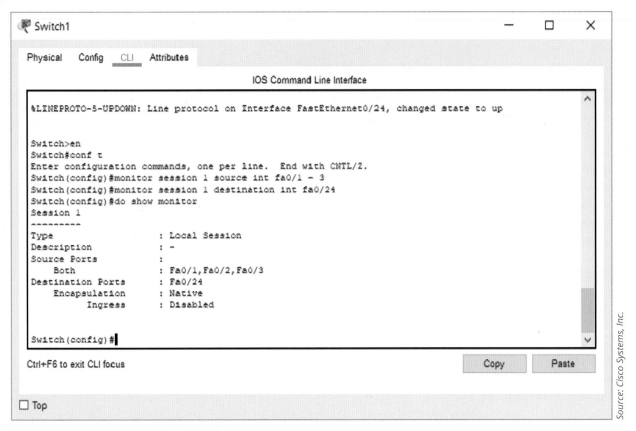

Figure 12-33   SPAN monitoring session from three interfaces to FastEthernet 0/24

12. To test your monitoring session, enter Simulation Mode and send a simple PDU from PC0 to PC1 again. Watch the traffic carefully. To which device(s) does the switch send the PDU this time? Why do you think this is?

13. To see the captured traffic, click the **Sniffer** and click its **GUI** tab. Apply the same filter here as the one you used for Simulation Mode in Step 4 and run the ping again. Click any of the captured ICMP messages. What are the source and destination IP addresses of the message you chose?

Syslog is another way to capture network traffic; however, syslog functions differently by capturing messages processed on a monitored device. To compare SPAN and syslog functionality, complete the following steps:

14. Add a 2901 router and a server to the workspace. Connect both to the switch.

15. On the server's **Services** tab, confirm the Syslog service is turned on. Configure the server with a static IP address on the same subnet as your PCs. What IP address did you give the server?

16. Configure the router with a static IP address and turn on the interface connected to the switch.

Syslog logging is enabled by default on the router, but additional information is needed to send the required logs to the server. Complete the following steps:

17. To configure syslog logging on the router's CLI, enter the commands listed in Table 12-2, starting in global configuration mode.

18. Check the logging configuration on your router. Where are the router's logs being sent? What port are these messages using?

19. To test your syslog configuration, ping one of your PCs from your router. Return to your syslog server to examine captured traffic. **Take a screenshot** of the Syslog Service window showing logged traffic; submit this visual with your answers to this project's questions. How many ICMP messages are logged?

Table 12-2   Configure syslog on a router

Command	Purpose
`logging <server IP address>`	Tells the router where to send syslog messages
`logging trap debugging`	Requires all messages from the debugging level (level 7, which is the lowest severity level) and above to be logged with the server; note that Packet Tracer only supports logging at level 7 (debugging), which includes all severity levels
`exit`	Returns to privileged EXEC mode
`debug ip icmp`	Enables debugging for ICMP messages
`show debugging`	Displays debugging configuration; confirm ICMP packet debugging is on
`show logging`	Displays syslog configuration

20. Syslog captured the ICMP messages for a ping between the router and a PC. Now ping between two PCs. Return to your syslog server to examine captured traffic. How many ICMP messages are logged now? Why do you think this is?

21. Save this Packet Tracer file in a safe place for future reference. Make some notes on your Wikidot website about your activities in Packet Tracer for this project.

Note to instructors: A Packet Tracer solution file is provided for each Packet Tracer project through the Instructors site.

Project 12-3: Test Network Throughput with iPerf

Estimated Time: 30 minutes
Objective: Given a scenario, use the appropriate network software tools and commands. (Obj. 5.3)
Resources:
- Windows computer
- A second device, such as a computer (Windows, Linux, or macOS) or smartphone (Android or iOS)
- Access to the same computer used to complete Capstone Project 1-1 or 1-2
- Internet access

Context: In this module, you read about iPerf, which is a CLI-based tool for testing throughput between two devices on your local network. In this project, you'll install iPerf on two devices and then test throughput between them. Complete the following steps:

1. On your primary computer, go to **iperf.fr**. Download the latest version of iperf3 for your computer and save the download in your Downloads folder. Extract the contents of the iperf download.
2. Create a new folder named **iperf** in the root folder for your Windows drive. For example, if Windows is installed on your C: drive, create the folder **C:/iperf**.
3. Move the iperf files from your Downloads folder to your new iperf folder. This will make it easier to find the iperf files from the CLI.
4. Open a Command Prompt window. Enter the command `cd c:/iperf` to navigate to the folder you just created.
5. Enter the command `iperf3.exe` to see the help files. Which command starts server mode?

Now you're ready to install iPerf on your secondary device. This device could be another computer (Windows, Linux, or macOS) or a smartphone (Android or Linux). Complete the following steps:

6. Make sure your secondary device is on the same network as your primary device.
7. If you're using a computer, repeat Steps 1 through 4 to prepare the computer.
8. If you're using a smartphone, find the free iPerf app for your phone and install it.

You're now ready to run iPerf between the two devices. Complete the following steps:

9. Your primary device will be the iperf server. On your iperf server, enter the command `ipconfig` to display your computer's IP address. Record this information for future use. Next, enter the command `iperf3.exe -s` so the server will start listening. In the Windows Security Alert window, click **Allow access**.

10. Your secondary device will be the iperf client:
    a. If your secondary device is a computer, enter the command `iperf3.exe -c <server's IP address>`. For example, if the server's IP address from Step 9 is 192.168.2.120, you would enter the command `iperf3.exe -c 192.168.2.120`.
    b. If your secondary device is a smartphone, enter the parameter `-c <server's IP address>`. For example, if the server's IP address from Step 9 is 192.168.2.120, you would enter the parameter `-c 192.168.2.120`. At the top of the screen, toggle the **Stopped** switch to **Started** (see Figure 12-34).

Figure 12-34   A free iPerf app on Android

11. Watch the output on both devices for several seconds. When you're ready, stop the test on the computer(s) by pressing **Ctrl+C**. On a smartphone, stop the test by toggling the **Started** switch to **Stopped**.
12. **Take a screenshot** of the client's output; submit this visual with your answers to this project's questions.
13. What are some of the speeds your test reported? Are these speeds what you expect on your network? What troubleshooting might you need to do to determine how to increase your network speeds?
14. Start your Windows VM that you created in Capstone Project 1-1 or 1-2. Repeat the steps needed to install iPerf on the VM. Then run the iperf server on your primary computer and the iperf client on your VM. How does the throughput for this connection differ from the throughput for the earlier test?
15. Document this application installation in your wikidot website.

Project 12-4: Organize Your Wikidot Website

Estimated Time: 45 minutes (+15 minutes for group work, if assigned)
Objective: Explain the purpose of organization documents and policies. (Obj. 3.2)
Group work: This project includes enhancements when assigned as a group project.
Resources:
• Internet access
Context: Throughout this course, you've kept notes on various projects in your Wikidot website. To finish up these projects, let's do some final cleanup and organization so these notes will continue to be useful and easily accessible for you as you move into your other IT classes and your career. You might decide to continue adding notes, pages, and categories, or create

new wikis as needed. Using good organization and adding thorough notes could make your wiki a valuable exhibit when applying for your first job in IT. Complete the following steps:

1. First, adjust the side navigation menu. On the All Pages page (click the gear icon and click **List All Pages**), click **Side Navigation** and then click **Edit**. You should see the text shown in Figure 12-35. Throughout this project, you can ignore any red, squiggly lines in the text unless they indicate a place where you've misspelled a word. Be sure to use correct spelling and good grammar in your wiki's content text.

```
[[div class="text-center" style ="margin-bottom: 12px;"]]
[[module Clone]]
[[/div]]

+ Site Navigation

* [[[help:_home|User Guide]]]
* [[[help:first-time-user|First Time User]]]
* [[[main:about|About]]]
* [[[main:contact|Contact]]]
* [[[legal:_home|Legal]]]
* [[[forum:start|Discussion Forums]]]
* [[[system:members|Members]]]

+ Create a Page
[[module NewPage size="20" button="New page"]]
```

Figure 12-35 **Side navigation bar coding**

2. Change the User Guide link to point to the list of all pages instead. On the User Guide line (the first line under "+ Site Navigation"), edit it to read as follows:

   `* [[[system:list-all-pages|All Pages]]]`

3. When you're finished, the edited text should match the first item in the Site Navigation list in Figure 12-36. Save your changes and test the new link under Site Navigation on the right.

```
[[div class="text-center" style="margin-bottom: 12px;"]]
[[module Clone]]
[[/div]]

+ Site Navigation

* [[[system:list-all-pages|All Pages]]]
* [[[help:first-time-user|First Time User]]]
* [[[main:about|About]]]
* [[[main:contact|Contact]]]
* [[[legal:_home|Legal]]]
* [[[forum:start|Discussion Forums]]]
* [[[system:members|Members]]]

+ Create a Page

[[module NewPage size="20" button="New page"]]
```

Figure 12-36 **Edited side navigation bar**

Each time you named a page with one part before the colon and another part after the colon, such as Applications:Wireshark, you added that page to a category. The first name, such as Applications, is the name of the category. The second name, such as Wireshark, is the name of the page. Complete the next step to display all available categories:

4. To see a list of all categories in your wiki, click the gear icon and then click **Site Manager**, **Appearance & Behaviour**, and **Navigation elements**. Click the drop-down arrow next to *Choose the category*.

Here, you can see the available categories, including the ones you've created. The trick now is to find a way to list pages according to each category. To do this, you'll first need to create a Categories page. Complete the following steps:

5. Go back to your wiki and create a new page called **system:All Categories**.
6. Add the text **[[module Categories]]** to your page and save it.
7. Go back to the All Pages list. The All Categories page is listed as "system:All Categories." To change page name to "All Categories" instead, click the **system:All Categories** page, click **Edit**, and change the title to **All Categories**. The *name* of the page still includes its category (system), but now the *title* of the page is simply "All Categories."

This module automatically creates a list of all the categories and all the pages within each category. If any page is listed in the wrong module, you can't edit the page's title to change its category. When you edit the page, you're editing the title of that page, not its name, which is what defines the page's category. Instead, use the following step to edit the page's category:

8. If a page is listed in the wrong category, go to the page and click **+ Options** and then click **Rename**. Change the page's category, which is the name *before* the colon, and click **Rename/move**. Repeat for any other miscategorized pages.

Now let's edit the top navigation bar so it shows one or more categories as an option, and each page within that category as an option. Complete the following steps:

9. Click the gear icon and click **Edit Top Bar**.
10. Click the **Edit** button on this page. You should see text similar to Figure 12-37.

```
[[ul class="nav navbar-nav"]]
[[li]][[a href="/main:about"]]About [[span class="fa fa-info-circle"]]@c[[/
span]][[/a]][[/li]]
[[li]][[a href="/main:layout"]]Layout [[span class="fa fa-code"]]
@< >@[[/span]][[/a]][[/li]]
[[li]][[a href="/system:join"]]Membership [[span class="fa fa-user"]]
@< >@[[/span]][[/a]][[/li]]
[[li]][[a href="/help:_home"]]User Guide [[span class="fa
fa-exclamation-circle"]]@< >@[[/span]]
[[/a]][[/li]]
[[li class="dropdown"]]
[[a href="#" class="dropdown-toggle" data-toggle="dropdown"]]Help Docs
[[span class="fa fa-question-circle"]]@< >@[[/span]][[/a]][[ul
class="dropdown-menu"]]
  [[li]][[a href="/help:_home"]]User Guide[[/a]][[/li]]
  [[li]][[a href="/help:first-time-user"]]First Time User[[/a]][[/li]]
  [[li]][[a href="/help:quick-reference"]]Quick Reference[[/a]][[/li]]
  [[li]][[a href="/help:creating-pages"]]Creating Pages[[/a]][[/li]]
  [[li]][[a href="/help:editing-pages"]]Editing Pages[[/a]][[/li]]
  [[li]][[a href="/help:navigation-bars"]]Navigation Bars[[/a]][[/li]]
  [[li]][[a href="/help:using-modules"]]Using Modules[[/a]][[/li]]
  [[li]][[a href="/help:templates"]]Templates[[/a]][[/li]]
  [[li]][[a href="/help:css-themes"]]CSS Themes[[/a]][[/li]]
[[/ul]]
[[/li]]
```

Source: Wikidot Inc.

Figure 12-37 Top navigation bar coding

Currently, the only link in the top navigation bar that gives a drop-down menu is the Help Docs link. In the next few steps, you'll remove some of the links in the top navigation bar and add a drop-down link for each category. Complete the following steps:

11. Delete the **Layout** and **Membership** lines in this text (lines 3 and 4).
12. On the next line, change the text **User Guide** to **All Categories**. Change its location to **system:all-categories**. The line should now read as follows:

```
[[li]][[a href="/system:all-categories"]]All Categories
[[span class="fa fa-exclamation-
circle"]]@< >@[[/span]][[/a]][[/li]]
```

13. On the dropdown-toggle line, change the text **Help Docs** to the name of one of your categories, such as **Applications**.

For this step, you'll create dropdown items for the dropdown link you just created. It might help to have two browser windows open—one showing the All Pages list for a reference and the other showing the top navigation menu editing page. Add extra lines if needed. Complete the next step:

14. For each sub-item, add the name and location of a page within that category. For example, the Wireshark page would be listed under Applications like this:

```
[[li]][[a
href="/applications:wireshark"]]Wireshark[[/a]][[/li]]
```

The Nmap line will look like this:

```
[[li]][[a href="/applications:nmap"]]Nmap[[/a]][[/li]]
```

Notice the small icons next to each item on the top navigation menu, such as an "i" in a circle, an exclamation mark in a circle, and a question mark in a circle. To change some of these icons, complete the following steps:

15. On the Applications line (the line that includes the dropdown-toggle text), change the text that reads "fa fa-question-circle" so it says **"fa fa-info-circle"**.
16. On the About line (line 2), change the text that reads "fa fa-info-circle" so it says **"fa fa-question-circle"**.
17. When you've made all these changes, review the navigation menu again and correct any typos or missed links. When you're ready, click **Save**. The new Top Navigation bar shows in the page's content area and at the top of the page.
18. Test each link to make sure it works correctly, and troubleshoot any problematic links. To make changes, go back to the **Top Navigation** page and click **Edit**. The edited text should look something like Figure 12-38. Make sure the page addresses are typed exactly right.
19. Add more categories and pages links, as desired, until you've listed all your categories and pages that you created for projects in this text.
20. On the top navigation bar, add a link to the All Pages page, with an information circle next to it. This link will make the All Pages page accessible directly from the Home page. What line of code must you add to the top navigation bar's code to accomplish this?
21. Edit the Home page text and the About page text to reflect what you've accomplished during this course and to describe the information available in your wiki. Make any other changes you would like to the navigation menus, categories, or pages. You might add screenshots or photos to some of the pages, add more detailed notes, or create new categories for other projects you've completed. If desired, research other editing options, themes, codes, and modules so this wiki reflects your interests and learning progress.
22. **For group assignments:** Invite a team member to check out your wiki and test your links. Correct any problems they find. In exchange, review your teammate's wiki and report any errors you find. Exchange notes and ideas for ways to improve your wikis.
23. When you're ready, **take a screenshot** of your wiki showing the top navigation and side navigation panes; submit this visual with your answers to this project's questions. Providing a link to your wiki when applying for an IT job could make a strong, positive first impression on a potential employer!

```
[[ul class="nav navbar-nav"]]
[[li]][[a href="/main:about"]]About [[span class="fa fa-question-circle"]]@< >@[[/span]][[/a]][[/li]]
[[li]][[a href="/system:all-categories"]]All Categories [[span class="fa fa-exclamation-
circle"]]@< >@[[/span]][[/a]][[/li]]
[[li class="dropdown"]]
[[a href="#" class="dropdown-toggle" data-toggle="dropdown"]]Applications [[span class="fa fa-info-
circle"]]@< >@[[/span]][[/a]][[ul class="dropdown-menu"]]
  [[li]][[a href="/applications:advancedipscanner"]]Advanced IP Scanner[[/a]][[/li]]
  [[li]][[a href="/applications:nmap"]]Nmap[[/a]][[/li]]
  [[li]][[a href="/applications:packettracer"]]Packet Tracer[[/a]][[/li]]
  [[li]][[a href="/applications:tamosoft-throughputtest"]]TamoSoft-Throughput Test[[/a]][[/li]]
  [[li]][[a href="/applications:totusoft-lanspeedtest"]]TotuSoft-LAN Speed Test[[/a]][[/li]]
  [[li]][[a href="/applications:wsl-ubuntu"]]WSL Ubuntu[[/a]][[/li]]
  [[li]][[a href="/applications:wireshark"]]Wireshark[[/a]][[/li]]
[[/ul]]
[[/li]]
[[li]][[a href="/main:contact"]]Contact [[span class="fa fa-envelope"]]@< >@[[/span]][[/a]][[/li]]
[[li class="dropdown admins-only"]]
[[a href="#" class="dropdown-toggle" data-toggle="dropdown"]][[span class="fa fa-
cog"]]@< >@[[/span]][[/a]][[ul class="dropdown-menu"]]
  [[li]][[a href="/_admin"]]Site Manager[[/a]][[/li]]
  [[li]][[a href="/nav:top"]]Edit Top Bar[[/a]][[/li]]
  [[li]][[a href="/nav:side"]]Edit Side Bar[[/a]][[/li]]
  [[li]][[a href="/css:_home"]]CSS Manager[[/a]][[/li]]
  [[li]][[a href="/system:recent-changes"]]Recent Changes[[/a]][[/li]]
  [[li]][[a href="/system:list-all-pages"]]List All Pages[[/a]][[/li]]
[[/ul]]
[[/li]]
[[/ul]]
```

Figure 12-38   The edited top navigation bar

Source: Wikidot Inc.

Capstone Projects

NOTE 12-11

Websites and applications change often. While the instructions given in these projects were accurate at the time of writing, you might need to adjust the steps or options according to later changes.

Note to Instructors and Students: A rubric is provided for evaluating student performance on these projects. Please see Appendix D.

Capstone Project 12-1: Use Syslog in Ubuntu Desktop

Estimated Time: 45 minutes

Objective: Explain common ports and protocols, their application, and encrypted alternatives. (Obj. 1.5)

Resources:

- Access to the same computer used to complete Capstone Project 2-1

Context: In this project, you will view and manipulate log file entries on a computer running the Linux operating system. Because Linux versions vary in the type of GUI application that allows you to open the system log, this exercise uses the CLI instead. For this exercise, you need a computer with a Linux operating system installed, such as the Ubuntu Desktop VM that you created in Module 2, Capstone Project 2-1. It need not be connected to a network, but for best results, it should be a computer that has been used in the past and not a fresh install. You must be logged on to the Linux computer as a user with administrator privileges. Complete the following steps:

1. Start your Ubuntu Desktop VM and open Terminal.
2. The syslog file contains information similar to that shown in Figure 12-39. The first step in viewing your Linux computer's system log is to find out where the file is located. Try each of these commands until you find the syslog file that contains information similar to that in Figure 12-39:

```
#
# First some standard log files.  Log by facility.
#
auth,authpriv.*                     /var/log/auth.log
*.*;auth,authpriv.none              -/var/log/syslog
#cron.*                             /var/log/cron.log
#daemon.*                           -/var/log/daemon.log
kern.*                              -/var/log/kern.log
#lpr.*                              -/var/log/lpr.log
mail.*                              -/var/log/mail.log
#user.*                             -/var/log/user.log
```

Source: Canonical Group Limited

Figure 12-39   Log files and their locations

```
more /etc/syslog.conf
more /etc/rsyslog.conf
more /etc/rsyslog.d/50-default.conf
```

3. The first part of the syslog file appears. In this part of the file, you should see a list of log types and their locations, similar to the listing shown in Figure 12-39. (If you don't see the listing in this part of the file, press the **Enter** or **Spacebar** key until you do see it.)

4. Write down the location and filename of the file that logs all events, as indicated by *.* in the first column. (For example, it might be /var/log/syslog or /var/adm/messages.)

5. Press the **Spacebar** enough times to view the entire log configuration file and return to the shell prompt.

6. Now that you know the name and location of your system log, you can view its messages. At the shell prompt, enter one of the following commands, depending on your log file's location:
   - If your log file is at /var/log/syslog, enter `tail /var/log/syslog`
   - If your log file is at /var/adm/messages, enter `tail /var/adm/messages`

7. The last 10 lines of your log file appear (assuming it is at least 10 lines long). What types of messages are recorded? When did the events occur?

8. Next find out all the types of log files your computer saves. Enter one of the following to change your working directory to the same directory where log files are kept:
   - If your log file is in the /var/log directory, enter `cd /var/log`
   - If your log file is in the /var/adm directory, enter `cd /var/adm`

9. To view a listing of the directory's contents, enter `ls -la`. List two types of log files that appear in this directory.

10. Suppose you want to find every message in the system log file that pertains to DHCP addressing. At the shell prompt, enter one of the following:
    - If your log file is named *syslog*, enter `grep DHCP syslog`
    - If your log file is named *messages*, enter `grep DHCP messages`

    A list of messages containing the term *DHCP* appears, if there are any.

11. Re-enter your command from Step 6 and then run a new search using a text string that appears in your results. What command did you use? **Take a screenshot** of your results showing successful location of the text string; submit this visual with your answers to this project's questions.

12. If your operating system is configured to start a new log file each day or each time the computer is restarted, your log file might be brief. Repeat Step 9 and this time, look for other versions of the syslog or messages file in your working directory. For example, Ubuntu Linux will save older system messages in a file called *syslog.1*, *syslog.2*, and so on (see Figure 12-40). If you find a larger, older log file, repeat Step 10 using this log file's name. How do the results differ?

13. Close the Terminal session window and power off your Ubuntu VM. Make some notes on your Wikidot website about your activities for this project.

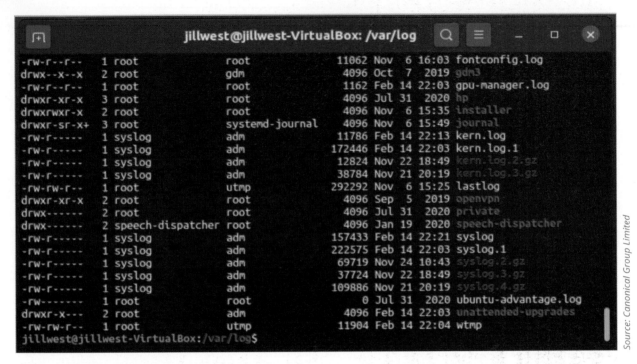

Figure 12-40 Several older syslog files are listed

Capstone Project 12-2: Manage Log Files in Ubuntu Server

Estimated Time: 30 minutes

Objective: Given a scenario, use the appropriate statistics and sensors to ensure network availability. (Obj. 3.1)

Resources:

- Access to the same computer used to complete Capstone Project 3-1

Context: Oftentimes it seems that working with Linux operating systems is like driving a stick shift while working with Windows is like driving an automatic. For example, to configure an installed program in Ubuntu, you must edit a text file.

Ubuntu creates various logs to track just about any event, and these logs are also stored as text files. By default, most are stored in the /var/log directory. For example, Ubuntu stores early initialization information for cloud instances (such as hostname and SSH keys) in a text file that, by default, is /var/log/cloud-init.log. (You can change the default path and filename by editing the /etc/cloud-init.conf file.) Using the installation of Ubuntu Server in a VM you created in Capstone Project 3-1, follow along to learn how to manage log files in Ubuntu:

1. Start Ubuntu Server and log on with your username and password. Refer to your LastPass vault if you don't remember that information.
2. Enter the commands shown in Table 12-3 to work with Ubuntu log files.
3. It's helpful to learn about other log files in the /var/log directory. Search the **help.ubuntu.com** website or do a general Google search on three log files you find in the directory (enter `ls -l` again if you need to see the list again). Write a one-sentence description of the type of information kept in each file and why a technician might find this information helpful.
4. Power off your Ubuntu Server VM and make some notes on your Wikidot website about your activities for this project.

Table 12-3   Manage Ubuntu log files

Command	Explanation
`cd /var/log`	Goes to the directory that contains log files.
`ls -l	less`	Lists all files and subdirectories, and details about each item, one page at a time. Look for log files that have gotten excessively large. If a technician doesn't monitor and control log files, they may get large enough to take up all available hard drive space and bring a system down. Press the **spacebar** to move to the next page and **q** to return to the prompt.
`ls -l cloud-init.log`	Lists details about cloud-init.log. Notice the file is owned by syslog. Also notice the file size. If it is 0, look for another large log file and view information about that one instead.
`less cloud-init.log`	Views and pages through the contents of the file. Note that if you want to view a file owned by root, you must use the `sudo` command in front of the `less` command. What are some common entries in this log?
`q`	Quits the less pager.
`grep "ownership" cloud-init.log`	Uses the `grep` command to narrow down a search in a text file for a particular string of text. Remember you must use the `sudo` command if you're trying to access a file owned by root. The `grep` command is particularly useful for large text files when you're searching for a particular username, event, or command. How many results did you get? If you didn't get any results, use a word that showed up frequently when you viewed the contents of the file.
`grep "OWNERSHIP" cloud-init.log`	Searches for the same text string except using all capital letters in the string. How many results do you see?
`grep -i "OWNERSHIP" cloud-init.log`	Ignores case when searching. **Take a screenshot** of the output; submit this visual with your answers to this project's questions.

Capstone Project 12-3: Use PRTG to Monitor Network Devices

Estimated Time: 60 minutes

Objective: Given a scenario, use the appropriate statistics and sensors to ensure network availability. (Obj. 3.1)

Resources:

- Access to the same computer used to complete Capstone Project 1-1 or 1-2
- Internet access

Context: Throughout this module, you've learned about tools to monitor network devices, including SNMP. In this project, you'll install a network monitor called PRTG (Paessler Router Traffic Grapher) on a VM and see what information you can gather about your network with no further configuration. You'll then enable SNMP on your Windows 10 host and see what additional information becomes available to you in the PRTG network monitor.

 **CAUTION**   Scanning a network you don't own or don't have permission to scan is illegal. Do not use PRTG on public Wi-Fi networks at all. Also don't use PRTG on any network you don't own unless you have written permission from the owner to do so.

Complete the following steps:

1. Ensure your Windows 10 VM that you created in Capstone Project 1-1 or 1-2 is configured with the bridged network mode. In Hyper-V, the VM should be connected to a vSwitch using the External network type. In VirtualBox, the VM should use the Bridged Adapter option. Start your Windows 10 VM.

2. In the VM, go to **paessler.com**. Download and install **PRTG**. You'll need to enter an email address—you can choose any of your email addresses for this purpose.

3. After installation, if PRTG doesn't open automatically, open it from your new desktop shortcut. The user interface will open in a browser. The default login name and password are **prtgadmin**.

4. You can skip the introduction and close all other information windows on the website. If you were setting this application up for use in a production network, what is the first task you would need to do to ensure its security?

5. PRTG Auto-discovery automatically begins populating the monitoring system with devices on the network. Before you perform any other configurations, which devices were discovered automatically?

6. In the top left corner, click the **Home** button. How many sensors are currently configured? How many trial days do you have left? How many sensors do you have available? Note that at the end of your trial, your PRTG will automatically revert to the free version, which supports only a few sensors, unless you pay for the full version.

7. Click the menu icon and click **Devices** to return to the earlier screen. Click the **2 days** tab to see metrics being mapped on charts. These charts give visual output of monitored sensors and can be customized. Return to the **Overview** tab.

You can manually add devices and their various sensors. To add your physical host computer, which is a Windows 10 computer, you must first enable SNMP. Complete the following steps on your physical host computer:

8. Open Settings and click **Apps**. Click **Optional features**. Click **Add a feature**. Select **Simple Network Management Protocol (SNMP)** and click **Install**. Click the back arrow to observe the installation progress.

9. After installation is complete, close Settings. In the Windows search box, type **services** and click the **Services** app. Find **SNMP Service** in the list and double-click it. Make the following changes:
   a. Click the **Agent** tab and select all checkboxes in the Service group.
   b. Click the **Security** tab, click **Add**, and make sure **READ ONLY** is selected. Add a Community Name, such as **public**. Click **Add**.
   c. Under *Accept SNMP packets from these hosts*, click **Add**. Type your VM's IP address and click **Add**. Click **OK** and then close the **Services** window.

You're now ready to add your physical Windows machine as a monitored device in PRTG. Complete the following steps:

10. Back in your VM's PRTG user interface, under Windows > Clients, click **Add Device**.

11. Give the device a name, such as **Windows10_host**. Add the physical host's IPv4 address. Choose a device icon, such as the Windows logo, and then click **OK**. The device is added to your list.

12. Click **Run Auto-Discovery**. This process will take a few minutes. When the process is complete, **take a screenshot** of the sensors discovered for the Windows10_host machine; submit this visual with your answers to this project's questions.

13. Which of these sensors are familiar to you? Which sensors are new to you?

14. If you decide to use PRTG long-term, you might want to install it instead on a physical computer with ample hardware resources to process incoming data. What other devices on your network would you like to monitor using PRTG?

15. If you decide not to continue using PRTG, be sure to disable SNMP on your host computer. Document the application installation in your wikidot website.

Solutions to Self-Check Questions

Collect Network Data

1. Which of the following would an environmental monitoring system *not* track?

Answer: b. User authentication

Explanation: Monitoring sensors can detect liquid such as when water floods a room, identify if a room's lights are on, and monitor voltage from a UPS. However, an environmental monitoring system would not be responsible for tracking **user authentication** to the network.

2. Which log type would most likely be used first to investigate the cause of high numbers of dropped packets?

Answer: a. Traffic log

Explanation: Historical **traffic logs** can be used to investigate security breaches, confirm regulatory compliance, and investigate network performance issues. A system log tracks information on a single device and will not be helpful until you know which device(s) to check. The data in an audit log is thorough enough to retroactively prove compliance and is often used in forensics investigations; due to the level of detail included, an audit log is not likely the best place to start investigating a network problem. There's no such thing as a jitter log.

3. Which of the following is *not* defined by syslog?

Answer: d. Message security

Explanation: The syslog standard addresses three primary components, including event message format, event message transmission, and event message handling. Syslog does not define or require **message security**.

4. Which of the following would be assigned an OID?

Answer: b. A switch's interface

Explanation: A device, such as a web server, can be managed by an NMS server, typically using UDP ports 161 and 162. Each managed device may contain several managed objects, which can be any characteristic of the device that is monitored, including components such as a **switch's interface**, processor temperature, or memory utilization. Each managed object is assigned an OID (object identifier).

Manage Network Traffic

5. Which bandwidth management technique limits traffic specifically between a single sender and a single receiver?

Answer: d. Flow control

Explanation: **Flow control** addresses the number of frames that can be handled from end-to-end between a single sender and a single receiver. Congestion control addresses traffic throughout the network. QoS (Quality of Service) techniques allow for more nuanced control of what happens to the traffic once it's on the network. Traffic shaping is a QoS technique.

6. Which flow control method resends a lost frame along with all frames sent with it?

Answer: c. Go-back-n sliding window

Explanation: With the **go-back-n sliding window** flow control method, the sender retransmits all frames in the window, even if only one frame was lost. With the stop-and-wait method, only one frame is sent at a time. With the selective repeat sliding window method, only the lost frame is resent while successive frames continue to be sent. Backpressure is a congestion control technique.

7. Which of the following statements is true? Choose *two*.

Answer: c. When streaming a movie, the transmission is sensitive to delays and tolerant of loss. And d. When sending an email, the transmission is sensitive to loss and tolerant of delays.

Explanation: Delayed traffic for a streaming movie results in reduced quality, while an occasional skipped video frame will likely not be noticeable. This means that, **when streaming a movie, the transmission is sensitive to delays and tolerant of loss**. An email, however, can tolerate a brief delay, but lost data can result in a corrupted message. Therefore, **when sending an email, the transmission is sensitive to loss and tolerant of delays**.

Plan Response and Recovery Strategies

8. When repairing a coworker's computer, you find some illegal files. What should you do next?

Answer: c. Disconnect the computer from the network and leave it running.

Explanation: First secure the area by **disconnecting the computer from the network** (remove the Ethernet cable or disable the Wi-Fi antenna). Ideally, you should **leave the device running** without closing any applications or files. Don't shut down the computer unless a destructive program is running, and then you would immediately unplug the computer. Don't change anything on the computer by taking screenshots and don't tamper with evidence by deleting files.

9. Which backup site includes a running server that does not have access to the latest backups?

Answer: a. Warm site

Explanation: At a **warm site**, you might have server duplicates configured, updated, and connected, but backed up data is applied only at regular intervals to reduce costs. At a cold site, devices aren't necessarily configured or connected. At a hot site, servers are constantly mirrored so they have access to the latest data. On site refers to the location of resources.

10. Which power device prevents a critical server from losing power, even for an instant?

Answer: d. UPS

Explanation: Because the server never needs to switch from the wall outlet's power to the **UPS's (uninterruptible power supply)** power, there is no risk of briefly losing service. A surge protector redirects excess voltage away from the device to a ground, thereby protecting the device from harm. A generator serves as a backup power source for many devices, providing power redundancy in the event of a total blackout. A PDU (power distribution unit) acts as a power strip to bring power from outlets, a generator, or a UPS closer to the devices on the rack.

COMPTIA NETWORK+ N10-008 CERTIFICATION EXAM OBJECTIVES

This text covers material related to all the examination objectives for the CompTIA Network+ exam N10-008, which was released by CompTIA (the Computing Technology Industry Association) in 2021. The official list of objectives is available at CompTIA's website, *comptia.org*. For your reference, the following tables list each exam objective and the module of this course that explains the objective, plus the amount of the exam that will cover each certification domain. Each objective belongs to one of five domains (or main categories) of networking expertise. For example, the task of comparing and contrasting different 802.11 standards belongs to Objective 2.4 in the "Network Implementations" domain, which altogether accounts for 19 percent of the exam's content.

Domain	Percentage of examination
1.0 Networking Fundamentals	24%
2.0 Network Implementations	19%
3.0 Network Operations	16%
4.0 Network Security	19%
5.0 Network Troubleshooting	22%
Total	**100%**

As you read through the exam objectives, pay close attention to the verbs used in each objective, as these words indicate how deeply you should know the content listed. For example, an objective that says, "Explain the purposes …" or "Compare and contrast …" expects you to understand the concepts listed, be able to identify those concepts in a scenario, and answer questions about the concepts. However, an objective that says, "Given a scenario, use …" or "Given a scenario, implement …" expects you to be able to put those concepts to work. Any objective that begins with the words "Given a scenario" is likely to show up on the exam as a performance-based question rather than simply as a multiple-choice question.

DOMAIN 1.0 NETWORKING FUNDAMENTALS—24% OF EXAMINATION

Objective	Section	Bloom's Taxonomy

1.1 Compare and contrast the Open Systems Interconnection (OSI) model layers and encapsulation concepts.
 	
• OSI model
  ○ Layer 1 – Physical
  ○ Layer 2 – Data link
  ○ Layer 3 – Network
  ○ Layer 4 – Transport
  ○ Layer 5 – Session
  ○ Layer 6 – Presentation
  ○ Layer 7 – Application
• Data encapsulation and decapsulation within the OSI model context
  ○ Ethernet header
  ○ Internet Protocol (IP) header
  ○ Transmission Control Protocol (TCP)/User Datagram Protocol (UDP) headers
  ○ TCP flags
  ○ Payload
  ○ Maximum transmission unit (MTU)
	1: The Seven-Layer OSI Model
	
	4: TCP/IP Core Protocols
	
	9: Routing Protocols
		Understand

1.2 Explain the characteristics of network topologies and network types.
 	
• Mesh
• Star/hub-and-spoke
• Bus
• Ring
• Hybrid
• Network types and characteristics
  ○ Peer-to-peer
  ○ Client-server
  ○ Local area network (LAN)
  ○ Metropolitan area network (MAN)
  ○ Wide area network (WAN)
  ○ Wireless local area network (WLAN)
  ○ Personal area network (PAN)
  ○ Campus area network (CAN)
  ○ Storage area network (SAN)
  ○ Software-defined wide area network (SDWAN)
  ○ Multiprotocol label switching (MPLS)
  ○ Multipoint generic routing encapsulation (mGRE)
• Service-related entry point
  ○ Demarcation point
  ○ Smartjack
• Virtual network concepts
  ○ vSwitch
  ○ Virtual network interface card (vNIC)
  ○ Network function virtualization (NFV)
  ○ Hypervisor
• Provider links
  ○ Satellite
  ○ Digital subscriber line (DSL)
  ○ Cable
  ○ Leased line
  ○ Metro-optical
	1: Network Models
	
	1: Network Hardware
	
	2: Components of Structured Cabling
	
	4: Remote Access Protocols
	
	6: Characteristics of Wireless Transmissions
	
	7: Physical Architecture
	
	7: Virtual Architecture
	
	9: WAN Essentials
	
	9: WAN Connectivity
	
	9: Wireless WANs
		Understand

Objective	Section	Bloom's Taxonomy

1.3 Summarize the types of cables and connectors and explain which is the appropriate type for a solution.
 	
• Copper
  ○ Twisted pair
    ▪ Cat 5
    ▪ Cat 5e
    ▪ Cat 6
    ▪ Cat 6a
    ▪ Cat 7
    ▪ Cat 8
  ○ Coaxial/RG-6
  ○ Twinaxial
  ○ Termination standards
    ▪ TIA/EIA-568A
    ▪ TIA/EIA-568B
• Fiber
  ○ Single-mode
  ○ Multimode
• Connector types
  ○ Local connector (LC), straight tip (ST), subscriber connector (SC), mechanical transfer (MT), registered jack (RJ)
    ▪ Angled physical contact (APC)
    ▪ Ultra-physical contact (UPC)
  ○ RJ11
  ○ RJ45
  ○ F-type connector
  ○ Transceivers/media converters
  ○ Transceiver type
    ▪ Small form-factor pluggable (SFP)
    ▪ Enhanced form-factor pluggable (SFP+)
    ▪ Quad small form-factor pluggable (QSFP)
    ▪ Enhanced quad small form-factor pluggable (QSFP+)
• Cable management
  ○ Patch panel/patch bay
  ○ Fiber distribution panel
  ○ Punchdown block
    ▪ 66
    ▪ 110
    ▪ Krone
    ▪ Bix
• Ethernet standards
  ○ Copper
    ▪ 10BASE-T
    ▪ 100BASE-TX
    ▪ 1000BASE-T
    ▪ 10GBASE-T
    ▪ 40GBASE-T
  ○ Fiber
    ▪ 100BASE-FX
    ▪ 100BASE-SX
    ▪ 1000BASE-SX
    ▪ 1000BASE-LX
    ▪ 10GBASE-SR
    ▪ 10GBASE-LR
    ▪ Coarse wavelength division multiplexing (CWDM)
    ▪ Dense wavelength division multiplexing (DWDM)
    ▪ Bidirectional wavelength division multiplexing (WDM)
	2: Components of Structured Cabling
	
	5: Transmission Basics
	
	5: Copper Cable
	
	5: Fiber-Optic Cable
		Understand

Objective	Section	Bloom's Taxonomy

1.4 Given a scenario, configure a subnet and use appropriate IP addressing schemes.
 	
• Public vs. private
  ○ RFC1918
  ○ Network address translation (NAT)
  ○ Port address translation (PAT)
• IPv4 vs. IPv6
  ○ Automatic Private IP Addressing (APIPA)
  ○ Extended unique identifier (EUI-64)
  ○ Multicast
  ○ Unicast
  ○ Anycast
  ○ Broadcast
  ○ Link local
  ○ Loopback
  ○ Default gateway
• IPv4 subnetting
  ○ Classless (variable-length subnet mask)
  ○ Classful
    ▪ A
    ▪ B
    ▪ C
    ▪ D
    ▪ E
  ○ Classless Inter-Domain Routing (CIDR) notation
• IPv6 concepts
  ○ Tunneling
  ○ Dual stack
  ○ Shorthand notation
  ○ Router advertisement
  ○ Stateless address autoconfiguration (SLAAC)
• Virtual IP (VIP)
• Subinterfaces
	3: IP Addresses
	
	7: Network Availability
	
	8: Subnet Masks
	
	8: Calculating Subnets
	
	8: Virtual LANs (VLANs)
		Apply

Objective	Section	Bloom's Taxonomy

1.5 Explain common ports and protocols, their application, and encrypted alternatives.
 	
Protocols and Ports
 	
• File Transfer Protocol (FTP)   20/21
• Secure Shell (SSH)   22
• Secure File Transfer Protocol (SFTP)   22
• Telnet   23
• Simple Mail Transfer Protocol (SMTP)   25
• Domain Name System (DNS)   53
• Dynamic Host Configuration Protocol (DHCP)   67/68
• Trivial File Transfer Protocol (TFTP)   69
• Hypertext Transfer Protocol (HTTP)   80
• Post Office Protocol v3 (POP3)   110
• Network Time Protocol (NTP)   123
• Internet Message Access Protocol (IMAP)   143
• Simple Network Management Protocol (SNMP)   161/162
• Lightweight Directory Access Protocol (LDAP)   389
• Hypertext Transfer Protocol Secure (HTTPS) [Secure Sockets Layer (SSL)]   443
• HTTPS [Transport Layer Security (TLS)]   443
• Server Message Block (SMB)   445
• Syslog   514
• SMTP TLS   587
• Lightweight Directory Access Protocol (over SSL) (LDAPS)   636
• IMAP over SSL   993
• POP3 over SSL   995
• Structured Query Language (SQL) Server   1433
• SQLnet   1521
• MySQL   3306
• Remote Desktop Protocol (RDP)   3389
• Session Initiation Protocol (SIP)   5060/5061
• IP protocol types
  ○ Internet Control Message Protocol (ICMP)
  ○ TCP
  ○ UDP
  ○ Generic Routing Encapsulation (GRE)
  ○ Internet Protocol Security (IPSec)
    ■ Authentication Header (AH)/Encapsulating Security Payload (ESP)
• Connectionless vs. connection-oriented
	1: Client-Server Applications
	
	2: Components of Structured Cabling
	
	3: Ports and Sockets
	
	3: Troubleshooting Address Problems
	
	4: TCP/IP Core Protocols
	
	4: Encryption Protocols
	
	4: Remote Access Protocols
	
	11: Authentication Technologies
	
	12: Collect Network Data
		Understand

Objective	Section	Bloom's Taxonomy
1.6 Explain the use and purpose of network services.	3: IP Addresses	Understand

• DHCP
 ○ Scope
 ○ Exclusion ranges
 ○ Reservation
 ○ Dynamic assignment
 ○ Static assignment
 ○ Lease time
 ○ Scope options
 ○ Available leases
 ○ DHCP relay
 ○ IP helper/UDP forwarding
• DNS
 ○ Record types
  ▪ Address (A)
  ▪ Canonical name (CNAME)
  ▪ Mail exchange (MX)
  ▪ Authentication, authorization, accounting, auditing (AAAA)
  ▪ Start of authority (SOA)
  ▪ Pointer (PTR)
  ▪ Text (TXT)
  ▪ Service (SRV)
  ▪ Name server (NS)
 ○ Global hierarchy
  ▪ Root DNS servers
  ▪ Internal vs. external
  ▪ Zone transfers
  ▪ Authoritative name servers
  ▪ Time to live (TTL)
  ▪ DNS caching
  ▪ Reverse DNS/reverse lookup/forward lookup
  ▪ Recursive lookup/iterative lookup
• NTP
 ○ Stratum
 ○ Clients
 ○ Servers
	3: Ports and Sockets
	
	3: Domain Names and DNS
	
	8: Calculating Subnets	

Objective	Section	Bloom's Taxonomy

1.7 Explain basic corporate and datacenter network architecture.
 	
• Three-tiered
  ○ Core
  ○ Distribution/aggregation layer
  ○ Access/edge
• Software-defined networking
  ○ Application layer
  ○ Control layer
  ○ Infrastructure layer
  ○ Management plane
• Spine and leaf
  ○ Software-defined network
  ○ Top-of-rack switching
  ○ Backbone
• Traffic flows
  ○ North-South
  ○ East-West
• Branch office vs. on-premises datacenter vs. colocation
• Storage area networks
  ○ Connection types
    ▪ Fibre Channel over Ethernet (FCoE)
    ▪ Fibre Channel
    ▪ Internet Small Computer Systems Interface (iSCSI)
	7: Physical Architecture
	
	7: Cloud Architecture
		Understand

1.8 Summarize cloud concepts and connectivity options.
 	
• Deployment models
  ○ Public
  ○ Private
  ○ Hybrid
  ○ Community
• Service models
  ○ Software as a service (SaaS)
  ○ Infrastructure as a service (IaaS)
  ○ Platform as a service (PaaS)
  ○ Desktop as a service (DaaS)
• Infrastructure as code
  ○ Automation/orchestration
• Connectivity options
  ○ Virtual private network (VPN)
  ○ Private-direct connection to cloud provider
• Multitenancy
• Elasticity
• Scalability
• Security implications
	7: Cloud Architecture
	
	9: WAN Connectivity
	
	11: Network Security Tools
		Understand

DOMAIN 2.0 NETWORK IMPLEMENTATIONS—19% OF EXAMINATION

Objective	Section	Bloom's Taxonomy

2.1 Compare and contrast various devices, their features, and their appropriate placement on the network.
 	
• Networking devices
 ○ Layer 2 switch
 ○ Layer 3 capable switch
 ○ Router
 ○ Hub
 ○ Access point
 ○ Bridge
 ○ Wireless LAN controller
 ○ Load balancer
 ○ Proxy server
 ○ Cable modem
 ○ DSL modem
 ○ Repeater
 ○ Voice gateway
 ○ Media converter
 ○ Intrusion prevention system (IPS)/intrusion detection system (IDS) device
 ○ Firewall
 ○ VPN headend
• Networked devices
 ○ Voice over Internet Protocol (VoIP) phone
 ○ Printer
 ○ Physical access control devices
 ○ Cameras
 ○ Heating, ventilation, and air conditioning (HVAC) sensors
 ○ Internet of Things (IoT)
  ▪ Refrigerator
  ▪ Smart speakers
  ▪ Smart thermostats
  ▪ Smart doorbells
 ○ Industrial control systems/supervisory control and data acquisition (SCADA)
	1: Network Hardware
	
	1: The Seven-Layer OSI Model
	
	2: Components of Structured Cabling
	
	3: Ports and Sockets
	
	4: Remote Access Protocols
	
	5: Transmission Basics
	
	5: Fiber-Optic Cable
	
	6: Characteristics of Wireless Transmissions
	
	7: Physical Architecture
	
	7: Network Availability
	
	9: WAN Connectivity
	
	10: Physical Security
	
	11: Network Security Tools
		Understand

2.2 Compare and contrast routing technologies and bandwidth management concepts.
 	
• Routing
 ○ Dynamic routing
  ▪ Protocols [Routing Internet Protocol (RIP), Open Shortest Path First (OSPF), Enhanced Interior Gateway Routing Protocol (EIGRP), Border Gateway Protocol (BGP)]
  ▪ Link state vs. distance vector vs. hybrid
 ○ Static routing
 ○ Default route
 ○ Administrative distance
 ○ Exterior vs. interior
 ○ Time to live
• Bandwidth management
 ○ Traffic shaping
 ○ Quality of service (QoS)
	9: Routing Protocols
	
	9: WAN Connectivity
	
	12: Manage Network Traffic
		Understand

Objective	Section	Bloom's Taxonomy

2.3 Given a scenario, configure and deploy common Ethernet switching features.
 	
• Data virtual local area network (VLAN)
• Voice VLAN
• Port configurations
  ○ Port tagging/802.1Q
  ○ Port aggregation
    ▪ Link Aggregation Control Protocol (LACP)
  ○ Duplex
  ○ Speed
  ○ Flow control
  ○ Port mirroring
  ○ Port security
  ○ Jumbo frames
  ○ Auto-medium-dependent interface crossover (MDI-X)
• Media access control (MAC) address tables
• Power over Ethernet (PoE)/Power over Ethernet plus (PoE+)
• Spanning Tree Protocol
• Carrier-sense multiple access with collision detection (CSMA/CD)
• Address Resolution Protocol (ARP)
• Neighbor Discovery Protocol
	3: Addressing Overview
	4: TCP/IP Core Protocols
	5: Transmission Basics
	5: Copper Cable
	7: Physical Architecture
	7: Network Availability
	8: Virtual LANs (VLANs)
	11: Network Security Tools
	12: Collect Network Data
	12: Manage Network Traffic
		Apply

2.4 Given a scenario, install and configure the appropriate wireless standards and technologies.
 	
• 802.11 standards
  ○ a
  ○ b
  ○ g
  ○ n (WiFi 4)
  ○ ac (WiFi 5)
  ○ ax (WiFi 6)
• Frequencies and range
  ○ 2.4GHz
  ○ 5GHz
• Channels
  ○ Regulatory impacts
• Channel bonding
• Service set identifier (SSID)
  ○ Basic service set
  ○ Extended service set
  ○ Independent basic service set (Ad-hoc)
  ○ Roaming
• Antenna types
  ○ Omni
  ○ Directional
• Encryption standards
  ○ WiFi Protected Access (WPA)/WPA2 Personal [Advanced Encryption Standard (AES)/Temporal Key Integrity Protocol (TKIP)]
  ○ WPA/WPA2 Enterprise (AES/TKIP)
• Cellular technologies
  ○ Code-division multiple access (CDMA)
  ○ Global System for Mobile Communications (GSM)
  ○ Long-Term Evolution (LTE)
  ○ 3G, 4G, 5G
• Multiple input, multiple output (MIMO) and multi-user MIMO (MU-MIMO)
	6: Characteristics of Wireless Transmissions
	9: Wireless WANs
		Apply

DOMAIN 3.0 NETWORK OPERATIONS—16% OF EXAMINATION

Objective	Section	Bloom's Taxonomy

3.1 Given a scenario, use the appropriate statistics and sensors to ensure network availability.
 	
• Performance metrics/sensors
  ○ Device/chassis
    ▪ Temperature
    ▪ Central processing unit (CPU) usage
    ▪ Memory
  ○ Network metrics
    ▪ Bandwidth
    ▪ Latency
    ▪ Jitter
• SNMP
  ○ Traps
  ○ Object identifiers (OIDs)
  ○ Management information bases (MIBs)
• Network device logs
  ○ Log reviews
    ▪ Traffic logs
    ▪ Audit logs
    ▪ Syslog
  ○ Logging levels/severity levels
• Interface statistics/status
  ○ Link state (up/down)
  ○ Speed/duplex
  ○ Send/receive traffic
  ○ Cyclic redundancy checks (CRCs)
  ○ Protocol packet and byte counts
• Interface errors or alerts
  ○ CRC errors
  ○ Giants
  ○ Runts
  ○ Encapsulation errors
• Environmental factors and sensors
  ○ Temperature
  ○ Humidity
  ○ Electrical
  ○ Flooding
• Baselines
• NetFlow data
• Uptime/downtime
	2: Components of Structured Cabling
	
	5: Transmission Basics
	
	7: Cloud Architecture
	
	9: Troubleshooting Connections
	
	12: Collect Network Data
	
	12: Manage Network Traffic
		Apply

Objective	Section	Bloom's Taxonomy

3.2 Explain the purpose of organizational documents and policies.
 	
• Plans and procedures
  ○ Change management
  ○ Incident response plan
  ○ Disaster recovery plan
  ○ Business continuity plan
  ○ System life cycle
  ○ Standard operating procedures
• Hardening and security policies
  ○ Password policy
  ○ Acceptable use policy
  ○ Bring your own device (BYOD) policy
  ○ Remote access policy
  ○ Onboarding and offboarding policy
  ○ Security policy
  ○ Data loss prevention
• Common documentation
  ○ Physical network diagram
    ▪ Floor plan
    ▪ Rack diagram
    ▪ Intermediate distribution frame (IDF)/main distribution frame (MDF) documentation
  ○ Logical network diagram
  ○ Wiring diagram
  ○ Site survey report
  ○ Audit and assessment report
  ○ Baseline configurations
• Common agreements
  ○ Non-disclosure agreement (NDA)
  ○ Service-level agreement (SLA)
  ○ Memorandum of understanding (MOU)
	2: Network Documentation
	
	2: Change Management
	
	4: Remote Access Protocols
	
	10: Security Risks
	
	10: Security Assessment
	
	10: Device Hardening
	
	10: Security Policies for Users
	
	12: Plan Response and Recovery Strategies
		Understand

Objective	Section	Bloom's Taxonomy

3.3 Explain high availability and disaster recovery concepts and summarize which is the best solution.
 	
• Load balancing
• Multipathing
• Network interface card (NIC) teaming
• Redundant hardware/clusters
  ° Switches
  ° Routers
  ° Firewalls
• Facilities and infrastructure support
  ° Uninterruptible power supply (UPS)
  ° Power distribution units (PDUs)
  ° Generator
  ° HVAC
  ° Fire suppression
• Redundancy and high availability (HA) concepts
  ° Cold site
  ° Warm site
  ° Hot site
  ° Cloud site
  ° Active-active vs. active-passive
    • Multiple Internet service providers (ISPs)/ diverse paths
    • Virtual Router Redundancy Protocol (VRRP)/ First Hop Redundancy Protocol (FHRP)
  ° Mean time to repair (MTTR)
  ° Mean time between failure (MTBF)
  ° Recovery time objective (RTO)
  ° Recovery point objective (RPO)
• Network device backup/restore
  ° State
  ° Configuration
	1: Safety Procedures and Policies
	
	2: Components of Structured Cabling
	
	7: Physical Architecture
	
	7: Network Availability
	
	9: Routing Protocols
	
	11: Network Security Tools
	
	12: Plan Response and Recovery Strategies
		Understand

DOMAIN 4.0 NETWORK SECURITY—19% OF EXAMINATION

Objective	Section	Bloom's Taxonomy
4.1 Explain common security concepts.	4: Encryption Protocols	Understand
• Confidentiality, integrity, availability (CIA)	4: Troubleshooting Network Issues	
• Threats		
○ Internal	6: Wi-Fi Network Security	
○ External	7: Physical Architecture	
• Vulnerabilities		
○ Common vulnerabilities and exposures (CVE)	8: Network Segmentation	
○ Zero-day	8: Virtual LANs (VLANs)	
• Exploits	10: Security Risks	
• Least privilege	10: Security Assessment	
• Role-based access		
• Zero Trust	10: Device Hardening	
• Defense in depth	11: Network Hardening by Design	
○ Network segmentation enforcement		
○ Screened subnet [previously known as demilitarized zone (DMZ)]	11: Network Security Tools	
○ Separation of duties	11: Authentication, Authorization, and Accounting (AAA)	
○ Network access control		
○ Honeypot	11: Authentication Technologies	
• Authentication methods		
○ Multifactor		
○ Terminal Access Controller Access-Control System Plus (TACACS+)		
○ Single sign-on (SSO)		
○ Remote Authentication Dial-in User Service (RADIUS)		
○ LDAP		
○ Kerberos		
○ Local authentication		
○ 802.1X		
○ Extensible Authentication Protocol (EAP)		
• Risk Management		
○ Security risk assessments		
■ Threat assessment		
■ Vulnerability assessment		
■ Penetration testing		
■ Posture assessment		
○ Business risk assessments		
■ Process assessment		
■ Vendor assessment		
• Security information and event management (SIEM)		

Objective	Section	Bloom's Taxonomy

4.2 Compare and contrast common types of attacks.
 	
• Technology-based
  ○ Denial-of-service (DoS)/distributed denial-of-service (DDoS)
    ▪ Botnet/command and control
  ○ On-path attack (previously known as man-in-the-middle attack)
  ○ DNS poisoning
  ○ VLAN hopping
  ○ ARP spoofing
  ○ Rogue DHCP
  ○ Rogue access point (AP)
  ○ Evil twin
  ○ Ransomware
  ○ Password attacks
    ▪ Brute-force
    ▪ Dictionary
  ○ MAC spoofing
  ○ IP spoofing
  ○ Deauthentication
  ○ Malware
• Human and environmental
  ○ Social engineering
    ▪ Phishing
    ▪ Tailgating
    ▪ Piggybacking
    ▪ Shoulder surfing
	4: Remote Access Protocols
	
	4: Troubleshooting Network Issues
	
	6: Wi-Fi Network Security
	
	8: Virtual LANs (VLANs)
	
	10: Security Risks
	
	10: Security Policies for Users
	
	11: Network Hardening by Design
		Understand

Objective	Section	Bloom's Taxonomy

4.3 Given a scenario, apply network hardening techniques.
 	
• Best practices
  ◦ Secure SNMP
  ◦ Router Advertisement (RA) Guard
  ◦ Port security
  ◦ Dynamic ARP inspection
  ◦ Control plane policing
  ◦ Private VLANs
  ◦ Disable unneeded switchports
  ◦ Disable unneeded network services
  ◦ Change default passwords
  ◦ Password complexity/length
  ◦ Enable DHCP snooping
  ◦ Change default VLAN
  ◦ Patch and firmware management
  ◦ Access control list
  ◦ Role-based access
  ◦ Firewall rules
    ▪ Explicit deny
    ▪ Implicit deny
• Wireless security
  ◦ MAC filtering
  ◦ Antenna placement
  ◦ Power levels
  ◦ Wireless client isolation
  ◦ Guest network isolation
  ◦ Preshared keys (PSKs)
  ◦ EAP
  ◦ Geofencing
  ◦ Captive portal
• IoT access considerations
	2: Change Management
	6: Wi-Fi Network Security
	7: Physical Architecture
	8: Virtual LANs (VLANs)
	10: Device Hardening
	10: Security Policies for Users
	11: Network Hardening by Design
	11: Network Security Tools
	11: Authentication, Authorization, and Accounting (AAA)
	12: Collect Network Data
		Apply

4.4 Compare and contrast remote access methods and security implications.
 	
• Site-to-site VPN
• Client-to-site VPN
  ◦ Clientless VPN
  ◦ Split tunnel vs. full tunnel
• Remote desktop connection
• Remote desktop gateway
• SSH
• Virtual network computing (VNC)
• Virtual desktop
• Authentication and authorization considerations
• In-band vs. out-of-band management
	4: Remote Access Protocols
	11: Authentication, Authorization, and Accounting (AAA)
		Understand

Objective	Section	Bloom's Taxonomy

4.5 Explain the importance of physical security.
 	
• Detection methods
  ○ Camera
  ○ Motion detection
  ○ Asset tags
  ○ Tamper detection
• Prevention methods
  ○ Employee training
  ○ Access control hardware
    ▪ Badge readers
    ▪ Biometrics
  ○ Locking racks
  ○ Locking cabinets
  ○ Access control vestibule (previously known as a mantrap)
  ○ Smart lockers
• Asset disposal
  ○ Factory reset/wipe configuration
  ○ Sanitize devices for disposal
	10: Security Risks
	
	10: Physical Security
	
	10: Device Hardening
		Understand

DOMAIN 5.0 NETWORK TROUBLESHOOTING—22% OF EXAMINATION

Objective	Section	Bloom's Taxonomy

5.1 Explain the network troubleshooting methodology.
 	
• Identify the problem
  ○ Gather information
  ○ Question users
  ○ Identify symptoms
  ○ Determine if anything has changed
  ○ Duplicate the problem, if possible
  ○ Approach multiple problems individually
• Establish a theory of probable cause
  ○ Question the obvious
  ○ Consider multiple approaches
    ▪ Top-to-bottom/bottom-to-top OSI model
    ▪ Divide and conquer
• Test the theory to determine the cause
  ○ If the theory is confirmed, determine the next steps to resolve the problem
  ○ If the theory is not confirmed, reestablish a new theory or escalate
• Establish a plan of action to resolve the problem and identify potential effects
• Implement the solution or escalate as necessary
• Verify full system functionality and, if applicable, implement preventive measures
• Document findings, actions, outcomes, and lessons learned
	1: Troubleshooting Network Problems	Understand

Objective	Section	Bloom's Taxonomy
5.2 Given a scenario, troubleshoot common cable connectivity issues and select the appropriate tools. • Specifications and limitations ○ Throughput ○ Speed ○ Distance • Cable considerations ○ Shielded and unshielded ○ Plenum and riser-rated • Cable application ○ Rollover cable/console cable ○ Crossover cable ○ Power over Ethernet • Common issues ○ Attenuation ○ Interference ○ Decibel (dB) loss ○ Incorrect pinout ○ Bad ports ○ Open/short ○ Light-emitting diode (LED) status indicators ○ Incorrect transceivers ○ Duplexing issues ○ Transmit and receive (TX/RX) reversed ○ Dirty optical cables • Common tools ○ Cable crimper ○ Punchdown tool ○ Tone generator ○ Loopback adapter ○ Optical time-domain reflectometer (OTDR) ○ Multimeter ○ Cable tester ○ Wire map ○ Tap ○ Fusion splicers ○ Spectrum analyzers ○ Snips/cutters ○ Cable stripper ○ Fiber light meter	2: Components of Structured Cabling 5: Transmission Basics 5: Copper Cable 5: Fiber-Optic Cable 5: Cable Troubleshooting Tools 6: Troubleshooting Wi-Fi Networks 11: Network Security Tools	Analyze

Objective	Section	Bloom's Taxonomy

5.3 Given a scenario, use the appropriate network software tools and commands.
 	
• Software tools
  ○ WiFi analyzer
  ○ Protocol analyzer/packet capture
  ○ Bandwidth speed tester
  ○ Port scanner
  ○ iperf
  ○ NetFlow analyzers
  ○ Trivial File Transfer Protocol (TFTP) server
  ○ Terminal emulator
  ○ IP scanner
• Command line tools
  ○ ping
  ○ ipconfig/ifconfig/ip
  ○ nslookup/dig
  ○ traceroute/tracert
  ○ arp
  ○ netstat
  ○ hostname
  ○ route
  ○ telnet
  ○ tcpdump
  ○ nmap
• Basic network platform commands
  ○ show interface
  ○ show config
  ○ show route
	2: Network Documentation
	
	3: Troubleshooting Address Problems
	
	4: TCP/IP Core Protocols
	
	4: Remote Access Protocols
	
	4: Troubleshooting Network Issues
	
	6: Troubleshooting Wi-Fi Networks
	
	9: Routing Protocols
	
	9: WAN Connectivity
	
	9: Troubleshooting Connections
	
	10: Security Assessment
	
	12: Collect Network Data
	
	12: Manage Network Traffic
		Apply

5.4 Given a scenario, troubleshoot common wireless connectivity issues.
 	
• Specifications and limitations
  ○ Throughput
  ○ Speed
  ○ Distance
  ○ Received signal strength indication (RSSI) signal strength
  ○ Effective isotropic radiated power (EIRP)/power settings
• Considerations
  ○ Antennas
    ▪ Placement
    ▪ Type
    ▪ Polarization
  ○ Channel utilization
  ○ AP association time
  ○ Site survey
• Common issues
  ○ Interference
    ▪ Channel overlap
  ○ Antenna cable attenuation/signal loss
  ○ RF attenuation/signal loss
  ○ Wrong SSID
  ○ Incorrect passphrase
  ○ Encryption protocol mismatch
  ○ Insufficient wireless coverage
  ○ Captive portal issues
  ○ Client disassociation issues
	6: Characteristics of Wireless Transmissions
	
	6: Wi-Fi Network Security
	
	6: Troubleshooting Wi-Fi Networks
		Analyze

Objective	Section	Bloom's Taxonomy
5.5 Given a scenario, troubleshoot general networking issues. • Considerations ○ Device configuration review ○ Routing tables ○ Interface status ○ VLAN assignment ○ Network performance baselines • Common issues ○ Collisions ○ Broadcast storm ○ Duplicate MAC address ○ Duplicate IP address ○ Multicast flooding ○ Asymmetrical routing ○ Switching loops ○ Routing loops ○ Rogue DHCP server ○ DHCP scope exhaustion ○ IP setting issues ▪ Incorrect gateway ▪ Incorrect subnet mask ▪ Incorrect IP address ▪ Incorrect DNS ○ Missing route ○ Low optical link budget ○ Certificate issues ○ Hardware failure ○ Host-based/network-based firewall settings ○ Blocked services, ports, or addresses ○ Incorrect VLAN ○ DNS issues ○ NTP issues ○ BYOD challenges ○ Licensed feature issues ○ Network performance issues	1: Troubleshooting Network Problems 3: IP Addresses 3: Troubleshooting Address Problems 4: TCP/IP Core Protocols 4: Troubleshooting Network Issues 5: Fiber-Optic Cable 7: Physical Architecture 8: Virtual LANs (VLANs) 9: Troubleshooting Connections 10: Device Hardening 10: Security Policies for Users 11: Network Hardening by Design 11: Network Security Tools 12: Manage Network Traffic	Analyze

VISUAL GUIDE TO CONNECTORS

Throughout this text, you learned about several different cabling and connector options that may be used on networks. Some, such as RJ-45 connectors, are very common, whereas others, such as MT-RJ connectors, are used only on high-speed optical networks. So that you can compare such connectors and ensure that you understand their differences, this appendix compiles drawings and photos of the connectors along with a brief summary of their uses in this simple table (see Table B-1). You must be familiar with the most popular types of connectors to qualify for CompTIA's Network+ certification. You can find more details about these connectors and the networks on which they are used in Module 5.

Table B-1 Cable connectors and their uses

Specification	Male connector (front view)	Male connector (side view)	Female receptacle (front view)	Application
BNC (Bayonet Neill-Concelman)				Used with coaxial cable for broadband cable connections
F-connector				Used on coaxial cable suitable for use with broadband video and data applications; more common than BNC connectors
RJ-11 (registered jack 11)				Used on twisted-pair cabling for telephone systems (and some older twisted-pair networks)
RJ-45 (registered jack 45)				Used on twisted-pair cabling for Ethernet (RJ-45) connections

(continues)

Table B-1 Cable connectors and their uses *(continued)*

Specification	Male connector (front view)	Male connector (side view)	Female receptacle (front view)	Application
ST (straight tip), usually multimode				Uses a bayonet locking mechanism; one of the first commercially available fiber connectors
SC (subscriber connector or standard connector)				Widely used; has a snap-in connector
LC (local connector), single-mode				Most common 2.5-mm ferrule; available in full-duplex mode
MT-RJ (Mechanical Transfer Registered Jack), multimode				Most common MMF; contains two strands of fiber per ferrule to provide full-duplex signaling

COMPTIA NETWORK+ PRACTICE EXAM

The following exam contains questions that are similar in content and format to the multiple-choice questions you will encounter on CompTIA's Network+ N10-008 certification exam, released in 2021. This practice exam consists of 100 questions, all of which are multiple choice. Some questions have more than one correct answer. The number of questions from each domain reflects the weighting that CompTIA assigned to these domains in its exam objectives. To simulate taking the CompTIA Network+ certification exam, allow yourself 90 minutes to answer all the questions.

1. To ensure that your private network is always protected, you decide to install three redundant firewalls. Which of the following would allow you to assign the same IP address to all three?
  a. SMTP
  b. CARP
  c. SNMPv3
  d. IMAP
  e. NTP

2. What Ethernet standard could use the connector shown here?

  a. 1000BASE-LX
  b. 10GBASE-T
  c. 100BASE-TX
  d. 1000BASE-T
  e. 5GBASE-T

3. While troubleshooting a workstation connectivity problem, you enter the following command: `ping 127.0.0.1`. The response indicates the test failed. What can you determine about that workstation?

  a. Its network cable is faulty or not connected to the wall jack.
  b. Its TCP/IP stack is not installed properly.
  c. It has been prevented from transmitting data past the default gateway.
  d. Its DHCP settings are incorrect.
  e. Its DNS name server specification is incorrect.

4. You have been asked to help improve network performance on a store's small office network. The network relies on two switches, two access points, and a router to connect its 18 employees to the Internet and other store locations. You decide to determine what type of traffic the network currently handles. In particular, you're interested in the volume of unnecessary broadcast traffic that might be bogging down shared segments. Which of the following tools will help you identify the percentage of traffic made up of broadcasts?
  a. Port scanner
  b. OTDR
  c. Protocol analyzer
  d. Multimeter
  e. Cable tester

5. Which of the following standards describes a security technique, often used on wireless networks, in which a port is prevented from receiving traffic until the transmitter's credentials are verified by an authentication server?

a. EAPoL

b. SSH

c. RADIUS

d. Kerberos

e. CCMP

6. Which of the following ports would be used during a domain name lookup?

a. 22

b. 23

c. 53

d. 110

e. 443

7. You are configuring a connection from a Windows server to a switch, and you want to make sure the connection doesn't fail or become overwhelmed by heavy traffic. Which of the following techniques would help you achieve both aims?

a. Multipathing

b. CARP

c. Clustering

d. Trunking

e. NIC teaming

8. As a network admin, you have decided to install additional physical security to the main office's data room. Due to the sensitivity of the data held in this room, you decide it's critical to ensure two-factor authentication before granting anyone access to the room. You already have a lock on the door. Which of the following physical security measures would provide 2FA?

a. Smart card

b. Fingerprint scanner

c. Keychain fob

d. Video surveillance

e. Proximity card

9. You have installed and configured two virtual web servers and a virtual mail server on a physical server. What networking mode will you assign to each server's vNIC to ensure that the virtual machines' clients on the Internet can access the virtual machines?

a. NAT

b. Bridged

c. Host-only

d. Internal

e. Grouped

10. At the beginning of the school year, students at your school must configure their computers and other devices to obtain trusted access to the student portion of the school's network. What is this process called?

a. Authenticating

b. Remote wiping

c. Associating

d. Onboarding

e. Social engineering

11. When using NAT, how does an IP gateway ensure that outgoing traffic can traverse public networks?

a. It modifies each outgoing frame's Type field to indicate that the transmission is destined for a public network.

b. It assigns each outgoing packet a masked ID via the Options field.

c. It replaces each outgoing packet's Source address field with a public IP address.

d. It interprets the contents of outgoing packets to ensure that they contain no client-identifying information.

e. It modifies the frame length to create uniformly sized frames, called cells, which are required for public network transmission.

12. Which of these authentication techniques only encrypts the password when transmitting sign-in credentials?

a. RADIUS

b. TACACS+

c. Kerberos

d. Single sign-on

e. Local authentication

13. You are a networking technician in a radiology clinic where physicians use the network to transmit and store patients' diagnostic results. Shortly after a new wing, which contains X-ray and MRI (magnetic resonance imaging) machines, is added to the building, computers in that area begin having intermittent problems saving data to the file server. After you have gathered information, identified the symptoms, questioned users, and determined what has changed, what is your next step in troubleshooting this problem?

a. Establish a plan of action to resolve the problem.

b. Escalate the problem.

c. Document findings, actions, and outcomes.

d. Establish a theory of probable cause.

e. Implement the solution.

14. The software on a firewall you recently installed on your network examines each incoming packet. It blocks or allows traffic based on a set of

criteria—including source IP address, destination ports, and TCP flags—and it does not evaluate traffic in relation to other traffic. What type of system is this? *Choose two.*

a. Host-based firewall
b. Stateful firewall
c. Stateless firewall
d. Packet-filtering firewall
e. Application layer firewall

15. Suppose you are creating six subnets on a network that leases a group of class C IPv4 addresses. What subnet mask must you specify in your clients' configurations to maximize the number of host addresses available on each subnet?

a. 255.255.255.6
b. 255.255.255.128
c. 255.255.255.192
d. 255.255.255.224
e. 255.255.255.0

16. What would the command `route del default gw 192.168.5.1 eth1` accomplish on your Linux workstation?

a. Delete the default gateway's route to the host whose IP address is 192.168.5.1.
b. Remove the assignment of IP address 192.168.5.1 from the eth1 interface.
c. Remove the workstation's route to the default gateway whose IP address is 192.168.5.1.
d. Add a route from the workstation to the default gateway whose IP address is 192.168.5.1.
e. Remove the designation of default gateway, but keep the route for the host whose IP address is 192.168.5.1.

17. From your laptop, you need to remote into a switch to make some configuration changes. Which transport layer protocol and TCP/IP port should you open in Windows Firewall to make this work using Telnet?

a. UDP, port 23
b. TCP, port 23
c. UDP, port 22
d. TCP, port 22
e. UDP, port 21

18. Recently, your company's WAN experienced a disabling DDoS attack. Which of the following devices could detect such an attack and prevent it from affecting your network in the future?

a. A honeypot
b. SIEM
c. HIPS
d. HIDS
e. NIPS

19. Which of the following routing protocols offer fast convergence times and can be used on both core and edge routers? *Choose two.*

a. RIPv2
b. IS-IS
c. OSPF
d. BGP
e. EIGRP

20. A friend calls you for help with his home office Internet connection. He is using an 802.11n wireless router connected to a DSL modem. The router's private IP address is 192.168.1.1, and it has been assigned an Internet routable IP address of 76.83.124.35. Your friend cannot connect to any resources on the Internet using his new Windows workstation. You ask him to run the `ipconfig` command and read the results to you. He says his workstation's IP address is 192.168.1.3, the subnet mask is 255.255.255.0, and the default gateway address is 192.168.1.10. What do you advise him to do next?

a. Display his DNS information.
b. Change his gateway address.
c. Change his subnet mask.
d. Try pinging the loopback address.
e. Use the `tracert` command to contact the access point/router.

21. Your organization contracts with a cloud service provider to store some backup data. The company promises 99.999 percent uptime. If it lives up to its claims, what is the maximum number of minutes each year you can expect your data to be unavailable?

a. Approximately 448 minutes
b. Approximately 199 minutes
c. Approximately 52 minutes
d. Approximately 14 minutes
e. Approximately 5 minutes

22. In a spine-and-leaf architecture, what type of switch is typically connected to a spine layer switch?

a. Core switch
b. Distribution switch
c. Access switch
d. Leaf switch
e. Spine switch

23. What STP configuration ensures that a laptop connected to a switch cannot alter the STP paths on the network?

a. BPDU filter
b. BPDU guard
c. Root bridge
d. BID
e. Designated port

24. What is the default subnet mask for the IP address 154.13.44.87?
    a. 255.255.255.255
    b. 255.255.255.0
    c. 255.255.0.0
    d. 255.0.0.0
    e. 0.0.0.0

25. Your CFO has approved installing new backbone cabling on your school's campus. One of the buildings is particularly far away from the others, nearly a kilometer. Which Ethernet standard will reach the distant building without the use of a repeater?
    a. 10GBASE-T
    b. 1000BASE-LX
    c. 1000BASE-SX
    d. 10GBASE-SR
    e. 1000BASE-T

26. Which of the following is often used to secure data traveling over VPNs that use L2TP?
    a. OpenVPN
    b. GRE
    c. Kerberos
    d. SSH
    e. IPsec

27. You are a support technician working in a data closet in a remote office. You suspect that a connectivity problem is related to a broken RJ-45 plug on a patch cable that connects a switch to a patch panel. You need to replace that connector, but you forgot to bring an extra patch cable. You decide to install a new RJ-45 connector to replace the broken connector. Which tools must you have to successfully accomplish this task? *Choose two.*
    a. Punchdown tool
    b. Cable crimper
    c. Wire cutter
    d. Cable tester
    e. Multimeter

28. You have purchased an outdoor access point capable of exchanging data via the 802.11n or 802.11ac wireless standard. According to these standards, what is the maximum distance, in meters, from the access point that wireless clients can travel and still reliably exchange data with the access point if there are no obstacles between them?
    a. 20
    b. 70
    c. 100
    d. 250
    e. 450

29. Which of the following is a single sign-on authentication method?
    a. IPsec
    b. EAPoL
    c. SSL
    d. Kerberos
    e. RADIUS

30. Your organization has just ordered its first leased line to the Internet. Prior to that, your organization relied on a DSL connection. Which of the following features will your subscription provide that no type of DSL offers?
    a. Dedicated bandwidth
    b. Low price
    c. Symmetrical bandwidth
    d. Local loop
    e. Modem

31. Your friend's printer isn't printing the document she just sent it. In what order should you perform the listed steps?
    a. Follow the OSI model from bottom to top to check possible causes, send a new document to the printer, and determine if anything has changed on her network.
    b. Send a new document to the printer, follow the OSI model from bottom to top to check possible causes, and ask your friend when the problem started.
    c. Take notes on the outcome, send a new document to the printer, and determine if anything has changed on her network.
    d. Determine if anything has changed on her network, follow the OSI model from bottom to top to check possible causes, and send a new document to the printer.
    e. Determine if anything has changed on her network, take notes on the outcome, and send a new document to the printer.

32. A CEO fires her administrative assistant after the assistant was caught stealing company funds. Over the weekend, the administrative assistant hacks into the CEO's private email account and steals some personal data. What type of attack did the former employee most likely use to accomplish this exploit?
    a. Brute force attack
    b. War driving
    c. Logic bomb
    d. Deauth attack
    e. On-path attack

33. What is the network ID for a class C network that contains the group of IP addresses from 194.73.44.10 through 194.73.44.254?
   a. 194.73.44.0
   b. 194.73.44.1
   c. 194.73.0.0
   d. 194.73.44.255
   e. 194.1.1.1

34. Your organization is reassessing its WAN connections to determine how much more bandwidth it will need to purchase in the next two years. As a network administrator, which of the following data can you share that will help management make the right decision?
   a. Wiring diagram
   b. Baseline
   c. Logical topology
   d. Syslog
   e. Change management documentation

35. You are creating a new Linux server as a virtual machine on your Windows workstation. Which of the following commands will tell you the IP address that is assigned to your virtual server?
   a. `ipconfig /all` at the Windows workstation's command prompt
   b. `ifconfig -a` at the Linux server's shell prompt
   c. `iptables` at the Linux server's shell prompt
   d. `ping` at the Linux server's shell prompt
   e. `ipconfig /all` at the Linux server's shell prompt

36. Which of the following requirements provide 2FA? *Choose two.*
   a. Iris pattern and typing pattern
   b. Password and name of first elementary school
   c. Location in a secured closet
   d. Smart card and key fob
   e. Fingerprint and name of first elementary school

37. You are rearranging nodes on your Gigabit Ethernet network. Due to a necessarily hasty expansion, you have decided to supply power to a wireless router in a makeshift data room using PoE. Which of the following is the cheapest cabling you could use to connect this wireless router to the network's backbone?
   a. RG-6
   b. RG-59
   c. Cat 5e
   d. SMF
   e. Cat 6

38. As you're setting up APs in your client's office space, you want to ensure that all work areas and the meeting room have adequate access to the network. What tool will give you the information you need?
   a. Geofencing
   b. Packet sniffer
   c. Bandwidth speed tester
   d. Wi-Fi analyzer
   e. Toner probe

39. Which of the following protocols encapsulates data for transmission over VPNs?
   a. SFTP
   b. L2TP
   c. VNC
   d. TCP
   e. TACACS+

40. Which of the following is a valid MAC address?
   a. C3:00:50:00:FF:FF
   b. 153.101.24.3
   c. ::9F53
   d. FE80::32:1CA3:B0E2
   e. D0:00:00:00

41. Which of the following services would be most important to disable on a Windows workstation? *Choose two.*
   a. SSH
   b. DHCP
   c. Telnet
   d. FTP
   e. RDP

42. It's Friday night, and you have just settled in with some hot cocoa and popcorn to watch one of your favorite movies on Netflix. Five minutes into the movie, you realize you're getting more stressed than relaxed, and then you realize the problem is that the movie keeps lagging, buffering, and skipping. What transmission flaw is probably the source of the problem?
   a. Crosstalk
   b. Jitter
   c. EMI
   d. Latency
   e. Attenuation

43. Where might you find publicized information about a backdoor to an application?
   a. CIA
   b. EAP
   c. SIEM
   d. CVE
   e. SSO

44. As you type in your PIN at the ATM, what risk can you protect yourself from by covering the keypad as you type?
    a. Piggybacking
    b. Phishing
    c. Tailgating
    d. Shoulder surfing
    e. Spoofing

45. After running the `show interface` command on a router, which field in the output indicates a damaged but minimally functioning cable?
    a. Giants
    b. BW
    c. CRC errors
    d. Runts
    e. Link state

46. You suspect that a machine on your network with the host name PRTSRV is issuing excessive broadcast traffic. What command can you use to determine this host's IP address?
    a. `netstat PRTSRV`
    b. `ipconfig PRTSRV`
    c. `ping -4 PRTSRV`
    d. `ifconfig -a PRTSRV`
    e. `ip address show PRTSRV`

47. You're installing a network management system and need to install software on various devices. What software must be installed on a managed device, such as a router?
    a. SIEM
    b. OID
    c. NMS
    d. Agent
    e. Syslog

48. You work for a small ISP. Several of your customers have called to complain about slow responses from a popular website. You suspect that network congestion is at fault. Which TCP/IP utility would help you determine where the congestion is occurring?
    a. ftp
    b. nslookup
    c. arp
    d. tracert
    e. telnet

49. You are a network administrator for a WAN that connects two regional insurance company offices—the main office and a branch office—to each other by a leased line. The main office is also connected to the Internet using a leased line. This leased line provides Internet access for both offices. To ensure that your private network is not compromised by unauthorized access through the Internet connection, you install a firewall between the main office and the Internet. Shortly thereafter, users in your branch office complain that they cannot access the file server in the main office, but users in the main office can still access the Internet. What configurations should you check? *Choose two.*
    a. Whether the firewall has been configured to run in promiscuous mode
    b. Whether the firewall is placed in the appropriate location on the network
    c. Whether the firewall has been configured to allow access from IP addresses in the branch office
    d. Whether the firewall has been configured to receive and transmit UDP-based packets
    e. Whether the firewall has been configured to allow Internet access over the main office's leased line

50. On an IPv6 network, which of the following is a host computer's loopback address?
    a. 1.0.0.1
    b. 127::1
    c. FE80::1
    d. ::1/128
    e. 127.0.0.1

51. In the process of troubleshooting an intermittent performance problem with your network's Internet connection, you attempt to run a tracert test to *microsoft.com*. The tracert response displays the first 12 hops in the route but then presents several "Request timed out" messages in a row. What is the most likely reason for this result?
    a. Your network's ISP is experiencing connectivity problems.
    b. Microsoft's network is bounded by firewalls that do not accept incoming ICMP traffic.
    c. The Internet backbone is experiencing traffic congestion.
    d. Your client's TCP/IP service limits the `tracert` command to a maximum of 12 hops.
    e. Your IP gateway failed while you were attempting the tracert test.

52. You are setting up a new Windows 10 client to connect with your LAN, which relies on DHCP. Which of the following must you do to ensure that the client obtains correct TCP/IP information via DHCP?
    a. Make certain the client's computer name and host name are identical.
    b. Enter the client's MAC address in the DHCP server's ARP table.

c. Enter the DHCP server address in the Windows TCP/IP configuration.

d. Nothing; in Windows 10, the DHCP option is selected by default.

e. Enter a default gateway address in the Windows TCP/IP configuration.

53. Due to popular demand from employees who need to roam from one floor of your office building to another, you are expanding your wireless network. You want to ensure that mobile users enjoy uninterrupted network connectivity without having to reconfigure their workstations' wireless network connection settings as they travel throughout the office space. Which of the following variables must you configure on your new access points to match the settings on existing access points?

a. Administrator password

b. Scanning rate

c. ESSID

d. IP address

e. RSSI

54. You have installed a protocol analyzer on your laptop and connected the laptop to a switch on your network's backbone. You want to monitor all traffic on a specific VLAN. Which feature must you configure on the switch to make this work?

a. Trunking

b. Port mirroring

c. Looping

d. Spanning Tree Protocol

e. Caching

55. Which of the following does *not* accurately describe TACACS+ in comparison to RADIUS?

a. TACACS+ relies on TCP, not UDP, at the transport layer.

b. TACACS+ is used to authenticate to a router or switch.

c. TACACS+ encrypts all information transmitted for AAA rather than just the password.

d. TACACS+ was developed for proprietary use on Cisco products.

e. TACACS+ operates as a software application on a remote access server.

56. You are part of a team participating in a posture assessment of your company's LAN. Which of the following tools or strategies will help you gain a broad understanding of your network's security vulnerabilities?

a. MIB

b. War driving

c. Nmap

d. DHCP snooping

e. CCMP

57. Which of the following devices can be used to separate broadcast domains? *Choose two.*

a. Router

b. Switch

c. Access point

d. Repeater

e. Hub

58. About a year ago, you purchased and installed a new router at one of your company's branch offices, and you have had nothing but problems with the router since. Today you called the vendor for the third time to have them send a technician to repair the router. They estimate the repair will be completed by the end of business tomorrow. In the meantime, you have decided that you would prefer to replace the router the next time it fails. What factor should you carefully investigate when shopping for a replacement, so you won't face this same scenario with the next router?

a. MTTR

b. UPS

c. MTBF

d. SLA

e. MIB

59. A 500-watt transmitted signal arrives at the receiver at 250 watts. What is the signal's dB loss?

a. 250 dB loss

b. 3 dB loss

c. 1000 dB loss

d. 6 dB loss

e. 1 dB loss

60. Which of the following figures reflects the type of physical topology most likely to be used on a 1000BASE-T network?

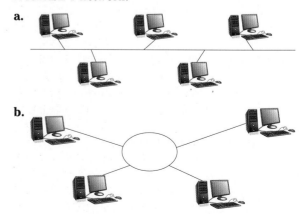

c.

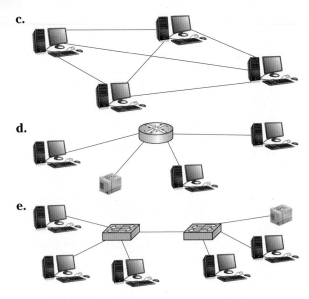

d.

e.

61. Your study partner is trying to access the Internet on her laptop, and it's not working. You offer to help, and you use her browser to try to go to google.com. That doesn't work. In a Command Prompt window, you ping google.com, which doesn't work either. You then ping 8.8.8.8, and it still doesn't work. You try to ping the network's gateway, and it fails. You ping your own computer, which is logged onto the same network, and it works. What is the most likely diagnosis of this problem?

   a. Exhausted DHCP scope

   b. Incorrect DNS server

   c. Incorrect gateway

   d. Duplicate IP address

   e. Incorrect subnet mask

62. You work for a small fashion design firm. Because of a video that recently went viral, your company has received national recognition. Within a few days, your web server crashes. What kind of attack most likely caused the crash?

   a. Phishing

   b. Friendly DoS

   c. Spoofing

   d. Ransomware

   e. Logic bomb

63. You have just installed Linux on an old laptop to bring it new life. Which of the following applications will provide the most protection for the computer when you connect it to the Internet?

   a. Defender

   b. Honeypot

   c. tcpdump

   d. iptables

   e. Wireshark

64. You are the network administrator for a large university whose network currently contains nearly 10,000 workstations, over 80 routers, 250 switches, and 500 printers. You are researching a proposal to upgrade the routers and switches on your network to primarily use multilayer switches instead. At the same time, you want to improve the management of your network devices. Which of the following protocols will help automate network management across all the new devices?

   a. TFTP

   b. SMTP

   c. NTP

   d. ICMP

   e. SNMP

65. Which of the following devices operate only at the physical layer of the OSI model? *Choose two.*

   a. Hub

   b. Switch

   c. Router

   d. Firewall

   e. Repeater

66. While making some configuration changes to a client's network, you need to connect your laptop to a router's console port. Which of the following connector types is most likely to be used for this purpose?

   a. RJ-11

   b. APC

   c. MT-RJ

   d. RJ-45

   e. F-connector

67. You have connected to your bank's home page. Its URL begins with *https://*. Based on this information, what type of security can you assume the bank employs for clients receiving and transmitting data to and from its web server?

   a. Kerberos

   b. TLS

   c. IPsec

   d. L2TP

   e. Packet-filtering firewall

68. Which of the following routing protocols has the poorest convergence time?

   a. EIGRP

   b. RIP

   c. BGP

   d. OSPF

   e. IS-IS

69. You need to gather some information about the traffic being broadcast and received on a Linux workstation. Unfortunately, you don't have time to install Wireshark. Which command can you use instead?

a. `tcpdump`

b. `telnet`

c. `traceroute`

d. `dig`

e. `nslookup`

70. To provide redundancy, you have to set up three links from a critical server to two redundant switches, both of which operate on the same subnet. Two connections from the server go to one switch, and the third link connects the other switch to the server. The server is running Windows Server 2019. What feature should you configure on the server to make these redundant links work together for load balancing and failover protection?

a. Port aggregation

b. NIC teaming

c. Flow control

d. Server cluster

e. Virtual IP address

71. A Windows workstation is configured to use DHCP, but it cannot find a DHCP server. You run `ipconfig` in PowerShell. Which of the following IP addresses is most likely reported by Windows?

a. 129.0.0.1

b. 255.255.255.0

c. 192.168.0.1

d. 169.254.1.120

e. 172.16.2.18

72. Used side-by-side with Kerberos, what service does LDAP provide Active Directory?

a. Accounting

b. Encryption

c. Auditing

d. Authorization

e. Authentication

73. In the following figure, if switch A suffers a failure, how will this failure affect nodes 1 through 3?

a. They will be unable to access the Internet or nodes 7 through 9.

b. They will be unable to access the Internet or any other nodes on the LAN.

c. They will only be unable to access the Internet.

d. They will be unable to access nodes 4 through 9.

e. Their connectivity will not be affected.

74. A file server on your network is running Ubuntu Server. You need to remote into it to make some configuration changes so that a new employee can access a group of files. The files are stored on an encrypted hard drive. Which of the following utilities will give you secure access to the server to make your reconfigurations?

a. RDP

b. SSH

c. SSL

d. SFTP

e. Telnet

75. You want to add five VMs on a server to the Staff VLAN at your office and two VMs to the Sales VLAN. Which of the following must your host machine's NIC support?

a. CSMA/CD

b. Channel bonding

c. MIMO

d. Trunking

e. OSPF

76. A regional bank manager asks you to help with an urgent network problem. Because of a sudden and severe network performance decline, the manager worries that the bank's network might be suffering a DoS attack. Viewing which of the following types of network documentation would probably give you the quickest insight into what's causing this problem?

a. Wiring diagram

b. Firewall log

c. Logical network diagram

d. The main file server's system log

e. Physical network diagram

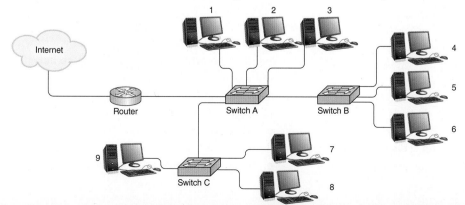

77. While troubleshooting a computer's connection to the network, you enter a command at the Command Prompt and see the following output. Which command did you enter?

```
Default Server:  google-public-dns-a.google.com
Address:  8.8.8.8

>
```

   a. `nslookup`
   b. `netstat`
   c. `arp -a`
   d. `tracert google.com`
   e. `ping 8.8.8.8`

78. Which of the following commands lists active TCP/IP connections on both Windows and Linux computers?
   a. `nslookup`
   b. `netstat`
   c. `hostname`
   d. `ipconfig`
   e. `route`

79. On which of the following devices would you *not* change the default administrative username and password when adding each device to your network?
   a. IP security camera
   b. Router
   c. Programmable thermostat
   d. Unmanaged switch
   e. Printer

80. Which of the following transmission media is most resistant to interference?
   a. Twinaxial cable
   b. Fiber-optic cable
   c. STP cable
   d. 802.11ac transmissions
   e. Coaxial cable

81. Which of the following cellular technologies uses time division to separate phone calls and Internet connections on a single channel?
   a. SIM
   b. GSM
   c. LTE
   d. CDMA
   e. LTE-Advanced

82. While troubleshooting a printer problem, you figured out the printer's static IP address had not been reserved on the DHCP server and so was mistakenly issued to a workstation. This caused a conflict and prevented users from accessing the printer. You have now configured the reservation in DHCP. What should you do next?
   a. Document the problem and your solution in your company's knowledge base.
   b. Close the service ticket.
   c. Report your findings to the network admin.
   d. Check that the printer is plugged into the wall outlet.
   e. Confirm that users can now print successfully.

83. How does STP prevent or stop broadcast storms?
   a. It examines the source IP address field in each broadcast packet and temporarily blocks traffic from that address.
   b. It enables routers to choose one set of best paths and ensures that alternate paths are used only when the best paths are obstructed.
   c. It enables switches to calculate paths that avoid potential loops and artificially blocks the links that would complete a loop.
   d. It allows switches to monitor IP address assignments on a network.
   e. It lets switches filter RA messages so these messages can only come from specific interfaces on the switch.

84. What is the function of protocols and services at the network layer of the OSI model?
   a. To manage the flow of communications in both directions during a session
   b. To add segmentation and assembly information
   c. To encode and encrypt data
   d. To add logical addresses and properly route data
   e. To apply electrical pulses to the wire

85. You have created a new web server on a computer running the Linux operating system. Some of the modules aren't loading correctly, and services are encountering errors. Which of the following applications should you check for information on these errors?
   a. Event Viewer
   b. IDS
   c. Packet sniffer
   d. NetFlow
   e. Syslog

86. Your 1000BASE-T network is wired following the TIA/EIA-568B standard. As you make your own patch cable, which wires do you crimp into pins 1 and 2 of the RJ-45 connector?
   a. White with green stripe and green
   b. White with brown stripe and brown
   c. White with blue stripe and blue
   d. White with red stripe and red
   e. White with orange stripe and orange

87. Which authentication technology issues tickets to give clients access to network services?
    a. Kerberos
    b. TACACS+
    c. RADIUS
    d. Multifactor authentication
    e. Diameter

88. Suppose your Windows laptop's wireless network adapter is configured to use the 802.11n wireless networking standard. Also, suppose a café you visit has a popular model of an 802.11ac access point. Assuming you have the correct SSID and logon credentials, what will most likely happen when you attempt to associate with the café's wireless network?
    a. Your wireless networking client will be able to see the access point but will be unable to associate with it.
    b. Your wireless networking client will not be able to see the access point.
    c. Your wireless networking client will be able to see the access point and attempt to associate with it, but the incompatible frequencies will prevent successful association.
    d. Your wireless networking client will be able to see the access point and attempt to associate with it, but the incompatible security techniques will prevent successful association.
    e. Your wireless networking client will be able to see the access point and successfully associate with it.

89. You have just rearranged the access points on your small office network. Now a group of employees complains that they cannot reliably get their workstations to connect with a new 802.11ac access point. You have confirmed that the workstations are using the correct SSID, security type, and passphrase. You have also confirmed that the access point is turned on and functioning properly because when you stand in the computer room where it's located, you can connect to the access point from your smartphone. Which of the following is likely preventing the other users' workstations from associating with the new access point?
    a. The users are attempting to log on using incorrect user IDs.
    b. The workstations are located beyond the access point's range.
    c. The workstations are set to use 802.11g.
    d. The users have turned off their wireless antennas.
    e. The workstations' wired NICs are causing addressing conflicts with their wireless NICs.

90. With which of these utilities can you require a Windows 10 Professional user to create a password of at least eight characters?
    a. Cmd
    b. Devmgmt.msc
    c. Virtmgmt.msc
    d. Gpedit.msc
    e. Netplwiz

91. Which protocol supports recovery of a router config file?
    a. UPS
    b. TFTP
    c. SSH
    d. SNMP
    e. OID

92. Which of the following is a likely reason for using VLANs?
    a. To facilitate easier migration from IPv4 to IPv6 addressing
    b. To enable DHCP on a network
    c. To limit broadcast domains
    d. To reduce the likelihood for user error when modifying TCP/IP properties
    e. To reduce the number of routing table entries

93. Which of the following wireless security techniques uses both RADIUS and AES?
    a. WPA2-Enterprise
    b. WPA
    c. WEP
    d. WPA-Enterprise
    e. WPA2

94. Your company is experiencing a growth spurt and is ready to invest in a more sophisticated disaster recovery plan. Currently the backup plan consists of a few spare computers in a storage closet, and data on the servers is duplicated weekly to an off-site backup service. The company owners have committed to acquiring additional servers to duplicate critical servers in their current network, and they want the servers to be configured identically to the servers now in use. The new servers will be stored at an off-site data center and updated every time the on-site servers are updated. What type of disaster recovery site is your company creating?
    a. Hot site
    b. Ambient site
    c. Cloud site
    d. Warm site
    e. Differential site

95. A virtual switch includes several virtual ports, each of which can be considered a _____.
    a. virtual bridge
    b. virtual router
    c. virtual gateway
    d. virtual hub
    e. virtual repeater

96. Which OSI layer(s) operate differently in wired versus wireless network connections?
    a. Layers 5, 6, and 7
    b. Layers 1, 2, and 3
    c. Layer 1
    d. Layer 2
    e. Layers 1 and 2

97. As a networking professional, you might use a multimeter to do which of the following? *Choose two.*
    a. Determine where the patch cable for a specific server terminates on the patch panel.
    b. Verify that the amount of resistance presented by terminators on coaxial cable networks is appropriate.
    c. Check for the presence of noise on a wire by detecting extraneous voltage.
    d. Confirm that a fiber-optic cable can transmit signals from one node to another.
    e. Validate the processing capabilities of a new router.

98. You're setting up a wireless network for a coffee shop and want to provide some liability protection for the shop owners when customers use their Wi-Fi Internet access. Which of the following tools will provide this protection while still allowing customers convenient access to the Internet?
    a. ACL
    b. WPA2
    c. MAC filter
    d. EAPoL
    e. Captive portal

99. What type of device does this icon represent on a network diagram?

    a. Router
    b. Access point
    c. Switch
    d. Firewall
    e. Internet

100. While configuring your new SOHO router, you're given several security options. Which one would provide the most secure encryption of your transmissions?
    a. PSK
    b. AES
    c. WEP
    d. TKIP
    e. RC4

RUBRIC FOR HANDS-ON PROJECTS AND CAPSTONE PROJECTS

Criteria	Beginning	Developing	Proficient	Exemplary	Score
Responses to questions	All missing or incorrect **[0 points]**	Most missing or incorrect **[15 points]**	Little missing or incorrect **[20 points]**	All complete **[25 points]**	
Other deliverables	Missing **[0 points]**	Present but missing most or all the required information **[15 points]**	Present but missing some of the required information **[20 points]**	Present and contains all the required information **[25 points]**	
Critical thinking and engagement	Student shows little to no evidence of attempting to meet the performance requirements of the assignment **[0 points]**	Student retains their existing understanding while attempting to meet the performance requirements of the assignment **[15 points]**	Student challenges their existing understanding and shows evidence of new learning **[20 points]**	Student challenges their existing understanding and displays creative and original insights **[25 points]**	
Mechanics	Grammar, spelling, punctuation, and formatting make student's message difficult to understand **[0 points]**	Grammar, spelling, punctuation, and formatting detract from student's message **[15 points]**	Grammar, spelling, punctuation, and formatting support student's message **[20 points]**	Grammar, spelling, punctuation, and formatting enhance student's message **[25 points]**	
				Total	

RUBRIC FOR DISCUSSION ASSIGNMENTS

Task	Developing	Proficient	Exemplary	Score
Initial post	Generalized statements **[30 points]**	Some specific statements with supporting evidence **[40 points]**	Self-reflective discussion with specific and thoughtful statements and supporting evidence **[50 points]**	
Initial post: Mechanics	• Length < 100 words • Several grammar and spelling errors **[5 points]**	• Length = 100 words • Occasional grammar and spelling errors **[7 points]**	• Length > 100 words • Appropriate grammar and spelling **[10 points]**	
Response 1	Brief response showing little engagement or critical thinking **[5 points]**	Detailed response with specific contributions to the discussion **[10 points]**	Thoughtful response with specific examples or details and open-ended questions that invite deeper discussion of the topic **[15 points]**	
Response 2	Brief response showing little engagement or critical thinking **[5 points]**	Detailed response with specific contributions to the discussion **[10 points]**	Thoughtful response with specific examples or details and open-ended questions that invite deeper discussion of the topic **[15 points]**	
Both responses: Mechanics	• Length < 50 words each • Several grammar and spelling errors **[5 points]**	• Length = 50 words each • Occasional grammar and spelling errors **[7 points]**	• Length > 50 words each • Appropriate grammar and spelling **[10 points]**	
			Total	

GLOSSARY

1000BASE-LX A physical layer standard for networks that specifies 1-Gbps transmission over fiber-optic cable using baseband transmission. The LX represents its reliance on long wavelengths of 1300 nanometers.

1000BASE-SX A physical layer standard for networks that specifies 1-Gbps transmission over fiber-optic cable using baseband transmission. The SX represents its reliance on short wavelengths of 850 nanometers.

1000BASE-T A physical layer standard for achieving 1 Gbps over twisted-pair cable.

100BASE-FX A physical layer standard for networks that specifies 100-Mbps transmission over fiber-optic cable using baseband transmission. The FX represents its support of Fast Ethernet speeds.

100BASE-SX A physical layer standard for networks that specifies 100-Mbps transmission over fiber-optic cable using baseband transmission. The SX represents its reliance on short wavelengths of 850 nanometers.

100BASE-T A physical layer standard for networks that specifies 100-Mbps transmission over twisted-pair cable. Also called 100BASE-TX.

100BASE-TX A physical layer standard for networks that specifies 100-Mbps transmission over twisted-pair cable. Also called 100BASE-T.

10BASE-T A physical layer standard for networks that specifies 10-Mbps transmission over twisted-pair cable.

10GBASE-LR A physical layer standard for networks that specifies 10-Gbps transmission over fiber-optic cable using baseband transmission. The LR represents its support of long-range transmissions.

10GBASE-SR A physical layer standard for networks that specifies 10-Gbps transmission over fiber-optic cable using baseband transmission. The SR represents its support of short-range transmissions.

10GBASE-T A physical layer standard for achieving 10-Gbps data transmission over twisted-pair cable.

110 block A type of punchdown block designed to terminate Cat 5 or better twisted-pair wires and typically used to handle data connections rather than telephone connections. The numeral *110* refers to the model number of the earliest blocks.

2FA (two-factor authentication) A form of identity verification where the user must provide something and know something.

3-2-1-1 Rule A collection of backup principles that requires at least three complete copies of the data, backups saved on at least two media types, with at least one copy stored offsite, and at least one copy stored offline.

3G (third generation) Third-generation mobile phone service released in the early 2000s that supported up to 384 Kbps.

40GBASE-T A physical layer standard for achieving 40-Gbps data transmission over twisted-pair cable.

4G (fourth generation) Fourth-generation mobile phone service that is characterized by an all-IP network for both data and voice transmission and throughput of 100 Mbps up to 1 Gbps.

5G (fifth generation) Fifth-generation mobile phone standard requiring minimal throughput of 1 Gbps and maxing out at 20 Gbps download and 10 Gbps upload. Actual speeds vary greatly depending on the bands, cell density, channels, and client volume.

66 block A type of punchdown block designed to terminate telephone connections. The numeral *66* refers to the model number of the earliest blocks.

802.11a The IEEE standard for a wireless networking technique that uses multiple frequency bands in the 5-GHz frequency range and provides a theoretical maximum throughput of 54 Mbps.

802.11ac The IEEE standard for a wireless networking technique that exceeds benchmarks set by earlier standards by increasing its useful bandwidth and amplitude. 802.11ac is the first Wi-Fi standard to approach Gigabit Ethernet capabilities. Also called Wi-Fi 5.

802.11ax The IEEE standard for a wireless networking technique that operates in both the 2.4-GHz and 5-GHz bands and improves on earlier standards through the implementation of modulation and multi-user technologies. Also called Wi-Fi 6.

802.11b   The IEEE standard for a wireless networking technique that uses DSSS (direct-sequence spread spectrum) signaling in the 2.4-GHz frequency range and provides a theoretical maximum throughput of 11 Mbps.

802.11g   The IEEE standard for a wireless networking technique designed to be compatible with 802.11b in the 2.4-GHz frequency range while using different data modulation techniques that allow it to reach a theoretical maximum capacity of 54 Mbps.

802.11n   The IEEE standard for a wireless networking technique that may issue signals in the 2.4-GHz or 5-GHz band and can achieve actual data throughput between 65 Mbps and 600 Mbps. Also called Wi-Fi 4.

802.1Q   The IEEE standard that specifies how VLAN and trunking information appears in frames and how switches and bridges interpret that information.

802.1X   A vendor-independent IEEE standard for securing transmission between nodes according to the transmission's port, whether physical or logical. 802.1X, also known as EAPoL, is commonly used with RADIUS authentication.

A

A (address) record   A type of DNS data record that maps the IPv4 address of an Internet-connected device to its domain name.

AAA (authentication, authorization, and accounting)   A category of protocols that establish a client's identity, authorize a user for certain privileges on a system or network, and keep an account of the client's system or network usage.

AAAA (address) record   A type of DNS data record that maps the IPv6 address of an Internet-connected device to its domain name. Pronounced "quad-A record."

AAAA (authentication, authorization, accounting, and auditing)   Similar to AAA, a category of protocols that establish a client's identity, authorize a user for certain privileges on a system or network, and keep an account of the client's system or network usage. AAAA adds the component of auditing, which consists of a posture assessment to analyze the network for vulnerabilities.

access badge   A security card that identifies a person by name and perhaps includes a photo, title, and other information.

access control   One or more security techniques for managing users' access to a network and its resources.

access control vestibule   A confined space between two locking doors where one door must lock closed before the other can open. Formerly called a mantrap.

access layer   Workgroup switches connected directly to hosts. Also called edge layer.

access port   The interface on a switch used for an endpoint. Devices connected to access ports are unaware of VLAN information.

accounting   In the context of network security, the process of logging users' access and activities on a network.

ACL (access control list)   A list of statements used by a router or other device to permit or deny the forwarding of traffic on a network based on one or more criteria.

active-active redundancy   A redundancy strategy in which all redundant resources are kept active at all times and work is distributed among them. If one resource fails, the other active resources continue handling the workload.

active-passive redundancy   A redundancy strategy in which only one or a few redundant resources are kept active at all times, with backup devices on standby ready to fill in if they're needed.

AD (Active Directory)   The centralized directory database that contains user account information and security for the entire group of computers on a network.

AD (administrative distance)   A number indicating a protocol's reliability, with lower values being given higher priority. This assignment can be changed by a network administrator.

AD DS (Active Directory Domain Services)   The Active Directory service that manages the process allowing a user to sign on to a network from any computer on the network and get access to the resources that Active Directory manages.

ad hoc topology   A type of wireless LAN in which stations communicate directly with each other (rather than using an access point).

AES (Advanced Encryption Standard) A private key encryption algorithm that uses a sophisticated family of ciphers along with multiple stages of data transformation.

aggregation layer A highly redundant mesh of connections between multilayer switches or routers that provides routing within the corporate network as well as traffic filtering and the network's connection to one or more WANs. Also called distributed layer.

AH (authentication header) In the context of IPsec, a type of encryption that provides authentication of the IP packet's data payload through public key techniques.

alert A message generated when a pre-defined event occurs, which is then logged by the system.

ANDing A logical process of combining bits.

ANSI (American National Standards Institute) A private, non-profit entity consisting of a membership of standards writers and users. ANSI oversees standards development and provides accreditation for approved standards for a period of five years, at which time the standards must be revised, rescinded, or reaffirmed.

ANT+ An open source wireless technology that gathers and tracks information from sensors typically embedded in heart rate monitors, GPS devices, and other activity monitoring devices.

anycast address A type of IPv6 address that represents a group of interfaces, any one of which (and usually the first available of which) can accept a transmission. At this time, anycast addresses are not designed to be assigned to hosts, such as servers or workstations, but rather to routers.

AP (access point) A device used on wireless LANs that accepts wireless signals from multiple nodes and retransmits them to the rest of the network.

APC (angled physical contact) The latest advancement in ferrule technology that uses the principles of reflection to its advantage by placing the end faces of the highly polished ferrules at an angle to each other, thus reducing the effect of back reflection.

API (application programming interface) An access point into a software's available processes through which a specific type of request generates a particular kind of response.

APIPA (Automatic Private IP Addressing) A service available on Windows computers that automatically assigns the computer's NIC a link local IPv4 address in the range of 169.254.0.1 through 169.254.255.254.

application layer The seventh layer of the OSI model. Application layer protocols enable software programs to negotiate formatting, procedural, security, synchronization, and other requirements with the network.

application layer firewall A firewall that can block designated types of traffic based on application data contained within packets.

application plane An SDN (software-defined networking) construct corresponding to the OSI model's application layer where network applications communicate with the network via APIs (application programming interfaces).

architecture The overall design of a device, network, or other system. In the context of a network, the architecture includes the devices involved, how they're configured, the services implemented to support the network, and the way devices are connected to the network.

ARP (Address Resolution Protocol) A core protocol in the TCP/IP suite that functions in the data link layer of the OSI model. ARP works in conjunction with IPv4 to discover the MAC address of a node on the local network and to maintain a database that maps local IP addresses to MAC addresses.

ARP spoofing An attack in which fake ARP replies are used to alter ARP tables in a network. Also called ARP poisoning.

ARP table A database of records that maps MAC addresses to IP addresses. The ARP table is stored on a computer's hard disk where it is used by the ARP utility to supply the MAC addresses of network nodes, given their IP addresses.

AS (autonomous system) A group of networks, often on the same domain, that are operated by the same organization.

asset tag A barcode or wireless-enabled transmitter used to track the movement or condition of equipment, inventory, or people.

association In the context of wireless networking, the communication that occurs between a wireless client and an access point enabling the client to connect to the network via that access point.

asymmetric encryption A type of encryption (such as public key encryption) that uses a different key for encoding data than is used for decoding the cipher text.

asymmetrical A characteristic of transmission technology that offers faster download speeds than upload speeds.

asymmetrical routing A routing challenge caused when messages going in one direction in a conversation travel a different path than messages going in the other direction. This is typically unavoidable (especially when using BGP on the Internet) and is not a problem. However, it can cause issues for NAT (network address translation) and for firewalls that need to see traffic in both directions of a conversation to properly apply filtering rules.

attenuation The loss of a signal's strength as it travels away from its source.

audit log A collection of data in logs that is consistent and thorough enough to retroactively prove compliance and also to defensibly prove user actions.

audit report A document generated after an IT audit that evaluates a business's operations, processes, infrastructure, and policies as related to its business goals and relevant laws or other standards.

audit trail A system of documentation that makes it possible for a third party to inspect evidence and understand the flow of events.

AUP (acceptable use policy) The portion of a security policy that explains to users what they can and cannot do while accessing a network's resources and the penalties for violations. It might also describe how these measures protect the network's security.

authentication The process of comparing and matching a client's credentials with the credentials in a client database to enable the client to log on to the network.

authoritative name server The authority on computer names and their IP addresses for computers in their domains.

authorization The process that determines what a user can and cannot do with network resources.

automatic failover In the event of a component failure, the ability of a redundant component to immediately assume the duties of the failed component.

automation The use of technology to perform a process or procedure with minimal human interaction.

auto-MDI-X Ports on newer devices that automatically negotiate the transmit and receive wires between devices.

availability A measure of how consistently and reliably a file, device, or connection can be accessed by authorized personnel.

B

back reflection The return of a light signal back into a fiber-optic cable that is transmitting the signal. Back reflection is measured as optical loss in dB (decibels).

backbone The central conduit of a network that connects network segments and significant shared devices (such as routers, switches, and servers) and is sometimes referred to as "a network of networks."

backup A copy of data or program files created for archiving or safekeeping.

badge reader A device that detects information embedded on a smart card.

band A specific frequency range on the wireless spectrum.

bandwidth A measure of the amount of data that could theoretically be transmitted during a given period of time.

bandwidth management A collection of strategies to optimize the volume of traffic a network can support.

bandwidth speed tester A website that tests the current upload and download speeds on a WAN connection.

baseline A record of how a network or resource operates under normal conditions.

baseline configuration A change-management concept that defines the desired stable state that must be achieved and maintained before future changes can be attempted.

BCP (business continuity plan) A document that details how an organization intends to maintain business operations during a disaster.

best path The most efficient route from one network to another, as calculated by a router.

BGP (Border Gateway Protocol) Dubbed the "protocol of the Internet," this path-vector routing protocol is the only current EGP (exterior gateway protocol) and is capable of considering many factors in its routing metrics.

bidirectional WDM A type of WDM multiplexing that supports full-duplex light transmissions.

biometrics   Unique physical characteristics of an individual, such as the color patterns in their iris or the geometry of their hand.

BIX (Building Industry Cross-connect) block   A compact type of punchdown block typically used to handle data connections rather than telephone connections.

Bluetooth   A low-power wireless technology that provides close-range communication between devices such as PCs, smartphones, tablets, and accessories.

BNC (British Naval Connector/Bayonet Neill-Concelman) connector   A coaxial cable connector type that uses a turn-and-lock (or bayonet) style of coupling.

border router   A router that connects an autonomous system with an outside network—for example, the router that connects a business to its ISP. Also called an edge router.

botnet   A collection of infected systems used in coordinated attacks against targets.

BPDU (Bridge Protocol Data Unit)   A type of network message that transmits STP information between switches.

branch office   A remote location within the corporation's network that is often connected over a WAN link or the open Internet.

bridged mode   A type of network connection in which a vNIC accesses a physical network using the host machine's NIC. The bridged vNIC obtains its own IP address, default gateway, and subnet mask information from the physical LAN's DHCP server.

broadband   A WAN technology where the network media and available bandwidth are shared between multiple customers.

broadcast   A message that is read by every node on a network.

broadcast domain   Logically grouped network nodes that can communicate directly via broadcast transmissions. By default, switches and repeating devices, such as hubs, extend broadcast domains. Routers and other layer 3 devices separate broadcast domains.

broadcast storm   Redundant broadcast transmissions that flood a network in switching loops that are not limited by some protective system such as STP (Spanning Tree Protocol).

brute force attack   An attempt to discover an encryption key or password by trying numerous possible character combinations until the correct combination is found.

BSS (basic service set)   In IEEE terminology, a group of stations that share an access point.

BSSID (basic service set identifier)   In IEEE terminology, the identifier for a BSS (basic service set).

buffering   A form of traffic shaping that delays less-important traffic during times of high bandwidth utilization.

bus topology   A topology in which a single cable connects all nodes on a network without intervening connectivity devices.

business continuity   The ability of a company to continue doing business with the least amount of interruption possible after a major outage or other disaster.

business process   A series of steps that accomplish a defined goal in a business context.

business risk assessment   An evaluation of the potential impact of various security threats on business processes.

BYOD (bring your own device)   The practice of allowing people to bring their personally owned smartphones, laptops, or other technology into a facility for the purpose of performing work or school responsibilities.

C

C&C (command-and-control) server   A central server commanding infected devices that have been recruited into a botnet.

CA (certificate authority)   An organization that issues and maintains digital certificates as part of the PKI (public-key infrastructure).

cable broadband   Broadband Internet access provided over the coaxial cable wiring used for TV signals.

cable crimper   A tool used to push the pins of a connector into the wires of a cable so they pierce the wire's insulation.

cable modem   A device that modulates and demodulates signals for transmission and reception via cable wiring.

cable performance tester   A troubleshooting tool that tests cables for continuity, but can also measure crosstalk, attenuation, and impedance; identify the location of faults; and store or print cable testing results. Also called line tester, certifier, or network tester.

cable stripper   A tool used to pull off the protective covering of a cable without damaging the wires inside.

cable tester   A device that tests cables for one or more of the following conditions: continuity, segment length, distance to a fault, attenuation along a cable, near-end crosstalk, and termination resistance and impedance.

caching DNS server   A server that accesses public DNS data and caches the DNS information it collects.

CAN (campus area network)   A network of connected LANs within a limited geographical area, such as the buildings on a university campus.

canonical name   The true name of a server, such as *www.example.com*, as opposed to one of many alias names a server might have, such as *ns1.example.com*.

captive portal   The first page displayed by a client's browser when the client connects to a guest network. This page usually requires the user to agree to a set of terms and conditions before gaining further access to the guest network.

CARP (Common Address Redundancy Protocol)   A protocol that allows a pool of computers or interfaces to share one or more IP addresses.

Cat 5 (Category 5)   A form of UTP that contains four wire pairs and supports up to 100-Mbps throughput and a 100-MHz signal rate. Required minimum standard for Fast Ethernet.

Cat 5e (Enhanced Category 5)   A higher-grade version of Cat 5 wiring that supports a signaling rate of up to 350 MHz and a maximum throughput of 1 Gbps, making it the required minimum standard for Gigabit Ethernet.

Cat 6 (Category 6)   A twisted-pair cable that contains four wire pairs, each wrapped in foil insulation. Additional foil insulation can cover the bundle of wire pairs, and a fire-resistant plastic sheath might cover the second foil layer. The foil insulation provides excellent resistance to crosstalk and enables Cat 6 to support a signaling rate of 250 MHz and throughput up to 10 Gbps.

Cat 6a (Augmented Category 6)   A higher-grade version of Cat 6 wiring that further reduces attenuation and crosstalk, and allows for potentially exceeding traditional network segment length limits.

Cat 7 (Category 7)   A twisted-pair cable that contains multiple wire pairs, each separately shielded then surrounded by another layer of shielding within the jacket, allowing throughput up to 100 Gbps at very short distances. Cat 7 is not included in the TIA/EIA standards.

Cat 7a (Augmented Category 7)   A higher-grade version of Cat 7 wiring that might support up to 100-Gbps throughput at short distances and up to 1000-MHz signal rate but has not been accepted as a TIA/EIA standard.

Cat 8 (Category 8)   A twisted-pair cable that relies on improved and extensive shielding and is optimized for short-distance backbone connections within the data center.

CCMP (Counter Mode with CBC [Cipher Block Chaining] MAC [Message Authentication Code] Protocol)   A security method used in WPA2 that helps ensure data confidentiality by providing message integrity and encryption services.

CCTV (closed-circuit TV)   A video surveillance system that monitors activity in secured areas.

CDMA (Code Division Multiple Access)   A cellular standard that uses spread-spectrum technology, in which a signal is spread over a wide bandwidth so that multiple users can occupy the same channel.

CEED (Certificate of Electronic Equipment Destruction)   Documentation provided by disposal services that serves as legal protection should data later be recovered from destroyed devices.

cell site   The combination of a cellular antenna array and its base station.

CFP (centum form-factor pluggable)   A fiber-optic transceiver intended for 100-Gbps network connections.

chain of custody   Documentation that describes evidence, including when it was collected, who collected it, its condition, and how it was secured and transferred from one responsible party to the next.

change management   Carefully defined processes to evaluate the need for a change, the cost of the change, a plan for making the change with minimal disruption, and a backup plan if the change doesn't work as expected.

channel bonding   In the context of 802.11 wireless technology, the combination of two or more adjacent 20-MHz frequency bands to create one 40-, 60-, 80-, or 120-MHz channel.

checksum   A method of error checking that determines if the contents of an arriving data unit match the contents of the data unit sent by the source.

CIA (confidentiality, integrity, and availability) triad   A three-tenet, standard security model describing the primary ways that encryption protects data. Confidentiality ensures that data can only be viewed by its intended recipient or at its intended destination. Integrity ensures that data was not modified after the sender transmitted it and before the receiver picked it up. Availability ensures that data is available to and accessible by the intended recipient when needed.

CIDR (Classless Interdomain Routing) notation   A shorthand method for identifying network and host bits in an IP address.

cladding   The glass or plastic shield around the core of a fiber-optic cable. Cladding reflects light back to the core in patterns that vary depending on the transmission mode.

classful addressing   An IP addressing convention that adheres to network class distinctions, in which the first 8 bits of a class A address, the first 16 bits of a class B address, and the first 24 bits of a class C address are used for network information.

classless addressing   An IP addressing convention that alters the rules of classful IPv4 addressing to create subnets in a network.

client   A computer or application that makes a request from another computer or application.

clientless VPN   A VPN accessed by the client system through a limited, web-based connection using a browser and secured by SSL/TLS.

client-server application   Data or a service requested by one computer from another.

client-server network model   A network where resources are managed by the NOS (network operating system) via a centralized directory database.

client-to-site VPN (virtual private network)   A type of VPN in which clients, servers, and other hosts establish tunnels with a private network using a VPN gateway at the edge of the private network.

cloud computing   The flexible provision of data storage, applications, or services to clients over a network.

cloud service model   Categories of cloud service types according to the division of labor between customer and cloud provider for each service.

cloud site   A highly scalable, inexpensive DR (disaster recovery) option of establishing a cloud configuration that could take over many or most business processes in the event of a disaster. Also called DRaaS (disaster recovery as a service).

clustering   A technique of grouping multiple devices so they appear as a single device to the rest of the network.

CNAME (canonical name) record   A type of DNS data record that holds alternative names for a host.

coaxial cable   A type of cable that consists of a central metal conducting core, surrounded by an insulator, shielding, and an outer cover. Today coaxial cable, called "coax" for short, is mostly used to connect cable Internet and cable TV systems.

cold site   A place where the computers, devices, and connectivity necessary to rebuild a network exist but are not appropriately configured, updated, or connected to match the network's current state.

collision   In Ethernet networks, the interference of one node's data transmission with the data transmission of another node sharing the same segment.

collision domain   The portion of an Ethernet network in which collisions could occur if two nodes transmit data at the same time. Today, switches and routers separate collision domains.

colocation facility   A data center facility that is shared by a variety of providers. Also called a carrier hotel.

community cloud   A cloud deployment model in which flexible data storage, applications, or services are shared between multiple organizations but are not available publicly.

congestion control   A bandwidth management technique used to adjust the way network devices respond to indications of network performance issues caused by traffic congestion, with the goal of ensuring devices don't make the problem worse.

connectionless protocol   A type of transport layer protocol that services a request without requiring a verified session and without guaranteeing delivery of data.

connection-oriented protocol   A type of transport layer protocol that requires the establishment of a connection between communicating nodes before it will transmit data.

console cable   A cable used to connect a computer to the console port of a router.

container A lightweight, self-contained environment that provides the services needed to run an application in nearly any OS environment.

continuity The ability of a cable to carry a signal to its destination.

continuity tester An instrument that tests whether voltage (or light, in the case of fiber-optic cable) issued at one end of a cable can be detected at the opposite end of the cable. Also called cable checker or cable tester.

control plane The process of decision making, such as routing, blocking, and forwarding, that is performed by protocols.

convergence time The time it takes for routers on a network to recognize and adjust to configuration changes or a network outage.

CoPP (control plane policing) An adaptation of QoS (quality of service) filters used to rate-limit traffic on the control plane and management plane of routers and switches.

core layer A group of highly efficient multilayer switches or routers that support the network's backbone traffic.

core router A router that directs data between networks within the same autonomous system. Also called an interior router.

CoS (Class of Service) Quality control techniques performed at layer 2 on Ethernet frames.

CRC (cyclic redundancy checking) error An error statistic that indicates messages are being damaged in transit.

crossover cable A twisted-pair patch cable in which the termination locations of the transmit and receive wires on one end of the cable are reversed as compared with the other end.

crosstalk A type of interference caused by signals traveling on nearby wire pairs infringing on another pair's signal.

CSMA/CA (Carrier Sense Multiple Access with Collision Avoidance) A network access method used on 802.11 wireless networks. CSMA/CA does not eliminate, but minimizes, the potential for collisions.

CSMA/CD (Carrier Sense Multiple Access with Collision Detection) A network access method specified for use by IEEE 802.3 (Ethernet) networks. In CSMA/CD, each node waits its turn before transmitting data to avoid interfering with other nodes' transmissions.

CSP (cloud service provider) A business that offers one or more cloud services to other businesses or individuals.

CVE (Common Vulnerabilities and Exposures) A dictionary project funded by the U.S. Department of Homeland Security and managed by The MITRE Corporation to index cybersecurity vulnerabilities.

CWDM (coarse wavelength division multiplexing or coarse WDM) A multiplexing technique used over single-mode or multimode fiber-optic cable in which each signal is assigned a different wavelength for its carrier wave.

D

DaaS (Desktop as a Service) A cloud-service model in which desktop services (that is, VDI) are provided virtually from a third-party provider.

DAC (discretionary access control) A method of access control where users decide for themselves who has access to that user's resources.

DAI (dynamic ARP inspection) A configuration on a switch that compares incoming messages with the switch's DHCP snooping binding table to determine whether the message's source IP address is appropriately matched with its source MAC address according to DHCP assignments on the network. DAI helps protect against ARP spoofing attacks.

data breach Unauthorized access or use of sensitive data.

data link layer The second layer in the OSI model. The data link layer, also called the link layer, bridges the physical layer's networking media with network layer processes.

data plane An SDN (software-defined networking) construct made up of physical or virtual devices that receive and send network messages. Also called infrastructure plane.

data VLAN A VLAN that carries user-generated traffic, such as email, web browsing, or database updates.

datagram A UDP message at the transport layer.

dB (decibel) loss A measure of the degradation or distortion of a signal.

DBMS (database management system) Software installed on a database server that is responsible for making requested changes to data and organizing data for viewing, reporting, or exporting.

DDoS (distributed DoS) attack   An attack in which multiple hosts simultaneously flood a target host with traffic, rendering the target unable to function.

deauth (deauthentication) attack   An attack on a wireless network in which the attacker sends faked deauthentication frames to the AP, the client, or both (or as a broadcast to the whole wireless network) to trigger the deauthentication process and knock one or more clients off the wireless network.

decapsulation   Removing a header or trailer from a lower OSI layer.

default gateway   The gateway device that nodes on the network turn to for access to the outside world.

default route   A backup route, usually to another router, used when a router cannot determine a path to a message's destination.

default VLAN   A preconfigured VLAN on a switch that cannot be renamed or deleted.

defense in depth   Layers of security implemented to protect a network from multiple attack vectors.

delay-sensitive   Transmissions that will suffer significantly compromised user experiences if portions of the transmission are delayed, such as with voice and video transmissions.

demarc (demarcation point)   The point of division between a telecommunications service carrier's network and a building's internal network.

device hardening   Preventive measures that can be taken to secure a device from network- or software-supported attacks.

device ID   A unique set of characters assigned to each NIC by its manufacturer. Also called extension identifier.

DHCP (Dynamic Host Configuration Protocol)   An application layer protocol in the TCP/IP suite that manages the dynamic distribution of IP addresses on a network.

DHCP reservation   An IP address that is set aside by a DHCP server for a specific network client, which is identified by its MAC address. Also called MAC reservation or IP reservation.

DHCP scope   The predefined range of addresses that can be leased to any network device on a particular segment.

DHCP scope exhaustion   A network problem caused by all available IP addresses being used up, and new clients cannot connect to the network.

DHCP snooping   A security feature on switches whereby DHCP messages on the network are checked and filtered.

DIA (dedicated Internet access)   A WAN service where the network media or a portion of its available bandwidth is dedicated to a single customer and comes with an SLA-defined guarantee of minimum uptime percentages and maximum recovery times if the service goes down.

dictionary attack   A technique in which attackers run a program that tries a combination of a known user ID and, for a password, every word in a dictionary to attempt to gain access to a network.

differential backup   A backup method in which only data that has changed since the last full or incremental backup is copied to a storage medium even if earlier differential backups have been made.

diffraction   In the context of wireless signal propagation, the phenomenon that occurs when an electromagnetic wave encounters an obstruction and splits into secondary waves.

DiffServ (Differentiated Services)   A technique for ensuring QoS by prioritizing traffic.

dig (domain information groper)   A utility available on Linux and macOS that provides more detailed domain information than nslookup. Use dig to query DNS nameservers for information about host addresses and other DNS records.

digital certificate   A small file containing verified identification information about the user and the user's public key.

directional antenna   A type of antenna that issues wireless signals along a single direction, or path. Also called a unidirectional antenna.

disaster   An extreme type of incident, involving a network outage that affects more than a single system or limited group of users.

disaster recovery plan   A part of the BCP (business continuity plan) that details the processes for restoring critical functionality and data to a network after an outage.

distance-vector routing protocol   The simplest type of routing protocols; used to determine the best route for data based on the distance to a destination.

distributed switching The centralized control of many VMs' access to a network across a server cluster.

distribution layer A highly redundant mesh of connections between multilayer switches or routers that provides routing within the corporate network as well as traffic filtering and the network's connection to one or more WANs. Also called aggregation layer.

DLP (data loss prevention) A security technique that uses software to monitor confidential data, track data access and ownership, and prevent it from being copied or transmitted off the network.

DMVPN (Dynamic Multipoint VPN) A particular type of enterprise VPN using Cisco devices that dynamically creates VPN tunnels between branch locations as needed rather than requiring constant, static tunnels for site-to-site connections.

DNS (Domain Name System) A hierarchical system for tracking domain names and their addresses, devised in the mid-1980s.

DNS poisoning An attack that alters DNS records on a DNS server, thereby redirecting traffic from a legitimate server to a malicious server, such as a phishing website.

DNS zone A portion of the DNS namespace for which one organization is assigned authority to manage.

DOCSIS (Data Over Cable Service Interface Specifications) An international, cooperative effort orchestrated by Cable-Labs that standardized cable broadband service.

domain In the context of Windows Server, a group of users, servers, and other resources that share account and security policies.

domain name The last two parts of an FQDN, such as *mycompany.com*. Usually, a domain name is associated with the company's name and its type of organization, such as a school or nonprofit organization.

DoS (denial-of-service) attack An attack in which a legitimate user is unable to access normal network resources because of an attacker's intervention. Most often, this type of attack is achieved by flooding a system with so many requests for services that it can't respond to any of them.

DRaaS (disaster recovery as a service) A highly scalable, inexpensive DR option of establishing a cloud configuration that could take over many or most business processes in the event of a disaster. Also called a cloud site.

DSCP (Differentiated Services Code Point) The first 6 bits of the 8-bit DiffServ field in an IPv4 packet, which indicates to network routers how the data stream should be forwarded.

DSL (digital subscriber line) A WAN connection technology that operates over the PSTN (public switched telephone network) and can support multiple data and voice channels over a single line.

DSL modem A device that modulates a DSL signal between the ISP's telephone line and the customer's Ethernet network.

DSSS (direct sequence spread spectrum) A modulation technique that, like other spread-spectrum technologies, distributes lower-level signals over several frequencies simultaneously.

dual stacked A type of network that supports both IPv4 and IPv6 traffic.

duplex A type of transmission in which signals may travel in both directions over a medium simultaneously.

durability A resource's ongoing existence.

DWDM (dense wavelength division multiplexing or dense WDM) A multiplexing technique used over single-mode or multimode fiber-optic cable in which each signal is assigned a different wavelength for its carrier wave.

dynamic ARP table entry A record in an ARP table that is created when a client makes an ARP request that cannot be satisfied by data already in the ARP table.

dynamic IP address An IP address that is assigned to a device upon request and may change when the DHCP lease expires or is terminated.

dynamic route A route automatically calculated by the router to determine the best path between two networks. As dynamic routes are identified and calculated, this information is collected in a routing table.

dynamic VLAN assignment A VLAN assignment based on various criteria, such as client device information, results of an authentication process in cooperation with a RADIUS server, or WLAN association.

E

EAP (Extensible Authentication Protocol) An authentication mechanism that provides the framework for authenticating clients and servers.

It does not perform encryption or authentication on its own, but rather works with other encryption and authentication schemes to verify the credentials of clients and servers.

EAPoL (EAP over LAN) A vendor-independent IEEE standard, numbered 802.1X, for securing transmission between nodes according to the transmission's port, whether physical or logical, and commonly used with RADIUS authentication.

east-west traffic The flow of traffic between peers within a network segment.

edge layer Workgroup switches connected directly to hosts. Also called access layer.

edge router A router that connects an autonomous system with an outside network—for example, the router that connects a business to its ISP. Also called a border router.

EF (entrance facility) The location where an incoming network service (whether phone, Internet, or long-distance service) enters a building and connects with the building's backbone cabling.

EGP (exterior gateway protocol) A type of routing protocol used by edge routers and exterior routers to distribute data outside of autonomous systems. BGP (Border Gateway Protocol) is the only modern example of an exterior gateway protocol.

EIGRP (Enhanced Interior Gateway Routing Protocol) An advanced distance-vector protocol developed by Cisco that combines some of the features of a link-state protocol and so is sometimes referred to as a hybrid protocol.

EIRP (effective isotropic radiated power) The calculation of net gain or loss of a signal's strength, taking into consideration the transmission power (dBm), cable loss (dB), and antenna gain (dBi).

elasticity The ability to quickly and dynamically upscale or downscale resources in response to changing demand.

EMI (electromagnetic interference) A type of interference that can be caused by motors, power lines, televisions, copiers, fluorescent lights, or other sources of electrical activity.

encapsulation The process of adding a header to data inherited from the layer above.

encoding The process of converting data into a digital signal for transmission.

encryption The use of an algorithm to scramble data into a format that can be read only by reversing the algorithm—that is, by decrypting the data—to keep the information private.

EoR (end of row) switching A rack architecture in which switches in a rack at the end of the row serve as the connection points to the network for all other devices in the row.

ESD (electrostatic discharge) The transfer of electrical charge between two bodies, such as when a technician touches a computer component.

ESP (Encapsulating Security Payload) In the context of IPsec, a type of encryption that provides authentication of the IP packet's data payload through public key techniques and encrypts the entire IP packet for added security.

ESS (extended service set) A group of access points and associated stations (or basic service sets) connected to the same LAN.

ESSID (extended service set identifier) A special identifier shared by BSSs that belong to the same ESS.

Ethernet II The most common Ethernet standard today. Ethernet II is distinguished from other Ethernet frame types in that it contains a 2-byte type field to identify the upper-layer protocol contained in the frame.

Ethernet standards Various standards used to rate the performance expectations of a cable, NIC, or other device.

EUI-64 (Extended Unique Identifier-64) The IEEE standard defining 64-bit physical addresses. In the EUI-64 scheme, the OUI portion of an address is 24 bits in length. A 40-bit extension identifier makes up the rest of the physical address, for a total of 64 bits.

Event Viewer A GUI application that allows users to easily view and sort events recorded in the event log on a computer running a Windows-based operating system.

evil twin An exploit in which a rogue access point masquerades as a legitimate access point, using the same SSID and potentially other identical settings.

exclusion range A range of IP addresses within a defined DHCP scope that are excluded from the pool because they're reserved for other devices.

exploit In the context of network security, the act of taking advantage of a vulnerability.

extension identifier A unique set of characters assigned to each NIC by its manufacturer. Also called device ID.

exterior router   A router that directs data between autonomous systems, for example, routers used on the Internet's backbone.

F

fading   A variation in a wireless signal's strength as a result of some of the electromagnetic energy being scattered, reflected, or diffracted after being issued by the transmitter.

fail close   System default that denies access during a system or network failure.

fail open   System default that allows access during a system or network failure.

failure   A deviation from a specified level of system performance for a given period of time.

Fast Ethernet   A type of Ethernet network that is capable of 100-Mbps throughput.

fault   The malfunction of one component of a system.

fault tolerance   The capacity of a system to continue performing despite an unexpected hardware or software malfunction.

FC (Fibre Channel)   A storage networking architecture that runs separately from Ethernet networks to maximize speed of data storage and access.

FCoE (Fibre Channel over Ethernet)   A technology that allows FC to travel over Ethernet hardware and connections.

F-connector   A connector used to terminate coaxial cable that transmits television and cable broadband signals.

FDM (frequency division multiplexing)   A type of multiplexing that assigns a unique frequency band to each communications subchannel. Signals are modulated with different carrier frequencies and then multiplexed to simultaneously travel over a single channel.

FDP (fiber distribution panel)   A device on a rack where fiber cables converge, connect with each other, and connect with fiber-optic terminal equipment from the ISP.

ferrule   The extended tip of a fiber-optic cable connector that encircles the fiber strand to keep it properly aligned and ensure that it makes contact with the receptacle in a jack or other connector.

FHRP (First Hop Redundancy Protocol)   A type of protocol configured on a router or layer 3 switch to provide a single VIP (Virtual IP) address as the default gateway that, in turn, potentially points to multiple routers. Popular FHRPs include VRRP (Virtual Router Redundancy Protocol), HSRP (Hot Standby Routing Protocol), and GLBP (Gateway Load Balancing Protocol).

FHSS (frequency hopping spread spectrum)   A wireless signaling technique in which a signal jumps between several frequencies within a band in a synchronization pattern known to the channel's receiver and transmitter.

fiber light meter   A device that measures the amount of light power transmitted on a fiber-optic line. Also called an OPM (optical power meter).

fiber-optic cable   A form of cable that contains one or several glass or plastic fibers in its core. Data is transmitted via a pulsing light sent from a laser or LED (light-emitting diode) through the central fiber or fibers.

FIM (file integrity monitoring)   A security technique that alerts the system of any changes made to files that shouldn't change, such as operating system files.

fire suppression system   Any system designed to combat the outbreak of a fire. A fire suppression system might include an emergency alert system, fire extinguishers, emergency power-off switch, and/or a suppression agent such as a foaming chemical, gas, or water.

firewall   A device (either a router, a dedicated device, or a computer running special software) that selectively filters or blocks traffic between networks.

firmware   Programs embedded into hardware devices.

first responder   A person with training or certifications in handling evidence in such a way as to preserve its admissibility in court.

flow control   A bandwidth management technique configured on interfaces to balance permitted traffic volume with a device's capability of handling that traffic.

forward lookup   A DNS query that provides an FQDN and requests an IP address.

forwarding DNS server   An optional server that receives queries from local clients but doesn't work to resolve the queries.

FQDN (fully qualified domain name)   A host name plus domain name that uniquely identifies a computer or location on a network.

fragmentation   A network layer service that subdivides packets into smaller packets when those packets exceed the maximum size for the network.

frame The entire data link layer message, including the header, payload, and trailer.

frequency A measure of the number of times an electrical signal changes state per second.

FTP (File Transfer Protocol) An application layer protocol used to send and receive files via TCP/IP.

FTP bounce An attack in which an FTP client specifies a different host's IP address and port for the requested data's destination. By commanding the FTP server to connect to a different computer, a hacker can scan the ports on other hosts and transmit malicious code.

FTPS (FTP Secure or FTP over SSL) A version of FTP that incorporates the SSL/TLS protocols for added security.

full backup A backup in which all data on all servers is copied to a storage medium, regardless of whether the data is new, changed, or unchanged.

full tunnel VPN A type of VPN that captures all network traffic, whether destined for the Internet or for the corporate network.

full-duplex A type of transmission in which signals may travel in both directions over a medium simultaneously; also called, simply, duplex.

fusion splicer A tool used to melt the tips of two fibers together so light can pass cleanly through the joint.

G

gateway A computer, router, or other device that a host uses to access another network. Gateways perform connectivity, session management, and data translation, so they must operate at multiple layers of the OSI model.

gateway of last resort The router on a network that accepts all unroutable messages from other routers.

geofencing An authentication restriction that determines a client's geographic location to enforce a virtual security perimeter.

giant A frame that is too large and is dropped.

Gigabit Ethernet A type of Ethernet network that is capable of 1000-Mbps, or 1-Gbps, throughput. Requires Cat 5e or higher cabling.

global address An IPv6 address that can be routed on the Internet. These addresses are similar to public IPv4 addresses. Most global addresses begin with the prefix 2000::/3, although other prefixes are being released.

global routing prefix The first four blocks or 64 bits of an IPv6 address that normally identify the network. Also called site prefix.

GRE (Generic Routing Encapsulation) A tunneling protocol developed by Cisco that is used to transmit IP and other kinds of messages through a tunnel.

grounding Connecting a device directly to the earth so that, in the event of a short circuit, the electricity flows into the earth rather than out of control through the device.

Group Policy (gpedit.msc) A Windows utility that is used to control what users can do and how the system can be used.

GSM (Global System for Mobile Communications) An open standard for cellular networks that uses digital communication of data separated by time slots on a channel.

guest In the context of virtualization, a virtual machine operated and managed by a virtualization program.

guest network A separate wireless network created through a Wi-Fi router or access point to protect a private network while still providing guests with access to the Internet.

H

HA (high availability) A system that functions reliably nearly all the time.

hacker Traditionally, a person who masters the inner workings of computer hardware and software in an effort to better understand them. More generally, an individual who gains unauthorized access to systems or networks with or without malicious intent.

hashing The transformation of data through an algorithm that is mathematically irreversible and generally reduces the amount of space needed for the data. Hashing is mostly used to ensure data integrity—that is, to verify the data has not been altered.

header An area at the beginning of a payload where protocols add control information.

HFC (hybrid fiber coaxial) A physical infrastructure where fiber-optic cabling connects the cable company's distribution center to distribution hubs and then to optical nodes near customers; either fiber-optic or coaxial cable then connects a node to each customer's business or residence.

HIDS (host-based intrusion detection system) A type of intrusion detection that runs on a single computer, such as a client or server, to alert about attacks against that one host.

HIPS (host-based intrusion prevention system)   A type of intrusion prevention that runs on a single computer, such as a client or server, to intercept and help prevent attacks against that one host.

honeynet   A network of honeypots.

honeypot   A decoy system isolated from legitimate systems and designed to be vulnerable to security exploits for the purposes of learning more about hacking techniques or nabbing a hacker in the act.

hop   The trip a unit of data takes from one connectivity device to another. Typically, hop is used in the context of router-to-router communications.

host   (1) Any computer or device on a network that provides or uses a resource such as an application or data. (2) In the context of virtualization, the physical computer on which virtualization software operates and manages guests.

host ID   The portion of an IP address that identifies the host on a network.

host name   The first part of an FQDN, such as *www* or *ftp*, which identifies the individual computer on the network.

host-based firewall   A firewall that only protects the computer on which it's installed.

hostname   The utility used to display a device's host name or, in UNIX/Linux systems, to alter the host name.

host-only mode   A type of network connection in which VMs on a host can exchange data with each other and with their host, but they cannot communicate with any nodes beyond the host. In host-only mode, VMs use the DHCP service in the host's virtualization software to obtain IP address assignments.

hot site   A place where the computers, devices, and connectivity necessary to rebuild a network exist, and all are appropriately configured, updated, and connected to match a network's current state.

hot-swappable   A component that can be installed or removed without disrupting operations.

HSRP (Hot Standby Routing Protocol)   Cisco's proprietary standard that assigns a virtual IP address to a group of routers.

HTTP (Hypertext Transfer Protocol)   An application layer protocol that formulates and interprets requests between web clients and servers.

HTTPS (HTTP Secure)   An extension to HTTP that requires data be exchanged between client and server using SSL or TLS encryption.

hub   An outdated connectivity device that belongs to the physical layer of the OSI model and retransmits incoming data signals to its multiple ports.

hub-and-spoke topology   A topology in which a central networking component, such as a switch, connects to multiple peripheral networking components that each connect to endpoint devices in their areas.

hybrid cloud   A cloud deployment model in which shared and flexible data storage, applications, or services are made available through a combination of other service models into a single deployment, or a collection of services connected within the cloud.

hybrid routing protocol   A routing protocol that exhibits characteristics of both distance-vector and link-state routing protocols.

hybrid topology   A physical topology that combines characteristics of more than one simple physical topology.

hypervisor   The element of virtualization software that manages multiple guest machines and their connections to the host (and by association, to a physical network).

I

IaaS (Infrastructure as a Service)   A cloud service model in which hardware services are provided virtually, including network infrastructure devices such as virtual servers.

IaC (infrastructure as code)   The process of using text-based commands in a computer-readable configuration file to create and manage cloud resources.

IANA (Internet Assigned Numbers Authority)   A nonprofit, U.S. government-funded group that was established at the University of Southern California and charged with managing IP address allocation and the Domain Name System. The oversight for many of IANA's functions was given to ICANN in 1998; however, IANA continues to perform Internet addressing and Domain Name System administration.

IB (InfiniBand) A storage networking architecture that serves a few niche markets and falls on the difficult end of the installation and configuration spectrum.

IBSS (independent basic service set) A small number of nodes closely positioned to transmit directly to each other without an intervening connectivity device.

ICANN (Internet Corporation for Assigned Names and Numbers) The nonprofit corporation currently designated by the U.S. government to maintain and assign IP addresses.

ICMP (Internet Control Message Protocol) A core protocol in the TCP/IP suite that notifies the sender when something has gone wrong in the transmission process and packets were not delivered.

IDF (intermediate distribution frame) A junction point between the MDF and concentrations of fewer connections—for example, those that terminate in a data closet.

IDS (intrusion detection system) A stand-alone device, an application, or a built-in feature running on a workstation, server, switch, router, or firewall. It monitors network traffic, generating alerts about suspicious activity.

ifconfig An interface configuration and management utility used with UNIX and Linux systems.

IGP (interior gateway protocol) A type of routing protocol, such as OSPF and IS-IS, used by core routers and edge routers within autonomous systems.

IMAP4 (Internet Message Access Protocol, version 4) A mail retrieval protocol that allows users to store messages on the mail server while reading, responding to, and organizing the messages. The most current version of IMAP is version 4 (IMAP4).

impedance A measure of the opposition to a current's flow through a cable, expressed in ohms.

implicit deny An ACL (access control list) rule that ensures that any traffic the ACL does not explicitly permit is denied by default.

in-band management A switch management option, such as Telnet, that uses the existing network and its protocols to interface with a switch.

incident Any event, large or small, that has adverse effects on a network's availability or resources.

incident response plan A document specifically defining the characteristics of an event that qualifies as a formal incident and the steps that should be followed as a result.

incremental backup A backup in which only data that has changed since the last full or incremental backup is copied to a storage medium.

industrial controls system A network that acquires real-time data from a physical system and manages the physical system or presents the data to humans, who monitor and manage the system. Also called SCADA (supervisory control and data acquisition).

infrastructure plane An SDN (software-defined networking) construct made up of physical or virtual devices that receive and send network messages. Also called data plane.

infrastructure topology A type of wireless network in which stations communicate through an access point and not directly with each other.

insider threat A security risk associated with someone who is or was trusted by an organization, such as an employee, former employee, contractor, or other associate.

interconnection A leased line from a customer's location or from their ISP to a PoP (point of presence), or colocation, which provides connection with other providers (such as cloud providers). Also called a private-direct connection.

interface A network connection made by a node or host on a network.

interface ID The last 64 bits, or four blocks, of an IPv6 address that uniquely identify the interface on the local link.

interference Degradation of a wireless signal caused by electromagnetic waves in the atmosphere.

interior router A router that directs data between networks within the same autonomous system. Also called a core router.

inventory management The process of monitoring and maintaining all the assets that make up a network.

IoT (Internet of Things) Any device connected to the Internet.

ip The utility used to display and alter TCP/IP addressing and domain name information in UNIX/Linux operating systems.

IP (Internet Protocol)   A core protocol in the TCP/IP suite that operates in the network layer of the OSI model and provides information about how and where data should be delivered. IP is the subprotocol that enables TCP/IP to internetwork.

IP address   A unique network layer address assigned to each node on a TCP/IP network. IPv4 addresses consist of 32 bits divided into four octets, or bytes. IPv6 addresses are composed of eight 16-bit fields, for a total of 128 bits.

IP helper address   An IP address or broadcast address configured on a relay agent to direct UDP messages in support of UDP forwarding for centralized network services, such as DHCP, DNS, NTP, and TFTP.

IP reservation   An IP address that is set aside by a DHCP server for a specific network client, which is identified by its MAC address. Also called MAC reservation or DHCP reservation.

IP scanner   A tool used to gather information about all devices connected to a network, including host names, manufacturer names, operating systems, IP addresses, MAC addresses, interfaces used, and open ports with running services.

IPAM (IP address management)   A standalone product or application embedded in another product, such as Windows Server, that provides a way to plan, deploy, and monitor a network's IP address space.

ipconfig   The utility used to display and alter TCP/IP addressing and domain name information in the Windows client operating systems.

iPerf   A command-line based tool that can measure throughput between two network hosts.

IPS (intrusion prevention system)   A stand-alone device, an application, or a built-in feature running on a workstation, server, switch, router, or firewall that stands in-line between an attacker and the targeted network or host and can prevent traffic from reaching that network or host.

IPsec (Internet Protocol Security)   A layer 3 protocol that defines encryption, authentication, and key management for TCP/IP transmissions. IPsec is an enhancement to IPv4 and is native to IPv6.

IPv4 (Internet Protocol version 4)   The Internet Protocol standard released in the 1980s and still commonly used on modern networks. It specifies 32-bit addresses composed of four octets.

IPv6 (Internet Protocol version 6)   A standard for IP addressing that is gradually replacing the current IPv4. Most notably, IPv6 uses a newer, more efficient header in its packets and allows for 128-bit source and destination IP addresses, which are usually written as eight blocks of hexadecimal numbers, such as 2001:0DB8:0B80:0000:0000:00D3:9C5A:00CC.

IR (infrared)   A wireless technology that uses a bandwidth just below the spectrum that is visible to the human eye, with longer wavelengths than red light.

iSCSI (Internet SCSI)   A transport layer protocol used by SANs that runs on top of TCP to allow fast transmission over LANs, WANs, and the Internet.

IS-IS (Intermediate System to Intermediate System)   A link-state routing protocol that uses a best-path algorithm. IS-IS was originally codified by ISO, which referred to routers as "intermediate systems," thus the protocol's name.

ISP (Internet service provider)   A company that provides Internet connectivity.

iterative lookup   A DNS query that does not demand a resolution, which means the server provides the information only if it already has that information available.

J

jitter   A transmission flaw caused by packets experiencing varying amounts of delay and arriving out of order. Also called PDV (packet delay variation).

jumbo frame   A setting on Ethernet network devices that allows the creation and transmission of extra-large frames, which can be as large as just over 9,000 bytes.

K

KDC (Key Distribution Center)   In Kerberos terminology, the server that issues keys to clients during initial client authentication.

Kerberos   A cross-platform authentication protocol that uses key encryption to verify the identity of client devices and to securely exchange information after a client logs on to a system.

key   A series of characters that is combined with a block of data during that data's encryption.

knowledge base   A collection of accumulated insights and solutions to the problems encountered on a particular network.

Krone (Krone LSA-Plus) block   A proprietary type of punchdown block developed and patented in Europe. Like the more common 110 block, it's typically used to handle data connections rather than telephone connections.

KVM (keyboard, video, and mouse) switch   A device that connects the equipment in a rack to a single console to provide a central control portal for all devices on the rack.

L

LACP (Link Aggregation Control Protocol)   A protocol currently defined by IEEE's 802.1AX standard that dynamically coordinates communications between two hosts on aggregated connections.

LAN (local area network)   A network of computers and other devices that typically is confined to a relatively small space, such as one building or even one office. Each node on a LAN can communicate directly with others on the same LAN.

latency   The delay between the transmission of a signal and its receipt.

layer 3 switch   A switch capable of interpreting layer 3 data and works much like a router in that it supports the same routing protocols and makes routing decisions.

layer 4 switch   A switch capable of interpreting layer 4 data, which means it can perform advanced filtering, keep statistics, and provide security functions.

LC (local connector)   The most common 1.25-mm ferrule connector, which is used with single-mode, fiber-optic cable.

LDAP (Lightweight Directory Access Protocol)   A standard protocol for accessing network directories.

LDAPS (Lightweight Directory Access Protocol over SSL)   A version of LDAP that uses SSL/TLS to encrypt its communications with network directories and clients.

lease time   A time limit on the validity of a DHCP-issued IP address.

leased line   Dedicated Internet bandwidth provided over fiber-optic connections.

least cost path   The most efficient path from each switch to the root bridge in an STP (Spanning Tree Protocol) environment.

LED (light-emitting diode)   A cool-burning, long-lasting technology that creates light by the release of photons as electrons move through a semiconductor material.

licensing restrictions   The portion of a software license that limits what a product can be used for.

link   Any LAN (local area network) bounded by routers.

link aggregation   The seamless combination of multiple network interfaces or ports to act as one logical interface.

link local address   An IP address that is automatically assigned by an operating system to allow a node to communicate over its local subnet if a routable IP address is not available.

link-layer address   The name for a MAC address on an IPv6 network.

link-state routing protocol   A type of routing protocol that enables routers to share performance and status information about their connected links with routers throughout the network, after which each router can independently map the network and determine the best path between itself and a message's destination node.

LLC (logical link control) sublayer   A sublayer of layer 2 that is primarily concerned with multiplexing, flow and error control, and reliability.

load balancer   A device that distributes traffic intelligently among multiple devices or connections.

load balancing   The distribution of traffic over multiple components or links to optimize performance and fault tolerance.

local loop   The part of a phone system that connects a customer site with a telecommunications carrier's switching facility.

locking cabinet   A storage container secured by a locked panel or door that might be used to store documents or hardware not in use.

locking rack   A data center rack secured by a locked panel or door.

log   A record of activities or state changes on a device or in an operating system.

logging level   An indication of priority that syslog assigns to each logged event. Also called severity level.

logic bomb   Code or a bug in code that will start when certain conditions are met.

logical topology   A characteristic of network transmission that reflects the way in which data is transmitted between nodes, including how access to the network is controlled and how specific resources are shared on the network. A network's logical topology may differ from its physical topology.

long-haul connection   A long-distance connection, such as across hundreds of miles, that supports the Internet backbone.

loopback adapter   A troubleshooting tool that plugs into a port (for example, an RJ-45 or fiber-optic port) and crosses the transmit line with the receive line, allowing outgoing signals to be redirected back into the computer for testing. Also called a loopback plug.

loopback address   An IP address reserved for communicating from a node to itself, used mostly for troubleshooting purposes.

LOS (line of sight)   A wireless signal or path that travels directly in a straight line from its transmitter to its intended receiver.

loss-tolerant   Transmissions that can tolerate occasional loss of data without compromising the user experience.

LTE (Long-Term Evolution)   A transitional cellular network technology between 3G and 4G that takes advantage of some improved 4G technologies to exceed 3G speeds but does not reach 4G throughput requirements.

LTE-Advanced   The latest version of LTE, with theoretical downlink rates approaching true 4G speeds up to 1 Gbps and uplink rates as high as 100 Mbps, although actual speeds are significantly less. Sometimes misleadingly called 5G E (5G Evolution).

M

MAC (mandatory access control)   A method of access control where resources are organized into hierarchical classifications, such as "confidential" or "top secret," and grouped into categories, perhaps by department. Users, then, are also classified and categorized. If a user's classification and category match those of a resource, then the user is given access.

MAC (Media Access Control) address   A 48- or 64-bit network interface identifier that includes two parts: the OUI, assigned by IEEE to the manufacturer, and the extension identifier, a unique number assigned to each NIC by the manufacturer.

MAC address table   A database configured manually or dynamically that in some cases stores a mapping of MAC addresses to switch ports and in other cases stores MAC addresses allowed on a network.

MAC filtering   A security measure that prevents an AP or a switch from authenticating any device whose MAC address is not listed by the network administrator as an approved device.

MAC reservation   An IP address that is set aside by a DHCP server for a specific network client, which is identified by its MAC address. Also called IP reservation or DHCP reservation.

MAC sublayer   The lower portion of the data link layer that is specifically involved with managing MAC addresses in message frames.

magic number   In the context of calculating subnets, the difference between 256 and the interesting octet (any octet in the subnet whose value is something other than 0 or 255). It can be used to calculate the network IDs in all the subnets of a larger network.

malware (malicious software)   A program or piece of code designed to intrude upon or harm a system or its resources.

MAN (metropolitan area network)   A network of connected LANs within a limited geographical area, such as multiple city government buildings around a city's center.

managed switch   A switch that can be configured via a command-line interface or a web-based management GUI, and sometimes can be configured in groups.

management plane   An SDN (software-defined networking) construct sometimes considered part of the control plane that allows network administrators to remotely manage and monitor network devices.

MDF (main distribution frame)   Also known as the main cross connect, the centralized point of interconnection between an organization's LAN or WAN and a service provider's network.

MDI (media dependent interface)   A connector used with twisted-pair wiring on an Ethernet network.

MDI-X (media dependent interface crossover)   An alternative connector used with twisted-pair wiring on an Ethernet network that reverses the transmit and receive wires.

MDM (mobile device management)   Software that automatically handles the process of configuring wireless clients for network access.

media converter   A device that enables networks or segments running on different media to interconnect and exchange signals.

mesh topology (1) A type of network in which several nodes are directly interconnected and no single node controls communications on the network. (2) A wireless network in which multiple APs work as peer devices on the same network, thereby providing more fault-tolerant network access to clients.

MFA (multifactor authentication) An authentication process that requires information from two or more categories of authentication factors.

mGRE (multipoint GRE) A tunneling protocol developed by Cisco that allows the configuration of multiple tunnel destinations on a single interface.

MIB (Management Information Base) The list of objects managed by an NMS (network management system), as well as the descriptions of these objects.

Microsoft SQL Server A DBMS (database management system) produced by Microsoft that is designed to handle large volumes of data.

MIMO (multiple input-multiple output) In the context of 802.11 wireless networking, the ability for access points to use multiple antennas to issue multiple signals to stations, thereby multiplying the signal's strength and increasing their range and data-carrying capacity.

MLA (master license agreement) A contract that grants a license from a creator, developer, or producer, such as a software producer, to a third party for the purposes of marketing, sublicensing, or distributing the product to consumers as a stand-alone product or as part of another product.

MMF (multimode fiber) A type of fiber-optic cable containing a core that is usually 50 or 62.5 microns in diameter, over which many pulses of light generated by a laser or LED (light-emitting diode) travel at different angles.

modal bandwidth A measure of the highest frequency of signal a multimode fiber-optic cable can support over a specific distance. Modal bandwidth is measured in MHz-km.

modem A modulation/demodulation device that converts between digital and analog signals.

modulation The process of altering an analog signal to carry data.

MON (metropolitan optical network) A dense, localized grid of junctions and fiber cables designed to make direct fiber connections available to as many customers as possible.

motion detection Technology that triggers an alarm when it detects movement within its field of view.

MOU (memorandum of understanding) A document presenting the intentions of two or more parties to enter into a binding agreement, or contract. The MOU is usually not a legally binding document (although there are exceptions), does not grant extensive rights to either party, provides no legal recourse, and is not intended to provide a thorough coverage of the agreement to come.

MPLS (multiprotocol label switching) A type of switching that enables multiple types of layer 3 protocols to travel over any one of several connection-oriented layer 2 protocols.

MSA (master service agreement) A contract that defines terms of future contracts.

MTBF (mean time between failures) The average amount of time that will pass before the next failure of a device or service is expected to occur.

MT-RJ (Mechanical Transfer-Registered Jack) The most common type of connector used with multimode fiber-optic cable.

MTTR (mean time to repair) The average amount of time required to repair a device or restore a service.

MTU (maximum transmission unit) The largest IP packet size in bytes that routers in a message's path will allow without fragmentation and excluding the frame.

multicast Transmissions in which one host sends messages to multiple hosts.

multicast address A type of IPv6 address that represents multiple interfaces, often on multiple nodes.

multicast flooding Traffic congestion on a network caused by a weakness in the way switches learn MAC addresses of network devices. To fix this problem, a switch that must handle multicast traffic should have IGMP snooping enabled on it, which allows the switch to detect IGMP (Internet Group Management Protocol) messages to add more accurate entries in its MAC address tables.

multicloud A cloud deployment model consisting of a combination of cloud platforms (such as AWS, Azure, and Salesforce) or a combination of other deployment models, such as private, public, and community cloud.

multimeter   A simple instrument that can measure multiple characteristics of an electric circuit, including its resistance, voltage, and impedance.

multipathing   The provision of multiple connections between servers and storage devices in a SAN (storage area network) to ensure quick failover and high-performance load balancing.

multiplexing   A form of transmission that allows multiple signals to travel simultaneously over one medium.

multitenancy   The provision of cloud services hosted on the same hardware for multiple customers.

MU-MIMO (multiuser MIMO)   In the context of 802.11 wireless networking, the ability for access points to use multiple antennas to issue multiple signals to different stations at the same time, thereby reducing congestion and contributing to faster data transmission.

MX (mail exchanger) record   A type of DNS data record that identifies a mail server and that is used for email traffic.

MySQL   A popular open source DBMS (database management system).

N

name resolution   The process of discovering the IP address of a host when the FQDN is known.

NAT (Network Address Translation)   A technique in which IP addresses used on a private network are assigned a public IP address by a gateway when accessing a public network.

NAT (network address translation) mode   A type of network connection in which a vNIC relies on the host machine to act as a NAT device. The virtualization software acts as a DHCP server.

NDA (non-disclosure agreement)   The part of a security policy that defines what *confidential* and *private* mean to the organization and, therefore, identifies what should not be shared outside a defined team or the organization itself.

NDP (Neighbor Discovery Protocol)   A data link layer protocol that works with ICMPv6 to detect neighboring devices on an IPv6 network, helps manage the SLAAC (stateless address autoconfiguration) process, and oversees router and network prefix discovery.

neighbor   Two or more nodes on the same link.

NetFlow   A proprietary traffic monitoring protocol from Cisco that tracks all IP traffic crossing any interface where NetFlow is enabled.

NetFlow analyzer   A device that collates flow records from throughout the network to provide insights into traffic patterns. Also called a NetFlow collector.

netstat   A TCP/IP troubleshooting utility that displays statistics and details about TCP/IP components and connections on a host. It also lists ports, which can signal whether services are using the correct ports.

network   A group of computers and other devices (such as printers) that are connected by and can exchange data via wired or wireless transmission media.

network diagram   A graphical representation of a network's devices and connections.

network ID   The portion of an IP address common to all nodes on the same network or subnet.

network layer   The third layer in the OSI model. The network layer, sometimes called the Internet layer, is responsible for moving messages between networks.

network management   The assessment, monitoring, and maintenance of all aspects of a network.

network service   A resource the network makes available to its users, including applications and the data provided by these applications.

network-based firewall   A firewall configured and positioned to protect an entire network or segment of a network.

NFC (near-field communication)   A form of radio communication that transfers data wirelessly over very short distances (usually 10 cm or less).

NFV (Network Functions Virtualization)   A network architecture that merges physical and virtual network devices.

NIC (network interface card)   The component in a computer or other networking device that enables the device to connect to the network and communicate with other devices. Also called network adapters.

NIC teaming   The seamless combination of multiple network interfaces or ports on Windows devices to act as one logical interface.

NIDS (network-based intrusion detection system)   A type of intrusion detection that protects an entire network and is situated at the edge of the network or in a network's screened subnet.

NIPS (network-based intrusion prevention system)   A type of intrusion prevention that protects an entire network and is situated at the edge of the network or in a network's screened subnet.

Nmap (Network Mapper) A scanning tool designed to assess large networks quickly and provide comprehensive, customized information about a network and its hosts.

NMS (network management system) server A server or workstation that collects data from multiple managed devices at regular intervals.

node Any computer or other device on a network that can be addressed on the local network.

node ID The portion of an IP address that identifies the node on a network.

north-south traffic Messages that must leave the local segment to reach their destinations.

NOS (network operating system) The software that runs on a server and enables the server to manage data, users, groups, security, applications, and other networking functions. Popular examples of network operating systems are Windows Server, Ubuntu Server, and Red Hat Enterprise Linux.

NS (name server) record A DNS lookup file that indicates the authoritative name server for a domain. It's mostly used for delegating subdomains to other name servers.

nslookup (name space lookup) A TCP/IP utility that allows a technician to query the DNS database from any computer on the network and find the host name of a network node by specifying its IP address, or vice versa. This ability is useful for verifying that a host is configured correctly and for troubleshooting DNS resolution problems.

NTP (Network Time Protocol) A simple application layer protocol in the TCP/IP suite used to synchronize the clocks of computers on a network. NTP depends on UDP for transport layer services.

O

octet One of 4 bytes that are separated by periods and together make up an IPv4 address.

OFDMA (Orthogonal Frequency Division Multiple Access) In the context of 802.11 wireless technology, a technique that supports more efficient multi-user functionality by allowing an AP to subdivide each channel into smaller frequency allocations for each client, such as 2 MHz or 4 MHz of each 20 MHz channel.

offboarding The reverse process of onboarding, involving the removal of programs that gave a device special permissions on the network.

OID (object identifier) A number assigned each object managed by an NMS (network management system).

omnidirectional antenna A type of antenna that issues and receives wireless signals with equal strength and clarity in all directions.

onboarding A process of configuring clients for wireless access to a network.

on-path attack An attack that relies on intercepted transmissions. It can take one of several forms, but in all cases a person redirects or captures secure data traffic while in transit. Formerly called MitM (man-in-the-middle) attack.

on-premises data center The physical location of the customer and the hardware they own.

open circuit A circuit in which necessary connections are missing, such as occurs when a wire breaks.

open source Software whose code is publicly available for use and modification.

OPM (optical power meter) A device that measures the amount of light power transmitted on a fiber-optic line. Also called a fiber light meter.

optical link budget The calculation of power a transceiver must use to overcome all anticipated losses along the length of a fiber-optic connection.

optical loss The degradation of a light signal on a fiber-optic network as it travels away from its source.

Oracle Database A proprietary DBMS (database management system) offered by Oracle.

orchestration The design, development, and optimization of automation processes into a single workflow.

OSHA (Occupational Safety and Health Administration) The main federal agency charged with regulating safety and health in the workplace.

OSI (Open Systems Interconnection) reference model A model for understanding, developing, and troubleshooting computer-to-computer communication that was developed in the 1980s by ISO. It divides networking functions among seven layers: physical, data link, network, transport, session, presentation, and application.

OSPF (Open Shortest Path First) An IGP (interior gateway protocol) and link-state routing protocol that improves on some of the limitations of RIP (Routing Information Protocol) and can coexist with RIP on a network.

OTDR (optical time domain reflectometer) A performance testing device for use with fiber-optic networks, which can accurately measure the length of the fiber, locations of faults, and many other characteristics.

OUI (Organizationally Unique Identifier) A 24-bit character sequence assigned by IEEE that appears at the beginning of a network interface's physical address and identifies the NIC's manufacturer.

out-of-band management A dedicated connection (either wired or wireless) from the network administrator's computer used to manage each critical network device, such as routers, firewalls, servers, power supplies, applications, and security cameras.

overhead The burden placed on the underlying network to support a routing protocol.

P

P2P (peer-to-peer) network model A network in which every computer can communicate directly with every other computer. By default, no computer on a P2P network has more authority than another.

PaaS (Platform as a Service) A cloud service model in which various platforms are provided virtually, enabling developers to build and test applications within virtual, online environments tailored to the specific needs of a project.

packet The entire network layer message, which includes the segment (TCP) or datagram (UDP) from the transport layer, plus the network layer header.

packet analysis The examination of information contained within packets to identify protocols, errors, and misconfigurations.

packet sniffer A software package or hardware-based tool that can capture data on a network.

packet-filtering firewall A network device or application that examines the header of every packet of data it receives on any of its interfaces to determine whether the packet should be allowed to continue traversing the network.

PAN (personal area network) A network of personal devices, such as a smartphone, laptop, and Bluetooth printer.

password manager An application that provides a secure means of storing and organizing passwords.

PAT (Port Address Translation) A form of address translation that assigns a separate TCP port to each ongoing conversation, or session, between a local host and an Internet host.

patch A correction, improvement, or enhancement to part of a software application, often distributed at no charge by software vendors to fix a bug in their code or to add slightly more functionality.

patch bay A wall- or rack-mounted panel where cables converge in one location. Also called a patch panel.

patch cable A relatively short section (usually between 3 and 25 feet) of cabling with connectors on both ends.

patch management The process of monitoring the release of new patches, testing them for use on networked devices, and installing them.

patch panel A wall- or rack-mounted panel where cables converge in one location. Also called a patch bay.

payload Data that is passed between applications or utility programs and the operating system, and that includes control information.

PDU (power distribution unit) A power management device that acts as a sophisticated power strip to bring power from outlets, a generator, or a UPS (uninterruptible power supply) closer to the devices on a rack.

pen (penetration) testing A process of scanning a network for vulnerabilities and investigating potential security flaws.

phishing A practice in which a person attempts to glean access or authentication information by posing as someone who needs that information.

physical layer The lowest, or first, layer of the OSI model. The physical layer is responsible only for sending bits via a wired or wireless transmission.

physical topology The physical layout of the media, nodes, and devices on a network. A physical topology does not specify device types, connectivity methods, or addressing schemes. A network's physical topology may differ from its logical topology.

piggybacking An attack type in which a person uses deception to follow an authorized employee into a restricted area.

ping (Packet Internet Groper) A TCP/IP troubleshooting utility that can verify TCP/IP is installed, bound to the NIC, configured correctly, and communicating with the network. Ping uses

ICMP (Internet Control Message Protocol) to send echo request and echo reply messages.

pinout The pin numbers and color-coded wire assignments used when terminating a cable or installing a jack, as determined by the TIA/EIA standard.

PKI (public-key infrastructure) The use of certificate authorities to associate public keys with certain users.

plenum The area above the ceiling tile or below the subfloor in a building.

plenum-grade cabling Cabling designed to withstand high temperatures, offers a highly fire-retardant jacket, and burns with less smoke that is nontoxic.

PoE (Power over Ethernet) A method of delivering up to 15.4 watts to devices using Ethernet connection cables.

PoE+ A method of delivering more current (up to 25.5 watts) than PoE does to devices using Ethernet connection cables.

polarization A characteristic of a wireless device's antenna that determines what axis the antenna's signals will follow, such as a vertical axis or horizontal axis.

PoP (Point of Presence) A data center facility at which a provider rents space to allow for dedicated connection services.

POP3 (Post Office Protocol, version 3) An application layer protocol used to retrieve messages from a mail server. When a client retrieves mail via POP, messages previously stored on the mail server are downloaded to the client's workstation, and then deleted from the mail server. The most commonly used form of POP is POP3.

port A number that identifies a process, such as an application or service, running on a computer. TCP and UDP ports ensure that data is transmitted to the correct process among multiple processes running on a computer.

port aggregation The seamless combination of multiple network interfaces or ports on Cisco devices to act as one logical interface.

port mirroring A monitoring technique in which one port on a switch is configured to send a copy of all the switch's traffic to the device connected to that port. Also called SPAN (switched port analyzer).

port scanner Software that searches a server, switch, router, or other device for open ports that might be vulnerable to attack.

posture assessment An evaluation of an organization's security vulnerabilities.

PPE (personal protective equipment) Wearable equipment such as goggles that might be required in the workplace to increase safety of workers.

presentation layer The sixth layer of the OSI model. Protocols in the presentation layer are responsible for reformatting, compressing, and/or encrypting data in a way that the application on the receiving end can read.

primary DNS server The authoritative name server for an organization, which holds the authoritative DNS database for the organization's zones. This server is contacted by clients, both local and over the Internet, to resolve DNS queries for the organization's domains.

principal In Kerberos terminology, a user or client.

principle of least privilege A security measure that ensures employees and contractors are only given enough access and privileges to do their jobs, and these privileges are terminated as soon as the person no longer needs them.

private cloud A cloud deployment model in which shared and flexible data storage, applications, or services are managed on and delivered via an organization's own network, or established virtually for a single organization's private use.

private IP address IP addresses that can be used on a private network but not on the Internet. IEEE recommends the following IP address ranges for private use: 10.0.0.0 through 10.255.255.255; 172.16.0.0 through 172.31.255.255; and 192.168.0.0 through 192.168.255.255.

private key encryption A type of key encryption in which the sender and receiver use a key to which only they have access. Also known as symmetric encryption.

private VLAN A VLAN partitioned into multiple broadcast domains, called secondary VLANs.

private-direct connection A leased line from a customer's location or from their ISP to a PoP (point of presence), or colocation, which provides connection with other providers (such as cloud providers). Also called an interconnection.

privileged access An administrative account on a device or network that gives high-level permissions to change configurations or access data.

probe (1) A repeated trial message transmitted by the tracert and traceroute utilities to trigger routers along a route to return specific information about the route. (2) A small electronic device that emits a tone when it detects electrical activity on a wire pair. When used in conjunction with a tone generator, it can help locate the termination of a wire pair. Also called a tone locator. (3) In 802.11 wireless networking, a type of frame issued by a station during active scanning to find nearby access points.

process   An instance of a running computer application or service.

process assessment   An evaluation of all business processes that might be impacted by various cybersecurity threats.

promiscuous port   A port within a private VLAN designed to communicate with all secondary VLAN ports within the primary VLAN.

propagation   The way in which a wave travels from one point to another.

protocol   A standard method or format for communication between network devices.

protocol analyzer   A software package or hardware-based tool that can capture and analyze data on a network.

proxy server   A server acting as an intermediary between the external and internal networks, screening all incoming and outgoing traffic.

PSK (Pre-Shared Key)   An authentication method for WPA or WPA2 that requires a passphrase for a device to be authenticated to the network.

PSTN (public switched telephone network)   The network of lines and carrier equipment that provides wired telephone service to most homes and businesses.

PTR (pointer) record   A type of DNS data record that is used for reverse lookups, to provide a host name when the IP address is known.

PUA (privileged user agreement)   A document that addresses the specific concerns related to privileged access given to administrators and certain support staff.

public cloud   A cloud deployment model in which shared and flexible data storage, applications, or services are managed centrally by service providers and delivered over public transmission lines, such as the Internet.

public IP address   An IP address that is valid for use on public networks, such as the Internet.

public key encryption   A form of key encryption in which data is encrypted using two keys: One is a key known only to a user (that is, a private key),

and the other is a key associated with the user and that can be obtained from a public source, such as a public key server. Public key encryption is also known as asymmetric encryption.

punchdown tool   A pointed tool used to insert twisted-pair wire into receptors in a punchdown block to complete a circuit.

Q

QoS (quality of service)   A group of techniques for adjusting the priority a network assigns to various types of transmissions.

QSFP (quad small form-factor pluggable)   A fiber-optic transceiver that complies with the 802.3ba standard, squeezing four channels in a single transceiver and supporting data rates up to 40 Gbps (4 × 10 Gbps).

QSFP+   Generally the same technology as QSFP while supporting data rates over 40 Gbps.

R

RA (router advertisement)   A message from a router in response to a client's solicitation and provides DHCP information.

RA guard   A feature that can be configured on switches to filter RA messages according to interface, MAC or IP address, router priority, or other factors.

rack diagram   A drawing that shows the devices stacked in a rack system and is typically drawn to scale.

radiation pattern   The relative strength over a three-dimensional area of all the electromagnetic energy an antenna sends or receives.

RADIUS (Remote Authentication Dial-In User Service)   A popular protocol for providing centralized AAA services for multiple users.

range   The geographical area in which signals issued from an antenna or wireless system can be consistently and accurately received.

ransomware   A program that locks a user's data or computer system until a ransom is paid.

RAS (remote access server)   A server that runs communications services enabling remote users to log on to a network and grant privileges to the network's resources.

RBAC (role-based access control)   A method of access control where a network administrator assigns only the privileges and permissions necessary for a user to perform the role required by an organization.

RC4 (Rivest Cipher 4)   An insecure encryption cipher that is still widely used.

rDNS (reverse DNS)   A DNS query that provides an IP address and requests an FQDN. Also called reverse lookup.

RDP (Remote Desktop Protocol)   An application layer protocol that uses TCP/IP to transmit graphics and text quickly over a remote client-host connection. RDP also carries session, licensing, and encryption information.

RDS (Remote Desktop Services)   A service offered by Windows Server that uses RDP (Remote Desktop Protocol) to allow multiple users to access the same virtual or physical Windows Server system at the same time.

reassociation   In the context of wireless networking, the process by which a station establishes a connection with (or associates with) a different access point.

recursive lookup   A DNS query that demands a resolution or the response that the information can't be found.

red team–blue team exercise   An attack simulation in which the red team conducts an attack and the blue team attempts to defend the network.

redundancy   The use of more than one identical component, device, or connection for storing, processing, or transporting data.

reflection   In the context of wireless signaling, the phenomenon that occurs when an electromagnetic wave encounters an obstacle and bounces back toward its source.

refraction   In the context of wireless signaling, the way in which a wave alters its direction, speed, and wavelength when it travels through different transmission mediums.

registered port   The TCP/IP ports in the range of 1024 to 49,151. These ports can be used by network users and processes that are not considered standard processes. Default assignments of these ports must be registered with IANA.

relay agent   A networking device (such as a router or firewall) configured to support UDP forwarding.

reliability   A measurement of how well a resource functions without errors.

remote access   A method for connecting and logging on to a server, LAN, or WAN from a workstation that is in a different geographical location.

remote desktop connection   Graphical-based access to a remote computer's desktop.

remote desktop gateway   A service on a Windows server that can manage high volumes of RDP (Remote Desktop Protocol) connections to a network's computers through a single public IP address.

remote wipe   A security procedure that clears a device of all important information, permissions, and applications without having physical access to the device.

repeater   A device used to regenerate a digital signal in its original form. Repeaters operate at the physical layer of the OSI model.

resiliency   The measurement of a resource's ability to recover from errors even when it becomes unavailable during an outage.

resource record   The element of a DNS database stored on a name server that contains information about TCP/IP host names and their addresses.

reverse lookup   A DNS query that provides an IP address and requests an FQDN. Also called rDNS (reverse DNS).

RFC1918 (Request for Comment 1918)   IANA's document that formally identified IP address ranges for private networks.

RFID (Radio Frequency Identification)   A wireless technology that uses electromagnetic fields to store data on a small chip in a tag, which includes an antenna that can both transmit and receive, and possibly a battery.

RFP (request for proposal)   A document requesting that vendors submit a proposal for a product or service that a company wants to purchase.

RG-6 (radio guide 6)   A type of coaxial cable with an impedance of 75 ohms and an 18 AWG core conductor. RG-6 is used for television, satellite, and broadband cable connections.

ring topology   A network layout in which each node is connected to the two nearest nodes so that the entire network forms a circle. Data is transmitted in one direction around the ring. Each node accepts and responds to packets addressed to it, then forwards the other packets to the next node in the ring.

RIP (Routing Information Protocol)   The oldest routing protocol that is still widely used. RIP is a distance-vector protocol that uses hop count as its routing metric and only allows up to 15 hops.

RIPv2 (Routing Information Protocol version 2)   An updated version of the original RIP routing protocol that generates less broadcast traffic and functions more securely than its predecessor. However, RIPv2's packet forwarding is still limited to a maximum 15 hops.

riser-rated cable   Cabling coated with a fire-retardant jacket that is thicker than typical network cables to ease the cable's insertion through risers in buildings or between floors.

RJ-11 (registered jack 11)   The standard connector used with unshielded twisted-pair cabling (usually Cat 3) to connect analog telephones.

RJ-45 (registered jack 45)   The standard connector used with shielded twisted-pair and unshielded twisted-pair cabling.

roam   The movement of a wireless client from one network or access point to another.

rogue access point   An unauthorized access point in the same vicinity as a legitimate network.

rogue DHCP server   A DHCP service running on a client device that could be used to implement an on-path attack by configuring the attacker's IP address as the victim computers' default gateway or DNS server.

rollback   The process of reverting to a previous version of a software application after attempting to patch or upgrade it.

rollover cable   A cable used to connect a computer to the console port of a router.

root bridge   The single bridge on a network selected by STP (Spanning Tree Protocol) to provide the basis for all subsequent path calculations.

root DNS server   A DNS server maintained by ICANN and IANA that is an authority on how to contact the top-level domains, such as those ending with .com, .edu, .net, .us, and so on. ICANN oversees the operation of 13 clusters of root servers around the world.

root port   The port on a switch designated as the interface facing the root bridge in an STP (Spanning Tree Protocol) switched environment.

route command   A command-line utility used to show or change a host's routing table.

router   A network layer device that uses logical addressing information to direct data between two or more networks and can help find the best path for traffic to get from one network to another.

routing cost   A value assigned to a particular route as judged by the network administrator—the more desirable the path, the lower its cost.

routing loop   A failure of a routing protocol that results in messages being transmitted continuously in a loop along the same paths and never reaching their destinations; commonly caused by making too many topology changes too quickly.

routing metrics   Properties of a route used by routing protocols to determine the best path to a destination when various paths are available. Routing metrics may be calculated using any of several variables, including hop count, bandwidth, delay, MTU, cost, and reliability.

routing protocol   A set of standards that determines how routers communicate with each other about network status and connections. Routing protocols determine the best path for data to take between networks.

routing table   A database stored in a router's memory that maintains information about the location of hosts and networks and the best paths for forwarding packets between them.

RPO (recovery point objective)   A metric that defines how much data loss is tolerable, depending on what backup methods and schedules are in place.

RS (router solicitation)   A message from a client to a router requesting network configuration information.

RSSI (received signal strength indicator)   The measure in dBm (decibels relative to one milliwatt) of the power of a transmitted signal at the point of the receiver.

RTO (recovery time objective)   A metric that defines the maximum tolerable outage time for an application or network service.

RTS/CTS (Request to Send/Clear to Send)   An exchange in which a source node requests the exclusive right to communicate with an access point and the access point confirms that it has granted that request.

RTT (round trip time)   The length of time it takes for a packet to go from sender to receiver, then back from receiver to sender. RTT is usually measured in milliseconds.

runt   A message that is so small it is dropped.

S

SaaS (Software as a Service)   A cloud service model in which applications are provided through an online user interface and are compatible with a multitude of devices and operating systems.

SAN (storage area network) A distinct network of storage devices that communicate directly with each other and with other networks.

SC (subscriber connector or standard connector) A connector with a 2.5-mm ferrule that is used with single-mode, fiber-optic cable.

SCADA (supervisory control and data acquisition) A network that acquires real-time data from a physical system and manages the physical system or presents the data to humans, who monitor and manage the system. Also called industrial control system.

scalable The property of a network that allows the addition of nodes or increasing its size easily.

scanning The process by which a wireless station finds an access point.

scattering The diffusion, or the reflection in multiple directions, of a wireless signal that results from hitting an object with a rough surface or small dimensions compared to the signal's wavelength.

scope option Specific configuration information, such as a time limit and a default gateway IP address, that is shared from a DHCP server along with an IP address assignment.

screened subnet An area on the perimeter of a network that is surrounded by two firewalls—an external firewall porous enough to allow more types of traffic, and a hardened internal firewall that provides greater protection to the internal network. Formerly called DMZ (demilitarized zone).

SDN (software-defined networking) A centralized approach to networking that removes most of the decision-making power from network devices and instead handles that responsibility at a software level.

SDN controller A product that integrates configuration and management control of all network devices, both physical and virtual, into one cohesive system that is overseen by the network administrator through a single dashboard.

SDS (safety data sheet) Instructions provided with dangerous substances that explain how to properly handle these substances and how to safely dispose of them. Formerly called MSDS (material safety data sheet).

SD-WAN (software-defined wide area network) Abstracted, centralized control of networking devices that manage network functions across a diverse infrastructure.

secondary DNS server The backup authoritative name server for an organization.

security audit An assessment of an organization's security vulnerabilities performed by an accredited network security firm. Also called an IT audit.

security camera A network or Internet connected video camera that sends alerts or video footage to a smartphone app where the user can remotely monitor covered areas.

security policy A document or plan that identifies an organization's security goals, risks, levels of authority, designated security coordinator and team members, responsibilities for each team member, and responsibilities for each employee. In addition, it specifies how to address security breaches.

security risk assessment An evaluation of threats to and vulnerabilities of a network.

security token A device or piece of software used for authentication that stores or generates information, such as a series of numbers or letters, known only to its authorized user.

segment (1) A TCP message at the transport layer. (2) A part of a network.

server Any computer or application that provides a service, such as data or other resources, to other devices.

server operating system An operating system designed to run on a server and provide network services to networked clients.

serverless compute A cloud-native, streamlined technology for hosting cloud-based applications where a server runs for short bursts only when needed by an application or service.

session An ongoing conversation between two hosts.

session layer The fifth layer in the OSI model. The session layer describes how data between applications is synced and recovered if messages don't arrive intact at the receiving application.

severity level An indication of priority that syslog assigns to each logged event. Also called logging level.

SFP (small form-factor pluggable) A standard hot-swappable network interface used to link a connectivity device's backplane with fiber-optic or copper cabling.

SFP+ A type of SFP that can send and receive data at rates of up to 16 Gbps.

SFTP (Secure File Transfer Protocol) A protocol available with the proprietary version of SSH (Secure Shell) that securely copies files between hosts.

SHA (Secure Hash Algorithm) A hash algorithm originally designed by the NSA to eliminate the inherent weaknesses of the older MD5 hash. The most recent iteration is SHA-3, developed by private designers for a public competition in 2012.

shared responsibility model A theoretical model that clarifies the division of responsibilities between cloud provider and cloud customer for the security of cloud resources.

short circuit An unwanted connection, such as when exposed wires touch each other.

shoulder surfing An attack type in which a person secretly observes an authorized person entering their credentials to access a secure area and then uses that information later.

SIEM (Security Information and Event Management) Software that can be configured to evaluate data logs from IDS, IPS, firewalls, and proxy servers to detect significant events that require the attention of IT staff according to predefined rules.

signature Identifiable patterns of code that are known to indicate specific vulnerabilities, exploits, or other undesirable traffic.

signature management The process of regularly updating the signatures used to monitor a network's traffic.

SIM (Subscriber Identity Module) card A microchip installed in a cellular device to hold data about the subscription a user has with the cellular carrier.

SIP (Session Initiation Protocol) A signaling protocol that is used to make an initial connection between hosts but that does not participate in data transfer during the session. SIP is a common application layer protocol used by voice gateways to initiate and maintain connections.

site prefix The first four blocks or 64 bits of an IPv6 address that normally identify the network. Also called global routing prefix.

site survey In the context of wireless networking, an assessment of client requirements, facility characteristics, and coverage areas to determine an access point arrangement that will ensure reliable wireless connectivity within a given area.

site-to-site VPN A type of VPN in which VPN gateways at multiple sites encrypt and encapsulate data to exchange over tunnels with other VPN gateways. Meanwhile, clients, servers, and other hosts on a site-to-site VPN communicate with the VPN gateway.

SLA (service-level agreement) A legally binding contract or part of a contract that defines, in plain language and in measurable terms, the aspects of a service provided to a customer. Specific details might include contract duration, guaranteed uptime, problem management, performance benchmarks, and termination options.

SLAAC (stateless address autoconfiguration) The process by which an IPv6 client collects the basic information required to configure its own IPv6 address on a network.

smart card An electronic access badge.

smart doorbell An Internet-connected doorbell with two-way audio and one- or two-way video capability that monitors an entryway and provides alerts when movement is detected.

smart locker An access-controlled locker that requires authentication, such as by providing a bar code from an email or a PIN.

smart refrigerator An Internet-connected refrigerator that uses RFID or barcode tracking to detect items in the refrigerator.

smart speaker A voice controlled IoT device that provides an embedded personal assistant app used to access information and control other IoT devices.

smart thermostat More sophisticated than a programmable thermostat, an Internet-connected thermostat device that can be controlled remotely through an app or can monitor environmental or behavioral information to automatically adjust temperature settings.

smartjack An intelligent type of NIU (network interface unit) located at the customer's demarc that can provide diagnostic information about the interface.

SMB (Server Message Block) A protocol for communications and resource access between systems, such as clients and servers.

SMF (single-mode fiber) A type of fiber-optic cable with a narrow core of 8 to 10 microns in diameter that carries light pulses along a single path from one end of the cable to the other end.

SMTP (Simple Mail Transfer Protocol) An application layer protocol responsible for moving messages from one email server to another.

snips Heavy-duty scissors that make a clean cut through a cable.

SNMP (Simple Network Management Protocol) An application layer protocol in the TCP/IP suite used to monitor and manage devices on a network.

SNR (signal-to-noise ratio) The proportion of noise to the strength of a signal.

SOA (start of authority) record A record in a DNS zone about that zone and the records within it.

social engineering The act of manipulating social relationships to circumvent network security measures and gain access to a system.

socket A logical address consisting of a host's IP address and the port of an application running on the host with a colon separating the two values.

SoD (separation of duties) A division of labor that ensures no one person can singlehandedly compromise the security of data, finances, or other resources.

SOHO (small office/home office) network A network consisting of fewer than 10 networked devices.

SOP (standard operating procedure) The steps defined for a specific process within an organization to maintain consistency and avoid errors.

SOW (statement of work) A document that details the work that must be completed for a particular project, including specifics such as tasks, deliverables, standards, payment schedule, and work timeline. An SOW is legally binding, meaning it can be enforced by a court of law. Many times, an SOW is used to define the terms of each new project as an addendum to an existing MSA.

spectrum analyzer A software tool that assesses the characteristics (for example, frequency, amplitude, and the effects of interference) of wireless signals.

speed and duplex mismatch A problem that occurs when neighboring devices are using different speed or duplex configurations and results in failed transmissions.

spine-and-leaf architecture A two-layer network architectural design where spine switches organize traffic and network segments using OSI layer 3 technologies while leaf switches manage traffic by either layer 2 or layer 3 principles.

split tunnel VPN A type of VPN that captures only the traffic destined for the corporate network. The client can communicate with local network resources directly and with Internet resources through a local Internet connection.

spoofing The act of impersonating fields of data in a transmission, such as when a source IP address is impersonated in a DRDoS attack.

SQL (Structured Query Language) A programming language used to configure and interact with a database's objects and data.

SQLnet A standard used by Oracle Database to communicate with other Oracle Databases or with database clients.

SRV (service) record A type of DNS data record that identifies the hostname and port of a computer hosting a specific network service besides email, such as FTP or SIP.

SSH (Secure Shell) A remote connection utility that provides authentication and encryption. SSH is often used to log onto a host, execute commands on that host, and copy files to or from the host.

SSID (service set identifier) A character string used to identify an access point on an 802.11 network.

SSL (Secure Sockets Layer) A method of encrypting TCP/IP transmissions—including web pages and data entered into web forms—en route between the client and server using public key encryption technology.

SSO (single sign-on) A form of authentication in which a client signs on once to access multiple systems or resources.

ST (straight tip) A connector with a 2.5-mm ferrule that is used with single-mode, fiber-optic cable.

star topology A physical topology in which every node on the network is connected through a central device.

stateful firewall A firewall capable of examining an incoming packet to determine whether it belongs to a currently active connection and is, therefore, a legitimate packet.

stateless firewall A firewall that manages each incoming packet as a stand-alone entity without regard to currently active connections.

static ARP table entry A record in an ARP table that someone has manually entered using the ARP utility.

static electricity An electrical charge at rest. When that charge is transferred between two bodies, it creates an electrostatic discharge, or ESD.

static IP address An IP address that is manually assigned to a device and remains constant until it is manually changed.

static route A route manually configured by a network administrator to direct messages along specific paths between networks.

static VLAN assignment A VLAN assignment based on the switch port a device is connected to.

STDM (statistical time division multiplexing) A type of multiplexing that assigns time slots to nodes (similar to TDM), but then adjusts these slots according to priority and need.

STP (shielded twisted pair) A type of copper-based cable containing twisted-pair wires with metallic shielding such as foil around each wire pair and/or shielding surrounding all four wire pairs.

STP (Spanning Tree Protocol) A switching protocol defined by the IEEE standard 802.1D that functions at the data link layer and prevents traffic loops by artificially blocking the links that would complete a loop.

straight-through cable A twisted-pair patch cable in which the wire terminations in both connectors follow the same scheme.

stratum A number that indicates an NTP (Network Time Protocol) server's location within the NTP hierarchy relative to a stratum-1 server.

structured cabling A method for uniform, enterprise-wide, multivendor cabling systems specified by the ANSI/TIA-568 family of standards. Structured cabling is based on a hierarchical design using a high-speed backbone.

subinterface Logical interfaces on a router that logically segment a single physical interface.

subnet A smaller network within a larger network in which all nodes share a network addressing component and a fixed amount of bandwidth.

subnet ID The 16 bits, or one block, in an IPv6 address that can be used to identify a subnet on a large corporate network.

subnet mask In IPv4 addressing, a 32-bit number that helps one computer find another by indicating what portion of an IP address is the network and subnet portion and what portion is the host portion.

subnetting The process of segmenting a network into smaller networks that requires calculations of IP address ranges within a larger IP address range.

surge protector A power management device that redirects excess voltage away from connected computing or networking devices to the ground, thereby protecting connected devices from harm.

switch A connectivity device that logically subdivides a network into smaller, individual collision domains.

symmetric encryption A method of encryption that requires the same key to encode the data as is used to decode the cipher text.

symmetrical A characteristic of transmission technology that offers the same download speeds as upload speeds.

syslog (system log) A standard for generating, storing, and processing messages about events on a system.

system life cycle The process of designing, implementing, and maintaining an entire network.

system log The location where syslog data is stored in the OS.

T

TACACS+ (Terminal Access Controller Access Control System Plus) A Cisco proprietary protocol that provides AAA services.

tag A VLAN identifier added to a frame's header according to specifications in the 802.1Q standard.

tailgating An attack type in which an unauthorized person follows an authorized person into a secure area without the authorized person's knowledge or cooperation.

tamper detection Sensors that can detect physical penetration, temperature extremes, input voltage variations, input frequency variations, or certain kinds of radiation.

TAP (test access point) A device connected between two devices on a network that can capture all traffic traversing the connection, for example, between a switch and a router.

TCP (Transmission Control Protocol) A core protocol of the TCP/IP suite that makes a connection with the end host, checks whether data is received, and resends it if it is not.

TCP/IP (Transmission Control Protocol/Internet Protocol) suite A suite of networking protocols that includes TCP, IP, UDP, and many others. TCP/IP provides the foundation for data exchange across the Internet.

tcpdump A free, command-line packet sniffer utility that runs on Linux and other UNIX operating systems.

TDM (time division multiplexing) A method of multiplexing that assigns a time slot in the flow of communications to every node on the network and, in that time slot, carries data from that node.

TDMA (time division multiple access) A method of multiplexing in which signals from several sources on a channel are separated by timeslots.

TDR (time domain reflectometer) A high-end instrument for testing the qualities of a cable.

Telnet A terminal emulation protocol used to log on to remote hosts using the TCP/IP protocol.

terminal emulator Software that allows a user on one computer, called the client, to control another computer, called the host or server, across a network connection.

TFTP (Trivial File Transfer Protocol) A TCP/IP application layer protocol that is seldom used by humans. Network devices, such as routers and switches, commonly use it as they are booting up to request configuration files from a TFTP server on the local network. Unlike FTP, TFTP relies on UDP at the transport layer using port 69.

TFTP server A file server used to remotely boot devices that don't have their own hard drives, to collect log files from devices, or to back up and update network device configuration files.

threat assessment An evaluation of specific security threats to a network and related risk factors.

three-tiered architecture A hierarchical network design that organizes switches and routers into three tiers: access layer or edge layer, distribution layer or aggregation layer, and core layer. This design increases both redundancy on the network and network performance.

three-way handshake A three-step process in which transport layer protocols establish a connection between nodes.

throughput The amount of data that a medium transmits during a given period of time. Throughput is usually measured in Mbps

(megabits per second, which is 1,000,000 bits) or Gbps (gigabits per second).

TIA (Telecommunications Industry Association) A subgroup of the former EIA that focuses on standards for information technology, wireless, satellite, fiber optics, and telephone equipment. EIA was dissolved in 2011, and its responsibilities were transferred to ECA (Electronic Components, Assemblies, Equipment & Supplies Association).

TIA/EIA-568A A standard pinout for RJ-45 plugs required by the federal government on all federal contracts. Also called T568A.

TIA/EIA-568B A standard pinout for RJ-45 plugs commonly used in homes and businesses. Also called T568B.

ticket In Kerberos terminology, a temporary set of credentials that a client uses to prove its identity has been validated by the authentication service.

TKIP (Temporal Key Integrity Protocol) An encryption key generation and management scheme used by WPA (Wi-Fi Protected Access).

TLD (top-level domain) The last part of an FQDN and the highest-level category used to distinguish domain names—for example, .org, .com, and .net. A TLD is also known as the domain suffix.

TLS (Transport Layer Security) An update to SSL (Secure Sockets Layer) standardized by the IETF (Internet Engineering Task Force). TLS uses slightly different encryption algorithms than SSL and is more secure, but otherwise is very similar to the most recent version of SSL.

tone generator A small electronic device that issues a signal on a wire pair. When used in conjunction with a tone locator, it can help locate the termination of a wire pair. Also called a toner.

tone locator A small electronic device that emits a tone when it detects electrical activity on a wire pair. When used in conjunction with a tone generator, it can help locate the termination of a wire pair. Also called a probe.

toner *See* tone generator.

topology How the parts of a whole work together.

ToR (top of rack) switching A rack architecture where one switch on each rack serves as the connection point to the network for all other devices on the rack.

traceroute A TCP/IP troubleshooting utility available in Linux, UNIX, and macOS systems that sends UDP messages to a random port on the destination node to trace the path from one networked node to another, identifying all intermediate hops between the two nodes.

tracert   A Windows utility that uses ICMP (Internet Control Message Protocol) echo requests to trace the path from one networked node to another, identifying all intermediate hops between the two nodes.

traffic analysis   The examination of network traffic for patterns and exceptions to those patterns.

traffic log   Historical records of network traffic primarily used to investigate network performance issues.

traffic policing   A traffic-shaping technique in which the volume or rate of traffic traversing an interface is limited to a predefined maximum.

traffic shaping   Manipulating certain characteristics of packets, data streams, or connections to manage the type and amount of traffic traversing a network or interface at any moment. Also called packet shaping.

trailer   Control information attached to the end of a packet by a data link layer protocol.

transceiver   A modular interface that can be inserted in a switch to connect its motherboard with an external, fiber-optic cable.

transport layer   The fourth layer of the OSI model. The transport layer is responsible for transporting application layer payloads from one application to another.

trap   A type of unsolicited SNMP (Simple Network Message Protocol) message sent from an agent to the NMS (network management system) once specified conditions on the managed device are met.

trunk port   The interface on a switch capable of managing traffic from multiple VLANs.

trunking   The aggregation of multiple logical connections in one physical connection between connectivity devices. In the case of VLANs, a trunk allows switches to manage and exchange data between multiple VLANs across a single interface.

TTL (Time to Live)   A field that indicates the maximum duration that an IPv4 packet can remain on the network before it is discarded, or a field in a DNS zone file that indicates how long the information can be considered valid in a DNS server's cache.

tunneling   The process of encapsulating one type of protocol in another. For example,

tunneling is the way higher-layer data is transported over VPNs by layer 2 protocols.

twinaxial cable   A type of copper cable that looks very similar to coaxial cable but has two or more cores, or conductors, inside the cable. Called twinax for short.

twist ratio   The number of twists per meter or foot in a twisted-pair cable.

twisted-pair   A type of cable similar to telephone wiring that consists of color-coded pairs of insulated copper wires, each with a diameter of 0.4 to 0.8 mm. Every two wires are twisted around each other to form pairs, and all the pairs are encased in a plastic sheath.

TX/RX reverse   A problem caused by mismatched pinout standards, resulting in near end crosstalk.

TXT (text) record   A type of DNS data record that holds any type of free-form text. It might contain text designed to be read by humans regarding network, server, or accounting issues.

type 1 hypervisor   A hypervisor that installs on a computer before any OS and is sometimes erroneously called a bare-metal hypervisor.

type 2 hypervisor   A hypervisor that installs in a host OS as an application and is called a hosted hypervisor.

U

UDP (User Datagram Protocol)   A core protocol in the TCP/ IP suite that does not guarantee delivery because it does not first make the connection before sending data or check to confirm that data is received.

UDP forwarding   The ability of a router, firewall, layer 3 switch, or other relay agent to forward UDP traffic to support centralized network services such as DHCP, DNS, NTP, and TFTP.

unicast address   A type of IPv6 address that represents a single node on a network.

unmanaged switch   A switch that provides plug-and-play simplicity with minimal configuration options and has no IP address assigned to it.

UPC (ultra-physical contact)   A type of ferrule in which the tip has been highly polished, thereby increasing the efficiency of the connection.

upgrade   A significant change to an application's existing code, typically designed to improve functionality or add new features while also correcting bugs and vulnerabilities.

UPS (uninterruptible power supply) A battery-operated power source directly attached to one or more devices and to a power supply (such as a wall outlet) that provides a backup power source in the event of a power outage and prevents undesired fluctuations of the wall outlet's AC power from harming the device or interrupting its services.

uptime The duration or percentage of time a system or network functions normally between failures.

URL (Uniform Resource Locator) An application layer addressing scheme that identifies where to find a particular resource on a network or across networks.

UTP (unshielded twisted pair) A type of copper-based cable that consists of one or more insulated twisted-pair wires encased in a plastic sheath, which does not contain additional shielding for the twisted pairs.

V

VDI (Virtual Desktop Infrastructure) A remote desktop implementation that offers VM instances for remote access clients.

vendor risk assessment An evaluation of security and compliance risks related to suppliers and vendors a company does business with. Also called a third-party risk assessment.

VIP (virtual IP address) A single IP address that represents a cluster of devices.

virtualization The emulation of all or part of a computer or network.

VLAN (virtual local area network or virtual LAN) A network within a network that is logically defined by grouping ports on a switch so that some of the local traffic on the switch is forced to go through a router, thereby limiting the traffic to a smaller broadcast domain.

VLAN hopping An attack in which the attacker generates transmissions that appear, to the switch, to belong to a protected VLAN.

VLSM (Variable Length Subnet Mask) A subnetting method that allows subnets to be further subdivided into smaller and smaller groupings until each subnet is about the same size as the needed IP address space.

VNC (Virtual Network Computing) Software that uses the cross-platform protocol RFB (remote frame buffer) to remotely control a workstation or server.

vNIC (virtual NIC) A logically defined network interface associated with a physical or virtual machine.

voice gateway A device that converts signals from a campus's analog phone equipment into IP data that can travel over the Internet, or that converts VoIP data from an internal IP network to travel over a phone company's analog telephone lines.

voice VLAN A VLAN designed specifically to support VoIP traffic, which requires high bandwidths, priority over other traffic, flexible routing, and minimized latency.

VoIP (Voice over IP) The provision of telephone service over a packet-switched network running the TCP/IP protocol suite.

VoIP phone An end user device or application that gives the user access to VoIP services on a network.

VPN (virtual private network) A virtual connection between a client and a remote network, two remote networks, or two remote hosts over the Internet or other types of networks, to remotely provide network resources.

VPN headend A VPN gateway that manages multiple tunnels from individual VPN clients.

VRRP (Virtual Router Redundancy Protocol) A standard that assigns a virtual IP address to a group of routers.

vSwitch (virtual switch) A logically defined device that operates at the data link layer to pass frames between physical and virtual nodes.

vulnerability A weakness of a system, process, or architecture that could lead to compromised information or unauthorized access to a network.

vulnerability assessment An evaluation of security weaknesses in a network.

W

WAN (wide area network) A network that spans a long distance and connects two or more LANs.

warm site A place where the computers, devices, and connectivity necessary to rebuild a network exist, though only some are appropriately configured, updated, or connected to match the network's current state.

wavelength The distance from the crest of one wave to the crest of the next wave.

WDM (wavelength division multiplexing) A multiplexing technique in which each signal on a fiber-optic cable is assigned a different wavelength, which equates to its own subchannel.

well-known port The TCP/IP ports numbered 0 to 1023, so named because they were long ago assigned by Internet authorities to popular services and are, therefore, well known and frequently used.

WEP (Wired Equivalent Privacy)   A key encryption technique for wireless networks that uses keys both to authenticate network clients and to encrypt data in transit.

Wi-Fi (wireless fidelity)   The IEEE standards and their amendments, extensions, and corrections for wireless networking.

Wi-Fi 4   The IEEE standard for a wireless networking technique that may issue signals in the 2.4-GHz or 5-GHz band and can achieve actual data throughput between 65 Mbps and 600 Mbps. Also called 802.11n.

Wi-Fi 5   The IEEE standard for a wireless networking technique that exceeds benchmarks set by earlier standards by increasing its useful bandwidth and amplitude. Wi-Fi 5 is the first Wi-Fi standard to approach Gigabit Ethernet capabilities. Also called 802.11ac.

Wi-Fi 6   The IEEE standard for a wireless networking technique that operates in both the 2.4-GHz and 5-GHz bands and improves on earlier standards through the implementation of modulation and multi-user technologies. Also called 802.11ax.

Wi-Fi 6E   An enhancement to the IEEE standard 802.11ax that uses the 6-GHz frequency range.

Wi-Fi analyzer   Software that can evaluate Wi-Fi network availability as well as help optimize Wi-Fi signal settings or help identify Wi-Fi security threats.

wiki   A website that can be edited by users.

wire cutter   A pliers-shaped tool that makes a clean cut through a cable.

wire map test   A test that indicates if each pin on one end of a cable is paired with the appropriate pin on the other end.

wireless bridge   An access point used to create remote wired access to a network.

wireless client isolation   A security technique for wireless networks that allows a wireless client onto the network but imposes firewall rules to restrict the client's ability to communicate with only the default gateway, not other devices on the network.

wireless LAN controller   A central management console for all the APs on a network.

wireless range extender   A device that extends the reach of a wireless signal by repeating the signal from a closer broadcast point.

wireless spectrum   A continuum of electromagnetic waves used for data and voice communication.

wiring diagram   A graphical representation of a network's wired infrastructure.

WLAN (wireless local area network)   A LAN that uses wireless connections for some or all of its transmissions.

WPA (Wi-Fi Protected Access or Wireless Protected Access)   A wireless security method that dynamically assigns every transmission its own key.

WPA2   A wireless security method that improves upon WPA by using a stronger encryption protocol called AES (Advanced Encryption Standard).

X

XaaS (Anything as a Service)   A type of cloud computing in which the cloud can provide any combination of functions depending on a client's exact needs, or assumes functions beyond networking including, for example, monitoring, storage, applications, and virtual desktops.

XFP (10 Gigabit small form-factor pluggable)   A type of SFP that can send and receive data at rates of up to 10 Gbps.

Z

zero trust   A security model where everything in the network is considered untrustworthy until proven otherwise.

zero-day exploit   An attack that takes advantage of a software vulnerability that hasn't yet or has only very recently become public.

ZigBee   A smart home protocol based on the 802.15.4 standard that requires little power and is designed to handle small amounts of data, which makes it ideal for ISM (industrial, scientific, and medical) sensors.

zone transfer   The process of updating a secondary DNS server with information from the primary DNS server's database.

Z-Wave   A smart home protocol that provides two basic types of functions: signaling, to manage wireless connections, and control, to transmit data and commands between devices.

INDEX